國際去來法

국제거래법

: 에너지

정영철 지음

Dedication

For Mi-Ryoung Kim

김미령에게

서 문

기업을 자문하면서 발전소 관련 지식을 얻었고 이를 기초로 에너지산업의 정책적 논의를 연구하고 해외자원탐사나 건설사업관련 계약을 검토할 기회가 있었다. 그런 과정에서 우리나라에도 에너지법 관련 소개책자가 있으면 앞으로 이 분야를 개척하려는 법률가들에게 도움이 될 것 같다는 생각을 한 적이 있다. 이제 법학전문대학원의 첫 졸업생들이 배출되면서 교육과정도 자리를 잡아 가는 것 같으니 학교에서의 생활을 마무리하면서 과거의 경험과 기억을 모아서 유망한 실무분야로서 그리고 우리의 법률가들이 처리하여야 할 미래의 중요한 분야로서 에너지법에 관한 간단한 casebook을 만들었다.

Ernest E. Smith의 International Petroleum Transactions (3rd, 2010)에서 출발, 우리 판례 및 계약사례와 함께 기존의 연구업적을 모아서 소개하였고 우리 행정부의 정책자료나 통계자료 등도 모았다. 판례는 국제 에너지거래에 관한 것뿐만 아니라 에너지산업의 이해에 도움이 될 것 같으면 관련성이 적은 것이라도 모두 포함시켰다. 우리나라가 체결한 에너지 관련 계약사례도 다양하게 소개하여 보려고 하였지만, 현재는 접근가능한 것이 거의 없었다. 판례와 마찬가지로 계약사례도 시간이 상당히 지나야만 보완가능할 것으로 보인다.

이 책은 5편 12장으로 구성되어 있다. 1편은 지구상에 에너지의 원천이 되는 자원, 그 중에서도 화석연료가 지구상에 어디에 얼마나 있으며 이들은 전세계적으로 그리로 우리나라에서 어떻게 소비되는지에 대한 현실을 살피고 석유와 천연가스에 관한 법체계의 출발점인 국가권력의 기초를 살핀다. 2편은 국가권력과 석유나 천연가스를 탐사·개발·생산하는 행위주체로서의 NOC와 IOC간의 법률관계와 이를 전제로 한 공동개발자, 운영자, 시추용역 제공자 등 제반 행위주체간 계약을 기초로 한 권리의무관계를 논한다. 3편은 이들 행위자들이 생산한 석유나 천연가스를 실제 수요자와 연결시키는 메커니즘으로서의 시장에서 어떤 일들이 벌어지는지 판례를 중심으로 들여다본다. 4편은 석유나 천연가스 개발을 둘러싼 분쟁으로서의 국유화, 그리고 구체적으로 계약상 분쟁의 해결방법과 해결의 준거법에 관한 것이며 마지막으로 5편에서 지금 현재의 법이 아닌 미래를 향하여 변하여 가는 법으로서 새로운 법원리를 제시한다.

이 책은 대학원에서의 강의에서 기본교재가 될 수 있고, 실무가들에게도 참고서가 될 수 있을 것이다. 이 책에서의 논의가 출발점이 되어 보다 많은 법률가들이 에너지법 분야에 관심을 가지고 연구와 실무를 계속한다면 조만간 우리의 공무원, 법률가와 사업가들이 세계의 에너지 정책결정과 국제거래에 적극적으로 참여할 수 있을 것이다. 이 책이 여러 모로 부족하지만 장기적 식견을 가진 인재를 키우는 데 조금이라도 도움이 되면 좋겠다는 마음에서 서둘러 출판하였다. 많은 질책을 기대한다.

2012. 9.

정 영 철

감사(Acknowledgement)

아래 논문 또는 책의 전재를 허락한 저자 또는 출판사에 감사한다.

Shalanda H. Baker, *Unmasking Project Finance: Risk Mitigation, Risk Inducement, and an Invitation to Development Disaster?* 6 TEX. J. OIL GAS & ENER. L. 273 (2010-11)

Peter Cameron, *North Sea Oil Licensing: Comparisons and Contracts,* 4 Oil & GAS L. TAX REV. 99 (1984-85)

Ana E. Bastida, Adaeze Ifesi-Okoye, Salim Mahmud, James Ross & Thomas Wälde, *Cross-Border Unitization and Joint Development Agreements: An International Law Perspective,* 29 HOUS. J. INT'L L. 355 (2006-07)

James A. Holtkamp/Richard M. Saines, *North American Approaches to Climate Change: Greenhouse Gas Emission Contral Strategies,* 51 ROCKY MT. MIN. INST. (2005)

Clifford D. Johnson, *Non-Operator's Rights Under the CAPL Operating Procedure,* 28 ALTA. L. REV. 1 (1989-90)

Lucinda A. Low/Thomas K. Sprange/Milos Barutciski, *Global Anti-corruption Standard and Enforcement: Implications for Energy Companies,* 3 J. WORLD ENER. L & BUS. 166 (2010)

C.R.K. Moore, *Perspectives on the Valuation of Upstream Oil and Gas Interests: An Overview,* 2 J. WORLD ENER. L & BUS. 24 (2009)

Richard J. Pierce, Jr., *The Past, Present, and Future of Energy Regulation,* 31 UTAH ENVT'L. L. REV. 291 (2011)

Ernest E. Smith & John S. Dzienkowski, *A Fifty-Year Perspective on World Petroleum Arrangements,* 24 TEX. INT'L L. J. 13 (1989)

류권홍, 자원소유권의 귀속, 25 원광법학 35 (2009)

신창훈, 대한민국의 대륙붕선언의 기원과 1974년 한일대륙붕공동개발협정의의의, 13 서울국제법연구 57 (2006)

염명천, 에너지시장, 산업 & 정책 173 (2006)

오정환, 원유가스탐사개발권의 취득에 관한 법적 연구 40 (2010 한양대학교 박사학위 논문)

이준기, 해외자원개발사업법 개선방안연구, 2010 자원 · 에너지 법제연구회연구논문집 230

최원목, 해외자원개발에 따른 투자분쟁방지 및 해결을 위한 지침, 2010 자원 · 에너지 법제연구회 연구논문집 11

최종일, IFRS도입에 따른 자원개발회계 개선방안, 2010 자원 · 에너지법제연구회 연구논문집 274

최 철, 해외자원프로젝트와 관련된 법적위험과 금융가능성에 관한 고찰, 34 외법논집 185 (2010)

홍종완/심어진, 동중국해에서의 한중일 대륙붕중첩주장수역의 공동개발에 관한 고찰, 16 서울국제법연구 279 (2009)

Rocky Mountain Mineral Law Foundation에서 scholarship grant를 보내 주어 RA를 활용할 수 있었고 또한 digital library에의 접근을 허락하여 많은 자료를 열람할 수 있었다. Barrows Company의 Mr. Barrows와 Mr. Nelson Pinero는 한국관련 개발계약서를 조사, 이를 제공하였을 뿐만 아니라 안정화조항, 분쟁해결조항과 준거법조항의 전재에 동의하여 주었다. K-EXIM의 변상완 부행장이 KOGAS 관련 자료를 찾는 데 커다란 도움을 주었다. 이들 모두에게 감사한다. 우리 정부와 기업, 연구소도 law school을 교육기관으로서뿐만 아니라 연구기관으로 인식하고 faculty와 학생들의 관심과 조사영역의 확대에 보다 많은 노력을 기울이는 날이 조만간 오기를 바란다.

법학도서관의 유희경 사서님은 교내 이용가능한 논문이나 전자책은 즉시 이메일로 보내 주었고, 책이 없으면 상호대차로, 논문이 없으면 복사신청으로, 그리고 추가로 책이 필요하면 구입요청으로 아낌없는 지원을 하여 주었다. 법학전문대학원 윤선우 학생이 TA로서, 최지원 · 민혜빈 · 서우영 학생이 RA로서, 이상후 학생이 MA로서 수고했다. 배정연 · 강지은 · 경우선 학생이 마지막 교정작업을 도왔다. 모두 한국을 짊어질 훌륭한 법률가로 클 것이라 믿는다.

law school 때문에 수험생이 줄어들어서 법학서적의 출판이 더 이상 수지가 맞지 않는다고 하면서도 사명감으로 이 책의 출판을 결정한 박영사의 안종만 회장님과 조성호 부장님, 조판·편집·오탈자수정 등 손이 많이 가는 작업을 끝까지 열심히 하여 주신 나경선 차장님에게 감사드린다.

학생들을 통하여 미래를 볼 수 있는 대신 현재와의 소통이 단절되어 있는 학교로 들어온 이후, 대부분의 지인이나 고객, 친구들과 연락이 끊겼지만 그래도 잊지 않고 소식을 물어온 선·후배들에게 감사한다. 경제인문사회연구회 김세원 이사장님의 연구프로젝트를 수행하면서 중동과 이란, 중앙아시아의 산유국을 돌아볼 기회가 있었다. 경영대학의 김인준 선생님 덕분에 금융/자본시장법에 대한 강의의 경험을 얻었고 파생상품에 대하여 보다 깊이 있는 이해가 가능하였다.

마지막으로 언제나 나를 지켜주고 있는 가족 — 김미령, 정헌직, 정원주 — 에게 감사의 마음을 전한다. 머리칼이 급속히 하얗게 변하는 늦은 시간에 품성과 능력에 어울리지 않는 쓸데없는 자존심과 지나친 허영심을 만족시키느라 가족들에게 너무 소홀하였다. 앞으로의 남은 시간은 가족들을 위하여 쓸 것을 약속한다.

간단한 목차

제 3 편 국제에너지자원—시장

제 4 편 국제에너지자원—분쟁

제 5 편 국제에너지자원—미래

Table of Contents

제 1 편 국제에너지자원—법과 정책

제 1 장 세계의 에너지자원

제 2 장 한국의 에너지자원

제 2 편 국제에너지자원—탐사개발생산

제 4 장 에너지자원 개발계약유형

제 4 편 국제에너지자원—분쟁

제 9 장 외국인투자와 정치경제적 위험

제10장 분쟁해결의 방법

제 5 편 국제에너지자원—미래

제12장 새로운 법의 형성

표 목 록

그림 목록

약어 목록

도시가스사업법	가스사업법
석유 및 석유대체연료 사업법	석유사업법
약관 규제에 관한 법률	약관법
액화석유가스의 안전관리 및 사업법	액화석유가스사업법
채무자회생 및 파산에 관한 법률	도산법
한국가스공사	KOGAS
한국석유공사	KNOC
해외자원개발사업법	해자사업법
해저광물자원개발법	해저개발법
United Nations Charter of Economic Rights and Duties of States (U.N.G.A. Res. 3281 (1975))	Charter
United Nations Declaration on the Establishment of a New International Economic Order (U.N.G.A. Res. 3201 (1974))	NIEO
United Nations General Assembly resolution 1803 (XVII) of 14 December 1962, Permanent Sovereignty Over Natural Resources	Res. 1803
1958 United Nations Convention on the Recognition and Enforcement of Foreign Arbitral Awards	뉴욕협약, New York 협약

°	degree
$	United States dolloar
$M	Thousands of dollars
$MM	Millions of dollars
2-D	Two-dimensional (as in seismic data)
3-D	Three-dimensional (as in seismic data)
AAA	American Arbitration Association
AAPG	American Association of Petroleum Geologists
AAPL	Asian Agricultural Products Limited

ACG	Azeri-Chirag-Guneshli (oilfiled)
ACIA	ASEAN Comprehensive Investment Agreement
ADMA	Abu Dahbi Marine Areas, Ltd.
ADPC	Abu Dahbi Petroleum Company
AFE	Authority(or Authorization) for Expenditures under a JOA
AG	German corporate designation
AGIP	Italian oil and gas company
AGR	Access to Gross Revenues
AHSTF	Alberta Heritage Savings Trust Fund
AIOC	Azerbaijan International Operating Company
AIPN	Association of International Petroleum Negotiators
AJIL	American Journal of International Law
ALBA	Alternativa Bolivariana para la América Latina y El Caribe
AMI	Area of Mutual Interest under a JOA or Farm-In Agreement
Aminoil	American Independent Oil Co.
AMPLA	Australian Mineral and Petroleum Law Association
AMT	American Manufacturing & Trading INC.
APF	Alaska's Permanent Fund
API	American Petroleum Institute
AOP	After payout
API	American Petroleum Institute
Aramco	Arabian American Oil Company
ASEAN	Association of South-East Asian Nations
B	Billion
Baht	Thai currency unit
BBL or bbl	Barrel ($1m^3$=6.3 barrels)
BCF	Billion Cubic Feet
BCM	Billion Cubic Metres
BCPD or pcpd	Barrels of condensate per day
BEE	Black Economic Empowerment
BIT	Bilateral Investment Treaty
BOE	Barrels of oil equivalent (including oil, natural gas and gas/

	hydrocarbon liquids)
BOO	Build Own and Operate
BOOT	Build Own Operate and Transfer
BOPD	Barrels of oil per day
BOT	Build Own and Transfer
BOTAS	Turkish State Oil Company
BP	British Petroleum Company Ltd.
BPD, bpd, b/p	Barrels per day
BPO	Before payout
BPPKA	Foreign Contractors Coordinating and Management Body (of Pertamina)
Bráspetro	Petrobrás International S.A.
BS&W	Basic Sediment and Water
BTC	Baku-Tbiliai-Ceyhan Pipeline
BTU	British Thermal Unit
b/d	Barrel per day
b/m	Barrel per month
C	Centigrade
C_1	Methane
C_2	Ethane
C_3	Propane
C_4	Butane
C_5	Pentane
C_6+	Hexanes plus
Caltex	California Texas Oil Company
CAMMESA	State regulator (Electricity wholesale market; Argentina)
Capex	Capital Expenditures
cbft/d	Cubic feet per day
CCS	Carbon Captures and Storage(or Sequestration)
CDM	Clean Development Mechanism
CEO	Chief Executive Officer
CEPMLP	Centre for Energy, Petroleum and Mineral Law and Policy
CFP/Total	Compagnie Français des Pétroles

CGT	The UK Capital Gains Tax
CICT	Consolidated Industrial and Commercial Tax
CIS	Commonwealth of Independent States
CIT	Corporate Income Tax
CLHB	Bolivian liquids pipeline and logistics company
CN	Cerro Negro (region in Venezuela)
CNG	Compressed Natural Gas
CNODC	China National Oil and Gas Exploration and Development Corporation
CNOOC	China National Offshore Oil Company
CNP	National Petroleum Council (Brazil)
CNPC	China National Petroleum Corporation
CO_3	Carbon dioxide
COE	Crude oil equivalent (Same as BOE)
CONELEC	State electricity regulatory authority (Ecuador)
COTCO	Cameroon Oil Transportation Company
CPC	Caspian Pipeline Consortium
CPI	Consumer Price Index (US)
CPR	Conflict Prevention and Resolution (Institute for Dispute Resolution)
CSR	Corporate Social Responsibilities
CVP	Subsidiary company of PDVSA
C/F	Carry Forward
C/R	Cost Recovery
DC	District of Columbia
DCF	Discounted Cash Flow
DD&A	Depreciation, Depletion, and Amortization(used in USA, Canada, etc
DEI	Duke Energy International
Dev.	Development
DHT	Direct Hydrocarbons Tax (in spanish : IDH)
DMO	Domestic Market Obligation
DMR	Department of Mineral Resources (Thailand)
DOE	US Department of Energy
DR-CA FTA	Dominican Republic-Central American Free Trade Association

DSU	Drilling Spacing Unit
DTI	Department of Trade and Industry of the UK
DTP	Draft Transit Protocol
EBO	Equivalent barrels of oil (same as BOE and COE)
EBR	Bolivian Refinery Company
EC	European Commission
ECHR	European Court of Human Rights
ECT	Energy Charter Treaty
EDF	Electricité de France
EGPC	Egypt General Petroleum Corporation
EI	Energy Institute
EIA	Environmental Impact Assessment
EIA	Energy Information Administration (USA)
EIB	European Investment Bank
EITI	Extractive Industries Transparency Initiative
EIU	Economist Intelligence Unit
ELEM	Macedonian power company
Elf	Société Nationale Elf Aquitaine
EMELEC	Empresa Eléctrica del Ecuador
EMG	East Mediterranean Gas
EMP	Energy Materials and Products
ENARGAS	State gas regulatory authority (Argentina)
ENARSA	Energía Argentina S.A.
ENEL	Ente Nazionale per l'Energia Elletrica
Eni	Ente Nazionale Idrocarburi
E.On	German energy group (Acronym used only)
EOR	Enhanced Oil Recovery
EPA	Economic Partnership Agreement
EPSA or EPSC	Exploration and Production Sharing Agreement or Contract
ERAP	Enterprise d'Activités et de Recherches Pétroliès (France)
ERBC	Energy Resources Board of Canada
ERR	Effective Royalty Rate

ESIA	Environmental and Social(or Socio-Economic) Impart Assessment
ETF	Energy Transit Facilities
EU	European Union
EV.	Expected Value (same as EMV)
EVN	Austrian energy supplier
EWC	East-West Center
E&P	Exploration and Production
F	Fahrenheit
ft	Feet
FASB	Financial Accounting Standards Board of the United States
FC	US Full Cost Accounting
FD	Finding and Development (Costs)
FDA	Finding and Development and Acquisition (Costs)
FDI	Foreign Direct Investment
FEED	Front End Engineering and Design
FERC	US Federal Energy Regulatory Commission
FET	Fair and Equitable Treatment
FI	Foreign Investment
FMV	Fair Market Value
F.o.b.	Free on board (used in transport of oil)
FPSO	Floating Production, Storage and Offloading System
FTA	Free Trade Agreement
FTP	First Tranche Petroleum
FVF	Formation Volume Factor
GA	General Assembly
GAAP	Generally Accepted Accounting Principles (e.g., the US GAAP)
GATT	General Agreement on Trade and Tariffs
GdF	Gaz de France
GGFR	Global Gas Flaring Reduction Partnership initiated by the World Bank
GHG	Greenhouse Gases
GNP	Gross National Product
GmbH	German corporate designation

GML	Yukos' shareholder company
GOR	Gas-Oil Ratio (typically cubic feet / BBL)
GTL	Gas to Liquids
Gvt.	Government
G&A	General and Administrative (Costs)
G&G	Geological and Geophysical
H_2S	Hydrogen sulfide
HC	Host Country
HC(s)	Hybrid contract(s)
HGA	Host Government Agreement
HSE	Health, Safety and Environment
HSSE	Health, Safety, Security and Environment
I-C_4	Iso-butane
I-C_5	Iso-pentane
IAS	International Accounting Standards
IBA	International Bar Association
IBRD	International Bank of Reconstruction & Development
ICAC	International Commercial Arbitration Court (Moscow)
ICC	International Chamber of Commerce
ICESCR	International Covenant on Economic, Social and Cultural Rights (UN)
ICJ	International Court of Justice
ICSID	International Centre for Settlement of International Disputes, (established by the ICSID Convention of March 18, 1965)
IDC	Intangible Drilling Costs (US concept)
IEA	International Energy Agency
IFC	International Finance Corporation
IGA	Inter-Governmental Agreement
IIA	International Investment Agreement
IIAPCO	Independent Indonesian American Petroleum Company
IIC	International Investment Claims
ILC	International Law Commission
ILM	International Legal Materials

ILO	International Labour Office
IMF	International Monetary Fund
IMO	International Maritime Organization
INECEL	State electricity utility (Ecuador)
INOC	Internationalized National Oil Company
INOGATE	Interstate Oil and Gas Transport to Europe
IOC	International Oil Company 국제석유회사
IOR	Improved Oil Recovery
IPA	International Petroleum E&P Agreement
IPC	Iraq Petroleum Company
IRCAN	Iranian Canada Oil Company
IRR	Internal Rate-of-Return
IRS	Internal Revenue Service (the US tax administrative agency)
ITC	(US) Investment Tax Credit
JENRL	Journal of Energy and Natural Resources Law
JI	Joint Interest under a JOA
JIB	Joint Interest Billing under a JOA
JMC	Joint Management Committee
JNOC	Japan National Oil Corporation
JOA	Joint Operating Agreement
JOB	Joint Operating Board
JOC	Joint Operating Committee
JSA	Joint Structure Agreement (Iran)
JSC	Joint Supervisory Committee
JV	Joint Venture (same as JVOA)
JVOA	Joint Venture Operating Agreement (same as JOA)
JWELB	Journal of World Energy Law & Business
km^2	Square kilometers
KCS	KazakhstanCaspieShelf
KEEI	Korea Energy Economy Institute 한국에너지경제연구원
KE-1	Kashagan East-1 well
KE-2	Kashagan East-2 well

KGM	Kyrgyzgazmunaizat (Petrobart case)
KMG	Kazmunaigaz
KOC	Kuwait Oil Company, the Kuwaiti NOC since the full nationalization of the initial KOC owned by BP and Gulf
KRG	Kurdistan Regional Government
KW-1	Kashagan West-1 well
LCIA	London Court of International Arbitration
LCM	Lower of Cost or Market
LDC	Local Distribution Company
LGR	Liquid Gas Ratio (typicall in BBLS/MMCF)
Liamco	Libyan American Oil Co.
LLC	Limited Company
LPG	Liquified Petroleum Gas
LNG	Liquified Natural Gas
LOE	Lease Operating Expenses
LSA	Legal Stability Agreement
m	Meters
m^3	Cubic meters
M	Thousand
MARPOL	International Convention for the Prevention of Pollution from Ships
MBBLS	Thousand barrels
MCC(s)	Modernized/modern concession contract(s)
MCF	Thousand cubic feet of gas at specified pressure and temperature conditions (1 BOE is equivalent to around 5.8/6 MCF)
MCFD	Thousand cubic feet of gas per day
MEP	Main Export Pipeline
MEPL	Marine Environmental Protection Law
MER	Maximum Efficient Rate
MFC	Most favored country
MFN	Most Favored Nation (treatment)
MFTEC	Ministry of Foreign Trade and Economic Cooperation (China)
MI	Mineral Interest

MIT	Multilateral Investment Treaty
MM	Million
mm	millimeter
MMBBLS	Million barrels
MMBOE	Million barrels of (Crude) oil equivalent
mmbpd	Million Barrels Per Day
MMBTU	One Million BTU
MMCFD	One million cubic feet per day at a specified pressure and temperature
MMS	US Mineral Management Service
MMT/yr	Millions of (metric) tons per year
mol	Molecular
mol vol	Molecular volume
% mol vol	Percent molecular volume
MPRDA	Mineral & Petroleum Resources Development Act
MSC	Maritime Safety Committee (of IMO)
MT(s)	Metric ton(s) 또는 millione tonnes
mw	Megawatt
MVM Rt	Hungarian electricity transmission utility
MVMT	Hungarian Electricity Trust
m^3/y	Cubic meters per year
N_2	Nitrogen (molecular nitrogen)
Nafta	North American Free Trade Association
$N-C_4$	Normal butane
$N-C_5$	Normal pentane
NGL	Natural Gas Liquids
NGO	Non-Governmental Organization
NEB	National Energy Board of Canada
NEI	Netherlands East Indies
NGL	Natural Gas Liquids
NGO	Non-Governmental Organization
NIOC	National Iranian Oil Company
NNPC	Nigerian National Petroleum Corporation, the NOC of Nigeria

No.	Number
NOC	National Oil and Gas Company, fully owned or primarily owned and controlled by a State (also called state-owned company)국영석유회사
NPC	National Petrochemical Company (Iran)
NPD	Norwegian Petroleum Directorate
NPV	Net percent value (Same as PV)
NT	National Treatment
NV	Netherlands Vereinigung(company designation = limited liability company)
N/A	Not applicable or not available
OAPEC	Organization of Arab Petroleum Exporting Countries
OAS	Organization of American States
ODIL	Ocean Development & International Law
OECD	Organization for Economic Cooperation and Development
OEPC	Occidental Exploration and Production Company
OGEL	Oil and Gas Energy Law (online journal)
OGJ	Oil and Gas Journal
OGJTR	Oil and Gas Law and Taxation Review
OGP	Oil and Gas Producers (association)
OKIOC	Offshore Kazakhstan International Operating Company
OLH	Organic Law of Hydrocarbons
ONGC	Oil and Natural Gas Company (India)
OPEC	Organization of Petroleum Exporting Countries
Opex	Operating Expenses
OPIC	Overseas Private Investment Corporation
OSA	Operating Services Agreement (Convenios Operativos)
OSPAR	Oslo Paris Convention (regional maritime treaty)
O&G	Oil and Gas
P_{50}	Probabilistic reserve figure-50th percentile
PCA	Permanent Court of Arbitration
PCIJ	Permanent Court of International Justice
PDVSA	Petróleo de Venezuela S.A.

PEMEX	Petróleos Mexicanos
Pertamina	Perusahaan Pertambangan Minjak dan Gas Bumi Negara (State Oil and Natural Gas Mining Enterprise)
Petrobrás	Petróleo Brasileiro S.A. (Brazilian Petroleum Corporation)
PIATO	Concessionnaire in Fraport case
PIR	Private Investment Regulations
PIW	Petroleum Intelligence Weekly
PLA	Petroleum Loan Agreement
PLN	Indonesian electricity utility
PPA	Power Purchase Agreement
PPI	Producer Price Index for industrial goods (US)
PSA	Production sharing agreement (same as PCS)
PSC	Production sharing contract (same as PCA)
psi	Pounds per square inch
PTT	Petroleum Authority of Thailand
PV	Present Value (same as NPV)
P&A	Plugged and abandoned
P/O	Profit Oil
P/R	Production to Reserves Ratio
QPC	Petroleum Development Company (Qatar)
Refican	Refining Associates, Ltd.
RF	Russian Federation
RFF	Resources for the Future Fund
RLI	Reserve Life Index
RMB	Ren Min Bi (Chinese currency unit)
RMMLF	Rocky Mountain Mineral Law Foundation
RMP	Revenue Management Plan
RO	Remainder Oil
ROR	Rate of Return (sometimes refers to IRR)
Rp	Rupiah (Indonesian currency unit)
RSA	Republic of South Africa
RSC(s)	Risk Services Contract(s)

RWE	Formerly Rhenisch-Westfälische Elektrizitätswerke AG (now known only by its acronym)
SA	Limited company status
SCC	Stockholm Chamber of Commerce (Arbitration Institute)
SCP	South Caucasus Pipeline (change in text from SPC)
SEIC	Sakhalin Energy Investment Company
SERL	Section on Energy and Natural Resources Law (of IBA)
SIA	Social Impact Assessment
SIAC	Singapore International Arbitration Center
SIAP	Social Impact Assessment Plan
SLD	Straight-line Decline
Socal	Standard Oil Company of California
SOCAR	Azeri state oil company
SPA	Sale and Purchase Agreement
SPE	Society of Petroleum Engineers
SRB	Special Remuneratory Benefit
SRC	Shared Risk Contract
SRI	Servicio de Rentas Internas
STOIIP	Stock Tank Oil Initially in Place
STOIP	Stock Tank Oil in Place
STPF	Severance Tax Permanent Fund
SUNAT	Peruvian tax authority
TAC	Technical Assistance Contract
TBD	Thousan barrels per day
TCF	Trillion Cubic Feet
TCO	Tenghiz Chevron Oil (company)
TDM	Transnational Dispute Management
TEA	Technical Evaluation Agreement
TFE	TotalFinaElf
TLCF	Tax Loss Carry Forward
TMB	thousand million barrels
TNCs	Transnational Corporations

TNK-BP	Joint venture between BP and Russian private entitytoeton of oil equivalent
TOPCO	Texaco Overseas Petroleum Co./ California Asiatic Oil Co.
TOTCO	Tchad Oil Transportation Company
TPA	Third Party Access
TRANSENER	Compañía de Transporte de Energía
TSA	Technical Service Agreement
t.s.c.f.	trillion standard cubic feet
TVO	Finnish nuclear power company
t/d	Tons/day
UAE	United Arab Emirates
UK	United Kingdom
UKOOA	UK Offshore Operators Association (now the Oil and Gas UK)
UN/U.N.	United Nations
UNCED	United Nations Conference on Environment and Development
UNCITRAL	United Nations Commission on International Trade Law
UNCLOS	United Convention on the Law of the Sea
UNCTAD	United Nations Center for Trade and Development
UNCTC	United Nations Center on Transnational Corporations
UNDP	United Nations Development Program
UNESCO	United Nations Educational, Scientific and Cultural Organization
UNFCCC	United Nations Framework Convention on Climate Change
UNIDROIT	United Nations International Law Association
UNTS	United Nations Treaty Series
US	United States
USGS	U.S. Geological Survey
USSR	Union of Soviet Socialist Republics
VAT	Value Added Tax
Vs. V. v.	Versus
WAGP	West African Gas Pipeline
WCED	World Commission on Environment and Development
WI	Working Interest

WPC	World Petroleum Congress
WMO	World Maritime Organization
WPT	US Windfall Profits Tax, repealed on August 23, 1988
WTO	World Trade Organization
Wt%	Weight percent
WWF	Name of NGO (formerly World Wildlife Fund)
YEPC	Yemen Exploration & Production Company
YPF	Yacimientos Petroliferos Fiscales, the former NOC of Argentina, now part of Repsol YPF
YPFB	Yacimientos Petroliferos Fiscales Bolivianos, the NOC of Bolibia
yr(s)	Year(s)
Z	Gas compressibility factor

Glossary(주요용어해설)

Abrogate: To officially abolish or repeal a treaty or contract through legislative authority or an authoritative act.

Abu Dahbi formula: A mechanism developed by OPEC in 1974 to recover the windfall profits accruing to international oil companies as a result of large price increase in crude oil.

Accelerated depreciation: Writing off an asset through depreciation or amortization at a rate that is faster than normal accounting straight-line depreciation. There are a number of methods of accelerated deprecation, but they are usually characterized by higher rates of deprecation in the early years than latter years in the life of the asset. Accelerated depreciation allows for lower tax rates in the early years.

Acreage: Amount of land area (or offshore area) under lease or associated with and/or governed by a production-sharing contract (PSC).

Ad valorem: Latin, meaning *according to value*. A tax on goods or property, based upon value rather than quantity or size. Royalties are typically and valorem, based upon value *at the wellhead*.

Affiliate: Two companies are affiliated when one owns less than a majority of the voting stock of the other or when they are both subsidiaries of a third parent company. A subsidiary is an affiliate of its parent company. (See **Subsidiary**)

amicus curiae: Friend of the court: advice formally offered to the court in a brief filed by an entity interested in, but not, a party.

Amortization: An accounting convention designed to emulate the cost or expense associated with reduction in value of an intangible asset (See **Depreciation**) over a period of time. Amortization is a non-cash expense. Similar to depreciation of tangible capital costs, there are several techniques for amortization of intangible capital costs:

- Straight Line Decline (SLD)
- Double Declining Balance (DDB)

- Declining Balance (DB)
- Sum of Year Digits (SYD)
- Unit-of-Production (UOP)

API: American Petroleum Institute.

API gravity: American Petroleum Institute measure of the density or weight of a crude oil. Measured in degrees as in "West Texas Intermediate is a 38°-40° API crude."

$$^{\circ}\mathrm{API} = \frac{141.5}{Sg} - 131.5$$

Sg=pecific gravity in grams per cubic centimeter.

Appraisal well: See **Delineation well.**

Aquifer: Porous water-bearing rock.

Arbitration: A process in which parties to a dispute agree to settle their differences by submitting their dispute to an independent individual arbitrator or group such as a *tribunal*. Typically, each side of the dispute chooses an arbitrator, and those two arbitrators choose a third. The third arbitrator acts as the chairman of the tribunal, which then hears and reviews both sides of the dispute. The tribunal then renders a decision that is final and binding.

Backwardation: When a commodity's current prices or spot price is greater than futures prices, the market is said to be *inverted* or in backwardation. (See **Contango**, which is the opposite of backwardation).

Basket: When term is often used to mean a hypothetical blend of crudes also referred to as a *coctail* for price reference purposes in the absence of arms-length sales.

Block: A license area or contract area; relates to each individual parcel of creage held by an oil company or a government.

Book value: (1) The value of the equity of a company. Book value per share is equal to the equity divided by the number of shares of common stock. Fully diluted book value is equal to the equity less any amount that preferred shareholders are entitled to, divided by the number of shares of common stock. (2) Book value of an asset or group of assets is equal to the initial cost less DD&A (effectively depreciation).

Branch: An extension of a parent company but not a separate independent entity. Subsidiary companies are normally taxed as profits and are distributed as opposed to branch profits, which are taxed as they accrue.

Brown tax: A tax that can be positive or negative. A *cash-flow based* Government (working interest) participation could be viewed this way. During the periods of investment, the government *pays*. During the periods or positive cash flow, the government *takes*.

Bubble point: Reservoir pressure at which gas in solution (in the oil) will bubble out of the host oil at the prevailing reservoir temperature.

Calvo clause: A relatively obsolete contract clause once promoted in Latin American countries where the contractor explicitly renounced the protection of its home government over its operation of the contract. THe objectives of the Calvo Doctrine were to direct disputes to local jurisdictions and avoid international arbitration.

Capitalization: All money invested in a company including long-term debt (bonds), equity capital (common and preferred stock), retained earings and other surplus funds. Market capitalization is stock price times the numbers of shares of common stock.

Capitalization rate: The rate of interest used to convert a series of future payments into a single present value.

Capitalize: (1) In an accounting sense, the periodic expending of capital costs such as through amortization, depreciation, or depletion. (2) To convert an (anticipated) income stream to a present value by dividing by an interest rate. (3) To record capital outlays as additions to asset value rather than as expenses.

Generally, expenditures that will yield benefits to future operations beyond the accounting period in which they are incurred are capitalized-that is, they are depreciated at either a statutory rate or a rate consistent with the useful life of the asset.

Carried interest: When a working interest partner in the exploration or development phase of a contract is paying a disproportionately lower share of costs and expenses than its working interest share. This occurs when government agencies such as the Oil Ministry or the National Oil Company (NOC) are *carried* through the exploration phase of a contract. In this case, the NOC is said to have a *back-in option*. Also in a farm-in agreement, typically, the company holding the original working interest will farm out a portion of the work obligation to another company and is carried through that portion of the work program. The company farming in then *carries* the original license holder through that phase, i.e. the original license holder then does not pay, or pays a disproportionately lower percentage.

Cash flow: Gross revenues less all associated capital and operating costs. Contractor cash flow is equal to gross revenues less all costs, government royalties, taxes, imposts, levies, duties and profit oil share, etc. It therefore represents contractor share of profits. Government cash flow typically consists of government royalties, taxes, imposts, duties, profit oil share, etc.

In a financial sense, net income plus depreciation, depletion and amortization and other non-cash expenses. Usually synonymous with cash earnings and operating cash flow. An analysis of all the changes that affect the cash account during an accounting period.

Central bank: The primary government-owned banking institution of a country. The central bank usually regulates all aspects of foreign exchange in and aout of the country. It actively intervenes in the acquisition and sale of its own currency in foreign exchange markets primarily to maintain stability in the value of the country's currency.

Commercial discovery: (Or commercial success) In popular usage, the term applies to any discovery that would be economically feasible to develop under a given fiscal system. As a contractual term, it often applies to the requirement on the part of the contractor to demonstrate to the government that a discovery would be sufficiently profitable to develop from both the contractor and government point of view. A filed that satisfied these conditions would then be *granted commercial status,* and the contractor would then have the right to develop the field.

Commingled production: Production of petroleum from more than one reservoir through a single wellbore or flowline without separate measurement.

Completion: Equipment and activities required after drilling a well in order to prepare the well for production of oil and/or gas.

Concession: An agreement between a government and a company that grants the company the right to explore for, develop, produce, transport, and market hydrocarbons or minerals within a fixed area for a specific amount of time. The concession and production and sale of hydro carbons from the concession are then subject to rentals, royalties, bonuses, and taxes. Under a concessionary agreement, the company would take title to gross production less government royalty oil *at the wellhead.*

Condensate: Light liquid hydrocarbons associated with gas, typically *pentanes plus*. (See **Hydrocarbon seires**).

Consortium: A group of companies operating jointly, usually in a partnership with one company as operator in a given permit, license contract area, block, etc.

Contango: The relationship between a commodity's futures prices and the current market price for the commodity. When futures prices are greater than current prices (such as spot prices or current contract prices), the market is said to be in *contango*. Contango is the opposite of *backwardation*.

Contractor: An oil company operating in a country under a PSC or a service contract on behalf of the host covernment for which it receives either a share of production or fees consisting of reimbursement of costs and remuneration.

Contractor take: Total contractor after-tax share of cash flow.

Cost insurance and Freight (CIF): is included in the contract price for a commodity. The seller fulfills his obligations when he delivers the merchandise to the shipper, pays the freight and insurance to the point of (buyer's) destination and sends the buyer the bill of lading, insurance policy, invoice, and receipt for payment of freight. The following example illustrates the difference between an FOB Jakarta price and a CIF Yokohama price for a ton of LNG. (See FOB)

FOB Jakarta $170/ton also called "netback price"

+ 30/ton freight Charge

CIF Yokohama $200/ton

Cost of capital: The minimum rate of return on capital required to compensate debt holders and equity investors for bearing risk. Cost of capital is computed by weighting the after tax cost of debt and equity according to their relative proportions in the corporate capital structure.

Cost oil: A term most commonly applied to PSCs that refers to the oil (or revenues) used to reimburse the contractor for exploration, development and operating costs incurred by the contractor.

Cost recovery: The means by which companies recover costs; same as deductions.

Cost recovery limit: Typically with PSCs in any given accounting period, there is a limit to the amount of deductions that can be taken for cost recovery purposes. The limit is usually quoted in terms of a percentage of gross revenues or gross production.

Unrecovered costs are carried forward and recovered in subsequent accounting periods if there is sufficient production.

Country risk: The risks and uncertainties of doing business in a foreign country, including political and commercial risks. (See **Sovereign Risk**)

Creeping nationalization or creeping expropriation: A subtle means of expropriation through expanding taxes, restrictive labor legislation, or labor strikes, withholding work permits, import restrictions, price controls, and tariff policies.

Crypto tax: This is a nontechnical reference to non-conventional (less direct) means by which governments may impose duties, levies, or financial requirements on an oil company. These elements rarely are captured in typical published *take* statistics. Examples include: social welfare development funds (written or unwritten), hostile audits, mandatory currency conversions, customs duty exemptions that are not honored, hiring and purchase quotas, inordinately long depreciation rates, inefficient procurement requirements, excessive immigration / visa requirements, etc.

damnum emergens: Loss, quantifiable in money, suffered to property and caused by extrinsic circumstances.

Debt service: Cash required in a given period, usually one year, for payments of interest and current maturities of principal on outstanding debt. In corporate bond issues, the annual interest plus annual sinking fund payments.

Delineation well: A well drilled in order to determine the extent of a reservoir also known as a *appraisal well.*

Depletion: (1) Economic depletion is the reduction in value of a wasting asset by the removal of minerals. (2) Depletion for tax purposes (depletion allowance) deals with the reduction of mineral resources due to removal by production from an oil or gas reservoir or a mineral deposit.

Depletion allowance: This is one type of *incentive* that a few governments use to encourage investment. Typically these allowances provide the companies a *deduction* for tax calculation purposes based on some percentage of gross revenues. The Filipino Participation Incentive Allowance (FPIA) in the Philippines has this characteristic. It allows the contractor group 7.5% of gross revenues as part of the service fee.

Depreciation: An accounting convention designed to emulate the cost or expense associated with reduction in value of a tangible asset due to wear and tear, deterioration or obsolescence over a period of time. Depreciation is a non-cash expense. There are several techniques for depreciation of capital costs:

- Straight-Line Decline
- Double-Declining Balance
- Declining Balance
- Sum-of-Year Digits
- Unit-of Production

Development cost: Costs associated with placing an oil or gas discovery into production. These costs typically consist of drilling, production facilities, and transportation costs.

Development drilling: Drilling that follows exploratory and appraisal drilling after a discovery.

Development well: A well drilled within a proven or known productive are a of an oil or gas reservoir.

Dew point pressure: The (gas) reservoir pressure below which liquids begin to condensate out of the gas at the prevailing reservoir temperature.

Dilution Clause: In a joint operating agreement, a clause that outlines a formula for the dilution of interest of a working interest partner, if that partner defaults on a financial obligation. (See **Withering Clause)**

Direct tax: A tax that is levied on corporations or individuals-the opposite of an indirect tax such as a value-added tax (VAT) or sales taxes.

Discounted cash flow analysis: Economic modeling of anticipated income versus expenditures over time. It is based upon estimated production rates, oil prices and costs, as well as royalties, taxes and other means of government take. The net result is a stream of cash flow over time. Cash received in the distant future is not as valuable as cash received now, so the time value of the cash flow is calculated factoring in time value of money to arrive at a *present value* equivalent.

Discounted rate: In discounted cash flow (DCF) analysis, the interest or cost of capital percentage used to calculate time value of money. The present value formula for a *payment* received at some future time n at a discount rate i is :

$$\text{Present value} = \text{future payment} \ / \ (1+i)^{n}$$

Where: present value of the future payment is a function of the discount rate i and time n.

For example, if a payment of $5 MM was to be received in 6 years (n=6) the present calue discounted at 10% (i=0.10) is.

Present value = $5 MM/$(1+0.10)^6$ = $5 mm/1.77156 = $2.82 MM

Disposal: This term usually refers to transportation and sales of crude or gas from the field.

Dividend withholding tax: A tax levied on dividends or repatriation of profits. Tax treaties normally try to reduce these taxes whether they are so named or simply operate in the same manner as a withholding tax.

Dollars-of-the-day: A term usually associated with cost estimates that indicate the effects of anticipated inflation have been taken into account. For example, if a well costs $5 MM right now in *today's dollars*- (the opposite of *dollars-of the-day)* then the cost of the well two years from now might be estimated at $5.51 MM in *dollars-of-the-day,* assuming a 5% inflation factor. Other associated terms:

- Dollars-of-the-day vs. Nominal Dollars
- Escalated vs. Non-escalated
- Current Dollars vs. Today's dollars
- Inflated vs. Real

Domestic market obligation (DMO): Some countries provide the state an option to purchase a certain portion of the contractor's share of production. This is called domestic market obligation or domestic requirement. Typically the purchase price for DMO crude is less than market price. Also local currency may be part of the price formula. There are many variations on this theme.

Domestication: A form of creeping nationalization where a host government enacts legislation that forces foreign-owned enterprises to surrender various degrees of ownership and/or control to nationals.

Double taxation: (1) In economics, a situation where income flow is subjected to more than one tier of taxation under the same domestic tax system-such as state/provincial taxes, then federal taxes or federal income taxes and then dividend taxes. (2) International double taxation is where profit is taxed under the system of more than one country. It arises when a taxpayer or taxpaying entity resident (for tax purposes) in one country generates income in another country. It can also occur when a taxpaying entity is resident for tax purposes in more than one country.

Double taxation treaty: Formal agreement between countries to reduce or eliminate double taxation. A bilateral tax treaty is a treaty between two countries to coordinate taxation provisions that would otherwise create double taxation. A multilateral tax treaty involves three or more countries fo rthe same purpose. The United States has few treaties with oil-producing nations.

Dual residence: When a taxpaying entity is resident for tax purposes in more than one country. This can happen when different countrieds apply the tests for determining residence, and the company passes the test in more than one country.

Dutch disease: When taxpaying entity is resident for tax purposes in more than one country. This can happen when different countries apply the tests for determining residence, and the company passes the test in more than one country.

Economic profit: Gross project revenues minus total costs that include exploration, development, and operating costs.

Economic rent: While there are a number of definitions, one common definition is: the difference between the value of production and the cost to extract it. The extraction cost consists of normal exploration, development, and operating costs as well as a share of profits for the industry. Economic rent is what the government try to extract as efficiently as possible.

Effective royalty rate: The minimum share of revenue (or production) the government will receive in any given accounting period from royalties and its share of profit oil.

Entitlements: The shares of production to which the operating company, the working interest partners, and the government or government agencies are authorized to lift. Entitlements are based on royalties, cost recovery, production sharing, working interest percentages, etc. (See **Lifting**)

Excise tax: A tax applied to a specific commodity such as tobacco, coffee, gasoline, or oil; based either on production, sale, or consumption.

Exclusion of areas: (See **Relinquishment**)

Expected monetary value (EMV): (See **Expected value**)

Expected value: A weighted average financial value of various possible outcomes such as either a discovery or a dry hole weighted according to the estimated likelihood (Estimated proability of success or failure) that either outcome might occur. (See

Expected monetary value)

Expense: (1) In a financial sense, a non-capital cost associated most often with operations or production. (2) In accounting, costs incurred in a given accounting period that are charged against revenues. To *expense* a particular cost is to charge it against income during the accounting period in which it was spent. The opposite would be *capitalize* the cost and charge it off through some depreciation schedule.

Exploration drilling: Drilling in an un-proved area. (See **Exploratory well**)

Exploratory well: A well drilled in an unproved area. This can include: (1) a well in a proved area seeking a new reservoir in a significantly deeper horizon, (2) a well drilled substantially beyond the limits of existing production. Exploratory wells are defined partly by distance from proved production and by degree of risk associated with the drilling. Wildcat wells involve a higher degree of risk than exploratory wells.

Expropriation: Similar to the concept of nationalization or outright seizure of confiscation of foreign assets by a host government. With expropriation, the confiscation is directed toward a particular company; nationalization is where a government confiscates a whole industry. Expropriation is legal but theoretically must be accompanied by prompt adequate and effective compensation and must be in the public interest.

Fair market value (FMV) of reserves: Often defined as a specific fraction of the present value of future net cash flow discounted at a specific discount rate. One common usage defines FMV at two-thirds to three-fourths of the present value of future net cash flow discounted at the prime interest rate plus 0.75 to 1 percentage point.

Fairway: (See **Trend**)

Farmee: The party farming-in.

Farm-in: (1) A lease or working interest obtained from another company in return for a consideration. (2) To receive a farm-in.

farmor: The party farming-out.

Farmout, farm out: (1) A lease or working interest granted to another company in return for a consideration. (2) To grant a farmout.

Farmout extension: Sometimes the NOC or the government will allow a contractor some additional time (an extension to the current contract phase) to find a partner.

Governments know that finding partners is an important way for companies to spread the risk of exploration.

Finding cost: The amount of money spent per unit (Barrel of oil or MCF of gas) in exploration divided by reserves added. There are numerous formulas but generally includes discoveries and revisions to previous reserve estimates. Some include acquisition costs of reserves.

Fiscal marksmanship: The ability of authorities to predict with any degree of accuracy or certainty the tax revenues that may fall due to be paid to the government. In the petroleum industry, it is particularly difficult to accurately estimate what revenues may be generated for countries with little or no exploration history.

Also the ability to determine the appropriate taxation scheme

Fiscal system: Technically the legislated taxation structure for a country including royalty payments. In popular usage, the term includes all aspects of contractual and fiscal elements that make up a given government-foreign oil company relationship.

Flare: Or "flaring"; burning of residue hydrocarbon gasses.

Flooding: Injection of water (*water flood)* or gas (*gas flood*) into or adjacent to a reservoir to increase oil recovery.

FOB (Free on Board): A transportation term that means the invoice price includes transportation charges to a specific destination. Title is usually transferred to the buyer at the FOB point by way of a bill of lading. For example, FOB New York means the buyer must pay all transportation cost from New York to the buyer's receiving point. FOB plus transportation costs equals CIF price. (See **Cost Insurance Freight [CIF]**)

FOB shipping point: Buyer bears transportation costs from point of origin.

FOB destination: Supplier bears transportation costs to the destination.

force majeure: An Act of God: performance of a legal obligation is prevented by a natural and unavoidable catastrophe that interrupts the expected course of events.

Foreign Corrupt Practices Act (FCPA): Sometimes referred to as *anti-bribery legislation*. It is illegal for a US company or individual to knowingly pay a bribe to a foreign official in order to obtain or retain business. This includes commissions or payments to agments or intermediaries with the knowledge that all or part of the payments will be given to a foreign official. The FCPA also has various recordkeeping and reporting requirements.

Foreign tax credit: Taxes paid by a company in a foreign country may sometimes be treated as *taxes paid* in the company's home country. These are creditable against taxes and represent a direct dollar-for-dollar reduction in tax liability. This usually applies to foreign income taxes paid and credited against home country income taxes. Other taxes that may not qualify for a tax credit may nevertheless qualify as deductions for home country income tax calculations.

Fork in the road: A cluase in an investment treaty which presents the investor with a choice between investment arbitration or litigation before the local courts of the host state. If the investor chooses the latter or an alternative procedure provided for in the contract, it loses forever the right to pursue its claim(s) in international investment arbitration.

Formation: A layer of rock or geological horizon that can be mapped. It has a distinct top and bottom. The formation is typically given a name such as the Red Wall Limestone or Kimmeridgian Shale.

Franked dividends: Dividends that have already been taxed at the corporate level and are therefore either not subject to withholding tax or the taxes paid are creditable against withholding taxes.

fumus boni juris: Appearance of good law or prima facie case.

Gas oil ratio (GOR): The number of cubic feet of natural gas produced with each barrel of oil produced. It is measured under surface conditions. Also known as *solution gas oil ratio.*

The engineer J.J.Arps had a rule of thumb; typically GOR for black oil is equal to reservoir depth divided by 10. For example, if oil was found at a reservoir depth of 7000 ft, then the amount of gas in solution would be equal to 700 cu ft per barrel (7000/10). This would not require substantial gas-handling facilities by world standards. However, some crudes can have a GOR of 3000 to 9000 cu ft per barrel or more.

Gazette: To officially announce license round offering or results, or publication of notification of acceptance of bids in official government publication (*gazette*). To gazette means to offer blocks-as in "The licenses have not been gazetted yet."

Geological horizon: A layer of rock that can be mapped. It has a distinct top and bottom. (See **Formation**)

Gold plating: When a company or contractor makes unreasonably large expenditure due to lack of cost cutting incentives. This kind of behavior could be encouraged where a contractor's compensation is based in part on the level of capital and operating expenditure, however, it is rare.

Government take: Government share of economic profits, typically expressed as percent. Total government share of production or gross cash flow from royalties, taxes, bonuses, profit oil.

There are a number of definitions, but the most succinct is: government take= government cash flow / gross project cash flow.

Graben: A block of rock that has dropped down (due to geologic faults) between two other blocks.

Gravity: (See **API gravity**)

Gravity-based structure (GBS): Concrete production or wellhead platform fixed to the sea floor by its own weight.

Gross benefits: In addition to the cash flow received by a government from petroleum operations, there are other benefits for a country to have foreign companies operating in-country, such as employment, added infrastructure, and technology transfer. The combination of these various economic benefits is known as the *gross benefits.*

Hard currency: Currency in which there is widespread confidence and a broad market such as that for the US dollar, the British pound, Swiss franc, or Japaneses yen. The opposite would be *soft currency,* where there is a thin market and the currency fluctuates erratically in value.

Heads up: When working interest partners are paying costs and expenses in proportion to their working interest percentages, they are said to be *heads up.* When one or more partners are being *carried,* they are *not* `heads up.

Hectare: Metric unit of are equal to 10,000 square meters, which also equals 2.471 acres.

High grade: A term used to describe the evaluation of acreage or a portfolio of prospects to determine which prospects or areas are best. It is used to determine which acreage to relinquish and or which prospects to drill first.

Horizon: A geological layer of rock or a formation (See **Formation**)

Hull formula: Compensation for expropriation in the language of many bilateral and multilateral investment treaties that states it should be "prompt, adequate and effective."

This is known as the *Hull formula*. Alternate wording found in other treaties includes, "fair and equitable", "reasonable", "market value at date of expropriation," etc.

Hurdle rate: Term used in investment analysis or capital budgeting that means that required rate of return in a discounted cash flow analysis. Projects to be considered viable must at least meet the hurdle rate should be equal to or greater than the incremental cost of capital.

Hydrocarbon series: The various components of crude oil and natural cas composed of carbon and hydrogen atoms, i.e. the praffin seried (a subset of the hydrocarbon series):

Paraffin Series (characterized by the formula CnH_{2n+2})

C_1	Methane	CH_4
C_2	Ethane	C_2H_6
C_3	Propane	C_3H_8
C_4	Butanes	C_4H_{10}
C_5	Pentanes	C_5H_{12}
C_6	Hexanes	C_6H_{14}
C_7	Heptanes	C_7H_{16}
C_8	Octanes	C_8H_{18}
C_9	Nonanes	C_9H_{20}
C_{10}	Decanes	$C_{10}H_{22}$

et cetera

Hydrocarbon system

in bonis: Solvent or not in receivership.

Incentives: Fiscal or contractual elements provided by host governments that make petroleum exploration or development more economically attractive. Includes such things as:

- Royalty holidays
- Tax holidays
- Tax credits
- Reduced government participation
- Lower government take
- Investment credits/ uplifts

- Accelerated depreciation
- Depletion allowances
- Interest expense deductions (cost recovery)

Inconvertibility: Inability of a foreign contractor to convert payments reveived in soft local currency into home country or hard currency such as dollars, pounds, or yen.

Indirect tax: A tax that is levied on consumption rather than income. Examples include value-added taxes, sales taxes, or excise taxes on luxury items. (See **Direct Tax**)

Injection: The process of pumping gas or water in a petroleum reservoir in order to maintain pressure and enhance production.

in statu nascendi: In the process of being born.

Intangible drilling and development costs (IDCs): Expenditures for wages, transportation, fuel, fungible supplies used in drilling and equipping wells for production.

Intangibles: All intangible assets such as goodwill, patents, trademarks, unamortized debt discounts, and deferred charges. Also, for example, for fixed assets the cost of transportation, labor, and fuel associated with construction, installation, and commissioning.

Internal rate of return (IRR): The discount rate used in discounted cash flow analysis that yields a present value of zero fo ra cash flow stream is known as the internal rate of return. Rate of return (ROR) systems are based on IRR thresholds and this causes some confusion-they are called ROR systems not IRR systems.

Investment credit: A fiscal incentive where the government allows a company to recover an additional percentage of tangible capital expenditure. For example, if a contractor spent $10MM on expenditures eligible for a 20% investment credit, then the contractor would actually be able to recover $12MM through cost recovery (See **Uplift**). These incentives can be taxable. Sometimes investment credits are mistakenly referred to as *investment tax credits.*

Jack-up rig: Offshore mobile drilling vessel with a drilling rig mounted on the hull and with at least 3 tall legs through the hull. It is floated into position like a barge and hoisted above the water when the legs are mechanically lowered to the see floor.

Joint operating agreement: Official contract between working interest partners (members of the contractor group) in a foreign concession or PSC. The JOA outlines rights and obligations of the operator and other working interest shareholders (members of the contractor group) and means by which partners will conduct themselves. It outlines the means by which an operating committee is established, authorizations for expenditure and budgets are governed, notification deadlines, lifting rules, cash calls, and so forth.

Joint venture: The term applies to a number of partnership arrangements between individual oil companies or between a company and a host government. Typically an oil company or consortium (contractor group) carries out sole risk exploration efforts with a right to devleop and discoveries made. Development and production costs then are shared pro rata between partners to the joint venture that may include the government.

jus cogens: A fundamental principle of international law which is accepted by the international community of states as a norm from which no derogation is ever permitted.

Lease option: A contractual right of an individual or a company to sign a lease, typically within a certain time frame and upon completion of some agreed-upon work such as a feasibility study, regional study, or regional data acquisition program.

Letter of credit: An instrument or document from a bank to another party indicating that a credit has been opened in that party's favor guaranteeing payment under certain contractual conditions. The conditions are based upon a contract between the two parties. Sometimes called a *performance letter of credit,* which is issued to guarantee performance under the contract.

Letter of intent: A formal letter of agreement signed by all parties to negotiations after negotiations have been completed, outlining the basic features of the agreement, but preliminary to formal contract signing.

Levy: To impose or collect a tax or fine.

License: An arrangement between an oil company and a host government regarding a specific geographical area and petroleum operations. In more precise usage, the term applies to the development phase of a contract after a commercial discovery has been made (See **Permit** or **Block**)

License area: A block or concession area governed by a PSC or other type of contract between an IOC and a host government.

License splitting: A company's option to segregate a license area into segments and find partners and negotiate farm-in/farm-out arrangements for a specific segment.

Lifting: When a company takes physical and legal possession of its entitlement of crude oil, which ordinarily consists of two components under a PSC, namely: cost oil and profit oil. Lifting agreements govern the rules by which partners will lift their respective shares and how adjustments are made if a party is over *lifter* or *under lifted*.

The liftings may actually be more or less than actual entitlements, which are based on royalties, working interest percentages, and a number of other factors. If an operator or partner has taken and sold more oil than it was actually entitled to, then it is in an *over lifter* position. Conversely, if a partner has not taken as much as it was entitled to it is in an *under lifted* position. (See **Nomination and Entitlements**)

Lifting agreement: (See **Lifting**)

Limitada: Business entity that resembles a partnership with liability of all members limited to their contribution and no general partner with unlimited liability. Normally treated as a partnership by the United States for tax purposes. Similar to a Limited Liability Company in the United States, although the limitada was the forereunner.

Liquid natural gas (LNG): Methane and ethane that is liquefied for shipment in specially designed refrigeration ships then re-gasified and distributed to customers through pipelines.

Liquid petroleum gas (LPG): A product of distillation and contains considerably more energy than natural gas. A cubic foot of natural gas contains roughly 100 BTUs of energy. A cubic foot of propane contains about 2500 BTUs.

London interbank offered rate (LIBOR): The rate most creditworthy international banks that deal in Eurodollars will charge each other. Thus, LIBOR is sometimes referred to as the Eurodollar Rate. International lending is often based on LIBOR rates. For example, a country may have a loan with interest pegged at LIBOR plus 1.5%.

Loss of bargain damages: In an action for breach of contract under English common law, the plaintiff is entitled to damages so as to put him in the same position, as far as money can do it, as he would have been in if the contract ahs ben performed.

lucrum cessans: Loss of a reasonable profit or earnings which may constitute part of a claim for damages or compensation.

Marginal government take: Same as government take but with costs assumed to be zero.

Marker crude: A *marker*, or *benchmark, crude*, is a widely traded crude oil used as a reference for setting prices for other crudes, (e.g., Brent, West Texas Intermediate, and Dubai are benchmark crudes).

Maximum cash impairment: Maximum negative cash balance in a cash flow projection.

Millenium wave: A pattern of unilateral state actions against investments of international energy companies which began in the early years of the twenty-first century.

Mixed companies: Latin American joint venture companies

Nationalization: Government confiscation of the assets held by foreign companies throughout an entire industry. (See **Expropriation**)

Net back: Many royalty calculations are based upon gross revenues from some point of valuation, usually the wellhead, the last valve off of a production platform, or at the boundary of a filed or license area. The point of sale, however may be different than the point of valuation, and the statutory royalty calculation may allow the transportation costs from the point of valuation to the point of sale to be deducted from the actual sale price-netted back. Downstream costs between the wellhead (point of valuation) and the point of sale are sometimes referred to as net back deductions.

Net book value: A method of valuing fixed assets on a balance sheet which reflects the original cost of the asset minus an allowance for depreciation.

Nomination: Under a lifting agreement, the amount of crude oil a working interest owner is expected to lift. Each working interest partner has a specific entitlement, depending upon the level of production, royalties, their working interest, and their relative position (i.e. under lifted or over lifted), etc. Ech working interest partner must notify the operator regarding the amount of oil it will lift. This is called *nominating*. Sometimes, depending upon the lifting agreement, the nomination may be more or less than the actual entitlement. (See **Lifting** and **Entitlements**)

Obsolescing bargain: The theory that a shift in bargaining power occurs between investor and host state after the investment has been made, creating the conditions for a demand for revisions by the state

Oil-in-place (OIP): Estimates of the quantity of liquid hydrocarbons held in the pore spaces of a reservoir rock. It is understood that it is virtually impossible to recover all of the oil in a reservoir. Therefore, an estimate of the percentage of the oil-in-place that might be recovered is required to estimate recoverable reserves. (See **Recovery**

factor)

OPEC (Organization of Petroleum Exporting Countries): Founded in 1960 to coordinate petroleum prices of the members. Members include:

Member	Date Joined	1993 Quota (1) MBOPD	June 2000 Production MBOPD
Abu Dhabi (UAE)	1967	2,161	2,280
Algeria	1969	750	1,250
Ecuador (2)	1960		
Gabon (3)	1975	287	
Indonesia	1962	1,330	1,490
Iran	1960	3,600	3,705
Iraq	1960	400	2,565
Kuwait	1960	2,000	2,150
Libya	1962	1,390	1,420
Neutral Zone		(4)	
Nigeria	1971	1,865	2,140
Qatar	1961	378	735
Saudi Arabia	1960	8,000	8,250
Venezuela	1960	2,359	2,940
		24,520	28,925

(1) Quota did not apply for the full year

(2) Dropped out at end of 1992

(3) Dropped out at end of 1996

(4) Quotas do not apply-production shared by Saudi Arabia and Kuwait and included in their production

Operator: The company directly responsible for day-to-day operations, maintaing a lease or license, and ensurin gthe rights and obligations of the other members of the contractor group are met.

Operating profit (or loss): The difference between business revenues and the associated costs and expenses exclusive of interest or other financing expenses, and extraordinary items or ancillary activities, Synonymous with net operating profit (or loss), operating income (or loss), and net operating income (or loss), economic profit (or loss) or cash flow.

OIPC (Overseas Private Investment Corporation): A US government agency founded under the Foreign Assistance Act of 1969 to administer the national investment guarantee program for investment in less developed countries (LDCs) through the issuance of insurance for risks associated with war, expropriation, and inconvertibility of payments in local currency.

Out-of round: A term that indicates licensing of particular blocks or licenses is conducted at a time other than during an official bid round. Usually these out-of-round situations occur when companies *nominate* particular acreage that is of interest due to recent discoveries or other situations.

Over lifting: Over/under lifting is the difference between actual contractor lifting during an accounting period and the contractor entitlements based upon cost recovery and profit oil in the case of a PSC. A lifting is the actual physical colume of crude oil taken and sold.

Overspill: In international taxation, a situation where a taxpaying company has a credit for foreign taxes that is greater than its corporate tzx liability in its home country so that it has an unused and/or unusable tax credit.

Pareto's law: The law of the trivial many and the critical few, is commonly known as the 80/20 rule. It has many applications and is an important analytical concept. It allows the analyst to maximize efficiency by concentrating efforts on key elements.

For example, in a portfolio of producing wells, if there is a large enough (statistically significant) sampling, 20% of the wells will likely produce 80% of the production. 20% of the wells will represent 80% of the value. In a given basin, it is likely that 20% of the fileds will hold 80% of the reserves.

pacta sunt servanda: Agreements must be kept; a basic principle of civil and international law.

periculum in mora: Danger in procedural delay.

Permit: In a loose sense, the term is used to describe any arrangement between a foreign contractor and a host government regarding a specific geographical area and petroleum operations. In a more precise usage, the term applies to the exploration phase of a contract before a commercial discovery has been made. (See **License**)

Pesification: Abandonment of the pegging of the peso to the dollar.

Petrophysics: The study of rock properties from either actual rock samples from the field, from coring and/or from logging methods.

Pood: Unit of measure of oil production (Azerbaijan). One pood equals 16 kilograms or roughly 62-62.5 poods per ton.

Posted price: The official government selling price of crude oil. Posted prices may or may not reflect actual market values or market prices.

Pour point: The lowest temperature at which a particular crude oil will flow. It is an indication of the wax content of the oil. Some of the famous Indonesian *waxy* crudes have pour points at nearly 100°F.

Present value: The value now of a future payment or stream of payments based on a specified discount rate.

Price cap formulas: A fiscal mechanism where government gets all or a significant portion of revenues above a certain oil or gas price. These formulas are typically characterized by a base price indexed to an inflation factor such as percentage change in the US Producer Price Index for example. The US windfall profits tax of the late 1970s and early 1980s was a variation on this theme. Malaysia and Angola have had such elements in their systems.

Prime lending rate: The interest rate on short-term loans banks charge to their most stable and creditworthy customers. The prime rate charged by major lending institutions is closely watched and is considered a benchmark by which other loans are based. For example, a less well-established company may borrow at prime plus 1%.

Produced water: Water associated with oil or gas that is produced along with the oil or gas.

Production platform: An offshore structure equipped for oil and gas production and processing. As opposed to a *wellhead platform* that is equipped for production only. Typically, production from a wellhead platform is piped to a production platform.

Production/Reserves ratio (P/R): The percentage of total ultimate recoverable reserves produced in a peak year of production (barrels divided by barrels=%). For example, the Murcheson filed in the UK sector of the North Sea produced at an average rate of 112,000 BOPD [40.8 MMBBLS] during 1983. With total ultimate recovery of 350 MMBBLS, this represented a P/R ratio of 11.6%.

This statistic is the inverse of the Reserves/Production ratio and/or the Reserve Life Index. These measures compare expected ultimate recovery with annual production rates (Barrels divided by barrels per year= years). For example, a company has 2400 MMBBBLS of oil reserves and produces 800 MBOPD [365 billion barrels per year]. The reserve life index is 8.2 years-about average for most wetern oil companies. This is a slightly abstract statistic because it represents how many *years* of production the company has *if* it produces at a constant rate with no decline.

Production sharing agreement (PSA): This is the same as a production-sharing contract (PSC). While at one time, this term was quite common, it is used elss frequently now; and the ter *PSC* is becoming more common-except in the former Soviet Union (FSLI) where *PSA* is preferred terminology.

Production sharing contract (PSC): A contractual agreement between a contractor and a host government whereby the contractor bears all exploration costs and risks and development and production costs in return for a stipulated share of the production resulting from this effort.

Productive horizon: A geological formation (horizon) that is known to be hydrocarbon-bearing in a given area or province.

pro forma: Latin for *as a matter of form*. A financial projection based upon assumptions and possible events that have not occurred. For example, a financial analyst may create a consolidated balance sheet of two non-related companies to see what the combination would look like if the companies had merged. Often a cash flow projection, for discounted cash flow analysis, is referred to as a pro forma cash flow.

Profit oil: In a PSC, the share of production remaining after royalty oil and cost oil have been allocated to the appropriate parties to the contract.

Progressive taxation: Where tax rates increase as the basis to which the applied tax increases, or, where tax rates decrease as the basis decreases; the opposite eof regressive taxation.

Prospect: A location where both geological and geophysical information and economic conditions indicate a feasible place to drill a well.

Prospectivity: This term deals with the exploration potential of an area and the chances for making commercial discoveries and the risks associated with exploration. An area with the potential for large discoveries and low costs and low risks would be considered highly *prospective*.

Protocol: (1) Culturally dictated forms of ceremony and etiquette that govern business relationships, meetings, and negotiations. (2) Formal document primarily used in republics of the FSU signed by parties who attend meetings or negotiations indicating various minor agreements or stages of agreement reached. These are not the same as a more formal letter of intent that usually signified that most of the negotiations have been concluded.

Rate of return (ROR) contracts: Sometimes referred to as *Resource rent royalties (or taxes), trigger taxes,* or the *World Bank Model.* The government collects a share of cash flows at specific threshold rate of return (using a method called *compound uplifting).* Once the accumulated value becomes positive, the government takes a specified share. An example is shown as follows:

ROR	Tax Rate
0-20%	0%
20-25%	30%
25-30%	50%
>30%	70%

rebus sic stantibus: A legal doctrine allowing for treaties to become inapplicable because of a fundamental change of circumstances.

Recoverable reserves: The hydrocarbon volumes expected to be produced economically and not left behind in the reservoir.

Recovery factor: The percentage of oil or gas in place expected to be produced. It is an estimate based upon consideration of the fluid properties such as viscosity and GOR, rock properties such as porosity and permeability, pressure gradients, well spacing, and the nature of the reservoir energy or drive mechanism.

Regressive tax: Where tax rates become lower as the basis to which the applied tax increases. Or, where tax rates increase as the basis decreases. This is the opposite of progressive taxation.

Relinquishment: This is a common contract term in exploration agreements that requires a certain percentage (often around 25%) of the original contract area be returned to the government at the end of the first phase of the exploration period. Usually additional relinquishment is required at the end of the second phase of the exploration period. Also referred to as *exclusion of areas.* Contracts typically have specific provisions for the timing and amount of relinquishment prior to entering the subsequent phases of the contract.

Reinvestment obligations: A fiscal term that requires the contractor/operator to set aside a specified percentage of profit oil or income after-tax that must be spent on domestic projects such as exploration.

Reserve life index: (See **Reserve/Production ratio**).

Reserve/Production ratio: This statistic compares expected ultimate recovery with annual production rate (barrels divided by barrels per year=years). For example, a company has 2400 MMBBBLS of oil reserves and produces 800 MBOPD [292 million barrels per year]. The reserves/production ratio (also called the reserve life index) is 8.2 years-about average for most western oil companies. This is a slightly abstract statistic because it represents how many *years* of production the company has *if* it produces at a constant rate with no decline.

This statistic is the inverse of the Production/Reserves ratio. (See **Production/ Reserves ratio**)

Reserve replacement ratio: The amount of oil and gas discovered in a goven period divided by the amount of production during that period.

Reservoir: A porous, permeable rock formation in which hydrocarbons have accumulated.

Reservoir pressure: The reservoir fluid pressure. (See **Hydrostatic Pressure**)

Resource rent tax (RRT): Some economists refer to additional profits taxes (peculiar to the oil industry) as a resource rent tax. Australia has a specific tax based upon profits, which is referred to as resource rent tax. Normally the RRT is levied after the contractor or oil company has recouped all capital costs plus a specified return on capital that supposedly will wield a fair return on investment. (See **Rate of Return Contract**)

restitutio in integrum: Remedy granted to erase the effects of specific circumstances such as duress or fraud on the performance of an obligation.

R factors: Some tax rates (and royalties, DMO, Gvt. Participation) are governed by pre-determined *payout* thresholds. stands for *ratio,* typically the contracts defines R as the ratio of X divided by Y. And X is defined as *cumulative receipts* and Y is defined as *cumulative expenditures.* Cumulative expenditures include both capital as well as operating cost. When I equals 1, this is the point at which the company has achived *payout*. Usually multiple thresholds are established. For example:

R	Tax Rate
0-1	40%
1-1.5	50%
1.5-2	60%
>2	70%

At the end of each accounting period, the R factor is calculated; and when a threshold is crossed, then the new tax rate would apply in the next accounting period.

Ringfencing: A cost-center-based fiscal (or contractual) device that forces contractors or concessionaires to restrict all cost recovery and/or deductions associated with a given license (or sometimes a given filed) to that particular cost center. The cost centers may be individual licenses or on a filed-byciled basis.

For example, with typical ringfencing, exploration expenses in one non=producing block could not be deducted against income for tax calculation purposes in another block. Under a PSC, ringfencing acts in the same way-cost incurred in one ringfenced block cannot be *recovered* from another block outside the ringfence. Most countries use ringfencing.

Risk capital: Typically the drilling, seismic, signature bonuses, and costs associated with the first phase of exploration. The money placed at risk to see if hydrocarbons can be found. Often these costs have very little chance of being recovered if hydrocarbons are not found.

Royalty holiday: A form of fiscal incentive to encourage investment and particularly marginal field development. A specified period of time, in years of months, during which royalties are not payable to the government. After the holiday period the standard royalty rates are applicable. (See **Tax Holiday)**

Royalty leakage: In Newfoundland the *incentive* payment portion of the fees for Halliburton services which would be deductible for calculating royalty was referred to as a possible source of *leakage* i.e. it would reduce government revenue from the royalty that allowed each deductions.

Royalty oil: A percentage of the production (or revenue) paid to the mineral rights owner (government typically) free and clear of the costs of production. This represents the government oil entitlement is a result of the royalty rate in the contract between the government and the international oil company (IOC).

Saturation: This term applies to accounting periods where there are unrecovered costs carried forward. The cost recovery mechanism is at its maximum (Saturated).

Seal: An impermeable rock capable of trapping hydrocarbons in a porous reservoir rock.

S curve: A mechanism in gas contracts with oil price linkage that limits the price response of gas when the linked oil prices fall outside fixed limits, using a floor and a ceiling (and thereby reduces the risk of a very large rise due to a spike in oil prices).

Seismic: A petroleum exploration method in which acoustic (sound) energy is put into the earth with a source such as dynamite, vibrating trucks, or air guns. The sound energy reflects off subsurface rock layers and is recorded by detectors (geophones) at the earth's surface. Images of the subsurface rock layers are made with seismic surveys to locate geological structures.

Two-dimensional (2-D) seismic is where data is =acquired along a single line of geophones. This has been the way data has been acquired for many years.

Three-dimensional (3-D) seismic is where data is acquired with a *grid* of multiple lines of geophones. This is a newer, more costly technology, but results have typically been quite good in terms of the quality of the data acquired.

Seismic option: A contractual arrangement between a host government and a contractor. The arrangement provides the contractor exclusive rights over a geographic area where it is obligated to shoot seismic data. After data acquisition, processing, and interpretation, the contractor has the right to enter into a additional phase of the agreement or a more formal contract with the government for the area, which usually includes a drilling commitment.

Seismic reflectors: When seismic data is acquired, there are some rocks in the subsurface that yield stronger responses *echoes* when the sound energy bounces back to the detectors (geophones) at the surface. These make it easier to *see* how the geological horizons or formations in the subsurface are folded or faulted.

Severance tax: A tax on the removal of minerals or petroleum from the ground, usually levied as a percentage of the gross value of the minerals removed. The tax can be levied on the basis of so many cents per barrel or per million cubic feet of gas.

Shelf company: An incorporated entity, which has no assets and/or income but has gone through the process of registration and licensing. Some operations in foreign countries are started with acquisition of a shelf company because of the long delays that can be experienced setting up and incorporating a company.

siège réel: The doctrine that a company is subject to the law of the country in which it has its real seat (usually where its central administration is located), rather than the law of the country in which it is incorporated.

siège social: A concept in international law for determining the nationality of companies where priority is given to effective rather than 'paper' nationality, requiring a genuine link to the corporate activity.

Sinking fund: Money accumulated on a regular basis in a separate account for the purpose of paying off an obligation or debt.

Sliding scales: A mechanism in a fiscal system that increase effective taxes, and/or royalties based upon profitability or some proxy for profitability such as increased levels of oil or gas production (most common). Ordinarily each tranche of production is subject to a specific rate and the term *incremental sliding scale* is sometimes used to further identify this.

Example :

Typical Sliding Scale Royalty:		Royalty
First Tranche	Up to 0,000 BOPD	5%
Second Tranche	10,001-20,000 BOPD	10%
Third Tranche	20,001-40,000 BOPD	15%
Fourth Tranche	>40,001 BOPD	20%

Sovereign risk: Also called country risk or political risk, this term refers to the risks of doing business in a foreign country where the government may not honor its obligations or may default on commitments. Encompasses a variety of possibilities including nationalization, confiscation, expropriation, etc.

Spot market: Commodities market where oil (or other commodities) is sold for cash, and the buyer takes physical delivery immediately. Futures trades for the current month are also called spot market trades. The spot market is mostly an over-the-counter market conducted by telephone and not on the floor of an organized commodity exchange.

Spot price: Also called the *cash price*. The delivery price of a commodity traded on the spot market.

Spud: The commencement of drilling operations when a drilling rig is in-place, and a drillbit begins to penetrate the earth.

State take: The government share of profits also referred to as government take. (Although there are some consulting firms that make a distinction between government take and state take.) There are a number of definitions but the most succinct is: state take=state cash flow/gross project cash flow.

Stay: The act of temporarily stopping a judicial proceeding by the order of a court or tribunal.

Subsidiary: A company legally separated from but controlled by a parent company who owns more than 50% of the voting shares. A subsidiary is always by definition an affiliate company. Subsidiary companies are normally taxed as profits are distributed as opposed to branch profits that are taxed as they accrue. (See **Affiliate)**

Sunk costs: Accumulated costs at any point in time or past costs. There are a number of categories of sunk costs.

- Tax loss carry forward (TLCF)
- Depreciation balance
- Amortization balance
- Cost recovery carry forward

Surrender: Surrender is often synonymous with relinquishment in the context of area reduction. However the term also is used to describe a contractor's option to withdraw from a license or contract at or after various stages in a contract (See **Relinquishment**).

Swanson's Rule: A statistical method for estimating the mean of distribution. The focus on the mean is because it is the one single value that best represents the complete distribution. And only the *means* from one distribution to another can be added. The mean is estimated by taking a *weighting* the 10th, 50th, and 90th percentile reserve estimates 30%, 40%, and 30% respectively and taking the weighted average.

Take-or-pay contract: A type of contract where specific quantities of gas (usually daily or annual rates) must be paid for, even if delivery is not taken. The purchaser may have the right in following years to take gas that 뭉 been paid for but not taken.

Tax: A compulsory payment pursuant to the authority of a foreign government. Fines, penalties, interest, and customs duties are not taxes.

Tax haven: A country where certain taxes are low or nonexistent, in order to increase commercial and financial activity.

Tax holiday: A form of fiscal incentive to encourage investment. A specified period of time, in years or months during which income taxes are not payable to the government. After the holiday period, the standard tax rates apply.

Tax loss carry forward (TLCF): In systems where expending of pre-production costs is allowed, a negative tax base can arise, referred to as a *tax loss carry forward (TLCF)*. Also a TLCF can originate in systems where bonuses are deductible for tax calculation purposes and may be expensed.

Tax treaty: A treaty between two (bilateral) or more (multilateral) nations that lowers or abolishes withholding taxes on interest and dividends or grants creditability of income taxes to avoid double taxation.

Technical cost factor: A cost index per unit such as barrels, mcf, or BOE at some parity between oil and gas. The index is based upon the capital costs per barrel plus one-half of all operating costs per barrel. For example, if a filed development is expected to cost US $300 MM for 100 MMBBLS of recoverable oil, the capital costs amount to $3/BBL. If operating costs over the life of the filed are expected to amount to $600 MM, then the technical cost factor would be $5/BBL. ($300 MM capital cost+$400 MM operating costs (full cycle)/2=$500 MM *technical costs)*. Technical costs factor then would be $500 MM/100 MMBBLS (or $5/BBL)

Thin capitalization rules: In countries where interest cost is recoverable or deductible, the government may introduce a backstop against the practice where overseas shareholders load the balance sheets of there in-country operations with debt, with the object of reducing host country tax exposure. Typically the government will impose an artificial (or *imputed)* capitalization structure such as 75% debt, or limit the debt/equity ratio to a certain percentage.

Tranche: Usually a quantity or percentage of oil or gas production that is subject to specific fiscal criteria. (1) The Indonesian first tranche production (FTP) of 20% means that the first 20% of production is subject to the profit oil split and taxation and this tranche of production is not available for cost recovery. (2) Sliding scale terms typically subject different levels of production (tranches) to different royalty rates, tax rates, or profit oil splits.

Transfer pricing: Integrated oil companies must establish a price at which upstream segments of the company sell crude oil production to the downstream refining and marketing segments. This is done for the purpose of accounting and tax purposes. Where intra-firm (transfer) prices are different than established market prices, governments will force companies to use a market price or a basket price for purposes of calculating cost oil and taxes.

Trap: A high area on the reservoir rock where oil and/or gas can accumulate. It is overlain by a cap rock (seal).

Treaty shopping: Seeking tax benefits and treaties in various countries in order to structure an appropriately situated business entity in a given country that would take advantage of benefits that would not ordinarily be available.

Trend: The area along which a petroleum play occurs. Sometimes referred to as a fairway.

Trigger letter: Formal notice of dispute under an international investment agreement, sent to host state by investor, specifically identifying alleged breaches (and opening up a period of amicable netotiations without prejudice to contractual rights).

Turnover: A financial term that means gross revenues. The term is commonly used outside of the United States.

Under lifting: (See **Over Lifting**)

Unit-of-production depreciation: Method of depreciation for capital costs. This method attempts to match the costs with the production those costs are associated with.

Formula for unit-of-production method

$$\text{Annual depreciation} = (C - AD - S)\ \frac{P}{R}$$

Where:

C = Capital costs of equipment

AD = Accumulated depreciation

S = Salvage value

P = Barrels of oil produced during the year*

R = Recoverable reserves remaining at the beginning of the tax year

* If there is both oil and gas production associated with the capital costs being depreciated, then the gas can be converted to oil on a thermal basis.

Uplift: Common terminology for a fiscal incentive whereby the government allows the contractor to recover some additional percentage of tangible capital expenditure. For example, if a contractor spent $10 MM on eligible expenditures and the government allowed a 20% uplift, then the contractor would be able to recover $12 MM. The uplift is similar to an investment credit. However, the term often implies that all costs are eligible where the investment credit applies to certain eligible costs, The term uplift is also used at times to refer to the built-in rate of return element in a rate of return contract.

Value-added tax (VAT): A tax that is levied at each stage of the production cycle or at the point of sale. Normally associated with consumer goods. The tax is assessed in proportion to the value added at any given stage.

Indirect taxes such as the VAT [or goods & services tax (GST)] place the company or contractor in the role of unpaid tax collector on behalf of the government. Sometimes referred to as a withholding tax.

Wildcat well: An exploratory well drilled far from any proven production. Wildcat wells involve a higher degree of risk than exploratory or development wells.

Windfall profit: A profit that results from an increase in the price of the product rather than from any increased effort on the part of the producer.

Withering Clause: (See **Dilution Clause)**

Withholding tax: A direct tax on a foreign corporation by a foreign government, levied on dividends or profits remitted to the parent company or to the home country, as well as interest paid on foreign loans.

Work commitment: The drilling and/or seismic data acquisition and processing obligation associated with any given phase of a PSC. This term is also used in the context of a farm-in agreement.

Working interest: The percentage interest ownership a company (or government) has in a joint venture, partnership, or consortium that bears 100% of the costs of production. The expense-bearing interests of various working interest owners during exploration, development, and production operations may change at certain stages of a contract or linces. For example, a partner with a 20% working interest in a concession may be required to pay 30% of exploration costs but only a 20% share of development costs (See **Carried interest**). with government participation, the host government usually pays no exploration expenses but will pay its pro rata working interest share of development and operating costs and expenses.

World Bank: A bank funded by approximately 130 countries and makes loans to LDCs. The official name of the World Bank is the International Bank for Reconstruction and Development.

각주달기와 인용방법에 관한 일러두기

- 아무런 표시없이 위 주 번호를 인용하면 같은 장 내의 자료이며 각주의 번호 앞에 숫자가 있으면 이는 해당인용문헌이 최초로 나오는 장을 표시한다.
- 동일한 문헌을 뒤에서 반복하는 경우 저자 뒤에 위 주 … 게재서, 게재논문 등으로 표시한다.
- 외국문헌의 인용은 blue book에 따라서, 한국문헌의 인용은 한국법학교수회에서 2000년 발행한 “논문작성 및 문헌인용에 관한 표준안”을 기초로 하나, 미국의 blue book에 따른 변형방법을 채택한다.
- 책인 경우 출판사는 표시하지 아니하였고 판수는 재판 이상의 경우에만 표시한다.
- 잡지에 게재된 논문의 경우 blue book과 같이 권수를 해당 잡지의 이름 앞에 아라비아숫자로만 표시하고 동일한 해에 발행된 잡지를 계속 면수를 매기지 않은 경우 권과 호 사이에 쌍점으로 권수와 호수를 구별한다. 면수는 잡지의 이름 뒤에 아라비아숫자로만 표시한다.
- 판례는 통상의 인용방법 뒤에 괄호로 가능한 한 범위 내에서 당사자의 이름을 표시하고 필요하면 사건의 내용도 간략하게 추가한다. 회사의 경우 주식회사나 Company, Inc. 등은 가능한 한 생략한다. 병합사건의 경우 사건번호 하나만 표시한다.
- 맞춤법과 띄어쓰기, 외래어표기, 문장부호는 문교부 맞춤법에 대한 고시, 국회사무처 법률용어의 표준화기준에 관한 예규, 법원행정처의 법률문장의 관행 및 용례, 법제처의 법문의 띄어쓰기 기준을 따르되 필요한 경우 이를 수정한다.
- 기존의 판례나 논문의 전제 시에 원문을 존중하지만, 일부 표현을 수정한 부분이 있고 각주는 일부만을 다시 알파벳으로 번호를 붙여서 편집하거나 전부 생략한다. 중간에 생략된 내용이 있는 경우 …으로 표시한다.

제01편

국제에너지자원—법과 정책

제1편은 국제에너지자원 자체에 대한 개관이다.

제1장에서 전세계를 기준으로 지금 어떤 에너지가 얼마만큼 소비되며 이러한 소비유형이 과거에 어떻게 변화하여 왔고 앞으로 어떻게 변화할 것으로 예상되는지를 논한다. 에너지의 생산에 관한 한 소비수요를 맞추기 위하여 생산된다고 보면 생산과 소비수요를 구분하여 별도로 논할 필요는 없을 것이다.

제2장은 제1장과 동일한 주제를 한국에 초점을 맞추어 살펴본다. 우리는 엄청한 에너지를 소비하지만 극히 미미한 양의 에너지를 생산하기 때문에 이러한 괴리에 따르는 국가정책적 고려가 필요하다. 따라서, 에너지의 원천별 정책목표는 무엇이어야 하며 이를 달성하기 위한 수단은 무엇인지 살펴본다. 에너지자립도 증진이 유일한 정책목표가 될 수는 없으며 이것이 과연 정당한 정책목표인지에 관하여서도 많은 논란이 있다는 점에서 정책목표 자체에 관한 보다 심각한 논의가 필요할 것이다.

제3장은 에너지의 여러 가지 원천 중에서 석유와 천연가스에 국한하여 이들 화석연료의 생산과 소비를 둘러싼 국가간 자본의 이동과 이를 규율하는 법체계의 기초를 논한다. 국가주권의 영토적 범위를 확정하고 국가주권이 그 지역적 범위내 화석연료에 대하여 가지는 권리는 무엇인지, 그리고 그 권리를 어떻게 행사할 수 있는지에 대하여 살펴본다.

제 1 장

세계의 에너지자원

1. 에너지자원의 현황

에너지는 통상 석탄 · 원유 · 천연가스를 포괄하는 화석연료에너지, 원자력에너지, 태양이나 바람 · 파도 · 조수간만의 차 등을 이용하는 재생에너지, 동식물 폐기물이나 자원작물 등을 이용하는 생물질에너지로 분류된다. 전기도 중요한 에너지원이지만 1차적인 에너지를 이용하여 만든 2차적인 에너지라는 점에서 독자적인 에너지로 분류되지 않는다. 에너지는 전기를 만드는 데에 필요하며 냉난방과 자동차, 석유화학산업 등에 사용되므로 인류의 생존과 성장에 필수불가결한 것이다. 그러나 에너지는 영원히 공급될 수는 없다. 따라서 인류는 미래의 에너지 수요와 공급을 전망하고 또한 계획하고자 한다. 미래에 대한 전망과 계획에는 과거와 현재에 대한 수치가 필요하다.

IEA, USEIA, 지경부 같은 공적 기구와 BP 같은 다국적기업, 한국에너지경제연구원(KEEI) 같은 연구소 등에서 많은 통계와 전망이 나오지만[1] 아래에서는 주로 BP의 수치를 기호로 한다.[2] 〈표 1-1〉에서와 같이 2010년은 2009년에 비하여 인류의 총에너지소비량이 5.6% 증가하여 2010년 총에너지 소비량은 12,000 million tonnes(MT)에 달한다. 이를 지역적으로 살펴보면 OECD가 5,568 MT로 46% 정도이며 중동은 5.8%, 아시아는 38.1%를 구성한다. 연료별로는 〈표 1-2〉에 따르면 석유가 4,028 MT로 34%, 천연가스가 2,858 MT로 24%, 석탄이 3,555 MT로 30%이므로 이들 화석연료가 전체 에너지소비량 중 차지하는 비율은 무려 88%에 달한다. 따라서 [그림 1-1], [그림 1-2]와 같이 과거 수십년간 인류의 화석연료에 대한 의존도는 절대적이라 할 수 있다. 앞으로를 전망하여 보면 [그림 1-3]과 [그림 1-4]에서 보듯이 2035년까지 매년 에너지수요는 40% 이상 증가할 것이며 생물질에너지와 재생에너지가

---

1) 우리나라 지경부는 미국의 US Energy Information Administration과 유사하게 국가에너지통계종합정보시스템(Korea Energy Statistics Information System)을 유지하고 있으며(www.kesis.net), KNOC이 Petronet.co.kr을, KORES가 KOMIS를 제공하고 있다.

2) BP Statistical Review of World Energy June 2011, 40 이하. bp.com에서 열람가능.

〈표 1-1〉 국가별/지역별 에너지소비량(00–10)(BP)

Million tonnes oil equivalent	2000	2001	2002	2003	2004	2005	2006	2007	2008	2009	2010	Change 2010 over 2009	2010 share of total
US	2313.7	2259.7	2295.5	2302.3	2348.8	2351.2	2332.7	2372.7	2320.2	2204.1	**2285.7**	3.7%	19.0%
Canada	302.3	298.2	303.1	312.3	315.2	325.3	323.6	329.0	326.6	312.5	**316.7**	1.3%	2.6%
Mexico	141.2	140.7	140.3	147.1	153.0	159.0	164.9	168.2	171.2	167.1	**169.1**	1.2%	1.4%
Total North America	2757.2	2698.5	2738.9	2761.8	2817.1	2835.4	2821.2	2870.0	2818.0	2683.7	**2771.5**	3.3%	23.1%
Argentina	59.3	58.6	55.3	59.8	63.1	67.6	71.3	74.6	77.5	75.1	**77.1**	2.6%	0.6%
Brazil	185.2	182.9	187.1	192.5	199.9	207.2	212.7	225.4	235.1	234.1	**253.9**	8.5%	2.1%
Chile	24.2	24.8	25.1	25.4	27.0	28.3	29.4	29.9	29.3	28.5	**28.4**	-0.4%	0.2%
Colombia	25.8	25.3	25.2	25.8	26.8	28.3	29.6	29.3	30.8	31.5	**32.2**	2.2%	0.3%
Ecuador	7.8	7.8	7.8	8.0	8.3	9.5	10.5	11.5	12.4	12.6	**13.0**	2.8%	0.1%
Peru	11.9	11.7	11.9	11.7	12.6	13.1	13.4	14.6	15.9	16.3	**18.3**	12.2%	0.2%
Trinidad & Tobago	11.4	11.9	13.1	14.6	13.9	15.8	20.6	20.6	21.9	20.8	**22.0**	5.4%	0.2%
Venezuela	65.2	69.2	69.4	61.4	68.6	71.3	77.3	77.0	80.9	80.6	**80.3**	-0.4%	0.7%
Other S. & Cent. America	73.7	75.7	77.1	80.2	80.2	81.3	83.4	86.7	86.0	85.4	**86.8**	1.6%	0.7%
Total S. & Cent. America	464.4	467.8	472.0	479.4	500.2	522.3	548.1	569.6	589.9	585.0	**611.9**	4.6%	5.1%
Austria	31.8	33.5	33.2	34.6	34.0	34.8	34.1	33.4	34.1	33.1	**33.3**	0.7%	0.3%
Azerbaijan	11.4	11.1	10.9	11.8	12.7	13.8	13.6	12.2	12.3	10.7	**10.0**	-6.9%	0.1%
Belarus	21.2	21.5	21.7	21.5	23.7	23.7	25.2	24.3	25.5	23.9	**24.4**	2.0%	0.2%
Belgium & Luxembourg	66.8	64.5	65.4	69.0	70.4	70.6	70.4	70.3	72.5	65.7	**69.8**	6.1%	0.6%
Bulgaria	17.9	18.5	18.4	19.8	19.2	19.9	20.7	19.8	20.1	18.3	**18.0**	-1.8%	0.2%
Czech Republic	40.1	41.6	41.6	43.7	44.9	44.8	44.4	43.6	42.0	40.6	**41.3**	1.7%	0.3%
Denmark	20.1	20.0	19.9	21.4	20.5	19.8	21.9	20.9	20.1	18.8	**19.5**	3.8%	0.2%
Finland	28.0	28.3	28.8	31.0	30.9	28.4	30.0	29.8	29.2	27.1	**29.1**	7.6%	0.2%
France	254.2	258.4	255.4	259.3	263.6	261.2	259.2	256.7	257.8	244.0	**252.4**	3.4%	2.1%
Germany	332.3	338.8	334.0	337.1	337.3	333.2	339.5	324.2	326.8	307.4	**319.5**	3.9%	2.7%
Greece	32.0	32.1	33.0	32.7	34.3	34.0	35.0	34.9	34.7	33.3	**32.5**	-2.3%	0.3%
Hungary	23.0	24.1	23.4	24.1	24.2	25.8	25.4	25.0	24.8	22.8	**23.4**	2.7%	0.2%
Republic of Ireland	13.7	14.7	14.5	14.1	14.6	15.0	15.5	15.8	15.7	14.6	**14.6**	◆	0.1%
Italy	176.5	177.5	176.3	182.3	185.8	186.2	185.4	182.4	180.7	168.3	**172.0**	2.3%	1.4%
Kazakhstan	41.3	42.1	47.4	53.1	61.6	64.5	66.7	68.2	73.0	67.5	**72.8**	7.9%	0.6%
Lithuania	7.0	8.1	8.6	9.1	9.2	8.4	8.1	8.7	8.7	8.0	**6.1**	-24.3%	0.1%
Netherlands	87.6	90.6	91.0	91.8	95.0	97.1	97.2	98.4	98.1	95.6	**100.1**	4.8%	0.8%
Norway	46.1	41.2	43.1	38.8	39.5	45.6	42.0	45.7	46.7	43.4	**41.8**	-3.7%	0.3%
Poland	88.5	88.9	87.7	90.1	91.7	91.5	94.9	95.8	95.4	91.3	**95.8**	4.9%	0.8%
Portugal	25.2	25.4	25.5	25.8	25.4	25.6	25.5	25.4	24.3	24.6	**27.1**	10.0%	0.2%
Romania	37.0	37.3	38.6	37.8	39.0	39.8	40.6	37.5	38.5	34.0	**34.5**	1.5%	0.3%
Russian Federation	620.4	631.4	633.1	649.9	657.8	657.4	675.3	685.8	691.0	654.7	**690.9**	5.5%	5.8%
Slovakia	18.1	18.6	18.7	18.1	17.6	18.8	17.8	17.2	17.7	16.0	**16.2**	0.8%	0.1%
Spain	130.2	134.0	135.9	144.4	151.1	153.4	154.1	158.6	157.1	146.1	**149.7**	2.5%	1.2%
Sweden	50.6	54.4	51.1	48.8	52.6	54.3	51.4	52.0	51.7	47.4	**50.7**	6.8%	0.4%
Switzerland	29.3	31.3	29.3	29.1	28.8	27.7	28.9	28.6	29.7	29.7	**29.0**	-2.4%	0.2%
Turkey	76.7	71.6	75.2	79.7	84.4	89.5	95.8	102.2	103.8	101.0	**110.9**	9.8%	0.9%
Turkmenistan	14.5	14.9	15.4	17.0	17.9	19.0	21.2	24.2	23.8	23.4	**26.0**	11.2%	0.2%
Ukraine	134.7	134.7	132.3	135.2	137.4	136.1	137.5	135.2	131.9	112.0	**118.0**	5.4%	1.0%
United Kingdom	224.1	226.7	221.9	225.6	227.4	228.3	225.6	218.4	214.9	203.6	**209.1**	2.7%	1.7%
Uzbekistan	50.9	54.0	55.5	51.4	48.8	46.2	45.6	49.0	52.6	48.0	**49.8**	3.9%	0.4%
Other Europe & Eurasia	70.0	71.4	73.8	77.3	81.4	81.0	79.2	80.9	82.4	79.0	**83.4**	5.6%	0.7%
Total Europe & Eurasia	2821.4	2861.3	2860.7	2925.4	2982.7	2995.4	3027.6	3025.6	3037.4	2853.8	**2971.5**	4.1%	24.8%
Iran	121.2	128.0	141.8	149.3	156.1	177.0	185.7	189.6	197.4	205.9	**212.5**	3.2%	1.8%
Israel	19.7	19.7	20.1	20.7	21.0	21.6	21.8	22.9	23.8	23.3	**23.7**	1.9%	0.2%
Kuwait	20.0	21.0	21.0	23.5	25.9	27.7	26.5	26.2	27.7	28.0	**30.6**	9.1%	0.3%
Qatar	10.7	12.3	13.0	14.1	17.0	20.8	22.3	22.8	23.6	24.2	**25.7**	6.1%	0.2%
Saudi Arabia	117.9	123.0	127.6	135.8	147.4	152.3	158.5	165.2	179.6	187.8	**201.0**	7.0%	1.7%
United Arab Emirates	48.4	54.0	53.5	57.3	61.0	64.6	67.4	74.3	85.5	83.0	**86.8**	4.6%	0.7%
Other Middle East	78.3	81.5	83.0	80.9	86.1	89.0	97.0	100.3	107.3	112.7	**120.7**	7.1%	1.0%
Total Middle East	416.2	439.5	460.0	481.5	514.5	553.0	579.1	601.4	644.9	664.9	**701.1**	5.4%	5.8%
Algeria	26.8	27.9	28.9	30.2	31.3	32.7	33.7	35.5	37.5	39.7	**41.1**	3.6%	0.3%
Egypt	49.8	52.6	53.6	57.0	59.6	62.5	65.8	69.9	74.1	76.5	**81.0**	6.0%	0.7%
South Africa	101.2	100.1	103.4	109.5	115.7	113.5	115.4	118.0	116.3	118.8	**120.9**	1.7%	1.0%
Other Africa	94.4	97.8	100.8	103.6	111.4	115.9	114.2	120.1	126.2	125.2	**129.5**	3.4%	1.1%
Total Africa	272.1	278.4	286.7	300.4	318.0	324.6	329.0	343.6	354.1	360.1	**372.6**	3.4%	3.1%
Australia	106.7	109.7	112.8	112.0	116.9	117.7	124.3	125.2	124.3	125.6	**118.2**	-5.8%	1.0%
Bangladesh	12.7	14.1	14.8	15.7	16.6	18.3	19.1	20.0	21.8	23.4	**23.6**	1.2%	0.2%
China	1038.2	1072.5	1140.4	1313.5	1531.3	1691.5	1858.1	1996.8	2079.9	2187.7	**2432.2**	11.2%	20.3%
China Hong Kong SAR	16.1	19.4	20.8	21.2	24.3	22.9	24.7	26.2	24.5	24.3	**25.9**	6.4%	0.2%
India	295.8	297.4	308.7	317.2	345.5	364.0	381.4	414.5	444.6	480.0	**524.2**	9.2%	4.4%
Indonesia	98.4	104.0	108.7	117.6	116.9	120.5	122.0	129.6	123.6	132.2	**140.0**	5.9%	1.2%
Japan	514.1	512.9	510.3	511.0	522.1	527.2	528.3	523.6	516.2	473.0	**500.9**	5.9%	4.2%
Malaysia	46.5	48.6	52.2	53.6	53.8	59.6	62.6	63.4	62.2	60.8	**62.9**	3.6%	0.5%
New Zealand	18.6	18.5	19.1	18.7	19.3	18.8	19.1	19.0	19.1	19.0	**18.9**	-0.5%	0.2%
Pakistan	44.3	45.5	47.4	52.4	56.8	58.9	61.8	65.1	64.8	66.9	**67.6**	1.1%	0.6%
Philippines	25.2	25.1	25.8	26.6	27.5	27.7	25.9	27.1	26.9	27.3	**27.6**	1.3%	0.2%
Singapore	33.4	37.2	38.7	37.5	42.7	48.4	51.5	56.8	59.4	63.4	**69.8**	10.2%	0.6%
South Korea	188.9	193.5	202.4	209.0	213.2	220.6	222.7	231.3	235.3	236.7	**255.0**	7.7%	2.1%
Taiwan	87.5	90.9	94.9	99.3	104.8	107.1	108.7	113.7	106.7	104.2	**110.5**	6.0%	0.9%
Thailand	68.0	70.9	76.3	81.3	87.7	93.1	95.0	97.9	100.6	102.4	**107.9**	5.4%	0.9%
Vietnam	17.7	19.9	21.4	22.5	28.7	29.8	32.3	34.9	36.7	42.1	**44.0**	4.5%	0.4%
Other Asia Pacific	39.0	39.9	38.8	40.2	41.5	44.0	45.4	43.2	44.6	46.9	**44.6**	-5.0%	0.4%
Total Asia Pacific	2651.2	2720.1	2833.5	3049.3	3349.5	3570.2	3782.8	3988.3	4091.5	4215.6	**4573.8**	8.5%	38.1%
Total World	**9382.4**	**9465.6**	**9651.8**	**9997.8**	**10482.0**	**10800.9**	**11087.8**	**11398.4**	**11535.8**	**11363.2**	**12002.4**	**5.6%**	**100.0%**
of which: OECD	5435.4	5405.0	5445.0	5511.4	5622.5	5667.3	5673.2	5714.6	5658.7	5378.4	**5568.3**	3.5%	46.4%
Non-OECD	3947.0	4060.6	4206.8	4486.4	4859.5	5133.7	5414.6	5683.8	5877.1	5984.8	**6434.1**	7.5%	53.6%
European Union	1720.4	1751.8	1738.9	1777.0	1805.9	1808.2	1814.0	1786.9	1783.9	1678.6	**1732.9**	3.2%	14.4%
Former Soviet Union	922.3	939.0	945.7	971.2	992.6	993.9	1018.2	1034.5	1044.1	972.1	**1023.3**	5.3%	8.5%

*In this Review, primary energy comprises commercially traded fuels, including modern renewables used to generate electricity.
◆Less than 0.05%.
Note: Oil consumption is measured in million tonnes; other fuels in million tonnes of oil equivalent.

〈표 1-2〉 국가별/지역별 에너지원별 소비량(09/10)(BP)

Million tonnes oil equivalent	2009 Oil	2009 Natural gas	2009 Coal	2009 Nuclear energy	2009 Hydro-electricity	2009 Renew-ables	2009 Total	2010 Oil	2010 Natural gas	2010 Coal	2010 Nuclear energy	2010 Hydro-electricity	2010 Renew-ables	2010 **Total**
US	833.2	588.3	496.2	190.3	62.5	33.6	2204.1	850.0	621.0	524.6	192.2	58.8	39.1	**2285.7**
Canada	97.1	85.0	23.3	20.2	83.6	3.3	312.5	102.3	84.5	23.4	20.3	82.9	3.3	**316.7**
Mexico	88.5	59.9	8.6	2.4	6.0	1.8	167.1	87.4	62.0	8.4	1.3	8.3	1.7	**169.1**
Total North America	1018.8	733.1	528.1	212.9	152.1	38.7	2683.7	1039.7	767.4	556.3	213.8	149.9	44.2	**2771.5**
Argentina	23.7	38.8	1.2	1.8	9.2	0.4	75.1	25.7	39.0	1.2	1.6	9.2	0.4	**77.1**
Brazil	107.0	17.8	11.7	2.9	88.5	6.2	234.1	116.9	23.8	12.4	3.3	89.6	7.9	**253.9**
Chile	15.6	2.8	3.7	–	5.6	0.7	28.5	14.7	4.2	3.7	–	4.9	0.8	**28.4**
Colombia	10.5	7.8	3.7	–	9.3	0.2	31.5	11.0	8.2	3.8	–	9.1	0.2	**32.2**
Ecuador	10.1	0.4	–	–	2.1	†	12.6	10.6	0.4	–	–	2.0	0.1	**13.0**
Peru	8.1	3.1	0.5	–	4.5	0.1	16.3	8.4	4.9	0.5	–	4.4	0.1	**18.3**
Trinidad & Tobago	2.1	18.8	–	–	–	†	20.8	2.1	19.8	–	–	–	†	**22.0**
Venezuela	33.7	27.5	†	–	19.5	–	80.6	35.2	27.6	†	–	17.4	–	**80.3**
Other S. & Cent. America	57.9	4.5	2.0	–	19.2	1.7	85.4	57.3	5.0	2.1	–	20.7	1.7	**86.8**
Total S. & Cent. America	268.6	121.6	22.9	4.7	157.9	9.3	585.0	282.0	132.9	23.8	4.9	157.2	11.1	**611.9**
Austria	13.0	8.4	2.2	–	8.2	1.4	33.1	13.0	9.1	2.0	–	7.8	1.4	**33.3**
Azerbaijan	3.2	7.0	†	–	0.5	†	10.7	3.3	5.9	†	–	0.8	†	**10.0**
Belarus	9.3	14.5	†	–	†	†	23.9	6.6	17.7	†	–	†	†	**24.4**
Belgium & Luxembourg	33.4	15.7	4.6	10.7	0.1	1.3	65.7	35.0	17.4	4.9	10.9	0.1	1.5	**69.8**
Bulgaria	5.6	2.1	6.3	3.4	0.8	0.1	18.3	4.2	2.3	6.6	3.5	1.3	0.2	**18.0**
Czech Republic	9.7	7.4	16.2	6.2	0.7	0.5	40.6	9.2	8.4	16.0	6.3	0.8	0.6	**41.3**
Denmark	8.5	4.0	4.0	–	†	2.3	18.8	8.7	4.5	3.8	–	†	2.5	**19.5**
Finland	9.9	3.2	3.7	5.4	2.9	2.0	27.1	10.4	3.5	4.6	5.2	3.2	2.2	**29.1**
France	87.5	38.0	9.9	92.8	13.1	2.8	244.0	83.4	42.2	12.1	96.9	14.3	3.4	**252.4**
Germany	113.9	70.2	71.7	30.5	4.2	16.9	307.4	115.1	73.2	76.5	31.8	4.3	18.6	**319.5**
Greece	20.2	3.0	8.1	–	1.3	0.6	33.3	18.5	3.3	8.5	–	1.7	0.6	**32.5**
Hungary	7.1	9.1	2.5	3.5	0.1	0.6	22.8	6.7	9.8	2.6	3.6	†	0.7	**23.4**
Republic of Ireland	8.0	4.3	1.3	–	0.2	0.7	14.6	7.6	4.8	1.4	–	0.1	0.7	**14.6**
Italy	75.1	64.4	13.1	–	11.1	4.6	168.3	73.1	68.5	13.7	–	11.2	5.6	**172.0**
Kazakhstan	12.1	22.1	31.7	–	1.6	–	67.5	12.5	22.7	36.1	–	1.5	–	**72.8**
Lithuania	2.6	2.5	0.1	2.5	0.3	0.1	8.0	2.7	2.8	0.2	–	0.3	0.1	**6.1**
Netherlands	49.4	35.0	7.9	1.0	†	2.3	95.6	49.8	39.2	7.9	0.9	†	2.2	**100.1**
Norway	10.3	3.7	0.3	–	28.8	0.3	43.4	10.7	3.7	0.5	–	26.7	0.3	**41.8**
Poland	25.3	12.0	51.9	–	0.7	1.4	91.3	26.3	12.9	54.0	–	0.8	1.9	**95.8**
Portugal	12.8	4.2	3.3	–	2.0	2.3	24.6	12.6	4.5	3.4	–	3.8	2.8	**27.1**
Romania	9.2	11.9	6.6	2.7	3.6	†	34.0	9.1	12.0	6.2	2.6	4.6	0.1	**34.5**
Russian Federation	135.2	350.7	91.9	37.0	39.9	0.1	654.7	147.6	372.7	93.8	38.5	38.1	0.1	**690.9**
Slovakia	3.7	4.4	3.5	3.2	1.0	0.1	16.0	3.7	5.1	2.7	3.3	1.3	0.1	**16.2**
Spain	75.7	31.1	10.5	11.9	6.0	10.9	146.1	74.5	31.0	8.3	13.9	9.6	12.4	**149.7**
Sweden	14.6	1.0	1.6	11.9	14.9	3.4	47.4	14.5	1.4	2.0	13.2	15.1	4.3	**50.7**
Switzerland	12.3	2.7	0.1	6.2	8.1	0.3	29.7	11.4	3.0	0.1	6.0	8.2	0.3	**29.0**
Turkey	28.2	32.1	32.0	–	8.1	0.5	101.0	28.7	35.1	34.4	–	11.7	1.0	**110.9**
Turkmenistan	5.4	17.9	–	–	–	–	23.4	5.6	20.4	–	–	–	–	**26.0**
Ukraine	13.3	42.3	35.0	18.8	2.7	†	112.0	11.6	46.9	36.4	20.2	2.9	†	**118.0**
United Kingdom	74.4	78.0	29.6	15.6	1.2	4.7	203.6	73.7	84.5	31.2	14.1	0.8	4.9	**209.1**
Uzbekistan	4.8	39.2	1.4	–	2.6	–	48.0	5.0	41.0	1.3	–	2.5	–	**49.8**
Other Europe & Eurasia	28.5	12.3	15.2	1.9	19.6	1.5	79.0	28.3	14.1	15.7	1.8	22.3	1.2	**83.4**
Total Europe & Eurasia	922.2	954.5	466.4	265.1	184.0	61.6	2853.8	922.9	1023.5	486.8	272.8	195.9	69.6	**2971.5**
Iran	85.1	118.2	1.1	–	1.5	†	205.9	86.0	123.2	1.1	–	2.2	0.1	**212.5**
Israel	11.5	4.1	7.7	–	–	†	23.3	11.2	4.8	7.7	–	–	†	**23.7**
Kuwait	17.2	10.9	–	–	–	–	28.0	17.7	12.9	–	–	–	–	**30.6**
Qatar	6.2	18.0	–	–	–	–	24.2	7.4	18.4	–	–	–	–	**25.7**
Saudi Arabia	117.2	70.6	–	–	–	–	187.8	125.5	75.5	–	–	–	–	**201.0**
United Arab Emirates	29.8	53.2	–	–	–	†	83.0	32.3	54.5	–	–	–	†	**86.8**
Other Middle East	77.3	34.7	–	–	0.7	†	112.7	80.2	39.6	–	–	0.9	†	**120.7**
Total Middle East	344.3	309.7	8.8	–	2.1	0.1	664.9	360.2	329.0	8.8	–	3.0	0.1	**701.1**
Algeria	14.9	24.5	0.2	–	0.1	–	39.7	14.9	26.0	0.3	–	†	–	**41.1**
Egypt	34.4	38.3	0.6	–	2.9	0.2	76.5	36.3	40.6	0.7	–	3.2	0.3	**81.0**
South Africa	24.7	3.0	87.7	3.1	0.2	0.1	118.8	25.3	3.4	88.7	3.1	0.3	0.1	**120.9**
Other Africa	77.0	23.2	5.5	–	18.9	0.6	125.2	79.0	24.4	5.7	–	19.6	0.7	**129.5**
Total Africa	150.9	89.0	94.1	3.1	22.2	0.9	360.1	155.5	94.5	95.3	3.1	23.2	1.1	**372.6**
Australia	42.2	27.7	51.7	–	2.6	1.3	125.6	42.6	27.3	43.4	–	3.4	1.5	**118.2**
Bangladesh	4.8	17.8	0.4	–	0.3	–	23.4	4.8	18.0	0.5	–	0.3	–	**23.6**
China	388.2	80.6	1556.8	15.9	139.3	6.9	2187.7	428.6	98.1	1713.5	16.7	163.1	12.1	**2432.2**
China Hong Kong SAR	14.0	2.8	7.6	–	–	†	24.3	16.1	3.4	6.3	–	–	†	**25.9**
India	151.0	45.9	250.6	3.8	24.0	4.6	480.0	155.5	55.7	277.6	5.2	25.2	5.0	**524.2**
Indonesia	59.2	33.6	34.6	–	2.6	2.1	132.2	59.6	36.3	39.4	–	2.6	2.1	**140.0**
Japan	198.7	78.7	108.8	65.0	16.5	5.4	473.0	201.6	85.1	123.7	66.2	19.3	5.1	**500.9**
Malaysia	24.5	30.3	4.0	–	2.0	†	60.8	25.3	32.2	3.4	–	2.1	†	**62.9**
New Zealand	6.8	3.5	1.6	–	5.5	1.6	19.0	6.9	3.7	1.0	–	5.5	1.8	**18.9**
Pakistan	20.6	34.6	4.7	0.6	6.4	–	66.9	20.5	35.5	4.6	0.6	6.4	–	**67.6**
Philippines	13.1	3.0	6.7	–	2.2	2.4	27.3	13.1	2.8	7.7	–	1.8	2.3	**27.6**
Singapore	56.1	7.3	–	–	–	–	63.4	62.2	7.6	–	–	–	–	**69.8**
South Korea	103.0	30.5	68.6	33.4	0.6	0.4	236.7	105.6	38.6	76.0	33.4	0.8	0.5	**255.0**
Taiwan	44.1	10.2	38.7	9.4	0.8	1.0	104.2	46.2	12.7	40.3	9.4	0.9	1.0	**110.5**
Thailand	49.9	35.3	14.5	–	1.6	1.1	102.4	50.2	40.6	14.8	–	1.2	1.1	**107.9**
Vietnam	14.1	7.2	14.0	–	6.8	–	42.1	15.6	8.4	13.7	–	6.3	–	**44.0**
Other Asia Pacific	13.4	4.6	22.1	–	6.8	†	46.9	13.5	4.8	18.9	–	7.4	†	**44.6**
Total Asia Pacific	1203.8	453.5	2185.3	128.2	218.0	26.7	4215.6	1267.8	510.8	2384.7	131.6	246.4	32.6	**4573.8**
Total World	**3908.7**	**2661.4**	**3305.6**	**614.0**	**736.3**	**137.4**	**11363.2**	**4028.1**	**2858.1**	**3555.8**	**626.2**	**775.6**	**158.6**	**12002.4**
of which: OECD	2094.8	1313.9	1049.5	511.5	299.4	109.5	5378.4	2113.8	1397.6	1103.6	520.9	309.5	123.0	**5568.3**
Non-OECD	1813.9	1347.5	2256.1	102.5	436.9	27.9	5984.8	1914.3	1460.5	2452.2	105.3	466.1	35.6	**6434.1**
European Union	670.2	412.6	259.9	202.5	74.1	59.3	1678.6	662.5	443.3	269.7	207.5	83.0	66.9	**1732.9**
Former Soviet Union	192.7	503.0	161.1	58.8	56.2	0.3	972.1	201.5	537.1	169.1	59.3	55.9	0.3	**1023.3**

*In this Review, primary energy comprises commercially traded fuels, including modern renewables used to generate electricity.
†Less than 0.05.
Note: Oil consumption is measured in million tonnes; other fuels in million tonnes of oil equivalent.

[그림 1-1] World Energy Consumption(85–10)(BP)

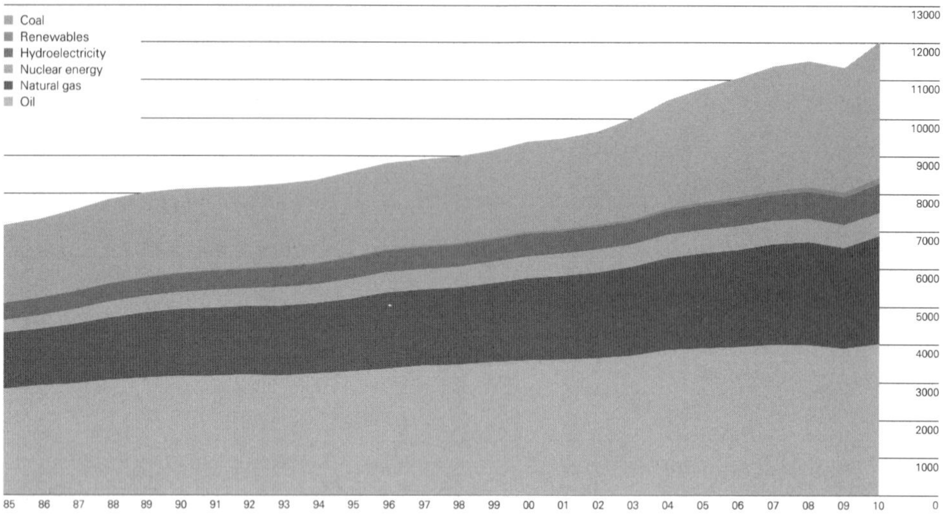

World primary energy consumption grew by 5.6% in 2010, the strongest growth since 1973. Growth was above average for oil, natural gas, coal, nuclear, hydroelectricity, as well as for renewables in power generation. Oil remains the dominant fuel (33.6% of the global total) but has lost share for 11 consecutive years. The share of coal in total energy consumption continues to rise, and the share of natural gas was the highest on record.

[그림 1-2] Regional Consumption Pattern(2010)(BP)

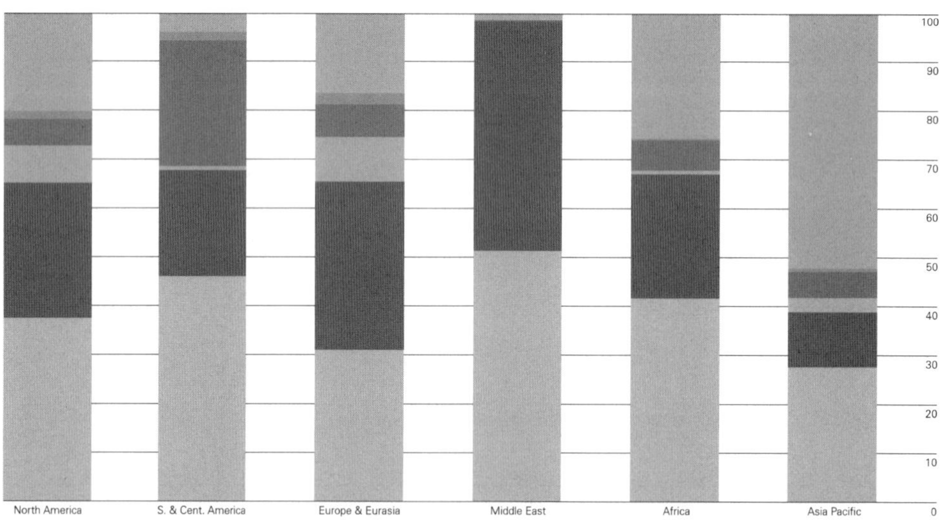

The Asia Pacific region continues to lead global energy consumption, accounting for 38.1% of the world total and for 67.1% of globa coal consumption. Within the Asia Pacific countries, coal is the dominant fuel, accounting for 52.1% of energy consumption.
Oil is the dominant fuel for all other regions except Europe and Eurasia, where natural gas is the leading fuel. In addition to being the largest consumer of coal, the Asia Pacific countries are also the leading users of oil and hydroelectric generation.
Europe and Eurasia are leading consumers of natural gas, nuclear power, and renewables in power generation.

차지하는 비중이 점차 증가하겠지만 석유와 천연가스가 여전히 주종을 이룰 것이다.[3)]

[그림 1-3] 2035년 세계 에너지원별 수요전망(IEA)

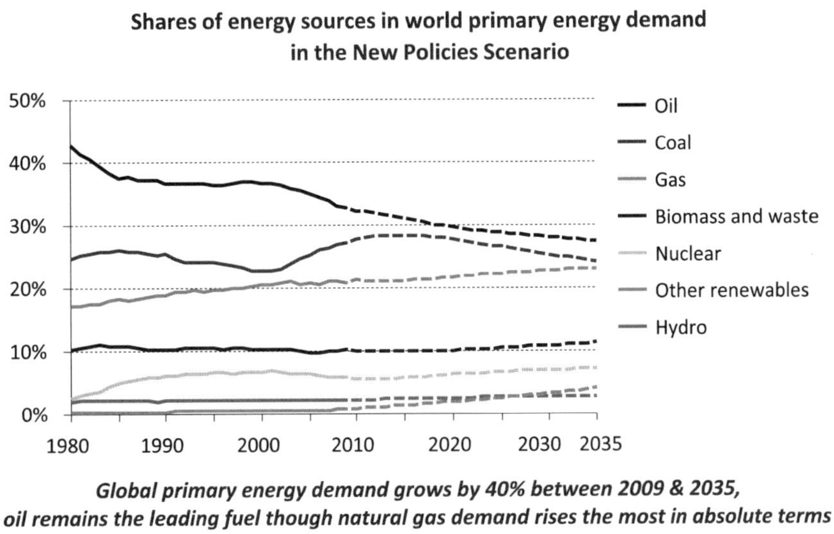

[그림 1-4] 2030년 세계 에너지원별 사용전망(BP)

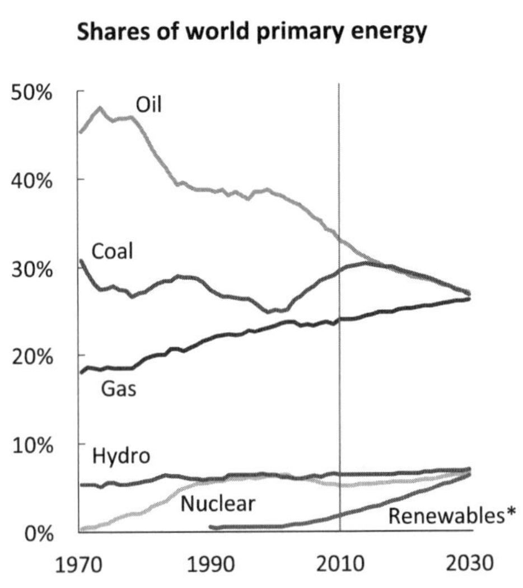

3) IEA, World Energy Outlook 2011, Key Graphics. iea.org에서 열람가능. BP Energy Outlook 2030 (Jan. 2012), 18페이지도 동일하게 전망.

노트와 질문

에너지분야의 법을 연구하려면 상당한 기술적 지식이 필요하다. 지질학적 기본지식은 물론[4] 측량단위나 각종 기관의 약어에 대하여도 익숙하여질 필요가 있다. 이런 필요에 대비하여 이 책의 모두에 약어표와 주요용어해설(glossary)을 첨부한다. www.iea.org상의 약어표, glossary, 측량단위에 대한 설명도 많은 도움이 된다.

2. 화석연료

가. 원유 매장량, 생산량, 소비량[5]

〈표 1-3〉에 따르면 2010년말 전세계의 확인된 원유매장량[6]은 총 1,383 TMB(thousand million barrels)로[7] 그 중 중동이 55%, 남미가 17%, 유럽이 10%, 아프리카가 9.5%, 아시아가 3.3%를 차지하고 있으며 과거 추세를 보면 확인매장량은 매년 100 내지 200 TMB씩 증가하고 있다. 〈표 1-4〉와 〈표 1-5〉는 전세계 국가/지역별 생산량과 소비량을 표시하고 있고 [그림 1-5]는 확인매장량과 생산량간 비율을 지역별로 표시하고 있다. 우리나라는 매장량이나 생산량은 0%이면서 2010년 하루 2,384 TBD를 소비, 전세계 소비량의 2.6%를 차지하여 미국, 중국, 인도, 사우디, 독일에 이어서 세계 6위이다.

4) Ernst E. Smith, et al, INTERNATIONAL PETROLEUM TRANSACTIONS 5-17 (3rd 2010).

5) BP, 위 주 1 자료, 6페이지 이하.

6) 확인매장량은 현재의 경제적 여건 및 운영조건하에서 합리적으로 확실한 정도로 추출될 수 있는 양을 의미하며 우리나라 금감원 표준공시기준상 확인가채매장량에 해당한다. 뒤 제2장 제3절 금감원, 유전(가스)개발사업 모범공시기준(2010. 3. 1. 개정)과 지경부고시 제2009-315호(2009. 12. 28.), 해외자원개발사업에 소요되는 자금의 융자기준 참조. 미국의 연방증권거래위원회 Reg. S-X, Rule 4-10와 Reg. S-K, Item 102, Subpart 1200도 참조, 자세한 배경설명은 17 CFR Parts 210, 211 et al. Modernization of Oil and Gas Reporting, 74 Fed. Reg. 2158 (Jan. 14, 2009). 확인매장량은 추정매장량, 가능매장량과 구별된다.

7) Tonnes와 Barrels 등 계량형간 전환표는 www.bp.com/conversionfactor.jsp 참조.

〈표 1-3〉 국가별/지역별 원유확인매장량(90/00/09/10)(BP)

	At end 1990 Thousand million barrels	At end 2000 Thousand million barrels	At end 2009 Thousand million barrels	At end 2010 Thousand million tonnes	At end 2010 Thousand million barrels	At end 2010 Share of total	At end 2010 R/P ratio
US	33.8	30.4	30.9	**3.7**	**30.9**	2.2%	11.3
Canada	11.2	18.3	32.1	**5.0**	**32.1**	2.3%	26.3
Mexico	51.3	20.2	11.7	**1.6**	**11.4**	0.8%	10.6
Total North America	96.3	68.9	74.6	**10.3**	**74.3**	5.4%	14.8
Argentina	1.6	3.0	2.5	**0.3**	**2.5**	0.2%	10.6
Brazil	4.5	8.5	12.9	**2.0**	**14.2**	1.0%	18.3
Colombia	2.0	2.0	1.4	**0.3**	**1.9**	0.1%	6.5
Ecuador	1.4	4.6	6.3	**0.9**	**6.2**	0.4%	34.1
Peru	0.8	0.9	1.1	**0.2**	**1.2**	0.1%	21.6
Trinidad & Tobago	0.6	0.9	0.8	**0.1**	**0.8**	0.1%	15.6
Venezuela	60.1	76.8	211.2	**30.4**	**211.2**	15.3%	*
Other S. & Cent. America	0.6	1.3	1.4	**0.2**	**1.4**	0.1%	28.9
Total S. & Cent. America	71.5	97.9	237.6	**34.3**	**239.4**	17.3%	93.9
Azerbaijan	n/a	1.2	7.0	**1.0**	**7.0**	0.5%	18.5
Denmark	0.6	1.1	0.9	**0.1**	**0.9**	0.1%	9.9
Italy	0.8	0.9	1.0	**0.1**	**1.0**	0.1%	25.0
Kazakhstan	n/a	25.0	39.8	**5.5**	**39.8**	2.9%	62.1
Norway	8.6	11.4	7.1	**0.8**	**6.7**	0.5%	8.5
Romania	1.5	1.2	0.5	**0.1**	**0.5**	◆	14.8
Russian Federation	n/a	59.0	76.7	**10.6**	**77.4**	5.6%	20.6
Turkmenistan	n/a	0.5	0.6	**0.1**	**0.6**	◆	7.6
United Kingdom	4.0	4.7	2.8	**0.4**	**2.8**	0.2%	5.8
Uzbekistan	n/a	0.6	0.6	**0.1**	**0.6**	◆	18.7
Other Europe & Eurasia	65.3	2.3	2.3	**0.3**	**2.4**	0.2%	17.5
Total Europe & Eurasia	80.8	107.9	139.2	**19.0**	**139.7**	10.1%	21.7
Iran	92.9	99.5	137.0	**18.8**	**137.0**	9.9%	88.4
Iraq	100.0	112.5	115.0	**15.5**	**115.0**	8.3%	*
Kuwait	97.0	96.5	101.5	**14.0**	**101.5**	7.3%	*
Oman	4.4	5.8	5.5	**0.7**	**5.5**	0.4%	17.4
Qatar	3.0	16.9	25.9	**2.7**	**25.9**	1.9%	45.2
Saudi Arabia	260.3	262.8	264.6	**36.3**	**264.5**	19.1%	72.4
Syria	1.9	2.3	2.5	**0.3**	**2.5**	0.2%	17.8
United Arab Emirates	98.1	97.8	97.8	**13.0**	**97.8**	7.1%	94.1
Yemen	2.0	2.4	2.7	**0.3**	**2.7**	0.2%	27.7
Other Middle East	0.1	0.2	0.1	**†**	**0.1**	◆	9.3
Total Middle East	659.6	696.7	752.6	**101.8**	**752.5**	54.4%	81.9
Algeria	9.2	11.3	12.2	**1.5**	**12.2**	0.9%	18.5
Angola	1.6	6.0	13.5	**1.8**	**13.5**	1.0%	20.0
Chad	–	0.9	1.5	**0.2**	**1.5**	0.1%	33.7
Republic of Congo (Brazzaville)	0.8	1.7	1.9	**0.3**	**1.9**	0.1%	18.2
Egypt	3.5	3.6	4.4	**0.6**	**4.5**	0.3%	16.7
Equatorial Guinea	–	0.8	1.7	**0.2**	**1.7**	0.1%	17.1
Gabon	0.9	2.4	3.7	**0.5**	**3.7**	0.3%	41.2
Libya	22.8	36.0	46.4	**6.0**	**46.4**	3.4%	76.7
Nigeria	17.1	29.0	37.2	**5.0**	**37.2**	2.7%	42.4
Sudan	0.3	0.6	6.7	**0.9**	**6.7**	0.5%	37.8
Tunisia	1.7	0.4	0.4	**0.1**	**0.4**	◆	14.6
Other Africa	0.9	0.7	0.7	**0.2**	**2.3**	0.2%	44.2
Total Africa	58.7	93.4	130.3	**17.4**	**132.1**	9.5%	35.8
Australia	3.2	4.9	4.1	**0.4**	**4.1**	0.3%	19.9
Brunei	1.1	1.2	1.1	**0.1**	**1.1**	0.1%	17.5
China	16.0	15.2	14.8	**2.0**	**14.8**	1.1%	9.9
India	5.6	5.3	5.8	**1.2**	**9.0**	0.7%	30.0
Indonesia	5.4	5.1	4.3	**0.6**	**4.2**	0.3%	11.8
Malaysia	3.6	4.5	5.8	**0.8**	**5.8**	0.4%	22.2
Thailand	0.3	0.5	0.4	**0.1**	**0.4**	◆	3.6
Vietnam	0.2	2.0	4.5	**0.6**	**4.4**	0.3%	32.6
Other Asia Pacific	1.0	1.3	1.3	**0.2**	**1.3**	0.1%	11.3
Total Asia Pacific	36.3	40.1	42.2	**6.0**	**45.2**	3.3%	14.8
Total World	**1003.2**	**1104.9**	**1376.6**	**188.8**	**1383.2**	**100.0%**	**46.2**
of which: OECD	115.4	93.3	92.0	**12.4**	**91.4**	6.6%	13.5
OPEC	763.4	849.7	1068.6	**146.0**	**1068.4**	77.2%	85.3
Non-OPEC‡	176.5	168.2	182.6	**25.5**	**188.7**	13.6%	15.1
European Union #	8.1	8.8	6.2	**0.8**	**6.3**	0.5%	8.8
Former Soviet Union	63.3	87.1	125.4	**17.3**	**126.1**	9.1%	25.6
Canadian oil sands•	n/a	163.3	143.1	**23.3**	**143.1**		
Proved reserves and oil sands	n/a	1268.2	1519.6	**212.0**	**1526.3**		

*More than 100 years.
◆Less than 0.05%.
†Less than 0.05.
‡Excludes Former Soviet Union.
#Excludes Lithuania and Slovenia in 1990.
•'Remaining established reserves', less reserves 'under active development'.

Notes: Proved reserves of oil – Generally taken to be those quantities that geological and engineering information indicates with reasonable certainty can be recovered in the future from known reservoirs under existing economic and operating conditions.
Reserves-to-production (R/P) ratio – If the reserves remaining at the end of any year are divided by the production in that year, the result is the length of time that those remaining reserves would last if production were to continue at that rate. **Source of data** – The estimates in this table have been compiled using a combination of primary official sources, third-party data from the OPEC Secretariat, *Oil & Gas Journal* and an independent estimate of Russian reserves based on information in the public domain. Canadian proved reserves include an official 26.5 billion barrels for oil sands 'under active development'. Venezuelan reserves are taken from the *OPEC Annual Statistical Bulletin*, that noted in 2008 that the figure included 'proven reserves of the Magna Reserve Project in the Orinoco Belt, which amounted to 94,168mb'. Reserves include gas condensate and natural gas liquids (NGLs) as well as crude oil.
Annual changes and shares of total are calculated using thousand million barrels figures.

〈표 1-4〉 국가별/지역별 원유생산량(00–10)(BP)

Thousand barrels daily	2000	2001	2002	2003	2004	2005	2006	2007	2008	2009	**2010**	Change 2010 over 2009	2010 share of total
US	7733	7669	7626	7400	7228	6895	6841	6847	6734	7271	**7513**	3.2%	8.7%
Canada	2721	2677	2858	3004	3085	3041	3208	3297	3251	3224	**3336**	4.3%	4.2%
Mexico	3450	3560	3585	3789	3824	3760	3683	3471	3167	2979	**2958**	-0.8%	3.7%
Total North America	13904	13906	14069	14193	14137	13696	13732	13616	13152	13474	**13808**	2.5%	16.6%
Argentina	819	830	818	806	754	725	716	699	682	676	**651**	-3.8%	0.8%
Brazil	1268	1337	1499	1555	1542	1716	1809	1833	1899	2029	**2137**	5.3%	2.7%
Colombia	711	627	601	564	551	554	559	561	616	685	**801**	16.9%	1.0%
Ecuador	409	416	401	427	535	541	545	520	514	495	**495**	◆	0.6%
Peru	100	98	98	92	94	111	116	114	120	145	**157**	8.2%	0.2%
Trinidad & Tobago	138	135	155	164	152	171	174	154	149	151	**146**	-4.3%	0.2%
Venezuela	3239	3142	2895	2554	2907	2937	2808	2613	2558	2438	**2471**	1.4%	3.2%
Other S. & Cent. America	130	137	152	153	144	142	139	141	139	133	**131**	-1.6%	0.2%
Total S. & Cent. America	6813	6722	6619	6314	6680	6898	6865	6635	6676	6753	**6989**	3.5%	8.9%
Azerbaijan	282	301	311	313	315	452	654	869	915	1033	**1037**	0.5%	1.3%
Denmark	363	348	371	368	390	377	342	311	287	265	**249**	-5.8%	0.3%
Italy	95	86	115	116	113	127	120	122	108	95	**106**	11.7%	0.1%
Kazakhstan	744	836	1018	1111	1297	1356	1426	1484	1554	1688	**1757**	4.4%	2.1%
Norway	3346	3418	3333	3264	3189	2969	2779	2551	2459	2358	**2137**	-9.4%	2.5%
Romania	131	130	127	123	119	114	105	99	98	93	**89**	-4.7%	0.1%
Russian Federation	6536	7056	7698	8544	9287	9552	9769	9978	9888	10035	**10270**	2.2%	12.9%
Turkmenistan	144	162	182	202	193	192	186	198	207	210	**216**	2.8%	0.3%
United Kingdom	2667	2476	2463	2257	2028	1809	1636	1638	1526	1452	**1339**	-7.7%	1.6%
Uzbekistan	177	171	171	166	152	126	125	114	114	107	**87**	-17.8%	0.1%
Other Europe & Eurasia	465	466	501	509	497	469	458	453	432	411	**374**	-7.0%	0.5%
Total Europe & Eurasia	14950	15450	16289	16973	17580	17542	17599	17815	17590	17745	**17661**	-0.4%	21.8%
Iran	3855	3892	3709	4183	4248	4234	4286	4322	4327	4199	**4245**	0.9%	5.2%
Iraq	2614	2523	2116	1344	2030	1833	1999	2143	2428	2442	**2460**	0.6%	3.1%
Kuwait	2206	2148	1995	2329	2475	2618	2690	2636	2782	2489	**2508**	0.6%	3.1%
Oman	959	960	904	824	786	778	742	715	754	813	**865**	5.9%	1.0%
Qatar	757	754	764	879	992	1028	1110	1197	1378	1345	**1569**	13.5%	1.7%
Saudi Arabia	9491	9209	8928	10164	10638	11114	10853	10449	10846	9893	**10007**	0.7%	12.0%
Syria	548	581	548	527	495	450	435	415	398	375	**385**	2.7%	0.5%
United Arab Emirates	2620	2551	2390	2695	2847	2983	3149	3053	3088	2750	**2849**	3.5%	3.3%
Yemen	450	455	457	448	420	416	380	345	304	287	**264**	-7.9%	0.3%
Other Middle East	48	47	48	48	48	34	32	35	33	37	**38**	0.6%	◆
Total Middle East	23547	23120	21858	23442	24981	25488	25675	25309	26338	24629	**25188**	1.7%	30.3%
Algeria	1578	1562	1680	1852	1946	2015	2003	2016	1993	1818	**1809**	-0.3%	2.0%
Angola	746	742	905	870	1103	1405	1421	1684	1875	1784	**1851**	3.8%	2.3%
Chad	–	–	–	24	168	173	153	144	127	118	**122**	3.5%	0.2%
Republic of Congo (Brazzaville)	254	234	238	217	223	245	278	228	241	270	**292**	8.1%	0.4%
Egypt	781	758	751	749	721	696	697	710	722	742	**736**	-0.6%	0.9%
Equatorial Guinea	91	177	230	266	351	358	342	350	347	307	**274**	-10.8%	0.3%
Gabon	327	301	295	240	235	234	235	230	235	230	**245**	6.5%	0.3%
Libya	1475	1427	1375	1485	1623	1745	1815	1820	1820	1652	**1659**	0.5%	2.0%
Nigeria	2155	2274	2103	2238	2431	2499	2420	2305	2113	2061	**2402**	16.2%	2.9%
Sudan	174	217	241	265	301	305	331	468	480	479	**486**	1.5%	0.6%
Tunisia	78	71	74	68	71	73	70	97	89	83	**80**	-4.7%	0.1%
Other Africa	144	134	135	138	164	154	153	166	162	155	**143**	-8.0%	0.2%
Total Africa	7804	7897	8028	8411	9336	9902	9918	10218	10204	9698	**10098**	4.2%	12.2%
Australia	809	733	730	624	582	580	551	555	555	520	**562**	8.9%	0.6%
Brunei	193	203	210	214	210	206	221	194	175	168	**172**	2.5%	0.2%
China	3252	3306	3346	3401	3481	3637	3705	3737	3809	3800	**4071**	7.1%	5.2%
India	726	727	753	756	773	738	762	769	768	754	**826**	9.8%	1.0%
Indonesia	1456	1387	1289	1176	1130	1090	996	972	1003	990	**986**	-0.3%	1.2%
Malaysia	735	719	757	776	793	759	747	763	768	739	**716**	-3.1%	0.8%
Thailand	176	191	204	236	223	265	286	305	321	331	**334**	0.9%	0.4%
Vietnam	328	350	354	364	427	398	367	337	317	345	**370**	6.9%	0.5%
Other Asia Pacific	200	195	193	195	235	286	305	320	340	329	**312**	-4.7%	0.3%
Total Asia Pacific	7874	7811	7837	7742	7854	7959	7940	7951	8054	7978	**8350**	4.9%	10.2%
Total World	**74893**	**74906**	**74700**	**77075**	**80568**	**81485**	**81729**	**81544**	**82015**	**80278**	**82095**	**2.2%**	**100.0%**
of which: OECD	21531	21314	21440	21174	20775	19870	19463	19114	18414	18471	**18490**	0.2%	22.1%
Non-OECD	53361	53592	53260	55900	59793	61616	62266	62430	63600	61807	**63605**	2.7%	77.9%
OPEC	31145	30640	29261	31020	33776	34951	35098	34757	35722	33365	**34324**	2.5%	41.5%
Non-OPEC‡	35734	35606	35907	35556	35385	34695	34315	33991	33466	33699	**34287**	1.9%	41.7%
European Union	3493	3285	3339	3128	2902	2659	2422	2388	2222	2088	**1951**	-6.5%	2.4%
Former Soviet Union	8014	8660	9533	10499	11407	11839	12316	12795	12827	13214	**13484**	2.0%	16.8%

*Includes crude oil, shale oil, oil sands and NGLs (the liquid content of natural gas where this is recovered separately). Excludes liquid fuels from other sources such as biomass and coal derivatives.

◆Less than 0.05%.

‡Excludes Former Soviet Union.

Note: Annual changes and shares of total are calculated using million tonnes per annum figures.

〈표 1-5〉 국가별/지역별 원유소비량(00-10)(BP)

Thousand barrels daily	2000	2001	2002	2003	2004	2005	2006	2007	2008	2009	**2010**	Change 2010 over 2009	2010 share of total
US	19701	19649	19761	20033	20732	20802	20687	20680	19498	18771	**19148**	2.0%	21.1%
Canada	1922	2008	2051	2115	2231	2229	2246	2323	2288	2179	**2276**	5.4%	2.5%
Mexico	1950	1939	1864	1909	1985	2032	2021	2070	2055	1996	**1994**	-1.2%	2.2%
Total North America	23574	23595	23676	24058	24947	25063	24955	25073	23841	22946	**23418**	2.1%	25.8%
Argentina	434	431	391	403	423	447	468	528	553	521	**557**	8.5%	0.6%
Brazil	2018	2047	2030	2010	2020	2078	2094	2234	2382	2399	**2604**	9.3%	2.9%
Chile	233	227	225	225	238	251	261	343	353	335	**314**	-6.0%	0.4%
Colombia	235	219	214	214	218	232	241	233	230	228	**238**	4.1%	0.3%
Ecuador	128	131	130	136	140	166	179	193	203	216	**226**	5.0%	0.3%
Peru	153	146	146	139	152	152	147	153	172	176	**184**	3.6%	0.2%
Trinidad & Tobago	36	28	33	31	36	41	46	47	43	41	**43**	4.4%	0.1%
Venezuela	559	622	660	535	582	628	661	682	712	729	**765**	4.7%	0.9%
Other S. & Cent. America	1060	1106	1112	1132	1138	1149	1173	1210	1186	1182	**1174**	-1.0%	1.4%
Total S. & Cent. America	4855	4956	4941	4825	4946	5144	5271	5622	5835	5827	**6104**	5.0%	7.0%
Austria	242	263	269	291	283	292	292	275	277	267	**269**	0.2%	0.3%
Azerbaijan	120	79	73	84	90	106	96	91	73	70	**73**	4.0%	0.1%
Belarus	140	146	142	146	151	145	162	150	166	188	**133**	-29.3%	0.2%
Belgium & Luxembourg	694	662	682	738	759	762	748	752	818	679	**715**	4.8%	0.9%
Bulgaria	88	92	96	111	104	110	117	114	119	124	**93**	-25.6%	0.1%
Czech Republic	167	177	172	184	202	210	207	205	209	204	**195**	-5.0%	0.2%
Denmark	212	202	197	189	186	194	198	200	196	178	**180**	2.0%	0.2%
Finland	220	218	222	235	221	229	222	223	222	209	**219**	4.9%	0.3%
France	1994	2010	1953	1952	1963	1946	1942	1911	1889	1822	**1744**	-4.7%	2.1%
Germany	2746	2787	2697	2648	2619	2592	2609	2380	2502	2409	**2441**	1.1%	2.9%
Greece	398	403	406	395	428	426	444	435	427	407	**372**	-8.7%	0.5%
Hungary	144	141	139	137	141	163	168	168	164	154	**146**	-5.2%	0.2%
Republic of Ireland	167	182	179	175	181	191	191	195	187	166	**158**	-5.0%	0.2%
Italy	1930	1920	1915	1900	1850	1798	1791	1740	1661	1563	**1532**	-2.7%	1.8%
Kazakhstan	162	179	191	209	223	236	239	247	266	253	**262**	3.2%	0.3%
Lithuania	48	55	51	50	53	57	58	58	63	54	**55**	3.0%	0.1%
Netherlands	879	922	933	943	984	1049	1070	1123	1069	1041	**1057**	0.9%	1.2%
Norway	204	216	211	229	219	221	226	235	225	230	**239**	3.5%	0.3%
Poland	426	419	430	441	469	487	512	531	549	549	**568**	3.9%	0.7%
Portugal	318	321	332	311	315	324	294	296	278	263	**261**	-1.6%	0.3%
Romania	197	211	220	194	224	218	214	218	216	195	**192**	-1.4%	0.2%
Russian Federation	2698	2688	2730	2755	2767	2777	2893	2913	3036	2936	**3199**	9.2%	3.7%
Slovakia	73	67	75	70	67	80	72	76	82	79	**78**	-0.3%	0.1%
Spain	1425	1469	1473	1533	1600	1623	1608	1629	1587	1525	**1505**	-1.6%	1.8%
Sweden	339	349	356	360	347	349	356	342	333	307	**305**	-0.1%	0.4%
Switzerland	260	278	264	257	255	260	266	241	256	260	**242**	-7.1%	0.3%
Turkey	668	636	647	653	658	648	629	651	657	615	**624**	1.7%	0.7%
Turkmenistan	78	82	85	94	96	101	103	111	117	120	**125**	3.6%	0.1%
Ukraine	253	284	282	295	310	296	308	338	323	288	**256**	-13.2%	0.3%
United Kingdom	1704	1704	1700	1723	1766	1806	1788	1716	1683	1610	**1590**	-1.0%	1.8%
Uzbekistan	154	148	145	156	144	111	112	103	101	101	**104**	2.8%	0.1%
Other Europe & Eurasia	433	461	483	509	526	553	562	602	608	581	**578**	-0.7%	0.7%
Total Europe & Eurasia	19582	19769	19750	19966	20198	20356	20498	20271	20358	19448	**19510**	0.1%	22.9%
Iran	1304	1322	1423	1509	1578	1641	1728	1718	1822	1787	**1799**	1.0%	2.1%
Israel	279	260	260	267	251	257	251	264	259	246	**242**	-2.2%	0.3%
Kuwait	249	253	273	296	327	359	333	338	359	399	**413**	2.8%	0.4%
Qatar	60	73	84	95	107	122	136	153	174	176	**220**	18.1%	0.2%
Saudi Arabia	1578	1622	1668	1780	1913	2001	2074	2200	2387	2624	**2812**	7.1%	3.1%
United Arab Emirates	396	400	439	488	515	553	584	617	654	616	**682**	8.4%	0.8%
Other Middle East	1155	1218	1228	1180	1255	1291	1390	1446	1499	1584	**1653**	3.8%	2.0%
Total Middle East	5021	5148	5374	5615	5946	6225	6497	6736	7153	7433	**7821**	4.6%	8.9%
Algeria	191	198	221	230	239	250	258	286	309	327	**327**	-0.1%	0.4%
Egypt	552	537	524	540	556	616	598	638	680	719	**757**	5.4%	0.9%
South Africa	457	468	480	497	513	514	528	549	528	517	**531**	2.7%	0.6%
Other Africa	1238	1278	1315	1344	1400	1455	1439	1501	1580	1632	**1676**	2.6%	2.0%
Total Africa	2439	2481	2540	2611	2708	2835	2824	2974	3097	3195	**3291**	3.0%	3.9%
Australia	831	839	839	844	855	886	918	925	936	931	**941**	0.8%	1.1%
Bangladesh	65	80	80	83	83	94	93	93	98	100	**101**	0.4%	0.1%
China	4766	4859	5262	5771	6738	6944	7437	7817	7937	8201	**9057**	10.4%	10.6%
China Hong Kong SAR	201	243	267	269	313	285	305	324	293	280	**324**	15.2%	0.4%
India	2261	2288	2376	2420	2574	2567	2571	2835	3068	3211	**3319**	2.9%	3.9%
Indonesia	1143	1160	1207	1232	1306	1295	1240	1270	1264	1289	**1304**	0.7%	1.5%
Japan	5530	5394	5320	5413	5238	5334	5203	5029	4836	4391	**4451**	1.5%	5.0%
Malaysia	460	479	521	513	533	523	512	542	544	538	**556**	3.3%	0.6%
New Zealand	131	131	136	147	148	152	155	155	156	147	**147**	0.1%	0.2%
Pakistan	371	365	356	319	324	311	354	385	386	412	**410**	-0.6%	0.5%
Philippines	347	345	329	329	338	315	285	300	265	281	**282**	0.1%	0.3%
Singapore	645	706	690	660	739	817	865	941	990	1067	**1185**	10.9%	1.5%
South Korea	2252	2259	2308	2326	2283	2308	2317	2389	2287	2326	**2384**	2.5%	2.6%
Taiwan	882	936	954	994	1039	1049	1039	1093	990	983	**1026**	4.7%	1.1%
Thailand	835	831	886	953	1040	1096	1097	1088	1090	1121	**1128**	0.5%	1.2%
Vietnam	171	186	205	220	263	258	254	283	300	304	**338**	10.4%	0.4%
Other Asia Pacific	242	252	251	256	268	269	270	284	275	283	**286**	0.9%	0.3%
Total Asia Pacific	21135	21353	21987	22750	24081	24503	24914	25753	25715	25866	**27237**	5.3%	31.5%
Total World	**76605**	**77304**	**78268**	**79823**	**82827**	**84126**	**84958**	**86428**	**85999**	**84714**	**87382**	**3.1%**	**100.0%**
of which: OECD	48128	48139	48106	48734	49566	49996	49794	49611	48053	45963	**46438**	0.9%	52.5%
Non-OECD	28477	29165	30162	31090	33262	34130	35164	36817	37946	38751	**40944**	5.5%	47.5%
European Union	14585	14754	14679	14769	14953	15101	15103	14801	14757	14016	**13890**	-1.1%	16.4%
Former Soviet Union	3743	3754	3799	3889	3942	3946	4095	4156	4291	4153	**4349**	4.6%	5.0%

*Inland demand plus international aviation and marine bunkers and refinery fuel and loss. Consumption of fuel ethanol and biodiesel is also included.
Notes: Annual changes and shares of total are calculated using million tonnes per annum figures.
Differences between these world consumption figures and world production statistics are accounted for by stock changes, consumption of non-petroleum additives and substitute fuels, and unavoidable disparities in the definition, measurement or conversion of oil supply and demand data.

[그림 1-5] 지역별 Reserve-to-production(R/P) ratio(90-10)(BP)

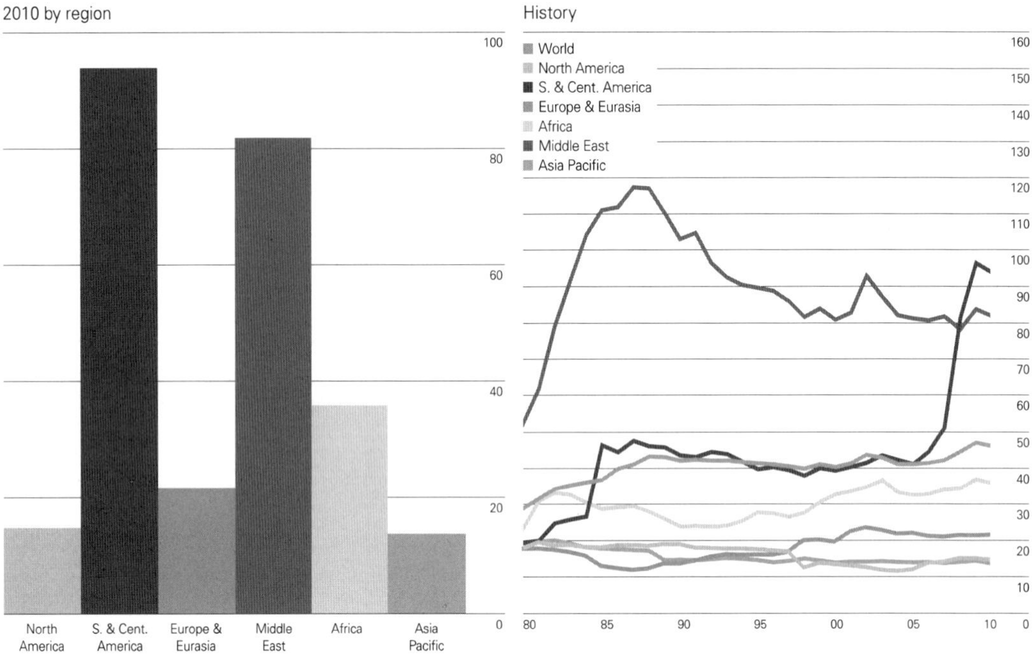

World proved oil reserves in 2010 were sufficient to meet 46.2 years of global production, down slightly from the 2009 R/P ratio because of a large increase in world production; global proved reserves rose slightly last year. An increase in Venezuelan official reserve estimates drove Latin America's R/P ratio to 93.9 years – the world's largest, surpassing the Middle East.

나. 천연가스 매장량, 생산량, 소비량

〈표 1-6〉에 따르면 전세계 천연가스 확인매장량은 187 TCM(Trillion cubic meters)로 중동이 40.5%, 유럽이 33.7%, 아시아가 8.7%를 차지하고 있다. 과거의 추세를 보면 매 10년 사이에 30 TCM 정도씩 확인매장량이 늘고 있다. 〈표 1-7〉, 〈표 1-8〉에 따르면 우리나라는 매장량이나 생산량은 0%이면서 2010년 소비량은 42.9 BCM(Billion cubic meters)로 전세계 천연가스 소비량의 1.4%를 차지하고 있다.

〈표 1-6〉 국가별/지역별 천연가스확인매장량(90/00/10)(BP)

	At end 1990 Trillion cubic metres	At end 2000 Trillion cubic metres	At end 2009 Trillion cubic metres	At end 2010 Trillion cubic feet	At end 2010 Trillion cubic metres	At end 2010 Share of total	At end 2010 R/P ratio
US	4.8	5.0	7.7	**272.5**	**7.7**	4.1%	12.6
Canada	2.7	1.7	1.7	**61.0**	**1.7**	0.9%	10.8
Mexico	2.0	0.8	0.5	**17.3**	**0.5**	0.3%	8.9
Total North America	9.5	7.5	9.9	**350.8**	**9.9**	5.3%	12.0
Argentina	0.7	0.8	0.4	**12.2**	**0.3**	0.2%	8.6
Bolivia	0.1	0.7	0.7	**9.9**	**0.3**	0.2%	19.5
Brazil	0.1	0.2	0.4	**14.7**	**0.4**	0.2%	28.9
Colombia	0.1	0.1	0.1	**4.4**	**0.1**	0.1%	11.0
Peru	0.3	0.2	0.4	**12.5**	**0.4**	0.2%	48.8
Trinidad & Tobago	0.3	0.6	0.4	**12.9**	**0.4**	0.2%	8.6
Venezuela	3.4	4.2	5.1	**192.7**	**5.5**	2.9%	*
Other S. & Cent. America	0.2	0.1	0.1	**2.3**	**0.1**	◆	22.4
Total S. & Cent. America	5.2	6.9	7.5	**261.6**	**7.4**	4.0%	45.9
Azerbaijan	n/a	1.2	1.3	**44.9**	**1.3**	0.7%	84.2
Denmark	0.1	0.1	0.1	**1.8**	**0.1**	◆	6.4
Germany	0.2	0.2	0.1	**2.4**	**0.1**	◆	6.5
Italy	0.3	0.2	0.1	**3.0**	**0.1**	◆	11.1
Kazakhstan	n/a	1.8	1.9	**65.2**	**1.8**	1.0%	54.9
Netherlands	1.8	1.5	1.2	**41.5**	**1.2**	0.6%	16.6
Norway	1.7	1.3	2.0	**72.1**	**2.0**	1.1%	19.2
Poland	0.2	0.1	0.1	**4.2**	**0.1**	0.1%	29.2
Romania	0.1	0.3	0.6	**21.0**	**0.6**	0.3%	54.4
Russian Federation	n/a	42.3	44.4	**1580.8**	**44.8**	23.9%	76.0
Turkmenistan	n/a	2.6	8.0	**283.6**	**8.0**	4.3%	*
Ukraine	n/a	1.0	1.0	**33.0**	**0.9**	0.5%	50.4
United Kingdom	0.5	1.2	0.3	**9.0**	**0.3**	0.1%	4.5
Uzbekistan	n/a	1.7	1.6	**55.1**	**1.6**	0.8%	26.4
Other Europe & Eurasia	49.7	0.5	0.4	**10.0**	**0.3**	0.2%	28.3
Total Europe & Eurasia	54.5	55.9	63.0	**2227.6**	**63.1**	33.7%	60.5
Bahrain	0.2	0.1	0.2	**7.7**	**0.2**	0.1%	16.7
Iran	17.0	26.0	29.6	**1045.7**	**29.6**	15.8%	*
Iraq	3.1	3.1	3.2	**111.9**	**3.2**	1.7%	*
Kuwait	1.5	1.6	1.8	**63.0**	**1.8**	1.0%	*
Oman	0.3	0.9	0.7	**24.4**	**0.7**	0.4%	25.5
Qatar	4.6	14.4	25.3	**894.2**	**25.3**	13.5%	*
Saudi Arabia	5.2	6.3	7.9	**283.1**	**8.0**	4.3%	95.5
Syria	0.2	0.2	0.3	**9.1**	**0.3**	0.1%	33.2
United Arab Emirates	5.6	6.0	6.1	**213.0**	**6.0**	3.2%	*
Yemen	0.2	0.5	0.5	**17.3**	**0.5**	0.3%	78.3
Other Middle East	†	0.1	0.1	**7.7**	**0.2**	0.1%	62.1
Total Middle East	38.0	59.1	75.7	**2677.0**	**75.8**	40.5%	*
Algeria	3.3	4.5	4.5	**159.1**	**4.5**	2.4%	56.0
Egypt	0.4	1.4	2.2	**78.0**	**2.2**	1.2%	36.0
Libya	1.2	1.3	1.5	**54.7**	**1.5**	0.8%	98.0
Nigeria	2.8	4.1	5.3	**186.9**	**5.3**	2.8%	*
Other Africa	0.8	1.1	1.2	**41.4**	**1.2**	0.6%	65.7
Total Africa	8.6	12.5	14.7	**520.1**	**14.7**	7.9%	70.5
Australia	0.9	2.2	2.9	**103.1**	**2.9**	1.6%	58.0
Bangladesh	0.7	0.3	0.4	**12.9**	**0.4**	0.2%	18.3
Brunei	0.3	0.4	0.3	**10.6**	**0.3**	0.2%	24.7
China	1.0	1.4	2.8	**99.2**	**2.8**	1.5%	29.0
India	0.7	0.8	1.1	**51.2**	**1.5**	0.8%	28.5
Indonesia	2.9	2.7	3.0	**108.4**	**3.1**	1.6%	37.4
Malaysia	1.6	2.3	2.4	**84.6**	**2.4**	1.3%	36.1
Myanmar	0.3	0.3	0.3	**11.8**	**0.3**	0.2%	27.5
Pakistan	0.6	0.7	0.8	**29.1**	**0.8**	0.4%	20.9
Papua New Guinea	0.2	0.4	0.4	**15.6**	**0.4**	0.2%	*
Thailand	0.2	0.4	0.3	**11.0**	**0.3**	0.2%	8.6
Vietnam	†	0.2	0.7	**21.8**	**0.6**	0.3%	66.0
Other Asia Pacific	0.3	0.3	0.4	**12.4**	**0.4**	0.2%	20.4
Total Asia Pacific	9.9	12.3	15.8	**571.8**	**16.2**	8.7%	32.8
Total World	**125.7**	**154.3**	**186.6**	**6608.9**	**187.1**	**100.0%**	**58.6**
of which: OECD	15.7	14.7	17.0	**603.8**	**17.1**	9.1%	14.7
Non-OECD	109.9	139.6	169.6	**6005.1**	**170.0**	90.9%	83.6
European Union	3.4	3.8	2.5	**86.2**	**2.4**	1.3%	14.0
Former Soviet Union	49.3	50.8	58.4	**2066.4**	**58.5**	31.3%	77.2

*More than 100 years.
†Less than 0.05.
◆Less than 0.05%.
n/a not available.
Notes: Proved reserves of natural gas – Generally taken to be those quantities that geological and engineering information indicates with reasonable certainty can be recovered in the future from known reservoirs under existing economic and operating conditions.
Reserves-to-production (R/P) ratio – If the reserves remaining at the end of any year are divided by the production in that year, the result is the length of time that those remaining reserves would last if production were to continue at that rate. **Source of data** – The estimates in this table have been compiled using a combination of primary official sources and third-party data from Cedigaz and the OPEC Secretariat.

〈표 1-7〉 국가별/지역별 천연가스생산량(00–10)(BP)

Billion cubic metres	2000	2001	2002	2003	2004	2005	2006	2007	2008	2009	**2010**	Change 2010 over 2009	2010 share of total
US	543.2	555.5	536.0	540.8	526.4	511.1	524.0	545.6	570.8	582.8	**611.0**	4.7%	19.3%
Canada	182.2	186.5	187.9	184.7	183.7	187.1	188.4	182.5	176.4	163.9	**159.8**	-2.5%	5.0%
Mexico	38.3	38.2	39.4	41.1	42.6	45.0	51.5	53.6	54.2	54.9	**55.3**	0.7%	1.7%
Total North America	763.7	780.1	763.3	766.6	752.8	743.3	763.9	781.6	801.5	801.6	**826.1**	3.0%	26.0%
Argentina	37.4	37.1	36.1	41.0	44.9	45.6	46.1	44.8	44.1	41.4	**40.1**	-3.0%	1.3%
Bolivia	3.2	4.7	4.9	6.4	9.8	11.9	12.9	13.8	14.3	12.3	**14.4**	16.8%	0.4%
Brazil	7.5	7.7	9.2	10.0	11.0	11.0	11.3	11.2	13.7	11.7	**14.4**	23.5%	0.5%
Colombia	5.9	6.1	6.2	6.1	6.4	6.7	7.0	7.5	9.1	10.5	**11.3**	7.2%	0.4%
Peru	0.3	0.4	0.4	0.5	0.9	1.5	1.8	2.7	3.4	3.5	**7.2**	108.4%	0.2%
Trinidad & Tobago	14.5	15.5	18.0	26.3	27.3	31.0	36.4	39.0	39.3	40.6	**42.4**	4.4%	1.3%
Venezuela	27.9	29.6	28.4	25.2	28.4	27.4	31.5	29.5	30.0	28.7	**28.5**	-0.7%	0.9%
Other S. & Cent. America	3.4	3.5	3.4	3.1	3.1	3.4	4.1	3.9	3.7	3.2	**2.9**	-9.9%	0.1%
Total S. & Cent. America	100.2	104.5	106.7	118.7	131.7	138.6	151.1	152.5	157.6	151.9	**161.2**	6.2%	5.0%
Azerbaijan	5.1	5.0	4.7	4.6	4.5	5.2	6.1	9.8	14.8	14.8	**15.1**	2.2%	0.5%
Denmark	8.2	8.4	8.4	8.0	9.4	10.4	10.4	9.2	10.1	8.4	**8.2**	-3.0%	0.3%
Germany	16.9	17.0	17.0	17.7	16.4	15.8	15.6	14.3	13.0	12.2	**10.6**	-12.7%	0.3%
Italy	15.2	14.0	13.4	12.7	11.9	11.1	10.1	8.9	8.5	7.3	**7.6**	3.6%	0.2%
Kazakhstan	10.4	10.5	10.2	12.6	20.0	22.6	23.9	26.8	29.8	32.5	**33.6**	3.3%	1.1%
Netherlands	58.1	62.4	60.3	58.1	68.5	62.5	61.6	60.5	66.6	62.7	**70.5**	12.4%	2.2%
Norway	49.7	53.9	65.5	73.1	78.5	85.0	87.6	89.7	99.3	103.7	**106.4**	2.5%	3.3%
Poland	3.7	3.9	4.0	4.0	4.4	4.3	4.3	4.3	4.1	4.1	**4.1**	0.5%	0.1%
Romania	13.8	13.6	13.2	13.0	12.8	12.4	11.9	11.5	11.4	11.3	**10.9**	-2.9%	0.3%
Russian Federation	528.5	526.2	538.8	561.5	573.3	580.1	595.2	592.0	601.7	527.7	**588.9**	11.6%	18.4%
Turkmenistan	42.5	46.4	48.4	53.5	52.8	57.0	60.4	65.4	66.1	36.4	**42.4**	16.4%	1.3%
Ukraine	16.2	16.6	17.0	17.6	18.4	18.6	18.7	18.7	19.0	19.3	**18.6**	-3.8%	0.6%
United Kingdom	108.4	105.8	103.6	102.9	96.4	88.2	80.0	72.1	69.6	59.7	**57.1**	-4.3%	1.8%
Uzbekistan	51.1	52.0	51.9	52.0	54.2	54.0	54.5	59.1	62.2	60.0	**59.1**	-1.5%	1.8%
Other Europe & Eurasia	11.1	10.9	11.2	10.6	11.0	10.9	11.5	10.8	10.3	9.7	**10.0**	3.0%	0.3%
Total Europe & Eurasia	938.9	946.6	967.6	1001.9	1032.3	1038.0	1051.7	1053.2	1086.5	969.8	**1043.1**	7.6%	32.6%
Bahrain	8.8	9.1	9.5	9.6	9.8	10.7	11.3	11.8	12.7	12.8	**13.1**	2.4%	0.4%
Iran	60.2	66.0	75.0	81.5	84.9	103.5	108.6	111.9	116.3	131.2	**138.5**	5.6%	4.3%
Iraq	3.2	2.8	2.4	1.6	1.0	1.5	1.5	1.5	1.9	1.2	**1.3**	8.7%	◆
Kuwait	9.6	10.5	9.5	11.0	11.9	12.2	12.5	12.1	12.8	11.2	**11.6**	3.5%	0.4%
Oman	8.7	14.0	15.0	16.5	18.5	19.8	23.7	24.0	24.1	24.8	**27.1**	9.4%	0.8%
Qatar	23.7	27.0	29.5	31.4	39.2	45.8	50.7	63.2	77.0	89.3	**116.7**	30.7%	3.6%
Saudi Arabia	49.8	53.7	56.7	60.1	65.7	71.2	73.5	74.4	80.4	78.5	**83.9**	7.0%	2.6%
Syria	5.5	5.0	6.1	6.2	6.4	5.5	5.7	5.6	5.3	5.7	**7.8**	37.3%	0.2%
United Arab Emirates	38.4	44.9	43.4	44.8	46.3	47.8	49.0	50.3	50.2	48.8	**51.0**	4.5%	1.6%
Yemen	–	–	–	–	–	–	–	–	–	0.8	**6.2**	704.6%	0.2%
Other Middle East	0.3	0.3	0.3	0.3	1.5	1.9	2.6	3.0	3.7	3.1	**3.5**	15.0%	0.1%
Total Middle East	208.1	233.3	247.2	262.9	285.1	319.9	339.1	357.8	384.3	407.1	**460.7**	13.2%	14.4%
Algeria	84.4	78.2	80.4	82.8	82.0	88.2	84.5	84.8	85.8	79.6	**80.4**	1.1%	2.5%
Egypt	21.0	25.2	27.3	30.1	33.0	42.5	54.7	55.7	59.0	62.7	**61.3**	-2.2%	1.9%
Libya	5.9	6.2	5.9	5.5	8.1	11.3	13.2	15.3	15.9	15.9	**15.8**	-0.6%	0.5%
Nigeria	12.5	14.9	14.2	19.2	22.8	22.4	28.4	35.0	35.0	24.8	**33.6**	35.7%	1.1%
Other Africa	6.5	6.9	6.6	7.2	8.9	9.9	10.4	12.3	15.8	16.3	**17.8**	9.4%	0.6%
Total Africa	130.3	131.5	134.4	144.9	154.7	174.3	191.2	203.1	211.5	199.2	**209.0**	4.9%	6.5%
Australia	31.2	32.1	32.2	32.7	35.8	37.2	40.2	41.9	41.6	47.9	**50.4**	5.1%	1.6%
Bangladesh	10.0	10.7	11.4	12.3	13.2	14.5	15.3	16.3	17.9	19.7	**20.0**	1.3%	0.6%
Brunei	11.3	11.4	11.5	12.4	12.2	12.0	12.6	12.3	12.2	11.4	**12.2**	6.7%	0.4%
China	27.2	30.3	32.7	35.0	41.5	49.3	58.6	69.2	80.3	85.3	**96.8**	13.5%	3.0%
India	26.4	26.4	27.6	29.5	29.2	29.6	29.3	30.1	30.5	39.2	**50.9**	29.7%	1.6%
Indonesia	65.2	63.3	69.7	73.2	70.3	71.2	70.3	67.6	69.7	71.9	**82.0**	14.0%	2.6%
Malaysia	45.3	46.9	48.3	51.8	53.9	61.1	63.3	64.6	64.7	64.1	**66.5**	3.7%	2.1%
Myanmar	3.4	7.0	8.4	9.6	10.2	12.2	12.6	13.5	12.4	11.5	**12.1**	4.9%	0.4%
Pakistan	21.5	22.7	24.6	30.4	34.5	35.5	36.1	36.8	37.5	38.4	**39.5**	2.7%	1.2%
Thailand	20.2	19.6	20.5	21.5	22.4	23.7	24.3	26.0	28.8	30.9	**36.3**	17.4%	1.1%
Vietnam	1.6	2.0	2.4	2.4	4.2	6.4	7.0	7.1	7.5	8.0	**9.4**	16.7%	0.3%
Other Asia Pacific	9.0	9.5	10.9	10.7	10.1	11.1	14.2	16.9	17.7	17.9	**17.3**	-3.4%	0.5%
Total Asia Pacific	272.1	282.0	300.2	321.6	337.4	363.9	383.7	402.2	420.7	446.4	**493.2**	10.5%	15.4%
Total World	**2413.4**	**2478.0**	**2519.4**	**2616.5**	**2694.0**	**2778.0**	**2880.7**	**2950.5**	**3062.1**	**2975.9**	**3193.3**	**7.3%**	**100.0%**
of which: OECD	1073.9	1096.6	1086.4	1092.8	1091.9	1076.4	1092.9	1102.2	1134.3	1126.3	**1159.8**	2.9%	36.5%
Non-OECD	1339.5	1381.4	1433.0	1523.7	1602.1	1701.6	1787.9	1848.3	1927.8	1849.5	**2033.5**	9.9%	63.5%
European Union	231.9	232.8	227.6	223.6	227.3	212.0	201.3	187.5	189.4	171.5	**174.9**	2.0%	5.5%
Former Soviet Union	654.2	657.1	671.4	702.1	723.4	737.7	759.0	772.1	793.8	690.9	**757.9**	9.7%	23.7%

*Excluding gas flared or recycled.

◆Less than 0.05%.

Source: Includes data from Cedigaz.

Notes: As far as possible, the data above represents standard cubic metres (measured at 15°C and 1013 mbar); because it is derived directly from tonnes of oil equivalent using an average conversion factor, it does not necessarily equate with gas volumes expressed in specific national terms.

Annual changes and shares of total are calculated using million tonnes of oil equivalent figures.

Natural gas production data expressed in billion cubic feet per day is available at *www.bp.com/statisticalreview*.

〈표 1-8〉 국가별/지역별 천연가스소비량(00-10)(BP)

Billion cubic metres	2000	2001	2002	2003	2004	2005	2006	2007	2008	2009	**2010**	Change 2010 over 2009	2010 share of total
US	660.7	629.7	651.5	630.8	634.0	623.3	614.1	654.0	658.9	646.7	**683.4**	5.6%	21.7%
Canada	92.7	88.2	90.2	97.7	95.1	97.8	96.9	95.2	95.5	94.4	**93.8**	-0.6%	3.0%
Mexico	41.0	41.7	45.3	50.1	53.4	53.8	60.9	62.8	66.4	66.6	**68.9**	3.4%	2.2%
Total North America	794.4	759.6	787.0	778.6	782.5	774.9	771.9	812.1	820.8	807.7	**846.1**	4.7%	26.9%
Argentina	33.2	31.1	30.3	34.6	37.9	40.4	41.8	43.9	44.4	43.2	**43.3**	0.4%	1.4%
Brazil	9.4	11.9	14.1	15.8	18.8	19.7	20.8	21.1	24.6	19.8	**26.5**	33.8%	0.8%
Chile	6.5	7.3	7.4	8.0	8.7	8.4	7.8	4.6	2.7	3.1	**4.7**	51.0%	0.1%
Colombia	5.9	6.1	6.1	6.0	6.3	6.7	7.0	7.4	7.6	8.7	**9.1**	4.3%	0.3%
Ecuador	0.3	0.3	0.2	0.3	0.3	0.4	0.7	0.5	0.5	0.5	**0.5**	-6.0%	◆
Peru	0.3	0.4	0.4	0.5	0.9	1.5	1.8	2.7	3.4	3.5	**5.4**	56.0%	0.2%
Trinidad & Tobago	10.6	11.6	12.7	14.4	13.4	15.1	20.2	20.3	21.9	20.9	**22.0**	5.5%	0.7%
Venezuela	27.9	29.6	28.4	25.2	28.4	27.4	31.5	29.6	31.5	30.5	**30.7**	0.6%	1.0%
Other S. & Cent. America	1.8	2.3	2.4	3.1	2.9	3.3	3.9	4.5	4.7	5.1	**5.6**	9.9%	0.2%
Total S. & Cent. America	96.0	100.7	102.1	107.9	117.5	122.9	135.5	134.6	141.3	135.1	**147.7**	9.3%	4.7%
Austria	8.1	8.6	8.5	9.4	9.5	10.0	9.4	8.9	9.5	9.3	**10.1**	8.6%	0.3%
Azerbaijan	5.2	7.5	7.5	7.7	8.3	8.6	9.1	8.0	9.2	7.8	**6.6**	-15.9%	0.2%
Belarus	15.7	15.7	16.1	15.8	17.9	18.4	19.0	18.8	19.2	16.1	**19.7**	22.3%	0.6%
Belgium & Luxembourg	15.6	15.4	15.7	16.6	16.9	17.1	17.1	17.0	17.2	17.5	**19.4**	10.9%	0.6%
Bulgaria	3.3	3.0	2.7	2.8	2.8	3.1	3.2	3.2	3.2	2.3	**2.6**	10.1%	0.1%
Czech Republic	8.3	8.9	8.7	8.7	9.1	9.6	9.3	8.7	8.7	8.2	**9.3**	13.7%	0.3%
Denmark	4.9	5.1	5.1	5.2	5.2	5.0	5.1	4.6	4.6	4.4	**4.9**	12.2%	0.2%
Finland	3.7	4.1	4.0	4.5	4.3	4.0	4.2	3.9	4.0	3.6	**3.9**	9.9%	0.1%
France	39.3	41.9	40.5	43.0	45.1	44.0	42.1	42.4	43.8	42.2	**46.9**	11.1%	1.5%
Germany	79.5	82.9	82.6	85.5	85.9	86.2	87.2	82.9	81.2	78.0	**81.3**	4.2%	2.6%
Greece	2.0	2.0	2.1	2.4	2.7	2.7	3.1	3.8	4.0	3.4	**3.7**	8.2%	0.1%
Hungary	10.7	11.9	11.8	13.2	13.0	13.4	12.7	11.9	11.8	10.1	**10.9**	7.7%	0.3%
Republic of Ireland	3.8	4.0	4.1	4.1	4.1	3.9	4.5	4.8	5.0	4.8	**5.3**	10.8%	0.2%
Italy	64.9	65.0	64.6	71.2	73.9	79.1	77.4	77.8	77.8	71.5	**76.1**	6.4%	2.4%
Kazakhstan	9.5	10.2	14.8	17.6	25.0	26.8	28.1	26.4	27.2	24.5	**25.3**	2.9%	0.8%
Lithuania	2.7	2.8	2.9	3.1	3.1	3.3	3.2	3.6	3.2	2.7	**3.1**	14.3%	0.1%
Netherlands	38.9	40.0	39.8	40.0	40.9	39.3	38.1	37.0	38.6	38.9	**43.6**	12.1%	1.4%
Norway	4.0	3.8	4.0	4.3	4.6	4.5	4.4	4.3	4.3	4.1	**4.1**	-0.5%	0.1%
Poland	11.1	11.5	11.2	12.5	13.2	13.6	13.7	13.8	13.9	13.4	**14.3**	7.1%	0.5%
Portugal	2.4	2.6	3.1	3.0	3.8	4.2	4.1	4.3	4.6	4.7	**5.0**	6.7%	0.2%
Romania	17.1	16.6	17.2	18.3	17.5	17.6	18.1	16.1	15.9	13.3	**13.3**	0.6%	0.4%
Russian Federation	354.0	366.2	367.7	384.9	394.1	400.3	408.5	422.1	416.0	389.6	**414.1**	6.3%	13.0%
Slovakia	6.5	6.9	6.5	6.3	6.1	6.6	6.0	5.7	5.7	4.9	**5.6**	14.5%	0.2%
Spain	16.9	18.2	20.8	23.6	27.4	32.4	33.7	35.1	38.6	34.6	**34.4**	-0.3%	1.1%
Sweden	0.7	0.7	0.8	0.8	0.8	0.8	0.9	1.0	0.9	1.1	**1.6**	38.9%	0.1%
Switzerland	2.7	2.8	2.8	2.9	3.0	3.1	3.0	2.9	3.1	3.0	**3.3**	10.5%	0.1%
Turkey	14.6	16.0	17.4	20.9	22.1	26.9	30.5	36.1	37.5	35.7	**39.0**	9.2%	1.2%
Turkmenistan	12.2	12.5	12.9	14.2	15.0	16.1	18.4	21.3	20.5	19.9	**22.6**	13.5%	0.7%
Ukraine	71.0	68.8	67.7	69.0	68.5	69.0	67.0	63.2	60.0	47.0	**52.1**	11.0%	1.6%
United Kingdom	96.9	96.4	95.1	95.4	97.4	95.0	90.1	91.1	93.8	86.7	**93.8**	8.3%	3.0%
Uzbekistan	45.7	49.6	50.9	45.8	43.4	42.7	41.9	45.9	48.7	43.5	**45.5**	4.6%	1.4%
Other Europe & Eurasia	13.2	14.5	13.6	14.1	15.6	15.9	16.4	17.0	16.1	13.7	**15.7**	14.9%	0.5%
Total Europe & Eurasia	985.3	1016.1	1023.2	1067.1	1100.1	1122.8	1129.5	1143.5	1148.2	1060.5	**1137.2**	7.2%	35.8%
Iran	62.9	70.1	79.2	82.9	86.5	105.0	108.7	113.0	119.3	131.4	**136.9**	4.2%	4.3%
Israel	†	†	†	†	1.2	1.7	2.3	2.8	4.1	4.5	**5.3**	17.5%	0.2%
Kuwait	9.6	10.5	9.5	11.0	11.9	12.2	12.5	12.1	12.8	12.1	**14.4**	18.8%	0.5%
Qatar	9.7	11.0	11.1	12.2	15.0	18.7	19.6	19.3	19.3	20.0	**20.4**	2.0%	0.6%
Saudi Arabia	49.8	53.7	56.7	60.1	65.7	71.2	73.5	74.4	80.4	78.5	**83.9**	7.0%	2.6%
United Arab Emirates	31.4	37.9	36.4	37.9	40.2	42.1	43.4	49.2	59.5	59.1	**60.5**	2.5%	1.9%
Other Middle East	23.3	23.7	24.6	25.0	26.5	28.4	31.5	32.3	36.5	38.6	**44.1**	14.1%	1.4%
Total Middle East	186.7	206.8	217.6	229.0	247.1	279.2	291.5	303.1	331.9	344.1	**365.5**	6.2%	11.5%
Algeria	19.8	20.5	20.2	21.4	22.0	23.2	23.7	24.3	25.4	27.2	**28.9**	6.0%	0.9%
Egypt	20.0	24.5	26.5	29.7	31.7	31.6	36.5	38.4	40.8	42.5	**45.1**	6.0%	1.4%
South Africa	1.2	1.2	1.0	1.0	2.1	3.1	3.5	3.5	3.7	3.4	**3.8**	13.8%	0.1%
Other Africa	17.4	17.6	18.0	20.4	23.8	25.0	24.4	28.3	30.2	25.7	**27.1**	5.5%	0.9%
Total Africa	58.4	63.8	65.8	72.6	79.7	83.0	88.1	94.4	100.1	98.9	**105.0**	6.1%	3.3%
Australia	20.5	21.6	22.0	22.0	23.4	22.0	25.3	27.6	28.8	30.7	**30.4**	-1.2%	1.0%
Bangladesh	10.0	10.7	11.4	12.3	13.2	14.5	15.3	16.3	17.9	19.7	**20.0**	1.3%	0.6%
China	24.5	27.4	29.2	33.9	39.7	46.8	56.1	70.5	81.3	89.5	**109.0**	21.8%	3.4%
China Hong Kong SAR	3.0	3.0	2.9	1.8	2.7	2.7	2.9	2.7	3.2	3.1	**3.8**	24.3%	0.1%
India	26.4	26.4	27.6	29.5	31.9	35.7	37.3	40.1	41.3	51.0	**61.9**	21.5%	1.9%
Indonesia	29.7	31.0	32.9	35.0	32.2	33.2	33.2	31.3	33.3	37.4	**40.3**	7.8%	1.3%
Japan	72.3	74.3	72.7	79.8	77.0	78.6	83.7	90.2	93.7	87.4	**94.5**	8.1%	3.0%
Malaysia	24.1	25.2	26.2	27.3	24.7	31.4	33.7	33.4	33.8	33.7	**35.7**	6.2%	1.1%
New Zealand	5.6	5.9	5.6	4.3	3.9	3.6	3.7	4.1	3.8	3.9	**4.1**	4.2%	0.1%
Pakistan	21.5	22.7	24.6	30.4	34.5	35.5	36.1	36.8	37.5	38.4	**39.5**	2.7%	1.2%
Philippines	†	0.1	1.8	2.7	2.5	3.3	2.6	3.2	3.3	3.3	**3.1**	-5.8%	0.1%
Singapore	†	0.9	3.6	4.0	5.0	6.8	7.1	8.6	8.2	8.1	**8.4**	4.2%	0.3%
South Korea	18.9	20.8	23.1	24.2	28.4	30.4	32.0	34.7	35.7	33.9	**42.9**	26.5%	1.4%
Taiwan	6.8	7.3	8.2	8.4	10.2	10.3	11.1	11.8	11.6	11.3	**14.1**	24.3%	0.4%
Thailand	22.0	24.8	26.9	28.6	29.9	32.5	33.3	35.4	37.4	39.2	**45.1**	15.0%	1.4%
Vietnam	1.6	2.0	2.4	2.4	4.2	6.4	7.0	7.1	7.5	8.0	**9.4**	16.7%	0.3%
Other Asia Pacific	3.9	3.8	3.6	4.2	4.5	5.2	5.5	6.0	5.7	5.2	**5.3**	3.6%	0.2%
Total Asia Pacific	290.8	308.0	324.6	350.8	367.7	398.9	426.0	459.6	484.0	503.9	**567.6**	12.6%	17.9%
Total World	**2411.7**	**2455.0**	**2520.3**	**2606.1**	**2694.5**	**2781.8**	**2842.4**	**2947.4**	**3026.4**	**2950.2**	**3169.0**	**7.4%**	**100.0%**
of which: OECD	1355.5	1340.1	1368.8	1392.4	1415.7	1422.5	1425.3	1475.9	1500.4	1453.0	**1546.2**	6.4%	48.9%
Non-OECD	1056.1	1114.9	1151.5	1213.7	1278.9	1359.2	1417.1	1471.5	1526.0	1497.2	**1622.8**	8.4%	51.1%
European Union	440.4	451.8	451.2	473.2	486.0	494.2	486.9	481.2	489.7	458.5	**492.5**	7.4%	15.5%
Former Soviet Union	523.6	541.6	547.8	565.9	583.9	594.4	604.7	619.0	613.1	558.9	**596.8**	6.8%	18.8%

†Less than 0.05.

◆Less than 0.05%.

Source: Includes data from Cedigaz.

Notes: As far as possible, the data above represent standard cubic metres (measured at 15°C and 1013 mbar); as they are derived directly from tonnes of oil equivalent using an average conversion factor, they do not necessarily equate with gas volumes expressed in specific national terms.
The difference between these world consumption figures and the world production statistics is due to variations in stocks at storage facilities and liquefaction plants, together with unavoidable disparities in the definition, measurement or conversion of gas supply and demand data.
Annual changes and shares of total are calculated using million tonnes oil equivalent figures.
Natural gas consumption data expressed in billion cubic feet per day is available at *www.bp.com/statisticalreview*.

노트와 질문

1. 매장량을 어떻게 측정할지에 관하여 다양한 의견이 있을 수 있기 때문에 용어의 사용을 통일하기 위하여 많은 국가의 자본시장 규율당국은 이의 기준과 용어의 사용에 관한 규정을 가지고 있다.[8] 확인매장량은 90% 이상, 추정매장량은 50% 이상, 가능매장량은 10% 이상 실제 회수가능성을 가진다.
2. 원유라고 모두 동일한 것이 아니고 이들 사이에도 많은 차이가 있고 천연가스 역시 이물질의 포함 정도에 따라서 천차만별이다. 이들을 측정하는 단위도 상이할 수 있으나 이는 서로 변환가능하다. 원유나 천연가스의 품질을 어떻게 측정하는지에 관한 기술적인 이해도 에너지법의 연구에 도움이 될 것이다.[9]

다. 석탄 매장량, 생산량, 소비량

〈표 1-9〉 국가별/지역별 석탄확인매장량(10)(BP)

Million tonnes	Anthracite and bituminous	Sub-bituminous and lignite	**Total**	Share of total	R/P ratio
US	108501	128794	**237295**	27.6%	241
Canada	3474	3108	**6582**	0.8%	97
Mexico	860	351	**1211**	0.1%	130
Total North America	112835	132253	**245088**	28.5%	231
Brazil	–	4559	**4559**	0.5%	*
Colombia	6366	380	**6746**	0.8%	91
Venezuela	479	–	**479**	0.1%	120
Other S. & Cent. America	45	679	**724**	0.1%	*
Total S. & Cent. America	6890	5618	**12508**	1.5%	148
Bulgaria	2	2364	**2366**	0.3%	82
Czech Republic	192	908	**1100**	0.1%	22
Germany	99	40600	**40699**	4.7%	223
Greece	–	3020	**3020**	0.4%	44
Hungary	13	1647	**1660**	0.2%	183
Kazakhstan	21500	12100	**33600**	3.9%	303
Poland	4338	1371	**5709**	0.7%	43
Romania	10	281	**291**	◆	9
Russian Federation	49088	107922	**157010**	18.2%	495
Spain	200	330	**530**	0.1%	73
Turkey	529	1814	**2343**	0.3%	27
Ukraine	15351	18522	**33873**	3.9%	462
United Kingdom	228	–	**228**	◆	13
Other Europe & Eurasia	1440	20735	**22175**	2.6%	317
Total Europe & Eurasia	92990	211614	**304604**	35.4%	257
South Africa	30156	–	**30156**	3.5%	119
Zimbabwe	502	–	**502**	0.1%	301
Other Africa	860	174	**1034**	0.1%	*
Middle East	1203	–	**1203**	0.1%	*
Total Middle East & Africa	32721	174	**32895**	3.8%	127
Australia	37100	39300	**76400**	8.9%	180
China	62200	52300	**114500**	13.3%	35
India	56100	4500	**60600**	7.0%	106
Indonesia	1520	4009	**5529**	0.6%	18
Japan	340	10	**350**	◆	382
New Zealand	33	538	**571**	0.1%	107
North Korea	300	300	**600**	0.1%	16
Pakistan	–	2070	**2070**	0.2%	*
South Korea	–	126	**126**	◆	60
Thailand	–	1239	**1239**	0.1%	69
Vietnam	150	–	**150**	◆	3
Other Asia Pacific	1582	2125	**3707**	0.4%	114
Total Asia Pacific	159326	106517	**265843**	30.9%	57
Total World	**404762**	**456176**	**860938**	**100.0%**	**118**
of which: OECD	155926	222603	**378529**	44.0%	184
Non-OECD	248836	233573	**482409**	56.0%	92
European Union	5101	51047	**56148**	6.5%	105
Former Soviet Union	86725	141309	**228034**	26.5%	452

*More than 500 years.
◆Less than 0.05%.

Source of reserves data: Survey of Energy Resources, World Energy Council 2010.

Notes: Proved reserves of coal – Generally taken to be those quantities that geological and engineering information indicates with reasonable certainty can be recovered in the future from known deposits under existing economic and operating conditions.
Reserves-to-production (R/P) ratio – If the reserves remaining at the end of the year are divided by the production in that year, the result is the length of time that those remaining reserves would last if production were to continue at that rate.

8) 위 주 6 참조.
9) Ernst E. Smith, 위 주 4 게재서, 1031-32. 유황함유량이나 질량의 차이에 따른 원유의 등급에 관하여는 Id., 1002-04.

〈표 1-10〉 국가별/지역별 석탄생산량(00-10)(BP)

Million tonnes oil equivalent	2000	2001	2002	2003	2004	2005	2006	2007	2008	2009	**2010**	Change 2010 over 2009	2010 share of total
US	570.1	590.3	570.1	553.6	572.4	580.2	595.1	587.7	596.7	540.9	**552.2**	2.1%	14.8%
Canada	36.1	36.6	34.2	31.7	33.8	33.5	33.9	36.0	35.6	32.5	**34.9**	7.2%	0.9%
Mexico	5.4	5.3	5.3	4.6	4.7	5.2	5.5	6.0	5.5	5.1	**4.5**	-11.4%	0.1%
Total North America	611.6	632.2	609.5	589.9	610.9	618.8	634.5	629.7	637.8	578.5	**591.6**	2.3%	15.9%
Brazil	2.9	2.1	1.9	1.8	2.0	2.4	2.2	2.3	2.5	1.9	**2.1**	8.2%	0.1%
Colombia	24.9	28.5	25.7	32.5	34.9	38.4	42.6	45.4	47.8	47.3	**48.3**	2.1%	1.3%
Venezuela	5.8	5.6	5.9	5.1	5.9	5.3	5.4	5.6	4.5	2.7	**2.9**	8.1%	0.1%
Other S. & Cent. America	0.4	0.5	0.4	0.5	0.2	0.3	0.6	0.3	0.4	0.5	**0.5**	-7.0%	◆
Total S. & Cent. America	33.9	36.8	33.9	39.9	43.0	46.3	50.8	53.6	55.2	52.4	**53.8**	2.6%	1.4%
Bulgaria	4.4	4.4	4.4	4.6	4.5	4.1	4.2	4.7	4.8	4.6	**4.8**	5.8%	0.1%
Czech Republic	25.0	25.4	24.3	24.2	23.5	23.5	23.7	23.3	21.1	19.5	**19.4**	-0.7%	0.5%
France	2.3	1.5	1.1	1.3	0.4	0.2	0.2	0.2	0.1	†	**†**	–	◆
Germany	56.5	54.1	55.0	54.1	54.7	53.2	50.3	51.5	47.7	44.4	**43.7**	-1.5%	1.2%
Greece	8.2	8.5	9.1	9.0	9.1	9.0	8.3	8.6	8.3	8.4	**8.8**	5.0%	0.2%
Hungary	2.9	2.9	2.7	2.8	2.4	2.0	2.1	2.0	1.9	1.9	**1.9**	1.0%	0.1%
Kazakhstan	38.5	40.7	37.8	43.3	44.4	44.2	49.1	50.0	56.8	51.5	**56.2**	9.2%	1.5%
Poland	71.3	71.7	71.3	71.4	70.5	68.7	67.0	62.3	60.5	56.4	**55.5**	-1.6%	1.5%
Romania	6.4	7.1	6.6	7.0	6.7	6.6	6.5	6.7	6.7	6.4	**5.8**	-9.2%	0.2%
Russian Federation	116.0	122.6	117.3	127.1	131.7	139.2	145.1	148.0	153.4	142.1	**148.8**	4.7%	4.0%
Spain	8.0	7.6	7.2	6.8	6.7	6.4	6.2	6.0	3.7	3.5	**3.3**	-6.3%	0.1%
Turkey	13.9	14.2	11.5	10.5	10.5	12.8	13.4	15.8	17.2	17.4	**17.4**	◆	0.5%
Ukraine	42.0	43.5	42.8	41.6	42.2	41.0	41.7	39.9	41.3	38.4	**38.1**	-0.8%	1.0%
United Kingdom	19.0	19.4	18.2	17.2	15.3	12.5	11.3	10.3	11.0	10.9	**11.0**	1.6%	0.3%
Other Europe & Eurasia	14.0	14.4	15.3	15.8	15.6	14.7	15.7	16.7	17.3	16.9	**16.1**	-4.3%	0.4%
Total Europe & Eurasia	428.6	438.2	424.7	436.7	438.2	438.1	444.9	446.1	452.0	422.1	**430.9**	2.1%	11.5%
Total Middle East	0.8	0.7	0.8	0.7	0.8	0.8	0.9	1.0	1.0	1.0	**1.0**	–	◆
South Africa	126.6	126.1	124.1	134.1	137.2	137.7	138.0	139.6	142.4	141.2	**143.0**	1.3%	3.8%
Zimbabwe	2.8	2.9	2.5	1.8	2.4	2.2	1.4	1.3	1.0	1.1	**1.1**	–	◆
Other Africa	1.2	1.2	1.3	1.5	1.2	1.1	1.0	0.9	0.9	0.8	**0.8**	–	◆
Total Africa	130.6	130.1	127.9	137.4	140.8	141.0	140.3	141.8	144.2	143.1	**144.9**	1.3%	3.9%
Australia	166.5	180.2	184.3	189.9	198.5	205.8	210.3	217.2	220.7	228.8	**235.4**	2.9%	6.3%
China	762.5	809.5	853.8	1013.4	1174.1	1302.2	1406.4	1501.1	1557.1	1652.1	**1800.4**	9.0%	48.3%
India	132.2	133.6	138.5	144.4	155.7	162.1	170.2	181.0	195.6	210.8	**216.1**	2.5%	5.8%
Indonesia	47.4	56.9	63.5	70.3	81.4	93.9	119.2	133.4	147.8	157.6	**188.1**	19.4%	5.0%
Japan	1.7	1.8	0.8	0.7	0.7	0.6	0.7	0.8	0.7	0.7	**0.5**	-28.4%	◆
New Zealand	2.2	2.4	2.7	3.2	3.2	3.2	3.5	3.0	3.0	2.8	**3.3**	16.8%	0.1%
Pakistan	1.4	1.5	1.6	1.5	1.5	1.6	1.7	1.6	1.8	1.6	**1.5**	-5.2%	◆
South Korea	1.9	1.7	1.5	1.5	1.4	1.3	1.3	1.3	1.2	1.1	**0.9**	-17.3%	◆
Thailand	5.1	5.6	5.7	5.3	5.6	5.8	5.3	5.1	5.0	5.0	**5.0**	0.5%	0.1%
Vietnam	6.5	7.5	9.2	10.8	14.7	18.3	21.8	22.4	23.0	25.2	**24.7**	-2.0%	0.7%
Other Asia Pacific	19.6	20.1	19.6	20.6	22.4	24.7	25.1	23.3	24.3	29.2	**33.4**	14.5%	0.9%
Total Asia Pacific	1147.1	1220.8	1281.0	1461.5	1659.2	1819.4	1965.6	2090.2	2180.1	2314.8	**2509.4**	8.4%	67.2%
Total World	**2352.5**	**2458.9**	**2477.7**	**2666.1**	**2893.0**	**3064.4**	**3237.1**	**3362.4**	**3470.3**	**3511.8**	**3731.4**	**6.3%**	**100.0%**
of which: OECD	994.2	1027.6	1003.5	987.3	1012.0	1021.0	1036.6	1036.6	1039.3	978.2	**996.0**	1.8%	26.7%
Non-OECD	1358.3	1431.3	1474.2	1678.8	1881.0	2043.4	2200.5	2325.8	2431.1	2533.7	**2735.5**	8.0%	73.3%
European Union	206.6	205.1	202.5	200.7	195.8	188.1	181.5	177.4	167.7	157.7	**156.0**	-1.1%	4.2%
Former Soviet Union	197.4	207.8	198.9	212.8	219.4	225.5	237.0	239.0	252.9	233.2	**244.4**	4.8%	6.5%

*Commercial solid fuels only, i.e. bituminous coal and anthracite (hard coal), and lignite and brown (sub-bituminous) coal.
†Less than 0.05.
◆Less than 0.05%.
Note: Coal production data expressed in million tonnes is available at *www.bp.com/statisticalreview.*

〈표 1-11〉 국가별/지역별 석탄소비량(00–10)(BP)

Million tonnes oil equivalent	2000	2001	2002	2003	2004	2005	2006	2007	2008	2009	**2010**	Change 2010 over 2009	2010 share of total
US	569.0	552.2	552.0	562.5	566.1	574.2	565.7	573.3	564.1	496.2	**524.6**	5.7%	14.8%
Canada	31.8	34.0	31.6	33.4	29.9	31.7	31.0	32.3	28.9	23.3	**23.4**	0.4%	0.7%
Mexico	6.2	6.8	7.6	8.6	7.0	9.1	9.4	9.1	6.9	8.6	**8.4**	-2.4%	0.2%
Total North America	606.9	593.0	591.1	604.5	603.0	614.9	606.1	614.7	599.9	528.1	**556.3**	5.3%	15.6%
Argentina	0.8	0.6	0.5	0.7	0.8	0.9	0.3	0.4	1.1	1.2	**1.2**	–	◆
Brazil	12.5	12.2	11.5	11.8	12.8	12.7	12.5	13.4	13.5	11.7	**12.4**	6.0%	0.3%
Chile	3.0	2.3	2.4	2.3	2.6	2.6	3.2	3.8	4.1	3.7	**3.7**	1.0%	0.1%
Colombia	2.7	2.7	2.2	2.4	2.0	2.7	2.4	2.4	2.8	3.7	**3.8**	2.1%	0.1%
Ecuador	–	–	–	–	–	–	–	–	–	–	–	–	–
Peru	0.5	0.4	0.4	0.4	0.5	0.5	0.4	0.5	0.5	0.5	**0.5**	6.3%	◆
Trinidad & Tobago	–	–	–	–	–	–	–	–	–	–	–	–	–
Venezuela	†	†	†	†	–	†	†	†	†	†	**†**	-1.9%	◆
Other S. & Cent. America	0.6	0.7	1.0	2.1	1.9	1.8	2.1	2.1	2.2	2.0	**2.1**	1.9%	0.1%
Total S. & Cent. America	20.1	19.0	18.0	19.6	20.5	21.2	21.0	22.6	24.2	22.9	**23.8**	3.9%	0.7%
Austria	2.8	3.1	3.0	3.3	3.3	3.1	3.1	2.9	2.7	2.2	**2.0**	-10.5%	0.1%
Azerbaijan	–	†	†	†	†	†	†	†	†	†	**†**	-7.8%	◆
Belarus	0.1	0.1	0.1	0.1	0.1	0.1	0.1	†	†	†	**†**	-23.0%	◆
Belgium & Luxembourg	7.6	7.6	6.7	6.5	6.4	6.1	6.1	5.5	4.8	4.6	**4.9**	6.2%	0.1%
Bulgaria	6.3	6.9	6.5	7.1	6.9	6.9	7.1	7.8	7.5	6.3	**6.6**	4.8%	0.2%
Czech Republic	21.0	21.2	20.6	20.8	20.5	19.8	19.4	19.3	17.4	16.2	**16.0**	-1.3%	0.5%
Denmark	4.0	4.2	4.2	5.7	4.6	3.7	5.6	4.7	4.1	4.0	**3.8**	-4.9%	0.1%
Finland	3.5	4.0	4.4	5.8	5.3	3.1	5.2	4.6	3.4	3.7	**4.6**	24.9%	0.1%
France	13.9	12.1	12.4	13.3	12.8	13.3	12.1	12.3	11.9	9.9	**12.1**	23.2%	0.3%
Germany	84.9	85.0	84.6	87.2	85.4	82.1	83.5	85.7	80.1	71.7	**76.5**	6.7%	2.2%
Greece	9.2	9.3	9.8	9.4	9.0	8.8	8.1	8.5	8.1	8.1	**8.5**	4.6%	0.2%
Hungary	3.2	3.4	3.1	3.4	3.1	2.7	2.9	2.9	2.8	2.5	**2.6**	6.0%	0.1%
Republic of Ireland	1.8	1.9	1.8	1.7	1.8	1.8	1.6	1.5	1.4	1.3	**1.4**	3.8%	◆
Italy	13.0	13.7	14.2	15.3	17.1	17.0	17.2	17.2	16.7	13.1	**13.7**	5.0%	0.4%
Kazakhstan	23.2	22.5	22.8	25.2	26.5	27.2	28.1	30.8	34.0	31.7	**36.1**	13.8%	1.0%
Lithuania	0.1	0.1	0.1	0.2	0.2	0.2	0.2	0.2	0.2	0.1	**0.2**	19.6%	◆
Netherlands	8.6	8.5	8.9	9.1	9.1	8.7	8.5	9.0	8.5	7.9	**7.9**	-0.1%	0.2%
Norway	0.7	0.6	0.5	0.5	0.6	0.5	0.4	0.4	0.5	0.3	**0.5**	32.0%	◆
Poland	57.6	58.0	56.7	57.7	57.3	55.7	58.0	57.9	56.0	51.9	**54.0**	3.9%	1.5%
Portugal	4.5	3.7	4.1	3.8	3.7	3.8	3.8	3.3	3.2	3.3	**3.4**	3.4%	0.1%
Romania	7.0	7.2	7.6	7.8	7.4	7.6	8.5	7.4	7.4	6.6	**6.2**	-6.6%	0.2%
Russian Federation	105.2	102.4	103.0	104.0	99.5	94.2	96.7	93.5	100.4	91.9	**93.8**	2.1%	2.6%
Slovakia	4.0	4.1	4.0	4.2	4.1	3.9	3.8	3.8	3.7	3.5	**2.7**	-24.3%	0.1%
Spain	21.6	19.5	21.9	20.5	21.0	21.2	18.5	20.2	15.6	10.5	**8.3**	-21.3%	0.2%
Sweden	1.9	2.0	2.2	2.2	2.3	2.2	2.3	2.2	2.0	1.6	**2.0**	23.6%	0.1%
Switzerland	0.1	0.1	0.1	0.1	0.1	0.1	0.1	0.1	0.1	0.1	**0.1**	5.7%	◆
Turkey	25.5	21.8	21.2	21.8	23.0	26.1	28.8	31.0	31.3	32.0	**34.4**	7.4%	1.0%
Turkmenistan	–	–	–	–	–	–	–	–	–	–	–	–	–
Ukraine	38.8	39.4	38.3	39.0	39.1	37.5	39.8	39.7	40.3	35.0	**36.4**	4.2%	1.0%
United Kingdom	36.7	38.9	35.7	38.1	36.6	37.4	40.9	38.4	35.6	29.6	**31.2**	5.2%	0.9%
Uzbekistan	1.0	1.1	1.0	1.0	1.2	1.1	1.1	1.4	1.4	1.4	**1.3**	-3.3%	◆
Other Europe & Eurasia	17.4	16.6	18.8	19.7	20.2	18.0	15.8	16.0	16.8	15.2	**15.7**	3.1%	0.4%
Total Europe & Eurasia	525.2	518.9	518.5	534.3	528.1	513.9	527.2	528.3	517.8	466.4	**486.8**	4.4%	13.7%
Iran	1.1	1.1	1.1	1.1	1.0	1.2	1.2	1.3	0.9	1.1	**1.1**	1.0%	◆
Israel	6.2	7.2	7.6	7.9	8.0	7.9	7.8	8.0	7.9	7.7	**7.7**	◆	0.2%
Kuwait	–	–	–	–	–	–	–	–	–	–	–	–	–
Qatar	–	–	–	–	–	–	–	–	–	–	–	–	–
Saudi Arabia	–	–	–	–	–	–	–	–	–	–	–	–	–
United Arab Emirates	–	–	–	–	–	–	–	–	–	–	–	–	–
Other Middle East	–	–	–	–	–	–	–	–	–	–	–	–	–
Total Middle East	7.3	8.3	8.7	9.0	9.0	9.1	9.1	9.3	8.7	8.8	**8.8**	0.1%	0.2%
Algeria	0.5	0.6	0.9	0.8	0.8	0.6	0.7	0.7	0.6	0.2	**0.3**	6.1%	◆
Egypt	1.4	1.2	1.3	1.4	1.3	1.3	1.2	1.2	1.2	0.6	**0.7**	5.1%	◆
South Africa	74.6	73.4	75.9	81.4	85.4	82.9	84.0	85.1	84.7	87.7	**88.7**	1.1%	2.5%
Other Africa	6.5	7.3	7.2	6.4	7.1	7.3	6.7	6.0	6.2	5.5	**5.7**	3.8%	0.2%
Total Africa	82.9	82.6	85.4	90.0	94.7	92.1	92.6	93.1	92.7	94.1	**95.3**	1.3%	2.7%
Australia	46.7	48.2	51.0	49.8	52.7	53.6	55.6	54.2	51.8	51.7	**43.4**	-16.1%	1.2%
Bangladesh	0.3	0.4	0.4	0.4	0.4	0.4	0.5	0.4	0.6	0.4	**0.5**	6.0%	◆
China	737.1	751.9	794.9	936.3	1084.3	1218.7	1343.9	1438.4	1479.3	1556.8	**1713.5**	10.1%	48.2%
China Hong Kong SAR	3.7	4.9	5.4	6.6	6.6	6.7	7.0	7.5	7.0	7.6	**6.3**	-16.3%	0.2%
India	144.2	145.2	151.8	156.8	172.3	184.4	195.4	210.3	230.4	250.6	**277.6**	10.8%	7.8%
Indonesia	13.7	16.8	18.0	24.2	22.2	25.4	30.1	37.8	30.1	34.6	**39.4**	13.7%	1.1%
Japan	98.9	103.0	106.6	112.2	120.8	121.3	119.1	125.3	128.7	108.8	**123.7**	13.7%	3.5%
Malaysia	1.9	2.6	3.6	4.2	5.7	6.3	7.3	7.1	5.0	4.0	**3.4**	-16.1%	0.1%
New Zealand	1.1	1.3	1.3	1.9	2.0	2.2	2.2	1.6	2.0	1.6	**1.0**	-37.3%	◆
Pakistan	2.0	2.1	2.4	2.9	3.8	4.1	4.2	5.1	5.3	4.7	**4.6**	-2.3%	0.1%
Philippines	4.3	4.5	4.7	4.7	5.0	5.7	5.5	5.9	7.0	6.7	**7.7**	15.8%	0.2%
Singapore	–	–	–	–	–	–	–	–	–	–	–	–	–
South Korea	43.0	45.7	49.1	51.1	53.1	54.8	54.8	59.7	66.1	68.6	**76.0**	10.8%	2.1%
Taiwan	28.7	30.6	32.7	35.1	36.6	38.1	39.6	41.8	40.2	38.7	**40.3**	4.0%	1.1%
Thailand	7.8	8.8	9.2	9.4	10.4	11.2	12.4	14.1	15.3	14.5	**14.8**	2.6%	0.4%
Vietnam	4.7	5.0	5.3	5.5	8.2	8.0	9.5	10.1	10.0	14.0	**13.7**	-2.0%	0.4%
Other Asia Pacific	18.9	19.5	18.6	18.9	19.2	20.7	21.4	18.0	19.7	22.1	**18.9**	-14.5%	0.5%
Total Asia Pacific	1157.1	1190.7	1254.9	1419.9	1603.1	1761.6	1908.6	2037.5	2098.4	2185.3	**2384.7**	9.1%	67.1%
Total World	**2399.7**	**2412.4**	**2476.7**	**2677.3**	**2858.4**	**3012.9**	**3164.5**	**3305.6**	**3341.7**	**3305.6**	**3555.8**	**7.6%**	**100.0%**
of which: OECD	1133.6	1124.9	1130.7	1161.4	1170.5	1179.7	1179.8	1200.2	1171.5	1049.5	**1103.6**	5.2%	31.0%
Non-OECD	1266.1	1287.5	1345.9	1515.9	1687.9	1833.2	1984.7	2105.4	2170.2	2256.1	**2452.2**	8.7%	69.0%
European Union	314.9	315.7	314.0	324.3	319.1	310.4	317.7	316.7	294.4	259.9	**269.7**	3.8%	7.6%
Former Soviet Union	169.1	166.1	166.0	170.3	167.6	161.1	166.8	166.4	177.2	161.1	**169.1**	5.0%	4.8%

*Commercial solid fuels only, i.e. bituminous coal and anthracite (hard coal), and lignite and brown (sub-bituminous) coal.
†Less than 0.05.
◆Less than 0.05%.

3. 대체에너지의 필요성

화석연료 에너지에 기초한 경제의 지속적 성장가능성에 대한 의문이 일찍이 M. King Hubbert에 의하여 제기된 이래[10)]그 시기가 문제일 뿐 화석연료는 어느 순간부터는 그 비중이 줄어들 것이라는 데 많은 이들이 대체로 동의한다. 아무리 과학기술이 발달하여도 매장량의 증가가 소비량의 증가보다 빠를 수는 없기 때문이다.[11)] 그럴 경우 지속적으로 성장가능한 경제체제를 위하여 정책적인 측면에서 필요한 것은 화석연료 에너지의 비중이 줄어드는 만큼 이를 대체할 만한 재생에너지의 개발이 받쳐주어야 한다는 것이다. 또한, 화석연료의 사용에 따른 배출 이산화탄소의 증가와 기후변화는 재생에너지의 비중을 조속히 늘려나갈 것을 요구하고 있다. 이런 이유에서 에너지의 사용분포를 어느 시점에 어떻게 조절하여야 할 것인가는 전 인류의 장래에 관계된 문제이다.[12)] 그러나, 앞으로의 지속적 성장을 위한 구체적 행동계획에 관하여 인류의 합의를 도출하는 데 현실적으로 많은 시간이 필요한 것으로 보인다.[13)]

Richard J. Pierce, Jr., *The Past, Present, and Future of Energy Regulation,* 31 UTAH ENVT'L. L. REV. 291 (2011)[14)]

Ⅰ. THE PAST

A. Oil — 1960 to 2011

The U.S. implemented poor fiscal and monetary policies in the 1960s that led to high and rising economy-wide inflation. President Nixon responded to that problem with economy-wide wage and price controls in 1971.[1] Wage and price controls had devastating effects on the economy that caused them to be the subject of near universal

10) M.K. Hubbert, *Nuclear Energy and the Fossil Fuels*, Presented before the Spring Meeting of the Southern District, AMERICAN PETROLEUM INSTITUTE(March 7-9, 1956). 최근의 논의는 N.E. "Skip" Maryan, *Peak Oil: The End of the Roller Coaster Ride? Implications for Law and Policy* 52 ROCKY MT. MIN. L. INST. (2006).

11) 확인매장량과 생산량의 비율에 관하여는 위 [그림 1-5] 참조.

12) Jacqueline Lang Weaver, *The Traditional Petroleum-Based Economy: An "Eventful" Future,* 36 CUMBERLAND L. REV. 505 (2005-06).

13) 뒤 12장 참조.

14) 1980-89까지는 J. ENER. L. & POL'Y로, 1990-96까지는 J. ENER. NAT'L RES. ENV'N L.로 발행되었다.

1. Exec. Order No. 11,615, 34 Fed. Reg. 15727 (Aug. 17, 1971).

criticism by 1973. At that time, they were eliminated for all sectors of the economy except oil and petroleum products.[2]

Several factors in addition to economy-wide inflation led to large increases in the price of oil and petroleum products. First, air quality rules implemented in the 1960s induced many electric utilities and industrial consumers to switch from coal to oil or gas, thereby increasing demand for oil. Second, the U.S. position on the 1973 Arab-Israeli War led the Arab members of the Organization of Petroleum Exporting Countries (OPEC) to impose an embargo on exports of oil to the U.S. for several months. That embargo produced shortages and increases in the price of petroleum products in the U.S. More important, the success of the embargo suggested to all members of OPEC that they could increase their wealth by withholding supplies from the market and thereby increasing the global price of oil. They began to do so, with a resulting four-fold increase in the price of oil.

The U.S. responded to this sequence of events by retaining price controls on oil and petroleum products when it eliminated economy-wide price controls in 1973. The U.S. imposed oil price controls continuously until 1981. Their effects included long lines at gas stations, implementation of a complicated rationing system, cross-subsidization of imports, increased dependence on imported oil, an increased global price of oil, and lots of work for lawyers. In 1981, President Reagan deregulated the price of oil and petroleum products.[3] With cross-subsidies of imports eliminated, the price of oil declined significantly. The oil market has performed well since, and OPEC has little power to increase prices artificially by withholding supplies today.

B. Natural Gas — 1960 to 2011

In 1954, a five-Justice majority of the U.S. Supreme Court held that the Federal Power Commission (FPC) was required to regulate the wellhead price of natural gas.[4] FPC began to impose price controls in the 1960s.[5] By the late 1960s, air quality rules had increased demand for gas by encouraging switching from coal to oil or gas, and price controls had reduced the supply of gas. The result was a shortage that grew through the 1970s.[6] The effects of the price controls and the shortage included millions

2. 38 Fed. Reg. 22,536 (Aug. 22, 1973) (to be codified at 6 C.F.R. pt. 150).
3. Exec. Order No. 12,287, 3 C.F.R. 124 (1982).
4. *Phillips Petroleum v. Wisconsin*, 347 U.S. 672 (1954).
5. Richard J. Pierce, *Reconstituting the Natural Gas Industry from Wellhead to Burnertip*, 9 ENERGY L.J. 1 (1988).
6. For detailed descriptions of the effects of controls on the wellhead price of gas, see Richard J. Pierce, *Reconsidering the Roles of Regulation and Competition on the Natural Gas Industry*, 97 HARV. L. REV. 345 (1983); Richard J. Pierce, *Natural Gas Regulation, Deregulation, and Contracts*,

of people out of work due to factory closings, cross-subsidization of imports, an increased global price of gas, and implementation of a complicated rationing system.

Congress responded by enacting the Natural Gas Policy Act of 1978[7](NGPA) — a statute that divided gas supplies into twenty-three categories, each subject to a different price ceiling. NGPA created a combination of conditions that most economists previously believed to be impossible — a surplus of gas combined with above market prices for many types of gas. NGPA also created a situation in which the artificially low regulated price of "old" domestic gas cross-subsidized "high cost gas" and imported gas. Gas in those categories sold for prices two to four times the market price of gas.

Beginning in 1985, the Federal Energy Regulatory Commission (FERC), FPC's successor, issued a series of orders in which it: (1) deintegrated the gas market vertically, separating the natural monopoly functions from the structurally competitive functions, (2) subjected the structurally competitive wholesale gas market to unregulated competition, and (3) imposed a common carrier form of regulation on the natural monopoly gas transportation function.[8] With competition in place and cross-subsidies eliminated, the price of gas declined significantly. The gas market has performed well since.

Over the period between 2007-2011, gas producers have combined two traditional practices — horizontal drilling and hydraulic fracturing of shale formations — with excellent results. The supply of gas has increased significantly, with a large resulting decrease in price. Gas is now less than half the price of oil. However, concern that some chemicals used in hydraulic fracturing are having adverse effects on water quality has resulted in pressure to increase regulation of hydraulic fracturing. It seems clear that regulation will (and should) increase to some uncertain extent with some uncertain resulting increase in cost and, hence, in the price of gas.

C. Electricity — 1960-2011

Air quality rules implemented in the 1960s encouraged utilities to install expensive pollution control technologies, to switch from coal to gas, and to begin construction of 200 nuclear generating plants. Economy-wide inflation combined with fuel switching and pollution controls significantly increased the cost of generating electricity.[9]

---

68 VA. L. REV. 63 (1982) [hereinafter Pierce, Natural Gas].

7. Natural Gas Policy Act of 1978, Pub. L. No. 95-621, 92 Stat. 3351 (1978).

8. Federal Energy Regulatory Commision, 50 Fed. Reg. 42,408 (Oct. 18, 1985) (to be codified at 18 C.F.R. pt. 2); Federal Energy Regulatory Commission, 57 Fed. Reg. 13,267 (Apr. 16, 1992) (to be codified at 18 C.F.R. pt. 284).

9. *See generally* Paul L. Joskow, *Inflation and Environmental Concern: Structural Change in the Process of Public Utility Price Regulation,* 17 J.L. &ECON. 291 (1974).

The oil and gas shortages of the 1970s and a desire to achieve energy independence induced Congress to enact two statutes in 1978. The first statute was the Powerplant and Industrial Fuel Use Act (PIFUA)[10] which required utilities and industrial consumers to switch from oil and gas to coal. PIFUA prohibited electric utilities from constructing new generating plants that were designed to burn oil or gas.[11] Congress later repealed PIFUA in 1987. By the late 1980s PIFUA was a counter-productive anachronism. The government-created shortages of oil and gas that had inspired enactment of the statute were long gone, and it seemed silly to require utilities to rely exclusively on the dirtiest fuel, coal, when they had access to abundant, clean, and inexpensive natural gas.

The second statute Congress enacted in 1978 was the Public Utility Regulatory Policies Act (PURPA).[12] PURPA encouraged utilities to buy electricity from non-utility generators (NUGS) at above market prices if the NUGS used specified preferred technologies that included cogeneration and low head hydro.[13] It also encouraged utilities to use customer funds to make purchases, such as insulation, high efficiency light bulbs, and high efficiency appliances, which were designed to increase their customers' energy efficiency. Some states, primarily California and then or the astern states, required utilities to enter into long-term contracts to purchase large quantities of electricity from NUGs at prices far above market, and rewarded utilities for using their customers' money to make large energy efficiency purchases on behalf of their customers.[14]

The unit price of electricity increased significantly as a result of: (1) economy-wide inflation, (2) higher costs of fuel and pollution controls, (3) higher than expected costs of constructing nuclear generating plants, (4) methods of regulation used to reflect the cost of new plants in prices that overstated the cost of those plants, and (5) a decline in demand caused partly by the increased price of electricity and partly by an economic downturn.[15] The price of electricity increased most in the states that required utilities to

---

10. Powerplant and Industrial Fuel Use Act of 1978, Pub. L. No. 95-620, 92 Stat. 3289 (1978).
11. For a description of PIFUA, see Richard J. Pierce, *Introduction: Symposium on the Powerplant and Industrial Fuel Use Act of 1978, 29* U. KAN. L. REV. 297 (1981).
12. Public Utility Regulatory Policy Act of 1978, Pub. L. No. 95-617, 93 Stat. 3117 (1978).
13. For a description of PURPA, see John T. Miller Jr., *Conscripting State Regulatory Authorities in a Federal Electric Rate Regulatory Regime: A Goal of PURPA Partially Realized,* 4 ENERGY L.J. 77 (1983).
14. Bernard S. Black & Richard J. Pierce, *The Choice Between Markets and Central Planning in Regulating the U.S. Electricity Market*, 93 COLUM. L. REV. 1339, 1347-48, 1354-89 (1993); Paul L. Joskow & Donald B. Marron, *What Does Utility-Subsidized Energy Efficiency Really Cost*? SCIENCE, Apr. 16, 1993, at 281..
15. Richard J. Pierce, *Public Utility Regulatory Takings: Should the Judiciary Attempt to Police the*

buy a lot of electricity from NUGS at above market prices and that rewarded utilities that used large quantities of their customers' money to make efficiency purchases on their behalf. The price of electricity was almost twice as high in those states as in the states that did not take those actions.

The increased price of electricity produced a consumer backlash that was particularly strong in the states with the highest electricity prices. State regulators used a variety of regulatory doctrines to disallow billions of dollars in investments in cancelled or completed nuclear generating plants.[16] One hundred plants were completed, while another one hundred partially completed plants were cancelled. No utility has been willing to invest in a new nuclear generating plant since the investment disallowances of the 1980s.

The large increases in the price of electricity also provided the impetus to attempt to restructure the electricity market in a manner similar to the successful restructuring of the gas market in the 1980s — vertical deintegration of structurally-competitive functions from monopoly functions, imposition of deregulated competition on the structurally-competitive wholesale market, and imposition of common carrier type regulation on the monopolistic transmission function. FERC initiated such a restructuring effort in 1996.[17]

After years of halting progress, FERC abandoned its attempt to restructure the electricity market. The failure of that restructuring effort was attributable to many factors, including: (1) inadequate FERC jurisdiction, (2) the fragmented corporate structure of the utility industry, (3) resistance from some states that wanted to retain complete control over their utilities, and from some utilities that did not want to confront competition, (4) low short term price elasticity of demand coupled with inability to store electricity, (5) serious errors made by FERC and by many states, (6) the combination of extraordinarily high prices and intermittent blackouts experienced in California in 2000-2001, and (7) the 2001 scandal involving the misconduct and ultimate demise of Enron, the largest participant in the nascent competitive electricity market.[18]

Political Institutions? 77 GEO. L. J. 2031, 2047-52 (1989) [hereinafter "Pierce, *Pubilc Utility*"].

16. Richard J. Pierce, *The Regulatory Treatment of Mistakes in Retrospect: Cancelled Plantsand Excess Capacity,* 132 U. PA. L. REV. 497-99, 519-21 (1984).

17. Richard J. Pierce, *Using the Gas Industry as a Guide to Reconstituting the Electricity Industry*, 13 RES. L. & ECON. 7, 16-17 (1991). Federal Energy Regulatory Commission, 61 Fed. Reg. 21,540 (May 10, 1996) (to be codified at 18 C.F.R. pts. 35 & 385).

18. Richard J. Pierce, *Completing the Process of Restructuring the Electricity Market,* 40 WAKE FOREST L. REV. 451, 479-93 (2005).

Ⅱ. THE PRESENT AND FUTURE

At present, we focus primarily on the use of energy regulation to pursue two goals — energy independence and mitigation of global warming. We rely mainly on three tools to pursue those goals — subsidies for domestic carbon-free sources of energy, mandates to electric utilities to increase the percentage of total electricity they generate from carbon-free fuels, and novel uses of the Clean Air Act (CAA).

I see two potential future courses of action — continuation of the status quo and substitution of a large carbon tax for the tools we are now attempting to use. Continuation of the status quo will produce a lot of work for lawyers but poor results for the nation and the world. By contrast, we can maximize the efficacy and efficiency of our efforts if we drop one of our goals — energy independence — and substitute a large carbon tax for the expensive and ineffective tools we are now using in an effort to mitigate global warming.

A. We Should Pursue Only the Goal of Mitigation of Global Warming

It makes no sense to pursue energy independence as a goal.[19] Any effective effort to replace all foreign sources of energy with domestic sources would cost trillions of dollars, with little, if any beneficial effects. We are dependent on foreign sources for many important goods. There is no more reason to be concerned about our dependence on foreign sources of energy than to be concerned about our dependence on foreign sources for a myriad other important resources.

Lithium is a particularly good example of a resource that is critical to the nation's future and that is, or should be, of greater concern than energy. Lithium is critical to any effort to manufacture efficient batteries. That, in turn, is critical to our ability to improve the efficiency with which we generate and consume electricity. The U.S. produces only a tiny fraction of the lithium we use. Most of the world's lithium supply is in Bolivia — a country with an unstable anti-American government and an economy based primarily on cocaine. By contrast, the largest sources of U.S. energy imports by far are our neighbors, Canada and Mexico, and we are much less dependent on foreign sources of energy than on foreign sources of lithium. Electric cars are being sold politically as a means of avoiding dependence on insecure foreign sources of oil, but a fleet of electric cars would render us dependent on far less secure foreign sources of lithium. I trust

---

19. For detailed explanations of the expense and futility of pursuing the goal of energy independence, see Richard J. Pierce, *Energy Independence and Global Warming,* 37 ENVTL. L. 595 (2007); Richard J. Pierce, *Dija Vu All Over Again-The Return of Project Independenceand Rate-PayerFundedDSM,* 16 ELECTRICITY J. 77 (2003).

Canada far more than I trust Bolivia.

Some people maintain that we could reduce threats to our national security and/or our level of defense spending if we attained energy independence. There is no evidence to support that widely held view, and it is inconsistent with a quick survey of the major threats that now concern us. We import no energy from any of the five countries that are of greatest concern to us today-North Korea, Afghanistan, Pakistan, Iran, and China. Indeed, four of the five are themselves dependent on foreign sources of energy, and even Iran must import large quantities of gasoline every year. Reducing our dependence on Canada and Mexico as our primary suppliers of energy would have no effect whatsoever on the potential threats to our national security posed by North Korea, Afghanistan, Pakistan, Iran, or China or on our need to devote large sums to national defense.

By contrast, there is overwhelming evidence that global warming will have catastrophic effects, including the death of millions of people and the displacement of hundreds of millions of people, primarily in impoverished areas like central Africa, central India, Bangladesh, and coastal Indonesia.[20] There is also persuasive evidence that global warming can be mitigated by reducing global emissions of green house gases (GHG), including carbon dioxide (CO_2), the most ubiquitous GHG. We should continue to embrace mitigation of global warming as an important goal of energy policy.

We can greatly simplify our choice of means to pursue our goals if we drop pursuit of the ill-conceived goal of energy independence and pursue only the goal of mitigation of global warming. As long as we continue to attempt to pursue both goals simultaneously, we will be forced to make tradeoffs that sacrifice one goal to further the other. Thus, for instance, President Carter's expensive and ill-fated attempt to obtain energy independence relied heavily on maximum substitution of coal for oil and gas. Such a policy would be terrible from a global warming perspective. Use of coal results in twice as much emissions of CO_2 as use of natural gas and about 50 percent more emissions than use of oil. Our present policy of providing massive subsidies for use of corn-based ethanol to replace gasoline is even worse from a global warming perspective. Substitution of corn-based ethanol for gasoline induces increases in deforestation to create land that can be used to cultivate corn and other food crops. When the effects of those land use changes are added to the CO_2 emissions that result from the process of growing corn and converting it into ethanol, substituting corn-based ethanol for gasoline has effects on global warming that are even worse than the effects of substituting coal for petroleum products.

---

20. The United Nations has collected a large body of publications that analyze the causes and consequences of global warming on its website. *See Climate Change,* UNITED NATIONS ENVTL. PROGRAMME, http://www.unep.org/climatechange/ (last visited Apr. 11, 2010).

B. We Should Replace Our Present Tools with a Carbon Tax

Once we focus on the single goal of mitigation of global warming, we can then identify and implement ways of taking the most important step to further that goal - reduction of CO_2 emissions by at least 80 percent by 2050. The present mix of tools used to further that goal is expensive, ineffective, and unsustainable. The Supreme Court has provided the foundation for EPA to use the CAA to reduce CO_2 emissions,[21] and the Obama Administration has taken a few modest steps in that direction, but there is a broad consensus that CAA is poorly designed to reduce CO_2 emissions. In the context of the other pollutants EPA has regulated,[22] it was possible to install pollution control devices that significantly reduced emissions produced by use of hydrocarbons, while continuing to consume the fuels. That is not an option in the case of CO_2. It is an inevitable byproduct of the process of using hydrocarbons. EPA can reduce CO_2 emissions only by reducing use of hydrocarbons. It is not clear how EPA could accomplish that result. The CAA is not designed to accomplish a result of that type.

Subsidies for carbon-free domestic fuels are extremely expensive, largely ineffective, and ultimately unsustainable. The subsidies needed to induce enough substitution of carbon-free fuels to reduce CO_2 emissions by 80 percent are enormous. Thus, for instance, since energy from windmills is almost twice as expensive as energy from coal or gas, wind farms would have to be assured of subsidies equal to the current price of coal or gas. Similarly, producers of solar energy would have to be assured of subsidies equal to three to four times the current price of coal or gas in order to induce a large scale transition to carbon-free fuels. We simply cannot afford carbon-free fuel subsidies of that magnitude.

Mandates to electric utilities to add enough carbon-free generation to mitigate global warming would be equally expensive, but the cost would be borne by consumers. The average price of electricity would increase significantly if utilities engaged in the massive fuel switching needed to reduce CO_2 emissions by 80 percent. Of course, consumers would revolt long before mandates could accomplish that result. For example, more modest increases in the price of electricity spawned a consumer revolt in the 1970s and 1980s.

There has long been a broad consensus that the massive reductions in CO_2 emissions needed to mitigate global warming can be attained through only one of two means — a global cap and trade system or a large global carbon tax. The failure of the Copenhagen meeting has left even many of the strongest proponents of a cap and trade

---

21. *Massachusetts v. EPA*, 549 U.S. 497, 556-60 (2007).

22. For a description of the steps EPA has taken to date, see ROBERT GLICKSMAN, ENVIRONMENTAL PROTECTION: LAW AND POLICY (2011).

system in despair. It seems highly unlikely that an effective global cap and trade system can be designed and implemented. That leaves a large carbon tax as the only potentially viable means of mitigating global warming.

Given the present political climate, it is hard to imagine the U.S. adopting a large carbon tax. Democrats are unwilling to increase taxes on people who earn less than $250,000 per year, while Republicans are unwilling to increase taxes on anyone. That aspect of the political environment must change in the near future, however, if the U.S. is to avoid the fate of Greece. Unless we make major changes in fiscal policy, we will experience large deficits for the indefinite future. Deficits of that magnitude are unsustainable. At some point in the near future, we must reduce spending and increase taxes.

A carbon tax is superior to an increase in income taxes or a value-added tax - the only alternatives to a carbon tax that offer the prospect of increasing revenues to the point at which our budget deficit will be tolerable. Taxes discourage the taxed activity. Thus, income taxes discourage work, while a value added tax discourages purchases of all types of goods and services. By contrast, a carbon tax discourages only what we need to discourage to mitigate global warming-emissions of CO_2.

A carbon tax is superior to subsidies for carbon-free energy sources in two important respects. First, it has the opposite effect on the budget deficit. While subsidies increase the deficit, a carbon tax would decrease the deficit. Second, it is much easier to design and to implement. To be effective, a carbon tax need only deter consumption of hydrocarbons. Consumers are left with complete discretion with respect to the ways in which they reduce their consumption of hydrocarbons. For example, by increasing the efficiency of their use of energy or by substituting for hydrocarbons some mix of carbon-free fuels like wind power, solar power, or nuclear power. It is important to give consumers that flexibility, both because the alternatives will be more or less attractive to different consumers in a variety of different situations, and because we cannot predict which of the alternatives to hydrocarbons will become more attractive in the future as a result of technological breakthroughs. By contrast, subsidies must be set at levels that are adequate to encourage optimal substitution of each subsidized alternative. By definition, they are always too high or too low, both because of the varying circumstances of consumers and because of the dynamic and unpredictable pace of technological progress.

1. Will a Carbon Tax Be Effective?

I am confident that a large carbon tax is the best policy the U.S. can implement in an effort to mitigate global warming. I am less confident, however, that a carbon tax implemented by the U.S. will be effective in mitigating global warming, given the daunting nature of the task. The climate experts tell us that we must reduce global CO_2 emissions by 80 percent by 2050. I am skeptical that there is anything the U.S. can do that can accomplish such a result. My skepticism has two sources — the likely behavior of some other countries, and the extreme difficulty of meeting this goal even in the U.S.

It is reasonable to assume that most other developed countries, for example, the members of the EU and Japan, would join the U.S. in an effort to reduce their CO_2 emissions by 80 percent. But it is not realistic to make such an assumption with respect to most developing countries, for example, China, India, and Russia. If the developed countries reduce their CO_2 emissions by reducing their consumption of hydrocarbons, developing countries are likely to *increase* their emissions by *increasing* their consumption of hydrocarbons. Any significant reduction in the quantity of hydrocarbons consumed in developed countries will reduce the global price of hydrocarbons. That, in turn, will yield increased consumption of hydrocarbons in the developing countries that already account for almost all of the increases in global CO_2 emissions in recent years.

The extent to which increased hydrocarbon consumption and increased CO_2 emissions in developing countries will offset decreased hydrocarbon consumption and decreased CO_2 emissions in developed countries, will depend on the price elasticity of demand for hydrocarbons in developing countries over the next forty years. Estimates of that metric range from 29 percent to 70 percent. So increased emissions in developing countries will offset about one-half of the decreased emissions in developed countries unless developing countries impose meaningful limits on their own emissions. That is why efforts must continue to implement an international agreement that imposes meaningful limits of some type on the emissions of GHGs in developing countries. Without such limits, nothing the U.S. does is likely to be effective in mitigating global warming.

Even a U.S. effort to reduce our CO_2 emissions by 80 percent would be extremely expensive and time-consuming. It also would produce uncertain and adverse effects on the environment. To illustrate the difficulty of the task, I will describe briefly each of the potential steps the U.S. might take to reduce CO_2 emissions in the electricity sector by 80 percent, and a few of the obstacles to implementation of each ofthose steps.

The electricity sector accounts for 40 percent of U.S. emissions of CO_2. The present composition of our sources of electricity are: 46 percent coal, 21 percent gas, 20 percent nuclear, 2 percent oil, 7 percent hydropower, and 4 percent other renewable sources. Since coal consumption produces twice as much CO_2 emissions as gas consumption, we would need to eliminate completely all emissions attributable to coal to reach the goal of an 80 percent reduction in CO_2 emissions in the electricity sector. That statistic illustrates a major political obstacle. Coal is mined throughout Appalachia and the Powder River Basin. Any effort to eliminate coal mining will face strong opposition from the many members of the House and Senate who represent states and districts in which coal accounts for a significant part of the economy. There are many paths we can take to move toward elimination of CO_2 emissions from use of coal in generating plants, but there are many obstacles on each of those paths. I will begin by describing the generic obstacles to the kinds of changes we need to make to reduce CO_2 emissions from electricity generation by 80 percent.

First, all carbon-free sources of electricity are more expensive than coal or gas. Thus, inducing consumers to switch sources will require either large subsidies or a large carbon tax. Second, electricity cannot be stored economically. That is important because some of the carbon-free sources of electricity are unpredictable in their availability. Thus, for instance, wind power is available only when the wind velocity falls within a particular range, and solar power is available only when the sun shines. This characteristic would be much less important if we could generate electricity in one period, store it economically, and consume it in another period. Since electricity cannot be stored economically, we can add only a modest amount of wind or solar energy to the grid without significantly impairing reliability. Third, the U.S. has traditionally relied on state and local governments to regulate the most important activities that are needed to generate, transmit, and distribute electricity. Some state and local governments are not likely to share the national government's interests in taking the actions needed to mitigate global warming, and even those that do are likely to have divergent preferences with respect to the best means to further that goal. No national plan to mitigate global warming can succeed if California and Oklahoma are free to adopt different policies with respect to the actions needed to mitigate global warming. Fourth, increased reliance on carbon-free sources like wind or solar will require large additions to our transmission grid. Most such additions provoke strong opposition on aesthetic grounds, and there is an ongoing controversy over the manner in which such expansions should be financed. Fifth, the U.S. is extremely litigious. Most of the projects needed to mitigate global warming will provoke opposition at regulatory agencies and in courts. The resulting litigation will slow the rate at which we can achieve the mitigation goal and increase the cost of achieving that goal.

(a) Conservation

Turning to particular steps that can be taken to mitigate global warming, I will begin with the step most people believe to be the most promising - conservation/ increased efficiency of use. Price is the most reliable and effective means of encouraging conservation and increased efficiency. If consumers confront electricity prices that reflect accurately the cost of electricity, including external costs like those attributable to global warming, they will decrease their consumption of electricity and increase the efficiency with which they use electricity. A large carbon tax would move the price of electricity in the right direction, but it is not enough.

Demand for electricity varies greatly over time. Since electricity cannot be stored economically, that widely varying demand must be met with contemporaneous variations in supply. The cost of supplying a kilowatt hour (kWh) of electricity to a particular location can vary by as much as a factor of twenty to one depending on the time when the electricity is supplied. Yet, most consumers pay a price for each kWh that does not vary as the cost of a kWh goes up or down. We can encourage consumers to engage in optimal efforts at conservation and efficiency enhancement only by changing the methods used to bill consumers. To accomplish that goal, we must install smart meters for all consumers. Smart meters allow consumers and utilities to observe the constantly changing cost of electricity and to measure consumption at each cost level. Smart meters will have no effect, however, unless we also change the method of billing all consumers so that the price they pay for each kWh varies greatly depending on the constantly changing cost of meeting their demand for electricity.

The federal government is attempting to implement a smart grid that would include smart meters and new billing methods. However, this attempt lacks the power to make the needed changes. Both the decision whether to authorize a utility to install smart meters, and the decision to change the method of billing consumers is subject to state regulation. The federal efforts to implement a smart grid have made little progress because many consumer advocacy groups and state regulators have objected on a wide variety of grounds. Unless consumer advocacy groups or state regulators change their attitudes dramatically, or Congress gives the federal government the power to require installation of smart meters and changes in billing methods, and the federal government exercises that power, the highly touted attempt to install a smart grid will go nowhere.

Some people believe that price provides an inadequate incentive for consumers to conserve because of various imperfections in the market. In order to overcome those imperfections, they urge adoption of state regulatory systems that reward utilities for using their customers' funds to make large payments for energy conservation purposes on behalf of their customers. Under a system of this type, a utility would pay for additional home insulation, high efficiency light bulbs, and high efficiency appliances, and add the cost of those acquisitions, plus a reward for their conservation-enhancing efforts, to their customers' bills.

Several states implemented regulatory systems of this type in the late 1970s and early 1980s with unfortunate effects. The new systems replaced one arguable market imperfection with another — utilities that are rewarded for making purchases on behalf of their customers do not have an incentive to insure that the purchases are cost effective. Audits of the customer-funded conservation acquisition programs consistently found that the efficiency enhancing claims for the goods and services purchased by the utilities were overstated. Ultimately, all of the state agencies that authorized programs of that type were forced by consumer backlash to abandon them.

(b) Switching to Natural Gas

We can achieve some part of our global warming mitigation goal by encouraging utilities to switch from coal to gas. At present, gas is available in abundance at about the same price as coal, and it emits only half as much CO_2 per kWh of electricity produced as coal. There are limits on our ability to switch to gas as a mitigation strategy, however. In the short term, only about 10 percent of generating capacity that uses coal can switch to gas. Over a longer period, of course, we could substitute gas for all of our present coal capacity. It is highly likely, however, that the price of gas will increase, perhaps significantly, as a result of increased regulation of hydraulic fracturing and increased demand attributable to fuel switching. Moreover, even a complete replacement of coal with gas would decrease emissions of CO_2. attributable to electricity generation by only about *45* percent - far short of the 80 percent needed to mitigate global warming.

(c) Switching to Nuclear

We could pursue a strategy of switching from coal to nuclear power. The obstacles to success in pursuing that strategy include: nuclear energy is approximately 20 percent more expensive than coal or gas; nuclear is controversial with the public; we have made no progress in solving the permanent nuclear waste disposal problem; nuclear generating plants are difficult to finance; and prospective investors remember the $100 billion dollars in losses investors suffered in the 1980S.

(d) Switching to Hydro

We could pursue a strategy of switching from coal to hydroelectric power. The obstacles to success in pursuing that strategy include: hydro is about 20 percent more expensive than coal or gas; the U.S. has limited untapped hydro potential; and hydro has become unpopular with the public because of the effects of dams on fisheries resources.

(e) Switching to Wind

We could pursue a strategy of switching from coal to wind. The obstacles to success in pursuing that strategy include: wind is 50-90 percent more expensive than coal or gas; wind farms kill large numbers of birds and bats; wind farms raise serious issues under the Endangered Species Act; windmills are extremely noisy; wind *farms* are aesthetically controversial; windmills have a low load factor; it takes about 1,000 windmills to equal the output of one standard-sized generator; wind power is unreliable because its availability depends on wind velocity; and because of its unreliability and low load factor, wind power requires construction of a disproportionately large number of new transmission lines. ...

(g) Switching to Solar

We could pursue a strategy of switching from coal to one of two forms of solar energy - central station thermal or decentralized photovoltaic. The obstacles to success in pursuing a solar thermal policy include: solar thermal is about 160 percent more expensive than coal or gas; it requires new transmission lines; and it requires a large amount of land that is rendered useless for any other purpose. The obstacles to success in pursuing decentralized photovoltaic include: photovoltaic is about 300 percent more expensive than coal or gas; it requires states to approve feed-in tariffs to allow solar producers to sell their excess electricity to the grid at generous prices; it is unpopular with many zoning boards and neighborhood associations; and unreliable because it is available only when the sun shines.

(h) Switching to Clean Coal

We could pursue a strategy of switching from coal to "clean coal" by implementing a program of carbon capture and storage (ccs). The obstacles to success in pursuing that strategy include: it has never been done on a large-scale basis; it would increase the cost of generating energy, with coal by about 30 percent; it would take decades to construct the required pipeline network and underground storage caverns; safe storage of CO_2 may be more difficult and risky than safe storage of spent nuclear fuel; a natural CO_2 leak in Cameroon killed 1,700 people in 1986; public awareness of the risks of CO_2 storage will cause major NIMBY problems; and none will embark on such a project without federal legislation that limits the project sponsor's liability in the event of a catastrophic leak.

CONCLUSION

I hope that my description of the limited options available to us to reduce CO_2 emissions by 80 percent and the formidable obstacles to success in attaining that goal persuade you both that the task is daunting and that a large carbon tax provides the best prospect for success in attaining the goal. A large carbon tax would offset to some extent the difference between the cost of continuing to rely primarily on hydrocarbons to generate electricity and the cost of switching to primary reliance on carbon-free sources of electricity. It would also spur investment in the research and development needed to enhance the efficiency with which we use electricity, reduce the cost of using carbon-free sources, improve the reliability of sources like wind and solar, and develop methods of storing electricity at tolerable cost. Perhaps most important, given the high variability of circumstances and the uncertain pace of technological progress, producers and consumers may be able to take steps needed to mitigate global warming, and at the same time take advantage of the evolving options that are best suited for them.

Our only hope of mitigating global warming lies in major technological breakthroughs. With the economic incentives created by a large carbon tax, we are likely to attain significant improvements in the technology needed to mitigate global warming. It is impossible to predict, however, whether the major advances will take place in the context of conservation/enhanced efficiency, reduced costs and/or increased reliability of specific carbon-free sources, or improved ability to store electricity economically. If we implement a large carbon tax, we do not have to engage in the hazardous process of predicting technological advances. If they take place primarily in the context of solar power, the tax will automatically channel most of our mitigation efforts in that direction. Conversely, if they take place primarily in the context of some other source — such as conservation/efficiency enhancement, cost of storage, wind, geothermal, clean coal, or nuclear — the tax will automatically channel most of our efforts down whatever path has become the most economic route to mitigate global warming.

노트와 질문

Pierce 교수는 다른 대체에너지의 개발을 위한 보조금으로 온실가스의 배출을 줄일 수 있는 화석연료의 사용비중 절감이 불가능하며 온실가스의 배출에 대한 탄소세를 부과, 탄소의 배출을 줄일 수 있는 기술개발이 유일한 해결책이라 본다. 우리나라는 온실가스의 배출을 줄이기 위하여 어떠한 정책적 노력을 하고 있는가?

제 2 장

한국의 에너지자원

1. 수요와 공급

BP자료에 의하면 우리나라는 2010년 하루 원유 2,384 TBD를 사용하여 전 세계 소비량의 2.6%를 차지하고 있으며 천연가스는 2010년 43 BCM를 사용, 전 세계 소비량의 1.4%를 차지하고 있다. 이를 보다 자세하게 한국에너지경제연구원 발표자료를 통하여 보면 아래와 같다.[1)]

[그림 2-1] 에너지 해외의존도 및 석유의존도(90-10)(KEEI)

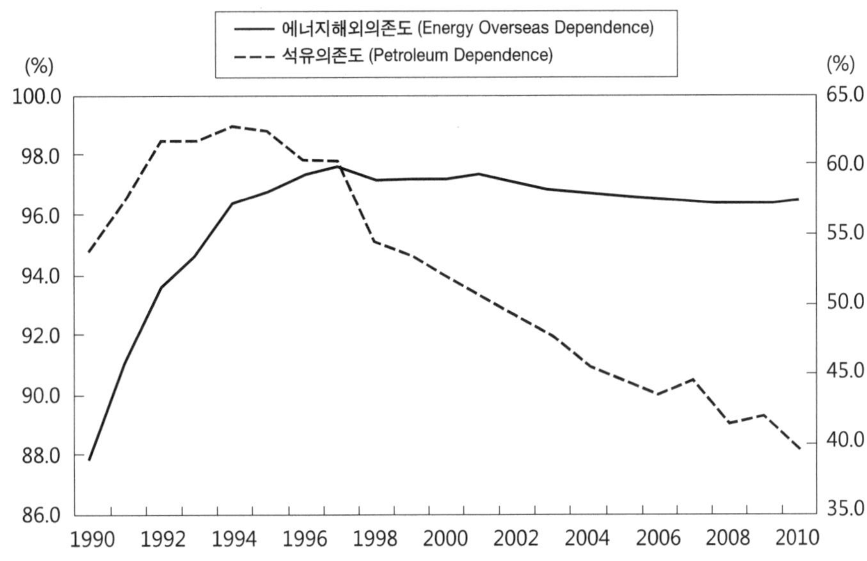

1) 한국에너지경제연구원, 2011 자주찾는 에너지통계, 3 이하 (2011). toe는 석유환산톤으로 원유 1톤이 갖는 열량 107kcal.

[그림 2-2] 에너지 밸런스 흐름(2010)(KEEI)

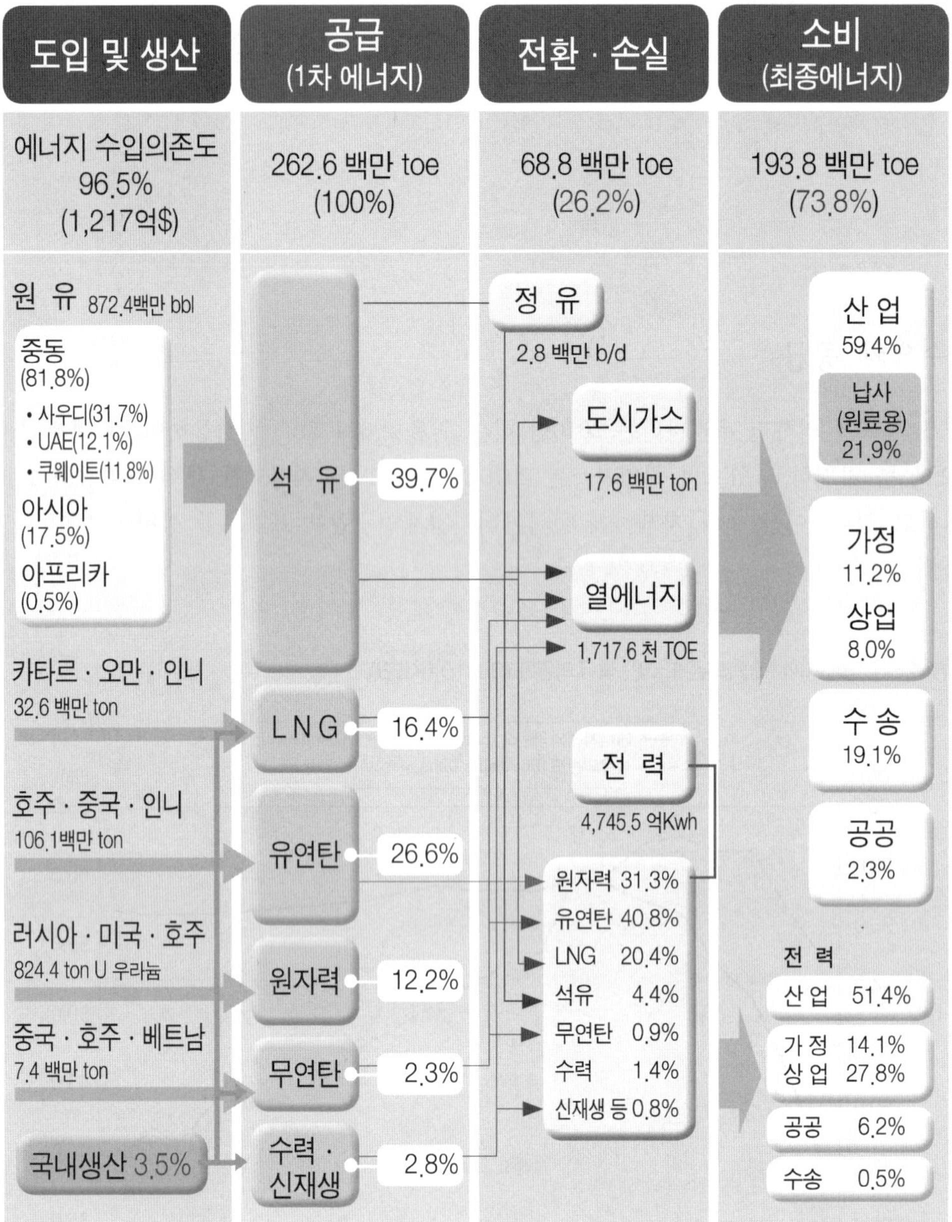

〈표 2-1〉 에너지 생산 및 수출입(90–10)(KEEI)

	국내생산				수입						수출	
	무연탄 (천톤)	천연가스 (천톤)	수력 (GWh)	신재생 (천toe)	석탄(천톤)		석유(천배럴)		원자력 (ton U)	천연가스 (천톤)	석유제품 (천배럴)	
					무연탄	유연탄	원유	석유제품				
1990	17,217	-	6,361	797	1,121	22,848	308,368	101,248	170	2,329	27,184	1990
1991	15,058	-	5,051	614	1,505	27,906	399,304	110,675	205	2,694	69,744	1991
1992	11,970	-	4,863	723	898	29,208	509,377	139,716	138	3,524	91,653	1992
1993	9,443	-	6,006	742	820	35,158	560,563	173,429	354	4,402	103,493	1993
1994	7,438	-	4,098	906	696	38,710	573,714	190,790	313	5,860	93,132	1994
1995	5,720	-	5,478	1,051	778	43,166	624,945	205,428	310	7,087	122,620	1995
1996	4,951	-	5,202	1,161	27	45,925	721,927	215,124	378	9,363	158,329	1996
1997	4,512	-	5,404	1,344	507	49,312	873,415	185,811	449	11,379	231,050	1997
1998	4,361	-	6,099	1,526	789	50,566	819,094	175,895	844	10,645	296,682	1998
1999	4,197	-	6,067	1,806	1,139	51,101	874,090	184,490	612	12,961	297,899	1999
2000	4,150	-	5,610	2,130	2,038	59,600	893,943	204,301	576	14,557	306,293	2000
2001	3,817	-	4,151	2,456	3,110	61,856	859,367	204,781	723	15,990	295,010	2001
2002	3,318	-	5,309	2,925	3,879	64,640	790,992	228,557	778	17,768	239,127	2002
2003	3,298	-	6,887	3,241	4,640	65,318	804,809	219,897	750	18,610	209,079	2003
2004	3,191	-	5,861	3,977	4,251	72,103	825,790	195,110	808	21,809	235,506	2004
2005	2,832	398	5,189	3,961	4,567	69,330	843,203	179,354	714	22,952	262,647	2005
2006	2,824	355	5,219	4,358	5,113	70,888	888,794	191,560	737	24,264	289,070	2006
2007	2,886	271	5,042	4,856	5,444	79,355	872,541	209,130	823	26,393	292,072	2007
2008	2,773	181	5,563	5,198	5,955	90,470	864,872	224,614	883	27,258	333,764	2008
2009	2,519	383	5,641	5,480	6,468	92,952	835,085	268,214	913	25,822	330,912	2009
2010	2,084	418	6,472	6,064	7,406	106,096	872,415	279,100	824	32,604	341,784	2010
	Anthracite (thou. ton)	LNG (thou. ton)	Hydro (GWh)	New & Renewable (thou. toe)	Anthracite	Bituminous	Crude Oil	Petroleum Products	Uranium (ton U)	LNG (thou. ton)	Petroleum Products (thou. bbl)	
					Coal(thou. ton)		Petroleum(thou. bbl)					
	Domestic Production				Imports						Exports	

〈표 2-2〉 지역별 원유수입(90–10)(KEEI)

(단위: 천배럴) (Unit: thou. bbl)

	수입							
	합 계	소 계	중동			아시아	아프리카	중남미
			사우디	UAE	쿠웨이트			
1990	308,368	229,017	-	-	-	62,530	9,689	7,132
1991	399,304	294,357	-	-	-	82,695	5,552	16,701
1992	509,377	380,452	155,104	53,206	14,372	95,032	12,822	21,071
1993	560,563	430,839	172,413	57,576	29,334	96,233	15,790	17,702
1994	573,714	439,330	177,619	48,598	27,239	91,083	23,225	20,075
1995	624,945	486,528	226,863	70,536	25,233	82,051	37,911	18,456
1996	721,927	561,098	252,665	91,620	41,134	98,629	37,024	25,174
1997	873,415	645,678	267,888	127,395	55,091	121,372	82,126	24,240
1998	819,094	622,005	234,450	122,022	66,894	113,494	61,907	21,689
1999	874,090	632,067	241,747	117,405	53,284	93,517	109,560	38,946
2000	893,943	686,916	264,925	128,064	66,627	112,669	67,749	26,610
2001	859,367	661,649	255,432	128,405	64,407	130,033	39,155	28,530
2002	790,992	579,865	240,765	105,905	56,996	136,756	35,877	38,494
2003	804,809	639,453	250,473	138,869	65,885	102,736	32,141	30,479
2004	825,790	645,183	253,849	145,598	64,659	116,287	42,874	21,447
2005	843,203	689,356	249,337	150,608	79,679	111,937	34,424	7,487
2006	888,794	730,843	261,563	158,865	92,620	110,306	42,814	4,831
2007	872,541	704,020	249,887	141,887	94,031	131,273	35,557	1,690
2008	864,872	746,458	262,637	158,109	104,593	108,482	9,932	-
2009	835,085	705,364	254,799	114,592	100,090	116,379	11,608	1,734
2010	872,415	713,646	276,787	105,656	103,079	152,354	4,592	1,823
	Total	Sub total	Saudi Arabia	UAE	Kuwait	Asia	Africa	Latin America
			Middle East					
	Imports							

• 주 : 97년 이후 자료는 석유류의 신분류체계에 의거 작성된 자료임.

• Note : From 1997, the classification of oil was revised.

〈표 2-3〉 국가별 LNG수입(90-10)(KEEI)

(단위: 천톤) (Unit: thou. ton)

	합 계	인도네시아	말레이시아	브루나이	카타르	오 만	호 주	기타
1990	2,291	2,291	-	-	-	-	-	-
1991	2,758	2,700	58	-	-	-	-	-
1992	3,425	3,308	117	-	-	-	-	-
1993	4,454	4,108	289	-	-	-	56	-
1994	5,928	5,366	291	271	-	-	-	-
1995	7,060	5,258	1,039	707	-	-	57	-
1996	9,595	6,262	2,572	705	-	-	56	-
1997	11,629	6,848	4,028	753	-	-	-	-
1998	10,600	7,050	2,893	596	-	-	-	61
1999	12,974	8,353	3,261	745	498	-	-	117
2000	14,578	6,124	2,435	800	3,268	1,593	54	304
2001	16,164	3,968	2,252	591	4,942	3,928	57	426
2002	17,993	5,127	2,325	540	5,253	3,970	176	604
2003	19,308	5,369	2,798	489	5,525	4,714	241	173
2004	21,781	5,290	4,638	838	5,818	4,411	285	501
2005	22,317	5,502	4,688	594	6,211	4,244	748	332
2006	25,256	5,060	5,546	850	6,458	5,221	701	1,421
2007	25,569	3,755	6,161	590	8,031	4,792	422	1,817
2008	27,259	3,053	6,247	738	8,744	4,544	397	3,536
2009	25,822	3,084	5,874	530	6,973	4,551	1,314	3,496
2010	32,603	5,451	4,745	787	7,448	4,557	1,030	8,585
	Total	Indonesia	Malaysia	Brunei Darussalam	Qatar	Oman	Australia	Others

〈표 2-4〉 1차에너지소비물량(90–10)(KEEI)

	석 탄(천톤)			석 유(천배럴)				천연가스 (천톤)	수 력 (GWh)	원자력 (GWh)	신재생 (천toe)	
	합 계	무연탄	유연탄	합 계	에너지유	LPG	비에너지유					
1990	43,405	21,529	21,876	356,348	267,514	35,712	53,123	2,329	6,361	52,887	797	1990
1991	42,392	17,557	24,835	424,667	308,487	43,131	73,048	2,694	5,051	56,311	614	1991
1992	39,814	13,597	26,217	514,224	352,828	53,917	107,479	3,524	4,863	56,530	723	1992
1993	42,419	10,867	31,552	564,575	386,698	59,437	118,440	4,402	6,006	58,138	742	1993
1994	42,660	7,549	35,111	621,498	424,675	63,452	133,371	5,860	4,098	58,651	906	1994
1995	44,352	6,263	38,089	677,210	469,010	66,468	141,731	7,087	5,478	67,029	1,051	1995
1996	50,277	5,370	44,907	721,065	499,962	68,441	152,662	9,363	5,202	73,925	1,161	1996
1997	53,942	4,230	49,712	793,899	507,218	71,623	215,059	11,379	5,404	77,086	1,344	1997
1998	55,892	4,631	51,262	670,278	370,853	67,992	231,433	10,645	6,099	89,689	1,526	1998
1999	59,129	4,992	54,137	719,657	405,864	77,007	236,786	12,961	6,067	103,064	1,806	1999
2000	66,525	6,196	60,329	742,557	409,673	84,688	248,196	14,557	5,610	108,964	2,130	2000
2001	70,823	7,137	63,686	743,667	404,727	84,377	254,563	15,990	4,151	112,133	2,456	2001
2002	75,952	7,687	68,264	762,868	402,143	91,415	269,310	17,768	5,309	119,102	2,925	2002
2003	79,120	8,581	70,540	762,941	395,124	88,606	279,211	18,610	6,887	129,659	3,241	2003
2004	82,116	8,138	73,978	752,329	371,241	88,432	292,655	21,809	5,861	130,715	3,977	2004
2005	84,822	9,034	75,788	761,080	367,053	91,668	302,359	23,350	5,189	146,779	3,961	2005
2006	87,827	9,829	77,998	765,520	355,881	93,451	316,189	24,619	5,219	148,749	4,358	2006
2007	94,128	9,698	84,430	794,945	352,955	97,143	344,848	26,664	5,042	142,937	4,828	2007
2008	104,198	10,215	93,983	760,641	320,153	101,881	338,607	27,439	5,563	150,958	5,198	2008
2009	108,378	9,777	98,602	778,480	319,864	106,320	352,296	26,083	5,641	147,771	5,480	2009
2010	119,321	10,104	109,218	794,278	326,416	105,175	362,688	33,083	6,472	148,596	6,064	2010
	Total	Anthracite	Bituminous	Total	Energy Use	LPG	Non-Energy Use	LNG (thou. ton)	Hydro (GWh)	Nuclear (GWh)	New & Renewable (thou. toe)	
	Coal(thou. ton)			Petroleum(thou. bbl)								

노트와 질문

KEEI의 2010년도 현황과 아래 2005년도 정책에 대한 설명, 2012년 지경부 업무계획을 비교하여 보고 우리의 석유/천연가스정책목표는 지난 5년간의 노력으로 2010년 달성되었는지, 달성되지 않은 정책목표가 있다면 무엇이며 그 원인은 무엇인지, 그리고 2012년 지경부의 업무계획은 제대로 목표를 잡고 있는 것인지 논평하여 보라.

2. 정책목표의 설정과 집행수단[2)]

가. 석유정책

염명천, 에너지시장, 산업 & 정책 173-189 (2006)[3)]

1) 석유비축 확대

가) 현황과 계획

정부는 1차 석유파동 직후인 74년도에 이미 비축사업 추진 구상이 있었으나, 관계 부처 등의 인식부족으로 지지부진하다가 78~79년 제2차 석유파동을 겪고 나서 80년도부터 비축사업을 추진해 왔다.

제1차 비축사업으로 80~88년간 4개의 비축기지(울산, 거제, 구리, 평택)를 건설하고 원유 36.3백만b, 석유제품 1.8백만b, LPG 1.9백만b을 비축하여 1988년도에 당초 목표인 국내소비량기준 지속일수 60일분을 넘는 66일분을 달성하였다.

그러나 석유소비가 계속 증가하면서 지속일수가 계속 줄어들자, 정부는 제2차 비축사업을 추진하여 90~03년간 6개의 비축기지를 추가건설(거제추가, 여수, 구리추가, 용인, 곡성, 평택추가)하여 원유 20.2백만b, 제품 1.9백만b, LPG 3.0백만b을 추가로 비축하면서, 민간 사업자에게도 비축의무를 새로이 부담시켜, 03년도 말 지속일수 106.1일분(정부 50.7일, 민간 55.4일)을 달성하였다.

민간비축의무는 93년 2월 원유와 석유제품은 판매량의 27일분으로 최초 부과하고 96년에 30일, 02년 5월에 40일이 된다. LPG는 93년 2월에 15일분으로 최초 부과 후, 96년에 17일, 2000년에 25일, 01년에 27일, 04년에 30일이 된다(〈표 A〉에서 보듯 08년에 민간비축 63일을

2) 일찍이 에너지정책법의 제정을 주장한 김성수, 국제에너지자원법 184-85 (2002) 참조.
3) 석유의 품질관리도 정책목표 중 하나로서 석유사업법 제24조 이하에서 규정하고 있다. 석유사업법 개정 전 유사석유제품 여부에 관한 판결로 대법 1997. 12. 12. 선고 97누15623 판결 등 참조.

〈표 A〉 우리나라 석유비축현황 및 목표 [단위: 백만b(지속일수)]

		04년말 현황			08년 목표		
		정부	민간	계	정부	민간	계
	원유	63.2(46.1)	31.6(23.0)	94.8(69.1)	101.1(62.5)	43.7(28.3)	144.8(90.8)
	제품	11.0(7.6)	53.6(32.2)	64.5(39.8)	15.6(9.7)	53.3(34.7)	68.9(44.4)
합계		74.2(53.7)	85.2(55.2)	159.4(108.9)	116.7(72.2)	97.0(63.0)	213.7(135.2)

달성하려면 비축의무를 원유, 석유제품, LPG 할 것 없이 모두 50일로 늘려야 가능하다).

우리나라가 2002년 가입한 IEA에서 요구하는 국가 비축수준은 정부와 민간을 합하여 90일이다. 한편, IEA 회원국 평균 비축일수는 04년 7월 기준 113일인데, 한국의 비축수준은 석유수요 증가에 따라 계속 저하될 것이 예상되어 정부는 95년 제3차 비축계획('95~'06)을 수립하였다. 내용은 8개의 기지를 추가건설(동해, 여수추가, 거제추가, 서산[원유], 서산[제품], 울산추가, 김천, 평택추가)하고 원유 37.9백만b, 제품 4.6백만b를 구입해 비축하는 것이다. 그러나 이 또한 예산부족으로 2년이 지연되어 08년까지 완성되는 것으로 수정되었다. 04년 말 우리나라 비축수준과 3차 계획달성 이후의 목표는 〈표 A〉와 같다. 예정대로 비축이 달성되면 우리나라는 08년에 그 당시의 예상 수요기준으로 135일분을 비축하게 된다.

〈표 A〉에서 정부비축은 현재 한국석유공사가 실시하고 있고, 민간비축은 석유사업법상 비축의무자 25개사의 민간재고와, 비축의무자는 아니지만 정부가 관리하는 발전회사 등 대수요처 16개사의 민간재고를 합한 것이다. 민간비축의무자는 석유사업자로서 석유사업법에 의해 비축의무가 부과되고 위반하면 처벌을 받는 회사로서, 정유사 5개, 제품수입사 18개, LPG 수입사 2개, 석유화학사 5개이다.

나) 평가 및 논의

04년 7월 기준 각국의 비축량과 비축수준은 OECD 전체가 3,898백만b(113일)이고, 순위는 ① 미국 1,631백만b(121일), ② 일본 622백만b(117일), ③ 독일 267백만b(114일), ④ 프랑스 184백만b(99일), ⑤ 캐나다 172백만b(n), ⑥ 한국 153백만b(113일), ⑦ 이태리 135백만b(95일), ⑧ 영국 98백만b(n), ⑨ 네덜란드 102백만b(185일) 등이다. 캐나다와 영국은 산유국으로 지속일수를 계산하지 않고 IEA에서 비축을 요구하지도 않는다. 미국은 산유국이지만 전략비축유(SPR; Strategic Petroleum Reserves)로 상업재고량과 구분하여 정부가 따로 비축한다. 미국의 상업재고량 수준은 매주단위 발표되므로 국제유가 등락에 큰 영향을 준다. 한국의 현재 비축물량이나 비축일수가 외국과 비교하여 분명 적은 수준은 아니다. 따라서 이제 비축은 더 이상 필요없다는 의견이 일부 제기되기도 한다. 그러나 유럽 국가는 수십 개의 나라가 한 덩어리로 뭉쳐있고, 각국 간 송유관, 가스 공급망, 송전망이 거미줄처럼 연결되어 있어 한국이나 일본에 비해 석유위기에 대한 위험도가 현저하게 적은 편임을 감안해야 한다. 석유공급 안정성에 관한 한 한국과 일본은 육지에서 멀리 떨어진 섬과 같다. 작은 투자를 아끼려다 몇 배 큰 곤욕을 치른 과거의 경험을 또 잊어버리는 처사일 수도 있다.

정부비축은 석유공사가 비축기지를 지어 비축유를 저장하는 형태이지만, 민간비축은 정부가 정유사, LPG수입사, 제품수입사, 석유화학회사 등 27개 업체에 원유나 석유제품은 40일분 이상, LPG는 30일분 이상의 재고를 보유하도록 의무화하고 있다. 그러나 대부분의 경우 정유사와 LPG 수입사는 의무일수 이상의 재고를 운영재고로 평소 보유하므로 유가급락이 예상되어 재고를 그 이하로 유지해야 할 경우가 아니면 추가부담을 갖는 것은 아니다.

반면 제품수입사나 석유화학사는 재고 보유기간이 평소 짧기 때문에 정부의 의무부과 때문에 추가적 자금 부담을 정유사에 비해 상대적으로 많이 지는 경우가 있어 형평성 문제가 제기될 수도 있다. 그러나 이 제도의 취지인 "석유 공급 단절시 국내 일정량 이상의 재고가 보유되어야 하고, 그 부담은 판매량에 따라 공평해야 한다"는 입장에서 보면 양자를 차별한다는 근거는 희박하다.

석유비축수준을 유지하는 것은 상당한 비용 지불을 요한다. 04년 말 기준 정부비축 74.2백만b은 가격을 35$/b씩 쳐도 2.6조원이다. 여기에 지금까지 투입된 기지 건설 비용은 1차 2,673억 원, 2차 7,726억 원으로 10,399억 원이다. 즉 거대 자금이 비축 목적을 위해 잠겨 있는 것이다. 석유공사는 1999년부터 비축유의 10% 범위 내에서 국제유가의 등락을 이용하여 해외의 트레이더(trader)와 스왑(swap)거래 등을 통해 수익을 얻고 있는데, 05년 말까지 1,314억 원의 세전 이익을 내었다. 또한 정유사의 유조선이 태풍·재해 등으로 입항이 지연되는 경우 정유사 등에 긴급 대여를 하여 수급 안정에 기여하는 측면도 있다. 이러한 수익 창출 폭을 확대하려는 시도, 즉 10% 범위를 늘리려는 시도가 있을 수 있는데, 그럴 경우 위기 시 대응 능력은 당연히 저하된다.

비축제도는 돈을 버는 제도가 아니라 비상시에 대비하는 값비싼 제도라는 면에서 주객이 바뀌는 일이 되어서는 곤란하다. 또, OECD 회원국 중 이렇게 비축유 트레이딩으로 수익을 내는 나라는 한국뿐이다.

2) 원유도입선 다변화

가) 제도의 추이와 현황

원유도입선 다변화제도는 74년 5월 장기에너지 종합계획에 처음 등장한다. 당시에는 국내도입 원유전량의 공급권을 Major가 가지면서, 중동에서 100% 도입되고 있었다. 제1차 석유파동으로 Major의 공급능력에 타격을 받자 한국도 피해를 입었다. 그럼에도 다변화제도의 시행은 지지부진, 78년 제2차 석유파동으로 다시 한 번 타격을 받고 나서 82년부터 제도화되었다. 78년까지는 기간계약의 경우 중동 의존도가 100%로 사우디, 쿠웨이트, 이란에서만 도입했다.

79년에 인도네시아에서 15.4만b이 들어와 중동 의존도가 최초로 99.92%가 되었고, 정부의 원유확보 노력으로 동남아, 에콰도르 등에서 원유도입이 늘면서 중동 의존도가 90% 수준으로 줄다가 82년에 이 제도의 시행으로 중동 의존도가 본격적으로 낮아지게 된다.

이 제도는 미주·아프리카에서 도입되는 원유에 대해서는 중동지역에 비해 불리한 수송비와 금융비 등을 정부가 재정으로 보전해 주어 중동 의존도를 줄이려는 정책이다.

이 제도는 약간의 변화를 거쳐 왔는데, 제1기는 82년 3월~86년 4월 동안 미주·아프리카에서 도입되는 기간계약이나 현물계약을 막론한 전체 원유도입에 대해 추가운송비, 추가금융비와 장려금까지 지급하는 제도였다. 그 결과 제도시행 전인 81년 중동 의존도 90.7%는 85년에 57.0%까지 축소된다. 제2기는 국제유가가 하락한 86년 4월~87년 5월 동안 지원 대상에서 현물계약은 제외하고, 지원 내용에서도 장려금을 제외하여 지원 폭을 상당히 줄였다. 이에 따라 87년도 중동 의존도는 63.7%까지 상승한다. 제3기는 국제유가가 더 하락한 87년 5월 이후 지원 내용에서 추가 금융비를 제외하고 추가 운송비만 지급하게 된다. 이에 따라 중동 의존도는 다시 70%대로 상승하게 된다. 제4기는 98년 이후 예산당국이 지원예산을 대폭 축소하면서 요건을 충족하는 지원 대상 원유의 60% 내외만 실제 지원이 되고, 나머지는 예산이 없어 지원을 못하는 모순을 보인다. 03년에 가서는 전체 도입물량 중 0.08%만 이 제도의 혜택을 보게 되고, GS정유를 제외한 다른 정유사는 이 제도를 외면하게 된다. 즉 예산부족으로 다변화제도가 극히 부실화된 것이다. 〈표 B〉는 중동의존도 변화 추이를 보여준다.

산업자원부는 제도의 부실에 대응, 다변화제도가 단기적인 예산 책정에 좌우되지 않도록 수송비차액을 석유수입 시 부과되는 석유수입 부과금에서 차감해 주는 제도로 변경(04. 2. 13 및 5. 11 고시개정)하여 04년도 도입분부터 적용하고 있다. 즉, 정유사가 확실하게 이 제도의 혜택을 신뢰할 수 있게 하여 2~3년 전부터 도입선 변경을 추진할 수 있도록 한 것이다.

이와 함께 지원 대상지역을 미주·아프리카에 구주·CIS 지역을 추가하고, 지원 대상계약에 산유국 정부뿐 아니라 Major나 Trading 회사와의 계약분도 포함하였다. 또한 부과금 감면 후 사후 불이행이 발견되면 지원액의 3배의 위약금을 물도록 하여 제도의 악용을 방지하였다. 새로운 제도로 원유도입선 다변화제도가 활성화될 것을 기대한다.

〈표 B〉 중동의존도 및 도입선다변화 지원예산추이(82–03)

	'82	'85	'88	'91	'94	'97	'00	'01	'02	'03
중동의존도(%)	76.0	57.0	64.2	73.7	76.6	73.9	76.9	77.0	73.3	79.5
지원물량비율(%)	4.0	19.0	6.4	3.4	4.5	1.1	0.65	0.68	0.56	0.08
지원금액(억원)	21.9	271.8	29.4	55.1	145.1	78.6	45.3	48.2	48.2	4.4

나) 평가 및 논의

이 제도의 필요성에 대한 논란이 있다. 세계석유매장량 분포로 보아 중동 의존도 증가는 불가피한데, 이를 저지하려고 예산을 들일 필요가 있는가? 또, 그간 수십 년 동안 지원을 했어도 중동의존도가 줄지 않고 75~80%에 있지 않는가? 하는 지적들이다. 한편, 이 제도는 연원을 갖고 있으며, 큰 역할을 했고, 분명 그 의미는 현재에도 퇴색되지 않는다는 설명이 있다. 또 지원액은 매년 지출하는 보험료의 성격을 갖고 있고, 그 보험료가 적립되지는 않으므로 수십 년 지원에 중동의존도 75~80%라는 지적은 부당하다는 설명이 있다.

한편, 석유위기에 대응하는 방안으로 세 가지 방법이 있는데, 비교대상인 석유비축, 석유개발에 비해 다변화제도는 값싼 제도라는 분석도 있다. 즉, 중동으로부터 원유공급 중단을 가정 시, 다변화원유는 비축원유나 자주개발원유와 동일 물량을 확보하면서도 비용은 추가운송비에 불과하므로 훨씬 적게 든다는 분석이다. 또한 동북아 프리미엄에 대한 근본적인 대책이 될 수도 있다. 일각에서 WTO 규정상 "최혜국 대우"에 위반될 가능성, 상계가능 보조금으로 분류될 가능성이 제기되나, 구체적 피해사실 입증이 어렵고, 석유거래 자체가 성격상 전략 물자로서 전반적으로 GATT나 WTO 규정의 적용에서 벗어나 있는 현실을 감안하면 기우로 볼 수도 있다. 그러나 양자협의에서는 문제될 가능성은 있다.

〈표 C〉 원유도입선다변화제도의 변경

구분	종전('03년)	개정안('04. 5. 11.)
지원방식 변경	추가운송비(World Scale 기준)의 80%를 예산범위 내 지원	추가운송비(World Scale기준)의 80%를 부과금에서 감면
지원지역 확대	미주+아프리카	미주+아프리카+구주(CIS포함)
지원대상 명확화	산유국정부·국영회사와 체결한 장기계약	산유국정부·국영회사, 석유 Major·Trading사와 체결한 1년 이상 장기계약으로 4개년 이상, 총 700만 배럴/년 이상, 가격조건 명시될 것
환수 및 가산금 징수	〈신설〉	부과금 감면 이후 장기계약 요건(1년 이상) 등 불이행시 위약금(3배) 징수 부당·허위 신청시 (지원액+가산금) 징수
지원금액 제한	예산범위 내로 지원 제한	재정상황 등 고려하여 지원제한 가능(예외적)

3) 국제유가 상승에 대응

가) 03년 3월 이라크전쟁 대응

2001년 9월 9.11테러 사건이 나고 미국은 01년 10~12월간 알카에다를 비호한다는 이유로 아프가니스탄의 탈레반정권을 공격하여 붕괴시킨다. 이어 02년 1월 북한, 이란, 이라크를 "악의 축"으로 규정하고, 이라크가 보유한 대량살상무기(WMD)를 제거한다는 명분으로 2003

년 3월 20일 이라크를 침공하여 4월 14일 점령을 끝내고 군정을 실시한다.

국제유가는 02년 3월부터 미국의 이라크 공격 예상과 베네수엘라 석유회사 파업 등으로 18~19$/b대로 상승세를 보이고, 미국의 공격이 임박한 03년 1월에는 28$/b 선까지 오른다. 이에 정부는 『국제유가상승에 따른 경제안정화대책(03. 1. 28.)』을 수립한다. 그 내용은 ① 원유가 32$/b대까지는 국내유가를 29$/b 선, 즉 국내 휘발유 가격을 1,340원/l 선으로 유지하고 29$/b을 넘는 상승분은 관세, 내국세 및 석유수입 부과금을 인하한다. ② 원유가가 33$/b을 상회 시 세금·석유수입 부과금을 추가 인하하고, 일부는 국내유가 상승으로 시장에 흡수하며, 필요시 비축유 방출과 석유수급 조정 명령으로 대처한다. ③ 에너지 소비절약은 1단계로 자발적으로 시행하고, 필요시 2단계로 의무적 절약대책을 추진한다는 내용이었다.

이에 따라 원유가가 29$/b을 상회하자 정부는 석유수입 부과금을 14원/l에서 8원/l으로 내리고(03. 2. 17.), 공공기관 승용차 10부제 등 자발적 에너지 절약시책을 시행한다. 유가가 추가 상승하자 부과금으로 다시 4원/l으로 내리고, 재경부는 석유관세를 5%에서 3%로 내린다(03. 3. 12.). 이렇게 하여 국내 유가는 29$/b대로 유지되며, 정부는 전국의 정유사, 대리점, 주유소의 출하가격을 감시하여 휘발유 소비자 가격기준으로 전국 평균 1,340원/l으로 억제시켰다. 미국의 이라크 점령 이후 국제유가가 안정되자 관세는 5%를 회복(03. 5. 3.)하고, 석유수입 부과금도 14원/l을 회복(04. 1. 1.)하게 된다.

나) 04년 고유가 대응

03년부터 중국의 석유수요가 예상외로 급증하면서 전세계적으로 수급 우려가 제기되었다. 베네수엘라의 석유파업으로 정정불안이 지속되면서 미국의 석유제품 가격이 상승하고, 04. 2. 10. OPEC이 100만b/d 감산을 결정하고, 달러화 약세와 유가상승을 예상한 투기자본이 석유시장에 대량 들어오면서 WTI의 급등이 인도한 국제원유가는 3월말 31$/b을 넘고, 5월에는 34$/b, 8월에는 38$/b을 넘어선다.

정부는 원유가가 30$/b를 넘자 『국제유가상승에 따른 상황별 대응 방안(04. 4. 6.)』을 작

〈표 D〉 국제유가상승에 따른 상황별 대응방안(04. 4. 6.)

유가안정 대책	32~35$/b 미만 시	• 32$/b 상회 시, 할당관세 3 → 1%, 석유수입부과금 14 → 8원/l • 33~35$/b 미만 시, 부과금·내국세를 적정수준으로 추가 인하
	35$/b 상회 시	• 추가상승분 50%는 내국세·유가완충자금으로 흡수, 50%는 시장가격에 반영
수급안정 대책	수급차질 우려 시	• 종합적 수급안정 대책 검토·수립 (상황주시 단계)
	부분적 수급차질 시	• 의무적 에너지 수요관리 조치, 부분적 수급조정·비축유 방출 조치
	전면적 수급차질 시	• 강제적 에너지 소비억제 조치, 최고가격제·유가완충지급 집행, 전면적 수급조정명령 등 (석유위기 대응계획 단계별 시행)

〈표 E〉 고유가 종합대책(05. 5. 18.)

에너지 저소비형 사회구조로 전환	• 단기; 공공부문 솔선수범+자율적 에너지절약 유도 • 중자기; 산업부문(2,157개 다소비사업장) 중심으로 에너지절약 시설투자 촉진
신생에너지보급확대	• 신재생에너지비중: (03년) 2.1% → (11년) 5% • 3대 기술분야(수소 · 연료전지, 태양광, 풍력) 집중지원 • 공공기관 설치 의무화, 태양광주택보급, 발전차액제도 등으로 단기 경제성 보완
해외자원개발 확대	• 자주개발 원유비중; (03년) 3.0% → (10년) 10% • 국가에너지위원회(대통령주재) 구성 · 운영+자원부국과 정상외교 → 국가적과제化

성한다. 그 내용은 03년도의 유가대책과 비슷한 것으로, ① 원유가가 32$/b을 넘으면 관세와 석유수입 부과금 인하로 국내유가를 32$/b 선으로 유지하고, ② 35$/b을 넘으면 추가 상승분의 1/2은 석유수입 부과금 추가 인하와 법인세 인하로 흡수하고, 나머지 1/2은 국내소비자 가격에 반영하기로 하였다. ③ 수급차질의 경우에는 단계에 따라 부분적 또는 전면적인 석유수급 조정명령, 비축유 방출로 대처하고, 자발적 또는 강제적인 에너지 소비절약을 시행하기로 하였다. ④ 전면수급 차질 발생 시 IEA와 공조하고, 에너지 수요억제 조치, 비축유 방출, 석유수급 조정명령, 최고가격제 실시와 유가 완충 자금을 집행하기로 하였다. 이에 따라 원유가가 10일 이동평균으로 32$/b을 넘자, 우선 석유 수입부과금을 14원/l에서 8원/l으로 내리고(04. 4. 30.) 시장을 감시하여 국내 제품가격을 32$/b대로 억제하였다. 전국 주유소에 대한 가격 감시 결과, 휘발유 가격은 전국 평균 1,360원/l 이하로 유지되었다.

그러나 원유가가 35$/b을 넘어서고, 향후 중국 등의 소비 급증의 지속으로 고유가가 고착화될 가능성이 커지자 산자부는『최근 국제유가 동향과 대책(04. 5. 18.)』을 수립하여 시행하게 된다. 이는 향후 국제유가가 장기간 고유가를 지속한다는 전제를 바탕으로 그 동안의 단기적 가격안정 대책을 버리고, 중장기 에너지 대책을 천명하는 내용이다. 즉 ① 에너지 저소비형사회로 전환, ② 신재생에너지 보급확대, ③ 해외자원개발 확대 등을 내용으로 한다.

이러한 시책은 당연히 대규모 자금조달을 전제로 하는 것으로, 에너지 특별회계의 세입 확보 방안을 현안으로 검토하게 된다. 이후 원유가는 11~12월에 34~35$/b, 6월 51$/b, 7월 53$/b을 차례로 상회한다. 과거 25년 간 유지되던 월별 최고 유가인 1980년 1월의 41.25$/b을 가볍게 넘어버린 것이다. 04. 4. 30.에 14원/l에서 8원/l으로 인하된 석유수입 부과금은 고유가 장기화에 따라 05. 1. 1.부로 14원/l으로 회복된다.

다) 평가 및 논의

가격이 자유화된 상황에서 원유가 상승에 따라 관세나 석유수입 부과금을 인하하여 국내가격을 안정시키는 것은 실제로는 불완전하고 정부의 노력이 많이 들어가는 정책이다. 국제 원유가격이 상승하면서 사회분위기는 이미 국내 가격 상승을 예상하여, 정부가 세금 등을 내려주어도 정유사나 판매상들이 분위기를 이용해 국내가격을 내리지 않아도 소비자들은 대부분 이를 수용하게 된다. 즉, 시장기능이 발휘되어 가격을 내리지 않은 사업자는 시장에서도 도태되어야 하는데, 현실은 그렇지 않다.

결국 세금 등을 내려준 정부가 가격을 감시하고 행정지도로 세금인하분이 가격에 반영되도록 해야 하는데, 이것이 쉽지 않고 결과가 확실하지도 않다. 따라서 단기 가격대책은 정교한 가격 통제시스템이 동반되어야 한다. 즉, 최고가격제를 동반 시행하는 경우에 효과가 확실하다.

03년과 04년 정부가 가격 안정대책을 시행했을 때 관세와 석유수입 부과금 인하분이 정유사의 출하가격에는 제대로 반영된 것으로 분석되었다. 정유사는 5개밖에 안 되므로 정부의 감시기능이 작동된 것이다. 그러나 매일 가격이 변동되는 51개의 수입사, 362개의 대리점과 11,005개의 주유소의 출하가격을 정부가 감시하는 것은 쉽지 않다. 여건에 따라 어떤 판매상은 정부의 관세 등 인하분을 출하가격에 반영할 수밖에 없겠지만, 여건에 따라 그렇게 하지 않는 판매상도 많을 것이다.

따라서 이런 경우에는 최고가격제를 병행하는 것이 바람직하다. 최고가격제에 3가지 방식이 있는데, 국민생활에 불편이 없는 방안을 선택해야 한다. 첫째는 전국균일 최고가격제로서, 전국의 정유사·수입사, 대리점, 주유소 단계별로 단일한 가격을 고시하는 것이다. 단순명료하고 통제가 쉬우나 현재 휘발유의 경우 전국의 주유소별로 최고 400원/l 정도의 가격차이가 있는 현실을 외면하는 것이다.

둘째는 전국의 각 대리점과 주유소별로 가격통제 전 일정기간 동안 가격을 조사하여 그 가격에서 얼마를 가감한 가격을 고시하는 것이다. 이것은 전국 대리점과 주유소의 최고가격이 모두 제각각 달라지게 된다. 시장 현실을 반영하고 있으나 1개 기초지자체당 평균 47개의 주유소, 30개의 일반판매소를 감시해야 하는 정부의 가격감시에 많은 비용이 들어갈 수 있다. 셋째는 지역별로 또는 평소의 가격대별로 전국의 대리점과 주유소를 A, B, C, D, E그룹 등으로 묶어 가격감시를 하는 것이다. 첫째와 둘째의 중간노선이고 현실적 방안이겠으나, 적절한 그룹핑이 과제가 된다. 이런 문제점과 부담을 감안하면, 이번 정부의 고유가 대책이 단기적 가격대책을 벗어나 중장기 근본적인 에너지대책으로 선회한 것은 매우 적절한 일이다.

4) 석유위기 대응계획

가) 석유위기 대응계획

제1차 또는 제2차 석유파동과 같은 공급위기가 발생할 경우 대응은 상황별로 다양하게 이루어질 수 있겠지만, 구체적 수단으로 채택 가능한 행동계획은 전시의 『충무계획』처럼 통일성 있고 구체성 있는 계획으로 미리 준비되어 있어야 한다. 정부는 아래와 같은 구체적인 계획을 갖고 있다.

그 연원은 과거 1, 2차 석유위기와 91년 걸프전쟁 등 위기가 발생할 때마다 대응계획을 세워 대처한 적이 있고 이를 종합·보강한 계획을 『석유위기 대응계획』을 작성하여 03. 3. 18.에 완성하였다. 이는 석유위기가 발생하거나 임박했을 때 구체적으로 시행될 내용으로, ① 에너지 비상대책반의 구성·운용, ② 단계적(자발적 혹은 강제적) 에너지 소비절약시책, ③ 비축유 방출, ④ 최고가격 고시제, ⑤ 유가완충자금 집행, ⑥ 단계적(부분적 혹은 전면적) 석유수급 조정명령, ⑦ 해외 유전생산석유 우선인수, ⑧ 석유 품질기준 완화조치, ⑨ 제한송전, ⑩ 석유배급제 등에 대한 상세한 절차와 시행방법을 담고 있다. 실제 상황이 발생하였을 때, 구체적인 대응의 결정이나 선택은 국무회의 등을 거쳐 종합적 판단이 이루어지겠지만, 결정이 있을 경우 시행할 세부내용과 절차 등을 미리 정해 놓은 것이다. 실제 사태가 발생하면

〈표 F〉 석유위기 대응방안 주요 내용(03. 3. 18.)

단계	대응방안	주요 내용
〈1단계〉 수급차질 우려시	석유 등『에너지비상대책반』설치, 가동	산자부-유관기관-관련업계를 5개 반으로 구성 ① 총괄, ② 석유, ③ 가스, ④ 전력, ⑤ 절약
	석유 수급·가격동향분석·점검	석유수급 일일 보고체제 유지(석유사업자-정부)
	민간업계의 협조유도 및 석유확보외교 강화	필수민생유류 수출·국제벙커링 자제 권고 (고위정부인사+업계대표)를 산유국에 파견
	자율적 에너지 소비절약시책 시행	공공기관 절약노력+인센티브 이용 소비절약, 절약홍보 광고(TV, 라디오, 신문 인터넷 등)
〈2단계〉 부분적 수급차질 발생시	부분적 석유수급조정·비축유 방출조치	일부지역·유종 대상, 민간비축 의무일수 축소
	의무적 에너지 소비 절감조치 시행	에너지사용 제한명령(골프장, 스키장, 주유소, 네온사인)
〈3단계〉 전면적 수급차질 발생시	정부 및 민간보유 비축유 방출	민간비축 의무일수축소 → 민간재고 감소로 방출 90일분까지 자율방축, 그 이하는 IEA와 공조
	석유류 최고가격고시제 및 유가완충자금 집행	유가연동제방식의 formula 적용하여 가격통제 정유사 손실은 유가완충자금으로 보전
	석유수급조정명령 발동	석유도입·수출입·정제생산, 지역별·사업자별 배정, 가동률·조업조정, 사업자간 교환·분배, 유통경로지정 등
	강제적 에너지 소비 절감조치	미리 정해진 우선순위에 따라 사용량 제한
	해외유전 생산 원유 우선인수권 발동	정부지원 받아 참여한 유전, 국내수요 9일분
	한-노르웨이 공동비축 물량 우선 구매	국제현물가로 여수기지 내 계약물량(6일분) 강제인수
	석유품질기준 완화조치	단계별로 제품 품질기준 완화 또는 폐지
	제한송전 실시	미리 정해진 우선순위에 따라 송전차단
	석유배급제 실시	1차로 민생유종·가정생필용 유류부터

시장의 기능이 상당부분 정지되고, 적지 않은 혼란과 가수요 등이 예상되므로, 상세한 대응 내용은 처음 충무계획처럼 대외보안이 엄격하게 유지되는 것이 중요하다. 이 내용은 국내외 에너지 시장상황의 변화에 따라 계속 보완되어야 할 것이다. 그 대강의 내용은 〈표 F〉와 같다.

5) 고유가 구조 고착화대책

가) 고유가 고착화 현상

2001년 9.11테러 사건으로 촉발된 아프간전쟁, 이라크전쟁 등 미국의 강경대응과 이슬람세력의 저항과 테러, 이스라엘-팔레스타인의 분쟁 지속, 거의 주기적으로 발생하는 베네수엘라와 나이지리아의 석유노동자 파업, 중국을 선두로 하는 아시아 개도국의 석유수요 급증과 그 지속 전망, 석유 선물시장의 확대로 인한 투기자금의 가세, OPEC의 고유가를 목표로 하는 감산정책 등이 엉켜 01년 9월 이후 국제유가는 급등하여, 최근 55$/b을 넘고 있다. 이는 분기단위로 보더라도 과거 월평균 최고치인 80년 1월의 41.25$/b을 연속으로 1년째 넘고 있는 것이다. 〈표 G〉는 2001년 이후 국제원유가 동향을 나타내고 있다.

〈표 G〉 Dubai유 분기별, 연도별 가격추이($/b)(01–05)

2001년				2002년				2003년				2004년				2005년			
1/4	2/4	3/4	4/4	1/4	2/4	3/4	4/4	1/4	2/4	3/4	4/4	1/4	2/4	3/4	4/4	1/4	2/4	3/4	4/4
23.7	25.2	24.1	18.5	20.2	24.4	25.6	25.2	28.5	24.5	26.7	27.7	29.5	33.2	36.2	35.8	41.6	48.0	55.1	52.9
22.84				23.88				26.80				33.74				49.37			

나) 고유가 고착화 전망의 근거

문제는 현재의 유가가 불변가격으로 비교 시 결코 과거에 비해 꼭 높은 수준이 아니라는 점이다. 과거 최고치인 80년도 연평균가격은 명목가격으로 36,01$/b이지만, 2003년 불변가격으로 환산하면 80.34$/b이 된다. 불변가격으로 50$/b이 넘는 해는 79년 74.02$/b, 80년 80.34$/b, 81년 68.48$/b, 82년 59.26$/b, 83년 52.03$/b로 만 5년간이나 된다. 따라서 현재 50~55$/b선의 원유가는 83년 이후에 나타나는 개도국의 지속적인 수요증가, 선물시장 확대에 따른 투기자금의 진입 등을 감안하면, 향후 현재수준에서 고착되거나 혹은 더 오를 수도 있다.

지금까지 원유가 상승은 수급문제보다는 대부분 중동지역의 정정불안이 그 원인이었다. 또한 장기적인 고유가는 산유국에도 결코 유리하지 않았다는 경험에 근거한 인식이 있었다. 따라서 짧으면 2~3개월, 길어야 6개월 내외의 기간이 지나면 안정을 찾는 수순을 밟아 왔다. 73년과 78년의 1, 2차 석유파동 때는 사태 이후 가격은 떨어지지 않았지만 일단 6개월

[그림 A] 01~05년 Dubai유 분기별 가격추이($/b)

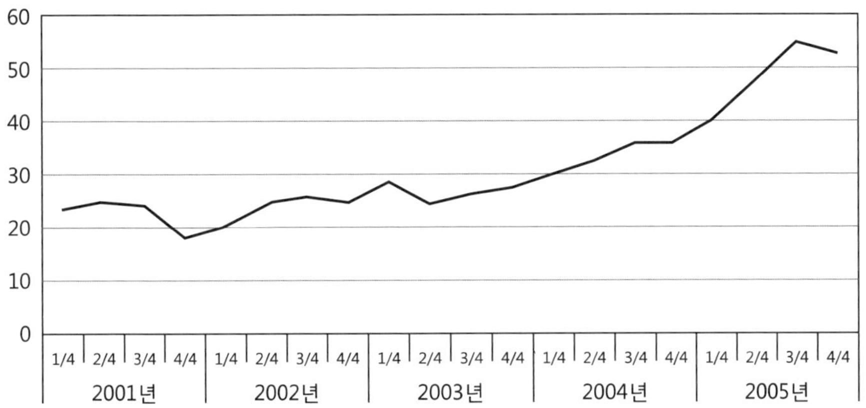

이나 지나 안정을 되찾았다. 91년 걸프사태 때는 3개월, 2000년 고유가 때도 2개월, 03년 이라크전쟁 때는 2개월 만에 가격하락과 함께 안정을 회복했다. 근본적 수급불균형이 없었고, 가격이 오르면 유전개발이 활성화되어 공급이 늘고, 수요는 소비절약 등으로 줄었기 때문이다.

이번 고유가의 특징은 중장기 수급불균형 전망을 배경에 두고 있다는 점이다. 중국의 석유소비는 03년 598만b/d로 세계 비중 7.6%이며, 일본(545만 b/d)을 제치고 세계 2위를 기록했다. 이는 1년 전보다 11.5%가 늘어난 것으로 04년도 고유가의 근본 원인으로 작용했다. 투기자금이 가세하는 것은 이러한 근본 원인에 편승하는 것이다. 따라서 투기자금의 가세가 근본원인이라고 보기는 어렵다. IEA는 향후 중국의 수요를 2010년 790만b/d, 2020년 1,060만b/d, 2030년 1,330만b/d로 보고 있다. EIA는 2010년 763만b/d, 2015년 920만b/d, 2020년 1,106만b/d, 2025년 1,279만b/d로 보고 있다. 약간 차이는 있지만 모두 엄청난 증가를 예상하는 것이다. 중국의 뒤를 인도, 브라질 등 개도국의 수요 증가가 잇고 있기 때문에 거대 개도국의 수요 증가는 고유가 고착화의 근본 원인이 된다. 인도는 대략 2034년이면 중국의 인구를 추월할 것으로 Goldman Sachs는 전망하고 있다. 전세계 석유는 2002년 현재 수송용으로 47%가 소비되는데, 2030년이면 54%로 늘어난다. 전세계 수송용 연료 중 석유의 비중은 현재도 95%가 넘는데, 향후 30년간 95% 이상을 유지할 것이다. 즉, biofuel이나 CNG(Compressed Natural Gas) 등이 수송 부문에서 석유대체를 하는 폭은 극히 작아서 무시해도 좋을 정도의 비중이다.

풍부한 매장량과 가채 연수로 보아 향후 세계 석유의 중동 의존도는 점점 심화될 전망인데, 중동의 정정불안이 단기간 내 해결될 전망은 거의 없다. 오히려 중동의 정정불안이 적정 수준에서 관리만 될 수 있다면 서방 Major에게는 아랍 민족주의나 이슬람주의의 발흥을 제어하고 중동의 석유를 지속적으로 장악하는 좋은 명분이 될 수도 있다. 한편, IEA는 04년 향후 장기 에너지 수급전망(World Energy Outlook)을 하면서 향후 장기적인 유가 전망을 2000년 불변가격으로 2010년 22$/b, 2020년 26$/b, 2030년 29$/b을 전제하고 평균 25$/b 정도로 보고 있다. 또한 유가가 35$/b 정도의 고유가로 지속되는 경우 OPEC의 시장점유율은 크게 줄어 2003~2030년간 누적수익은 7% 정도 줄어드는 것으로 보고 있다. 이는 현재의 고유가가 장기적으로 지속되기 어렵다는 것을 전제로 하고 있다. 따라서 현재의 고유가를 너무 단기적으로 판단하여 오랫동안 지속된다고 단정하기도 어렵다.

다) 정부의 대책

04년 초 원유가가 급등할 때 6개월 이내의 기간을 대상으로 하는 단기 가격 안정대책을 세워 시행한 적이 있으나, 곧 고유가 고착화를 인지하고, 중장기 대책으로 전환한 바 있다. 즉, 중국 석유 소비 급증세, OPEC의 목표유가 조정 주장, 중동지역 정정불안 지속 등을 근거로 고유가 고착화 가능성이 국제 석유시장에서 제기되자, 정책을 전환하여 중장기 에너지 정책의 착실한 추진으로 체질개선이 필요하다는 데 의견이 모아졌다.

이에 따라 고유가 종합대책이 수립되었는데, 그 내용은 크게 ① 에너지 저소비형 사회구조로의 전환, ② 신재생에너지 확대, ③ 해외 자원개발사업 활성화 등이다.

첫째, 우리나라가 아직도 경제규모에 비해 에너지를 많이 쓰는 부문을 찾아내어 같은 소득을 내면서도 에너지를 덜 쓰는 사회 구조로 바꿔나가는 것이다. 에너지 다소비의 사회 분위기는 결국 값싼 에너지가 뒷받침되기 때문이다. 이는 에너지가격의 지속 인상할 필요성을 제기하는 것이기도 하다.

둘째, 04년 현재 신재생에너지 에너지 구성비율 2.3%를 2010년까지 5%로 확대하는 시책을 추진하는 것이다. 단기적으로 5%의 비중은 미미하겠지만, 수소·연료전지, 태양광, 풍력 등 신재생에너지 기술이 장기적으로 에너지기술의 패권시대를 열 수 있기 때문에 자원빈국인 우리에게 중요하다.

셋째, 한국은 석유수입량이 세계 4위인 것에 비해 석유개발실적은 03년 국내수요의 3%(24백만b)에 불과하다. 석유개발에 대규모 투자로 원유 자주개발율을 08년까지 10%(1억b)로 높이는 것이 목표다.

이러한 목표 달성을 위해 소요되는 자금의 조달을 위해 광범위한 제도의 전반적인 개편 작업이 필요하다. 즉 기본 재원인 에너지 특별 회계의 징수 대상을 확대하여 세입을 늘리고 불필요한 환급, 면제 등 누락분을 제거하며, 일반회계나 다른 금융자금의 이용을 확대하는 등의 내용이다.

■ 지경부 2012년 업무보고

나. 안정적인 에너지 공급체계 실현

(석유) 국내 석유제품의 소비패턴 변화(등유 수요 감소, 휘발유 수요 증가)를 반영하여 제3차 정부비축계획 조정* 추진

* 등유(45일, 2,477천B) → (16일, 883천B), 휘발유(4일, 891천B) → (6일, 1,340천B)

- 동북아 오일허브 구축을 위해 상업적 저장 시설(여수·울산) 건설

3. 국내외 에너지·자원 개발·확보

가. 해외자원 자주개발 확대

◇ 자주개발률 목표* 달성으로 국정과제를 차질 없이 마무리하고 인프라를 새로이 정비하여 해외자원개발 역량 강화

* (석유·가스) ('10) 10.8% → ('12) 20%,
(6대 광물) ('10) 27% → ('12) 32%

□ 전통적인 전략 지역 진출 확대와 유망 지역과의 협력 강화

- 旣확보 이라크 광구 생산·증산* 추진과 함께 4차 입찰참여('12. 4), 쿠르드 탐사광구 시추와 UAE 미개발 광구 탐사작업 지속 추진

  * 주바이르는 '11년 25만b/d에서 35만b/d로 증산, 바스라는 '13년, 아카스·만수리아는 '15년 생산 개시 목표로 추진

- 중요성이 높아진 비전통 자원 선점을 위해 「비전통 자원 개발전략」 수립, 중국(셰일가스), 베네수엘라(초중질유) 등과 협력 강화

□ 석유공사 대형화의 성공적 마무리와 포스트 「3020」 전략 수립

- 신규 자산인수, 기존 자산 생산성 제고 등을 통해 '12년 말까지 일일 생산량 30만 배럴, 매장량 20억 배럴 목표 달성
- 탐사역량 강화, 피인수 기업 성과 제고, 추가 자산인수 등 대형화 이후 글로벌 석유기업으로서 자립기반 구축을 위한 전략* 마련

  * 석유공사 대형화 성과평가와 이를 활용한 「포스트 3020」 전략 수립('12. 상)

□ 미래 산업구조 변화를 감안한 광물 자원개발 경쟁력 강화

- 광물공사를 글로벌 메이저 기업으로 육성하고 우리기업의 경쟁력 제고를 위해 '광물개발강국 도약을 위한 마스터플랜' 수립('12. 상)
- 희토류 등 광물자원의 분리·정제 소재화 기술 확보를 위해 Pilot Plant 건립 등 인프라 마련

나. 국내 자급능력 확대

◇ 국내 자원에 대한 탐사활동을 확대하고, 도시광산을 활성화 하여 해외 에너지 자원 개발 성과를 보완

□ 국내 자원에 대한 탐사 활동을 강화

• 제2의 '동해 가스전' 발견을 위해 국내 대륙붕 탐사* 추진, 국내 최초 심해지역 시추** 를 통해 원유 탐사의 지평 확대

* 6-1광구 남부지역(대우인터내셔널), 6-1광구 중부지역(STX에너지)

** 석유공사와 호주 우드사이드社 8광구 심해시추 추진 예정('12. 4)

■ 공정위 2007. 4. 11. 의결 제2007-232호(2006서카4707)

1. 기초사실

가. 피심인들의 적격성 및 일반현황

피심인 에스케이 주식회사(이하 "SK"라 한다), 피심인 지에스칼텍스 주식회사(이하 "GS"라 한다), 피심인 현대오일뱅크 주식회사(이하 "현대"라 한다), 피심인 에쓰-오일 주식회사(이하 "S-Oil"이라 한다)는 원유를 정제·가공하여 휘발유, 등유, 경유 등의 석유제품을 제조·판매하는 자들로서 각각 '독점규제 및 공정거래에 관한 법률(이하 "법"이라 한다)' 제2조 제1호의 규정에 의한 사업자에 해당된다. 위 피심인들의 2005. 12. 31. 기준 일반현황은 아래 〈표 A〉와 같다.

〈표 A〉 피심인 일반현황 (2005. 12. 31. 기준, 단위: 십억 원, 명)

피심인	자본금	매출액	영업이익	경상이익	당기순이익	상시종업원수	설립일자
SK	653	21,914	1,205	2,210	1,686	5,077	1962. 10. 13.
GS	260	16,234	848	979	729	2,722	1967. 05. 19.
현대	1,225	7,927	399	374	277	1,653	1964. 11. 19.
S-Oil	291	12,232	888	913	655	2,437	1976. 01. 06.

* 자료출처: 피심인들 감사보고서

나. 시장구조 및 실태

(1) 석유산업의 특징

(가) 석유제품의 종류 및 특징

원유는 탄소와 수소의 화합물인 탄화수소가 주성분이고 기타 황, 질소, 산소 등의 화합

물이 소량 함유되어 있다. 탄화수소는 증류에 의해 분리가능하고 끓는점이 달라 이런 특성을 이용한 정제과정을 거쳐 원유에서 휘발유, 등유, 경유, 중유, 나프타, 아스팔트, 윤활유, LPG 등의 석유제품이 추출된다.

한 종류의 원자재로부터 다수의 제품이 연쇄적·자동적으로 생산되는 연산품의 특성상 특정 석유제품에 대한 수요증가에 대응하기 위하여 그 제품의 공급량을 증가시키면 다른 제품들의 공급 또한 해당제품의 수요와 관계없이 증가되는바, 이로 인해 발생하는 국내시장에서의 일시적인 수급불균형은 수입·수출을 통하여 해소된다.

경질유제품[1]에 속하는 휘발유, 등유, 경유의 경우 대체재가 희소한 필수재적 특성을 지니고 있어 수요의 탄력성이 매우 낮고 품질은 고도로 표준화되어 있어 실질적으로 제품의 차별화가 어렵다.

(나) 석유산업의 특성

석유제품은 국가의 경제와 산업 및 안보에 미치는 영향이 클 뿐만 아니라, 원유의 매장량이 한정되어 있고 이를 전량 수입에 의존할 수밖에 없는 전략 물자의 성격을 지니고 있는바, 제품의 가격·품질·비축·유통 등에 관하여 정부의 지속적인 규제를 받아 왔다. 제품 가격의 경우, 1990년대 이후 규제 완화가 급속도로 진행되어 1997년도에는 완전한 가격 자유화가 이루어졌다.

국내 석유정제업시장은 법적 진입규제[2]와 초기투자비용이 큰 장치산업의 특성상 약 30년에 걸쳐 타사업자의 신규진입이 없이 5개(2005년도 이후 4개) 정유사들의 과점형태로 유지되어 왔다. 2000년도 초반에 석유수입사들이 내수시장에 진출하여 국내 정유사들과 경쟁체제를 유지하여 오다가 국제 제품 가격 상승 등으로 인한 시장여건 악화로 2004년도에는 수입사의 시장점유율이 극히 미미한 수준으로 감소하였다.

(2) 석유제품의 시장현황

(가) 석유제품 전체 시장현황

국내 석유제품시장은 1980년대 후반부터 급격한 경제성장 및 소득수준 향상으로 수송부문의 휘발유와 경유 등 경질유제품 중심으로 내수가 증가해 왔으나, 2000년대 이후에는 정유사들의 생산능력 향상 및 국내수요 침체로 공급 과잉현상이 지속되고 있다. 그럼에도 불구하고 중국 등 석유소비 증가에 따른 대아시아 수출증가로 제품생산은 꾸준히 증가하고 있는 추세를 나타내고 있다. 국내 석유제품 시장현황은 아래 〈표 B〉와 같다.

---

1. API(미국석유협회가 정한 비중측정단위) 비중이 낮은 원유를 경질유라고 하고, 원유의 비중이 낮을수록 휘발유·등유·경유와 같이 사용가치가 높은 제품이 많이 추출된다. 국내 정유사들은 원유의 종류에 상관없이 휘발유·등유·경유를 경질유제품으로 분류하고 있다.
2. 1998. 10월 정제업이 허가제에서 등록제로 전환되면서 진입장벽이 완화되었다.

〈표 B〉 국내 석유제품의 시장상황 (2004년도 말 기준, 단위: 천Barrel per Day, B/D)

참여업체	생산능력		생산량		국내판매량		수출량	
	수량	%	수량	%	수량	%	수량	%
SK	840	31.57	801	32.99	562	27.27	243	30.13
GS	650	24.43	637	26.23	493	23.90	165	20.49
S-Oil	580	21.80	560	23.06	243	11.80	283	35.10
현대	390	14.66	297	12.21	228	11.04	73	9.02
인천	200	7.52	116	4.76	92	4.45	38	4.76
기 타	-	-	18	0.75	444	21.53	4	0.51
합 계	2,660	100.0	2,429	100.0	2,061	100.0	805	100.0

* 자료: 한국석유공사

정유사들의 2004년 법인 영업이익은 SK와 S-Oil이 1조원을 넘어서는 등 전체적으로 전년대비 132.5%의 증가율을 나타내고 있으며 특히 석유제품 사업부문의 영업이익은 전년대비 188.1%의 증가율을 나타내었다. 2002년 이후 정유사별 석유제품 부문 영업이익의 변동추이는 아래의 〈표 C〉와 같다.

〈표 C〉 피심인 영업이익(석유제품 부문) (단위: 십억 원)

피심인	2002년	2003년(전년대비(%))	2004년(전년대비(%))	2005년(전년대비(%))
SK	103	156 (51.4)	723 (363.4)	458 (-36.6)
GS	223	326 (46.2)	427 (31.0)	336 (-21.3)
현대	142	183 (28.8)	461 (151.2)	399 (-13.4)
S-Oil	71	124 (74.6)	662 (433.9)	427 (-35.5)
계	539	789 (46.4)	2,273 (188.1)	1620 (-28.7)

※ 자료: 피심인 사업보고서
※ 현대는 석유외 사업부문이 없으므로 법인전체의 영업이익과 동일

(나) 경질유제품의 시장현황

1) 경질유제품의 시장규모

2004년도 국내 석유제품시장에서 경질유제품의 매출액은 156,026억 원으로 전체 263,902억 원 석유제품시장의 약 59%에 해당하며, 생산량 기준으로는 전체의 약 38.1%를 차지한다. 경질유제품의 유종별 시장규모는 아래 〈표 D〉와 같다.

〈표 D〉 경질유제품의 유종별 시장규모 (2004년도 기준, 단위: 억 원)

유 종		용 도	시장규모
휘발유		자동차용 연료	37,468
등유	실내	가정용 스토브, 온풍기 등의 난방연료	31,844
	보일러	가정용 난방보일러 연료	
경유		디젤엔진의 연료로 사용	86,714
총계		156,026	

원유와 석유제품에 대한 수입부과금 및 관세율의 차이가 확대되고, 국제 석유제품 시장가격이 급격히 상승함에 따라 수입사의 가격경쟁력 약화되어 최근 3년간 경질유제품시장에서 수입사의 시장점유율은 아래 〈표 E〉와 같이 지속적인 감소 추세를 보이고 있다.

〈표 E〉 석유수입사 시장점유율 추이(%)

구 분	2002년	2003년	2004년
휘발유	6.5	3.7	1.6
등 유	6.5	4.8	3.4
경 유	9.0	7.4	3.5

2) 경질유제품의 유통구조

경질유제품은 정유사가 도매업자인 대리점에 공급하고 대리점이 최종 판매업자인 주유소 또는 일반 판매소에 판매하는 형태와, 정유사가 대리점 등을 거치지 않고 주유소 또는 일반판매소에 직접 공급하는 형태로 구분된다.[3]

대리점은 전속계약에 따라 특정 정유사와 고정 거래하는 자영대리점과 시장가격에 따라 다양한 공급자로부터 물량을 공급받는 현물대리점으로 구분된다.

주유소는 특정 정유사의 상표를 게시하고 해당 정유사의 제품만을 공급하는 상표표시주유소와 상표를 게시하지 않고 여러 정유사 또는 수입사들로부터 공급받은 제품을 판매하는 무상표주유소로 구분된다. 무상표주유소는 전체 주유소의 약 4%에 불과하며, 상표표시주유소는 정유사가 직접 소유 및 위탁·운영하는 직영 주유소와 정유사의 상표를 임차하여 독립 자영업자가 운영하는 자영 주유소로 구분된다. 경질유 제품시장의 유통구조는 아래의 [그림 A]와 같다.

3. 석유사업법상 수평거래금지조항에 의해 유통단계상 수평적 위치에 있는 유통업자간의 거래는 금지됨 (예: 일반판매소가 주유소에 휘발유를 공급하는 행위).

[그림 A] 경질유 제품시장의 유통구조(2004년 기준)

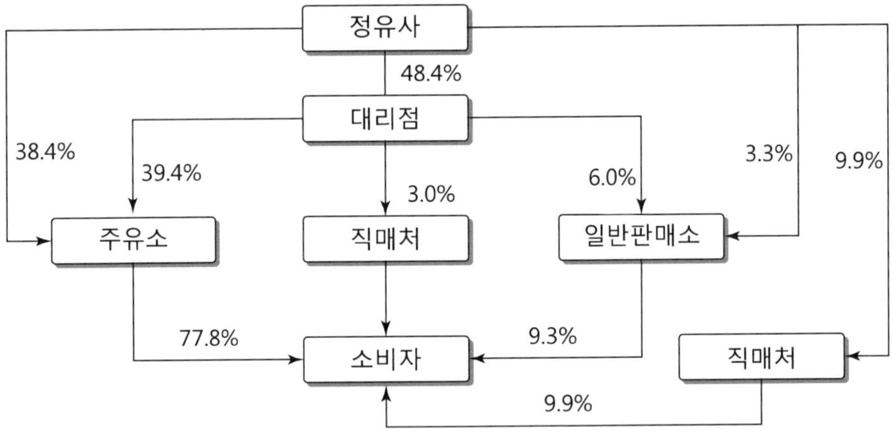

※ 자료: 한국석유공사

상표표시주유소의 경우 「주유소상표표시제」[4]에 따라서 해당상표 정유사로부터 구입한 제품만을 판매할 수 있으므로 정유사들은 자사의 상표표시주유소의 수를 유지 또는 확대하는 것이 정유사의 손익제고 및 시장점유율 증대에 절대적인 영향을 미친다고 할 수 있다. 실제로 각 사별 상표표시주유소의 구성비와 석유 제품 시장에서의 시장점유율 구성비가 유사하게 나타나고 있다. 정유사별 계열주유소 현황은 아래 〈표 F〉과 같다.

〈표 F〉 정유사 계열주유소 현황(2002년도~2004년도) (단위: 개소)

연도 \ 업체	SK		GS		현대		S-Oil		무상표	기타	계
	직영	자영	직영	자영	직영	자영	직영	자영			
2002년	882	2,929	664	2,167	402	1,797	124	1255	397	41	10,655
	3,808		2,831		2,199		1,379				
	35.7%		26.5%		20.6%		13.0%		3.7%	0.3%	100%
2003년	795	3,057	563	2,343	367	1,848	122	1,319	391	45	10,850
	3,852		2,906		2,215		1,441				
	35.5%		26.8%		20.4%		13.3%		3.6%	0.4%	100%
2004년	779	3,139	560	2,457	378	1,866	124	1,374	405	41	11,123
	3,918		3,017		2,244		1,498				
	35.2%		27.1%		20.2%		13.4%		3.6%	0.4%	100%

※ 자료출처: 한국주유소협회

4. 공정거래위원회 고시(제2001-2호).

3) 경질유제품의 가격체계

경질유제품의 가격은 원유가, 세금 및 부과금, 정제비용, 유통마진 등으로 구성된다. 경질유제품은 정부에 의해 가격결정이 이루어지다가 1991년도 이후 가격 자유화가 단계적으로 시행되었고 1997년도에 이르러 정부의 가격 상한제 및 유가 연동제가 폐지됨으로써 완전한 자유화가 이루어졌다. 이에 따라 정유사들은 원유가, 국제 제품 가격, 환율, 세금 등의 비용요인 및 시장 수급상황 등을 감안하여 자율적으로 공급가격을 결정하고 있으며, 정기적으로 공장도가격을 공개하고 있다.

① 공장도가격

공장도가격은 정유사가 유통 시장에 공급하는 가격의 기준이 되는 가격으로 국제 제품가격, 환율, 세금의 변동에 따라 연동하여 변동한다. 일반적으로 각 유통단계의 판매업자들이 실제 시장가격을 표현할 때, SK 공장도가격(MP)이 원용된다.[5] 1997년 가격자유화 이후 정유사들은 매월 언론을 통하여 석유제품가격을 발표해 왔으며, 2004년 2월부터 가격 변동 요인의 즉각적인 반영을 위하여 발표주기를 월단위에서 주단위로 변경한 바 있다.[6]

공장도가격은 정유사가 대리점 또는 주유소 등에 공급할 때 적용하는 명목상 기준가격으로 언론 등을 통하여 간헐적으로 발표되며, SK와 GS의 인터넷 홈페이지에 게시되고 있다. 이러한 공장도 가격을 대외적으로 공시하는 이유는 최종 소비자들에게 주유소가격 등 최종판매가격의 변동요인을 참고할 수 있도록 도움을 주기 위한 것이라고 정유사들은 설명하고 있다.

그러나 이러한 공장도가격은 실제 정유사가 대리점 등에 공급하는 가격보다 상당히 높은 수준에 형성되어 있다. 따라서 이러한 사정을 모르는 소비자에게는 이렇게 부풀려진 공장도가격을 보게 되면 자신이 구입하는 석유제품이 싸다고 오인할 수 있다. 그리고 사업자가 이러한 공장도가격을 공시하는 행위 자체가 각 사 제품 간 품질차이가 거의 없는 시장에서는 가격담합의 '신호'로 기능할 수도 있는 측면이 있다.

② 일일판매 기준가격

일일판매 기준가격은 석유 제품 시장에서 정유사가 대리점 및 주유소 등에 적용하는 시장가격의 실질적인 기준이 되는 가격으로 본사가 당일의 수출가격 대비 경제성, 시장수급현황 및 현물 시장 가격 등을 종합하여 결정한 후 지역본부 또는 지사로 매일 통보한다.

③ 실거래가격

지역본부 및 지사는 일일 판매 기준 가격에서 일정한 범위 내에서 할인·할증하여 개별대리점, 주유소 및 일반판매소 등에 제품을 공급하게 된다. 일반적으로 정유사가 대리점 등

5. MP는 maker price를 의미함. 예) "SK MP △40원/리터," "SK MP △8,000원/드럼"는 각각 SK 공장도가격보다 리터당 40원 낮은 가격, SK 공장도가격보다 드럼당 8,000원 낮은 가격이라는 의미로 사용된다.

6. GS는 월요일(화요일 시행), SK는 수요일(목요일 시행)에 공장도가격을 공시한다. S-Oil은 2001년 2월, 현대는 2004년 8월에 공장도가격 공시를 각각 중단하였다.

에 공급하는 실거래가격은 아래와 같이 거래 상대방의 유형 및 거래 조건에 따라 다르게 결정된다.

첫째, 유통 단계상 상위에 있는 대리점의 경우 하위 유통업자인 주유소 또는 일반판매소에 비해 상대적으로 정유사의 할인율이 더 크게 나타나고 이에 따라 실거래 가격은 다소 낮은 수준으로 결정된다.

둘째, 정유사와 고정적으로 거래하는 자영대리점 또는 상표표시주유소의 경우 정유사의 외상채권에 대한 이자비용, 시설투자비용, 상표가치 등 추가적인 비용요인이 반영되기 때문에 이러한 추가 비용 요인이 없는 현물대리점, 무상표주유소, 일반 석유판매소 등의 경우에서보다 할인율이 낮으며 이에 따라 실거래가격은 다소 높은 수준으로 결정된다.

셋째, 같은 유형의 거래 상대방이라고 하더라도 거래 조건에 따라 실거래 가격이 다르게 나타나는데, 상표표시주유소의 경우에도 외상채권이 없는 상태의 현금 구매조건[7]으로 거래할 때에는 외상으로 거래할 때에 비하여 할인율이 더 크게 나타나고 이에 따라 실거래가격은 다소 낮은 수준으로 결정된다.

실거래가격이 일일 판매 가격과 일치하지 않는 이유는 위에 설명한 바와 같이 지역별로 거래 단계, 거래 상대방 및 거래 조건에 따라 다양한 할인이 적용되기 때문이기도 하지만 정유사 지사(지역본부)의 추가적인 가격 결정권 보유 여부에 따라 더 차이가 날 수 있다. 실제 판매가격의 결정 권한이 지사에 많이 주어지는 경우, 지사가 본부로부터 통보받는 일일판매기준가격을 더 큰 폭으로 할인하여 판매함으로써 실제 거래가격의 변동폭이 커질 수 있다.

그리고 지사는 판매 목표를 달성하기 위해 본사 일일판매기준가격에서 직접 할인을 하는 방법으로 매출을 증가시키기도 하지만 본사의 일일판매 기준가격은 그대로 수용하더라도 사후 매출 조정을 통해서 거래상대방에 실제 할인의 효과를 부여하는 방법으로 판매할 수 있다. 이러한 여러 가지 사정으로 실거래가격은 정유사별로 다를 수밖에 없으며 같은 정유사 내에서도 지역 본부별로 일일판매기준가격조차도 다를 수 있다. 정유사의 가격 결정 체계는 아래의 [그림 B]와 같다.[8]

---

7. 정유업계에서는 "무채권현금조건"이라 한다.

8. GS의 경우 2004년 4월~6월 당시 본사가 일일판매기준가격을 결정하지 않고 지역본부가 개별적으로 가격을 결정하였다고 주장한다. 그러나 증거자료를 종합해 볼 때 본사차원의 결정이 있었던 것으로 보인다. 설사 본사가 결정하지 않고 지역본부 차원에서 결정·운용하였다 하더라도 이를 기준으로 개별 거래처별로 실거래가격이 결정되는 방식과 그 효과는 본사차원의 결정이 이루어질 때와 크게 다르지 않다. 그 이유는 GS의 지역본부가 7개로서 소수이며 본사차원의 일일판매기준 가격결정이 이루어지는 SK의 경우에도 각 지역본부·지사별로 어느 정도의 재량을 가지고 실거래가격을 결정하고 있기 때문이다. 따라서 양사의 가격결정방식은 GS의 지역본부가 SK의 지역본부·지사에 비해 다소 더 넓은 재량을 가지고 실거래가격을 결정하는 정도의 차이만 있다고 보인다. p. 13의 2004년 5월초 경 SK 작성「정유사별 시장가격 운영현황」참고.

[그림 B] 정유사의 가격 결정 체계

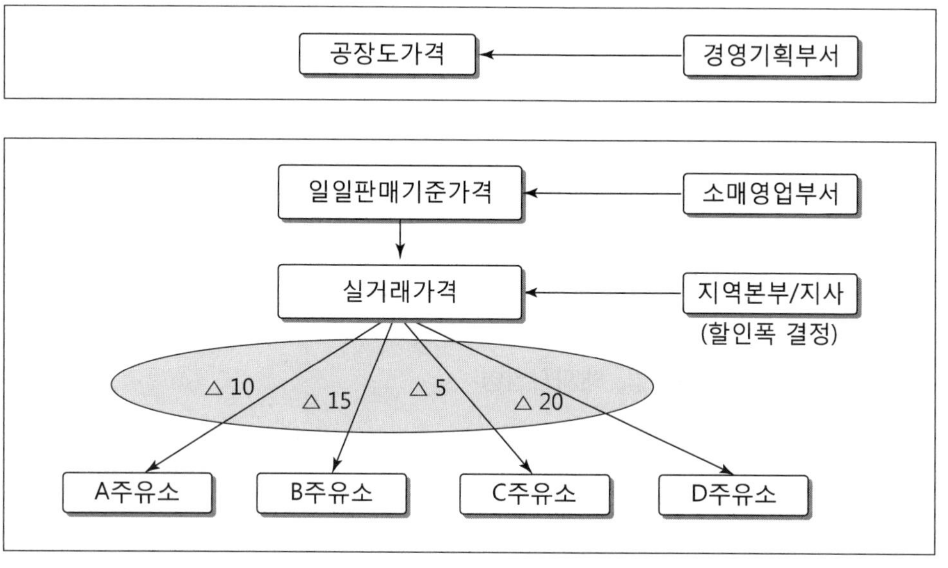

④ 현물 시장 가격

복수의 정유사 또는 수입사와 거래하는 현물 대리점이 주유소 및 일반판매소 등에 공급할 때 적용하는 판매가격을 현물가격 또는 부판가격이라 한다. 현물 시장 가격은 수송비용을 제외하고는 별도의 판매 비용(외상채권, 상표가치, 시설투자 등) 부담이 없기 때문에 국내 유통가격 중에서는 최저 가격에 해당한다.

현물 대리점들은 매일 오전 주유소에 휴대폰 문자 메시지 등을 이용하여 판매가격을 제시하며, 주유소들은 이 현물가격 정보를 근거로 정유사에 희망 공급 가격을 제시하고, 정유사는 현물 가격에 추가적인 비용요소를 고려하여 주유소 등에 적용할 일일 판매 기준가격을 정하고 있다.

노트와 질문

석유제품의 산업구조를 개선하기 위한 정책은 어떤 것들이 있으며 그러한 정책이 지경부의 업무의 일부가 아니라면 어느 부서의 업무일까?

나. 석유정책의 집행수단

1) 한국석유공사(KNOC)

KNOC은 한국석유공사법에 의하여 설립된 100% 정부가 자본금을 출자한 법인이다. 정부출자금만이 아니라 정부의 보조금, 정부의 보증에 기초한 사채 및 차관을 사업자금으로 한다. 법과 정관이 정한 사업목적은 석유자원의 탐사 및 개발, 원유와 석유제품의 수출입·비축·수송·대여 및 판매, 석유비축시설의 건설·관리·운영 및 대여, 석유의 유통구조개선, 에너지 및 자원관련사업법인에 대한 투자·융자·채무보증 등이다.

2) 석유사업법, 해저개발법, 해자사업법

석유사업법은 석유수출입업을 하려는 자는 지경부장관에 등록할 것을 요구하고 있다. 다만, 석유정제업의 등록을 한 자가 해당연도 수입 석유가스의 양이 5만톤 이하인 경우나 자기가 사용할 목적으로 해당연도 수입석유의 양이 10만 킬로리터 이하인 경우 등은 예외로 한다. 등록을 위하여는 석유저장시설의 현황자료 또는 건설 및 보유 계획과 해당연도 이후 5년간의 석유수급계획을 포함한 사업계획서와 수입 대행 계약서를 한국석유관리원에 제출하여야 한다.

석유정제업을 하려는 자도 지경부장관에게 등록하여야 한다. 다만, 윤활유 등의 정제를 위하여는 신고로 족하다. 정제업 등록을 위하여는 압증류시설, 감압증류시설 등 중 하나 이상의 시설을 갖추고, 개시연도 내수 판매계획량의 60일분에 해당하는 양과 생산계획량의 45일분에 해당하는 양 중 많은 양을 저장할 수 있는 저장시설을 갖추어야 한다. 또한, 석유판매업을 하려는 자는 일반대리점, 주유소, 일반판매소 등 판매업의 종류에 따라서 요건을 구비하여 해당 지방자치단체의 장에게 신고 또는 등록하여야 한다.

이들은 석유비축의무가 있으며 또한 수입·판매부과금을 납부하여야 한다. 부과금은 에너지 및 자원사업특별회계에 귀속하며 이들 부과징수에 관한 사무는 KNOC에 위탁되어 있다. 석유사업법에 따르면 석유수출입업, 석유정제업, 석유판매업은 지경부에 등록을 필요로 하며 법이 정한 의무를 이행하지 아니하는 경우 등록의 취소나 과징금의 부과 대상이 된다. 법이 요구하는 대표적인 의무로서 석유 비축의무와 석유의 수입·판매부과금의 납부의무를 들 수 있다.

해저개발법은 우리 영해 및 대륙붕의 개발과 관련된 것으로 제3장에서 자세히 논의한다. 해자사업법의 개관을 살펴보면 동법은 해자사업을 정의하고 해자사업을 위한 사업계획의 신고, 영업보고서의 제출, 반입명령의 이행 등을 요구하면서, 이에 대한 반대급부로서 자금의 지원, 융자, 조세혜택을 규정하고 있다. KNOC 중심의 해자사업에 시장을 통한 사업참여를 추가하자는 것이 제도의 취지로 보이며 2012년초 현재 석유/가스사업에 170여 건의 신고가, 광물사업에 210여 건의 신고가[4] 접수되어 있다.

국내 유일의 석유개발 전문회사인 KNOC는 2010년 12월말 기준 기준으로 현재 24개국 189개 해외 유망 석유개발 프로젝트에 참여하여 일일 평균 약 180천 배럴('10년 12월말 기준)을 생산하고 있으며 확보한 매장량은 석유환산 약 11.3억 배럴('10년 12월말 기준)에 이르고 있다. KNOC는 기술력과 사업 운영 능력을 확보하여 직접 광권을 취득하여 운영하고 있는 광구가 베트남 11-2 등 51개이고 공동운영은 11개 광구로 단순 지분참여 위주의 기존 민간 기업들과는 다른 차원의 석유개발사업을 추진하고 있다. 최근에는 해외 M&A를 벌여서 2011년 영국의 Dana사, 캐나다 Harvest사, 페루 Savia Peru사, 미국 Ankor사, 카자흐스탄 Sumbe사 등을 인수한 바 있다.[5]

다. 천연가스정책

염명천, 에너지시장, 산업 & 정책 255-274 (2006)

1) 가스산업에 경쟁도입

가스산업은 전통적으로 ① 장기공급계약과 의무물량인수의무(Take or Pay), ② LNG의 경우 한국과 일본의 큰 비중, ③ 배관을 기초로 한 지역독점 허용 등을 특징으로 하여 왔다. 즉, 장기공급계약과 TOP 조항이 없이는 대규모 투자가 소요되는 가스개발, 배관, 수송, 액화와 재기화 등이 불가능하였기 때문이다. 또한 대규모 투자를 뒷받침하기 위해 지역독점을 허용하여 투자비 회수를 보장해야 했다.

이제 여건이 바뀌고 있다. 우선, ① LNG의 경우 단기·현물거래 등 시장의 유연성이 확대되고 있다. 이는 기본적으로 공급량의 증가와 각국의 여유시설의 보유가 가져다준 것이다. ② 국제 LNG 시장의 중심축이던 한국·일본의 역할이 감소하고, 신규 LNG 수요국으로 중국, 인도, 미국, EU(U.K., Spain, Italy 등)의 비중이 커지고 있다. ③ 배관에 따라 지역독점이 불가피하다는 전통적 견해가 바뀌어 경쟁이 가능한 부분은 경쟁체제로 변화하는 추세에 있다. 특히 배관을 소유하지 않고도 배관을 공동 이용하는 시스템이 도입되고 있다. ④ 마지막으로 국제유가 상승과 중동정세 불안으로 천연가스 비중 증가를 전망하면서, 최근 에너지 수입 의존국들은 천연가스의 개발·생산부문 참여, 국가 간 자원협력 강화, 주력기업 육성 등 에너지안보 차원의 역량을 집중하는 추세에 있다. 이러한 여건의 변화가 세계적인 가스산업

4) http://www.mke.go.kr/info/resource/resource_04.jsp?div=1 참조.
5) www.knoc.co.kr 설명.

〈표 A〉 가스공사 구조개편 찬성 및 반대논거

찬성	반대
기업의 사업참여 자율권 보장차원에서 가스 산업분야에도 자유로운 진입 허용 필요	천연가스는 민생연료로서 공공성이 중시되므로 수익성, 효율성 위주의 경쟁도입은 특정기업에 이윤귀속 우려
시장개방화 등 세계적인 가스산업 구조개편 조류에 따라 경쟁도입은 당연한 정책방향	우리나라는 98% 에너지 수입국이며 열악한 수급구조, 에너지 안보 중요성 등 고려 시, 외국과 국내여건을 같이 보는 것은 곤란

구조개편을 가져오고 있다. 한국의 경우는 이에 더하여 가스산업이 이미 20년이 되어 성숙단계에 진입하였고, 최근 대수요처가 자가소비용 LNG의 직도입을 요구하여 도입판매부문 경쟁이 시작되었으며, 전력부문 구조개편으로 발전원간 치열한 경쟁이 발전용 천연가스 수급조절에 애로를 발생시켜, 직도입의 필요성을 키우고 있으며, WTO, 한미투자협정 및 각국과의 FTA 협상 등에서 에너지 시장 개방 압력이 가시화되고 있어 사전준비가 불가피하다. 따라서 한국도 가스산업의 구조개편은 불가피한 것으로 보이나, 〈표 A〉에서 보듯 가스공사의 구조개편에 대한 국내의 찬반의견은 아직 정리되지 않고 있다.

2) LNG의 안정적 공급

가스산업에 경쟁을 도입하는 것이 정책과제로는 중심에 있지만, 현실적으로는 단기적으로나 중장기적으로나 LNG 안정도입을 확보하는 것이 그보다 더 중요하다. 이를 위해서 중장기적으로 필요한 물량을 중장기계약을 좋은 조건에 맺어 해당 물량을 적기에 확실하게 확보하는 것이고, 단기적으로는 동절기수요 또는 2002. 12~2003. 3.간 발생한 것 같은 LNG 수급위기에 발빠르게 대처하여 소요물량을 단기적으로 충당하는 것이 중요하다.

중장기물량은 대략 7~8년 전부터 시장을 탐색하여 장기계약을 추진하게 된다. 현재 도입중인 중장기계약물량 1,948만 톤 중 950만 톤이 2015년 이전에 계약이 종료된다. 그 계약의 규모는 매우 크다. 예를 들어 200만 톤/년 계약을 20년 장기계약에 도입단가 300$/톤을 가정하면 계약금액은 120억 달러로 12조 원 정도가 된다. 가스공사는 추가계약 소요 950만 톤 중 550만톤에 대해 예멘, 말레이시아, 러시아로부터 장기도입계약을 2005년 7월 체결한 바 있다.

단기적으로 수급차질이 예상되면 신속한 대응으로 단기물량을 확보하는 것이 필요하다. 중요한 것은 조기경보시스템이다. 대부분의 경우 수급차질이 발생하였을 때 가스공사 등 현장의 실무자에게 책임을 묻게 되면 어떻게 스스로 해결해 보려다 조기경보가 되지 않고 사태가 악화된 다음에야 정부에 보고되고 정부의 개입이 때늦을 수가 있다. 따라서 조기경보가 무엇보다 중요하다. 또 단기적 수급차질 가능성을 줄이기 위해서는 도입선을 다원화하는 것이 필요하다. 최근 발전사를 포함한 민간기업 등 대수요처의 직도입추세의 증가는 이러한 수급위기의 가능성을 줄일 수 있다.

3) LNG전국공급사업의 지속적 추진

LNG 수요증가율을 87~97년간 연 21.4%, 97~04년간 연 9.7%로 증가해 왔다. 이러한 증가추세는 앞으로도 지속될 것으로 보인다. 따라서 인수기지와 전국배관망을 수요증가에 맞추어 지속적으로 확충해야 할 필요가 있다. 〈표 B〉는 2017년까지 정부의 LNG 인수기지 저장설비와 배관망 확충계획을 요약한 것이다.

즉, 04년 말 현재 전국 3개 기지에 있는 33기, 418만kl의 저장시설을 2017년까지 4개기지, 64기, 864만 kl로 확장하고, 전국배관망을 04년 말 2,415km에서 07년 말까지 2,685km로 확장하는 것이다. 이를 위한 투자비는 대략 2017년까지 12조 3천억 원 정도로 추산되는데, 에너지특별회계 융자로 34,285억 원을 조달하고 나머지 78,550억 원은 별도의 재원대책을 마련해야 한다.

〈표 B〉 LNG 공급설비 확충계획

		인수기지 (저장탱크)					전국 배관망	도시가스 배관망
		인천	평택	통영	추가기지	소계		
04말	탱크수	18기	10기	5기	-	33기	2,451km (155개 관리소)	22,734km
	용량	248만kl	100만kl	70만kl	-	418만kl		
추가 건설	탱크수	2기	14기	10기	5기	31기	234km (18개 관리소)	
	용량	40만kl	196만kl	140만kl	70만kl	446만kl		
17년	탱크수	20기	24기	14기	5기	64기	2,685km* (173개 관리소)	
	용량	288만kl	296만kl	210만kl	70만kl	864만kl		

* 전국배관망은 2007년까지 2,685km로 확장계획

4) 도시가스보급확대

서울시가 1972년 5월 시험적으로 용산구 이촌동에 LPG를 이용한 설비로 약 3,000가구에 도시가스를 공급한 것이 한국도시가스 산업의 효시이다. 이어 1972년 11월 서울시가 강서고 남창동에 납사분해방식으로 본격적인 도시가스 공급이 시작되었다. 1987년 12월 5일 도시가스사업법이 제정·공포되어 민영도시가스회사의 설립기반이 마련되었다.

1980년 2월 15일 대한도시가스(주)가 민간최초로 도시가스 사업을 시작했고, 이어 (주)부산도시가스, (주)삼천리가 도시가스사업에 진입했다.

처음에는 주로 LPG와 납사분해방식으로 도시가스를 공급하였으나, 1987년 LNG가 도입되면서 LNG가 도시가스 공급의 주류를 차지한다. 현재 전국 33개 도시가스회사 중 29개는 LNG, 4개(속초, 강릉, 충주, 안동)만 LPG로 도시가스를 공급한다. 이들 지역은 LNG 공급망이 아직 미치지 않는 곳으로 실제 공급가구 비중은 전국의 0.69%에 불과하다.

04년 말 기준 전국가구 18,538천 가구 중 58.7%인 10,815천 가구가 도시가스를 사용한다. LNG에 의한 도시가스가 10,371천 가구로 대부분이며, LPG에 의한 도시가스는 75천 가구에 불과하다. 기타 상업용이 369천 가구이다. 도시가스 배관망은 04년 말 22,734km이다.

가구당 배관망 길이는 2.1m로 수용가들이 매우 밀집되어 있음을 알 수있다. 도시가스회사의 배관망 건설에는 에너지특별회계에서 자금이 융자지원된다. 87~94년간에는 석유사업기금으로 1,850억 원, 95~04년간에는 에너지특별회계로 2,142억 원이 융자지원되었다.

도시가스요금은 도시가스의 원료가 되는 LNG의 도매요금은 정부(산자부)가 조정하고, 각 시도별 도시가스 소매요금은 관할 시도지사가 주택난방용, 업무난방용, 영업용, 산업용으로 나누어 결정한다. 따라서 도시가스 소비자 가격은 지역별로 상이하다. 정부가 조정하고 있는 LNG 도매요금은 그동안 물가안정 등의 이유로 원가변동이 제대로 반영되지 못한 경험이 있어, LNG 국제가격 변동 시 국내 도매요금이 자동 조정되는 "도시가스요금 원료비 연동제"를 시행하고 있다. 98. 8. 1.부터 매 3개월 주기로 조정하다, 02. 1. 1.부터는 매 2개월을 주기로 조정하고 있다.

5) LPG공급안정성과 경쟁력강화

가) LPG 비축

1980년 들어 LPG 수요가 증가하자 정부는 석유비축사업의 일환으로 LPG 비축기지를 건설하여 85년부터 정부비축을 실시하게 된다. 04년 말 기준 정부(석유공사)는 360천 톤의 비축시설을 평택에 보유하고 14.3일분인 303천 톤의 LPG를 비축하고 있다. 그러나 LPG 수요 증가세가 꺾이고 있으므로 추가적인 비축기지 증설계획은 현재 갖고 있지 않다.

일반 석유제품의 민간비축은 93년 2월부터 시행되었는데, LPG도 동시에 시행되었다. SK 가스 평택기지(18만 톤)가 99년 7월에, E1 인천기지(24만 톤)가 2000년 7월에 완공되어 비축시설은 큰 여유를 갖게 되었다. 04년 말 민간비축 시설은 95만 톤으로 정부 비축 시설까지 합하면 131만 톤이 되는데, 이는 국내수요의 61.9일분이다. 한편, LPG를 국내에서 공급하는 정유사와 석유화학사는 상대적으로 적은 규모의 LPG 저장시설을 갖고 있다. 정유사는 원유와 석유제품 전체로 비축의무를 달성하면 되므로 상대적으로 건설비가 비싼 LPG 비축설비를 적게 유지하는 것이고, 석유화학사는 의무달성에 필수적인 최소규모의 저장시설만을 유지하고 있다.

LPG 민간비축의무는 93년 최초로 15일 의무비축을 부과하다 96년 17일, 2000년 25일로 증가하고, 01년 27일에서 2004년 이후 현재까지 30일이다. 현재 일반 석유제품의 비축의무일수는 40일인데, 2008년까지 135일을 달성하려면 민간비축의무일수를 50일로 올려야 한다. 따라서 LPG 비축의무일수도 조만간 40일을 거쳐 50일로 조정되어야 할 것이다. LPG 저장탱크 건설비가 일반 석유제품보다 비싸다는 이유로 비축의무일수를 낮게 유지하는 것은 타당하지 않다. 저장탱크 건설비가 비싼 제품이 공급차질에서 특별히 더 자유롭지는 않기 때문이다.

나) LPG 산업 경쟁력 강화

LPG는 LNG에 비해 각종의 세금이 많이 부과되고, 수입 · 정유사-충전소-판매소 등 유통단계가 길어 LNG 대비 가격이 1.8배 이상 고가가 되어 가격경쟁력에서 취약하다. 또한 유통체계가 낙후된 상태로 인건비, 배송비용상승 등으로 경쟁력이 더욱 악화되는 현실이다. 이에 따라 LPG 소비는 87년 이후 연평균 8.9%의 증가율을 보였으나, 03년부터 미세한 감소세를 시현하고 있는데, 이 감소세는 향후 LNG의 보급 확대로 점점 커질 것으로 예상된다. 〈표 C〉는 그 추세를 보여준다.

특히 가정 · 상업용으로 사용되는 프로판은 도시가스 보급확대, 복잡한 유통구조 및 높은 국제가격에 따른 가격경쟁력 저하로 '97년 이후 감소세를 지속하고 있다. 즉, 도시가스 보급률을 97년 39.5%에서 04년에는 58.7%로 늘었다. 이 추세는 지속될 것이다. 가격도 LPG는 115원/Kcal이나 도시가스는 69원/Kcal으로 훨씬 낮다.

나아가 LPG 수요증가세를 유지시켜 온 부탄(LPG자동차연료)은 00년 7월 에너지가격체계 개편 이후 그 증가세가 크게 둔화되고 있다. 즉, 경쟁연료인 경유에 비해 부탄특소세는 00년 7월의 40원/kg에서 06년 7월의 704원/kg으로 크게 오르나, 경유는 같은 기간에 183원/l에서 497원/l으로 오른다. 이에 따라 향후 수송용 LPG(부탄)의 수요도 크게 늘지 않을 것이라는 예상을 할 수 있다. LPG 수요가 LNG를 사용하는 도시가스 수요로 전환되는 것은 자연스러운 일이지만 현실적으로 도시가스 배관이 들어가지 않는 지역이 아직도 가구기준으로 전국에 약 40% 이상이 있으므로 LPG 산업의 경쟁력을 제고하기 위한 대책은 도시가스 보급 확대와 함께 역시 필요하다.

〈표 C〉 LPG 소비증가율 연도별추이(%)

구분	95	96	97	98	99	00	01	02	03	04 (잠정)
프로판	10.5	2.7	3.3	-12.3	9.4	-0.6	-12.1	8.7	-9.1	-6.7
부탄	-6.7	3.6	7.8	10.7	20.0	26.6	14.3	8.0	2.8	5.4
합계	4.2	3.0	4.8	-4.4	13.6	10.8	0.5	8.3	-2.7	0.2

LPG 산업의 경쟁력 제고방안으로 제시되는 것은 ① 집단배송센터의 도입, ② 체적거래 활성화, ③ 벌크공급 활성화, ④ LPG 특소세 조정으로 가격인하, ⑤ Peak Shaving System 등이다.

① 집단배송센터 도입방안은 상승하는 유통비용 절감을 위한 대안이다. 즉, 기존의 유통구조는 충전소(도매업자)-판매점(소매업자)-소비자의 구조였으나, 이제 판매점단계에 집단배송센터를 두어 여기서 대부분의 소비자에게 직접 배송하는 구조이다. 이는 배송전문회사를 도입하여 소규모의 판매점을 통폐합하는 개념으로 유통단계를 축소하고 물류효율화를 이루기 위한 것이다. 그 장점은 배송에 의한 인력과 시설비 등 절감과 안전 관리의 강화가 강점이나, 소규모 판매점의 소멸 등이 문제점이다. 즉, 많은 판매상의 이해관계 조정이 과제이다.

② 체적거래제는 기존의 중량거래방식의 대안이다. 중량거래방식은 가스를 무게단위로 판매하는 방식으로 실제로는 가장 정확한 판매방식이나 일반 소비자 입장에서는 무게를 알기 어렵고 가스가 얼마나 소진되었는지를 미리 알기 어려워 안전성과 편이성에서 소비자의 불만요인이 되어 왔다.

즉, 중량거래방식은 정량시비문제, 사용중 중단, 잔가스 손실 등 문제가 제기되어 왔다. 체적거래방식은 무게가 아니라 부피를 단위로 가스를 판매하는 방식으로 온도에 따라 체적의 증감이 있어 사실 정확한 판매방식은 아니나 계량기를 설치하면 도시가스와 같이 계획배달이 가능하여 안전하고 편리하게 소비자가 사용할 수 있는 방식이다. 문제는 계량기 설치부담과 소비자들이 그 부담을 지면서까지 체적거래를 할 필요성을 느끼지 못한다는 것이다. 정부는 당초 업무용건축물은 2000년 말까지, 공동주택은 01년 말까지, 단독주택은 03년 말까지 체적거래를 하도록 했으나 04년 말 기준 실제 이행은 각 80%, 73%, 3%에 머무르고 있다.

③ 현재 대부분 난방취사용 LPG는 용기에 넣어 판매되는데, 안전관리와 함께 가스가 얼마나 남았는지 알 수 없는 문제점 등이 지적되어 왔다. 따라서 용기에 넣어 공급하는 대신 소형가스탱크(탱크로리)로 각 가정·업소에 있는 탱크에 직접 공급하는 방안이 벌크공급제도이다. 장점은 용기 값이 절감되며, 사고발생 시 책임소재 규명이 가능해 보험혜택을 받을 수 있고, 가스가 얼마나 남았는지 알 수 있는 점 등이다.

④ 수송용 LPG(부탄)의 경우, 정부는 00년 7월 결정하여 시행하던 수송용 연료간 가격체제개편계획을 04년 12월 수정하여, 수송용 LPG의 가격경쟁력을 키워주었다. 즉, LPG업계와 영업용 택시업계의 요구를 반영하여, 06년 7월까지 휘발유 : 경유 : LPG 가격비를 당초목표 100 : 75 : 60에서 100 : 85 : 50으로 완화하기로 수정하였다. 이는 LPG 산업의 경쟁력을 강화한다는 명분에는 좋으나, 정부가 어떻든 7개년 계획을 결정한 다음, 4년간 잘 추진하던 계획을 업계의 압력에 밀려 중도에 변경하는 바람직하지 못한 사례를 남겼다는 점도 부인할 수는 없다.

⑤ 또한 LPG 수요개발과 가스 안정공급을 위해 비상시 Peak Shaving System 도입을 중장기적으로 검토할 필요가 있다. Peak Shaving System이란 LNG 공급차질이 우려되는 비상시에 LPG를 LNG에 일부혼합 또는 대체공급함으로써 LNG의 공급안정성을 제고하는 시스템을 말한다.

다) LPG 품질관리

LPG는 청정연료로 2001년까지는 품질문제가 제기되지 않았다. 00년 7월 수송용연료 간 가격체계 개편계획으로 휘발유 : 경유 : LPG(부탄)의 소비자 가격 상대가격비율을 00년 7월 현재 100 : 47 : 26에서 2006년 7월까지 100 : 75 : 65로 완화하기로 하고, 소비자가격 조정을 위해 특소세를 매년 조정해 가기로 하였다. 이에 따라 수송용 LPG(부탄)의 특소세가 대폭 인상되고, 난방취사용 LPG(프로판)는 특소세가 변하지 않아 상대적으로 소비자가격이 낮아지게 되고, 소비자가격이 상대적으로 낮아진 프로판을 부탄에 혼합하여 판매하는 탈세행위가 발생하게 된다. 이에 따라 2002년부터 정부는 LPG에 대한 품질검사를 시행하게 된다. 품질검사는 당초 석유품질검사소가 담당하였으나, 2002년 하반기부터는 가스안전공사도 공인검사기관으로 같이 참여하고 있다. 이 품질 검사는 일반 석유제품의 품질검사와 마찬가지로 품질검사와 탈세단속이라는 두 가지 성격을 갖고 있다.

품질검사 결과를 보면 2002년에는 2,226건 검사에 27건 위반, 2003년에는 2,693건에 54건 위반, 2004년에는 3,775건에 77건 위반으로 수송용 LPG(부탄)의 특소세가 늘어나면서 위반비율이 증가하는 추세이다.

6) 도시가스와 지역난방간 분쟁처리

도시가스 사업은 LNG가 도입되는 1986년부터 전국의 도시지역에 배관을 매설하여 도시가스 공급사업을 시작하였고, 지역난방사업은 1991년부터 대규모 아파트단지와 신도시를 중심으로 난방용 배관을 매설하면서 급속도로 확장되고 있는데, 저렴한 요금과 안정적인 공급이 그 강점이다. 문제는 기존 도시가스배관이 깔려 도시가스로 난방이 이루어지고 있는 지역에 주민들이 보다 저렴한 지역난방의 공급을 요구하는 경우, 도시가스업체와 지역난방업체간 분쟁이 발생하게 된다.

기존 도시가스가 공급되는 지역은 도시가스로 난방과 취사가 동시에 이루어지나, 지역난방은 난방만이 공급되므로, 지역난방 공급구역에서는 난방은 지역난방, 취사는 도시가스로 하는 이중구조를 갖게 된다. 따라서 기존 도시가스로 난방과 취사가 이뤄지는 지역에 지역난방이 진출하는 경우, 도시가스업체는 난방수요를 잃어 수익성이 저하된다. 따라서 도시가스회사는 지역난방 진출저지를 위해 취사용만 사용하는 도시가스는 공급을 중단하겠다고 위협하는 사례가 발생하는 것이다. 즉, 도시가스회사는 도시가스가 공급되는 지역이나 배관이 완료된 지역에 대해서는 기투자된 배관의 사장화(死藏化) 및 중복투자 문제를 거론하며 지역난방의 진출을 저지하려고 한다.

현재 양사업자 간 분쟁지역은, ① 지역난방이 기존 공급지역에서 인근으로 확대되는 지역으로서, 부천, 광명, 화성, 용인 등 11개 지구(5만 세대)가 있으며, ② 지역난방 공급예정인 택지개발계획지구인 인천, 용인, 화성, 안산 등 11개 지구(20만 세대)이다.

분쟁 해소를 위한 방안은 뚜렷하게 없다. 장기적 결론은 도시가스는 취사만 담당하고, 난방은 저렴한 지역난방이 담당하는 것이다. 그러나 현실은 양 업계간 이해가 대립되는 부문이라 해결은 쉽지 않다. 지역난방의 진출에 따른 도시가스 시설의 유휴화 문제도 있고, 도시가스에 부과되는 각종의 세금감면 문제도 논의가 될 수 있다. 이 문제는 이런 사항을 종합적으로 검토해야 할 것이나 그 해결책이 명확하게 재단될 수 있는 것은 아니다.

■ 지경부, 2012년 업무보고

나. 안정적인 에너지 공급체계 실현

(가스) 저장탱크 3기(평택2, 통영1, 54만kℓ)를 완공하여 저장 비율을 확대(10.4% → 12.3%)하고 삼척기지 5기(100만kℓ) 착공

* '16년까지 15기를 추가 건설하여 저장 능력을 1,106만kℓ로 확대할 계획

- 다수의 공급선과 LNG 도입협상을 추진하고 남북러 가스관 사업 추진**을 통해 도입국가·방식 다변화 도모

  ** '17년 북한경유 러시아 PNG 도입개시 목표로 가스공사와 가즈프롬간 서명('11. 9)

라. 천연가스정책의 집행수단

1) 한국가스공사(KOGAS)

KOGAS는 한국가스공사법에 따라 설립된 주식회사로서 사업목적은 천연가스의 제조·공급, 천연가스 인수기지 및 공급망의 건설·운영, 천연가스의 개발 및 수출입, 석유자원의 탐사·개발사업을 포함한다. 사업자금조달을 위하여 사채를 발행할 수 있으며 자본금 3,865억 원에 장단기차입금 14조 원의 재무구조를 가지고있다. 1999년 상장하여 정부 및 지자체가 60%, 일반투자자가 40% 정도 주식을 보유하고 있다.[6]

---

6) kogas.or.kr 참조.

2) 도시가스사업법 등[7)]

도시가스사업법에 따르면 천연가스수출입업을 하려는 자는 지경부장관에게 등록하여야 하며 등록을 위하여는 일정한 저장시설만 갖추면 된다. 다만, 수급을 총괄하는 지경부에 수입계약 체결 30일 전에 통보하고 계약이 체결되면 이를 신고하여야 한다.

천연가스의 수출입계약이 인수기지 및 공급망은 과거 KOGAS가 독점하였으나 이제는 일정한 시설기준을 갖추면 수출입업 등록을 할 수 있다. 따라서 발전자회사나 민자사업자, 자가용전기설비를 구비한 자 등도 KOGAS를 통함이 없이 자가소비용 수출입업자로서 천연가스를 직접 수출입할 수 있다. 다만 도시가스사업자는 지경부장관으로부터 수입 또는 운송계약의 승인을, 자가소비용직수입자는 사전에 지경부장관에게 계약의 통고를, 사후에 계약을 신고하여야 한다. 이는 가스의 원활한 수급을 책임지는 지경부장관이 전체적인 도입물량이나 가격을 조정하도록 하게 하기 위함이다.

KOGAS는 보다 적극적인 안정적 수급확보책의 일환으로 미얀마, 캐나다, 호주, 모잠비크, 우즈베키스탄, 인도네시아, 이라크 등에서 광구를 탐사하거나 개발·생산하고 있다.[8)] 천연가스는 KOGAS가 해외산지에서 액화된 LNG를 국내인수기지로 운송, 국내연결망을 통하여 수요지로 이동, 다시 기화시키지만 PNG에 대하여는 아직 본격적인 법적인 논의가 되고 있지 않다. 다만, 최근에 자기소비용직수입자가 독자적인 국내인수기지를 건설하여 이를 수입하여도 KOGAS의 연결망을 사용할 수밖에 없는 까닭에 순전히 상업적인 차원에서 이의 사용료 문제가 제기되고 있을 뿐이다.[9)]

노트와 질문

1. 자가소비용 천연가스의 도입이 자유화되었음에도 불구하고 KOGAS의 수입독점이 깨지지 않는 이유는 무엇일까? 수입을 자유화함으로써 자가소비자들이 필요로 하는 천연가스의 가격인하라는 정책적 목표를 달성할 수 있는 방안은 무엇일까?
2. 비축률과 자급률의 상승에도 불구하고 국내석유가의 안정이나 이의 인상률 통제라는 정책적 목표를 이루지 못한 이유는 무엇일까? 국내정유산업의 공급자독점 상황을 변화시키면 이러한 정책적 목표달성이 가능할까? 구체적으로 어떠한 정책수단이 있을까?

---

7) 천연가스와 구별되는 액화석유가스(LPG)는 석유제품의 일종으로 액화석유가스의 안전관리 및 사업법에 의하여 규율된다.

8) dart.fss.or.kr KOGAS분기보고서 참조.

9) 방선혁, 배관을 통한 국제천연가스경유운송 및 경유운송요금에 관한 연구(한국산업기술대학교 박사학위 논문).

3. 자금의 조달

가. 국가의 자금

국가재정은 통일성의 원칙에 따라서 특정한 세입을 특정한 세출에 연결시키지 않은 것이 바람직하지만, 사업의 완성에 장기간이 소요되는 경우 기금이나 특별회계를 운용, 특정한 세출에 필요한 자금의 조달을 보장하기도 한다.[10] 에너지특별회계는 1977년 이래 여러 에너지관련법안에 근거하여 운용되던 기금을 에너지 및 자원사업특별회계법("에특법")에 근거하여 하나로 통합, 설립된 것이다.

기금의 재원은 융자계정수입 이외에 석유의 수입·판매부과금, 가스안전관리부담금, 기타보유자산의 매각으로 얻어진 투자계정수입이 있다. 이의 징수 및 부과는 KNOC에 위임되어 있는바, 실제 매년 2조에서 4조 원 정도의 세수가 기록되고 있다. 세출은 에너지개발사업에 투자하거나 KNOC, KORES 등을 통하여 해외유전이나 자원개발사업자에 융자하는 데 사용되고 있다.[11]

천연가스의 안정적 공급을 위하여 이를 비축하고 수입선을 다변화하며 직접 해외자원개발사업에 뛰어들거나 또는 해외기업을 인수하는 것은 올바른 정책방향으로 보인다. 그러나, 이러한 정책추진기구로서 정부투자기관인 KNOC/KOGAS를 설립하고 이들을 통하여 에특세입을 사용하는 것이 가장 효과적인 방법인가? 이들 세입은 정부에서 정한 융자지원기준에 따라서 투명하게 집행되지만, KNOC는 정부가 전액출자한 법인으로서 정부의 감독과 통제를 받는 이상 융자대상을 선정함에 있어서 시장에서의 성공가능성과 융자대금의 회수가능성 이외의 정치적 요소를 고려할 가능성이 없지 않다. 또한 에특법상의 세입만으로 다양한 정책목표를 달성하기에 충분한 자금을 조달할 수 있는지 의문이다.

이를 보완할 수 있는 방안은 시장에서의 평가를 통하여 효과적인 자원배분을 시도하는 것일 것이다. 따라서, 정부는 에특을 시장에서의 평가가 어렵거나 정확하지 못할 가능성이 많은 단계의 사업에 국한하여 일종의 벤처자본으로서 최소한 투입되어야 할 것이며, 시장에서의 평가가 가능하도록 보다 명확한 회계원칙과 사업의 규율을 정해 나가야 할 것이다. 지식경제부 고시 제2009-315호, 해외자원개발사업에 소요되는 자금의 융자기준(2009. 12. 28.)은 융자대상을 조사(탐사)사업, 개발사업, 생산사업, 투자위험보증사업으로 구분하고 조사와 보증사업의 경우 성공불융자가 가능하도록 정하고 있다. 또한 이들의 경우에는 상업적 생산을

10) 염명천, 에너지시장, 산업 & 정책 646 (2006). 우리나라는 2012년의 경우 특별회계가 51조, 일반회계가 223조로 특별회계의 비중이 너무 높다는 문제점이 있다.
https://www.digitalbrain.go.kr/kor/view/statis/statis01_01_02.jsp?code=DB01010102에서 재정통계열람 가능.

11) www.knoc.co.kr 참조.

개시한 경우 원리금뿐만 아니라 특별부담금의 반환도 요구하고 있는 것은 타당하여 보인다. 보다 근본적으로 개발사업과 생산사업을 위하여는 금융시장에서의 자금조달이 가능하니 에특자금의 융자를 탐사에 국한하는 것도 고려하여 볼 만하다.

■ 지식경제부고시 제2011-24호 에너지및자원사업특별회계운용요령(2011. 2. 11.)

제1장 총 칙

제1조(목적) 이 요령은 에너지및자원사업특별회계(이하 "이 회계"라 한다)의 효율적 운영을 위하여 에너지및자원사업특별회계법(이하 "법"이라 한다) 및 동법 시행령(이하 "영"이라 한다)에서 위임된 사항과 그 시행에 관하여 필요한 사항을 규정함을 목적으로 한다.

제2조(용어의 정의) 이 요령에서 사용하는 용어의 정의는 다음과 같다.

1. "에너지 및 자원 관련사업자"라 함은 에너지 및 자원 관련사업을 수행하는 자(이하 "관련사업자"라 한다)를 말한다.
2. "회계운용부서"라 함은 이 회계의 운용·관리를 총괄하는 지식경제부 소관부서를 말한다.
3. "사업담당부서"라 함은 에너지 및 자원관련 사업의 수행을 담당하는 지식경제부 소관부서를 말한다.

제3조(다른 고시와의 관계 등) ① 이 회계의 예산편성·집행 및 관리에 관하여는 다른 법령에 특별한 규정이 있는 경우를 제외하고는 이 고시가 다른 고시, 공고, 지침 등에 우선하여 적용된다.

② 각 사업담당부서가 이 회계의 세입·세출 및 관리에 관련된 세부사항을 정하고자 할 경우에는 회계운용부서와 사전에 협의하여야 한다.

③ 법 및 영에 따라 회계사무를 위탁받은 기관, 융자대상기관과 보조금의 예산 및 관리에 관한 법률에 의한 간접보조사업자가 위탁받은 사무의 처리, 융자금의 대출 및 보조금의 집행에 관하여 필요한 사항을 정하고자 하는 경우에는 지식경제부장관의 승인을 받아야 한다.

제2장 회계관계직원의 임명 등

제4조(회계관계직원) ① 이 회계의 운용·관리를 위한 국가재정법 및 법 제14조의 규정에 의한 회계관계직원은 "별표 1"과 같으며, 필요한 경우 별도의 회계관계직원을 임명할 수 있다.

② 제1항의 규정에 의한 회계관계직원의 임명은 당해 관서장에게 위임한다.

③ 이 규정에 의하여 각 관서장이 회계관계직원을 임명하였을 때에는 지식경제부 장관에게 보고하고, 이를 관련기관에 통보하여야 한다.

④ 〈삭제〉

제5조(회계관계직원의 임무) ① 회계관계 직원은 국가재정법 등 관련법령의 규정에 따라 장부의 비치·기록 및 자료의 제출·보고를 이행하여야 한다.

② 제1항의 규정에 의한 자료의 제출 및 보고는 지식경제부장관을 경유하여야 한다.

제3장 예산의 편성 및 집행

제6조(사업계획의 수립) ① 관련사업자가 이 회계예산의 지원을 수반하는 중·장기계획을 수립할 때에는 국가재정법 제7조 제6항 및 동법시행령 제2조 제3항의 규정에 의한 기획재정부장관과의 협의를 위하여 그 사업규모, 총사업비 및 사업기간 등을 정하여 지식경제부장관에게 제출하여야 한다. 사업규모, 총사업비 또는 사업기간을 변경하고자 할 때에도 또한 같다.

② 관련사업자는 매년 1월 말까지 다음연도 신규사업 및 주요 계속사업에 대한 사업계획서를 지식경제부장

관에게 제출하여야 한다.

제7조(예산편성지침 및 예산요구서 제출) ① 회계운용부서는 매년 3월 31일까지 시달된 다음연도 예산안 편성지침을 사업담당부서에 통보하여야 하며 사업담당부서는 이를 관련사업자에게 통보하여야 한다.

② 사업담당부서는 제1항의 규정에 의한 예산안 편성지침에 따라 그 소관에 속하는 다음연도의 예산요구서를 작성하여 매년 4월 20일까지 회계운용부서로 제출하여야 한다.

제8조(예산의 배정) ① 예산이 성립되면 각 사업담당부서는 사업운영계획과 예산배정 요구서를 4분기별로 구분·작성하여 즉시 회계운용부서로 제출하여야 한다.

② 지식경제부장관은 제1항의 규정에 의한 사업운영계획 및 이에 의한 세입세출예산·계속비와 국고채무부담행위를 포함한 예산배정요구서를 기획재정부장관에게 제출하여야 한다.

③ 지식경제부장관은 배정된 세출예산의 범위안에서 재무관별로 세출예산 재배정계획서를 작성하고 이에 따라 세출예산을 재배정하여야 한다.

④ 지식경제부장관은 세출예산을 재배정한 때에는 이를 지출관과 기획기획재정부장관에게 통지하여야 한다.

제4장 수입 및 지출

제9조(월별징수계획서 제출 등) ① 예산이 성립되면 즉시 각 사업담당부서는 소관세입의 월별징수계획서 및 세출예산사업별 월별지출계획서를 작성하여 회계운용부서에 제출하여야 한다.

② 지식경제부장관은 제8조의 규정에 의한 예산배정요구서에 의거하여 세입예산월별징수계획서와 세출예산 월별 지출계획서를 기획재정부장관에게 제출하여야 한다.

③ 지식경제부장관은 기획재정부장관으로부터 지출한도액의 통지를 받은 때에는 지출관에게 지출한도액을 지시하고, 이를 기획재정부장관과 한국은행에 통지하여야한다.

제10조(수납절차) ① 분임수입징수관은 소관세 입금에 대한 징수결정 관계서류를 징수결정명세서에 첨부하여 징수결정일부터 5일이내로 주임 수입징수관에게 송부하여야 한다.

② 분임수입징수관은 징수부에 기재를 마친 영수필 통지서 또는 세입금 영수내역서에 기재필임을 표시하고, 이를 수납액 합계표에 첨부하여 주임수입징수관에게 송부하여야 한다.

③ 분임수입징수관은 월별 세입징수명세서를 작성하여 주임수입징수관에게 다음달 10일까지 보고하여야 한다.

④ 수입징수관은 매월 말일에 징수부를 마감하고, 세입징수보고서를 작성하여야 한다.

제11조(환급금의 지급) ① 부과금의 환급은 이 회계의 세입계정에서 지급하며, 환급금 지급명령관이 이를 관장한다.

② 환급금은 부과금을 납부한 자가 환급을 신청한 날로부터 25일이내에 지급하여야 하며, 기타 지급절차 등에 대해서도 별도 고시에 정하는 바에 따른다.

제12조(지출절차) ① 지출원인행위는 배정된 예산 및 자금의 범위내에서 하여야 한다.

② 보조금 및 출연금에 대해서는 각 사업담당부서에서 승인한 내용에 따라 지출을 수행한다.

제5장 융 자

제13조(융자약정 및 융자절차) ① 융자는 소관부처의 장관과 융자대상기관의 장이 체결한 융자약정에 의한다.

② 제1항의 융자약정은 지식경제부장관이 정하는 융자약정서에 의한다.

③ 융자대상기관의 장이 융자를 받고자 할 때에는 융자신청서를 제출하여야 하며, 융자금을 수령한 때에는 영수증을 제출하여야 한다.

제14조(융자금의 계리 및 관리) ① 융자대상기관의 장은 융자금을 다른 자금과 구분하여 계리하여야 한다.

② 융자대상기관은 융자금을 융자받은 목적외의 용도에 대출하거나 사용할 수 없다.

제15조(융자기간 등) ① 융자기간은 융자금 지급일자로부터 기산한다.

② 융자대상기관의 장은 이 회계를 통하여 대출받은 자가 대출기간 만료일까지 대출금의 상환이 곤란하여 대출금의 상환을 연기하고자 할 때에는 미리 소관부처 장관의 승인을 얻어야 한다. 다만, 하계저탄 및 연탄

공장 시설자금은 대한석탄공사사장의 승인을 얻어 대출금상환을 연기할 수 있고, 이 경우 소관부처의 장관에게 그 내용을 보고하여야 하며 이 회계의 위탁관리기관인 한국석유공사에 통보하여야 한다.

③ 지식경제부장관은 석유개발사업의 경우 제2항에 의한 대출금의 상환 연기와 동시에 융자금상환도 연기할 수 있다.

제16조(융자금의 원리금 상환) ① 융자금의 원금은 일시상환 조건부 대출인 경우를 제외하고는 연 4회 균등분할하여 상환한다.

② 융자금의 원리금상환일은 3월, 6월, 9월, 12월의 각 15일로 하되, 최초의 상환일은 융자금의 거치기간 만료후 최초로 도래하는 상환일로 한다.

③ 융자대상기관이 융자금상환을 지체한 때에는 상환하여야 할 원리금에 대하여 당해 상환기일의 다음날로부터 이를 납입한 날까지의 일수에 따라 지식경제부장관이 정하는 금융기관의 대출연체 이자율을 적용한 연체금을 납부하여야 한다.

④ 융자대상기관이 납부하는 원리금과 연체금은 납입일 현재의 연체금, 이자, 원금의 순으로 충당한다.

⑤ 융자금의 원리금은 그 상환일이 토요일 또는 공휴일인 경우에는 그 다음날에 이를 납입하여야 한다.

⑥ 융자대상기관은 융자금의 대출 후 이를 회수한 경우 또는 정당한 사유 없이 융자금의 대출이 2개월 이내 실행되지 않을 경우 융자기간 만료전이라도 이를 상환하여야 한다. 다만, 융자대상기관이 소관부처의 장관에게 보고하여 승인을 받은 경우에는 그러하지 아니한다.

⑦ 석유개발사업의 융자원리금 상환방법에 대해서는 제1항 및 제2항의 규정에도 불구하고 별도 고시에 정하는 바에 따른다.

⑧ 융자대상기관은 원리금을 상환한 후, 그 내역을 지체없이 소관부처의 장관에게 보고하여야 하며, 이 회계의 위탁관리기관인 한국석유공사에 통보하여야 한다.

제17조(융자금의 이자계산) 융자금의 이자는 융자금에 약정이자율과 융자된 다음날부터 상환되는 날까지의 일수를 곱하여 산출한다.

제18조(융자조건 등) ① 융자사업별 융자이자율 및 융자기간 등은 "별표 2"와 같다.

② 융자대상기관에 대한 융자취급수수료는 융자이자율과 대출이자율의 차이로 하되, 금융기관을 통하여 대출하는 경우의 융자취급수수료는 금융기관에 귀속된다. 다만, 융자대상기관이 직접 대출받는 경우와 성공불융자사업과 같이 융자원리금 감면대상사업의 경우에는 융자취급수수료를 지급하지 아니한다.

제19조(제재) ① 소관부처의 장관은 융자대상기관 또는 대출받은 자가 이 규정에 위반하여 융자금 또는 대출금을 운용한 때에는 융자기간만료전이라도 당해 자금을 즉시 회수하여야 하며, 그 융자금 또는 대출금에 대하여는 제16조 제3항의 규정에 의하여 금융기관의 대출연체이자율을 적용할 수 있다.

② 융자대상기관은 대출금을 다른 목적에 유용하거나 원리금의 상환을 연기한 사례가 있는 관련사업자에 대하여는 추가적인 대출을 중단할 수 있다.

제6장 결산 및 보고

제20조(결산보고서 작성 및 제출) ① 한국석유공사사장은 정부결산지침에 의거 매회계연도마다 이 회계의 세입·세출 결산보고서 및 부속서류를 작성하여 다음연도 1월 25일까지 지식경제부장관에게 제출한다.

② 지식경제부장관은 제1항의 규정에 의하여 제출된 결산보고서 등을 반영한 "중앙관서결산보고서"를 작성하여 다음연도 2월말일까지 기획재정부장관에게 제출하여야 한다.

제21조(보고) ① 영 제8조 제1항 제1호의 사무를 위탁받은 한국석유공사 사장은 위탁받은 사무의 운용·관리상황에 대하여 매월의 실적을 다음달 15일까지 지식경제부장관에게 보고하여야 한다.

② 제1항의 규정에 의한 보고를 위하여 융자대상기관 및 간접보조사업자, 기타 이 회계로부터 예산의 지원을 받은 기관, 단체는 매월의 예산집행실적을 다음달 10일까지 한국석유공사에 제출하여야 한다.

대법 1994. 10. 7. 선고 93다43064 판결

가. 원심판결 이유에 의하면, 원심은, 거시증거들을 종합하여 원고들이 1988. 4. 25. 도시가스판매업을 하고자 하는 피고들과의 사이에 원고들 소유의 소외 공단도시가스주식회사(법인명이 1988. 5. 12. 대화에너지주식회사로 변경되었다. 이 뒤에서는 소외 회사라고 한다)의 주식 일체(위 회사의 자산과 부채 일체)를 피고들에게 대금 1,920,000,000원에 매도하고, 계약금은 금 218,000,000원으로 하되 그 중 금 18,000,000원은 계약 당일 지급받고, 나머지 금 200,000,000원은 피고들이 소외 회사의 도시가스공급시설의 시험가동을 완료할 때까지 보관하면서 소외 회사의 시급한 채무가 나타나면 이를 직접 갚아가며 나머지는 원고들에게 반환하기로 하고, 잔금 1,702,000,000원은 같은 해 8. 30.까지 피고들이 소외 회사의 도시가스공급시설을 담보로 석유사업기금으로부터 융자를 받아 소외 풍림산업주식회사(이 뒤에서는 풍림산업이라고 한다)에 대한 공사대금채무금 1,236,059,000원 등 원심판결의 별지 목록 기재와 같은 소외 회사의 채무합계금 1,585,815,000원을 원고들과 상호 협의하여 변제하고 그 후에 위 채무의 변제금을 위 매매대금에서 공제하고 정산하기로 하는 내용의 매매계약을 체결한 사실, 피고들은 위 매매대금에서 피고들이 변제하였다는 소외 회사의 채무합계금 1,585,815,000원 등을 공제한 나머지 금원만을 지급한 사실을 인정한 다음, 원고들의 다음과 같은 주장, 즉 풍림산업에 대한 공사대금 채무금 1,236,059,000원의 채무 중 금 50,000,000원은 1987. 8. 7. 변제하였는데 위 매매계약 당시에 착오로 위 공사대금 채무액을 위 변제금을 공제하지 아니한 채 위 별지 목록 기재와 같이 금 1,236,059,000원으로 기재한 것이므로, 피고들은 위 변제금 50,000,000원을 공제하고 나머지 공사대금만을 풍림산업에 지급하여야 할 것임에도 불구하고 다시 위 공사대금 전액을 풍림산업에 지급하여, 위 금 50,000,000원은 이중변제가 되었고, 이는 결국 피고들의 과실로 말미암아 풍림산업에 부당이득을 주게 된 것일 뿐 원고들에게 변제한 것은 아니어서 이를 위 매매대금에서 공제할 수는 없으므로 위 금원에 해당하는 매매대금의 지급을 구한다는 주장에 대하여는, 원고들이 1987. 8. 7. 풍림산업에 위 공사대금의 일부로서 금 50,000,000원을 지급하였다고 인정할 증거가 없고 오히려 원고 오세칠이 1987. 8. 7. 위 풍림산업의 현장소장이던 위 심규대에게 위 공사대금에 대한 이자 내지 부가가치세환급금 등으로 금 50,000,000원을 지급한 사실이 인정되고 가사 위 돈이 원고들의 주장처럼 위 공사대금의 일부로 지급된 것이라 한들 원고들이 이 사실을 이 사건 매매계약 당시는 물론 피고들이 원고들과의 약정에 따라 풍림산업에 대한 채무를 변제할 때까지도 피고측에 통보하거나 갑 제2호증을 보여준 바도 없어 피고측이 결국 이 사실을 모른 채 위 돈을 변제한 터에 신의칙이나 공평의 원칙상 이중변제로 인한 불이익을 원고측이 부담하여야 하지 이를 피고측에 부담시킬 수는 없다고 할 것이므로, 원고들의 위 주장은 어느 모로 보나 이유 없다고

판단하였다.

그러나, 소외 회사와 풍림산업 사이에 1987. 8. 27.자로 작성된 갑 제2호증(인증서)에는 소외 회사의 풍림산업에 대한 공사대금 잔액이 당초의 금 1,236,059.000원에서 금 50,000,000원이 감액된 금 1,186,059,000원으로 기재되어 있고, 풍림산업의 현장소장으로서 위 금 50,000,000원을 직접 수령한 소외 심규대도 제1심 증인으로 나와 위 금 50,000,000원을 공사대금으로 수령하였다고 증언하고 있는바, 갑 제2호증은 채권자인 풍림산업에 의하여 작성된 것이고,위 증인 심규대는 그 담당직원이므로 원고들이 위 매매계약 당시에 위 변제사실을 피고들에게 고지하지 아니한 점과 갑 제2호증을 피고들에게 제시하지 아니한 점 등 원심판결설시의 사정만으로는 위 증거들이 그 신빙성이 없다고 할 수 없다 할 것이다. 그럼에도 불구하고 원심은 합리적인 이유의 설시 없이 위 증거들을 배척하고 원고의 주장사실을 인정하지 아니하였으니 원심판결에는 채증법칙을 위반하여 사실을 잘못 인정한 위법이 있다고 할 것이다.

그리고, 기록에 의하면, 원고들과 피고들은 이 사건 매매계약서의 별지에 기재된 소외 회사의 채무는 원고들의 일단의 제시액으로서 쌍방의 협의를 거쳐 채무를 확정한 다음 피고들이 그 확정채무의 변제를 위하여 지급한 금액을 매매대금에서 공제하기로 약정한 것으로 인정되는바, 사실관계가 이와 같다면 피고들이 그 변제를 위하여 지급한 금원 중 일부에 해당하는 채무가 존재하지 아니하여 변제가 성립하지 아니하는 임의지급금까지 이 사건 매매대금에서 공제하기로 약정한 것으로 볼 수는 없으므로 위 이중지급금을 이 사건 매매대금에서 공제할 수는 없다 할 것이고, 비록 원고들이 피고들에게 위 변제사실을 통보하지 아니하였다고 하더라도 당초 매매계약서 별지에 기재된 소외 회사의 채무액은 원고들의 일단의 제시액에 불과한 것으로서 쌍방의 협의를 거쳐 채무를 확정하여 변제하기로 약정한 이상 원고들이 변제사실의 통보를 해태하였다고 하여 피고들이 이중으로 지급한 위 금 50,000,000원을 이 사건 매매대금에서 공제할 것이 아니고, 신의칙이나 공평의 원칙상 이러한 이중변제로 인한 불이익을 원고측이 부담하여야 한다고 볼 수도 없다. 그럼에도 불구하고 원심은 그 설시의 이유로 위와 같은 이중변제로 인한 불이익을 원고측이 부담하여야 한다 하여 원고들의 위 주장을 받아들이지 아니하였으니 원심판결에는 법령의 해석적용을 잘못한 위법이 있다고 할 것이다. 원심판결의 위와 같은 위법은 판결에 영향을 미친 것임이 명백하므로 논지는 이유가 있다.

대법 2008. 11. 13. 선고 2008다46531 판결

1. 원심의 판단

원심은 그 채택증거들을 종합하여, 대한민국 정부가 1970년대 말 제2차 석유파동 직후 석유자원의 안정적 확보를 위하여 당시 인도네시아에서 영업하던 소외 1 주식회사의 창업자 소외 2에게 사업비 80%의 지원을 약속하면서 국책사업의 일환으로 인도네시아 서마두라 광구의 유전개발사업에 참여하도록 종용하자 이에 소외 1 주식회사가 1981. 4. 1. 현지에 피고 법인을 설립하여 유전개발사업에 착수하여 같은 해 5. 7. 피고가 인도네시아 국영석유회사와 사이에 서마두라 광구 유전개발사업에 관한 생산물분배계약을 체결하고 위 사업의 지분 50%를 취득한 사실, 수출입과 해외투자 및 해외자원개발에 필요한 금융제공을 목적으로 설립된 원고 은행은 1981. 4. 23. 정부 경제장관협의회에서 이루어진 서마두라 광구 유전개발사업의 초기 3년간 소요자금 미화 38,518,000달러 지원결정에 따라 같은 해 5. 26. 피고에게 미화 38,518,000달러를 원금은 최초 대출취급일부터 8년 거치 후 10년간 연 1회 균등 분할 상환의, 이자는 연 8%를 최초 대출취급일부터 매 1년 후취의, 각 조건으로 무담보로 대여한 데 이어 정부의 추가지원결정에 따라 1982. 11. 29.경 미화 4,155,000달러, 1983. 9. 2.경 미화 7,336,000달러를 각 추가 대여한 후 위 1983. 9. 2.자 대여금은 대여당시 약정에 따라 1984. 12. 29. 피고의 석유개발기금 대출금으로 변제받아 1985. 12. 30. 무렵 미상환 대출원금은 미화 42,673,000달러, 그때까지 발생한 이자로서 원·피고 합의로 원금에 산입한 이자액이 미화 12,175,731.44달러(이하 '원금화된 이자'라고 한다)에 이른 사실, 1986년경부터 서마두라 광구의 석유생산량 격감 및 세계 유가의 하락으로 피고의 경영상태가 어려워지자 원고는 1986. 11. 6.자 정부 경제장관협의회결정에 따라 1986. 5. 27. 이후 발생하는 이자 및 1986. 5. 30.자로 지급유예된 이자액 미화 5,016,000달러에 관하여 1989년 말까지 상환유예의 조치를 취하였으나, 1989. 12. 30.자 원리금 상환의 곤란을 이유로 피고가 정부에 대출원금의 대환과 이자의 확정 혹은 감면과 분할 상환 등의 조치를 수차 건의하자 이에 1990. 3. 19.경 정부가 작성하여 원고에게 통보한 위 차입금 대책방안을 참고하여 원고가 같은 해 5. 26. "대출원금 미화 42,673,000달러는 1995년까지 상환을 유예하되 1996년부터 가스전 개발로 발생하는 수익금으로 2001. 5. 26.까지 연차적으로 상환한다. 원금화된 이자는 대출원금 상환 후 가스전 및 기타 광구 등의 개발로 얻는 수익금으로 상환가능시 2001. 5. 26.까지 연차적으로 상환하고, 1985. 12. 31.부터 1989. 12. 30.까지 기발생된 이자(미화 18,005,421.54달러, 이하 '기발생 이자'라고 한다)는 원금과 원금화된 이자 상환후 추가 수익이 발생하여 상환이 가능할 때부터 연차적으로 상환하고, 1989. 12. 31. 이후에는 이자를 부과하지 않되 추가 유전의 발견 등으로 본사업의 정상화가 가능한 수익이 발생한 경우에는 이자를 부과할 수 있다(이하 '1990년 이후 이자'

라고 한다)"라는 내용으로 대출조건을 변경함과 아울러 한국석유공사로부터 대출원금 채무에 대한 지급보증을 받은 사실, 그러나 피고가 1996. 9. 4. 위 변경된 대출조건에 따른 최초 분할 상환액 미화 1,500,000달러를 상환한 후 다시 상환약정을 이행할 수 없는 처지가 되자 원고는 1997. 2. 27. 미상환 대출원금 미화 41,173,000달러는 2001. 4. 30.에 일시 상환하고 원금화된 이자는 상환가능시 2001. 5. 26.까지 상환하는 내용으로 재차 대출조건을 변경하면서 소외 1 주식회사와 한국석유공사로부터 위 미상환 대출원금 채무에 대한 추가 지급보증 및 그 담보로서 약속어음을 발행, 교부받은 사실, 원고는 2001. 5. 9. 피고로부터 위 대출원금과 원금화된 이자의 상환기일을 2002년 이후로 유예해 달라는 요청을 받고 이를 거절한 후 2002. 4. 29. 피고의 보증인인 한국석유공사와 위 대출원금에 관한 5년간 분할변제계약을 체결하여 현재까지 위 대출원금 미화 41,173,000달러 전액을 변제받은 사실 등을 인정하였다.

위 인정 사실을 토대로 원심은, 이 사건 대출금은 피고가 유전개발사업에서 성공하여 다른 일반융자를 모두 상환하는 등 상환조건이 충족되면 원리금 전액을 상환하는 반면 사업에 실패할 경우에는 전액 면제받는 성공불융자인데, 위 상환조건의 불성취로 이 사건 대출금 채무가 면제로 소멸하였고, 그렇지 않다 해도 위 원금화된 이자는 가스전 등의 개발수익금으로 2001. 5. 26.까지 피고에게 상환능력 있음을 정지조건으로 상환하기로 약정하였는데, 위 상환조건의 불성취로 그 상환채무가 존재하지 아니한다는 피고의 항변에 대하여, 정부의 논의과정 및 일부 정부문서에 이 사건 대출금이 성공불융자라는 언급 혹은 기재가 있은 사실은 인정되지만, 이 사건 대출에 관한 차입금신청서, 어음거래약정서 등에 그러한 내용의 특약이 기재된 바 없는데다가 1990. 5. 26.자 대출조건 변경 당시 한국석유공사가 대출원금채무의 지급을 보증한 점 등의 사정에 비추어 원금화된 이자를 포함한 원리금 전부의 상환면제에 관한 구체적 감면약정이 있었다고 보기 어렵고, 또한 ① 1990. 5. 26.자 대출조건 변경 당시 정부의 대책방안을 일부 수정하여 대출원금 및 원금화된 이자의 대출조건에 '2001. 5. 26.까지'라는 구체적인 기한을 설정한 바 있고, 위 상환기한은 한국수출입은행법 제25조 제3항에서 정한 해외투자 지원자금의 대출기간 만료일에 해당하는 점, ② 변경된 대출조건에서 대출원금 부분은 '상환가능시'라는 문구 외에는 원금화된 이자 부분과 차이가 없는 반면, 1985. 12. 31.부터 1989. 12. 30.까지 기발생 이자 부분과 1990년 이후 이자 부분은 원금화된 이자와 별도로 구분하고 있고 그 내용상으로도 차이가 있는 점, ③ 피고의 상환능력이 거의 없는 상황에서 원금화된 이자의 상환조건을 피고 주장과 같은 내용의 정지조건으로 변경하는 것은 사실상 채무를 면제하는 것과 마찬가지이나, 이를 인정하기는 어려운 점 등의 사정에 비추어, 피고가 가스전개발 등의 개발수익금으로 2001. 5. 26.까지 상환능력 있음을 정지조건으로 원금화된 이자를 상환하기로 하는 약정이 있었다고 보기도 어렵다고 판단함으로써, 피고의 항변을 모두 배척하고 원고의 청구를 인용한 제1심판결을 그대로 유지하였다.

2. 상고이유 제1점에 대하여

원심의 인정 사실에 의하면, 설령 이 사건 대출의 결정 및 그 대출조건의 변경에 주도적으로 관여한 정부의 입장에서는 피고의 주장처럼 성공불융자의 의도를 가진 것으로 볼 수 있다 하더라도 이 사건 대출계약의 법률상 당사자인 원·피고 사이의 관련 계약서에 그러한 특약의 기재가 없는 이상 위 대출계약이 처음부터 성공불융자라고 인정하기 어려울 뿐만 아니라 피고의 요청에 따른 1990. 5. 26.자 대출조건 변경 및 1997. 2. 27.자 대출조건 변경 당시 그 대가로 이 사건 대출의 주된 부분인 대출원금 채무에 대하여 한국석유공사 혹은 소외 1 주식회사에 의한 조건 없는 보증이 이루어지고, 나아가 원·피고 사이의 위 변경된 대출조건에서도 이자 부분에 관하여 규정한 '(수익금으로) 상환가능시'라는 조건적 문언을 대출원금 부분에는 두지 아니한 이상 적어도 대출원금 부분에 대하여는 그 시점에 이르러 확정적인 채무상환의 의사를 밝힌 셈이 되어, 그 이전의 사실관계를 들어 달리 주장할 수도 없다 할 것이다.

같은 취지에서 피고의 이 부분 항변을 배척한 원심판단은 정당하고, 상고이유의 주장처럼 원심이 그 판단의 논거로 든 그 밖의 사유에 일부 부적절한 점이 있다 하더라도 위에서 적시한 사유들만으로도 피고의 주장을 인정하기 어려운 이상 그 부분 원심판단의 당부는 결론에 영향을 미치지 아니한다.

이 부분 상고이유의 주장은 이유 없다.

3. 상고이유 제2점에 대하여

계약당사자 사이에 어떠한 계약내용을 처분문서인 서면으로 작성한 경우에 문언의 객관적인 의미가 명확하다면 특별한 사정이 없는 한 문언대로의 의사표시의 존재와 내용을 인정하여야 하고, 그 문언의 객관적인 의미가 명확하게 드러나지 않는 경우에는 그 문언의 내용과 계약이 이루어지게 된 동기 및 경위, 당사자가 계약에 의하여 달성하려고 하는 목적과 진정한 의사, 거래의 관행 등을 종합적으로 고찰하여 사회정의와 형평의 이념에 맞도록 논리와 경험의 법칙, 그리고 사회일반의 상식과 거래의 통념에 따라 계약내용을 합리적으로 해석하여야 하는바(대법원 2002. 5. 24. 선고 2000다72572 판결, 대법원 2008. 3. 14. 선고 2007다11996 판결 등 참조), 특히 문언의 객관적 의미와 달리 해석함으로써 당사자 사이의 법률관계에 중대한 영향을 초래하게 되는 경우에는 그 문언의 내용을 더욱 엄격하게 해석하여야 할 것이다.

그런데 원·피고 사이의 이 사건 대출은 최초 계약 이래 1990. 5. 26.경 및 1997. 2. 27.경 그 대출조건이 일부 변경되었으므로 위 1997. 2. 27.자 최종 대출조건에 따라 작성된 금전소비대차약정서(갑 제1호증)의 기재 내용과 처분문서 해석의 법리를 바탕으로 관련 사정들을 참작하여 그 약정의 객관적·합리적 의미를 도출하여야 할 것인바, 위 금전소비대차약정서에는 이 사건 대출원금의 경우 단순히 '2001. 4. 30.에 상환'하는 것으로 규정한 것과 달리, 원금화된 이자는 '대출원금 상환 후 가스전 및 기타 광구 수익금으로 상환가능시' 2001. 5. 26.까지 상환하도록 명시적으로 달리 규정한 이상, 위 예상 수익방안에 따른 상환가능한 수익금의 발생을 조건으로 그 상환의무가 발생한다고 보는 것이 위 금전소비대차약정서의 문언에 객관적으로 가장 부합하는 해석이라 할 것이고, 이와 달리 위 상환가능한 수익금의 발생 여부와 상관없이 확정적인 상환의무가 성립한 것으로 보는 원심과 같은 해석을 하기 위해서는 이를 수긍할 수 있는 특별한 사정이 존재하여야만 할 것이다.

그러나 이 점에 관하여 원심이 앞서 본 바와 같이 들고 있는 논거 중 ②의 점은, 전문금융기관인 원고가 작성한 금전소비대차약정서에서 대출원금 부분과 원금화된 이자 부분 사이에 위 '상환가능시'라는 조건적 문언을 달리 규정한 것 자체에 중요한 차이점이 존재한다고 보아야 할 것이고(원고가 작성한 대출조건 변경내역표에서도 원금화된 이자 부분 중 다른 부분의 기재는 생략하면서도 '상환가능시 2001. 5. 26.까지 상환'이라는 부분은 기재하고 있다. 기록 193면 참조), 한편 위 원금화된 이자와 기발생 이자 및 더 나아가 1990년 이후 이자 부분은 위 조건적 문언을 공통으로 두고 있어 그 대출조건의 본질적 유사성이 인정된다 할 것임에도 이와 정반대로 본 원심의 해석은 합리적이라고 보기 어렵고, 원심의 논거 중 ③의 점 역시, 원심의 인정 사실에 의하더라도 당초 목표로 한 유전개발사업은 실패로 돌아간 반면 가스전개발사업의 성공가능성을 믿고 위 대출조건의 변경 및 대출원금의 보증이 이루어진 것으로 보일 뿐만 아니라 기록에 의하더라도 그러한 사정이 명백히 인정되는바(기록상 많은 관련 자료들이 있지만 가령, 1990. 5. 26.자 대출조건 변경에 앞서 1989년 11월경 동력자원부장관이 정부 경제장관협의회에 안건으로 제출한 '인니 서마두라광구 수은차입금 상환대책'(을 제8호증의8)에서 그 대책안의 논거로, "90년 말부터 위 광구의 가스전에서 수입전망이 확실시되고 있으나 본 사업 추진에 소요된 자금의 차입금 원리금상환을 현실적이고 합리적으로 대치할 필요성이 있고, 원고 자금은 정책적 결정에 의해 성공불융자 자금으로 지원되어 90년부터 원리금상환이 도래되었으나 가스전개발로 발생하는 수입금으로는 적기상환이 불가능하며 특히 이자상환은 본 사업에 투자된 차입금전액을 감안할 때 불가능한 실정이므로 이를 해결하기 위해 별첨과 같은 대책을 수립하여 추진하고자 한다. 현재 원고 차입금은 성공시는 원리금상환과 특별부담금 지불, 실패시는 원리금회수불능액은 원고 자체 결손으로 처리하고 이에 따른 연불수출자금 부족문제는 그 시점에서 정부가 대처한다. 차입원리금 상환에 관한 당사자 견해는, 원고는 89년 말 기일 도래되는 대출원리금 등이 기일에 상환될 수 있도록 협조를 구하고 대출금을 석유사업기금에서 지급보증하거나 대환할 수 있는 방안강구를 요청하고, 한국석유공사 및 피고는, 현재로선 피고의 상환능력이 전무하고 90년 말부터 가스전 생산수입이 예상되나 시티은행 등 타 차입금을 감안하면 원고 차입금의 조기상환은 불가능하며, 원고 차입원금은 석유사업기금에서 대환하고 이자는 감면조치를 요망한다는 것이다. 대책은, 원금 42,673,000달러는 석유사업기금에서 대체상환하고, 현재까지 발생된 차입금이자 30,181,000달러는 원고가 자체 결손처리하고 다만 가스전의 판매량 증가 또는 타지역에서 성공하여 이자지불이 가능하게 될 때에는 원고에게 이자를 상환한다"라고 적고 있는 것이 한 예이다), 그럼에도 위 가스전개발 수익금으로 원금화된 이자를 상환하기로 하는 내용의 위 조건적 문언의 성취가 사실상 불가능하여 채무면제나 마찬가지임을 전제로 하는 원심의 해석도 합리적이라고 보기 어렵다.

원심의 논거 중 마지막으로 ①의 점을 살펴보면, 이 사건 대출조건 변경 당시 원금화된 이자 부분에 2001. 5. 26.이라는 상환기한의 규정을 둔 경위는 한국수출입은행법상 대출기간 제한규정을 고려하였기 때문임은 기록상 명백하고 쌍방 모두 인정하지만, 위 변경된 대출조건 중 '수익금으로 상환가능시'라는 문언은 그 성질상 법률행위의 효력의 발생 또는 소멸을 장래의 불확실한 사실의 성부에 의존하게 하는 것이란 점에서 법률상 조건임이 분명하다 할 것인데, 조건부 법률행위를 함에 있어서 조건의 성취를 가정하여 그 조건의 성취시와는 별도로 이행기한을 설정한다 하여 그 조건부 법률행위와 모순된다거나 그 조건설정의 효력이 당연히 상실되는 것은 아니라 할 것이고, 다만 그 경우 당해 약정에 나타난 당사자 의사의 합리적 해석상 그러한 조건의 성취 여부를 불문하고 별도로 정한 기한에 확정적으로 채무를 이행하기로 하는 취지로 인정할 수 있다면 그로써 위 조건에 관한 약정이 실효된 것으로 볼 수는 있을 것이다.

그러나 이 점과 관련하여 원심이 제시한 위 ②, ③의 사정은 모두 합리적 근거가 되지 못함은 위에서 본 바와 같고, 오히려 앞서 본 위 조건적 문언의 객관적 의미와 계약당사자인 원고의 신분 등의 사정에다가, 기록에 의하여 인정되는 그 밖의 사정들, 즉 '2001. 5. 26.'이라는 상환기한 이외에는 변경된 대출조건이 그 계기가 된 정부의 대책방안과 차이가 없다 할 것인데, 위 정부의 대책방안은 앞서 본 '인니 서마두라광구 수은차입금 상환대책'에 나타난 바와 같이 기본적으로 원금화된 이자와 기발생 이자를 차별하지 않고 가스전개발 수익금으로 상환가능시에 지급하고자 하는 계획이었음이 분명한 점, 당초 무담보대출로서 유전개발사업의 실패에 따라 거액의 결손처리를 하여야 할 형편에 있던 원고의 입장에서는(원고가 대출조건 변경에 앞서 1989년 9월경 법률회사에 자문을 의뢰한 결과도 그러하다. 갑 제3호증) 정부의 위 대책방안에 따르면 그 중 대출원금에 대하여 정부측의 보증을 받아 확실한 상환방안을 확보하게 될 뿐만 아니라 원금화된 이자의 상환 역시 가망성이 있다고 알려진 가스전개발사업의 성공과 연계할 수 있게 되어, 이를 받아들이는 것이 원고에게 불리하다거나 이례적인 조치라고 할 수는 없고, 따라서 원고가 정부의 대책방안에 반하여 독자적 계산하에 실질적인 수정을 가하고자 하는 의도에서 위 상환기한에 관한 규정을 둔 것으로 보기는 어렵다는 점, 정부 대책방안의 계기가 된 피고의 정부에 대한 요구사항 또한 1990. 2. 21.자 건의서(을 제3호증의 9)에 나타나듯이 "가스전 수입금으로는 원고 차입금 중 원금상환만 가능하므로 원금에 가산된 개발이자 12,176,000달러와 기발생 이자 18,006,000달러 합계 30,182,000달러와 1990년 이후 발생 이자는 감면하고 차입원금 42,673,000달러는 정부 혹은 공신력 있는 국내기관의 보증하에 1996년부터 2001년까지 분할상환하겠다"는 내용으로서 위와 동일한 취지인 점, 원금화된 이자의 경우 이미 대출원금에 편입된 데다가 2차에 걸친 대출조건 변경을 통해 사실상 그 상환기한이 대출원금의 경우와 실질적인 차이가 없게 된 이상 만약 이를 조건부채권이 아닌 위 상환기일의 확정채권으로 취급할 요량이었다면 대출원금과 함께 규정, 처리하였을 터임에도 각 처리방안을 따로 마련하고 그 규정상 중요한 차이마저 둔 것은 양자를 달리 취급하겠다는 의사로 해석할 수밖에 없고, 나아가 당장의 상환능력은 없는 것으로 드러난 피고에 대하여 위와 같이 각 상환기한에 특별한 차이를 두지 않은 것은, 향후 개발사업의 성공에 따른 새로운 상환능력 창출이라는 실질적인 사정변경을 전제로 하지 않고서는 합리적 설명이 어렵고, 2차에 걸친 대출조건 변경 당시 대출원금에 대해서만 보증 및 담보어음의 발행이 이루어졌지 원금화된 이자 부분에 대해서는 어떠한 담보방안도 강구되지 않은 것도 같은 맥락에서 이해된다는 점, 위 각 대출조건 변경의 중간에 제정된 1993. 2. 26.자 '석유개발사업에 소요되는 자금의 융자기준'에서 "융자대상사업이 상업적 생산에 못 이르고 사업종료하게 된 경우 융자금전액을 감면하고, 융자대상사업이 상업적 생산에 이른 경우라도 융자원리금의 전부나 일부를 상환하지 못하고 사업을 종료하게 된 경우에는 미상환잔액을 감면한다"는 규정을 정식으로 둔 것도 같은 성격의 이 사건 대출금의 일부 감면조치가 이례적인 조치가 아님을 반증하는 점, 앞서 본 것처럼 1차 대출조건 변경 이전에 원고가 이미 이 사건 대출의 처리에 관한 전문적인 법률검토까지 마친 상태이었음에도 위 조건적 문언을 계약서에 명시하였음에 비추어 그것이 원고의 부주의 혹은 무사려 때문이라고 볼 수는 없고, 이는 원고가 1996. 3. 11. 피고에게 보낸 대출원금 분납금 상환통지서에서 원금화된 이자부분에 대해 "대출원금 상환 후 가스전 및 기타 광구 등의 개발로 얻은 수익금으로 상환가능시 2001. 5. 26.까지 연차적으로 상환"하도록 요구하고(기록 161면), 2002. 4. 30. 피고에게 보낸 통보서에서 "이 사건 대출금 중 원금화된 이자를 제외한 대출원금 41,173,000달러는 지급보증인인 한국석유공사가 대지급하기로 함에 따라 위 대출채권을 한국석유공사에게 양도하고, 원금화된 이자의 경우, 광구 개발수익금 등 귀사의 유동성으로 타 차입금을 상환할 경우 채권자 동등원칙에 따라 이를 상환해야 하며, 당행 요청시 위 사업의 진행상황, 수익금 발생현황 및 사용내역의 제출에 적극 협조해 주기 바란다"라고 요구한(기록 220면) 사실에 비추어도 그러하다는 점 등의 사정들을 종합하여 보면, 위 2001. 5. 26.이라는 기한의 설정은 20년이라는 법정 대출기간을 감안해서 그때까지 위 조건이 성취되는 경우를 가정하여 잠정적인 상환기한을 위 법정 대출기간 만기에 맞추어 정해 놓은 것으로 이해될 뿐, 위 조건의 성취 여부를 불문하고 확정적으로 위 기한까지 채무를 이행하기로 한다는 취지라고 보기는 어렵다 할 것이니, 이와 다른 취지의 이 점에 관한 원심의 해석 역시 합리적이라고 보기 어렵다.

이상과 같은 해석에 의할 경우, 위 조건의 성취가 위 잠정적인 상환기한 이전에 이루어진 경우에도 위 상환기한까지는 상환의무의 이행이 유예된 것으로 보아야 할 것인 반면, 위 조건의 성취가 그 이후에 이루어진 경우에 그 채무의 성립을 부정할 것인지 여부는 당사자 의사해석의 문제라 할 것인데, 이 사건 변경된 대출조건의 근간이 된 위 정부 대책방안에서 원금화된 이자의 상환일을 대출원금의 상환 이후로 하면서도 구체적 일시를 따로 특정하지 않은 것은 위 개발수익금의 발생을 조건으로 하되 그 발생기간에는 제한을 두지 않음으로써 수익발생의 원천인 위 개발사업의 종료시점을 기한으로 설정한 것으로 볼 수 있고, 위 2001. 5. 26. 이후에도 피고가 상환의 가능성을 거론하면서 상환기한의 유예를 요청한 사실 또한 이에 부합한다 할 것인바, 그렇다면 위 조건적 문언에 함축된 당사자들의 의사는 위 상환기한 이후에도 피고의 광구개발사업 종료 이전까지 조건의 성취가 있는 한 상환채무의 성립을 긍정하기로 한 것으로 볼 여지가 많다 할 것이다.

그럼에도 불구하고, 이 사건 최종 변경된 금전소비대차약정서에 기재된 '가스전 등의 개발수익금으로 상환가능시'라는 조건의 성취 여부와 상관없이 2001. 5. 26.까지 확정적으로 위 원금화된 이자를 상환하기로 약정한 것으로 본 원심판단은 처분문서의 해석에 관한 법리를 오해하여 판결 결과에 영향을 미친 위법이 있다 할 것이다.

이 점을 지적하는 취지의 상고이유의 주장은 이유 있다.

4. 결　론

그러므로 원심판결을 파기하고, 사건을 다시 심리·판단하게 하기 위하여 원심법원에 환송하기로 하여 관여 대법관의 일치된 의견으로 주문과 같이 판결한다.

서울고법 2007. 6. 28. 선고 2005노2499 판결

(가) 원심은 그 거시 증거에 의하여 그 판시와 같은 사실을 인정한 다음, 그 인정사실을 종합하여 인정되는 사정, 즉 ① 사할린 유전 인수사업의 사업성을 검토함에 있어 피고인 왕영용 및 철도청이 유전사업에 대하여 전혀 경험이 없음에도 유전 전문기관에 자문이나 사업성 검토를 의뢰한 바 없이 한국석유공사 출장보고서 및 슐럼버거보고서에 나와 있는 러시아 정부의 승인매장량만을 기준으로 사업성을 판단하고, 또한 피고인 전대월 측이 제공하는 관련자료를 뒷받침할 수 있는 객관적인 자료가 전혀 없는 상태에서 그들이 제공하는 자료상의 수치만으로 사할린 유전 인수사업의 사업성을 평가한 점, ② 사할린 유전 인수사업을 제안한

민간사업참여자로서 위 사업의 최대지분권자인 피고인 전대월이 운영하는 하이앤드가 2003. 12. 31. 기준으로 자본잠식상태에 빠져 자금난으로 2004. 8. 30.에는 최종 부도처리되었음에도 하이앤드의 재무상태, 하이앤드가 유전인수사업을 수행할 능력이 있는지 여부에 대하여도 검토하지 않은 점, ③ 비록 슐럼버거보고서나 한국석유공사의 사할린 출장보고서를 받아보고 페트로사흐가 존재하는지는 알 수 있었을 것이나, 사업성을 검토함에 있어 철도청 입장에서 사할린 현지 출장 등으로 페트로사흐가 실제 존재하는지, 페트로사흐의 주식을 소유하고 있는 니미르사가 실제 존재하는 회사인지 등에 관하여 전혀 조사를 해 본 적이 없는 점, ④ 한국석유공사의 사할린 출장보고서를 피고인 전대월 측으로부터 받아 보았으므로 당시 한국석유공사가 사할린 유전 인수사업에 대하여 검토를 한 적이 있다는 것을 충분히 알 수 있었음에도 같은 공공기관인 한국석유공사에조차 사할린 유전 인수사업에 대하여 자문을 의뢰한 적이 없는 점, ⑤ 사할린 유전 인수사업의 수익성 평가와 관련하여 중요한 요소 중의 하나인 연간 영업이익을 산정함에 있어, 처음에는 비용 등에 관하여 객관적인 자료나 수치에 근거하지 않은 채 극히 피상적으로 198억 원이라고 계산하였다가 그 후 직원이 문제점을 제기하여 120억 원이라고 수정하였으나 그 기초가 된 자료 또한 비용 등에 관하여 구체적인 산정근거가 없고, 또 그 자료를 객관적으로 뒷받침할 만한 구체적인 근거도 없는 상태인바, 비록 유전사업에 대하여 전혀 경험이 없다는 사정을 감안하더라도 수익성 평가로서는 상당히 미흡한 점(더욱이, 철도재단은 페트로사흐의 유전자체를 인수하는 것이 아니라, 철도재단이 코리아크루드오일의 주주가 되고, 코리아크루드오일이 니미르사가 소유하고 있는 페트로사흐의 주식을 인수하여 페트로사흐의 주주가 됨으로써 순차로 주주로서 이익배당을 받을 수 있을 뿐이지 페트로사흐가 석유를 생산하여 얻을 수 있는 영업이익 전부가 그대로 철도재단의 이익이 되는 것은 아니다), ⑥ 이광재 의원이 추천한 사업으로 믿고 2004. 9. 20.경에 예정되어 있던 대통령의 러시아 방문시 한·러 정상회담 의제에 포함시키고, 철도청장인 피고인 김세호가 수행하여 사할린유전 인수계약 체결 조인식을 거행할 수 있도록 하기 위하여 페트로사흐에 대한 실사도 하지 않은 채 일반적인 M&A 관행과는 달리 계약금 지급 후 실사하는 방식으로 사할린 유전 인수사업을 추진하려고 한 점, ⑦ 정책심의회의의 담당부서 직원으로부터 사할린 유전 인수사업의 사업성 및 수익성을 판단할 수 있는 자료가 미비하여 정책심의회의를 개최할 수 없다는 반대의견을 듣고도 위 ⑥과 같은 목적 등으로 피고인 신광순에게 보고한 후 바로 당일 아침 여전히 사업성 및 수익성을 판단할 수 있는 자료가 갖추어지지 않은 상태에서 사업설명회를 열어 삼일회계법인이 600만 톤의 매장량을 확인하였다거나 향후 사업추진 주체에 미국석유회사 등이 참여할 예정이라는 등의 전혀 확인되지 아니한 사실을 설명하고, 사할린 유전 인수사업은 연간 120억 원의 수익이 나는 사업이라고 주장하면서 사업참여의 필요성을 강조하고, 철도청 간부들이 여러 가지 문제점을 제기하였으나 사할린 유전 인수사업을 추진함에 있어 그와 같은 문제점을 보완하지 아니한 채 사업을 진행한 점, ⑧ 2004. 9. 10. 사할린 유전 인수사업 실무자들이 피고인 전대월 등의 신용문제와 사할린 유전 인수사업의 계약금은 제3국 은행에 계좌를 개설하여 실사 후에 지급하는 것이 바람직하다는 점을 지적하면서 사할린 유전 인수사업에 대하여 재검토를 요구하였음에도 이를 받아들이지 않고 오히려 그들을 사할린 유전 인수사업에서 배제시킨 점, ⑨ 페트로사흐의 실체 및 코리아크루드오일과 니미르사 사이에 실제로 주식구매계약이 체결되었는지 등을 알아보기 위하여 사할린 현지 출장을 다녀온 이재성 등이 작성한 출장보고서에 의하면, 페트로사흐에 대해 상당한 부정적인 의견이 기재되어 있음에도 2004. 9. 30. 열린 회의에서 위 보고서의 내용을 제대로 보고하지 아니하고 '6광구 개발권은 판매하고, 정유공장은 공동운영'하는 방식으로 사할린 유전 인수사업을 계속 추진할 것을 적극 주장하여 위 사업을 계속 추진하는 것으로 결론을 얻은 후 2004. 10. 4. 페트로사흐에 대한 실사도 없이 철도재단이 코리아크루드오일을 통하여 니미르사에 계약금 620만 불을 현금으로 지급하게 한 점, ⑩ 페트로사흐는 러시아 정부가 승인한 매장량이 약 4,520만 배럴(누적생산량을 제외하면 약 3,100만 배럴이고, Miller & Lents가 2002년 7월 평가한 바에 따르면 확인매장량이 약 1,246만 5천 배럴이며, 한국석유공사는 Miller & Lents가 평가한 매장량에 근거하여 사업성을 평가하였다)인 오크루즈노예유전에서 원유를 생산하고 있는데, 1997년에는 유정 1개당 1일 115톤을 생산하였으나 동일한 기간에 작업효율이 50%에서 90%로 개선되었음에도 2002년에는 1일 50톤을 생산하는 수준이며, 2002년에는 9개의 유정에서 1일 평균 약 3,800배럴을 생산하였으나, 2003년에는 유정을 14개로 증가시켰음에도 1일 평균 약 3,300배럴로, 2004년 7월경에는 1일 평균 약 2,700배럴로 원유생산량이 점차 감소하는 추세이고, 생산량을 증대시키기 위해서는 추가 생산정의 시추가 필요하나 생산정 시추에 적지 않은 비용이 들어가며, 생산정 시추를 통하여 생산량의 증대를 가져올 지는 실사를 통해서만 검증할 수 있고, 생산초기 수년간은 투수도가 높은 저류층 균열대에서 비교적 양호한 생산성을 보이나 균열대 시스템과 연결되어 생산 중·후반기의 생산성에 중요한 영향을 주게 되는 저류층 모암의 공극률과 투수율이 매우 낮아 이론적인 회수율인 38%에 이르기까지는 47년 정도 걸릴 것으로 예측되며, 또 육상광구에서는 34개의 탐사정이 시추되어 1개의 탐사정에서 1일 156㎥ 정도의 석유가 나왔으나 다른 탐사정에서는 전반적으로 낮은 생산량을 보이거나 관심을 가질 만한 양의 석유나 가스가 나오지 않았고, 또 해상광구는 2005년도에 면허를 유지하기 위해 최소한 2개의 탐사정을 의무적으로 시추하여야 하는데 그 비용도 적지 않게 들어갈 것으로 보이며, 또한 페트로사흐 유전은 1년에 6개월은 얼어 있는 동토지역으로 그 기간 동안 생산은 가능하나 바다가 얼기 때문에 수출을 할 수 없는데 이를 운영하기 위하여는 동토지역에 대한 경험 및 운영기술이 별도로 필요한 것으로 보이는바, 위와 같은 이유 등으로 한국석유공사는 사업추진타당성을 낮다고 판단하여 페트로사흐 인수검토를 포기하였고, 에스케이(SK) 주식회사는 많은 돈을 벌기는 어렵다고 판단하고 알파에코사에서 페트로사흐를 6,500만 불 정도에 내놓을 것이라는 소문을 듣고 그 정도의 가치에는 이르지 않는다고 보아 페트로사흐 인수검토를 포기하였으며, 세계적인 석유개발용역전문회사인 슐럼버거는 페트로사흐가 보유하고 있는 3개의 허가구역 내에서 추가적인 탐사작업에 투자하는 것이 어떤 것인지에 대하여 검토한 결과 페트로사흐 투자사업은 '위험성은 높고 수익성은 낮다'라는 결론을 내렸으며, 또 페트로사흐는 1996년도부터 2002년도까지 순자산가치가 마이너스여서 러시아법에 따르면 청산절차에 들어가야 할 정도였고, 2003년도의 경우 2억 루블을 보험료로 납부하는 등 보험료를 과다하게 납부하여 경영 및 현금왜곡을 하고 있으며, 이후에도 1억 루블의 보험료 납부가 예정되어 있었고, 페트로사흐는 2004년도부터 2005년도까지 사이에 오호츠크해 사업권(해상광구)의 허가조건을 충족시키기 위한 작업을 완료하여야 하는데, 이를 위하여는 약 1,675만 불의 투자가 필요하며, 또 2006. 2. 1.까지 위 사업권을 보유할 수 있으나 그 기간 내에 작업프로그램을 완료하고 필요한 경우 상업적인 발견허가를 신청하는 것이 불가능할 수도 있는 상태였음을 고려하고, 한편 당시 철도청은 2005. 1. 1. 공사화되면 기존 부채에 10조 4천억 원에 달하는 고속철도 부채도 인수하여야 할 상황에서 만성적인 적자를 해결하기 위하여 수익사업을 수행하는 경우에는 보다 더 안정적인 수익사업이 필요한 것으로 보이는데, 철도청은 페트로사흐 유전 인수자금을 철도청이 보유하고 있는 여유자금이 아닌 대출금으로 모두 충당하려고 한 점 등에 비추어, 유가상승의 가능성(유가는 여러 가지 복합요인에 의하여 내려갈 수도 올라갈 수도 있는 것으로 유가예측 및 적용은 사업성 평가 당시를 기준으로 향후 유가변화 위험도를 고려하여 유가동향 분석에 근거하여 적절한 유가를 적용하여야 한다. 곽재휘 법정진술)과 페트로사흐의 보험과다가입으로 인한 과다납부한 보험료 금액만큼이 영업이익으로 전환될 가능성이 있는 점 등을 감안한다고 하더라도, 당시 철도청으로서는 사할린 유전 인수사업의 사업성을 충분히 검토하였다면 철도청의 기존 사업과 무관하고 경험도 없으며 고도의 위험성을 수반하는 해외유전사업인 사할린 유전 인수사업에 철도재단을 통하여 참여하지 않았을 것이라고 봄이 상당한 점 등의 여러 사정을 종합하여 보면, 피고인 왕영용은 사업성 판단을 충분히 하기보다는 이광재 의원이 추천한 사업이라는 등의 사업외적인 요소를 고려하여 사할린 유전 인수사업에 대한 사업성 검토를 소홀히하고 실무진들이 사할린 유전 인수사업에 대한 문제점을 지적하며 재검토를 요구하였음에도 이를 무시한 채 통상적인 거래관행과 달리 페트로사흐에 대한 실사도 없이 계약금을 먼저 직접 지급함으로써 니미르사에게 이익을 주고 철도재단에 손해를 가하여 배임행위를 저질렀다고 판단하였다.

기록에 의하여 살펴보면, 원심의 위 사실인정과 판단은 대체로 수긍할 수 있고, 변호인들이 당심 법원에 제출한 증거서류들만으로 이를 번복하기는 어렵다.

(나) 또, 피고인들의 당심법정에서의 각 일부 진술과 증인 김천환, 나승권, 유희복, 신승

호, 이정래, 이재붕의 당심법정에서의 각 진술 및 원심이 적법하게 조사·채택한 증거들에 의하면, ① 당시 철도청은 책임경영제를 도입하여 본부장에게 권한을 대폭 위임하고 있었는바, 피고인 왕영용은 2004년 5월경 철도청의 공개모집에서 사업개발본부장으로 선정되어 철도청의 총무이사 겸 사업개발본부장으로서 주도적으로 철도청 내 개발사업을 총괄하여 진행시키는 임무를 담당하게 되었는데, 이 사건 사할린 유전 인수사업도 피고인 김세호, 피고인 신광순 등 상부의 지시에 의해서가 아니라, 피고인 왕영용이 2004년 7월 중순경 허문석 등과 접촉하면서 허문석의 제안을 받고 이를 철도청의 사업으로 추진하기로 하였던 것일 뿐만 아니라, 피고인 왕영용은 이를 관철하기 위하여 피고인 김세호, 피고인 신광순과 철도청 내 다른 간부들에게 사업성이 있을 뿐만 아니라 이광재 의원이 추천한 사업으로서 대통령의 방러일정에도 포함될 수 있는 것처럼 보고한 사실, ② 피고인 왕영용은 위와 같이 허문석의 제안을 받을 당시 허문석으로부터 기존사업자들에 대한 보상차원에서 1,000만 불을 지급하라는 요구를 받고 임의로 이를 수용하고도 그 뒤 피고인 김세호, 피고인 신광순이나 철도청의 어느 누구에게도 이에 관하여 보고하거나 알리지 않은 사실, ③ 당초 니미르사와 페트로사흐 주식인수계약을 체결하기 전에 계약상대방으로 되어 있는 니미르사의 실체에 관하여 확인하지 않았는데, 뒤늦게 확인한 결과 니미르사는 세금회피를 위하여 싸이프러스에 만든 페이퍼컴퍼니였던 사실(그 때문에 계약해제 과정에서도 어려움을 겪었다), ④ 피고인 왕영용은 2004. 8. 12. 사업설명회에서 사할린 유전 인수사업을 추진하는 쪽으로 간부들의 의견이 모아지도록 유도하기 위하여, 이광재 의원이 철도청에 사업 참여를 제의하였고, 페트로사흐 인수는 하이앤드그룹과 한국석유공사가 공동으로 추진할 계획이었으나 지분율 다툼으로 한국석유공사가 불참을 표명하였으며, 하이앤드 그룹은 일본기업을 물리치고 경쟁입찰에 성공한 1차 우선협상대상자로서 우선협상 시한이 2004. 8. 15.까지이고, 사업리스크 부담을 없애기 위하여 철도청(35%), 하이앤드그룹(35%), 외국석유회사(Exxon, Texaco, BP: 30%)가 컨소시엄을 형성한 신설법인이 향후 직접 계약 및 자산인수의 주체가 될 것이라고 하면서 확인되지 않거나 허위인 내용을 보고한 사실, ⑤ 사할린 유전 인수사업을 서둘러 추진한 이유로 2004. 8. 18.까지 계약을 체결하지 않을 경우 영국이나 일본기업으로 사업권이 넘어가고, 대통령의 러시아 방문시 의제에 포함되도록 하기 위한 것이라고 주장하면서도, 위와 같은 사항에 대하여 그 진위여부를 확인하고자 하는 노력을 전혀 기울이지 않은 채 피고인 전대월이나 허문석의 말을 확인도 없이 사실인 것처럼 강조한 사실, ⑥ 피고인 왕영용은 2004. 8. 12.에 개최된 사업설명회에서 다른 본부장들이 제기한 계약금 송금 후 실사에 따른 리스크 감소대책 등의 각종 문제점에 대하여 보완하겠다고 보고하고도 아무런 보완조치를 취하지 않았고, 민간사업참여자로부터 충분한 담보를 제공받도록 하라는 피고인 김세호의 지시를 받고도 이를 제대로 이행하지 않았으며, 2004. 9. 10. 사업개발본부 실무자들인 고재철, 장홍진, 신상철이 제기한 사할린 유전 인수사업의 각종 문제점에 대하여도 이를 대부분 외면하였고, 2004. 9. 30.에 개최된 간부회의에서 코리아크루드오일의 주주구성을 보완하여 대한석유공사, 한국전력, 에스케이 주식회사 등이 주식의 65%를 보유하고 사할린 유전 인수사업에 참여하도록 하겠다고 전혀 검토한 바도 없고 실현 가능성도 없는 내용을 보고하고 실제로는 주주구성 변경을 위하여 아무런 조치도 취하지 않은 사실, ⑦ 피고인 왕영용은 2004. 8. 17. 코리아크루드오일을 설립하면서 발기인 및 주식인수 청약인을 철도재단 명의로 하지 않고 피고인 왕영용 개인 명의로 해 둔 사실, ⑧ 2004. 9. 7. 철도청 서울청사에서 열린 회의에서 피고인 전대월과 허문석이 철도청에 2,400만 불의 분담을 요구하였으나, 장흥진, 신상철 등 철도청 실무진과 우리은행의 김의식과 김웅렬 등이 위 돈의 사용처를 명확히 밝히기 전에는 위 요구에 응할 수 없다고 하여 회의가 결렬되었음에도, 피고인 왕영용은 2004. 9. 9. 철도재단 이사회가 개최된 것으로 임의로 의사록을 작성한 후 다음날 우리은행에 2,400만 불의 대출신청을 한 사실, ⑨ 철도재단이 코리아크루드오일의 35%의 지분만 가지고 사할린 유전 인수사업에 관여하는 것으로 되어 있다가 피고인 전대월과 권광진의 주식을 철도재단이 모두 인수하게 됨으로써 그 지분 비율이 95%로 증가된 것은 위험부담의 대폭 증가를 초래하는 등 사업의 근본적인 틀이 달라지는 중대한 사정변경 사유임에도 이를 철도청의 다른 간부들에게 제대로 알리지 않았으며, 특히 철도재단이 피고인 전대월과 권광진의 코리아크루드오일 주식을 인수하는 것에 대하여 피고인 신광순으로부터 승낙을 받기도 전인 2004. 9. 14.에 철도재단이 코리아크루드오일 주식의 95%를 우리은행에 양도담보로 제공한다는 공문을 임의로 피고인 왕영용의 전결로 처리하고, 철도재단의 이사회를 거치지도 않고 철도재단 이사장인 피고인 신광순의 위임장을 받지도 않은 상태에서 임의로 주식인수대금을 120억 원으로 정하고, 철도재단이 피고인 전대월과 권광진의 코리아크루드오일 주식을 120억 원에 인수하는 계약을 체결하였으며, 코리아크루드오일 주식인수 대금이 120억 원이라는 것은 페트로사흐 주식인수계약이 해지될 때까지도 당시 철도청장인 피고인 신광순을 포함한 다른 철도청 간부들에게 알리지 않은 사실, ⑩ 하이앤드의 부도 등으로 사할린 유전 인수사업에 대하여 부정적인 의견이 많아짐에 따라 사할린 유전 인수사업의 계속 추진 여부를 결정하기 위하여 열린 2004. 9. 30. 회의에서도 피고인 왕영용은 철도재단이 피고인 전대월과 권광진의 코리아크루드오일 주식을 120억 원에 인수하는 계약을 체결한 사실에 대하여 다른 철도청 간부들에게 알리지 않은 채 사할린 유전 인수사업을 계속 추진할 목적으로 코리아크루드오일의 주주구성을 보완하여 대한석유공사, 한국전력, 에스케이 주식회사 등이 주식의 65%를 보유하고 사할린 유전 인수사업에 참여하도록 하겠다고 검토되지도 않은 사실을 보고한 사실 등을 각 인정할 수 있다.

(다) 한편, 피고인 김세호의 변호인이 제출한 제32호증의 1, 2부터 제42호증의 1 내지

3(공판기록 제5186쪽부터 제5242쪽)의 각 기재내용에 의하면, 피고인 왕영용은 이 사건 사할린 유전 인수사업을 추진하기 전인 2002년경부터 개인적으로 3,000만 원 가량을 투자하여 허문석, 전영석, 곽영태 등과 함께 인도네시아 철광석개발 사업에 관여하는 등 오래 전부터 허문석과 사업상 관계가 있었음을 알 수 있는바, 피고인 왕영용 스스로도 자신은 허문석이 도와달라고 하여 도와준 적은 있다고 한다(공판기록 제1938쪽).

(라) 앞서 본 바와 같이, 피고인 왕영용은 소극적으로 사할린 유전 인수사업의 사업성과 수익성이나 이를 추진할 사업주체가 되는 하이앤드의 재무상태는 물론이고 페트로사흐와 니미르사의 실재 여부 및 선지급 후실사 방식의 위험성 등에 관하여 제대로 확인·점검하는 등의 임무를 제대로 이행하지 않은 데 그치지 않고, 평소 사업상 관계가 있던 허문석의 제안을 받고 사할린 유전 인수사업을 철도청의 사업으로 추진하기로 하면서 허문석의 요청대로 기존사업자에게 1,000만 불을 지급할 것을 임의로 약속하였으며, 나아가 사업개발본부장으로서 철도청 내 개발사업의 추진에 관하여 주도적인 위치에 있음을 이용하여 사할린 유전 인수사업을 조속히 관철시키기 위하여 담당직원으로부터 자료가 미비하여 정책심의회의를 개최할 수 없다는 반대의견을 듣게 되자 여전히 자료를 갖추지 않은 상태에서 서둘러 사업설명회를 개최하였을 뿐만 아니라, 그밖에 상관 및 동료 간부들에게 보고를 하거나 회의를 하는 과정에서 사업참여의 필요성을 강조하기 위하여 객관적 자료나 근거도 없이 매장량과 사업성 및 영업이익은 물론이고, 국내외의 유력 업체가 함께 참여하는 것처럼 과장하고, 관련 자료 가운데 부정적이거나 불리한 내용은 일부러 제외하고, 확인되지 않은 내용이나 전혀 검토도 않고 실현 가능성도 없는 내용은 물론이고 심지어 허위사실을 보고하고, 임의로 의사록을 작성하였으며, 보고 및 회의과정에서 지적된 각종 문제점을 보완하지도 않고 담보를 제공받지도 않았을 뿐만 아니라, 장홍진 등의 재검토 요구를 묵살하고 오히려 이들을 배제한 후 계속하여 사업을 추진하는 등의 적극적인 임무위배 행위를 하였는바, 피고인 왕영용의 위와 같은 행위는 철도청이나 철도재단의 재산을 적정하게 유지·관리하여야 할 임무에 위배되는 행위에 해당하고, 또 이러한 사정에 비추어 보면, 피고인 왕영용에게는 적어도 미필적으로나마 철도재단에 손해가 발생할 우려가 있다는 점에 관한 인식이 있었다고 봄이 상당하며, 철도재단에 손해가 발생하면 그 거래상대방인 니미르사가 그 상당의 이익을 얻는다는 인식 또한 있었다고 할 것이므로, 업무상배임죄의 성립에 요구되는 불법이득의 의사도 있었다고 인정된다.

(마) 다만, 피고인 왕영용은 철도청의 공개모집에서 사업개발본부장으로 선정된 후 당시 대량 에너지 수급기관으로서 만성적인 적자에 시달리던 철도청의 적자를 해결하고 철도청의 수익구조를 개선시켜 철도청이나 철도재단에게 이익을 얻게 하려는 동기에서 사할린 유전 인수사업을 추진한 측면이 있었다고 하더라도, 앞서 본 바와 같이 피고인 왕영용은 소

극적으로 임무이행을 제대로 하지 않은 데 그치지 않고 허위사실을 보고하는 등의 방법으로 적극적인 배임행위를 하였으므로, 위와 같은 동기가 있었다는 것만으로는 그 죄책을 면할 수 없다.

(바) 한편, 피고인 왕영용은 변호사 등 전문가들을 통하여 페트로사흐의 수익구조에 문제가 있고 이를 시정할 수 없는 경우 등에는 계약을 해제하고 계약금을 반환받을 수 있는 것으로 확인하고 계약금을 송금한 것이므로 배임의 고의를 인정할 수 없다고 주장한다. 그러나 원심이 적절하게 설명한 바와 같이, 코리아크루드오일과 니미르사 사이에 2004. 9. 3. 체결된 주식구매계약서의 규정 자체에 의하더라도 '코리아크루드오일은 실사결과에 합리적으로 만족할 수 없는 경우에는 위 계약을 종결하고, 니미르사로부터 계약금을 반환받을 수 있다'고만 되어 있어 실사결과에 합리적으로 만족할 수 없는 경우의 기준이 불분명하여 그 기준에 관하여 분쟁의 소지가 있을 수 있는 상황에서, 앞서 본 바와 같이 피고인 왕영용이 사할린 유전 인수사업의 사업성 검토를 소홀히 한 채 허위사실을 보고하기까지 하면서 사업을 추진하기로 하는 결론을 이끌어 낸 다음, 통상의 거래관행과는 달리 계약금 지급 후 실사의 방식으로 체결된 계약내용을 용인하고, 실무직원들로부터 사할린 유전 인수사업의 재검토를 요구받고도 이를 무시한 채 페트로사흐에 대한 실사도 하지 아니하고 계약금을 직접 지급하였다면, 가사 계약체결을 담당한 변호사로부터 위와 같은 설명을 듣고 계약금을 지급하였다고 하더라도 배임의 고의를 인정하는 데 장애가 되지 않는다.

(사) 그리고 피고인 왕영용은, 페트로사흐가 브리티쉬 페트롤리움에 철도재단의 인수예정금액의 2배에 해당하는 1억 3,000만 불에 인수되었을 뿐만 아니라 실제가치도 상승한 것을 보더라도 이 사건 사할린 유전 인수사업은 경제성 및 수익성이 있는 사업이어서 피고인 왕영용의 배임행위가 성립되지 않는다고 주장한다. 그러나 위 피고인의 변호인이 제출한 자료(런던주식시장 AIM부 상장신청서)에 의하더라도 우랄스 에너지(Urals Energy)가 2004. 11. 19.경 페트로사흐의 지분 97.2%를 코리아크루드오일이 계약시 약정한 금액보다 훨씬 적은 미화 44,899,000불에 인수한 것으로 되어 있을 뿐이고, 달리 변호인이 제출한 자료만으로 페트로사흐가 다른 회사에 위 주장과 같은 가격에 인수되었거나 그 실제가치가 상승되었음을 인정하기에는 부족하다. 또, 배임죄에 있어서는 범행 당시를 기준으로 하여 손해 발생의 위험이 있으면 범죄는 성립하고 그 뒤에 더 높은 가격에 처분되었거나 실제가치가 상승했더라도 이는 이미 성립한 범죄의 사후정상에 불과하다(피고인 왕영용은 페트로사흐 주식인수대금을 일단 6,200만 불로 정해 놓고 나중에 실사를 통하여 1,800만 불까지 감액할 예정이었다고도 주장하나, 앞서 본 바와 같이 충분한 사전검토 없이 계약을 체결한 상태에서 나중에 실제로 감액할 수 있는지 그 결과를 전혀 예측할 수 없는 막연하고도 일방적인 희망사항에 불과하다).

(아) 따라서, 피고인 왕영용의 이 부분 공소사실에 관한 사실오인 또는 법리오해 주장은 이유 없다.

나. 시장의 자금

자원개발사업이 다른 사업에 비하여 장기성, 위험성, 대규모성이라는 면에서 차이가 있다고는 하지만, 모든 자금을 국가가 제공할 수는 없다. 자금의 규모도 문제이지만 효율성면에서 국가가 언제나 최적의 판단자인지도 의문이다. 따라서 궁극적으로 시장이 보완적으로 또는 주도적으로 자금을 공급하여야 할 것이다. 문제는 이러한 자금조달을 위하여는 어떠한 법적 장치가 뒷받침되어야 할 것인가이다.

시장에서의 player를 단계별로 나누면 최종 player인 석유개발업체, 이들 산업에 자금을 지원하는 은행이나 중간 투자 기구인 펀드운용사, 그리고 이들 업체에 대한 직간접 투자자가 있을 것인바, 자금의 수요자인 석유개발업체와 자금보유자인 투자자간 중개기능을 하는 은행과 자산운용사에 대한 정책이 문제일 것이다. 금융공공기관인 수출입은행, 중소기업은행, 정책금융공사, 산은지주, 산은을 별론으로 하고 민영화된 은행에 대한 정책은 이들이 자금의 수요처를 정함에 있어서 우선 순위를 두도록 하는 방법이 있을 것이고, 자산 운용사의 경우에는 자원개발로부터의 투자수익률이 올라가도록 감세를 하거나 매칭펀드를 설정하여 주는 방법이 있을 것이다. 에너지 정책의 주무부처인 지경부는 과거 특정 산업에의 자금 지원을 위하여 특정펀드를 새로이 정의하고 펀드의 자산 운용에 제약을 가하는 식의 정책을[12] 에너지 정책에서도 시행하고 있다.

통상 시장에서는 탐사개발이나 건설 프로젝트별로 모회사에 대한 상환없이 당해 프로젝트의 현금흐름과 자산을 기초로 대출하는 프로젝트자금조달방식이 정석이다.[13] 프로젝트자금조달방식은 저축은행 사태이후 불법적인 것이거나 지극히 위험한 것으로 간주되는 경향이 있으나 이는 프로젝트자금조달에 대한 오해에 기인한 것으로 앞으로 우리의 기업들도 국가의 에특자금이나 수출입은행에 기대지 말고 독자적인 자금조달방식으로서의 프로젝트자금조달방식에 보다 익숙하여져야만 언젠가 북한의 변화시 국민과 국가에 의존하지 말고 국제자금시장에서 자금을 조달할 수 있을 것이다.

---

12) 예를 들면 부품소재전문기업등의 육성에 관한 특별조치법, 산업발전법 등에서 정하고 있는 전문회사, 사모투자전문회사 규정.

13) John Teolis, *Issues in Project Finance*, in ECONOMIC DEVELOPMENT,FOREIGN INVESTMENT AND THE LAW (Robert Pritchard ed. 1996) 197, 201-207은 completion, technology, operational, supply, sales, political, environmental, currency, force majeure risk를 열거. John D. Finnerty, PROJECT FINANCE (1996)는 pipeline건설을, Benjamin C. Esty, MODERN PROJECT FINANCE (2004)는 PDVSA를 예로 열거.

자원개발의 문제를 단순히 효과적인 자금조달의 문제에 국한하지 말고 자원개발의 결과 그 효과가 실제 국가나 사회의 모든 구성원에 어떻게 배분되는지, 그리고 실제 경제적 측면 이외에 어떤 사회적 영향을 받았는지에 대한 시각도 분석이 필요하다는 견해는 소위 자원이 풍부한 나라가 자원개발의 결과 더 빈곤하여지는 자원의 저주를 방지하여야 한다는 측면에서 귀기울여 볼 만하다.[14)]

최철, 해외자원프로젝트와 관련된 법적위험과 금융가능성에 관한 고찰, 34 외법논집 185 (2010)

1) 해외자원개발 프로젝트와 금융 가능성

가) 해외자원개발 프로젝트의 금융방법의 변천

해외자원개발사업은 자원의 탐사에서 개발·생산 및 수송을 위한 건설 사업까지 포함되는 대규모의 프로젝트로 대규모의 투자가 요구되고 다양한 위험요소가 내재되어 있는 장기 프로젝트로서의 성격을 갖는다. 이러한 대규모 자원개발프로젝트는 투자회수기간도 장기화되어, 자원의 발견에서 개발, 생산까지 10년 정도가 소요되며 동 기간 중에도 지속적인 투자가 요구된다. 또한 프로젝트의 구조도 복잡화되어 특정기업이 독자적으로 사업을 추진하며 리스크를 단독으로 부담하는 것이 점차 어려워져 가고 있는 상황이다. 따라서 복수의 기업이 컨소시엄을 구성하여 자원보유국의 국영회사나 현지기업들과 합작투자를 하는 경우가 증가하고 있으며, 이러한 구조적 변화는 프로젝트에 참여하는 다수 당사자 간의 법적 계약구조를 복잡화시키며, 특히 현지국 정부나 공기업이 프로젝트에 개입하게 되는 법적 환경에 대한 이해의 중요성이 증대하게 된다.

해외자원개발 프로젝트의 금융조달구조의 변천을 국제적인 자원개발 프로젝트의 중심으로서 성장해 온 석유개발 프로젝트와 관련하여 Hussein Razavi는 다음과 같이 3단계의 시기로 구분하고 있는데 각 단계의 특성은 다음과 같다.[1]

A: **1970년대 이전**(Financing Oil Project: Pre-1970)

1970년대 이전의 경우 대부분의 석유개발 프로젝트에 소요되는 자금조달은 국제적인 석

14) S Scott Gaille, *Mitigating the Resource Curse: A Proposal for a Microfiance and Educational Lending Royalty Law,* 32 ENERG. L. J. 81, 89-92 (2011)(주민들에 대한 직접지급, microfinance lending, 교육비지급/대차를 제안).

1. Hussein Razavi, Financing Energy Projects in Developing Countries, PennWell, 2007, pp. 30-33 참조.

유회사(International Oil Company: IOC)가 내부유보자금을 사용하거나 자사의 높은 재무신용도를 이용하여 기업금융형태로 장기차입을 통하여 조달하였다. 이 시기의 IOC의 투자행태(investment behavior)는 엄격한 재무적 기준보다는 전략적 동기에 의하여 결정되는 경우가 많았다.[2]

[그림 A] 1970년대 이전 프로젝트 금융

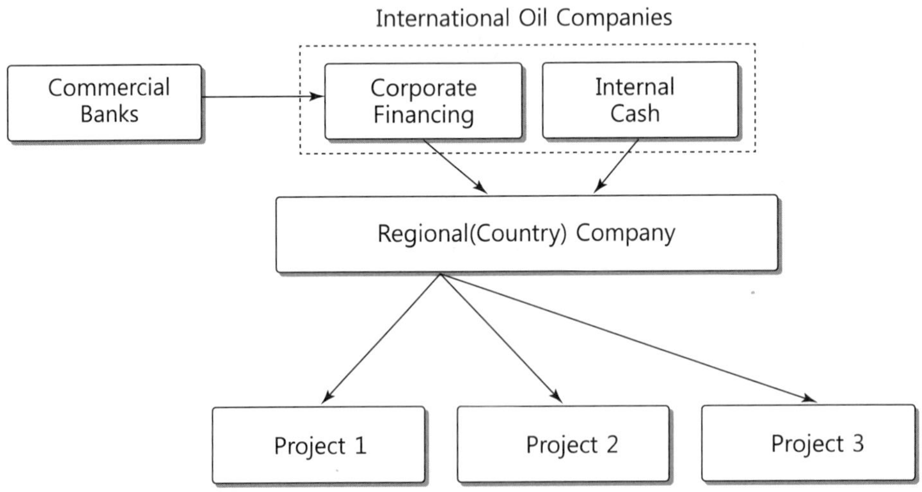

B: **1970년대와 1980년대**(Financing Oil Project in 1970s and 1980s)

70년대 Oil Shock 등을 거치면서 국제적 석유개발 프로젝트에 있어서 전통적인 IOC 역할과 함께, 석유 수출국과 수입국의 정부가 석유 개발에 적극적으로 참여하기 시작했다. 산유국 정부의 경우 국영석유회사(National Oil Company: NOC)의 역할을 강화하여 조인트 벤쳐 등의 형태로 석유개발 사업에 참가하였고, IOC, 정부, 국제금융기구 등이 프로젝트에 소요되는 자금원을 제공하게 되어 자원개발 프로젝트 참가자의 범위가 확대되고 참가자의 성격과 이해관계도 다원화되기 시작했다.[3]

2. Ibid.
3. Ibid.

[그림 B] 1970/80년대 프로젝트 금융

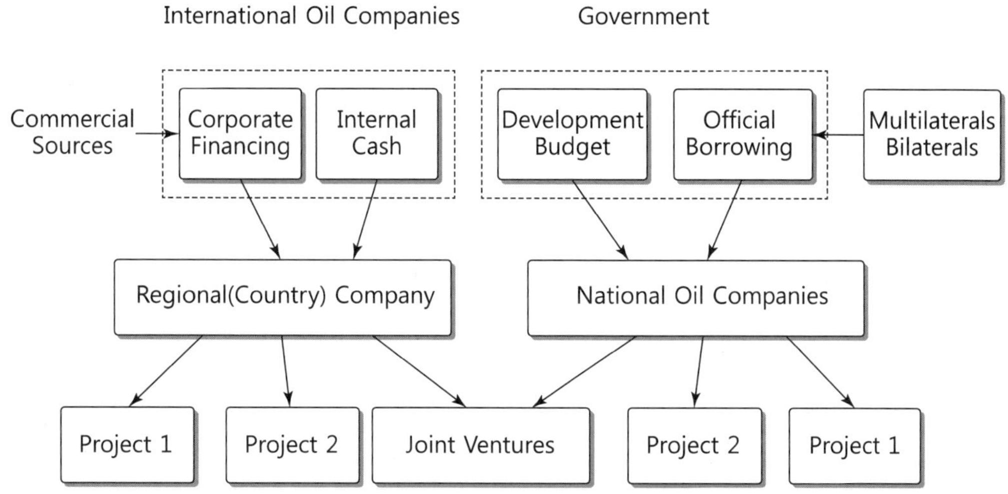

C: 1990년대 이후(Financing Oil Projects since 1990s)

1986년 국제 석유가격 붕괴이후 1990년대에 걸쳐 저유가 시대가 지속되면서 IOC들은 자체 자금조달의 한계에 직면하게 되었고 석유개발 프로젝트 진행에 있어 엄격한 재무적 기준을 도입하게 되었다. 공적자금을 통하여 자금지원을 하였던 정부기관도 지속적 자금지원에 대한 한계를 느끼게 되어, 자금원(funding source)의 다각화와 함께 석유개발사업과 관련된 다양한 금융기법이 도입되게 되었다. 전통적인 메이저 IOC뿐만 아니라 신흥경제국의 보다 작은 규모의 IOC들도 국제 석유개발 사업에 참여하게 되고, 프로젝트도 대형화하여, 투자자들이 컨소시엄을 구성하고, 구조화 금융(structured financing) 을 통한 자금조달도 활발해졌다.[4]

4. Ibid.

[그림 C] 1990년대 프로젝트 금융

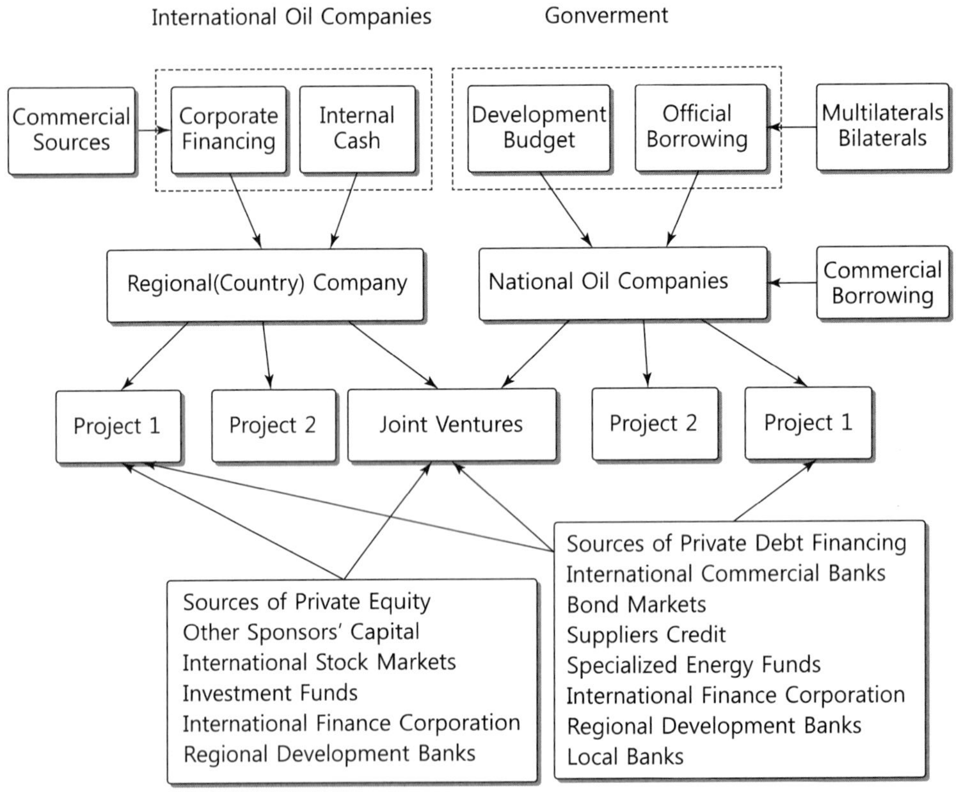

나) 자원개발 프로젝트와 프로젝트 파이낸스

이상에서 본 바와 같이 에너지자원개발 프로젝트의 대형화, 복잡화로 소요자금 조달을 위한 금융기법도 발전하였는데, 프로젝트 파이낸스(project finance)를 통한 자금조달이 대표적인 예이다. 광의의 프로젝트 파이낸스는 대규모 개발 투자사업에 대한 자금조달로서 기업 단위가 아닌 프로젝트 단위의 구조화된 금융조달 방식을 의미한다. 프로젝트기간과 투하자본 회수기간이 장기이고, 사업의 성공 가능성에 대한 불확실성이 높은 프로젝트에 대하여 특정 기업이 아닌 신규의 대규모 특정 프로젝트에 대한 장기 금융조달의 형태가 된다. 프로젝트 파이낸스의 대상이 되는 사업은 대부분의 경우 사업규모가 방대하여 거대한 소요자금이 요구될 뿐만 아니라 계획사업에 내재하는 위험성이 매우 크므로 금융기관이 단독으로 자금을 공여하고 리스크를 부담하기보다는 복수의 금융기관이 차관단을 구성하여 신디케이트 방식으로 필요자금을 대출해 주는 것이 일반적이다.[5]

5. 반기로, 프로젝트파이낸스, 한국금융연수원, 2008, pp. 4-10; Graham Vinter, Project Finance, Sweet &

프로젝트 파이낸스는 프로젝트 자체로부터 발생할 미래의 현금흐름(cash flow)만을 대출원리금상환재원으로 보고, 프로젝트의 유무형의 자산만을 담보로 하여, 별도로 설립된 프로젝트 회사(project company)에 자금을 공급하는 금융형태가 되므로, 이 같은 금융 방법은 자원개발 프로젝트와 같이 장기 고위험 프로젝트에 대한 자금조달 수단으로서 중요한 의미가 있다 일반 기업금융(corporate finance) 방식에 의한 대출은 채권확보의 수단으로 차주나 보증인에게 대출원리금 상환에 대하여 전적인 책임(full-recourse) 을 지우는 데 반해, 프로젝트 파이낸스 방식에 의한 대출에서는 대출원리금의 상환책임이 대상 프로젝트 자체가 갖는 경제적 가치와 미래 현금흐름의 범위 내로 한정되는 비소구(non-recourse) 금융이 되거나, 출자자 등에게 일정 범위 내에서 추가로 상환책임을 부담하도록 하는 제한적 소구(limited recourse) 금융의 형태가 된다. 프로젝트 파이낸스에서는 프로젝트 사업주는 단독 또는 공동으로 출자하여 법률적·회계적으로 독립된 특수목적(special purpose vehicle)인 프로젝트 회사를 설립하고, 이 회사가 차입주체가 됨으로써 사업주(sponsor)는 프로젝트와 분리되어 프로젝트 회사에 대한 출자와 보증을 통해 프로젝트를 지원하는 입장에 서게 되므로, 사업추진에 대한 직접적 위험을 줄일 수 있다. 또한 프로젝트 추진에 소요되는 차입금이 출자자의 대차대조표에 표시되지 않는 부외금융거래(off-balance sheet financing)의 형태가 되어, 프로젝트가 실패하더라도 출자자의 신용에 미치는 영향이 기업금융에 비하여 제한적인 측면이 있다. 따라서 프로젝트 파이낸스는 특정된 프로젝트의 추진이라는 제한된 목적에 적합한 특수목적회사를 설립하여 그 목적에 부합하는 금융구조를 기초로 한다는 점에서 구조화금융(structured finance)으로서의 특징을 가지고 있다.[6]

다) 자원개발 프로젝트의 금융가능성(bankability)

프로젝트 파이낸스는 위와 같이 상환재원과 담보를 대상 프로젝트의 가치와 미래현금흐름에 의존하는 파이낸스 방식이기 때문에, 프로젝트 파이낸스에 참여하는 대출은행은 대상 프로젝트의 수익성과 위험 분석을 엄밀히 행하고 충분한 확신이들 때 프로젝트를 추진하는 SPV인 프로젝트 회사에 대한 대출을 결정하게 된다. 이와 같이 자금을 제공하는 금융기관(project financier)이 프로젝트 자체의 사업성을 종합적으로 검토한 결과 대출이 가능한 프로젝트로 판정하게 되는데, 프로젝트의 경제적, 기술적 사업성과 위험 분산 구조를 포함한 프로젝트의 구조가 자금을 대출 받을 수 있을 정도로 금융기관이 평가되는 사업을 금융가능한(bankable 또는 financeable)[7] 프로젝트라고 하며 이러한 금융가능성(bankability)이라는 개념[8]은

Maxwell (London), 1998, p. 85.

6. Ibid.

7. Scott Hoffman, The Law and Business of International Project Finance, Cambridge, 2008, p. 19.

8. 금융가능성(bankability)라는 개념을 일의적으로 정의하기는 어려운데, 이것은 각 프로젝트의 사업특성

대상프로젝트의 사업성 및 위험성을 검토하는 데 있어서 유용한 개념이 될 수 있다. 자원개발 프로젝트의 경우에도 장기의 프로젝트 진행기간 동안 현금흐름의 창출 가능성과 관련하여 자원개발 회사, 현지국 정부, 대주단 등 프로젝트에 이해관계를 갖고 있는 다양한 관련 당사자들 간의 협상에 기초하여 성립되기 때문에 관련계약이 많고 계약서류 및 절차가 복잡하며, 프로젝트의 구조화 단계에서부터 대주단의 구성, 참여자들의 위험배분 및 참여조건의 결정에 많은 시간과 비용이 소요된다. 이렇게 형성된 계약구조(contractual framework)는 경제적 기술적 측면에서의 사업타당성 검토와 함께 프로젝트의 사업성 평가의 중요한 요소로서 프로젝트의 지속가능성의 전제조건이 되므로 자금을 제공하는 금융기관은 이러한 프로젝트의 계약구조와 법적측면을 면밀히 검토하게 된다. 따라서 대규모 장기 프로젝트이며 다수의 상이한 이해관계를 갖는 프로젝트 참가자가 참여하며, 진행 단계별로 다양한 위험요소가 평가되어야 하는 자원개발 프로젝트에 있어서, 금융가능성(bankability)이라는 관점에서의 평가는 경제적, 기술적 분석뿐만 아니라 정치적 위험, 법률, 규제위험 등 자원개발 프로젝트가 내포하고 있는 다양한 위험을 종합적으로 고려하는 과정이라 할 수 있다.

2) 해외자원개발 프로젝트의 특성과 법적위험

가) 법적·정치적 위험의 형태

해외자원개발 프로젝트는 현지국의 경제개발에 중요한 전략적 사업인 경우가 대부분으로 현지국 정부는 다양한 방법으로 프로젝트의 초기 단계에서부터 개입하고 있으며, 개입형태로는 각종 인허가 제도를 통하여 프로젝트의 허가·감독기관으로서 개입하거나, 정부유관기관을 통한 지원 또는 공기업을 통한 지분참여 등으로 프로젝트의 당사자로 프로젝트의 운영 및 생산물 분배에 직접 참여하는 경우, 조세정책, 환경정책, 노동정책 등을 통하여 개입하는 경우 등 자원개발 프로젝트의 시행에 있어서 현지국 정부의 역할은 프로젝트의 성공적 진행에 매우 중요한 변수가 되고 있다.

특히 사회주의 경제체제에서 시장경제체제로 전환한 체제전환국에서 진행되는 자원개발 프로젝트의 경우 시장경제체제 구현을 위한 정책적, 제도적 체제 정비의 불완정성과 법체제의 안정성 결여로 법적·규제적 위험, 정치적 위험 등이 프로젝트의 사업가능성 평가에 있어 중요한 위험요소로서 검토가 이루어져야 하는데, 법적·규제적·정치적 위험의 예로 일반적으로 제시되는 것은 아래와 같다.

에 따라 사례별로 적용되어야 하는 기준 또는 평가요소의 충족을 전제로 하는 개념이기 때문이다.

법적 위험(Legal Risk)

- 준거법으로 국제적으로 통용되는 법률을 적용하지 않고 현지국법을 적용하여 분쟁발생 시 조정이 어려운 경우
- 프로젝트와 관련된 계약상 권리 이전이 제한되는 경우
- 관련 법률의 사후적 개정에 따른 계약내용의 변경 등 법적 안정성이 인정되지 않는 경우
- 부동산에 대한 담보권 설정이 법적으로 부인되거나, 동산, 현금흐름 및 각종 권리에 대한 채권실행이 어려운 경우
- 신탁의 개념이 인정되지 않아 담보의 분배 및 대주 금융기관들의 지분양도가 어려운 경우
- 사업권, 탐사 채굴권, 또는 사용권 등의 취소 가능성

규제적 위험(Regulatory Risk)[9]

- 환경보호와 관련된 소재지 정부의 각종 규제사항
- 현지국 정부가 국내산업 보호를 위해 국내산 원자재 사용을 의무화하고 해외로부터의 수입을 규제하거나 관세를 부과할 가능성
- 현지국 정부가 생산물에 대해 생산 및 수출에 대한 제한을 가할 위험
- 배당이나 원리금 상환에 대한 제한이나 세금 부과의 위험

정치적 위험(Political Risk)

- 프로젝트의 국유화, 대상시설의 수용 가능성
- 외환거래 및 외화송금통제 위험
- 전쟁, 내란, 테러의 위험

국유화, 과실송금제한, 외환통제, 전쟁, 내란 등과 같은 전형적인 정치적 위험에 대해서는 OPIC, ECGD, Coface와 같은 각국의 공적수출신용기관(Export Credit Agency: ECA)이나 일반 보험사가 제공하는 보험(Political Risk Insurance: PRI)을 통하여 위험을 완화할 수 있는 방안이 있으나, 이러한 보험이 적용 가능한 대상 위험의 범위가 제한적이고, 보험에 의한 보호는 사후적이 것으로 프로젝트가 더 이상 진행되기 어려운 종국적 단계에서 사용되는 위험관

9. 여기서 제시된 내용을 정치적 위험의 사례로 포함시키는 경우도 있으나, 상당 부분이 현지국 정부의 정책적·법제도적 변경에 의해 이루어지는 것이 많아 정치적 위험, 법적 위험이 성격상 중첩되는 요소가 있으며, 규제적 위험으로 파악하는 것이 더 적합할 수 있다.

리 방안이라 할 수 있다. 한편 위에 예시된 전형적 정치적 위험요소와 같은 정부의 강제적이고 직접적인 개입이 아니라, 프로젝트의 진행단계에서 환경, 노동정책 관련법령의 개정이나 수입 원자재 조달제한과 같은 행정조치를 통한 제도적, 간접적 개입은 프로젝트 수행 자체를 불가능하게 하지는 않으나 프로젝트의 수입과 원가 흐름에 상당한 영향을 미쳐 프로젝트 참여자들이 추구하는 경제적 목표 달성에 영향을 미친다는 점에서 다른 차원에서 관리가 요구되는 위험을 창출되고 있다. 따라서 과거 해외프로젝트의 수행에 있어서 중요 위험요소로 고려되었던 현지국 정부에 의한 국유화, 외환통제 등과 같은 전형적 위험보다는 환경·노동 등과 관련한 법적 규제적 변화에서 발생하는 각종 위험요인들에 대한 분석이 이루어져야 하며 이러한 위험요소의 관리를 위한 계약적 대응방안과 위험분산을 위한 다양한 구조적 장치를 강구해야 한다.

나) 금융가능성과 법적·정치적 위험

자원개발 프로젝트의 사업타당성 분석에 있어서 금융가능성이라는 개념을 고려하는 것은 금융가능성을 기초로 한 사업타당성 분석이 프로젝트의 장기적 현금흐름의 통하여 원리금 상황능력을 판단하는 데 중점을 두고 현금의 유출입을 결정짓는 다양한 요인들을 파악하여 프로젝트에 영향을 미치는 다양한 위험 요소를 종합하여 검토하기 때문이다. 프로젝트와 관련된 법적·정치적 위험과 계약구조에 대한 평가도 궁극적으로는 프로젝트의 현금흐름의 지속가능성이라는 측면에서 고려할 수 있다고 본다. [그림 D]는 프로젝트의 수입과 원가의 현금흐름에 관한 요소와 법률·규제 및 계약구조가 프로젝트에 영향을 미치는 경로에 대한 개념적 구조를 나타내고 있는데, 이러한 내용은 아래에서 살펴 볼 현지국의 법적 규제적 환경 변화가 프로젝트의 원가와 수입구조에 어떠한 경로를 거쳐 프로젝트의 금융가능성에 영향을 미칠 수 있는지를 개념적으로 보여주고 있다.[10]

10. 여기에 제시된 개념도는 Hussein Razavi, Financing Energy Project in Developing Countries에서 제시된 도표를 프로젝트에 대한 법·규제 요소와 법·정치적 위험의 영향이라는 관점에서 수정한 것이다.

[그림 D] 국제 프로젝트 개념도

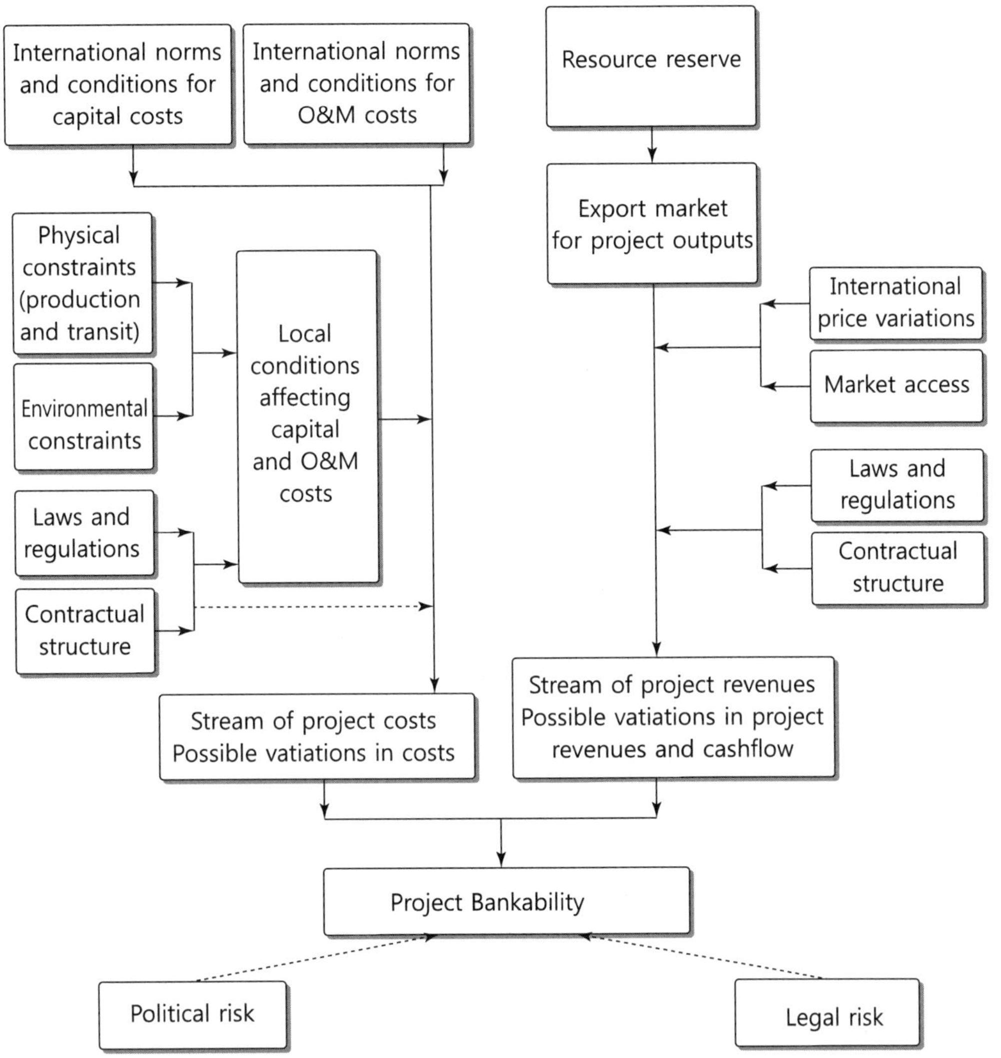

이준기, 해외자원개발사업법 개선방안연구, 2010 자원·에너지 법제연구회 연구논문집 230

3) 해외자원개발펀드의 도입과 현황

가) 해외자원개발펀드의 도입[1]

가)-1. 도입경위

해외자원개발펀드는 2006. 10. 27. 개정 해외자원개발 사업법에 의하여 도입된 제도이다. 이와 같이 해외자원개발펀드를 도입한 취지는 국제적으로 자원확보를 둘러싼 경쟁이 심화됨에 따라 에너지자원의 안정적 확보가 국가적 과제로 대두되는 상황에서 향후 에너지 확보를 위한 재원으로 민간의 풍부한 유동자금을 활용하기 위한 것이다. 즉, 우리나라의 경우 석유, 가스 등 주요 해외자원에 대한 국내 소비량의 대부분을 주로 수입에 의존하고 있음에 따라 자주개발률 제고를 통한 주요 해외자원의 안정적 확보가 국가적 당면과제로 대두되었고, 그에 따라 민간의 풍부한 유동자금이 펀드 형태로 해외자원개발사업에 투자될 수 있도록 함으로써 해외자원개발사업이 활발하게 전개될 수 있는 금융여건을 조성하고자 하였던 것이다.

가)-2. 왜 펀드였는가?

나아가, 해외자원개발 사업법이 위와 같이 해외자원 개발 사업에 대한 민간자금 조달의 수단으로 펀드 형태를 도입, 활용하고자 했던 것은 펀드 형태가 다른 자금조달방법에 비하여 대규모 자금을 확보할 수 있고, 특히 투자대상사업 및 투자자의 특성에 따라 펀드구조를 신축적으로 설계함으로써 수익과 위험에 관하여 각기 다른 입장을 가지고 있는 다양한 투자자로부터 투자를 유치할 수 있게 되어 해외자원개발사업 추진을 위한 자금조달 규모를 극대화할 수 있다는 판단이 있었던 것으로 보인다.

나) 해외자원개발펀드의 현황

이와 같이 2006년 해외자원개발 사업법의 개정을 통해 해외자원개발펀드가 도입되었으나 해외자원개발펀드는 활성화되고 있지 않은 상황이다.

---

1. 산업자원위원회 수석전문위원 도재문, 해외자원개발사업법 일부개정법률안 검토보고서(2006. 8.), 1, 4~6면 참조.

〈표 A〉 해외자원개발펀드의 현황표(2010. 6. 기준)

연도	펀드명	최초규모	현재규모	투자자
2006	베트남 15-1 유전펀드	2,041억 원	437억 원	기관 및 개인 투자자
2007	니켈펀드 사할린석탄펀드	1,302억 원 210억 원	1,302억 원 210억 원	기관 및 개인 투자자 기관투자자
2008	텍사스유전펀드 카자흐스탄유전펀드 동광펀드	304억 원 101억 원 88억 원원	304억 원 101억 원 90억 원	기관투자자 개인투자자 일반기업
2009	미국 G유전펀드 지경부 자원 Blind 펀드	648억 원 –	648억 원 –	기관투자자 기관, 일반기업
2010	천연자원펀드	357억 원	357억 원	기관투자자
	합계	5,051억 원	3,409억 원	

위 〈표 A〉에서 나타난 해외자원개발펀드의 규모는 해외 유수의 에너지펀드에 비하여 미미한 수준에 불과하다. 예컨대, 미국의 대표적 에너지 PEF인 Natural Gas Partners와 Quantum Energy Partners는 현재 자산운용규모가 각각 73억 달러와 57억 달러에 이른다.[2] 그나마 비교적 대규모 조성된 베트남 15-1 유전펀드와 암바토비 니켈펀드는 한국석유공사와 한국광물자원공사가 주도하는 해외자원개발사업에 참여하는 형태이며, 지경부 지원 blind 펀드(트로이카해외자원개발투자전문회사 등) 또한 지식경제부의 주도로 조성된 점을 고려할 때, 우리나라에서 해외자원개발 펀드 주도의 해외자원개발사업 탐색 및 funding은 매우 제한적으로 이루어지고 있다고 할 수 있다.

또한, 신규 해외자원개발펀드의 수와 규모가 지속적으로 하락하고 있는 점을 〈표 A〉를 통해 확인할 수 있다.

다) 해외 자원개발펀드 부진의 원인

대내외적 평가

이와 같이 해외자원개발펀드가 활성화되지 않고 있는 이유에 대하여는, 해외자원개발펀드의 조성규모가 작아 소규모 투자만이 가능함에 따라 우량의 big deal 참여가 어려운 점, 자원개발펀드에 대한 성공사례가 부족하여 주요 투자자들이 내부 투자심의를 통과하는 데에 어려움을 겪고 있다는 점 및 기관투자자들이 시장 유동성이 풍부하고 단기 투자가 가능한 원자재 관련 파생상품펀드와 같은 증권형 투자를 선호하고 있는 점 등이 지적되고 있다.[3] 또한,

---

2. 해당 인터넷 홈페이지 참조.
3. 서철수, "자원개발펀드의 현황 및 활성화 방안," 해외자원개발 금융제도 발전 방안에 관한 세미나 자료 (2010. 6. 1.), 71면.

한 유력한 외국자산 운용사는 국민연금, 한국투자공사 등 국내의 top-tier 투자자는 해외자원개발펀드보다는 외국펀드를 통하여 해외자원에 투자하는 것을 선호하고 있고 기타 국내 재무적 투자자들은 해외자원 토자에 대하여 큰 관심이 없는 점을 문제로 지적하고 있다.

이상의 논의 및 관련 실무자들의 논의에 의할 때, 해외자원개발펀드가 부진한 이유는 다음과 같이 정리할 수 있을 것이다.

다)-1. 국내 자산운용인력의 전문성 부족

국내 자산운용인력이 광구운영 등 해외자원개발사업에 투자하거나 관련 펀드를 운용한 경험이나 지식이 전반적으로 부족함으로 인하여, 안정된 고수익이 보장되는 광구 등 해외자원개발사업기회를 물색하고 또한 이를 다양한 투자자에게 적합한 투자상품으로 설계, 가공할 수 있는 전문성이 상대적으로 부족한 점이 해외자원개발펀드가 부진한 이유로 지적될 수 있을 것이다.

실제로 해외자원개발펀드를 통해 미국 E&P 기업으로부터 유전의 지분(working interest)을 인수하려고 하였으나 기관투자자들이 요구하는 안정적인 투자구조를 도출하지 못하여 funding에 실패한 사례가 보고된 바 있다.[4]

다)-2. 국내투자자의 투자분석 능력 부족

아울러, 국내 투자자들 또한 해외자원개발사업에 대한 투자 경험 부족으로 해외 자원개발사업의 수익성과 위험성을 전문적으로 평가할 능력을 제대로 갖추지 못하여 해외자원개발사업을 아예 기피하거나 또는 운용능력이 검증된 외국의 선진 펀드만을 선호하는 현상도 해외자원개발펀드 부진의 이유라 할 수 있다.

예컨대, 탐사광구에 대해서는 초기 현금흐름이 없고 사업 성공에 대한 합리적 예측이 불가능하다는 이유로 자금조달이 실패한 사례가 보고된 바 있다.[5]

다)-3. 법제도적 문제점

해외자원개발펀드 법제 또한 해외자원개발펀드를 통하여 다양한 해외자원개발 사업기회를 물색하고 다양한 투자자들에게 적합한 투자상품을 만들어 내는 데에 제약적으로 사용하고 있다. 해외자원개발펀드의 자산운용인력은 다양하고 선진적인 투자구조를 통해 해외자원개발사업에 투자하는 방안을 검토하고 있으나, 해외자원개발 사업법이 정하고 있는 자산운용방법 등이 상당히 제한적으로 규정되어 있어 투자자들의 수요를 충족시키는 투자구조를 만들어 내는 데에 어려움을 겪는 경우가 많다. 이는 투자대상사업 및 투자자의 특성에 따라 펀드구조를 신축적으로 설계함으로써 다양한 투자자들로부터 자금을 조달할 수 있도록 하고자

4. 서철수, 각주 3 발표자료, 75면.
5. 서철수, "금융기관의 투자전략 및 자금조달," 해외자원개발심포지엄 자료집(2009), 39면.

하였던 해외자원개발펀드 법제의 당초 취지에 부합하지 않는 것이다.

라) 펀드형태 설정상 개선방안

① 해외자원개발집합투자기구의 법적 형태는 자본시장법상 허용되는 집합투자기구의 법적 형태를 취할 수 있도록 하고, 해외자원개발펀드 설정자가 해외자원개발펀드의 법적 형태와 투자자모집방법을 설계함에 있어서 재량을 가지도록 할 필요가 있다.

② 해외자원개발투자회사를 환매금지형 집합투자기구로 설립하도록 한 현행 해외자원개발 사업법 제14조를 삭제하거나, 적어도 해외자원개발투자회사가 적격투자자만을 대상으로 하는 사모집합투자기구로 설립되는 경우에는 환매금지제한을 받지 않도록 규정하는 것이 바람직하다.

③ 해외자원개발투자회사 또한 blind 펀드로 설정할 수 있도록 허용하여야 한다.

마) 자금조달 관련 개선방안

① 해외자원개발개발펀드에 대하여 원칙적으로 일정한 비율의 차입, 담보제공 내지 채무보증을 허용하는 것이 바람직하다. 특히, 해외자원개발투자전문회사와 적격투자자만을 대상으로 하는 사모집합 투자기구로 설립되는 해외자원개발투자회사에 대해서는 leverage 비율을 적어도 100% 이상으로 대폭 상향하는 것이 적절하다.

② 장기적으로는 해외자원개발개발사업의 위험을 우려하는 투자자들도 비교적 낮은 위험으로 해외자원개발펀드에 투자할 수 있도록 해외자원개발펀드에 대한 채무투자(debt investment)방식도 허용하는 방안을 검토할 필요가 있다.

바) 자산운용방법상 개선방안

① 해외자원개발을 정의함에 있어서 해외자원의 생산 및 판매가 핵심과정임을 분명하게 규정하고, 기술용역제공 거래와 개발자금융자 거래는 전형적인 해외자원개발과 다른 형태인 것으로 규정하는 것이 바람직하다. 아울러, 광구 등에 관한 권리(working interest, production payment, net profit interest 등)를 취득하는 것도 해외자원개발의 한 유형으로 규정하는 것이 바람직 하다. 또한, 특수목적 회사를 통해 해외자원개발을 할 수 있음을 명시할 필요가 있다.

② 해외자원개발 사업법상 해외자원개발 전담회사의 정의를 “해외자원개발사업의 투자 및 시행을 주된 사업목적으로 하는 법인”으로 변경하는 것이 필요하다.

③ 해외자원개발펀드가 자원개발기업의 주식 및 지분 외에 전환사채, 신주인수권부사채 등 주식연계증권을 인수할 수 있도록 허용하여야 한다. 해외자원개발펀드가 영업양수도 방식

으로 자원개발기업을 인수하는 경우에는 자원개발기업의 해외자원분야 매출액 요건을 인수 대상 사업의 종전 매출액을 기준으로 산정할 수 있도록 하는 예외 규정을 마련할 필요가 있다. 해외자원개발 펀드에 의한 국내 자원개발기업의 주식 및 지분 인수를 허용함이 바람직하다.

④ 해외자원개발펀드가 특수목적회사를 통하여 해외자원개발 전담회사 또는 외국자원개발기업에 투자할 수 있도록 하는 명시적인 규정을 두는 것이 필요하다.

⑤ 장기적으로, 해외자원개발펀드의 투자대상자산을 다각화할 수 있도록 해외 자원개발 펀드가 해외자원개발과 관련된 다양한 증권 등에 투자할 수 있도록 하는 방안을 검토해 볼 필요가 있다.

사) 존립기간 관련 개선방안

해외자원개발펀드의 활성화를 위해서 해외자원개발펀드가 프로젝트 portfolio를 보유하고 있는 영속적인 펀드로 설정될 수 있도록 적어도 (향후 법개정을 통해) 환매가 허용되는 해외자원개발투자회사 및 해외자원개발투자전문회사에 대해서는 존립기간의 제한을 받지 않도록 할 필요가 있다.

Shalanda H. Baker, *Unmasking Project Finance: Risk Mitigation, Risk Inducement, and an Invitation to Development Disaster?* 6 TEX. J. OIL GAS & ENER. L. 273 (2010-11)

Ⅳ. UNDERSTANDING PROJECT FINANCE

On learning of the situation in La Ventosa, I was immediately drawn into the story. It is compelling and complex. However, one of the most intriguing aspects of this story, so full of fascinating elements, is that the project sponsors relied on project financing for the transactions. We have seen this before. The situation playing out in La Ventosa replicates itself in all corners of the world and across development industries. Indeed, the people of Peru,[1] India,[2] Argentina,[3] Burma,[4] Azerbaijan, Turkey, Georgia,[5] *inter*

1. The Camisea natural gas project is a thirty-year project that is touted by the Inter-American Development Bank as enabling Peru to become one of the few Latin American countries to meet its internal energy needs and eventually export natural gas outside of the country. It involves the exploration and processing of gas deposits in the Camisea field in Peru; the transportation of the processed natural gas through over 1200 kilometers of pipeline; and the distribution of the gas. *See*

Inter-American Development Bank, Camisea Project: Fact Sheet (Feb. 5, 2007), http://idbdocs.iadb.org/wsdocs/getdocument.aspx?docnum=837877 (last visited May. 20, 2011). The project is the subject of intense scrutiny because it requirespipeline construction in sensitive areas of the Andes, development of the natural gas in areas inhabited by indigenous groups, and the construction of a processing facility in an environmentally sensitive marine national park. *See id.* The complex project received financing through a consortium of banks and sponsors using project finance. *See Latin American Oil & Gas Deal of the Year 2004,* EUROMONEY INSTITUTIONAL INVESTOR PLC, Mar. 1, 2005, 2005 WLNR 27364850. *See also* Chloe Hayward, *Project Finance: Record Financing for Peruvian LNG Project,* EUROMONEY, Aug. 5, 2008, 2008 WLNR 27704713 (discussing related liquid natural gas pipeline that will export gas from Camisea field). Despite much attention paid to promoting the sustainability of the project, it has been troubled since inception, experiencing a number of pipeline spills and damaging the ecosystem of the surrounding area. *See Bowen, supra* note 91, at 737-38. The project also appears to be part of a larger effort on the part of the Peruvian government to openup large swaths of rain forest to private energy and agriculture investment, resulting in the large-scale displacement of indigenous people. *See* Kelly Hearn, *Peru Indians', Demands Seen as Stoked by Chavez U.S.-backed President Pressured by Protesters*, THE WASHINGTON TIMES, July 6, 2009, at Al.

2. In 1992, the Dabhol Power Corporation ("DPC"), a joint venture of the Enron Corporation, General Electric, and the Bechtel Corporation, contracted with the government of Maharashtra state in India to build a $3 billion electricity generating plant, the largest in the world. HUMAN RIGHTS WATCH, THE ENRON CORPORATION CORPORATE COMPLICITY IN HUMAN RIGHTS VIOLATIONS (1999), *available at* http://www.hrw.org/legacy/reports/1999/enronlindex.htm/. The project was heavily opposed by environmental activists and communities affected by the development. Id. In 1999, Human Rights Watch issued an extensive report detailing DPC's alleged complicity in human rights abuses carried out by state police that were paid to provide security for the company. *Id.* The report also claims that contractors of DPC "engaged in a pattern of harassment, intimidation, and attacks on individuals opposed" to the project. *Id.*
3. An Argentine NGO has been engaged in a pitched battle against the developer ofa paper mill on the Uruguay-Argentina border. The project is one of the largest capital investments in Uruguay's history, and is financed by project finance. *See* Vivian Lee, Note & Comment, *Enforcing the Equator Principles: An NGO's Principled Effort to Stop the Financing of a Paper Pulp Mill in Uruguay,* 6 NW. U. J. INT'L HUM. RTS. 354, 359-60 (2008). The complaint alleged that the mill would cause damage to the local environment and fisheries relied on by local populations. *See id.* at 360-61.
4. Unocal Corporation, a California oil company, acting with an international consortium,participated in the development of the Yadana oil field in the Andaman Sea off the southern coast of Burma. The consortium allegedly paid the Burma military to provide security for the project. Residents of Burma claimed that they "were relocated against their will, subjected to forced labor, assault, rape, torture, and saw friends and family murdered by the Myanmar State." *See* Eric Marcks, *Avoiding Liability for Human Rights Violations in Project Finance,*22 ENERGY L.J. 301, 306-08 (2001). The pipeline, at $1.2 billion, was the largest cross-border transaction ever conducted by the Burmese government, which was constructed using project finance. *Id.*
5. The Baku-Thlisi-Ceyhan Pipeline, financed by the IFC, the European Bank for Reconstruction and Development, and a group of private lenders, cost over $3.6 billion and, according to IFC documents, "traverses 17,700 individual land parcels with a total of 60,000 landowners" and reaches from the Caspian Sea to the Mediterranean Sea. IFC, IFC SUSTAINABILITY REPORT 2004

alia, have borne acute witness to the degradation of their environment, exploitation of their natural resources, wholesale disregard for traditional land rights, and other well-documented abuses. These harms were all facilitated by project finance-based development.

Project finance transactions may assume many different configurations; however, the basic project finance form is well understood and generally consistent across industries. By definition, project finance effectively relies on an income-generating asset and is self-financing as to debt service-hence the name, project finance. High amounts of non-recourse debt, low initial equity contributions, and the use of a special purpose vehicle to conduct the affairs of the project further characterize project finance.[6] The form has roots dating back to the medieval period, and the simplicity of the name obfuscates a world of complexity. Despite this complexity, there is an underlying form, which is the subject of this article.

A. Theoretical Underpinnings

Project finance locates itself in the larger law and development narrative constructed by legal and political science scholars in the Global North,'" and advanced **by** the Bretton Woods agencies. In *The New Law and Economic Development*[7] Professors David Trubek and Alvaro Santos describe the law and development movement in terms of "moments," which provides a useful, if simplified, lens through which to view the discourse. The First Moment, initiated in the 1960's, assumed that import substitution in

---

33 (2004), *available at* http://www.ifc.org/ifcext/sustain ability.nsf/Content/PublicationsReport Sustainability 2004. The bank indicates that no physical displacement resulted from the pipeline, but thirty-three complaints to the IFC's ombudsmen indicate a host of other grievances, including, *inter alia,* issues with compensation for land acquisition, proper assessment of the environment in an area prone to landslides, and losses to fishing stocks. Compliance Advisor Ombudsman, *Georgia/BTCPipeline-30/Vale,* http://www.cao-ombudsman.org/cases/case-detail.aspx?id=71. Non-governmental agencies also report serious concerns related to worker rights and the environment. Press Release, CEE Bankwatch Network, *BTC Outraged By Oil Company's Violations. Promised Highest Standards Are Sorely Lacking in Georgia* (Feb. 6, 2004) (claiming that pipeline workers are required to work twelve to fourteen hours per day, including weekends and holidays); *BP Accused Of Cover-up In Pipeline Deal,* THE SUNDAY TIMES, Feb. 15, 2004, http://www.bakuceyhan.org.uk/BP%20accused %20of%20cover-up%20over%20pipeline%2Odeal.htm (discussing a document leak which indicated that British Petroleum failed to disclose safety design faults that could lead to an environmentally catastrophic leak in the pipeline).

6. For a lengthy discussion of project finance and its variations, see generally SCOTT L. HOFFMAN, THE LAW AND BUSINESS OF INTERNATIONAL PROJECT FINANCE (Cambridge Univ. Press 2008).

7. DAVID M. TRUBEK & ALVARO SANTOS, THE "RULE OF LAW" IN DEVELOPMENT ASSISTANCE: PAST, PRESENT, AND FUTURE, IN THE NEW LAW AND ECONOMIC DEVELOPMENT A CRITICAL APPRAISAL 79 (2006).

the internal markets of states would facilitate growth, and states must direct limited financial resources to specified investment targets. This moment emphasized the importation of public and regulatory law from more advanced states to "developmental" states in order to manage an increasingly complex legal and economic environment and remove limitations to natural macroeconomic processes. The focus in this moment was on capacity building within public agencies and modernization of the legal profession in order to support the dynamics of the "developmental" state, with an inherent suspicion in the abilities of private markets and foreign capital to create sustainable growth.

In the so-called Second Moment, beginning in the late 1980s, post-Cold War period,[8] the tenor shifted away from a focus on capacity building in the public sector and toward neoliberalism. By some accounts, the move toward privatization began as early as the 1970s with Margaret Thatcher, and continued with President Ronald Reagan in the1980s.[9] In this moment, state intervention was seen as limiting the natural progression of development, and foreign investment became the overriding goal. The development of the law of private property and contract regimes would foster these goals, coupled with an emphasis on the judiciary as a way to limit the role of the state and promote markets." In this moment, as Professors Trubek and Santos note, there was a belief that "markets were markets, and the same legal foundations would be needed and could operate anywhere."[10] The concept of "project lending" also gained prominence in development circles, for industry could not be developed without infrastructure-a consistent supply of electricity and the roads to allow for the transport of finished products."

According to Trubek and Santos, in the Third, and current moment, the neo-liberal development is critiqued and disrupted. In particular, critics point to the limitations of transplanting laws without fully understanding the local institutions in place or the particular cultural context in which such transplantation takes place.[11] Moreover, the overemphasis on economic development and poverty alleviation at the expense of other development goals, such as freedom, is seen as ignoring the human aspects of development. The World Bank has weighed in to critique policies it has supported as well, noting that transplantation of a "formalistic rule of law to developing and/or

8. MICHAEL B. LIKOSKY, LAW, INFRASTRUCTURE, AND HUMAN RIGHTS 36 (Cambridge Univ. Press 2006); HOSSEIN RAZAVI, FINANCING ENERGY PROJECTS IN DEVELOPING COUNTRIES *51 (1996)*.

9. Tamara Lothian & Katharina Pistor, *Local Institutions, Foreign Investment and Alternative Strategies of Development: Some Views from Practice,* 42 COLUM. J. TRANSNAT'L L. 101, 113-14 (2003).

10. *See* TRUBEK & SANTOS, *supra* note 7, at 6-7

11. *See generally* AMARTYA SEN, DEVELOPMENT AS FREEDOM (1999) (recharacterizing development in more human terms).

democratizing countries could actually be counterproductive for economic, institutional, and political development, especially when informal mechanisms would be more effective and efficient."[12] Other critics push the inquiry further, querying the notion of the linear arc of development as a viable or even desired outcome with respect to "developing" the Third World.[13] Still others take an even more critical view, questioning the very dialectic frame that produced the development discourse.[14] Scholars such as Ruth Gordon and Jon Sylvester argue that the discursive production of the development frame has obfuscated the reality that the rules relating to development were and have always been a Northern construct.[15] The exportation of legal models and privatization mechanisms from North to South takes for granted that those in the Global South actually accept the underlying methodologies and psychologies supporting such importation. This, such scholars argue, is flawed reasoning, and the underlying rules that produced the linear development model should be exposed and evaluated.

Project finance locates itself near the nucleus of this rich discourse. The discursive production of the development framework that evolved through the three so-called moments produced the same flawed theoretical understandings of development finance, specifically project finance. Similar to the development discourse, the more pervasive the use of project finance, the less penetrable, as a form, it became. Outsiders assumed that the outcomes resulting from infrastructure development were attributable to other causes-

---

12. TRUBEK & SANTOS, *supra* note 7, at 90 *(citing* World Bank, Legal Institutions of a Global Economy Home Page, http://wwwl.worldbank.org/publicsector/legallindex.htm).

13. TRUBEK & SANTOS, *supra* note 7, at 80 (discussing linear development as the presupposition that "all nations [go] through similar states to reach a common end, represented in this kind of thought by the legal, economic, and social structures of the United States and Western Europe").

14. Joel M. Ngugi, *The World Bank and the Ideology of Reform and Development in International Economic Development Discourse,* 14 CARDOZO J. INT'L & COMP. L. 313, 320 (2006) (quoting Duncan Kennedy, "the World Bank's attitudes toward development seen as a whole are 'the product of the underlying structure of economic forces and relations, which it legitimizes.' That 'underlying structure' is the current system of international economic relations, including the international division of labor, extraction of natural resources, banking and trading systems and supposedly supported by a world of liberal democracies."). *See also* Gordon & Sylvester, *Deconstracting Development*, 22 WIS. INTL L.J. 31, at 82 ("The post war development discourse established a discursive practice that in turn established the rules of the game. This discourse permits 'the systematic creation of object, concepts and strategies,' as it determines who can speak, from what points of view, and with what authority. It establishes the criteria that define expertise and that expertise was deemed to reside in Western systems of thought, values and ways of life.").

15. Tayyab Mahmud, *Postcolonial Imaginaries: Alternative Development or Alternatives to Development?,* 9 TRANSNAT'L. L. & CONTEMP. PROBS. 25, 26 (1999) (noting that critiques of development "remain imprisoned within the imaginary of development" and therefore "radical critique must move beyond the discourse of alternative development and begin to imagine alternatives to development.").

the corruption of transition states in the Global South, market imperfections, and necessary evils in the messy business of creating infrastructure. I suggest that the answer is hidden in plain sight, in the form itself. ...

C. Structural Components

The key features of a project finance transaction include: (1) an equity investment by project sponsors into a special purpose legal entity formed to build the project; (2) a high debt-to-equity ratio, where debt of the project ranges from seventy to ninety percent of the total project cost; (3) no recourse or limited recourse to the project sponsors for defaults related to the project debt; (4) lender reliance on cash flows from the project to service the project debt; and (5) lender reliance on project contracts and assets, rather than the sponsor's assets, as security for the project debt. 151Each feature is described in more detail below, along with a brief description of the principal project contracts.

The typical project finance transaction begins with an equity investment by a project sponsor or sponsors into a project company. The sponsors serve as the project promoters and principal developers for the project. In modern project finance transactions, the number of equity investors ranges from one to three. These investors are corporations with recognizable names, such as Texaco, Pemex, Shell, and BP. Project finance may also involve a co-investment by a sovereign (e.g., a public-private partnership); however, the analysis herein is limited to private investments that involve agreements with the sovereign for the provision of services, but in which the sovereign is not an initial co-investor. Sovereign involvement would significantly alter the analysis. A sovereign possesses obligations to its polity, and even dictatorial regimes are subjected to a level of scrutiny not yet faced by transnational actors in the international community.

The principal agreement to which the project sponsors are party is the shareholder agreement. The shareholder agreement governs the relationship between the joint venture (e.g., the sponsors, as equity) in the creation of a special-purpose entity ("SPE") project company whose sole purpose (in the corporate sense) is to develop the project. The project company therefore serves as the borrower and contracting party for all transactions related to the project. The project company also engages a political risk insurer to insure against political and other host-country risks that may arise throughout the course of the project. In addition, the debt of the project company does not appear on the balance sheet of sponsors with less than a majority stake in the company.

At the outset, the project company enters into a government support agreement or concession agreement concerning the goods the project will provide. The government support agreement essentially provides that "in exchange for the building of the project, the sovereign shall provide to the project company certain compensation. Such compensation may involve beneficial tax treatment, guaranteed payment rates for project output, performance guarantees, permits," and other favorable treatment. In countries where the private investment in an industry is novel, the government services agreement will provide the legal framework for the transaction, including debt-to-equity ratio requirements, share retention requirements for equity investors, provision of work permits, a waiver of sovereign immunity, and consent to arbitration. The concession agreement is a major project document that allows the project company to construct and earn revenues from the project in exchange for providing a public service. It is similar to, but distinct from, the government services agreement, which governs the relationship between the project company and the government.

The project company also engages a contractor to design and construct the project. This is usually a private entity, called the engineering, procurement, and construction contractor (the "EPC Contractor," the underlying contract, the "EPC Contract"). The EPC Contractor agrees to design, engineer, and construct the project at a fixed-price, on a fixed dated, and on a turn-key, basis, meaning that the EPC Contractor shall deliver the keys to the fully-constructed, fully-operable project by a date certain to the project company. EPC Contracts are preferred by lenders to most infrastructure and energy transactions because of their ability to shift the risk of construction delay to the EPC Contractor. They are inapplicable in extraction projects (e.g., oil and mining) or projects that rely on the creation of a network (such as telecommunications).

Most large projects also involve an operation and maintenance contract (the "O&M Contract"), wherein a contractor agrees to provide general operations and maintenance services to the project to ensure that the project's operations and management-related fees stay within budget. The operations and maintenance contractor ("O&M Contractor") provides key personnel, such as the project manager, and sometimes other human resources to train project employees regarding the start up of the facility.5 The O&M Contractor receives incentive payments for efficient operation of a project that exceeds projected operation targets.

If the project requires a fuel input, the project company must enter into a fuel supply contract (the "Supply Contract") in order to supply the project with the fuel (e.g., oil, gas, or coal) required to run the facility. The process of negotiating the Supply Contract requires an understanding of prevailing fuel rates and projected supply; securing price guarantees for the fuel input becomes a critical aspect of the overall financial picture of the project. The input requirements of the project are closely linked to the output requirements and the negotiated rates set forth in the output contract; the timeline of the Supply Contract should match the term of the output contract.

The output contract is arguably the most important document among the project contracts, and may take the form of a power purchase agreement, which is sometimes also confusingly called a concession agreement (the "Offtake Agreement"). This principal project document dictates the revenue stream that will be generated by the output of the project. The parties to this agreement are usually the project company and a utility, which may be a government entity (the "Offtaker"). The Offtake Agreement contains several features related to pricing. A common feature is the "take or pay" arrangement, where the utility agrees to purchase the project's capacity, or pay the project company in lieu of purchasing the project's output. Other payment methods include the long-term sales contract, the hedging contract, the contract for differences, and the throughput contract. The Offtake Agreement, and the pricing mechanisms therein, provide the critical justification for the project's financing. In the case of the Mexico wind developments, Wal-Mart, Cemex, and CFE are the offtakers of the electricity generated by the wind farms. The stability of these entities provides significant security to theproject sponsors, and comfort to the lenders regarding the future income stream of the projects.

With respect to financing, project finance transactions are typically non-recourse, which means that in the event of a default, the lenders' recourse is only as to the project assets, and not the assets of the sponsor. During the initial, riskier phases of the project development, lenders may also request a sponsor guarantee of the project company debt or allow some recourse to the sponsor's assets ("limited recourse"). As in the La Mata-La Ventosa wind project, these limited recourse features often dissolve after completion of the initial phase of the project, after which time the project reverts back to a non-recourse project.

When the parent does not own more than fifty percent of the project company, the project debt does not appear on the balance sheet of the project sponsor. This arrangement frees up the sponsor to invest in multiple projects without carrying their respective liabilities. There is some indication that reliance on this benefit of project finance transaction is declining in the U.S. and the United Kingdom; however, scholars still point to the availability of off-balance sheet financing as a critical incentive to electing the project finance form over standard corporate finance, where debt appears on the project sponsor's balance sheet.

Because of the capital requirements of infrastructure projects, the debt-to-equity ratio of project finance transactions is high, meaning there is typically a low initial equity investment and substantial debt required to finance the cost of the project. The debt-to-equity ratio varies, but could be as low as 75% in some cases, or as high as 100% in others. Ratios between 80-90% are common, with lenders, and sometimes host governments, requiring more of an equity commitment in the Global South. In general, the lenders set forth the equity requirements, understanding that the more a project sponsor has at stake in a particular project, the more likely it is that such sponsor will be committed to see the project through. Because wind had never been privately developed in Oaxaca, the debt-to-equity ratios of the Oaxaca projects were lower than anticipated in future projects, which are expected to be financed almost entirely by private debt.6 Given that the players in Oaxaca wind development are consistent, such investors were presumably willing to advance more of an initial cash outlay in early projects-La Venta, Eurus, and La Mata-La Ventosa-in anticipation of higher debt-to-equity ratios in future projects.

Project lenders also obtain collateral security in the form of contract assignments and project revenue in order to step into the shoes of the project company in the event of default and to support the underlying debt obligations of the project. This is standard and largely seen as an advantage to sponsors, whose assets are not placed in jeopardy as a result of the financing.

Notably absent from the transaction are members of the community that hosts the project. Although the World Bank Inspection Panel aims to integrate the voices of individuals affected by large-scale development into discussions regarding a project, such engagement is limited to state-led projects involving the World Bank. In the private development context, such community involvement is at the discretion of the developers. For highly controversial projects, engaging the community is critical to prevent construction delay or disruption to plant operations, but for outsiders to a region, determining whose voice should be added to the negotiations can be daunting. Moreover, as illustrated by the difficulties faced by wind developers in El Istmo, such engagement is typically limited in its ability to affect, on any meaningful level, the trajectory of a well-financed project.

This highly complex transactional structure brings with it substantial

transaction costs; however, developers, lenders, and host governments rely on several rationales to support its continued popularity. Such rationales can be viewed from both outside and within the transaction form. I begin by examining the external rationales.

D. External Rationales for Project Finance

The rationale underlying the discursive shift from public to private financing of infrastructure consists of two main points, one practical, and the other a bit more nuanced. Practically speaking, post-conflict and transition states following the linear modernization track emerged from the 1960s and 1970s saddled with debt and unable to finance large, expensive infrastructure projects, seen as risky investments by private enterprises. This created quite a conundrum, but to no surprise, the same parties involved in the lending and structural adjustment programs that led to many of the sovereign debt problems emerged with solutions to the liquidity crisis facing states in the Global South. The proposed solution? Private financing of public infrastructure projects. The more nuanced argument proffered by the development community, including the World Bank and other multilateral lenders, in support of private infrastructure development, is that the market is better positioned to bear the costs of development and, in the case of infrastructure, the professional expertise provided by international developers allows for more efficient project development. Evaluating the efficiency argument provides a useful starting point.

Project finance, development proponents argue, is a relatively "efficient" way to bring public works projects to fruition. As illustrated by Mexico's efforts to provide a legal framework that is attractive to wind development, host countries buy into this rationale by providing incentives for various types of development and making investment more attractive. Project developers benefit from this arrangement, which is sometimes critiqued as providing a reverse subsidy that flows from a developing country to a corporation that resides in a developed economy, because the host government is unlikely to resist the activities of the project developers.19 In theory, host governments also benefit by importing capital that would otherwise be unavailable to furnish public goods. In the end, the theory provides, the country as a whole is benefited by the efficiency of development experts.

This "efficiency" argument does not fully account for all of the harm that accompanies project development. Moreover, the argument purports to distribute comprehensively the costs and benefits of the project. Once again, Oaxaca provides a useful illustration. On its face, the development in Oaxaca appears to be a win-win situation, and perhaps a net gain. The energy produced is clean; the wind is virtually free, save land rental fees; and the corporations purchasing the energy are no longer relying on carbon-dioxide-producing elements to power certain portions of their operations. Looking deeper, however, the social and environmental externalities emerge. Although our Northern lens prevents full understanding and quantification of the true social costs of the project, they are probative of a less-definite balance of costs and benefits.

Also included in the efficiency rationale is the suggestion that project finance allows the economic integration of developed and developing economies because a number of the projects involve the exploration of commodities that are exported to developed countries. This is certainly the argument promoted in Oaxaca; however, as seen in certain Amazonian regions, such integration could result in the widespread devastation of previously pristine environments and the traumatic disruption of the community in which such projects are located. In this context, project finance, as a tool to aid the shift from public to privately-led development, provides the path of least resistance.

The private development of infrastructure allows host governments to move away from the prominent role of project developer and bridge capital shortfalls. In doing so, host governments are also able to shift development risks away from public entities and toward private actors and thus avoid many of the negative reputational and political outcomes associated with state-led development. If project finance is the chosen method of delivering infrastructure, these shifted risks are further shifted by private developers onto third parties through the contractual mechanisms discussed in Part V. In many cases, the sovereign is among the group bearing the risk of development, but in the end, the sovereign still avoids holding the bag; any risk it bears is ultimately borne by the people, and private actors may be blamed for any resulting negative externalities. The end result is a circular game of finger pointing, where adversely affected persons are left without a clear avenue for redress.

Underlying the cost and efficiency rationales is a subtle, but related, rationale. Project finance is unique in its ability to allow corporate actors to engage in the foregoing risky and profit-maximizing public-goods producing behavior under the full protective guise of private activity. Currently a growing body of scholarship attempts to create a human rights framework around such transnational corporate behavior, but for now, the elusive quality of private behavior in the public context continues to evade meaningful review. Human rights advocates have also identified the private nature of project contracts as significantly limiting with respect to achieving accountability for various atrocities that occur in the development context.[16] Michael B. Likosky alludes to this difficulty in his work, *Law, Infrastructure and Human Rights,* noting that the penumbra of project finance creates a gray area of activity wherein actors are difficult to identify.[17] This is evident in Oaxaca, where farmers allege that access to their own land

---

16. *See, e.g.,* Jena Martin Amerson, *What's in a Name? Transnational Corporations As Bystanders Under International Law,* 85 ST. JOHN'S L. REV. (forthcoming 2011) (using "bystander" framework to discuss transnational actors' assumed role under international law); Rachel J. Anderson, *Reimagining Human Rights Law: Toward Global Regulation of Transnational Corporations,* 88 DENv. U.L. REV. (forthcoming 2011) ("Failure to regulate the power, wealth, and influence of transnational corporations is a weakness in human rights law that should be remedied."); David Kinley & Rachel Chambers, *The UN Human Rights Norms for Corporations: The Private Implications of Public International Law,* 6 HUM. RTS. L. REV. 447, 450 (2006) (discussing the need for uniform and enforceable international standards for transnational corporations).

17. In addition, the lack of transparency with respect to such contracts prevents sovereigns from

leases, in which they serve as landlords, were not provided. Moreover, Inter-American Development bank and IFC each declined to provide this author with detailed information regarding the Eurus wind project, the largest wind project ever developed in the Americas. In this development context, accountability is a significant challenge.

E. Internal Rationale for Project Finance

Full consideration of the efficiency rationales espoused by project finance proponents suggests that external rationales provide the most support for deploying project finance; however, the internal rationales provide more compelling evidence for the proliferation of the form. Project finance can be viewed as a revenue-generating mechanism. The name suggests as much. The project *finances* itself. Investors continue to see this as a viable option because if the project fails, the banks typically only seek recourse through the project's assets, not the assets of the sponsors. If the project succeeds, the project will generate proceeds to pay down the underlying project debt and eventually provide sponsors with an attractive return. Thus, the prevailing literature states, project finance, as a form, provides an avenue for developers to engage in infrastructure transactions that, from a risk-management perspective, would otherwise be cost prohibitive. This provides useful cover for parties conducting project finance transactions because it allows such actors to justify their risk-mitigating activities, which comprise the core of the project finance form and which may have harmful effects on third parties. Inside the transaction form, project finance fundamentally serves as a risk-allocation structure. In addition, its perceived profitability and self-governing features all provide attractive incentives to rely on this method of finance. Each rationale is addressed in turn.

Infrastructure and energy projects carry certain risks, and project finance is designed to mitigate the risks to project sponsors without affecting their creditworthiness. The long-term debt received by the project affects neither the balance sheet nor assets of the project sponsors. These benefits are well known, and as Scott Hoffman, author of a comprehensive treatise on project finance, states, "[p]roject financing is used by companies that desire any or all of several objectives. Established, well-capitalized corporations often select a project finance structure to assist in undertaking large debt commitments with a minimum of risk."[18] This creates an interesting paradox. The risks

---

negotiating market terms with respect to their individual extractive projects. *See generally,* PETER ROSENBLUM & SUSAN MAPLES, CONTRACTS CONFIDENTIAL: ENDING SECRET DEALS IN THE EXTRACTIVE INDUSTRIES (2009) (including a comprehensive review of host country contracts with corporations in the extractive industries and arguing for greater transparency).

18. *See* HOFFMAN, *supra* note 6, at 15 (illustrating that in low leverage scenarios, profits are divided

inherent in infrastructure development do not go away on initiation of a development project. Rather, in project finance, such risk is distributed throughout the structure through various contractual mechanisms, described more fully in Part These mechanisms diffuse risk as to the sponsors and developers, making it difficult, if not impossible, to correlate negative outcomes to their original source and thus lead to an externalization of these inherent risks.

With respect to internal economics, project finance is profitable when compared with low leverage transactions. The financestructure of a project finance deal rewards equity investors for taking on more project debt (at the special purpose entity level), given that lenders generally accept lower returns than equity investors. Interest is also tax deductible, which further cheapens the value of debt as compared to equity.

Finally, project finance is a self-contained, self-regulated, mechanism that relies on its own highly negotiated terms to deliver the goods. Project financiers are famously creative, and while the basic components of a project finance transaction are fairly standardized, no two deals are alike. The advantage of this framework is that developers may push the transactional boundaries to maximize revenue. In emerging markets, creativity is critical to managing unknown risks. Also, given that the transactions involve mostly private parties, the legal framework of the host state is less outcome determinative; more important is a party's leverage. This can create tension between the host government and the project developers, especially with respect to waiving sovereign immunity and submitting to an arbitration tribunal. More troubling, however, is the inability of parties likely to be affected by the transaction to penetrate the form in any meaningful way to affect its terms. This disenfranchisement is not the subject of this article, but is closely connected to the most well-understood aspect of project finance-its ability to diffuse risk.

Ⅴ. PROJECT FINANCE AS A RISK DIFFUSION MECHANISM

Early proponents of project finance as a mechanism for foreign direct investment believed that no single external legal framework was outcome determinative with respect to the decision to invest. Instead, access to raw materials, receptiveness of the foreign market to the product to be exported, and geographical location of the host country with respect to other markets were believed more important to investors. The instability of the legal regimes in the Global South was also viewed as a liability to early investors, but through project finance, investors could control the terms of their investment through

---

by a greater amount of equity, whereas in a high leverage situation profits are divided against a lower equity number, increasing the overall return).

reliance on private contract. Risks inherent in the development project were therefore handled within the project structure, rather than vis-a-vis a corporate legal schema that distributes risks. As such, the parties imported a form with the ability to create a quasi-governmental, but private, legal framework, replete with the requisite checks and balances.

The foregoing reflects a fundamental shift from reliance on a public forum to manage and distribute risks to a private, contractual mechanism for such tasks. While the private management of risks has yielded substantial rewards for developers, it has effectively excluded the public from meaningful, consensual, participation in large-scale projects. The features highlighted below indicate the specific ways in which project finance provides a unique shield to distribute risk within the form and, subsequently, away from investors.

A. High Debt-to-equity Ratio

As discussed, in contrast to corporate financing, project finance provides sponsors with the unique benefit of limiting risk exposure to the initial equity investment in the project, while offering such equity investors theopportunity to enjoy the benefits of a successful project. Sponsors may spread the financial risk by sharing the initial equity contribution with other parties. As previously stated, the lenders or the host government may dictate the amount of equity contribution. A project identified as having strong potential cash flows might be structured with a debt-to-equity ratio of 90% to 100%, while a higher risk project might involve upwards of 40% initial equity investment.

Although a failure to develop the project would mean a loss of the equity investment, such losses pale in comparison to losses suffered when a project is financed almost exclusively from a project promoter's coffers. The high debt-to-equity ratio shifts the risk of project failure to debtholders sophisticated multilateral lenders.

B. Use of Stand-Alone Project Company

Special purpose entities ("SPE's") provide a key element of project finance transactions. The rationale is straightforward. In the vast majority of cases, project sponsors are experienced developers with consistent and expert global engagement in project finance transactions. SPEs allow prolific project sponsors to obtain financing for numerous projects without such debt appearing on the balance sheet of the project sponsor or affecting the sponsor's ability to obtain its own financing or engage in other development projects. This parent-subsidiary structure also protects the SPE by preventing contamination of the SPE's financial status by the sponsor's other liabilities.

SPEs are bankruptcy remote entities, which means that a parent's bankruptcy will not affect the SPEs operations. These entities also allow the sponsor to minimize exposure to risk, including environmental and human rights risks associated with the project, because the sponsor does not participate directly in the project. All financing, development, operation, and maintenance are handled through the SPE.

C. Non-Recourse Financing

The availability of non-recourse financing provides project sponsors a key incentive in project financing. As previously discussed, in the classic form of project finance transactions, loans are extended on a non-recourse basis, which means that in the event of default the lender's recourse is only to the assets of the project itself, not the assets of the project sponsor. Such financing does not appear on the sponsor's financial statements unless the sponsor and financial auditors view the investment as material to the sponsor's overall financial picture. Non-recourse financing thus provides project sponsors with the flexibility to invest in multiple, risky projects without any such project affecting its balance sheet.

In awarding financing, lenders evaluate the economic viability of the project to determine whether the key feature of project finance, the self-financing aspect of the transaction, will indeed be realized throughout the life of the loan. Lenders therefore scrutinize deal documents to determine whether risks have been adequately transferred to third parties or assumed by project participants that are best able to absorb the risk. As Professor Wendy Duong notes in her case study regarding a power project in Vietnam, lenders react to "untreated or uncovered risk of loss" by turning down requests for financing or by requesting additional collateral support for the loan.[19] These fiercely negotiated contractual arrangements give lenders the comfort required to extend loans on a non-recourse basis. The resulting contractual framework for cross-border project finance transactions is one of the most complex and extensive of any type of financial arrangement.

Under most loan documents, in the event of default, the agent of the lending syndicate has the right to step into the shoes of the project company and protect its most valuable asset, the project itself. In some instances the loan is extended on a limited recourse basis, allowing for some encumbrance on the balance sheet of the sponsor. The collateral, in most cases, consists of any project contracts and the physical assets of the project, thereby further isolating the sponsors' assets from the activities of

---

19. Wendy N. Duong, Partnership with Monarchs—Two Case Studies ... 26 U. PA. J. INT'L ECON. L. 69 (2005), at 82/*See also* Carl S. Bjerre, *Project Finance, Securitization and Consensuality,* 12 DUKE J. COMP. & INT'L. L.J. 411 (2002).

the project. As such, during project negotiations, significant energy goes into developing a cross collateralization framework that allows the lender to take over the project if the project company defaults on its loan. The other recourse available to the lender is to obtain possession of and operate the project. This allows the lender to maintain the operation of the project, thus increasing the likelihood that the asset will generate income to service the outstanding debt.

While some empirical studies point to a trend toward limited recourse financing to provide lenders with additional collateral in the event of a default (e.g., the assets of the sponsor), the trend in project finance remains closely linked to non-recourse financing.

D. Risk Shifting in Project Contracts

To borrow a property law analogy, project finance transactions are composed of a bundle of risks. As Scott Hoffman notes, "contracts form the framework for project viability and control the allocation of risks."[20] Contract serves as a critical risk mitigation mechanism within the overall risk mitigation mechanism of project finance. Under general contractual principles, risks are shifted to parties best able to bear them.[21] Usually this means that the parties who control the causal mechanism responsible for bringing the risk to fruition as a harm or loss also bear the contractual burden of the risk. In a complex infrastructure development transaction, multiple causes may produce various risks within the project, and therefore the project company must disaggregate and isolate individual risks and their associated causation in order to distribute them through the project documents. As such, risk shifting becomes a key component of the project negotiations, which include identifying the party best situated to assume the risk and translating such risk into a premium paid by the party shifting the risk.

Scholars and practitioners engaged in project finance routinely identify two primary categories of risks with respect to infrastructure development: (1) commercial, or economic, risks, including (a) construction risks, which generally take the form of delays and cost overruns, (b) fuel supply risks, including price increases and supply shortfalls, (c) market risks, such as weak demand for output, lower prices for the project output, and changes in the exchange rate and inflation, and (d) operating risks, which include risks relating to the day-to-day operations of a project, such as environmental damage or regulatory interference; and (2) political risks such as government expropriation, currency inconvertibility, and war. The foregoing risks are typically evaluated and incorporated into highly negotiated transaction documents. If these risks are not covered

20. *See* HOFFMAN, *supra* note 6, at 7.

21. John G. Mauel, *Common Contractual Risk Allocations in International Power Projects,* 1996 COLUM. BUS. L. REV. 37, 41 (1996).

via risk shifting, the project developer will bear both the risks and associated costs. The following sections outline the key mechanisms utilized to diffuse the two primary categories of risk commonly associated with infrastructure development.

1. Commercial Risks

The key commercial risks are risk of construction delay and operational risk. Construction delay is the death knell of a project finance transaction reliant on the income generated by the project under construction, and is the most frequently referenced commercial risk. The party best able to absorb the risk of delay is the EPC Contractor. The project company passes along any construction-delay risks to the EPC Contractor as reflected in the financial terms of the fixed-price, turn-key, EPC Contract. The EPC Contractor then completes the construction, bearing any costs associated with delay. The project company pays the EPC Contractor a premium to absorb the risk associated with a delay, and thereby shifts the risk of delay to the contractor and away from the project company. When the project company or operations and maintenance contractor receives the keys to the project, the EPC Contractor may walk way from the project, save the honoring of various warranty obligations.

Performance difficulties in the project fall into the category of operation risk. The party to whom such risks are shifted is the O&M Contractor. The O&M Contractor oversees the daily operations of the plant, and is therefore well situated to control factors that may lead to performance difficulties at the plant. Accordingly, the project company shifts operation risks to the O&M Contractor via the terms of the O&M Contract.

In each of the foregoing cases, the party absorbing the risk is paid a premium for accepting it.

2. Political Risks

Political risks generally fall into three categories: expropriation, currency inconvertibility, and war. Project companies have become quite adept at obtaining political risk insurance [246] to cover the risk of government expropriation of a project or political unrest. Both the build-own-operate-transfer ("BOOT") and build-operate-transfer ("BOT") models also effectively displace expropriation risks associated with risky development projects, because they are structured to provide for the eventual public take over of the project.

To avoid currency-related risks, the project company has several options. It may designate a purportedly stable currency, such as the U.S. dollar, as the dominant currency for the transaction. To create stability within the transaction, the Offtaker and project company may agree to use a certain exchange rate throughout the course of the transaction to avoid significant variations in the revenue generated by the project and to provide comfort to lenders regarding the project's ability to service the debt. If availability of currency poses a threat, the project company establishes an offshore account with a certain amount of the required currency and requires that the Offtaker maintain the currency at certain levels within the account until the project debt is paid.

These risk mitigation tools allow the project company to better manage the most precious commodity at stake in a project finance transaction: the revenue stream. Moreover, as illustrated in Part IV, they combine to create an environment where certain risks are passed on to third parties.

다. 공시/회계기준의 정립

자금조달이 은행을 통한 간접금융이건, 자본시장을 통한 직접금융이건, 사모펀드와 벤처자본을 통한 초기금융이건, 자금조달을 위한 기초는 자원개발사업의 성과 및 전망을 일관성있는 기준에 따라서 반영한 재무제표라고 할 수 있다. 따라서, 추출산업에 적용되는 회계기준을 정립하기 위하여 많은 논의가 진행되고 있으나 아직 확립된 기준은 없는 것으로 보인다.

대법 2009. 7. 9. 선고 2009도1374 판결[15](에이치앤티 사건)

1. 증권거래법위반 부분

가. 구 증권거래법(2007. 8. 3. 법률 제8635호로 공포되어 2009. 2. 4. 시행된 자본시장과 금융투자업에 관한 법률에 의하여 폐지되기 전의 것. 아래에서도 같다.) **제188조의4 제4항 제1호 적용에 관한 주장에 대하여**

구 증권거래법 제188조의4 제4항은 "누구든지 유가증권의 매매 기타 거래와 관련하여 다음 각 호의 1에 해당하는 행위를 하지 못한다."고 하면서, 그 제1호로 "부당한 이득을 얻기 위하여 고의로 허위의 시세 또는 허위의 사실 기타 풍설을 유포하거나 위계를 쓰는 행위"를 들고 있다. 구 증권거래법이 위와 같이 사기적 부정거래행위를 금지하는 것은 증권거래에 관한 사기적 부정거래가 다수인에게 영향을 미치고 증권시장 전체를 불건전하게 할 수 있기 때

15) 파기환송후 서울고법 2009. 11. 26. 선고 2009노1838 판결, 대법 2010. 4. 5. 선고 2009도13890 판결로 확정.

문에 증권거래에 참가하는 개개의 투자자의 이익을 보호함과 함께 투자자 일반의 증권시장에 대한 신뢰를 보호하여 증권시장이 국민경제의 발전에 기여할 수 있도록 함에 그 목적이 있다고 할 것인바(대법원 2003. 11. 14. 선고 2003도686 판결 등 참조), **언론을 통하여 기업의 사업 추진 현황이나 전망 등에 관한 인터뷰 기사 등이 보도되도록 한 경우** 그것이 단순히 사업과 관련된 의견 또는 평가 내지 단순한 홍보성 발언에 불과한 것이 아니라 허위의 사실을 유포하는 행위에 해당하는지 및 그러한 행위가 부당한 이익을 얻기 위한 것인지 등은 위 금지 조항의 취지를 염두에 두고 행위자의 지위, 해당 기업의 경영 상태와 그 주가의 동향, 인터뷰 및 보도 내용의 구체적인 표현과 전체적인 취지, 보도의 계기 및 그 계속·반복성 여부, 보도 내용과 관련된 기업의 여러 실제 사정 등을 전체적·종합적으로 고려하여 객관적인 기준에 의하여 판단하여야 한다. 또, 위 조항에서 정한 고의란 행위자가 허위의 시세 또는 허위의 사실 기타 풍설을 유포하거나 위계를 쓰는 행위라는 객관적 구성요건을 충족하였음을 인식하면서도 이를 용인한다는 주관적 구성요건을 의미한다. 나아가 구 증권거래법의 목적과 위 조항의 입법 취지 등에 비추어 위 조항이 정한 부당한 이득은 유가증권의 처분으로 인한 행위자의 개인적이고 유형적인 경제적 이익에 한정되지 않고, 기업의 경영권 획득, 지배권 확보, 회사 내에서의 지위 상승 등 무형적 이익 및 적극적 이득뿐 아니라 손실을 회피하는 경우와 같은 소극적 이득, 아직 현실화되지 않는 장래의 이득도 모두 포함하는 포괄적인 개념으로 해석하는 것이 상당하고, 허위의 사실을 유포하는 행위 당시 위와 같은 포괄적인 의미의 부당한 이득을 얻으려는 목적이 있으면 족하며 그 행위 당시부터 장차 유가증권을 처분하여 이득을 얻겠다는 목적이 구체적이고 확정적으로 존재하여야 하는 것은 아니다. 또, 위와 같은 부당한 이익을 얻으려는 목적은 그것이 행위의 유일한 동기일 필요는 없는 것이므로 다른 목적과 함께 존재하여도 무방하고 그 경우 어떤 목적이 행위의 주된 원인인지는 문제되지 아니하며(대법원 2003. 12. 12. 선고 2001도606 판결 등 참조), 피고인이 목적의 존재를 부인하는 경우에는 이러한 주관적 구성요건 요소인 사실은 그 성질상 상당한 관련성이 있는 간접사실 또는 정황사실을 분석하는 방법에 의하여 그 존부를 판단할 수밖에 없으며, 이때 무엇이 목적의 존재를 뒷받침할 수 있는 상당한 관련성이 있는 간접사실 또는 정황사실에 해당하는 것인지는 정상적인 경험칙에 바탕을 두고 치밀한 관찰력 및 분석력에 의하여 합리적으로 판단하여야 한다.

같은 취지의 원심 판단은 정당하고 거기에 상고이유에서 주장하는 바와 같은 법리오해 등의 위법은 없다. 그리고, 위 법리에 비추어 볼 때 원심이 판시한 바와 같은 여러 상세한 이유를 들어 피고인이 이 사건 인터뷰 등을 통하여 자신이 대표이사 겸 대주주인 공소외 1 주식회사가 추진 중인 우즈베키스탄 내 규사광산 개발사업의 추진 현황과 전망에 관하여 실제와 다른 내용을 계속·반복적으로 언론에 보도되도록 한 행위가 공소외 1 주식회사의 주가 상승을 통한 부당한 이익을 얻기 위한 허위사실 유포행위로서 구 증권거래법 제188조의4 제

4항 제1호에 해당한다고 판단한 조치는 정당하고, 증거에 의하지 아니하거나 합리적인 의심이 없는 정도의 증명에 이르지 아니하였음에도 공소사실을 인정한 위법 또는 증거평가에 관한 논리법칙·경험법칙을 위반하여 자유심증의 한계를 넘어선 위법은 보이지 아니한다. 그 밖에 피고인이 원심의 이 부분 사실인정에 관하여 내세우는 사유들은 결국 구체적인 논리법칙·경험법칙 위반 사실을 특정하지 아니한 채 원심의 사실인정을 다투는 취지에 불과하므로 이는 적법한 상고이유에 해당하지 아니한다. 이 부분 상고이유는 모두 받아들이지 아니한다.

나. 구 증권거래법 제188조의4 제4항 제2호 적용에 관한 주장에 대하여

구 증권거래법 제188조의4 제4항 제2호는 "중요한 사항에 관하여 허위의 표시를 하거나 필요한 사실의 표시가 누락된 문서를 이용하여 타인에게 오해를 유발하게 함으로써 금전 기타 재산상의 이익을 얻고자 하는 행위" 역시 사기적 부정거래행위로 정하여 이를 금지하고 있다. 위와 같은 사기적 부정거래행위를 근절하여 투자자의 이익과 증권시장에 대한 신뢰를 보호함으로써 증권시장이 국민경제의 발전에 기여할 수 있도록 하려는 취지에 비추어 볼 때, 위 조항의 '중요한 사항'이란 미공개정보 이용행위 금지 조항인 구 증권거래법 제188조의2 제2항에서 정한 '일반인에게 공개되지 아니한 중요한 정보'와 궤를 같이 하는 것으로서 당해 법인의 재산·경영에 관하여 중대한 영향을 미치거나 유가증권의 공정거래와 투자자 보호를 위하여 필요한 사항으로서 투자자의 투자 판단에 영향을 미칠 수 있는 사항을 의미한다고 할 것이다(대법원 2006. 2. 9. 선고 2005도8652 판결). 그리고 위와 같은 중요한 사항에 관하여 허위 또는 부실 표시된 문서를 증권선물거래소를 통하여 이미 공시한 상태에서 이를 단순히 시정하지 않고 방치하는 데 그치는 것이 아니라, 구체적인 상황에서 그 문서가 투자자의 투자 판단에 영향을 미칠 수 있는 사항에 관하여 오해를 유발할 수 있는 상황임을 알면서도 이를 금전 기타 재산상의 이익을 얻는 기회로 삼기 위해서 유사한 취지의 허위 또는 부실 표시 문서를 계속 증권선물거래소에 보고하는 등의 방법으로 적극적으로 활용하는 행위는 위 조항에서 정한 문서의 이용행위에 포함될 수 있다(대법원 2002. 12. 10. 선고 2002도5407 판결, 대법원 2003. 11. 14. 선고 2003도686 판결 참조). 나아가 위 조항의 문언 해석상 일단 '타인에게 오해를 유발하게 함으로써 금전 기타 재산상의 이익을 얻기 위하여' 중요한 사항에 관한 허위·부실 표시 문서를 이용한 이상 그로써 바로 위 조항 위반죄가 성립하는 것이고, 문서 이용행위로 인하여 실제 '타인에게 오해를 유발'하거나 '금전 기타 재산상의 이익을 얻을 것'을 요하지 않는 것이므로, 허위 또는 부실 표시 문서 이용행위와 타인의 오해 사이의 인과관계 여부는 위 죄의 성립에 아무런 영향을 미치지 않는다(대법원 2006. 4. 14. 선고 2003도6759 판결).

같은 취지의 원심 판단은 정당하고 거기에 상고이유에서 주장하는 바와 같은 법리오해 등의 위법은 없다. 그리고 위 법리에 비추어 볼 때 원심이 판시한 바와 같은 여러 상세한 이유를 들어 경영 상황이 점차 악화되고 있던 공소외 1 주식회사가 새로운 사업으로 추진 중이라고 홍보한 규사광산 개발사업 계속 진행 의지와 전망 등에 대하여 투자자들의 관심이 집중된 상황에서, 피고인이 차명주식을 누락한 채 공시되어 있던 임원·주요주주 소유 주식 보고서의 내용을 바로 잡지 않고 여전히 차명주식을 누락한 추가 보고서를 제출하는 방법으로 투자자들로 하여금 피고인이 보유 중이던 주식을 순차 처분하고 있다는 사정을 알지 못하게 함으로써, 주가에 영향을 미치지 아니한 채 보유 주식을 처분하여 상당한 이익을 취한 행위가 허위 또는 부실 표시된 위 보고서들을 이용한 행위로서 구 증권거래법 제188조의4 제4항 제2호에 해당한다고 판단한 조치는 정당하고, 증거에 의하지 아니하거나 합리적인 의심이 없는 정도의 증명에 이르지 아니하였음에도 공소사실을 인정한 위법 또는 증거평가에 관한 논리법칙·경험법칙을 위반하여 자유심증의 한계를 넘어선 위법은 보이지 아니한다.

그 밖에 피고인이 원심의 이 부분 사실인정에 관하여 내세우는 사유들이나 검사의 이 부분에 관한 상고이유 주장은 모두 결국 구체적인 논리법칙·경험법칙 위반 사실을 특정하지 아니한 채 원심의 사실인정을 다투는 취지에 불과하므로 이는 적법한 상고이유에 해당하지 아니한다. 이 부분 피고인과 검사의 상고이유는 모두 받아들이지 아니한다.

금감원, 유전(가스)개발사업 모범공시기준 (2008. 1. 1)

〈목 차〉

4.4. 회계처리 현황

제5편 유전개발사업의 평가
5.1. 자원량(매장량)의 산정기준
5.1.1. 가채매장량의 산정기준
5.1.1.1 확인 가채매장량의 산정기준
5.1.1.2 개발 가채매장량의 산정기준
5.1.1.3 가채매장량의 상업성 평가기준
5.1.2. 매장량의 단독 산정 및 합산기준
5.2. 유전개발사업의 경제성 평가
5.3. 외부평가

제1편 목　　적

이 모범기준은 유전(가스)개발사업(이하 "유전개발사업"이라 한다)의 공시방법에 대한 모범적인 기준을 설정하는 것으로서, 유전개발사업에 대한 상장법인 등의 공시업무 수행 시 고려해야 할 사항들을 권고함을 목적으로 한다.

제2편 유전개발사업에 대한 공시개요

2.1 일반원칙

(1) 공시의무자는 증권거래법(이하 "법"이라 한다), 증권거래법 시행령 및 증권거래법시행규칙의 규정에 따라 금융감독위원회 또는 금융감독원에 제출하는 공시서류를 작성함에 있어서 관련법규를 준수하여야 하며, 신의에 따라 성실하게 작성하되, 이 기준에 따라 알기 쉽고 충실하게 작성하여야 한다.
(2) 공시서류를 작성함에 있어서는 투자자 등 이용자가 이해하기 쉽도록 알기 쉬운 용어를 사용하여 서술식으로 기재하는 것을 원칙으로 하되, 관련 규정 및 이 지침에서 특정 형태의 도표나 그림을 기재할 것을 요구하는 경우에는 이에 따라야 한다. 다만, 중요한 정보를 빠짐없이 전달하거나 쉽고 정확하게 정보를 전달하기 위하여 당해 도표 등을 수정 또는 보완하여 기재하거나 별도의 그래프, 도표, 그림 등을 이용하여 작성할 수 있다.
(3) 모든 기재사항은 객관적인 자료나 사실 또는 합리적 추론이나 분석에 근거하여 기술하여야 하고, 예측·추정·전망·계획 등을 기재하는 경우에도 단정적인 주장이나 표현을 피하고 애매모호한 표현이나 용어 등을 삼가는 등 이용자의 오해를 일으키지 않도록 작성하여야 한다.
(4) 이 기준에서 기재를 요구하는 항목에 있어 각 조 또는 작성지침에서 기재내용이나 방법을 구체적으로 정하고 있지 아니하였더라도 투자자 등 이용자의 의사결정에 영향을 미칠 수 있는 중요한 정보가 있는 경우에는 가장 관련 깊은 항목에 이를 기재하여야 한다.
(5) 이 기준에서 기재를 요구하는 항목이 계약상 비밀유지의무가 있거나 기업경영상 비밀에 해당되어 공시하는 것이 곤란한 경우에는 회사는 자료를 확보하되 공시서류에 기재하지 아니할 수 있다. 또한 이 기준에서 확보하도록 요구한 자료 중 거래상대방의 경영상 비밀사항에 해당하는 등의 이유로 거래상대방으로부터 확보하지 못한 경우에는 그러한 사실을 기재하여야 한다.

2.2 적용범위

(1) 이 기준은 법 제8조의 규정에 의한 유가증권신고서, 제186조의 규정에 의한 상장법인 등의 신고·공시의무 등, 제186조의2 및 제186조의3의 규정에 의한 사업보고서, 반기보고서 및 분기보고서, 제190조의2의 규정에 의한 합병신고서, 분할신고서, 영업 양수·양도신고서, 주식의 포괄적 이전·교환신고서, 자산양수·양도신고서에 대하여 이를 적용한다.

(2) 이 기준 제4편(유전개발사업의 공시내용)은 다음에 해당하는 경우에만 적용한다.
   (a) 제8조의 규정에 의한 유가증권신고서, 제190조의2의 규정에 의한 합병신고서, 분할신고서, 영업양수·양도신고서, 주식의 포괄적 이전·교환신고서, 자산양수·양도신고서의 경우에는 유전개발사업별 투자금액이 자기자본의 100분의 30이상 투자하는 경우
   (b) 법 제186조의2 및 제186조의3의 규정에 의한 사업보고서, 반기보고서 및 분기보고서의 경우에는 상기 (a)조문에 따라 유전개발사업을 공시한 사실이 있는 경우
(3) 이 기준 제4편(유전개발사업의 공시내용)은 법 제186조의 규정에 의한 상장법인 등의 신고·공시의무 등에 따라 주요경영사항 등을 공시하는 경우에는 해당 공시내용과 분량에 적절하게 필요한 내용만을 발췌·요약하여 기재하되 아래의 사항은 반드시 기재한다.
   - 회사의 유전개발사업 추진내역 개요
   - 유전개발사업 대상지역의 개요 및 추진단계
   - 유전개발사업 대상지역의 확인 가채매장량 및 해당국 정부에 보고된 확인·추정·가능 가채매장량
   - 유전개발사업 대상지역에 대한 경제성평가내역 개요
(4) 법 제186조의 규정 등에 따라 유전개발사업과 관련하여 주요경영사항을 신고나 자율·공정공시 등을 통하여 공시한 사항이 있는 경우, 법 제186조의2 및 제186조의3의 규정에 의한 사업보고서, 반기보고서 및 분기보고서, 제8조의 규정에 의한 유가증권신고서에는 제출일 현재 기 공시된 사항의 진행현황을 기재한다.
   - 기 공시한 내용에 대하여 사업추진 현황 및 가채매장량 등에 중요한 수정사항이 발생한 경우 그 내용 및 사유를 기재

2.3 이사회와 경영진의 역할

(1) 이사회는 유전개발사업 추진에 필요한 주요 사항을 심의·의결하며, 경영진은 유전개발사업을 수립·변경하는 경우 상장기업에 발생 가능한 위험요인을 고려하여 의사결정을 하여야 한다.
(2) 이사회와 경영진은 유전개발사업의 매장량/생산리스크, 법적리스크 등 계량화하기 힘든 리스크를 포함하여 발생가능한 모든 위험요인을 종합적·체계적으로 관리할 수 있는 체제를 구축하여야 한다.

제3편 유전개발사업의 용어정의

3.1. 용어사용의 기본원칙

(1) 신고서등에 사용한 유전개발관련 전문용어는 적절한 용어정의를 기재하여야 하며, 용어정의는 원유업계에서 일반적으로 통용되는 의미와 일관성이 훼손되지 않아야 한다.
(2) 회사는 유전개발관련 전문용어에 대하여 세계석유협회(World Petroleum Council) 등 국제적 공신력이 있는 기관이 사용하는 용어의 해설*을 참고하여 기술할 수 있다.
   * 석유 매장량/자원의 정의에 사용되는 용어의 해설(Glossary of Terms Used in Petroleum Reserves/Resources, Society of Petroleum Engineering/World Petroleum Congress) 참조
(3) 원유자원의 인식은 일반적으로 통용되는 분류 및 산출체계에 따라 구분하여 기재한다(석유자원의 분류체계 개요는 붙임 1 참조).

3.2 용어정의

이 기준에서 사용하는 용어의 정의는 다음과 같다.

3.2.1. 매장량 관련 용어

(1) "확인 가채매장량(Proved reserves)"이라 함은 지질학적·공학적 자료의 분석에 의해, 현재의 경제적 조건(Current Economic Conditions)·운영방법·정부규제상황을 고려할 때에, 이미 발견(Discovered)

된 저류층으로부터 상업적(Commercial)으로 회수가능(Recoverable)할 것이 합리적으로 확실시되는 매장량이다. 합리적으로 확실시된다는 것은 회수가능성에 대한 신뢰수준이 높거나 또는 실제 회수될 매장량이 예측한 매장량 이상일 확률이 90% 이상인 경우를 말한다. 확인 가채매장량은 개발여부에 따라 아래와 같이 분류한다.

가. 확인 개발 가채매장량(Proved developed reserves)

－기존 시추정에서 상업적으로 회수할 수 있을 것으로 기대되는 매장량으로, 1차 회수후 추가회수의 경우는 추가회수를 위해 필요한 장비가 설치완료되었거나, 설치를 위해 소요될 비용이 상대적으로 적은 경우 개발로 분류된다.

나. 확인 미개발 가채매장량(Proved undeveloped reserves)

－시추되지 않은 지역의 새로운 유정, 기존 저류층보다 더 깊게 파서 새로운 저류층까지 확대된 기존 유정, 매장량 회수를 위한 생산 또는 이동 설비 설치에 상대적으로 많은 비용이 필요하거나 기존 유정의 추가 생산을 위해 상대적으로 많은 비용이 필요한 유정으로부터 회수될 것으로 기대되는 확인 원유 가채매장량을 말한다.

(2) "추정 가채매장량(Probable reserves)"이라 함은 지질학적·공학적 자료의 분석에 의해, 상업적으로 회수되지 않을 가능성보다 상업적으로 회수될 가능성이 큰 매장량이다. 즉, 실제 회수될 매장량이 예측한 매장량 이상일 확률이 50% 이상인 경우를 말한다.

(3) "가능 가채매장량(Possible reserves)"이라 함은 지질학적·공학적 자료의 분석에 의해, 상업적 회수 가능성이 추정 가채매장량보다 적은 매장량이다. 확률적으로는 실제 회수될 매장량이 예측한 매장량 이상일 확률이 10% 이상인 경우를 말한다.

(4) "발견(Discovered)" 이라 함은 실제 시추를 통해 지표로 분출된 석유 또는 표본 추출을 통해 유동 석유의 존재가 확인된 석유 퇴적층·저류층에 적용될 수 있는 용어이다.

(5) "회수가능 자원(Recoverable Resources)"이라 함은 기술적으로 퇴적구조로부터 퍼 올릴 수 있을 것으로 예측되는 탄화수소자원양을 말한다.

(6) "개발(Development)"이라 함은 생산중이거나 생산을 위한 준비가 완료된 상태를 말한다. 1차 회수후 추가 회수의 경우에는 필요한 장비의 설치가 완료되거나 그러한 설치에 소요될 비용이 상대적으로 적을 때 개발된 것으로 본다.

(7) "상업적(Commercial)"이라 함은 합리적인 시간안에 개발되어 생산될 것으로 기대되는 것을 말하며, 합리적인 시간은 상황에 따라 다르지만 일반적으로 5년 이내로 제한된다.

(8) "현재의 경제적 조건(Current Economic Conditions)"이라 함은 과거 원유 가격과 관련 원가, 평균 소요기간, 계약상의 의무, 관련 가채 매장량보고와 관련된 정부의 규제 등을 포함한다.

(9) "경제적(Economic)"이라 함은 석유 자원이나 가채매장량과 관련하여 수익이 운영과 관련된 비용을 초과할 때를 말한다.

3.2.2. 유전개발사업 관련 용어

(1) "유전개발"이라 함은 국내·외에서 아래의 방법 등에 따라 유전을 개발(개발을 위한 조사 및 개발에 부대되는 사업을 포함한다)하는 것을 말한다. 다만, 원유·가스의 수송·정제·마케팅, 부산물로 얻어지는 석유자원 생산 등은 제외한다.

－유전을 단독 또는 외국인과 합작으로 유전을 개발하는 방법

－유전을 개발하는 자에게 기술용역을 제공하여 유전개발에 참여하는 방법

－유전을 개발하는 자에게 개발자금의 전부 또는 일부를 융자하여 유전개발에 참여하는 방법

(2) "조사(탐사)사업"이라 함은 광구에서 원유의 부존을 확인하기 위하여 행하는 지질조사, 지질광상조사, 물리탐사, 지화학탐사, 탐사시추, 평가시추, 탐광시추, 시굴, 탐광굴진, 사업타당성 조사 등의 사업(상업적 생산에 도달되지 못한 경우에 동일 광구 내에서 매장량 확보를 위한 조사(탐사)작업을 포함한다)을 말한다.

(3) "개발사업"이라 함은 원유의 부존이 확인된 광구 또는 개발단계에 있는 광구의 권리 취득 및 지분을

매입하거나, 상업적 생산을 위한 생산시설과 부대시설 건설 등의 모든 사업을 말한다.

(4) "생산사업"이라 함은 운영권자 또는 비운영권자로서 경제적(Economic) 생산단계에 있는 광구의 권리취득 및 지분매입, 생산설비 건설, 추가매장량 확보를 위한 시추 등의 사업을 말한다.

(5) "경제적(Economic) 생산"이라 함은 경제적 생산개시일 이후부터의 생산을 말하며, 경제적 생산개시일은 원유개발의 경우 운영권자가 "경제적 생산"으로 제시하는 일자 또는 시험생산중 생산물량 판매수입이 생산에 필요한 인건비 및 생산설비 유지비를 초과하는 회계연도 말일을 기준으로 하며, 해외광물자원개발의 경우는 연간 사업수익금이 생산에 필요한 매출원가와 판매비 및 일반관리비를 초과하는 회계연도 초일을 기준으로 한다.

(6) "기술용역제공사업," "개발자금융자사업," "투자위험보증사업" 등 기타 유전개발사업과 관련하여 별도로 정하지 않은 용어는 "해외자원개발사업에 소요되는 자금의 융자기준(산업자원부 고시 제2007-120호)"의 규정을 참고하여 기재할 수 있다.

제4편 유전개발사업의 공시내용

4.1. 회사의 유전개발사업 추진 현황

(1) 회사의 유전개발사업에 대한 과거 추진내역 및 향후 추진계획, 신규로 추진하는 경우 사업 참여 경위를 기재한다.
- 사업운영 체계 및 유전개발관련 기술인력 보유 현황을 기재
- 회사가 직접 유전개발사업에 참여하는지 여부를 기재

(2) 유전개발사업 관련 계약의 형태 및 구조를 투자자가 알기 쉽게 그림 또는 도표를 이용하여 기재하고, 주요 계약내용을 기술한다.
- 수익배분 구조도를 기재
- 광권계약, 생산분배계약, 서비스계약 등 계약의 세부형태를 기재
- 계약상대방의 주요현황, 계약기간, 공동참여자 및 지분내역을 기재
- 보증각서 또는 은행보증서, 의무이행 보증서 등 계약상대방의 계약이행 보장내용을 기재하고 증빙자료를 확보*

* 자료를 확보하도록 규정된 사항은 공시서류에는 기재하거나 첨부하지 아니하며 사후 검증을 위하여 회사에서 증빙자료를 확보하여 보관함(이하 같음)

(3) 유전개발 사업의 착공, 완공 및 운영 등과 관련한 해당국 정부의 승인, 인허가 취득 여부 및 기타 의무부담사항을 기재한다.

(4) 회사의 유전개발사업에 대한 과거 투자금액 현황 및 향후 투자하게 될 자금의 조달계획을 기재한다.
- 기간별 과거 투자금액 및 향후 투자예정금액(매입비, 탐사비, 개발비, 운영비, 기타로 구분 기재)을 기재
- 과거의 자금조달 내역 및 향후 조달계획을 기재

(5) 회사의 유전개발사업 참여에 대한 수익성 평가내역을 투자기간별로 구분하여 기재한다.
- 수익구조 및 투자금액 회수시점(기간)을 기재
- 유전개발사업에 대한 향후 예상 재무제표 추정자료를 확보
- 생산량 및 판매량, 유가전망 등에 대한 분석내용을 확보
- 자본비용, 운영비용, 감가상각비, 의무작업량, 로열티, 세제 등 세부적인 비용지출 분석자료를 확보

(6) 회사의 유전개발사업 추진 사업(회사)의 주식, 지분, 수익권 등을 취득하여 유전개발사업에 투자하는 경우 해당 주식, 지분, 권리 등의 가치평가 내역을 기재한다.
- 주식, 지분, 수익권 등에 대한 평가방법과 해당 평가방법을 채택한 이유를 기재
- 주식 등에 대한 가치평가에 필요한 세부자료를 확보
- 현금흐름할인법(Discounted Cash Flow)을 적용하는 경우 현금흐름가정에 대한 주요추정 근거 및

내역을 확보
- 비교가치를 통하여 가치를 평가한 경우 비교대상 주식 등의 상장 및 거래현황과 시장가치 산출내역을 확보

(7) 회사는 해당 유전개발사업에 대하여 독립적인 외부평가기관의 평가를 받았는지 여부와 평가를 받은 경우 평가의견의 개요를 기재한다.
- 평가기관의 신인도를 판별할 수 있도록 평가기관의 현황 및 해당 평가기관이 과거에 평가한 사례에 대한 분석자료를 확보

(8) 회사는 해당 유전개발사업의 추진과 자원 및 매장량 등과 관련하여 정부기관에 신고한 내역을 기재한다.

4.2. 유전개발 대상지역의 사업 추진현황

(1) 회사는 유전개발사업 대상지역(이하 '대상지역')의 명칭, 면적, 위치, 지도를 상세하게 기재한다.
- 지질학적 지형과 원유의 매장 가능한 구조를 비교하여 분석한 자료를 확보

(2) 대상지역의 매장자원에 대한 매장량 등을 기재하는 경우 확인 가채매장량을 기준으로 기재한다.

(3) 확인 가채매장량이 확인되지 않는 경우에는 동 사실을 기재하고 참고사항으로 추정 가채매장량 또는 가능 가채매장량을 기재할 수 있으나, 기타의 자원량 또는 매장량 등은 기재할 수 없다.
- 추정 가채매장량과 가능 가채매장량을 기재하는 경우에는 투자자의 판단에 도움이 되도록 해당 가채매장량과 확인 가채매장량의 산정기준상 차이를 간략하게 기재
- 상세한 매장량 및 상업성 분석자료를 확보

(4) 대상지역의 유전개발사업 추진, 매장량 등과 관련하여 해당국 정부기관에 보고한 내역을 기재한다.

(5) 대상지역의 매장량과 관련하여 매장량을 추정한 기관의 현황 및 과거 평가내역의 개요를 기재한다.
- 매장량 평가기관의 신인도를 확인 할 수 있도록 평가기관의 과거 평가내역 등 세부 증빙서류를 확보

(6) 회사는 대상지역 해당국에서 유전개발대상지역에 대한 개발사업에 대한 승인 여부 및 조건의 개요를 기재한다.
- 소재국의 사업승인신청 서류 및 승인문서를 확보

(7) 대상지역에 대한 전체 운영권을 확보한 자(이하 "운영자")의 현황을 기재한다.
- 운영자의 주요재무현황 및 주요주주, 임직원 현황을 기재

(8) 운영자의 유전개발사업 관련 계약의 형태 및 구조를 투자자가 알기 쉽게 그림 또는 도표를 이용하여 기재하고, 주요 계약내용을 기술한다.
- 광권계약, 생산분배계약, 서비스계약 등 계약의 세부형태를 기재
- 주요 지분참여자 및 지분내역, 주요 지분참여자와의 계약기간을 기재
- 주요 지분참여자의 주요재무현황 및 주요주주, 임직원 현황을 확보
- 계약상대방의 계약이행을 보장하기 위한 보증각서 또는 은행보증서, 의무이행 보증서 등의 보장내역을 확보
- 생산물 판매계약 및 수익의 배분 구조를 기재

(9) 대상지역 유전개발사업 운영자의 과거 유전개발사업 추진내역과 향후 사업추진일정을 연도별로 구분 기재한다(5개년 이상).
- 기간별 과거 투자금액 및 향후 투자예정금액(매입비, 탐사비, 개발비, 운영비, 기타로 구분 기재)을 기재
- 과거의 자금조달 내역 및 향후 조달계획을 기재
- 회사가 분담하게 되는 금액 내역 및 비중을 기재
- 전년도 사업계획 대비 당해연도 실적을 확보
- 당해연도 사업계획(작업범위 및 내용, 당해연도 월별 수행일정)을 확보

(10) 대상지역 운영자가 과거 유사한 유전개발사업의 운영/유지에 대한 검증된 경험을 보유하고 있는지 평가하고 기재한다.
- 과거 유전개발사업 운영경력을 기재하고 운영경력을 증빙할 수 있는 자료를 확보
- 운영권자가 직접 개발사업 관련 시설의 관리·유지에 대해 책임이 있는지 여부를 기재하고 별도의 관리·유지 계약자가 있는 경우 동 계약자의 현황을 확보
- 운영권자가 개발사업 시설을 직접 운영한다면 필요한 기술과 인력의 확보내역을 확보

(11) 회사는 운영권자의 대상지역 유전개발사업에 대한 경제성 평가내역을 기재한다.
- 수익구조 및 투자금액 회수시점(기간)을 기재
- 경제성 평가에 필요한 세부자료를 확보
- 유전개발사업에 대한 향후 예상 재무제표 추정자료를 확보
- 생산량 및 판매량, 유가전망 등에 대한 분석내용을 확보
- 자본비용, 운영비용, 감가상각비, 의무작업량, 로열티, 세제 등 세부적인 비용지출 분석자료를 확보
- 현금흐름할인법(Discounted Cash Flow)을 적용하는 경우 현금흐름가정에 대한 주요추정 근거 및 내역을 확보
- 법적·환경적·사회적요인, 정부의 규제변경, 정부와의 계약내용 등 기타 제반 사업환경에 대한 조사내역을 확보하고 경제성 평가시 고려한 내역을 확보

4.2.1. 대상지역의 개발사업 추진단계

(1) 회사는 용어정의 및 아래의 개발순서 구분을 참고하여 대상지역에 대한 현재 유전개발사업 추진단계를 ① 대상지역에 대한 개발(운영)권 확보 단계, ② 조사(탐사)사업단계, ③ 개발사업단계, ④ 생산사업단계으로 구분하여 기재한다.

〈유전개발순서 개요(한국석유공사)〉

개발순서 구분		내 용
조사(탐사)단계	탄성파 탐사	탄성파 탐사
	자료처리	컴퓨터 이용
	지질조사	대상지역에 대한 지질조사
	자료해석	지질조사 자료해석 및 시추위치 확정
	시추선 및 용역계약	기자재 구입, 보급기지 설치
개발단계	시추	원유부존여부 직접확인
	유전평가	원유부존량 확인(10~20공), 경제성 평가
	생산시설 설치 및 굴착	플랫폼 건설, 생산정 굴착, 파이프라인 설치(약 3년, 파이프라인 제외)
생산단계		원유 생산

(2) 각 추진단계별로 운영자의 해당국 정부 인허가 보유 내역, 예상되는 소요시간, 운영자의 사업추진관련 주요 계약사항을 기재한다.

4.2.2. 대상지역의 탐사 및 개발현황

(1) 대상지역의 탐사 및 개발현황(4.2.2)은 유전개발순서에 따라 대상지역이 해당하는 사업단계에서 일반적으로 추진되는 사업내용을 모두 기재하여야 하며, 다음 단계에서 추진하게 되는 사업내용은 기재하지 아니할 수 있다.

(2) 운영자가 대상지역을 탐사/개발지역으로 선정하게 된 경위에 대하여 기재한다.
- 광구탐사 연혁 및 현황자료를 확보

(3) 분지개요 및 석유지질의 개요를 기재한다.

- 퇴적 환경, 분지의 발달사, 형태, 층서 분석자료를 확보

(4) 석유시스템(Petroleum System) 분석 및 석유포텐셜 평가의 개요를 기재한다.
- 근원암의 분포상황, 유기물 함량, 성숙도 등 분석자료를 확보
- 저류암의 구성, 공극률, 투수율 등 평가자료를 확보
- 덮개암, 트랩의 종류, 구조 등 트랩형성 분석자료를 확보
- 탄화수소의 생성·방출·이동·보존 등 석유시스템 모델링내역을 확보
- 석유시스템 모델링에 사용된 소프트웨어 및 분석내용을 확보
- 가채매장량을 기재하는 경우 계산 시 사용한 방법(결정론적 방식, 확률론적 방식 등), 계산내역, 상업성 평가내역의 개요를 기재
  • 결정론적 방식을 사용한 경우 유추계산법, 용적법, 물질수지법, 감퇴곡선법, 시뮬레이션법 등 분석자료를 확보
  • 확률론적 방식을 사용한 경우 면적, 두께, 공극률, 수포화도 등 입력변수에 대한 확률적 분포 및 시뮬레이션 분석자료를 확보
  • 기타 방식을 사용한 경우 사용방식의 세부내역 및 계산내역을 확보
  • 상업성 평가와 관련한 세부 분석자료를 확보

(5) 대상지역에 대한 과거 지질학적, 지구물리학적 조사내역 및 과거 탄성파 탐사 등 탐사실적 및 시추실적을 기재한다.
- 지표지질, 중자력 탐사, 물리탐사, 위성탐사 자료, 인접광구 기술자료를 확보

(6) 대상지역에 대한 과거 탄성파 탐사 등 탐사실적 및 시추실적을 기재한다.
- 탄성파 탐사 내역의 개요를 기재하고 탐사측선 및 위치도, 해석도면을 확보
- 탐사정 시추 지역 및 개수, 시추자, 시추결과, 산출시험에 따른 생산내역을 기재
- 시추보고서, 고생물, 지화학 및 저류암보고서를 확보
- SP검층, GR검층, 비저항검층, 공극율 검층 등 물리검층내역을 확보
- 반복지층시험기, 생산성시험 결과를 확보
- 유망구조 및 유망구조별 가채매장량(확인·추정·가능) 산정내역을 확보
- 탐사 후 가채매장량을 기재하는 경우 계산내역 및 상업성 분석자료를 확보

(7) 대상지역에 대한 향후 지질 및 물리 조사계획 및 탐사계획, 탐사정 시추계획을 기재한다.
- 향후 추가적인 조사 및 탐사비용 산정자료를 확보

(8) 대상지역에 대한 과거 평가정 시추실적, 향후 평가정 시추계획, 연도별 개발계획을 기재한다.
- 평가정 시추 지역 및 개수, 시추자, 시추결과, 산출시험에 따른 생산내역을 기재
- 시추시스템 및 생산시설 확보내역을 확보
- 평가정 시추후 가채매장량을 기재하는 경우 계산내역 및 상업성 분석자료를 확보
- 기간별 시추계획 및 시추비용 산정자료를 확보

(9) 대상지역에 대한 생산정 시추 등 과거개발·생산실적 및 향후 개발·생산계획을 기재한다.
- 생산정 시추 지역 및 개수, 시추자, 시추결과를 기재
- 원유 생산, 운송, 출하시설 구축현황 및 계획을 확보
- 기간별 생산설비 설치계획 및 투자비 산정자료를 확보
- 기간별 생산량자료, 저류층시뮬레이션, 회수증진법(EOR)계획서를 확보

4.2.3. 생산된 원유의 판매방안

(1) 회사는 계획된 생산량에 대한 판매계획, 시장 존재여부, 마케팅 계획에 대하여 기재한다. 다만, 대상지역의 유전개발사업이 조사(탐사)단계인 경우 생산된 원유의 판매방안(4.2.3)은 기재하지 아니할 수 있다.

(2) 대상지역 생산량에 대한 운영자와 구매자간 인수도계약 또는 의무구매계약 등 사전 판매처를 확보하기 위한 계약내용을 기재한다.

4.3. 유전개발사업 추진관련 위험(Risk)요인

(1) 회사는 유전개발사업에 대하여 가채매장량의 크기가 변동하거나 생산의 난이도가 증가하는 등의 매장량/생산 위험(Reserve/Production Risks)을 평가하고 위험요인을 기재한다.
(2) 회사는 개발시설의 적기완공, 예산준수, 시방사항과 공사 진행의 적정성 여부 등 건설관련 위험과 생산개시시점에서 완공이 지체되는 준공위험(Construction/Completion Risk)을 평가하고 위험요인을 기재한다.
(3) 회사는 생산시설이 설계대로 잘 운영되고 유지되는가에 대한 운영위험(Operating Risk)을 평가하고 위험요인을 기재한다.
(4) 회사는 생산원유를 흡수할 만한 충분한 시장의 존재와 판매가격의 변동성 등과 관련한 시장위험(Market Risk)을 평가하고 위험요인을 기재한다.
(5) 회사는 광구 운영권자와 각종의 계약 당사자가 각각의 계약이행을 거부하는 등의 계약당사자 위험(Counterpart Risk)을 평가하고 위험요인을 기재한다.
(6) 회사는 투자대상국의 정치, 재무적 불안정성과 관련한 정치적 위험(Political Risk)을 평가하고 위험요인을 기재한다.
(7) 회사는 회사 및 운영권자의 유전개발에 대한 전문적인 능력 부족, 개발시간의 지연 등 기타 비계량적인 위험을 평가하고 위험요인을 기재한다.

4.4. 회계처리 현황

(1) 회사는 유전개발사업과 관련하여 발생된 비용이나 수익에 대한 회계처리기준 및 내역을 기재한다.
(2) 회사는 유전개발사업과 관련하여 적용한 주요한 회계처리기준을 채택하게 된 사유를 기재하고, 주요한 회계처리기준이 변경된 경우에도 변경사유를 기재한다.

제5편 유전개발사업의 평가

(1) 회사는 개발사업 및 매장량의 평가업무 등을 수행함에 있어 석유업계에서 일반적으로 통용되는 평가 및 보고기준에 따라 업무를 수행하여야 한다.
(2) 회사는 원유개발사업에 대한 평가 시 이 기준 제5편에 기재된 사항, 세계석유협회 등*이 정한 석유자원 관리체계(Petroleum Resources Management System)(2007), 석유 가채매장량 및 자원량 평가를 위한 가이드라인(Guidelines for the Evaluation of Petroleum Reserves and Resources)을 참고하여 평가할 수 있다.
  * (SPE/WPC/AAPG/SPEE)

5.1. 자원량(매장량)의 산정기준

5.1.1. 가채매장량의 산정기준

5.1.1.1. 확인 가채매장량의 산정기준

(1) 회사 등 유전개발자는 확인가채매장량의 산정을 위한 현재의 경제적 조건(Current economic condition)을 알기 위해서 가채매장량이 회수되는 기간 동안 정부의 관련 규제 현황, 회사의 운영상황, 개발계약의 효력존재 여부, 유가와 운영비의 공정한 산출에 대한 충분한 자료를 확보한다.
(2) 일반적으로 해당 저류층의 상업적 회수가능성이 실제 생산 또는 유층시험에 의해 검증되는 경우에 확인가채매장량으로 분류되며, 저류층의 생산성만으로는 확인가채매장량으로 분류될 수 없다. 또한 검층이나 코아분석으로 해당 저류층이 원유를 포함하고 있으며 동일 지역 내의 저류층이 생산중이거나 유층시험에 의해 생산가능성이 입증된 경우에도 확인가채매장량으로 분류할 수 있다.
(3) 기존에 확립된 회수증진법을 사용하는 경우에는 시험생산이 성공적인 경우와 회수증진법을 적용하여 성공적인 결과를 얻은 경우에 확인가채매장량으로 분류가 된다. 그러나 새로운 회수증진법을 사

용하는 경우에는 해당 저류층에 대한 대표적인 시험생산으로부터 성공적인 결과를 얻은 경우에만 확인가채매장량으로 분류할 수 있다.

5.1.1.2. 개발 가채매장량의 산정기준

(1) 개발 가채매장량은 필요한 장비의 설치가 완료된 후 또는 설치를 완료하기 위하여 투입될 비용이 상대적으로 미미한 경우에 분류할 수 있다. 요구되는 설비가 사용가능하지 않은 경우에는 미개발로 재분류하여야 한다. 개발된 가채매장량은 생산중인 또는 미생산중인 개발 가채매장량으로 하위 분류할 수 있다.

(2) 미개발 가채매장량은 아래로부터 미래투자를 통하여 회수될 것으로 기대되는 양이다.
- 알려진 퇴적지역 안의 미시추지역에 있는 새로운 유정
- 다른(알려진) 저류층으로 기존 유정을 더 깊이 파들어 가는 것
- 회수를 높이는 추가유정(Infill wells)
- 주요한 또는 개량된 회수프로젝트를 위해 생산이나 수송설비를 설치하거나 기존 유정을 재건설하기 위해 상대적으로(새로운 유정을 시추하는 비용과 비교할 때) 큰 규모의 지출이 요구되는 경우

5.1.1.3. 가채매장량의 상업성(commerciality) 평가기준

(1) 가채매장량의 상업성을 주장하는 자는 개발에 대한 확고한 의사를 견지하고 그러한 의사가 다음의 모든 기준을 충족하여야 한다.
- 개발을 위한 합리적인 시간계획표를 뒷받침하는 증거
- 세부적인 투자 및 운영기준을 만족하는 개발계획의 미래 경제성에 대한 합리적인 평가
- 개발을 보장하기 위해 요구되는 생산량의 기대매출(최소) 또는 모든 생산량에 대한 시장이 존재할 것이라는 합리적인 기대
- 필요한 생산과 수송설비가 사용가능하거나 가능하여질 수 있다는 증거
- 법적, 계약상의, 환경과 다른 사회·경제적 관련사항이 평가되는 회수프로젝트의 실제수행을 허용할 것이라는 증거
- 현재의 허가기간(Duration of licence)이 만료하는 경우에는, 개발권자(the licence holder)가 현 허가권을 갱신하는 권한을 가지고 있고 허가권을 갱신하여 온 과거 역사적인 경력을 명확하게 증명하기 전에는 가채매장량이 회수가능한 것으로 평가되지 않음

5.1.2. 매장량의 단독 산정 및 합산기준

(1) 단일구조에 대한 매장량은 확률론적 방식이 사용된 경우에는 평균값을 최적값으로 사용할 수 있으며, 결정론적인 방식 특히 용적법에 의해 계산된 경우에는 확인가채매장량에(0.8~1.0), 추정가채매장량(0.4~0.6), 가능가채매장량(0~0.2)의 계수를 곱하여 그 합을 최적값으로 사용할 수 있다(붙임2 가채매장량 예측방법의 비교 참조).

(2) 하나의 광구에 포함된 여러 유전의 매장량을 합산하거나, 한 회사가 보유하고 있는 전체 매장량을 계산하는 경우, Level 단위간의 매장량 합산은 원칙적으로는 결정론적 또는 확률적인 방식에 따라 해당 저류층의 동일부류끼리 각각 합산하여 계산할 수 있다.
- 평가자, Data의 양과 질, Field의 성숙도 등의 차이로 인해 일관성이 결여될 수 있는 경우에는 세계석유협회의 석유 가채매장량 및 자원량 평가를 위한 가이드라인(Guidelines for the Evaluation of Petroleum Reserves and Resources)을 참고하여 평가하여야 한다.

5.2. 유전개발사업의 경제성 평가

(1) 개발사업의 경제성은 재무적요인(생산(자본비용, 운영비용), 생산종료비용, 원가, 가격, 기간, 세금) 뿐 아니라, 마케팅, 법적, 환경적, 사회적, 정부의 요인들을 고려하여 평가한다.

(2) 개발사업의 평가는 역사적 원가법, 시장 비교가치 등 여러가지 방법을 사용하여 평가할 수 있다.

(3) 현금흐름기준 자원의 평가(Cash-flow-based resources evaluations)는 아래의 조건을 고려한다.

- 예정된 기간 동안 계획된 기대 생산량
- 미래기간 동안에 적용이 기대되는 원가에 대한 평가자의 관점에서, 생산인식시점(Reference point)에 생산량을 개발, 회수, 생산하는 프로젝트와 관련된 예상원가(환경, 사업포기, 교정원가를 포함)
- 미래기간 동안 각 상품에 적용이 예상되는 가격에 대한 평가자의 관점에서의 생산량으로부터 기대되는 수익(회사에 부과되는 원가와 수익 부분을 포함)
- 미래의 계획된 생산 및 수익과 관련하여 회사가 부담하게 되는 세금 및 로열티
- 권한과 그로부터 합리적으로 기대되는 기간으로 한정된 프로젝트 수행기간
- 평가시점에서 회사에 적용가능한 가중평균 자본비용 또는 최소 필수 수익률을 합리적으로 반영하는 적절한 할인율의 적용

(4) 회사는 특정한 투자기준을 정할 수 있으나 일반적으로 프로젝트는 최선의 예측 케이스가 회사의 기준할인율에 따라 양의 현재가치를 가지거나 최소한 양의 미할인 현금흐름을 가지는 경우 "경제적(economic)"으로 간주될 수 있다.

5.3. 외부평가

(1) 회사는 회사와 독립적인 유전개발관련 전문 감사인 또는 평가인을 선임할 수 있다.
- 회사는 이들 감사인이나 평가인이 평가업무 등을 수행하는데 필요한 모든 정보를 제공하여야 한다.

〈붙임〉

[그림 A] 석유자원의 분류체계 개요*

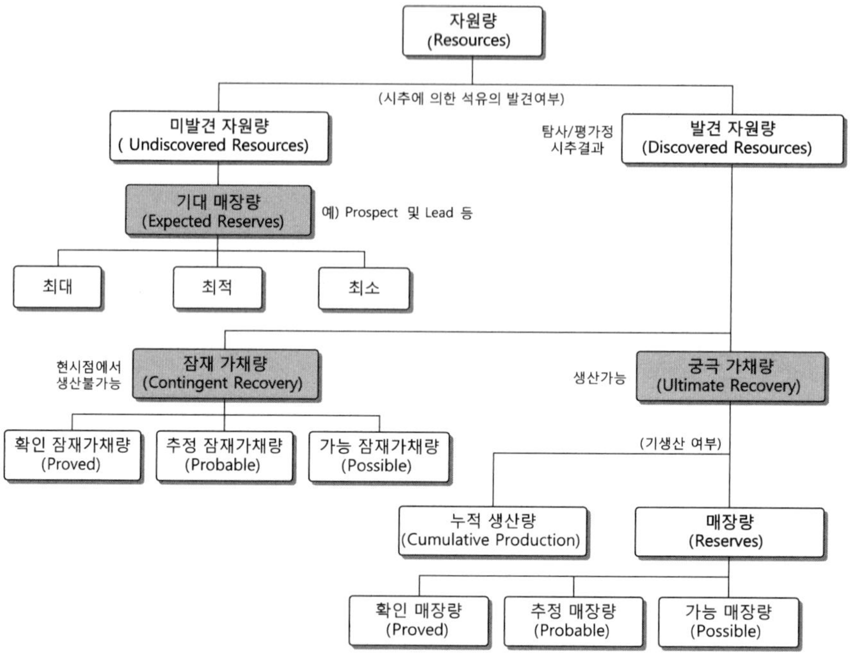

* A classification system of petroleum resoures(Zainul, A, J. et al., 1997), 석유 매장량의 분류체계 및 산출법(한국석유공사 유상수 등 4인, 2000)

– 유전개발 관련 전문 감사인 또는 평가인은 자원의 매장량 및 관련 정보에 대한 전문자격을 보유하거나 관련분야에 대한 적정한 경험 및 경력을 갖추어야 한다.

(2) 회사는 유전개발사업과 관련하여 합병, 주식교환, 중요한 영업양수도, 자산양수도 등의 신고서를 제출하는 경우 외부평가기관이 관련전문가의 의견을 참고하여 평가하도록 요구할 수 있다.

– 회사는 공정한 평가에 도움이 되도록 유전개발사업에 대한 전문가의 의견을 평가인에게 제출할 수 있다.

〈표 A〉 석유자원 분류체계 국제비교 및 한국의 분류체계(안)*

분류 항목	SPE/WPC/AAPG	SPE/WPC/AAPG (세부)	USA SEC	Korea(안)	(번역)
Petroleum Resources	total PIIP			total PIIP**	총 원시석유부존량**
Discovered	Discovered PIIP			Discovered PIIP	발견 원시석유부존량
Produced	commercial	production	produced	cumulative production	누적 생산량
Discovered Commercial		reserves	reserves	reserves**	가채 매장량**
		proved	proved	proved	확인 가채매장량
		probable		probable	추정 가채매장량
		possible		possible	가능 가채매장량
Discovered Sub-commercial	sub-commercial	contingent resources		potential resources	잠재 자원량
Discovered Unrecoverable		Unrecoverable		unrecoverable resources	회수불능 발견자원량
Undiscovered	undiscovered PIIP			undiscovered PIIP	미발견 석유부존량
Undiscovered recoverable	prospective resources			hypothetical	가상 자원량
				speculative	의심 자원량
Undiscovered unrecoverable	unrecoverable			unrecoverable resources	회수불능 미발견자원량

* 한국의 석유자원량 분류체계 제안(허대기, 한국지질자원연구원).

** 석유매장량의 분류체계 및 산출법(류상수 등 4인, 한국시스템공학회, 2000) 참조.

〈표 B〉 가채매장량(Reserve)의 세부 분류*

구분	확인(Proved) 매장량	추정(Probable) 매장량	가능(Possible) 매장량
일반적 정의	지질학적 및 공학적 자료의 평가 결과 • 현재의 경제적 조건, 운영방법, 국가의 법체계 하에서 회수가능성에 대해 타당하고 확실한 예측이 가능한 평가량	지질학적 및 공학적 자료의 평가결과 • 회수가 안 될 가능성보다 될 가능성이 큰 평가량	지질학적 및 공학적 자료의 평가결과 • 개발여부에 대한 확실성 조차 부족한 평가량
경제적 기준	• 평가시점에 있어서의 가격, 비용 등 현재의 경제적 조건	• 현재 또는 미래의 평가된 경제적 조건	• 현재 또는 미래의 평가된 경제적 조건
운영 및 설비	• 처리 및 운반에 필요한 설비가 운영 중이거나 • 이러한 설비의 설치에 대한 합의 또는 확실한 기대가 가능		
상업적 생산성	• 실제 생산 또는 생산시험에 의해 상업적인 생산가능성이 증명된 매장량 • 생산 또는 생산시험이 수행되지 않은 경우 • 검층 및 코아 자료로부터 탄화수소의 부존이 확인되고 • 생산성이 확인된 저류층과 지질학적으로 연결된 곳에 포함되는 매장량	• 검층자료의 분석결과 생산성이 확인매장량과 동일하지 않는 경우	• 탄화수소는 있어 보이나, 상업적수준의 생산에 못 미칠 수도 있는 경우
세부기준	생략	생략	생략

* Detailed reserve classification(Zainul, A.J. et al, 1997).

〈표 C〉 가채매장량(Reserve) 예측방법의 비교

구분	확인(Proved) 매장량	추정(Probable) 매장량	가능(Possible) 매장량
결정론적 방식 (Deterministic)	지질학적 및 공학적 자료의 검토결과, 현재의 경제적 조건하에서 회수가능성에 대한 타당성이 있는 평가량	지질학적 및 공학적 자료의 검토결과, 현재의 경제적 조건하에서 회수 안 될 가능성보다 될 가능성이 큰 평가량	지질학적 및 공학적 자료의 검토결과, 현재의 경제적조건하에서 개발여부에 대한 확실성 조차 부족한 평가량
확률론적 방식 (Probabilistic)	P90 = 확인매장량 = 1P 또는 최소 기대매장량	P50 = 확인 + 추정 매장량 = 2P 또는 적정 기대매장량	P10 = 확인 + 추정 + 가능매장량 = 3P 또는 최대 기대매장량
	실제 가채매장량이 예측한 매장량과 같거나 많을 확률이 90% 이상일 경우	실제 가채매장량이 예측한 매장량과 같거나 많을 확률이 50% 이상일 경우	실제 가채매장량이 예측한 매장량과 같거나 많을 확률이 10% 이상일 경우

A comparison of reserve estimation approaches(Zainul, A.J. et al, 1997).

최종일, IFRS도입에 따른 자원개발회계 개선방안, 2010 자원·에너지법제연구회 연구논문집 262

가) 광물자원개발 지출의 자본화의 범위

한국채택국제회계기준 제1106호는 IFRS 전환 이전에 회사가 적용하였던 회계기준을 수용하고자 하는 관점에서 작성되었으므로, 향후 관련된 기준서가 발표되기 전까지 자원개발과 관련된 지출의 자본화 여부는 개별 회사의 회계정책에 따르는 것으로 봐야 한다. 자원개발지출은 탐사권 매입이전 단계에서의 지출, 탐사 및 평가 단계에서의 지출, 개발 및 생산단계에서의 지출로 구분되며, 단계별 지출액의 자본화에 대한 회계처리이슈는 다음과 같다.

가)-1. 탐사권 매입 이전단계의 지출

앞서 언급한 바와 같이 한국채택국제회계기준 제1106호는 탐사 및 평가단계에서의 발생된 지출을 기준서의 범위로 하고 있으며, 특정지역을 탐사할 수 있는 법적 권리를 취득하기 전에 발생한 지출의 회계처리에 대해서는 언급을 하고 있지 않다. 탐사 및 평가단계 이전에 발생한 지출은 탐사활동 수행의 타당성 검토 비용으로서, 향후 탐사권 획득을 통한 탐사활동 수행, 매장량의 발견 등과 직접적 상관관계 및 실질적 기여도를 규명하기 어려운 것이 일반적이다. 이에 따라 대부분의 국내외 광물자원개발기업은 탐사권 매입 이전의 지출이 자산인식요건을 충족시키지 않는다고 보아 발생하는 시점에 당기 비용으로 처리하고 있다. 최근 IASB가 발표한 Discussion Paper "Extractive Activities"는 자원개발과 관련된 자산은 탐사 및 추출에 대한 법적인 권리를 취득할 때 최초로 인식되는 것이며, 석유나 광물을 발견하고 추출하기 위해 투입되는 탐사, 평가, 개발과 관련된 비용은 이러한 법적인 권리에 가산되는 것으로 보고 있다. 이러한 의견은 법적인 권리인 탐사권을 취득하기 이전에는 관련 지출을 자산으로 인식할 수 없다는 의미로 해석할 수 있다. 다만, 사전단계에서 이루어지는 지출이라고 할지라도 제3자로부터 구입한 탐사 관련 정보, 탐사작업을 진행하기 위해 필요한 유형자산 등 회사가 통제할 수 있는 정보 및 자산에 대해서는 자산화하는 것이 타당하다고 볼 수 있다.

가)-2. 탐사 및 평가단계에서의 지출

IFRS에서는 이 단계에서 발생하는 거래와 사건에 대한 기준을 제공하고 있으나, 자본화될 수 있는 지출의 개략적인 예시만을 제공하고 있을 뿐이며, 지출항목별 자본화 대상여부에 대해서는 회사가 관련 회계정책을 정하여 적용하는 것을 인정하고 있다.

탐사 및 평가단계에서의 지출은 탐사권 취득을 위한 지출, 광구에서의 부존자원여부를 확인하여 기술 및 상업적 실현가능성의 여부를 평가하기 위한 지출로 구분할 수 있다. 탐사권 취득을 위한 지출은 탐사권 취득을 위한 사전 조사 후, 특정광구의 매입을 결정하기 위한 실질적인 활동에 소요되는 비용으로서 Signing Bonus, 광권취득비용 및 각종 자문수수료 등이 해당된다. 탐사권의 취득과 관련된 비용은 탐사평가무형자산으로 자본화하는 것이 일반적이다.

탐사 및 평가를 위한 지출은 탐사 및 평가활동과 직접적인 관련이 있는지에 따라 직접원가와 간접원가로 구분될 수 있다. 직접원가는 탐사를 위한 설비의 취득, 지질 및 지구물리탐사비용(G&G: Geological and Geophysical), 탐사를 위한 시추비용, 굴착비용, 기술 및 상업적 타당성을 평가하는 비용 등이 포함되며, 간접원가는 관리부서의 인건비 등 탐사 및 평가활동을 간접적으로 지원하기 위한 관리원가 및 일반간접원가(G&A: General and administrative) 성격의 원가이다.

직접원가는 탐사 및 평가활동과 직접적으로 관련된 원가이므로 대부분의 광물자원개발회사의 경우 탐사 및 평가단계에서의 지출을 자본화하고 있다. 그러나 간접원가의 경우에는 탐사·평가활동에 귀속될 수 있는지를 확인하여 자본화 여부를 결정하여야 하나 이를 실무적으로 정확히 구분하는 것이 쉽지 않으며, 비용 대비 효익이 크지 않은 것이 사실이다. 한국채택국제회계기준 제1106호는 이러한 간접원가의 자본화가 IAS 2 "재고자산" 및 IAS 38 "무형자산"에서 정한 원가의 구성요소와는 일치하나 IAS 16 "유형자산"과는 일치하지 않는 것처럼 보여질 수 있다는 이유로 기준서에서 간접원가에 대한 자본화 여부를 결정하지 아니하였으며, 이에 따라 각 회사가 관련한 회계정책을 선택하도록 규정하고 있다.

참고로 미국의 경우, FASB(Financial Accounting Standards Board)에서 성공원가법과 전부원가법에 따른 탐사 및 평가비용의 자본화 범위를 다음과 같이 정하고 있다.

〈표 A〉 미국회계기준에 따른 탐사·평가비용의 자본화 범위

구분	성공원가법	전부원가법
Acquisition Cost	자산화	자산화
G&G Cost	비용화	자산화
G&A Cost	비용화	자산화
Exploratory dry hole	비용화	자산화
Exploratory well, Successful	자산화	자산화

자본화된 지출은 생산이 개시되는 시점까지 상각을 하지 않는 것이 타당하다. 그러나 설비의 취득 등으로 인해 발생한 탐사평가유형자산은 생산개시 이전에라도 경제적 내용연수에 따라 상각하며, 감가상각비는 탐사평가무형자산에 가산하여 다시 자본화한다. 결론적으로, 탐사·평가단계에서 자본화된 지출은 손상이 발생하는 경우를 제외하고는 생산개시시점까지

비용이 이연된다.

가)-3. 개발단계에서의 지출

개발비는 탐사결과 경제성 있는 매장량을 발견하여 개발시추 및 생산/공급 시설을 건설하는 활동을 위해 지출되는 비용을 의미한다. 개발비는 개발활동이 자원 존재 유무를 확인하기보다는 생산시스템을 건설하는 것과 관련이 있기 때문에 성공이든 실패든 모든 비용이 자원개발비용으로 인정된다. IFRS를 적용하는 외국 광물자원 기업의 사례를 살펴보면 파이프 및 펌프, 탱크 등 생산에 필요한 제반 시추설비의 취득 및 설치비용에 대해서 성공하지 않은 개발관련 비용도 모두 자본화하고 생산이 개시되는 시점에 상각을 하고 있다.

나) 감가상각 회계처리

나)-1. 감가상각 방법의 적용

감가상각은 고정자산의 취득원가에서 법존가액을 차감한 금액을 그 자산의 추정내용연수(또는 채굴가능기간)동안 합리적인 방법으로 배분하는 것으로 이는 자산에 대한 평가과정은 아니다. IFRS에서는 감가상각에 대한 일반적인 규정을 언급하고 있을 뿐, 광물자원개발회사에 대한 감가상각방법에 대해서는 별도로 규정하고 있지 않으므로 각 회사의 회계정책에 따라 합리적이라고 판단되는 감가상각방법을 적용하면 될 것이다.

탐사·평가·개발 및 생산 과정에서 자본화된 원가는 대부분 생산량비례법(a Unit of Production, UOP)에 의해 상각하는 것이 일반적이나 일부 회사는 정액법으로 상각하고 있다. 조사대상회사 중 현재 자원개발과 관련된 유·무형자산에 대해 감가상각을 하고 있는 회사는 8곳이었으며, 이들 중 1곳을 제외한 나머지 회사는 모두 생산량비례법에 의해 감가상각을 하는 것으로 조사되었다. 외국의 광물자원개발회사의 경우도 거의 대부분 생산량비례법을 사용하고 있으며 정액법을 사용하는 것은 매우 예외적인 것으로 인식되고 있다.

나)-2. 상각기준의 결정

현재 대부분의 광물자원개발회사가 적용하고 있는 생산량비례법과 관련하여 IFRS에서는 구체적인 상각방법을 규정하고 있지는 않다. 현재 IFRS를 적용하는 외국 광물자원개발회사들의 사례를 살펴보면, 성공원가법을 적용하는 경우 일반적으로 자원의 탐사·개발과 관련된 원가에 대해 확인개발 가채매장량(Proved Developed Reserve)을 기준으로 상각을 하고 있다. 다만, 탐사권의 취득과 관련된 원가는 확인 가채매장량(Proved Reserve) 또는 확인·추정 가채매장량(Proved Plus Probable Reserve)을 기준으로 상각하는 것이 타당하다고 판단되며, 실제로 대다수의 외국 기업들이 이 방식을 따르고 있다. 전부원가법을 적용하는 회사는 일반적으로 각각의 원가중심점별로 자본화된 모든 원가에 대해 확인 가채매장량 (Proved Reserve) 또는 확인 · 추정 가채매장량(Proved Plus Probable Reserve)을 기준으로 상각을 실시하고 있다.

다) 정부대여금의 회계처리

해외자원개발을 위해 조달하는 자금 중 '해외자원개발사업에 소요되는 자금의 융자기준'(지식경제부 고시)에 따라 융자받는 자금(이하 에특기금)은 시장이자율보다 낮은 이자율로 대여받는 것이 일반적이며, 성공불 융자의 경우에는 실패 확정시 원리금을 감면받는 상환면제가능대출(forgivable loan)이므로 대여를 받는 자는 일반 시장에서의 대여에 비해 상대적으로 효익을 얻게 된다. 이는 일종의 정부보조금으로 볼 수 있으므로 일정 요건을 만족하는 경우 한국채택국제회계기준 제1020호 '정부보조금의 회계처리와 정부지원의 공시'에 따라 정부보조금을 인식하여야 한다. 또한, 에특기금도 IFRS상 차입금의 정의를 충족하므로 원칙적으로 공정가치평가 및 차입기간 중의 이자인식 및 외화환산 등의 회계처리를 수행하여야 한다. 기존 한국회계기준과 IFRS에서의 에특기금에 대한 회계처리는 다음과 같다.

〈표 B〉 정부대여금의 회계처리

구분	한국회계기준(기존)	한국채택국제회계기준
차입시	• 차입금액을 부채로 계상	• 공정가치를 부채로 계상 • 차입금액과 공정가치의 차이는 정부 보조금으로 인식
차입기간 중	• 이자 및 원금상환 인식 • 외화환산 인식 • 성공불 융자의 경우 거치기간 동안 회계처리 없음	• 이자 및 원금상환 인식 • 외화환산 인식 • 현재가치할인차금 상각 • 정부보조금은 원본자산의 상각형태에 따라 상각비에서 차감 • 성공불 융자의 경우 거치기간 중에도 이자 및 환산 손익을 인식
기타	• 원리금 감면시 자산 감액 및 채무면제 인식 • 특별부담금 지급시 비용인식	

IFRS에서는 정부로부터 시장이자율보다 낮은 이자율로 자금을 조달함에 따른 효익을 정부보조금으로 처리하도록 하고 있으며, 동 차입금은 한국채택국제회계기준 제1039호 '금융상품: 인식과 측정'에 따라 공정가치로 측정하도록 하고 있다. 시장이자율보다 낮은 이자율의 효익은 에특기금의 공정가치와 차입금액의 차이로 계산되며, 관련 효익은 보조금으로 취득한 자산이 비용으로 인식되는 기간에 걸쳐 체계적인 기준에 따라 당기손익으로 인식한다.

융자금 차입시 공정가치의 측정은 상환 스케줄표에 따른 원금 및 이자의 지급스케줄을 유효이자율로 할인하여 계산된다. 그러나, 일부 광물자원개발회사는 에특기금의 공정가치와 차입금액의 차이가 중요하지 않다고 판단하여 공정가치를 평가하지 않고, 이에 따라 정부보조금을 인식하지 않고 있다. 이러한 회사는 정부보조금과 관련된 시장은 일반 채권시장과 구분하여 보는 것이 타당하며, 이 경우 계약상 표면이자율은 정부보조금시장의 이자율과 중요한 차이가 없을 것이므로 에특기금의 장부가액과 공정가액 간에도 중요한 차이가 없을 것이라고 판단한다. 또한, 성공불 융자의 경우에는 특별부담금 지급시 실질 지급이자율이 시장이자율과 크게 다르지 않을 것이므로 에특기금의 공정가치가 중요하지 않다는 입장이다.

성공불 융자와 관련하여, 한국채택국제회계기준 제1020호에서는 정부의 상환면제가능대출은 당해 기업이 대출의 상환면제조건을 충족할 것이라는 합리적인 확신이 있을 때 정부보조금으로 처리하도록 하고 있다. 이에 따라 성공불 융자는 탐사가 실패로 판명될 때 채무면제금액을 정부보조금으로 인식하며, 그 이전까지는 공정가치로 평가하는 것이 타당하다. 실제 정부로부터 상환의무면제와 관련된 승인을 받기 이전이라도 탐사의 실패가 확정적이고 정부로부터 상환의무면제를 받을 것이 확실시되는 경우에 관련 금액을 정부보조금으로 인식할 수 있을 것이다.

라) 공시사항에 대한 개선방향

재무보고(financial reporting)의 목적은 기업 외부에 있는 이해관계자에게 그들의 경제적 의사결정에 유용한 정보를 제공하는 것이다. 그러나 재무제표에 포함된 손익계산서, 현금흐름표의 내용으로는 회사가 투자한 광물자원개발자산에 대해 제한된 정보만을 확인할 수밖에 없으므로 추가적인 정보의 주석 공시를 통해 이해관계자의 경제적 의사결정을 돕고 경영진에 대한 평가를 할 수 있도록 하는 것은 매우 중요하다.

IFRS를 적용하는 다수의 외국 광물자원개발회사는 그들이 투자한 자산에 대해서 폭넓은 정보를 주석으로 공시하고 있다. 이러한 공시는 정부기관 등의 규제에 의해서 이루어지는 경우도 있으나, 관련 정보의 공시가 중요하다고 생각하는 회사의 자발적인 의지에 의해서 이루어지기도 한다. 이와는 대조적으로, 대부분의 국내 광물자원개발회사는 광구취득사실, 자원개발과 관련된 지출 정도만을 간략하게 주석으로 공시하고 있을 뿐이며, 설문결과 향후 추가적인 정보의 공시 여부에 대해서도 구체적인 계획을 갖고 있지 않는 것으로 조사되었다.

현재 광물자원개발회사의 주석공시와 관련된 국제적인 기준은 존재하지 않으며, IFRS에서도 광물자원의 탐사 및 평가와 관련한 회계정책, 탐사와 평가단계에서 발생한 자산, 부채, 수익, 비용, 영업 및 투자 현금흐름을 공시하도록 규정하고 있을 뿐이다. 최근 IASB가 발표한 Discussion Paper "Extractive Activities"는 추출산업에 대한 회계기준 및 공시사항에 대한 제안을 담고 있다. 물론 Discussion Paper는 기준서로서의 효력이 없으며, 향후 토론과정에서 많은 부분이 수정될 수 있으나, 추출산업에 대한 심도있는 연구 내용을 담고 있어 이를 통해 공시사항에 대한 기본적인 가이드라인을 고민해 볼 수 있을 것으로 판단된다. Discussion Paper에서 제안하고 있는 주석공시사항은 매장량 및 매장량의 공정가치 평가, 영업성과에 대한 평가를 포함하고 있으며 구체적인 공시사항은 다음과 같다.

〈표 C〉 주요공시사항 (Discussion Paper, "Extractive Activities")

구분	주요 공시 사항
매장량에 대한 가치평가	1) 매장량 (Quantity of reserve) 2) 추출활동을 통해 발생될 것으로 예측되는 현금흐름 및 Fair Value 3) 매장량 및 매장량의 공정가치평가를 위해 사용된 주요 가정 및 이러한 가정에 대한 민감도 분석 4) 연도별 매장량 및 매장량의 공정가치 변동에 대한 설명
영업성과 평가	1) 생산단계에서 발생한 수익 및 생산원가 2) 탐사, 평가 및 개발과 관련하여 비용으로 인식한 금액 3) 탐사, 평가 및 개발과 관련하여 자산으로 인식한 금액

라)-1. 매장량의 공시

광물자원개발회사의 재무적 상황 및 미래 현금유입을 평가함에 있어서 가장 중요한 요소는 매장량이므로 이에 대한 정보는 이해관계자의 의사결정에 있어 필수적이라고 할 수 있다. 매장량의 정의 및 평가에 대해서 여러기관의 다양한 의견과 방법이 존재하므로 이 중 어떤 것을 공통의 기준으로 선정해야 할지를 결정할 필요가 있다. Discussion Paper에서는 광물(Mineral)의 매장량을 추정하고 분류하는 데에는 Committee for Mineral Reserves International Reporting Standards(CRIRSCO) Template을 사용하고 석유 및 가스 매장량을 추정하고 분류하는 데에는 Society of Petroleum Engineers(SPE)에서 발행된 Petroleum Resource Management System(PRMS)을 사용하여, 확인 가채매장량과 및 추정 가채매장량을 공시할 것을 제안하고 있다. IFRS를 적용하고 있는 외국의 광물자원개발회사들은 자신들이 추정하는 가채매장량의 범위와 연도별 추이 변화, 재무제표에 미치는 영향 등을 연차보고서 등에 기재하고 있으며, 향후 국내 회사들도 투자자들의 이해 증진을 위하여 매장량에 대한 공시를 적극적으로 검토하여야 할 것이다.

라)-2. 매장량의 공정가치 공시

회사가 투자한 광물 및 석유 등으로부터 발생할 향후 현금흐름과 이를 기초로 계산된 매장량에 대한 공정가치는 정보이용자가 자신이 투자한 회사의 가치와 경영진의 능력을 평가하는 데 매우 중요한 자료로서 활용될 수 있다. 매장량의 공정가치를 공시하는 것은 정보

이용자에게 정확한 공정가치에 대한 정보를 제공하는 목적보다는 경영진이 수립한 가정에 따라 가장 적정하다고 판단하는 공정가치를 정보 이용자가 참고할 수 있다는 점에서 그 의미를 찾을 수 있을 것이다. 또한, 공정가치에 대한 결과와 함께 공정가치를 산정함에 있어 고려한 주요 가정들에 대한 민감도 분석을 함께 공시함으로써 공정가치의 불확실성 평가를 위한 정보를 제공하는 것도 적극적으로 검토할 필요가 있다. IFRS를 적용하고 있는 외국 광물자원 개발회사들은 지역별로 미래의 현금흐름 및 매장량의 공정가치를 공시하고 있다.

또한, 일부 IFRS 적용 회사들은 주석에서 당기 중 공정가치의 변동 원인을 설명하여, 매장량, 판매가격 및 생산원가 등 주요 요인의 변동으로 인한 공정가치의 민감도 정보를 제공하고 있다. 이를 통해 정보이용자는 어떤 요소가 매장량의 공정가치변동에 가장 큰 영향을 주는지를 확인하고 이러한 요소들에 대한 분석을 통해 향후 회사에 대한 투자의사결정에 참고할 수 있다. 회계기간 중의 공정가치의 변동과 관련하여 매장량의 변동, 판매가격의 변동, 추정생산 및 개발원가의 변동, 할인율의 변동, 세금효과의 변동 등으로 구분하여 설명하고 있다.

라)-3. 영업성과에 대한 공시

IFRS 적용 기업은 기업에서 수행하는 정유사업, 석유화학사업 등 다른 업무부문과는 별도로 광물자원의 생산·판매 활동의 결과로 발생된 영업성과를 별도로 구분하여 공시하기도 한다. 구분된 영업성과에 대한 정보를 바탕으로 정보이용자는 해당 회사와 산업에 대한 이해를 높이고 수익 및 생산원가의 분석을 용이하게 할 수 있다. 일반적으로 외국의 IFRS 적용 기업은 수익의 경우 제3자에 대한 수익 금액과 관계사간의 수익금액을 구분해서 표시하고 있으며, 원가는 탐사, 개발 및 생산단계별 지출액을 지역별로 공시하고 있다.

노트와 질문

KOGAS의 공시서류를 통하여 해외사업에 대한 투자나 이를 위한 자금조달에 대한 공시의 정도를 살펴보고 이를 개선할 점이 있다면 어떻게 개선할 수 있을지에 대하여 논의하여 보라.

제 3 장

에너지자원보유국과 투자국

1. 국가주권이 미치는 범위

우리 헌법은 "대한민국의 영토는 한반도와 그 부속도서로 한다"고 정하고 있다. 주권이 미치는 범위는 영토뿐만 아니라 영해도 포함하는바, 영해에 관하여는 아무런 언급이 없지만 헌법에 의하여 체결·공포된 조약과 일반적으로 승인된 국제법규가 국내법과 동일한 효력이 미치므로 영해의 범위를 정하기 위하여는 조약과 국제법규를 살펴야 한다. 1982년 UN해양법은 기저선으로부터 12해리의 영해와,[1] 12해리의 접속수역,[2] 200해리의 해저광물개발권을 포함한 제한된 주권을 행사할 수 있는 배타적 경제수역을[3] 규정하고 있다. 또한 대륙붕에 관한 한 200해리를 초과하더라도 최소한 대륙붕의 외부경계까지의 해저자원개발권을 규정하고 있다.[4] 우리는 이에 따라 "영해 및 접속수역법"과 "배타적 경제수역법"을 제정, 직선기선으로부터 12해리, 24해리, 200해리를 각각 영해, 접속수역, 배타적 경제수역으로 정하였다. 또한 우리나라는 일찍이 1970. 1. 해저광물자원개발법을 제정하고 그 시행령에서 해저광물인 석유와 천연가스의 개발구역인 해저광구를 정하며 해저광업권은 국가만 가질 수 있음을 명확히 하였다. 이어서 1974년 한일간에 인접한 대륙붕 공동개발에 관한 협정을 체결하였으나 그 효력이 2028년 만료될 것이므로 그 이후에 일본과 공동개발광구를 둘러싸고, 한국과 중국간에는 해자법상 제4해저광구를 둘러싸고 다툼이 발생할 여지가 있다.

1) UNCLOS 3조.
2) Id., 66조.
3) Id., 56조.
4) Id., 76조.

신창훈, 대한민국의 대륙붕선언의 기원과 1974년 한일대륙붕공동개발협정의 의의, 13 서울국제법연구 57 (2006)[1]

가. 대한민국의 대륙붕선언의 기원과 의의

비록 대륙붕제도에 대한 포괄적 권리 선언이라 하기에는 다소 애매한 점도 존재하지만 대한민국의 대륙붕선언의 기원은 1952년 "인접해양의 주권에 관한 대통령선언"으로 거슬러 올라갈 수 있을 것이다. 또한 한일 간의 대륙붕을 둘러싼 분쟁의 직접적 시발점이 되었던 것은 1970년 1월 1일에 제정된 해저광물자원개발법[2]과 같은 해 5월 30일에 공포된 동법시행령[3]이라 할 수 있다. 따라서 이 장에서는 1952년 선언과 1970년 동법 및 그 시행령의 의의에 관해 개괄적으로 분석해 볼 것이다.

1) 1952년 인접해양의 주권에 관한 대통령 선언

1945년 9월 28일 미국의 트루먼 대통령이 "보존수역에 관한 선언"[4]과 "대륙붕의 지하 및 해저 천연자원에 관한 미합중국선언"[5]을 한 이래 중남미 국가들을 포함한 다수의 국가들이 어업보존수역과 대륙붕을 선언하게 된 관행을 따라, 대한민국 정부는 1952년 1월 18일 "인접해양의 주권에 관한 대통령선언"(동선언에 의해 획정된 선을 소위 평화선 또는 평화주권선, 일본에서는 이승만라인이라 함)을 선포하였다. 당해 선언에서 대한민국 정부는 "국가의 영토인 한반도 및 도서의 연안에 인접한 해붕의 상하에 기지되고 또는 장래에 발견될 모든 자원광물 및 수산물을 국가에 가장 이롭게 보호, 보존 및 이용하기 위하여 그 심도 여하를 불문하고 인접 해붕에 대한 국가의 주권을 보존하며 또 시행한다"[6]라고 하여 비록 명칭은 "해붕"이라는 용어를 사용하였지만 대륙붕과 그 상부수역의 생물 및 무생물 자원에 관한 보호, 보존 및 이용을 위해 한반도와 도서연안에 인접한 해붕의 상하에 대한민국의 주권(sovereignty)을 선

---

1. 박창건, 국제해양레짐의 변화에서 한일대륙붕협정의 재조명, 45 한국정치학회보 165(2008) 참고.
2. 대한민국, 해저광물자원개발법, 법률 제2184호, 1970. 1. 1. 제정, 법률5781호 1999. 2. 5. 일부개정, 법률 제6756호 2002. 12. 5. 일부개정.
3. 대한민국, 해저광물자원개발법 시행령, 최종개정 — 대통령령 제10645호 법제명변경 및 일부개정 2006. 8. 17.("해저광물자원개발법시행령"에서 변경).
4. 당해 선언의 정식명칭은 "Policy of the United States with Respect to Coastal Fisheries in Certain Areas of High Seas," Presidental Proclamation No. 2668 (1945. 9. 28.). 선언의 내용은 http://www.oceanlaw.net/tests/truman2.htm에서 찾아볼 수 있음.
5. 당해 선언의 정식명칭은 "Policy of the United States with Respect to the Natural Resources of the Subsoil and Sea Bed of the Continental Shelf," Presidental Proclamation No. 2667 (1945. 9. 28.). 선언의 내용은 http://www.oceanlaw.net/texts/truman1.htm에서 찾아볼 수 있음.
6. 국무원고시 제14호(1952. 1. 18.). 당해 선언의 구체적 내용은 김석우, "대륙붕에 대한 연안국의 권리" (서울대 석사학위논문, 1970. 5.), pp. 167-169 참조.

포하였다. 비록 해붕의 상부수역과 관련하여서는 동선언 4항이 "인접해양에 대한 본 주권의 선언은 공해상의 자유 통항권을 방해하지 않는다"라고 규정하고 있으며, 미국과 중국 등의 항의각서에 대한 회답각서에서 "동 평화선이 영해의 확장을 의미하지 아니한다"라고 답변함으로써 영해적 성격을 지닌 것임을 부인하고 있지만,[7] 대륙붕과 관련하여서는 자원의 보호, 보존 및 이용을 위한 관할권 (jurisdiction) 및 통제권(control)을 선포한 트루먼 선언,[8] 칠레, 에콰도르, 페루 등의 산티아고 선언상의 대륙붕의 관념[9] 및 1958년 대륙붕에 관한 제네바협약[10] 등과 비교해 볼 경우 배타적 주권과 관할권을 선포한 산티아고 선언에 가까운 법리를 나타낸 셈이 되었다.

평화선 선포이후 일본의 끈질긴 항의 끝에 해붕의 상부수역과 관련한 어업보존으로서의 조치는 결국 한일국교정상화 직후 체결되어 1965년 12월 18일에 발효한 한일어업협정에 의해 양국간의 어업문제에 관한 한 평화선이 효력을 정지하는 셈이 되었다.[11] 그러나 주의를 요하는 것은 대륙붕에 관한 권리에 관하여서는 동 선언에 의해 창설된 평화선이 양국 간에 여전히 효력을 발생하고 있었다고 보아야 할 것이다.

2) 1970년 해저광물자원개발법 및 동법 시행령

서해와 동지나해에 위치한 대륙붕을 둘러싼 주변국간의 긴장관계는 1968년 이후부터 본격화되기 시작하였다. 1966년 UN의 극동경제위원회(ECAFE)는 동아시아의 잠재적 광물자원을 탐사할 목적으로 "아시아 연안지역 광물자원 공동탐사조정위원회"(Committee for Coordination of Joint Prospecting for Mineral Resources in Asia Offshore)를 설치하여 서해와 동지나해의 광범위한 지질학적 탐사작업을 후원하였다. 그 결과 작성된 1969년 보고서는 "이 지역중에 석유와 가스 매장이 가장 유망시되는 구역은 대만 동북부의 20만 평방킬로미터의 해저이다. 이 지역의 침전물의 두께는 거의 2km를 초과하고 있고 대만에서는 5km의 신세기 침전

---

7. Ibid, pp. 122-123.

8. 당해 선언은 "the Government of the United States regards the natural resources of the subsoil and sea bed of the continental shelf beneath the high seas but contiguous to the coasts of the United States as appertaining to the United States, subject to its jurisdiction and control"이라고 하여 천연자원을 미국의 관할권과 통제하에 있는 것으로 선포함.

9. 1952년 8월 18일 칠레, 에콰도르, 페루가 선포한 산티아고 선언은 200해리까지의 인접수역과 해저에 대해 주권적 권리가 아니라 "배타적 주권과 관할권"(exclusive sovereignty and jurisdiction)을 선포하고 있다. 당해 선언의 구체적 내용은 U.S. Department of State, *Limits in the Seas, No. 88. Maritime Boundary: Ecuador-Peru (1979),* pp. 4-5 참조.

10. 1958년 대륙붕에 관한 제네바협약 제2조 1항에서는 연안국이 보유하는 권리를 주권적 권리(sovereign rights)로 표현하고 있다. "연안국은 대륙붕에 대해 이를 탐사하고, 그 천연자원을 개발하기 위하여 주권적 권리를 행사한다."(The coastal State exercises over the continental shelf sovereign rights for the purpose of exploring it and exploiting its naural resources).

11. 김석우, *supra note 6*, p. 122.

물을 포함하여 9km에 달하고 있다. 대만과 일본간의 대륙붕은 세계에서 가장 비옥한 석유 매장지대일 개연성이 크다. 석유 및 가스에 대한 두 번째 유망 구역은 세 개의 광대한 해분이 있는 서해 해저이다. 이들 해분은 상호 연결되어 있으며, 그 중간 해분은 한국근처에 있고 나머지 두 개의 해분은 중국 근처에 있다. 이들 해분은 약 1.5km 두께의 침전물을 내포하고 있으며, 이 침전물은 보통 대륙붕하의 침전물보다 고도의 유기물질을 포함하고 있다. 하층토의 수평선을 나타내는 지층은 유기물질이 풍성한 하층토 간의 석유 매장층으로서의 역할을 하는 사층일 가능성이 크다"[12]라고 하여 주변국의 대륙붕에 대한 관심과 개발참여에 촉발점이 되었다.

대한민국은 국내법의 정비를 통해 발빠른 행보를 내딛었다. 대한민국 정부는 1970년 1월 한반도와 그 부속도서의 해안에 인접한 대륙붕에 존재하는 석유 및 천연가스 등 천연자원을 합리적으로 개발함으로써 산업발전에 기여할 목적으로 해저광물자원개발법[13]을 제정하였다. 또한 같은 해 5월에 동법시행령을 공포하면서 제3항에 근거하여 면적이 약 30만 평방킬로미터에 달하는 7개의 해저개발광구를 일방적으로 설정하였으며, 이후 서구 석유개발회사들과 개발계약 등을 체결[14]하였다. 1952년 인접해양의 주권에 관한 대통령선언 3항에 의해 창설된 평화선에 의한 대륙붕의 외측한계는 1958년 대륙붕에 관한 제네바협약상의 대륙붕의 정의와 1969년 북해대륙붕사건에서 국제사법재판소(ICJ)가 판단한 대륙붕의 정의에 비추어 볼 때 다소 작위적이었다고 평가할 수 있을 것이다. 이에 비해 1970년 해저광물자원개발법과 동법시행령에 의해 설정된 7개 해저개발광구가 형성하는 기하학적 다면체는 남동해안의 일본과의 관계에 있어서는 대만 북부와 유구열도 부근에서 시작하여 일본 규슈 앞바다에까지 이르는 상부 수심 400미터 이상의 대한민국 영토의 자연적 연장의 종단인 오키나와 해구를 외측한계로 함으로써 1969년 북해대륙붕사건에서 확립된 "육지영토의 자연적 연장 원칙"에 부합하고 서해안의 중국과의 관계에 있어서는 "등거리선 원칙"에 부합하는 외측한계를 지니고 있다고 평가할 수 있다.[15]

동법의 목적에서 볼 수 있듯이, 비록 개발대상을 대륙붕에 부존하는 천연자원 중 석유

---

12. ECAFE(Economic Commission of Asia and Far East), *Technical Bulletin,* Vol. 2, pp. 3-43. 인용문은 김동조, "한일 대륙붕협정 체결의 의의와 전망," 국민회의보(1974. 3.), pp. 113-4에서 재인용.

13. 해저광물개발법 제1조.

14. "대한민국은 1969. 4. 15. 제 2, 4광구에 대한 채광계약을 미국의 Gulf회사와, 1970. 1. 28. 제 3, 6광구에 대한 탐사계약을 Royal Dutch Shell 회사와 1970. 2. 27. 제 1, 5광구에 대한 채광계약을 Caltex회사와 1970. 9. 24. 제7광구에 대한 계약을 Wendell Phillips(그 후 Koam회사로 이양)와 체결하여 동해저 광구의 탐사와 개발에 대한 구체적 조치를 취하였다." 외무부, 한일간대륙붕공동개발협정 및 경계선협정에 관한 해설(1978. 11), p. 91.

15. 노명준, "한일간의 대륙붕 공동개발에 관련된 법적 문제," 외교·안보 제1권(1978. 1), p. 170; 백진현, "우리의 해양관할권과 그 관리방안," 해양 21세기(나남, 1998), p. 4; 외교통상부 오윤경 외 20인, 현대국제법 —외교실무자들이 본 이론과 실제— (2000), pp. 308-309 등 참조.

및 천연가스 등 광물자원에 한정하여 대륙붕의 또 다른 천연자원인 정착성 어종 등을 포함하고 있지는 않기 때문에, 해저개발광구의 설정이 연안국의 온전한 주권적 권리를 모두 포함하는 대륙붕선언으로 취급하기에는 부족한 측면도 존재한다.[16] 그러나 해저광물자원의 개발, 보존 및 탐사 등에 관한 주권적 권리를 명백히 함으로써 특정 자원과 관련한 대륙붕의 선포라는 기능적 측면을 지니고 있다고 보아도 큰 무리가 없을 것이다.

동법의 제정을 통한 국내법의 정비와 7개 해저개발광구의 설정 등 대한민국 정부의 1969년 CAFE 보고서에 대한 민첩한 대응은 한일대륙봉협정의 협상과정에서 일본보다 우위에 서서 협상을 주도하는 외교적 성과를 달성하는 밑거름이 되었다고 평가할 수 있다. 대한민국의 이와 같은 조치는 결국 1969년 3월 대한민국에서 성안중이던 대륙붕광물자원개발법안의 개요 통보 요청과 1971년 6월 한일간 대륙붕경계획정을 위한 정부간 협의 요청 등[17] 일본 정부를 부산하게 만드는 계기가 되었다.

나. 한일대륙봉공동개발협정 체결과 그 배경

1972년 10월부터 1973년 7월까지 불과 9개월여 만에 양국은 실무접촉을 통하여 1974년 1월 30일 "한일간에 인접한 대륙봉 남부구역 공동개발에 관한 협정"과 그 부속 "의사합의록," "굴착의무에 관한 교환각서," "해상충돌 예방에 관한 교환각서," "해상오염제거 및 방지에 관한 교환각서," "한일간에 인접한 대륙봉 북부구역 경계획정에 관한 협정" 및 그 부속 "의사합의록"이라는 일련의 협정을 조인하였다. 대륙봉문제와 관련하여 9개월이라는 짧은 기간 내에 일련의 협정이 조인된 전례를 찾기가 곤란하여 협정 체결 후 국내에서는 졸속에 대한 우려도 존재하였지만,[18] 이는 양국 간의 대륙봉 개발에 대한 절실함과 상호선린관계의 돈독이라는 측면에서 이해할 수도 있는 문제라 할 수 있다. 협상의 시기는 짧았지만 당해 협정은 많은 문제를 미결의 상태로 남겨두고 개발이라는 기능적 실리적 측면에서 합의를 달성하였으며 중국의 강력한 항의가 있었던 터라 일본에서는 협정의 비준안이 통과되는 데 무려 4년의 시간이 흘러가고 말았듯이 체결과정과 발효시에 흥미로운 여러 배경이 존재하는데 지면관계상 정치적, 경제적 및 국제법적 배경에 대해 개괄적으로 논해 보고자 한다.

---

16. 참고로 1958년 대륙붕에 관한 제네바 협약의 제2조 4항은 "본협약에서 언급되는 천연자원이란 해상 및 해저지하의 광물과 그 밖의 비생산자원 및 정착성어종에 속하는 생물, 즉 심취기에 해상의 표면 또는 하부에 정지하고 있거나 해상 또는 해저지하에 줄곧 밀착해 있지 않으면 움직일 수 없는 생물로써 구성된다"라고 규정하여 정착성 어종을 대륙붕의 천연자원에 포함시키고 있다.

17. 김동조, *supra note 12,* pp. 114-115 참조.

18. 이강열, "한일대륙봉협정과 그 문제점," 자유공론(1973.9), p. 75.

1) 협정 체결의 국제정치적 및 경제적 배경

한일 양국간의 대륙붕 문제는 단순한 양국 간의 문제에 국한된다기보다는 국제적 성격을 지닌 문제로서 국제정치의 영향과 동아시아의 경제발전과도 밀접한 관계를 지니고 있는 문제로 인식될 수 있다. 국제정치적 배경과 관련하여 비록 관련 논문에서 출처가 명확히 밝혀지고 있지는 않지만, 당시 수년 동안의 세계적 에너지 위기로 인해 복잡한 국제정치 역관계를 새로이 조성하는 요인으로 자원주권의 문제가 대두되는 국제정치의 현실과 1972년 2월 미국 닉슨대통령의 북경방문으로 조성된 미국과 중국간의 화해와 관계진전을 위한 정치적 배려 속에서 미국무성은 분쟁요소를 안고 있는 해역의 해상에 미국인 상사나 회사 또는 개인이 끼어들지 말도록 신중히 권고함으로써 미국과 중국이 한국과 일본 및 대만의 해저개발문제에 간섭할 의도를 지니고 있었다는 보도에 영향을 받아 대륙붕 개발에 우선적 지위를 확보하기 위해, 한국 및 대만 등이 개발문제에 적극적으로 참여할 수밖에 없었다는 설도 제기되었다.[19] 또한 1972년 5월 15일 오키나와 반환에 즈음하여 15세기 초에 성립되어 16세기까지 국제무역으로 번성했던 류큐왕국의 재건을 꿈꾸는 독립운동을 저지하기 위해 일본 정부가 서둘러 대한민국 정부와 대륙붕문제를 해결하는 데 총력을 기울일 수밖에 없었다는 설득력 있는 주장도 제기되었다.

국제정치적 배경에 의한 역관계의 조정 측면도 무시할 수 없지만 한일 간의 대륙붕협정 체결의 가장 직접적인 요인은 주변국의 경제적 실리에 있다는 분석이 가장 정확하다고 할 수 있다. 1969년 ECAFE 보고서에 가장 민감한 반응을 보였던 대한민국, 일본 및 대만은 모두 많은 석유를 소비함에도 불구하고 그 수요를 거의 수입에 의존하고 있었다는 공통점을 지니고 있었기 때문에 산유국이 될 수 있다는 꿈을 현실화시킬 수 있는 개연성을 지닌 동 보고서에 흥분하지 않을 수 없었다.[20] 이로 인해 대한민국, 일본 및 대만 간의 양립 불가능한 국제법 원칙에 근거한 관할권 주장과 인근 섬에 대한 영유권 주장이 이어져 많은 구역이 관할권 중복구역이 되어 결국 각국이 설정한 총 17개 해저광구 중 4개를 제외한 13개 광구에서 관할권이 중첩되는 결과를 초래하게 되었다.[21]

관할권 주장과 인근 섬에 대한 영유권 주장의 중첩은 법적 측면에서의 분석에서도 많은 시사점을 가져다 줄 수 있지만 대만문제 및 한반도 문제와 관련하여 필연적으로 중국의 정치적 혹은 선전적 개입을 야기할 수밖에 없었다는 국제정치적 측면에서의 분석도 흥미로운 시사점을 제공해 준다. 1969년 ECAFE 보고서가 야기한 서해와 동지나해에서의 석유개발경쟁과 관련하여 중국은 대륙붕개발이라는 경제적 실리에 관심을 두었다기보다는 대륙붕문제를

19. Ibid., pp. 70-71 참조.
20. 박춘호, "한국의 대륙붕경계 문제," 해법회지 Vol. 6, No. 1(1984), pp. 62-64 참조.
21. 김동조, *supra* note 12, p. 114; 박춘호, ibid., p. 68 참조.

대미, 대일 및 대한반도 외교의 수단으로 활용한 측면도 존재하기 때문이다. 당시 일본과 중국은 국교정상화의 목전에 있었으므로 일본은 중국과의 관계에 주의를 기울이지 않을 수 없는 입장이었고, 중국은 당시 북한과의 관계 때문에 대륙붕문제의 협상 파트너로 대한민국을 생각할 수 없었다. 이러한 현실은 추후 중국과 일본의 태도에 충분히 반영되었다. 우선 1970년 11월 대한민국, 일본, 대만은 국가 간의 관계를 설정하려는 정치적 부담 때문에 공동개발을 위한 민간기업으로 구성된 협력위원회를 서울에서 조직한 적이 있었다. 그러나 대륙붕에 대한 관할권 문제는 연안국의 주권적 권리에 속하기 때문에 민간기업으로 구성된 단체의 비정부 간 조치에는 당연히 한계를 내포하고 있었고, 공동개발에 성공하더라도 개발된 석유의 분배문제를 비정부 간 단체에 의해 해결하기에는 미흡하다는 문제점과 공동개발 시도자체가 중국을 자극할 우려가 있었는데 결국은 같은 해 12월 중국의 강력한 항의 등 다분히 정치적 문제로 공동개발 시도가 무산되고 말았다.[22] 물론 이러한 공동개발시도 실패의 또 다른 배경에는 1971년 4월 미국무성이 중국이 서해나 동지나해에서 미국 탐사선을 나포하더라도 미국정부는 외교적 보호권의 행사 등과 같이 이 문제에 개입하는 일은 없을 것이라는 입장을 천명한 적이 있었다는 점도 존재했다.[23]

한편 대만문제를 통해 중국을 자극할 필요가 없다는 점에 대해서 대한민국과 일본간에 공감대가 형성되어, 2년 후인 1972년부터 대만을 제외하고 한일 양국만이 협상을 진행키로 합의하여, 1972년 9월 제6차 한일 정기각료회의에 즈음하여 자원 개발의 긴급성과 양국의 공동이익 추구라는 대국적 견지에서 관할권 주장이 중첩되는 구역을 공동개발하자는 데 원칙적으로 합의하게 되었고, 이러한 원칙합의를 기초로 하여 양국의 실무자는 1972년 10월부터 서울과 동경을 오가며 총 9차례에 이르는 회담 끝에 1973년 7월 공동개발협정안을 확정하고, 1974년 1월 30일에는 이 협정안이 서울에서 정식 서명되었다.[24]

더구나 1973년 10월 6일부터 시작된 중동전쟁이 10월 17일부터 석유전쟁으로 비화되어 제1차 석유파동이 불어 닥친 국제정세 역시 한일대륙붕공동개발협정의 조인에 영향을 미친 것도 사실이다. 대한민국 정부는 공동개발협정이 조인된 후 머지않아 국회의 비준동의를 얻었으나, 일본은 의회의 비준동의를 얻는 데 무려 4년의 시일이 소요되었으며 1978년 6월 22일에 이르러서야 동협정의 비준서를 교환하여 발효할 수 있었다. 일본 의회에서 동협정의 비준안은 절차의 지연으로 인한 자동승인의 방식으로 통과되었는데, 지연이유와 관련해서는 당시 일본의 사회당, 공명당, 공산당이 영해를 12해리로 확대할 경우 공동개발구역의 일부가 영해로 편입되기 때문에 협정을 보완해야 한다는 주장과 1972년 국교를 정상화한 중국이 심

22. 박춘호, *supra* note 20, p. 70 참조.

23. Ibid., p. 71.

24. 김동조, *supra* note 12, p. 115 참조.

하게 반발하고 있다는 고려 등을 들 수 있다.[25]

2) 협정체결의 국제법적 배경

한일간의 대륙붕공동개발협정의 체결과 관련한 국제법적 배경으로는 1958년 대륙붕에 관한 제네바협약을 가장 먼저 들 수 있지만, 협정 체결당시 한일 양국은 동협약의 당사국이 아니었으므로, 보다 중요한 국제법적 배경에는 ICJ의 1969년 북해대륙붕사건에서의 판결내용[26]이 있다고 할 것이다. 당해 사건에서 ICJ는 1958년 대륙붕에 관한 제네바협약에서 규정하고 있지 않은 "육지영토의 자연적 연장"(natural prolongation of the land territory)이라는 기준을 제시하였고, 경계획정에 적용될 법원칙과 관련하여 경계획정은 형평의 원칙에 입각하여 당사국 간 합의에 의해 이루어져야 하며 합의가 되지 않는 중첩지역은 공동 관할, 이용 혹은 개발을 권고하였다. 또한 형평한 해결을 위해 협의과정에서 고려되어야 할 사정으로 연안의 일반적 형태와 특수한 형태의 존재, 해당 대륙붕지역의 지형학적, 지질학적 구조 및 자연자원의 분포, 특정 연안국에 귀속되는 대륙붕지역의 범위와 그 연안국 해안선의 길이 간의 합리적 비례성 요소 및 동일지역의 다른 연안국과 획정될 경계선에 대한 고려 등을 예시하였다.[27] 따라서 한일간의 대륙붕공동개발협정은 이러한 ICJ의 판시사항을 적절히 반영하여 공동개발에 관한 합의를 달성한 사례라 할 것이다.

---

25. 송석환, "대한민국과 일본국간의 대륙붕 협정에 관한 연구"(연세대 석사학위논문), 1977. 7.), pp. 27-31; 일본 각 당의 입장에 관한 구체적 분석은 김동기, "한일 대륙붕 공동개발 협정의 일본 국회 비준" (고려대 석사학위논문, 1980. 1), pp. 23-35 참조; 특히 중국측의 반발에 관해서는 이상면 "한일 대륙붕 공동개발에 대한 중공의 간섭," 사회과학정책연구(1983. 10), pp. 240-241 참조.

26. *North Sea Continental Shelf Cases*, ICJ Reports (1969).

27. 당해 사건에 대한 개략적 분석은 김은수, "한국과 일본간 남부대륙붕 경계획정에 관한 법적 문제점 소고," 국제법학회논총 제44권 제2호(1999), pp. 40-41 참조.

성조환, 대륙붕 해저광물자원 개발정책의 문제점과 개선방안—해저광물자원개발법을 중심으로, 12 한독사회과학논총 51 (2002)

〈표 A〉 국내대륙붕광구별 탐사실적 현황 (2001. 9월말 현재)**

구분 \ 단위	물리탐사 L-km	시추탐사 공	투자액 천불	주요작업
I	6,477	1	8,977 (8,618)*	• '70 미Texaco 물탐(1,000L-km) • '91 공사 시추
II	19,114	4	38,664 (17,987)	• '69, '71 미Gulf 물탐(6,700L-Km) • '73 미Gulf 시추(2공) • '89, '91 미Mrathon과 공동시추(2공)
III	8,193	–	5,157 (4,665)	• '70, '71 화란Shell 물탐(2,000L-Km)
IV	11,314	1	9,721 (2,491)	• '69, '71 미Gulf 물탐(6,600L-Km) • '83 미Zapex와 공동시추
V	11,995	4	26,793 (9,680)	• '70, '71 미Texaco 물탐(3,400L-Km) • '72 미Texaco 시추 • '90 미Hadson과 공동시추 • '91 영Ultramar와 공동시추 • '98 영Kirkland와 공동시추
VI – 1	80,497	15	159,036 (151,441)	• '70, '71 화란Shell 물탐(5,100L-Km) • '72 화란Shell 시추(1공) • '87~'98 공사 시추(14공) –가스발견 5공 • '98~'99 공사 시추(4공) –양질의 가스층 발견
VI – 2	10,998	2	13,776 (4,324)	• '70 화란Shell 물탐(5,300L-Km) • '75 화란Shell 시추(2공) –석유징후 1공 –석유 · 가스징후 1공
한일공동	19,571	7	79,401 (7,306)	• '79~'84 미Texaco 시추(2공) –석유 · 가스징후 1공 • '79~'85 KOAM 시추(4공) –석유 · 가스징후 1공 • '86 일본석유와 공동시추(1공)
기타지역	2,585	–	1,421 (1,421)	
계	170,744 (114,934)	34 (15)	342,946 (207,933)	• 시추 34개공 중 –가스발견 9공 –석유 · 가스징후 5공

* ( )는 국내외 탐사 및 투자실적
** 보다 최근까지의 현황은 KNOC홈피 www.knoc.co.kr/subo3(subo3_1_2jsp) 참조.

나. 국내 대륙붕 개발사업 추진에 따른 문제점

1) 대륙붕개발에 대한 석유개발회사의 투자유인 부족

외국의 주요 석유회사들은 국제유가가 중·장기적으로 안정적인 추세를 보일 것으로 전망됨에 따라 투자위험이 상대적으로 큰 탐사광구에 대한 투자를 억제하고 있는 실정이다.[1] 그리고 기존 석유생산국가 중 석유탐사작업이 별로 이루어지지 않은 미탐사지역에 대한 개방이 급속하게 진행되고 있어 석유의 부존 가능성이 확인되지 않은 우리로서는 경쟁력이 그만큼 약화되고 있다. 현재 한국석유공사를 제외한 국내 민간사나 외국 석유회사는 대륙붕 탐사에 참여 열의가 미약하여 국내 대륙붕 탐사 활성화에 장애가 되고 있다. 이러한 이유를 구체적으로 분석하여 보면 다음과 같다.

첫째로 국내 대륙붕이 석유부존 유망지역으로 분류되어 있지 않은데다 기초적인 탐사작업이 체계적으로 이루어져 있지 않다. 따라서 외국 석유회사들이 국내 대륙붕에 대한 참여를 결정할 때에 활용할 수 있는 자료가 충분하지 못하다는 것이다. 그러므로 외국사에게 기초적인 자료를 제공하기 위해서는 현재 분류되어 있는 3개분지의 탐사자료를 명확히 정리하여 투자사에게 제공할 필요가 있다. 그리고 과거 조광권의 부여의 대가로 받은 관련탐사 및 개발지역의 자료를 DB화하여 제공할 필요가 있다. 이를 위해서는 대륙붕 개발과 관련하여 수집된 각종자료와 탐사시 의무적으로 보고하게 된 관련자료를 전문적으로 관리 운영할 수 있는 기관이 필요하다. 현재 대륙붕개발과 관련된 자료는 정부귀속 하에 있어 이를 효율적으로 관리할 수 있는 방안이 강구되어야 한다.

둘째, 해저법이 석유회사에게 투자유인을 제공하기에는 미흡하다는 것이다. 현행의 해저법은 1970년에 제정된 것으로서 당시는 국내대륙붕에서의 석유발견 가능성이 상당히 높은 것으로 평가되어 외국 석유회사의 관심이 집중되었던 시기이다. 그러나 이제까지의 국내 대륙붕에 대한 탐사작업 결과에 의하면 대규모 유전보다는 소규모 유전의 발견 가능성이 높은 것으로 분석된다. 최근의 동해 가스전을 제외하고는 충분한 경제규모의 유전이 발견되지 못하였다는 것이다. 이 결과 현재 외국 석유회사들이 국내 대륙붕을 보는 시각은 1970년대의 그것과는 현저히 다르다. 이러한 점에서 해저법을 개정하여 투자유인을 제공할 수 있도록 해야 한다.

구체적으로 살펴보면, 해저법에서는 생산규모와 관계없이 우선적으로 생산물의 12.5% 이상을 조광료로 납부하도록 규정하고 있다(해저법 시행령 제8조). 이는 중·소규모 유전의 발견 가능성이 높은 국내 대륙붕을 전제로 할 때 조광료 부과 수준이 높아 투자를 유인하기에 미흡한 것이다. 더욱이 한계유전에 대하여는 이 수준의 조광료는 매우 높은 것이어서 그 개

1. 석유개발시 석유가 개발되거나 탐사되지 않은 지역에서 유전개발의 성공률은 3~4%에 불과한 것으로 나타나고 있다.

발을 곤란하게 하고 있어 이의 개정이 시급한 실정이다.

2) 성공적인 사업 수행을 위한 전략체계 부족

석유개발사업은 대규모 자금을 필요로 하는 동시에 높은 불확실성과 장기간의 투자회임 기간을 가진 사업이다. 따라서 석유개발사업에 대한 성급한 기대보다는 장기적인 시각에서 큰 인내를 가지고 지속적으로 그리고 체계적으로 석유개발사업을 추진하는 것이 성공적인 사업수행의 요건이다.

그러나 우리나라는 과거 뚜렷한 성과에 대한 성급한 기대를 바탕으로 대륙붕 개발 사업을 담당하는 기관을 지나치게 채근하였다. 정부가 국내 대륙붕 개발사업의 추진을 위한 예산을 책정함에 있어서도 성과의 미흡으로 인하여 그 규모가 감소하는 추세이다. 그러나 역으로 말하면 성과가 미흡하기 때문에 더 많은 예산이 요구되는 것이다.

이러한 국내의 전반적인 여건 하에서 석유개발 담당기관은 성과위주의 사업추진 방식을 채택하게 되었다. 이 결과 해당시점에서의 정보를 바탕으로 가능성이 가장 큰 광구만을 집중적으로 탐사하게 되었다. 또한 대규모 석유부존 유망 구조에만 관심을 갖고 탐사작업을 수행하였다. 그러나 이는 국내 대륙붕에서의 중소규모 퇴적분지에 대한 명확한 규명을 위해 지속적인 탐사가 필요한 점을 고려해 볼 때 적절한 접근방법이 아니라고 할 수 있다.[2]

이러한 작업 추진 방식은 대륙붕 전체를 대상으로 체계적인 전략하에서 탐사작업을 추진하기에는 곤란한 결과를 초래했다. 거시적인 시각에서 체계적인 탐사작업을 추진할 때 양질의 탐사자료를 얻을 수 있다. 이 양질의 자료를 정확히 해석하면 국지적인 탐사자료를 바탕으로 한 해석결과와는 상이한 결론을 얻을 수 있으며 보다 정확한 향후의 작업계획을 수립할 수 있다.

결국 국내 대륙붕 개발사업의 성공적인 추진을 위하여 긴급히 요청되는 것은 성급한 성과를 요구하지 않는 것이다. 석유개발사업의 성공률이 3% 이내라는 사실을 인정한다면 성급한 성과의 요구는 장기적인 측면에서 석유개발사업 투자를 저해하는 요인으로 등장할 것이다. 이는 국내대륙붕 개발보다는 국외 석유발견 유망지역으로 투자를 집중시키는 결과를 초

2. 이는 표에 제시된 인접국의 대륙붕 면적과 탐사량을 비교해 보면 명백히 드러난다.

〈표 B〉 인접국의 대륙붕 면적 대비 탐사량 비교

구분	대륙붕 면적	시추공 수	만㎢당 시추공수
한국	30만㎢	34공	1.1
일본	38만㎢	175공	4.6
대만	24만㎢	126공	5.3

자료: 부범석(2000. 11. 7.), 국내 대륙붕 석유/가스 개발현황 및 활성화 대책, p. 48.

(저자주: KNOC에 따르면 2011년말 현재 44개 시추공으로 지난 10년간 10개 추가가 되었음을 알 수 있다)

래할 것이다. 따라서 정부와 관련기관은 장기적인 시각에서 기초적인 탐사작업이 체계적으로 이루어질 수 있도록 지원저액이 마련되어야 한다. 이렇게 될 때 작업수행기관은 보다 전략적으로 탐사작업을 추진하게 될 것이다.

3) 인접국과의 대륙붕 경계 미합의

석유개발사업을 활성화하기 위해서는 우리의 주변국과 대륙붕경계 문제가 시급해 해결되어야 한다. 대륙붕경계 문제가 해결되지 않음으로써 이 경계지역에서의 유전 개발사업이 원활히 추진되지 못하고 있다. 일본과 대륙붕경계는 남부지역에 대해서는 한·일 공동 대륙붕개발 협정이 체결되어 양국이 공동으로 유전개발사업을 추진하기로 합의한 바 있다. 그러나 제6-1광구의 북부지역인 동해구역에 관하여는 아직까지 대륙붕 경계문제를 해결하지 못하고 있다.

중국과 대륙붕 경계는 1989년에 4광구에서 시추작업을 계획할 때에 시추지점의 위치가 중국과의 경계에 근접하고 있어 경계에 대한 당사국간의 합의가 없는 상황에서 시추작업을 실시할 경우 당사국 간에 외교적 마찰이 우려되어 당시의 시추작업을 유보하게 되었다. 중국은 동도를 기점으로 하여 자연연장원칙을 주장하고 있다. 그러나 동도는 작은 바위섬으로서 사람이 살지 않는 무인도이며 따라서 기준점이 될 수 없다. 국제해양법에 의하면 무인도는 대륙붕경계 획정의 기준점이 될 수 없다. 그 예로서 한·일간 대륙붕경계를 획정할 때에 일본의 조도나 남녀군도는 무인도로서 이들 섬에 대하여는 12해리 영해만 인정하고 대륙붕경계 획정시 중간선의 기점으로는 삼지 아니하였다. 따라서 무인도인 동도를 기점으로 하는 것은 합당한 주장이 아니라고 볼 수 있다.

이에 더하여 중국이 주장하고 있는 자연연장원칙도 합리적이지 못한 점이 발견된다. 왜냐하면 수심이 최고 125m 이하이므로 한·중 양국간의 대륙붕은 동일한 것으로 인정되기 때문이다. 이 결과 제네바협약 제6조에 의하여 중간선 원칙을 적용하는 것이 타당하다고 볼 수 있다. 특히 중국은 북한과의 대륙붕경계를 획정할 때 중간선을 광구경계로 하였던 것을 적극 고려해야 한다는 것이다.

이와 같이 현재 주변국들 간의 대륙붕 경계문제에서 한국 측은 대륙붕의 자연 연장에 의한 최심선을 주장하고 있고, 일본은 한·일 간의 중간선이 되어야 한다는 등거리 중간선론을 주장하고 있다. 중국은 대륙붕 자연연장론을 주장하고 있는 반면, 우리는 중간선을 주장하는 상태에서 원만한 해결을 위해서는 국가 간에 타협의 조정점을 찾아야만 대륙붕개발의 활성화를 도모할 수 있다.

4) 대륙붕 석유개발사업에 대한 긍정적 인식 제고

최근의 동해-1 가스전 발견을 제외하고 과거 탐사결과가 가시적인 성과가 없이 진행됨에 따라 대륙붕 석유개발 사업에 대한 국민적 인식이 부정적인 실정이고, 기술력이 높은 외국회사들이 실패했기 때문에 기술이나 경험이 일천한 우리나라 기업의 탐사수행에 대한 불신의 시각이 있는 것도 사실이다.

그러나 과거 북해지역은 40여 공을 뚫어 원유개발에 성공한 예를 보더라도 석유개발사업은 장기적인 시간과 리스크 부담이 높은 사업이라는 것을 알 수 있다. 우리의 경우 지금까지 시추한 34공 중 국내에서 독자적으로 시추한 것은 15공이고, 대륙붕탐사 총 투자액이 2억 불 정도에 불과한 실정인데, 현 단계에서 성급하게 부정적인 결론을 내리는 것은 무리라는 것이다.

대륙붕 석유·가스 개발사업의 투자는 낭비라는 근시안적인 인식을 불식하고, 장기적으로 에너지공급확보라는 안보 전략적인 관점 이외에도, 기술과 자본집약적인 사업으로 연관산업효과가 높아 국가적 부가가치가 매우 큰 투자 사업이라는 인식의 전환이 필요하다.

다. 대륙붕개발 활성화를 위한 해저법 개선사항

1) 조광권 부여의 문제

현행 조광권부여는 정부가 외국사간에 조광협약을 통해 조광계약을 체결하고, 국영석유회사와는 출원·설정을 통해 조광권을 부여하고 있다. 현행 해저법상에는 국내 대륙붕은 7개의 해저광구로 구성되어 있어 해저광구의 평균면적이 매우 넓으나, 지금까지는 해저광구 전체를 대상으로 조광권이 부여되어 왔다. 따라서 사업수행시 실질적인 어려움이 발생하고 있다. 현 6-1광구의 경우 채취권 설정지역 이외의 반납문제뿐만 아니라, 기존에 조광권이 부여된 광구 내에 외국사 등 타사가 탐사를 희망할 경우 관심지역을 별도 분리하여 탐사 허가를 내주기도 어렵게 되어 있다.*

현행 조광권의 부여기간은 탐사권 10년 채취권 30년으로 규정하고 특별한 사유발생시 연장 가능하도록 되어 있다. 이러한 조광권의 부여기간은 산유국에 비해 길지 않지만 우리의 경우 선진국과는 유전규모 면에서 많은 차이를 보이고 있어 이를 탄력적으로 운영할 필요가 있다. 특히 유전의 수명은 다른 자원과는 달리 매우 짧다는 것이다. 중동의 거대유전과 같은 것을 별도로 하면 보통 중간정도 규모인 유전(5억 배럴 이하)의 수명은 보통 20년 정도이다. 이에 비해 우리의 경우 소규모 유전이다. 따라서 조광권 부여기간을 탄력적으로 운영할 필요가 있다. 왜냐하면 채취권이 기존 탐사권이 설정되어 있는 광구 내에 설정되어 있다면 이는

---

* 저자주: barrowscompany.com의 계약서 library에서 1970년 Wendell Phillips Oil과의 계약서, Chevron Oil과의 계약서, 1981년 Zapata와의 계약서 열람가능.

별도의 채취권허가를 받은 것이므로, 기존 탐사권은 채취권역을 제외한 지역으로 새롭게 탐사권을 조정, 설정하여야 할 필요성이 제기될 수 있고, 동해 6-1가스전 사업의 경우 매장량을 약 2000억 입방피트(천연가스의 경우 6000입방피트를 원유 1배럴로 환산하면 약 3천 3백만 배럴)로 보고 석유공사가 일일생산량을 50백만 입방피트를 생산 공급한다고 할 때 수명은 약 10년 정도로 추산되기 때문에 조광권 부여기간을 탄력적으로 운영하는 것이 오히려 다른 광구 개발에 대한 유인책으로 제공될 수 있을 것이다.

2) 광구의 기준 설정의 문제

현행 해저법 제3조(해저광구 등) 제3항에 따르면 해저조광권의 구역(이하 "해저광구"라 한다)은 제3조 제1항의 규정을 준용한다고 명시하고 있다. 해저광구의 경계는 직선으로 정하고 해저의 경계는 직하를 한계로 한다라고 규정하고 있다.

해저광구의 설정은 1970년 5월 30일 대통령령 제5020호로 동법 시행령을 제정하여 한반도와 그 부속도서의 해안에 연접한 대륙붕의 개발구역으로 7개 해저광구를 설정하였는바(동 시행령 제3조), 동 광구는 대략 북위 28°~38°와 동경 121°~130°사이의 해저에 걸쳐 총면적 약 30만㎢을 설정하여 오늘에 이르고 있다.

이때 대륙붕 광구의 설정에 있어서 우리 정부가 취한 기본적 입장은 대체로 다음과 같았다. 즉 황해에 위치한 제1, 2, 3광구와 동중국해의 북해에 위치한 제4광구는 전 해역의 수심이 200m 이하로 이루어져 있으므로 중간선 원칙에 따라 경계를 설정하였으며, 제5광구는 제4, 6, 7광구의 내측에 있으므로 대륙붕의 경계와는 직접적인 관계가 없고 제6광구는 대략 중간선 원칙에 의거했으며, 끝으로 동중국해 북부의 제7광구는 오키나와 해구가 우리나라와 일본의 대륙붕을 각각 양분하고 있으므로 이 해역에서는 대륙붕 자연연장의 원칙에 의거하여 우리 대륙붕의 자연적 연장이 끝나는 28° 36′의 오키나와 해구에 의하여 경계를 획정한 것으로 나타났다.

그러나 경계선을 획정하는 것은 분쟁을 방지하고 관할권 수행을 분명하고 효율적으로 하기 위해서인데, 이중적 경계선을 그으면 실제로 관할권 행사에 지장이 있을 뿐만 아니라 분쟁이 자주 발생할 가능성이 높다. 또 메인만 사건[3] 판결에서도 볼 수 있듯이 단일경계선에

3. 메인만 해양경계확정사건은 미국의 메사추세츠 주 Cape Cod에서 캐나다의 Nova Scotia 사이의 상부수역과 대륙붕에 대한 관할권을 두고 의견의 대립으로 1981년 이 사건을 ICJ에 제소하여 미국과 캐나다간의 대륙붕 및 어업수역과 동시에 구별하여 달라는 재판이었다. 동 법원은 메인만의 해양경계선을 확정하는 데 적용할 방법은 형평에 맞고 구체적 상황에 적합하여야 한다고 하면서 북미 동북부수역의 대륙붕은 지형적으로 하나의 대륙붕을 형성하고 있어서 자연적 경계선은 없고 인위적으로 확정해야 한다고 판단하였다. 더구나 대륙붕과 상부수역과 동일한 경계선으로 확정해야 하는데 양 국가의 해안선이 거의90°를 이루고 있어서 수직선 방법도 형평스럽지 못하기 때문에 결국 등거리 방법을 적용하고 특례상황을 고려하면서 중복되는 수역과 이등분하는 방법을 사용하여 이 수역의 경계선을 확정하였다.

의하여 해양관할권의 경계를 획정하는 것이 국제사회의 추세이므로 주변국과의 경계설정시 단일경계선에 의한 경계가 획정되도록 정부는 노력해야 할 것이다.

3) 광구의 관리체계문제

현행 우리나라는 조광제도를 바탕으로 조광권을 부여하고, 제반 조건들은 정부와 투자사 간의 협약에 의하여 조광계약을 체결하고 있다. 이러한 조광권제도 하에서는 계약자가 정부임으로 모든 권리를 정부가 소유하고 있고 국영석유회사는 단지 위탁기관의 역할만 수행할 뿐 실질적인 권한의 주체가 되지 못하고 있다. 또한 위탁기관의 역할과 임무가 법률에 명시되어 있지 않아 실제 운영에 있어서는 정부의 업무를 대신하고 있는 실정이다. 그러므로 현행 조광제도 하에서는 효율적으로 사업을 관리운영하기가 힘든 실정이다. 특히 제도적 미비점(계약조건 및 운영조건)으로 인하여 실제 사업수행에는 많은 애로사항을 겪고 있다.

생산분배계약시스템은 전술할 조광계약의 내용을 대부분 그대로 채택하고 있으나, 사업관리의 책임은 외국석유회사가 지지만 산유국 정부가 석유사업의 전반적인 경영권을 장악하고 있다는 점 및 석유회사는 조광계약의 경우와는 달리 허가취득자로서가 아니라 계약자로서의 지위만 보유하게 되는 점이 근본적으로 다르다.

생산분배계약제도 운영시 다음과 같은 장점을 가질 수 있다.

첫째, 투자비 회수(cost recovery)허용으로서 생산량의 20~40% 범위 내에서 계약자가 부담한 이전의 탐사 및 개발비용은 생산 즉시 우선 회수가 가능토록 되어 있다. 이는 조광계약의 조광료를 우선 납부해야 하는 의무와는 반대로 석유회사에 매우 유리한 조건이며, 소규모 유전에 대해서도 석유회사에 대한 투자비 회수가 보장되는 장점을 제공하게 된다. 둘째, 계약자와 정부간에 생산분배(production split)로서 생산 분배계약의 대표적인 인도네시아의 경우 정부가 85%, 계약자가 15% 정도이나 국가마다 외국석유회사 유치를 목적으로 약간씩 달리하고 있으며, 대부분 생산량의 규모에 따라 분배율을 차등 적용한다. 그러나 칠레의 경우 정부는 15%, 계약자 85%로서 반대로 되어 있으나 국가의 취득분 조절은 높은 수입세 징수에 의해 가능하다. 본제도는 석유회사와 정부간의 상호협의에 의하여 분배율을 적절히 조정한 후 탐사투자 의무를 결정하게 함으로서 합리적인 계약체결이 가능하다는 장점이 있으나 유망성이 높은 지역일수록 산유국이 유리한 조건의 계약이 되는 경우가 대부분이다. 셋째, 소득세(income tax)로서 계약자에게 일반적으로 순이익의 50% 이상을 부과하는데, 이는 조광계약의 법인세와 동일한 국가의 조세수입에 해당한다.

이러한 생산분배계약시스템은 정부가 가지고 있는 일반적인 권한 위임을 통하여 외국석유회사와 계약 주체가 될 수 있어 실질적인 운영주체가 될 수 있다.

그러나 현재의 여건 하에서 생산분배제도를 도입하는 것은 아직은 시기상조로서 향후 중장기적으로 국내 대륙붕개발이 일정궤도에 진입한 후에 현재의 조광제도를 생산분배계약 시스템으로 전환하는 방안을 검토해 볼 필요가 있을 것이다.

그리고 조광권의 분할 설정에 대한 명확한 규정이 필요하다. 현행 광구의 평균면적이 4만 ㎢에 이르고 있어 이에 대한 관리가 효율적으로 이루어지지 못하고 있다. 따라서 조광권 부여시 출원인이 출원한 부분만 가능하도록 분할 설정을 가능케 하는 규정이 필요하다. 그리고 해저법상 해저광구로 설정되지 않은 지역에 대한 탐사 근거 조항을 삽입하여 광구가 설정되지 않은 지역에 대한 조광권을 부여할 수 있도록 명시해야 한다.

4) 조광권의 양도 및 반납 처리문제

현행 해저법에서는 조광권의 양도 및 반납규정이 삭제되었지만 정부는 외국회사와 조광협약시 이에 대한 내용을 협약서에 명시하고 있다. 제5해저 광구 내에서의 석유탐사 및 생산에 관한 조광협약서 제16조의 양도규정을 살펴보면 다음과 같다. 조광권자들은 정부의 승인 없이는 그들 각자의 권리 및 의무 또는 협약구역의 전부 혹은 일부라도 양도, 이전 또는 처분하여서는 아니 된다고 규정하고 있다. 만일 정부가 요청할 경우 양도된 모든 의무를 관계회사가 이행할 수 있다면 조광권자들은 정부에 통고함으로써 정기의 양도, 이전 또는 기타의 처분을 관계회사에 할 수 있다고 명시하고 있다. 또한 생산기간이 종료 혹은 만료되었을 경우에는 해당 조광권자는 건물, 플랫폼, 저유탱크, 파이프라인, 펌프, 터미널, 정유장, 공장, 항구, 통신시설, 전기 및 수도 등의 공급시설 또는 협약구역 내에 정부가 석유산업에 관한 작업을 계속함에 필요한 협약구역 내의 기타 시설 또는 기타 부동산 등에 대하여 조광권자들이 가지는 권리 및 소유권의 일체를 정부에 양도해야 한다. 정부에 양도하는 모든 자산의 미상각잔고(취득가격－감가상각비)는 조광권자들이 본 양도에 따른 총조세 이익을 산정하기 위해 요구되는 바에 따라 조광권자들의 과세소득에서 공제될 수 있다. 또한 협약구역 내의 동산을 취득가격에서 적절한 상각비를 공제한 가격으로 구매할 수 있는 선택권을 갖는다고 명시하고 있다.

그러나 문제는 우리의 경우 지금까지 대륙붕에서 경제적 가치가 있는 유전을 발견하지 못함으로써 기존의 외국투자회사가 모두 철수한 상태에서 반납된 광구를 전부 관리하는 데는 한계가 있고, '99. 2. 해저법 개정 이후 반납 및 양도조항이 불분명해져서 사업수행에 실질적인 어려움이 발생하고 있다. 특히 기존에 조광권이 부여된 광구 내에 외국사 등 타사가 탐사를 희망할 경우 외국회사의 관심지역을 별도 분리하여 탐사권 허가를 해 주기도 어렵게 되어 있다.

따라서 해저조광구의 반납 및 양도가 원활이 이루어질 수 있도록 현행 해저법에 삭제된 제6조와 제19조의 규정을 부활하거나 새로운 조항을 신설하여 운영할 필요가 있다. 이에 대해서 개정 해저법에서는 다음과 같은 조항을 삽입해야 할 것이다.

탐사권이 설정된 해저조광구의 조광권자는 탐사권의 존속기간 중 해저 조광구의 일정부분에 대한 조광권을 반납할 수 있으며, 산업자원부장관은 반납된 지역에 대하여 추가 출원이 있을 경우 새로운 조광권을 부여할 수 있다고 명시하여야 할 것이다. 또한 해저조광권자는 해저광구의 부분 또는 전부를 정부의 승인 하에 양도할 수 있으며, 양도시 양도된 구역에 한하여 해저조광권자의 권리·의무는 포괄 승계된다고 명시해야 할 것이다.

5) 조광료 및 관련세제의 개선

우리나라의 대륙붕 석유개발 사업은 외국회사가 투자매력을 가질 만큼 유망한 지역이 아니며 민간기업도 별 관심을 갖지 않을 만큼 열악한 지역이다. 그러나 현행 석유개발사업과 관련한 법인세는 일반법인세율(28%)보다 훨씬 높은 50%로 규정되어 있어 외국회사나 민간기업의 투자를 가로막는 조항이 되고 있다.

외국의 경우 석유개발사업에 대하여 적용되는 소득세는 자국 내 일반법인세와 같은 수준이며 비산유국의 경우에는 일반법인세율을 적용하는 것이 보통이다. 이와 같은 열악한 산업환경에 해저법상의 법인세까지도 일반법인세보다 훨씬 높아 민간사의 관심유도나 외국회사의 투자유치가 어려운 실정인바 관련제도의 개선의 시급히 요구되고 있다.

조광료의 경우는 현행법상 판매가액의 12.5% 이상으로 규정되어 있어 한계가 불명확하고 현행 법규상의 최저 조광료율인 12.5%도 외국에 비하여 상대적으로 높은 편이다. 특히 산유국 및 비산유국을 포함한 외국의 경우 전반적으로 조광료율을 하향함으로서 자국 내 민간사 및 외국회사의 투자를 유치하기 위한 투자환경을 조성하고 있고, 우리나라와 같이 석유가스 생산이 없거나 미미한 나라의 경우에는 조광료율이 더욱 낮아지거나 부과하지 않는 추세에 있어 이의 개정이 필요하다.

특히 현행법상 조광료는 탐사권 또는 채취권 설정시에 산업자원부 장관이 정하도록 되어 있어서 외국투자자 입장에서 볼 때 투자시 매우 불확실한 규정으로 볼 수 있다. 따라서 조광료율을 정확히 명시함으로써 이와 같은 불확실성을 제거해 줄 필요가 있다.*

* 저자주: 이용국, 국내대륙붕 석유자원개발 활성화방안(한국산업기술대학원 석사논문 2005) 87-105은 대륙붕 개발 활성화 방안으로 중/일과의 공동개발구역설정, 북한의 참여, 전문기술인력개발을 열거. Barrows Company의 자료실은 북한과 러시아간 양허계약을 제공.

대법 1972. 4. 11. 선고 71누98 판결

소론과 같이 원고의 이 사건 광업권출원이 불수리 요건에 해당되지 아니하여 수리되었다고 하더라도 광업권의 설정은 출원만에 의하여 되는 것이 아니고, 허가를 받아야 되는 것이므로 피고가 허가처분을 하기 전에 원심판시와 같이 해저광물자원 개발법이 공포 시행되어 1970. 1. 1. 이후에 있어서, 해저광업권은 정부만이 가질 수 있게 되었는 만큼, 원고가 이 사건에서 소구하는바 피고의 광업권설정출원을 반려한 처분이 취소되었다 한들 원고는 광업법에 따른 석유광업권설정의 출원을 한 상태에 돌아갈 뿐 허가처분에 이르지 아니할 것이므로 원고에게 해저석유광업권이 설정 허가될 여지가 없다 할 것이니 원고의 소는 소의 이익이 없다고 할 것이고 이와 같은 취지에서 원고의 소를 각하한 원심판결 이유는 정당하고 논지는 이유없다.

2. 국가주권의 범위에 관한 분쟁과 해결책

가. 조약/판결

석유개발지역을 둘러싼 영토분쟁의 예는 수없이 많다. 사우디와 쿠웨이트 간 분쟁은 사우디과 쿠웨이트 간 중립지역으로부터의 석유개발수익을 1968년까지 균등하게 분할하도록 하였으며[5] 터키와 이란 사이의 국경분쟁은 이라크가 자리잡기까지는 1639년 Zohab 조약에서부터 시작, 1847년 2차 Erzeroam 조약을 거쳐서 1913년 Constantinople 의정서로 마무리되기까지 200년 가까운 시간이 걸렸다. 물론 1932년 이라크가 독립한 이후에도 분쟁은 지속되어 1937년 Saadabad조약, 1975년 State Boundary and Good-Neighborliness Treaty로 국경다툼을 마무리지으려 하였으나 이라크에 만족스럽지 못하여 결국 1980-88년 이란-이라크 전쟁의 원인이 되기도 하였다.[6] 예멘과 사우디도 2000년 조약을 체결할 때까지 국경분쟁이 있었다.[7] 아프리카에서는 나이지리아와 그 주변국인 카메룬, 니제르, 차드와의 국경이 명확하지 않아서 2002년 국제사법재판소에 의하여[8] 해결되었다.

---

5) Aileen Keating, MIRAGE: POWER, POLITICS, AND THE HIDDEN HISTORY OF ARABIAN OIL (2005)

6) R. Schofield, THE IRAN-IRAQ BORDER 1840-1958 (1989). 총 12권의 외교자료집으로 1840-1958간 Shatt-al-'Arab강을 둘러싼 이란/이라크 간 분쟁기록.

7) Ernst E. Smith, 위 주 1-4 게재서, 104.

8) Judgment of 10 October 2002, *Case Concerning the Land and Maritime Boundary Between Cameroon and Nigeria*. http://www.icj-cij.org/docket/files/94/7453.pdf.

나. 광구단일화(Unitization)

분쟁의 해결을 위하여 국제사법재판소로 가는 것도 한 가지 해결방법이기는 하지만, 보다 바람직하게는 광구단일화협정을[9] 체결하거나 공동개발구역으로 합의하는 것이다. 국경을 달리하기 이전에 지하의 매장량은 서로 연결되어 있으나 그 지상의 토지소유권 내지 개발권자가 다른 경우 미국의 보통법에 따르면 선점의 법리가 적용되었다. 선점의 법리에 따르면 자원이 해저로 서로 연결되어 있건 말건 이를 먼저 지상으로 추출한 자가 석유소유권자가 된다. 이 법리에 따르면 첫째 손해배상의 소가 제기된 경우 이를 정산하기 어려운 실질적 문제점을 해결할 수 있다는 편의, 둘째 먼저 추출하기 위한 경쟁 때문에 최대한의 석유개발을 촉진시킬 수 있다는 정책적 효과, 셋째 석유의 원천을 판별하기 어려운 기술적 문제점에 대한 적절한 해결책이라는 점에서 바람직한 법리였다. 그러나, 한편으로 선점의 법리는 남보다 먼저 석유를 추출하기 위한 시공작업이 지나쳐 결국 석유자원의 낭비라는 결과를 가져오는 문제점이 있었고 또한 기술의 발전은 하나의 지하매장석유에 대하여 복수의 개발권을 부여하는 사태를 막을 수 있게 되어 현재 다수의 석유사업법은 공동개발을 법적으로 강제하고 있다.[10] 국제법적으로 이러한 사태를 해결하는 방법이 광구단일화협정이나 공동개발구역설정이다.[11]

광구단일화는 하나의 저유지에 대하여 이해관계를 가진 자들이 저유지를 공동소유하고 있는 것처럼 하나의 단일체를 구성, 저유지를 개발하는 것이다. 미국의 국내법은 통상 2단계 추출작업시 토지임대인과 토지임차인들 모두의 단일체구성을 강제하는 경우가 많으며 임의적 합의도 주위원회의 승인을 필요로 한다.[12] 국가 간에는 공동저유지를 하나의 광구로 단일화하여 운용할 법적인 의무가 있는지 여부에 대하여는 의견이 일치하지 않지만 많은 광구단

---

9) unitization agreement를 류권홍, 국제석유·가스개발과 거래계약 228 (2011) 이하에서는 광구통합협정으로 번역한다.

10) 캐나다의 입법에 관하여는 Cecilia A. Low, *The Rule of Capture: Its Current Status and Some Issues to Consider*, 46 ALTA. L. REV. 799, 816-22 (2009). 네덜란드 판결로 *Unocal Netherlands B.V.et al. v. Continental Netherlands Oil Company et al.*, The Supreme Court of the Netherlands. No. C04/127HR, LJN AT537 (14 Oct. 2005) Smith, 위 주 1-4 게재서 160-64.

11) Rainer Lagoni, *Oil and Gas Deposits Across National Frontier*, 73 AM. J. INT'L. L. 215, 243 (1979) 선의로 협상할 의무와 산출물을 형평의 원칙에 따라서 배분할 의무는 국제법상 확립된 관습이라고 본다. David M. Ong, *Joint Development of Common Offshore Oil and Gas Deposits Mere State Practice or Customary International Law?*, 93 AM. J. INT'L L. 771, 802 (1999)는 일방적인 행동전에 상대방에 협상할 의사가 있음을 통지한 의무 정도로 본다. 계속 협상할 의무 정도라는 견해는 Peter D. Cameron, *The Rules of Engagement: Development Cross-Border Petroleum Deposits in the North Sea and the Caribbean,* 55 I.C.L.Q. 559, 561 (2006).

12) Jackqueline Lang Weaver/David F. Asmus, *Unitization and Gas Fields Around the World: A Comparative Analysis of National Laws and Private Contracts,* 26 HOUS. J. OF INT'L L. 3, 18 (2006). 12개국의 국내법비교는 23페이지 이하.

일화조약이 체결되었음을 기초로 협상의 의무를 인정하는 이가 많으며 따라서 새로이 국경을 확정하면서 앞으로의 광구단일화를 예정하는 조항을 포함하기도 한다.[13] 통상 석유가 발견되면 최적의 개발계획을 공동으로 작성한 후 생산비용분담비율, 생산물분담비율, 주기적 재평가의무 등을 규정한 공동광구운영계약을 체결한다.[14]

다. 공동개발구역(Joint Development Zone)

광구단일화는 통상 경계확정과 공동저유지를 전제로 한 것이라면 공동개발구역의 설정은 배타적 경계를 확정하기 위한 다툼 자체를 피하고 일정한 구역을 공동으로 개발하기 위한 것이다. 통상 공동저유지보다 광범위하며 탐사작업 개시 전단계로서 하나의 관리기구가 설립된다. 공동개발구역 운영계약은 그 내용이 지극히 다양하지만 자원을 어떻게 나눌지, 경영에 관한 결정을 누가 어떻게 할지, 적용법규는 무엇으로 할지, 개발자의 법적인 지위와 조세의무, 그리고 분쟁해결방법에 관하여는 합의가 필요하다. 경영에 관한 결정을 하나의 국가에 전적으로 맡겨 놓을 수도 있고, 두 국가가 각자 결정할 수도 있으며 하나의 공동결정기구를 설립할 수도 있다.[15]

Agreement Concerning Joint Development of the Southern Part of the Continental Shelf Adjacent to S. Korea－Japan－S. Korea on Jan. 30, 1974

DESIRING to promote the friendly relations existing between the two countries,

CONSIDERING their mutual interest in carrying out jointly exploration and exploitation of petroleum resources in the southern part of the continental shelf adjacent to the two countries,

RESOLVING to reach a final practical solution to the question of the develop ment of such resources,

HAVE AGREED as follows

Article I

For the purposes of this Agreement

(1) The term "natural resources" means petroleum (including natural gas) resources and other underground minerals which are produced in association with such resources;

(2) The term "concessionaire" means a person authorized by either Party under the laws and regulations of that Party to explore and/or exploit natural resources in the Joint

13) Ana E. Bastida et al., *Cross-Border Unitization and Joint Development Agreements: An Internatioinal Law Perspective,* 29 HOUS. J. OF INT'L L. 355, 381-99 (2007).

14) AIPN은 2006년 모델계약서를 제시. 이상면, 해양경계선상의 에너지개발에 있어서의 UNITIZATION원칙의 적용, 31 법학 122(1990).

15) Bastida, 위 주 13 게재논문, 415-17.

Development Zone;

(3) The term "concessionaires of both Parties" means a concessionaire of one Party and a concessionaire of the other Party respectively authorized with respect to the same subzone of the Joint Development Zone;

(4) The term "operating agreement" means a contract concluded between concessionaires of both Parties for the purpose of exploring and exploiting natural resources in the Joint Development Zone;

(5) The term "operator" means a concessionaire designated and acting as such under the operating agreement with respect to a subzone of the Joint Development Zone.

Article II

1. The Joint Development Zone shall be the area of the continental shelf bounded by straight lines connecting the following points in the sequence given below:

2. The straight lines bounding the Joint Development Zone are shown on the map annexed to this Agreement.

Article III

1. The Joint Development Zone may be divided into subzones, each of which shall be explored and exploited by concessionaires of both Parties.

2. Each subzone shall be numbered and defined by reference to geographical coordinates in the appendix to this Agreement. The appendix may be amended by mutual consent of the Parties without modification of this Agreement.

Article IV

1. Each Party shall authorize one or more concessionaires with respect to each subzone within three months after the date of entry into force of this Agreement. When one Party authorizes more than one concessionaire with respect to one subzone, all such concessionaires shall have an undivided interest and shall be represented, for the purposes of this Agreement, by one concessionaire. In case of any change in concessionaire or in subzone, the Party concerned shall authorize one or more new concessionaires as soon as possible.

2. Each Party shall notify the other Party of its concessionaire or concessionaires without delay.

Article V

1. Concessionaires of both Parties shall enter into an operating agreement to carry out jointly exploration and exploitation of natural resources in the Joint Development Zone. Such operating agreement shall provide, *inter alia*, for the following:

(a) Details relating to the sharing of natural resources and expenses in accordance with article IX;

(b) Designation of operator;

(c) Treatment of sole risk operations;

(d) Adjustment of fisheries interests;

(e) Settlement of disputes.

2. The operating agreement and modifications thereof shall enter into force upon approval by the Parties. Approval of the Parties shall be deemed to have been given unless either Party explicitly disapproves the operating agreement or modifications thereof within two months after such operating agreement or modifications thereof have been submitted to the Parties for approval.

3. The Parties shall endeavour to ensure that the operating agreement enter into force within six months after concessionaires of both Parties have been authorized under paragraph 1 of article IV.

Article VI

1. The operator shall be designated by agreement between concessionaires of both Parties. If concessionaires of both Parties fail to reach agreement between themselves as to the designation of the operator within three months after such concessionaires have been authorized, the Parties shall hold consultations concerning the designation of the operator. If the operator is not designated within two months after such consultations have started, concessionaires of both Parties shall determine the operator by lot-drawing.

2. The operator shall have exclusive control of all operations under the operating agreement and employ all personnel required for such operations, pay and discharge all expenses incurred in connection with such operations, and obtain all assets, including equipment, materials and supplies, necessary for carrying out such operations.

Article VII

A concessionaire of one Party may acquire, construct, maintain, use and dispose of, in the territory of the other Party, buildings, platforms, tanks, pipelines, terminals and other facilities necessary for exploration or exploitation of natural resources in the Joint Development Zone in accordance with the laws and regulations of that other Party.

Article VIII

A concessionaire of one Party shall not interfere with the discharging by a concessionaire of the other Party of its obligations under the laws and regulations of that other Party, insofar as such obligations are consistent with the provisions of this Agreement.

Article IX

1. Concessionaires of both Parties shall be respectively entitled to an equal share of natural resources extracted in the Joint Development Zone.

2. Expenses reasonably attributable to exploration and exploitation of such natural resources shall be shared in equal proportions between concessionaires of both Parties.

Article X

1. The right of concessionaires under this Agreement shall be exploration right and exploitation right.

2. The duration of exploration right shall be eight years from the date of entry into force of the operating agreement, subject to the provisions of paragraph 4 (3) of this article.

3. The duration of exploitation right shall be thirty years from the date of the establishment of such right. Concessionaires of both Parties may apply to the respective Parties for an extension of an additional period of five years. Such application may be made as many times as necessary. The Parties shall, upon receipt of such application, consult with each other to decide whether to approve such application.

4. (1) When commercial discovery of natural resources is made during the period of exploration right, concessionaires of both Parties may apply to the respective Parties for the establishment of exploitation right. When the Parties receive such application, they shall promptly hold consultations and shall without delay approve such application.

(2) When the Parties recognize that commercial discovery is made, each Party may request its concessionaire concerned to present an application for the establishment of exploitation right. Such concessionaire shall present such application within three months after receiving the request.

(3) If exploitation right is established during the period of exploration right, the period of exploration right shall expire on the date of the establishment of exploitation right.

5. In case of any change in concessionaire of one Party, the period of exploration

right or exploitation right of a new concessionaire shall expire on the date of expiration of the period of exploration right or exploitation right of the original concessionaire.

6. Exploration right or exploitation right of a concessionaire may be transferred in its entirety subject to the approval of the Party that has authorized it and to the consent of the other concessionaire authorized with respect to the same subzone, provided that the rights and obligations of that concessionaire under this Agreement and the operating agreement are transferred in whole.

Article XI

1. Concessionaires of both Parties shall be required to drill a certain number of wells during the period of exploration right in accordance with a separate arrangement to be made between the Parties. However, the minimum number of wells to be drilled in each subzone shall not exceed two respectively for the first three-year period, the following three-year period and the remaining two-year period, from the date of entry into force of the operating agreement. The Parties shall, when agreeing upon the minimum number of wells to be drilled in each subzone, take into account the depths of the superjacent waters and the size of each subzone.

2. If concessionaires of both Parties have drilled wells in excess of the requirements during any of the periods referred to in paragraph 1 of this article, such excess wells shall be regarded as having been drilled in the succeeding period or periods.

Article XII

Concessionaires of both Parties shall start operations within six months from the date of the establishment of exploration right or exploitation right and shall not suspend operations for more than six consecutive months.

Article XIII

1. Subject to the provisions of paragraph 2 of this article, concessionaires of both Parties shall release twenty-five percent of the original subzone concerned within three years, fifty percent of such subzone within six years, and seventy-five percent of such subzone within eight years, from the date of entry into force of the operating agreement.

2. The size, shape and location of the area to be released and the time of release shall be determined by agreement between concessionaires of both Parties. However, no single area smaller than seventy-five square kilometres shall be released except under paragraph 3 of this article.

3. (1) If concessionaires of both Parties are unable to agree on the area to be released under paragraph 1 of this article, concessionaires of both Parties shall release, on the date of the expiration of the release period concerned, the area mutually proposed for release and fifty percent of the areas respectively proposed for release in such a way that the total area to be released will be a single area whenever possible.

(2) If there is no area mutually proposed for release, concessionaires of both Parties shall release fifty percent of the areas respectively proposed for release.

4. Concessionaires of both Parties may release voluntarily any area subject to the provisions of paragraph 2 of this article.

5. Notwithstanding the provisions of paragraph 2 of this article, a concessionaire may unilaterally release the total subzone concerned after two years have elapsed from the date of entry into force of the operating agreement.

Article XIV

1. Either Party may, by pertinent procedures laid down in its laws and regulations concerning the protection of concessionaires, cancel exploration right or exploitation right of its concessionaire after consultations with the other Party if such concessionaire fails to discharge any of its obligations under this Agreement or the operating agreement.

2. When either Party intends to cancel in accordance with its laws and regulations

exploration right or exploitation right of its concessionaire, that Party shall notify the other Party of its intention at least fifteen days prior to such cancellation, except under paragraph 1 of this article.

3. The cancellation of exploration right or exploitation right by one Party shall be notified to the other Party without delay.

Article XV

1. When a concessionaire of one Party has unilaterally released a subzone under paragraph 5 of article XIII, when exploration right or exploitation right of a concessionaire of one Party has been cancelled under article XIV or when a concessionaire of one Party has ceased to exist (any such concessionaire hereinafter referred to as "the former concessionaire"), the remaining concessionaire in the subzone concerned may, until such time as the Party that has authorized the former concessionaire authorizes a new concessionaire, carry out exploration or exploitation of natural resources under the terms of the sole risk operation clauses and under other relevant provisions of the operating agreement to which such remaining concessionaire and the former concessionaire were parties, subject to the approval of the Party that has authorized the former concessionaire.

2. For the purposes of paragraph 1 of this article, the remaining concessionaire shall be regarded as a concessionaire of the Party that has authorized the former concessionaire in respect of rights and obligations of a concessionaire, while retaining its own concessionaireship. The provisions of the above sentence shall not apply to taxation upon the remaining concessionaire with respect to its income derived from exploration or exploitation of natural resources under paragraph 1 of this article.

3. When a new concessionaire is authorized by one Party, the new concessionaire and the remaining concessionaire shall be bound by the operating agreement to which the remaining concessionaire and the former concessionaire were parties until such time as a new operating agreement enters into force. The remaining concessionaire who has started exploration or exploitation of natural resources under paragraph 1 of this article may continue such exploration or exploitation under the terms of the sole risk operation clauses of the operating agreement to which such remaining concessionaire and the former concessionaire were parties until such time as the new operating agreement referred to above enters into force.

Article XVI

In the application of the laws and regulations of each Party to natural resources extracted in the Joint Development Zone, the share of such natural resources to which concessionaires of one Party are entitled under article IX shall be regarded as natural resources extracted in the continental shelf over which that Party has sovereign rights.

Article XVII

1. Neither Party (including local authorities) shall impose taxes or other charges upon concessionaires of the other Party with respect to:

(a) Exploration or exploitation activities in the Joint Development Zone;

(b) Income derived from such activities;

(c) The possession of fixed assets in the Joint Development Zone necessary for carrying out such activities; or

(d) The subzones with respect to which such concessionaires are authorized.

2. Each Party (including local authorities) may impose taxes and other charges upon its concessionaires with respect to:

(a) Exploration or exploitation activities in the Joint Development Zone;

(b) The possession of fixed assets in the Joint Development Zone necessary for carrying out such activities; and

(c) The subzones with respect to which such concessionaires are authorized. **Article**

XVIII

In the application of the laws and regulations of each Party on customs duties, imports and exports:

(1) The introduction of equipment, materials and other goods necessary for exploration or exploitation of natural resources in the Joint Development Zone (hereinafter referred to as "equipment") into the Joint Development Zone, the subsequent use of equipment therein or the shipment of equipment therefrom shall not be regarded as imports or exports;

(2) The shipment of equipment from areas under the jurisdiction of one Party to the Joint Development Zone shall not be regarded as imports or exports by that Party;

(3) The users of equipment in the Joint Development Zone which has been introduced into the Joint Development Zone from areas under the jurisdiction of either Party may be required to submit reports to that Party on the use of such equipment;

(4) Notwithstanding the provisions of (1) of this article, the shipment of the equipment referred to in (3) of this article from the Joint Development Zone to areas other than those under the jurisdiction of that Party shall be regarded as exports by that Party.

Article XIX

Except where otherwise provided in this Agreement, the laws and regulations of one Party shall apply with respect to matters relating to exploration or exploitation of natural resources in the subzones with respect to which that Party has authorized concessionaires designated and acting as operators.

Article XX

The Parties shall agree on measures to be taken to prevent collisions at sea and to prevent and remove pollution of the sea resulting from activities relating to exploration or exploitation of natural resources in the Joint Development Zone.

Article XXI

1. When damage resulting from exploration or exploitation of natural resources in the Joint Development Zone has been sustained by nationals of either Party or other persons who are resident in the territory of either Party, actions for compensation for such damage may be brought by such nationals or persons in the court of one Party (a) in the territory of which such damage has occurred, (b) in the territory of which such nationals or persons are resident, or (c) which has authorized the concessionaire designated and acting as the operator in the subzone where the incident causing such damage has occurred.

2. The court of one Party in which actions for compensation for such damage have been brought under paragraph 1 of this article shall apply the laws and regulations of that Party.

3. (1) When damage referred to in paragraph 1 of this article has been caused by digging operations of seabed and subsoil, or discharging of mine water or used water:

(a) Concessionaires of both Parties who have exploration right or exploitation right with respect to the subzone concerned at the time of occurrence of such damage,

(b) In case no concessionaire has exploration right or exploitation right with respect to the subzone concerned at the time of occurrence of such damage, the concessionaires who had exploration right or exploitation right most recently with respect to the subzone concerned or

(c) In case only one concessionaire has exploration right or exploitation right with respect to the subzone concerned at the time of occurrence of such damage, such concessionaire and the former concessionaire as defined in paragraph 1 of article XV, shall be jointly and severally liable for the compensation for such damage in accordance with the laws and regulations applicable under paragraph 2 of this article.

(2) For the purposes of (1) of this paragraph, when exploration right or exploitation right has been transferred after the occurrence of the damage referred to in (1) of this paragraph, the concessionaire who has transferred exploration right or exploitation right and the concessionaire who has obtained exploration right or exploitation right by such transfer shall be jointly and severally liable for the compensation.

Article XXII

1. Each Party shall, when assigning a frequency or frequencies to a radio station on a fixed installation for exploration or exploitation of natural resources in the Joint Development Zone, inform as soon as possible prior to such assignment the other Party of such frequency or frequencies, class of emission, antenna power, location of the station and other particulars deemed necessary. Each Party shall likewise inform the other Party of any subsequent changes in the above particulars.

2. The Parties shall hold consultations at the request of either Party for necessary coordination concerning the above particulars.

Article XXIII

1. If any single geological structure or field of natural resources extends across any of the lines specified in paragraph 1 of article II and the part of such structure or field which is situated on one side of such lines is exploitable, wholly or in part, from the other side of such lines, concessionaires and other persons authorized by either Party to exploit such structure or field (hereinafter referred to as "concessionaires and other persons") shall, through consultations, seek to reach agreement as to the most effective method of exploiting such structure or field.

2. (1) If concessionaires and other persons fail to reach agreement as to the method referred to in paragraph 1 of this article within six months after such consultations have started, the Parties shall, through consultations, endeavour to make a joint proposal concerning such method to concessionaires and other persons within a reasonable period of time.

(2) When agreement concerning such method is reached among all or some of concessionaires and other persons, the agreement (including modifications thereof) shall enter into force upon approval by the Parties. Such agreement shall provide for details relating to the sharing, in accordance with paragraph 3 of this article, of natural resources and expenses.

3. In cases of exploitation under the agreement referred to in paragraph 2 (2) of this article, natural resources extracted from such structure or field and expenses reasonably attributable to exploitation of such natural resources shall be shared among concessionaires and other persons in proportion to the quantities of producible reserves in the respective parts of such structure or field which are situated in the area with respect to which they have been authorized by either Party.

4. The provisions of the foregoing paragraphs of this article shall apply *mutatis mutandis* with respect to exploitation of a single geological structure or field of natural resources extending across lines bounding the subzones of the Joint Development Zone.

5. (1) For the purposes of article XVI, the share of natural resources extracted in the Joint Development Zone to which persons (other than concessionaires) authorized by one Party are entitled under paragraph 3 of this article and the agreement referred to in paragraph 2 (2) of this article shall be regarded as the share of natural resources to which concessionaires of that Party are entitled.

(2) For the purposes of article XVII, persons (other than concessionaires) authorized by one Party who are parties to the agreement referred to in paragraph 2 (2) of this article shall be regarded as concessionaires of that Party.

(3) Neither Party (including local authorities) shall impose taxes or other charges upon concessionaires of the other Party with respect to:

(a) Exploitation activities carried out outside the Joint Development Zone in accordance with the agreement referred to in paragraph 2 (2) of this article;

(b) Income derived from such activities; or
(c) The possession of fixed assets necessary for carrying out such activities.

Article XXIV

1. The Parties shall establish and maintain the Japan-Republic of Korea Joint Commission (hereinafter referred to as "the Commission") as a means for consultations on matters concerning the implementation of this Agreement.

2. The Commission shall be composed of two national sections, each consisting of two members appointed by the respective Parties.

3. All resolutions, recommendations and other decisions of the Commission shall be made only by agreement between the national sections.

4. The Commission may adopt and amend, when necessary, rules of procedure for its meetings.

5. The Commission shall meet at least once each year and whenever requested by either national section.

6. At its first meeting, the Commission shall select its Chairman and Vice-Chairman from different national sections. The Chairman and the Vice-Chairman shall hold office for a period of one year. Selection of the Chairman and the Vice-Chairman from the national sections shall be made in such a manner as will provide in turn each Party with representation in these offices.

7. A permanent secretariat may be established under the Commission to carry out the clerical work of the Commission.

8. The official languages of the Commission shall be Japanese, Korean and English. Proposals and data may be submitted in any official language.

9. In case the Commission decides that joint expenses are necessary, such expenses shall be paid by the Commission through contributions made by the Parties as recommended by the Commission and approved by the Parties.

Article XXV

1. The Commission shall perform the following functions:

(a) To review the operation of this Agreement and, when necessary, deliberate on and recommend to the Parties measures to be taken to improve the operation of this Agreement;

(b) To receive technical and financial reports of concessionaires, which shall be submitted annually by the Parties;

(c) To recommend to the Parties measures to be taken to settle disputes incapable of solution by concessionaires;

(d) To observe operations of operators and installations and other facilities for exploration or exploitation of natural resources in the Joint Development Zone;

(e) To study problems, including those relating to the application of laws and regulations of the Parties, unexpected at the time of entry into force of this Agreement, and, when necessary, recommend to the Parties appropriate measures to solve such problems;

(f) To receive notices concerning the laws and regulations promulgated by the Parties relating to exploration or exploitation of natural resources in the Joint Development Zone, which shall be submitted by the Parties;

(g) To discuss any other matter relating to the implementation of this Agreement.

2. The Parties shall respect to the extent possible recommendations made by the Commission under paragraph 1 of this article.

Article XXVI

1. Any dispute between the Parties concerning the interpretation and implementation of this Agreement shall be settled, first of all, through diplomatic channels.

2. Any dispute which fails to be settled under paragraph 1 of this article shall be

referred for decision to an arbitration board composed of three arbitrators, with each Party appointing one arbitrator within a period of thirty days from the date of receipt by either Party from the other Party of a note requesting arbitration of the dispute, and the third arbitrator to be agreed upon by the two arbitrators so chosen within a further period of thirty days or the third arbitrator to be appointed by the government of a third country agreed upon within such further period by the two arbitrators, provided that the third arbitrator shall not be a national of either Party.

3. If the third arbitrator or the third country is not agreed upon between the arbitrators appointed by each Party within a period referred to in paragraph 2 of this article, the Parties shall request the President of the International Court of Justice to appoint the third arbitrator who shall not be a national of either Party.

4. At the request of either Party, the arbitration board may in urgent cases issue a provisional order, which shall be respected by the Parties, before an award is made.

5. The Parties shall abide by any award made by the arbitration board under this article.

Article XXVII

Exploration and exploitation of natural resources in the Joint Development Zone shall be carried out in such a manner that other legitimate activities in the Joint Development Zone and its superjacent waters such as navigation and fisheries will not be unduly affected.

Article XXVIII

Nothing in this Agreement shall be regarded as determining the question of sovereign rights over all or any portion of the Joint Development Zone or as prejudicing the positions of the respective Parties with respect to the delimitation of the continental shelf.

Article XXIX

Upon the request of either Party, the Parties shall hold consultations regarding the implementation of this Agreement.

Article XXX

The Parties shall take all necessary internal measures to implement this Agreement.

Article XXXI

1. This Agreement shall be ratified. The instruments of ratification shall be exchanged at Tokyo as soon as possible. This Agreement shall enter into force as from the date on which such instruments of ratification are exchanged.

2. This Agreement shall remain in force for a period of fifty years and shall continue in force thereafter until terminated in accordance with paragraph 3 of this article.

3. Either Party may, by giving three years' written notice to the other Party, terminate this Agreement at the end of the initial fifty-year period or at any time thereafter.

4. Notwithstanding the provisions of paragraph 2 of this article, when either Party recognizes that natural resources are no longer economically exploitable in the Joint Development Zone, the Parties shall consult with each other whether to revise or terminate this Agreement. If no agreement is reached as to the revision or termination of this Agreement, this Agreement shall remain in force during the period as provided for in paragraph 2 of this article.

IN WITNESS WHEREOF, the undersigned, being duly authorized by their respective Governments, have signed this Agreement.

DONE in duplicate at Seoul in the English language, this thirtieth day of January of the year one thousand nine hundred and seventy-four.

For Japan:
TORAO USHIROKU

For the Republic of Korea:
DONG-JO KIM

[그림 A] Joint Development Zone

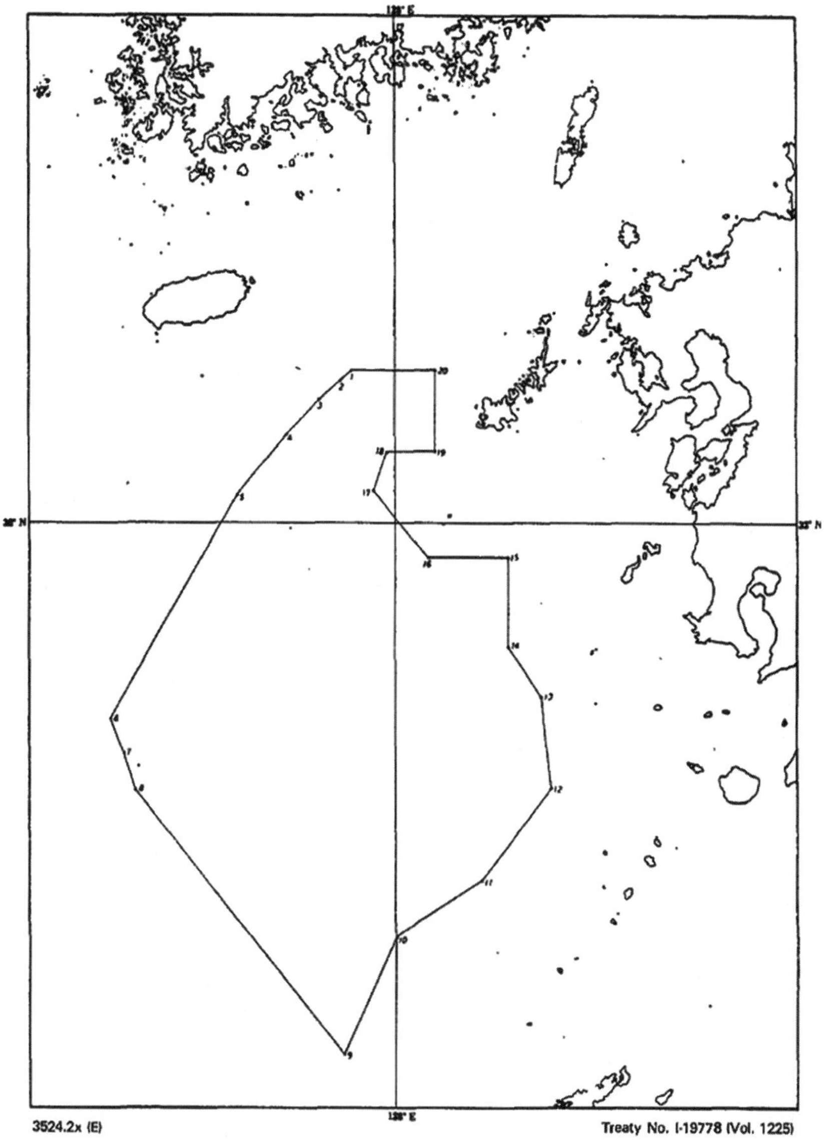

3524.2x (E) Treaty No. I-19778 (Vol. 1225)

Appendix

The Subzones shall be those areas of the Joint Development Zone bounded respectively by straight lines connecting the following points in the sequence given below:

Subzone I
Subzone II
Subzone III
Subzone IV
Subzone V
Subzone VI
Subzone VII
Subzone VIII
Subzone IX

AGREED MINUTES TO THE AGREEMENT BETWEEN JAPAN AND THE REPUBLIC OF KOREA CONCERNING JOINT DEVELOPMENT OF THE SOUTHERN PART OF THE CONTINENTAL SHELF ADJACENT TO THE TWO COUNTRIES

The representatives of the Government of Japan and the Government of the Republic of Korea wish to record the following understanding which has been reached during the negotiations for the Agreement between Japan and the Republic of Korea concerning joint development of the southern part of the continental shelf adjacent to the two countries signed today (hereinafter referred to as "the Agreement"):

1. "The laws and regulations" referred to in the Agreement shall be construed, unless the context otherwise requires, to include concession agreements between the Government of the Republic of Korea and its concessionaires.

2. The geographical coordinates as specified in paragraph 1 of article II and the appendix to the Agreement are based on Japan Maritime Safety Agency Chart No. 210 of December 1955, New Edition.

3. (1) Regardless of whether the sole risk party is the operator, sole risk operations referred to in paragraph 1 of article V shall be carried out by the operator of the subzone concerned.

(2) Natural resources extracted through sole risk operations shall be equally shared between the concessionaires concerned in accordance with article IX.

(3) The non-sole risk party shall pay in money to the sole risk party the reasonable price for the portion of natural resources equal to the half of the sole risk bonus, less expenses incurred in connection with the sale of such portion and tax or other charges paid in connection with such portion.

4. As regards "adjustment of fisheries interests" referred to in paragraph 1 of article V, the Government of each Party shall give administrative guidance to its concessionaires so that they will, before operations for exploration or exploitation of natural resources begin in the subzones with respect to which they have been authorized, endeavour to adjust fisheries interests of nationals concerned of that Party.

5. As regards paragraph 2 of article V, the two Governments shall notify each other of the date on which the operating agreement was submitted to them and the date on which they intend to approve or disapprove the operating agreement.

6. As regards article VI, the two Governments shall endeavour to ensure that the designation of operators be made in such a way as to be equitable to the greatest possible extent.

7. "Expenses reasonably attributable to exploration and exploitation" referred to in paragraph 2 of article IX shall include expenses incurred for the purposes of survey in the Joint Development Zone prior to the date of entry into force of the Agreement.

8. The provisions of paragraph 2 of article IX shall not apply to expenses incurred by sole risk operations.

9. As regards paragraph 3 of article X, application for an extension of the period of exploitation right shall be made at least six months prior to the expiration of each of such periods.

10. As regards paragraph 4 of article X, the two Governments shall, after consultations, grant exploitation right respectively to concessionaires of both Parties on the same date.

11. As regards paragraph 5 of article X, the new concessionaire may apply for an extension of the period of exploitation right under paragraph 3 of article X.

12. For the purposes of article XII, sole risk operations shall be regarded as having been carried out by concessionaires of both Parties.

13. When concessionaires of both Parties are unable to comply with the provisions of article XII for unavoidable reasons, they shall submit for approval a statement setting forth reasons for, and the period of, such delay or suspension to the respective Governments authorizing them. The two Governments shall consult with each other before giving such approval.

14. The approval of the Party referred to in paragraph 1 of article XV shall not be withheld without justifiable reasons.

15. As regards paragraph 2 of article XV, when the remaining concessionaire of one Party who was not the operator under the operating agreement to which such concessionaire and the former concessionaire were parties carries out exploration or exploitation of natural resources under paragraph 1 of article XV, such concessionaire shall be regarded as the concessionaire of the other Party designated and acting as the operator, while retaining its own concessionaireship.

16. As regards paragraph 2 of article XV, taxes on income shall not include royalty.

17. Taxes and other charges to be imposed under paragraph 2 of article XVII include

(1) For Japan:
 (a) Mineral product tax,
 (b) Fixed assets tax and
 (c) Mine lot tax;
(2) For the Republic of Korea:
 (a) Royalty,
 (b) Property tax and
 (c) Rental.

18. (1) "Damage caused by digging operations of seabed and subsoil" referred to in paragraph 3 of article XXI include damage caused by blow-out of oil or natural gas.

(2) "Mine water" referred to in paragraph 3 of article XXI means water flowing out in the course of drilling wells for exploration or exploitation of natural resources, and oil and other substances flowing out together with such water.

19. The provisions of paragraph 3(1) (a) of article XXI shall apply when a concessionaire of one Party carries out exploration or exploitation of natural resources under paragraph 1 of article XV. In such a case, the provisions of paragraph 3 (1) (c) of article XXI shall not apply.

20. As regards paragraph 2 (1) of article XXIII, each Government shall take, within its powers, necessary measures so that its concessionaires and other persons will not exploit independently the structure or field referred to in paragraph 1 of article XXIII during the six-month period referred to in paragraph 2 (1) of article XXIII or during the period in which the two Governments hold consultations for the purpose of making a joint proposal.

21. A concessionaire shall not enter into the agreement referred to in paragraph 2 (2) of article XXIII unless the other concessionaire authorized with respect to the same

subzone also enters into such agreement.

EXCHANGES OF NOTES

Ia

Seoul, January 30, 1974

Excellency,

I have the honour to refer to article XI of the Agreement between the Republic of Korea and Japan concerning joint development of the southern part of the continental shelf adjacent to the two countries signed today (hereinafter referred to as "the Agreement") and to confirm, on behalf of the Government of the Republic of Korea, the following arrangements concerning drilling obligations of concessionaires to be performed during the period of exploration right.

1. (1) Concessionaires of both Parties authorized with respect to each subzone as specified in the appendix to the Agreement shall drill one well during the first three-year period, the following three-year period and the remaining two-year period respectively.

(2) For the purposes of (1), sole risk operations shall be regarded as having been performed by concessionaires of both Parties.

(3) Subzones I and IX shall be deemed to constitute a single subzone for the purposes

(4) Notwithstanding the provisions of (1), concessionaires authorized with respect to Subzone VIII shall be exempted from the obligations under (1) during the first three-year period and concessionaires authorized with respect to Subzones II, III, IV and VI shall be exempted from the obligations under (1).

2. The present arrangements shall become applicable as from the date of entry into force of the Agreement.

I have further the honour to propose that the present Note and Your Excellency's Note in reply thereto confirming the foregoing arrangements on behalf of the Government of Japan shall be regarded as constituting an agreement between the two Governments.

I avail myself of this opportunity to renew to Your Excellency the assurance of my highest consideration.

DONG-JO KIM
Minister of Foreign
Affairs

His Excellency Torao Ushiroku
Ambassador Extraordinary and Plenipotentiary
of Japan to the Republic of Korea

IIa

Seoul, January 30, 1974

Excellency,

I have the honour to acknowledge the receipt of Your Excellency's Note of today's date which reads as follows:

[*See note* Ia]

I have further the honour to confirm, on behalf of the Government of Japan, the arrangements embodied in Your Excellency's Note and to agree that Your Excellency's Note and this Note shall be regarded as constituting an agreement between the two Governments.

I avail myself of this opportunity to renew to Your Excellency the assurance of my highest consideration.

TORAO USHIROKU
Ambassador Extraordinary and Plenipotentiary
of Japan to the Republic of Korea

His Excellency Mr. Dong-Jo Kim
Minister of Foreign Affairs of the Republic of Korea

Ib

Seoul, January 30, 1974

Excellency,

I have the honour to refer to article XX of the Agreement between the Republic of Korea and Japan concerning joint development of the southern part of the continental shelf adjacent to the two countries signed today (hereinafter referred to as "the Agreement") and to confirm, on behalf of the Government of the Republic of Korea, the following arrangements concerning the prevention of collisions at sea.

1. The Government of either Party shall take the following measures in the subzones of the Joint Development Zone with respect to which that Party has authorized concessionaires designated and acting as operators:

(1) (a) When the exploration under the Agreement is carried out in such subzones by surface vessels, that Government shall promptly inform the other Government and mariners of the areas covered by, and the durations of, such exploration activities.

(b) When a fixed installation hazardous to navigation (hereinafter referred to as "fixed installation") is erected, that Government shall promptly inform the other Government and mariners of the exact location of the fixed installation and other particulars necessary for the safety of navigation, such as markings to be fixed to such installation while being erected. That Government shall take similar measures when a fixed installation is dismantled or removed.

(2) When a fixed installation has been erected which rises above the water, that Government shall ensure that:

(a) The fixed installation is marked at night by one or more white lights so constructed that at least one light is visible from any direction. Such lights shall be placed not less than 15 metres above Mean High Water and shall flash Morse letter U (.. -) every 15 seconds or less. The intensity of such lights shall be not less than 6,000 candelas;

(b) The horizontal and vertical extremities of the fixed installation are marked at night by red lights having intensity of not less than 300 candelas;

(c) The fixed installation is equipped with one or more sound signals so constructed and fixed as to be audible from any direction. The sound signals shall have a rated range of not less than 2 nautical miles and shall emit blasts corresponding to Morse letter U (• —) every 30 seconds. The signals shall be operated when the meterological visibility is less than 2 nautical miles;

(d) A radar reflector is so fixed as to enable vessels approaching the fixed installation from any direction to clearly detect the presence of the fixed installation on their radar from a distance of not less than 10 nautical miles;

(e) The fixed installation is equipped with appropriate markings to prevent collisions with aircraft.

(3) When an underwater fixed installation such as submerged well or pipe-line has been erected, that Government shall ensure that it is adequately marked.

(4) (a) When a number of fixed installations are situated in close proximity to one another and when safety of navigation can be secured without each of fixed installations being individually equipped with signals referred to in (2) (a), (b), (c) and (d), such fixed installations may be regarded as constituting a single fixed installation for the

purposes of (2) (a), (b), (c) and (d).

(b) When a fixed installation itself possesses radar reflectory capability which meets the requirements of (2) (d), the fixing of a radar reflector may be omitted.

2. The present arrangements shall become applicable as from the date of entry into force of the Agreement.

3. The present arrangements may be terminated by either Government by giving one year's written notice to the other Government.

4. The two Governments shall meet before the present arrangements are terminated in accordance with 3 to decide on future arrangements.

I have further the honour to propose that the present Note and Your Excellency's Note in reply thereto confirming the foregoing arrangements on behalf of the Government of Japan shall be regarded as constituting an agreement between the two Governments.

I avail myself of this opportunity to renew to Your Excellency the assurance of my highest consideration.

DONG-JO KIM
Minister of Foreign Affairs

His Excellency Torao Ushiroku
Ambassador Extraordinary and Plenipotentiary
of Japan to the Republic of Korea

IIb

Seoul, January 30, 1974

Excellency,

I have the honour to acknowledge the receipt of Your Excellency's Note of today's date which reads as follows:

[*See note* Ib]

I have further the honour to confirm, on behalf of the Government of Japan, the arrangements embodied in Your Excellency's Note and to agree that Your Excellency's Note and this Note shall be regarded as constituting an agreement between the two Governments.

I avail myself of this opportunity to renew to Your Excellency the assurance of my highest consideration.

TORAO USHIROKU
Ambassador Extraordinary and Plenipotentiary
of Japan to the Republic of Korea

His Excellency Mr. Dong-Jo Kim
Minister of Foreign Affairs of the Republic of Korea

Ic

Seoul, January 30, 1974

Excellency,

I have the honour to refer to article XX of the Agreement between Japan and the Republic of Korea concerning joint development of the southern part of the continental shelf adjacent to the two countries signed today (hereinafter referred to as "the Agreement") and to confirm, on behalf of the Government of Japan, the following arrangements concerning the prevention and removal of pollution of the sea resulting from activities relating to exploration or exploitation of natural resources in the Joint Development Zone.

I

The Government of either Party shall ensure that the following measures are taken with respect to (a) a well or a marine facility relating to exploration or exploitation of natural resources in the subzones of the Joint Development Zone with respect to which that Party has authorized concessionaires designated and acting as operators, or (h) a vessel under the flag of that Party engaged in activities relating to exploration or exploitation of natural resources in the Joint Development Zone (hereinafter referred to as "ship"):

1. Blow-out preventer, etc.

(1) (a) A well which is being drilled shall be equipped with blow-out preventer in case blow-out of oil or natural gas is likely to occur.

(b) The provisions of (a) shall not apply when oil testing or repair works are performed and automatic oil- or gas-collecting devices for blow-out have been installed.

(2) The blow-out preventer referred to in (1) shall meet the following requirements:

(a) The blow-out preventer installed at the entrance of a well shall be of an open-and-close type, and of a remote control type which can be promptly operated, with an independent power source;

(b) The operating gear or warning devices for emergency use of such blow-out preventer shall be located close to the person who operates the draw-works;

(c) Flow-bean or other devices shall be installed to control the quantity of oil or natural gas flowing from the outlet of such blow-out preventer;

(d) Devices capable of prevention of blow-out of oil or natural gas from inside drilling pipes, tubing pipes or casing pipes shall be installed.

(3) (a) When drilling of a well or oil testing is performed, muddy water or its materials for emergency use and such materials as are necessary for making heavy muddy water or for controlling the quality of muddy water shall be stocked at the drilling site.

(b) The provisions of (a) shall not apply when automatic oil- or gas-collecting devices for blow-out have been installed.

(4) The blow-out preventer, automatic oil- or gas-collecting devices for blow-out and other devices installed at the entrance of a well shall be such that they can withstand at least the pressures prescribed in the Schedule attached to this Note.

(5) In the course of drilling operations, the following requirements shall be met:

(a) When a well has been drilled to an appropriate depth, the insertion of casing pipes and cementing shall be performed promptly;

(b) When cementing has been performed, its effectiveness shall be confirmed by applying pressure or by other means;

(c) Devices capable of immediate detection of any unusual increases or decreases in the quantity of muddy water in the tank for circulating muddy water shall be installed.

(6) Pressure proof tests of the blow-out preventer shall be conducted at least once a month by applying appropriate pressures.

(7) The blow-out preventer shall be closed when drilling operations are suspended because of difficulties arising from meteorological conditions in maintaining the position of a drilling facility or because of the occurrence, or the danger, of an accident.

2. Discharge of oil

(1) (a) Crude oil, fuel oil, heavy diesel oil, lubricating oil or a mixture containing such oils (hereinafter referred to as "oil") shall not be discharged from a ship or a marine facility.

(b) The provisions of (a) shall not apply to:

(i) The discharge of oil from a ship other than a tanker or the discharge of bilge from a tanker, when the following conditions are all satisfied:

i) The ship or tanker is proceeding en route;

ii) The instantaneous rate of discharge of oil content does not exceed 60 litres per nautical mile;

iii) The oil content of the discharge is less than 100/1,000,000 of the discharge;

(ii) The discharge of oil from a tanker, when the following conditions are all satisfied:

i) The tanker is proceeding en route;

ii) The instantaneous rate of discharge of oil content does not exceed 60 litres per nautical mile;

iii) The total quantity of oil discharged on a ballast voyage does not exceed 1/15,000 of the total cargo-carrying capacity;

iv) The tanker is more than 50 nautical miles from the nearest land;

(iii) The discharge of water ballast from a cargo tank which has been so cleaned that any effluent therefrom would produce no visible traces of oil on the surface of the water, if it were discharged from a stationary tanker into clean calm water on a clear day.

(2) The provisions of (1) shall not apply to:

(a) The discharge of oil for the purpose of securing the safety of a ship or a marine facility, preventing damage to a ship or a marine facility or cargo of a ship or saving life at sea;

(b) The escape of oil resulting from damage to a ship or a marine facility or unavoidable leakage, if all reasonable precautions have been taken after the occurrence of the damage or discovery of the leakage for the purpose of preventing or minimizing the escape;

(c) The discharge of oil from a marine facility if the oil content of such discharge is less than 10/1,000,000 of the discharge;

(d) The discharge of oil from tankers of under 150 tons gross tonnage and other ships of under 500 tons gross tonnage.

3. Discharge of waste

(1) Waste shall not be discharged from a ship or a marine facility.

(2) The provisions of (1) shall not apply to:

(a) The discharge of refuse, excretion, sewage or similar waste resulting from daily life of the personnel aboard a ship or a marine facility;

(b) The discharge of cuttings or dirty water in a manner in which pollution of the sea is not likely to occur;

(c) The discharge of waste other than cuttings or dirty water from a ship in a manner in which pollution of the sea is not likely to occur, and at a location where such discharge is not likely to hinder the maintenance of the sea-environment;

(d) The discharge of waste for the purpose of securing the safety of a ship or a marine facility, preventing damage to a ship or a marine facility or cargo of a ship or saving life at sea;

(e) The discharge of waste resulting from damage to a ship or a marine facility or unavoidable discharge, if all reasonable precautions have been taken after the occurrence of the damage or discovery of the discharge for the purpose of preventing or minimizing the discharge.

4. Prevention and removal of pollution

When large quantities of oil have been discharged from a ship or a marine facility, measures shall be taken promptly to prevent the spread of such pollution, to prevent the continued discharge of oil and to remove the discharged oil.

5. Abandonment of a well

When a well is abandoned, measures such as sealing of the well shall be taken to prevent leakage of mine water or other substances from such well.

II

1. One Government shall promptly provide the other Government with all available information when any of the following occurs:

(a) Discharge of large quantities of oil from a ship or a marine facility;

(b) Collisions between a marine facility and a ship or other objects;

(c) Evacuation of personnel from a marine facility due to dangerous meteorological conditions or other emergencies.

2. When information concerning 1 («) is provided, the Government concerned shall also inform the other Government of the measures taken in accordance with 1.4.

III

1. Under special circumstances, each Government may authorize exceptions to the provisions of I. 1 (2) (a), (b), (c) or (d).

2. With respect to a well exceeding 1,500 metres in depth, each Government may authorize exceptions to the provisions of I. 1 (4).

IV

Either Government may take necessary measures to prevent and remove pollution of the sea when measures are not taken in accordance with I. 4 or when that Government considers that such measures are not sufficient to prevent or remove pollution of the sea.

V

The two Governments shall cooperate closely for the effective implementation of the present arrangements.

VI

1. The present arrangements shall become applicable six months after the date of entry into force of the Agreement or on an earlier date as may be mutually agreed upon between the two Governments.

2. The present arrangements may be terminated by either Government by giving one year's written notice to the other Government.

3. The two Governments shall meet before the present arrangements are terminated in accordance with 2 to decide on future arrangements.

I have further the honour to propose that the present Note and Your Excellency's Note in reply thereto confirming the foregoing arrangements on behalf of the Government of the Republic of Korea shall be regarded as constituting an agreement between the two Governments.

I avail myself of this opportunity to renew to Your Excellency the assurance of my highest consideration.

TORAO USHIROKU
Ambassador Extraordinary and Plenipotentiary
of Japan to the Republic of Korea

His Excellency Mr. Dong-Jo Kim
Minister of Foreign Affairs of the Republic of Korea

SCHEDULE

	Pressure	
Nature of oil or natural gas stratum to be drilled	*Blow-out preventor*	*Devices other than blow-out preventor*
Oil stratum or isolated natural gas stratum with known pressure	1.5 times the pressure at the bottom of an airtight well	Twice the pressure at the entrance of an airtight well
Oil stratum or isolated natural gas stratum with unknown pressure	Kilogram weight per square centimetre equivalent to the figure computed by multiplying by 1.5 the number of metres of the depth of the stratum divided by 10	Twice the pressure at the entrance of an airtight well

Stratum of natural gas dissolved in water	Kilogram weight per square centimetre equivalent to the figure computed by multiplying by 0.5 the number of metres of the depth of the stratum divided by 10	Twice the pressure at the entrance of an airtight well

IIc

Seoul, January 30, 1974

Excellency,

I have the honour to acknowledge the receipt of Your Excellency's Note of today's date which reads as follows:

[*See note* Ic]

I have further the honour to confirm, on behalf of the Government of the Republic of Korea, the arrangements embodied in Your Excellency's Note and to agree that Your Excellency's Note and this Note shall be regarded as constituting an agreement between the two Governments.

I avail myself of this opportunity to renew to Your Excellency the assurance of my highest consideration.

DONG-JO KIM
Minister of Foreign Affairs

His Excellency Torao Ushiroku
Ambassador Extraordinary and Plenipotentiary
of Japan to the Republic of Korea

홍종완/심어진, 동중국해에서의 한·중·일 대륙붕 중첩주장수역의 공동개발에 관한 고찰, 16 서울국제법연구 279 (2009)[1]

한·중·일 대륙붕 중첩주장수역의 공동개발

1) 논의의 필요성

만일 2028년 한·일 공동개발협정이 종료한다면, 한국입장에서는 제7광구가 위치한 수역 중 상당부분이 어떤 합의된 관할약정도 없는 한·중·일 삼국의 대륙붕 중첩주장수역이 된다. 1970년대 초반처럼, 중첩주장수역에 관련국들이 분명한 경계확정에의 합의 내지는 공

1. Sun Pyo Kim, *Legal Relations between States with Opposite or Adjacent Coasts pending Ultimate Delimitation of the Exclusive Economic Zone/Continental Shelf with Particular Reference to North East Sea* (THESIS FOR UNIVERSITY OF EDINBURGH 2001); 양희철/박성욱/박세헌, 동중국해 중일유전개발분쟁을 통해 본 양국의 해영경계획정에 대한 입장연구, 28 OCEAN AND POLAR RESEARCH 175 (Jun. 2006); 김현수, 한일간 동중국해 해양획정에 관한 일본주장의 대응논리, 52 국제법학회논총 43 (2007).

동개별협정이 존재하지 않게 되는 상황이 다시 도래하는 것이다. 대응방법은 크게 두 가지로 전망된다. 하나는 대륙붕 경계선을 정하는 것이고, 다른 하나는 경계획정은 뒤로 미루고 공동개발을 추진하는 것이다. 앞서 살폈듯이, 삼국이 그들의 중첩 대륙붕의 경계를 정하는 문제는 결코 쉬운 문제가 아니다. 기본적으로 대륙붕 경계획정을 위한 법원칙, 어떤 섬을 기점으로 정할지의 문제 등 서로 양보하기 어려운 요인들이 많기 때문이다. 또 경계획정협정이 체결된다고 해도, 만약 경계선상에 자원이 걸쳐 있거나 실질적인 자원의 이동을 초래하는 경우[2] 그런 수역별로 관련국이 합의하여 어떤 방식으로든 공동개발 문제는 분명 반영될 것으로 보인다.[3] 이하에서는 의무적 합작투자모델(Compulsory Joint Venture Model), 초국가적 공동기구모델(Supra-National Joint Authority Model), 단일국 관리모델(Single State Managing Model)의 세 가지 유형[4]을 중심으로 향후 공동개발의 모습을 전망하고자 한다.

---

2. 중 · 일간 핑후(平湖), 춘샤오(春曉), 촨쉐(殘雪), 돤차오(斷橋), 렁취안(冷泉), 룽징(龍井)유전 등이 바다 및 자원의 실질적 이동을 초래하는 그런 유전지역이다.

3. 예컨대, 중국과 베트남 간 체결된 해양경계협정은 경계선에 걸쳐 존재하는 자원에 대해 협의를 통해 개발이익이 동등하게 공유되도록 하는 개발합의를 규정하고 있다(중 · 월간 해양경계협정 제7조). 상세는 최진모, "중국 · 베트남간 통킹만 어업협정 및 해양경계협정 사례에 관한 소고," 해양정책연구, 제21권 제1호(2006) 참조.

4. 공동개발협정은 주권적 권리의 향유주체, 공동위원회 내지 공동기구의 권한과 독립성 등에 따라 다양한 모델이 존재하는바, 'British Institute of International and Comparative Law' 연구팀이 분류한 모델은 아래와 같다.

〈표 A〉 공동개발모델의 분류

구분	의무적 합작투자모델	초국가적 공동기구모델	단일국 관리모델
개념	관련국이 공동수역에 주권적 권리를 향유하며, 일정한 공동운영방식과 수익배분구조를 추구하는 모델	관련국이 그들의 주권적 권리를 공동개발을 위해 만들어진 초국가적 공동기구에 위임하는 모델	일국이 대표하여 공동개발 구역의 자원개발을 담당하는 모델
주권적 권리의 주체	각 협정 당사국	초국가적 공동기구	협정의 일방 당사국
결정방식	당사국간의 합의에 의함 (합의에 의해 운영자 내지 개발권자 결정)	공동기구에 의함 (공동기구가 운영자 내지 개발권자 결정)	일방 당사국이 주도적으로 결정
운영기구	공동위원회	초국가적 공동기구	일방당사국의 운영기구
특징	합의에 이르지 못하면 사실상 개발 불가	공동기구가 실질적 규제권한을 가짐	해양경계가 일국으로 많이 치우친 경우에 주로 체결
대표사례	1974년 한 · 일 공동개발협정	1974년 수단 · 사우디아라비아 협정	1969년 아부다비 · 카타르 협정

위의 표는 상기한 영국 연구팀의 저서와 David M. Ong 교수의 논문을 참고하여 필자에 의해 작성되었음. 각 모델의 특징에 관한 상세는 Hazel Fox et al., *Joint Development of Offshore Oil and Gas* (BR. INS. INT'L & CMP. L., 1989), pp. 115-153; 각 모델에 관한 상세는 David M. Ong, "Joint Development of Common Offshore Oil and Gas Deposits: "Mere" State Practice or Customary International Law?," THE AMERICAN JOURNAL OF INTERNATIONAL LAW, pp. 788-796 (1999) 참조.

2) 한·중·일 삼국간 공동개발

가) 공동개발에 협력할 의무가 존재하는가?

북해대륙붕사건에서 국제사법재판소는 중첩수역이 존재할 경우 관련국에 공동개발을 권고하고 있다. 또한, 현재 삼국은 모두 유엔해양법협약의 당사국으로서, 유엔해양법협약 제83조 제3항을 통해 대륙붕 경계획정의 최종합의에 대한 잠정조치로 공동개발을 추진할 수 있다. 한편, 중첩수역의 석유 및 가스에 관한 공동개발의 여러 국제사례[5]를 통하여 국가가 공동개발협정을 체결할 국제관습법상의 규범이 확립되어 간다고 보는 견해[6]도 있다. 그러나 현재까지는 삼국이 양자 혹은 삼자 간 공동개발을 체결한 명시적인 국제법적 의무가 있다고 말하기는 어렵다. 오히려 분쟁을 피하고 실질적으로 자원을 개발한다는 실리적 관점에서 관련국들이 합의에 의해 공동개발을 진행하는 것으로 이해하는 것이 국제현실에 가깝다고 하겠다.

나) 공동개발구역의 범위

삼자간 공동개발의 문제에 있어 가장 먼저 문제되는 것은 어디서부터 어디까지를 삼국간의 공동개발구역으로 규정할 것인가 하는 공동개발구역의 범위문제이다. 이는 삼국의 배타적 경제수역 경계획정과의 조화 문제로도 이어질 수 있는데, 동중국해는 마주보는 수역이 400 해리가 되지 않아 필연적으로 삼국 접합지점(Tri-junction)을 정해야 하는 문제가 대두된다. 이에 대한 합의는 동중국해의 대륙붕 경계문제에 어떤 식으로든 영향을 미칠 것이다. 이와 관련해 지난 1997년 한·일 배타적경제수역 협상 시 일본은 한·중·일 삼국 간 배타적 경제수역 교차점을 특히 북위 30도43분50초, 동경 125도56분19초라고 제시한 바 있는데, 이는 한국 입장에서 보면 한·일 공동개발구역 거의 전부가 일본의 배타적 경제수역으로 편입되는 것을 뜻한다. 물론 이 교차점이 국제법상 인정받을 수 있는 섬을 기점으로 사용했는지, 또 반드시 배타적 경제수역과 대륙붕을 하나의 경계로 고려해야 하는지는 재차 생각해 봐야 할 쟁점이지만, 배타적 경제수역 경계획정이나 삼국접합지점 문제는 지리적 측면으로 보면 한국에 이로울 것이 없는 게 현실이다.

다행히 한·일 공동개발협정은 협정 체결당시의 지배적인 경계획정원칙이었던 '육지영토의 자연적 연장원칙'을 원용하여 한국에 유리하게 체결된 협정이다. 따라서 적어도 2028년

---

5. 1958년 바레인·사우디아라비아 간 공동개발협정에서부터 1999년 덴마크·영국 간 공동개발협정에 이르기까지 약 20여 건의 공동개발사례가 있었다.

6. David M. Ong 교수는 국가가 공동개발 협정을 체결할 국제관습법상의 규범(rule)이 존재하느냐의 문제에 대해, 유엔총회 결의·국제한례·국가관행 등을 고려해 볼 때, '그렇다'고 결론짓고 있다. 상세는 David M. Ong (전게주 4), pp. 771-804 참조.

까지의 50년 간 관행으로 한·일 양국이 이를 유지한다면 동 협정은 추후 동 지역에의 삼국 간 공동개발 논의 시 쉽사리 무시할 수 없는 요인이 된다. 따라서 한국은 추후 협상과정에서 그 부분을 강조해야 하고, 그리하여 제주 남쪽으로 중국과 일본이 자국 대륙붕이라고 주장하는 수역에 한국의 제7광구가 뻗어나가 중첩되는 수역 전부에 대해 삼자 간 공동개발을 추진하는 것이 한국의 전략이 된다.

다) 각 모델에 따른 전망

삼국이 어떤 모델의 공동개발을 진행하는가에 따라 추후 개발상황이나 속도, 그리고 분쟁해결방법의 판도는 사뭇 달라질 것이다. 첫째, 의무적 합작투자모델로 공동개발을 진행하게 되면, 현재 한·일 대륙붕 공동개발과 비슷한 상황이 초래될 가능성이 있다. 왜냐하면 전술한 바와 같이, 한·일 공동개발협정은 협정시행에 있어 문제의 해결수단으로 공동위원회(제24조)를 두지만, 위원회의 기능은 문제를 접수하고 이를 당사국에 권고하는 것에 국한되며(제25조). 협정이행과 당사국간 분쟁은 일차적으로 외교경로를 통하여 해결되는 구조이다(제26조). 따라서 외교채널에 장애가 발생하거나 원활한 조정이 이루어지지 않는다면 실질적인 공동개발이 속도감 있게 진행되지 않는다. 물론 공동위원회의 구성과 기능, 문제해결수단과 관련한 조항을 어떻게 만드느냐에 따라 일정부분 달라질 수 있지만, 당사국이 각자 주권적 권리를 가지고 그 합의에 의해 개발권자가 정해지고 운영계약이 체결되는 것이 이 모델의 특징이므로, 공동개발협정은 체결했지만 운영과정에서 합의도출이 안 된다면, 실질적인 개발은 더디게 진행될 우려가 크다. 다만, 삼국간 민감한 해역에서 강대국들과의 불필요한 마찰과 긴장을 줄여준다는 점, 추후 자국에 유리한 국제법 논리를 개발할 시간적 여유를 제공한다는 점, 협정기간 동안 삼국 간 공동개발구역으로 존재했다는 사실이 적어도 추후 한국이 동 지역의 이해당사국이라는 권리주장을 할 수 있게 해주는 관행이 된다는 점은 이점으로 볼 수 있겠다.

둘째, 초국가적 공동기구모델의 경우다. 이 모델은 실리적 관점에서 중첩수역의 석유자원을 개발하는 최적의 모델이 될 수 있다. 삼국이 초국가적 공동기구를 두고 실질적인 권한을 모두 위임하게 되면, 외교적 마찰이나 기타 개발협력에 장애를 줄 수 있는 외부적 변수를 최소화할 수 있기 때문이다. 한국 입장에서 보면 이 모델은 다른 모델보다 협정기간 중 긴장이나 불안요인이 적다는 이점이 있다. 그러나 이 모델은 체결되기 전 단계에 많은 노력이 요구된다. 단순히 경계획정의 문제와 자원개발의 문제를 양분해서 경계획정문제를 뒤로 미루고 대신 자원개발을 통해 실질적 이해를 도모한다는 관련국 간의 공동의 이해만으로는 불충분하다. 공동운영과정에서 발생할 수 있는 운영상의 마찰은 그 근본적 이유가 국가의 영유권 욕심에 기인하기 때문이다. 따라서 이 모델이 성공하기 위해서는 기본적으로 관련국 모두가

협정기간동안 공동개발구역을 자국의 바다가 아닌 별개의 공간이라고 인식하는 자세가 필요하다. 역사적으로 볼 때, 한·중·일 삼국은 통합을 꾀하기보다는 서로 경쟁하면서 발전해 온 국가들이라는 특징이 있다. 그랬기에 2000년대 초 한·중·일 에너지 공동기구 설립과 같은 한국측 제안이 제대로 받아들여지지 못했고, 각국이 중동지역 등 산유국들과 개별적으로 협력하는 외부적 방법으로 에너지 전략을 추진해 오고 있는 것이다. 그러나 현재 그리고 미래의 에너지자원의 확보 측면에서 삼국 모두 서로 협력해야 한다는 점을 인식하고 있다. 이와 관련해 지난해 중·일 간 가스전 공동개발합의[7]는 동중국해에서 양국이 실리를 위해 협력할 수 있다는 것을 보여준 상징적인 사례이다.

셋째, 단일국 관리모델이다. 만약 삼국 대륙붕의 가상 경계선이 명백히 한 국가 쪽으로 기울었다면, 나머지 국가들의 합의에 따라 개발은 한 국가가 담당하고 나머지 국가들은 개발이익에 지분참여 하는 방법으로 진행될 수도 있을 것이다. 그러나 오키나와 해구에 대한 입장이 다르고, 설혹 공동개발 논의에 도달하더라도 이 모델은 상대국의 주권적 권리가 타국에 의해 행사된다는 점에서 사실상 주권적 권리를 타국에 이양하는 형태가 되어 합의를 도출하기가 쉽지 않을 것이다. 특히, 일본과 중국은 자국 해양 영토 확장에 팽팽히 맞서고 있어 양국 모두 받아들이기 어려운 모델이라 하겠다.

3) 양자 간 공동개발

가) 개　　관

삼국의 주장수역이 중첩하고 있는 수역이기에 삼자가 아닌 양자 공동개발은 어떤 식으로든 나머지 한 국가의 강력한 항의가 뒤따르게 될 것이다. 더욱이 삼국 모두 상호간 외교관계가 성립되어 있고, 유엔해양법협약 가입국이며, 동중국해의 자원개발에 국가정책으로서의 상당한 무게를 두고 팽팽한 긴장감을 유지하고 있기에 양자 협정의 가능성은 그리 높다고 할 수 없다. 특히, 한·일 간 공동개발의 경우 이제까지 일본이 보여준 소극적 태도로 판단하건대, 한·일 공동개발 협정은 연장되지 않을 것으로 보인다. 또한, 한·중 간 공동개발의 경우 일본이 차지하는 수역의 범위로 보아 일본을 배제한다는 것은 현실적으로 불가능하다. 이하에서는 중·일 간 공동개발에 따른 각 모델의 모습을 전망해 본다.

나) 중·일간 공동개발의 각 모델에 따른 전망

지난 2008년 6월, 중국과 일본 양국은 춘샤오(일본명 '시라카바') 유전의 공동개발과 룽징

7. 중·일 간 춘사오 가스전 공동개발은 가스유전이 중·일 가상경계선의 중국 측 해역에 속하며 이미 중국이 개발 중인 상황에서 일본이 참여하는 방식으로 그 유형으로 따진다면 단일국 관리모델과 가깝다고 하겠다.

[그림 A] 중·일 동중국해 가스전 공동개발구역

(일본명 '아스나로') 남부해역의 공동탐사에 합의했다. 이 중 중국이 이미 개발 중인 춘샤오 유전에 관하여는 일본 법인이 중국 법률에 따라 출자하여 그 비율에 따라 이익을 배분하는 것이며, 룽징 유전에 있어서는 한국과 중국의 경계선이 되는 중간선과 한·일 공동개발구역에 근접해 있다는 점을 고려하여, 이 유전의 남부 수역을 중·일 양국이 공동으로 탐사하는 것으로 합의하였다.[8] 이는 중국과 일본이 주권문제는 일단 유보하고 공동개발을 추진하자는 공통의 이해의 결과이며, 이 같은 이해가 강화된다면 협력대상지역은 더욱 늘어날 것이다. 특히, 중국 측이 일본에 제안한 것으로 알려진 양국 간 공동개발구역이 현재의 한·일 공동개발구역과 지리적으로 매우 근접하고 있다.[9] 이와 관련하여 2028년 한·일 공동개발협정이 종료된다고 가정할 때, 우려되는 상황은 한국을 배제하고, 중국과 일본 양국이 공동개발을

8. 김경신, "중·일 동중국해 가스전 공동개발의 의미와 시사점," 해양수산동향 제1275권(2008), p. 2.

9. 중국과 일본은 2000년대 들어와 한국을 배제한 양국만의 공동개발안을 논의하고 있다. 물론 한·일 공동개발구역에 대한 현실적인 침해는 없었지만, 중국은 지속적으로 공동개발논의에서 한국을 배제하고 있어 한·일 공동개발협정이 종료된 수의 상황은 낙관적이지 않다는 관측도 있다. 구체적으로, 2005년 5월, 중국은 중·일 중간선으로부터 오키나와 해구해역까지 공동개발을 제안한 바 있고, 동년 10월 일본은 중·일 중간선을 포함한 양측해역의 공동개발안을 제안하였으며, 2006년 3월 중국은 한·일 공동개발구역 부근의 공동개발은 제안하였고, 2007년 12월 후구다 총리가 방중, 2008년 5월 후진타오 주석이 방일하였다. 상세는 최수정/홍성걸 "동중국해 한·중·일 자원개발 경쟁," 해양수산 현안분석, 2008-14 (2008), pp. 7-8.

체결하는 것이다. 물론 이 경우에 제7광구 전 지역을 협상수역으로 할 수는 없을 것이며, 제7광구의 남서쪽 경계선 일대이거나 제7광구 중 일부 남측 지역을 대상으로 할 공산이 크다.

중·일 양국이 채택할 공동개발모델에 관하여는, 공동개발협정은 기본적으로 경계획정과는 별개로 취급되는 잠정적 협정이기는 하지만 단일국 관리모델은 일국이 개발을 담당하므로 개발의 주도권과 향후 경계획정 문제에도 유리한 위치를 점하는 상황이 야기될 수 있는 측면이 있어 중·일 양국 모두 쉽게 이 모델을 택하지는 않을 것으로 보인다. 한편, 의무적 합작투자모델은 양국이 군사문제, 해상수송문제, 관련 국내법의 정비문제, 기타 외교적 실리문제 등을 넘어서는 실질적 자원개발이라는 목표가 뚜렷하고, 양국 모두 배분비율과 구조에 만족한다는 전제하에 힘을 발휘할 것이다. 이 경우에 공동운영을 위한 공동위원회가 만들어질 수 있는데, 만약 중요한 사항에 있어 양국간 합의가 원활히 이루어지지 못한다면, 위원회는 제 기능을 못할 가능성이 크다. 이 경우 현재 한·일 대륙붕 공동개발과 같은 부진한 상황이 연출될 수 있다. 가장 우려되는 상황은 중·일 양국이 초국가적 공동기구모델을 채택하는 경우이다. 이 모델은 당사국 정부의 자치권은 줄어들고 협정상의 운영기관이 법인격을 가지며 실질적인 개발활동을 수행하므로, 의사결정이 신속하고 또한 그 권한 행사에 있어 한국의 외교적 의사표시는 힘을 발휘하기 힘들어진다.

4) 소 결

양자 혹은 삼자 협정 중 어떤 경우든 단일국 관리모델은 실현가능성이 높지 않다. 의무적 합작투자모델의 경우는 공동위원회의 권한과 기능이 사실상 운영과정과 문제해결에 있어 권고적 역할을 할 뿐이므로 협정을 체결하더라도 실질적인 개발에는 어려움이 있다. 반면, 체결이 힘들기는 하지만, 한국에 가장 유리한 상황은 삼국이 초국가적 공동기구모델을 택하는 것이다. 이를 위해서는 2000년대 들어 마찰과 합의를 번갈아가며 평행선을 달리고 있는 중·일 양국을 한국이 삼국 논의의 장으로 끌어들여 문제되는 사안별로 논의하는 노력이 필요하다. 반면, 가장 우려되는 시나리오는 중·일 양국만의 초국가적 공동기구모델이다. 이상의 논의를 정리하면 아래 표와 같다.

〈표 B〉 당사국과 모델에 따른 각 경우의 전망

	중·일 간 공동개발	한·중·일 간 공동개발
의무적 합작투자 모델	–공동위원회의 권한과 기능이 중요 –중·일 간 실질적 협력 전제되지 않으면 한·일 공동개발협정과 같은 미온적 결과가 예상됨	–당사국이 주권적 권리를 가지고 합의에 의해 개발권자가 정해짐 –운영상 중요결정은 삼국 합의에 의함 –삼국 외교관계에 영향을 받음
초국가적 공동기구 모델	–초국가적 공동기구가 관리운영주도 –중·일 간 외교마찰의 영향을 덜 받게 됨 –한국으로서는 가장 우려되는 상황	–초국가적 공동기구가 관리운영주도 –협정기간 중 긴장이나 불안요인이 적음 –삼국 외교관계에 큰 영향을 받지 않음
단일국 관리모델	–중·일 간 해양주권 경쟁으로 인해 실현가능성이 낮음	–관리국에 사실상의 관할권을 이양 –실현가능성 낮음
대응방안	–공동개발구역의 범위가 제7광구의 남측 일부에서만 진행될 것임 –한국의 강력한 항의가 필요함	–한국에 가장 유리한 모델임 –삼국협의체 구성노력이 필요함

Ana E. Bastida, Adaeze Ifesi–Okoye, Salim Mahmud, James Ross & Thomas Wälde, *Cross–Border Unitization and Joint Development Agreements: An International Law Perspective,* 29 HOUS. J. INT'L L. 355 (2006–07)

C. General Structure of Agreements

Establishing the area to be covered by a joint development agreement is not a trivial exercise. Although such agreements are invariably without prejudice to subsequent delimitation, it is important that each state ensures that its claim is reflected in the area covered by the JDZ, to the extent that the claim is valid under international law. In some cases, it may be appropriate to establish more than one zone in the agreement, with different terms applying to each area.

Existing joint petroleum development agreements show a wide variation in structure. However, six major issues can be identified as being particularly important for any such agreement. These key issues are the (i) sharing of resources, (ii) management of joint development, (iii) applicable law, (iv) operator and position of contractors, (v) financial provisions, and (vi) dispute resolution.

1. Sharing of Resources

The sharing of resources from the JDZ is a key element to the success of the joint agreement as the perception that the basis for sharing is equitable and fundamental to the ongoing relationship between the two states. There is overwhelming support for the principle of equal sharing. In practice, this is the most common arrangement, though variations do exist. For example, the Senegal-Guinea-Bissau agreement of 1993 (85:15 split in favor of Senegal for petroleum resources, but 50:50 for fishing rights); the 2001 Nigeria-Sdo Tome Principe JDZ (60:40 split in favor of Nigeria) and the 2002 Australia-Timor-Leste Timor Sea Treaty (90:10 split in favor of Timor-Leste).

2. Management

Since the JDZ is generally an area where jurisdiction is disputed, the management structure must provide a satisfactory basis for the protection of the rights (and obligations) of both states. This includes the management of exploration and exploitation activities within the JDZ. Three categories of management structure have been identified:

(i) Single state model: One state managing on behalf of both states. An example of this arrangement is the Bahrain-Saudi Arabia agreement of 1958. As part of the delimitation agreement, the border was positioned to avoid crossing the Fasht Abu-Sa'fah field which, as a result, became wholly within the jurisdiction of Saudi Arabia. However, in return, Saudi Arabia was obliged to grant to Bahrain fifty percent of the net revenues from the field;

(ii) Two states/joint venture model: Each state nominates its own concessionaire, which enters into a joint venture with the concessionaire of the other state. An example of this type of agreement is the Japan-South Korea JDZ;

(iii) Joint Authority model: Both states delegate power to a single body, which becomes responsible for the overall supervision of petroleum activities in the zone. It may be given a legal personality. This model can vary significantly with respect to the powers given to the Joint Authority: it can be strong, almost like a separate state, or a weaker, purely administrative entity. Developing international practice has favored the Joint Authority approach, including the Thailand-Malaysia agreement (1979/1990), the Australia-Indonesia Timor Gap Treaty (1989), the Nigeria-Sdo Tome Principe JDZ (2001) and the Australia-East Timor Sea Treaty (2002). This model may also contain more than one level of authority. For example, administration of the Timor Sea Treaty is based on a three-tier structure: a ministerial council, a Joint Commission and a designated authority.

The Timor Gap Treaty of 1989 is noteworthy in that it actually combines two of the above models. The area covered by the agreement is subdivided into three parts of which Area A is a JDZ based on the Joint Authority model. Areas B and C, however, are consistent with the single-state model described above. In these two areas, jurisdiction is exercised solely by one state but with an obligation to share with the other state a proportion of benefits (ten percent of petroleum taxation revenues) arising from petroleum activities in that area.

3. Applicable Law

Because each state will have its own legal system, including a petroleum fiscal regime that encompasses production sharing contracts, which will very likely be significantly different from each other, it is necessary to establish the legal system that will apply within the JDZ in the agreement. This should include the petroleum licensing regime, laws governing civil and criminal jurisdiction over individuals in the zone, and rules and regulations governing health, safety and environmental issues.

The petroleum licensing guidelines and other regulations may be specified in the agreement or could be left to the Joint Authority to establish. Criminal jurisdiction is generally handled by applying the criminal law of the state corresponding to the nationality of the individual if that individual is a national of either of the two states, or by other agreement between states, but it may be applied by separating the JDZ into two parts with each state exercising criminal jurisdiction in its side of that boundary line.

4. Operator/Position of Contractors

The joint petroleum development agreement will either specify the basis for licensing the area of the JDZ or will designate to some body, for example the Joint Authority, the obligation to develop the rules for selecting contractors to undertake petroleum exploration and exploitation activities on behalf of the two states.

For example, the Nigeria-Sdo Tome Principe JDZ agreement defines "contractor" as a party to a development contract other than the Joint Authority. "Development contract" means any agreement, including leases, licenses, production sharing contracts, and concessions entered into between the Joint Authority and a contractor in relation to a development activity. It also defines "operator" as a contractor appointed and acting as operator under the terms of an operating agreement. In this JDZ agreement, the functions of the Joint Authority include, for example:

(i) [T]he division of the Zone into contract areas, and the negotiation, tendering for and issue and supervision of contracts with respect to such areas;
(ii) [E]ntering into development contracts with contractors, subject to the approval of the [joint ministerial council];
(iii) Oversight and control of the activities of contractors

5. Financial Provisions

States may agree to adopt the taxation regime of the other or apply a contractor to the regime of the state that approved the contractor. Alternatively, they may delegate to the Joint Authority the obligation to formulate and negotiate the fiscal terms applying to petroleum activities. In the latter case, the Joint Authority will develop and apply its own tax regime. Where this is not the case, and the contractor has financial obligations to both states, taxation will apply at a discounted rate, such that the contractor is liable for taxes only on a proportion of its profits to one state and the remainder to the other state.

6. Dispute Resolution

Each joint petroleum development agreement should provide for a dispute resolution mechanism. This will usually involve internal mechanisms that should be pursued prior to resorting to external or third party resolution. These agreements and treaties utilize a wide range of mechanisms, including consultation, negotiation, conciliation, and binding commercial arbitration.

The Nigeria-Sdo Tome Principe JDZ agreement of 2001 illustrates a possible approach. The Treaty covers the resolution of deadlocks and settlement of disputes in Articles 47, 48, and Article 47 refers to the "settlement of disputes between the [joint] authority and private interests. "This is subject to binding commercial arbitration under the UNCITRAL rules sitting in Lagos, Nigeria. Article 48 refers to the resolution of disputes arising in the work of the Joint Authority or Joint Ministerial Council. Where such a dispute arises (with respect to the functioning of the treaty), the first attempt to resolve it should be by the board that governs the Joint Authority. If this is unsuccessful the matter is to be referred to the Joint Ministerial Council, and if it is still unsuccessful it is referred to the heads of the states. Under Article 49, where there are unresolved disputes between states, it will be referred to an arbitral tribunal for a decision that is final and binding on the states. This tribunal is expected to sit at the Permanent Court of Arbitration in The Hague. Each state is to appoint an arbitrator and then both arbitrators appoint a third to act as president. Where this is not possible, it falls to the president of the ICJ to appoint the third arbitrator.

IV. SUMMARY AND CONCLUSIONS

The concept of cross-border unitization is the outcome of two principles:

(i) [T]he principle of unitization as developed in the domestic law of the U.S. and subsequently practiced in other parts of the world; and,

(ii) [T]he principle of cooperation between neighboring states that is emerging in international law and the provisions of international law relating to exploitation of cross-border common natural resources having physical properties analogous to those of petroleum.

There are no binding rules or customs under international law governing unitization, but there is a trend towards an international consensus on an acceptable practice to that end. Unitization is a specialized form of cooperative development where "[a] strong degree of political consensus is a prerequisite for [its implementation]. Under international law, states are not obligated to develop a disputed zone jointly. There is a general obligation, however, to consult and negotiate, with encouragement to "enter into provisional arrangements of a practical nature pending final delimitation. But, it remains the prerogative of each state to choose to consent to a joint development agreement.

Several international cases decided before the ICJ and persistent international practice indicate that JDZs are strongly recommended as suitable provisional arrangements to avoid inaction or the uncertainty of third party dispute resolution on boundary delimitation where petroleum resource potential is known or believed to exist.

The law and practice of cross-boundary petroleum development continues to evolve. Though unitization is a concept largely developed in the United States, it is typically utilized only late in the life of oil and gas fields, and sometimes only on a partial basis because of the unique regulatory history there. The international setting is not burdened by these shortcomings.

Over the last three decades, as petroleum exploration activity has moved outside of North America to states where the State holds the mineral rights, the fundamental principle of unitization has also been widely adopted in the remainder of the world, but with modifications to better reflect the local setting. Outside the United States, unitization is commonly undertaken at the time of initial field development, and may be supplemented by a redetermination of the relative interests of the parties later in the field's life. The widespread development of unitization in the international context is further evidenced by the twelve-state comparative analysis presented in this Article, which provides many examples of the application of unitization in an international setting. A rule of international customary law requiring unitization is not yet established because states are only obligated to negotiate, but not to reach a successful conclusion. Where states decide to cooperate, cross-border unitization and joint development agreements are among several possible legal outcomes.

This detailed analysis of the legal framework for unitization sets the stage for the oil and gas practitioner to successfully apply the practical advice presented in this Article on the necessary elements of a unitization agreement and on the interaction between the unitization agreement and the existing contractual structure in a typical petroleum development.

In conclusion, the evolving trend in international practice is moving toward unitization in situations where common petroleum reservoirs straddle the boundary between ownership interests of two or more parties. This trend is true regardless of whether these parties are foreign oil companies or government oil companies in one state or if the parties are two or more separate sovereign states. The practicalities, motivations, operational efficiencies, and near-term viability of unitization or joint development will continue to drive oil companies and sovereign nations alike to the same ultimate conclusion: unitization of a common reservoir makes the most sense. In light of this growing trend, the Authors hope that this Article can be a guidepost through the challenges facing anyone negotiating a unitization or joint development agreement.

춘천지법 2009. 10. 29. 선고 2007구합632 판결

1. 기초사실

가. 온천의 개발 및 이용 과정[별지 관계 법령 중 구 온천법(2007. 4. 6. 법률 제8337호로 개정되기 전의 것, 이하 '2007. 4. 6. 개정 전 온천법'이라고 한다) 참조]

온천의 개발·이용은, ① 온천징후의 조사·시추(법 제12조) → ② 온천발견신고·수리(법 제21조) → ③ 온천원보호지구 또는 온천공보호구역의 지정(법 제4조, 제5조) → ④ 토지용도별 조치(법 제10조 제5항) → ⑤ 온천개발계획의 수립·승인(법 제10조 제1항) → ⑥ 온천수 이용허가(법 제16조) → ⑦ 온천자원의 보전·관리(법 제24조)의 순서로 이루어진다.

나. 척산온천원보호지구의 지정경과

(1) 소외 1은 1971. 10.경 속초시 노학동 (지번 1 생략) 일대에서 온천공을 발견하여 '□□온천장'이라는 상호의 여관을 설립·운영해 오던 중, 온천법이 제정되어 1981. 6. 1.부터 시행되자 위 법률에 따라 온천굴착허가, 동력장치허가, 온천이용허가를 취득하였다.

(2) 피고는, 1981. 9. 1. 위 온천공 일대 91만㎡를 '척산온천지구'(2001. 1. 26. 온천법이 개정되어 '척산온천원보호지구'로 명칭이 변경되었다)로 지정·고시하였다.

(3) 그 후 설악산 국립공원구역이 지나치게 광범위하여 주민들의 생활 및 재산권 행사에 지장을 초래한다는 지적이 계속됨에 따라 환경부장관은 2003. 8. 30. 설악산 국립공원구역 중 척산온천원보호지구를 포함한 765,000㎡를 국립공원구역에서 해제하였고, 이에 척산온천원

보호지구 내의 주민들이 온천원보호지구도 변경해 줄 것을 지속적으로 요구하자, 속초시장은 2004. 12. 24. 척산온천원보호지구의 면적을 253,425㎡로 축소하는 내용의 척산온천원 보호지구변경처분을 하였다.

(4) 한편, 소외 1은 1985. 4.경 소외 2 주식회사를 설립하여 온천 및 호텔 영업을 하다가 2003. 6. 30. 온천 · 숙박업을 목적으로 하는 원고를 설립하여 대표이사로 취임한 다음, 소외 2 주식회사를 흡수 · 합병함으로써 척산온천원보호지구에 관한 모든 권리 · 의무를 포괄승계하였고, 현재 척산온천원보호지구 내에는 원고가 운영하는 척산온천휴양촌 외에 350m가량 떨어진 곳에 타인이 영업중인 □□온천장이 있다.

(5) 척산온천원보호지구 내에는 원고 소유의 척산온천휴양촌 1, 2호, 소학 1 내지 7호 온천공이 있는데, 2007. 12. 현재 척산온천휴양촌 1, 2호와 소학 7호 온천공만이 사용중이고 나머지 온천공은 사용되지 않고 있으며, 그 이외에 □□온천장이 사용중인 □□온천장 1, 2호공이 있다.

다. 노학온천원보호지구의 지정경과

(1) 참가인은 강원 고성군 토성면에 위치한 ○○대학교와 속초시 노학동에 위치한 □□대학을 설립 · 운영하고 있는 학교법인이다.

(2) 참가인은 □□대학의 부지인 참가인 소유의 속초시 노학동 (지번 2 생략) 일대에서 온천공이 발견되자 2002. 8. 22. 속초시장에게 온천발견신고서를 제출하였고, 속초시장은 온천전문검사기관인 주식회사 한국건업엔지니어링(이하 '한국건업엔지니어링'이라고 한다)의 검사를 거친 다음 2002. 12. 30. 위 신고를 수리하였다.

(3) 참가인은 속초시장으로부터 굴착허가를 얻어 속초시 노학동 (지번 3 생략)과 같은 동 (지번 4 생략)에 온천공 2개를 추가로 굴착하여 온천보조공 인정을 받은 다음, 한국건업엔지니어링의 온천자원조사를 거쳐 2004. 7. 16. 속초시장에게 위 온천공들이 위치한 속초시 노학동 (지번 3 생략) 일대를 온천원보호지구로 지정해 줄 것을 신청하였다.

(4) 이에 속초시장은 온천자원조사 결과를 바탕으로 검토를 마친 다음, 2004. 10. 18. 피고에게 온천부존지역인 속초시 노학동 (지번 4 생략) 일대 98,560㎡를 온천원보호지구로 지정해 줄 것을 신청하였다.

(5) 피고는 신청서류를 검토한 다음 속초시장에게 인근 온천과의 영향 유무 조사 필요성 및 지역 주민의 반대에 대한 의견에 관한 자료를 보완하도록 한 후 행정자치부장관에게 협의를 요청하였는데, 행정자치부장관은 피고에게 "지정예정 지구는 이미 온천원보호지구로 지정된 척산온천원보호지구의 온천부존지역 범위 내에 위치하고 있으므로, 온천의 적절한 보호 · 관리와 효율적인 개발을 위해 온천원보호지구의 지정이 불가하다"는 내용의 의견을 회신하

였다.

(6) 피고는 행정자치부장관의 의견회신을 근거로 "지정신청한 온천 부존구역이 기존의 척산온천 부존구역과 50%가량 중첩된다"는 이유로 속초시장의 온천원보호지구지정신청을 반려하였다.

(7) 참가인은 피고의 온천원보호지구 지정신청 반려처분이 부당하다는 이유로 감사원법 제43조에 따라 감사원에 심사청구를 하였고, 감사원은 2006. 8. 31. "온천원보호지구 지정절차에 아무런 하자가 없고, 법률상 근거가 없는 온천원 부존구역이 기존의 온천원보호지구와 중첩된다는 이유만으로 온천원보호지구지정신청을 거부한 것은 위법하다"는 이유로 피고에게 온천원보호지구 지정거부처분을 취소할 것을 결정하였다.

(8) 이에 속초시장은 2006. 11. 24. 피고에게 다시 노학온천원보호지구 지정신청을 하였고, 피고는 2006. 12. 29. 속초시 노학동 (지번 4 생략) 일원 93,080㎡를 노학온천원보호지구로 지정(이하 '이 사건 처분'이라고 한다)하고 이를 고시하였다.

라. 2007. 4. 6. 개정 전 온천법 제4조 제5항 위반 여부

(1) 원고의 주장

원고는 아래와 같은 이유로 이 사건 처분이 위법하다고 주장한다.

• 2007. 4. 6. 개정 전 온천법 제4조 제5항은 '동일한 온천원이 부존되어 있는 지역'에서는 2개 이상의 온천원보호지구를 지정할 수 없도록 규정하고 있는데, 피고는 척산온천원보호지구의 온천부존지역에 노학온천원보호지구를 중복 지정함으로써 위 온천법의 규정을 위반하였다.

• 척산온천원보호지구와 노학온천원보호지구는 동일한 온천원 부존지역 내에 위치하고 있으므로, 노학온천원보호지구를 지정하여 온천을 개발할 경우 척산온천원보호지구의 온천용출량에 큰 영향을 미치게 됨이 분명한데, 이는 동일한 온천원 부존지역 내에서 온천원보호지구 지정을 받아 온천영업을 해 온 원고의 이익을 부당하게 침해하는 결과를 가져와 온천법의 취지에 반한다.

(2) 2007. 4. 6. 개정 전 온천법 제4조 제5항의 취지

(가) 논의의 필요성

이 사건 처분 당시 시행되던 2007. 4. 6. 개정 전 온천법 제4조 제5항은 "동일한 온천원이 부존되어 있는 지역에서는 2개 이상의 온천원보호지구를 지정할 수 없다"고 규정하고 있는데, 여기서 '동일한 온천원이 부존되어 있는 지역'의 정의에 관하여는 아무런 규정이 없으므로, 관련 규정의 유기적인 해석과 전문가들의 의견 등 제반 사정을 종합하여 그 취지를 확정해야 할 것이다.

(나) 관련 규정

2007. 4. 6. 개정 전 온천법 및 2008. 2. 29. 개정 전 온천법 시행령에 의하면, 온천법은 온천에 대한 적절한 보호와 온천의 효율적인 개발·이용을 도모함으로써 공공의 복지증진과 지역경제 활성화 등에 이바지함을 목적으로 하고(법 제1조), 시·도지사는 온천에 대한 적절한 보호와 온천의 공공적 이용증진 및 효율적인 개발을 위하여 필요하다고 인정하는 때에는 시장·군수의 신청에 의하여 온천원이 부존되어 있는 지역을 온천원보호지구로 지정하거나 온천원보호지구의 범위를 변경할 수 있으며(법 제4조 제1항), 시·도지사가 온천원보호지구를 지정 또는 변경하거나 온천원보호지구의 지정을 해제함에 있어서는 온천전문검사기관의 검사를 거쳐야 하고(법 제4조 제3항), 공중의 목욕용 또는 음용에 제공하거나 산업용 또는 난방용으로 사용하기 위해 온천을 이용하고자 하는 자는 대통령령이 정하는 바에 의하여 시장·군수의 허가를 받아야 하되, 이 경우 이용을 허가할 수 있는 온천수의 수량은 적정한 양수량을 초과할 수 없으며(법 제16조 제1항), 시·도지사가 온천원보호지구를 지정하고자 할 때는 온천원의 부존지역 및 부존량, 온천의 효율적인 이용을 위한 시설 등의 배치, 주변 환경과의 적합성, 다른 지역 개발계획과의 관련성 등을 고려해야 하고(시행령 제2조 제1항), 온천 부존량의 감소 등으로 온천원보호지구의 범위 축소가 바람직하다고 인정되는 경우, 지정 당시의 여건에 현저한 변동이 있어 조정이 불가피한 경우 등에는 온천원보호지구의 범위를 변경할 수 있으며(시행령 제2조 제2항), 온천전문검사기관의 검사에는 온천원 보존실태 및 변화상황, 온천의 온도·수질 및 성분, 부존량 및 1일 적정양수량이 반드시 포함되어야 한다(시행령 제3조 제2항)고 각 규정하고 있다.

(다) 온천법에 의해 지정된 온천전문검사기관 또는 감독관청의 '온천원 부존지역' 개념에 관한 의견

• 행정자치부가 작성한 온천전문검사의 합리화 방안(한국지질자원연구원에 의뢰하여 작성, 갑 3호증): "온천원은 한 곳에 고정되기보다는 순환되고 있기 때문에 온천자원조사에서의 부존량은 실제로 산정할 수 없는 가상적인 개념이며, 온천자원조사(평가)시에는 당해 지구 전체의 지하수·온천수 총사용량에 대한 수위변동 상황을 고려할 수 있으므로 그 지구 전체의 채수가능수량(즉, 부존량)을 평가할 수 있다"라고 기재되어 있다.

• 행정자치부 발간 2004년 온천교육 교재(을 5호증의 1): 온천원보호지구의 지정은 온천법의 규정에 의해 온천원이 부존되어 있는 지역에 대하여 온천원 보호와 향후 온천원보호지구 안에서 1일 적정양수량의 판단에 의한 개발적지를 산정하고 온천 개발을 위해 지정하는 것이고, 온천원보호지구 지정 자체가 온천원 부존지구에 대한 온천원 보호와 향후 개발적지에 대한 온천개발계획의 적정한 수립과 관계되는 것으로서 온천법령상 당해 온천원보호지구

안에서만 온천개발계획이 이루어진다. 따라서 온천원보호지구로 지정된 이상 온천원보호지구의 바깥지역에서는 법제적으로는 온천공 간의 상호 영향이 없을 뿐만 아니라 영향권으로 인한 개발제한범위가 미치지 아니하므로, 설령 기존 온천공에 영향이 있다고 하더라도 온천법의 취지 및 온천개발계획의 성격을 고려해 볼 때 온천원보호지구를 벗어나서는 그 영향권은 인정되지 않는다.

• 강원도지사(갑 3호증): 온천원보호지구에 포함되지 않은 나머지 온천부존지역 내에서는 행위제한 등의 규제규정을 마련하고 있지 않고, 법령에 근거하지 않은 규제는 할 수 없다

• 속초시장(갑 3호증): 부존지역은 온천원보호지구를 지정 · 변경할 때 고려해야 할 사항으로만 명문화되어 있고, 지정 후에는 부존지역의 관리에 대한 명문규정이 없다.

• 한국지질자원연구원(갑 3호증, 감정촉탁 결과): 온천원보호지구는 각 시 · 군에서 온천부존지역을 고려하여 결정하므로 온천원보호지구와 온천부존지역은 많은 범위를 공유하게 되고, 따라서 별도의 지역을 따로 온천부존지역으로 지정하는 것은 필요하지 않다. 온천원 부존범위 조사는 1개 지구 내에 있는 온천공들에서 1일 적정양수량으로 양수할 때 수위가 발생하는 범위를 조사하는 것으로서, 대수층 특성, 지질구조 등을 고려하여 부존범위를 정하고 있는데, 온천원보호지구는 기술적 · 법적 · 행정적 개발의 타당성 등을 고려하여 설정된 범위이고, 부존지역은 기술적(수리지질학적)인 면을 고려한 범위로서 부존지역은 온천원보호지구를 지정하는 데 고려하는 하나의 요소이다.

• 한국수자원공사(갑 3호증): 온천원보호지구란 온천이 부존하는 지역과 그 온천에 영향을 줄 수 있는 지구를 포함하는 개념이므로, 온천원보호지구 밖에 별도의 온천부존지역을 설정하는 것은 적절하지 않다.

• 한국농촌공사(갑 3호증): 별도의 온천부존지역에 대한 범위를 정하여 관리하려 한다면 해당 유역 전체의 지표 · 지하 물수지 관계를 정확히 밝혀야 하나 이는 사실상 불가능한 일이며, 현행 온천법 시행령은 온천원보호지구 지정시 부존구역을 고려하여 지정토록 규정되어 있으므로 별도의 관리지역을 설정한다는 것은 그 근거가 없고 분쟁의 소지가 있다.

• 대한광업진흥공사(갑 3호증): 온천부존지역의 경계를 과학적으로 정확하게 설정한다는 것은 불가능하고, 온천부존지역은 행정적으로 온천원보호지구를 지정하기 위한 기초 또는 참고자료이므로, 온천원보호지구가 지정된 후의 온천부존지역은 관리측면에서 실익이 없다.

• 사단법인 한국수맥협회(갑 3호증): 온천은 지하수라 할 수 있고, 열을 간직한 암반이 넓게 분포되어 끊임 없이 연결되어 있으며, 대맥은 시 · 군 간 또는 도와 도 간에 계속적으로 연결되어 있으므로, 기존 온천원 보호를 위해 온천부존지역을 추가로 지정하는 것은 타당하지 않고, 지구의 과다책정은 그 지구 내 토지 소유자들에게 지하수 개발을 못하게 하는 등 불필요한 제한을 줄 뿐이다.

[인정 근거] 다툼 없는 사실, 갑 3호증, 을 5호증의 1 내지 4의 각 기재, 이 법원의 한국지질자원연구원장에 대한 감정촉탁 결과 및 사실조회 결과, 변론 전체의 취지

(라) 판 단

앞서 살펴본 바와 같이, 온천에 대한 적절한 보호와 온천의 효율적인 개발·이용을 도모하고자 하는 온천법의 목적과 그러한 목적을 위해 필요한 경우 온천원보호지구를 지정하고 그 범위를 변경하거나 해제할 수 있는 점, 온천에 대한 이용허가를 함에 있어서 온천수의 적절한 양수량을 초과하지 않도록 해야 하는 점, 온천원보호지구를 지정할 때는 온천원의 부존지역 및 부존량, 온천의 효율적인 이용을 위한 시설 등의 배치, 주변 환경과의 적합성, 다른 지역 개발계획과의 관련성 등을 고려해야 하고, 온천전문검사기관의 검사에는 온천원 보존실태 및 변화상황, 부존량 및 1일 적정양수량 등이 반드시 포함되어야 하며, 온천 부존량의 감소 등으로 온천원보호지구의 범위 축소가 바람직하다고 인정되거나 지정 당시의 여건에 현저한 변동이 있어 조정이 불가피한 경우 등에는 온천원보호지구의 범위를 변경할 수 있는 점 등 온천법령의 관련 규정들과 온천전문검사기관 등의 '온천원 부존지역' 개념에 관한 의견, 그리고 2007. 4. 6. 개정 전 온천법 제4조 제5항은 기존의 온천원보호지구가 설정되어 있는 경우 새로운 온천원보호지구를 지정함으로써 기존의 온천원보호지구에서 온천을 운영하고 있는 기득권자가 손해를 입지 않도록 하는 한편, 중복된 온천원보호지구 지정으로 온천의 이용·개발계획에 혼란이 야기되는 것을 방지하기 위함에 목적이 있는 것으로 보이는 점 등 제반 사정을 고려해 보면, 2007. 4. 6. 개정 전 온천법 제4조 제5항 소정의 "동일한 온천원이 부존되어 있는 지역으로서 2개 이상의 온천원보호지구를 지정할 수 없는 경우"에 해당하는지 여부는, 새로운 온천원보호지구를 지정함으로써 기존 온천원보호지구 안의 온천에 조금이라도 영향이 있는 모든 경우를 말하는 것이 아니라, 새로운 온천원보호지구를 지정함으로써 기존 온천원보호지구 안의 온천에 대한 적절한 보호와 온천의 효율적인 개발·이용을 도모하는 데 방해가 되거나 온천수의 적절한 양수량을 양수하는 데 상당한 정도로 방해가 되는 경우를 말하는 것으로 해석함이 타당하다(대법원 2008. 5. 29. 선고 2007두23941 판결은 온천발견신고의 수리 여부를 판단하는 기준에 관한 것이기는 하나, 이 사건에도 참고가 될 수 있을 것이다).

따라서 이 사건 처분이 위 온천법 규정에 위배되는지 여부는, 노학온천원보호지구의 지정·이용으로 인해 척산온천원보호지구 내 원고의 기존 온천에 대한 적절한 보호와 온천의 효율적인 개발·이용을 도모하는 데 방해가 되거나 온천수의 적절한 양수량을 양수하는 데 상당한 정도로 방해가 되는지 여부에 따라 판단해야 한다.

(3) 척산온천원보호지구의 온천공에 영향이 미치는지 여부

(가) 인정 사실

① 이 법원의 현장검증 결과: 참가인의 온천공 중 보조공의 하나인 SC-3호공만이 척산온천원보호지구 내에 있고, 척산온천휴양촌 내 온천공과는 800m 정도 떨어져 있다.

② 2002. 11.경 한국건업엔지니어링의 속초 노학지구 온천공 검사보고서 및 온천공 영향조사보고서

• 속초시 노학동(지번 2 생략)에 개발된 시추공(SC-1호공)은 투수량 계수 68.28㎡/일, 적정양수량 763㎥/일, 수위강하량 41.7m, 수온 41.2° C이고, 수질검사결과 대장균이 검출되지 않았으며 수질의 특성은 pH 8.84 정도의 알칼리성이다.

• SC-1호공의 장기 양수에 따른 인근 지하수공(노학동(지번 4 생략)에 있는 PW-4호공 및 노학동(지번 5 생략)에 있는 PW-5호공)의 수위 변동을 조사하였는데, SC-1호공의 경우 케이싱을 인근 지하수공의 케이싱 설치 심도보다 깊게 설치하여 온천수의 용출을 위한 상부 대수층의 냉수대를 철저히 차단하였기 때문에 온천공의 양수시 인근 지하수의 유입은 불가능하고, 장기대수성 시험결과 인근 지하수공인 PW-4호공, PW-5호공의 수위 강하도 발생하지 않는 것으로 측정되어 온천공의 양수에 의한 영향은 없을 것으로 생각된다.

• WHPA module을 이용한 지하수 유동 모델링 결과 온천공에서 3년 간 지속적으로 채수할 경우 온천공의 포획구간은 상류구배 구간 108m, 하류구배 구간 58m로 나타나고 있고, 인근 지하수공은 모두 온천공의 포획구간 외부에 위치하고 있어 온천공의 장기양수에 의한 영향은 없는 것으로 판단된다(다만, 위 보고서는 온천공과 인근 지하수공의 영향에 대한 조사이고, 온천공과 인근 온천공 사이의 직접적인 영향에 대한 조사는 이루어지지 않았다).

③ 2005. 1.경 한국건업엔지니어링의 속초 노학지구 인근 온천의 영향 유무에 대한 정황 분석

• 노학온천원보호지구 내에 개발된 온천공은 모두 3개로 인근에 위치하는 척산온천원보호지구의 온천공 중 가장 근거리에 위치하는 온천공과의 거리는 최소 662m 내지 최대 872m의 거리를 두고 있고, 굴착심도는 거의 비슷한 심도로 개발되어 있으나 척산온천원보호지구의 온천공들이 약 100m 정도 깊게 개발되었다.

• Schultze식 및 Weber식(온천공의 영향반경 산정방식으로서 구체적인 내용은 생략한다)에 의하여 산정된 노학온천원보호지구 온천공의 영향반경은 SC-1호공이 최대 110.86m, SC-2호공이 최대 117.74m, SC-3호공이 최대 41.42m로 나타났다.

• SC-1, 2, 3호공의 포획구간(양수정의 양수로 인해 인근 온천수가 유입될 때 유입되는 구역을 의미한다)은, SC-1호공의 경우 상류구배 구간 151m, 하류구배 구간 71m, SC-2호공은 상류구배 구간 196m, 하류구배 구간 85m, SC-3호공은 상류구배 구간 89m, 하류구배 구간 80m로

산정되었다(이 결과는 온천수를 3년 동안 지속적으로 채수한다는 극단적인 가정 아래 산출된 결과로서, 실제 온천수를 이용할 때는 필요시 온천공을 가동하고 불필요시 온천공의 가동을 중단하는 단속적인 채수를 하기 때문에 실제 포획구간은 감소할 것으로 예상된다).

• 노학온천원보호지구의 온천공 포획구간 내에 다른 온천공은 존재하지 않는다.

• 따라서 노학온천원보호지구의 온천공은 인근 지역에 위치하는 척산온천원보호지구의 기존 온천공에는 영향이 없을 것으로 판단된다.

④ 2004. 3.경 하나엔지니어링의 속초 척산온천원보호지구 온천부존량 조사보고서

• 척산온천원보호지구 내 온천공의 동시양수시험 결과 총양수량은 4,211㎥/일, 평균수위강하는 47.13㎥로 조사되었다.

• 조사지역 선구조선의 분포특성은 상기 북서-남동 방향의 조선누층군 및 공주-음성 단층과 매우 밀접한 구조지질학적 연관성을 가지고, 이로부터 예상되는 암반 단열계의 분포 양상과 그에 따른 지하수의 부존 및 수리지질학적 특성 역시 직·간접적으로 이들 단층대의 영향권에 포함될 것이다.

• 물리탐사 및 지질조사결과 부존면적은 290만㎡로 산출되었고, 조사지역의 채수가능량은 약 4,211㎥/일로 산출되었으나 이는 동시양수시험시의 자료이며, 전체적인 개발계획을 위한 본 지구의 적정양수량은 위 조사 값의 70%인 2,948㎥/일로 하는 것이 적당한 것으로 판단된다.

⑤ 이 법원의 한국지질자원연구원장에 대한 감정촉탁 결과 및 사실조회 결과

• 2002. 11.경 한국건업엔지니어링의 속초 노학지구 온천공 검사보고서 및 온천공 영향조사보고서는, 온천공 검사 및 주변 지하수공과의 영향조사로서 각 조사항목, 조사내용 및 그 결과에 있어서 타당하다.

• 2005. 1.경 속초 노학지구 인근 온천의 영향유무에 대한 정황분석 보고서는, 온천공의 영향반경 계산에서 시간인자를 1로 하여 축소한 경향이 있고, 현장에서 구한 수리상수가 많아 지하수 유동 모델링을 통하여 영향반경을 구하는 것이 보다 효율적인 정도의 약간의 오류가 있다.

• 2004. 3.경 하나엔지니어링의 온천부존량 조사보고서는, 적정양수량이 변경되려면 각 온천공에 대한 단계양수시험이 수행되어야 하나 이에 대한 시험자료가 없는 등 온천에서 중요한 적정양수량을 근거 자료 없이 변경함으로써 신뢰성이 떨어지고, 온천의 부존범위는 온천공에서 양수시 수위 강하가 발생되는 범위와 관련하여 해석해야 하는데 그렇게 하지 않았다.

• 결론: 온천조사의 표준화는 2003. 4. 1. 굴착허가신청서 접수분부터 시행되었는데, 노학온천보호지구의 온천공들은 2003. 4. 1. 전후에 굴착되었고 온천조사도 기관별로 상이하거

나 미숙한 점이 많으나, 전체적인 맥락에서 본다면 한국건업엔지니어링에서 수행한 온천조사가 약간 틀릴 수는 있어도 온천의 3대 요소인 수량, 수온, 수질의 평가에 있어서 온천공으로 합당하다고 판단된다.

(나) 판 단

위와 같이 노학온천원보호지구의 온천공들과 척산온천원보호지구의 온천공들 사이의 거리, 온천공들의 심도, 장기 양수에 따른 영향범위, 포획구간 등 제반 사정을 종합해 보면, 노학온천원보호지구의 지정·이용으로 인해 척산온천원보호지구 내 원고의 기존 온천에 대한 적절한 보호와 온천의 효율적인 개발·이용을 도모하는 데 방해가 되거나 온천수의 적절한 양수량을 양수하는 데 상당한 정도로 방해가 된다고 보기는 어렵고, 이에 반하는 듯한 2004. 3.경 하나엔지니어링의 온천부존량 조사보고서는 온천에서 중요한 적정양수량을 근거 자료 없이 변경하였고, 온천의 부존범위를 온천공에서 양수시 수위 강하가 발생되는 범위와 관련하여 해석하지 않는 등 신뢰성이 떨어지므로 이를 믿기 어려우며, 달리 노학온천원보호지구의 지정·이용으로 인해 척산온천원보호지구 내 원고의 기존 온천에 대한 적절한 보호와 온천의 효율적인 개발·이용을 도모하는 데 방해가 되거나 온천수의 적절한 양수량을 양수하는 데 상당한 정도로 방해가 된다는 점을 인정할 만한 증거가 없으므로(위 한국지질자원연구원장에 대한 사실조회 결과에 의하면, 노학온천원보호지구 내의 온천공과 척산온천원보호지구 내의 온천공들 사이에 직접적인 영향조사를 실시하는 것이 가장 합리적이라 할 것인데, 원고는 참가인이 2008. 3. 25.자 준비서면 및 2008. 4. 12.자 원고 신청 감정에 대한 의견서의 각 진술을 통해 "원고가 속초시의 직접적인 영향조사에 협조하거나, 이 사건 소송에서 직접적인 영향조사를 실시할 것"을 주장하였음에도 불구하고, 이를 거부한 채 감정비용 등을 이유로 위 한국건업엔지니어링 보고서의 타당성 감정 등 간접적인 영향조사만을 신청하였다가, 막상 그 감정촉탁 결과와 사실조회 결과가 자신에게 불리하게 나오자 소 제기일로부터 2년 6개월 정도가 경과하여 변론종결이 임박한 시점에 이르러서야 비로소 직접적인 영향조사를 요구하는 등 적기에 적절한 입증 방법을 신청·제출하지 않았다), 결국 원고의 이 부분 주장은 이유 없다.

3. 국가주권의 행사

가. 소유권 귀속

에너지자원에 대한 소유권 내지 에너지를 개발할 권리를 부여할 수 있는 권한이 국가주권의 일부라는 것에 모든 국가가 동의한다. 예외적으로 미국과 캐나다의 경우에만 토지 내지 해저면의 지하에 있는 광물에 대한 개발권 내지 채취권이 토지소유권 내지 수면이용권의 일부를 구성하는 것으로 보고 있으나 이런 권리 역시 국가주권의 행사로 인한 법으로 인정된다는 면에서 국가주권원칙과 배치되는 것은 아닌 것으로 보인다. 우리는 토지 내지 수면의 소유권 내지 이용권이 누구에게 속하는지에 관계없이 석유와 가스의 경우 이들을 개발할 권리 내지 이들의 소유권은 국가에 속하는 것으로 보고 있다.

류권홍, 자원소유권의 귀속, 25 원광법학 35 (2009)

가) 자원소유권의 귀속문제와 관련된 위험

해외에서 자원을 개발하려고 하는 회사가 가장 먼저 검토해야 하는 것은 자원 보유국의 헌법이나, 자원관련 법령들이 자원의 소유권 관계를 어떻게 정하고 있는지에 대한 법률적 검토이다. 물론 현지 변호사들의 의견서를 사전에 받는 것이 좋고, 자원의 소유권 귀속문제와 더불어 자원 개발권의 취득과 관련된 절차와 개발권의 기간, 등기 또는 등록 여부 및 대항력 그리고 조달에 관한 법, 세법, 노동법, 외환관련법 등에 대한 검토를 거치는 것이 대규모 자본을 투자가 뒤따르는 자원개발에 관련된 위험을 방지할 수 있는 방법이다. 그런 다음 또는 동시에 기술적 탕당성, 금융 가능성 등에 대한 분석이 수행된다.[1]

대부분의 나라들이 석유와 가스를 비롯한 중요 자원은 국유임을 밝히고 있으나, 북미 대륙의 미국과 캐나다 그리고 극히 소수의 몇몇 나라들의 경우는 토지 소유자에게 자원의 소유권이 귀속되어 있다. 그렇다 하더라도 자원의 국유를 선언한 나라들뿐 아니라, 자원의 사유를 인정하는 북미 국가들도 자국 영토 내의 자원에 대한 배타적 개발 및 처분에 관한 권리는 앞에서 본 바와 같이 주권[2]에 속하는 것으로 인식하고 있음은 물론이다.

자원의 소유권과 관련된 현실적인 문제는 ① 국경에 대한 분쟁은 없으나 석유나 가스가 두 국가 이상의 영역 아래에 존재하는 경우[3]와 ② 국경에 대한 분쟁이 존재하면서 동시에 두 국가 이상의 영역 아래에 존재하는 경우에 발생하며, 후자의 경우가 훨씬 해결되기 어렵다.[4] 이렇게 두 국가 이상의 영역 아래에 존재하는 경우 당사자들의 합의가 이루어지지 않아 자원

1. Rovert Pritchard, *Safeguards for Foreign Investment in Mining*, in INTERNATIONAL AND COMPARA - TIVE MINERAL LAW AND POLICY; TRENDS AND PROSPECTS (2005) 76.
2. 주권이라는 것이 반드시 국가기관만의 것이 아니라 국민 개인의 것이기도 하므로 자원의 사유권을 인정하는 국가라 하더라도 자원 주권주의를 부정하는 것은 아니다.
3. 북해 석유개발의 경우가 그 예이며, 영국과 노르웨이가 공동개발에 대한 협정을 체결했다.
4. 국경 분쟁이 발생하는 주된 이유는 과거 식민지 제국주의 하에서 식민지 국가들의 국경 획정이 역사적, 문화적, 종교적 그리고 인류학적 검토 없이 침략국들이 독자적으로 경계선을 획정했기 때문이다. 과거 석유나 가스가 중요한 국부의 원천으로 여겨지지 않았을 때는 커다란 문제가 되지 않았지만, 현재는 두 나라의 영역 아래에 석유나 가스가 매장되어 있음이 확인되는 경우 그 개발을 둘러싼 분쟁이 발생하며, 많은 경우 국가 간 또는 국가 내부에서의 전쟁으로 이어지기도 한다.

개발이 불가능한 경우도 있고, 비록 분쟁이 존재하더라도 공동개발의 형식을 통해 개발이 이루어지는 경우가 있다.[5]

특히 심해저 지역에 존재하는 자원에 대한 소유권(또는 주권)의 주체가 명확하지 않다. 영토 및 영해의 범위 획정에 관한 문제는 국제법의 쟁점이지만, 에너지 개발에 있어서 실질적인 의의를 가지게 되는 것도 이 때문이다.[6]

그리고 과거에는 소홀히 다루어졌으나 새로이 현실적인 문제로 전개되고 있는 것이 원주민들의 자원에 대한 권한 문제이다. 미국, 캐나다 및 호주 등의 경우 원주민들의 자원에 대한 권리를 어떻게 부여할 것인지가 중요한 쟁점이며, 따라서 이들 나라에서 자원을 개발하려는 회사들이 사전에 충분한 검토를 거쳐야만 하는 대상이기도 하다.[7]

이와 더불어, 연방정부와 지방정부 중 누가 자원을 소유하는가, 개발에 대한 관리권이 누구에게 있는가의 문제와 자원개발에 대한 권한을 국영석유회사에 위임했을 경우 그 법률관계에 대한 검토 또한 필요하다. 전자의 경우와 관련된 구체적 사례는 이라크 쿠르드 자치정부와 한국의 석유공사가 체결한 계약과 관련하여 쟁점이 된 사안이며, 이라크 헌법과 쿠르드 자치정부 석유법 그리고 현재까지 입법화되지는 않았지만 사안의 해결에 하나의 기준이 될 수 있는 연방정부의 석유법(안)의 해석문제이기도 하다. 연방정부의 승인 없이 독자적으로 쿠르드 자치정부가 석유의 개발권을 부여할 수 있는 권한이 없다고 해석된다면, 쿠르드 자치정부와 체결한 개발권 부여 계약은 하자있는 계약이 될 것이다.

나) 우리나라

나)–1. 헌법, 광물법, 해저광물자원개발법 및 민법의 규정

우리나라의 경우, 헌법 제120조 제1항에 '광물 기타 중요한 지하자원 · 수산자원 · 수력과 경제상 이용할 수 있는 자연력은 법률이 정하는 바에 의하여 일정한 기간 그 채취 · 개발 또는 이용을 특허할 수 있다'라고 되어 있으며 이에 대한 해석으로 자연자원의 사유화를 전제로 한 특허제도를 규정하고 있다는 견해[8]와, 국토개발상 필요한 국토 · 자원 등에 대한 제한으로 해석하는 견해[9] 등이 있다. 즉, 중요한 천연자원의 특허주의를 정하고 있을 뿐, 헌법적 차원에서

---

5. 해역에서의 공동개발에 관하여는 Hazel Fox, JOINT DEVELOPMENT OF OFFSHORE OIL AND GAS (1990) 가모델 계약서와 이에 대한 법적 검토 자료 및 호주 · 동티모르(과거의 인도네시아), 한국 · 일본 사이의 공동개발협정 등에 대한 분석을 제공하고 있다.

6. 영해, 대륙붕, 배타적 경제수역의 범위 획정에 관하여는 국제해양법협약(International Convention on the Law of the Sea 1982)이 적용되지만, 국제해양법협약의 법적 구속력 문제는 여전히 국제법적 검토 대상이다.

7. Ernst E. Smith, Joh, S. Dzienkowski, Owen L. Anderson, Gary B. Conine, John S. Lowe, Bruce M. Kramer, International Petroleum Transaction (2000), 275-299.

8. 권영성, 헌법학원론, 법문사, 2008, 168면.

든 법률적 차원에서 그 소유권의 귀속에 대한 법적 정리가 이루어지고 있지 않은 것이다.

한편 광업법 제2조는 '국가는 채굴되지 아니한 광물[10]에 대하여 채굴하고 취득할 권리를 부여할 권능을 갖는다'라고 하여, 광물의 소유권에 관한 내용은 없고 광물을 채굴하고 취득할 권리를 부여할 권능을 가진다는 것만 분명히 하고 있다. 또한 석유와 관련하여 광업법은 제9조 제1항에서 '석유에 관한 광업권은 정부만이 가질 수 있다'고 광업권 국유의 원칙을 밝히고 있다. 해저광물자원 개발법 또한 제4조 제1항에서 '해저광업권은 국가만이 가질 수 있다'라고 하여 해저광물의 소유권 귀속에 관한 내용은 없이 단지 국가만이 해저광업권의 귀속자라는 것을 정하고 있다. 한편 민법은 제212조는 '토지의 소유권은 정당한 이익 있는 범위 내에서 토지의 상하에 미친다'라고 정하고 있다.

나)-3. 우리법제의 문제점

위에서 본 우리 법률들이 가지고 있는 문제점을 구체적으로 지적할 필요가 있으며 이들은 입법적으로 해결되어야 할 사항들이다. 물론 아래의 지적사항 중 일부가 소유권의 쟁점과 직접 관련된 문제가 아닐 수도 있지만, 소유권과 석유에 대한 기본적 정의에 관한 문제가 복합적으로 해결되어야 할 필요가 있기 때문에 그런 부분까지 지적해 보고자 한다.

첫째, 석유가스를 포함한 광물의 소유권 귀속에 관한 명시적 규정이 없다. 일부 견해는 광업법상 또는 해저광물자원 개발법상 해저광물이 국유라고 전제하고 있거나,[11] 광물의 소유권에 관한 원칙을 소유자취득주의, 광업(국가)독점주의 및 특허주의로 구분하면서 우리나라는 특허주의를 택한 국가로 해석되는 견해가 있다.[12] 그러나 이런 견해들은 ① 헌법과 관계법들이 명시적으로 소유권의 귀속에 관한 규정을 두고 있지 않은 점, ② 헌법과 자원법 등은 국가가 광물(해저광물 포함)을 채굴하고 취득할 권리를 가진다는 점만을 분명히 하고 있는 점, ③ 특허주의는 소유권의 귀속문제와 차원을 달리한다는 점들 때문에 너무 앞서 나간 해석이라고 하지 않을 수 없다. 위에서 본 것처럼 헌법학자들도 단지 특허주의를 정하고 있다는 표현을 하고 있을 뿐 소유권이 국가에 속한다고 주장하지 않고 있는 이유도 이 때문일 것이다.

그렇다면 광물의 소유권은 토지의 소유권에 귀속되어서 광물이 존재하는 대지의 소유권자에게 귀속하되, 그 개발을 위해서는 국가의 특허를 부여받아야 한다고 해석하는 것도 현행법상 충분히 가능한 것이다. 이런 문제에 대하여 위에서 본 바와 같이, 미국은 소유권의 사적 귀속을 법적으로 인정하고 있는 것이며, 영국이나 호주, 터키[13] 등은 이런 문제를 해결하기

---

9. 허영, 한국헌법론, 박영사, 2008, 163면.

10. 광물의 정의는 광업법 제3조 제1호에 정해져 있다.

11. 이경한 외 5인, 광업권 관리제도 개선연구, 한국지질자원연구원, 2005, 20면.

12. 이연승, 광업법축조연구, 한국동력자원연구소, 1998, 42면.

13. 터키의 경우도 석유법(Petroleum Law) 제1조에서 '터키의 모든 석유자원인 국가의 소유에 속하며 그 지배하에 있다'고 명시하고 있다.

위해 입법적으로 국가의 소유임을 밝히고 있는 것이다. 따라서 우리나라도 석유, 가스 등 중요 자원의 소유권 문제를 헌법 또는 개별법에서 명시적으로 국유로 정하고, 그 개발권의 취득은 국가와의 계약[14]에 의해 이루어지는 방식으로 전환되어야 한다.

둘째, 석유·가스에 대해 명확한 개념이 정해져 있지 않다. 이로 인해 광업법의 적용과 해석에서 어려운 문제가 발생할 수 있다. 예를 들어, 우리나라 영토 내에서 가스개발에 성공하는 경우 현행 광업법 제9조는 '석유'에 대한 광업권만 정하고 있기 때문에 가스는 어떤 법에 따라 개발되어야 하는지에 대하여 법률 공백 상태가 발생한다. 근원적으로는 광업법과 해저광물자원 개발법이 석유(여기서는 'petroleum'을 의미한다)에 대한 정의를 분명히 하지 않아서 발생하는 문제이다. 만약 석유의 개념을 명확히 하고 가스도 포함하도록 한다면 이상의 문제는 해결될 수 있다. 예를 들어, 호주 빅토리아주의 자원개발법(Mineral Resources Sustainable Development Act 1990) 제4조는 '그것이 기체이든, 액체이든 또는 고체이든 그 상태를 묻지 않고 자연적으로 발생하는 탄화수소'를 석유라 정의하여[15] 그 개념이 포괄적이며, 터키 석유법 제3조 제1호[16]도 유사한 개념을 사용하고 있다. 이런 방식으로 개념이 정의되면, 가스 또는 향후 개발이 예상되는 가스 하이드레이트(Hydrate)의 경우까지 포섭하게 되므로 석유나 가스의 개념에 대한 해석에서 발생하는 어려움을 사전에 제거할 수 있게 된다.

셋째, 석유 등 자원개발 제도의 선진화가 필요하다. 우리나라는 석유나 가스의 개발을 독려할 필요성이 다른 어느 나라보다 강하게 요구되므로, 개발권의 취득 절차·개발권의 기간·조세·개발에 필요한 장비나 재료의 구입관련 혜택·기타 필요 토지, 시설이나 서비스의 취득·외국인 채용 등 자유로운 노동계약·대출 및 수익의 자국 송금 등 자원의 개발과 관련

---

14. 특허주의는 설권적 행정행위로 특정인에게 권리를 부여하는 것이지만, 현실적으로 특허장(허가증)을 부여하면서 별도의 계약을 체결하고 이에 따라 권리와 의무의 내용이 정해지고 있으므로 실질적으로는 계약으로 해석될 수 있다. 물론 이 계약의 방식은 양허방식(Concession Agreement), 생산물분배협정(Production Sharing Agreement), 역무제공계약(Service Contract) 등 다양하며, 계약을 입찰 방식으로 할 것인지 아니면 개별 협상 방식으로 할 것인지 등의 문제는 또 다른 정책적 결정 사항이다.

15. petroleum means-

(a) any naturally occurring hydrocarbon, whether in a gaseous, liquid or solid state; or

(b) any naturally occurring mixture of hydrocarbons, whether in a gaseous, liquid or solid state; or

(c) any naturally occurring mixture of one or more hydrocarbons, whether in an gaseous, liquid or solid state, and one or more of the following, that is to say, hydrocarbon sulphide, nitrogen, helium and carbon dioxide-and includes any petroleum as defined by paragraph (a), (b) or (c) or any prescribed petroleum product that has been returned to a natural reservoir in Victoria, but excludes any naturally occurring hydrocarbon or mixture of hydrocarbons within a deposit of coal or oil shale;

16. "Petroleum" means (a) all natural hydrocarbons, liquid or gaseous, produced or producible from the ground, (b) all asphalt and other solid hydrocarbons suitable for production with or dissolved in liquid petroleum or gas, or (c) all hydrocarbons suitable for products derived from the substances mentioned in the foregoing sub-paragraphs.

된 제도적 틀을 정비하고, 우리나라가 요구할 최소역무방위 · 탐사결과 취득한 정보의 취득 · 매장량 평가 방법 및 개발을 시행할 최소한의 매장량에 대한 규정 · 노하우의 취득 · 기술이전 등 국가 정책적으로 필요한 부분들을 사전에 정리하고 제도화하여 투자자들로 하여금 예측 가능성을 확보할 수 있게 해 줄 필요가 있다. …

* * *

국가가 석유와 가스에 대한 소유권을 가지고 있는 경우에도 이를 확인하고 개발권을 부여하는 절차에 관한 법적 형식은 다양하다. 우선 헌법에 이를 명시한 국가들이 있다. 멕시코 헌법 제27조가 대표적인 예이다.[16] 이는 당시 멕시코 석유산업이 외국인자본에 의하여 지배된데 대한 반발로서 1925년 석유법으로 보다 구체적인 집행절차가 마련되었으나 석유산업이 이에 불응, 1938년 최초의 국유화, PEMEX라는 최초의 국영석유회사(National Oil Company, "NOC")로 이어지게 되었다.[17] 헌법에 석유나 천연가스 등 광물자원에 대한 국가소유를 명시하더라도 그 구체적인 내용은 석유법에 정하여야 할 것이고 따라서 석유법에 국영석유회사와 탐사권의 성격이나 그 부여에 관한 방법과 광업권면허나 계약의 주된 내용을 규정하고 있는 경우가 대부분이다.

연방국가의 경우에는 연방정부와 주정부간 주권이 분할된다. 석유와 천연가스에 대한 소유권 내지 개발권이 연방정부에 전속적으로 귀속된다면 탐사 · 개발권을 둘러싼 법적 · 정치적 위험이 없겠지만, 이들 정부간 관계가 명확하지 않은 경우 문제는 복잡하여진다. 1991년 구 소련연방이 무너지면서 러시아와 중앙아시아의 독립국가 간에는[18] 순조롭게 개발권에 대한 권한이 명확하여졌지만 러시아 중앙정부와 지방정부간 권한분쟁은 심각하여졌고 그 대표적인 예가 1992년 사할린섬의 석유개발을 위한 입찰로서 당시 3개의 지방정부가 권한을 주장하고 나섰다. 1992년 러시아 지방정부들이 러시아공화국을 위한 연방조약을 체결하고 1993년 헌법에서 러시아 연방정부과 그 지방정부가 공동으로 광업권을 가진다고 규정하면서 이의 하위규범으로서 1995년 수개의 법률이 통과되었으나 러시아 내 지방정부와 중앙정부간 자원개발을 둘러싼 권한관계는 여전히 불확실하다.[19]

16) Jonathan C. Brown, OIL AND REVOLUTION IN MEXICO 224-29 (1993).

17) Ernest E. Smith/John S. Dzienkowski, *A Fifth-Year Perspective on World Petroleum Agrrangements,* 24 TEX. INT'L L. J. 13, 23-26 (1989).

18) 이현복, 카자흐스탄 지하자원개발 관련법에 관한 고찰, 7 한국시베리안연구 29 (2007); 박원석, 우즈베키스탄의 생산물분배계약법제 분석 19, 법학연구 221-45 (2009).

19) Smith, 위 주 1-4 상게서, 191-201. 이라크에 관하여는 송무현/박찬국, 이라크 석유법을 통해본 자원개발전망과 시사점, 29 한국중동학회 79 (2009).

나. 국영석유회사(NOC) 설립

국가가 자신의 주권이 미치는 자원에 대한 관리를 NOC를 통할 것인지, 아니면 정부의 일부인 에너지부에서 직접 운영할 것인지는 각 국가의 정치체제에 따라서 다를 것이다. 기존의 국제석유개발 회사(IOC)가 있는 영국이나 네덜란드 같은 국가의 경우 별도의 NOC를 설립하지 않지만, 대부분의 자원보유국은 NOC를 설립, 이들을 통하여 탐사·개발권을 부여하고 자원수요국도 이들을 통하여 수급을 조절하려고 한다.[20] 또한 해외자원개발이나 파이프라인 건설, 국제적인 downstream사업에까지 진출하려면 PDVSA나 CNOOC, CNPC의 설립이 필요할 것이다.

NOC는 Pemex나 NIOC, PDVSA와 같이 기존의 석유자산을 국유화하여 설립되기도 하지만 석유자원의 개발을 위하여 처음부터 자원보유국의 석유법에 기초하여 설립되는 경우가 대부분이고 예외적으로 Saudi Arabia나 Abu Dhabi처럼 기존의 IOC지분을 국가가 점차 매입하여 NOC가 되기도 한다. NOC는 국가가 100% 지분을 소유하는 것이 통상의 예이지만, 보다 효율적인 운영이나 자본조달을 위하여 YPF나 Petrobras처럼 일부 민영화된 것도 있다.[21]

다. 탐사개발권 부여

Peme와 같이 NOC가 국가내 유일한 개발생산권자인 경우도 있지만 이는 예외에 속하고, 대부분의 NOC는 독자적으로 개발·생산함과 동시에 또는 전적으로 IOC에게 이들 권리를 부여한다. 다음 장에서 보는 것처럼 지난 세기 초반 절대권력을 보유한 자와의 사적인 협상을 통하여 탐사개발권이 주어진 예도 있으나 오늘날 이런 예는 거의 없고 정부가 직접 또는 NOC를 통하여 입찰의 방법으로 IOC에게 탐사개발권을 부여한다.

입찰도 미국이나 브라질과 같이 서명보너스의 금액 다과에 따라 낙찰자가 결정되며 탐사개발권의 조건과 내용은 법과 하위규정이 정하는 방식이 있는가 하면 영국처럼 북해석유개발시 북해의 기후조건, 매장량의 불확실성 등을 이유로 개별 라운드마다 입찰자의 기술·재정적 능력, 과거의 탐사경험, 국가경제에의 기여도, 외국사업자의 경우 영국기업에 대한 형평성, 영국내 하도급업체의 사용계획 등을 고려하여 에너지성이 평가기준을 마련, 광범위한 재량권의 행사를 허용하는 방법도 있다.[22]

---

20) 노르웨이의 경우 에너지부가 있고 그 산하에 Statoil사가 있어서 정책적 결정과 상업적 집행을 나누어 하는 것이 대표적인 예이다. Bernard Taverne, AN INTRODUCTION TO THE REGULATION OF THE PETROLEUM INDUSTRY: LAWS, CONTRACTS AND CONVENTIONS 58-60 (1994).

21) Marilda Rosado, *New Upstrem Legal Environment,* 16 ENER. & NAT. RES. L. 417-419 (1998). Sam Fletcher, *Pemex, PDVSA, Petrobras: how strategies, results differ*, OIL & GAS J (Aug. 3, 2009). 조희문, 브라질 석유자원개발의 법률제도와 개정논의에 대한 소고, 22 라틴아메리카연구 43 (2009).

22) Smith, 위 주 1-4 상게서, 415-28.

Woodside Press Release (2007)

Block 8 & Block 6-1N, Ulleung Basin, Korea
Investment Opportunity in Frontier Deepwater Acreage

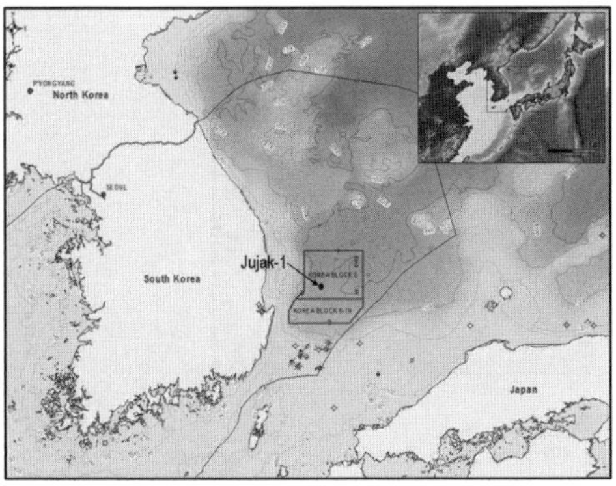

Introduction

Woodside Energy Korea (WEKo) has a 50% operating interest in 2 blocks (~10,000km^2) in the deepwater portion of the Ulleung Basin. Woodside and its partner, Korean National Oil Corporation (KNOC), are planning to drill the exploration well Jujak-1 in Q4 2011 to test the extension of the petroleum system that is proven by the producing fields on the shelf to the south (operated by KNOC). Woodside is offering up to 24% equity to a farminee in return for a promote on the well.

Location

Block 8 & Block 6-1N are located about 40 km north of the Donghae gas-condensate platform and about 50 km east of the city of Pohang in the East Sea of Korea. The Donghae platform started gas-condensate production in 2004 from Early-Middle Miocene shallow marine-deltaic reservoirs.

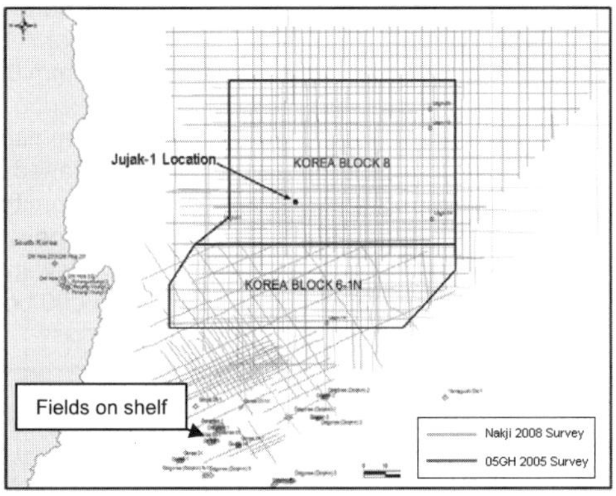

Permit History

Woodside and KNOC signed a Joint Study Agreement (JSA) in 2005 to explore the extension of the proven petroleum system in the gas fields on the shelf into the deepwater portion of the Ulleung Basin. The JSA was converted into a concession contract in 2007. The Joint Venture acquired more than 5000 line km of good quality 2D seismic data in 2008, thereby fulfilling the work commitment of the First Exploration Period. The subsequent technical evaluation confirmed the likely presence of reservoirs, seals and source rocks. An attractive portfolio of prospects and leads was mapped and the Second Exploration Period was entered in August 2009, which carries one well commitment in either of the blocks.

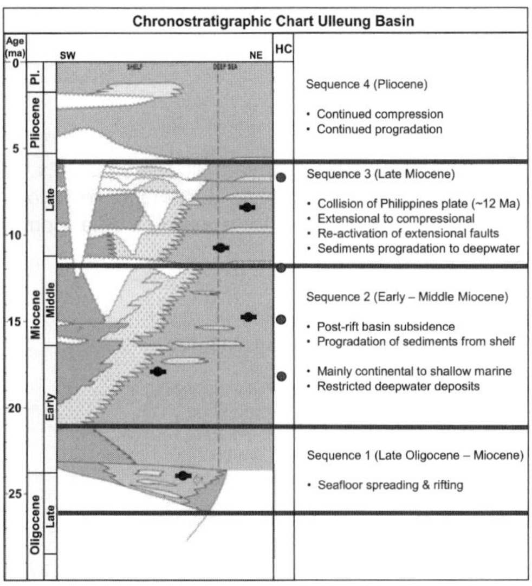

Geology & Plays

Primary Play: Turbidite reservoirs were deposited in the deeper part of the basin following erosion of the sand-rich shelf in the Middle-Late Miocene, as evidenced by numerous canyons and shelfal wells. A variety of traps are present, including four-way dip closures that formed due to compression, which began in the late Miocene. Hydrocarbon charge comes from present day mature, marine to pro-delta source rocks of Early-Middle Miocene age. Regional seals are provided by a major Pliocene flooding event and from intra-formational shales.

Secondary Play: Oligocene to Early Miocene shallow marine to deltaic reservoirs, charged from intra-formational deltaic source rocks or from the Oligocene lacustrine rift sequence. Seals are intra-formational and structures are both anticlines and fault blocks.

For both plays oil or gas are considered possible and realistic outcomes.

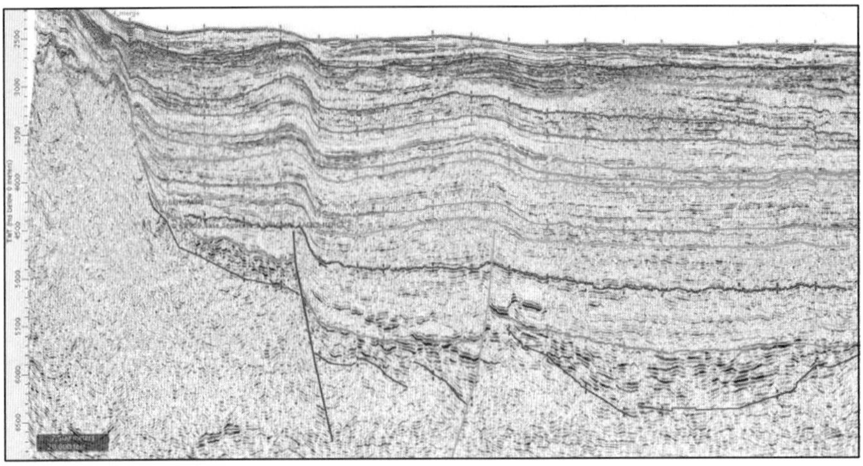

Prospectivity

Prospects: A portfolio of undrilled structural prospects has been identified in the blocks, within the Middle to Late Miocene turbidite reservoirs. Total un-risked mean recoverable volumes for these four way dip-closed prospects are 1.1 BBbbls oil or 6.1 Tcf gas.

Leads: Three-way closed traps, basin floor fans, and stratigraphic onlap traps are also identified in the blocks. Total un-risked mean recoverable volumes for these stratigraphic leads are 1.2 BBbbls oil or 5.7 Tcf gas.

Deep Leads: Most of the mapped structural prospects have deeper closures at Oligocene to Early Miocene levels, similar in age to the reservoir sequences in the fields on the shelf.

Development Concepts

Both oil and gas are considered realistic outcomes in this basin. An oil discovery will likely be developed via a FPSO, with the associated gas piped to the Donghae platform to the south. Larger gas volumes can conceptually be developed with a remotely controlled subsea manifold and an export pipeline to an onshore gas processing facility. The domestic gas price is highly attractive in South Korea.

Fiscal Terms

The terms of the Concession Contract is as follows :

• Period 1 - Feb 2007 - Aug 2009 (2yrs + 6 month extension)
Commitments: 2000 line km of 2D seismic. *(fulfilled)*

• Period 2 - Current, Aug 2009 – Aug 2012
(2yrs + 12 month extension requested)
Commitments: 1 well

• Period 3 - 2 years
Commitments: One well or 400 km^2 3D seismic

• Period 3 - 2 year extension upon request
Commitments: One well or 100 km^2 3D seismic

• Production period: 30+10 years

• Royalty: Sliding scale payable on production (3% at 2,000 – 5,000 bopd to 12% at >30,000 bopd).

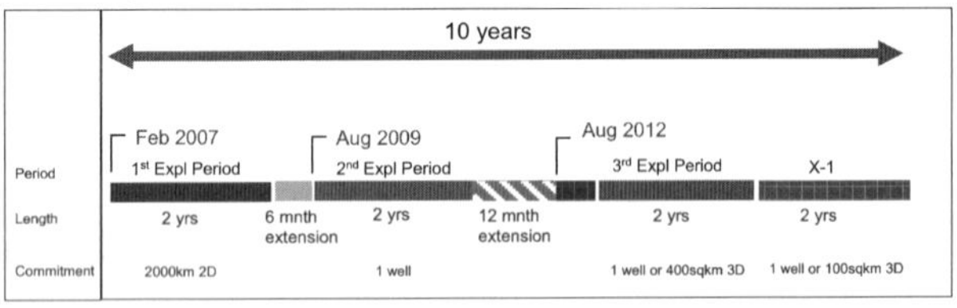

Data Room

Interested parties are requested to contact Mr Jeroen Bruins. All relevant technical, commercial and legal documents relating to the concession area will be available for review in a data room in Woodside's office in Perth.

Contacts:

Mr Peter Grant
General Manager,
International Exploration,
Woodside Energy Ltd.,
240 St Georges Terrace,
Perth WA 6000,
Western Australia.

t: +61 8 9348 6947
f: +61 8 9214 2633
e: peter.grant@woodside.com.au

Mr Jeroen Bruins
Manager,
International Evaluation,
Woodside Energy Ltd.,
240 St Georges Terrace,
Perth WA 6000,
Western Australia.

t: +61 8 9348 5411
f: +61 8 9214 2750
e: jeroen.bruins@woodside.com.au

머니투데이, 대우인터, 동해대륙붕 탐사작업 나선다 (2011. 9. 22.)

대우인터내셔널은 22일 서울 반포동 JW메리어트호텔에서 지식경제부, 한국석유공사와 국내 대륙붕 6-1 해저광구 남부지역에 대한 탐사권 계약을 체결했다고 밝혔다. 이번 계약식에는 이동희 대우인터내셔널 부회장과 최중경 지식경제부 장관, 강영원 한국석유공사 사장이 참석했다.

이번 계약으로 대우인터내셔널은 탐사작업 지분 70%를 갖고 운영권자로 사업을 주관하게 된다. 한국석유공사가 나머지 30% 지분으로 공동 참여한다. 이는 탐사작업에 소요되는 제반비용의 70%를 대우인터내셔널에서 부담한다는 얘기로, 향후 자원개발 수익의 상당부분도 대우인터내셔널 몫으로 돌아가게 될 전망이다. 민간기업이 해저유전 및 가스전 개발 운영권자로 나서기는 이번이 처음이다.

대우인터내셔널이 이처럼 국내 대륙붕 개발사업을 주도하게 된 것은 미얀마 가스전 탐사경험을 갖고 있기 때문이다. 이 회사는 프랑스, 미국, 일본의 유력 기업들이 발굴에 실패한 미얀마 서부 해상 지역에서 자체 기술력으로 가채매장량 4조5000억 입방피트(원유 8억 배럴, 액화천연가스 9000만톤)의 대규모 가스전을 발견했다. 미얀마 가스전에는 현재 생산시설 설치 작업이 진행 중이며 2013년 본격 생산에 돌입할 예정이다.

[그림 3-1] 광구 개발권

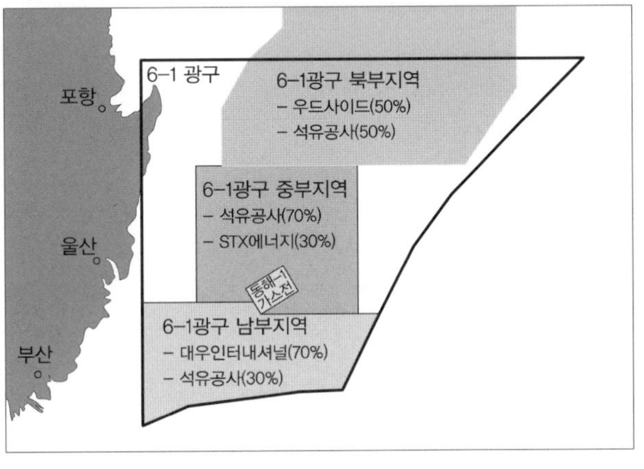

라. 다운스트림 프로젝트

석유나 가스의 탐사개발권의 부여는 이를 위한 해상시추선, 파이프라인, 정유시설, 또는 천연가스액화시설 등의 건설까지 포함하는 경우가 있다. 이럴 경우 에너지성이나 NOC는 탐사개발권과 동시에 이들 시설의 건설사업자를 선정, 계약을 체결하여야 할 것이다. 이럴 경우 EPC계약(Engineeing, procurement and construction contract) 또는 EPCM계약이 많이 사용된다. EPC계약이라 함은 주계약자가 시설의 설계, 시공, 자재조달, 건설까지 통틀어서 책임을 지는 일종의 턴키계약이다. 계약자는 하도급을 줄 수 있지만 발주자에 대한 관계에서는 계약자만이 책임을 진다. 계약자는 프로젝트 진행일정표를 제시하고 이를 완공할 것을 보증하는 한편, 발주자는 프로젝트의 진행과 관련된 의사결정에 관여할 필요가 없다. EPCM은 EPC와는 달리 설계나 시공, 건설의 감리를 담당하지만, 실제 시공, 조달, 건설을 포함, 일체의 결정은 발주자가 책임지는 경우를 말한다. 일반적으로 NOC는 프로젝트의 위험을 계약자에게 넘기기를 선호하며 또한 신용장, 모회사의 보증, 지급대금의 유보 등의 수단으로 프로젝트의 수행을 확실하게 보장받기를 원할 것이다. 그러나, 시장상황이나 건설현장의 실제 위험정도, 지역에 특수한 법규범, 현지정부의 부패정도, 산업관행, 프로젝트의 성격 등에 따라서 종국적인 계약형태가 결정될 것이다.[23)]

23) Id., 59-65.

[그림 3-2] 우즈베키스탄 수르길 가스전/석유화학단지개발사업 거래구조도[24)]

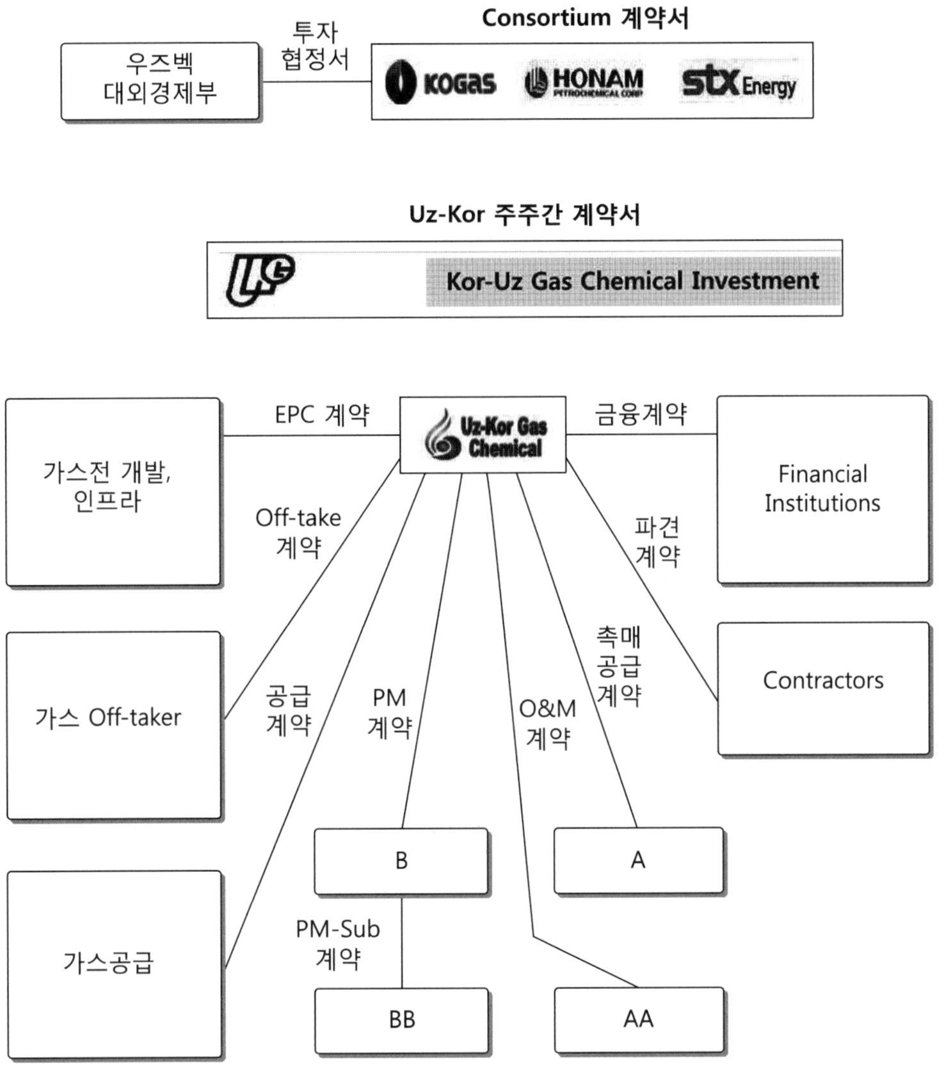

24) K-EXIM과 KOGAS의 동의를 받아서 게재함.

석유화학공장건설 EPC Heads of Terms

JV "UZ-KOR CAS CHEMICAL LLC"
("COMPANY")
and
("CONTRACTOR")

ENGINEER, PROCURE
AND
CONSTRUCT CONTRACT
relating to
THE ETHYLENE PLANT AT
THE USTYURT GAS CHEMICAL COMPLEX

CONTENTS

발전소건설 RFP-EPC Heads of Terms

Notes to Tenderers:

- These terms and conditions have been prepared on the basis of information available as at [ ]. Amendments may need to be made to these terms and conditions, including: in order to reflect requirements of other Project Documents as and when those requirements become known; to take account of whether the Contractor will act through a consortium of contractors on a joint and several basis, or as a single contractor; to deal with specific ECA requirements; and to take account of the incorporation of additional infrastructure into the original scope of work under the EPC contract.
- The Contract may be split between on-shore and off-shore components for tax reasons. If this is the case, the Contractor will be required to enter into an umbrella guarantee drawing-together the on-shore and off-shore components (including in relation to LDs, limits of liability, etc) to ensure that there is no dilution of the Contractor's obligations and liabilities to the Owner with respect to both on-shore and off-shore components.[The concept of an umbrella guarantee is acceptable although that would have to be reviewed and commented by the Contractor by the time of execution of this EPC Contract.]

CONTENTS

4.5 Testing And Commissioning
4.6 Owner's Scope Of Supply
5. Contractor's Responsibilities
5.1 Commencement, Progress And Target Dates
5.2 Standards Of Execution
5.3 Full Acquaintance
5.4 Permits
5.5 Prohibited Practices
5.6 Project Documents
6. Owner's Representatives
6.1 Designation
6.2 Authority
6.3 Delegation
7. Contractor's Representatives And Supervisory Staff
7.1 Contractor's Representative
7.2 Construction Manager
7.3 Other Key Personnel And Organisation Chart
7.4 Objection To Personnel
8. Programme, Progress Reports, Qa Scheme
8.1 Programme
8.2 Progress Reports
8.3 Quality Assurance
9. Subcontracting
9.1 Permitted Subcontracting
9.2 Responsibility For Subcontractors
9.3 Requirements Relating To Subcontractors
10. Project Implementation
10.1 Setting Out
10.2 Design Development
10.3 Transportation
10.4 Safety And Site Regulations
10.5 Nuisance, Trespass Etc
10.6 Contractor's Supervision
10.7 Labour
10.8 Construction Equipment
10.9 Co-Ordination With Associated Works Contractors
10.10 Emergency Work
10.11 Site Clearance
10.12 Security And Lighting
10.13 Royalties
10.14 Training
10.15 Manuals
10.16 Hazardous Materials
10.17 Antiquities
10.18 Consumables
10.19 Supplies And Equipment
11. Access To The Works In Progress
11.1 Access For Authorised Personnel
12. Transfer Of Title
12.1 Ownership
12.2 Liens

13. Care Of Works
    - 13.1 Duration Of Responsibility
    - 13.2 Excepted Risks
    - 13.3 Construction Equipment
    - 13.4 Combination Of Risks
    - 13.5 Funders' Non-Reinstatement Rights
14. Spare Parts
    - 14.1 Initial Spare Parts And Strategic Spares
    - 14.2 Spare Parts During Commissioning
    - 14.3 Spare Parts After Taking Over
15. Tests Generally
    - 15.1 Contractor To Conduct
    - 15.2 Attendances
    - 15.3 Notice And Reporting
    - 15.4 Covering Up
    - 15.5 Additional Tests
    - 15.6 Test Failures
16. Commissioning, Tests On Completion And Performance Tests
    - 16.1 Pre-Conditions To Tests On Completion
    - 16.2 Time For Tests On Completion
    - 16.3 Procedures For Tests On Completion
    - 16.4 Raw Materials Supply Nomination
    - 16.5 Cessation Of Tests On Completion
    - 16.6 Failures, Repetitions, Adjustments And Modifications
    - 16.7 Evaluation Of Results Of Tests On Completion
    - 16.8 Delayed Tests On Completion
    - 16.9 Creation Of Punch List
17. Taking Over
    - 17.1 Taking Over Definitions
    - 17.2 Taking Over Certificate
    - 17.3 Completion Of Punch List Items
18. Final Completion
    - 18.1 Final Completion Certificate
    - 18.2 Non-Release
19. Defects Liability Period
    - 19.1 Remedial Obligation
    - 19.2 Notification
    - 19.3 Extension
    - 19.4 Failure To Remedy
    - 19.5 Repetition Of Tests
    - 19.6 Removal For Repairs
    - 19.7 Search For Defects
    - 19.8 Expiry Of Defects Liability Period
20. Latent Defects
    - 20.1 Remedial Obligation
    - 20.2 Repetition Of Tests
21. Contract Price
    - 21.1 Amount And Adjustment
    - 21.2 Sufficiency Of Contract Price
    - 21.3 Eca Sourcing
22. Payment

22.1 Payment Mechanics
22.2 Advance Payment
22.3 Method Of Application For Payments Other Than The Advance Payment And Final Payment
22.4 Approval Of An Interim Payment Certificate
22.5 Corrections To Certificates Of Payment
22.6 Method Of Payment
22.7 Date Of Payment
22.8 Payment Profile
22.9 Set Off
22.10 Repayment Of Excess
22.11 Interest On Late Payment
22.12 Final Payment Certificate
22.13 Eca Requirements

23. Taxes And Duties
    23.1 Contractor To Bear Own Taxes
    23.2 Assistance In Tax Mitigation
    23.3 Tax Withholding
24. Performance Security
    24.1 Bonds
    24.2 Parent Company Guarantee
    24.3 Bond And Guarantee Expenses
    24.4 Direct Agreement
25. Supply Of Documents And Intellectual Property
    25.1 Access To Documents
    25.2 License
    25.3 No Infringement
    25.4 Contractor Indemnity
    25.5 Notice
    25.6 Owner Indemnity
    25.7 Survival
26. Confidential Information
    26.1 Obligation To Keep Confidential
    26.2 Permitted Disclosure
    26.3 Other Disclosure
    26.4 Restrictions On Use
    26.5 Survival
27. Not Used
28. Delay Damages
    28.1 Contracted Date For Taking Over
    28.2 Liquidated Damages For Delay
    28.3 Effect Of Delay Damages
29. Absolute Performance Levels, Guaranteed Performance Levels And Performance Liquidated Damages
    29.1 Performance Guarantees
    29.2 Liquidated Damages For Performance
    29.3 Failure To Attain Minimum Performance Levels And Absolute Performance Levels
30. Limitations On Liability
    30.1 Cap On Liability
    30.2 Excluded Loss

30.3 Caps On Liquidated Damages
31. Loss Or Damage To Property/Accident Or Injury To Workmen/Indemnification
    31.1 Contractor's Indemnity
    31.2 Scope Of Property Indemnity
    31.3 Owner's Indemnity
    31.4 Indemnity Proceedings
32. Insurance
    32.1 Owner Insurances
    32.2 Contractor Insurances
    32.3 Disclosure Requirements
    32.4 Alteration To Insurances
    32.5 Claims Assistance
    32.6 Continuance Of Underlying Responsibilities
    32.7 Failure To Insure
    32.8 Language
33. Changes
    33.1 Owner Right To Instruct Changes
    33.2 Owner Changes Procedure
    33.3 Implementation
    33.4 Contractor's Default
    33.5 Contractor-Proposed Changes
34. Change In Law
    34.1 Notice Of Statutory Modification
    34.2 Statutory Modification Procedure
    34.3 I Implementation
35. Not Used
36. Extension Of Time
    36.1 Extension Of Time: Grounds
    36.2 Extension Of Time: Procedures
    36.3 Award Of Extensions
    36.4 Acceleration
    36.5 Mitigation Of Delay
37. Claims For Additional Payments
    37.1 Additional Payment Grounds
    37.2 Additional Payment Procedures
38. Force Majeure
    38.1 Force Majeure Events
    38.2 Notification Of Force Majeure
    38.3 Relief From Force Majeure
    38.4 Termination
39. Suspension
    39.1 Right To Suspend And Entitlements
    39.2 Prolonged Suspension—Deemed Termination
    39.3 No Removal
    39.4 Resumption
40. Termination For Owner Convenience
    40.1 Termination At Will
    40.2 Consequences Of Termination-Owner Convenience
41. Termination For Contractor Default
    41.1 Events Of Default
    41.2 Remedy And Termination Rights

41.3 Consequences Of Termination－Contractor Default
42. Termination For Owner Default
    42.1 Owner Termination Events
    42.2 Consequences Of Termination－Owner Default Or Convenience
43. No Fault Termination
    43.1 Consequences Of Termination－No Fault
44. Settlement Of Disputes
    44.1 Early Warning
    44.2 Expert Resolution
    44.3 Arbitration
    44.4 Joinder Of Arbitrations
    44.5 Continuing Obligations
45. Assignment
    45.1 Owner Assignment
    45.2 Contractor Assignment
46. Notices
    46.1 Method Of Delivery
    46.2 Addresses
47. Remedies
    47.1 Sole And Exclusive Remedies
    47.2 Non-Waiver And Preservation Of Remedies
    47.3 Waiver
    47.4 Duty To Mitigate
    47.5 No Winding Up
48. Miscellaneous
    48.1 Successors
    48.2 Owner Assistance
    48.3 Independent Contractor
    48.4 Privity
    48.5 Entire Agreement
    48.6 Amendment
    48.7 Severability
    48.8 Costs And Expenses
    48.9 Counterparts
    48.10 Failure Of Liquidated Damages

Exhibit 1 Form Of Performance Bond
Exhibit 2 Parent Company Guarantee
Exhibit 3 Forms Of Legal Opinions
Exhibit 4 Direct Agreement
Exhibit 5 Insurances
    Part A Insurances To Be Effected By The Owner
    Part B Insurance To Be Effected By The Contractor
Exhibit 6 Guaranteed Performance Levels And Liquidated Damages
    Part A: Guaranteed Performance Levels
    Part B: Minimum Performance Levels
    Part C: Absolute Performance Levels
    Part D: Metering And Testing
    Part E: Performance Liquidated Damages
    Part F: Delay Liquidated Damages
Exhibit 7 Subcontractor Warranties
    Part A: Subcontractors To Provide Warranties

Part B: Form Of Warranty
Exhibit 8 Payment
Part A: Terms Of Payment
Part B: Interim Payment Certificate
Part C: Breakdown Of Contract Price
Part D: Milestone Schedule
Part E: Payment Profile
Part F: Schedule Of Prices
Exhibit 9 Completion And Testing
Exhibit 10 Taking Over Certificate
Exhibit 11 Spare Parts
Exhibit 12 Approved Subcontractors
Exhibit 13 Owner Warranted Information
Exhibit 14 Permits
Exhibit 15 Reference Programme
Exhibit 16 Description Of Sections
Part A: Section 1
Part B: Section 2
Part C: Section 3
Exhibit 17 The Specification

마. 탐사개발자금의 조달

자원보유국 내지 그 나라의 NOC가 탐사개발권 내지 다운스트림프로젝트에 필요한 자금까지 제공하는 경우는 거의 없을 것이고[25] 대부분은 IOC가 탐사개발권을 기초로 외부에서 자금을 구하여야 한다. 개발자금을 제공하는 국제적 금융기관으로 World Bank, IFC, MIGA가, 지역적 금융기관으로 ADB, Corporation Andina de Fomento, 미국의 EXIM, 일본의 J-EXIM 등이 있다. 국가자본주의를 경제운용의 기초로 하는 중국의 경우 중국의 은행들이 자국의 NOC 해외진출에 필요한 자금을 융자하여 주며 우리나라의 경우 수출입은행이 이러한 기능을 수행하고 있다. 예를 들어 KOGAS가 우즈베키스탄 수르길가스전 개발의 경우 우즈베키스탄과 합작투자법인을 설립한 후 이의 개발비용 상당부분을 수출입은행이 융자하여 주고 있다.

국제적 자본시장에서 장래 석유나 가스의 판매대금을 자산유동화 증권으로 바꾸어 자금을 조달하지만[26] 이는 이미 생산·판매단계에서만 가능한 자금조달수단일 것이다. 개발 이전 단계에서도 탐사의 결과 매장량이 증명되는 시점에서 생산, 분배될 장래의 석유를 기초로 하는 금융수법이 토지임대차를 자원개발의 기본법리로 하는 미국에서는 발달되어 있으니[27] 국

25) 중국의 해외자원개발을 목표로 설립된 국영석유회사나 Petrobras와 같이 공격적으로 해외개발에 나서는 NOC의 경우 사내자금으로 가능할 것이나 이 역시 엄격히 자원보유국의 NOC가 아니라는 점에서 외부금융이다.

26) Charles E. Harrell/James L. Rice, III./W. Robert Shearer, *Securitization of Oil, Gas, and Other Natural Resource Assets: Emerging Financing Technique,* 52 BUS. LAWYER 885 (1997).

제적인 광업권계약이나 생산물분배계약하에서도 앞으로 귀속될 이익석유를 기초로 확인매장량 단계에서 가능하여 보인다.

최근 중동의 석유자금이 쌓이는 반면 이의 투자기회는 제한되어 있음에 착안, 석유나 가스개발자금, 또는 인프라건설비용의 조달에 중동의 자금을 이용할 가능성이 논의되고 있다. 이슬람의 율법인 Shari'a에 따라서 이자와 도박이 금지되며 기초자산에 대한 소유권취득이 선호되는 것을 고려, 개발단계에 필요한 거액의 설비조달에 활용될 수 있을 것이다.[28] 아직 이에 대한 연구나 협의가 부족하지만, 앞으로 커다란 자금공급원천이 될 수 있다는 면에서 보다 심각한 고려가 필요하여 보인다.

노트와 질문

거대한 자금이 필요한 개발프로젝트의 경우 프로젝트자금조달 방법 이외에 어떤 방법이 사업의 추진에 필요한 자금조달을 위하여 가능할까? 점진적으로 일부씩 완성하여 가면서 일부 완성으로 인하여 들어오는 수입으로 다시 추가 투자를 하는 식으로 점차 프로젝트의 크기를 확대하는 방안은 어떨까? 초기에 가장 수익률이 좋을 것 같은 프로젝트부터 시작, 점차 수익률이 떨어지는 프로젝트로 확대하는 방안은 어떨까? 프로젝트가 한 국가의 경제개발이라면 그 방법론은 달라질까?

27) Jeffrey S. Munoz, *Financing of Oil and Gas Transactions,* 4 TEX. J. OIL, GAS & ENERG. L. 223, 228-40의 volumetric production payment나 net profits interest에 기초한 자금조달이 그 예.

28) Id., 259-65. Christopher F. Richardson, *Islamic Finance Opportunities in the Oil and Gas Sector: An Introduction to an Emerging Field,* 42 TEX. INT'L L. J. 119 (2006-07).

제02편

국제에너지자원—탐사개발생산

제2편은 자원을 보유한 국가와 자원을 개발하고자 하는 기업간 어떤 절차를 걸쳐서 어떤 거래가 이루어지는지에 관한 논의이다. 국제적 거래는 상업조건을 협상, 합의가 이루어지고 합의된 상업적 조건이 결국 계약에 반영되어야 한다. 자원탐사와 개발, 생산을 위한 개발계약도 모든 국제거래와 마찬가지로 국가와 개발기업간 합의를 바탕으로 이루어진다.

제4장은 탐사개발생산을 위한 최초단계로서 자원보유국과 IOC간 탐사와 개발·생산을 위한 비용 내지 위험의 부담과 수익의 분배를 정하는 탐사계약의 역사와 법적인 성격, 유형을 살핀다. 탐사계약은 과거 중동지역의 권력자로부터 광범위한 지역에 걸쳐서 장기간 동안 석유가격의 등락에 관계없이 일정한 금액을 지급하고 백지수표식으로 아무런 통제없는 개발권을 부여받거나 개발의 결과인 석유 자체에 대한 소유권을 양도받는 양허계약에서 시작되었다. 그 후 산유국이 많아지면서 각자 독특한 양식을 취하지만 이들을 크게 양허계약, 생산분배계약, 위험용역계약, 참여계약의 4가지 유형으로 나누어 각각의 중요한 특징과 실제사례를 살펴본다.

제5장은 공동운용계약상 논의되어야 할 사항들을 검토한다. 탐사계약에 따라 탐사권을 부여받은 IOC는 석유탐사에 수반되는 위험을 분산시키고 필요한 자금을 확보하기 위하여 다른 국제적 에너지업체에게 탐사권의 일부 지분을 양도한다. 그럴 경우 다수의 에너지업체간 권리의무를 정하는 공동운용계약이 필요하다. 일종의 동업계약 내지 합작사업계약이라고 할 수 있으며 따라서 합의하여야 할 많은 항목이 있다. IOC의 지분양도가 중요한 자금조달방법이지만 이 외에 다른 자금조달방안도 이 장에서 살펴본다.

제6장은 공동운용계약상 운용자와 그 하도급자인 용역업체간 권리의무에 관한 검토이다. 공동운용계약에 따라서 운용자가 결정되면 운용자는 실제 구체적 탐사작업을 수행할 많은 하도급업체와 개별 용역계약을 체결한다. 석유의 탐사·개발이라는 하나의 목적을 위하여 다수의 용역업체가 동시에 또는 순차적으로 용역을 제공하면서 이들간 책임의 분담과 위험귀속의 문제가 발생한다. 대규모프로젝트에 언제나 수반하는 문제이기도 하다.

제 4 장

에너지자원 개발계약유형[1)]

1. 역사적 배경

석유는 1858년 미국 펜실베이니아주 Titusville에서 시추공을 통하여 본격적으로 생산되었고 그 이후 러시아의 바쿠,[2)] 인도네시아의 수마트라에서[3)] 대규모로 개발되었다. 그 후 전통적 양허계약에[4)] 기초하여 본격적으로 석유가 개발된 것은 페르시아와 중동지역이었다. 1901년 William D'Arch는 페르시아의 황제와 양허계약을 체결하였는데, 그 특징은 권리가 광대한 지역에 걸쳐 있다는 것, 권리가 장기간 부여되었다는 것, IOC가 생산일정이나 방법에 관하여 절대적 결정권한을 가진다는 것, 그리고 자원보유국은 탐사·개발권에 대한 대가의 지급을 요구할 권한 이외의 아무런 권한이 없다는 것이 특징이었다. 1901년 양허계약에서 페르시아는 서명보너스로 미화 10만 불, 미화 10만 불 상당 IOC의 주식과 16% 로열티의 대가로 10만평방마일의 땅에 대하여 60년 동안 독점적으로 석유를 개발할 권리를 부여했다.[5)] 이러한 유형의 양허계약은 1933년 사우디의 동부지역, 1934년 쿠웨이트, 1939년 아부다비에서[6)] 반복되었다.[7)] 기간은 각각 66년, 75년, 75년이었다. 이들이 미국에서 1858년 이후 사용

---

1) 제2장 제3절 금감원모범공시기준에서 본 것처럼 탐사, 개발, 생산은 구별되지만 이러한 과정을 통틀어서 탐사 또는 개발로, 이를 위한 계약은 개발계약 또는 탐사계약으로 총칭한다. 아래 주 17 참조.

2) 1871년부터 시추, 1873년에는 20여 개의 정유소가 있었다. Daniel Yergin, THE PRIZE 58 (1991). 물론 그 이전부터 원유가 여러가지 용도로 사용된 기록은 있다.

3) 1880년 Sumatra 북동부 Telaga Said에서 시추 시작. Id., 73-75.

4) concession을 양허, 양허계약, 조광계약, 조광권계약, 조광권특허 등으로 번역한다. 절대군주가 일정한 부분의 토지에 관한 주권을 포기한다는 의미에서 양허라는 용어가 행위의 실질에 보다 가까운 것으로 보인다. E&P계약은 양허를 포함한 개발계약 일체를 의미한다. 통상적으로 양허보다는 양허계약이라는 용어가 사용되지만 계약인지 여부에 관하여 논란이 있다.

5) Smith, 위 주 3-16 전게논문, 17-18.

6) Atef Suleiman, *The Oil Experience of the United Arab Emirates and Its Legal Framework,* 6 J. ENER. & NAT'L RES. L. 1 (1988). 1937년 오만과 머스캇에 관한 양허계약서 본문은 Smith, 위 주 1-4 전게서, 431-32.

7) 아랍석유개발의 주연이라는 Frank Holmes에 관하여는 Aileen Keating, POWER, POLITICS AND THE HIDDEN HISTORY OF ARABIAN OIL (2006).

된 석유개발을 위한 임대차계약과 크게 다르지는 않았지만 동시대 미국에서 사용된 계약들은 석유의 생산여부에 따라서 임대인에게 지급하여야 할 금액이 달라지는 점과 임차기간이 훨씬 단기간이었다는 점에서 이들과 차이가 난다.[8] 또한 미국의 법원은 임차인의 묵시적 의무(implied covenant)로서 매장량을 탐색할 의무, 매장량을 발견하면 근면하고 적정하게 운용할 의무 등을 인정, 임대인을 보호한 것 또한 국제양허계약과 구별되는 점이다. 임차인의 의무를 인정할 법원이 없는 상황에서 산유국들은 과거의 양허계약을 개선하기 위한 여러 가지 시도를 행하였다.

멕시코는 토지소유권자가 지하의 석유에 대한 절대적 권리가 있었기 때문에 토지 내지 석유를 국유화하지 않는 이상 외국인이지만 토지를 소유 내지 임차하여 석유를 개발하고 있는 IOC의 절대적 지배권을 변화시킬 방법이 없었다.[9] 따라서 멕시코는 1938년 국유화조치를 단행할 수밖에 없었다. 한편, 중동제국에서는 권력자가 토지소유권을 가지고 있었기 때문에 권력자 자신의 권한으로 또는 협상을 통하여 과거 체결된 장기간의 양허계약을 점진적으로 수정하는 방법이 가능하였다. 이는 OPEC을 통한 산유국들의 집단행동과 산유국간 정보교환의 가능성, 그리고 새로운 탐사개발업자의 진입가능성 때문에 더욱 효과적이었다. 따라서, 1950년대와 60년대를 거쳐서 1970년대 이르러 과거의 양허계약조건은 자원보유국의 로열티수입 이외에 소득세의 부과, 인플레이션에 따른 석유가격의 조정, 최소생산량, 미개발지역의 환수일정부과 자원보유국의 지분보유분 증가일정과 경영에의 참여 권한 등 여러 측면에서 대폭 수정되었다.[10] 이런 일련의 변화는 "양허에서 참여로" 이름지을 수 있을 것이다.[11]

---

8) 임차인의 권리에 대한 제한은 미국의 경우 석유개발이 토지임대차형식을 취하고 있다는 점과 법원의 임대차계약조건에 대한 개입때문에 가능하였다. 통상 임대차는 임차인의 보호를 위하여 강행규정을 두고 있는데, 석유개발업자와 토지소유자간 임대차의 경우는 임대인의 보호를 위하여 법원이 개입하였다. 즉 법원은 기한이 제한이 없는 경우라거나 다른 이유로 계약조건이 임차인에 일방적으로 유리한 경우 약인이 없다는 이유로 집행할 수 없다고 하거나 임차인은 임대인과 임차인의 공동이익을 위하여 토지를 사용할 묵시적 의무가 있는 이론으로 계약조건의 수정을 가하였다. Smith, 위 주 3-16 논문, 20-23.

9) 멕시코와 마찬가지로 스페인법제에 근거한 라틴아메리카 여러 나라가 1968-76년 국유화한 것도 동일한 문맥에서 이해된다. Id., 31, fn. 127. Lybia의 잠행성 국유화에 대하여는 Note, *Unilateral Action by Oil Producing Countries: Possible Contractual Remedies of Foreign Petroleum Companies,* 9 FORDHAM INT'L L.J. 63, 65 (1985-1986). 국제적 국유화사태에 대한 요약은 *Libian American Oil Co. (Liamco) v. Government of the Libyan Arab Republic,* 20 I.L.M. 30, 96 "Iran in 1951, Egypt in 1956, Indonesia in 1957, Irak, Ceylon and Cuba in 1961, Algeria from 1963, Syria in 1964, Peru in 1968, Bolivia and Zambia in 1969, Chile in 1970, Lybia from 1970, Saudi Arabia in 1972, and Kuweit since 1973" (1981).

10) Id., 32-34.

11) Note, *From Concession to Participation: Restructuring the Middle East Oil Industry,* 48 N.Y.U.L.REV. 774, 776-777(1973). 1970년대 양허계약이 수정이 가능하였던 것은 국제정치의 역학관계와, 자원민족주의도 원인이지만 직접적인 원인은 중동제국의 왕실이 기존의 양허계약에 따른 로열티수입이 줄어든 데 대하여 반발, 소득세를 부과하고 또한 로열티계산을 위한 석유가격에 소득세를 포함시

Ernest E. Smith & John S. Dzienkowski, *A Fifty-Year Perspective on World Petroleum Arrangements,* 24 TEX. INT'L L. J. 13 (1989)

Ⅲ. CHANGES IN THE CONCESSION SYSTEM

In the United States, the doctrine of implied covenants helped to balance the rights of the oil companies and the lessors. Lacking such judicial redress, foreign sovereigns inevitably turned to other methods to establish more equitable arrangements. Two principal options appeared available to accomplish this result: expropriation or renegotiation. In some instances no bright line existed between these two methods. Renegotiation under political duress may appear to a company as differing only marginally from outright nationalization; expropriation can take place so gradually that the process may not seem significantly different from ongoing renegotiation. Typically, however, both the changes in petroleum arrangements and the methods used to change them differed markedly. In many ways, the methods of change in Mexico and in the Middle East were at opposite ends of the spectrum of options that sovereigns could use to obtain control over the exploitation of their natural resources.

A. Mexico's Expropriation of Oil Company Assets

In 1911, the Mexican Revolution brought the long reign of Porfirio Diaz to an end and, with it, the policies that had strongly encouraged and attracted foreign investment in Mexico. Indeed, the extraordinary concentration of Mexico's wealth in the hands of foreigners was one of the precipitating causes of the Revolution. Little overt hostility was displayed toward the oil companies during the revolutionary period, however, and for a time they continued to operate much as they had during the Diaz regime. Investment in the Mexican petroleum industry continued to increase, and new concessions were granted. The new taxes on petroleum, imposed in 1912 and again in 1914, and laws requiring the companies to register and value their property were widely resisted or simply ignored. Nonetheless, the revolutionary government's new laws clearly signaled that the Mexican government would henceforth attempt to obtain some return on the nation's oil wealth. The controversy between the oil companies and President Venustiano Carranza over the enforcement of these laws foreshadowed the more serious dispute that would occur with President Lazaro Cardenas twenty years later.

The legal controversy between the companies and the Mexican government focused upon article 27 of the Constitution of 1917. This article, an early precursor of the United

---

키고자 하는 바람이었다고 분석한다.

Nations Resolution on Permanent Sovereignty over Natural Resources, provided that direct ownership *(dominio directo)* of all natural resources, such as solid, liquid, or gaseous hydrocarbons, whose character is distinct from the components of the soil, was vested in the nation. The registration requirement contained in legislation enacted during Carranza's presidency was widely seen as an attempt to force the oil companies into an implicit endorsement of this constitutional principle.

The Petroleum Law of 1925 was even more explicit. It required that the companies confirm "by means of concessions" all rights derived from lands on which oil production had begun before May 1, 1917, and all rights "derived from contracts entered into before May 1, 1917, by the surface owner or his agents with the express intention of exploiting oil." The confirmation of rights granted under this statute was limited to a period of fifty years. Although this legislation was modified three years later to provide for confirmation of rights in favor of the surface owner "without limitation of time" and in other instances "for the term stipulated in the contracts," it still retained the concept of a concession rather than outright title to the oil in place.

Not surprisingly, the oil companies viewed these statutes as direct threats to their claims and refused to acknowledge their validity. The companies advanced two interrelated arguments in support of their position. The first rested upon article 14 of the Mexican Constitution, which provides that no law will be given retroactive effect to the prejudice of any person. The companies argued that the legislation imposing a new condition (i.e., confirmation) upon previously granted property rights was retroactive and thus conflicted with this provision of the 1917 Constitution. The second argument was based upon the oil companies' interpretation of the types of rights they had acquired. They argued that since their rights amounted to ownership of the subsoil, they had no "concessions" to confirm. Compliance with the statutory requirement would be tantamount to conceding that their rights fell short of absolute ownership.

The post-revolutionary government sharply disagreed with the oil companies' interpretation of the legal nature of their rights. The Diaz legislation upon which the companies based their arguments ran counter to a legal process that had begun in Spanish law at least as early as 1387. In that year a royal decree provided that all gold, silver, and quicksilver mines belonged to the Spanish Crown. The royal prerogatives over mines steadily expanded over the next several centuries, and the Spanish mineral regime unquestionably applied to Mexico. The Leyes de Indias and the Nueva Recopilacin de las Leyes de Indias made it clear that all mines in Mexico, whether or not discovered, passed to the Spanish Crown. Given the hostility felt by the new Mexican government toward the Diaz dictatorship it supplanted, it is hardly surprising that the government rejected the oil companies' literal reading of Diaz's mining legislation that appeared to reverse 500 years of legal history overnight.

During the twenty-year period following the adoption of the 1917 Constitution, the dispute between the government and the oil companies intensified as both sides became increasingly intractable. The government imposed new taxes, which the companies resisted. The government-controlled labor unions demanded higher wages and better working conditions, which the companies claimed would bankrupt them. Curiously, it was the labor dispute, not the tax laws or the concept of "confirmatory concessions," that finally led to the expropriation. In 1937, the oil companies' refusal to accede to the unions' demands for higher wages, better conditions, and increased fringe benefits led to a strike by the oil workers. The contract dispute was submitted to the Board of Conciliation and Arbitration. The Board's decision, which went entirely against the companies, was upheld by the Mexican Supreme Court. On March 14, 1938, the oil companies notified the government that they were unable to comply with the decision. The Board, in turn, announced that the new contracts established by its award were cancelled, thereby entitling the workers to three months' discharge pay.

On March 18, 1938, the blow fell. Asserting that the contract cancellation would bring the entire oil industry to a halt, President Lazaro Cardenas announced the expropriation of the oil industry. From that point on, the multinational oil companies were effectively banished from Mexico. The multinationals, however, remained in firm control of virtually all refining, transporting, and marketing activities outside of Mexico. They responded to the government's action with an international boycott of Mexican oil. Deprived of international markets and ready access to new technology and equipment, Mexico, which had been the second largest oil producer in the world in the early years of the century, saw its position in the world oil market decline steadily for twenty-five years following the expropriation. Indeed, eight years passed before Mexican production even regained the levels achieved in 1937, and the country did not again achieve status as a major oil producer until the discovery of the Reforma field in 1972 and the massive offshore reserves in the mid-1970s. In spite of the expropriation's initial negative impact upon its oil industry, Mexico had achieved two major accomplishments. First, Mexico demonstrated that a sovereign could effectively reclaim the right to its oil and mineral resources from the largest and most powerful international corporations in the world. Second, Mexico showed that it could develop those resources itself. Although Argentina's Yacimientos Petrolfferos Fiscales may claim to be the first "true" state oil company, Petrleos Mexicanos (Pemex) was the first such company formed to take over assets seized from foreign oil companies and forced to operate them without external aid. Although questions have been raised about its efficiency and its operational standards, no real doubts exist as to Pemex's ability to explore and develop Mexico's oil reserves.

B. The Middle East: From Concession to Participation

Although a few countries ultimately followed Mexico's lead in using expropriation to regain control over their domestic reserves, their actions generally did not take place until thirty or more years after the Mexican expropriation. Most countries turned to less drastic means of altering the existing agreements. In much of the Middle East, the original concessions were transformed by a process of renegotiation that ultimately resulted in the implementation of entirely new and significantly different arrangements. Today, although some countries both in the Middle East and elsewhere still use the concession format, the provisions are much different from those of the original agreements.

Several factors may explain the turn toward renegotiation in the Middle East. The willingness of the oil companies to renegotiate the original Middle Eastern concessions may be partially attributable to their fear that other countries would take the same step as Mexico; however, other factors proved to be even more influential. First, several oil-producing nations joined together to form the Organization of Petroleum Exporting Countries (OPEC). The existence of one entity representing the interests of all similarly situated countries helped coordinate efforts to renegotiate the original concessions. Second, it became increasingly obvious that it was unfair to tie the countries' royalties and other benefits to the "posted prices" controlled by the multinational oil companies. Finally, OPEC facilitated the sharing of information among its members, and thus, as some members entered into newer agreements with terms more favorable to the host country, other members were able to use their knowledge of these agreements as further leverage to complain about the original concessions. While the OPEC countries' bargaining power was steadily increasing, that of the original seven multinational companies was in decline as they faced increased competition from other United States oil companies and the national oil companies of several Western European nations. Although several countries managed to renegotiate their concessions in the 1950s and the 1960s, the major restructuring of the original arrangements occurred in the 1970s. In 1971, the OPEC renegotiations resulted in an increase in the countries' share of income through additional income taxes (averaging 55%) and an inflation-indexed system for determining the posted price of oil. In some instances, the companies agreed to maintain a minimum level of production. Further, the oil companies agreed to establish schedules to release undeveloped acreage held by the concessions over a period of years. These released fields gave the countries new and productive acreage, which became the subject of completely new petroleum arrangements that in many instances were more favorable to the countries than the renegotiated concessions.

Even more significant, in 1972 the multinational corporations agreed to amend the existing concessions to provide for host country participation. Thus, beginning in 1972, the companies gave 25% of their ownership share to a state-owned oil company and further agreed that the country's share would increase 5% a year until it reached 51%. The effect of this agreement was to convert many of the original concession agreements into participation agreements.

C. Politics, Changing Circumstances, and the Evolution of the Early Concessions and Leases

A casual observer of the international energy market may assume that the renegotiations of the early concessions resulted merely from international politics and the emergence of nationalism among developing nations and that any comparison between the evolution of the oil and gas lease in the United States and the change in foreign agreements is misplaced; however, one can view the lease as having undergone a similar transformation for at least some of the same reasons.

World politics, nationalism, and oil wealth have openly contributed to the bargaining strength of petroleum-producing nations and their ability to force favorable changes in the original concessions. United States domestic politics has played a powerful role in the development of the rights of lessors, but its presence has been less obvious. This difference results in part from the different legal mechanisms by which similar goals are achieved. In the United States, matters such as the rate at which a well is allowed to produce and whether development must be done on a fieldwide or a leasewide basis are deemed appropriate subjects of regulation, rather than of private contractual arrangements. In most other countries, matters of this magnitude are typically incorporated into the agreement entered into between the government and the oil company. For example, field-wide unitization, which is compelled by regulatory agencies in many United States oil-producing states, is imposed by licensing agreements upon the oil companies receiving North Sea licenses from the United Kingdom.

The regulation of oil and gas in the United States is subject to political pressure, and this pressure has frequently come from landowners as well as from large and small oil companies; that the regulatory and legislative action (or inaction) resulting from such political pressure is not part of the "text" of the leases does not diminish its importance to the lessor. Political pressure contributed to the ability of United States lessors and foreign sovereigns to force modifications in their rights, but the need for change resulted in part from the failure of the original agreements. The early concessions and leases inevitably failed to address situations that arose in future years. One principal rationale for implying covenants in oil and gas leases was the inability of the parties to foresee future events and thus to include provisions relating to matters such as the number of wells to be drilled, the rate of production, the existence and size of a market, and the means of transportation to market. These subjects were rationally left to the implication that the further prosecution of the work should be along such lines as would be reasonably calculated to effectuate the controlling intention of the parties as manifested in the lease, which was to make the extraction of oil and gas from the premises of mutual advantage and profit. The absence of provisions in leases and concessions to deal with such matters, and a widely held perception that the original arrangements did not adequately protect the interests of the landowner or foreign sovereign, contributed strongly to the revision of the rights of the parties to those arrangements.

1. The Modern Concession

The modem concession, exemplified by the concession agreement developed by Abu Dhabi, grants "the exclusive rights to explore, search, and drill for, produce, store, transport, and sell Petroleum" within the designated concession acreage for a specified number of years. This period is generally far shorter than the period of the early concessions. In some instances, however, countries wishing to encourage development of areas requiring expensive technology or presenting difficult engineering, meteorological, or geographical problems have granted terms approaching fifty years. In contrast, the United States oil and gas lease will last for so long as oil or gas is produced, deferring the lessor's resumption of control indefinitely.

Unlike the earlier agreements, the modem concession contains clauses specifically imposing a scheme of development based upon a monetary commitment for each year of the term. A company holding the concession is obligated to a work program and to the relinquishment of a portion of the acreage on a specified schedule. This scheme has a partial parallel in some modem oil and gas leases that incorporate provisions imposing some development obligations upon the lessee. Such provisions, often added to printed form leases by the lessor, are of two basic types. The retained acreage clause provides that a well will maintain the lease only as to a specified number of acres. The continuous drilling clause is a more complex provision that commits the lessee to a drilling program and terminates the lease as to undrilled acreage after a specified time period elapses. The use of such clauses is far from universal, however, and their scope is relatively limited when compared with the work programs imposed upon oil companies under modem concessions.

The modem concession's terms for compensation are considerably more generous than those of the early concessions and more sophisticated than the provisions in a typical modem lease. The Abu Dhabi concession provides for bonus payments at the beginning of the concession and later upon attaining certain levels of production. In addition, the concession provides for annual rental payments and a royalty based upon levels of production. The government has the option to receive all or part of the oil royalty in kind rather than in cash. Another provision relating to compensation, which is necessarily absent from a lease between two private parties, requires that the concessionaire pay to the host country a specified amount of tax on the income earned in the country.

2. The Production-Sharing Agreement

In the late 1950s and early 1960s Iran and Indonesia turned to the production-sharing agreement. Although a concession system can be carried out without the use of a state oil company, a production-sharing agreement virtually requires the creation of such an entity. A production-sharing agreement bears some resemblance to a farmout transaction or carried interest arrangement in the United States. The country grants a company a contractual right to explore and develop a specified area in exchange for the opportunity to recover its costs and a specified profit. The country contributes the acreage and receives a share of production. If the acreage is unproductive, however, the company receives no guaranteed profit.

Indonesia, which has had production-sharing agreements since the 1960s, is viewed as a leader in this type of arrangement. In the current version of the Indonesian Model Production Sharing Contract, a state-owned oil company, Pertamina, maintains control over all of the petroleum-producing properties in the country. Pertamina enters into the contract with a contractor for a thirty-year period. The contractor agrees to contribute a specified amount of money to a work program for a six-year period. During each of the six years, the contractor must submit a proposal to Pertamina for its approval. The country maintains much closer continuing control through this approval system than in many modem concessions. In addition, the Indonesian contract requires that the contractor pay Pertamina a management fee for facilitating the work program; thus, the state oil company retains management control over the manner in which the work is performed. This feature creates a resemblance between the production-sharing agreement and the typical joint venture.

As compensation, the Indonesian production-sharing agreement allows a contractor to deduct from gross production all operating costs plus an amount equal to 20% of the capital investments made by the contractor in production facilities. The remaining production is then divided by giving Indonesia 65.9091% and the contractor 34.0909%. In addition, the contractor shall pay Indonesia for information held by Pertamina and certain bonus payments once production reaches a certain specified level. As in the case of the concession agreement, the company must pay taxes upon income earned from the production-sharing agreement.

In theory, no reason exists why landowners in the United States could not enter into arrangements analogous to the production-sharing agreements used internationally. Indeed, some sophisticated leases contain express obligations to drill a test well, provisions for an increased royalty upon well payout, clauses giving the lessor access to well information and permitting the lessor to conduct his own well tests, and provisions for extensive development; these come reasonably close to the typical production-sharing arrangement. One commentator has recommended joint development agreements, under which the landowner will share in net profits rather than receive a royalty, as a viable and possibly desirable alternative to the traditional oil and gas lease, but these more complex arrangements represent a very small percentage of the arrangements in place for developing United States petroleum reserves.

3. The Participation Agreement

In both the concession and the production-sharing agreements, the country (or its state oil company) and the multinational corporation (or a subsidiary) have maintained separate entities. In contrast, in a participation agreement a joint operating company is formed between the country and the company to develop the petroleum reserves. Although it is difficult to generalize in the context of existing participation agreements, in theory the country contributes the acreage and the company contributes technology and expertise as well as a certain sum of capital to the jointly formed entity. This entity is then operated by a management committee composed of representatives from both the country and the company. In some cases, ownership and management are equally divided and in other cases the country retains a 1% advantage.

In theory, one could view a participation agreement as a partnership or corporation between the country and the multinational company. Historically, however, the participation arrangements have developed from the original concession agreements in the Middle East; thus, their structure has developed through compromise rather than an initial decision to create such an arrangement. Since very few of the participation agreements began with undeveloped and nonproducing properties, it is difficult to determine how such agreements would handle the risks and uncertainties of exploration. Furthermore, participation is commonly included as an option to existing concession and production-sharing agreements. For example, the Indonesian production-sharing agreement provides that Pertamina may elect to purchase a certain percentage of the contract area for a share of the operating expenses already incurred by the contractor.

Although this option lapses within three months after the first discovery in the contract area, it nevertheless gives the Indonesian government a valuable right to participate in a significant discovery.

4. The Service Contract

In proceeding from concession to production sharing to participation, this discussion has been moving from arrangements permitting the most foreign involvement to the least, or alternatively, from the least host country participation in developing its resources to the most. The final form of arrangement in this analysis involves a service agreement between the country and a company. Essentially, under a service arrangement, the company agrees for a fee or a share of production to provide the country and its state oil company with services and information to help the country develop its own resources. Three basic types of arrangements have been developed to take advantage of the multinationals' technological and managerial expertise and capital resources while allowing the host country to maintain the appearance that its state oil company has control and ownership: (1) the pure service contract, (2) the technical assistance agreement, and (3) the risk service contract.

Under a pure service contract, the country's state oil company would contract with a foreign company to perform a specified service for a flat fee. Although pure service contracts are widely used in the United States, they are unattractive to multinational oil companies as opportunities for the development of foreign petroleum reserves because they provide no right to production. To make them more attractive, various nations refine the contracts to include buyback arrangements that allow the oil company to obtain crude oil instead of a flat fee. Some of these agreements resemble the arrangements used in the United States in which a geologist or other person or company performs services in exchange for the right to a specified fraction of production or an amount of production limited by a dollar sum or number of barrels.

The second form of service agreement, a technical assistance agreement, is in some ways a more sophisticated version of the service contract. In these agreements, the contractor agrees to provide technical assistance in the exploration, development, production, and, in some cases, refining of oil. The contractor's services may include providing equipment and training employees to operate the petroleum facilities. In return, the country agrees to reimburse the company for the expenses incurred plus a fee based upon the production obtained. For example, Venezuela, as part of its plan for nationalizing its oil industry, entered into technical assistance agreements under which several of the multinational oil companies agreed to help operate the facilities they had constructed in return for a per-barrel-produced fee.

The third form of agreement for developing petroleum reserves, the risk service contract, finds its widest use in Latin America. Under the risk service agreement, the oil company agrees to explore a specific area and evaluate its potential for discoveries. If the existence of petroleum reserves is suspected, the company is obligated to develop the reservoir. Throughout this period, the company invests only its own money with no expectation of payment unless commercial production results. Thus, the company bears the entire financial risk without receiving any rights in the explored territory. If and when commercial production commences, the company has a right to be paid for its services with cash, or frequently has a right to take oil at a discounted price instead. Although the risk service agreement contains features similar to a production-sharing arrangement, it gives the oil company fewer rights in the acreage that is explored.

Modern arrangements, no matter what their form or conceptual basis, often include provisions designed to require reinvestment in the country for petroleum-related projects and to favor domestic suppliers and employees. The purpose of these additional clauses is to integrate the petroleum operations into the national economy and to maintain control over the reserves.

2. 양허계약

전통적 양허계약은 오늘날 조광권 특허(license)라는 형태로 유지되고 있다.[12] 이들이 과거의 전통적 양허와 다른 점은 자원보유국과 조광권자간 권리의무의 균형이다. 조광권자는 조광권을 행사함에 있어서 작업프로그램을 제시하고 최소한 탐사의무, 광구반환의무 등을 이행하여야 하며 심지어는 현지인력의 훈련의무와 기술이전의무를 부담하기도 한다.[13] 최소한의 탐사의무를 시추공의 수나 깊이, 면적 등으로 특정할 수 있는가 하면 일정한 금액으로 정할 수도 있을 것이다. 조광권만 부여받고 시장상황이나 자금사정을 이유로 탐사나 생산을 게을리하는 것을 막기 위한 것으로 광구반환의무나 상업성의 판단기준과 절차에 관한 규정도 동일한 우려에 기인한 조항들이다.

조광권자는 서명보너스, 로열티, 소득세를 납부하여야 하며 최소한 탐사의무의 내용으로

12) 유럽 여러나라가 이 제도를 유지하고 있다. 예를 들어 네덜란드에 관하여는 Taverne, 위 주 3-19 상게서, 70-84.

13) Smith, 위 주 1-4 상게서, 448-53. 류권홍, 국제석유·가스개발과 거래계약, 162-87 (2011) 참조. 이는 외국의 가맹점사업업자가 franchise계약을 통하여 국내업자에게 가맹사업을 시작할 권리를 부여하면서 일정에 따라서 개설하여야 할 가맹점수를 정하는 것과 유사하다. 반대로 국내업자는 기술의 이전이나 교육훈련에 관한 조항을 추가하고자 한다.

일정한 비용지출의 의무를 부담하기도 한다. 영국의 석유사업법과 그 하위법규인 에너지성규정은 조광권허가시 부가되어야 할 모범규정을 자세하게 규정하고 있으나,[14] 우리나라 해저사업법은 조광권과 광업권을 개념상 구분하여 그 기간, 조광료, 포기, 취소를 정하고 있을 뿐, 설정허가시의 구체적인 조건과 부담은 지경부장관에게 위임하고 있다.[15] 해저사업법을 실시, 운용함에 있어서 몇 가지 법적인 의문점이 있다.

우선 국가를 당사자로 하는 계약에 관한 법률("국가계약법")과의 관계가 명확하지 않다. 이는 조광권 실사허가는 계약이 아니기 때문에 동 법률이 전혀 적용되지 아니한다고 해석할 수 있다. 한편 다른 해석은 해저사업법이 국가계약법의 특별법이고 이에 반하지 않는 범위내에서 국가계약법이 적용된다고 볼 수도 있다. 이는 결국 조광권 허가가 행정처분에 불과한 것인지, 아니면 일종의 행정계약인지에 따라서 결정될 것이다. 이는 조광권허가를 경쟁입찰이 아닌 방식으로 지경부가 부여할 수 있는지와 직결되는 문제이기도 하다. 현재 해저사업법은 허가기준과 위원회의 심의를 언급하고 있을 뿐이며 경쟁입찰방식이 채택되고 있지는 않는 듯하다.[16]

또한, 해저사업법은 조광권허가만을 해저광구의 개발방법으로 정하고 있는데, 그렇다면 개발계약의 다른 형태, 예를 들면 생산물분배계약이나 위험용역계약방식으로 개발할 수는 없는 것인지 명확하지 않다. 해저사업법 시행령 제8조와 별표 2에서 정하고 있는 조광료가 언제나 해저광구의 개발에 적정한 수준인지 의문이며 따라서 광구나 시장상황, 석유가격, 탐사비용 등에 따라서 보다 탄력성있는 유인과 대가를 요구할 수 있는 다양한 개발계약체결 가능성을 규정하는 것이 바람직하여 보인다.

다양한 형태의 탐사개발계약을 포함하여 조광권허가로서의 양허계약(concession)의 법적 성질에 관하여 다양한 논의가 있다.[17] 대부분 행정계약으로서 또는 행정행위와 사법상 계약의 중간적인 특수한 계약으로서 이해하며[18] 이는 주로 석유개발업체와 국가간 분쟁시 국가

---

14) 영국에 관하여는 Terrence Daintith, RIGHTS TO EXPLORE FOR AND EXPLOIT PETROLEUM: THE LICENSE *in* UNITED KINGDOM OIL & GAS LAW 1045-78/8 (Terence Daintith/Geoffrey Willo-wughby/Adrian Hill eds. 3rd ed. 2012).

15) 해저사업법 제16조.

16) 이러한 논의는 사회기반시설에 대한 민간투자법 제2조 제6호 실시협약에 관하여도 논의될 수 있을 것이다. 그러나, 우리 법원은 실시협약은 사법적, 일반적 계약관계로 보지 않고 따라서 우선협상자지정은 행정처분으로 본다. 예를 들면 서울고법 2004. 6. 24. 선고 2003누6483 판결.

17) 양허계약뿐만 아니라 모든 탐사개발권계약, 우리나라의 실시협약에 해당하는 BOT계약 등을 통틀어 development agreement(개발계약)으로 총칭, 국가와 다국적기업간의 특수한 계약형태로 관념짓기도 한다. Piero Bernardini, *Development Agreements with Host Governments*, in ECONOMIC DEVELOP-MENT, FOREIGN INVESTMENTAN THE LAW 161, 165-69 (Robert Prichard ed., 1996). Detlev F. Vagts/William S.Dodge/Harold Hongju Koh, TRANSNATIONAL BUSINESS PROBLEMS 528-70 (4th ed. 2008)도 동일한 용어 사용.

18) Zhiguo Gao, INTERNATIONAL PETROLEUM CONTRACTS: CURRENT TRENDS AND NEW DIRECTIONS,

가 주장할 수 있는 항변과 관련된다. 계약상 이행되어야 할 급부의 내용으로 보아서 행정계약으로서의 특성을 인정하여야 할지 의문이며 조광권이라는 단어를 사용한다고 한들 그 법적 성격이 달라지는 것은 아니라고 볼 수도 있다.19) 법적 성격에 관한 논의에 관계없이 많은 중재판정은 계약의 일방당사자인 국가나 NOC는 공공의 이익을 위하여 또는 중대한 상황변화를 이유로 권리의 내용을 변경할 수는 있다고 본다.20)

Pluspetrol Group Contract of 1996 for Exploration & Exploitation of Hydrocarbons (Ucayali Basin, Block 79) between PeruPetro S.A. & Pluspetrol Peru Corporation, KNOC & Yukong*

---

209 (1994).

19) Henry Cattan, THE LAW OF OIL CONCESSIONS IN THE MIDDLE EAST AND NORTH AFRICA 4 (the doctrine of imprevision을 언급) (1967). 기본적 사정변경(fundamental change of circumstances/*rebus sic stantibus*)은 계약의 일반원칙으로 받아들여지기도 한다. UNDROIT Principles of International Commericla Contracts (2004) Article 6. 2. 1 참조.

20) *Governmnet of Kuwait v. American Independent Oil Co. (Aminoil),* 21 I.L.M. 976, 1001 (1982).

* Barrows Company의 동의를 받아서 게재.

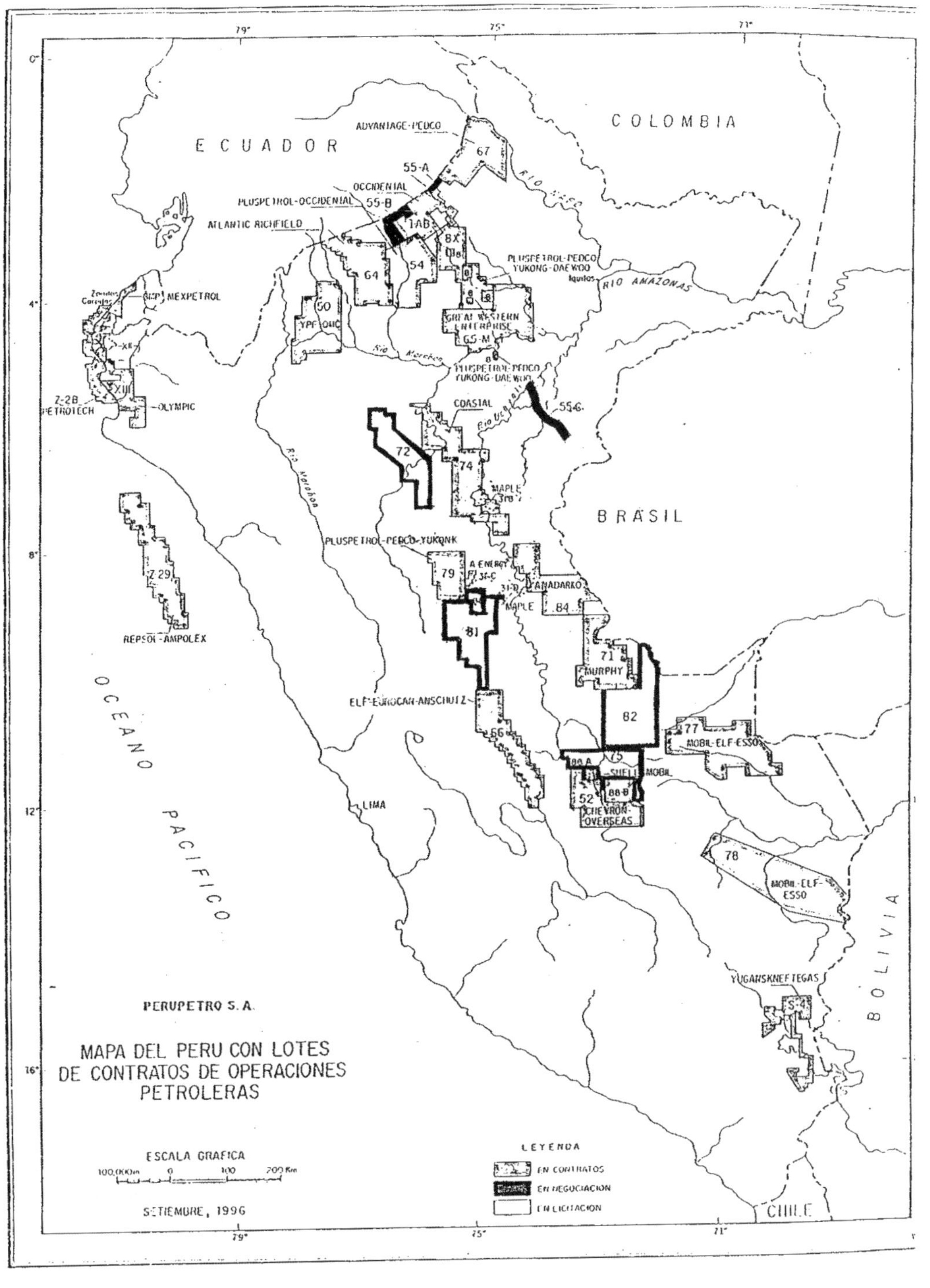

ECUADOR
COLOMBIA
BRASIL
BOLIVIA
CHILE
OCEANO PACIFICO
LIMA
RIO AMAZONAS
PERUPETRO S.A.
MAPA DEL PERU CON LOTES DE CONTRATOS DE OPERACIONES PETROLERAS
ESCALA GRAFICA
SETIEMBRE, 1996
LEYENDA
EN CONTRATOS
EN NEGOCIACION
EN LICITACION

EXHIBIT "B" MAP OF BLOCK
EXHIBIT (C, Cl/..C-x) LETTER OF GUARANTY FOR THE..OF THE MINIMUM WORK PROGRAM
EXHIBIT "D" CORPORATE GUARANTY

PRELIMINARY

Ⅰ. PERUPETRO participates, according to faculties granted by Law 26221, to celebrate "the License Contract for the Exploration and Exploitation of Hydrocarbons in the Ucayali Basin-Block 79." The Hydrocarbons "in situ" are the property of the state. The property right over the Hydrocarbons extracted is transfered by PERUPETRO to the Contractor in the Subscription Date, according to the Contract and the Article 8 of the Law N° 26221. The Contractor is obligated to pay to the Government the regalia in cash, in the conditions and the opportunities according to the Contract.

Ⅱ. Pursuant to the provisions of Law No. 26221, Article 12, this Contract is governed by Peruvian private law.

Ⅲ. For all purposes related to and arising from this Contract, the Parties agree that the captions of the Clauses are irrelevant to the interpretation of the contents thereof.

Ⅳ. Any reference to the Contract includes the Exhibits. In case of discrepancy, the provisions of the Contract shall prevail.

CLAUSE ONE: DEFINITIONS

The definitions agreed upon by the Parties in this clause are aimed at giving the required meaning to the terms used herein, and such meaning will be the only one accepted for the purposes of interpretation of the execution hereof, unless otherwise expressly agreed by the Parties in writing.

The terms defined and used in the Contract, whether in singular or plural, shall be written in capital letters and shall have the following meaning:

1.1 Affiliated

Any entity, fifty (50%) or more of the voting share capital of which, is owned, either directly or indirectly, by either of the Parties, or any entity or person who owns, either directly or indirectly, more than fifty percent (50%) of the voting share capital of one of the Parties, or any entity, fifty (50%) or more of the voting share capital of which, is owned, whether directly or indirectly, by the same shareholder or shareholders who own, either directly or indirectly, more than fifty percent (50%) of the voting share capital of any of the Parties hereto.

1.2 Year

A period of twelve (12) consecutive Months, according to the Gregorian Calendar, counted from a specific date.

1.3 Contract Area

The area described in Exhibit "A", appearing in Exhibit "B", defined as Block 79 located in the Padre Abad province and Coronel Portillo of Ucayali Department, Bellavista Province of San Martin Department and Ucayali Province of Loreto Department with an area of four hundred eighty two thousand (482,000) hectares.

The Contract Area will also be the one resulting after excluding the areas relinquished by the Contractor from time to time, according to the terms of the Contract.

In case of discrepancy, between the contents of Exhibit "B" and the description contained in Exhibit "A", the description contained in the latter shall prevail.

1.4 Barrel

Forty-two (42) United States of America gallons liquid measure, capacity, without water, mud or other sediments (BS&W), corrected to a temperature of sixty (60°) degrees Fahrenheit at sea level barometric pressure.

1.4 Acts of God or Force Majeure

Acts of God or Force Majeure shall be understood to be, among others, the following: fire, earthquakes, seaquakes, tremors, landslides, avalanches, floods, hurricanes, storms, explosions, unforeseeable acts of God, wars, guerrilla and terrorist activities, sabotage, civil commotion, blockades, uncontrollable delays in transportation, impossibility of obtaining, despite having foreseen it, adequate facilities for the transportation of materials, equipment and services, licenses or permits, or any other reason, whether similar to or different from those specifically listed herein, which are beyond the reasonable control of, and could not be foreseen by said Party, or if foreseen, could not be avoided.

1.5 Supervisory Committee

The body which supervises compliance with and execution of this Contract, the composition and powers of which are established in Clause 7 hereof.

1.6 Conciliation Committee

A non-permanent body established to pronounce over any discrepancies that may arise in connection with the Operations the issue to be settled pursuant to the provisions of Clause 21.3.

1.7 Condensate Hydrocarbons

The liquid formed by the condensation of the Hydrocarbons separated from Natural Gas, due to pressure and temperature changes when Natural Gas of the Reservoirs is released, and the liquid hydrocarbon recovered from one or more compression stages of Natural Gas.

1.8 Condensate

Condensate produced in the Contract Area and measured.

1.9 Contractor

Pluspetrol Peru Corporation, Peru Branch, registered in the Public Register of Hydrocarbons in Entry..., Page...,Volume...of the Operations Contractors' Book.

Korea Petroleum Development Corporation, Peruvian Branch registered in the Public Register of Hydrocarbons in Entry..., Page...,Volume...of the Operations Contractors' Book.

Yukong Limited, Peru Branch registered in the Public Register of Hydrocarbons in Entry..., Page..., Volume...of the Operations Contractors' Book.

The participating interest the Contractor at the Date of companies making is as follows:

Pluspetrol Peru Corporation, Peru Branch	66 2/3%
Korea Petroleum Development Corporation, Peruvian Branch	16 2/3%
Yukong Limited, Peru Branch	16 2/3%

1.10 Contract

This agreement which the Parties have entered, which stipulates the terms and conditions contained in this document and in exhibits that compromise it, and the amendments agreed upon and approved by the Parties pursuant to the law.

1.11 Development

The drilling, deepening, reconditioning and completion of wells, and also the design, construction, installation of equipment, piping, storage tanks and other types of installations and facilities, and the performance of any other activity appropriate to the Production of Hydrocarbons, including the use of methods for artificial production and the system of primary and improved recovery within the Contract Area and outside it whenever necessary. It includes the construction of the Transportation and Storage System, facilities at the Fiscalization Point and the plant for primary distilling for manufacturing products to be used in Operations.

1.12 Commercial Discovery

The discovery of Hydrocarbon reserves, which, in the Contractor's opinion, enables commercial exploitation.

1.13 Day

A period of twenty-four (24) hours, which starts at zero (0.00) hours and ends at twenty-four (24.00) hours.

1.14 Business Day

All working Days from Monday to Friday inclusive, except for those Days declared non-working or partially non-working in the city of Lima by the competent authority.

1.15 Dollar

The US legal unit of currency.

1.16 Exploration

The planning, execution and evaluation of all types of geological, geophysical, geochemical and other studies, the drilling of stratigraphic and Exploratory Wells and related activities necessary to discover Hydrocarbons, and including the drilling of Confirmation pitfalls for the purpose of evaluating any Reservoirs so discovered.

1.17 Exploitation

Development and Production

1.18 Date of Commencement of Commercial Extraction

The date on which the first measurement of Hydrocarbons is made at a Production Fiscalization Point giving rise to the subsequent payment of royalties. For the purpose of this definition, quantities produced for testing or for other reasons specifically agreed by the Parties hereto shall not be considered.

1.19 Date of Signing

... 1995 date on which the Parties sign this Contract.

1.20 Fiscalization

The action taken by the General Bureau of Hydrocarbons to control the Operations conducted by the Contractor as provided for herein.

1.21 Natural Gas

Hydrocarbons which, under Reservoir conditions, are in a gaseous state or diluted with oil. It comprises Associated Natural Gas and Non-Associated Natural Gas.

1.22 Associated Natural Gas

The Natural Gas produced together with Liquid Hydrocarbons of the Reservoir.

1.23 Non-Associated Natural Gas

Gas found in a natural Reservoir containing no Liquid Hydrocarbons.

1.24 Hydrocarbons

Every organic, gaseous, liquid or solid compound, consisting mainly of carbon and hydrogen.

1.25 Fiscalized Hydrocarbons

The Hydrocarbons of the Contract Area, measured at a Production Fiscalization Point.

1.26 Liquid Hydrocarbons

Petroleum, Condensate Hydrocarbons, which under pressure at any measurement and, in general, any and atmospheric temperature point are liquid.

1.27 Fiscalized Liquid Hydrocarbons

All Liquid Hydrocarbons produced in the Contract Area and measured at a Production Fiscalization Point.

1.28 Law 26221

Organic Hydrocarbon Law 26221, amendments and regulations included.

1.29 Month

Period counted as from any given Day in a calendar Month, which ends on the Day before the same Day of the following calendar Month or, if there is no such Day, the last Day of that Month.

1.30 TSCF

Means one thousand (1,000) standard cubic feet ("TSCF"). One (1) "SCF" is the volume of gas filling a space of one (1) cubic foot at 14.7 pounds per square inch of absolute pressure and a temperature of sixty (60) degrees Fahrenheit.

1.31 Operations

All activities related to the Exploration and Exploitation of Hydrocarbons as well as those related to the Transportation and Storage System together with any and all activities subject matter hereof or related herewith.

1.32 Operator

Any of the companies making up the Contractor, appointed by such companies to carry out Operations on behalf of and on account of the Contractor. On the Date of Signing ... was appointed Operator.

1.33 Parties

PERUPETRO and the Contractor

1.34 PERUPETRO

PERUPETRO S.A. is a State owned Corporation of the Energy and Mines Sector, that was incorporated by Law 26221, and is subject to private law.

1.35 Petroleum

Hydrocarbons found in a liquid state under Reservoir pressure and temperture conditions.

1.36 Confirmation Well

Well drilled to evaluate the Hydrocarbons in any Reservoir discovered.

1.37 Development Well

Well drilled to exploit the Hydrocarbons discovered.

1.38 Exploratory Well

Well drilled to discover a new Reservoir or to determine the stratigraphy in a particular area.

1.39 Production

Any and all activities inside or outside the Contract Area, as necessary, the main purpose of which is to extract and handle Hydrocarbons, including the operation and reconditioning of wells, equipment, piping, Transportation and Storage System, treatment and measurement of Hydrocarbons, as well as any type of primary, secondary and tertiary recovery methods.

1.40 Production Fiscalization Point

Place or places agreed upon by the Parties, located inside or outside of the Contract Area and where volumetric measurements and determinations, determinations of water and sediment contents, and other measurements are carried out in order to establish the volume of Fiscalized Hydrocarbons according to API and ASTM standards.

1.41 Reservoir

Underground stratum or strata having a common pressure system throughout and forming part of the same field, which are producing or have been proved to have the capacity to produce Hydrocarbons.

1.42 Transportation and Storage System

The pipework, pumping stations, compression stations, storage tanks and, if required, river facilities, as well as delivery systems, roads, other facilities and means necessary and useful for the transportation of Hydrocarbons produced inside the Contract Area up to the Production Fiscalization Point together with the design, construction, maintenance and equipping thereof.

1.43 Subcontractor

Every individual or body corporate domiciled in Peru or abroad, hired by the Contractor to render services related to Operations.

1.44 Supervision

The actions taken by PERUPETRO to verify compliance with Contractor's obligations during the term hereof.

1.45 Taxes

Includes taxes, contributions and rates, provided for by Tax Codes.

1.46 Term of Contract

Period between the Date of the Contract and the end of the term as established in Point 3.1.

1.47 Field

A surface area under which there are one or more Reservoirs which are producing or have been proved to have the capacity of producing Hydrocarbons.

CLAUSE TWO: PURPOSE OF THE CONTRACT

2.1 PERUPETRO authorizes the Contractor to conduct Operations, according to the provisions set forth by Law 26221, rules, regulations and amendments, pertinent legislation and Contract stipulations with the common purpose to discover and produce Hydrocarbons inside the Contract Area.

2.2 The Hydrocarbons "in situ" are the property of the State. The Contractor shall have the right of ownership of Hydrocarbons extracted from the Contract Area.

2.3 The Contractor shall perform the Operations according to the terms stipulated herein and shall conduct them directly or through Subcontractors. Any Operations outside the Contract Area must be previously approved by PERUPETRO.

2.4 PERUPETRO will be in charge of the Supervision of the Operations and the General Bureau of Hydrocarbons will be responsible for the Fiscalization thereof. The representatives of PERUPETRO and the General Bureau of Hydrocarbons may perform their duties at any time, by giving prior notice but must identify themselves and be expressly authorized in writing by PERUPETRO and the General Bureau of Hydrocarbons, respectively. The Contractor shall provide all the necessary facilities in the Contract Area to enable said representatives to carry out their responsibilities, which shall be executed without interfering with the Operations. All resulting costs and expenses incurred by such representatives shall be for PERUPETRO, the General Bureau of Hydrocarbons or the Contractor's account, according to law.

2.5 The Contractor shall furnish and be responsible for all the technical, financial and economic resources which may be required for the Operations hereunder.

2.6 The obligations assumed by the Contractor or Operator hereunder shall be joint and several with respect to each and every individual or body corporate forming part of the Contractor. Notwithstanding the foregoing, it is hereby understood that each and every individual or body corporate making up the Contractor is individually responsible for its tax obligations or any and all liabilities resulting therefrom. The same applies to the financial rights established in Clause 11 hereof, which as far as applicable, shall be enjoyed by them either on a several and a pro rata basis. Each and every individual or body corporate forming part of the Contractor shall individually comply with the provisions relating to the transfer of interest referred to in Clause 16 hereof.

CLAUSE THREE: TERM, CONDITIONS AND GUARANTY

3.1 The maximum term for the Hydrocarbons exploration stage is seven (7) Years, counted as from the Date of Signing hereof unless this term is modified in accordance with other provisions of the Contract. The maximum term for the Petroleum exploitation stage is that term remaining after the exploration stage up to the end of the thirty (30) Years term, counted as from the Date of Signing, unless it is modified in accordance with other provisions of the Contract. The maximum term for the exploitation stage of Non-Associated Natural Gas and Non-Associated Natural Gas and Condensates is that term remaining after the exploration stage up to the end of the forty (40) Years term, counted as from the Date of Signing, unless it is modified in accordance with other provisions of the Contract.

3.2 The exploration stage is divided into . (...) periods:

3.2.1 A first period lasting ... ( ) Months as from the Date of Signing.

3.2.2 A second period lasting ... ( ) Months as from the end of the term indicated in 3.2.1.

3.2.X A... period lasting ... ( ) Months as form the end of the term indicated in 3.2.(X-l).

3.3 During the exploration phase:

3.3.1 The Contractor may start the second, ... and X periods to which 3.2.2, ... and 3.2.X referred to respectively, unless it has not fulfilled obligations corresponding to the period previous to the one which it is about to begin, in which event the provisions set forth in Subpoint 22. 3.3 shall apply with the corresponding execution of the guaranty.

3.3.2 The Contractor shall notify PERUPETRO of its intention to continue with the next period, thirty (30) Days in advance of the expiration of the term.

3.4 If during the prescribed period of time indicated in Point 3.2 the Contractor fails to comply with the Minimum Work Program for each block referred to in Subpoints 4.6.1 and 4.6.2, ...and 4.6.X because of technical reasons, the Contractor shall have the right to extend the term by maximum period of six (6) Months, provided the contractor presents to PERUPETRO a new guaranty or extends the existing one sixty (60) Days before the expiry date thereof and the reasons supporting thereto have been verified and approved by PERUPETRO. In this case the Contractor before the expiration of the period shall submit a new guaranty or extend the existing ... only by the new established term, according to the provisions stipulated in 3.9. In no case whatsoever may the extensions result in a prolongation of the total term established for the exploration stage. The approval by PERUPETRO referred to in this Point shall be granted at the sole discretion of PERUPETRO.

3.5 The exploration stage may continue after the Date of Commencement of Commercial Extraction until expiry of the term indicated in Point 3.1, if the Contractor so requires. Should this be the case, Point 10.3 shall be applicable until the Exploration stage expires. The straight-line method of amortization referred to in Point 9.6 shall be applied until the Date of Commencement of Commercial Extraction.

3.6 Should the Contractor make a discovery of Hydrocarbons at any time of the Exploration stage, it may request a "retention period" of up to five (5) Years for the Field or Fields discovered in order to facilitate the transport of the hydrocarbons produced. The right to such retention shall be subject to at least the following requirements:

a) The Contractor must prove to the satisfaction of PERUPETRO that the volumes of Hydrocarbons discovered in the contract area are insufficient to economically justify the construction of the main pipeline;
b) The whole of the discoveries made in both adjacent areas and those of the Contractor are insufficient to economically justify the construction of the main pipeline; and
c) The Contractor must prove, based on economic grounds, that the Hydrocarbons discovered can not be transported from the Contract Area to any marketing place by any means of transport whatsoever.

3.7 Should the Contractor make a discovery of Non-Associated Natural Gas or Non-Associated Natural Gas and Condensates at any time at the Exploration stage, it may request a retention period up to ten (10) Years for the Field or Fields discovered in order to develop the market.

3.8 In the event the Contractor discovers Petroleum and Non-Associated Natural Gas or Non-Associated Natural Gas and Condensates during any period of the Exploration stage, and the cases stipulated in Points 3.6 and 3.7, the Contractor may require a retention period for Petroleum, Non-Associated Natural Gas or Non-Associated Natural Gas and Condensates, for the purposes indicated in the said Points. The retention periods may not exceed ten (10) Years.

3.9 The period of retention referred to Points 3.6 and 3.7 shall extend the Contract term for a time equal to the retention period granted by PERUPETRO. The period of retention shall be established in writing. To this end, the Contractor shall apply for such a period by submitting to PERUPETRO the supporting documentation, including a schedule containing any and all activities to be carried out. Upon commencement of the retention period, the Exploration stage shall end. The Exploitation stage shall start immediately after the Declaration of Commercial Discovery made during the aforementioned period. The period of retention referred to the Points 3.6 and 3.7 and the term thereof shall be determined at the sole discretion of PERUPETRO.

3.10 The Contractor shall guaranty compliance with each Minimum Work Program of Exploration by a joint and several, unconditional and irrevocable guaranty automatically executable in Peru, without the benefit of excussion, issued by a duly qualified entity of the financial system, established in Peru and accepted by PERUPETRO, in accordance with Points 3.2 and 4.6 hereof. PERUPETRO may request the Contractor that a guaranty be substituted whenever there is the justified risk that the guarantor might fail to honor the guaranty, and the Contractor shall have to deliver a new guaranty within fifteen (15) Business Days following the date on which it received the request made by PERUPETRO. The amount of the guaranty to cover Minimum Work Program for the first period established in Subpoint 4.6.1 shall be US$... (... US Dollars). The amount of the guaranty to cover Minimum Work Program for the second period established in Subpoint 4.6.2 shall be US$ ...(... US Dollars). The amount of the guaranty to cover Minimum Work Program for the X period established in Subpoint 4.6.X shall be US$...(... US Dollars). The first guaranty for the Minimum Work Program referred to in Subpoint 4.6.1 shall be delivered to PERUPETRO on the Date of Signing. The guaranties for the Minimum Work Program specified in Subpoints 4.6.2, ... and 4.6.X shall be delivered to PERUPETRO before the beginning of each period; otherwise, Subpoint 22.3.3 shall apply. The guaranties for each period of "the Minimum Work Program" shall remain in force for thirty(30) Business Days after the date on which the Minimum Work Program was completed. If any of the guaranties furnished by the Contractor does not remain in force during the agreed term, PERUPETRO shall advise the Contractor thereof and the Contractor must deliver a new guaranty or extend the existing one within a term of fifteen (15) Business Days following receipt of PERUPETRO's notice informing it of the matter. Otherwise, Subpoint 22.3.3 shall apply. Upon compliance with the guarantied obligation, PERUPETRO shall proceed to release the guaranty referred to. The guaranties indicated in Exhibits "C-1" to "C-X" shall be issued for each period of the Minimum Work Program. The execution of any and all guaranty shall extinguish the obligation of the Contractor to carry out the Minimum Work Program without prejudice to the application of the provisions set forth in Subpoint 22.3.3

3.11 ... and ... intervene in this Contract to furnish the Corporate Guaranties referred to in Exhibits "D" and "D-X", which shall be delivered to PERUPETRO as of the Date of Signing.

CLAUSE FOUR: EXPLORATION

4.1 The Contractor shall start the Exploration activities as from the Date of Signing hereof.

4.2 The Contractor may relinquish the whole of the Contract Area without being subject to fine or penalty whatsoever by serving written notice thereof to PERUPETRO at least thirty (30) Days in advance, provided the Minimum Work Program for entire current period of the Exploration stage has been completed. Should the Contractor relinquish the whole Contract Area, abandon it or should the current period expire without completion of the Minimum Work Program, without there being technical reasons approved by PERUPETRO, the guaranty shall be executed, without prejudice to the application of the provisions of Subpoint 22.3.3. The Contractor may partially relinquish the Contract Area by serving written notice thereof to PERUPETRO at least thirty (30) Days in advance without any fine or penalty whatsoever, but without this affecting or reducing its obligation to complete the Minimum Work Program for the current period of Operations. The Parties shall keep a record of the areas relinquished by the Contractor in the minutes of the Supervisory Committee meetings. The Contractor may continue using the ground of the relinquished areas, if there are installations constructed which are in use in connection with the Operations.

4.3 During the execution of the Contract, the areas shall be relinquished as follows:

a) 25% of the original area as to ... counted from the Date of Signing.
b) 25% of the original area as to ... counted from the Date of Signing.
c) At the end of the Exploitation stage, the Contractor shall only keep the Fields under Development, in Production or under retention plus surrounding area of five (5) kilometers.

4.4 For the purposes indicated in Points 4.2 and 4.3, the Contract Area has been divided into rectangular lots, as far as is possible with an area of twenty thousand (20,000) Has. each, and where not possible, into different areas. The description of these lots is in Exhibit "A" and they are shown in Exhibit "B". It is not necessary that areas relinquished by the Contractor should be adjoining.

4.5 Any area relinquished by the Contractor including Fields therein shall revert to the State at no charge whatsoever to it nor to PERUPETRO.

4.6 The Minimum Work Program for each of the periods of the exploration stage, that the Contractor must carry out is as follows:

4.6.1 First Period:
4.6.2 Second Period:
4.6.X "X" Period:

4.7 The Exploratory Wells referred to in point 4.6 shall be considered to be drilled and therefore the task of the Contractor completed, when they reach the geological objectives ... or a minimum depth of ...m. If, before the commencement of drilling of any Exploratory Well referred to in point 4.6, the Contractor demonstrates to the satisfaction of PERUPETRO, on the basis of the results of its geological and geophysical assessments, that it cannot comply with the objectives agreed in paragraph one of this Point, the Parties may agree another geological objective and/or depth. In addition, if during drilling of Exploratory Wells referred to in Point 4.6, insuperable geological or mechanical problems encountered, the Contractor may request that its drilling obligation be considered as satisfied, by submitting a substantiating report, subject to the approval of PERUPETRO.

4.8 In the event that for technical and geological reasons arising during the Exploration stage the Contractor request, through a supporting report approved by PERUPETRO, the drilling of any well shall not proceed, the investment scheduled for any such undrilled Exploratory Well shall be diverted to additional Exploration work upon execution of which the obligations of the Contractor shall be considered fulfilled. The approval for such substitution shall be granted at the sole discretion of PERUPETRO.

4.9 In the event the Contractor decides to declare a Commercial Discovery, this must be notified to PERUPETRO, and an "Initial Development Plan" to enable Exploitation of the Hydrocarbons discovery shall be submitted to PERUPETRO within 180 (one hundred and eighty) Days of the said declaration, indicating:

a) Physical and chemical characteristics of the Hydrocarbons discovered and the percentages of associated products and impurities they contain.
b) Estimated production rates during the Term of the Contract for the Field or Fields.

c) The estimated number of Development Wells and their productive capacity.
d) Transport and Storage System and Production Fiscalization Points.
e) Main pipeline, if necessary.
f) Safety measures and terms of reference of the "Environmental Impact Study" applicable to Exploitation in accordance with the "Environmental Regulations for Hydrocarbon Activities approved by Supreme Decree 046-93-EM, as amended."
g) Provisional schedule of all proposed activities.
h) Estimated Date of Commencement of Commercial Extraction.

The "Initial Development Plan" must include the specific investments, expenses and costs estimated for exploiting the Commercial Discovery as well as any other information the Contractor considers appropriate.

4.10 PERUPETRO shall advise the Contractor of its comments on the "Initial Development Plan" within sixty (60) Days of its receipt, stating whether or not the Date of Commencement of Commercial Extraction is satisfactory. In the event of any dispute over this, the Conciliation Committee shall be called.

4.11 If the Contractor makes a declaration of Commercial Discovery, it shall be obliged to initiate development thereof within one hundred and eighty (180) Days following the expiry of the sixty (60) Days mentioned in Point 4.10. The declaration of Commercial Discovery shall not imply any reduction or suspension of the obligation to complete the Minimum Work Program.

4.12 The development of any Hydrocarbons discovered shall be done in accordance with the work programs submitted by the Contractor to PERUPETRO, as stipulated in Point 5.3. The Parties hereby agree that should it be appropriate and necessary, the term for the submission of the "Initial Development Plan" or the annual work programs may be adjusted, extended or modified as the case may be. For this purpose, the Contractor shall submit the necessary proposals to PERUPETRO for it to approve such adjustments, extensions or modifications.

4.13 The expiry of the Exploration stage shall in no way affect the terms and conditions of the previously described activities that are being carried out.

4.14 The obligations of the Minimum Work Program for any of the periods referred to in Point 4.6 may be reduced, if the Contractor has completed them previously, and provided that the said work has been done in excess to that established in the Minimum Work Program for the previous periods.

CLAUSE FIVE: EXPLOITATION

5.1 The Exploitation stage shall commence the Day following the end of the exploration stage, provided a declaration of Commercial Discovery has been made during the exploration stage. However, if the Contractor deems it suitable, the Exploitation stage may be started in advance and the Exploration stage shall be concluded on the Date of Commencement of Commercial Extraction. In case of a retention period, the Exploitation stage shall be commenced based on the pertinent declaration of Commercial Discovery.

5.2 The Contractor shall be obliged to ensure that the Date of Commencement of Commercial Extraction falls within the term to be established in the "Initial Development Plan", which term may be extended by mutual consent of the Parties, if so required.

5.3 Within ninety (90) Days prior to the end of each calendar Year from the Date of Commencement of Commercial Extraction, the Contractor shall submit to PERUPETRO the following:

a) An annual work program and a detailed Exploitation budget of income, costs, expenses and investments for the following calendar Year of Exploitation.
b) A work program and an estimate of costs, expenses and investments for Exploration aimed at looking for additional reserves, if necessary.
c) A work program and an estimate of income, costs, expenses and investments for Development and Production for the next five (5) calendar Years.

The Contractor is entitled to readjust or change the said programs at any time provided such decision has been justified and submitted to PERUPETRO.

5.4 In order to carry out each program, the Contractor shall use the necessary and appropriate equipment and/or methods to allow a continuous evaluation of:

a) Reservoir pressure.
b) Productivity rate.
c) Well and Reservoir characteristics.
d) Physical and chemical characteristics of the Hydrocarbons.
e) Typical Reservoir rock and fluid parameters.
f) Recovery efficiency.
g) Proven, probable, and possible Hydrocarbons reserves.

This includes, but is not limited to, the items listed above.

5.5 The Contractor is obligated to exploit the Hydrocarbons reserves of the Contract Area and ensure their economic recovery in accordance with the programs referred to in this Clause Five, both of which shall be made pursuant to technical and economic principles generally accepted and used in the international Hydrocarbon industry.

5.6 The Contractor shall use the Hydrocarbons produced within the Contract Area for its Operations, free of charge.

5.7 The Contractor shall have the right to recover the Liquid Hydrocarbons from any Natural Gas produced within the Contract Area and to extract Liquid Hydrocarbons from any handling stage of Natural Gas. The liquids thus separated shall be considered as Liquid Hydrocarbons for determining the royalty of the Contractor.

5.8 The Natural Gas not used by the Contractor in the Operations pursuant to the stipulations in Point 5.6, shall be marketed or reinjected into the Reservoir or both by the Contractor. To the extent the Natural Gas is not used, distributed or reinjected, the Contractor may flare the gas with prior approval from the Ministry of Energy and Mines.

5.9 When a commercially exploitable Field or Fields extends continuously from the Contract Area to another area or areas, the Contractor and the other contractors shall establish a single Exploitation plan or a common Exploitation plan. Should no such agreement be reached, the Ministry of Energy and Mines shall submit the controversial issues to the Conciliation Committee referred to in Law 26221, Article 3.2, and its resolution shall be binding upon the Parties. If the area next to the commercially exploitable Field is not assigned to a contractor or is not in a negotiation process, bid or tender and there is no limitation regarding environmental protection, the Contractor shall have the first option to negotiate and incorporate such adjacent area as long as the request is made during the Exploration stage.

5.10 Once the drilling of a well has been completed, the Contractor must inform PERUPETRO of the date on which the well shall be tested, and of the production program and the estimated production volumes.

5.11 PERUPETRO may at any time inspect and test any and all equipment and instruments used to measure the volume and determine the quality of Hydrocarbons produced in the Contract Area. The measuring equipment and instruments shall be calibrated from time to time according to the legal provisions currently in force. The representatives of PERUPETRO shall be present when this is done.

5.12 Before the Commencement Date of Commercial Extraction and in order to determine the volume and quality of Fiscalized Hydrocarbons, the Supervisory Committee shall agree on the following:

a) The frequency of and opportunity on which measurements will take place.
b) Methods to be used for measuring the production volume, determination of the Hydrocarbon quality and Hydrocarbon volume for consumption or personal use.
c) Frequency of inspection, tests and calibration of measuring equipment.
d) The action to be taken for correction in case of determining an error in measurement.

CLAUSE SIX: INFORMATION AND STUDIES PRESENTATION

6.1 The Contractor shall continuously, promptly and regularly keep PERUPETRO informed on the Operations, providing it with all the information foreseen in this Clause and any regulations appliable. Moreover, the Contractor shall furnish any information on other natural or archaeological resources it may find or discover in the Contract area during the term hereof.

6.2 The Contractor shall provide a copy of any and all basic studies relating to the Development of the Fields it prepares based on the technical information obtained from the Contract Area. The Contractor shall also furnish any clarification PERUPETRO may request in relation to such studies.

6.3 Within ninety (90) Days following the end of each period established in 3.2.1, 3.2.X, the Contractor shall submit to PERUPETRO an evaluation report with studies containing geological, geophysical, geochemical, petrophysical and Reservoirs analysis prepared for the Minimum Work Program of each period.

6.4 The Contractor shall deliver the following reports to PERUPETRO:

6.4.1 "Monthly Production Report", by Reservoir no later than fifteen (15) Days after each calendar Month, indicating the following:

a) The quantity and quality of each class of Liquid Hydrocarbons produced in the calendar Month.
b) The quantity and quality of each class of Liquid Hydrocarbons produced from the Date of Commencement of Commercial Extraction until the end of the pertinent calendar Month.
c) Quantity and quality of Natural Gas reinjected and flared in each calendar Month, as well as the quantity accumulated as from the Date of Commencement of Commercial Extraction until the end of the pertinent calendar Month.
d) Quantity and quality of each class of Hydrocarbons used during the calendar Month in the Operations as well as the quantity accumulated as from the Date of Commencement of Commercial Extraction until the end of the corresponding calendar Month.
e) Inventory of Hydrocarbons in the Transportation and Storage System at the beginning of each calendar Month.
f) Quantity and quality of each class of Hydrocarbons exported as from the Date of

Commencement of Commercial Extraction until the end of the pertinent calendar Month.

g) Cumulative quantity and quality of each class of Hydrocarbons exported from the Date of Commencement of Commercial Extraction until the end of the pertinent calendar Month.

6.4.2 "Monthly Report of Income and Expenditure", no later than thirty (30) Days following the end of each calendar Month. This report. shall distinguish between Exploration and Exploitation investments, operating expenses and costs, overheads and administrative costs, and shall identify the main investments and expenses within these categories.

6.5 The Contractor shall deliver to PERUPETRO a copy of all the information it must submit to the Banco Central de Reserva del Peru pursuant to the provisions set forth in Point 11 on the same dates, and in the form and substance stipulated therein.

6.6 Within fifteen (15) Days following the end of each calendar Month, the Contractor shall deliever to PERUPETRO the list of contracts entered into with its Subcontractors in the said month and provide PERUPETRO, if so required, with a copy of all the contracts requested.

6.7 Any of the Parties may disclose such information without prior approval of the other Party, in the following cases:

a) To an Affiliate of such Party;
b) In relation to financing, obtaining a similar confidentiality commitment;
c) To the extent required by law, regulations or resolutions issued by a pertinent authority, including, without limitation, the regulations or resolutions issued by governmental authorities, underwriters or the Stock Exchange in which the securities of such Party or its Affiliates are registered;
d) To consultants, accountants, auditors, financiers, professionals, potential purchasers of the Parties or of a Contract sharing, to the extent necessary in relation to the Operations, obtaining the same confidentiality commitment.

If the Parties agree to disclose certain confidential information to third Parties, they must expressly state the confidential nature of such information so that it will not be further disclosed.

CLAUSE SEVEN: SUPERVISORY COMMITTEE

7.1 Without prejudice to the provisions set forth in Point 2.2 hereof, a Supervisory Committee shall supervise compliance with the Contract. The Supervisory Committee shall consist of three (3) members appointed by the Contractor, or its representatives, as one Party, and three (3) members designated by PERUPETRO, or its representatives, as the other party.

The Supervisory Committee shall be established and prepare its Operating Regulations within thirty (30) Days following the Date of Signing.

7.2 The Supervisory Committee shall have the following responsibilities:

a) Exchange and discuss among its members all the information in connection with the Operations hereunder.
b) Evaluate the minimum Exploration Program, referred to in Point 4.6.
c) Evaluate and supervise the work plans and programs, referred to in Points 4.9 and 5.3.
d) Supervise the Operations hereunder, for which purpose the representatives of the Parties accredited before the Supervisory Committee may consult the necessary advisory services.

e) Supervise compliance with all the obligations related to the Operations provided for in this Contract or agreed upon between the Parties through any other document.
f) Any other responsibilities provided for in this Contract or agreed upon between the Parties through any other document.

7.3 The Supervisory Committee shall be presided over by one (1) representative of PERUPETRO. It shall meet whenever requested by any of the Parties and from time to time as established in its regulations. The representatives of both Parties shall be required to attend in order for the Supervisory Committee to be considered as installed, and validly functioning. Each of the Parties shall assume the expenses incurred to maintain its respective members on the Supervisory Committee.

7.4 The decisions of the Supervisory Committee shall be adopted by the unanimous vote of the Parties. Each Party shall issue its vote. Should a disagreement between the Parties occur and persist in the Supervisory Committee, each of the Parties may request the technical, financial or legal opinions it may deem convenient and shall submit them for the consideration of the Supervisory Committee in a special meeting. Should the disagreement continue once the special meeting has ended, it shall be submitted to the Conciliation Committee.

7.5 The Contractor shall submit and explain to the Supervisory Committee the production profile programs for each Field for the purposes of fulfilling the responsibilities set forth in Point 7.2.

CLAUSE EIGHT: ROYALTY AND VALUATION

8.1 The royalty to be paid by the Contractor in cash — which for the purposes of Point 8.4 shall be considered an expense — based on the Hydrocarbons produced in the Contract Area, valued at one of the Production Fiscalization Points, in accordance with Points 8.3, 3.4 and 8.5.

8.2 For the purposes of this Clause, the terms indicated hereafter shall have the following meanings:

8.2.1 Transport and Storage Costs means the tariff estimated or paid for transport and storage necessary for exportation or normal sale, including handling and delivery fees to the fixed connecting flange on the vessel or to the installations required for carrying on the said activity.

8.2.2 Basket Price means the price expressed in Dollars and determined by the price\basket defined in accordance with Subpoint 8.6.1.

8.2.3 Realized Price means the price expressed in Dollars actually paid or payable by a buyer to the Contractor for the Hydrocarbons produced in the Contract Area and valued at the point of sale.

8.2.4 Estimated Tariff means the cost of transporting Fiscalized Hydrocarbons from the Production Fiscalization Point to the point of sale or Exploitation. This cost shall be established according to the pertinent provisions and regulations.

8.3 The royalty to be paid by the Contractor shall be determined by using the “R” Factor method, which factor shall be calculated pursuant to Subpoint 8.4 hereof. The “R” Factor establishes the percentage of the royalty, which shall be applied to the different classes of Fiscalized Hydrocarbons, as indicated in the following table, and valued in accordance with Subpoint 8.6.

Table

"R" Factor	Fiscalized Hydrocarbons Royalty Percentage		
	≤$15/BBL	$25/BBL	≥$35/BBL
From 0 to 0.99999	……	……	……
From 1.0 to 1.49999	……	……	……
From 1.5 to 1.99999	……	……	……
From 2 to more	……	……	……

In order to determine the royalty percentage for each Petroleum Basket Price higher than US$15/BBL and lower than US$25/BBL as well as any other Petroleum Basket Price higher than US$25/BBL and lower than US$35/BBL, the straight-line method of interpolation shall be used.

8.4 The calculation of the "R" factor shall be made monthly, within the first five (5) Days of each calendar Month, based on the information of the previous calendar Month. The "R" Factor shall be applied as from the Day of the calendar Month during which it is calculated. Only one "R" Factor shall be determined which shall be used to establish the compensation percentage for any and all Hydrocarbons produced in the Contract Area. This single "R" factor shall be determined by the following equation:

R=X/Y

Where:

X = Income accumulated according to the following
Acum[PFP(PC-CTAP)]+Acum[PFG(PR-CTAG)]+Acum[OI]

PFP = Fiscalized Petroleum Production

PC = Basket Price

CTAP = Transport and Storage Cost for Petroleum or Estimated Tariff from the Production Fiscalization Point to the point of sale or exportation

PFG = Fiscalized Production of Gas

PR = Realized Price

CTAG = Transport and Storage Cost from the Production Fiscalization Point to the point of sale or exportation.

OI = Other Income

Y = Expenditures accumulated according to the following:
Acum (Investment+Expenses+Royalty+Other Expenditures)

Both income and expenditure details as well as the date of recording "R" Factor components are specified in Exhibit "E", Accounting Procedure.

8.5 Without prejudice to the provisions of Exhibit "E", Point 2.5, paragraph d), Accounting Procedure, should the Parties at any time establish that 'the "R" Factor calculation was mistaken and said mistake results in the application of an "R" Factor other than that applied or which had to be applied at any time distinct from that on which it was applied, with the pertinent correction shall be for the calendar Month in which the mistake took place, the Royalty percentage being readjusted as from this calendar Month. Any adjustment resulting from a lower payment of the Royalty shall be subject to interest in favor of the Party affected, as from the moment in which the mistake was made.

8.6 For the purpose of the Contract, the valuation of each and every class of Fiscalized Hydrocarbons shall be expressed in Dollars and be determined as indicated hereinbelow:

8.6.1 The value of Liquid Hydrocarbons shall be that prevailing on the international market, to be determined as follows:

a) At least ninety (90) Days prior to the Date of Commencement of Commercial

Extract the quality of the Liquid Hydrocarbons to be produced in the Contract Area.

b) Within thirty (30) Days following the determination referred to in the preceding paragraph a), the Parties shall choose a Liquid Hydrocarbons basket of up to four (4) components as a maximum, which shall meet the following requirements:
   1. Have a quality similar to that of the Liquid Hydrocarbons to be produced in the Contract Area.
   2. Be regularly quoted in the "Platts Oilgramm Price Report" or in any other sources recognized by the Petroleum Industry and agreed upon by the Parties hereto.
   3. Be competitive on the market or markets where the Liquid Hydrocarbons to be produced in the Contract Area could be sold.

   Every six (6) Months or earlier if so requested by either Party, the Parties shall revise the basket determined to valuate the production in order to verify that the above mentioned conditions are being met. If it is found that any of the said conditions is no longer fulfilled, the Parties shall change the basket within thirty (30) Days following the date on which revision of the basket was commenced. If upon expiry of this term the Parties have not agreed upon a new basket, the provisions set forth in Subpoint 8.6.3 hereof shall be applied. If, with respect to quality, it is found that the API gravity (weighted average), sulphur content or any other element measuring the quality of the Liquid Hydrocarbons produced in the Contract Area have significantly changed in relation to the Liquid Hydrocarbons making up the basket (simple arithmetic average), the Parties shall change the basket composition so that it always reflects the quality of the Hydrocarbons produced in the Contract Area.

c) Once the quality of the Liquid Hydrocarbons referred to in the foregoing paragraph has been determined, the Parties shall sign a "Valuation Agreement" establishing the terms and conditions additional to those detailed in this Subpoint and required for its correct application. In the "Valuation Agreement", the adjustment procedures necessary for quality and transport purposes shall be defined. Quality adjustments shall foresee premiums and/or penalties for improving and/or degrading the quality of the Liquid Hydrocarbons produced in the Contract Area in relation to the quality of the Hydrocarbons which make up the basket. In addition, the "Valuation Agreement" shall establish both term and periods in which the methods and procedures agreed upon shall be revised in order to ensure that the determination of the prices of the Hydrocarbons produced in the Contract Area is at any time realistic. Should either Party at any time consider that the application of the methods and procedures stipulated in the "Valuation Agreement" do not result in a realistic determination of the value of any or all the Liquid Hydrocarbons produced in the Contract Area, the Parties may agreed to apply other methods and procedures to actually bring about said result.

d) In the event that in the future, the price of one or more of the Liquid Hydrocarbons which make up the basket of crude oil is quoted in a currency other than Dollars, said prices shall be converted into Dollars, taking into account the exchange rates in force on the date of each of the quotations of the Liquid Hydrocarbons considered for the calculations at the average exchange rates quoted by the Citibank N.A. of New York, New York, and by the Chase Manhattan Bank N.A. of New York, New York.

e) The Parties hereby agree that the valuation period to be used for valuing the

Liquid Hydrocarbons shall be the fortnight of each calendar Month, it being understood that the first fortnight covers the period from the first to the fifteenth Day of the said calendar Month, and the second fortnight is the period which is missing to complete the said calendar Month. Upon mutual consent of the Parties and to the extent permitted by the pertinent legal provisions, the valuation period may be extended or reduced.

f) The average price to be used to value the Liquid Hydrocarbons produced in the Contract Area during a valuation period shall be determined as follows:

1. The average price of each and every Liquid Hydrocarbon making up the basket is determined by calculating the arithmetic mean of its quotation published in relation to the valuation period. Only the Days on which each and every Liquid Hydrocarbons making up the basket were quoted shall be considered.
2. The average prices resulting from any Hydrocarbons making up the basket shall in turn be averaged in order to obtain the value of the Liquid Hydrocarbons produced in the Contract Area.

8.6.2 The value of Natural Gas produced in the Contract Area shall be determined based on the basic principles of international pricing, taking into account factors such as the market, quality and quantity of Natural Gas, as well as its calorific value compared with that of Liquid Hydrocarbons substitutes in Peru.

8.6.3 Should the Parties fail to reach any of the agreements stipulated in this Point, the Technical Conciliation Committee shall be called.

8.7 The compensation amount shall be calculated for each fortnight of each calendar Month. Payment thereof shall be made in Dollars no later than the second Business Day after the fortnight concerned. The production volume of each fortnight shall be supported by the fiscalization vouchers which PERUPETRO is obliged to deliver to the Contractor duly signed and acknowledged. In the event that on the date on which the compensation for the first fortnight of a determined calendar Month (Month "n") must be paid, the "R"Factor to be used in the said Month is as yet unknown, the compensation amount for the said first fortnight shall be calculated based upon the "R" Factor applied in the previous calendar Month (Month "n-l"). Once the "R" Factor to be applied in the said calendar Month (Month "n") has been determined, any adjustments applicable to the first fortnight shall be made together with the payment of the compensation for the second fortnight, of the same calendar Month (Month "n").

8.8 In the event that the Contractor fails to pay or only partially pays to PERUPETRO the royalty for the extraction of Hydrocarbons belonging to it from the Contract Area within the term stipulated in Point 8.7, PERUPETRO shall keep a payment in kind the quantity of Hydrocarbons equivalent to the amount due plus expenses and interest in accordance with Point 19.7.

CLAUSE NINE: TAXES

9.1 Any and all companies making up the Contractor are subject to the common Tax regulations of the Republic of Peru, which include the common Income Tax Regulations as well as the specific provisions established in relation thereto in Law 26221, as complemented, amended and regulated, in force on the Date of Signing. The Peruvian State, through the Ministry of Economy and Finance, guarantees each and every company making up the Contractor tax stability during the term of the Contract so that they shall be subject exclusively to the tax regulations in force on the Date of Signing.

9.2 The Hydrocarbons produced in the Contract Area and exported by each and every company making up the Contractor are exempt from any Tax whatsoever, including those requiring special mention.

9.3 Payment of any tax, surplus tax and profit-sharing shall be for PERUPETRO's own cost and account.

9.4 According to the legal provisions currently in force, the Contractor shall pay Taxes applicable to the import of capital goods and inputs required by the Contractor to carry out the Operations pursuant to Law.

9.5 In accordance with the Tax Code, Article 87, each and every company making up the Contractor may keep its accounting books and records in Dollars and, accordingly are the assessment of the taxable base of the Taxes, to which the said companies reliable, as well as the amount and payment thereof, shall be made pursuant to Law.

9.6 It is hereby expressly understood that each and every company making the Contractor shall use the straight-line method of depreciation over a period of five (5) Fiscal Years, counted as from the Fiscal Year corresponding to the Date of Commencement of Commercial Extraction. The straight-line method of depreciation referred to above shall be applied to all the Exploration and Development costs and expenses as well as all investments incurred and made by the Contractor from the Date of Signing until Date of Commencement of Commercial Extraction. It is hereby expressly understood that the foregoing depreciation term shall be extended, without exceeding the term of the Contract, if for price or any other reason agreed by the Parties and after application of the straight-line depreciation referred to in the preceding paragraph, the financial statements of any of the companies making up the Contractor show a negative result or a trading loss which, at the discretion of said company, is unlikely to be compensated for tax purposes by the Tax provisions currently in force. The extension of the depreciation term shall previously be the National Superintendency of Tax Administration.

CLAUSE TEN: CUSTOM DUTIES

10.1 In accordance with legal provisions currently in force, the Contractor is authorized to import, either permanently or temporarily, any goods necessary for the economical and efficient performance of the Operations.

10.2 The Contractor may import on a temporary basis, for a two (2) Year term, goods required for its activities, without payment of any import duty whatsoever, including the requiring special mention. Should an extension be necessary, the Contractor may request same from PERUPETRO twice each time for one (1) Year, in which case PERUPETRO shall arrange for the pertinent Directoral Resolution from the Bureau of Hydrocarbons. Based on said documentation, the National Superintendency of Tax Administration shall authorize an extension of the temporary import regime. The procedures, requirements and guaranties necessary for the temporary import regime shall be governed by the provisions contained in the General Customs Law, as amended and regulated.

10.3 The import of goods and inputs needed by the Contractor during the Exploration stage for the Exploration activities is exempt from any Tax whatsoever, including those requiring special mention, provided they are contained in the list of goods subject to this tax benefit, in accordance with Law 26221, Article 56, as regulated. The said benefits shall be applied to the term of this stage.

10.4 The import of goods and inputs needed by the Contractor for the Exploitation activities and for Exploration activities during the Exploitation stage shall be at the cost and expense of the importer.

10.5 PERUPETRO shall be entitled to inspect the goods imported under this Clause on a permanent or temporary basis for the Exploration activities of the Exploration stage, in order to verify whether said goods have been imported exclusively for the Operations.

10.6 The Contractor shall inform PERUPETRO from time to time of the goods and inputs which, according to Law 26221, Article 56, as regulated, are tax-exempt. The Contractor shall not be entitled to re-export or dispose otherwise of the good and inputs indicated in the foregoing paragraph, without authorization from PERUPETRO. Upon the granting of such authorization, the Contractor shall apply the Taxes payable according to the provisions set forth in Law. 26221, Article 57.

CLAUSE ELEVEN: FINANCIAL RIGHTS

11.1 STATE GUARANTY

In accordance with the provisions set forth in Law 26221 and Legislative Decree 668, the Banco Central de Reserva del Peru participates herein in order to grant the Contractor on behalf of the State the guaranties indicated in this Clause, pursuant to the Legal System in force on the Date Signing. In case of concessions, the guaranties granted under this Clause shall also apply to the Concessionaire, subject to the Law of Hydrocarbons and this Contract.

11.2 EXCHANGE RATE REGULATIONS

Pursuant to the legal provisions in force on the Date of Signing, the Banco Central de Reserva del Peru, acting by and through the State, guarantees that the Contractor shall be subject to the Exchange Rate Regulations prevailing on the Date of Signing, and therefore will have the right to freely dispose of, hold, use and deposit in the country or abroad, foreign currency, as well as to freely exchange its local currency into foreign currency in the supply and demand exchange market, under the terms and conditions indicated in this Clause.

To this end, the Banco Central de Reserva del Peru, acting by and through the State, guaranties the following to the Contractor, according to the legal regulations in force on the Date of Signing.

a) Free disposal by the contractor of up to one hundred percent (100%) of the foreign currency generated from its exports of Fiscalized Hydrocarbons, which may be directly deposited in its bank accounts in the country or abroad.
b) Contractor's right to freely dispose of and convert up to one hundred percent (100%) of the local currency obtained from its sales of Fiscalized Hydrocarbons for the domestic market supply into foreign currency and the right to directly deposit both the foreign currency and local currency in its bank accounts in the country or abroad.
c) Contractor's right to maintain, control and operate bank accounts in any currency, both in the country and abroad, control and freely use such accounts, and freely maintain and dispose of the funds of such accounts abroad, with no restriction whatsoever.
d) Notwithstanding the foregoing provisions, Contractor's right to freely dispose of, distribute, remit or retain its annual net profits abroad, with no restriction whatsoever.

It is hereby agreed that the Contractor will invoke to the financial system existing in the country, in order to make use of the foreign currency available to make any exchanges referred to in paragraph b), Point 11.2.

In the event that the aforementioned foreign currency is not available, in whole or in part, from the entities previously noted, the Banco Central de Reserva del Peru shall secure the provision of the necessary foreign currency. For this purpose, the Contractor shall send to the Banco Central de Reserva del Peru to PERUPETRO, a copy of the correspondence from three (3) financial institutions, by which the Contractor is informed that the requested funds in foreign currency cannot be supplied in whole or in part on such state. The communications of the entities belonging to the financial system shall be effective for two (2) Business Days following their Date of issue. Before 11:00 hours of the Business Day following the presentation of the aforementioned documents the Banco Central de Reserva del Peru shall inform the Contractor of the exchange rate in force for the transaction requested by the Contractor, which rate shall be effective provided the Contractor delivers the equivalent amount in local currency on the same Day. If, for any reason whatsoever, this equivalent amount is not delivered by the Contractor on the indicated Day, the Banco Central de Reserva del Peru shall inform the Contractor, at the same time of the following Business Day, of the exchange rate for the conversion of currency, provided such transaction is made on this Day. Without prejudice to the foregoing, if the Banco Central de Reserva del Peru verifies, in due time, that the entities referred to herein are not able to provide, in whole or in part, the necessary foreign exchange, it shall notify the Contractor to go to the Banco Central de Reserva del Peru with the necessary local currency, in order to carry out the foreign currency conversion. The Banco Central de Reserva del Peru, as representative of the State, shall ensure that the Regulations contained in this Clause continue in force for the Contractor during the Term of Contract.

Whenever the exchange rate cannot be fixed by the supply and demand, the following exchange rate shall be applicable to the Contractor:

a) If a Single exchange rate were in force in the country with the same value for all foreign currency or foreign currency-related Operations, as from the date of application of the Single Exchange Rate, such rate shall be used hereunder.
b) If different values were in force for the above Single Exchange Rate, or if there were two or more exchange rates or any other system with different values resulting from the application thereof, the exchange rate to be used for all contractual Operations shall be the most favorable exchange rate with respect to foreign currency.

The guaranties furnished by the Banco Central de Reserva del Peru to the Contractor shall remain in force during the Term of Contract. The Contractor shall have the right to opt, in whole or in part, when appropriate, for new legal exchange regulations enacted during the Term of Contract, including those dealing with exchange aspects not contemplated in this Clause, provided such regulations are of general application or apply directly to the Hydrocarbons activity. Opting for the aforementioned new provisions or regulations shall not affect the validity of the guaranties referred to in this Clause, nor the enforcement of guaranties related to aspects other than those contemplated in the new provisions or regulations to which the Contractor may have submitted itself.

It is expressly agreed that the Contractor may, at any time, resume the guaranties it decided not to use on a temporary basis, and that the fact of reassuming such guaranties does not create rights or obligations for the Contractor, with respect to the period in which it was subject to the aforementioned provisions or regulations. Similarly, it is hereby stated that the fact of resuming such guarantees does not affect all such guaranties or other guaranties in any manner whatsoever, nor does it create any further rights or obligations for the Contractor. The Banco Central de Reserva del Peru and PERUPETRO must be informed in Writing in the event that the Contractor opts for the new legal exchange regulations and in case the Contractor decides to resume the guaranties if decided not to use on a temporary basis. The rules established in this Point do not affect the provisions contained in the first paragraph of Point 11.4.

11.6 ECONOMIC INFORMATION

The Contractor shall provide the Banco Central de Reserva del Peru with monthly information on its economic activity, according to Article 74 of the Organic Banking Law, approved by Decree Law 26123.

CLAUSE TWELVE: EMPLOYEES

12.1 The Parties hereby agree that by the end of the fifth Year counted from the Date of Commencement of Commercial Extraction, the Contractor will have replaced all its foreign employees with Peruvian personnel of equal qualifications, except for foreign employees in management positions. The Contractor undertakes to train the Peruvian personnel in technically specialized works so that they may gradually replace the foreign employees in these works.

12.2 At the beginning of the Operations and at the end of each calendar Year, the Contractor shall provide PERUPETRO with a list of personnel rendering services for the operations hereunder including its Subcontractors and indicating place of work, personal details, nationality, date of engagement and technical or professional qualifications.

CLAUSE THIRTEEN: PROTECTION OF THE ENVIRONMENT

13.1 The Contractor undertakesto comply with the rules and provisions set forth in the "Environmental Regulations for Hydrocarbon Activities", approved by Supreme Decree 046-93-EM as amended, Legislative Decree 613, Code of the Environment and Natural Resources, as well as any other pertinent Law.

CLAUSE FOURTEEN: CONSERVATION OF HYDROCARBONS AND LOSS PREVENTION

14.1 The Contractor must adopt all reasonable measures to avoid any form of loss or waste of Hydrocarbons on the surface or subsurface during Exploration and Exploitation activities.

14.2 In the event of loss, the Operator must immediately advise PERUPETRO thereof, indicating the estimated volume of the loss and the actions taken to correct the causes thereof. PERUPETRO shall be entitled to verify the volume lost and analyze the pertinent causes thereof. Without prejudice to the provisions set forth in Point 13.1, in case of loss on the surface, before the Production Fiscalization Point, occasioned by gross negligence or misconduct on the part of the Contractor, the volume lost shall be valued and included in the calculation of the royalty. Without prejudice to the provisions set forth in Point 13.1, in case of loss before the Fiscalization Point, due to situations other than those detailed in the foregoing paragraph, which result in a compensation for the Contractor by third parties, the volume lost as well as its valuation shall be included in the calculation of the royalty.

CLAUSE FIFTEEN: TRAINING AND TRANSFER OF TECHNOLOGY

15.1 In compliance with the provisions of Law 26221, Article 29, the Contractor binds itself to make available to PERUPETRO the amounts indicated hereinbelow, on an annual basis during the Term of Contract: ANNUAL CONTRIBUTION (US$)

a) Until the calendar Year in which the Date of Commencement of Commercial Extraction takes place: 50,000.00
b) As from the calendar Year following the Date of Commencement of Commercial Extraction for the Hydrocarbons Fiscalized in the previous calendar Year,

in barrels per Day Barrels per Day
From 0 to 30,000:
From 30,001 to 50,000:
From 50,001 or more

The first payment shall be made on the Date of Signing, the amount of which shall be fixed by multiplying the annual contribution referred to in paragraph a) by the result from dividing the number of Days remaining until the end of the current calendar Year by three hundred and sixty five (365). The annual training contribution indicated in paragraph b) shall be that corresponding to the tranche of the average daily production of the Fiscalized Hydrocarbons in the previous calendar Year. The payments referred to in this Point, excepting the first, shall be made in each calendar Year, in accordance with the average daily production of the Fiscalized Hydrocarbons in the previous calendar Year the amount of which will be obtained by dividing the total volume of Fisca lized Hydrocarbons in the said Year by three hundred and sixty five (365) Days. In order to determine the Barrels/Day equivalence in case of Natural Gas production, the following formula shall be used: Barrels shall be equivalent to the volume of Natural Gas expressed in standard cubic feet divided by the factor 5,626.

15.2 The Contractor shall comply with its obligations set forth in Point 15.1 by depositing Dollars or its equivalent in local currency into an account to be designated by PERUPETRO. The Contractor, at PERUPETRO's request made before the corresponding annual payment has been made, may import training and research equipment and materials and may contract for training and research services abroad. The cost of these goods and services shall be deducted from the Contractor's annual contribution, in accordance with the agreement reached by the Parties. PERUPETRO shall deliver the pertinent certificates to the Contractor within five (5) Business Days after having received the contributions for either of the operations described in this Point.

15.3 The Contractor and PERUPETRO shall agree upon the execution of technical cooperation programs for the research and development of matters of mutual interest. Within ninety (90) Days prior to the end of each calendar Year, the Parties shall submit to the Supervision Committee the projects that will be implemented in the following calendar Year.

15.4 The Contractor commits itself to implement training programs for its personnel in PERU and, if necessary, abroad. PERUPETRO shall be advised of such training programs.

CLAUSE SIXTEEN: ASSIGNMENT

16.1 If any of the companies making up the Contractor enters into an agreement in order to assign its interest in the Contract to a third party, whether in whole or in part, it shall notify PERUPETRO thereof. Such notice shall indicate any complementary information required for qualification of both the third party and the petroleum Contractor, as established by law. If PERUPETRO grants the requested qualification, the assignment shall be carried out through amendment to the Contract, subject to Law, providing the inclusion of the third party. The assignment must be carried out in Peru, under Peruvian law.

16.2 Each and every company making up the Contractor shall be entitled to assign its interest in the Contract, in whole or in part, to an Affiliate, with prior notice to PERUPETRO. The assignment shall be made by amending the Contract, according to Law, in order to include the Affiliate in the Contractor, to which end the provisions set forth in the last paragraph of Point 16.1 shall be applied.

16.3 Each and every company making up the Contractor shall be entitled to assign its interest in the Contract, in whole or in part, to another company making up the Contractor. For this purpose, the provisions stipulated in Point. 16.1, second and third paragraph shall be applied.

16.4 If any of the companies making up the Contractor makes an assignment under this Contract, the assignee shall furnish all the necessary guarantees and shall assume any and all rights, responsibilities and obligations of the assignor.

16.5 __________ was appointed Operator pursuant to a "Joint Operating Agreement" entered into by and between the Operator and ____________________, a copy of which shall be delivered to PERUPETRO on the state of Signing. Copies of the amendments and extensions of the "Joint Operating Agreement" or new "Joint Operating Agreements" shall be delivered to PERUPETRO within fifteen (15) Business Days after signing thereof. The individual or body corporate having been appointed Operator shall keep a special account system for the record of the issues relating to the Operations. If the companies making up the Contractor decide to change the Operator, such appointment must be previously approved by PERUPETRO in writing, and any disapproval thereof must be duly supported.

CLAUSE SEVENTEEN: ACT OF GOD OR FORCE MAJEURE

17.1 None of the Parties shall be held liable for the non-compliance or partial, late, or deficient compliance with an obligation during the term in which such obliged Party is affected by reason of Acts of God or Force Majeure. Upon the termination of twelve (12) consecutive Months counted as from the moment at which the Force Majeure or Act of God occurred, the Contractor may terminate this Contract.

17.2 The provisions set forth in this Clause are not applicable to obligations consisting of money payments.

CLAUSE EIGHTEEN: ACCOUNTING PROCEDURE

18.1 Each and every company making up the Contractor shall keep its accounts in accordance with the accounting principles generally established and accepted in Peru. Furthermore, it shall keep and maintain detailed books and records as well as documents necessary to account or control the activities carried out in Peru or abroad in connection with the purpose of the Contract, and shall keep appropriate evidence of the income, investment costs, expenses and taxes incurred during each fiscal Year. On the other hand, within one hundred and twenty (120) Days from the Date of Signing, each and every company making up the Contractor shall deliver to PERUPETRO a copy of the "Manual on Accounting Principles", which it decided to use for recording its economic and financial operations.

The "Manual on Accounting Procedures" shall, among others, contain the following:

a) Language and currency of the accounting books and records.
b) Applicable accounting principles and practices.
c) Accounting structure and plan, in accordance with the requirements of CONASEV (National Supervisory Committee of Companies and Securities).
d) Codification of the Contract accounts and those of the other petroleum contracts as well as related and other activities.
e) Mechanisms of attributing income, investments, costs and overheads to the Contract as well as related and other activities.
f) Determination of revenue and expenditure accounts as well as the detailed records for calculating the "R" factor, including the procedures detailed in Exhibit "E" hereof.

PERUPETRO shall be responsible for approving the information to be included in the detailed records kept by the Operator as well as the accounting procedures of the "R" factor referred to in paragraph f) above, within the term indicated in point 18.2.

18.2 No later than thirty (30) Days after having received the "Manual on Accounting Procedures", PERUPETRO shall advise the Contractor that it approved the "R" factor accounting procedure referred to in Point 18.1, paragraph f), or otherwise make suggestions and/or observations to improve, extend or eliminate any or other accounting procedure(s) proposed in said manual.

18.3 The accounting books of the Contract, financial statements and supporting evidence thereof shall be made available for inspection of PERUPETRO, prior notice thereof. PERUPETRO shall make its best effects to ensure that the aforesaid inspection and supervision be carried out in a coordinate manner.

18.4 The Contractor shall make inventories of properties related to the Operations, classifying them according to their owners, that is, either the Contractor or third parties. The inventories shall be made at reasonable intervals, but no less than each calendar Year in the case of materials, supplies and other movable property; and every two calendar Years in the case of immovable property. The parties shall coordinate the date on which said inventories shall be made, being entitled to change this date only once, at the request of either Party. Said request must be forwarded to the other Party no less than thirty (30) Days prior to the date of commencement of such inventory. PERUPETRO, at its sole discretion, shall exercise its right to be represented during the inventories referred in this Point. Should the results of these inventories differ substantially from the accounting records, each company making up the Contractor shall make the pertinent conciliations and adjustments, the details of which shall be notified and explained in writing to PERUPETRO. If such reconciliations and adjustments do not satisfy PERUPETRO, the discrepancies shall be submitted to an auditors firm accepted by PERUPETRO which should give its opinion no later than three months counted from the date on which the said audit was commissioned to it. The opinion of this independent auditors firm shall be binding and final.

18.5 Each and every company making up the Contractor undertakes to submit to PERUPETRO on an annual basis and within thirty (30) Days after the issue of the independent auditors opinion for the previous Fiscal Year, and within the subsequent ninety (90) Days thereof, a report with comments on the observations made by the internal auditors, if any, and the actions taken to overcome or correct the said observations.

18.6 Should the Contractor or any of the companies making it up have entered into more than one contract with PERUPETRO, or carry out activities other than those stipulated in the Contract, both shall be obliged to keep separate accounts in order to prepare independent financial statements for each contract and/or activity.

CLAUSE NINETEEN: MISCELLANEOUS

19.1 Should any of the Parties, once or repeatedly, fail to invoke or insist on the compliance of any of the provisions in this Contract, or in the exercise of any right granted hereunder, this shall not be construed as a waiver of the said provisions or rights.

19.2 In the execution of the Operations, the Contractor should comply with all the resolutions issued by the pertinent authorities by virtue of their legal faculties. Furthermore, the Contractor undertakes to comply with any and all provisions prescribed by the pertinent authorities in relation to national defense and security.

19.3 The Contractor is entitled to enter and leave the Contract Area without any restriction whatsoever.

19.4 In accordance with the laws currently in force, the Contractor shall have the right to use, for the purpose of carrying out the Operations, the water, the timber, and other construction materials located within the Contract Area, free of any charge, license or permit whatsoever, observing any and all third party rights, if applicable.

19.5 Any technical information regarding the Contract or other areas, which the Contractor wishes to acquire, should be requested from PERUPETRO, which will provide it according to the valuation established in the sales policy and use of technical information from PERUPETRO, for which purpose the Parties signed a "Letter of Agreement".

19.6 Should any of the Parties fail to make payments within the term agreed herein, the amount to be paid shall be subject to interest, which will take effect. from the Day following the date of maturity, at the following rates:

a) For accounts expressed and payable in local currency, the interest rate applicable shall be the lending rate in local currency for credits up to the period of the three hundred and sixty (360) Days, published by the Superintendency of Banking and Insurance Companies, or any rate which substitutes it, applicable to the period elapsed from the Day of maturity until the actual date of payment.
b) For accounts expressed in dollars and payable in local currency or Dollars, the interest rate shall be the weighted average lending rate of the market (TAMEX), or any rate which substitutes it, applicable to the period elapsed from the maturity date until the actual date of payment.

19.7 The provisions set forth in Point 19.6 shall be applicable to any and all accounts established between the Parties hereunder, or under any other agreement or transaction entered into by the Parties. By mutual consent in writing, the Parties may establish other conditions for payment of interests. In no case whatsoever shall the provisions governing the application of interest rates hereunder change the legal rights and resources of the Parties regarding compliance with payment of the amounts owed.

19.8 In the event of a national emergency declared by law, by which the State must acquire Hydrocarbons from local producers, this shall be based on international prices, as stipulated in Clause 8, and be paid within thirty (30) Days following delivery.

19.9 The State, through the Ministries of Defense and Home Affairs, shall provide the Contractor, as far as possible, with the necessary security measures for the Operations.

19.10 The Contractor shall hold PERUPETRO and the State, as the case may be, harmless from any claim, legal action or other third party charges or encumbrances which might result from both the Operations and relationships maintained hereunder as a consequence of any contractual or extra-contractual relation, except for those occasioned by actions undertaken by PERUPETRO itself or by the State.

CLAUSE TWENTY: NOTICES AND COMMUNICATIONS

20.1 All notices or communications relating to this Contract shall be considered as effectively sent if in writing and delivered and signed for, or if received by registered mail, telegraph, telex or facsimile sent to the addressee on a Business Day to the following addresses:

PERUPETRO S.A. Gerencia General
Paseo de la Republica 3361, piso 20 Lima 27, Peru Fax: 4 25572
Contractor________________________
Corporative Guarantor ___________________________

20.2 Any of the Parties and the Corporative Guarantor may change its address or facsimile number for notices and communications by informing the other Party of the proposed date of change with at least five (5) Business Days notice. Any change in the address of Corporative Guarantors must be notified in good time to PERUPETRO.

20.3 If the Contractor comprises two or more bodies corporate, notices and communications shall be sent to the person designated "Operator", and shall be considered as effectively sent to all the persons which form part of the Contractor, except when the notices and communications relate to Clauses 9, 11, 17 and 23, which shall be sent by PERUPETRO to each and every body corporate comprising the Contractor.

CLAUSE TWENTY-ONE: SUBMISSION TO PERUVIAN LAW AND THE ARBITRATION AGREEMENT

21.1 SUBMISSION TO PERUVIAN LAW

This Contract has been negotiated, written and signed according to the legal provisions of Peru and its contents, interpretation, execution and consequences emanating therefrom shall be governed by Peruvian law.

21.2 ARBITRATION AGREEMENT

Any litigation, controversy, discrepancy or claim arising herefrom or in relation hereto, such as the construction, enforcement, termination, efficency which may arise between the Contractor and PERUPETRO and cannot be resolved by mutual agreement between the Parties, must be resolved by international legal arbitration, in accordance with the provisions contained in the last paragraph of Article 85 of the General Arbitration Law No. 25935. Arbitration shall be conducted in the Spanish language and as agreed in this Clause, and will be administered by... As to anything which has not been contemplated in this Clause, the arbitration shall be organized and conducted in accordance with the rules of ..., in force on the Date of Signing. In addition, the rules contained in the General Arbitration Law No. 25935 or any law replacing it shall be applied on a supplementary basis. There will be three arbitrators, with each party appointing one and the third being appointed by the previous two. If, after a period of thirty (30) Days from the date of appointment of the arbitrators by the Parties, a third member has not been appointed, either of the Parties may resort to ... to make the appointment. The arbitrators shall apply the internal laws of the Republic of Peru as a basis for resolving any litigation, controversy, difference or claim submitted for arbitration. Arbitration will be held in the city of Lima, Peru. However, if the amount of the issue submitted to arbitration exceeds US$500,000 (Five Hundred Thousand Dollars) and one of the Parties considers that the city of Lima is not convenient to hold the arbitration, it must so state and propose a new city or country in the first notice addressed to the other Party advising it of its decision to resort to arbitration. If after fifteen (15) Days from the aforementioned notice the Parties have not reached an agreement on the new place to carry out arbitration, ________ shall fix the place. In the event of a discrepancy as to the amount of the issue, or if it cannot be determined, ... shall establish the place of the arbitration taking into account the provisions contained in the foregoing paragraph. The Parties hereby waive any remedies of appeal, annulment or any other remedy against the arbitration award, which shall be binding and final and for immediate execution. The Parties are obliged to carry out all such acts as are necessary to accomplish the arbitration process from start to finish. The maximum period that the arbitration process may last shall be one hundred and eighty (180) Business Days, which shall be counted from the date of appointment of the Arbitration Tribunal or any other analogous act. The Arbitration Tribunal may extend this term if there are justifiable reasons. In the event that the arbitral award is made outside Peru, its recognition and execution shall be governed by the "Recognition and Execution of Foreign Arbitration Awards Agreement." made in New York on June 10, 1958 (The New York Convention), or the "Interamerican Agreement on International Commercial Arbitration" made in Panama on January 30, 1975 (The Panama Convention), or the provisions contained on this matter in the General Law of Arbitration 25935 or any rules which substitute it, as determined by the Party requesting recognition and execution of the judgement. During the arbitration proceedings the Parties shall continue with the performance of their contractual obligations, including those that are subject matters of the arbitration. If the arbitration were the compliance with the contractual obligations guaranteed by the bank guaranties referred to in Point 3.9, said guaranties may be executed and shall be kept in force during the arbitration proceedings.

21.3 The Parties hereby waive any diplomatic claim.

21.4 This Contract has been drawn up and shall be construed in the spanish language; therefore, the Parties agree that this is the only and official version.

CLAUSE TWENTY-TWO: TERMINATION

22.1 The termination of this contract shall be governed by the provisions contained therein, and in addition, by the regulations of Law 26221; in the event of anything not covered by these regulations, the rules of the Civil Code shall be applied. Except for those cases indicated in Point 22.3, when one of the Parties fails to comply with the provisions of the Contract for reasons other than force majeure or Acts of God, one Party may notify the other Party in writing of the non-compliance, and of its intention to terminate the Contract at the end of a sixty (60) Day term, if by the end of this time, the said non-compliance has not been corrected or is not in process of being corrected. If the Party receiving such notification questions or denies the existence of such default, it may refer the matter to arbitration in accordance with the provisions of Point 21, within thirty (30) Days following the receipt of said notification. In such a case, the sixty (60) Day period will be held in suspense until the arbitration judgement is issued to the Parties; and the Contract shall terminate if the non-compliance is confirmed and has not been rectified within the said term. The Contract may be terminated before its expiry date by mutual agreement between the Parties.

22.2 On the termination of the Contract, all rights and obligations of the parties thereto completely cease and the following shall be taken into consideration.

a) The rights and obligations of the Parties arising herefrom before the termination date shall be respected, including, among others, the Contractor's right to any Hydrocarbons extracted and to all the guarantees stipulated in Points 9, 10 and 11 and,
b) In the event of non-compliance and responsibilities incurred prior to the termination by any of the Parties of any of the obligations stipulated therein, these shall be rectified by the infringing Party, except for those specified in the Contract as being cancelled upon termination of the same.

22.3 The Contract shall be terminated by law and without previous notice in the following cases:

22.3.1 If the Contractor has not complied with the execution of the Minimum Work Program for any period of the Exploration phase after having utilized the extensions stipulated in point 3.4 and without reasons satisfactory to PERUPETRO, provided that the provisions of points 4.7 and 4.8 are complied with.

22.3.2 If, upon expiry of the Exploration period or retention period, whichever occurs later, no declaration of Commercial Discovery has been made.

22.3.3 In the specific cases indicated in Points 3.10, 4.2 and 17.5.

22.3.4 If any individual or body corporate comprising part of the Contractor has been declared in dissolution, liquidation or bankrupt and the other parties or a third party duly qualified by PERUPETRO does not assume the participation of the dissolved, liquidated or bankrupt individual or body corporate.

22.3.5 If any entity which has granted a guarantee in accordance with point 3.11 is declared in dissolution, liquidation or bankrupt, and the said guarantee is not assumed by a third party and accepted by PERUPETRO.

22.3.6 If the corporative guarantees referred to in point 3.11 have expired.

22.3.7 By the unappealable mandate of an arbitration award.

22.3.8 At the expiry of the Term of Contract.

22.4 The Contract may also be terminated by applying the provisions of Article 87 of Law 26221 and Article 49 of the Environmental Protection Regulations in Hydrocarbon Activities, approved by Supreme Decree 046-93-EM.

22.5 If any individual or body corporate comprising the contractor, or any entity which has granted a guarantee as referred to in point 3.11 requests judicial protection against the action of creditors, PERUPETRO may terminate the Contract in the event it considers its Contract rights are insufficiently protected.

22.6 On the termination of the Contract, the Contractor shall deliver in ownership of the State, at no cost to it whatsoever, through PERUPETRO, all property, power equipment, camps, means of communication, pipelines and other production equipment which will enable operations to continue, apart from that which it still requires, in a satisfactory state of conservation, maintenance and operating condition, taking into account fair wear and tear due to normal use. In the event of having exploited petroleum, together with Non-associated Natural Gas and/or Non-associated Natural Gas and Condensates, at the termination of the term established in point 3.1 for the Exploitation phase for petroleum Contractor shall deliver in ownership of the state whatsoever, through PERUPETRO all goods and installations belonging to it used in the Exploitation of Petroleum, and which are not necessary for the Exploitation of Non-associated Natural Gas and/or Non-associated Natural Gas and Condensates, in a satisfactory state of conservation, maintenance and operating condition, taking into account fair wear and tear due to normal use. The goods and installations that the Contractor keeps for the Exploitation of Non-associated Natural Gas and/or Non-associated Natural Gas and Condensates, which have also been used in the Exploitation of Petroleum, even though continuing in the ownership of the Contractor, shall be applied to serve both Exploitations, this being subject of a contract between the Parties. In the event that the Contractor has been using the goods and installations described in the first paragraph of this point, but are not connected with nor are accessories exclusively for the Operations, that is, that they have also been used for operations in other areas having a contract in force for the Exploration or Exploitation of Hydrocarbons in Peru, the Contractor shall continue with ownership of the said goods, and making use of them.

22.7 For the purpose of making the provisions of point 22.6 effective, during the last year of the Contract term, the Contractor shall carry out all that is necessary and enter into all reasonable agreements required by PERUPETRO to ensure an ordered and uninterrupted transfer of the operations being carried out on the date and time of termination of the Contract.

ADDITIONAL CLAUSE

Pursuant to the legal provisions in force, the Contract and the Public Deed resulting in this document are not subject to the payment of any Tax whatsoever.

EXHIBIT "A" DESCRIPTION OF THE CONTRACT AREA
EXHIBIT "B" MAP OF BLOCK
EXHIBIT (C, C-l/...C-x) LETTER OF GUARANTY FOR THE..OF THE MINIMUM WORK PROGRAM
EXHIBIT "D" CORPORATE GUARANTY

Form LETTER OF GUARANTY No.

Lima,
Messrs.
PERUPETRO S.A.
LIMA
Dear Sirs,

We, the ..., hereby constitute ourselves as joint and several guarantors for ...hereinafter referred to as Contractor, in favor of PERUPETRO S.A. hereinafter referred to as PERUPETRO for the amount of US$... (... US Dollars) in order to guaranty the faithful compliance with the obligations of the faithful work program of the Contractor contained in Subpoint 4.6.1 of Clause 4 of the License Contract for Exploration and Exploitation of Hydrocarbons in block ... of the ... Basin, signed with PERUPETRO, hereinafter referred to as the Contract. The obligation which ... assumes under the present guaranty is limited to pay PERUPETRO the amount of US$ ...(US Dollars) applied for in your payment request.

1. This is a joint and several, irrevocable, unconditional, and automatically collectable guaranty, payable during the period it is in effect, upon presentation of a notarial letter addressed by PERUPETRO to ..., requesting payment of an amount no higher than the amount of the guaranty then in effect, declaring that the Contractor has not complied, in whole or in part., with the obligations of the aforementioned work program under the Contract and attaching to said letter, as sole precaution and justification, a notarially certified copy of the notarial letter sent by PERUPETRO to the Contractor giving notice of its intention of cashing the guaranty. Said notarial letter from PERUPETRO to the Contractor must have been delivered to the latter at least thirty (30) calendar Days before the date on which PERUPETRO files its claim with for payment.

2. This guaranty shall expire no later than ... (...) Months and ... (...) Business Days from the date on which the guaranty was issued, that is, on ..., unless prior to this date, ... receives a letter from PERUPETRO, releasing ... the Contractor from any responsibility hereunder, in which case this guaranty shall be paid on the date of the above mentioned letter sent by PERUPETRO.

3. Any delay on our part in paying this guarantee in your favor, shall be subject to an interest equivalent to the interest rate authorized by the Banco Central de Reserva del Peru fair lending operations of the institutions belonging to the financial system, plus expenses at the rates applied by you. Interests and expenses shall be calculated as from the date of the afore-mentioned notarial request.

As from the expiry or payment date no claim whatsoever may be filed regarding this guaranty and the ... and the Contractor shall be released from any responsibility or obligation hereunder.

Yours truly, ______________________________
(Entity of the Financial System)

FORM CORPORATE GUARANTY

Messrs.
PERUPETRO S.A.
Las Begonias 441-Of. 801
Lima, 27
PERU

In accordance with Point 3.10 of the License Contract for the Exploration and Exploitation and Hydrocarbons on Block ...to be signed by PERUPETRO, S.A. and ... does hereby jointly and severally guaranty in favor of PERUPETRO, compliance by ... any and all obligations the latter assumes in the minimum work program described in Point 4.6 of the contracts as well as execution by... of any all annual Exploitation programs, as readjusted or changed, which ... may submit to PERUPETRO in fulfillment of Point 5.3 of the Contract.

This guaranty shall continue in effect for as long as the obligations of ... resulting from the Contract remain in force. For the purposes of this guaranty, ... submits itself to the laws and courts of the Republic of Peru, expressly waiving any diplomatic claim.

Any communication relating to this guaranty shall be considered validly served, if in writing and delivered to. ...Any change of our address shall be reported to PERUPETRO five (5) Business Days prior to the date on which such change is actually made.

Yours truly,
(Corporate Guarantor)

(Authorized Executive)

Peter Cameron, *North Sea Oil Licensing: Comparisons and Contracts,* 4 OIL & GAS L. TAX. REV. 99 (1984-85)

〈표 4-1〉 북해 석유개발권 비교표

Terms	Denmark	Netherlands	Norway	UK
Duration	6 yrs renewable for a further 30 yrs for production or for 2+2 yrs for further exploration	Exploration licence: 10 yrs; production licence: 40 yrs maximum	6 yrs renewable for a further 30 yrs	6 yrs renewable for a further 30 yrs; in frontier areas, 8 yrs, renew able for a further 40 yrs
Obligations*	Performance of work programme	Performance of work programme	Performance of work programme	Performance of work programme
Relinquish-ment	If licence extended at end of 6 yr period, area is delimited by Minister & includes deposits found	Between 47.5 and 50 percent of area surrendered after 6 yrs (exploration licence)	At least 50 percent of area surrendered after 6 yrs	At least 50 percent of area surrendered after 6 yrs
State participation	Sliding scale, with min. 20% state interest in each licence. Occurs on a carried interest basis, DONG [Danish Oil and Natural Gas] is national oil company.	Maximum of 50% participation in production of oil. Vehicle is at present the DSM(Dutch State Mines), now Danish North Sea partner.	Sliding scale, beginning at 50% and rising to 85% as production increases. Carried interest basis. Statoil is national oil company.	State is grant-ed right to take 51% of any oil produced, payable at market price. BNOC is vehicle for participation.
Applicants' qualifications	Financial and technical capability.	Proof of adequate financial and technical resources required; no limit on foreign ownership.	Incorporation in Norway; financial and technical capability to be shown.	Any person may apply for a production licence; financial and technical capability to be shown.
Disposition	No landing requirement, but state company has option to purchase up to 50 percent of oil and natural gas produced, and all producing companies required to link up with pipeline system.	Ministerial approval required before licensee may sell petroleum or natural gas outside the Netherlands. Natural gas for domestic consumption must be sold to state gas company.	Landing requirement, but dispensations may be granted.	Landing requirement. but ministerial consent may be given for export (and usually is).
Method of award	General invitation to apply in rounds; award by ministerial discretion on basis of published criteria.	General invitation to apply in rounds; award by ministerial discretion on basis of published criteria.	General invitation to apply in rounds; award by ministerial discretion to consortia organised by Minister, not companies.	General invitation to apply in rounds; award by ministerial discretion on basis of published criteria. Some awards may be made by tender method.
Royalty	Sliding scale: from 2%(up to 5,000 b/d) to 16%(more than 20,000 b/d). May be taken in cash or in kind.	Sliding scale: from 0 to 15%. according to production.	Sliding scale: from 8% to 16%, according to production. May be taken in cash or in kind.	Two-tier system: no royalty on production from fields approved on or after 1 April 1982; flat rate of 12.5% on rest, including Southern Basin fields. Usually taken in kind, not cash.

* The full range of legal obligations which the licensee accepts is much wider than the working obligations.

Concessionary System Flow Diagram[21)]

〈표 4-2〉 양허계약 IOC/NOC 배분표

CONCESSIONARY SYSTEM FLOW DIAGRAM

Contractor Share	One Barrel of Oil $20.00	Royalties & Taxes
	20% Royalty →	$4.00
	$16.00	(Next revenue)
	Deductions (Operating costs, DD&A, IDCs, etc.)	
$9.00 ←		
	$7.00(Taxable income)	
	Provincial Taxes (Ad valorem, severance, income)	
	10% →	$ .70
	$6.30	
	Federal Income Taxes 40% →	$2.52
$3.78 ←	Net Income after Tax	
$12.78		$7.22
64%		36%

21) Daniel Johnson, INTERNATIONAL PETROLEUM FISCAL SYSTEMS AND PRODUCTION SHARING CONTRACTS, 30 (1994).

3. 생산분배계약[22)]

양허계약하에서는 IOC가 양허구역 내 석유에 대한 소유권을 가지지만, 생산분배계약하에서는 IOC가 석유에 대한 소유권이 없다. 다만, 개발이 성공할 경우 개발비를 석유로 보상받을 수 있는 권리(cost oil)와 석유로 이익을 분배받을 수 있는 권리(profit oil)만을 가진다.[23)] NOC와 IOC의 권한배분에 있어서도 양허계약에서의 경우보다 NOC의 권한이 좀더 강화되어 IOC에게 단순한 작업계획의 제출요구나 최소투자금액의 이행요구에 그치지 않고 IOC의 활동을 감시하고 승인할 권한을 가지며 탐색이 성공적이지 못한 경우의 위험은 IOC만이 부담한다. 또한 성공적인 경우에도 기간이 만료되면 모든 장비나 기술을 NOC에게 넘겨주어야 할 의무가 있는 것이 보통이다.

이러한 관계설정의 원형은 미국의 farmout으로서 임차인이 임차받은 토지를 제3자에게 양도, 제3자가 이를 성공적으로 개발하여 비용을 받고 나가면, 임차인과 임대인이 생산물을 기존의 합의에 따라 분배하는 것이다.[24)] 국제생산분배계약의 경우는 NOC가 임대인의 역할을 수행, 궁극적으로 NOC가 독자적으로 석유를 생산, 운영할 수 있도록 하는 것이 목표이다.[25)] 연혁적으로 1966년 Pertamina가 처음으로 NOC의 경영권 개념을 제시하였으며 초기 IOC는 NOC가 경험이 없거나 적대적이며 위험과 권한이 분리되는 것이 바람직하지 않다는 이유로 회의적이었다. 그러나, 생산분배계약을 체결한 IOC는 실질에 있어서 NOC의 경영권 행사가 적어도 개발단계에서는 형식적이라는 것을 발견하였으며[26)] 또한 비용보상범위를 확정하기 위하여도 제한된 경영권한의 공유가 필요하다는 것을 인정하게 되었다. 그리하여 이제는 북유럽과 미국을 제외한 대부분의 자원탐사 내지 보유국에서 애용되는 석유개발계약이 되었다.[27)]

탐사와 개발이 성공적이어서 생산단계에 들어가게 되면 탐사·개발비용은 통상 보너스

---

22) 생산물분배계약, 생산물분배협정 등으로 번역된다. contract가 agreement와 다르지 않듯이 협정은 계약, 조약과 동일한 의미이다.

23) 인도네시아 PSC의 역사에 관하여는 Tengku Nathan Machmud, THE INDONESIAN PRODUCTION SHARING CONTRACT, 51-53 (2000). PSA의 시계열분석은 Kirsten Bindemann, PRODUCTION-SHARING AGREEMENTS: AN ECONOMIC ANALYSIS 87 (1999)(한계수익이 IOC에 귀속되지 않는다는 면에서 경제적으로는 비효율적이며 따라서 정치적 문서로 규정).

24) John S. Lowe, *Analyxing Oil and Gas Farmout Agreemeents,* 41 SW. L. J. 759 (1987).

25) 오정환, 원유가스탐사개발권의 취득에 관한 법적 연구 40 (2010 한양대학교 박사학위논문).

26) Robert Fabrikant, *Production Sharing Contracts in the Indonesian Petroleum Industry,* 16 HARV. INT'L L.J. 303, 316 (1975).

27) Daniel Johnston, INTERNATIONAL EXPLORATION, ECONOMICS, RISK, AND CONTRACT ANALYSIS, 281-327 (2003); Daniel Johnston, 주16 상게서, 207-55. 러시아의 경험에 대하여는 Conference Proceedings, *Investing in Russia under the Law on Production Sharing Agreements,* 20 HOUST. J. INT'L L 517 (1998).

를 제외하고 전부 보상된다. 개발단계에서 NOC가 비용의 일부를 분담하는 경우에도 NOC는 실제 비용을 지급하지 않고 ICO가 이를 대신 지급하고 추후 생산단계에서 NOC로부터 보상받는다.[28] 생산단계의 운용비용은 우선적으로 cost oil로 보상받으며 자본비용은 수년에 걸쳐서 감가상각금액만큼 보상된다. NOC는 통상 산출석유의 일정부분을 로열티 또는 간주수익으로 우선적으로 할당하고 나머지 석유를 IOC에 대한 비용보상에 충당할 것이지만 보상부분이 산출석유의 일정비율을 넘지 않도록 정하므로 IOC의 비용보상은 상당한 시간에 걸친다. 비용은 또한 IOC 전체로 계산되기 보다는 하나의 블락 또는 저유지단위로 계산한다.[29] 비용을 공제한 후에 이익을 나누는 공식은 비용보상방식만큼이나 다양하다. 일정한 비율을 정하면 가장 간단하겠지만, 생산량, 수심, 투자수익률에 따라서 비율이 달라지게 정할 수도 있다.[30]

Production Sharing Agreement dated 21 Jun. 2008 between Kurdistan Regional Government of Iraq and KNOC[31]

TABLE OF CONTENTS

28) 영어로 carried cost, 우리말로 이전비용이라고 한다. 사모펀드가 투자대상으로부터 투자에 대한 대가를 즉시 지급받지 않고 추후 투자대상이 다시 매각되거나 기업공개되는 경우 지급받는 부분을 carried interest라고 하는 것과 유사한 개념이다. 전자는 NOC가 지급하여야 하나 나중에 지급하는 이전비용이고 후자는 사모펀드가 지급받아야 하지만 나중에 지급받는 이전수익이다.

29) Smith, 위 주 1-4 상게서, 473-76. 류권홍 위 주 10 상게서, 145는 ring-fencing을 구역단위 투자비회수로 번역한다.

30) Id., 145-47.

31) Kurdistan Regional Government 홈페이지 http://www.krg.org/pages/page.asp?lngnr=12&rnr=296&PageNr=1을 살피면 Bazian과 Hawler 지역에서 KNOC가 체결한 PSC도 열람가능.

BETWEEN

The KURDISTAN REGIONAL GOVERNMENT OF IRAQ (hereafter referred to as the "GOVERNMENT"), duty represented by the Minister of Natural Resources:

AND

KOREA NATIONAL OIL CORPORATION, a company established and existing under the laws of the Republic of Korea, whose registered office is at 1588-14I Gwanyang-dong, Dongan-gu. Anyang. Gyeonggi-do, 431-711, Republic of Korea, duty represented by its Executive Vice President, Dr. Seong-Hoon Kim (hereafter referred to as the "CONTRACTOR");

WHEREAS

(A) The GOVERNMENT wishes to develop the petroleum wealth of the Kurdistan Region (as defined in this Contract) in a way that achieves the highest benefit to the people of the Kurdistan Region and all of Iraq, using the most advanced techniques of market principles and encouraging investment, consistent with the Constitution of Iraq including Article 112 thereof;

(B) In accordance with the Constitution of Iraq, and the prevailing law of the Kurdistan Region, the Kurdistan Region Law (as defined in this Contract) except with regard to a matter wholly within the exclusive jurisdiction of the Government of Iraq;

(C) The GOVERNMENT intends to present to the National Assembly of the Kurdistan Region a law or laws to authorize the GOVERNMENT, by contract or other authorization, to attemp investors in long term projects relating to the conduct of petroleum operations in the Kurdistan Region from Kurdistan Region taxation, to indemnify such holders against liability to pay such taxation, and/or to guarantee the stability of the applicable legal, fiscal and economic environment of such projects;

(D) The CONTRACTOR is a company, (i) with the financial capability, and the technical knowledge and technical ability, to carry out Petroleum Operations in the Contract Area (as defined in this Contract) under the terms of this Contract; (ii) having a record of compliance with the principles of good corporate citizenship; and (iii) willing to cooperate with the GOVERNMENT by entering into this Contract, thereby assisting the GOVERNMENT to develop the Kurdistan Region petroleum industry, thereby promoting the economic development of the Kurdistan Region and Iraq and the social welfare of its people; and

(E) the CONTRACTOR, in recognition of the needs of the people of the Kurdistan Region of Iraq, has entered into an agreement with GOVERNMENT to implement certain infrastructure and capacity building projects in the Capacity Building Support Agreement (as defined in this Contract);

NOW, THEREFORE, THE PARTIES HAVE AGREED AS FOLLOWS,

ARTICLE 1 – DEFINITIONS

1.1 Capitalized terms and expressions in this Contrant shall have the following meaning, unless otherwise specified.

Abroad means outside of the Kurdistan Region and other parts of lraq.

Access Authorization is defined in Article 17.9.

Accounts is defined in Article 15.1.

Accounting Procedure means the Accounting Procedure attached to this Contract as Annex B and constituting an integral part of this Contract.

Adjacent Contract Area is defined in Article 34.1.

Adjustment Date is definel in Article 27.6.

Affiliated Company or Affiliate means, as regards any of the companies or entities constituting the CONTRACTOR, a company or other legal entity which (a) controls a CONTRACTOR Entity; or (b) is controlled by a CONTRACTOR Entity; or (c) controls or is controlled by a company or entity which controls a CONTRACTOR Entity. but shall not include the GOVERNMENT in respect of the Public Company. For the purpose of this definition, "control" means direct or indirect ownership or control of the majority of the voting rights of the applicable entity at its shareholders' meetings or their equivalent.

Agreed Terms is defined in Article 14.10 (a).

Appraisal Area means the area defined in Article 12.2.

Appraisal Work Program and Budget is defined in Article 12.2.

Appraisal Report is defined in Article 12.4

Appraisal Well means a well drilled for the purpose of evaluating the commercial potential of a geological feature or a geological structure in which Petroleum has been discovered.

Arm's Length Sales means sales of Petroleum in freely convertible currencies between sellers and buyers having no direct or indirect relationship or common interest whatsoever with each other that could reasonably influence the sales price. Such Arm's Length shall exclude: (a) sales between or among any of the CONTRACTOR Entities and their respective Affiliates; (b) sales involving the GOVERNMENT or the Government of Iraq; and (c) sales involving exchanges and any transactions not relating to normal commercial practices

Assets means all land, platforms, pipelines, plant, equipment, machinery, wells, facilities and all other installations and structures and all Materials and Equipment.

Associated Natural Gas means (i) any Natural Gas dissolved in Crude Oil under reservoir conditions and (ii) any residue gas remaining after the extraction of Crude Oil from a reservoir.

Audit Request Period is defined in Article 15.3(a).

Available Associated Natural Gas is defined in Article 25.1.

Available Crude Oil is defined in Article 25.1.

Available Non-Associated Natural Gas is defined in Article 25.1

Available Petroleum is defined in Article 25.1.

Barrel means a quantity of forty-two (42) US gallons as a unit to measure liquids, at a temperature of sixty degrees (60°) Fahrenheit and pressure of fourteen point seven (14.7) psi.

Budgets means any budgets prepared by or on behalf of the CONTRACTOR pursuant to this Contract and forming part of an Exploration Work Program and Budget and/or an Appraisal Work Program and Budget and/or a Gas Marketing Work Program and Budget and/or a Development Work Program and Budget and/or a Production Work Program and Budget.

Calendar Year means a period of twelve (12) consecutive Months, commencing 1 January and ending on 31 December of the same year.

Capacity Building Support Agreement means the agreement entered into on 21 June 2008 between the GOVERNMENT and the CONTRACTOR for infrastructure and capacity building in the Kurdistan Regions.

Chairman is defined in Article 8.1.

Commercial Discovery means a Discovery which is potentially commercial when taking into account all technical, operational, commercial and financial data collected when carrying out appraisal works or similar operations, including recoverable reserves of Petroleum, sustainable regular production levels and other material technical, operational, commercial and financial parameters, all in accordance with prudent international petroleum industry practice.

Commercial Production means the production of Petroleum from the Production Area in accordance with annual Production Work Program and Budget.

Constitution of Iraq means the permanent constitution of Iraq approved by the people of Iraq in the general referendum of 15 October 2005.

Contract means this production sharing contract, including its Annexes A and B that are integral part hereof, as well as any extension, renewal, substitution or amendment of this production sharing contract that may be agreed in writing by the Parties in accordance with Article 43.7 and Capacity Building Support Agreement.

Contract Area means the area described and defined in Annex A attached to this Contract and constituting an integral part of this Contract, and any modifications made to that Annex in accordance with the provisions of this Contract, through amendments, surrender, withdrawal, extension or otherwise.

Contract Year means a period of twelve (12) consecutive Months starting from the Effective Date or any anniversary of the said Effective Date.

CONTRACTOR includes and composes each and all CONTRACTOR Entities, including any Third Party participant nominated by the GOVERNMENT pursuant to Article 4, and/or any assigned of all or part of the rights and obligations of a CONTRACTOR Entity under this Contract in accordance with Article 39, but not including any bolder of the Government Interest.

CONTRACTOR Entity means any Person which is for the time being a component of the CONTRACTOR, and/or any assignee of all the part of the rights and obligations of such Person under this Contract in accordance with Article 39, but not including any holder of the Government Interest. For the avoidance of doubt, at any time when there is only one entity constituting the CONTRACTOR any reference made in this contract to "the entities constituting the CONTRACTOR" or the "CONTRACTOR entities" or similar reference, shall be deemed to mean "the entity constituting the CONTRACTOR". KOREA NATIONAL OIL CORPORATION and the GOVERNMENT (the GOVERNMENT owning the Third Party Interest until a whole or partial assignment of such Third Party Interest pursuant to Article 4 as the CONTRACTOR Entity as the Effective Date, owns an undivided interest in the Petroleum Operations in respect of the entire Contract Area in the following percentage at the Effective Date.

KOREA NATIONAL OIL CORPORATION	60%
GOVERNMENT (Third Party Interest)	20%

The balance of the interest in Petroleum Operations in respect of the entire Contract Area, being twenty percent (20%) is the Government Interest as defined in Article 4.1.

Crude Oil means ail liquid hydrocarbons in their unprocessed state or obtained from Natural Gas by condensation or any other means of extraction.

Decommissioning Costs means all the costs and expenditures incurred by the CONTRACTOR when carrying out Decommissioning Operations, including those defined in the Accounting Procedure.

Decommissioning Operations means any works, together with all related and auxiliary activities, for decommissioning and/or removal and/or abandonment and making safe all of the Assets and site restoration and remediation related thereto in relation to any Production Area.

Decommissioning Plan is defined in Article 38.7.

Decommissioning Reserve Fund is defined in Article 38.1 and includes all contributions paid into such fund and all interest accumulated such fund.

Deductible Amount is defined in Article 35.12.

Delivery Point means the point after extraction, specified in the approved Development Plan for a Production Area, at which the Crude Oil, Associated Natural Gas and/or Non-Associated Natural Gas is metered for the purposes of Article 27.5. valued for the purposes of Article 27.1 and ready to be taken and disposed of, consistent with prudent international petroleum industry practice, and at which a Party may acquire title to its share of Petroleum under this Contract or such other point which may be agreed by the Parties.

Development Costs means all the costs und expenditures incurred by the

CONTRACTOR when carrying out Development Operations, including those defined in the Accounting Procedure.

Development Operations means all development operations or works conducted in accordance with a Development Plan up to the Delivery Point with a view to developing a Production Area, including: drilling of wells; primary and subsequent recovery projects and pressure maintenance; survey, engineering, building and erecting or laying of production plants and facilities (including separators, compressors, generators, pumps and tankage, gathering lines, pipelines and all facilities required to be installed for production, pressure maintenance, and treatment, storage and transportation of Petroleum); obtaining of such materials, equipment, machinery, items and supplies as may be required or expected for the foregoing activities, and all auxiliary operations and activities required or expected for the production of Petroleum from the Production Area.

Development Period is defined in Article 6.

Development Plan means a plan for development defined in Article 12.8.

Development Well means any well drilled after the date of approval of the Development Plan for the purpose of producing Petroleum, increasing or accelerating production of Petroleum, including injection wells and dry holes. Any well drilled within a Production Area shall be deemed a Development Well.

Development Work Program and Budget means the development work program and budget prepared pursuant to Article 13.2.

Discovery means a discovery of Petroleum within the limits of the Contract Area resulting from Petroleum Operations carried out under this Contract, provided such Petroleum is recoverable at the surface with a measurable flow utilizing techniques used in prudent international petroleum industry practice.

Dispute is defined in Article 42.1.

Dollar (USS) means the legal currency (dollar) at the United States of America (USA).

Effective Date means the date on which the conditions referred to in Article 47 have been fulfilled.

Environment Fund is defined in Article 23.9.

Equipment and Materials is defined in Article 19.1.

Exploration Costs means all the costs and expenditure incurred by the CONTRACTOR when carrying out Exploration Operations, including those defined in the Accounting Procedure.

Exploration Operations means any and all operations conducted with a view to discovering Petroleum, including any activities necessary to commence operations any topographical, hydrographical, geological, geophysical, acrial and other surveys the subsurface for the location of Petroleum, drilling of short holes, core holes and stratigraphic test holes, spud, drilling, testing coring, logging and equipping of equipment, machinery, items, and supplies as may be required or expected for the foregoing activities, and all auxiliary operations and activities required or expected for the conduct of the foregoing activities.

Exploration Period is defined in Article 6.

Exploration Rental is defined in Article 6.3.

Exploration Well means any well drilled for the purpose of confirming a geological structure or stratigraphic unit in which no Discovery has previously been made by the CONTRACTOR.

Exploration Work Program and Budget means the exploration work program and budget prepared pursuant to Article 11.1.

Export Crude Oil is defined in Article 24.2.

Export Non-Associated Natural Gas is defined in Article 24.2.

Export Petroleum is dctincd in Article 24.2.

First Commercial Declaration Date Is defined in Article 4.I.

First Exploration Well is defined in Article 10.2(c).

First Production means the moment when Commercial Production of Crude Oil or Non-Associated Natural Gas (as the case may be) first commences, by flowing at the rate forecast in the Development Plan without interruption for a minimum of forty eight (48) hours.

Force Majeure is defined in Article 40.2.

Gas Development is defined in Article 14.10.

Gas Marketing Costs means all costs and expenditure incurred by the CONTRACTOR when carrying out Gas Marketing Operations, including those defined in the Accounting Procedure.

Gas Marketing Operations means any and all of the activities and operations contemplated by Article 14.6.

Gas Marketing Work Program and Budget means the marketing work program and budget prepared pursuant to Article 14.8.

Government Interest is defined in Article 4.1.

Government of Iraq means the Federal Government of the Republic of Iraq, which holds office under the Constitution of Iraq and any minister, ministry, department, sub-division, agency, authority, council committee, or other constituent element thereof and shall, without limitation, include any corporation owned and/or controlled by any of the foregoing.

International Market Price is defined in Article 27.2.

Iraq means the entirety of the Republic of Iraq, including the Kurdistan Region.

Joint Operating Agreement means the agreement executed by the CONTRACTOR Entities for the purpose of regulating between such entities the terms under which the Petroleum Operations will be conducted, which agreement shall be: (a) consistent with prudent international petroleum industry practice; (b) as between such entities, supplementary to this Contract; and (c) consistent with the provisions of the contract.

Kurdistan Region means the Federal Region of Kurdistan recognized by the Constitution of Iraq and having the same meaning as 'Region' in the Kurdistan Region Oil and Gas law.

Kurdistan Region Law means all statutes, degrees, edicts, codes, orders, rules, ordinances and regulations of the GOVERNMENT or of any other local, municipal, territorial, provincial, or any duty constituted governmental authority or agency in the Kurdistan Region.

Kurdistan Region Oil and Gas Law means the Oil and Gas Law of the Kurdistan Region-Iraq (Law No. 22 of 2007) as the same may be amended.

Law means all applicable laws including the following: constitutional law, civil law, common law, international law, equity, treaties. statutes, decrees, edicts, codes, orders, judgements, rules, ordinances, and regulation of any local, municipal, territorial, provincial, federated, national or any other duty constituted governmental authority or agency.

LCIA Is defined in Article 42.1.(b).

LIBOR means the London Inter-Bank Offered Rate at which Dollar deposits for one (1) Month are offered in the inter-bank market in London, as quoted in the Financial Times of London for the day in question. In the event that such rate is not published in the Financial Times, it shall mean the London Inter-bank Offered Rate at which Dollar deposits for one (1) Month are offered for the nearest day as quoted by National Westminster Bank ptc.

Management Committee is defined in Article 8.

Maximum Efficient Rate ("MER") is defined in Article 16.12.

Minimum Exploration Obligations iS defined in Article 10.J.

Minimum Financial Commitment means
(a) in respect of the First Sub-Period, the total of the amounts set out in Articles10.2(d) and 10.2(e), and
(b) in respect of the Second Sub-Period, the amount set out in Article 10.3(b).

Month means a calendar month according to the Gregorian calender.

Natural Gas means all gaseous Petroleum and inerts.

Non-Associated Natural Gas means any Natural Gas which is not any Associated Natural Gas.

Notice of Dispute is defined in Article 42.1.

Operator means the entity designated by the CONTRACTOR pursuant to Article 5 which, in the name and on behalf of the CONTRACTOR, shall carry out all Petroleum Operations. If at any time there exists more than one (1) Operator under this Contract, any reference herein to the term "Operator" shall be to each Operator with respect to the parts of the Contract Area in which such Operator conducts Petroleum Operations.

Option of Government Participation is defined in Article 4.1.

Option of Third Party Participation is defined in Article 4.6.

Party or Parties means the GOVERNMENT and/or each CONTRACTOR Entity and/or the CONTRACTOR.

Permits means all licences, permits, consents, authorizations or other permissions, as the context requires.

Person shall include natural and juristic persons (including corporations and governmental agencies).

Petroleum means:
(a) any naturally occurring hydrocarbon in a gaseous or liquid state;
(b) any mixture of naturally occurring hydrocarbons in a gaseous or liquid state; or
(c) any Petroleum (as defined in paragraphs (a) and (b) above) that has been returned to a Reservoir.

Petroleum Costs means all costs and expenditure incurred by the CONTRACTOR for the Petroleum Operations, and which the CONTRACTOR is entitled to recover under this Contract and its Accounting Procedure, including Decommissioning Costs, Development

Costs, Exploration Costs, Gas Marketing Costs and Production Costs.

Petroleum Field means a Reservoir or group of Reservoirs within a common geological structure or stratigraphic unit, which may become part of a Production Area pursuant to a Development Plan.

Petroleum Operations means all Exploration Operations, Gas Marketing Operations, Development Operations, Production Operations and Decommissioning Operations, as well as any other activities or operations directly or indirectly related or connected with the said operations (including health, safely and environmental operations and activities) and authorized or contemplated by. or performed in accordance with, this Contract.

Pipeline Costs is defined in Article 33.5.

Production Area means such areas within the Contract Area designated as a production area in an approved Development Plan prepared pursuant to Article 1.2. For the avoidance of doubt, all superjacent or subjacent strata of the Reservoir in which a Commercial Discovery is located are automatically included in the relevant Production Area.

Production Bonus means any bonus due pursuant to Article 32.3 or 32.4.

Production Costs means all the costs and expenditure incurred by the CONTRACTOR in carrying out the Production Operations, including those defined in the Accounting Procedure.

Production Operations means any works, together with all related and auxiliary activities, for the production of Petroleum from the start of Commercial Production, including: extraction, injection, stimulation, pumping, treatment, storage, engineering, operating, servicing, repairing, and maintaining any wells, plants, equipment, pipelines, terminals and any other installations and facilities, and any related operations and auxiliary operations, and storage and transportation of Petroleum from the Production Area to the Delivery Point.

Production Rental is defined in Article 13.10.

Production Work Program and Budget shall mean the production work program and budget prepared pursuant to Article 13.6.

Profit Crude Oil is defined in Article 26.1.

Profit Natural Gas is defined in Article 26.1.

Profit Petroleum is defined in Article 26.1.

Proposed Contract is defined in Article 14.10(a).

Public Company means a public company duty registered and incorporated in the Kurdistan Region and regulated by the GOVERNMENT under the Kurdistan Region Oil and Gas Law.

Public Officer means a civil servant, including a member or employee of a public entity, a member of the Kurdistan National Assembly or a member of the GOVERNMENT.

Quarter means a period of three (3) consecutive Months starting on the first day of January, April, July or October, respectively.

Reservoir means a subsurface rock formation containing an individual and separate natural accumulation of producible Petroleum characterized by a single natural pressure system.

"R" Factor is defined in Article 26.4.

Royalty is defined in Article 24.

Second Exploration Wells is defined in Article 10.3.(b).

Semester means a period of six (6) consecutive Months starting from the first day of January or July, respectively.

Senior Representatives is defined in Article 42.3 (a).

Subcontractor means any entity of any contracting tier providing services and/or undertaking works relating to the Petroleum Operations directly or indirectly on behalf of the CONTRACTOR or any CONTRACTOR Entity.

Sub-Period and Sub-Periods are defined in Article 6.2.

Tax or Taxes means all current or future levies, duties, payments, charges, impositions, imposts, withholdings, fees, taxes (including value added tax or other sales or transaction based tax, corporation tax, income lax, capital gains tax, stamp duty, land tax, registration tax, capital and wealth tax, profit tax, dividend tax or withholdings, transfer tax, customs duties, branch or permanent establishment tax or withholdings, tax on income from movable capital and fixed tax on transfers) or contributions payable to or imposed by the GOVERNMENT.

Third Party Interest is defined in Article 4.6.

Third Party Participant means the holder of a Third Party Interest.

Work Program means any work program prepared by, or on behalf of, the CONTRACTOR pursuant to this Contract and forming part of an Exploration Work Program and Budget and/or art Appraisal Work Program and Budget and/or a Gas Marketing Work Program and Budget and/or a Development Work Program and Budget and/or a Production Work Program and Budget.

Vice-Chairman is defined in Article 8.1.

1.2 In this Contract, unless the context otherwise requires or is specifically otherwise stated:
(a) headings are to be ignored;
(b) "including" and similar words do not imply any limitations;
(c) singular includes plural and vice versa; and
(d) reference to an "Article" is to an article of this Contract and to a "Paragraph" is to a paragraph in the Accounting Procedure.

ARTICLE 2－SCOPE OF THE CONTRACT

2.1 This Contract is a production sharing arrangement with respect to the Contract Area, whereby the GOVERNMENT has the right, pursuant to the Constitution of Iraq, to regulate and oversee Petroleum Operations within the Contract Area. The purpose of this Contract is to define the respective rights and obligations of the Parties and the terms and conditions under which the CONTRACTOR shall carry out all the Petroleum Operations. By entering into this Contract, the GOVERNMENT grants the exclusive right and authority to conduct all Petroleum Operations in the Contract Area as detailed in Article 3.

2.2 Upon the CONTRACTOR'S request, the GOVERNMENT shall provide and/or procure all Permits relating to the Petroleum Operations required by the CONTRACTOR to fulfill its obligations under this Contract, including those relating to any extension and renewal periods and including those required by the Government of Iraq. The GOVERNMENT (i) represents and warrants to the CONTRACTOR that it has not done and has not omitted to do anything that would cause the cancellation or suspension of this Contract or any Permit granted under this Article 2.2 or pursuant to this Contract, and (ii) covenants that it will not do, or omit to do, anything that would cause the cancellation or suspension of this Contract or any Permit granted under this Article 2.2 or pursuant to this Contract. For the avoidance of doubt, nothing in this Article shall affect the rights and obligations of the Parties pursuant to Article 43.

2.3 The CONTRACTOR shall conduct all Petroleum Operations within the Contract Area at its sole cost, risk and peril on behalf of the GOVERNMENT, pursuant to this Contract, including the following operations.

(a) Technical Services
Implementation of all technical, human and material resources reasonably required for execution of the petroleum Operations, in accordance with prudent international petroleum industry practice.

(b) Financial Services
The responsibility for funding the Exploration Operations and in the event of a Commercial Discovery, Development, Production and Decommissioning Operations pursuant to this Contract. For the funding of Petroleum Operations, each CONTRACTOR Entity shall be entitled to have recourse to external financing from either its Affiliated Companies or from any third parties.

(c) Administrative Services
Implementation of all appropriate management and administration techniques for execution of the Petroleum Operations under this Contract, in accordance with prudent international petroleum industry practice.

2.4 During the term of this Contract, the CONTRACTOR shall he responsible to the GOVERNMENT for the conduct of Petroleum Operations within the Contract Area pursuant to the terms of this Contract.

2.5 Natural resources other than Petroleum shall be excluded from the scope of this Contract, even if the CONTRACTOR discovers any such resources when executing its obligations pursuant to this Contract.

2.6 The CONTRACTOR shall only be entitled to recover Petroleum Costs incurred under this Contract in the event of a Commercial Discovery. Recovery of Petroleum Costs shall occur within the limits provided under Article 25.

2.7 During the term of this Contract, Profit Crude Oil and/or Profit Natural Gas produced from Petroleum Operations shall be shared between the Parties in accordance with the provisions of Article 26.

2.8 For the execution of Petroleum Operations under this Contract, the CONTRACTOR shall have the right to;

(a) freely access and operate within the Contract Area, as well as any facilities associated with the Petroleum Operations, wherever they may be located;
(b) freely use access roads located within the Contract Area and outside the Contract Area for the construction, installation, maintenance, operation and removal of pipelines and other facilities required for the Petroleum Operations;
(c) freely use sand, water, electricity and any other natural resources located inside or outside the Contract Area for the Petroleum Operations;
(d) use any qualified foreign and local personnel and/or Subcontractors required for the conduct of Petroleum Operations in accordance with Articles 22 and 23. Any foreign personnel Working in the Kurdistan Region shall require prior

authorization of the GOVERNMENT (such authorization not to be unreasonably delayed or withheld) and the GOVERNMENT shall obtain any authorization required by the Government of Iraq;

(e) import any goods, materials, equipment and/or services required for the Petroleum Operations in accordance with Articles 19. 22 and 30; and

(f) freely use land or property belonging to the Kurdistan Region, and the GOVERNMENT will assist of the CONTRACTOR with facilitating the use by the CONTRACTOR of any private property in the Kurdistan Region.

ARTICLE 3 – CONTRACT AREA

The initial Contract Area covers the Sangaw South Block and extends over an area of extends over an area of three hundred and fifty-four square kilometers (354㎢), as detailed and indicated on the map attached in Annex A and is delimited by the following coordinates

Points	X-Easting	Y-Nothing	Longitude-E	Latitude-N
A	519 410	3907 007	45 12 49	35 18 22
B	538 210	3883 689	45 25 09	35 05 43
C	532 347	3880 313	45 21 17	35 03 54
D	518 327	3883 273	45 12 04	35 05 32
E	511 145	3891 192	45 07 21	35 09 49

The GOVERNMENT, by execution of this Contract. hereby validates and approves the foregoing co-ordinates of the Contract Area. The total area of the Contract Area may be reduced only in accordance with the provisions of this Contract.

ARTICLE 4 – GOVERNMENT PARTICIPATION AND THIRD PARTY PARTICIPATION

GOVERNMENT INTEREST

4.1 The GOVERNMENT shall participate in this Contract through a Public Company, effective from the Effective Date in respect of the entire Contract Area with an undivided interest in the Petroleum Operations and all the other rights, duties, obligations and liabilities of the CONTRACTOR (save as provided in and subject to this Article 4) under this Contract in respect of Contract Area of twenty percent (20%) (the "Government Interest").

4.2 The Public Company shall not have any liability to the CONTRACTOR to contribute its Government Interest share of all Petroleum Costs, whenever those Petroleum Costs may be inclined, and its Government Interest share of such Petroleum Costs shall be the responsibility of KOREA NATIONAL OIL CORPORATION for the duration of this Contract, provided always that KOREA NATIONAL OIL CORPORATION shall be entitled (through the CONTRACTOR) to recover all such Petroleum Costs in accordance with Article 25. For the avoidance of doubt, the Public Company shall contribute its share of Production Bonuses attributable to the Government Interest and payable pursuant to Article 32.3 and 32.4. For the purposes of Article 37 of the Kurdistan Region Oil and Gas Law the Government Interest shall be deemed to be held by the GOVERNMENT and in accordance with the principle in Article 16.13. The Public Company will be individually and separately liable (and not jointly and severally liable with the CONTRACTOR Entities) to the GOVERNMENT for its obligations, duties and liabilities under this Contract and the provisions of Article 4.5 shall apply.

4.3 The Public Company may, at its discretion, assign part or all of its Government

Interest to a third party or parties which is another Public Company duly authorized by the GOVERNMENT, provided that in no event shall a transfer made which would result in the transferor or transferee holding less than a five percent (5%) participating interest. In the event of such an assignment to another Public Company, for the purposes of Article 37 of the Kurdistan Region Oil and Gas Law, the Government Interest so assigned shall be deemed to be held by the GOVERNMENT and in accordance with the principle in Article 16.13. The Public Company to which such Government Interest is transferred will be individually and separately liable (and not jointly and severally liable with the CONTRACTOR Entities) to the GOVERNMENT for its obligations, duties and liabilities under tins Contract and the provisions of Article 4.4 shall apply.

4.4 Any failure by the Public Company to perform any of its obligations or to satisfy any of its duties or liabilities under this Contract shall not be considered as a default of the CONTRACTOR Entities and shall in no case be invoked by the GOVERNMENT to terminate this Contract or exercise any other rights or remedies in respect of such default that may be available to it. The capacity of a Public Company, as it may arise pursuant to the provisions of this Contract, shall in no event cancel or affect the rights of the CONTRACTOR Entities to seek to settle a dispute or to refer such dispute to arbitration or expert determination in accordance with the provisions of Article 42.

4.5 A Public Company may assign part or all of its Government Interest to a third party or parties (not being a Public Company) and for the avoidance of doubt the provisions of Articles 39.1, 39.2 and 39.3 shall not apply. Any such assignee shall have the same rights and responsibilities held by the Public Company prior to the assignment. For the avoidance of doubt, following any assignment by a Public Company part or all of a Government Interest to a third party which is not a Public Company, in accordance with the provisions of this Article 4, the provisions of Articles 39.1, 39.2, and 39.3 shall apply to any subsequent assignment of such interest.

THIRD PARTY INTEREST

4.6 The GOVERNMENT shall have the option of assigning to a third party, or third parties, in respect of the Contract Area, as a CONTRACTOR Entity or CONTRACTOR Entities, an undivided interest in the Petroleum Operations in respect of the entire Contract Area and which option, when exercised, shall assign and novate all the other rights, duties, obligations and liabilities of the CONTRACTOR (save as provided in and subject to this Article 4). under this Contract, of an aggregate of twenty percent (20%) (the "Third Party Interest"), such option being referred to herein as the "Option of Third Party Participation." Until the later of the exercise of the Option of Third Party Participation or the assignment by the GOVERNMENT of the Third Party Interest (or part thereof) to a Public Company in accordance with Article 4.9, or the expiry of the eight (8) month period contemplated by Article 4.7, KOREA NATIONAL OIL CORPORATION shall undertake ail necessary work under this Contract, provided always that KOREA NATIONAL OIL. CORPORATION shall be entitled (through the CONTRACTOR) to recover all such Petroleum Costs in accordance with Article 25.

4.7 The GOVERNMENT may exercise the Option of Third Party Participation at any time prior to the date eight (8) months following the Effective Date by notifying the CONTRACTOR Entities, in writing, of a company which has. or companies which have, adequate resources and capacity to discharge the obligations of a CONTRACTOR Entity under this Contract and a Joint Operating Agreement in respect thereof.

4.8 If the GOVERNMENT notifies the CONTRACTOR Entities of a Third Party Participant in accordance with Articles 4.6 and 4.7, that Third Party Participant shall have the Third Party Interest or such part of the Third Party Interest as the GOVERNMENT may decide.

4.9 If (a) the GOVERNMENT does not notify the CONTRACTOR Entities of a Third Party Participant in accordance with Articles 4.6 and 4.7 for all or part of the Third Party Interest, and/or (b) if the Third Party Participant does not complete the exercise of the option as contemplated in Article 4.10 within sixty (60) days following its assignment by the GOVERNMENT of a Third Party Interest, then the Third Party Interest and/or that part of the Third Party Interest not assigned by the GOVERNMENT in accordance with Articles 4.6 and 4.7 shall be held by a Public Company to be identified by the GOVERNMENT, which Public Company shall act as a Third Party Participant. For the avoidance of doubt, for the purposes of this Article 4.9, a Public Company shall be a wholly-owned entity of the GOVERNMENT.

4.10 If the Option of Third Party Participation is exercised in accordance with Articles 4.6 and 4.7, or if the Public Company holds all or part of the Third Party Interest under Article 4.9, (a) the effective date of such participation shall be the Effective Date, notwithstanding that the exercise of the Option of Third Party Participation under Articles 4.6. and 4.7, or the date on which the Public Company acquires the Third Party Interest under Articles 4.9 occurs after such date; (b) a Third Party Participant, upon signature of a binding and enforceable instrument of assignment and novation in respect of this Contract referred to in Article 39.3, shall pay to the CONTRACTOR by way of cleared funds to a bank account nominated by the CONTRACTOR an amount equivalent to the proportion of Petroleum Costs incurred by the CONTRACTOR Entities as at the date of such payment attributable to the interest held by such Third Party Participant (which Petroleum Costs, for the avoidance of doubt, shall not include the Signature Bonus or the Capacity Building Bonus payable or paid (as the case may be) under this Contract; and (i) if the Option of Third Party Participation is exercised in accordance with Articles 4.6 and 4.7 the CONTRACTOR Entities (excluding the Third Party Participant) shall within fourteen (14) days of the notification, purpose to the GOVERNMENT a statement of Petroleum Costs Within thirty (30) days of the notification, the GOVERNMENT shall present the Third Party Participant with a statement, agreed as between the GOVERNMENT and the CONTRACTOR (excluding the Third Party Participant) of Petroleum Costs. Within sixty (60) days of the notification, the GOVERNMENT shall cause the Third Party Participation to pay the full amount due in accordance with this Article 4.10(b), (ii) if the Public Company holds all or part of the Third Party Interest under Article 4.9, the GOVERNMENT shall cause the payment of the amount in accordance with this Article 4.10(b) to be made by the Public Company to the CONTRACTOR within sixty (60) days of the Public Company acquiring the Third Party Interest under Article 4.9; (c) upon payment pursuant to and in accordance with Article 4.10(b) and the execution of the instrument referred to in Article. 4.10(b) a Third Party Participant shall participate as a CONTRACTOR Entity (or, where a Third Party Participant constitutes a group of companies, as CONTRACTOR Entities) under this Contract as if it had been a CONTRACTOR Entity (or as if they had been CONTRACTOR Entities) from the Effective Date, with all the rights, duties, obligations and liabilities under this Contract, including the obligation to pay the relevant pro rata share of any and all Production Bonuses due at any time under the Contract, and a Third Party Participant shall not become a CONTRACTOR Entity until payment pursuant to and in accordance with Article 4.10(b) has been completed; and (d) where a Joint Operating Agreement has been executed by the CONTRACTOR Entities prior to any exercise of the Option of Third Party Participation pursuant to Articles 4.6 and 4.7, a Third Party Participant shall, upon signature of the instrument referred to in Article 4.10 (b), become a party or parties to such Joint Operating Agreement on the terms thereof.

4.11 If the Public Company shall hold all or part of the Third Party Interest under Article 4.9, and shall fail to make the payment referred to in Article 4.10(b) by the due date of payment, or if the GOVERNMENT and the Public Company have not completed the assignment of all or part of the Third Party Interest under Article 4.9 within ninety

(90) days of the expiry of the eight (8) Month period contemplated by Article 4.7, then upon the day following that date, the GOVERNMENT will with immediate effect therefrom take all contractual and procedural measures (enforceable under applicable law) to procure that: (a) fifty percent (50%) of the interest so held by the Public Company holding such Third Party Interest shall, notwithstanding any other Article in this Contract, be automatically deemed to be assigned and be assigned by such Public Company to the extant CONTRACTOR Entities; and (b) fifty percent (50%) of the interest so held by the Public Company holding such Third Party Interest shall, notwithstanding the provisions of Article 39.2 or any other Article in this Contract, be automatically deemed to be assigned and be assigned to that Public Company which holds the Government Interest pursuant to Article 4.1, and shall for the purposes of this Article 4 be part of the Government Interest and shall be subject to the rights and obligations of Article 4.2 and the other provisions of this Contract relating the Government Interest.

JOINT OPERATING AGREEMENT PROVISIONS

4.12 Any Joint Operating Agreement entered into in relation to this Contract shall be consistent with the principles of this Article 4 and shall provide as follows: (a) all decisions of any operating committee established under such Joint Operating Agreement shall require the affirmative vote of an agreed percentage of participating interests held thereunder, which in any event shall be not more than seventy five percent (75%); and (b) in the event of a proposed transfer by any CONTRACTOR Entity of part of a participating interest under such Joint Operating Agreement, including any Third Party Interest, (i) no transfer may be made which would result in the transferor or transferee holding less than a five percent (5%) participating interest, (ii) the proposed third party assignee must demonstrate to the reasonable satisfaction of each of the extant CONTRACTOR Entities that it has the financial capability to perform its payment obligations under the Contract and under the Joint Operating Agreement, and (iii) the proposed third party assignee shall enter into instrument satisfactory to each of the extant CONTRACTOR Entities so as to assume and to perform the obligations of the transferor.

ARTICLE 5 – OPERATOR

5.1 The CONTRACTOR hereby designates KOREA NATIONAL OIL CORPORATION to act at the operator on behalf of the CONTRACTOR for the execution of the Petroleum operations. The CONTRACTOR shall at any time have the right to appoint another entity as the Operator, upon giving the GOVERNMENT not less thirty (30) days prior written notice of such appointment.

5.2 The CONTRACTOR shall submit to the GOVERNMENT for comment any agreement to amend the Joint Operating Agreement regarding or regulating the Operator's appointment and its conduct of Petroleum Operations on behalf of the CONTRACTOR pursuant to this Contract prior to execution of such agreement.

5.3 In the event of the occurrence of either of the following, the GOVERNMENT may require the CONTRACTOR to appeal another entity as Operator as soon as is reasonably practicable: (a) if an order has been passed in court declaring the bankruptcy, liquidation. or dissolution of the Operator; or (b) if the Operator terminates the activities under this Contract delegated to it by this CONTRACTOR or a material proportion thereof, and, as a result the CONTRACTOR fails to fulfill its obligations under the Contract.

ARTICLE 6 – TERM OF THE CONTRACT

6.1 This Contract comprises an Exploration Period and a Development Period, as defined below:

EXPLORATION PERIOD

6.2 The Exploration Period shall be for an initial term of five (5) Contract Years, extendable on a yearly basis (as provided in Articles 6.5. and 6.6) up to a maximum period of seven (7) Contract Years. The initial term of five (5) years shall be subdivided in two (2) sub-periods as follows: (a) an initial sub-period of three (3) Contract Years ("First Sub-Period"); and (b) a second sub-period of two (2) Contract Years ("Second Sub-Period"), each a "Sub-Periods" and collectively "Sub-Periods". It is understood that the right of the CONTRACTOR to accede to the next Sub-Period or any extension thereof pursuant to Article 6.6 shall be subject to fulfillment of the Minimum Exploration Obligations or minimum work obligations applicable to the previous Sub-Period or extension thereof pursuant to Article 6.6 (as case may be).

6.3 During the Exploration Period, the CONTRACTOR shall pay to the GOVERNMENT, in arrears, an annual surface rental for the Contract Area, as may be reduced by relinquishment from time to time pursuant to Article 7, of ten Dollars (US$10) per square kilometer per Contract Year ("Exploration Rental"). Such Exploration Rental shall be considered as a Petroleum Cost and shall be recovered by the CONTRACTOR in accordance with the provisions of Articles 1 and 25.

6.4 If the CONTRACTOR decides not to enter into the Second Sub-Period, it shall notify the GOVERNMENT at least thirty (30) days prior to the expiry of the First Sub-period and provided that the data from the First Exploration Well demonstrates that there is no reasonable technical case for drilling the Second Exploration Well in the Contract Area, the Exploration Period shall expire at the end of the First Sub-Period, unless the First Sub-Period has been extended pursuant to Article 6.5 and/or Article 6.6.

6.5 If the CONTRACTOR has fulfilled its Minimum Exploration Obligations for a Sub-Period of the Exploration Period but considers that additional work as required prior: (a) to deciding to submit an Appraisal Work Program and Budget as provided under Article 12.2 in respect of a Discovery; or (b) to deciding to declare a Discovery as a Commercial Discovery in accordance with Article 12.6(a) or 14.5(a), which additional work may include the preparation and/or execution of an Appraisal Work Program and Budget as provided under Article 12.2 and/or Gas Marketing Operations, the CONTRACTOR will automatically be entitled to extensions each of one (1) Contract Year of the then current Sub-Period, up to the end of the maximum Exploration Period of seven (7) Contract Years (as provided in Article 6.2). The CONTRACTOR'S notification of its intention to exercise such extension and its duration shall be submitted in writing to the GOVERNMENT at least thirty (30) days prior to the end of the then current Sub-Period or the end of the then current extension (as the case may be).

6.6 Without prejudice to Article 6.5, upon expiry of the initial term of the Exploration Periods, if it considers it has not completed its exploration evaluation of the Contract Area, the CONTRACTOR shall be entitled to an extension of the Second Sub-Period, provided it notifies the GOVERNMENT in writing at least thirty (30) days prior to the end of such Sub-Period, together with a proposal for a minimum work obligation for such extension. Any such extension shall not exceed one (1) Contract Year. Upon the expiry of such extension, if it considers it has still not completed its evaluation of the Contract Area, the CONTRACTOR shall be entitled to a further extension of one (1) Contract Year provided that it notifies the GOVERNMENT in writing at least thirty (30) days prior to the end of the original extension. The right of the. CONTRACTOR to accede to the further extension shall be subject to fulfillment of the minimum work obligations applicable to the original extension.

6.7 Subject to Article 6.4, at any time during the Exploration Period, upon thirty (30) days prior notice to the GOVERNMENT, the CONTRACTOR shall have the right to withdraw from this Contract provided that the outstanding Minimum Exploration

Obligations relating to the then current Sub-Period have been completed in accordance with the Contract, or it has paid to the GOVERNMENT the amounts specified in Article 10.2. or Article 10.3, whichever is applicable to the then current Sub-Period.

6.8 If no Commercial Discovery has been made at the end of the Exploration Period (including any extension of), this Contract shall expire.

6.9 If a Discovery is made within the maximum Exploration Period of seven (7) Contract Years (as provided in Article 6.2), and if the CONTRACTOR considers it has not had time to complete sufficient Gas Marketing Operations to declare the Discovery a Commercial Discovery pursuant to Articles 12.6(a) or 14.5(a), the CONTRACTOR shall be entitled to request an extension of the Exploration Period (notwithstanding the maximum period provided in Article 6.2, provided it so requests the GOVERNMENT in writing at least thirty (30) days prior to the end of the maximum Exploration Period, together with a proposal for Gas Marketing Operations to be undertaken during such extension. If granted by the GOVERNMENT, any such extension, if it considers it has still not completed its Gas Marketing Operation, shall not exceed two (2) Contract Years. Upon the expiry of such extension if it considers it has still not completed its Gas Marketing Operations relating to such Discovery, the CONTRACTOR shall be entitled to request a further extension of two (2) Contract Years provided that it so requests the GOVERNMENT in writing at least thirty (30) days priot to the end of the original extension together with a proposal for Gas Marketing Operations to be undertaken during such extension.

DEVELOPMENT PERIOD

6.10 If the CONTRACTOR considers that a Discovery of Crude Oil and any Associated Natural Gas is a Commercial Discovery, the CONTRACTOR shall have the exclusive right to develop and produce such Commercial Discovery, pursuant to the terms of this Contract. The Development Period for a Commercial Discovery of Crude Oil and any Associated Natural Gas shall be twenty (20) years commencing on the declaration of such Commercial Discovery by CONTRACTOR, in accordance with Article 12.6(a), with an automatic right to a five (5) year extension.

6.11 If the CONTRACTOR considers that a Discovery of Non-Associated Natural Gas is a Commercial Discovery, the CONTRACTOR shall have the exclusive right to develop and produce such Commercial Discovery, pursuant to the terms of this Contract. The Development Period for a Commercial Discovery of Non-Associated Natural Gas shall be twenty (20) years, commencing on the declaration of such Commercial Discovery by CONTRACTOR, in accordance with Article 12.6(a) or Article 14.5 (a) with an automatic right to a five (5) year extension..

6.12 If Commercial Production from a Production Area is still possible at the end of its Development Period as defined in Articles 6.10 or 6.11 then, upon its request, the CONTRACTOR shall be entitled to an extension of such Development Period under the same terms as those provided in this Contract. Such request shall be made in writing by the CONTRACTOR at least six (6) Months before the end of the said Development Period. The term of any such extension of the Development Period shall be (a) five (5) years for Crude Oil and any Associated Natural Gas, and/or (b) five (5) years for Non-Associated Natural Gas.

6.13 The CONTRACTOR shall have the right to terminate Production Operations for any Production Area at any time during the term of this Contract, subject to giving notice to the GOVERNMENT of at least ninety (90) days. This Contract shall terminate on the expiry date of the last Production Area or when Production Operations for all Production Areas have terminated.

ARTICLE 7 – RELINQUISHMENTS

7.1 Subject to the provisions of Articles 7.2. and 7.3, the CONTRACTOR shall surrender portions of the Contract Area as follow:

(a) at the end of the initial term of the Exploration Period referred to in Article 6.2, twenty five percent (25%) of the net area determined by subtracting the Production Areas from the initial Contract Area;
(b) at the end of the first extension period entered into under this Contract after the end of the initial term of the Exploration Period referred to in Article 6.2, an additional twenty five percent (25%) of the net area determined by subtracting the Production Areas from the remaining part of the Contract Area, and not a Production Area;
(c) at the end of the Exploration Period (including all extensions thereof), all of the remaining area that is not to a Production Area.

7.2 For the application of Article 7.1:
(a) any areas already relinquished pursuant to Article 7.4 shall be deducted from areas to be surrendered; and
(b) the CONTRACTOR shall have the right to determine the area, shape and location of the Contract Area to be kept, provided that such surrendered portions of the Contract Area shall be in contiguous blocks.

7.3 If the relinquishment referred to in Article 7.1 can only be achieved by including part of an Appraisal Area, then these percentages shall be reduced to exclude such Appraisal Area.

7.4 During the Exploration Period, the CONTRACTOR may at the end of each Contract Year surrender all or any part of the Contract Area by written notice sent to the GOVERNMENT at least thirty (30) days in advance of the proposed date of surrender, subject to the provisions of this Article 7.4. Such voluntary surrenders during the Exploration Period shall be deemed equal to the obligatory relinquishments referred to under Article 7.1. This Contract shall terminate in the event of the surrender of the entire Contract Area.

7.5 No surrender provided under Article 7.4 shall exempt the CONTRACTOR from its outstanding obligations under this Contract. In the event the CONTRACTOR elects to surrender the entire Contract Area without having fulfilled the Minimum Exploration Obligations relating to the then current Sub-Period as provided in Article 10.2 or Article 10.3, the CONTRACTOR shall pay to the GOVERNMENT the relevant outstanding amount as detailed in Article 10.2 or Article 10.3, as the case may be.

7.6 The boundaries of the portion of the Contract Area to be relinquished by the CONTRACTOR shall be communicated to the GOVERNMENT by written notice at least thirty (30) days in advance of the relevant date for relinquishment, pursuant to Article 7.1.

ARTICLE 8 – MANAGEMENT COMMITTEE

8.1 A Management Committee shall be established within thirty (30) days following the Effective Date for the purpose of providing orderly direction of all matters pertaining to the Petroleum Operations and the Work Programs. Within such period, each of the GOVERNMENT and the CONTRACTOR shall by written notice nominate its respective members of the Management Committee and their deputies. The Management Committee shall comprise two (2) members designated by the GOVERNMENT and two (2) members designated by the CONTRACTOR. Upon ten (10) days notice, each of she GOVERNMENT and the CONTRACTOR may substitute any of its members of the Management Committee. The chairman of the Management Committee shall be one of the members designated by the GOVERNMENT (the "Chairman"). The vice-chairman of the Management Committee shall be one of the members designated by the CONTRACTOR (the "Vice-Chairman"). In the absence of the Chairman, the Vice-Chairman shall chair the meeting. Each Party shall have the right to invite a reasonable number of observers as deemed necessary to attend the meetings of the Management Committee in a non-voting capacity.

8.2 The Management Committee shall review, deliberate, decide and give advice suggestions and recommendations to the Parties regarding the following subject matters:
(a) Work Programs and Budgets;
(b) the CONTRACTOR's activity reports;
(c) production levels submitted by the CONTRACTOR, based on prudent international petroleum industry practice;
(d) Accounts of Petroleum Costs:
(e) procurement procedures for potential Subcontractors, with an estimated sub-contract value in excess of one million Dollars ($1,000,000), submitted by the CONTRACTOR in accordance with Article 19.3;
(f) Development Plan and Budget for each Production Area;
(g) any matter having a material adverse effect on Petroleum Operations;
(h) any other subject matter of a material nature that the Parties are willing to consider.

8.3 Each of the GOVERNMENT and the CONTRACTOR shall have one (1) vote in the Management Committee. The Management Committee cannot validly deliberate unless each of the GOVERNMENT and the CONTRACTOR is represented by at least one (1) of its members or its deputy. The Management Committee shall attempt to reach unanimous agreement on any subject matter being submitted. In the event the Management Committee cannot reach unanimous agreement, a second meeting shall be held within fourteen (14) days to discuss the same subject matter and attempt to reach a unanimous decision. Except as provided for in Article 8.4 and Article 8.5, in the event that no agreement is reached at the second meeting, the Chairman shall have the tie-breaking vote.

8.4 In the event that during the Exploration Period, no agreement is reached at the second meeting of the Management Committee, as provided for in Article 8.3, or unanimous approval is not obtained, as required pursuant to Article 8.5, then the proposal made by the CONTRACTOR shall be deemed adopted by the Management Committee.

8.5 Notwithstanding the provisions of Article 8.3 and subject to Article 8.4, unanimous approval of the Management Committee shall be required for:
(a) approval of, and any material revision to, any Exploration Work Program and Budget prepared after the first Commercial Discovery in the Production Area relating to such Commercial Discovery,
(b) approval of, and any material revision to, the Development Plan, the production schedule, lifting schedule and Development and Production Work Programs and Budgets,
(c) establishment of rules of procedure for the Management Committee,
(d) any insurance issues over which the Management Committee has authority,
(e) approval of, and any material revision to, procurement procedures for goods and/or services, submitted by the CONTRACTOR in accordance with Article 19.3

(unless such procedures have been deemed approved by the Management Committee in accordance with Article 19.3),

(f) approval of, and any material revision to, any proposed pipeline project submitted by CONTRACTOR in accordance with Article 3.3.3,

(g) approval of a first rate bank in which to place the Decommissioning Reserve Fund, in accordance with Article 38.1,

(h) approval of, and any material revision to, any proposed Decommissioning Plan submitted pursuant to Article 38.7 on any Decommissioning Work Program and Budget or Gas Marketing Work Program and Budget,

(i) any Terms of Reference which are required to be prepared and agreed for the purposes of expert determination, pursuant to Article 42.2,

(j) approval of any costs in excess of the ten percent (10%) above any Budget, and

(k) any matter having a material adverse effect on Petroleum Operations.

8.6 Ordinary meetings of the Management Committee shall take place in the Kurdistan Region, alternately at the offices of the GOVERNMENT and those of the CONTRACTOR, or at any other location agreed between Parties, at least twice a Contract Year prior to the date of the first Commercial Discovery and three times a Contract Year thereafter.

8.7 Either the GOVERNMENT or the CONTRACTOR may call an extraordinary meeting of the Management Committee to discuss important issues or developments related to Petroleum Operations, subject to giving reasonable prior notice, specifying the matters to be discussed at the meeting, to the other Party. The Management Committee may from time to time make decisions by correspondence provided all the members have indicated their approval of such decisions in such correspondence.

8.8 Unless at least one (1) member or its deputy of each of the GOVERNMENT the CONTRACTOR is present, the Management Committee shall be adjourned for a period not to exceed eight (8) days. The Party being present shall then notify the other Party of the new date, time and location for the meeting.

8.9 The agenda for meetings of the Management Committee shall be prepared by the CONTRACTOR in accordance with instructions of the Chairman and communicated to the Parties at least fifteen (15) days prior to the date of the meeting. The agenda shall include any subject matter proposed by either the GOVERNMENT or the CONTRACTOR. Decisions of the Management Committee will be made at the meetings. The CONTRACTOR shall be responsible for preparing and keeping minutes of the decisions made at the meetings. Copies of such minutes shall be forwarded to each Party for review and approval. Each Party shall review and approve such minutes within ten (10) days of receipt of the draft minutes. A Party who fails to notify in writing its approval or disapproval of such minutes within such ten (10) days shall be deemed to have approved the minutes.

8.10 If required, the Management Committee may request the creation of a technical sub-committee or any other sub-committee to assist it. Any such sub-committee shall be composed of a reasonable number of expers from the GOVERNMENT and the CONTRACTOR.

8.11 Any costs and expenditure incurred by the CONTRACTOR for meetings of the Management Committee or any technical sub-committee or any other sub-committee shall be considered as Petroleum Costs and shall be recovered by the CONTRACTOR in accordance with the provisions of Articles 1 and 25.

ARTICLE 9 – GUARANTEES

9.1 Each CONTRACTOR Entity shall provide the GOVERNMENT, if so required by the latter pursuant to written notice received by the CONTRACTOR Entity within thirty (30) days of the Effective Date, with a corporate guarantee in a form as shall be agreed in good faith between the GOVERNMENT and each CONTRACTOR Entity not later than ninety (90) days after the Effective Date, provided that such corporate guarantee shall be given only in respect of the Minimum Financial Commitment for the First Sub-Period and shall expire automatically upon completion of the performance of the Minimum Exploration Obligations set out in Article 10.2(d) and (e) or expenditure of such Minimum Financial Commitment, whichever is the earlier.

9.2 Not later than sixty (60) days after the commencement of the Second Sub-Period, each CONTRACTOR Entity shall provide the GOVERNMENT, if so required by the latter pursuant to written notice received by the CONTRACTOR Entity within thirty (30) days of such commencement date, with a corporate guarantee in (a) the form substantially agreed between the GOVERNMENT and each CONTRACTOR Entity for the First Sub-Period, if any, subject to making the changes necessary in order for the corporate guarantee to apply only to the Second Sub-Period or (b) if there is no agreed form in a form as shall be agreed in good faith between the GOVERNMENT and each CONTRACTOR Entity not later than ninety (90) days after the GOVERNMENT'S notice, and provided in each case that such corporate guarantee shall be given only respect of the Minimum Financial Commitment for the Second Sub-Period and that such corporate guarantee shall expire automatically upon completion of the performance of the Minimum Exploration Obligations set out in Article 10.3 (b) or expenditure of such Minimum Financial Commitment, whichever is the earlier.

9.3 In the event of an assignment by a CONTRACTOR Entity in accordance with Article 39, the relevant third party assignee shall provide the GOVERNMENT, if so required by the latter pursuant to written notice given to such assignee within thirty (30) days of the Effective Date, with a corporate guarantee in the form agreed pursuant to Articles 9.1 or 9.2, applicable to the then current Sub-Period or, in the absence of any such agreed form of corporate guarantees, in a form as shall be agreed in good faith between the GOVERNMENT and such assignee not later than ninety (90) days after the effective date of the assignment, provided that such corporate guarantee shall be given only in respect of the Minimum Financial Commitment for the then current Sub-Period, and shall expire automatically upon completion of the performance of the Minimum Exploration Obligations set out in Articles 10.2(d) and (e) or Article 10.3(b), as the case may be, or expenditure of such Minimum Financial Commitment, whichever is the earlier.

ARTICLE 10 – MINIMUM EXPLORATION WORK OBLIGATIONS

10.1 The CONTRACTOR shall start Exploration Operations within thirty (30) days of Management Committee approval of the Exploration Work Program and Budget in accordance with Article 8. The CONTRACTOR shall perform geological, geophysical and/or drilling works as provided under Articles 10.2 to 10.3 (the "Minimum Exploration Obligations"). If applicable, the said Minimum Exploration Obligations shall be performed during each Sub-Period in accordance with prudent international petroleum industry practice.

10.2 During the First Sub-Period, the CONTRACTOR shall,

(a) carry out geological and geophysical studies, comprising the following

(i) the compilation of a technical database;

(ii) the performance of a remote sensing study;

(iii) a field visit to verify initial geological and geological and geophysical;

(b) carry out a data search for existing data specific to this Contract Area, comprising the following:
(i) well data, if available, for example, electric logs;
(ii) seismic data and gravity data, if available; and
(iii) reprocess seismic data, if available;
(c) perform field work comprising structural, stratigraphic and lithologic mapping and sampling;
(d) acquire, process and interpret two hundred (200) line kilometres of two dimensional seismic data, committing for this Purpose a minimum financial amount of five million Dollars (US$5,000,000), or a three dimensional seismic data program by agreement between the Parties; and
(e) drill one (1) Exploration Well (the "First Exploration Well"), including testing and coring as appropriate, committing for this purpose a minimum financial amount of ten million Dollars. (US$10,000,000).

10.3 During the Second Sub-Period, the CONTRACTOR shall:
(a) acquire, process and interpret further seismic data (being either two dimensional or three dimension), if the CONTRACTOR considers that the result from the First Exploration Well justify the acquisition of further seismic data; and
(b) drill one (1) Exploration Well (the "Second Exploration Well"), including testing and coring as appropriate, committing for this purpose a minimum financial amount of ten million Dollars (US$10,000,000), unless the data from the First Exploration Well demonstrates that there is not a reasonable technical case for drilling the Second Exploration Well in the Contract Area.

10.4 Notwithstanding the provisions in Articles 10.2 to 10.3, for the execution of the Minimum Exploration Obligations under Articles 10.2 to 10.3, it is agreed as follows:
(a) Minimum Exploration Obligations in the Second Sub-Period shall only apply in the event the CONTRACTOR has not elected to notify the GOVERNMENT that it will not enter into the Second Sub-Period, in accordance with and subject to Article 6.4.
(b) Subject to Article 10.4(a), the CONTRACTOR shall be required to meet its Minimum Exploration Obligations for the applicable Sub-Period, even if this entails exceeding the Minimum Financial Commitment for such Sub-Period. If the CONTRACTOR has satisfied its Minimum Exploration Obligations without having spent the total Minimum Financial Commitment for such Sub-Period, it shall be deemed to have satisfied its Minimum Exploration Obligations for such Sub-Period.
(c) Each Exploration Well shall be drilled to the depth agreed by the Management Committee unless: (i) the formation is encountered at a lesser depth than originally anticipated; (ii) basement is encountered at a lesser depth than originally anticipated; (iii) in the CONTRACTOR'S sole opinion continued drilling of the relevant Exploration Well presents a hazard due to the presence of abnormal or unforeseen conditions; (iv) insurmountable technical problems are encountered rendering it impractical to continue drilling with standard equipment; or (v) petroleum formations are encountered whose penetration requires laying protective casing that does not enable the depth agreed by the Management Committee to be reached. If drilling is stopped for any of the foregoing reasons, the Exploration Well shall be deemed to have been drilled to the depth agreed by the Management Committee and the CONTRACTOR shall

be deemed to have satisfied its Minimum Exploration Obligations in respect of the Exploration Well.

(d) Any geological or geophysical work carried out or any seismic data acquired, processed or interpreted or any Exploration Well drilled or any other work performed its excess of the Minimum Exploration Obligations and/or any amounts spent in excess of the total Minimum Financial Commitment in any given Sub-Period shall be carried forward to the next Sub-Period or any extension period and shall be taken into account to satisfy the Minimum Exploration Obligations and/or the total Minimum Financial Commitment for such subsequent Sub-Period or extension period.

(e) For the avoidance of doubt, if (i) in the First Sub-Period, the CONTRACTOR performs any of the Minimum Exploration Obligations prescribed for the Second Sub-Period in Article 10.3; and (ii) the CONTRACTOR has not elected to notify the GOVERNMENT that it will not enter into the Second Sub-Period (in accordance with and subject to Article 6.4), the performance of such Minimum Exploration Obligations shall be deemed to satisfy the same Minimum Exploration Obligations for the Second Sub-Period.

ARTICLE 11 – EXPLORATION WORK PROGRAMS AND BUDGETS

11.1 Within forty-five (45) days following the Effective Date, the CONTRACTOR shall prepare and submit to the Management Committee a proposed work program and budget relating to Exploration Operations (the "Exploration Work Program and Budget") for the remainder of the Calendar year. Thereafter, no later than 1 October in each Calendar Year, the CONTRACTOR shall submit a proposed Exploration Work Program and Budget to the Management Committee for the following Calendar Year.

11.2 Each Exploration Work Program and Budget shall include details of, but not be limited to, the following: (a) work to be undertaken; (b) materials, goods and equipment to be acquired; (c) cost estimate of services to be provided, including services by third parties and/or Affiliated Companies of any CONTRACTOR Entity; and (d) estimated expenditures, broken down by cost centre in accordance with the Accounting Procedure.

11.3 The Management Committee shall meet within sixty (60) days following its receipt of CONTRACTOR'S proposal to examine and approve the Exploration Work Program and Budget.

11.4 If the GOVERNMENT requests any modification of the Exploration Work Program and Budget, the Management Committee shall meet to discuss the Exploration Work Program and Budget and proposed modifications thereto within the sixty (60) day period referred to in Article 11.3. The CONTRACTOR shall communicate its comments on any such requested modifications to the GOVERNMENT at the meeting of the Management Committee or in writing prior to such meeting.

11.5 The CONTRACTOR shall be authorized to make expenditures not budgeted in an approved Exploration Work Program and Budget provided that the aggregate amount of such expenditures shall not exceed ten percent (10%) of the approved Exploration Work Program and Budget in any Calendar Year and provided further that such excess expenditures shall be reported as soon as is reasonably practicable to the Management Committee. For the avoidance of doubt all excess expenditures shall be recovered by the CONTRACTOR in accordance with the provisions of Articles 1 and 25, provided that any excess expenditures above the ten percent (10%) limit shall only be recovered with the unanimous approval of the Management Committee.

11.6 In cases of emergency, the CONTRACTOR may incur such Additional expenditures as it deems necessary to protect life, environment or property. Such additional expenditures shall be reported promptly to the Management Committee. For the avoidance of doubt, such additional expenditure shall be considered Petroleum Costs and shall be recovered by the CONTRACTOR in accordance with the provisions of Articles 1 and 25.

ARTICLE 12 – DISCOVERY AND DEVELOPMENT

12.1 If the drilling of an Exploration Well results in a Discovery, the CONTRACTOR shall notify the GOVERNMENT within forty-eight (48) hours of completing tests confirming the presumed existence of such Discovery or within such longer period as the CONTRACTOR reasonably requires to determine whether or not there is a Discovery. Within thirty (30) days following notification of the said Discovery, the CONTRACTOR shall present to the Management Committee all technical data then available together with its opinion on the commercial potential of the said Discovery (the "Discovery Report"). The CONTRACTOR shall provide in a timely manner such other information relating to the Discovery as the GOVERNMENT may reasonably request.

APPRAISAL WORK PROGRAM AND BUDGET

12.2 If, pursuant to Article 12.1, the CONTRACTOR considers that the Discovery has commercial potential, it shall, within ninety (90) days following notification to the GOVERNMENT of the Discovery, submit an appraisal program in respect of the Discovery (the "Appraisal Work Program and Budget") to the Management Committee. The Management Committee shall examine the Appraisal Work Program and Budget within thirty (30) days of its receipt. If the GOVERNMENT requests any modification to the Appraisal Work Program and Budget, the Management Committee shall meet to discuss the Appraisal Work Program and Budget and the requested modifications thereto within sixty (60) days from its receipt of the proposed Appraisal Work Program and Budget. The CONTRACTOR shall communicate its comments on any such requested modifications to the GOVERNMENT at the meeting of the Management Committee or in writing prior to such meeting. The Appraisal Work Program and Budget shall include the following: (a) an appraisal works program and budget in accordance with prudent international petroleum industry practice; (b) an estimated time-frame for completion of appraisal works; and (c) the delimitation of the area to be evaluated, the surface of which shall not exceed twice (x2) the surface of the geological structure or prospect to be appraised (the "Appraisal Area").

12.3 If, following a Discovery, a rig acceptable to the CONTRACTOR is available to drill a well, the CONTRACTOR may drill any additional Exploration Well or any Appraisal Well deemed necessary by the CONTRACTOR before or during the Management Committee's review of the Discovery Report provided in accordance with Article 12.1 or its review of the Appraisal Work Program and Budget. The CONTRACTOR shall be authorized to incur expenditures not budgeted in an approved Appraisal Work Program and Budget, provided that the aggregate amount of such expenditures shall not exceed ten percent (10%) of the approved Appraisal Work Program and Budget in any Calendar Year, and provided further that such excess expenditures shall be reported as soon as is reasonably practicable to the Management Committee. For the avoidance of doubt, all excess expenditures shall be recovered by the CONTRACTOR in accordance with the provisions of Articles 1 and 25, provided that any excess expenditures above the ten percent (10%) limit shall only be recovered with the unanimous approval of the Management Committee.

APPRAISAL REPORT

12.4 The CONTRACTOR shall submit a detailed report relating to the Discovery (the "Appraisal Report") to the Management Committee within ninety (90) days following completion of the Appraisal Work Program and Budget.

12.5 The Appraisal Report shall include the following: (a) geological conditions; (b) physical properties of any liquids; (c) sulphur, sediment and water content; (d) type of substances obtained; (e) Natural Gas composition; (f) production forecast per well; and (g) a preliminary estimate of recoverable reserves.

DECLARATION OF COMMERCIAL DISCOVERY

12.6 Together with its Appraisal Report, the CONTRACTOR shall submit a written statement to the Management Committee specifying that: (a) the CONTRACTOR has determined that the Discovery is a Commercial Discovery; (b) the CONTRACTOR has determined that the Discovery is not a Commercial Discovery; (c) the CONTRACTOR has determined that the Discovery is a significant Discovery, which may become a Commercial Discovery subject to additional exploration and/or appraisal works within or outside of the Appraisal Area; or (d) the CONTRACTOR has determined that the Discovery is a significant Discovery of Non-Associated Natural Gas, which may become a Commercial Discovery subject to Gas Marketing Operations, in accordance with Article 14.5.

12.7 In case of the statement of the CONTRACTOR corresponds to Article 12.6(c), the CONTRACTOR shall submit a Work Program and Budget to the Management Committee within thirty (30) days following such statement. Any well drilled to evaluate the said significant Discovery shall be considered an Exploration Well.

DEVELOPMENT PLAN

12.8 If the Discovery has been declared a Commercial Discovery by the CONTRACTOR pursuant to Article 12.6(a) or Article 14.5(a), the CONTRACTOR shall submit a proposed Development Plan to the Management Committee within one hundred eighty (180) days following such declaration. The Development Plan shall be in accordance with prudent international petroleum industry practice. Except with the consent of the GOVERNMENT, such Development Plan shall include details of the following as applicable:

(a) the delimitation of the Production Area, taking into account the results of the Appraisal Report regarding the importance of the Petroleum Field within the Appraisal Area;
(b) drilling and completion of Development Wells;
(c) drilling and completion of water or Natural Gas injection wells;
(d) laying of gathering pipelines;
(e) installation of separators, tanks, pumps and any other associated production and injection facilities for the production;
(f) treatment and transportation of Petroleum to the processing and storage facilities onshore or offshore;
(g) laying of export pipelines inside or outside the Contract Area to the storage facility or Delivery Point;
(h) construction of storage facilities for Petroleum;
(i) plan for the utilisation of Associated Natural Gas;
(j) training commitment in accordance with Article 23;
(k) a preliminary decommissioning and site restoration plan;
(l) all contracts and arrangements made or to be made by the CONTRACTOR for the sale of Natural Gas;
(m) to the extent available, all contracts and arrangements made or to be made by Persons in respect of that Natural Gas downstream of the point at which it is to be sold by the CONTRACTOR and which are relevant to the price at which

(and other terms on which) it is to be sold by the CONTRACTOR or are otherwise relevant to the determination of the value of it for the purposes of this Contract, but not beyond the point at which it is first disposed of in an Arm's Length Sale;

(n) each CONTRACTOR Entity's plans for financing its interest, if any; and

(o) any other operations not expressly provided for in this Contract but reasonably necessary for Development Operations, Production Operations and delivery of Petroleum produced, in accordance with prudent international petroleum industry practice.

12.9 The Management Committee shall use its best efforts to approve the Development Plan within sixty (60) days after its receipt of such plan. The Development Period for each Commercial Discovery within a Development Plan shall be extended for the number of days in excess of such sixty (60) day period that it takes for the Management Committee to approve the Development Plan. The Development Plan shall be considered approved by the GOVERNMENT if the GOVERNMENT, through its representatives on the Management Committee, indicates its approval in writing.

12.10 If the GOVERNMENT requests any modification to the Development Plan, then the Management Committee shall meet within sixty (60) days of receipt by the CONTRACTOR of the GOVERNMENT'S written notification of requested modifications accompanied by all the documents justifying such request, and shall discuss such request. The CONTRACTOR shall communicate its comments on any such requested modifications to the GOVERNMENT at such meeting or in writing prior to such meeting. Any modification approved by the Management Committee at such meeting or within a further period of thirty (30) days from the date of such meeting shall be incorporated into the Development Plan which shall then be deemed approved and adopted.

12.11 If the CONTRACTOR makes several Commercial Discoveries within the Contract Area, each such Commercial Discovery will have a separate Production Area. The CONTRACTOR shall be entitled to develop and to produce each Commercial Discovery and the GOVERNMENT shall provide the appropriate Permits covering each Production Area. In case the area covered by the Commercial Discovery extends beyond the boundaries of the Contract Area, and to the extent such area outside the Contract Area is not the Subject of a Petroleum Contract (as defined in the Kurdistan Region Oil and Gas Law) with a third party, the provisions of Article 34.2 shall apply.

ARTICLE 13－DEVELOPMENT AND PRODUCTION WORK PROGRAMS AND BUDGET

13.1 Upon the approval of the Development Plan by the Management Committee, the CONTRACTOR shall start the Development Operations for the Commercial Discovery in accordance with the Development Plan and prudent international petroleum industry practice.

APPROVAL OF DEVELOPMENT WORKS PROGRAM AND BUDGET

13.2 Within ninety (90) days following approval of the Development Plan by the Management Committee, the CONTRACTOR shall prepare and submit to the Management Committee a proposed work program and budget for Development Operations (the "Development Work Program and Budget") to be carried out in the Production Area for the duration of the Development Operations. Thereafter, no later than 1 October in each Calendar Year, the CONTRACTOR shall submit to the Management Committee updates in respect of its Development Work Program and Budget. To enable the Management Committee to forecast expenditures, each Development Work Program and Budget shall include details of the following: (a) works to be carried out; (b) material and equipment to be acquired by main categories; (c) type of services to be provided, distinguishing between third parties and Affiliated Companies of any CONTRACTOR Entity; and (d) categories of general and administrative expenditure.

13.3 If any modification to the Development Work Program and Budget is requested by the GOVERNMENT, the Management Committee shall meet to discuss the Development Work Program and Budget and proposed modifications thereto within sixty (60) day from its receipt of the proposed Development Work Program and budget. The CONTRACTOR shall communicate its comments on any such requested modifications to the GOVERNMENT at the meeting of the Management Committee or in writing prior to such meeting.

13.4 The CONTRACTOR shall be authorized to incur expenditures not budgeted in an approved Development Work Program and Budget, provided that the aggregate amount of such expenditures shall not exceed ten percent (10%) of the approved Development Work Program and Budget in any Calendar Year, and provided further that such excess expenditures shall be reported as soon as is reasonably practicable to the Management Committee. For the avoidance of doubt, all excess expenditures shall be recovered by the CONTRACTOR in accordance with the provisions of Articles 1 and 25, provided that any excess expenditures above the ten percent (10%) limit shall only be recovered with the unanimous approval of the Management Committee.

13.5 In cases of emergency, the CONTRACTOR may incur such additional expenditures as it deems necessary to protect life, environment or property. Such additional expenditures shall be reported promptly to the Management Committee. For the avoidance of doubt, such additional expenditure shall be considered Petroleum Costs and shall be recovered by the CONTRACTOR in accordance with the provisions of Articles 1 and 25.

APPROVAL OF ANNUAL PRODUCTION WORKS PROGRAMS AND BUDGET

13.6 No later than 1 October of the Calendar Year preceding the estimated commencement of production pursuant to an approved Development Plan and thereafter no later than 1 October in each Calendar Year, the CONTRACTOR shall prepare and submit to the Management Committee a proposed work program and budget for Production Operations (the "'Production Work Program and Budget") for the following Calendar Year. To enable the Management Committee to forecast expenditures, the Production Work Program and Budget shall include details of the following: (a) works to be carried out; (b) material and equipment to be acquired by main categories; (c) type of services to be provided, distinguishing between third parties and Affiliated Companies of any CONTRACTOR Entity; and (d) categories of general and administrative expenditure.

13.7 If any modification to the Production Work Program and Budget is requested by the GOVERNMENT, the Management Committee shall meet to discuss the Production Work Program and Budget and proposed modifications thereto within sixty (60) days from its receipt of the proposed Production Work Program and Budget. The CONTRACTOR shall communicate its comments on any such requested modifications to the GOVERNMENT at the meeting of the Management Committee or in writing prior to such meeting.

13.8 The CONTRACTOR shall be authorized to incur expenditures not budgeted in an approved Production Work Program and Budget, provided that the aggregate amount of such expenditures shall not exceed ten percent (10%) of the approved Production Work Program and Budget in any Calendar Year, and provided further that such excess expenditures shall be reported as soon as reasonably practicable to the Management Committee. For the avoidance of doubt, all excess expenditures shall be recovered by the CONTRACTOR in accordance with the provisions of Articles 1 and 25, provided that any excess expenditure above the ten percent (10%) limit shall only be recovered with the unanimous approval of the Management Committee.

13.9 In cases of emergency, the CONTRACTOR may incur such additional expenditure as it deems necessary to protect life, environment or property. Such additional expenditures shall be reported promptly to the Management Committee. For the avoidance of doubt, such additional expenditure shall be considered Petroleum Costs and shall be recovered by the CONTRACTOR in accordance with the provisions of Articles 1 and 25.

13.10 After the commencement of Commercial Production the CONTRACTOR shall pay to the GOVERNMENT, in arrears an annual surface rental for the Production Area of one hundred Dollars (US $ 100) per square kilometre per Contract Year ("Production Rental"). Such Production Rental shall be considered as a Petroleum Cost and shall be recovered by the CONTRACTOR in accordance with the provisions of Articles 1 and 25.

ARTICLE 14 – NATURAL GAS

USE FOR THE PETROLEUM OPERATIONS

14.1 To take account of specific conditions relating to Natural Gas and to promote its development in the Kurdistan Region, the GOVERNMENT will grant specific benefits to the CONTRACTOR on principles materially similar to those contained in this Contract, including, consistent with the Kurdistan Region Oil and Gas Law, more generous provisions in respect of the recovery of Petroleum Costs and the sharing of Profit Petroleum than in respect of Crude Oil.

14.2 The CONTRACTOR may freely use any Natural Gas required for the petroleum operations. If technically and economically justified, the CONTRACTOR shall in priority use any Natural Gas for the purpose of enhancing recovery of Crude Oil in accordance with prudent international petroleum industry practice as follows.

ASSOCIATED NATURAL GAS

14.3 Any excess Associated Natural Gas produced that is neither used in the Petroleum Operations nor developed and sold by the CONTRACTOR shall, upon the GOVERNMENT'S written request, be transferred at the first practicable delivery point as agreed between the Parties, free of charge to the GOVERNMENT. In such case, the GOVERNMENT shall be solely responsible for collecting, treating, compressing and transporting such Natural Gas from such agreed delivery point and shall be solely liable for any additional direct and indirect costs associated therewith. The construction and operation of required facilities as well as the offtake of such excess Associated Natural Gas by the GOVERNMENT shall occur in accordance with prudent international petroleum industry practice and shall not interfere with the production, lifting and transportation of the Crude Oil by the CONTRACTOR. For the avoidance of doubt, all expenditure incurred by the CONTRACTOR up to such agreed delivery point shall be considered Petroleum Costs and shall be recovered by the CONTRACTOR in accordance with the provisions of Articles 1 and 25. In the event the GOVERNMENT finds a market for Associated Natural Gas, it shall promptly give written notice to the CONTRACTOR, and the CONTRACTOR may elect to participate in supplying such Associated Natural Gas within ninety (90) days following notification thereof by the GOVERNMENT. If the CONTRACTOR elects to participate in supplying Associated Natural Gas to such market, all expenditures associated with any necessary facilities shall be paid for by the CONTRACTOR. For the avoidance of doubt, such expenditure incurred shall be considered Petroleum Costs and shall be recovered by the CONTRACTOR in accordance with the provisions of Articles 1 and 25.

NON-ASSOCIATED NATURAL GAS

14.4 Until an approved Natural Gas sales contract is executed in respect of all volumes of Natural Gas expected to be produced, the CONTRACTOR shall be entitled during the Exploration Period and the Development Period to carry out Gas Marketing Operations.

14.5 If, pursuant to Article 12.6(d), the CONTRACTOR has determined that the Discovery is a significant Discovery of Non-Associated Natural Gas, which may become a Commercial Discovery subject to Gas Marketing Operations, it shall carry out Gas Marketing Operations, at the end of which it shall submit a written statement to the Management Committee specifying that: (a) the CONTRACTOR has determined that the Discovery is a Commercial Discovery; or (b) the CONTRACTOR has determined that the Discovery is a Commercial Discovery.

14.6 For the purpose of this Contract "Gas Marketing Operations" means any activity under this Contract relating to the marketing of Non-Associated Natural Gas, including any evaluation to find a commercial market for such Non-Associated Natural Gas and/or to find a commercially viable technical means of extraction of such Non-Associated Natural Gas and may include activities related to evaluating the quantities of Non-Associated Natural Gas to be sold, its quality, the geographic location of potential markets to he supplied as well as evaluating the costs of production, transportation and distribution of the Non-Associated Natural Gas from the Delivery Point to the relevant market.

14.7 All costs and expenditure incurred by the CONTRACTOR in the performance of the activities in relation to the Gas Marketing Operations shall be considered Petroleum Costs.

14.8 No later than 1 October of the Calendar Year preceding the Calendar Year in which any Gas Marketing Operations are due to occur, the CONTRACTOR shall prepare and submit to the Management Committee its Gas Marketing Work Program and Budget for the following Calendar Year. To enable the Management Committee to forecast expenditures, the Gas Marketing Work Program and Budget shall include the following: (a) works to be carried out; (b) type of services to be provided, distinguishing between third parties and Affiliated companies of any CONTRACTOR Entity; and (c) categories of general and administrative expenditure. If any modification to the Gas Marketing Work Program and Budget is requested by the GOVERNMENT, the Management Committee shall meet to discuss the Gas Marketing Work Program and Budget and proposed modifications thereto within sixty (60) days from its receipt of the proposed Gas Marketing Work Program and Budget. The CONTRACTOR shall communicate its comments on any such requested modifications to the GOVERNMENT at the meeting of the Management Committee or in writing prior to such meeting.

14.9 The CONTRACTOR shall be authorized to incur expenditures not budgeted in an approved Gas Marketing Work Program and Budget, provided that the aggregate amount of such expenditure shall not exceed ten percent (10%) of the approved Gas Marketing Work Program and Budget in any Calendar Year, and provided further that such excess expenditures shall be reported as soon as reasonably practicable to the Management Committee. For the avoidance of doubt, all excess expenditures shall be recovered by the CONTRACTOR in accordance with the provisions of Articles 1 and 25, provided that any excess expenditure above the ten percent (10%) limit shall only be recovered with the unanimous approval of the Management Committee.

14.10 If any Non-Associated Natural Gas is discovered within the Contract Area, and the CONTRACTOR reasonably considers that the Non-Associated Natural Gas Discovery will only be a Commercial Discovery if certain terms of this Contract are amended, it shall be entitled to request amendments to this Contract, with its reasons. The GOVERNMENT shall in good faith give reasonable consideration to the CONTRACTOR's proposed amendment and reasons and the Parties shall in good faith attempt to agree on live necessary amendments to the Contract.

If the Parties are unable to agree on such amendments, and the Exploration Period expires without the CONTRACTOR having declared such Discovery to be a Commercial Discovery in accordance with Article 12.6(a) or Article 14.5(a), and subsequently within a period of eight (8) years from the end of such Exploration Period, the GOVERNMENT reaches agreement with any third party to develop such Discovery (the "Gas development"), then the following provisions shall apply:

(a) either before or upon agreement in relation to the Gas Development having been reached (and whether or not such agreement is recorded in a fully termed production sharing and/or operating or other like agreement), but before such agreement is signed (the "Proposed Contract") (subject only to the rights of each CONTRACTOR Entity to pre-empt such Proposed Contract pursuant to Article 14.10(b) and such conditions as may be applicable), the GOVERNMENT shall, as soon as reasonably practicable after the occurrence of such circumstances, serve on each of the CONTRACTOR Entities, a notice to that effect and shall with such information and main terms of such agreement as the CONTRACTOR Entities may reasonably request to determine if they will exercise their rights (the "Agreed Terms"), including: (i) the identity of such third party; (ii) the effective date of the Proposed Contract; (iii) the applicable commercial terms, including bonuses, royalties, cost recovery, profit sharing, taxation and any other similar terms; and (iv) all and any material conditions to which the Proposed Contract is subject.

(b) Under a request from any CONTRACTOR Entity, the GOVERNMENT will provide all the CONTRACTOR Entities with such further information and terms as may be reasonably requested by any CONTRACTOR Entity. Within one hundred and eighty days (I80) days after receipt of a notice and any further information under Article 14.10(a) in relation to a Proposed Contract, each of the CONTRACTOR Entities shall elect either: (i) to enter into the Proposed Contract on the same or substantially similar terms to the Agreed Terms, with the right to cost recover all Petroleum Costs incurred under this Contract against all Petroleum revenues received under the Proposed Contract, up to any cost recovery limits set out therein; or (ii) to waive the aforesaid right of pre-emption in relation to the Proposed Contract; and shall serve notice accordingly upon the GOVERNMENT and all the CONTRACTOR Entities and in default of receipt by the GOVERNMENT of any such notice within such period of one hundred and eighty (180) days, such CONTRACTOR Entity shall be deemed conclusively to have served a notice electing to waive its aforesaid right of pre-emption in relation to the Proposed Contract.

(c) In the event that more than one of the CONTRACTOR Entities exercises its rights under Article 14.10(b)(i) in relation to the Proposed Contract, then the GOVERNMENT shall transfer or grant each such CONTRACTOR Entity an interest in the Proposed Contract upon the Agreed Terms in accordance with Article 14.10(b)(i) in the proportions in which their respective percentage interests bear to the aggregate of their respective percentage interests under the relevant Joint Operating Agreement (as it applied at the end of the Exploration Period) or in such other proportions as such CONTRACTOR Entities shall agree between them.

(d) In the event that one of the CONTRACTOR Entities exercises its rights under

Article 14.10(b)(i) in relation to the Proposed Contract, then the GOVERNMENT shall transfer or grant the whole of the interest in the Proposed Contract upon the Agreed Terms (in accordance with 14.10(b)(i) to such CONTRACTOR Entity.

(e) In the event that none of the CONTRACTOR Entitles exercises its rights under Article 14.10(b)(i), then the GOVERNMENT may enter into the Proposed Contract on terms no more favourable to its counter-party than the Agreed Terms and. in such case, the aforesaid rights of pre-emption shall thereupon cease to apply in relation to the Proposed Contract.

14.11 If the pre-emption rights in Article 14.10 are not exercised and the GOVERNMENT enters into the Proposed Contract with the third party concerned, the GOVERNMENT will use its best endeavours to avoid any effect which may hamper the Petroleum Operations of the CONTRACTOR while producing Petroleum.

FLARING

14.12 Flaring of Natural Gas in the course of activities provided for under this Contract is prohibited except (i) short-term flaring up to twelve (12) Months necessary for testing or other operational reasons in accordance with prudent international petroleum industry practice (which shall include the flaring of Associated Natural Gas to the extent the CONTRACTOR considers that re-injecting Associated Natural Gas is not justified technically and economically and provided the GOVERNMENT decides not to take such Associated Natural Gas), or (ii) with the prior authorization of the GOVERNMENT, such authorization not to be unreasonably withheld or delayed. The CONTRACTOR shall submit such request to the GOVERNMENT, which shall include an evaluation of reasonable alternatives to flaring that have been considered along with information on the amount and quality of Natural Gas involved and the duration of the requested flaring.

ARTICLE 15 – ACCOUNTING AND AUDITS

15.1 The CONTRACTOR shall keep in its offices in the Kurdistan Region copies of all books and accounts of all revenues relating to the Petroleum Operations and all Petroleum Costs (the "Accounts"), except during the Exploration Period, when the CONTRACTOR shall be entitled to keep the Accounts at its headquarters abroad. The Accounts shall reflect in detail expenditure incurred as a function of the quantities and value of Petroleum produced, and shall be kept for a period of five (5) years. All Accounts which are made available to the GOVERNMENT in accordance with the provisions of this Contract shall be prepared in the English language. The Accounts shall be kept in accordance with prudent international petroleum industry practice and in accordance with the provisions of the Accoutring Procedure. The Accounts shall be kept in Dollars, which shall be the reference currency for the purposes of this Contract.

15.2 Within ninety (90) days following the end of each Calendar Year, the CONTRACTOR shall submit to the GOVERNMENT a summary statement of all Petroleum Costs incurred during the said Calendar Year. The summary statement shall also include a profit calculation pursuant to the provisions of Article 26.

15.3 The GOVERNMENT shall have the right (a) to request an audit of the Accounts with respect to each Calendar Year within a period of two (2) Calendar Years following the end of such Calendar Year (the "Audit Request Period"), and (b) to retain an auditor of international standing familiar with international petroleum industry accounting practice to undertake or assist the GOVERNMENT to undertake the audit. Notwithstanding paragraphs (a) and (b) of this Article 15.3, the GOVERNMENT shall have the right to audit the Accounts with respect to each Calendar Year at any time in the case of manifest error or fraud.

15.4 The reasonable cost of retaining an auditor pursuant to Article 15.3 shall be borne by the CONTRACTOR and treated as a Petroleum Cost for the purpose of coat recovery under Articles 1 and 25.

15.5 During the Audit Request Period for any Calendar Year but not thereafter, the GOVERNMENT, acting reasonably and in accordance with prudent international petroleum industry practice, may request in writing all reasonably available information and justifications for its audit of Petroleum Costs.

15.6 Should the GOVERNMENT consider, on the basis of data and information available, that the CONTRACTOR made a material mistake or there is any irregularity in respect of the Account and considers that any corrections, adjustments or amendments should be made, the GOVERNMENT shall make any audit exceptions in writing and notify to the CONTRACTOR within six (6) Months of the date of request referred to in Article 15.3 and failure to give such written exception within ...

ARTICLE 16 – CONTRACTOR'S RIGHTS AND OBLIGATIONS

INFORMATION AND REPORTS

16.3 The CONTRACTOR shall provide the GOVERNMENT with periodic data and activity reports relating to Petroleum Operations. Said reports shall include details of the following: (a) information and data regarding all Exploration Operations, Development Operations and Production Operations (as applicable) performed during the Calendar Year, including any quantities of Petroleum produced and sold; (b) data and information regarding any transportation facilities built and operated by the CONTRACTOR; (c) a statement specifying the number of personnel, their title, their nationality as well as a report on any medical services and equipment made available to such personnel; and (d) a descriptive statement of all capital assets acquired for the Petroleum Operations, indicating the date and price or cost of their acquisition.

REQUIREMENT FOR PETROLEUM OPERATIONS

16.4 The CONTRACTOR may freely use any Petroleum produced within the Contract Area for the Petroleum Operations.

16.5 The CONTRACTOR shall at all times provide reasonable assistance as may reasonably be requested by the GOVERNMENT during its review and verification of records and of any other information relating to Petroleum Operations at the offices, worksites or any other facilities of the CONTRACTOR. Upon giving reasonable prior notice to the CONTRACTOR, the GOVERNMENT may send a reasonable number of representatives to the work-sites or any other facilities of the CONTRACTOR in the Kurdistan Region to perform such reviews and verifications. The representatives of the GOVERNMENT shall at all times comply with any safety regulations imposed by the CONTRACTOR and such reviews and verifications shall not hinder the smooth progress of the Petroleum Operations.

ACCESS TO FACILITIES

16.6 For the performance of the Petroleum Operations, the CONTRACTOR, any Affiliate of each CONTRACTOR Entity, its and their Subcontractors and the employees, consultants and agents of each of the foregoing shall at all times be granted free access to the Contract Area and to any facilities for the Petroleum Operations located within or outside of the Contract Area or within or outside the Production Area, for the purpose of carrying out the Petroleum Operations.

USE OF FACILITIES

16.7 Upon notice from the GOVERNMENT, the CONTRACTOR shall make available to a reasonable number of representatives of the GOVERNMENT those of the

CONTRACTOR's facilities which are necessary to enable such representatives to perform their tasks related to this Contract and the Kurdistan Region Oil and Gas Law including, in case of works to be performed on work sites, transportation, accommodation and board, under the same conditions as those provided by the CONTRACTOR for its own personnel. Notwithstanding Article 16.8, the GOVERNMENT shall indemnify and hold harmless each CONTRACTOR Entity against all losses, damages und liability arising under any claim, demand, action or proceeding brought or initiated against any CONTRACTOR Entity by any representative of the GOVERNMENT in connection with the access to or use of the facilities by such representatives.

LOSS OR DAMAGE

16.8 The CONTRACTOR shall be responsible for any loss or damage caused to third parties by its or its Subcontractors personnel solely and directly resulting from their negligence, errors or omissions in accordance with applicable Kurdistan Region Law.

INTELLECTUAL PROPERTY RIGHTS

16.9 In its Petroleum Operations, the CONTRACTOR shall respect any patents belonging to third parties.

LITIGATION

16.10 The CONTRACTOR shall as soon as reasonably practicable inform the GOVERNMENT of any material litigation relating to this Contract.

SAFETY

16.11 The CONTRACTOR shall implement a health, safety and environment program and take necessary measures to ensure hygiene, health and safety of its personnel carrying out Petroleum Operations in accordance with prudent international petroleum industry practice.

Said measures shall include the following:

(a) supplying first aid safety equipment for each work area and maintaining a healthy environment for personnel;

(b) reporting to the GOVERNMENT within seventy-two (72) hours of such accident, any accident where personnel has been injured while engaged in Petroleum Operations and resulting in such personnel being unable to return to work;

(c) implementing a permit-to-work procedure around hazardous equipment and installations;

(d) providing safe storage areas for explosives, detonators and any other dangerous products used in the operations;

(e) supplying fire-extinguishing equipment in each work area;

(f) for the purpose of taking control of any blow out or fire which could damage the environment of Petroleum Field, in accordance with prudent international petroleum industry practice; and

(g) for the purpose of preventing any involuntary injection of fluids in petroleum formations and production of Crude Oil and Natural Gas at rates that do not conform to prudent international petroleum industry practice.

PRODUCTING RATES

16.12 Subject to Article 43.2, in the event the production rate of the individual wells and Reservoir of a Petroleum Field is to be set below the Maximum Efficient Rate ("MER") for the Reservoir, as provided for in the Development Plan, as a consequence of a decision by the GOVERNMENT or any federal or international regulatory body, the GOVERNMENT undertakes to allocate any such reduction fairly and equitably among the various operators (including the GOVERNMENT) then producing in the Kurdistan Region, pro rata their respective production rates. In such event, the GOVERNMENT shall grant an extension of the Development Period of any Production Area so affected for reasonable period of time in order to produce the Petroleum which would otherwise have already been produced, had the MER for the individual wells and Reservoir of the Petroleum Field been maintained.

LEGAL STATUS

16.13 The respective rights, duties, obligations and liabilities of the CONTRACTOR and the GOVERNMENT under this Contract are to be understood as being separate and individual and not joint and several. The Parties agree that this Contract shall not create and shall not be deemed to have created a partnership or other form of association between them.

LIFTING

16.14 The GOVERNMENT and each CONTRACTOR Entity shall have the right and the obligation to take in kind and separately sell or otherwise dispose of their respective shares of Petroleum. Upon approval of the Development Plan, the Parties shall meet as soon as practicable to reach a detailed agreement governing the lifting of Petroleum by each such CONTRACTOR Entity. Such lilting agreement shall include the following: (a) the obligation of the GOVERNMENT and each CONTRACTOR Entity to lift, regularly throughout each Calendar Year, their share of Petroleum produced from the Production Area; (b) notification procedures by the Operator to the GOVERNMENT and each CONTRACTOR Entity regarding entitlements and availability of Petroleum for lifting by each Party during each lifting period and nominations by each Party; and (c) the right of the Parties to lift any Available Petroleum not scheduled for lifting and/or not lifted by the other Party during each such lifting period.

KURDISTAN REGION CONSUMPTION REQUIREMENTS

16.15 The CONTRACTOR Entities shall sell and transfer to the GOVERNMENT, upon written request of the GOVERNMENT, any amounts of Crude Oil that the GOVERNMENT shall deem necessary to meet Kurdistan Region internal consumption requirements. The sales price of such Crude Oil shall be the International Market Price. The GOVERNMENT shall provide the CONTRACTOR Entities with not less than six (6) Months' advance written notice of its intention to buy such Crude Oil. Payments shall be made in Dollars and otherwise on terms consistent with prudent international petroleum industry practice. The CONTRACTOR Entities' obligation to sell Crude Oil to the GOVERNMENT shall be, with the other operators (including the GOVERNMENT) then producing in the Kurdistan Region, pro rata to their respective production rates. The provisions of this Article 16.15 shall not apply to Non-Associated Natural Gas.

ARTICLE 17－USE OF LAND AND EXISTING INFRASTRUCTURE

17.1 The GOVERNMENT shall make available to the CONTRACTOR any land or property in the Kurdistan Region required for the Petroleum Operations, provided, however, the CONTRACTOR shall not request to use any such land unless there is a real need for it. The CONTRACTOR shall have the right to build and maintain, above and below ground, any facilities required for the Petroleum Operations.

17.2 If it becomes necessary for conduct of the Petroleum Operations to occupy and use any land or property in the Kurdistan Region belonging to third parties, the CONTRACTOR shall endeavour to reach amicable agreement with the owners of such land. If such amicable agreement cannot be reachcd, the CONTRACTOR shall notify the GOVERNMENT. On receipt of such notification: (a) the GOVERNMENT shall determine the amount of compensation to be paid by the CONTRACTOR to the owner, if occupation will be for a short duration; or (b) the GOVERNMENT shall expropriate the land or property in accordance with applicable Kurdistan Region Law, if such occupation will be long lasting or makes it henceforth impossible to resume original usage of such land or property. Any property rights shall be acquired by and recorded in the name of the GOVERNMENT, but the CONTRACTOR shall be entitled free use of the land or property for the Petroleum Operations for the entire duration of this Contract. The amount of the compensation in Article 17.2(a) shall be fair and reasonable in accordance with Article 29 of the Kurdistan Region Oil and Gas Law, and shall take into account the rights of the owner and any effective use of the land or property by its owner at the time of occupation by the CONTRACTOR. All reasonable costs, expenditures, and fair and reasonable compensation (as required pursuant to Article 29 of the Kurdistan Region Oil and Gas Law) which results from such expropriation shall be borne by the CONTRACTOR. For the avoidance of doubt, such costs, expenses and compensation incurred by the CONTRACTOR shall be considered Petroleum Costs and shall he recovered by the CONTRACTOR in accordance with the provisions of Articles 1 and 25.

17.3 For its Petroleum Operations, the CONTRACTOR shall have the right in the Kurdistan Region to use, subject to applicable Law, any railway, tramway, road, airport, landing field, canal, river, bridge or waterway, any telecommunications network and any existing pipelines or transportation infrastructure, on terms no less favourable than those offered to other entities and, unless generally in force, to be mutually agreed.

17.4 Under national emergencies due to environmental catastrophe or disaster, or internal or external war, the GOVERNMENT shall have the right to request to use any transportation and communication facilities installed by the CONTRACTOR. In such cases, the request shall originate from the Minister of Natural Resources. For the avoidance of doubt, such costs, expenses or liabilities incurred by the CONTRACTOR hereunder shall be considered Petroleum Costs and shall be recovered by the CONTRACTOR in accordance with the provisions of Articles 1 and 25.

17.5 For its Petroleum Operations, the CONTRACTOR shall have the right in the Kurdistan Region to clear land, excavate, drill, bore, construct, erect, place, procure, operate, emit and discharge, manage and maintain ditches, tanks, wells, trenches, access roads, excavations, dams, canals, water mains, plants, reservoirs, basins, storage and disposal facilities, primary distillation units, extraction and processing units, separation units, sulphur plants and any other facilities or installations for the Petroleum Operations, in addition to pipelines, pumping stations, generators, power plants, high voltage lines, telephone, radio and any other telecommunications systems, as well as warehouses, offices, sheds, houses for personnel, hospitals, school, premises, dikes, vehicles, railways, roads, bridges, airlines, airports and any other transportation facilities, garages, hangars, workshops, foundries, repair shops and any other auxiliary facilities for the Petroleum Operations and, generally, everything which is required for its performance of the Petroleum Operations. The CONTRACTOR shall have the right to select the location for these facilities.

17.6 For its Petroleum Operations, the CONTRACTOR shall have the right in the Kurdistan Region, subject to compliance with applicable Kurdistan Region Law, to remove and use the topsoil, fully-grown timber, clay, sand, lime, gypsum, stones (other than precious stones) and other similar substances as required for its Petroleum Operations. The CONTRACTOR shall have the right in the Kurdistan Region to take or use any water necessary for the Petroleum Operations provided it does not damage any existing irrigating or navigating systems and that land, houses or watering points belonging to third parties are not deprived of their use.

17.7 The GOVERNMENT shall have the right in the Kurdistan Region to build, operate and maintain roads, railways, airports, landing strips, canals, bridges, protection dams, police stations, military installations, pipelines and telecommunications networks in the Contract Area, provided this does not increase the costs, or compromise or have a material adverse effect on the performance of the Petroleum Operations. If the construction, operation and maintenance of such facilities by the GOVERNMENT results in increased cost or expense for the CONTRACTOR then, for the avoidance of doubt, such cost and expense shall be considered Petroleum Costs and shall be recovered by the CONTRACTOR in accordance with the provisions of Articles 1 and 25.

17.8 Upon request of the CONTRACTOR, the GOVERNMENT shall prohibit the construction of residential or commercial buildings in the vicinity of facilities used for the Petroleum Operations that may be declared dangerous due to the Petroleum Operations and to prohibit any interference with the use of any facilities required for the Petroleum Operations.

17.9 Access to the Contract Area may be granted pursuant to an Access Authorisation, as shall be defined in, and consistent with, the Region Oil and Gas Law, to authorised third parties on reasonable terms and conditions (including coordination), including Persons authorised to construct, install and operate structures, facilities and installations, and to carry out other works, provided that nothing in the Access Authorisation or in this Article 17.9 authorises the holder to drill a Well or to perform any Petroleum Operations in Contract Area. The GOVERNMENT shall give the CONTRACTOR adequate advance notice of any Access Authorisation in respect of the Contract Area and shall not grant any Access Authorisation in respect of the Contract Area until it has taken into account any submissions made by the CONTRACTOR nor in such a way that there is undue interference with or hindrance of the rights and activities of the CONTRACTOR.

ARTICLE 18 – ASSISTANCE FROM THE GOVERNMENT

18.1 To the extent allowed by Kurdistan Region Law and Iraqi Law and at the specific request of the CONTRACTOR, the GOVERNMENT shall take all necessary steps to assist the CONTRACTOR Entities in, but not limited to, the following areas;

(a) securing any necessary Permits for the use and installation of means of transportation and communications;
(b) securing regulatory Permits in matters of customs or import/expert;
(c) securing entry and exit visas, work and residence permits as well as any other administrative Permits for each CONTRACTOR Entity's, its Affiliates' and its Subcontractors' foreign personnel (including their family members) working in the Kurdistan Region and any other part of Iraq during the implementation of this Contract;
(d) securing any necessary Permits to send abroad documents, data or samples for analysis or processing for the petroleum Operations;
(e) relations with federal and local authorities and administrations, including for the purposes of the remainder of this Article 18.1;
(f) securing any necessary environmental Permits;
(g) obtaining any other Permits requested by any CONTRACTOR Entity for the Petroleum Operations;
(h) access to any existing data and information, including data and information relating to the Contract Area held by previous operators or contractors; and
(i) providing all necessary security for Petroleum Operations.

18.2 Within the scope of services to be provided under this Article 18, reasonable and duly justified expenses incurred by the GOVERNMENT or paid to third parties shall be charged to the CONTRACTOR and shall be considered Petroleum Costs and shall be recovered by tte CONTRACTOR as Petroleum Costs in accordance with the provisions of Articles 1 and 25.

ARTICLE 19 – EQUIPMENT AND MATERIALS

19.1 The CONTRACTOR shall supply, or procure the supply of, all materials, equipment, machinery, tools, spare parts and any other items or goods required for the Petroleum Operations ("Equipment and Materials").

19.2 Said Equipment and Materials shall be provided by the CONTRACTOR in accordance with the relevant Work Programs and Budgets.

19.3 As soon as possible after the Effective Date, the CONTRACTOR shall provide the Management Committee with a copy of its procedures for procurement of Equipment and Materials and/or services for the Petroleum Operations as required by the provisions of Article 8.2(c), including the criteria for tender evaluation, which procedures and criteria shall be in accordance with prudent international petroleum industry practice. If the Management Committee does not request any modifications to the procurement procedures within thirty (30) days after receiving such procedures, the procedures shall be deemed approved by the Management Committee.

19.4 The CONTRACTOR shall give priority to Equipment and Materials that are readily available in the Kurdistan Region and other parts of Iraq to the extent their price, grade, quality, quantity, specifications, purchase, delivery and other commercial and technical terms are comparable in all material respects with those generally available in the international petroleum industry.

ARTICLE 20 – TITLE TO ASSETS

20.1 During the Exploration Period, any Assets acquired by the CONTRACTOR for the Petroleum Operations shall remain the property of the CONTRACTOR, the CONTRACTOR Entities, their Affiliates or their Subcontractors, as the case may be.

20.2 During the Development Period, subject to Article 21, all Assets acquired by the CONTRACTOR for the Petroleum Operations shall become the property of the GOVERNMENT, upon the completion of the recovery of the costs, of all such as assets by the CONTRACTOR, or the end of the Contract, whichever is the earlier.

20.3 The provisions of Article 20.2 shall not apply to any Assets leased by the CONTRACTOR or belonging to an Affiliated Company of a CONTRACTOR Entity or belonging to its or their Subcontractors or its or their employees.

ARTICLE 21 – USE OF THE ASSETS

21.1 Each CONTRACTOR Entity shall have the exclusive right to use, free of any charge, all Assets described in Article 20, both before and after recovery of the cost of the same, for the Petroleum Operations, as well as for any petroleum operations under other agreements in the Kurdistan Region to which it or any of its Affiliates is a party, provided that the Petroleum Operations take priority. The GOVERNMENT agrees not to transfer or otherwise dispose of any of such Assets without the CONTRACTOR's prior written approval.

21.2 The CONTRACTOR may freely move to the Contract Area any Assets from any relinquished portion of the Contract Area, or from any other area in the Kurdistan Region.

ARTICLE 22 – SUBCONTRACTING

22.1 The CONTRACTOR shall ensure that any Subcontractors it engages have all the requisite experience and qualifications.

22.2 The CONTRACTOR shall give priority to Subcontractors from the Kurdistan Region and other parts of Iraq to the extent their competence, rates, experience, reputation, qualifications, specialties, credit rating and terms of availability, delivery and other commercial terms are, in the CONTRACTOR's sole opinion, comparable in all material respects with those provided by foreign companies operating in the international petroleum industry. Such Subcontractors must be bona fide Kurdistan Region companies not related to any Public Officer, directly or indirectly, and must have all necessary resources and capacity.

22.3 Selection of Subcontractors shall take place in accordance with the procurement procedures submitted by the CONTRACTOR in the Management Committer in accordance with Article 19.3 and approved by the Management Committee.

22.4 The CONTRACTOR shall provide the GOVERNMENT with copies of agreements entered into with Subcontractors, where their amount exceeds the limit set by the Management Committee from time to time.

ARTICLE 23 – PERSONNEL, TRAINING. AND TECHNOLOGICAL ASSISTANCE

PERSONNEL

23.1 For the Petroleum Operations, the CONTRACTOR shall give, and shall require its Subcontractors to give, preference to personnel from the Kurdistan Region and other parts of Iraq to the extent such personnel have the technical capability, qualifications, competence and experience required to perform the work.

23.2 The CONTRACTOR Entities shall give due consideration to the secondment of GOVERNMENT personnel to the CONTRACTOR Entities and of the CONTRACTOR. Entities' personnel to the GOVERNMENT during the various phases of the Petroleum Operations. Terms and conditions for such secondment shall be mutually agreed by the Parties and any costs associated therewith shall he considered Petroleum Costs and shall be recovered by the CONTRACTOR in accordance with the provisions of Articles 1 and 15.

23.3 Each CONTRACTOR Entity and its Affiliates and Subcontractors shall have the right to hire foreign personnel whenever the personnel from the Kurdistan Region and other parts of Iraq do not have the requisite technical capability, qualifications or experience for positions to be filled as required pursuant to Article 23.1. In the event any such foreign personnel and/or a member of their family engage in activities or commit acts which breach Kurdistan Region Law, the CONTRACTOR shall, at the request of the Management Committee, take the necessary steps to repatriate such individual(s).

23.4 For the first five(5) Contract Years, the CONTRACTOR shall provide two hundred and fifty thousand Dollars (US$250,000) in advance each Contract Year to the GOVERNMENT for the recruitment or secondment of personnel, whether from the Kurdistan Region, other parts of Iraq or Abroad, to the Ministry of Natural Resources. The selection of such personnel shall be at the discretion of the Minister of Natural Resources. Such costs shall he considered as Petroleum Costs and shall be recovered in accordance with the provisions of Articles 1 and 25.

TRAINING

23.5 In a planned way, in accordance with the provisions of this Article 23.5 and Articles 23.6 and 23.7, the CONTRACTOR shall train all its personnel from the Kurdistan Region and other parts of Iraq directly or indirectly involved in the Petroleum Operations for the purpose of improving their knowledge and professional qualifications in order that such personnel gradually reach the level of knowledge and professional qualification held by the CONTRACTOR Entities' foriegn workers with an equivalent résumé. Such training shall also include the transfer of knowledge of petroleum technology and the necessary management experience so as to enable the personnel from the Kurdistan Region and other parts of Iraq to apply advanced and appropriate technology in the Petroleum Operations, to the extent permitted by applicable Law and agreements with third parties, and subject to appropriate confidentiality agreements.

23.6 In addition to the requirements of Article 23.1, the recruitment, integration and training of the CONTRACTOR Entities' personnel from the Kurdistan Region and other parts of Iraq shall be planned, which plans shall be submitted to the Management Committee for its approval. The training plan shall take into consideration the requirements of Article 23.5 and may include training for the GOVERNMENT's personnel, depending on the extent to which the amount allocated to the training plan, as prescribed by Article 23.7 is available after taking into consideration the training of the CONTRACTOR Entities' Kurdisun Region and other lraqi personnel. Within ninety (90) days of the Effective Date, the CONTRACTOR shall submit to the Management Committee a proposed training plan for the remainder of the Calendar Year. Thereafter, no later than 1 October in each Calendar Year, the CONTRACTOR shall submit a proposed training plan to the Management Committee for the following Calendar Year.

23.7 The training plan referred to in Article 23.6 shall provide the the allocation to the GOVERNMENT of the amount of one hundred and fifty thousand Dollars (US$150,000) in advance for each Contract Year during the Exploration Period and three hundred thousand Dollors (US$300,000) in advance for each Contract Year during the Development Period.

23.8 Each CONTRACTOR Entity shall be responsible for the training coats which it may incur in respect of the personnel it employs from the Kurdistan Region and other parts of Iraq. All such reasonable costs shall be considered as Petroleum Costs and shall be recovered in accordance with the provisions of Articles 1 and 25. Costs incurred by the CONTRACTOR for training programs for the GOVERNMENT's personnel shall be borne by the CONTRACTOR only to the extent that they are included in the CONTRACTOR's training plan, pursuant to Article 23.6 and shall also be considered as Petroleum Costs and shall be recovered in accordance with the provisions of Articles 1 and 25. The cost of all other training programs for the GOVERNMENT's personnel shall be the GOVERNMENT's responsibility.

THE ENVIRONMENT FUND

23.9 The CONTRACTOR shall contribute the amount of one hundred and fifty Dollars (US$150,000) in advance each Contract Year during the Exploration Period and three hundred thousand Dollars (US$300,000) in advance for each Contract Year during the Development Period into the environment fund established by the GOVERNMENT for the benefit of the natural environment of the Kurdistan Region, pursuant to the Kurdistan Region Oil and Gas Law (the "Environment Fund") Such amounts shall be deemed to be Petroleum Costs and shall be recovered in accordance with Article 1 and 25.

23.10 Any expenditure incurred by the CONTRACTOR under this Article 23 shall be considered Petroleum Costs and shall be recovered in accordance with Articles 1 and 25.

TECHNOLOGICAL AND LOGISTICAL ASSISTANCE

21.11 Before the end of the first Control Year, the CONTRACTOR shall provide to the GOVERNMENT technological and logistical assistance to the Kurdistan Region petroleum sector, including geological computing hardware and software and such other equipment as the Minister of Natural Resources may require, up to the value of two million Dollars (US$2,000,000). The form of such assistants shall be mutually agreed by the Parties and any costs associated therewith shall be considered Petroleum Costs and shall be recovered by the CONTRACTOR in accordance with the provisions of Articles 1 and 25.

ARTICLE 24 – ROYALTY

24.1 The CONTRACTOR shall pay to the GOVERNMENT a portion of Petroleum produced and saved from the Contract Area, as provided in this Article 24 (the "Royalty").

24.2 The Royalty shall be applied on all Petroleum produced and saved from the Contract Area which is Crude Oil or Non-Associated Natural Gas, except for Petroleum used in Petroleum Operations, re-injected in a Petroleum Field, lost, flared or for Petroleum that cannot be used or sold and such Crude Oil and Non-Associated Natural Gas (excluding the excepted Petroleum) shall be referred to collectively as "Export Petroleum" and separately and respectively as "Export Crude Oil" and "Export Non-Associated Natural Gas".

24.3 If payable in each the amount of the Royalty calculated by applying the Royalty rates provided under Article 24.4 shall be paid by the CONTRACTOR as directed by the GOVERNMENT, in accordance with Article 24.7. If payable in kind, the quantity of Export Petroleum corresponding to the Royally and calculated by applying the Royalty rates provided under Article 24.4 shall be delivered in kind by the CONTRACTOR to the GOVERNMENT at the Delivery Point. Title and risk of loss of the Royalty paid in kind shall be transferred at the Delivery Point. Unless the GOVERNMENT requires the Royalty to be paid in kind, by giving the CONTRACTOR not less than ninety (90) days prior written notice prior to the commencement of the relevant Quarter, the GOVERNMENT shall be deemed to have elected to receive the Royalty in full and in cash for the relevant Quarter.

24.4 The Royalty due on any Export Petroleum produced and saved in the Contract Area shall be determined daily by applying the following relevant Royalty rate, to the Export Crude Oil or to the Export Non-Associated Natural Gas (as the case may be) produced and saved on that day.

(a) For Export Crude Oil:
the Royalty rate for Export Crude Oil shall be ten percent (10%), which, for the avoidance of doubt, shall apply regardless of the gravity of the oil, and

(b) For Export Non-Associated Natural Gas:
the Royalty rate for Export Non-Associated Natural Gas shall be ten percent (10%).

24.5 Associated Natural Gas and any other Petroleum shall be exempt from any Royalty.

24.6 If, pursuant to Article 24.3, the GOVERNMENT receives the Royalty in kind, and pursuant to Article 28, the GOVERNMENT requests assistance for the sale of all or part of the Royalty received in kind, each CONTRACTOR Entity shall assist the GOVERNMENT in selling all or part of such Royalty received in kind (belonging to the GOVERNMENT) in consideration of a commission payable to such CONTRACTOR Entity, in accordance with Article 28.

24.7 If, pursuant to Article 24.3, the GOVERNMENT receives the Royalty in cash, (a) any Export Crude Oil shall be valued at the International Market Price obtained at the Delivery Point, as defined in Article 27.2; (b) any Export Non-Associated Natural Gas shall be valued at the actual price obtained at the Delivery Point under and approved contract, as provided in Article 27.3; (c) the CONTRACTOR shall pay such Royalty each Quarter, in arrears, within thirty (30) days of the end of each Quarter, and shall calculate the payment due for the relevant Quartet by reference to the price for the Export Petroleum at the Delivery Point, determined in accordance with paragraphs (a) and (b) above, and the Royalty due on the Export Petroleum, determined in accordance with Article 24.4, for the said Quarter; and (d) the CONTRACTOR Entities shall be entitled to export freely the volume of Export Petroleum corresponding to the Royally determined in accordance with Article 24.4 for the purpose of paying the Royally in cash.

ARTICLE 25 – RECOVERY OF PETROLEUM COSTS

25.1 All Expert Crude Oil produced and saved from the Contract Area shall, after deduction of any quantities of Export Crude Oil due for Royalty pursuant to Article 24, be considered as "Available Crude Oil". All Associated Natural Gas produced and saved from the Contract Area, except for Associated Natural Gas which is used in Petroleum Operations, re-injected in a Petroleum Field, lost, flared or cannot be used or sold, shall be considered as "Available Associated Natural Gas". All Export Non-Associated Natural Gas produced and saved from the Contract Area shall, after deduction of any quantities of Export Non-Associated Natural Gas due for Royalty pursuant to Article 24, be considered as "Available Non-Associated Natural Gas". "Available Petroleum" means Available Crude Oil, Available Associated Natural Gas and Available Non-Associated Natural Gas.

25.2 For the purpose of this Article 25,
(a) any Available Crude Oil shall be valued at the International Market Price obtained at the Delivery Point, as defined in Article 27.2, and (b) any Available Associated Natural Gas and any Available Non-Associated Natural Gas shall be valued at the actual price obtained at the Delivery Point under an approved contract, as provided in Article 27.3.

25.3 Subject to the provisions of this Contract, from the First Production in the Contract Area, the CONTRACTOR shall at all times be entitled to recover all Petroleum Costs incurred under this Contract, of up to forty per cent (40%) of Available Crude Oil (which, for the avoidance of doubt, shall apply regardless of the gravity of the oil) and Available Associated Natural Gas, produced and saved within any Calendar Year. Available Crude Oil above this percentage or otherwise not used for the recovery of Petroleum Costs shall be Profit Crude Oil.

25.4 Subject to the provisions of this Contract, from First Production in the Contract Area, the CONTRACTOR shall at all times be entitled to recover all Petroleum Costs incurred under this Contract of up to fifty per cent (50%) of Available Non-Associated Natural Gas produced and saved within any Calendar Year. Available Non-Associated Natural Gas above this percentage or otherwise not used for the recovery of Petroleum Costs shall be Profit Natural Gas.

25.5 For the application of Article 25.3 and 25.4, the CONTRACTOR shall keep a detailed account of Petroleum Costs in accordance with the provisions detailed in the Accounting Procedure. Recovery of Petroleum Costs shall occur in the following order: (a) Production Costs; (b) Exploration Costs (including appraisal costs and further exploration within the Contract Area); (C) Gas Marketing Costs; (d) Development Costs; and (e) Decommissioning Costs.

25.6 Total recovery of Petroleum Costs during any Calendar Year, expressed in quantities of Petroleum, shall not exceed the relevant percentages indicated in Articles 25.3 and 25.4. If in any Calendar Year, the Available Crude Oil and/or Available Non-Associated Natural Gas do not allow the CONTRACTOR to recover all its Petroleum Costs pursuant to this Article 25, the amount of un-recovered Petroleum Costs in such

Calendar Year shall be carried forward indefinitely to the subsequent Calendar Years until all Petroleum Costs are fully recovered, but, save as provided in Articles 14.10 and 38.4, in no other case after the termination of the Contract.

25.7 The provisions of Articles 27.5 and 27.6 shall be applied to determine the quantities of Available Crude Oil and/or Available Non-Associated Natural Gas due to the CONTRACTOR for the recovery of its Petroleum Costs.

25.8 The quantities of Petroleum corresponding to the share of Available Petroleum due to the CONTRACTOR for the recovery of its Petroleum Costs shall be delivered to the CONTRACTOR at the Delivery Point. Title and risk of loss of such Available Petroleum shall be transferred at the Delivery Point.

25.9 Each CONTRACT Entity shall be entitled to receive, take in kind and to export freely all Available Petroleum to which it is entitled for recovery of its Petroleum Costs in accordance with the provisions of this Contract and to retain Abroad any proceeds from the sale of all such Available Petroleum. Petroleum Costs in each Production Area shall be recovered from Available Petroleum from the Contract Area.

25.10 Subject to Article 38.4, for the avoidance of doubt, Petroleum Costs under this Contract are not recoverable against other contract areas held by the CONTRACTOR.

ARTICLE 26 – SHARING OF PROFIT PETROLEUM

26.1 Under this Contract, (a) '"Profit Petroleum" means Profit Crude Oil and Profit Natural Gas; (b) "Profit Crude Oil" means the quantities of Available Crude Oil and Available Associated Natural Gas produced from the Contract Area, after the recovery of Petroleum Costs, in accordance with Articles 1 and 25; and (c) "Profit Natural Gas" means the quantities of Available Non-Associated Natural Gas produced from the Contract Area, after the recovery of Petroleum Costs in accordance with Articles 1 and 25.

26.2 From first Production and as and when Petroleum is being produced, the CONTRACTOR shall be entitled to take a percentage share of Profit Crude Oil and/or Profit Natural Gas, in consideration for its investment in the Petroleum Operations, which percentage share shall be determined in accordance with Article 26.5.

26.3 To determine the percentage share of Profit Crude Oil and/or Profit Natural Gas to which the CONTRACTOR is entitled, the "R" factor shall be calculated in accordance with Article 26.4 and shall be applied to the Contract Area.

26.4 The "R" factor shall be calculated as follows:

$R = X/Y$

where:

X: is equal to Cumulative Revenues actually received by the CONTRACTOR.

Y: is equal to Cumulative Costs actually incurred by the CONTRACTOR.

For the purpose of this Article 26.4, "Cumulative Revenues" means total Revenues, as defined below, received by the CONTRACTOR until the end of the relevant Semester, determined in accordance with Article 26.7. "Revenues" means the total amount actually received by the CONTRACTOR for recovery of its Petroleum Costs and its share of Profit Petroleum in the Contract Area. "Cumulative Costs" means all Petroleum Costs actually incurred pursuant to this Contract by the CONTRACTOR until the end of the relevant Semester, determined in accordance with Article 26.7. Notwithstanding the foregoing provisions of this Article 26.4, for the period from First Production until the end of the Calendar Year in which First Production occurs, the "R" Factor shall be deemed to less than one (1).

26.5 The share of Profit Petroleum to which the CONTRACTOR shall be entitled from First Production is:

(a) for Profit Crude Oil, equal to the quantities of Petroleum resulting from the application of the relevant percentage as indicated below to the daily volume of production of Profit Crude Oil within the Contract Area at the corresponding Delivery Point.

"R" Factor	CONTRACTOR's % Share of Profit Crude Oil
R < or=1	30%
1 < R < or=2	30% − (30% − 15%) × (R − 1)
R > 2	15%

and

(b) for Profit Natural Gas, equal to the quantities of Non-Associated Natural Gas resulting from the application of the relevant percentage as indicated below to the daily volume of production of Profit Natural Gas within the Contract Area at the corresponding Delivery Point.

"R" Factor	CONTRACTOR's % Share of Profit Natural Gas
R < or=1	40%
1 < R < or=2	40% − (40% − 35%) × (R − 1)
R > 2	20%

26.6 The CONTRACTOR's accounting shall account separately for all components for the calculation of "X" and "Y" values in the formula provided in Article 26.4.

26.7 For each Semester, starting from the 1st of January of the Calendar Year following the Calendar Year in which first Production occurs, the CONTRACTOR shall calculate the "R" Factor applicable to the relevant Semester within thirty (30) days of the beginning of such Semester. The "R" Factor to be applied during a Semester shall be that determined by applying the Cumulative Revenues actually received and the Cumulative Costs actually incurred up to and including the last day of the preceding Semester. If the CONTRACTOR is unable to calculate the "R" Factor for the relevant Semester before an allocation of Profit Petroleum for such Semester must be made, then the allocation of Profit Petroleum for the previous Semester shall be used for the relevant Semester. Upon the calculation of the "R" Factor for the relevant Semester,

(a) if the allocation of Profit Petroleum in the previous Semester and the relevant Semester is the same, then no adjustment shall be made, and

(b) if the allocation of the Profit Petroleum in the two Semesters is different, then the CONTRACTOR shall make any adjustments to the Parties' respective shares of Profit Petroleum to restore them to the position that they would have been in had the "R" Factor for the relevant Semester been available from the start of such Semester.

26.8 If at any time an error occurs in the calculation of the "R" Factor, resulting in a change in the CONTRACTOR's percentage share of Profit Crude Oil and/or Profit Natural Gas, the necessary correction shall be made and any adjustments shall apply from the Semester in which the error occurred. The Party having benefited from a surplus of Profit Petroleum shall surrender such surplus to the other Party, beginning from the first day of the Semester following the Semester in which the error was recognised. However, each lifting of Petroleum relating to such error by the Party receiving the surplus shall not exceed twenty-five percent (25%) of the share of Profit Petroleum to which such surrendering Party is entitled. For the avoidance of doubt, if at any time an error occurs in the calculation of the “R” Factor, which does not result in a change in the CONTRACTOR'S percentage share of Profit Crude Oil and or Profit Natural Gas, no correction shall be made.

26.9 The quantities of Profit Petroleum due to the CONTRACTOR shall be delivered to the CONTRACTOR Entities at the Delivery Point. Title and risk of loss of such Profit Petroleum shall be transferred to the CONTRACTOR Entities at the Delivery Point. Each CONTRACTOR Entity shall be entitled to receive, take in kind and to export freely its share of Profit Petroleum in accordance with the provisions of this Contract and to retain Abroad any proceeds from the sale of all such Profit Petroleum.

26.10 The share of the Profit Petroleum to which the GOVERNMENT is entitled in any Calendar Year in accordance with Article 26.5 shall be deemed to include a portion representing the corporate income tax imposed upon and due by each CONTRACTOR Entity, and which will be paid directly by the GOVERNMENT on behalf of each such entity representing the CONTRACTOR to the appropriate tax authorities in accordance with Article 31.2. The GOVERNMENT shall provide the CONTRACTOR Entities with all written documentation and evidence reasonably required by the CONTRACTOR Entities to confirm that such corporate income tax has been paid by the GOVERNMENT.

26.11 The quantities of Profit Petroleum due to the GOVERNMENT shall be delivered to the GOVERNMENT at the Delivery Point. Title and risk of loss of such Profit Petroleum shall be transferred at the Delivery Point.

26.12 At least twenty-one (21) days prior to CONTRACTOR's estimated date of First Production and, subsequently, thirty (30) days prior to the beginning of each Semester, the CONTRACTOR shall prepare and deliver to the GOVERNMENT a production program comprising the production forecast for the next Semester and the forecast of the quantities of Crude Oil and Natural Gas to which each Party shall be entitled during the said Semester.

26.13 Within ninety (90) days following the end of each Calendar Year, the CONTRACTOR shall prepare and deliver an annual production report to the GOVERNMEMT, stating the quantities of Crude Oil and Natural Gas to which each Party is entitled, the quantities of Crude Oil and Natural Gas lifted by each Party and the resulting over-lift or under-lift position of each Party, pursuant to the lifting agreement entered into pursuant to Article 16.14.

26.14 Any costs or expenditure incurred by the CONTRACTOR, its Subcontractors or suppliers, relating to the lifting of the GOVERNMENT's share of Petroleum by the CONTRACTOR shall not be considered Petroleum Costs, and shall be charged to the GOVERNMENT according to terms to be mutually agreed between the CONTRACTOR and the GOVERNMENT.

ARTICLE 27 – VALUATION AND METERING OF CRUDE OIL AND NATURAL GAS

VALUATION

27.1 For the purpose of this Contract, any Crude Oil produced in the Contract Area shall be valued at the end of each Quarter at the Delivery Point based on the International Market Price, as defined in Article 27.2.

27.2 The “International Marker Price” referred to in Article 27.1 shall be the weighted average price per Barrel, expressed in Dollars, obtained by the CONTRACTOR at the Delivery Point, by ..., if necessary, during the Quarter ending on the date of valuation for Arm's Length Sales of Crude Oil. The CONTRACTOR shall provide evidence to the GOVERNMENT that the sales of Crude Oil referred to in Article 27.2 are

Arm's Length Sales. If the GOVERNMENT considers that any such sale of Crude Oil is not on the basis of an Arm's Length Sale, then the GOVERNMENT has the right to refer the matter to an expert pursuant to Article 42.2. In the event that there is no lifting of Crude Oil in the relevant Quarter or no Arm's Length Sales, the applicable "International Market Price" for such Quarter shall be the weighted average price per Barrel obtained during that Quarter from Arm's Length Sales of Crude Oil of the same or similar gravity and quality from other production areas sold in markets competing with Crude Oil produced from the Contract Area, taking into account gravity and quality differences and transportation and other post Delivery Point costs. To determine such price, the Parties shall, prior to the commencement of Production, agree on a basket of Crude Oil comparable to those produced in the Contract Area and sold in the international market. Prices obtained shall be adjusted to account for any variations such as quality, specific gravity, sulphur content, transportation costs, product yield, seasonal variations in price and demand, general market trends and other terms of sale.

27.3 The price of Natural Gas shall be the actual price obtained at the Delivery Point, (which may take into account quantities to be sold, quality, geographic location of markets to be supplied as well as costs of production, transportation and distribution of Natural Gas from the Delivery Point to the relevant market, in accordance with standard international petroleum industry practice). The GOVERNMENT shall have the right to review and approve Natural Gas sales contracts.

ACCOUNTING STATEMENT

27.4 In accordance with the Article 27.4, the GOVERNMENT and the CONTRACTOR shall establish a statement showing calculations of the value of Petroleum produced and sold from the Contract Area. Such statement shall include following information: (a) quantities of Crude Oil sold by the CONTRACTOR Entities during the preceding Month constituting Arm's Length Sales together with corresponding sale prices; (b) quantities of Crude Oil sold by the CONTRACTOR Entities during the preceding Month that do not fall in the category referred to in paragraph (a) above, together with sale prices applied during such Month; (c) inventory in storage belonging to the CONTRACTOR Entities at the beginning and at the end of the Month; and (d) quantities of Natural Gas sold by the CONTRACTOR Entities and the GOVERNMENT together with sale prices realised.

27.5 All Export Petroleum shall be metered at the Delivery Point in accordance with prudent international petroleum industry practice and such meters shall be to fiscal meter standards. All metering equipment shall be installed and operated by the CONTRACTOR. The GOVERNMENT shall, upon receipt by the CONTRACTOR of reasonable prior written notice, have the right to inspect any such metering equipment installed by the CONTRACTOR, as well as all relevant documents and supporting information reasonably necessary to validate the accuracy of such metering. All metering equipment shall be subject to periodic technical inspections in accordance with prudent international petroleum industry practice.

27.6 If any metering equipment is defective, the CONTRACTOR shall use all reasonable endeavours to repair it within fifteen (15) days or, if deemed necessary by the CONTRACTOR, replace it as soon as reasonably practicable from the date the defect became known. The "Adjustment Date" shall be the last date that the metering equipment was known or agreed to have been measuring correctly, or if not known or agreed, the date that is midway between the date the defect was discovered and the last date the equipment was known to have measured correctly. The results from the defective equipment shall be disregarded for the period from the Adjustment Date until the date the defective equipment is repaired or replaced and the measurement for such period shall be estimated (a) if check measuring equipment is installed and registering accurately, then by using the measurements recorded by such check measuring equipment, (b) if check measuring equipment is not installed or not registering accurately, then by correcting the error if the percentage of error is ascertainable by verification, calibration or mathematical calculation, or (c) if neither method is feasible, then by estimating the volume and/or quantity delivered based on deliveries during the preceding comparable period of time when the metering equipment was registered accurately.

27.7 Any disputes arising under this Article shall be settled by expert determination in accordance with the provisions of Article 42.2.

ARTICLE 28 – SALE OF GOVERNMENT SHARE

Upon the GOVERNMENT's prior written notice of at least ninety (90) days, each CONTRACTOR Entity shall provide all reasonably necessary assistance to the GOVERNMENT for the sale of all or part of the quantities of Crude Oil to which the GOVERNMENT is entitled, in consideration of a sales commission per Barrel to be established with reference to prudent international petroleum practice and to be mutually agreed upon between the Parties.

ARTICLE 29 – FINANCIAL PROVISIONS

29.1 Any payment to be made by a CONTRACTOR Entity to the GOVERNMENT pursuant to this Contract shall be in Dollars and shall be offset against any outstanding payments due by the GOVERNMENT to the CONTRACTOR Entity, or paid into the bank account duly designated by the GOVERNMENT in writing and shall be paid within thirty (30) days of the due date, after which interest compounded monthly at the rate of LIBOR plus two (2) percentage points shall be applied.

29.2 The GOVERNMENT may, at its sole discretion, direct the CONTRACTOR Entities to pay: (a) any Royalty in cash due to the GOVERNMENT pursuant to the provisions of Article 24; and/or (b) any proceeds from the sale undertaken by the CONTRACTOR Entity on behalf of the GOVERNMENT pursuant to Article 28 of any Crude Oil to which the GOVERNMENT is entitled pursuant to Article 25; and/or (c) any Production Bonus, to a fund for revenue sharing, which may in due course be established by legislation consistent with the Constitution of Iraq, between the Government of Iraq and other regions (including the Kurdistan Region) and governorates of Iraq. Nothing in this Article 29.2 shall be understood of implying any contractual relationship or other relationship between the CONTRACTOR and/or any CONTRACTOR Entity and the Government of Iraq and/or the regions of Iraq (other than the Kurdistan Region) and/or and governorates of Iraq.

29.3 Any payment due by the GOVERNMENT to a CONTRACTOR Entity shall be offset against future payments due by such CONTRACTOR Entity to the GOVERNMENT or paid in Dollars to the bank account designated by the CONTACTOR Entity in writing and shall be paid within thirty (30) days of the date of invoice, after which interest compounded monthly at the rate of LIBOR plus two (2) percentage points shall be applied.

29.4 Any currency conversion to be made under this Contract shall be at the exchange rate of the Central Bank of Iraq, provided such exchange rate applied to the CONTRACTOR Entities shall not be less favourable than the rate offered by other private, commercial or industrial banks in the international market. In the absence of the Central Bank of Iraq or in the event that the Central Bank of Iraq is unable to provide the relevant exchange rate, any currency conversion to be made under this Contract shall be at the exchange rate of a reputable commercial bank carrying on business in the international market and approved by the Parties.

29.5 The CONTRACTOR shall not realise any gain or loss due to exchange rate fluctuations and, consequently, any gain or loss resulting from the exchange of currency shall be either considered as revenue and credited to the Accounts or shall be considered as a Petroleum Cost and shall be recovered by the CONTRACTOR in accordance with Articles 1 and 25, as the case may be.

29.6 Each CONTRACTOR Entity shall at all times be entitled to freely convert into Dollars or any other foreign currency any Iraqi dinars received in the framework of the Petroleum Operations and to freely transfer the same Abroad. The conversion rate shall be as provided under Article 29.4.

29.7 Each CONTRACTOR Entity shall have the right to be paid, receive, keep, transfer and use Abroad, without any restrictions, all proceeds of its share of Petroleum.

29.8 Each CONTRACTOR Entity and its Subcontractors shall have the right to freely open and maintain bank accounts for Petroleum Operations within or outside the Kurdistan Region and other parts of Iraq.

29.9 Each CONTRACTOR Entity shall have the right to pay in any freely convertible currency all its financial requirements for the Petroleum Operations and to convert these currencies to Iraqi dinars in any bank in the Kurdistan Region or other parts of Iraq, at the same exchange rate as provided under Article 29.4.

29.10 Each CONTRACTOR Entity shall have the right, without any restrictions, to freely repatriate Abroad and to freely dispose of (a) any proceeds received in the Kurdistan Region or other parts of Iraq from the sale of Petroleum, and (b) any proceeds received from other operations and activities carried out under this Contract in the Kurdistan Region or other parts of Iraq.

29.11 Each CONTRACTOR Entity shall have the right to pay in any foreign currency its Subcontractors and its expatriate personnel, either in the Kurdistan Region, other parts of Iraq, or Abroad. Said Subcontractors and expatriate personnel shall be obliged to transfer to the Kurdistan Region the amount of foreign currency required for their local needs and they shall have the right to repatriate the proceeds of the sale of their belongings in accordance with the regulations in force in the Kurdistan Region.

29.12 Each CONTRACTOR Entity's Affiliates, Subcontractors and their personnel shall equally benefit from the same rights as such CONTRACTOR Entity and its personnel as regard this Article 29.

29.13 For the financing of Petroleum Operations, each CONTRACTOR Entity shall have the right to have recourse to external financing from third parties or from its Affiliated Companies on an arm's length basis.

ARTICLE 30 – CUSTOMS PROVISIONS

30.1 All services, material, equipment, goods, consumables and products imported into the Kurdistan Region and other parts of Iraq by the CONTRACTOR, any CONTRACTOR Entity, its Affiliates, any Subcontractor or any agent of any of the foregoing, for use or consumption in the Petroleum Operations shall be admitted free and exempt from any and all Taxes on import. The CONTRACTOR, any CONTRACTOR Entity, its Affiliates, any Subcontractor or any agent of any of the foregoing shall have the right to re-export from the Kurdistan Region and other parts of Iraq free from all Taxes on export any material, equipment, goods, consumables and products that are no longer required for the Petroleum Operations, except where title has passed to the GOVERNMENT in accordance with Article 20, in which case re-export shall be approved by the Management Committee.

30.2 The CONTRACTOR any CONTRACTOR Entity, its Affiliates, any Subcontractor or any agent of any of the foregoing, and their personnel (including their family members) shall have the right to freely import into the Kurdistan Region and other parts of Iraq and re-export from the Kurdistan Region and other parts of Iraq any personal belongings and furniture free and exempt from any Taxes on import or export. The sale in the Kurdistan Region and other parts of Iraq of personal belongings and furniture of expatriate personnel shall comply with Kurdistan Region Law.

30.3 Each CONTRACTOR Entity and its Affiliates shall be entitled to freely export from the Kurdistan Region and other parts of Iraq, free of any Taxes, any Petroleum to which it is entitled pursuant to the provisions of this Contract.

30.4 The GOVERNMENT shall indemnity the CONTRACTOR, any CONTRACTOR Entity, its Affiliates, any Subcontractor or any agent of any of the foregoing, and their personnel (including their family members) for any import or export Taxes referred to in Articles 30.1, 30.2 or 30.3.

ARTICLE 31 – TAX PROVISIONS

31.1 Except as expressly provided in this Article 31, and without prejudice to the exemptions expressly provided for in Article 30 and in this Article 31, each CONTRACTOR Entity, its Affiliates and any Subcontractor shall, for the entire duration of this Contract, be exempt from all Taxes as a result of its income, assets and activities under the Contract. The GOVERNMENT shall indemnify each CONTRACTOR Entity upon demand against any liability to pay any Taxes assessed or imposed upon such entity which relate to any of the exemptions granted by the GOVERNMENT under this Article 31.1, and under Articles 31.4 to 31.11.

31.2 Each CONTRACTOR Entity shall be subject to corporate income tax on its income from Petroleum Operations as provided in Article 31.3, which shall be deemed to be inclusive and in full and total discharge of any Tax on income, receipts, revenues, gains or profits of each such entity. Payment of the said corporate income tax shall be made for the entire duration of this Contract directly to the official Kurdistan Region tux authorities by the GOVERNMENT, for the account of each CONTRACTOR Entity, from the GOVERNMENT's share of the Profit Petroleum received pursuant to Article 26. Each CONTRACTOR Entity shall, within sixty (60) days after the end of each tax year, provide a statement to the appropriate Kurdistan Region tax authorities of its profits which are subject to corporate income tax, together with a calculation of the amount of corporate income tax due on those profits. The GOVERNMENT shall, within ninety (90) days alter the each of each tax year, provide to each CONTRACTOR Entity (i) the appropriate official tax receipts from the appropriate Kurdistan Region tax authorities or other relevant authority certifying the payment of its corporate income tax, as determined in the said statement, and that such entity has met all its Tax obligations in the preceding tax year, and (ii) a copy of any return or other filing made by the GOVERNMENT in respect of its payment of corporate income tax on behalf of such CONTRACTOR Entity.

31.3 For the purposes of Article 31.2,

(a) The rate of corporate income tax to be applied to each CONTRACTOR Entity shall be the generally applicable rate prescribed in the Law of Taxation (Law No. 5 of 1999), passed by the National Assembly of the Kurdistan Region, as has been amended by Law No. 26 of 2007, and as may be amended from time to time or substituted in respect of Petroleum Operations (as defined under the Kurdistan Region Oil and Gas Law) by a petroleum operations taxation law for the Kurdistan Region, but in no event in excess of forty percent (40%). The Parties acknowledge and agree that at the Effective Date of this Contract, the corporate income tax rate is fifteen percent (15%) for all net taxable profits.

(b) The GOVERNMENT and the CONTRACTOR agree that corporate income tax shall be calculated for each CONTRACTOR Entity on its net taxable profits under the Contract, as calculated in accordance with the provisions relating thereto in the Accounting Procedure.

31.4 Each CONTRACTOR Entity, its Affiliates as well as any Subcontractors shall be exempt from any withholding tax applicable on any payments made to then or by them to or from Affiliates or third parties, whether inside or outside the Kurdistan Region and/or Iraq, for the entire duration of this Contract.

31.5 Each CONTRACTOR Entity and its Affiliates shall be exempt from Additional Profits Tax, as referred to in Article 40 of the Kurdistan Region Oil and Gas Law or any successor Tax.

31.6 Each CONTRACTOR Entity and its Affiliates shall be exempt from Surface Tax, as referred to in Article 40 of the Kurdistan Region Oil and Gas Law or any successor Tax.

31.7 Each CONTRACTOR Entity and its Affiliates shall be exempt from Windfall Profits Taxes, as referred to in Article 40 of the Kurdistan Region Oil and Gas Law or any successor Tax.

31.8 Each CONTRACTOR Entity and any Subcontractor shall be subject to the payment or withholding of the personal income tax and social security contributions for which such entity or Subcontractor is liable to pay or withhold in respect of its employees who are Iraqi nationals, pursuant to the Law of Taxation (Law No. 5 of 1^1) passed by the National Assembly of the Kurdistan Region, as may be amended from time to time, in the same manner as the same shall be generally applied to all other industries, except that a CONTRACTOR Entity or Subcontractor shall not be liable for such taxes or contributions with respect to employees of another Person.

31.9 It is acknowledged that double tax treaties will have effect to give relief from taxes to, but not limited to, the CONTRACTOR, CONTRACTOR Entities, Subcontractors and employees and other Persons in accordance with the provisions of such double tax treaties, but shall not impose an additional burden of taxation.

31.10 Any value added tax ("VAT") shall be considered as a Petroleum Cost and shall be cost recovered in accordance with the provisions of Articles 1 and 25.

31.11 Any value added tax ("VAT"), not otherwise recoverable by the CONTRACTOR under VAT law, shall be considered as a Petroleum Cost and shall be cost recovered in accordance with the provisions of Articles 1 and 25.

31.12 Notwithstanding any other provision to the contrary in this Contract, the Parties acknowledge and agree that the provisions of this Article 31 shall apply individually and separately to all CONTRACTOR Entities under this Contract and that there shall be no joint and several liability in respect of any liability, duty or obligation referred to in this Article 31.

ARTICLE 32 – BONUSES

SIGNATURE BONUS

32.1 A signature bonus of five million Dollars (US$5,000,000) ("Signature Bonus") shall be payable to the GOVERNMENT by KOREA NATIONAL OIL CORPORATION on or before the Effective Date.

CAPACITY BUILDING BONUS

32.2 A capacity building bonus of forty-five million Dollars (US$45,000,000) ("Capacity Building Bonus") shall be payable to the GOVERNMENT by KOREA NATIONAL OIL CORPORATION on or before the Effective Date.

PRODUCTION BONUSES

32.3 In the event of a Crude Oil Commercial Discovery, the CONTRACTOR and the holder of the Government Interest shall pay, pro rata the relevant percentage participation interest in the Contract, the following relevant Crude Oil Production Bonus to the GOVERNMENT within thirty (30) days of the following relevant occurrence:

(a) two million five hundred thousand Dollars (US$2,500,000) when First Production of Crude Oil from the Contract Area commences;

(b) five million Dollars (US$5,000,000) when production of Crude Oil from the Contract Area reaches a cumulative amount of ten million Barrels of Crude Oil (10mmbo);

(c) ten million Dollars (US$10,000,000) when production of Crude Oil from the Contract Area reaches a cumulative amount of twenty five million Barrels of Crude Oil (25mmbo); and

(d) twenty million Dollars (US$20,000,000) when production of Crude Oil from the Contract Area reaches a cumulative amount of fifty million Barrels of Crude Oil (50mmbo).

32.4 In the event of a Non-Associated Natural Gas Commercial Discovery, the CONTRACTOR and the holder of the Government Interest shall pay, pro rata the relevant percentage participation interest in the Contract, the following relevant Non-Associated Natural Gas Production Bonus to the GOVERNMENT within thirty (30) days of the following relevant occurrence:

(a) two million five hundred thousand Dollars (US$2,500,000) when First Production of Non-Associated Natural Gas from the Contract Area commences;

(b) five million Dollars (US$5,000,000) when production of Non-Associated Natural Gas from the Contract Area reaches a cumulative amount of ten million barrels of oil equivalent (10 mmboe);

(c) ten million Dollars (US$10,000,000) when production of Non-Associated Natural Gas from the Contract Area reaches a cumulative amount of twenty five million barrels of oil equivalent (25 mmboe); and

(d) twenty million Dollars (US$20,000,000) when production of Non-Associated Natural Gas from the Contract Area reaches a cumulative amount of fifty million barrels of oil equivalent (50 mmboe).

32.5 For the purposes of this Article 32, a Commercial Discovery shall be declared by the CONTRACTOR to be either a Crude Oil Commercial Discovery or a Non-Associated Gas Commercial Discovery and under no circumstances shall a Production Bonus be due in respect of both Crude Oil and Non-Associated Natural Gas for the same Commercial Discovery.

BONUS COST RECOVERY AND PAYMENT

32.6 No bonus due pursuant to this Article 32 shall be deemed to be a Petroleum Cost.

32.7 Payment by the CONTRACTOR (and, where applicable, the holder of the Government Interest) of any bonus due pursuant to this Article 32 shall be made in Dollars by wire transfer to a specified bank account of the GOVERNMENT or by banker's draft and on receipt thereof the GOVERNMENT shall forthwith issue a written receipt to the CONTRACTOR duly executed by the Minister of Natural Resources of the GOVERNMENT or such other officer or the GOVERNMENT who shall be duly authorised to issue such receipt under Kurdistan Region Law.

ARTICLE 33 – PIPELINES

33.1 The GOVERNMENT shall obtain any required Permits for the transportation of Petroleum in the Kurdistan Region and in Iraq, as well as any necessary Permits and easement rights for the construction of any pipelines and related facilities required for the Petroleum Operations, as provided in Article 33.2.

33.2 The GOVERNMENT undertakes to transfer to the CONTRACTOR its rights for transportation of Petroleum by pipeline. The CONTRACTOR shall have the right to design, construct, operate and maintain pipelines and any related facilities for the transportation of Petroleum produced under this Contract.

33.3 Prior to the construction of any pipeline and related facilities as provided in Article 33.2, the CONTRACTOR shall submit following information to the Management Committee: (a) proposed pipeline route and related facilities; (b) forecasted pipeline flow rate and capacity; (c) estimate of financial investment and operating costs of the pipeline and related facilities; (d) proposed financing schedule; (e) construction schedule; (f) general technical description of the pipeline and related facilities; (g) construction plans and tests; (h) preventive measures for damage to the environment and third parties; and (i) any other information relating to the pipeline project. The Management Committee shall examine all the above information, and shall, within ninety (90) days, approve the proposed pipeline project in accordance with the provisions of Article 8.5.

33.4 Subject to spare capacity being available and to their Petroleum being compatible, third parties shall be entitled to transport their Petroleum through any pipeline constructed by the CONTRACTOR in accordance with this Article 33 on terms to be agreed between the CONTRACTOR and such third party. Those terms shall be reasonable commercial terms and shall not discriminate among third party users. The CONTRACTOR shall always have priority of access to such pipelines.

33.5 To the extent that they are incurred upstream of the Delivery Point, any costs associated with the design, construction, operation and maintenance of the pipelines and related facilities by CONTRACTOR under this Article 33 ("Pipeline Costs") shall be considered Petroleum Costs and shall be recovered by the CONTRACTOR in accordance with the provisions of Articles 1 and 25.

33.6 The CONTRACTOR shall have the absolute right, without any exceptions and for the entire duration of this Contract, to use, free of charge, any pipeline and related facilities constructed by CONTRACTOR under this Article 33 and to transport Petroleum produced from any Production Area and to operate and maintain any pipeline and its related facilities, freely and without any additional costs.

33.7 To the extent related to transportation upstream of the Delivery Point, any tariffs received from third parties for use of any pipeline and related facilities by CONTRACTOR under this Article 33 shall be applied to the recovery of Petroleum Costs until all Pipeline Costs have been fully recovered by the CONTRACTOR pursuant to the provisions of Articles 1 and 25, and shall not be included in income for corporate income tax purposes. The GOVERNMENT shall be entitled to receive any such tariffs from third parties for their use of such pipeline and related facilities when the said Pipeline Costs have been fully recovered by the CONTRACTOR. The costs associated with providing such transportation services for third parties up to the Delivery Point shall be considered Pipeline Costs and therefore Petroleum Costs and shall be recovered by the CONTRACTOR in accordance with the provisions of Articles 1 and 25.

33.8 Upon recovery by the CONTRACTOR of all the Pipeline Costs, the operating and maintenance costs of any pipeline and its related facilities shall be borne by the CONTRACTOR and shall be considered Petroleum Costs and shall be recovered by the CONTRACTOR in accordance with the provisions of Articles 1 and 25.

33.9 The GOVERNMENT shall have the same rights as the CONTRACTOR for use, free of charge, of any pipeline and related facilities constructed by CONTRACTOR under this Article 33 for the transportation of the share of Petroleum to which the GOVERNMENT is entitled under this Contract up to the Delivery Point, provided that where the GOVERNMENT is participating in its capacity as a CONTRACTOR Entity pursuant to Article 4, it shall be liable for its share of Petroleum Costs.

33.10 The CONTRACTOR shall bear the cost of operation and maintenance of any pipeline and related facilities constructed by CONTRACTOR under this Article 33 and all risks of accidental loss or damage to such pipeline and related facilities while they are required for Petroleum Operations.

ARTICLE 34 – UNITISATION

34.1 In the event a Reservoir extends beyond the Contract Area into an adjacent area which is the subject of another Petroleum Contract (as defined by the Kurdistan Region Oil and Gas Law) (an "Adjacent Contract Area"), or in the event a Reservoir of an Adjacent Contract Area extends into the Contract Area, the provisions of Article 47, Paragraph Second of the Kurdistan Region Oil and Gas Law shall apply and the GOVERNMENT shall require the CONTRACTOR and the contractor of the Adjacent Contract Area to agree upon a schedule for reaching agreement of the terms of the unitisation of the Reservoir, which terms shall be based on reliable technical, operational and economical parameters, all in accordance with prudent international petroleum industry practice. In the event that the Minister of Natural Resources decides the unitisation pursuant to Article 47, Paragraph Third of the Kurdistan Region Oil and Gas Law, and if the CONTRACTOR does not agree with the decision of the Minister or Natural Resources, the CONTRACTOR shall be entitled to arbitration pursuant to the provisions of Article 42.1.

34.2 For clarification and the avoidance of doubt and notwithstanding Article 47 of the Kurdistan Region Oil and Gas Law, in the event that a Reservoir extends beyond the boundaries of the Contract Area into an adjacent area which is not the subject of another Petroleum Contract (as defined by the Kurdistan Region Oil and Gas Law), the GOVERNMENT shall, upon the CONTRACTOR's request, take the necessary steps to extend the boundaries of Contract Area so as to include the entire Reservoir within the Contract Area, provided that the CONTRACTOR can offer the GOVERNMENT a competitive minimum work program for such adjacent area.

ARTICLE 35 – LIABILITY AND INSURANCE

LIABILITY

35.1 Subject to other provisions of this Contract, the CONTRACTOR, in as capacity as the entity responsible for the execution of the Petroleum Operations within the Contract Area, shall be liable to third parties to the extent provided under applicable Law for any losses and damage it may cause to them in conducting the Petroleum Operations, and shall defend, indemnify and hold harmless the GOVERNMENT with respect to all claims for such loss or damage.

35.2 Notwithstanding the other provisions of this Contract, the CONTRACTOR and the CONTRACTOR Entities shall not be liable to the GOVERNMENT in the Public Company or other government agencies, authorities or bodies, courts or political subdivisions for any damage or loss or claims of any kind resulting from its conduct of the Petroleum Operations unless such damage or loss is the result of wilful misconduct or a material failure to conduct Petroleum Operations in accordance with the terms of this Contract; provided, however, that such liability cannot result in the event of any omissions, errors or mistakes committed in good faith by the CONTRACTOR in the exercise of the powers and authorisations conferred upon the CONTRACTOR by virtue of this Contract, and further provided that in no event shall the CONTRACTOR and the CONTRACTOR Entities be liable for any indirect or consequential loss or damage whatsoever or any loss, damages, costs, expenses or liabilities caused (directly or indirectly) by any of the following arising out of, relating to, or connected with this Contract or the Petroleum Operations carried out under this Contract: (i) reservoir or formation damage; (ii) inability to produce, use or dispose of Petroleum; (iii) loss or deferment of income; (iv) special or punitive damages; or (v) other indirect damages or losses whether or not similar to the foregoing.

35.3 The CONTRACTOR shall indemnify and hold harmless the GOVERNMENT against all losses, damages and liability arising under any claim, demand, action or proceeding brought or instituted against the GOVERNMENT by any employee of the CONTRACTOR or of any Subcontractor or by any dependent thereof, for personal injuries, industrial illness, death or damage to personal property sustained in connection with, related to or arising out of the performance or non-performance of this Contract regardless of the fault or negligence in whole or in party of any entity or individual.

35.4 Notwithstanding Article 35.1, the GOVERNMENT shall indemnify and hold harmless the CONTRACTOR and the CONTRACTOR Entities against all losses, damages and liability arising under any claim, demand, action or proceeding brought or instituted against the CONTRACTOR or any CONTRACTOR Entity by any employee of the GOVERNMENT or of any Public Company or of any subcontractor of the foregoing or by any dependent of any such employee, for personal injuries, industrial illness, death or damage to personal property sustained in connection with, related to or arising out of the performance or non-performance of this Contract regardless of the fault or negligence in whole or in part of any entity or individual.

35.5 The CONTRACTOR shall take all necessary steps to respond to, and shall promptly notify the GOVERNMENT of, all emergency and other events (including explosions, leaks and spills), occurring in relation to the Petroleum Operations which are causing or likely to cause material environmental damage or material risk to health and safety. Such notice shall include a summary description of the circumstances and steps taken and planned by the CONTRACTOR to control and remedy the situation. The CONTRACTOR shall provide such additional reports to the GOVERNMENT as are reasonably necessary in respect of the effects of such events and the course of all actions taken to prevent further loss and to irrigate deleterious effects.

35.6 In the event of emergency situations as set out in Article 35.4, at the request of the CONTRACTOR, the GOVERNMENT, without prejudice and in addition to any indemnification obligations the GOVERNMENT may have, shall assist the CONTRACTOR, to the extent possible, in any emergency response, remedial or repair effort by making available any labour, materials and equipment in reasonable quantities requested by the CONTRACTOR which are not otherwise readily available to the CONTRACTOR and by facilitating the measures taken by the CONTRACTOR to bring into the Kurdistan Region personnel, materials and equipment to be used in any such emergency response or remedial or repair effort. The CONTRACTOR shall reimburse the GOVERNMENT's reasonable and necessary costs incurred in such efforts, which reimbursed amounts shall be considered Petroleum Costs and shall be recovered by the CONTRACTOR in accordance with the provisions of Articles 1 and 25.

35.7 The GOVERNMENT shall indemnify and hold harmless the CONTRACTOR and each CONTRACTOR Entity from and against all costs (including legal costs) expenses, losses, damages and liability which such Person may suffer or incur, or may result from such Person being denied, hindered or prevented from fully exercising its rights or taking the full benefit of Articles 29.4, and 29.6 to 29.11.

35.8 In accordance with prudent international petroleum industry practice, each CONTRACTOR Entity shall maintain any insurance required by applicable Kurdistan Region Law, as well as any insurance approved by the Management Committee. Such insurance policies may cover: (a) loss of and damage to material and equipment used in the Petroleum Operations; and (b) personal injury, damage to third parties and risks of pollution associated with Petroleum Operations for reasonable amounts, within the limits approved by the Management Committee.

35.9 Any insurance policy relating to this Contract shall name the GOVERNMENT as an additional insured party and shall include a waiver of subrogation protecting the GOVERNMENT against any claim, loss and damage resulting from any Petroleum Operation conducted by or on behalf of the CONTRACTOR under this Contract, to the extent that the CONTRACTOR is liable for such claim, loss or damage under this Contract. The CONTRACTOR shall not be liable for and shall not purchase insurance cover for any claims arising from negligence or wilful misconduct of the GOVERNMENT or of any Public Company or of any of its or their subcontractors or of any personnel of any of the foregoing.

35.10 Upon its written request, the GOVERNMENT shall be provided with insurance certificates, including necessary details, for any insurance policy maintained by the CONTRACTOR which relates to this Contract.

35.11 Each CONTRACTOR Entity shall be responsible for the filing of all claims made under any insurance policy maintained by such CONTRACTOR Entity which relates to this Contract. Any premiums and payments relating to such insurance policies shall be considered Petroleum Costs and shall be recovered by the CONTRACTOR in accordance with the provisions of Articles 1 and 25.

35.12 In any insurance policy maintained by a CONTRACTOR Entity which relates to this Contract, the amount for which the CONTRACTOR itself is liable (the "Deductible Amount") shall be reasonably determined between the CONTRACTOR Entity and the insurer and such Deductible Amount shall in the event of any insurance claim be considered a Petroleum Cost and shall be recovered by the CONTRACTOR in accordance with the provisions of Articles 1 and 25.

ARTICLE 36 – INFORMATION AND CONFIDENTIALITY

36.1 The CONTRACTOR shall keep all records, data and information relating to the Petroleum Operations in accordance with the Kurdistan Region Oil and Gas Law and prudent international petroleum industry practice. In addition, it shall provide the GOVERNMENT with such information and data as it is obliged to provide under this Contract.

36.2 Upon the GOVERNMENT's written request, the CONTRACTOR shall provide the GOVERNMENT with samples of any rocks or any other items extracted during the Petroleum Operations.

36.3 The GOVERNMENT snall have title to all data and information, whether raw derived, processed, interpreted or analysed, obtained pursuant to this Contract.

36.4 Each CONTRACTOR Entity shall have the right, without any limitation, to send Abroad copies of all reports and technical data, magnetic tapes and other data relating to the Petroleum Operations. Magnetic tapes or other data, the original of which must be analysed and processed Abroad, may be transported out of the Kurdistan Region.

36.5 Any representatives authorised by the GOVERNMENT and notified to the CONTRACTOR shall, upon reasonable prior written notice, have reasonable access to any information and data relating to the Contract Area in the possession of the CONTRACTOR which the CONTRACTOR is obliged to provide to the GOVERNMENT pursuant to this Contract. It is understood that, when exercising such right, the GOVERNMENT shall ensure it does not unduly interfere with or hinder the CONTRACTOR's rights and activities.

36.6 The CONTRACTOR shall provide the GOVERNMENT upon the GOVERNMENT's written request any analysis information, reports, tapes or other data (geological, geophysical, logs, interpretations, drilling reports, etc.) related to the Petroleum Operations in the possession of the CONTRACTOR. All available originals of such data shall be transferred to the GOVERNMENT at the end of this Contract.

36.7 Apart from the exceptions stated in this Article 36, the Parties undertake to keep all data and information relating to this Contract and the Petroleum Operations confidential during the entire term of this Contract and not to divulge or disclose such data or information to third parties without the specific consent of the other Parties, such consent not to be unreasonably withheld or delayed. The foregoing confidentiality obligation shall not apply to information or data which: (a) is or, through no fault of any Party, becomes part of the public domain; (b) is known to the recipient at the date of disclosure; (c) is required to be furnished in compliance with any applicable Law, by a government agency having jurisdiction over a CONTRACTOR Entity, by a court order or any other legal proceedings; or (d) is required to be disclosed pursuant to the rules or regulations of any government or recognised stock exchange having jurisdiction over a CONTRACTOR Entity.

36.8 Notwithstanding the foregoing in Article 36.7, in accordance with prudent international petroleum industry practice, such data and information may be disclosed to: (a) Affiliates of each CONTRACTOR Entity; (b) employees, officers and directors of each CONTRACTOR Entity and their respective Affiliated Companies for the purpose of the Petroleum Operations, subject to each such entity taking customary precautions to ensure such information is kept confidential; (c) consultants or agents retained by any CONTRACTOR Entity or its Affiliates for the purpose of analysing or equating information or data; (d) banks or financial institution retained by any CONTRACTOR Entity or its Affiliates with a view to financing Petroleum operations, including any professional consultants retained by such bank or financial institution; (e) bona fide prospective assignees of a participating interest under this Contract (including any entity with whom a CONTRACTOR Entity and/or its Affiliates are conducting bona fide negotiation directed towards a merger, consolidation or the sale of a material portion of its or an Affiliates shares); (f) prospective or actual Subcontractors and suppliers engaged by a Party where disclosure of such information is essential to such Subcontractor's or supplier's work for such Party; and (g) any other Person or entity, upon the prior written approval of the non-disclosing Parties: provided that disclosure shall not be made pursuant to paragraphs (c), (d), (e) and (f), unless such third party has entered into a confidentiality undertaking.

36.9 Any data and information relating to relinquished or surrendered areas under this Contract shall become the exclusive property of the GOVERNMENT, who shall have the right to use same for any purpose in particular for the purpose of promoting said areas. Each CONTRACTOR Entity shall be entitled to keep copies of such data and information and to use such data and information for any purpose.

36.10 Subject to the provisions of this Article 36, the CONTRACTOR may not sell nor exchange any data related to the Petroleum Operations without the approval of the GOVERNMENT, which approval shall not be unreasonably withheld or delayed where, in the CONTRACTOR's reasonable opinion, such sale or exchange would benefit the Petroleum Operations.

ARTICLE 37 – ENVIRONMENTAL PROVISIONS

37.1 During the performance of the Petroleum Operations, the CONTRACTOR shall take reasonable measures to ensure that it, the Operator, its Subcontractors and agents attend to the protection of the environment and prevention of pollution, in accordance with prudent international petroleum industry practice in similar physical and ecological environments and any then applicable Kurdistan Region Law.

37.2 Prior to surrendering a portion of the Contract Area, the CONTRACTOR shall take reasonable measures to abandon the area to be surrendered in accordance with prudent international petroleum industry practice in similar physical and ecological environments. Such measures shall include removal or closure in place of facilities, material and equipment together with reasonable measures necessary for the preservation of fauna, flora and ecosystems, all in accordance with prudent international petroleum industry practice in similar physical and ecological environments. The CONTRACTOR shall only be responsible for site restoration or environmental damage to the extent the same pertains solely and directly to Petroleum Operations conducted pursuant to this Contract.

37.3 The CONTRACTOR shall take reasonable precautions and measures in accordance with prudent international petroleum industry practice in similar physical and ecological environments to prevent any pollution which may arise directly as a result of the Petroleum Operations and to protect the environment (fauna and flora), water sources and any other natural resources when carrying out Petroleum Operations.

37.4 The CONTRACTOR shall, in accordance with prudent international petroleum industry practice in similar physical and ecological environments, respect the preservation of property, agricultural ureas, and fisheries, when carrying out Petroleum Operations.

37.5 The CONTRACTOR shall conduct and submit an environmental impact assessment to the GOVERNMENT within six (6) months after the Effective Date.

NATIONAL PARKS AND NATURE RESERVE AREA

37.6 The CONTRACTOR shall take reasonable measures to minimise any adverse material impact on national parks and nature reserves which may arise directly as a result of the Petroleum Operations, in accordance with prudent International petroleum industry practice in similar physical and ecological environments.

37.7 The GOVERNMENT: (i) represents and warrants that, on the Effective Date, there are no national parks, nature reserves or other protected areas located in whole or in part within the Contract Area where the CONTRACTOR shall not be entitled to carry out Petroleum Operations; and (ii) covenants that during the term of this Contract will not designate or create or permit the creation of any national parks, nature reserves or other projected areas, located in whole or in part within the Contract Area.

EXPENDITURES

37.8 Any reasonable expenditure incurred by the CONTRACTOR in relation with this Article 37 shall be deemed Petroleum Costs and shall be recovered by the CONTRACTOR in accordance with the provisions of Articles 1 and 25.

PRE-EXISTING CONDITIONS

37.9 The CONTRACTOR is not responsible for any pre-existing environmental conditions or any acts of unrelated third parties.

ARTICLE 38 – DECOMMISSIONING

38.1 To enable the CONTRACTOR to recover the costs associated with future Contract Area Decommissioning Operations under this Contract, the CONTRACTOR shall have the right to establish a reserve fund for future decommissioning and site restoration (a "Decommissioning Reserve Fund." The Decommissioning Reserve Fund may be established at any time during the final ten (10) Calendar Years of the term of the Production Operations of a Production Area but, upon the reasonable request by the CONTRACTOR, the GOVERNMENT shall allow the CONTRACTOR to establish such fund over a longer period. Once established, the CONTRACTOR shall make regular contributions to the Decommissioning Reserve Fund based upon estimated Petroleum field decommissioning and site restoration costs in accordance with prudent international petroleum industry practice, and taking into account interest received and future interest expected to be earned on the Decommissioning Reserve Fund. Any contributions by the CONTRACTOR to the Decommissioning Reserve Fund shall be made in Dollars and shall be deemed Petroleum Costs when paid into the reserve fund, and shall be recovered by the CONTRACTOR in accordance with the provisions of Article 1 and 25. Contributions to the Decommissioning Reserve Fund shall be placed with a first rate bank approved by the Management Committee in accordance with Article 8.5.

38.2 If, at the end of the term of the Production Operations of the Production Area, the GOVERNMENT decides to take over production operations in the Production Area: (a) the GOVERNMENT shall become liable for its future Decommissioning Operations; (b) the contributions and any interest accumulated in the Decommissioning Reserve Fund, to the extent that such contributions have been recovered as Petroleum Costs, shall be paid to the GOVERNMENT; and (c) the GOVERNMENT shall release the CONTRACTOR and the CONTRACTOR Entities from any obligations relating to Decommissioning Operations and shall indemnify the CONTRACTOR and the CONTRACTOR Entities for any costs, liabilities, expenses, claims or obligations associated therewith.

38.3 If the CONTRACTOR undertakes the Production Area Decommissioning Operations, the contributions and any interest accumulated in the Decommissioning Reserve Fund shall be paid to the CONTRACTOR and shall be used for the Decommissioning Operations. The CONTRACTOR shall undertake any such Decommissioning Operations in accordance with prudent international petroleum industry practice in similar physical and ecological environments.

38.4 If the Decommissioning Reserve Fund Is paid to the CONTRACTOR and the Decommissioning Reserve Fund is not sufficient to cover all Decommissioning Costs for the Contract Area, the balance shall be paid by the CONTRACTOR and may be recovered, if applicable, by the CONTRACTOR Entities or any of their Affiliates from any other area which is the subject of another Petroleum Contract (as defined by the Kurdistan Region Oil and Gas Law) anywhere in the Kurdistan Region and, to the extent the balance is not recoverable as aforesaid, such remaining balance shall be paid by the GOVERNMENT to the CONTRACTOR.

38.5 If the Decommissioning Reserve fund is paid to the CONTRACTOR and the Decommissioning Reserve Fund exceeds all Decommissioning Costs for the Contract Area, the balance shall be transferred to the GOVERNMENT.

38.6 Any expenditure incurred by the CONTRACTOR in relation with this Article 38, including any contributions to the Decommissioning Reserve Fund, shall be deemed Petroleum Costs and shall be recovered by the CONTRACTOR in accordance with the provisions of Articles 1 and 25.

38.7 The CONTRACTOR shall submit to the Management Committee for approval in accordance with Article 8.5 a detailed plan for decommissioning the Contract Area facilities and site restoration (the "Decommissioning Plan"), such Decommissioning Plan to be submitted no later than twenty four (24) Mouths, prior to the date estimated by the CONTRACTOR for the end of Commercial Production from the Contract Area. The Management Committee shall provide comments, if any, on the Decommissioning Plan within ninety (90) days after receipt. The CONTRACTOR's completion of the Decommissioning Operations in accordance, in all material respects, with the Decommissioning Plan for a Production Area approved by the Management Committee shall satisfy all of the CONTRACTOR's obligations with respect to the performance of Decommissioning Operations for such Production Area in the event the GOVERNMENT does not agree that Decommissioning Operations for a Production Area were carried out in accordance with the approved Decommissioning Plan, it must advise the CONTRACTOR within six (6) months of CONTRACTOR's completion of such operation.

ARTICLE 39 – ASSIGNMENT AND CHANGE OF CONTROL

ASSIGNMENT TO AFFILIATES

39.1 Each CONTRACTOR Entity shall be free to sell, assign, transfer or otherwise dispose of all or part of its rights, obligations and interests under this Contract to an Affiliated Company or to another CONTRACTOR Entity with the prior consent of the GOVERNMENT, which consent shall not be unreasonably delayed or withheld.

39.2 Each CONTRACTOR Entity shall have the right to sell, assign, transfer or otherwise dispose of all or part of its rights and interests under this Contract to any thud party (not being an Affiliated Company or another CONTRACTOR Entity) with the prior consent of GOVERNMENT, and each other CONTRACTOR Entity (if any) which consent shall not be unreasonably delayed or withheld. Any CONTRACTOR Entity proposing to sell, assign, transfer or otherwise dispose of all or part of its rights and interests under thus Contract to any such third party shall request such consent in writing, which request shall be accompanied by reasonable evidence of the technical and financial capability of the proposed third party assignee. In the event that the Third Party Participant with a Third Party Interest subject to Article 4.8 proposes to sell, assign, transfer or otherwise dispose of all or part of such Third Party Interest to a person that is not an Affiliate, such Third Party Participant shall first offer to both the other CONTRACTOR Entity (or, if applicable, CONTRACTOR Entities) and to the GOVERNMENT pre-eruption rights in relation to such Third Party Interest, or part thereof. Such pre-eruption rights shall be offered on terms that are at least as favourable as the terms upon which the Third Party Interest (or parts thereof) has been offered to the interested Person. Any option by the GOVERNMENT to utilise such pre-eruption rights shall be subject to the maximum participation limit imposed upon a Government Interest by Article 4.1.

39.3 In order for any deed of sale, assignment, transfer or other disposal as provided under Articles 39.1 or 39.2 to be effective, the Parties and the relevant third party, if any, shall enter into a binding and enforceable instrumental of assignment and novation, which shall include an undertaking by the transferee or assignee to fulfil the obligations under this Contract which correspond to the interest transferred or assigned.

39.4 By way of clarification, and not in limitation of the foregoing provisions of this Article 39, the GOVERNMENT shall not be considered be acting unreasonably in withholding consent to any such assignment if the assignment in such proposed assignee is deemed contrary to the GOVERNMENT's interests, as evidenced in writing to that effect signed by the duly authorised representative of the GOVERNMENT below.

39.5 In the event a CONTRACTOR Entity assists or any other way transfers its rights and interests under this Contract, including through the exercise of the Option of Government Participation or the Option of Third Party Participation, whether in whole or in part, such assignment or transfer shall not give rise to any Tax, including on the consideration paid or received or on the income or gain therefrom.

39.6 The GOVERNMENT may not at any time transfer any or all its rights and obligations under this Contract to any Person, including to a Public Company or any other company or entity, except in accordance with Article 4.

CHANGE OF CONTROL

39.7 "Change of Control" for the purpose of this Article 39.7 means any direct or indirect change of the identity to the Person who Controls a CONTRACTOR Entity (whether through merger, sale of shares or of other equity interests, or otherwise) through a single transaction or series of transactions, from one or more transferors to one or more transferees, in which the market value of such entity's participating interest (which shall be as specified in the Joint Operating Agreement relating to this Contract, or where there is only one CONTRACTOR Entity, one hundred percent (100%) in this Contract) represents more than seventy five percent (75%) of the aggregate market value of the assets of such entity and its Affiliates that are subject to the Change in Control. For the purpose of this definition "Control" means the direct or indirect ownership or control of the majority of the voting rights of the applicable entity at its shareholders' meetings or there equivalent; and "market value" shall be determined based upon the amount in cash a willing buyer would pay a willing seller in an Arm's Length transaction. Each CONTRACTOR Entity which is or anticipates with a reasonable degree of certainty that it will be subject to a Change in Control, other than to an Affiliated Company or a CONTRACTOR Entity, shall notify the GOVERNMENT as soon as practicable after it becomes aware of the Change in Control or anticipated Change in Control and request the consent of GOVERNMENT, which consent shall not be unreasonably delayed or withheld. A Change in Control shall not give rise to any Tax including on the consideration paid or received or on the income or gain therefrom.

ARTICLE 40 – FORCE MAJEURE

40.1 No delay, default, breach or omission of the CONTRACTOR in the execution of any of its obligations under this Contract shall be considered a failure to perform this Contract or be the subject of a dispute if such delay, default, breach or omission is due to a case of Force Majeure. In such event the CONTRACTOR shall promptly notify the GOVERNMENT in writing and take all reasonably appropriate measures to perform its obligations under this Contract to the extent possible. The time resulting from any such delay or curtailment in the execution of such obligations, increased by the time necessary to repair any damage resulting from or occurred during such delay or curtailment, shall be added to any time period provided under this Contract (including the Exploration Period and any extension thereto, any Sub-Period and any extension thereto and any Development Period and any extension thereto). The Parties shall meet as soon as possible after the notification of Force Majeure with a view to using reasonable endeavours to mitigate the effects thereof.

40.2 For the purpose of this Contract, "Force Majeure" means any event that is unforeseeable, insurmountable and irresistible, not due to any error or omission by the CONTRACTOR but due to circumstances beyond its control, which prevents or impedes execution of all or part of its obligations under this Contract. Such events shall include the following: (a) war, whether declared or not, civil war. insurrection, riots, civil commotion, terrorism, any other hostile acts, whether internal or external; (b) strikes or other labour conflicts; (c) accidents or blowouts; (d) quarantine restrictions or epidemics; (e) any act, event, happening or occurrence due to natural causes, in particular, but without limitation, floods, storms, cyclones, fires, lightning, or earthquakes; (f) environmental restrictions, which the GOVERNMENT has not notified to the CONTRACTOR; (g) except in respect of the GOVERNMENT and/or any Public Company which may be a CONTRACTOR Entity, any acts or orders of the GOVERNMENT, any minister, ministry, department, sub-division, agency, authority, council, committee, or other constituent element thereof, any corporation owned and/or controlled by the any of the foregoing; and (h) any acts or orders of any other government claiming or asserting jurisdiction over the subject matter of this Contract, any minister, ministry, department, sub-division, agency, authority, council. committee, or other constituent element thereof, or any corporation owned and.or controlled by any of the foregoing.

40.3 The intention of the Parties is that force Majeure shall receive the interpretation that complies most with prudent international petroleum industry practice. Force Majeure affecting a CONTRACTOR Entity or an Affiliated Company of a CONTRACTOR Entity shall be deemed Force Majeure affecting the CONTRACTOR if the consequence of such Force Majeure prevents the performance of any of the CONTRACTOR's obligations under this Contract.

ARTICLE 41 – WAIVER OF SOVEREIGN IMMUNITY

The GOVERNMENT and any Public Company which may be a CONTRACTOR Entity at any time hereby fully and inevocably waives any claim to immunity for itself and or its assets. This waiver includes any claim to immunity from: (a) any expert determination, mediation, or arbitration proceedings commenced pursuant to Article 42; (b) any judicial, administrative or other proceedings to aid the expert determination, mediation, or arbitration proceedings commenced pursuant to Article 42; and (c) any effort to confirm, enforce or execute any decision, settlement, award, judgment, service of process, execution order or attachment (including pre-judgment attachment) that results from an expert determination, mediation, arbitration or any judicial, administrative or other proceedings commenced pursuant to this Contract.

ARTICLE 42 – ARBITRATION AND EXPERT DETERMINATION

NEGOTIATION, MEDIATION AND ARBITRATION

42.1 For the purpose of this Article 42.1, "Dispute" shall mean any dispute, controversy or claim (of any and every kind or type, whether based on contract, tort, statute, regulation or otherwise) arising out of, relating to, or connected with the Contract or the operations carried out under this Contract, including any dispute as the construction, existence, validity, interpretation. enforceability, breach or termination of this Contract, which arises between the Parties (or between any one or more entities constituting the CONTRACTOR and the GOVERNMENT). In the event of a Dispute, the parties to the Dispute shall use their reasonable endeavours to negotiate promptly in good faith a mutually acceptable resolution of such Dispute. Subject to the provisions of Article 42.2, a Party who desires to submit a Dispute for resolution which has not been promptly revolved as aforesaid shall commence the dispute resolution process by providing the other parties to the Dispute written notice of the Dispute ("Notice of Dispute"). The Notice of Dispute shall identify the parties to the Dispute, shall contain a brief statement of the nature of the Dispute and the relief requested and shall request negotiations among Senior Representatives.

(a) In the event that any Notice of Dispute is given in accordance with this Article 42.1, the parties to the Dispute shall first seek settlement of the dispute by negotiation between Senior Representatives. "Senior Representative" means any individual who has authority to negotiate the settlement of the Dispute for a party to the Dispute, which for the GOVERNMENT shall mean the Minister of Natural Resources. Within thirty (30) days after the date of delivery of the Notice of Dispute, the Senior Representatives representing the parties to the Dispute shall meet at a mutually acceptable date, time and place to exchange relevant information in an attempt to resolve the Dispute. If a Senior Representative intends to be accompanied at the meeting by a legal adviser, each other party shall be given written notice of such intention and its Senior Representative may also be accompanied at the meeting by a legal adviser.

(b) If the Dispute cannot be resolved by negotiation in accordance with Article 42.1 (a) within sixty (60) days after the date of the receipt by each party to the Dispute of the Notice of Dispute or such further period as the parties to the Dispute may agree in writing, any party to the Dispute may seek settlement of the dispute by mediation in accordance with the London Court of International Arbitration ("LCIA") Mediation Procedure, which Procedure shall be deemed to be incorporated by reference into this Article, and the parties to such Dispute shall submit to such mediation procedure.

(c) If the Dispute is not settled within the earlier of (A) sixty (60) days of the appointment of the mediator, or such further period as the parties to the Dispute may otherwise agree in writing under the mediation procedure under Article 42.1 (b), and (B) one hundred and twenty (120) days after the delivery of the Dispute Notice, any party to the Dispute may refer the Dispute to, and seek final resolution by, arbitration under the LCIA Rules, which Rules shall be deemed to be incorporated by reference into this Article.

  (i) Any arbitration shall be conducted by three (3) arbitrators.

  (ii) If parties to the Dispute are the GOVERNMENT and all the CONTRACTOR Entities, the GOVERNMENT and the CONTRACTOR shall each appoint one (1) arbitrator. If the parties to the Dispute are the GOVERNMENT and more than one, but not all the CONTRACTOR Entities, the GOVERNMENT shall appoint one (1) arbitrator and such CONTRACTOR Entities shall appoint one (1) arbitrator. If the parties to the Dispute are the GOVERNMENT and one CONTRACTOR Entity, the GOVERNMENT and such CONTRACTOR Entity shall each appoint one (1) arbitrator.

  (iii) In any event, the two arbitrators so appointed shall, in good faith, use all reasonable endeavours to agree on the appointment of the third arbitrator, who will chair the arbitral tribunal. In case of failure to appoint an arbitrator or to agree on the appointment of the third arbitrator, Rules of the LCIA shall apply.

  (vi) Arbitration shall take place in London, England. The language to be used in any prior negotiation, mediation and in the arbitration shall be English. During the arbitration procedure and until the arbitral decision, the Parties shall continue to perform their obligations and take no actions that would impair the Contract. The arbitral award may be enforced by any court of competent jurisdiction, including in the Kurdistan Region. Any award shall be expressed in Dollars.

  (v) The Parties agree that the arbitral award shall be final and not subject to any appeal, including to the Courts of England on issues of Law.

(vi) With respect to any matter referred to arbitration under Article 43.4, the arbitral tribunal shall have the authority to amend this Contract to restore the economic position referred to in Article 43.3.

EXPERT DETERMINATION

42.2 Any disagreement between the Parties bearing to Articles 15.9, 27.2 and 27.7, as well as any disagreement the Parties agree to refer to an expert, shall be submitted to an expert. The Management Committee shall prepare and agree appropriate terms of reference relating to a disagreement to be submitted to the expert, in accordance with Article 8.5 ("Terms of Reference"), as soon as possible after the Effective Date.

(a) The disagreement shall be submitted to an expert appointed by mutual agreement of the Parties within thirty (30) days following the date of preparation and agreement of the Terms of Reference by the Management Committee. If the Parties cannot agree on the choice of the expert within such thirty (30) day period, at the request of either Party, the expert shall be appointed by the President of the Energy Institute in London, England. Any expert appointed must have the necessary qualifications for reviewing and deciding on the subject matter of the disagreement.

(b) The duties of the expert shall be stated in the Terms of Reference prepared and agreed by the Management Committee. The Management Committee shall promptly provide the expert with the agreed Terms of Reference relating to the disagreement. Each Party shall have the right to give to the expert in writing any information which it considers useful, provided it does so within forty-five (45) days after the expert's appointment. Such information shall be provided to the other Party at the same time and such other Party shall be entitled to provide comments on such information to the first Party and the expert within thirty (30) days after receiving such information. The expert shall have the right to review and verify any information he deems useful to assist him in his review of the disagreement.

(c) The expert shall render his decision within forty-five (45) days of his receipt of the Terms of Reference and the information referred to in Article 42.2. Subject to the provisions of Article 15.9, any decision of the expert shall be final and shall not be subject to any appeal, except in the case of manifest error, fraud or malpractice. Any costs and expenses associated with the expert determination shall be shared equally between the Parties.

GENERAL

42.3 No negotiation, mediation, arbitration or expert determination procedure under this Article 42 shall exempt the Parties from fulfilling then respective legal and/or contractual obligations.

ARTICLE 43 – GOVERNING LAW, FISCAL STABILITY AND AMENDMENTS

GOVERNING LAW

43.1 This Contract, including any dispute arising therefrom, thereunder or in relation thereto and the agreement to arbitrate in Article 42, shall be governed by English law (except any rule of English law which would refer the matter to another jurisdiction), together with any relevant rules, customs and practices of international law, as well as by principles and practice generally accepted in petroleum producing countries and in the international petroleum industry.

43.2 The obligations of the CONTRACTOR in respect of this Contract shall not be changed by the GOVERNMENT and the general and overall equilibrium between the

Parties under this Contract shall not be affected in a substantial and lasting manner.

43.3 The GOVERNMENT guarantees to the CONTRACTOR, for the entire duration of this Contract, that it will maintain the stability of the legal, fiscal and economic conditions of this Contract, as they result from this Contract and as they result from the laws and regulations in force on the date of signature of this Contract. The CONTRACTOR has entered into this Contract on the basis of the legal, fiscal and economic framework prevailing at the Effective Date. If, at any time after the Effective Date, there is any change in the legal, fiscal and economic framework under the Kurdistan Region Law or other Law applicable in or to the Kurdistan Region which detrimentally affects the CONTRACTOR, the CONTRACTOR Entities or any other Person entitled to benefits under this Contract, the terms and conditions of the Contract shall be altered so as to restore the CONTRACTOR, the CONTRACTOR Entities and any other Person entitled to benefits under this Contract to the same overall economic position (taking into account home country taxes) as that which such Person would have been in, had no such change in the legal, fiscal and/or economic framework occurred.

43.4 If the CONTRACTOR believes that its economic position, or the economic position of a CONTRACTOR Entity or any other Person entitled to benefits under this Contract, has been detrimentally affected as provided in Article 43.3, upon the CONTRACTOR's written request, the Parties shall meet to agree on any necessary measures or making any appropriate amendments to the terms of this Contract to re-establishing the equilibrium between the Parties and restoring the CONTRACTOR, the CONTRACTOR Entities or any other Person entitled to benefits under this Contract to the position (taking into account home country taxes) it was in prior to the occurrence of the change having such detrimental effect. Should the Parties be unable to agree on the merit of amending this Contract and/or on any amendments to be made to this Contract within ninety (90) days of the CONTRACTOR's request for such other period as may be agreed by the Parties, the CONTRACTOR may refer the matter in dispute to arbitration as provided in Article 42.1 without the necessity of first referring the matter to negotiation and mediation.

43.5 Without prejudice to the generality of the foregoing, the CONTRACTOR shall be entitled to the benefit of any future changes to the petroleum legislation or any other legislation complementing, amending or replacing it.

43.6 The Parties agree to cooperate in all possible ways which a view to fully achieving the objectives of this Contract. The GOVERNMENT shall facilitate the performance of the Petroleum Operations by promptly granting to the CONTRACTOR any necessary authorisation, permit, licence or access right and making available any existing facilities and services with a view to the Parties obtaining maximum mutual benefit from the Contract.

AMENDMENTS

43.7 Any amendment to this Contract shall be the subject of a formal amendment, duly approved in writing by the Parties and subject to the same conditions of validity as this Contract. Notwithstanding the foregoing, the GOVERNMENT has the right and authority to waive the application of the provisions of this Contract on a case-by-case basis without having to fulfil the conditions of validity of this Contract, should CONTRACTOR so request.

43.8 This Contract constitutes the entire agreement of the Parties and supersedes any and all prior understandings or agreements in respect of the subject matter of this Contract, including the Original Contract.

43.9 Unless otherwise expressly stated elsewhere in this Contract, no failure or delay of any Party to exercise any right, power or remedy under this Contract shall operate as a waiver thereof; nor shall any single or partial exercise of any such right, power or remedy preclude any other or future exercise thereof or the exercise of any other right, power of remedy.

VALIDITY

43.10 As signatories to this Contract for and on behalf of the GOVERNMENT, the Ministry of Natural Resources in the Kurdistan Region and the Regional Council for the Oil and Gas Affairs of the Kurdistan Region — Iraq hereby represent that they agree and approve this Contract for the purposes of the Kurdistan Region Oil and Gas Law.

ARTICLE 44 – NOTICES

44.1 All notices, demands, instructions, waivers, consents or other communications to be provided pursuant to this Contract shall be in writing in English, shall be effective upon receipt, and shall be sent by receipted hand delivery or by email (followed by delivery by reputable international air courier company with an establishment in Erbil in the Kurdistan Region) to the following addresses: ______________________________.
A notice delivered by email (followed by air courier) shall, save for manifest error, be deemed to have been delivered upon its transmission by email.

44.2 The above address and/or designated representative of any of the Parties may be changed on giving ten (10) days prior notice to the other Party delivered pursuant to Article 44.1.

ARTICLE 45 – TERMINATION

45.1 Subject to the provisions of Article 45.5, the government shall have the right to terminate this Contract in the event the CONTRACTOR (a) fails to meet a material financial obligation expressly stated in this Contract; or (b) during the First Sub-Period does not carry out drilling and seismic acquisition, as detailed in Article 10.2 or, during the Second Sub-Period (or earlier), does not carry out drilling and seismic acquisition, as detailed in Article 10.3; or (c) interrupts Production for a period of more than ninety (90) consecutive days with no cause or justification acceptable in accordance with this Contract or under prudent international petroleum industry practice, it being recognised that Force Majeure is an acceptable justification for such interruptions; or (d) intentionally extracts or produces any mineral which is not covered by the object of this Contract, unless such extraction or production is expressly authorised or unavoidable as a result of operations carried out in accordance with prudent international petroleum industry practice; (e) if the CONTRACTOR comprises solely one entity, is declared bankrupt in accordance with applicable Law; (f) wilfully refuses to abide by negotiation, mediation, arbitration or expert decision under Article 42; or (g) breaches the Capacity Building Support Agreement.

45.2 The GOVERNMENT may also terminate the Contract only in respect of one CONTRACTOR Entity if such entity is subject to a Change of Control for which the GOVERNMENT has not given its authorisation in accordance with Article 39.7.

45.3 At any time prior to the Development the CONTRACTOR shall have the right to terminate this Contract by surrendering the entire Contract Area in accordance with the provisions of Article 7.

45.4 During the Development Period, the CONTRACTOR shall have the right in terminate this Contract at any time by surrendering all Production Areas, provided its then current obligations have been satisfied in accordance with this Contract.

45.5 If the GOVERNMENT intends to exercise its right to terminate this Contract pursuant to Article 45.1, it shall first comply with the following provisions: (a) the GOVERNMENT shall notify the CONTRACTOR of its intention to terminate this Contract stating the reasons for such termination and requesting the latter: (i) to remedy the default; or (ii) to propose acceptable compensation; (b) if, within three (3) Months after the notice referred to in Article 45.5(a), the CONTRACTOR has not remedied the situation complained of by the GOVERNMENT to its satisfaction or offered compensation acceptable to the GOVERNMENT in each case acting reasonably, the GOVERNMENT shall notify the CONTACTOR in writing that the Contract shall be terminated from the termination date detailed in such notice. This Contract shall terminate on such termination due unless the CONTRACTOR issues a notice of dispute as provided under Article 42, in which case this Contract shall remain in force until a final settlement of the dispute has been reached in accordance with the dispute resolution provisions of Article 42. The foregoing provisions of this Article 45.5 are subject to the proviso that, in case of a dispute where there has been breach of the Contract which has been submitted to dispute revolution pursuant to Article 42, the GOVERNMENT shall not be entitled to exercise its right to terminate this Contract prior to a final determination under Article 42 in favour of the GOVERNMENT.

45.6 If the GOVERNMENT terminates this Contract pursuant to the provisions of Articles 45.1 and 45.5, the CONTRACTOR shall lose all its rights and interest under this Contract. Notwithstanding the foregoing, the provisions of Articles 14.10, 16.7, 30, 31, 35.1, 35.3, 35.4, 35.7, 36, 38.2(c), 41, 42, 43.1 to 43.6 shall survive the termination or expiry of this Contract.

45.7 If a CONTRACTOR Entity breaches Article 46.1 or 46.2, the GOVERNMENT or another CONTRACTOR Entity may terminate this Contract in respect of the first CONTRACTOR Entity.

45.8 If the Contract is terminated under Article 45.2 or 45.7, the interest of the relevant CONTRACTOR Entity shall be transferred from the other CONTRACTOR Entities in the proportions in which their respective percentage interests bear to the aggregate of their reactive percentage interests under the relevant Joint Operating Agreement or in such other proportions as such CONTRACTOR Entities shall agree between them for the market value thereof (as such term is defined in Article 39.7). Such transfer shall not give rise to any tax including on the consideration paid or received or on the income or gain therefrom.

ARTICLE 46 – APPLICATION OF CORRUPTION LAWS

46.1 If this Contract is reasonably proven to have been obtained to violation of Kurdistan Region Law concerning corruption, this Contract is void ab initio.

46.2 Each CONTRACTOR Entity agrees that if it is, or any time, reasonably proven to be in breach of Kurdistan Region law concerning corruption, the provisions of Article 45.7 apply.

This Contract shall become effective and be binding on the parties when both of the following conditions have been satisfied: (a) the duly authorized representatives of the GOVERNMENT and the CONTRACTOR have signed the Contract as provided below; and (b) the Capacity Building Support Agreement Commencement Date (a the term 'Commencement Date' is defined in that Agreement) has occurred.

Entered into three (3) originals in Erbil, the Kurdistan Region on [ ]

Annex A CONTRACT AREA MAP AND LIST OF COORDINATES
Annex B ACCOUNTING PROCEDURE

PARAGRAPH 1 – GENERAL PROVISIONS

1.1 Purpose

To classify expenditures, define further Petroleum Costs (in addition to those defined as such in the Articles of the Contract), and prescribe the manner in which the CONTRACTOR'S Accounts shall be prepared and approved.

1.2 Definitions

Words and phrases to which a meaning has been assigned in Article 1 or other Articles of the Contract shall have the name meaning when used in this Annex.

1.3 Inconsistency

In the event of any inconsistency or conflict between the provisions of this Annex and the other provisions of the Contract, then the other provisions of the Contract shall prevail.

1.4 Accounting Records and Reports

1.4.1 The CONTRACTOR shall maintain the Accounts in accordance with Article 15.1 and in accordance with this Accounting Procedure, including in accordance with the charts of Accounts agreed under Paragraph 1.4.

1.4.2 Within sixty (60) days of the Effective Date, the CONTRACTOR shall submit to and discuss with the GOVERNMENT a proposed or line of charts of Accounts, which outline shall be in accordance with generally accepted standards and recognized accounting systems and consistent with normal petroleum industry practice and procedures. Within ninety (90) days of receiving the above submission, the GOVERNMENT shall either provide written notification of its approval of the proposal or request in writing revisions to the proposal. Within one hundred and eighty (180) days after the Effective Date, the CONTRACTOR and the GOVERNMENT shall agree on the outline of charts of Accounts which shall describe the basis of the accounting system and procedures to be developed and used under this Contract. Following such agreement, the CONTRACTOR shall expeditiously prepare and provide the GOVERNMENT with format copies of the comprehensive charts of Accounts and manuals related to the accounting, recording and reporting functions, and procedures which are, and shall be observed under the Contract.

1.4.3 Notwithstanding the generality of the foregoing, the CONTRACTOR shall make regular Statements relating to the Petroleum Operations. These Statements are as shown:

(a) Production Statement (as indicated in Paragraph 6)
(b) Value of Production and Pricing Statement (as indicated in Paragraph 7)
(c) Cost Recovery and Share Account Statement (as indicated in Paragraph 8)
(d) Statement of Expenditures and Receipts (as indicated in Paragraph 9).
(e) Final End-of-Year Statement (as indicated in Paragraph 10).
(F) Budget Statement (as indicated in Paragraph 12).

1.4.4 All reports and statements shall be prepared in accordance with the Contract, Kurdistan Region Law and where there are no provisions of either of these, in accordance with prudent international petroleum industry practice.

1.5 Language and Units of Account

All Accounts shall be maintained and prepared into English language and shall be recorded in Dollars. Where necessary for clarification, the CONTRACTOR may also maintain Accounts in other currencies.

1.6 Audit and Inspection Rights of the GOVERNMENT

In addition to the provisions of Articles 15.3 to 15.7 and 15.9, the following provisions shall apply to any audit entered or in accordance with Articles 15.3 to 15.7;

1.6.1 For purposes of auditing, the GOVERNMENT, acting reasonably and in accordance with prudent international petroleum industry practice, may expand and verity, at reasonable times upon reasonable prior written notice to the CONTRACTOR, all charges and credits relating to the Petroleum Operations, such as books of account, accounting entries, material records and inventories, vouchers, payrolls, invoices and any other documents, correspondence and records including electronic records reasonably considered necessary by the GOVERNMENT to audit and verify the charges and credits, values and treatments.

1.6.2 Furthermore, the auditors shall have the right, in connection with such audit, to visit and inspect at reasonable times all sites, plants, facilities, warehouses and offices of the CONTRACTOR directly or indirectly serving the Petroleum Operations and to question personnel associated with those Petroleum Operations.

1.6.3 Where the GOVERNMENT requires verification of charges made by an Affiliated Company of the CONTRACTOR, the GOVERNMENT shall have the right to obtain an audit certificate for such changes from an internationally recognized firm of public accountants acceptable to both the GOVERNMENT and the CONTRACTOR, which may be the CONTRACTOR's statutory auditor.

1.6.4 All agreed adjustments resulting from an audit shall be promptly made in the CONTRACTOR'S Accounts and any consequential adjustments to payments due to the CONTRACTOR or to the GOVERNMENT, as the ease may be, shall be made promptly.

1.6.5 When issues are outstanding with respect to an audit, the CONTRACTOR shall maintain the relevant documents and permit inspection thereof until the issue is resolved.

1.7 Payments

Unless as otherwise provided in Article 24, Article 29 or other Articles of the Contract:

1.7.1 All payments between the Parties shall, unless otherwise agreed, be in Dollars and be made through a bank designated in writing by each receiving party; and all sums due under the Contract shall be paid within thirty (30) days following the end of the Month in which the obligation to make such payment occurred.

1.7.2 All sums due by one party to the other under the Contract shall, for each day such sums are overdue, bear interest compounded monthly at LIBOR plus two per cent (2%).

1.8 Currency Exchange Rates

In addition to the provisions of Article 29, the following provisions shall apply to any exchanges of currency carried or in accordance with Article 29:

1.8.1 Accounts received and Petroleum Costs incurred shall be converted from other currencies in Dollars in accordance with the CONTRACTOR's usual accounting procedures which shall reflect generally accepted accounting practices in the international petroleum industry, and with accordance to exchange rates obtained in accordance with Article 29.

1.9 Accrual Basis, Cash Flow Basis and Reports

All books and Accounts shall be prepared on an accrual basis in accordance with generally accepted accounting principles used in the international petroleum industry.

1.10 Values and Treatments

Values and treatments proposed by the CONTRACTOR relating to all Petroleum Costs shall be subject to challenge by the GOVERNMENT in the course of audit to ensure that they are in accordance with the provisions of this Accounting Procedure.

PARAGRAPH 2

2.1 Segregation of Costs and Expenses

Petroleum Costs shall be segregated in accordance with the purposes for which such

Petroleum Costs are made. The purposes which shall qualify are: (a) those which have been included in the approved Work Program and Budget for the year in which the Costs and Expenditures are made; (b) expenditures incurred in cases of emergency as set forth in Articles 11.7, 13.5, 13.9, 35.5, 35.6 and any other Articles of the Contract; (c) any other purposes agreed in the Articles of the Contract; and (d) other items which have been agreed by the Parties from time to time. All Petroleum Costs recoverable under Paragraph 3 relating to Petroleum Operations shall be classified, defined and allocated as set forth below.

2.2 **Exploration Costs**

Exploration costs are all direct and allocated indirect costs and expenditures incurred in carrying on the Exploration Operations, including all direct and allocated indirect costs and expenditures incurred in the search for Petroleum in an area which is or was, at the time when such costs and expenses were incurred, part of the Contract Area including:

2.2.1 Aerial, geophysical, geochemical, paleontological, geological, topographical and seismic surveys and studies and their interpretation and purchased geological and geophysical information;

2.2.2 Stratigraphic test hole drilling and wafer well drilling;

2.2.3 Labour, materials, supplies, and services used in drilling and formation testing of wells with the object of finding Petroleum or Appraisal Wells excluding any costs of the subsequent completion of such wells at producing wells;

2.2.4 Facilities to the extent used in the support of the purposes described In Paragraphs 2.2.1, 2.2.2, and 2.2.3, including access roads;

2.2.5 That portion of all service expenditures and that portion of all general and administrative expenditures directly attributable to Exploration Costs or allocated thereto in a consistent and equitable basis; and

2.2.6 Any other expenditures incurred in the search for and appraisal of Petroleum after 14 January 2005 and not otherwise covered under this Paragraph 2.2. and including any and all costs incurred in the search for and appraisal of Petroleum at the area known as the Pulkhona area pursuant to the Original Contract.

2.3 **Gas Marketing Costs**

Gas Marketing Costs are all direct und allocated indirect costs and expenditures incurred in carrying out Gas Marketing Operations and include that portion of all service expenditures and that portion of all general and administrative expenditures directly attributable to Gas Marketing Costs or allocated thereto on a consistent and equitable basis.

2.4 **Development Costs**

Development Costs are all direct and allocated indirect costs and expenditures incurred in carrying out Development Operations Including, all direct and allocated indirect costs and expenditures incurred in:

2.4.1 Drilling wells which are completed as producing wells and drilling wells for purposes of producing from a Petroleum reservoir, whether these wells are dry or producing and drilling wells for the injection of water or gas to enhance recovery of Petroleum;

2.4.2 Completing wells by way of installation of casing or equipment or otherwise after a well has been drilled for the purpose of bringing the well into use as a producing well or as a well for the injection of water or gas to enhance recovers of Petroleum;

2.4.3 The costs of Petroleum production, transport and storage facilities such as pipelines, flow lines, production and treatment units, wellhead equipment, subsurface equipment, enhanced recovery systems, Petroleum storage facilities, and access roads for production activities;

2.4.5 Engineering and design studies for dry wells and facilities referred to in Paragraphs 2.4.1, 2.4.2 and 2.4.3; and including that portion of all service expenditures and that portion of all general and administrative expenditures directly attributable to Development Costs or allocated thereto on a consistent and equitable basis; and any other expenditure inclined in the Development Operations and not otherwise covered under Paragraph 2.3.

2.5 Production Costs

Production Costs are all direct and allocated indirect costs and expenditures incurred in carrying out Production Operations, including all direct and allocated indirect costs and expenses incurred in Petroleum Operations after First Production which are other than Exploration Costs, Gas Marketing Costs, Development Costs and Decommissioning Costs. Production Costs include that portion of all service expenditures and that portion of all general and administrative expenditures directly attributable to Production Costs or allocated thereto on a consistent and equitable basis.

2.6 Decommissioning Costs

Decommissioning Costs are all direct and allocated indirect costs and expenditures incurred tn carrying out Decommissioning Operations and include that portion of all service expenditures and that potion of all general and administrative expenditures directly attributable to Decommissioning Costs or allocated thereto on a consistent and equitable basis, and the Decommissioning Reserve Fund shall be determined on such basis, in advance of incurring such costs, as provided in Article 38 and, for the purposes of cost recovery, the contributions to the Decommissioning Reserve Fund shall be recovered in accordance with Article 38.

2.7 Service Expenditures

Service expenditures are expenditures in support of Petroleum Operations including warehouses, vehicles, motorized rolling equipment, aircraft, fire and security stations, workshops, water and sewerage plants, power plants, housing, community and recreational facilities and furniture, tools and equipment used in these activities. Service expenditures in any Calendar Year shall include the costs incurred in such year to purchase and/or construct the said facilities as well as the annual costs of maintaining and operating the same. All service expenditures shall be regularly allocated as specified in Paragraphs 2.2.5, 2.3, 2.4, 2.5 and 2.6 to Exploration Costs, Gas Marketing Coats, Development Costs, Production Costs and Decommissioning Costs, respectively, and shall be separately shown under each of these categories. Where service expenditures are made in respect of shared facilities, the basis of allocation of costs to Petroleum Operations shall be consistent and equitable and shall be specified.

2.8 General and Administrative Expenditures

General and administrative expenditures are:

2.8.1 All main office, field office and general administrative expenditures in the Kurdistan Region including supervisory, accounting, procurement and employee relations services.

2.8.2 Where the CONTRACTOR is an Affiliate of a group of companies whose headquarters is Abroad (a "Foreign CONTRACTORS"), an annual overhead charge shall be made for services tendered (excluding the direct expenditures as referred in Paragraph 3.1.2.(b)) by any Affiliate of the foreign CONTRACTOR outside the Kurdistan Region to support and manage Petroleum Operations under the Contract, or where the CONTRACTOR, not being a Foreign CONTRACTOR, draws upon the Services of an Affiliate within the Kurdistan Region, an annual overhead charge shall be made for services rendered (excluding the direct expenditures as referred in Paragraphs 3.1.2 (a) and (b) by such Affiliate to support and manage Petroleum Operations under the Contract Parent Company Overhead). Parent Company Overhead will be deemed to cover the actual cost (being salaries, wages and labour burden, employee benefits, travel, hotel and other normally reimbursable expenses paid by the Affiliate of a CONTRACTOR in accordance with its standard personnel policy in force in the relevant period, provision of office accommodation and provision of services reasonably necessary for operation and maintaining such staff offices) incurred for services rendered by those functions of CONTRACTOR' s Affiliate, such as, but not limited to, international production headquarters, international exploration headquarters, treasury, payroll, taxation, insurance, legal, communications, computer services, controllers, personnel, executive administrative management, research and development, central engineering and process engineering which: (a) cannot, without unreasonable effort and/or expenditure or without the release of confidential data proprietary to any of the CONTRACTOR's Affiliates, be charged under any other section of this Annex; and (b) are properly allocable to Petroleum Operations under the Contract. It is understood, however, that services performed by the departments listed above and under corporate departments which directly benefit Petroleum Operations under the Contract shall be charged as direct costs in accordance with Paragraph 3. In respect of the costs of the CONTRACTOR's Parent Company Overhead, as described above, the CONTRACTOR shall charge monthly to Petroleum Operations an amount equal to the total of the following:

2.8.2.1 Exploration Overhead

The CONTRACTOR shall be entitled to an annual charge based on a sliding scale percentage and charged monthly to Petroleum Operations. The basis for applying this percentage shall be the total of Exploration Costs and Gas Marketing Costs during each Calendar Year (exclusive of this Exploration Overhead) or faction thereof less expenditures which have been subjected to the two (2) percent fee, referred to in paragraph 3,1.8(b). The sliding scale percentage shall be the following.

For the first four million Dollars (US$ 4,000,000) four percent (4%)

For the next four million Dollars (US$4,000,000) three percent (3%)

Over eight million Dollars (US$8,000,000) two percent (2%)

The foregoing percentages may be reviewed bor not more often than annually, and any approved appropriate adjustment shall be made, if necessary, prospectively.

2.8.2.2 Development, Production and Decommissioning Operations Overhead

The overhead rates applicable to Development, Production and Decommissioning Operations shall be agreed between the Parties in due course and shall incorporate the following guidelines: (a) The CONTRACTOR's charges must be charged as direct charges whenever possible. Overhead charges exist only to compensate the CONTRAC- TOR's Affiliates for costs which are properly allocable to Petroleum Operations under the Contract for which cannot, without unreasonable effort and/or release of confidential data proprietary to the CONTRACTOR's Affiliates, be charged under any other section. Overhead coats are billed monthly. Overhead must be commensurate with services rendered and based on actual cost but may not exceed an amount calculated as a percentage of certain annual expenditures excluding Exploration Costs; and (b) That percentage as well as the types of expenditures, which affect overhead and those, which do not, shall be agreed among the Parties; (c) The maximum percentage rates may be revised by mutual agreement not more often than annually. The initial maximum percentage rates and the types of expenditures to which they apply shall be agreed as soon the Parties possess reasonably reliable cost estimates for the relevant Production Area; (d) Overhead charges are not subject to audit by GOVERNMENT; (e) The CONTRACTOR shall upon request furnish at the end of each relevant Calendar Year to the GOVERNMENT a confirmation by its statutory auditor that the overhead costs actually charged do not duplicate any other charges and that the method used in allocating overhead to Petroleum Operations hereunder as opposed to other activities is reasonable and in accordance with generally accepted accounting practices; (f) The CONTRACTOR must budget for overhead charges.

2.8.3 All general and administrative expenditures shall be regularly allocated as specified in Paragraphs 2.2.5, 2.3, 2.4, 2.5 and 2.6 to Exploration Costs, Gas Marketing

Costs, Development Costs, Production Costs and Decommissioning Costs, respectively, and shall be separately shown under each of these categories.

PARAGRAPH 3 – COSTS, EXPENSES, EXPENDITURES AND CREDITS OF THE CONTRACTOR

3.1 Costs Recoverable Without Further Approval of the GOVERNMENT

The following Petroleum Costs incurred by the CONTRACTOR pursuant to the Contract as classified under the headings referred to in Paragraph 2 shall be recoverable for the purpose of Article 25 of the Contract (except lo the extent provided in Paragraph 2 or elsewhere in this Annex) without the requirement for obtaining any further approval of the GOVERNMENT, subject to audit as provided for in Article 15 and in Paragraph 1.6.

3.1.1 Surface Rights

All direct Costs necessary for the acquisition, renewal or relinquishment of surface right acquired and maintained in force for the purposes of the Contract.

3.1.2 Labour and Associated Labour Costs

(a) The CONTRACTOR's locally recruited employees based in the Kurdistan Region: Costs of all CONTRACTOR'S locally recruited employees who are directly engaged in the conduct of Petroleum Operations under the Contract in the Kurdistan Region. Such costs shall include the costs of whines, wages, bonuses, overtime, employee benefits and GOVERNMENT benefits for employees and levies imposed on the CONTRACTOR as in employee's transportation and relocation costs within the Kurdistan Region of the employee and such members of the employee's family (limited to spouse and dependent children) as required by law or customary practice in the Kurdistan Region. If such employees are engaged in other activities in the Kurdistan Region, in addition to Petroleum Operations, the cost of such employees shall be apportioned on a time sheet basis according to sound and acceptable accounting principles.

(b) Assigned Personnel: Costs of salaries and wages including bonuses of the CONTRACTOR'S employees directly engaged in the conduct of the Petroleum Operations under the Contract, whether temporarily or permanently assigned, irrespective of the location of such employees, it being understood that in the case of those personnel only a portion of whose time is wholly dedicated to Petroleum Operations under the Contract, only that pro-rata portion of applicable salaries, wages, and other costs as delineated in Paragraphs 3.1.2(c). (d), (c), (f) and (g), shall be charged and the bails of such pro-rata allocation shall he specified.

(c) The CONTRACTOR's costs regarding holiday, vacation, sickness and disability benefits and living and housing and other customary allowances applicable to the salaries and wages chargeable under Paragraph 3.1.2(b).

(d) Expenses or contributions made pursuant to assessments or obligations imposed under Law which are applicable to the CONTRACTOR's cost of salaries and wages chargeable under Paragraph 3.1.2(b).

(e) The CONTRACTOR'S cost of established plow for employees' group life insurance, hospitalization, pension, stock purchases, savings, bonus, and other benefit plans of a like nature customarily granted to the CONTRACTOR's employees, provided however that such costs are in accordance with generally acceptable standards in the international petroleum industry applicable to salaries and wages chargeable to Petroleum Operations under Paragraph 3.1.2(b).

(f) Actual transportation and travel expenses of employees of CONTRACTOR, including those made for travel and relocation of the expatriate employees, including their families and personal effects, assigned to the Kurdistan Region whose salaries and wages are chargeable to Petroleum Operations under Paragraph 3.1.2 (b). Actual Transportation expenses of expatriate personnel transferred to Petroleum Operations from their country of origin shall be charged to the Petroleum Operations. Transportation expenses of personnel transferred from Petroleum Operations to a country other than the country of their origin shall not be charged to the Petroleum Operations. Transportation cost as used in this section shall mean the cost of freight and passenger service, meals, folds, insurance and other expenditures related tn vacation and transfer travel and authorized under the CONTRACTOR standard personnel policies. The CONTRACTOR shall ensure that all expenditures related to transportation costs are equitably allocated to the activities, which have benefited from the personnel concerned.

(g) Reasonable personal expenses of personnel whose salaries and wages are chargeable to Petroleum Operations under Paragraph 3.1.(b) and for which expenses such personnel are reimbursed under the CONTRACTOR'S standard personnel policies. In the event such expenses are not wholly attributable to Petroleum Operations, the petroleum Operations shall be charged with only the applicable portion thereof, which shall be determined on an equitable basis.

3.1.3 Transportation and Employee Relocation Costs

The cost of transportation of employees, equipment, materials and supplies other than as provided in Paragraph 3.1.2(f) necessary for the conduct of the Petroleum Operations under the Contract along with other related coats such as, but not limited to, import duties, customs fees, unloading charges, dock fees, and inland and ocean freight charges.

(a) Third Parties

The actual costs of contract services, services of professional consultants. utilities, and other services necessary for the conduct of the Petroleum Operations under the Contract performed by third parties other than an Affiliate of the CONTRACTOR

(b) Affiliates of the CONTRACTOR

(i) Professional and Administrative Services Expenses; cost of professional and administrative services provided by any Affiliates of the CONTRACTOR for the direct benefit of Petroleum Operations, including services provided by the production, exploration, legal, procurement, financial, insurance, accounting and computer services divisions other than those covered by paragraphs 3 1.4 (b) (ii), 3.1.6 and 3.1.8 (b) which CONTRACTOR may use in lieu of having its own employees. Such charges shall reflect the cost of providing their services. Such charges shall not include any element of profit and shall be no more or less favourable than similar charges for other operations carried on by the CONTRACTOR and its Affiliates. The chargeout rate shall include all costs incurred by Affiliates incidental to the employment of such personnel including Associated labour Costs and the cost of maintaining and operating offices and providing all support services for such personnel. Costs of travel of such personnel in respect of Petroleum Operations will be directly charged. The charges for such services shall not exceed those prevailing if performed by non-Affiliated third parties, taking into account the quality and availability of such services. Where the work is performed outside the home office base of such personnel, the daily rate shall be charged from the date such personnel leave the home office base where they usually work up to their return thereto, including days which are not working days in the location where the work is performed, excluding any holiday entitlements derived by such personnel from their employment at their home office base.

(ii) Scientific or Technical Personnel; cost of scientific or technical personnel services provided by any Affiliate of the CONTRACTOR for the direct benefit of Petroleum Operations, which cost shall be charged on a cost of service basis and shall not include any element of profit. The chargeout rate shall include all costs incurred by Affiliates incidental to the employment of such personnel including all Labour and Associated Labour Costs and the costs of maintaining und operating offices and providing all support services for such personnel costs of travel of such personnel in respect of Petroleum Operations will be directly charged. The charges for such services shall not exceed those prevailing if performed by nonaffiliated third parties, taking into account the quality and availability of such services. Unless the work to be done by such personnel is covered by an approved Work Program and Budget, the CONTRACTOR shall not authorize work by such personnel without approval of the GOVERNMENT,

(iii) Equipment and facilities use of equipment and facilities owned and furnished by the CONTRACTOR'S Affiliates at rates commensurate with the cost of ownership and operation; provided, however, that such rates shall not exceed those currently prevailing for the supply of like equipment and facilities on comparable terms in the area where the Petroleum Operations are being conducted and shall be on an arm's length basis. On the request of the GOVERNMENT, the CONTRACTOR shall provide the GOVERNMENT with evidence of such rates being on an arm's length basis If the GOVERNMENT considers that any such rate is not on the arm's length basis, then the GOVERNMENT has the right to refer the matter to an expert pursuant to Article 42.2 of the Contract. The equipment and facilities referred to herein shall exclude major investment items such as (but not limited to) drilling rigs, producing platforms, oil treating facilities, oil and gas loading and transportation systems, storage and terminal facilities and other major facilities, rates for which shall be subject to separate agreement with the GOVERNMENT.

3.1.5 Communications

Cost of acquiring, leasing, installing, operating, repairing and maintaining communication systems including radio and microwave facilities within and between the Contract Area and the CONTRACTOR's nearest base facility.

3.1.6 Office and Miscellaneous Facilities

Net cost to the CONTRACTOR of establishing maintaining and operating any office. sub-office, warehouse, housing or other facility directly serving the Petroleum Operations. If any such facility services more than one contract area, the net costs thereof shall be allocated on an equitable basis in accordance with prudent international petroleum industry practice.

(a) Costs incurred in the Contract Area as a result of legislation for archeological and geophysical surveys relating to identification and protection of cultural sites or resources;

(b) Costs incurred in environmental or ecological surveys requited by regulatory authorities, including an environmental impact assessment commissioned pursuant to Article 37.5 of the Contract and any other costs incurred in complying with the requirements of Article 37;

(c) Costs to provide or have available pollution containment and removal equipment;

(d) Costs of actual control and cleanup of oil spills, and of such further responsibilities resulting therefrom as may be required by applicable laws and regulations;

(e) Costs of restoration of the operating environment incurred pursuant to an approval scheme prepared in accordance with Article of the Contract;

(f) Any costs incurred for the decommissioning of facilities and site restoration, including any related activity required by the GOVERNMENT or other competent authority or by the Contract; and

(g) Any contributions made by the CONTRACTOR to the Decommissioning Reserve Fund in accordance with Article 38, when such contributions are made.

3.1.8 Costs of materials and supplies, equipment, machines, tools and any other goods of a similar nature used or consumed in Petroleum Operations subject to the following:

(a) Acquisition — the CONTRACTOR shall only supply or purchase materials for use in Petroleum Operations that may be used in the foreseeable future. The accumulation of surplus stocks and inventory shall be avoided so far as is reasonably practical and consistent with efficient und economical operations. Inventory levels shall, however, take into account the time lag for replacement, emergency needs, weather conditions affecting operations and similar considerations.

(b) Components of costs, arm's length transactions — except as otherwise provided in paragraph 3.1.8(d), material purchased by the CONTRACTOR in arm's length transaction in the open market for use in the Petroleum Operations under the Contract shall be valued to include invoice price less trade and cash discounts (if any), licence fees, purchase and procurement fees plus freight and forwarding charges between point of supply and point of shipment. freight to port of destination, insurance, taxes, customs duties, consular fees, excise taxes, other items chargeable against imported materials and, where applicable, handling and transportation expenses from point of importation to warehouse or operating site. Where an Affiliate of the CONTRACTOR has arranged the purchase, coordinated the forwarding and expediting effort, its costs should not exceed those currently prevailing in normal arm's length transactions on the open market and in any case shall not exceed a. fee equal to two percent (2%) of the value of the materials added to the cost of the materials purchased.

(c) Accounting-such material costs shall be charged lo the accounting records and books in accordance with the "First In, First out" (FIFO)method,

(d) Material purchased from or sold to Affiliates of the CONTRACTOR or transferred from other activities of the CONTRACTOR to or from Petroleum Operations under this Contract shall be valued and charged or credited at the prices specified in Paragraphs 3.I.8(d)(i), 3.1.8(d)(ii) and 3.I.8(iii).

(i) New material, including used new material moved from inventory (Condition "A"), shall be valued at the current international net price which shall not exceed the price prevailing in normal arm's length transactions in the open market.

(ii) Used material (Conditions "B" "C" and "D")

(A) Material which is in sound and serviceable condition and is suitable for re-use without reconditioning shall be classified as Condition "B" and priced at seventy five percent (75%) of the current fee of new material defined in Paragraph 3 l.8,(d)(i);

(B) Material which cannot be classified as Condition "B" but which after reconditioning will be further serviceable for its original function shall be classified as Condition "C" and priced of not more than fifty percent (50%) of the current fee of new material as defined in Paragraph 3.1.8(d)(i). The cost of reconditioning shall be charged to the reconditioned material provided that the value of Condition "C" material plus the cost of reconditioning do not exceed the value of Condition "B" material;

(C) Material which cannot be classified as Condition "B" or Condition "C" shall be classified as Condition "D" and priced at a value commensurate with its use by the CONTRACTOR. If material is not fit for use by the CONTRACTOR, it shall be deposed of as junk.

(iii) Material involving erection costs shall be charged at the applicable condition percentage of the current knocked-down price of new material as defined in Paragraph 3.1.8(d)(i).

(iv) When the use of material is temporary and its service to the Petroleum Operations under the Contract does not justify the reduction in price as provided for in paragraph 3.1.8(d)(ii)(B), such material shall be priced on a basis that will result in a net charge to the accounts under the Contract consistent with the value of the service rendered.

(v) Premium prices — whenever material is not readily obtainable at published or listed prices because of national emergencies, strikes or other unusual causes over which the CONTRACTOR has no control, the CONTRACTOR may charge Petroleum Operations for the required material at the CONTRACTOR'S actual cost incurred in providing such material, in making it suitable for use. and in moving it to the Contract Area, provided notice in writing is furnished to the GOVERNMENT or the proposed charge prior to charging Petroleum Operations for such material and the GOVERNMENT shall have the right to challenge the transaction on audit.

(vi) Warranty of material furnished by the CONTRACTOR — the CONTRACTOR does not warrant the material furnished. In case of defective material, credit shall not be passed to Petroleum Operations until adjustment has been received by the CONTRACTOR from the manufacturers of the material or their agents.

(vii) Adjustments arising from material inventories conducted in accordance with Paragraph 5.2.

(e) Equipment of the CONTRACTOR charged at rates not to exceed the average commercial rates of non-affiliated third parties for equipment, facilities, installations and utilities for use in the area where the same are used. On request, the CONTRACTOR shall finish a list of rates and the basis of application. Such rates stall be revised when found to be either excessive or insufficient, not more than once every six (6) Months. Drilling tools and ether equipment lost in the hole or damaged beyond repair may be charged at replacement cost less depreciation plus transportation costs to deliver like equipment to the location where used.

(f) Use of leased or hired machinery and/or a equipment in the Petroleum Operations shall be charged at full cost to the CONTRACTOR. This may include mobilization and de-mobilization charges, lease and hire fees, as well as other contractual costs.

3.1.9 Rentals and Taxes

All rentals of every and nature levied by any GOVERNMENT and all Taxes imposed in connection with the CONTRACTOR'S assets, income or activities under the Contract and paid directly by the CONTRACTOR or any CONTRACTOR Entity (save where the contrary is expressly provided in the Contract) with the exception of Taxes described in Article 31.2 and bonus payments made under Article 32. If the CONTRACTOR, any CONTRACTOR Entity or any of its Affiliated Companies is subject to income or withholding tax as a result of services performed at cost for the Petroleum Operations under the Contract, its charges for such services may be increased by the amount required to cover such taxes (grossed up) including taxes on such gross up.

3.1.10 Insurance and Losses

Insurance premiums and costs incurred for insurance carried for the benefit of the Petroleum Operations, provided that such insurance is customary, affords prudent protection against risk and is at a premium no higher than that charged on a competitive basis by insurance companies which are not Affiliated Companies of the CONTRACTOR. Except in cases or failure to insure where insurance coverage is required pursuant to the Contract, actual costs and losses incurred shall be recoverable to the extent not made good by insurance unless such losses result solely from an act of wilful misconduct by the CONTRACTOR. Such costs may include repair and replacement of property in the Contract Area resulting from damages or losses incurred by fire, flood, storm, theft, accident or such oilier cause.

3.1.11 Legal Expenses

All reasonable costs and expenses resulting from the handling, investigating, asserting, defending, or settling of any claim or legal action necessary or expediant for the procuring, perfecting, retention and protection of the Contract Area, and in defending or prosecuting lawsuits involving the Contract Area or any third party claim arising out of the Petroleum Operations under the Contract or sums paid in respect of legal services necessary for the protection of the joint interest of the GOVERNMENT and the CONTRACTOR shall be recoverable. Such expenditures shall include attorney's fees, court costs, arbitration costs of investigation, and procurement of evidence and amounts paid in settlement or satisfaction of any such litigation and claims, provided such costs are not covered elsewhere in the Annex. Where legal services are rendered to such matters by salaried or regularly retained lawyers of the CONTRACTOR or an Affiliated Company of the CONTRACTOR, such compensation shall be included instead under Paragraph 3.1.2 or 3.1.4(b) as applicable.

3.1.12 Claims

Expenditures made in the settlement or satisfaction of any loss, claim, damage, judgement or other expense arising out of or relating to Petroleum Operations, except as may otherwise be covered elsewhere in the Annex.

3.1.13 Training Costs

All costs and expenses incurred by the CONTRACTOR in the training of its employees engaged in Petroleum Operations under the Contract.

3.1.14 General and Administrative Costs

The costs described in Paragraph 2.8.1 and the charge described in Paragraph 2.8 2.

3.1.15 Banking Charges and Currency Exchange Losses

Charges and fees by the banks for money transfers, payments and foreign exchange transactions, as well as currency exchange losses incurred by the CONTRACTOR in connection with the Petroleum Operations.

3.1.16 Other Expenditures

Other reasonable expenditures not Covered or dealt with in the foregoing provisions of Paragraph 3 which are necessarily incurred by the CONTRACTOR for the proper, economical and efficient conduct of Petroleum Operations

3.2 Credit Under the Contract

The proceeds, other than the proceeds from the sale of Petroleum received from Petroleum Operations under the Contract, including the items listed below shall be credited to the Accounts under the Contract for the purposes of Article 25 of the Contract:

3.2.1 The proceeds of any insurance or claim or judicial awards in connection with

Petroleum Operations under the Contract or any assets charged to the Accounts under the Contract where such operations or assets have been insured and the premia charged to the Accounts under the Contract.

3.2.2 Legal costs charged to the accounts under Paragraph 3.1.11 and subsequently recovered by the CONTRACTOR

3.2.3 Revenue received from third parties for the use of property or assets the cost of which has been charged to the Accounts under the Contract.

3.2.4 Any adjustment received by the CONTRACTOR from the suppliers' manufacturers or their agents in connection with a defective material the cost of which was previously charged by the CONTRACTOR to the Accounts under the Contract.

3.2.5 Rentals, refunds, including refunds of taxes paid, or other credits received by the CONTRACTOR which apply to any charge which has been made to the Accounts under the Contract, but excluding any award granted to the CONTRACTOR under arbitration or expert proceedings.

3.2.6 Costs originally charged to the Accounts under the Contract for materials subsequently exported from the Kurdistan Region or transferred to another Contract Area within the Kurdistan Region.

3.2.7 Proceeds from the sale or exchange by the CONTRACTOR of plant or facilities used in Petroleum Operations the acquisition costs of which have been charged to the Accounts under the Contract.

3.2.8 Proceeds derived from the sale or license of any intellectual property the development costs of which were incurred pursuant to and are recoverable under the Contract

3.2.9 Proceeds derived from the sale, exchange, lease, hire, transfer or disposal in any manner whatsoever of any other item the costs of which have been charged to Petroleum Operations.

3.3 Duplication of Charges and Credits

Notwithstanding any provision to the contrary in this Accounting Procedure, there shall be no duplication of charges or credits to the Accounts under the Contract

PARAGRAPH 4－COSTS AND EXPENSES NOT TO BE TREATED AS IRRECOVERABLE

The following costs and expenditures shall not be included in the Petroleum Costs recoverable under Article 25:

4.1 Taxes on income or profit paid to any GOVERNMENT authority except taxes and duties that may be included in the costs of material and equipment purchased for the Petroleum Operations;

4.2 Any payment made to the GOVERNMENT by reason of the failure of the CONTRACTOR to fulfil its Minimum Exploration Obligations in respect of the relevant Sub-Period under the Contract;

4.3 The cost of any letter of guarantee, if any, required under the Contract;

4.4 The bonuses set out in Article 32 of the Contract;

4.5 Coats of marketing or translation of Petroleum beyond the Delivery Point (excluding Gas Marketing Costs);

4.6 Attorney's fees and other coats of proceedings in connection with arbitration under Article 42 of the Contract or internationally recognised independent expert determination as provided in the Contract or this Accounting Procedure;

4.7 Any interests, fees, costs and expenses paid by the CONTRACTOR for loans and any other form of financing or advances for the financing of the Petroleum Costs entered into by the CONTRACTOR with third parties or Affiliated Companies;

4.8 Any accounting provision for depreciation and/or amortization, excluding any adjustments in value pursuant to Paragraph 3.1.8;

4.9 Dividends, repayment of equity or repayment of intercompany loans; and

4.10 Fines and penalties imposed under Law.

PARAGRAPH 5 – RECORDS AND VALUATION OF ASSETS

5.1 Records

The CONTRACTOR shall maintain detailed records of property in use for Petroleum Operations under the Contract in accordance with prudent international petroleum industry practice for exploration and production activities.

5.2 Inventories

Inventories of property in use in Petroleum Operations shall be taken at reasonable intervals but at least once a year with respect to movable assets and once every three (3) years with respect to immovable assets. The CONTRACTOR shall give the GOVERNMENT at least thirty (30) days written notice of its intention to take such inventory and the GOVERNMENT shall have the right to be represented when such inventory is taken. Failure of the GOVERNMENT to be represented at an inventory shall bind the GOVERNMENT to accept the inventory taken by the CONTRACTOR. The CONTRACTOR shall clearly inform GOVERNMENT about the principles upon which valuation of the inventory has been based. The CONTRACTOR shall make every effort to provide to the GOVERNMENT a full report on such inventory within thirty (30) days of the taking of the inventory. When an assignment of rights under the Contract takes place, the CONTACTOR may, at the request of the assignee, take a special inventory, provided that the costs of such inventory are borne by the assignee.

PARAGRAPH 6 – PRODUCTION STATEMENT

6.1 Production Information

Without prejudice to the rights and obligations of the Parties under Article 16 of the Contract, from the date of First Production from the Contract Area, the CONTRACTOR shall submit a monthly production statement to the GOVERNMENT showing the following information separately for each producing Development Area and in aggregate for the Contract Area:

6.1.1 The quantity of Crude Oil produced and saved;
6.1.2 The quality characteristics of such Crude Oil produced and saved;
6.1.3 The quantity of Natural Gas produced and saved;
6.1.4 The quality characteristics of such Natural Gas produced and saved;
6.1.5 The quantities of Crude Oil anil Natural Gas used for the purposes of carrying on drilling and production operations and pumping to field storage;
6.1.6 The quantities of Crude Oil and Natural Gas unavoidably lost;
6.1.7 The quantities of Natural Gas flared and vented;
6.1.8 The site of Petroleum stocks held at the beginning of the calendar Month in question;
6.1.9 The size of Petroleum stocks held at the end of the calendar Month in question;
6.1.10 the quantities of Natural Gas reinjected into the Reservoir; and
6.1.11 In respect of the Contract Area as a whole, the quantities of Petroleum transferred at the Measurement Point. All quantities shown in this Statement shall be expressed in both volumetric terms (Barrels of oil and cubic meters of gas) and in

weight (metric tones).

6.2 Submission of Production Statement

The Production Statement for each calendar Month shall be submitted to the GOVERNMENT no later than ten (10) days after the end of such calendar Month.

PARAGRAPH 7 – VALUE OF PRODUCTION AND PRICING STATEMENT

7.1 Value of Production and Pricing Statement Information

The CONTRACTOR shall, for purposes of Article 25 of the Contract, prepare a statement providing calculations of the value of Crude Oil produced and saved during each Quarter.

This "Value of Production and Pricing Statement" shall contain the following information:

7.1.1 The quantities and prices realized therefor by the CONTRACTOR in respect of sales of Natural Gas and Crude Oil delivered to third parties made during the Quarter in question; and

7.1.2 The quantities and prices realized therefor by the CONTRACTOR in respect of sales of Natural Gas and Crude Oil delivered during the Quarter in question, other than to Third Parties.

7.2 Submission of Value of Production and Pricing Statement

The Value of Production and Pricing Statement for each Quarter shall be submitted to the GOVERNMENT not later than twenty-one (21) days after the end of such Quarter.

PARAGRAPH 8 – COST RECOVERY AND SHARE ACCOUNT STATEMENT

8.1 Cost Recovery Statement

The CONTRACTOR shall prepare with respect to each Quarter a Cost Recovery Statement containing the following information:

8.1.1 Recoverable Petroleum Costs carried forward from the previous Quarter, if any;

8.1.2 Recoverable Petroleum Costs for the Quarter in question;

8.1.3 Credits under the Contract for the Quarter in question;

8.1.4 Total Recoverable Petroleum Costs for the Quarter in question (Paragraph 8.1.1 plus Paragraph 8.1.2 set of Paragraph 8.1.3);

8.1.5 Quantity and value of Petroleum applied to cost recovery pursuant lo Article 25 taken by the CONTRACTOR for the Quarter in question; and

8.1.6 Amount of recoverable Petroleum Costs to be earned forward into the real Quarter (Paragraph 8.1 4 net of Paragraph 8.1.5).

8.2 Cumulative Production Statement

The CONTRACTOR shall prepare with respect to each Quarter a Cumulative Production Statement containing the following information:

8.2.1 The cumulative production position at the end of the Quarter preceding the Quarter in question;

8.2.2 Production of Export Petroleum for the Quarter in question;

8.2.4 The cumulative production position at the end of the Quarter in question;

8.2.5 The amount of Petroleum applied to Royalty pursued to Article 24 cost recovery pursuant to Article 25 and Profit Petroleum pursuant to Article 26, taken by the GOVERNMENT and by the CONTRACTOR, respectively, during the Quarter in question; and

8.2.6 the forecast of production and the share of Petroleum applied to Royalty pursuant to Article 24, cost recovery pursuant to Article and Profit Oil pursuant to Article 26 due to the GOVERNMENT and to the CONTRACTOR, respectively, for the next succeeding Quarter.

8.3 Preparation and Submission of Cost Recovery and Cumulative Production Statements

8.3.1 Provisional Cost Recovery and Cumulative Production Statements, containing estimated information where necessity, shall be submitted by the CONTRACTOR on the last day of each Quarter for the purposes of Article 25 of the Contract.

8.3.2 Final quarterly Cost Recovery and Cumulative Production Statements shall be submitted within thirty (30) days of the end of the Quarter in question.

8.4 Annual Statement

For the purposes of Article 25 of the Contract, an Annual Cost Recovery and Cumulative. Production Statement shall be submitted within ninety (90) days of the end of each Year. The Annual Statement shall contain the categories of information listed in Paragraphs 8.1 and 8.2 for the Year in question, separated into the Quarters of the Year in question and showing the cumulative positions at the end of the Year in question with respect to cumulative unrecovered Petroleum costs and Cumulative Production.

PARAGRAPH 9 – STATEMENT OF EXPENDITURE AND RECEIPTS

9.1 The CONTRACTOR shall prepare with respect to each Quarter a Statement of Expenditure and Receipts under the Contract. The Statement will distinguish between Exploration Costs, Gas Marketing Costs, Development Costs, Production Costs and Decommissioning Costs, and will identity major items of expenditures within these categories. The Statement will show the following:

9.1.1 Actual expenditures and receipts for the Quarter in question;

9.1.2 Cumulative expenditure and receipts for the budget Calender Year in question;

9.1.3 Latest forecast cumulative expenditures at the Calendar Year end; and

9.1.4 Variations between budget forecast and latest forecast and explanation thereof.

9.2 The Statement of expenditure and Receipts of each Quarter shall be submitted to the GOVERNMENT no later than thirty (30) days after the end of such Quarter.

PARAGRAPH 10 – FINAL END-OF-YEAR STATEMENT

The CONTRACTOR will prepare a Final End-of-Year Statement. The Statement will contain information as provided in the Production Statement, Value of Production and Pricing Statement, Cost Recovery and Cumulative Production Statements and Statement of Expenditures and Receipts, but will he based on actual quantities of Petroleum produced and expenses incurred. This Statement will be used to make any adjustments that are necessary to the payments made by the CONTRACTOR under the Contract. The Final End- of-Year Statement of each Calendar Year shall be submitted to the GOVERNMENT within ninety (90) days of the end of such Calendar Year.

PARAGRAPH 11 – AUDITS

Each such report and statement provided for in Paragraphs 6 through 10 shall be considered true and correct, unless the GOVERNMENT raises an exception thereto within the timeframe and under the process set out in Article 15 of the Contract.

PARAGRAPH 12 – ANNUAL WORK PROGRAM AND BUDGET

12.1 Each annual work Program and Budget to be prepared in accordance with Articles 11.12 and 14 of the Contract, in respect of Exploration Oils, Gas Marketing Costs, Development Costs and Production Costs, respectively, will show the following:

12.1.1 Forecast expenditures for the budget Calendar Year in question including a quarterly classification of such expenditures;

12.1.2 Cumulative expenditures to the end of said budget Calendar Year; and

12.1.3 A schedule showing the most important individual items of Development Costs (if applicable) for said budget Year.

PARAGRAPH 13 – CONTRACTOR ENTITY INCOME COMPUTATION

13.1 For the purpose of Article 31.3(b) of the Contract, the net taxable profits of each CONTRACTOR Entity from all the Petroleum Operations earned out under this Contract shall be calculated in accordance with this Paragraph.

13.2 Each CONTRACTOR Entity Shall maintain for each Calendar Year separate Accounts with respect to the Petroleum Operations which shall be used, inter alia, to establish a profit and loss account and a balance sheet which will show the results of the Petroleum Operation carried out in such Calendar Year as well as the assets and liabilities assigned or directly related hereto. The profit and lots account will be maintained under the accrual method of accounting.

13.3 For purposes of determining the net taxable profits of each CONTRACTOR Entity for corporate income tax purposes,

13.3.1 The profit and loss account of such CONTRACTOR Entity shall be credited with the following:

(a) if the Royalty is paid in cash pursuant to Article 24, revenues arising from the disposal of Royalty volumes as recorded in such entity's Accounts and determined in accordance with the provisions of Article 24;
(b) revenues arising from the disposal of any available Petroleum to which such entity is entitled for recovery of its Petroleum Costs as recorded in its Accounts and determined in accordance with the provisions of Article 25;
(c) revenues from the disposal of any Profit Petroleum to which such entity is entitled under Article 26 as is recorded in its Accounts and determined in accordance with the provisions of Article 26;
(d) any other revenues or proceeds directly connected to the Petroleum Operations including those arising from the disposal of related Petroleum substances, or from the treatment storage and transportation of products for third partie; and
(e) any exchange gains realised or other financial income earned by such entity in connection with the Petroleum Operations.

13.3.2 The profit and loss account for such CONTRACTOR Entity shall be debited with all charges incurred for the purposes of the Petroleum Operations whether incurred inside or outside the Kurdistan Region, which charges shall include the following:

(a) in addition to the charges specifically set forth below in this Paragraph, all other Petroleum Costs, including the costs of supplies, personnel and manpower expenses, and the cost of services provided to the CONTRACTOR in connection with the Petroleum Costs;
(b) if the Royalty is paid in cash pursuant to Article 24, royalty payments made and as recorded in such entity's Accounts and determined in accordance with the provisions of Article 24;
(c) general and administrative expenditures related to the Petroleum Operations performed under this Contract;
(d) depreciation of capital expenditure in accordance with the following provisions
    (i) capital expenditures incurred by the CONTRACTOR for the purposes of the Petroleum Operations shall be depreciated on a reducing balance basis;
    (ii) the depreciation rates, which shall be applicable from the Calendar Year during which such capital expenditures are incurred, or from the Calendar Year during which the assets corresponding to said capital expenditures are put into normal service, whichever is later, for the first Calendar Year in

question and for each subsequent Calendar Year, are as follows:

Nature of the capital asset to be depreciated	Annual depreciation Rate
Permanent buildings	10.0%
Temporary buildings	20.0%
Office and house furniture and fixtures	20.0%
Productive wells	10.0%
Production and delivery equipment	20.0%
Drilling equipment	20.0%
Pipelines	20.0%
Automotive equipment	20.0%
Marine and aviation equipment	20.0%
All other capital assets	20.0%

(e) Expeditation Costs (which for the avoidance of doubt include appraisal expenditures) shall be deductible on a reducing balance basis at the rate of 20% per annum;
(f) interest and fees paid to creditors of the CONTRACTOR for their actual amount;
(g) losses of assets resulting from destruction or damage, assets which are renounced or abandoned during the year, assets which are transferred under Article 20.2, bad debts, indemnities paid to third parties as compensation for damage;
(h) any other costs, expenses, losses or charges directly related to the Petroleum Operations, including exchange losses realised in connection with the Petroleum Operations as well as the bonuses provided in Article 32, the Exploration Rental provided in Article 6.3, the Production Rental provided in Article 13.10, the allocation to training, provided in Article 23.7 and the allocation to the Environment Fund provided in Article 23.9, the costs specified in Articles 23.11, 38.1 and 38.6 and transportation and marketing costs beyond the Delivery Point; and
(i) the amount of non-offset losses relating to the previous Calendar Years, which shall be carried forward for an indefinite period until full settlement of said losses or termination of this Contract,

13.3.3 The net profit of such CONTRACTOR Entity shall be equal to the difference between all the amounts credited and all the amounts debited in the profit and loss account; and

(a) if this amount is negative, it shall constitute a loss.
(b) if the amount is positive, it shall be grossed up to take account of the fact that such entity's corporate income tax is being settled out of the GOVERNMENT'S share of the Profit Petroleum in accordance with Article 31.2 by applying the following formula in order to provide such entity's net taxable profits for corporate income tax purposes

Net Taxable

$$\text{Net Profits}\ \frac{(100\text{-Applicable Rate of Corporate Income Tax})}{100}$$

13.4 For purposes of determining each CONTRACTOR Entity's liability to corporate income tax for a tax year in respect of the Petroleum Operations carried out under this Contract, the net taxable profits (if any) for such tax year shall be multiplied by the applicable rate of corporate income tax, us provided in Article 31.3(a).

KNOC E&P Operations 공시자료 (As of Jun. 2011)[32]

Indonesia

Block	Contract	Acreage (km^2)	Working Interest	Operator	Production 2011 (boped)	Phase
South East Sumatra	PSC	8,098	8.91%	CNOOC SES (China)	57,363	Production

SES

The South East Sumatra(referenced as 'SES' below) is one of oil development offshore of Indonesia. The SES is located in shallow water(20~50m) in the Java Sea off the southeastern coast of Sumatra. The SES covers approximately 8,098 sq.km, and is consist of 34 fields and 360 production wells.

The SES was first awarded to IIAPCO in 1968 under PSC contract and has been produced since 1971. KNOC acquired a 8.91% interest in the SES in 2002, and the contact will be valid until 2018.

After the gas contract with Indonesia PLN in 2004, the SES Block began to produce the gas in ZELDA and BANUWATI field in 2006. And a gas project has been conducted to increase the gas reserve and productivity.

Despite the long production period, oil and gas reserve amounts are estimated 66 million barrels and 374,425 million cubic feet as of Jun 2011. Those are result from the work programs which comprise secondary recovery water flood schemes, infill drilling, well maintenance and workover programmes as well as marginal field additions.

In 2011, production of the SES Block will be approximately 38,000 bopd of oil and 101 mmcfd of gas from over 360 producing wells. Also, three exploration and ten development wells are scheduled to be drilled.

Uzbekistsan

Block	Contract	Acreage (km^2)	Working Interest	Operator	Phase
Aral	PSA	18,000	10.2%	Aral Sea Operating Co.	Exploration
Namangan/ Chust	Explorat'n	4,800	50%	KNOC	Exploration

Aral

"Production Sharing Agreement" for Aral Sea block exploration project was concluded. The participating companies are KNOC (Korea), Uzbekneftegaz (Uzbekistan), Lukoil (Russia) and CNPC (China). During the Initial stage from January 2007 to April 2011, two exploratory drillings and seismic acquisition (2D 2,940 L-km) was completed and in the 1st exploratory drilling gas was discovered. Currently, the partners are making preparation for the Main stage.

Namangan/Chust

Namangan/Chust block is located in the Northern part of Fergana Basin in the Republic of Uzbekistan near to Kyrgyzstan. The acreage of the block is approximately 4,800 square kilometers. KNOC was proposed to participate in the project of the block in May 2005. Having performed the tech. and feasibility evaluation, KNOC(50%) organized consortium which consist of SK Gas(18.75%), POSCO(12.5%), Samchully

32) http://www.knoc.co.kr/ENG/sub03/sub03_1_1_1.jsp.

(12.5%), and SK E&S(6.25%), and KNOC concluded an exploration agreement with UNG in November 2008.

The partners are in preparation for exploration drilling planned on Dec. 2011.

Viet Nam

Block	Contract	Acreage (km^2)	Working Interest	Operator	Production 2006(boped)	Phase
15-1	PSC	800	14.25%	CLJOC	66,000	Production
11-2	PSC	691	39.75%	KNOC	33,949	Production

Block 11-2

(History)

KNOC obtained operatorship of this block in May 1992. The Rong Doi(Twin Dragon) and Rong Doi Tay(Twin Dragon West) gas fields were discovered by KNOC in March 1998. KNOC signed an interim gas sales and purchase agreement with PetroVietnam in December 2004, which was finalised shortly thereafter and commenced construction works for the development of the gas field, which was completed on schedule less than two years.

May 1992 Acquirement of Block
Mar. 1998 Discovery Announcement of Rong Doi & Rong Doi Tay Gas Fields
Mar. 2003 Commercial Discovery Declaration for RD/RDT gas fields
Jul. 2004 Gas Sales and Purchase Agreement(GSPA)
Dec. 2004 Installation, Procurement, and Construction Agreement
Apr. 2005 Commencement of Construction of Production Facilities
Dec. 2006 First Gas Production
Oct. 2010 Current production of 169mmcf/d of natural gas

(Business Outline)

KNOC is the sole operator that carries out exploration, development and production activities in Block 11-2, located 320km offshore Vietnam. KNOC holds 75% participating interest in this block on behalf of itself and a Korean Consortium which consists of LG International Corp., Daesung Industrial Com., Daewoo International Corp., Hyundai Corp., Samwhan Corp., and Seoul City Gas Co. Ltd. PetroVietnam Exploration and Production Company(PVEP) holds 25% participating interest in Block 11-2. This field commenced production on December 25, 2006. Now 6 Production Wells in the fields are producing the average 153 million standard cubic feet of natural gas per day upon the buyer's gas nomination. The recoverable volume of this block is 856 billion standard cubic feet and production will continue by 2030.

Total Reserves	Daily production	Production Period
856 billion cubic feet	160 million cubic feet	23 years, 2007-2030

Block 15-1

(History)

CLJOC is a joint operating company for the Block 15-1, located 50km offshore Vietnam. Petroleum Contract was entered into in September 1998. Contractor Parties consist of PetroVietnam Exploration and Production Company(PVEP)(50%), ConocoPhillips (23.25%), Korean National Oil Corporation(KNOC) (14.25%), SK Energy (9%) and Geopetrol (3.5%).

Sep. 1998 Acquirement of Block 15-1
Oct. 2000 Discovery of Su Tu Den Field

Aug. 2001 Commercial Discovery Declaration for Su Tu Den Field
Oct. 2001 Discovery of Su Tu Vang Field
Oct. 2003 First Oil Production in Su Tu Den Southwest Field
Nov. 2003 Discovery of Su Tu Trang Field
Sep. 2005 Discovery of Su Tu Nau Field
Oct. 2008 First Oil Production in Su Tu Vang Field
Apr. 2010 First Oil Production in Su Tu Den Northeast
Jun. 2011 Current Production of 66,000 boed

(Business Outline)

After the first discovery of Su Tu Den Field, CLJOC had consecutively successful results from Su Tu Vang(Gold Lion) in October 2001, from Su Tu Trang(White Lion) in November 2003, and from Su Tu Nau(Brown Lion) in September 2005. In Su Tu Den field 24 production wells are now producing average 31 thousand barrels per day. The Su Tu Den offshore facilities consist of the Cuulong Thai Binh FPSO, a 28 well slots wellhead platform(WHP-A), and over 2.4 km of pipelines(from WHP-A to PLEM). The oil produced from Su Tu Den field is processed and stored on boarding the FPSO, a Floating Production Storage and Offloading vessel (FPSO) purchased from Modec in 2008. The Thai Binh FPSO has 1 million barrels of storage capacity. The oil produced from Su Tu Den Field is exported to FPSO. In Su Tu Vang field 10 production wells are now producing average 13 thousand barrels per day. The Su Tu Vang offshore facilities consist of the central processing platform(CPP) and a Floating Storage and Offloading vessel(FSO) leased from Danashe Shipping Inc. The oil produced from Su Tu Vang field is exported from CPP(100 thousand barrels of processing capacity per day) to FSO(1.1 million barrels of storage capacity). Also the new development of Su Tu Den Northeast field was completed in Apr 2010 and this field is producing average 22 thousand barrels per day now. Su Tu Trang and Su Tu Nau field will commence production one after another in 2012 and 2015. The recoverable volume of Su Tu Den, Su Tu Vang, Su Tu Trang and Su Tu Nau fields is 621 million barrels and Production will last by 2023.

Estimated Ultimate Reserves	Daily production	Production Period
621MMboe	66Mbbl	20 years, 2003~2023

Block 11-2 &15-1 (Futures)

Block 11-2 is the first overseas operating project of KNOC. The successful production in RD/RDT fields is a milestone not only for KNOC but also for Korean oil and gas industry. Korean personnel were involved in all stages of the project, from evaluation of drilling prospects, to discovery of the accumulations of gas, to negotiating all the required commercial arrangements and designing and overseeing construction of the production facilities, which were constructed and installed by a Korean company. A successful discovery and production in Block 15-1 is also a great achievement of KNOC. KNOC actively participated from exploration to production in developing the fields. These blocks are of great significance in securing energy resources for Korea by developing overseas fields.

Azerbaijan

Block	Contract	Acreage (km^2)	Working Interest	Operator	Phase
Inam	PSC	450	8%	BP	Exploration

Overview

KNOC possesses 8% and Korean Consortium total 20% of working interest on Azerbaijan Inam project. The field area covers 450 km^2 (offshore). BP has operatorship on this field.

Inam block

The Inam block is located in South Caspian basin between Kura subsidence zone and deepsea small basin. There exists Northwest-southeast anticline formed by tectonic movement during Cenozoic age, and most of oil and gas field are located in relatively shallow anticline. 3D seismic over an area of 513 km^2 was acquired and INX-1 exploration well was drilled in 2001. INX-2 exploration well was drilled in 2007~08. PSA was terminated in 2008~12 and all participants are in the process of withdrawal of the project.

Kazahkstan

Block	Contract	Acreage (km^2)	SH%	Operator	Production (2011 boepd)	Phase
ADA	Concession	1,976	40%	KNOC	N/A	Developm't
S. Karpovsky	Concession	1,880	42.5%	KKM	N/A	Explorat'n
Zhambyl	Concession	2,000	9.45%	ZPL	N/A	Explorat'n
Arystan	Concession	623	85%	KNOC	1,930	Developm't
Kulzhan	Concession	34	85%	KNOC	1,054	Developm't

ADA

ADA block is located on the south-west from Kenkiyak, Zhanazhol oil fields, which are one of the main producing well, in Aktyubinsk region, Kazakhstan. The acreage of the block is 1,969 sq. km. KNOC began to participate in the project with the interests of 22.5% on 18 November 2005 after performing technology and feasibility evaluation around the end of 2005. And KNOC purchased an additional 17.5% interests to hold 40.0% in the field. Pilot production has begun on June 2010. Around 3,000b/d crude oil is being produced as of Feb. 2011. Furthermore, increase in crude oil production is anticipated with the plan of the additional production wells in the future.

South Karpovsky

South Karpovsky block is located near to Ural city, Kazkhstan north-west and this block is near to Karachaganak. The acreage of the block is 1,880 sq. km. KNOC was proposed to participate in the project of the block in June 2006. Having performed the tech. and feasibility evaluation, KNOC organized a consortium which consists of GS Holdings, Kyeongnam Enterprise, Hyundai Heavy Industry, Kaznergy. The Korean consortium acquired a 50% interest in the South Karpovsky Block pursuant to a share purchase agreement with Central Asian Energy Holdings B.V.("CAEH") in November 2006. Also KNOC acquired an additional 25% interest in this Block pursuant to a share purchase agreement with CAEH in December 2009. The first exploratory drilling was finished on April, 2011. The company and its exploration partners are conducting the evaluation of the result of the first drilling

Zhambyl

The Company acquired a 9.45% interest in the Zhambyl Block pursuant to an Supplement agreement with KazMunaiGas in January 2009. Pursuant to the exploration agreement, the exploration period will last for 6 years, starting in April 2008. KazMunaiGas, Kazakhstan's national oil corporation, owns a 73% interest in the Zhambyl Block, with KC Kazakh B.V., a consortium comprised of the Company and seven other Korean companies, owning the remaining 27%. The Zhambyl Block, covering an area of about 2,000 square kilometers, is located in the northwestern part of the Caspian Sea. The Company is currently conducting the site survey for exploration drilling planned in

2012

Sumbe

KNOC recently acquired two blocks (Arystan and Kulzhan) in western Kazakhstan as it merged Sumbe JSC in December, 2009, taking a working interest of 85%. Both of the Arystan and Kulzhan are under exploration contract and being under pilot production with field development activities and each of their registered reserves is 81.8MMbbl and 15.6MMbbl.

Equator Exploration Limited 공시자료[33)]

History

Equator holds a 30% participating interest in each of the highly prospective deep water blocks, OPL 323 and OPL 321 offshore Nigeria.

Equator and its bidding group won the blocks in the Nigerian 2005 licensing round with bids comprising signature bonuses (US$161.7 million net), work programmes and level of local content. However, the Korean National Oil Corporation ('KNOC') exercised a right of first refusal and was awarded a 60% interest in the blocks and was appointed operator. Equator's main bidding partner, ONGC Videsh elected not to participate in the blocks allowing Equator to take a 30% interest. The remaining 10% was awarded to Local Content Vehicles ('LCVs'), Tulip Energy Resources Nigeria Limited for OPL 321 and NJ Exploration Limited for OPL 323. Equator and KNOC carry the costs of the two LCV's in proportion to their participating interests. The two Production Sharing Contracts ('PSC's') were signed with the Nigeria National Petroleum Corporation ('NNPC') on 10 March 2006. The Joint Operating Agreements were signed on 7 June 2007.

Since the award of operatorship to KNOC made it impractical for the Company's remaining bidding partners to enter the PSC's directly, the Company granted them carried interests amounting to 4% out of its 30% participation in the PSC's. During 2008, the Company entered into agreements to eliminate these carried interests for a combination of warrants and contingent cash payments. Equator now holds the full economic rights to its 30% participating interest in each PSC.

In August 2007, the Company executed a farm-out agreement to assign a 20% interest in OPL 323 to BG Exploration and Production Nigeria Limited. The total consideration to be paid by BG was US$75 million, comprising both cash and a carry on the future expenditure on the remaining 10% interest. The Company worked diligently to secure the approval of NNPC and the Federal Government of Nigeria. However, this was withheld due to a number of public and private government inquiries into the allocation of the blocks to KNOC.

In January 2009, the Nigerian government voided the allocations of OPL 323 and OPL 321 to KNOC. The blocks were simultaneously offered to the winning group of the 2005 licensing round, which includes ONGC Videsh and Equator. KNOC brought a lawsuit against the government parties in the Federal High Court in Abuja and, in August 2009, judgment was given in their favour. Although the government has appealed the judgment, we believe that the government and KNOC both seek a settlement. Equator is lobbying the government to give the matter the highest of priorities.

33) www.equatorexploration.com.

In September 2009, the government refunded the signature bonuses of US$ 161.7 million which Equator paid for OPL 323 and OPL 321. The Company had requested the return of the signature bonuses because, due to the ongoing litigation, it was being denied its right to explore the blocks and faced severe economic hardship. The Company has notified the government of its intention to maintain its interests in the two blocks until such time that the court disposes of the matter and beyond. This notification was acknowledged by the government.

In August 2010 BG terminated the farm out agreement.

Under the terms of the PSC's, Equator provides performance bonds of US$41 million each to cover its share of the minimum work programmes of two wells on each of the blocks. These bonds have been provided by a Nigerian bank which has taken security over the wholly owned subsidiaries that hold the PSC's.

Operational status

Starting with Equator's studies, KNOC developed the interpretation of the 3D seismic survey and identified several prospect horizons in a number of geological structures in each block. The prospect horizons were ranked and optimum drilling locations were selected for each geological structure. The final step was to rank the geological structures and select the locations of the two commitment wells on each block. Equator took a full part in the direction of all this work by participating in the joint venture's regular Technical and Operating Committee meetings.

The Deepwater Pathfinder was contracted to drill the four obligation wells under the two PSC's. Drilling would have commenced in 3Q 2009. However, to avoid a large early termination penalty in light of the ongoing litigation, the rig contract had to be assigned to Addax for use in the Joint Development Zone between Nigeria and São Tomé & Príncipe.

Prospectivity

OPL 323

OPL 323 is located 80 kilometres offshore and lies in water depths of between 890 metres and 2,080 metres. A number of large structures have been identified by interpretation of the 3D seismic survey. Within each of the geological structures there are several prospective horizons. Many of the prospect horizons are supported by seismic amplitude anomalies. Furthermore, the proximity of the block to large oil fields on adjacent acreage supports the presence of source rocks and abundant reservoir sands. OPL 323 is to the west of the Abo Field in OML 125 and immediately to the north of the large Bosi and Erha Fields in OML 133. Erha has proved reserves reported by ExxonMobil to be in excess of 500 million barrels and 5 trillion cubic feet of gas and, with its satellite development Erha North, produces in excess of 200,000 barrels of oil per day. Bosi, the second field development on OML 133, produces 135,000 barrels of oil per day.

In October 2006, Netherland, Sewell & Associates, Inc. ('NSAI'), Independent Petroleum Engineers, made an assessment of the prospective resources within the four largest structures using a statistical 'Monte Carlo' approach. At the time, they quoted the mean value as the Best Estimate. In 2007, the Society of Petroleum Engineers specified that the median P50 value has to be used. Under this definition, NSAI's Best Estimate of Gross Unrisked Prospective Resources on OPL 323 is 1.1 billion barrels of oil and 4.9 trillion standard cubic feet of gas (Tables 1 & 2). The subsequent evaluation of five structures by the operator has given a best estimate of 1.3 billion barrels for oil.

During 2006, Agip made a discovery of both oil and gas in the Okodo-1 well on OML 125, adjacent to OPL 323. This discovery had a direct impact on the prospectivity of one structure on OPL 323, located only 7 kilometres away. It appears to lie in the same channel as the Okodo discovery, which proved that the hanging wall of the common major bounding fault forms a trap for hydrocarbons and that the immediate area has sources of oil and gas and migration paths.

OPL 321

OPL 321 is located immediately to the west of OPL 323, lying in deeper water in the range 1,900 to 2,600 metres. The block lies on trend with block OPL 322 to the south, where Shell's discovery well, Bobo-1, encountered a significant column of hydrocarbons. It has access to the same hydrocarbon sources as the giant Bosi and Erha Fields located nearby to the southeast. NSAI assessed the Best Estimate, under the new definition, of the Gross Unrisked Prospective Resources in the largest prospect to be 0.57 billion barrels of oil and 0.67 trillion standard cubic feet of gas (Tables 1 & 2).

The operator, in its subsequent and more detailed evaluation, has identified a total of four structures and has calculated the best estimate of the total gross unrisked prospective resources of oil to be 1.6 billion barrels.

Table 1. OPL 321 & OPL 323

Unrisked Recoverable Oil Resources (million barrels)* as at 1 October 2006

	Gross (100 percent)				Equator Interest (30 percent)				POS**
Prospect Cluster	Low	Median (Best)	Mean	High	Low	Median (Best)	Mean	High	percent
323-G	115	507	992	2,611	34	152	298	783	36
323-O	52	157	265	643	16	47	80	193	25
323-W	100	278	401	889	30	84	120	267	34
323-L	55	165	261	617	16	49	78	185	33
321-E	156	574	1,005	2,506	47	172	302	752	27
Total	478	1,682	2,924	7,266	143	504	878	2,180	

Table 2. OPL 321 & OPL 323

Unrisked Recoverable Gas Resources (billion cubic feet)* as at 1 October 2006

	Gross (100 percent)				Equator Interest (30 percent)				POS**
Prospect Cluster	Low	Median (Best)	Mean	High	Low	Median (Best)	Mean	High	percent
323-G	834	3,487	6,392	16,271	250	1,046	1,840	4,881	36
323-O	279	896	1,431	3,401	84	269	362	1,020	25
323-W	89	316	524	1,291	27	95	187	387	34
323-L	57	232	449	1,186	17	70	150	356	33
321-E	147	670	1,351	3,623	44	201	369	1,087	27
Total	1,406	5,601	10,147	25,772	422	1,681	2,908	7,731	

Totals may not add due to rounding
* Netherland, Sewell & Associates, Inc
** Probability of geological success

Production Sharing Contract Flow Diagram[34)]

〈표 4-3〉 생산분배계약 IOC/NOC 배분표

PRODUCTION SHARING SYSTEM FLOW DIAGRAM

Contractor Share	One Barrel of Oil $20.00	Government Share
	10% Royalty →	$2.00
	$18.00	
$8.00 ←	Cost Recovery (Operating costs, DD&A, IDCs, etc.) 40% (Limit)	
	$10.00	
$4.00 ←	Profit Oil split (40%/60%) →	$6.00
($1.60) ←	Taxes 40% →	$1.60
$10.40		$9.60
52%		48%

34) Daniel Johnson, 위 주 20 상게서, 43 (1994).

4. 위험용역계약[35)]

위험용역계약은 양허계약이나 생산분배계약보다도 훨씬 자원보유국의 통제권한을 확대하여 IOC가 NOC의 하도급업체로 작동하는 것이다. IOC는 자신의 자금과 위험으로 탐사·생산작업을 하되 탐사가 성공적인 경우 탐사·개발비용을 보상받지만 생산분배계약의 경우과 같이 일정한 profit oil에 대한 권리가 없는 것이 특징이다. 멕시코, 베네주엘라, 브라질, 아르헨티나(예를 들면 PETROVEN)와 이란 등지에서 국유화 이후 단기적으로 시도된 계약유형으로서 외국의 IOC는 위험용역계약하에서 국제하도급업체로 전락하였다.[36)] 요즈음은 기술용역계약은 WILDCAT 탐사작업이 아니라 기존의 유전의 생산성을 높이기 위한 경우에 주로 체결된다.

Iraq Oil Ministry, FORM TECHNICAL SERVICE CONTRACT[37)]

TABLE OF CONTENTS

35) 서비스계약, 모험용역계약, 서비스제공계약 등으로 번역된다.

36) 참여계약이나 리스계약, 하이브리드 PSC, 기술지원계약, 기술서비스제공계약 등을 추가적인 대표적 자원개발생산계약 유형으로 열거하기도 하나 이들은 3가지 전형적 계약유형의 변형으로 보면 충분하다. Smith, 위 주 1-4 상게서, 492-501.

37) Republic of Iraq, Ministry of Oil 홈페이지 http://www.oil.gov.iq/moo/feeds.php?lang=en&page_name=news&start=16에서 열람가능.

This Technical Service Contract ("Contract") is made and entered into this ____ day of _____ yyyy, by and between: _____________, an Iraqi State oil company, the Republic of Iraq ("Regional Operating Company or ROC") of the First Part, and ___________, a ___________ company established and existing under the laws of ___________, having its registered head office at___________("__________"); and ___________, a ___________ company established and existing under the laws of ___________, having its registered head office at___________("__________"); and (individually a "Company" and collectively the "Companies"); together with _________, an Iraqi State entity established and existing under the laws of the Republic of Iraq ("State Partner"),

Companies and State Partner are collectively referred to as "Contractor", of the Second Part;

ROC and Contractor are referred to, individually, as "Party", or, collectively, as "Parties".

WITNESSETH

WHEREAS, all oil and gas resources within the territory and offshore areas of the Republic of Iraq are owned by all the people of the Republic of Iraq; and the Iraqi Government, representing the whole Iraqi people, has sole right to explore, develop, extract, exploit and utilize such natural resources, therefrom; and

WHEREAS, ROC, in its role as an Iraqi State oil and gas company, is exclusively entrusted with and authorized for development and production of the __________ Field, in accordance with the Law; and

WHEREAS, Contractor has sound financial standing, technical competency, and professional skills to provide any and all of the technical services warranted for rehabilitation, improved production, enhanced recovery, and generally all and any Petroleum Operations as defined herein; and

WHEREAS, the Parties mutually represent that they have the power, authority and desire to enter into this Technical Service Contract for the __________ Field as defined herein.

NOW THEREFORE, and in consideration of the promises and the mutual covenants hereinafter set out, it is agreed as follows:

ARTICLE 1 – DEFINITIONS

Except as specifically provided otherwise herein, any reference to an Article, Annex or Addendum shall be construed as reference to an Article, Annex or Addendum of this Contract. In this Contract, including its Annexes and Addenda, words in the singular include the plural and vice versa and except where the context otherwise requires, the following terms shall have the meanings set out as follows:

1.1 "Accounting Procedure" means the accounting procedures and requirements set out in Annex C.

1.2 "Additional Appraisal Program" means as defined in Article 11.1(b).

1.3 "Affiliate" in relation to any entity constituting Contractor, means:
(a) a company which controls such entity; or
(b) a company which is controlled by such entity; or
(c) a company which is controlled by a company which controls such entity.

For the purpose of this definition, "control" means the power to dictate and conduct the policy of a company through the control, directly or indirectly, of more than fifty percent (50%) of the shares or voting rights in such company. For the purposes of this Contract, subsidiaries of ROC as well as companies and enterprises of Iraq's Ministry of Oil or Iraq National Oil Company (when established) shall be considered as ROC's Affiliates.

1.4 "Appraisal" or "Appraisal Operations" shall include, but not be limited to, such geological, geophysical, aerial and any other surveys and any interpretation of data relating thereto and the drilling of such shot-holes, core holes, stratigraphic tests, holes for the appraisal of Petroleum and other related holes and wells, the production testing and the purchase or acquisition of such supplies, materials and equipment therefore, as may be contained in approved Plans and Work Programs.

1.5 "Associated Gas" means Gas, occurring as gas-cap gas, which overlies and is in contact with crude oil in a reservoir and/or solution gas dissolved in crude oil in a reservoir.

1.6 "Barrel" means a liquid quantity consisting of forty-two (42) United States gallons under a pressure of one (1) atmosphere and a temperature of sixty (60) degrees Fahrenheit.

1.7 "Baseline Production" for any Quarter means the deemed Net Production for the said Quarter, at the deemed Baseline Production Rate.

1.8 "Baseline Production Rate" for any Quarter constitutes the amount for any Incremental Production under this Contract in such Quarter, being derived from an assumed decline from the Initial Production Rate at a compounded annual rate of five percent (5%) as from the Quarter following the Quarter in which the Effective Date occurs, calculated in accordance with Article 19.5(c).

1.9 "Best International Petroleum Industry Practices" means all those uses and practices that are, at the time in question, generally accepted in the international petroleum industry as being good, safe, economical, environmentally sound and efficient in exploring for, developing, producing, processing and transporting Petroleum. They should reflect standards of service and technology that are either state-of-the-art or otherwise economically appropriate to the operations in question in respect of new facilities and should be applied using standards in all matters that are no less rigorous than those in use by the Companies in other global operations.

1.10 "Budget" means the estimates of the expenditure expected to be incurred for implementing an approved Work Program for any Calendar Year or part thereof.

1.11 "Calendar Month" or "Month" means, in respect of any Month in a Calendar Year, a period commencing on the first day of such Month and ending on the last day of the same Month.

1.12 "Calendar Quarter" or "Quarter" means a period of three consecutive Months commencing on the first day of January, April, July or October in any Calendar Year.

1.13 "Calendar Year" means a period of twelve (12) consecutive Months commencing with the first day of January and ending with the last day of December, according to the Gregorian calendar.

1.14 "Capital Cost" means all costs and expenditures, excluding Operating Cost, related to Petroleum Operations pursuant to Annex C.

1.15 "Cash Receipts" means as defined in Article 19.5(d).

1.16 "Company" means any entity that is a signatory party to this Contract and that forms part of the Contractor, excluding the State Partner, and at any time thereafter shall include their legal successors and permitted assignees.

1.17 "Companies" means, collectively, each Company that comprises the ontractor, excluding the State Partner, and at any time thereafter shall include their legal successors and permitted assignees.

1.18 "Contract" means this agreement between the Parties, including the Annexes and Addenda attached hereto, as amended or supplemented from time to time in accordance with this Contract.

1.19 "Contract Area" means the __________ Field area covered by this Contract, the coordinates of which are described in Annex A and outlined in Annex B.

1.20 "Contractor" means, on the Effective Date, Companies and State Partner, and at any time thereafter shall include their legal successors and permitted assignees.

1.21 "Crude Oil" means all hydrocarbons regardless of gravity which are produced and saved from the Field in the liquid state at an absolute pressure of fourteen decimal six nine six (14.696) pounds per square inch and a temperature of sixty (60) degrees Fahrenheit, including asphalt, tar, distillates or condensates obtained from oil-gas separation facilities within the Contract Area.

1.22 "Data" means as defined in Article 14.2.

1.23 "Delivery Measurement Point" or "DMP" means the point, immediately upstream of the Delivery Point, where the volume and quality of Export Oil that may be lifted by Contractor under this Contract is measured.

1.24 "Delivery Point" or "DP" means the point(s) where Contractor may lift Export Oil in lieu of its due and payable Supplementary Fees and Service Fees.

1.25 "Development or Redevelopment Operations" means any and all Petroleum Operations other than Appraisal and Production Operations, including primary and subsequent (secondary, tertiary or other) recovery projects and pressure maintenance, conducted with a view to redeveloping the Field including, but without limitations: the drilling, deepening, completing, plugging, side-tracking, re-completing and equipping of evaluation and development wells; the engineering, building and erecting or laying of production plants and facilities (such as, without limitation, separators, compressors, generators, pumps and tankage, gathering lines, pipelines, and all facilities required to be installed for production, pressure maintenance, treatment, storage and transportation of Petroleum, and loading the same into seagoing tankers); the obtaining of such materials, equipment, machinery, articles and supplies as may be required or expedient for the above activities; and all auxiliary operations, activities and services required or expedient for the better conduct or result of the above activities, including decommissioning and abandonment operations, all in accordance with approved Plans and Work Programs and Best International Petroleum Industry Practices.

1.26 "Development Plan" or "Plan" means a scheduled program and cost estimate specifying the Development or Redevelopment Operations required for developing and/or increasing the production capacity of the Field, which includes the Rehabilitation Plan, Enhanced Redevelopment Plan, and any subsequent Revisions thereof.

1.27 "Dinar" or "IQD" means the Iraqi Dinar.

1.28 "Dollar" or "USD" means the United States Dollar.

1.29 "Effective Date" means the date when all the conditions listed in Article 39 are satisfied.

1.30 "Enhanced Redevelopment Plan" means, pursuant to Article 11.3, the full Field redevelopment plan, based on all knowledge existing on the Effective Date as well as additional knowledge derived from the execution of the Rehabilitation Plan; all with the objective of increased and optimized production and enhanced recovery of Petroleum from the Field.

1.31 "Expenditure" means as defined in Article 19.5(d).

1.32 "Export Oil" means Crude Oil of standard Iraqi export blend.

1.33 "Export Oil Price" means the price per Barrel of Export Oil Free on Board ("FOB") at the Delivery Point, determined in accordance with the provisions of Article 18.

1.34 "Field" means the __________ Field within the Contract Area as defined in Annexes A, B and D, subject to the provisions of Article 5 hereof.

1.35 "Field Operating Division" or "FOD" means a non-profit, unincorporated, joint operating entity, administratively and financially independent of the ROC; established in accordance with Articles 9.1, 9.10 and Addendum Three, exclusively to serve as Operator of the Field for conducting Petroleum Operations under the supervision, direction and management of the Contractor as well as the general supervision and control of the Joint Management Committee in accordance with the authorities set out in Article 13.2.

1.36 "Financial Year" means the Calendar Year starting on January 1st and ending on December 31st of the same year, both dates being inclusive.

1.37 "Force Majeure" means as defined in Article 31.

1.38 "Gas" means a mixture of hydrocarbons and varying quantities of non-hydrocarbons that exist either in the gaseous phase or in solution with Crude Oil in natural underground reservoirs and when produced remain in gaseous phase at atmospheric conditions of temperature and pressure, and is classified as either "Associated Gas" or "Non-Associated Gas".

1.39 "Government" means the Government of the Republic of Iraq.

1.40 "Gross Negligence or Wilful Misconduct" means any unjustifiable act or omission, but not mere negligence, that constitutes an intentional, deliberate, reckless or conscious disregard of Best International Petroleum Industry Practices or the terms of this Contract, where such act or omission results in loss, damage or harm by the Senior Supervisory Personnel of a Party or the FOD.

1.41 "Improved Production Target" means that Net Production Rate in Barrels of Crude Oil per day defined in Article 2.2(a)(i) measured by the same methodology and the same or equivalent equipment used for measuring the Initial Production Rate regardless of the installation of new or improved methods of measurement or equipment.

1.42 "Incremental Production", during a certain period of time, means the incremental volume of Net Production from the Field during the said period that is realized in excess of the deemed Net Production volume at the Baseline Production Rate.

1.43 "Incremental Production Rate" in Barrels of Crude Oil per day, means the Incremental Production of Crude Oil for a certain period of time divided by the number of calendar days in that period of time.

1.44 "Initial Production Rate" means a Net Production Rate to be determined by the Parties before or on the Effective Date, in accordance with the methodology and the equipment for measuring such Net Production Rate, to be agreed by the Parties, that fairly represents the Net Production Rate as of the Effective Date.

1.45 "Joint Management Committee" or "JMC" means the committee formed pursuant to Article 13.

1.46 "Law" means any constitution, law, decree, resolution, statute, ordinance, rule, directive, order, treaty, code or regulation and any injunction or final non-appealable judgment, as adopted, enacted, issued, promulgated or ratified by the Republic of Iraq or, unless otherwise provided for herein, as such may, from time to time, be amended or repealed.

1.47 "Lead Contractor" means the Company that is appointed as from the Effective Date as the representative of Contractor and which is authorized to act on Contractor's behalf in the conduct of Petroleum Operations.

1.48 "LIBOR" or "London Inter-Bank Offered Rate" means the interest rate determined as the arithmetic average (rounded upward to the nearest one thousandth of a percentage point) of the offered rates for deposits in Dollars for a period of three (3) Months as published by the Financial Times (London Edition) on the date which is one (1) business day prior to the beginning of the said three (3) Months period corresponding to each interest period. Should the Financial Times rate not be published for a period of seven (7) consecutive days, the Wall Street Journal (New York Edition) shall be used.

1.49 "Lifting Quarter" means the Quarter during which Export Oil is available for lifting by Contractor at the Delivery Point under this Contract and Addendum Four, where any Lifting Quarter shall be the Quarter in which Service Fees and Supplementary Fees are due and payable.

1.50 "Measurement Point" means the place(s) at which volumes and qualities of Crude Oil pumped out, received, transmitted or delivered shall be measured, such as the Production Measurement Point and Delivery Measurement Point.

1.51 "Minimum Expenditure Obligation" means that amount which shall be the minimum amount to be spent by the Contractor as specified in Article 6.2.

1.52 "Minimum Work Obligation" means the minimum work commitment undertaken by Contractor under Article 6 and Annex E.

1.53 "Natural Gas Liquids" or "NGL" means the propane and heavier (C3+) components of natural gas that can be classified according to their vapour pressures as low vapour pressure (Condensate), intermediate vapour pressure (Natural Gasoline) and high vapour pressure (LPG).

1.54 "Net Production", over a certain period of time, means all Barrels of Crude Oil and NGL actually produced from the Field over the said period of time, less base sediments and water, saved, measured at the Production Measurement Point, and received by Transporter at the Transfer Point.

1.55 "Net Production Rate", in Barrels of Crude Oil per day, means the Net Production of Crude Oil and NGL for a certain period of time divided by the number of calendar days in that period of time.

1.56 "Official Selling Price" or "OSP" means SOMO's declared price for each of the Iraqi crude oil blends.

1.57 "Operating Account" means the account or set of accounts maintained by Contractor and Operator to record Petroleum Costs and Supplementary Costs.

1.58 "Operating Cost" means recoverable Contractor's costs, expenses, duties, fees, and charges related to Production Operations pursuant to Annex C.

1.59 "Operator" means the entity designated to conduct Petroleum Operations in accordance with Article 9, namely the ROC until the FOD takes responsibility for Petroleum Operations and thereafter the FOD.

1.60 "Participating Interest" means, in respect of each Contractor's entity, the undivided share expressed as a percentage as defined in Article 27.1 for such party's participation in the rights, benefits, privileges, duties, liabilities and obligations of Contractor.

1.61 "Performance Factor", for the purposes of Article 19.5(e), means the ratio of the Net Production Rate to the bid Plateau Production Target, although in no event shall it exceed one point zero (1.0).

1.62 "Petroleum" means all hydrocarbons including liquid and gaseous hydrocarbons produced and saved from the Field under this Contract.

1.63 "Petroleum Costs" means recoverable costs and expenditures incurred and/or payments made by Contractor in connection with or in relation to the conduct of Petroleum Operations (except corporate income taxes paid in the Republic of Iraq or as otherwise stipulated herein) determined in accordance with the provisions of this Contract, including Annex C.

1.64 "Petroleum Operations" means all Appraisal, Development, Redevelopment, Production Operations, and any other activities related thereto.

1.65 "Plateau Production Period" means a period of seven (7) Years starting with the earlier of three (3) Years from the approval date of the Enhanced Redevelopment Plan or the date on which the Plateau Production Target has been achieved for a continuous period of thirty (30) days, but in no event shall such period commence either earlier than the approval date of the Enhanced Redevelopment Plan or, subject to Article 12.2, no later than six (6) Years from the Effective Date.

1.66 "Plateau Production Target" means the Net Production Rate that is to be achieved and sustained for the Plateau Production Period, as bid and as specified in Article 2.2(a)(ii).

1.67 "Production Measurement Point" or "PMP" means the point, immediately upstream of the Transfer Point within or close to the Contract Area, where the volume and quality of Net Production is measured.

1.68 "Production Operations" means, in respect of Contractor, any and all operations related to production of Petroleum, including (but not limited to) workovers, stimulations, remediation, restoration, operating, staffing, supervising, servicing, repairing, decommissioning and maintaining of any and all wells, plants, equipment, pipelines, tank-farms, terminals and all other installations and facilities.

1.69 "Provisional Export Oil Price" means the arithmetic average of SOMO's declared OSPs for the Delivery Point for the following destinations, the Americas, Europe and the Far East, for the Month preceding the Month in which the Forward Quantity Statement under Addendum Four is provided or the preceding Month to such Month if the price is not available.

1.70 "Rehabilitation Period" means the period starting from the Effective Date and ending thirty-six (36) Months after the approval date of the Rehabilitation Plan.

1.71 "Rehabilitation Plan" means, pursuant to Article 11.1, the plan to be submitted by Contractor, based on existing knowledge of the Field on Effective Date, for the rehabilitation and improved/optimized production therefrom.

1.72 "R-Factor" is the ratio of cumulative Cash Receipts to cumulative Expenditures in the conduct of Petroleum Operations as defined in Article 19.5(d).

1.73 "Remedial Program" means as defined in Article 11.1(a).

1.74 "Remuneration Fee" means the fee paid to Contractor for Incremental Production as calculated pursuant to Article 19.5.

1.75 "Remuneration Fee Bid" or "RFB" USD ________ ($x.yy) per Barrel of Crude Oil as utilized in Article 19.5.

1.76 "Revision", in respect of a Development Plan or Work Program and Budget, has the meaning given in Articles 12.4 and 12.3, respectively.

1.77 "Senior Supervisory Personnel" means any individual who functions as its senior resident manager who directs all operations and activities of such Party in the country or region in which he is resident, and any manager who directly reports to such senior resident manager in such country or region, but excluding all managers or supervisors who are responsible for or in charge of installations or facilities, onsite drilling, construction or production and related operations, or any other field operations.

1.78 "Service Fees" means those Petroleum Costs and the Remuneration Fee as defined in Article 19.6.

1.79 "Service Fees Eligibility Date" means the earlier of the end of the Rehabilitation Period or the date when the Improved Production Target is first achieved over thirty (30) consecutive days, provided that in no event can this date be earlier than the approval date of the Rehabilitation Plan.

1.80 "SOMO" means the Iraq State entity, Oil Marketing Company.

1.81 "__________________" or "ROC" means an Iraqi State oil company operating the Field prior to the Effective Date.

1.82 "State Partner" means __________________ in its capacity as an Iraqi State entity established and existing under the Law holding a share of Contractor's total Participating Interest as set out in this Contract.

1.83 "Sub-Contractor" means any company or person contracted by the Contractor and/or Operator to provide goods or services with respect to Petroleum Operations.

1.84 "Supplementary Costs" means recoverable costs and expenditures incurred by Contractor, other than those costs defined as Petroleum Costs in Article 19 and as determined in accordance with the provisions of this Contract.

1.85 "Supplementary Fees" means those Supplementary Costs invoiced by Contractor as defined in Article 19.3 and Annex C.

1.86 "Tax" means Iraqi corporate income tax pursuant to Article 23.

1.87 "Tax Year" means the period of twelve (12) consecutive Months according to the Gregorian calendar for which tax returns or reports are required according to the Law.

1.88 "Term" means the term of this Contract as defined in Article 3.2.

1.89 "Training, Technology and Scholarship Fund" or "Fund" means the fund established as defined in Article 26.2.

1.90 "Transfer Point" or "TP" means the inlet flange(s) of the outgoing pipeline(s), immediately downstream of the Production Measurement Point, where Transporter shall receive Net Production from Operator.

1.91 "Transportation Facilities" means the pipelines, pumps, compressors, tanks, meters, and other transportation facilities for Crude Oil that are built by Contractor beyond the Transfer Point(s) or as otherwise provided and integrated into the Transportation System pursuant to this Contract.

1.92 "Transportation System" means, at any time, any and all transportation facilities beyond the Transfer Point(s) that are operated by or under control of the Transporter.

1.93 "Transporter" means the entity designated by ROC to operate the Transportation System for transporting Crude Oil beyond the Transfer Point(s) pursuant to Article 17 and Addendum Two, all on behalf of ROC.

1.94 "Work Program" means an itemisation and time schedule of Petroleum Operations.

1.95 "Year" means a period of twelve (12) consecutive Months to the Gregorian calendar, starting at some date and ending at the anniversary thereof.

ARTICLE 2 – SCOPE OF CONTRACT

2.1 This Contract is a Technical Service Contract for the rehabilitation of improved production and enhanced recovery of Petroleum from the __________ Field in accordance with the provisions herein. It includes 43 Articles, Annexes A, B, C, D, E, and F, and Addenda One, Two, Three, and Four; all attached hereto and made part hereof. In the event of a conflict between the Contract Articles and the Annexes or Addenda, the provisions of the Contract Articles shall prevail. Any reference to an Addendum herein shall be deemed to include the fully-termed agreement which replaces such Addendum, unless the context requires otherwise.

2.2 Contractor, subject to the provisions of this Contract and in accordance with Best International Petroleum Industry Practices, shall:

(a) provide or arrange to perform its obligations set out in this Contract through the Operator to carry out Petroleum Operations to rehabilitate, to further appraise, and to re-develop the Field for improved production and to carry out enhanced recovery of Petroleum from the Field in order to achieve the production targets set out below:
   (i) the Improved Production Target being a Net Production Rate of 10% above the Initial Production Rate, to be achieved as soon as possible after the approval date of the Rehabilitation Plan; and
   (ii) the Plateau Production Target at the Net Production Rate of __________

Barrels of Crude Oil and NGL per day for the Plateau Production Period. It is understood that the Plateau Production Target shall only include production from producing reservoirs as defined in Annex D, and is to be achieved, subject to Article 12.2, not later than six (6) Years from the Effective Date.

(b) annually assess and determine the maximum volume of reserves and resources of Petroleum in the Contract Area;

(c) provide or arrange to provide all capital, machinery, equipment, technology, personnel and services necessary to conduct Petroleum Operations through the Operator;

(d) incur all costs and expenses required for carrying out Petroleum Operations in accordance with approved Plans, Work Programs and Budgets in order to achieve the production levels set out in this Article 2; and

(e) fulfil all financial and other obligations of Contractor and enjoy all rights and benefits, in accordance with the provisions of this Contract.

2.3 Discovered but undeveloped reservoirs, as defined in Annex D, may be developed and produced under this Contract but shall be subject to a separately agreed remuneration fee which the Parties undertake to, in good faith, agree. If no such agreement is reached within the period set forth in Article 5, ROC shall be free to develop such reservoirs in any manner it may deem appropriate, taking care not to hinder or unduly interfere with Petroleum Operations.

2.4 For a period of six (6) years from the Effective Date Contractor shall have the right to negotiate a separate agreement to explore for and develop the undiscovered potential reservoirs, as defined in Annex D. If no such agreement is reached in this time period, ROC shall be free to explore and develop such reservoirs in any manner it may deem appropriate, taking care not to hinder or unduly interfere with Petroleum Operations.

2.5 In the event of unintentional infringement on the undeveloped or undiscovered reservoirs, the Parties shall convene to agree in good faith on a proper course of action, taking into consideration the quantities of petroleum involved, safeguarding the interests of both Parties.

2.6 At any time, the entities then constituting Contractor shall be jointly and severally liable to ROC for all obligations of Contractor.

ARTICLE 3 – TERM OF CONTRACT

3.1 This Contract shall come into force on the Effective Date.

3.2 The basic term of this Contract ("Term") shall be twenty (20) Years from the Effective Date. This Term is extendable pursuant to Article 31 or elsewhere in this Contract.

3.3 No later than one (1) Year prior to this Contract's expiry date, Contractor may submit a written request to ROC for an extension of the Term for a maximum period of five (5) Years, subject to newly negotiated terms and conditions.

ARTICLE 4 – SIGNATURE BONUS

4.1 Within thirty (30) days from the Effective Date the Companies shall deposit in cash into a bank account designated by ROC, their respective pro-rated Participating Interest share of a signature bonus of __________ USD (US$__________).

4.2 The signature bonus paid shall be considered Supplementary Costs and shall be recovered pursuant to and in accordance with Article 19.2(a).

ARTICLE 5 – RELINQUISHMENT

Contractor shall relinquish to ROC, within six (6) Years from the approval date of the Enhanced Redevelopment Plan, any discovered but undeveloped reservoir(s) not targeted in or for which Development Operations have not effectively started in accordance with the Enhanced Redevelopment Plan.

ARTICLE 6 – MINIMUM WORK OBLIGATION

6.1 No later than thirty-six (36) Months from the approval of the Rehabilitation Plan and according to the provisions set out in Annex E, to fulfil the Minimum Work Obligation specified therein, Contractor shall itself or through the Operator prepare or provide the following activities:

(a) preparation of the Rehabilitation Plan, Enhanced Redevelopment Plan, and Revisions;
(b) conduct of 3-D seismic surveys, including processing and interpretation thereof;
(c) conduct of detailed geological and reservoir engineering studies, including 3-D simulation for the reservoirs targeted for enhanced production;
(d) drilling appraisal and/or development wells with the aim of further Appraisal of the relevant reservoirs defined in Annex D, and achieving planned production in accordance with the Rehabilitation Plan;
(e) conduct of detailed laboratory and reservoir engineering studies to evaluate most suitable secondary and/or enhanced recovery mechanisms for the reservoirs targeted under the Rehabilitation Plan and Enhanced Redevelopment Plan; and
(f) performing engineering studies and building/upgrading all necessary surface installations required under the Rehabilitation Plan, and initiation of engineering work and infrastructure facilities expected to be incorporated in the Enhanced Redevelopment Plan.

6.2 Contractor shall spend a minimum amount of __________ USD (US$__________) in the course of the Operator implementing the Minimum Work Obligation specified in Annex E. The Minimum Expenditure Obligation shall be deemed to have been met provided that the Minimum Work Obligations under Annex E are fulfilled.

6.3 Notwithstanding Article 6.2, Contractor shall invest the sums consistent with the amounts and timing contemplated in the relevant approved Plans, subject to the terms and conditions set forth in this Contract.

6.4 The performance of each Company and the fulfilment of its contractual and financial obligations under this Contract shall be guaranteed by an Affiliate in the form set out in Annex F where in the case of

(a) __________ this shall be ______________________;
(b) __________ this shall be ______________________; and
(c) __________ this shall be ______________________.

Each such guarantee shall be effective as of the Effective Date and must be delivered to ROC at Contract signing, and as provided in Article 28 in respect of assignees. Any such guarantee may be called by ROC on notice describing the default and issued to either Company in accordance with Annex F.

6.5 Ministry of Oil shall provide to Companies a guarantee through an instrument in the form set out in Annex F, to guarantee the performance of the State Partner, Transporter, ROC, SOMO and any other Iraqi State company in their fulfillment of their respective contractual and financial obligations under this Contract. Such guarantee shall be effective as of the Effective Date and must be delivered to Companies at Contract signing.

6.6 Substantial failure of Contractor to perform timely the levels of investment and to carry out the work contemplated in any approved Plan through the Operator shall lead to Contract termination in accordance with the provisions of Article 8.

ARTICLE 7－ROC'S ASSISTANCE

The Parties acknowledge that time is of the essence and as permitted by the Law ROC shall, in good faith, provide or procure the provisions of any approval, consent or review required under this Contract in a timely manner. In the event that Petroleum Operations are delayed, curtailed or prevented due to extended delays in acquiring necessary approvals, consents, entry visas, work permits or reviews under this Contract, clearing or demining operations, the Parties shall meet and agree appropriate remediation measures.

ROC shall:

7.1 provide Contractor with all available pertinent technical data, if any, (in addition to information provided to Companies during the bidding process) which may become available from time to time to be used exclusively for Petroleum Operations;

7.2 provide Contractor with the inventory and equipment in its possession used in maintaining petroleum operations prior to the Effective Date;

7.3 provide Contractor within thirty (30) days of the Effective Date the available technical data, not already provided, related to the discovered but undeveloped reservoirs;

7.4 ensure that the Contract Area, including all other areas where Petroleum Operations are required under this Contract, shall be free of any mines or hazardous war remnants and free of any claims by third parties. However, in the event that a clearing operation is deemed necessary by either Party, Contractor shall prepare the respective work program for discussion with ROC prior to submission to the JMC for approval. Once such work program is approved by the JMC, Operator shall execute the de-mining work program through competent service providers and Contractor shall fund the related costs, which shall be considered as Supplementary Costs and recovered pursuant to Article 19;

7.5 provide adequate security, through the Iraqi armed forces within the Contract Area and any other areas in the Republic of Iraq in which Petroleum Operations or operations related to the Transportation Facilities are conducted including during travel to and from such areas. ROC shall be solely liable for the conduct of all operations by the Iraqi armed forces and shall indemnify and hold Contractor harmless in respect of any liability or obligation due to any loss, damage, fee, compensation to any party for any acts or activities of the Iraqi armed forces or from being obliged to the cost and expense of providing security as contemplated herein. However, in the event that the Contractor, in its reasonable opinion and following consultation with ROC, considers the security provided for its personnel is inconsistent with its HSE policies, Best International Petroleum Industry Practices or inadequate to allow Petroleum Operations to be conducted safely and without threat to life, the Parties hereby agree supplementary measures shall be implemented by Contractor and FOD, as the case may be, including, but not limited to, the engagement of competent private security providers licensed to operate in the Republic of Iraq, such costs being considered Petroleum Costs. Such arrangements shall be revised from time to time in response to changes in security conditions;

7.6 provide assistance, and shall use its best efforts to seek the assistance of and/or cooperation by any regional, district and/or local government, or other representative, agency or authority of the Government to Contractor and Operator as may reasonably be required to secure and renew all entry visas or work permits for employees of Contractor and Operator or Sub-Contractors and their dependents, all permits and registrations required for Contractor to open and maintain a branch office in the Republic of Iraq, all customs and other clearances required for imports and exports of equipment and supplies required for Petroleum Operations and assist Contractor and Operator in obtaining the office space, its equipment, accommodation, communication facilities and permits, way-leaves, easements, rights of way, licences and renewals thereof, all for the purpose of conducting Petroleum Operations;

7.7 provide Contractor and Operator free of charge:

(a) access to the Contract Area and to any other areas where Petroleum Operations are required;
(b) access to, and use of, water, including water for injection requirements, within or outside the Contract Area for the purpose of Petroleum Operations, provided that all installations for off-take, treatment, distribution, and disposal of water shall be the responsibility of Contractor it being agreed that costs relating to access to, and use of, water, including water for injection incurred outside the Contract Area shall be considered Supplementary Costs and recovered pursuant to Article 19.2 (c), or, at Contractor's option, could be considered Petroleum Costs. The Contractor shall be under no obligation to fund investments related to quantities of water in excess of those required for Petroleum Operations unless agreed otherwise;
(c) use of Petroleum for Petroleum Operations; and
(d) use of all existing wells and facilities related to the Field within the Contract Area.

7.8 In the event of unintentional infringement on Petroleum Operations of either Party, the Parties shall convene to agree in good faith on a proper course of action, safeguarding the interests of the Parties.

ARTICLE 8 – TERMINATION

8.1 Termination by ROC

(a) ROC may terminate this Contract (i) by giving Contractor written notice if the last remaining Company (or its parent company that provides a guarantee) becomes bankrupt or is declared insolvent, or (ii) by giving Contractor three (3) Months written notice if Contractor commits a breach of a material obligation of this Contract, including but not limited to:
    (i) Contractor knowingly submits a false statement to ROC which is of material consideration for the execution of this Contract;
    (ii) the last remaining Company assigns any interest, right or obligation under this Contract contrary to the provisions of Article 28; and
    (iii) Contractor fails substantially to comply with approved Plans, Work Programs and Budgets.

(b) If Contractor has remedied its breach pursuant to Article 8.1(a) within the three (3) Months' notice period, ROC shall consider the notice as ineffective and automatically revoked. If ROC reasonably believes that Contractor is doing its best to remedy the breach and its efforts look promising, then ROC shall extend the notice period accordingly.

(c) If ROC terminates this Contract in accordance with Article 8.1(a), Contractor shall:
   (i) forfeit all its future rights and interests under this Contract as from the date of termination;
   (ii) release ROC from any and all actions, claims, demands and proceedings that may arise out of such termination other than in respect of a dispute in relation to such termination; and
   (iii) pay ROC any unspent portion of the Minimum Expenditure Obligation, otherwise, ROC shall be entitled to recover such balance from Contractor by any means it may deem proper.

(d) If Petroleum Operations are suspended or seriously jeopardized for a period exceeding twelve (12) consecutive Months due to Force Majeure, either ROC or Contractor may terminate this Contract by giving two (2) Months written notice. Upon such termination, the provisions of Articles 8.1(c)(i) and 8.1(c)(ii) shall apply, and ROC shall compensate Contractor for accrued but unpaid Supplementary Fees and Service Fees up to the date of termination.

(e) If Contractor suspends its obligations in respect of Petroleum Operations by order or decree of the government of the home country of any of the Companies or their parent companies, ROC shall have the right to assume full responsibility for Petroleum Operations in any way it deems appropriate after giving Contractor one (1) Month written notice to this effect. However, if such suspension continues for a period exceeding one (1) Year, either Party shall have the right to terminate this Contract after giving the other Party two (2) Months written notice. Upon such termination, the provisions of Articles 8.1(c)(i), 8.1(c)(ii) and 8.1(c)(iii) shall apply and Contractor shall be entitled to no compensation whatsoever. However, if at any time during the period when Contractor has suspended its obligations and prior to the end of termination notice, Contractor gives ROC notice that it is able and willing to resume its obligations toward Petroleum Operations, ROC and Contractor shall agree on the best course of action to resume Contractor's obligations and on the payment by ROC of the outstanding Supplementary Fees and Service Fees that were due and payable to Contractor prior to the period of suspension. It is understood that Contractor shall not be entitled to any Supplementary Fees or Service Fees during the period of suspension.

(f) Subject to Article 7, if Contractor fails to establish a normal presence in the Republic of Iraq, as manifested by the necessary personnel and equipment required to conduct Petroleum Operations within six (6) Months after the approval date of the Rehabilitation Plan, and in due consideration of Article 31.5, ROC shall have the right to terminate this Contract after giving Contractor two (2) Months written notice. Upon such termination, the provisions of Article 8.1(c) shall apply and Contractor shall be entitled to no compensation.

(g) The provisions of this Article 8.1 shall not prejudice Contractor's rights to refer any dispute in relation to the termination of this Contract to be resolved in accordance with Article 37.

8.2 Termination by Contractor:

(a) If Contractor elects to terminate this Contract before the end of the Term, Contractor shall give ROC three (3) Months written notice to this effect giving reasons for such election. If by the end of the said notice period the Parties have not agreed on a course of action other than termination, then Contractor may terminate this Contract after giving ROC a further written notice of one (1) Month. Upon such termination the provisions of Article 8.1(c) shall apply.

(b) In the event of termination of this Contract (whether by ROC or by Contractor), in accordance with this Article 8, Contractor hereby warrants that it shall not obstruct, hinder or otherwise interfere in any way with Petroleum Operations by ROC or any third party.

(c) The provisions of this Article 8.2 shall not prejudice ROC's rights to refer any dispute in relation to the termination of this Contract to be resolved in accordance with Article 37.

8.3 The provisions of this Contract that by their nature survive termination or expiry of this Contract (including indemnities, liabilities, audit, confidentiality, governing law and arbitration) shall remain in full force and effect for a period of three (3) Years after such termination or expiry.

8.4 In the event of the Contract being declared by any competent Iraqi authority invalid or voided under the Law, ROC hereby indemnifies and holds Contractor harmless for any and all costs actually incurred by Contractor, including, demobilisation costs, Petroleum Costs, Supplementary Costs paid by Contractor but not recovered, Remuneration Fees accrued but not paid at the date this Contract is declared invalid or voided and penalties, fines, levies, if any, imposed on Contractor under the Law.

ARTICLE 9 – CONDUCT OF PETROLEUM OPERATIONS

9.1 The Parties acknowledge that all measures and precautions shall be taken to safeguard against any possibility of interruption in the ongoing production from the Field as a result of activities under this Contract. For this purpose and for building upon the long experience of the existing operating manpower unit in the Field, and for securing the continuity of the necessary support by ROC, Contractor and ROC agree to the set up of the Field Operating Division or FOD. The FOD shall inherit the existing manpower unit, which shall be detached from ROC, to conduct Petroleum Operations.

9.2 To guard against any interruption in production from the Field, ROC shall continue to conduct Petroleum Operations until the FOD is established and takes over the conduct of Petroleum Operations. As from the Effective Date, ROC shall operate the Field in close coordination and consultation with Contractor; all under the supervision and control of the JMC. During the interim period while ROC is continuing to operate the Field, ROC shall hold Contractor harmless against any loss or damage caused by non-performance or breach by ROC of Best International Petroleum Industry Practices or the terms of this Contract. All costs paid by ROC for activities related to the Petroleum Operations after the Effective Date shall be reimbursed by the Contractor. The Contractor shall treat such reimbursements as Petroleum Costs.

9.3 Should permission be granted to third parties to operate within the Contract Area, such as for operations that are not related to Petroleum Operations and/or petroleum operations for the reservoir(s) that are excluded under Article 2.3 or those relinquished pursuant to Article 5, or for sole-risk operations under Article 12.6, if any, ROC shall take necessary measures to ensure that such operations within the Contract Area shall not obstruct, hinder, or unduly interfere with Petroleum Operations. ROC shall indemnify and hold Contractor harmless of any damage, cost, or delay caused by or resulting from any such third party operations.

9.4 Contractor shall appoint one of the Companies to serve as Lead Contractor. Hence, the Lead Contractor upon the Effective Date shall be __________. Contractor shall not change the Lead Contractor without prior written consent of ROC. As from the Effective Date, the Lead Contractor shall take a substantial role in all planning, decision-making and activities to ensure the efficient conduct of Petroleum Operations by ROC and shall represent Contractor in all matters related to the set-up of the FOD, all in accordance with approved Development Plans, Work Programs and Budgets, and Addendum Three.

9.5 Immediately following the Effective Date the ROC shall deliver to the Contractor and shall co-operate to refine, and agree no later than thirty (30) days thereafter, an interim Work Program and Budget capable of lasting until sixty (60) days after the approval of the Rehabilitation Plan.

9.6 Within thirty (30) days of the Effective Date, the Parties shall jointly commence setting up the FOD, which shall take over the conduct of Petroleum Operations under the general supervision and control of the JMC; all in accordance with this Contract, approved Plans, Work Programs and Budgets, and Addendum Three.

9.7 Promptly following the setting up of the FOD, the Contractor and ROC shall commence preparation of a plan and procedure for the transfer of direct operatorship from ROC to FOD, taking into consideration that the transfer plan shall include but not be limited to:

(a) a list of the various positions to be taken over by the FOD;
(b) a schedule of transfer stages pursuant to which transfer shall be completed within twelve (12) Months of the Effective Date;
(c) inventories of the relevant facilities, equipment, documents, manuals, data and information necessary for the Petroleum Operations; and
(d) a list of the activities, facilities and infrastructure that will remain under the direct management and responsibility of ROC.

9.8 In accordance with the transfer schedule established in Article 9.7(b), ROC shall transfer to and do all things necessary to allow FOD to operate all facilities and equipment relating to Petroleum Operations and retain all documents, manuals, data and information regarding the use and operation of such facilities and equipment so that FOD personnel are able to manage and handle such facilities and equipment in accordance with Best International Petroleum Industry Practices applicable on the date on which such facilities and equipment are transferred. ROC shall keep managing and funding the common activities and facilities that remain under its direct responsibility, as per Article 9.7(d) above, in close coordination and consultation with the FOD.

9.9 The transfer of the accounting and financial aspects shall be handled in accordance with Article 12 of Annex C attached hereto.

9.10 After the FOD has taken over conduct of Petroleum Operations and has become Operator and in accordance with the authorities of the Joint Management Committee as set out in Article 13.2, Contractor shall supervise, direct and manage all the planning, decisions, surveillance, and day-to-day conduct of Petroleum Operations by the FOD, as set forth in more detail in Addendum Three. In general, Contractor shall make available appropriate managerial and technological skills and personnel to the FOD to ensure that Petroleum Operations can be performed in accordance with Best International Petroleum Industry Practices. In particular, Contractor shall prepare and submit for approval the Rehabilitation Plan and Enhanced Redevelopment Plan and their Revisions, and all annual Work Programs and Budgets and their Revisions. The establishment of the FOD shall in no way relieve Contractor of its obligations to achieve the production targets under this Contract.

9.11 It is understood that any commitments entered into by ROC prior to the Effective Date that cover activity in support of the Minimum Work Obligations shall be funded by Contractor, which funding shall be Petroleum Costs. However, Contractor shall have the right to review these commitments and, following consultation with ROC, may request ROC to terminate such commitments subject to the provision of suitable alternative arrangements put in place by Contractor or FOD, as the case may be.

9.12 Not later than the twentieth (20th) day of each Calendar Month, the Operator shall furnish Contractor with a detailed written estimate of its total cash requirements for the succeeding Calendar Month expressed in Dollars, in accordance with approved Work Programs and Budgets.

9.13 Such estimate shall take into consideration any forecast cash balance at Calendar Month end. Payment by Contractor for the succeeding Calendar Month shall be made directly to the correspondent bank designated in Article 9.14 below on the first (1st) day of the Month, or the next following working day, if such day is not a working day.

9.14 Each of Operator and Contractor are authorized to keep, at their own disposal, abroad the foreign funds advanced by Contractor, in an account opened with a first class international bank. Interest or similar income generated by the account shall be credited to the account. Withdrawals from said account shall be used to pay for goods and services abroad and to transfer to a local bank in the Republic of Iraq the required amounts to meet expenditures in Dinars for the Operator in connection with Petroleum Operations, converted at the applicable rate of exchange available as published by the Iraqi Central Bank on the date of conversion. Within sixty (60) days after the end of each Financial Year, Operator shall submit to the appropriate exchange control authorities in the Republic of Iraq a statement, duly certified by a recognized firm of independent auditors, showing the funds credited to the account, the disbursements made out of the account and the balance outstanding at the end of such Financial Year.

9.15 Operator shall diligently conduct Petroleum Operations in compliance with the Law, and in accordance with Best International Petroleum Industry Practices.

9.16 Operator's activities above ground and underground shall be designed to achieve efficient and safe production of Petroleum. Operator shall ensure that all materials, equipment, and facilities used in Petroleum Operations comply with generally accepted engineering norms, are of proper and acceptable construction, and are kept in good working order throughout the Term. The Parties shall at least one (1) Year before the expiry of this Contract agree on a detailed procedure for handing-over the Field and related facilities to ROC as a going concern.

9.17 Operator shall in accordance with the Law and Article 41 take all appropriate and necessary measures to safeguard the environment and prevent or minimise the effect of any pollution which may result from Petroleum Operations.

9.18 Each of Contractor, ROC and Operator shall take all appropriate and necessary measures, in accordance with the Law and international standards, to uphold transparency, accountability, and the strict observance of general business ethics and anti-corruption laws and regulations. Contractor and Operator shall develop procedures and guidance documents to secure compliance with the above.

9.19 Operator shall conduct Petroleum Operations in accordance with the provisions of this Contract, and under the general supervision and control of the JMC.

9.20 Operator shall:

(a) provide all personnel required for the Petroleum Operations, giving first priority to Iraqi nationals, provided the Iraqi nationals have the required qualifications and experience;

(b) without prejudice to the Contractor's right to occupy positions in FOD, adhere to employment and training programs which shall aim at the Iraqization of Operator's manpower pursuant to a plan to be submitted by the Operator and approved by the JMC no later than three (3) Years from the Effective Date;

(c) utilize Sub-Contractors and suppliers of proven capability and professional experience on competitive basis, and in accordance with the tendering procedures established pursuant to Article 9.22(c), subject to the provisions of Article 29, keeping JMC informed accordingly. Any purchase order and sub-contract shall be in accordance with approved Work Programs and Budgets; However, prior approval shall be obtained before an award of any individual purchase order or sub-contract as follows, giving details of bids received and the basis for recommended award:

 (i) by FOD up to or equal to twenty million USD(US$20,000,000) in value;

 (ii) by JMC if exceeding twenty million USD(US$20,000,000) and up to or equal to one hundred million USD (US$100,000,000) in value;

 (iii) by ROC if exceeding one hundred million USD (US$100,000,000) in value, where such written approval shall not to be unreasonably withheld, provided if the total period taken by ROC exceeds forty five (45) days then approval of any such purchase order or sub-contract is deemed to have been provided by ROC. If ROC communicates within the specified period its non-approval of the award in question, then the matter shall be promptly referred to the senior management of the Parties for resolution; and

(d) prepare and issue reports pursuant to Article 15, and provide any further information as may reasonably be required by ROC.

9.21 Operator shall place fixtures and installations inside and outside the Contract Area, as shall be necessary to carry out Petroleum Operations, in accordance with the approved Plans. Fixtures and installations relating to the Transportation System shall be handed over upon completion and commissioning to the Transporter which will thereafter be responsible for the operation and maintenance thereof in accordance with the provisions of Addendum Two and the subsequent Crude Oil Transfer Agreement.

9.22 Promptly after the Effective Date, but not later than six (6) Months thereafter, Contractor shall prepare and submit for JMC approval, in accordance with Article 12, the following operating procedures:

(a) employment procedures and personnel regulations for locally recruited personnel including scales of salaries, wages, benefits, and all allowances applicable to the respective grade of staff and employees, together with employment requirements such as standard job descriptions and qualifications to fill the jobs, all in accordance with the Law and local market conditions. Salaries and terms of employment of Iraqis shall be determined by consultation between ROC and Contractor subject to the Law;

(b) benefits and allowances to be paid in the Republic of Iraq to assigned personnel referred to in Annex C during the assignment for Petroleum Operations;

(c) tendering, bidding and contract awarding procedures for engineering, drilling, construction and other service contracts, and procedures for purchasing materials and equipment, all on a competitive basis (unless otherwise agreed by the JMC), taking into account, where applicable, the provisions of this Contract, Best International Petroleum Industry Practices, and the Law; and

(d) detailed accounting system to be adopted by Contractor and Operator based on the provisions of Annex C.

ARTICLE 10 – ASSOCIATED GAS

10.1 Associated Gas shall not be flared except pursuant to the Law, and as provided herein.

10.2 Operator may use, free of charge and on a priority basis, the quantity of Associated Gas necessary for Petroleum Operations including for re-injection into the reservoir(s) for the purpose of pressure maintenance, enhanced recovery or temporary storage, and for power generation.

10.3 All Associated Gas produced from the Field, which is not used in Petroleum Operations pursuant to Article 10.2 shall be delivered unprocessed to ROC, at the outlet of the relevant crude oil separators or such other point as Contractor and ROC may agree. Contractor shall be under no obligation to provide compression or treatment facilities for Associated Gas, unless otherwise agreed by the Parties in an approved Plan.

10.4 If requested by ROC Contractor shall submit to the JMC, as part of any Plan, a proposal for economically and technically feasible schemes for the utilisation, and/or disposal of all the excess Associated Gas not used in Petroleum Operations. Contractor shall be under no obligation to implement such schemes unless otherwise agreed by the Parties in an approved Plan.

10.5 Quantities of Associated Gas made available to, but not received by ROC, may be flared. Upon prior consent of ROC, Operator may flare Associated Gas; provided, however, that the period and volume of Associated Gas flaring shall be kept to the absolute minimum. Associated Gas may also be flared in limited quantities for testing and maintenance purposes and in emergency cases.

10.6 If agreed in an approved Plan Contractor shall finance and/or through the Operator build Transportation Facilities downstream of the delivery point set out in Article 10.3. Transportation Facilities built by Operator related to the transportation of Associated Gas beyond the delivery point set out in Article 10.3 shall be handed over upon completion and commissioning to the relevant Iraqi entity designated by ROC, which shall thereafter be responsible for the operation and maintenance thereof.

10.7 All costs and expenses incurred by Contractor in connection with the production, re-injection, treatment, transportation, delivery, and disposal of Associated Gas within the Contract Area shall be recovered as Petroleum Costs. All costs and expenses incurred by Contractor in connection with Articles 10.3, 10.4 and 10.6 shall be considered Supplementary Costs.

10.8 The Natural Gas Liquids (NGL) resulting from infield Associated Gas condensation or extraction processes, if any, that are delivered to ROC where one Barrel of NGL is equivalent to one Barrel of Crude Oil for the purposes of Remuneration Fee under Article 19.5.

ARTICLE 11 – DEVELOPMENT PLANS AND WORK PROGRAMS

11.1 Promptly after the Effective Date, and in any case not later than six (6) Months thereafter, Contractor shall prepare and submit for JMC approval the Rehabilitation Plan, based on the available knowledge of the Field including a detailed Work Program and Budget for the remainder of the current Calendar Year. While focusing on near-term Petroleum Operations related to additional Appraisal activities and increased production from the Field, the said Plan shall also anticipate the overall targets and phases of redevelopment of the Field for the Term. The Rehabilitation Plan shall particularly include:

(a) a "Remedial Program" for the immediate and near-term actions to be taken to halt any non-optimal operations, to arrest production decline, and to achieve a sustainable and improved production rate pursuant to Article 2.2(a)(i), all in accordance with Best International Petroleum Industry Practices; and
(b) an "Additional Appraisal Program" for the currently producing as well as the discovered but undeveloped reservoir(s) in the Contract Area which require and justify further Appraisal works, including a time schedule for geophysical surveys and any interpretations of data relating thereto, geological and reservoir engineering studies, as well as laboratory work and Field data gathering programs. The Additional Appraisal Program is aimed at acquiring technical data required to conceive the Enhanced Redevelopment Plan.

11.2 Contractor shall prepare annual Work Programs and Budgets, including production schedules for the succeeding Calendar Years, not later than the first of October of each Calendar Year. Each annual Work Program and Budget shall set out in detail by Quarter all aspects of proposed Petroleum Operations to be carried out including all relevant data and information, estimated cost, duration of each operation, estimated monthly rate of production for each reservoir in the Contract Area. Annual Work Programs shall also include forecasts of yearly activities including costs for the four (4) year period following the end of the relevant Calendar Year or the period up to the expiry of this Contract, whichever is shorter.

11.3 Within six (6) Months after the completion of the Additional Appraisal Program, but no later than three (3) Years from Effective Date, Contractor shall submit for approval the Enhanced Redevelopment Plan, which shall, upon endorsement by ROC, supersede the Rehabilitation Plan.

11.4 Contractor and Operator each in accordance with their respective roles under the provisions of this Contract shall conduct Petroleum Operations in a manner that is designed to achieve the Improved Production Target as soon as possible but no later than the end of the Rehabilitation Period, and the Plateau Production Target no later than six (6) Years after the Effective Date. The Enhanced Redevelopment Plan (and any Revision) submitted by Contractor for approval must contemplate achieving the Plateau Production Target within the designated time periods.

11.5 Contractor may further prepare and submit for ROC's endorsement Revisions of the Enhanced Redevelopment Plan as deemed necessary.

11.6 All Plans and production schedules shall be based on sound geological, reservoir, engineering and economical principles, all in accordance with Best International Petroleum Industry Practices and with the objective of optimizing production and maximizing the volume of Petroleum to be produced from the Contract Area.

ARTICLE 12 – APPROVAL OF DEVELOPMENT PLANS AND WORK PROGRAMS

12.1 Following the establishment of the FOD, no Petroleum Operations shall be carried out unless and until the relevant Work Program and Budget Plan, or their Revisions have been duly approved.

12.2 Contractor shall prepare and submit to the JMC in a timely manner its proposals concerning the Plans, or their Revisions, as well as the associated annual Work Programs and Budgets, and any administrative, accounting or other operating procedures, complete with supporting studies, data and information, for approval in accordance with the following procedure:

(a) within fourteen (14) days of receiving Contractor's proposal or revised proposal, in respect of annual Work Programs and Budgets, and any administrative, accounting or other operating procedures, the JMC shall review and shall either approve the proposal or return it to Contractor with recommended changes. Contractor shall, within a further fourteen (14) days of receiving recommended changes, amend and re-submit the proposal to the JMC for approval;

(b) within twenty (20) days of receiving Contractor's proposal or proposed Revision in respect of Development Plans, the JMC shall review the proposal and pass it to ROC for endorsement or return to the Contractor with recommended changes. Contractor shall amend the proposal and re-submit it to the JMC for approval no later than thirty (30) days thereafter;

(c) within thirty (30) days of receiving a Development Plan from the JMC, the ROC shall advise Contractor and the JMC of its endorsement or rejection. In the event of a rejection, ROC shall provide written advice as to the reasons for its rejection;

(d) it is understood that the Parties shall use their best endeavours to expedite the approval process through close interaction and consultation, and, if necessary, through the intervention of their senior managements;

(e) if line items of an annual Work Program or Budget remain unresolved after submission to senior management, the Parties agree that the Operator will be authorized to act as though the most recent submission by the Contractor has been approved until such time as final resolution of disputed items has occurred; and

(f) time periods in this Article 12.2 shall be subject to appropriate extensions corresponding to any delay resulting from Force Majeure or as otherwise agreed between the Parties. In either case, if the total period taken for approval and endorsement by ROC of the Rehabilitation Plan or the Enhanced Redevelopment Plan exceeds one hundred and twenty (120) days, then the Term together with all rights and obligations hereunder shall be extended to reflect the additional time taken for approvals.

12.3 After the approval of the annual Work Program and Budget by the JMC, it shall be implemented by Operator under the general supervision and control of the JMC in accordance with the authorities set out in Article 13.2. Operator may make minor changes to the details of an approved Work Program and Budget, provided, however, such changes shall not change the budgeted amount for each major line item by more than ten percent (10%), change the total approved Budget by more than five percent (5%), or alter the general objectives of the Work Program. Otherwise, the change shall be considered a Revision of said Work Program or Budget requiring JMC's prior approval unless such changes are warranted due to emergency or extraordinary circumstances requiring immediate action, including but not limited to safeguarding lives or property, protection of the environment or health reasons. Such changes shall be reported by Operator to the Parties and the JMC within five (5) working days.

12.4 Any modification to an approved Plan that alters its general objectives or changes its total estimated cost by more than ten percent (10%) shall be considered a Revision of said Plan and shall be subject to approval in accordance with this Article 12.

12.5 ROC shall have the right to review the proposed or target level of production in respect of any proposed or approved annual Work Program and may, with reasonable justification and upon written notification, require Contractor and Operator to increase or decrease the rate of production from the Contract Area for any of the following reasons:

(a) to avoid material damage to reservoirs;
(b) to minimize Associated Gas wastage; provided, however, ROC shall, at all times, use best endeavours to take all Associated Gas;
(c) for safety consideration;
(d) for operational consideration;
(e) for Government imposed curtailment; and
(f) for curtailments due to failure of Transporter to receive Net Production at the Transfer Point through no fault of Contractor or Operator.

In case reduction of production of Crude Oil is applied as per Articles 12.5(e), ROC shall apply such reduction in a non-discriminatory manner to all of its and its Affiliates' production from the Republic of Iraq. Contractor and Operator shall comply with such reduction upon receipt of notification from ROC to this effect. During the periods when the rate of production is decreased due to minimising Associated Gas wastage under Article 12.5(b), production curtailment imposed under Article 12.5(e) or Article 12.5(f), the Remuneration Fee Bid adjustment under Article 19.5(e) shall cease to apply. Immediately after such ROC notice of minimizing Associated Gas wastage or production curtailment the Parties shall agree in good faith a mechanism to fully compensate Contractor as soon as practicable, which may include, amongst other things, a revised Field production schedule or an extension to the Term or payment of lost income to Contractor in respect of the estimated volumes not produced during the period for which the production levels are decreased under Article 12.5(b) or curtailed under Article 12.5(e) or Article 12.5(f).

12.6 ROC may, at any time, by written notice, request Contractor and Operator to execute specific works or build specific facilities not included in the currently approved Plan or Work Program. Within ninety (90) days of receiving such notice, Contractor and Operator shall amend the relevant Plan or Work Program and Budget accordingly. All costs associated with the construction and operation of the additional facilities or works paid for by the Contractor shall be considered Supplementary Costs. If Contractor decides not to share the possible risks and rewards of such works and facilities in accordance with this Contract, the expenditure incurred shall be borne by ROC, and the said works shall be conducted by and for ROC's sole risk and reward.

ARTICLE 13 – JOINT MANAGEMENT OF PETROLEUM OPERATIONS

13.1 The Parties shall establish, within thirty (30) days from the Effective Date, a joint management committee, referred to herein as the "Joint Management Committee" or "JMC", for the purpose of general supervision and control of Petroleum Operations. The JMC shall consist of eight (8) members. ROC shall nominate four (4) members, including the Chairman. Contractor shall nominate four (4) members, including the Deputy Chairman and the Secretary. The Parties shall also designate one alternate to each of their members and shall promptly inform each other in writing of any change of the members or alternates.

13.2 The JMC shall have the following duties and authorities related to Petroleum Operations:

(a) review and recommendation of Plans and any Revisions thereof;
(b) review and approval of annual Work Programs, Budgets and production schedules, and any Revisions thereof;
(c) review and approval of operating procedures prepared pursuant to Article 9;
(d) review and/or approval of the award of sub-contracts and purchase orders as applicable pursuant to Article 9;
(e) approval of training programs and Iraqization plans for developing Iraqi personnel pursuant to Articles 9 and 26;
(f) supervision and control of the implementation of approved Plans and Work Programs and the overall policy of Operator in accordance with Article 9.10;
(g) review and approval of manpower strength and organisation chart of Operator;
(h) review of Quarterly statements, annual accounts and other financial statements;
(i) review of periodical and other reports submitted by Contractor or Operator and issue of comments and recommendations to ensure proper implementation of Petroleum Operations; and
(j) recommendation of the appointment of the independent international auditor as per Article 20.

13.3 Decisions of the JMC shall be taken by unanimous vote of the members or their alternates present at the meeting or by proxy. In the event that the JMC is unable to reach unanimous decision in respect of any issue, then the issue shall be promptly referred to the senior management of the Parties for resolution. Quorum shall be at least three (3) members or alternates of each Party. Decisions taken by the JMC shall be recorded in official minutes signed by the members present and communicated by Operator to the Parties.

13.4 The JMC shall meet whenever necessary or expedient for the implementation of this Contract and at any time a Party requests a meeting to be held. In any event the JMC shall meet at least four (4) times each Calendar Year. A meeting of the JMC may be convened by either Party giving not less than twenty (20) days prior written notice to the other Party or, in a case requiring urgent action, by giving reasonable shorter notice, with decisions by way of circulated written resolutions. Contractor through the Operator shall prepare the agenda and necessary documents prior to such meetings and communicate the same to the members of the JMC. Either Party may, on seven (7) days prior notice other than in the case of an urgent action, add any matter related to Petroleum Operations not listed by Operator to any JMC meeting agenda.

13.5 The JMC may adopt such procedures as it deems appropriate regarding the conduct of its functions, meetings, and other related matters. For the purpose of facilitating the conduct of its functions, the JMC may appoint such appropriate sub-committees as shall from time to time be required.

13.6 All costs incurred by Contractor and approved by the JMC for carrying out JMC or sub-committee duties shall be considered as Petroleum Costs.

13.7 Decisions made by JMC shall not release the Contractor from its obligations under this Contract.

ARTICLE 14 – DATA AND SAMPLES

14.1 All original data and samples obtained by Contractor or the Operator shall be the property of ROC.

14.2 Contractor and Operator shall provide ROC, free of charge, with copies of any and all data obtained as a result of Petroleum Operations including, but not limited to, geological, geophysical, geochemical, petrophysical, engineering, well logs, maps, magnetic tapes, cores, cuttings and production data as well as all interpretative and derivative data, including reports, analyses, interpretations and evaluation prepared in respect of Petroleum Operations (hereinafter referred to as "Data"). Contractor and Operator shall have the right to make use of such Data, free of charge, for the purpose of Petroleum Operations.

14.3 Contractor and Operator may, for use in Petroleum Operations, retain copies or samples of material or information constituting the Data and, with the approval of ROC, original material. Where such material is capable of reproduction or division and originals have been delivered to ROC, Contractor and Operator may export samples or other reproduced material for processing or laboratory examination or analysis, taking into consideration whether such analysis can be conducted in the Republic of Iraq. Contractor and Operator shall guarantee their proper handling and keeping, and that such exports shall be returned to the Republic of Iraq within a maximum period of three (3) Months from the date of completion of any study, analysis or processing thereof, except for the consumable samples and materials.

14.4 Contractor and Operator shall save and keep in the Republic of Iraq, for a minimum period of one (1) Year, representative portions of each sample of cores and cuttings taken from drilled wells, to be disposed of or forwarded in a manner directed by ROC.

14.5 Contractor shall work with ROC to establish entities in the Republic of Iraq capable of analyzing and processing Data obtained during Petroleum Operations.

ARTICLE 15 – REPORTS AND RECORDS

15.1 Operator shall, once the FOD is established, report in writing to ROC the progress of Petroleum Operations according to the following schedule:

(a) within one (1) Month of the last day of March, June, September and December covering the previous Quarter; and

(b) within three (3) Months of the last day of December covering the previous Calendar Year.

15.2 A report under Article 15.1 shall contain, without limitation, the following in respect of the period which it covers:

(a) details of Petroleum Operations and the factual information obtained;

(b) description of the area in which Operator has operated;

(c) account of the expenditure on Petroleum Operations in accordance with the Accounting Procedure; and

(d) maps indicating all bore-holes, wells and other Petroleum Operations.

15.3 Contractor and Operator shall prepare at all times during the Term accurate and current records of their operations. Such records shall be maintained by Contractor and Operator in accordance with procedures to be established by the JMC in accordance with Best International Petroleum Industry Practices.

15.4 Operator's reports on Petroleum Operations shall comply with the Law.

ARTICLE 16 – ACCESS AND INSPECTION

16.1 Duly authorised inspectors of ROC shall, upon written prior notice to the Operator and Contractor, have access to the Contract Area and any other area where Petroleum Operations are being carried out, for the purpose of inspection of the same. Such inspectors may examine the books, registers and records of Operator and may require Operator to make a reasonable number of surveys, drawings, tests and the like for the purpose of enforcing the provisions of this Contract. They shall, for this purpose, be entitled to make reasonable use or inspection of devices, machinery and instruments used for measurement and other Petroleum Operations. The inspectors shall make all reasonable efforts to conduct any inspection in a manner that will result in a minimum of inconvenience and interruption to the Petroleum Operations, and the inspectors shall always take due account of the advice from the Operator and the Contractor when conducting the inspections. Such inspectors shall be given assistance by the agents and employees of Operator to facilitate the objectives of their task and to avoid endangering or hindering the safety or efficiency of Petroleum Operations. Operator shall offer such inspectors all privileges and facilities afforded to its own staff in the Field and shall provide them, free of charge, with reasonable office space and adequately furnished housing and lodging while they are in the Field whether on temporary or permanent basis.

16.2 Competent Government authorities shall have access to the Contract Area and to the operations conducted thereon by Operator, in the course of carrying out their duties in accordance with the Law. Operator shall offer the necessary assistance and services to such officials free of charge in order to facilitate their objectives.

16.3 Reasonable costs and expenses incurred by Contractor or Operator in implementing the provisions of this Article shall be considered as Petroleum Costs.

ARTICLE 17 – MEASUREMENT, TRANSFER, AND DELIVERY OF CRUDE OIL/EXPORT OIL

17.1 The volume and quality of Crude Oil shall be measured at a Production Measurement Point, immediately upstream of the Transfer Point. The location of the PMP and TP shall be specified in the approved Rehabilitation Plan so as to be within or close to the Contract Area.

17.2 In accordance with Addendum Two, the Operator shall deliver Net Production to Transporter at the Transfer Point. The transportation of crude Oil from the Transfer Point to the Delivery Point shall be carried out by the Transporter, under the terms of Addendum Two and the Crude Oil Transfer Agreement. Transporter shall act exclusively on behalf of ROC, and the Contractor and Operator shall have no liability or obligations in respect of the transportation of Crude Oil from the Transfer Point to the Delivery Point, except as set forth in Annex E.

Where production from the Contract Area is curtailed or suspended, other than for minor service outages, through failure of Transporter to receive the same at the Transfer Point through no fault of the Operator or Contractor, the Parties shall meet and agree, as soon as possible, appropriate measures to compensate the Contractor in accordance with Article 12.5.

17.3 Methods and procedures for measurement of volume and quality of Crude Oil at the Transfer Point shall be as per Addendum Two and the Crude Oil Transfer Agreement. Methods and procedures for measurement of volume and quality of Export Oil at the Delivery Point shall be as per standard practice of SOMO in respect of the

Export Oil.

17.4 Crude Oil may be commingled with crude oil produced from other fields. If Contractor chooses to receive Supplementary Fees or Service Fees in the form of Export Oil, the quality of Export Oil that may be lifted by Contractor at the Delivery Point shall be any available standard Iraqi export blend of nearest quality to that produced from the Field.

17.5 The volume of Export Oil that may be lifted by Contractor at the Delivery Point shall be determined in accordance with Articles 18 and 19, Annex C and Addendum Four.

17.6 If agreed in an approved Plan, Contractor shall finance and/or through the Operator build Transportation Facilities downstream of the Transfer Point. In the event that Contractor finances and/or builds such Transportation Facilities, they shall be handed over to the Transporter upon completion and commissioning.

17.7 Any cost and expenses incurred by Contractor pursuant to Article 17.6 shall be considered as Supplementary Costs.

ARTICLE 18 – VALUATION OF EXPORT OIL

18.1 It is the intent of both Parties that the pricing of Export Oil for all purposes under this Contract shall reflect the prevailing export market price FOB Delivery Point.

18.2 The Export Oil Price for each quantity and quality of Export Oil that may be lifted by Contractor, during any Month in a Lifting Quarter, shall be SOMO's declared OSP for:

18.2.1 the Month of loading for such quantity;
18.2.2 the quality and Delivery Point for such quantity; and
18.2.3 the final destination to which such Export Oil is delivered by the Contractor.

For the avoidance of doubt in calculating the Export Oil Price for any quantity of Export Oil, the standard provisions stipulated in SOMO's standard crude oil sales agreements shall be applied including provisions relating to (a) API escalation/de-escalation, and (b) freight protection.

18.3 In the event that Export Oil market conditions oblige SOMO to adopt a different pricing mechanism, SOMO shall promptly advise Contractor of the new pricing mechanism.

18.4 The determination of the Export Oil Price, as above, (used for actualising the quantities of Export Oil that may be lifted by Contractor in each Month of the said Lifting Quarter) as well as adjustments required to the quantity of Export Oil to be lifted (due to the timing between estimated and actual dates of liftings) shall be pursuant to Addendum Four and Annex C (Article 9.6).

18.5 Contractor shall cooperate with SOMO in areas such as:

(a) assessment of worldwide evolution in export qualities of crude oil;
(b) market studies and outlet forecasts in various market areas; and
(c) other information concerning Export Oil market conditions.

The costs of such cooperation shall be paid by Contractor.

ARTICLE 19 – SUPPLEMENTARY FEES AND SERVICE FEES

19.1 For the Petroleum Operations performed under this Contract, Contractor is entitled to Supplementary Fees and Service Fees. In accordance with this Article 19, Supplementary Fees shall be comprised of Supplementary Costs. Service Fees shall be comprised of Petroleum Costs and a Remuneration Fee.

19.2 Supplementary Costs

Contractor shall start charging Supplementary Costs to the Operating Account as from the Effective Date, in accordance with this Contract and the Accounting Procedure but the same shall be due and payable according to the following:

(a) the signature bonus paid under Article 4 shall be amortized and recovered over twenty (20) equal Quarterly payments beginning with the ninth Quarter following the Quarter in which the Effective Date occurs;
(b) de-mining costs incurred pursuant to Article 7.4 shall accrue and be recovered over eight (8) equal Quarterly payments beginning with the first Quarter following the date on which de-mining costs start being incurred;
(c) costs or expenses incurred pursuant to Articles 7.7 (b), 10.4, 10.6, 12.6, and 17.6 for additional facilities shall accrue and be payable beginning in the first Month of the Calendar Quarter following their payment date;
(d) costs or expenditures incurred pursuant to Article 41.16 for remediation of pre-existing environmental conditions shall accrue and be payable beginning in the first Month of the Calendar Quarter following their payment date; and
(e) outstanding balances on all Supplementary Costs shall bear interest at LIBOR plus one percent (1%) from the date when Supplementary Costs are first invoiced until the date when they are received; provided, that interest shall be fixed for each tranche of Supplementary Costs based on LIBOR prevailing as at the first invoice date.

19.3 Supplementary Fees

The Supplementary Fees due to Contractor shall be paid in Export Oil at the Delivery Point or, at ROC's option, in cash, in USD, within sixty (60) days of the submission of an invoice pursuant to Article 9 of the Accounting Procedure. For payment in Export Oil, the Export Oil Price shall be in accordance with Article 18. ROC shall notify Contractor of its election whether to pay Supplementary Fees in cash or in Export Oil within ten (10) days of receipt of Contractor's first invoice for payment of Supplementary Fees. Such election shall remain in effect for the remainder of this Contract, unless otherwise agreed by the Parties or ROC is unable to pay the Supplementary Fees in Export Oil for any reason whatsoever then payment shall be made in cash.

(a) Supplementary Fees shall be deemed to cover all amounts due to Contractor for Supplementary Costs.
(b) Supplementary Fees shall become due and payable as detailed in Article 19.2 and shall be paid to the extent of ten percent (10%) of the deemed revenues of the Baseline Production.
(c) Any due and payable Supplementary Fees that remain unpaid in respect of any Calendar Quarter shall be carried forward and paid in succeeding Quarter(s) until fully paid.
(d) ROC reserves the right at any time by notice to Contractor to decrease the amortization periods specified in Articles 19.2(a) and 19.2(b), and/or increase the percentage of Baseline Production specified in Article 19.3(b).

19.4 Petroleum Costs

Contractor shall start charging Petroleum Costs to the Operating Account as from the Effective Date, in accordance with this Contract and the Accounting Procedure, but the same shall be due and payable only after the Service Fees Eligibility Date.

19.5 Remuneration Fee

Contractor shall become entitled to the Remuneration Fee and shall start charging the same to the Operating Account only after the Service Fees Eligibility Date.

(a) For each Calendar Quarter, commencing with the Calendar Quarter following the Quarter in which the Service Fees Eligibility Date occurs, the Remuneration Fee shall be an amount equal to the product of the Remuneration Fee per Barrel applicable to such Quarter, multiplied by the Incremental Production applicable to such Quarter and subject to the performance adjustment in Article 19.5(e).

R-Factor	Remuneration Fee per Barrel (USD)
Less than 1.0	Remuneration Fee Bid (RFB)
1.0 to less than 1.25	80%*RFB
1.25 to less than 1.5	60%*RFB
1.5 to less than 2.0	50%*RFB
2.0 and above	30%*RFB

(b) The Remuneration Fee per Barrel of Crude Oil applicable for all Calendar Quarters during any given Calendar Year shall be determined on the basis of the R-Factor calculated at the end of the preceding Calendar Year for the Field as follows:

(c) For the purposes of calculating Baseline Production and Incremental Production, the Baseline Production Rate for any Quarter, expressed to the nearest Barrel of oil per day, will be calculated according to the product of the Initial Production Rate and a Decline Factor for that Quarter according to the formulae:

BPRn = IPR * DFn

and

DFn = DF raised to the power ((n)/4)

where:

BPRn	=	Baseline Production Rate for Quarter n
IPR	=	Initial Production Rate
DFn	=	Decline Factor for Quarter n
n	=	Number of the Quarter following the Quarter in which the Effective Date occurs
DF	=	0.95

(d) The R-Factor achieved by Contractor as at the end of any Calendar Year shall be calculated by dividing the aggregate value of Cash Receipts from the Effective Date up to and including that Calendar Year by the aggregate of Expenditure over that same time frame.

For the purposes of calculating the R-Factor: Aggregate "Cash Receipts" of Contractor from Petroleum Operations as of the end of any Calendar Year is the aggregate value from the Effective Date up to and including that Year of:

(i) Service Fees paid to Contractor as provided in Articles 19.6; plus

(ii) any Contractor's incidental income (of the type specified in the Accounting Procedure) arising from Petroleum Operations; and

Aggregate "Expenditure" made by Contractor for Petroleum Operations as of the end of any Calendar Year is the aggregate value from the Effective Date up to and including that Year of:

(i) Petroleum Costs; plus

(ii) Training, Technology and Scholarship Fund as per Article 26. For the avoidance of doubt, this expense is included as Expenditures for purposes of determining the R-Factor, but shall not be Petroleum Costs.

(e) During the Plateau Production Period the Remuneration Fee payable in respect of any Quarter shall be adjusted by multiplying it by the Performance Factor. However, any adjustment to the Remuneration Fee under this Article may cease to apply in accordance with Article 12.5 in relation to: (i) minimizing Associated Gas wastage (under Article 12.5(b)); (ii) Government imposed production curtailment (under Article 12.5(e)); and/or (iii) where normal production is curtailed or suspended through failure of Transporter to receive the same at the Transfer Point through no fault of the Operator or Contractor (under Article 12.5(f)).

19.6 Service Fees

(a) The Service Fees due to Contractor shall be paid without interest, in Export Oil at the Delivery Point or, at Contractor's option, in cash, in USD, within sixty (60) days of the submission of an invoice pursuant to Article 9 of the Accounting Procedure. For payment of Contractor's entitlement in Export Oil, the Export Oil Price shall be determined in accordance with Article 18. Contractor shall notify ROC of its election whether to receive Service Fees in cash or in Export Oil no later than the end of the Rehabilitation Period and thereafter annually seven (7) months prior to the commencement of each Calendar Year or ROC is unable to pay the Service Fees in Export Oil for any reason whatsoever then payment shall be made in cash.

(b) The Service Fees and Supplementary Fees shall be deemed to cover all costs, expenses, liabilities and remuneration to Contractor under this Contract. ROC shall not be obliged to pay any other compensation whatsoever to the Contractor for the fulfilment of its obligations under this Contract unless otherwise provided for under this Contract.

(c) Service Fees shall become due and payable starting with the first Calendar Quarter following the Quarter in which the Service Fees Eligibility Date occurs and shall be paid to the extent of fifty percent (50%) of the deemed revenues of the Incremental Production. It is understood that payment of due and payable Petroleum Costs shall have priority over the payment of due and payable Remuneration Fees.

(d) Any due and payable Service Fees that remain unpaid in respect of any Calendar Quarter shall be carried forward and paid in succeeding Quarter(s) until fully paid.

19.7 For the purpose of calculating the Supplementary Fees and Service Fees only, the Baseline Production and Incremental Production of Crude Oil under Articles 19.3 (b) and 19.6 (c) shall be valued at the Provisional Export Oil Price, pursuant to Articles 17 and 18.

19.8 Subject to Article 8, any due and payable Supplementary Fees and Service

Fees that remain outstanding at the expiry or termination of this Contract shall become immediately due and payable within thirty (30) days thereof, or under such other terms as may be agreed by the Parties.

19.9 In case the Supplementary Fees or Service Fees are paid in Export Oil, ROC shall arrange with SOMO to deliver to Contractor at the Delivery Point an amount of Export Oil, at the relevant Export Oil Price, equivalent to the amount of Supplementary Fees or Service Fees owed and payable hereunder. Contractor's Quarterly lifting of Export Oil shall be estimated in advance on the basis of Supplementary Fees and Service Fees due and payable in the Lifting Quarter, unpaid Supplementary Fees or Service Fees carried forward, production schedule and Provisional Export Oil Price.

Contractor's final lifting shall be adjusted on the basis of actual amounts of Supplementary Fees or Service Fees owed as computed under this Article 19, and on the applicable Export Oil Price in accordance with the provisions of Article 18, Annex C and Addendum Four.

ARTICLE 20 – BOOKS OF ACCOUNT, ACCOUNTING AND AUDIT

20.1 Contractor and Operator shall maintain at their business offices in the Republic of Iraq books of account, in accordance with the Accounting Procedure, generally accepted accounting principles used in the international petroleum industry, and such other books, records and original supporting documents necessary to show the work performed and expenditures and costs incurred including the quantity and value of all Petroleum produced, saved, and delivered as well as the quantity and value of Export Oil received by Contractor at the Delivery Point.

20.2 Contractor and Operator shall keep books of account and accounting records in Dollars and in the English language. Contractor and Operator shall also prepare and keep an Arabic summary of the main items of these books of account and accounting records.

20.3 Operator shall furnish to the Parties or their designees monthly reports showing the quantity of Petroleum produced and saved from the Contract Area. Such reports shall be prepared in accordance with practices generally used in the international petroleum industry and in a form agreed upon with the Parties and shall be signed by the authorised representative of Operator or his deputy and delivered to the Parties or their designees within thirty (30) days after the end of the Month covered by such report.

20.4 The Parties shall jointly appoint an independent auditor of international qualification and standing to audit all the books and accounts of Contractor and Operator on an annual basis and report thereon. The costs of such audit shall be considered as Petroleum Costs. The auditors shall confirm, inter alia, that:

(a) the record of costs is correct;
(b) the costs are in accordance with this Contract;
(c) the costs are properly classified in accordance with the expenditure classification;
(d) documentation exists to justify such costs and expenditures; and
(e) no evidence exists of fraudulent records and accounts in respect of the costs incurred.

20.5 Contractor shall, within forty five (45) days after the end of each Quarter, submit to ROC a statement of Supplementary Costs and Petroleum Costs showing costs incurred by Contractor during such Quarter, and when applicable a statement for cost recovery for that Quarter as per Annex C.

20.6 Contractor and Operator shall submit to ROC a set of accounts audited by the independent auditor for each Calendar Year within three (3) Months from the last day of said Calendar Year to show the results of Petroleum Operations.

20.7 Contractor's and Operator's books, records and necessary supporting documents shall be made available for auditing by ROC at any time during regular working hours for twelve (12) Months from the end of each Quarter to which such documents relate. If within such twelve (12) Months, ROC has not advised Contractor and Operator of its objections, the said books, records and supporting documents shall be considered approved. Audits conducted by auditors appointed under Article 20.4, the Iraqi Supreme Auditing Board or ROC shall be conducted in accordance with generally accepted accounting principles used in the international petroleum industry.

20.8 If the ROC has an objection to any costs or expenses as reported and invoiced by the Contractor, the ROC will notify the Contractor of its objection in writing but shall pay both the disputed and undisputed amounts pending resolution of the matter. Within one (1) Month from the date of Contractor's receipt of ROC's objection, Contractor and ROC shall mutually agree to either seek in good faith an acceptable solution or nominate one (1) or more Experts to settle the matter. If the matter is referred to an Expert, the Expert shall, within three (3) Months following their appointment, provide their solution to the dispute that is in line with the provisions of this Contract and Annex C. Failing such settlement, either Party may refer the matter to arbitration pursuant to Article 37.

20.9 During, and for a period of three (3) Years after the Term, the books of account and other books and records referred to above shall be made available by Contractor and Operator at all reasonable times for auditing by duly authorised representatives of the Government, in accordance with the Law.

ARTICLE 21 – EXCHANGE AND CURRENCY CONTROL

21.1 Contractor and Operator shall have the right of availability, free possession, use of, and internal and external disposal of foreign currency.

21.2 Contractor shall provide funds necessary for Petroleum Operations in the Republic of Iraq under this Contract in freely convertible foreign currencies supplied from abroad.

21.3 Contractor and Operator are authorized to open and operate accounts in foreign banks outside the Republic of Iraq and shall have the right to make payments out of the said accounts directly in foreign currencies for goods and services obtained for Petroleum Operations in the Republic of Iraq and to charge such payments in accordance with the provisions of this Contract without having first to transfer the funds for such payments to the Republic of Iraq.

21.4 Contractor and Operator and any non-Iraqi Sub-Contractors shall have the right to open and maintain bank accounts in foreign and/or local currencies in the Republic of Iraq in accordance with Central Bank of Iraq regulations and retain or dispose of any funds therein for its Petroleum Operations in the Republic of Iraq in accordance with Central Bank of Iraq regulations.

ARTICLE 22 – TITLE TO ASSETS

22.1 All assets acquired and/or provided by Contractor or Operator, in connection with or in relation to Petroleum Operations, the costs of which are subject to cost recovery in accordance with the provisions of this Contract, shall become the property of ROC upon their landing in the Republic of Iraq.

22.2 Notwithstanding the above, Contractor and Operator shall be entitled to the full and free use of such assets for the purpose and Term of this Contract. During the Term, ROC and Contractor shall not assign, sell or otherwise dispose of such fixed and/or movable assets except by mutual agreement.

22.3 The provisions of Article 22.1 shall not apply to equipment leased by Contractor or Operator or belonging to Sub-Contractors who perform services or carry out works in connection with Petroleum Operations. Contractor and Operator and non-Iraqi Sub-Contractors may import such equipment on a temporary basis. Unless otherwise agreed by ROC, such equipment shall be re-exported from the Republic of Iraq subject to the provisions of Article 25, as and when they are no longer required for Petroleum Operations.

ARTICLE 23 – TAXES

23.1 Each entity constituting Contractor shall keep books of account and be individually liable for and shall pay corporate income tax in accordance with the Law.

23.2 In no event shall ROC be liable under this Contract for any taxes payable by Companies outside of the Republic of Iraq.

23.3 For the avoidance of doubt, it is the understanding of the Parties that the sole tax liability of Contractor under this Contract shall not exceed corporate income tax levied at a rate not to exceed thirty five percent (35%) of Contractor's taxable profit under the Law which shall, as between the Contractor and ROC, be deemed to be the Remuneration Fee received during the relevant Tax Year calculated in accordance with Article 19.5 ("Contractor's Income Tax Liability").

23.4 In the event Contractor is subject to any demand to pay other taxes (other than or in excess of Contractor's Income Tax Liability) ROC shall bear and pay on behalf of each entity constituting Contractor all such other or additional taxes and shall indemnify and hold each entity constituting Contractor harmless against any and all liabilities relating to the payment of such other or additional taxes.

ARTICLE 24 – PARTNERSHIP, INDEMNITY AND INSURANCE

24.1 It is expressly agreed that it is not the purpose or intention of this Contract to create, nor shall this Contract be construed as creating, any mining partnership, joint venture, commercial partnership or other partnership between the Parties.

24.2 Except for the period when ROC is Operator or as otherwise provided in this Contract, Contractor shall indemnify and hold ROC harmless against all and any claims, actions, demands and proceedings made by third parties arising out of any loss or damage, resulting from an act or omission of Contractor and/or Operator and/or their Sub-Contractors in their conduct of Petroleum Operations. All costs incurred by Contractor to indemnify and hold ROC harmless as aforesaid shall be considered as Petroleum Costs except in the case of Gross Negligence or Wilful Misconduct on the part of the Contractor and/or Operator and/or their Sub-Contractors.

24.3 Except for the period when ROC is Operator and in respect of the Contract Area, Contractor shall be liable for any loss of or damage to any installations belonging to ROC or any third party arising from Gross Negligence or Wilful Misconduct of Contractor and/or Operator or their Sub-Contractors.

24.4 Notwithstanding the foregoing, under no circumstances shall Contractor, its Affiliates or Operator be liable to ROC, its Affiliates or any third party, for consequential or indirect damages, losses, expenses or liabilities, loss of profit, loss of production, reservoir or formation damage or other losses whether or not similar to the foregoing and howsoever arising.

24.5 Contractor shall establish an insurance plan, to be approved by the ROC, for its operations hereunder and obtain the insurance policies in favour of ROC and/or Contractor, as provided for in accordance therewith. Such insurances shall cover the types of exposure that are normally covered in the international petroleum industry, including but not limited to damage to equipment, installations and third party liabilities. Contractor and/or Operator shall ensure that Sub-Contractors adequately insure their risks under their relevant sub-contracts.

24.6 Such insurance plan shall require that the Contractor obtains and maintains insurance from an Iraqi insurance company or foreign insurance company permitted to conduct business in the Republic of Iraq to cover the risks associated with the Petroleum Operations and any other activities related thereto and as may be required by Law during the Term, including third party liability and environmental damage and injury, where such coverage is available in the Republic of Iraq and available on commercially reasonable terms. If such coverage is unavailable in the Republic of Iraq, insurance shall be obtained from a foreign insurance company. The insurance company shall arrange, in co-operation with Contractor to the extent needed, re-insurance placement for coverages on the international market for the part of exposure in excess of the insurance company's net retention.

24.7 The cost of insurance or reinsurance obtained and maintained by Contractor and/or Operator whether obtained inside or outside the Republic of Iraq and any amounts paid for deductibles, losses, or claims in excess of such insurances and not attributable to the Gross Negligence or Wilful Misconduct of Contractor or Operator or their Sub-Contractors under this Contract shall be considered as Petroleum Costs.

24.8 Contractor and/or Operator shall notify ROC of the issue and terms of all insurance policies obtained by it under this Contract.

ARTICLE 25 – IMPORTS AND EXPORTS

25.1 Contractor, Operator and Sub-Contractors engaged in carrying out Petroleum Operations shall be permitted to import machinery, equipment, vehicles, materials, supplies,consumables and movable property to be used solely for the purpose of carrying out Petroleum Operations and supporting activities. Importation of machinery, equipment, vehicles, materials, supplies, consumables and movable property to be used solely for the purpose of carrying out Petroleum Operations and supporting activities shall be exempted from customs duties to the extent they are imported in the name of ROC. Any other customs duties relevant to carrying out of Petroleum Operations and supporting activities shall be recoverable as Petroleum Costs. Contractor, Operator and Sub-Contractors shall comply with the applicable administrative formalities in this respect.

25.2 Expatriate employees of Contractor, Operator and Sub-Contractors shall be permitted to import and shall be exempted from customs duties with respect to the reasonable importation of household goods and personal effects, provided that such property is imported for the sole use of the employee and his family and provided further that such imported property shall be re-exported by employee, without any export duty or impost upon termination of his employment, or be disposed of in the Republic of Iraq in accordance with the Law.

25.3 Items imported by Contractor, Operator or Sub-Contractors on temporary basis and no longer required for Petroleum Operations or supporting activities shall, unless otherwise agreed by ROC, be re-exported without any export duty or impost in accordance with the Law.

25.4 The sale in the Republic of Iraq of any items imported under this Contract shall be subject to ROC's prior consent and to the Law.

25.5 Customs duties, as used herein, shall include all duties, taxes and other financial imposts which may be due as a result of the importation of the above-mentioned items but, shall not include charges, dues or fees of general application to be paid to Governmental entities for services rendered.

25.6 Contractor shall be exempted from any export duty or impost with respect to the Export Oil that Contractor may lift under this Contract, except for port dues of general application to all buyers which are payable for services rendered by the port authorities in accordance with the Law. Such port dues shall not be considered Petroleum Costs.

ARTICLE 26 – EMPLOYMENT, TRAINING, AND TECHNOLOGY TRANSFER

26.1 Without prejudice to the right of Contractor and Operator to select and employ such number of personnel as, in the opinion of the Contractor or Operator, are required for carrying out Petroleum Operations in a safe, cost effective and efficient manner, Contractor and Operator shall, to the maximum extent possible, employ, and require Sub-Contractors to employ Iraqi nationals having the requisite qualifications and experience.

26.2 Through a Training, Technology and Scholarship Fund, Contractor and Operator shall offer and facilitate for an agreed number of Iraqi nationals, as designated by ROC in consultation with Contractor, the opportunity, both inside and/or outside of the Republic of Iraq, for on-the-job training and practical experience in Petroleum Operations, and academic education. The Fund shall also be used for supporting oil and gas related technology and research including the establishment or upgrading of research institutes inside the Republic of Iraq.

26.3 As a minimum, Contractor shall allocate during the Term an annual amount of five million USD (US$ 5,000,000) to the Training, Technology and Scholarship Fund. The Fund payment shall not be recoverable as Petroleum Costs.

26.4 Not later than twelve (12) Months after the Effective Date, Contractor shall, in consultation with ROC, establish and implement training programs for staff positions in each phase and level of Petroleum Operations including skilled, technical, executive and management positions, with a view to ensuring increased employment of Iraqi nationals and a commensurate reduction of expatriate employees.

26.5 Each Company may separately negotiate, in good faith, technical assistance agreements with ROC to make available, on commercially agreeable terms, technology and information of a proprietary nature for use in the Republic of Iraq by ROC and its Affiliates.

ARTICLE 27 – PARTICIPATION

27.1 The State Partner shall have twenty-five percent (25%) of Contractor's total Participating Interest and the remaining Participating Interest of seventy-five percent (75%) shall be apportioned between the Companies as follows:

____________: ____________________ (______%);
____________: ____________________ (______%);
____________: ____________________ (______%);

27.2 Companies shall pay for all of the State Partner's share of Petroleum Costs and Supplementary Costs during the Term and any extension thereto. The Companies shall have all Petroleum Costs paid as Service Fees and Supplementary Costs paid as Supplementary Fees, however, the State Partner shall be entitled to receive its twenty-five percent (25%) Participating Interest of any Remuneration Fee paid to Contractor.

27.3 Participation shall further be subject to the provisions of Addendum One.

ARTICLE 28 – ASSIGNMENT

28.1 No Company may assign its rights or obligations under this Contract, in whole or in part, without the prior written consent of ROC. The direct or indirect transfer of shares or other ownership interests in any Company (except for the transfer of shares in a listed parent company) shall constitute an assignment of rights and obligations under this Contract and shall be subject to this Article 28.

28.2 By providing ROC one (1) Month prior written notice of its intent, any Company shall have the right to assign any of its Participating Interest, shares, rights, privileges, duties or obligations under this Contract to a wholly-owned and controlled Affiliate. Such assignment shall not release said Company from its obligations under this Contract and it shall remain jointly responsible together with the assignee Affiliate for the proper and timely execution of this Contract.

28.3 In the event that any Company wishes to assign, in whole or in part, any of its Participating Interest, shares, rights, privileges, duties or obligations under this Contract to a third party or an Affiliate that is not wholly-owned and controlled, the Company shall submit to ROC a request to this effect giving detailed evidence of the technical and financial competence of the recommended assignee. ROC shall consider the said request and notify Company of its approval or otherwise within three (3) Months of receipt thereof. Before such assignment becomes effective, the foreign assignee shall first provide ROC with a guarantee acceptable to ROC in the form set out in Annex F after which ROC shall, to the extent of the assigned Participating Interest, release assignor from its obligations under this Contract and any guarantee provided to it by assignor.

28.4 If any Company wishes to assign part of its Participating Interest in this Contract to a third party pursuant to Article 28.3, ROC shall within the period set out under Article 28.3 have the option to take such part and assign it to a nominated Iraqi entity on the same terms and conditions offered to the third party.

28.5 Notwithstanding the foregoing, for the purpose of financing Petroleum Operations, any entity constituting Contractor may pledge, or otherwise encumber, totally or partially, its rights under this Contract to an internationally recognized bank and/or financing institution acceptable to ROC (such acceptance not to be unreasonably withheld) provided that such pledge or encumbrance shall not in any way affect the rights or interests of ROC.

28.6 Without prejudice to the provisions of the Heads of Joint Operating Agreement (Addendum One) between the entities constituting Contractor, in the event that any Company (or the Affiliated company that provides a guarantee) becomes bankrupt, or makes an arrangement with or assignment in favour of its creditors or makes a composition with creditors, or if it assigns to a third party any of its interests/shares in this Contract contrary to the provisions herein, or goes into liquidation other than for reconstruction or amalgamation with a wholly-owned and controlled Affiliate, ROC shall have the right to terminate the participation of such Company in this Contract by a written notice to Contractor. The rights and obligations of such Company shall be assigned to the remaining Companies proportionately to their respective Participating Interests or as they may otherwise mutually agree.

28.7 The State Partner shall have the right to assign its Participating Interest only to an entity that is entirely owned and controlled by the Government; otherwise, any assignment by the State Partner of its Participating Interest shall require the consent of the Companies.

ARTICLE 29 – LAWS AND REGULATIONS

29.1 Contractor and Operator shall be bound by and shall comply, in all respects, with the provisions of the Law. Unless otherwise provided in this Contract, Contractor shall indemnify and save harmless ROC against all penalties, fines and other liabilities of every kind for breach of the Law by Contractor or Operator.

29.2 Notwithstanding the provisions of Article 29.1, Contractor, Operator and their Sub-Contractors shall, in accordance with the Law, be exempted from customs and stamp duties on the execution of this Contract, and from restrictions concerning work licences and employment of expatriates, subject to the provisions of Article 9.22. However, Contractor, Operator and their Sub-Contractors shall submit all data and information required by the relevant Iraqi authorities in this respect.

29.3 Contractor and Operator shall, in all their sub-contracts, include a provision whereby Sub-Contractors shall undertake to abide by and comply with the Law.

29.4 Subject to Article 29.5, if, after the Effective Date, the financial interests of Contractor are adversely and substantially affected by a change to the Law that was in force on the Effective Date, or by revocation, modification, or non-renewal of any approvals, consents or exemptions granted to Contractor pursuant to this Contract (other than as a result of Gross Negligence or Wilful Misconduct of Contractor or Operator), the Parties shall, within ninety (90) days, agree on necessary adjustments to the relevant provisions of this Contract in order to maintain Contractor's financial interests under this Contract reasonably unchanged.

29.5 It is the understanding of the Parties that the income tax payable by Contractor for any Tax Year shall not exceed Contractor's Income Tax Liability for such Tax Year. Contractor shall bear such income tax once applicable, according to the Law, provided, however, in the event the Contractor's income tax liability due under the Law exceeds Contractor's Income Tax Liability, then ROC shall assume, pay and discharge, in the name and on behalf of each entity constituting Contractor, any excess tax liability arising under the Law over Contractor's Income Tax Liability. ROC shall reimburse the same entities for the amount exceeding the Contractor's Income Tax Liability, should said excess amount be paid by them.

29.6 Should the Parties be unable to agree within ninety (90) days on any amendments to be made in respect of Articles 29.4 and 29.5, or such other period as may be agreed by the Parties, the dispute may be resolved in accordance with Article 37.

ARTICLE 30 – LOCAL GOODS AND SERVICES

30.1 Works and services performed in the Republic of Iraq through sub-contracts shall be carried out on a competitive basis. Preference shall always be given to Iraqi entities and firms, or foreign firms in association therewith, provided that their relevant capabilities and prices are competitive with those available in the international market.

30.2 Preference shall be given to locally manufactured and/or available goods, materials, equipment, consumables and the like, provided that their technical specifications, availability, prices, and time of delivery are comparable to those available in the international market.

30.3 Contractor and Operator shall ensure that contracts with Sub-Contractors, agents, assignees and employees shall strictly adhere to the provisions of this Article 30.

ARTICLE 31 – FORCE MAJEURE

31.1 The non-performance or delay in performance by either Party of its obligations or duties under this Contract shall be excused if and to the extent that such non-performance or delay is caused by Force Majeure.

31.2 The Party affected by Force Majeure shall notify the other Party thereof, in writing within fourteen (14) days, stating the cause and the extent of effect of such Force Majeure and shall keep the other Party informed of significant developments. The affected Party shall use all reasonable diligence to remove or overcome the Force Majeure situation as quickly as possible in a cost-effective manner.

31.3 Force Majeure shall mean any cause or event, unforeseen or beyond the reasonable control of the Party claiming to be affected by such event, and shall include, but without limitation, Acts of God, war (whether declared or undeclared), force of nature, insurrection, riot, fire, and with respect to Contractor only legislation/order of the Government and other acts or circumstances beyond the control of either Party affected by it, provided always that such acts or circumstances are not attributable to the Party invoking Force Majeure or its Affiliates. The inability to pay monies due shall not constitute a condition of Force Majeure.

31.4 In the event that the Petroleum Operations are delayed, curtailed or prevented due to Force Majeure for a period exceeding ninety (90) consecutive days, then the Term together with all rights and obligations hereunder shall be extended accordingly, subject to the provisions of Article 8, and the Parties shall meet shortly after a notice sent by the Contractor to ROC to, in good faith, agree on modifications to this Contract which will enable the Contractor's rights and obligations to be restored. If the Parties are unable to reach an agreement on the possible modifications to be made to this Contract within thirty (30) days, such disagreement shall be submitted to arbitration in accordance with the provisions of Articles 37.4 to 37.8.

31.5 It is agreed by the Parties that the security conditions prevailing in the Contract Area on Contract signing date shall not constitute a condition of Force Majeure for either Party. The Parties also agree that the political and security conditions generally prevailing in the Republic of Iraq on the Contract signing date shall not constitute a condition of Force Majeure for either Party unless these conditions prevent the implementation of Petroleum Operations.

ARTICLE 32 – ENTIRE AGREEMENT AND AMENDMENTS

32.1 This Contract constitutes the entire agreement between ROC and Contractor relating to the Field. Hence it supersedes any previous representations, whether explicit or implicit, and any prior agreement of any kind or nature, whether oral or written, in this respect.

32.2 This Contract shall not be amended or supplemented except by an instrument in writing signed by duly authorized representatives of both Parties.

32.3 If any provision of this Contract shall be found by any court, tribunal or administrative body of competent jurisdiction to be invalid or unenforceable, the invalidity or unenforceability shall not affect the other provisions of this Contract and all provisions not affected by such invalidity or unenforceability shall remain in full force and effect. The Parties shall attempt to substitute, for any invalid or unenforceable provision, a valid and enforceable provision that achieves, to the greatest possible extent, the principal objectives of the invalid or unenforceable provisions.

32.4 The provisions of this Contract shall inure to the benefit of and be binding upon the successors and permitted assignees of the Parties.

ARTICLE 33 – CONFIDENTIALITY AND TECHNOLOGY OWNERSHIP

33.1 All information and data obtained in connection with or in relation to this Contract shall be kept confidential by the Parties and their Affiliates and shall not be disclosed or communicated to any third party without the other Party's prior written consent, except: (i) to Affiliates; (ii) to any professional consultant retained by a Party; or (iii) where it is necessary for the approval, implementation and/or financing of Petroleum Operations; provided that in all cases of disclosure the party to whom the information is disclosed shall agree to the same confidentiality obligation as contained herein.

33.2 The confidentiality undertaking in Article 33.1 shall not apply:

(a) upon the confidential information becoming public knowledge other than by default on the part of a Party;
(b) upon such confidential information becoming available to a Party from a third party (unless the third party acts in violation of a confidentiality obligation of which the Party is aware);
(c) if such confidential information is independently developed by a Party or its Affiliates; or
(d) to the extent that such confidential information is required by the Law, judicial proceedings or applicable stock exchange regulations to be disclosed.

33.3 The foregoing provisions of Articles 33.1 and 33.2 shall continue in force for three (3) Years following termination or expiry of this Contract.

33.4 To the fullest extent permitted by applicable laws or agreements, the entities constituting Contractor agree to make available on reasonable terms the benefits of their most appropriate technical expertise and technology (and that of their Affiliates) for application in the conduct of Petroleum Operations, including such technology as can best improve the economic yield or performance of the Petroleum reservoirs operated by the Operator under this Contract. Any such technology shall remain the property of the relevant entities constituting Contractor (or their Affiliates), subject to any licensing or other appropriate arrangements entered into in connection with Petroleum Operations. The Operator shall be entitled to use such technology only for Petroleum Operations, subject to the terms of such licensing or other arrangements.

33.5 Any technology specifically developed by the Contractor or the Operator in the course of their activities under this Contract shall be owned by both the entities constituting Contractor and ROC and, except in the case of disclosure of such to, or use by, a third party, may be used by any of them or their Affiliates in their own operations without the consent of the other and without making any payment to the other.

ARTICLE 34 – HEADINGS OF ARTICLES

Headings of Articles herein are inserted for convenience only and shall not affect the construction and/or interpretation thereof.

ARTICLE 35 – LANGUAGE

35.1 This Contract is executed in the Arabic and English languages, both having equal force. However, if there shall be any conflict between the two versions the English version shall prevail to the extent of the conflict.

35.2 Communication between the Parties may be in English. However, Contractor and Operator shall use the Arabic language or both Arabic and English in all their correspondence and dealings with Government entities in the Republic of Iraq.

35.3 Contractor and Operator shall have no obligation to use any language other than English in their contractual relationships with Sub-Contractors and vendors in connection with Petroleum Operations.

ARTICLE 36 – CONTRACTOR'S OFFICE IN THE REPUBLIC OF IRAQ

36.1 Each Company shall establish a presence in the Republic of Iraq as required by the Law.

36.2 Lead Contractor shall, within ninety (90) days of the Effective Date, establish an office in Baghdad, Iraq, and shall maintain such office for the Term. ROC shall assist Lead Contractor in establishing and maintaining the said office.

36.3 Lead Contractor shall notify ROC of the address of its office in Baghdad and of the name of its authorised representative in the Republic of Iraq who shall be assigned on full time resident status. The said representative shall be entrusted with sufficient powers and authorities to represent and bind Contractor in all dealings with the Government, ROC and third parties in the Republic of Iraq, to receive legal notices served on Contractor, and to comply with lawful directions and orders given by the competent Government authorities and ROC in connection with or in relation to this Contract.

36.4 Lead Contractor shall notify ROC of any change in the address of its office or the appointment of its representative at least ten (10) days prior to the effective date of such change.

ARTICLE 37 – GOVERNING LAW, CONCILIATION AND ARBITRATION

37.1 This Contract and the rights and obligations of the Parties shall be governed, interpreted and construed in accordance with the Law.

37.2 The Parties shall endeavour to settle amicably any dispute ("the Dispute") arising out of or in connection with or in relation to this Contract or any provision or agreement related thereto. Where no such settlement is reached within thirty (30) days of the date when one Party notifies the other Party of the Dispute, then the matter may, as appropriate, be referred by the Parties to their senior management for resolution. Where no such settlement is reached within thirty (30) days of such referral to management, any Party to the Dispute may refer the matter, as appropriate, to an independent expert or, by giving sixty (60) days notice to the other Party, refer the matter to arbitration as stipulated hereunder. It is understood that the rights and obligations under this Contract constitute commercial rather than sovereign rights or obligations.

EXPERT

37.3 If any Dispute arises between the Parties with respect to relevant technical matters, such Dispute may, at the election of either Party, be referred to an independent expert ("Expert") for determination. Such Expert shall be agreed upon by the Parties to the Dispute and shall be willing to undertake such evaluation, and shall be independent, shall not be originated from, or have been at any time a citizen of, the country in which any of the Parties to the Dispute is incorporated, and shall have no interest in or relation to either Party or with any of the entities constituting the Parties and shall be qualified by education, experience and training to evaluate the matter in Dispute. The Expert shall render its decision within one (1) Month following the Expert's formal acceptance of its appointment, or within such further time as the Parties may agree in writing. The Expert shall act as an expert and not as an arbitrator. The costs of the Expert determination shall be shared equally by the Parties in Dispute.

ARBITRATION

37.4 All Disputes arising out of or in connection with this Contract, other than those Disputes that have been finally settled by reference to either senior management or Expert, shall be finally settled under the Rules of Arbitration of the International Chamber of Commerce by three arbitrators appointed in accordance with the said Rules.

37.5 The seat of the arbitration shall be Paris, France, unless agreed otherwise by the Parties to the Dispute.

37.6 The language of arbitration shall be the English language. The award of arbitration shall be in English and shall be final and binding on the Parties to the Dispute. Judgment on the award rendered may be entered and enforced in any court having jurisdiction in recognition and enforcement thereof.

37.7 Unless otherwise agreed by the Parties, the operations and the activities of the Parties with respect to the performance of this Contract shall not be stopped or delayed pending the award of arbitration.

37.8 Any arbitration under this Contract must be initiated within two (2) Years of the date on which one Party notifies the other Party of the Dispute, and in any event within three (3) Years of the date of the expiry or termination of this Contract.

ARTICLE 40 – WAIVER

40.1 Failure or delay on the part of either Party to exercise any right, power or privilege under this Contract shall not operate as a waiver thereof.

40.2 No waiver by either Party of any one or more obligations or defaults by the other Party in the performance of this Contract shall operate or be construed as a waiver of any other obligations or defaults whether of a like or of a different character.

ARTICLE 41 – PROTECTION OF THE ENVIRONMENT

41.1 In performance of this Contract, Operator shall conduct Petroleum Operations with due regard to the protection of the environment and conservation of natural resources and shall in particular:

(a) adopt Best International Petroleum Industry Practices in conducting and monitoring its Petroleum Operations and take necessary and adequate steps to:
 (i) prevent environmental damage and, should such environmental damage occur, minimize such damage and the consequential effects thereof on property and people;

(ii) prevent harm to or degradation of livelihood or quality of life of surrounding communities and, should some adverse impact occur, minimize such impact and ensure proper compensation for injury to persons or damage to property caused by the effect of Petroleum Operations; and

(b) comply with the requirements of the Law and reasonable requirements of ROC.

41.2 If Operator fails to comply with the provisions of Article 41.1(a)(i) or contravenes any relevant Law relating to the environment, and such failure or contravention results in any environmental damage, Operator shall forthwith take all necessary and reasonable measures to remedy the failure and the effects thereof.

41.3 If ROC in its reasonable opinion believes that any works or installations erected by Operator or any operations conducted by Operator are not in accordance with the Law and are damaging or may damage the environment, or are causing or may cause pollution, ROC shall give notice to Contractor and Operator to promptly consider and develop for JMC approval a remedial action plan and measures to mitigate such damage within a reasonable period as may be agreed in the remedial action plan to repair any such damage. If ROC deems it necessary, it may also require Operator to suspend Petroleum Operations in whole or in part until Operator has commenced such remedial measures or has repaired any damage caused.

41.4 The measures and methods to be used by Operator for the purpose of complying with the terms of Article 41.1(a)(i) shall be determined in timely consultation with ROC and Contractor upon the commencement of Petroleum Operations by the FOD or later when there is a significant change in the scope or method of conducting Petroleum Operations and shall take into account the international standards applicable in similar circumstances and the relevant environmental impact study carried out in accordance with Article 41.5. Contractor shall notify ROC and Operator, in writing, of the measures and methods finally determined by Contractor and approved in accordance with Article 12 and shall cause such measures and methods to be reviewed from time to time in the light of prevailing circumstances.

41.5 Contractor shall cause a person or persons with special knowledge on environmental matters, to carry out two environmental impact studies in order:

(a) to determine at the time of the studies the prevailing conditions relating to the environment, human beings and local communities, the flora and fauna in the Contract Area and in the adjoining or neighbouring areas; and

(b) to establish the likely effect on the environment, human beings and local communities, the flora and fauna in the Contract Area and in the adjoining or neighbouring areas in consequence of the relevant phase of Petroleum Operations, and to submit, for consideration by the Parties, methods and measures contemplated in Article 41.4 for minimizing environmental damage and carrying out site restoration activities.

41.6 The first of these environmental impact studies shall act as the baseline study for purposes of Article 41.14 and shall be concluded promptly after the Effective Date but in any event before commencement of any fieldwork by the FOD.

41.7 The second environmental impact study shall be submitted by Contractor as part of the Enhanced Redevelopment Plan.

41.8 The studies mentioned in Article 41.5 above shall contain proposed environmental guidelines to be followed in order to minimize environmental damage and shall include, but not be limited to, the following, to the extent appropriate to the respective study taking into account the phase of operations to which the study relates:

(a) proposed access cutting;
(b) clearing and timber salvage;
(c) wildlife and habitat protection;
(d) fuel storage and handling;
(e) use of explosives;
(f) camps and staging;
(g) liquid and solid waste disposal;
(h) cultural and archaeological sites;
(i) selection of drilling sites;
(j) terrain stabilization;
(k) protection of freshwater horizons;
(l) blow-out prevention plan;
(m) flaring during completion and testing of Gas and Crude Oil wells;
(n) abandonment of wells;
(o) rig dismantling and site completion;
(p) reclamation for abandonment;
(q) noise control;
(r) debris disposal; and
(s) protection of natural drainage and water flow.

41.9 Subject to the provisions of the Law on the protection of the environment, any new project or expansion or modernization projects for Petroleum Operations for which a proposal, other than a Plan, is submitted by Contractor, ROC shall consider the assessment of the project and convey a decision with respect to environment clearance within a period of ninety (90) days from the receipt of the requisite documents and data. Subject to actual or pending receipt of the necessary environmental clearance, the JMC shall decide upon the proposal of Contractor within thirty (30) days thereafter.

41.10 Contractor and/or Operator shall ensure that:
(a) the pertinent completed results of the environmental impact studies are made available to its employees and to Sub-Contractors to develop adequate and proper awareness of the measures and methods of environmental protection to be used in carrying out Petroleum Operations; and
(b) the contracts entered into between Contractor and/or Operator and Sub-Contractors relating to Petroleum Operations shall include the provisions stipulated herein and any established measures and methods for the implementation of Contractor's and Operator's obligations in relation to the environment under this Contract.

41.11 Operator shall, in cooperation with Contractor, prior to conducting any drilling activities, prepare and submit for review by ROC contingency plans for dealing with crude oil spills, blowouts, fires, accidents and emergencies, designed to achieve rapid and effective emergency response. The plans referred to above shall be discussed with ROC and concerns expressed shall be taken into account.

(a) In the event of an emergency, accident, oil spill or fire arising from Petroleum Operations affecting the environment, Operator shall forthwith notify ROC and Contractor and shall promptly implement the relevant contingency plan and perform such site restoration as may be necessary in accordance with Best

International Petroleum Industry Practices.

(b) In the event of any other emergency or accident arising from the Petroleum Operations affecting the environment, Operator shall, in consultation with Contractor, take such action as may be prudent and necessary in accordance with Best International Petroleum Industry Practices.

41.12 In the event that Contractor and Operator fail to comply with any of the terms contained in Article 41.11, ROC, after giving Contractor and Operator reasonable notice in the circumstances, may take any emergency response action which may be necessary to ensure compliance with the terms of the relevant contingency plan and to recover from Contractor, immediately after having taken such action, all costs and expenditures incurred in connection with such action together with such interest as may be determined in accordance with Annex C.

41.13 Where the Contract Area is partly located in areas forming part of formally designated national parks, sanctuaries, mangroves, wetlands of national importance, biosphere reserves and other biologically sensitive areas, passage through these areas shall generally not be permitted unless permitted by the Law. However, if there is no passage, other than through these areas to reach a particular point beyond these areas, permission of the appropriate authorities shall be obtained by ROC for the benefit of Operator.

41.14 In accordance with Article 41.6, the environmental impact study shall act as the baseline study to determine the obligations and liability of Contractor and Operator for the environment which shall be limited to damage to the environment which:

(a) occurs after the Effective Date and prior to the expiry or termination of this Contract; and

(b) results from an act or omission of Contractor or Operator.

41.15 Except for cases of Gross Negligence and Wilful Misconduct on the part of Contractor and/or Operator, all costs incurred towards protection of or damage to the environment shall be treated as Petroleum Costs.

41.16 Any costs approved by ROC and incurred by the Contractor in remediation of conditions existing prior to the Effective Date and identified in the first study noted in Article 41.6 shall be considered Supplementary Costs.

41.17 In the event that Petroleum Operations are delayed, curtailed or prevented due to extended delays in acquiring necessary environmental approvals, the Parties shall meet and agree an appropriate extension of the Term together with all rights and obligations hereunder, subject to the provisions of Article 8.

ARTICLE 42 – SITE RESTORATION AND DECOMMISSIONING

42.1 On expiry or termination of this Contract or relinquishment of part of the Contract Area, Contractor shall, subject to Article 5, remove all equipment and installations from the relinquished area or former Contract Area in a manner agreed with ROC pursuant to an abandonment plan.

42.2 Around mid-Term, Contractor shall prepare a proposal for JMC approval relating to site restoration including a decommissioning plan.

ARTICLE 43 – GENERAL BUSINESS ETHICS

43.1 In the performance of this Contract, Contractor, Operator, ROC or any of their Affiliates and every other person acting on their behalf ("Related Person") shall ensure that they each strictly comply with general business ethics, the provisions of the United Nations Convention against Corruption and any provision of any act, rule or regulation of the laws of the country of incorporation of such entity or such entity's ultimate parent company pertaining to anti-bribery, anti-corruption, anti-money laundering, the export or import of technical data, restrictive trade practices regardless of their technical applicability to the relevant person (the "Business Ethics Laws").

43.2 Contractor and Operator shall in their sub-contracts stipulate their right to terminate the sub-contracts with immediate effect in case of violation of the general business ethics or Business Ethics Laws by Sub-Contractor or suppliers, and Contractor and/or Operator shall terminate a sub-contract in case of such a violation at their discretion or if ROC requests Contractor or Operator to do so.

43.3 Neither Contractor, Operator, ROC nor their Related Persons shall, in relation to or in the performance of this Contract, give or receive from any director, employee or agent of the other or its Affiliates, any gift, entertainment or other benefit of more than minimal cost or value or any commission, fee or rebate, and any hospitality shall be held within reasonable limits.

43.4 Each of ROC and the entities constituting Contractor warrant that neither they nor any of their Related Persons has taken or will take any action or failed to take or will fail to take any action where such action or failure to act would result in a violation of any Business Ethics Law by any Party and that each of them or their Related Persons have not made, offered, or authorized, requested, received, or accepted and will not make, offer, or authorize, request, receive, or accept with respect to the matters which are the subject of or related to the signing of this Contract, any ancillary document related to this Contract or any matter arising out or related to the Petroleum Operations, any payment, gift, promise or other advantage, whether directly or indirectly through any other person or entity, to or for the use or benefit of any public official (i.e. any person holding a legislative, administrative or judicial office, including any person employed by or acting on behalf of a public agency, a public enterprise or a public international organization) or any political party or political party official or candidate for office, or any other person, where such payment, gift, promise or advantage would violate (i) the Law; (ii) the laws of the country of incorporation of such entity or such entity's ultimate parent company and of the principal place of business of such ultimate parent company; or (iii) the principles described in the Convention on Combating Bribery of Foreign Public Officials in International Business Transactions, signed in Paris on December 17, 1997, which entered into force on February 15, 1999. Each entity shall defend, indemnify and hold the others harmless from and against any and all claims, damages, losses, penalties, costs and expenses arising from or related to, any breach by such first entity of such warranty. Such indemnity obligation shall survive termination or expiration of this Contract. ...

ANNEX C-ACCOUNTING PROCEDURE

This Annex C shall be attached to and made part of the Technical Service Contract of the __________ Field ("Contract"). Terms defined in the Contract shall have the same meanings for the purpose of this Annex C.

ARTICLE 1 – GENERAL PROVISIONS

1.1 Definitions

Terms used in this Accounting Procedure shall have the meanings ascribed to them in this Contract. In addition:

"Material" shall mean and include any and all materials, equipment, machinery, articles and supplies; and

"Operating Account" shall mean the account or set of accounts maintained by Contractor and Operator to record Petroleum Costs and Supplementary Costs.

1.2 Purpose of Accounting Procedure

The purpose of this Accounting Procedure is to establish methods and rules of accounting for Petroleum Operations. Any procedure established herein may only be modified by mutual agreement of the Parties.

1.3 Operating Account and Records

Contractor and Operator shall open and maintain all accounts and records necessary to document in reasonable detail and in separate accounts the transactions relating to Petroleum Operations, in accordance with generally accepted accounting principles, all in accordance with and subject to the provisions of this Contract.

(a) The accounts and records shall show, among other things, the following:
  (i) Costs of assets including:
    1. drilling in general and cost of each well;
    2. production facilities such as flow lines and degassing stations in sufficient details;
    3. Crude Oil and Associated Gas Transportation Facilities;
    4. tank-farms and pumping stations; and
    5. infrastructure facilities and industrial centres.
  (ii) Cost of Materials showing in detail the cost and quantity of each item. The method of pricing should be stated.
  (iii) Operating Costs analysed by main items such as salaries, Materials and services as defined or described in this Accounting Procedure.
(b) Contractor's and Operator's books shall be kept in the Republic of Iraq in English language (with Arabic language summary). All transactions shall be recorded in Dollars, in accordance with the provisions of Article 20 of this Contract.
(c) Accounts shall be kept according to the accounting system approved by the JMC pursuant to Article 9.22(d) of this Contract.
(d) Contractor and Operator shall maintain appropriate cost control records to meet the requirements and obligations under this Contract.
(e) Petroleum production, storage and transfer records shall be maintained according to this Contract and consistent with Best International Petroleum Industry Practices.
(f) Expenditures shall be charged in Dollars as follows:
  (i) all Dollar Expenditures shall be charged in the amount incurred;
  (ii) for accounting purposes, all Dinar Expenditures shall be translated into Dollars at the exchange rate prevailing on the date of the relevant Expenditure in accordance with the regulations of the Central Bank of Iraq;
  (iii) Expenditures in currencies other than Dollars or Dinars, shall be charged in the equivalent amount in Dollars, using the actual exchange rate applied by

the relevant first class international bank on the date of payment;

(iv) a record shall be kept of the exchange rates actually used in converting Dinars and other non-Dollar Expenditures into Dollars; and

(v) on the date of each balance sheet, monetary items in currencies other than Dollars shall be translated to Dollars at the rate of exchange applicable on such balance sheet date.

1.4 Statements

(a) Quarterly Statements

Contractor and Operator shall submit to ROC within forty five (45) days from the end of each Quarter, a statement of Petroleum Costs and Supplementary Costs together with reports and statement of the Operating Account of the said Quarter.

(b) Yearly Statements

Contractor and Operator shall submit to ROC within three (3) Months from the last day of each Calendar Year, a statement of Petroleum Costs and Supplementary Costs together with reports and statement of the Operating Account of the said Calendar Year.

1.5 Audits

Yearly statements shall be supported by a report issued by an independent auditor of international qualification appointed according to Article 20.4 of this Contract. The auditor's report shall include a statement that the accounts and statements are prepared according to the terms and conditions of this Contract and this Accounting Procedure.

ARTICLE 2－OPERATING ACCOUNT

Subject to the provisions of this Contract, Article 19 of this Contract, and this Accounting Procedure, Contractor shall charge the Operating Account with Service Fees and Supplementary Fees. Petroleum Costs and Supplementary Costs shall start being charged as from the Effective Date, while Remuneration Fees shall start being charged as from the Service Fees Eligibility Date.

The Remuneration Fee per Barrel shall be computed pursuant to Article 19.5 of this Contract and charged accordingly to the Operating Account. Petroleum Costs incurred inside or outside the Republic of Iraq shall be prepared on a cash basis for cost recovery purposes and shall include, but not be limited to, the following items unless such items would otherwise qualify as Supplementary Costs:

2.1 Personnel

(a) Operator's Locally Recruited Personnel

The actual cost of all of Operator's locally recruited personnel who are engaged in Petroleum Operations shall be charged as Petroleum Costs. Such costs shall include gross pay, all personnel benefits, employer contributions, taxes and other assessments levied on Operator as an employer by Government authorities, transportation and relocation costs of the personnel and such personnel's family within the Republic of Iraq or elsewhere on temporary assignment in the interest of Petroleum Operations (provided that no relocation costs for the personnel's family shall be charged if the temporary assignment is for less than six (6) consecutive Months) and such other costs that are statutory or customary for Operator. This procedure shall also be applied with respect to personnel of ROC seconded to Operator.

(b) Assigned Personnel

The cost of the personnel of Contractor's Affiliates working in the Republic of Iraq or in other countries (hereafter referred to as "Countries of Assignment") for Petroleum Operations on a long-term assignment (more than six (6) consecutive Months). The cost of these personnel shall be as per rates or actual cost as the case may be, representing the Contractor's Affiliates actual cost which is consistent with the standard employment policies of the head office Affiliate or of other Affiliates employing such personnel.
These rates shall include all costs of salaries, wages, benefits, indemnities and ROCial charges according to laws, regulations or contractual agreements applicable to such personnel. In addition, they shall include reimbursement of personnel administrative charges according to the standard practice of Contractor's Affiliates.
The charges for personnel assigned on a temporary basis (less than six (6) consecutive Months) shall be made in accordance with Article 2.5(c) of this Annex C.

(c) Personnel Engaged in Other Activities
If local personnel or assigned personnel are engaged in other activities in the Republic of Iraq in addition to Petroleum Operations, the cost of such personnel or assigned personnel shall be allocated on a time sheet or pro rata basis according to sound and acceptable accounting principles.

(d) Training Costs
All costs and expenses incurred by Contractor or Operator in organising, setting up and conducting training activities for their Iraqi personnel engaged in Petroleum Operations or Contractor's training activities under Addendum Three, including the planning, designing, constructing, commissioning and running training facilities and the related software. All such training costs shall be subject to JMC prior approval.

2.2 Materials and Stock

The cost of Materials and stock purchased for or furnished to Petroleum Operations as detailed under Article 4.1 of this Annex C hereinafter.

2.3 Transportation

(a) Transportation of Personnel and Materials
Transportation of Materials necessary for the performance of Petroleum Operations, including costs of packaging, brokerage, insurance and other related costs. Personnel transportation costs, to the extent covered by the established policy of Operator, shall include travel expenses for personnel and their immediate families to and from the personnel's points of origin at the time employment commences, at the time of final departure and for vacations, as well as travel expenses in the Republic of Iraq for personnel and their immediate families incurred as a result of transfers from one location to another, and travel expenses relating to the periodical recuperation leaves of field personnel. Costs related to immediate families shall be charged for personnel assigned to work in the Republic of Iraq for periods exceeding six (6) consecutive Months.

(b) Transportation Facilities
All costs and expenses for the Transportation Facilities according to Article 17.7 of this Contract and Addendum Two attached thereto.

2.4 Buildings and Equipment

(a) Costs of buildings, equipment, furniture and fixtures and their maintenance and related costs and rents paid for all offices, houses, warehouses and other types of buildings and costs of supplies necessary for the operation of such buildings and facilities, all in the Republic of Iraq.

(b) Costs of vehicles and their maintenance and operation.

(c) Costs of computers and software and their maintenance and operation.

2.5 Services

The services required by Contractor or Operator for Petroleum Operations which may include but are not limited to:

(a) outside services of consultants, contract services, utilities and other services procured from outside sources, rentals or compensation paid for the use of any equipment and facilities;

(b) use of equipment and facilities of Operator for Petroleum Operations on rental basis at rates to be approved by the JMC;

(c) all Specific Services performed under an assistance agreement between Contractor and any Affiliate:

"Specific Services" shall mean services, activities, studies and projects of a technical nature as well as computer services, carried out or procured by the Affiliate at the Contractor or Operator's specific request under a purchase order procedure, for the benefit of Petroleum Operations. Specific Services shall also include studies and specific tasks such as, administrative, accounting, financial, tax, legal or other services when requested by Contractor or Operator under a purchase order; and Specific Services shall be charged at cost in accordance with the tariffs and price lists established each Year by the Affiliate and approved by the JMC for each Calendar Year.

2.6 Damages and Losses

All costs or expenses necessary to replace or repair damages or losses incurred by fire, flood, storm, theft, accident or any other cause not controllable by Contractor through exercise of reasonable care and diligence in operations and not resulting from Contractor's failure to timely file and diligently pursue claims against insurance companies. Contractor shall furnish ROC with written notice with details of damages or losses sustained in excess of ten thousand USD (US$10,000) per occurrence as soon as practicable.

2.7 Legal Expenses

All costs and expenses of actual or potential litigation or arbitration or legal services necessary or expedient for the protection of the Contract Area against third party claims, including attorney's fees and expenses as hereinafter provided, together with all judgements obtained against the Parties or any of them on account of Petroleum Operations, and actual expenses incurred by Contractor and/or Operator and/or ROC in securing evidence or expert advice for the purpose of defending any such action or claim pursued or urged in connection with operations under this Contract.

In the event actions or claims affecting the Parties' interests under this Contract shall be handled by the legal staff of ROC in the Republic of Iraq, an agreed compensation commensurate with cost of providing and furnishing such services shall be paid to ROC and charged to the Operating Account.

2.8 Taxes

Pursuant to Article 23 and subject to other provisions of this Contract, taxes (other than corporate income tax), levies, duties, imposts (if any) and/or charges and fees paid by Contractor (but not previously paid directly by ROC) to Government authorities as assessed or levied upon or in connection with Petroleum Operations.

2.9 Insurance and Claims

(a) The premium of any insurance policy secured by Contractor or Operator pursuant to this Contract.

(b) Any costs sustained by Contractor or Operator arising out of an event covered by insurance. Such costs include, but are not limited to, repairs and replacements of Materials in the Contract Area resulting from damage or loss incurred because of fire, flood, storm, theft, accident, or any other similar risk.

(c) All costs and expenses associated with suing, working or travelling for, or any other cost incurred in consequence of, or because of insurance related disputes, claims or litigation with any party including any insurer and/or any insurer's representatives or agents to the extent that such costs and expenses are not refunded for whatever reasons, by insurance and/or not awarded by an arbitrator or a court of law.

(d) Any compensation received, or any claim collected from insurers or third parties shall be credited to the Operating Account. If no insurance is carried for a particular risk, all related actual expenditures incurred and paid by Contractor or Operator in settling any and all losses, claims, damages, judgement and other expenses, including related legal expenditures. Any such loss, claim or damage shall be charged to the Operating Account unless otherwise provided for under Article 24.7 of this Contract.

2.10 Currency Exchange

The gain or loss, if any, through currency translation or exchange pursuant to the provisions of Article 21 of this Contract and Article 1.3(f) of this Accounting Procedure.

2.11 Tariffs

Subject to the provision of Article 3 of this Annex C, all sums paid to ROC inside or outside the Contract Area, contractor(s) on petroleum fields outside the Contract Area, or any third party in compensation for the use of facilities in connection with Petroleum Operations such as, but not limited to, pipelines, hydrocarbon treatment plants and storage facilities, on a basis of a mutually agreed tariff.

2.12 Surface Rights

All direct costs attributable to the acquisition, renewal or relinquishment of surface rights acquired and maintained in force for Petroleum Operations in the Republic of Iraq.

2.13 Environment

All costs incurred for the protection, cleanup or restoration of the environment pursuant to the Law or this Contract.

2.14 Administrative Overhead and General Expenses

The services of all personnel of Contractor's head office or its Affiliates not otherwise chargeable, as well as the contribution of Contractor's head office or its Affiliates to Petroleum Operations of an intangible nature and any overhead or its indirect cost incurred by a Company's head office or its Affiliates shall be compensated by a charge based on one percent (1%) of Petroleum Costs and Supplementary Costs (excluding the signature bonus paid under Article 4 of the Contract) during each Calendar Year or a fraction thereof.

The basis of applying this percentage shall be the total of Supplementary Costs (excluding the signature bonus paid under Article 4 of the Contract) and Petroleum Costs incurred in respect of Petroleum Operations and charged under this Accounting Procedure to the Operating Account during each Financial Year or fraction thereof, excluding administrative overhead as allowed in this section.

The above administrative overhead charges shall be paid I) while ROC is Operator 50% to ROC and fifty (50)% to Companies, and ii) once FOD becomes Operator 100% to Companies pursuant to Article 19 of this Contract.

2.15 To the extent any of the costs identified in Article 2 of this Annex C would qualify as eligible costs pursuant to Articles 4, 7.4, 7.7(b) 10.4,10.7, 12.6, 17.6, or 41.16 of this Contract, such costs shall be considered Supplementary Costs and not Petroleum Costs, unless Contractor indicates that it elects to include said costs as Petroleum Costs.

2.16 All the other costs and expenses incurred in connection with and for the benefit of Petroleum Operations shall, unless expressly excluded as Petroleum Costs, be chargeable to Petroleum Costs.

ARTICLE 3 – INFORMATION TO JMC AND ROC

Upon submitting the annual Work Program and Budget for approval in accordance with Article 12 of this Contract, Operator shall provide in writing the following details in respect of personnel, Specific Services and tariffs in connection with Petroleum Operations to be charged during the relevant Year.

3.1 Regarding Personnel Costs:

(a) estimate of the overall amount thereof;
(b) analysis and explanation of the applicable personnel policy and practice of Contractor or Operator and Contractor or Operator's Affiliates;
(c) reasonable breakdown of the aforesaid Expenditures as per details stated in this Accounting Procedure; and
(d) rates and/or methods of apportionment of such costs.

3.2 Regarding Specific Services:

(a) Estimate of the overall amount thereof;
(b) Reasonable breakdown of such services by major type; and
(c) Tariffs and rates expected to apply in respect to such services, especially to assigned personnel.

3.3 Regarding Tariffs:

(a) Estimate of the overall amount to be paid; and
(b) Reasonable breakdown of the tariff expenditures.

ARTICLE 4 – CHARGING PRINCIPLES

4.1 Purchases

(a) All Materials purchased for Petroleum Operations shall be purchased at competitive prices from reputable manufacturers or suppliers. Materials purchased from third parties shall be charged at net cost paid by Contractor after deduction of all discounts received. Net cost shall include but not be limited to such items as transportation, insurance, licence fees and purchasing and forwarding costs.

(b) The Parties may furnish new Materials from their own stock provided that the new Material transferred from the warehouses or other facilities of entities constituting Contractor or their respective Affiliates, shall be priced at cost, and provided that such cost is not higher than the price for new Material of the same quality, obtained on comparable terms and conditions, prevailing in the international market at the time such new Material was supplied to Contractor.

4.2 Direct and Indirect Costs

Costs shall be charged to the Operating Account using consistent methods from Year to Year, and such methods shall be agreed upon by the Parties subject to the following principles:

(a) costs that may be directly charged to a relevant subdivision of the Operating Account shall be so charged; and

(b) costs that cannot easily be charged directly to any subdivision of the Operating Account shall be apportioned either on a time basis or on a pro rata basis. Costs of services that cannot be assessed accurately may be charged according to standard rates and adjusted to actual costs at Year end.

4.3 Use of Equipment and Facilities Owned By Entities Constituting Contractor

For the use of any equipment or facilities that are wholly owned by entities constituting Contractor, the Operating Account shall be charged a rental commensurate with the cost of ownership.

The rental rates, which will not include any profit element, will be approved by the JMC each Calendar Year. Such rates should be in line with those currently prevailing in the area where Petroleum Operations are located for equipment and facilities comparable in terms of availability, safety, efficiency and quality.

ARTICLE 5 – INVENTORIES

At all times, Contractor shall maintain inventories of Materials at optimum levels required for Petroleum Operations and shall be subject to:

5.1 Periodic Inventories, Notices and Representation

At reasonable intervals, and at least once annually, inventories shall be taken by Contractor and Operator of the Materials charged to the Operating Account, which shall include all such Materials as are ordinarily considered controllable by operators in the international petroleum industry. Written notice of intention to take inventory shall be given by Contractor and Operator at least ninety (90) days before any inventory is to begin so that ROC may be represented when any inventory is to be carried out.

5.2 Reconciliation and Adjustment of Inventories

Reconciliation of inventory with the Operating Account shall be made and a list of overages and shortages shall be furnished to ROC. Inventory adjustments shall be made by Contractor and Operator to the Operating Account if required; provided, however, that any inventory adjustment exceeding a value of ten thousand USD (US$10,000) shall be reported to ROC.

ARTICLE 6 – DISPOSAL OF MATERIALS

Contractor and Operator shall inform the JMC and ROC of any excess or disposable Materials. ROC shall instruct Operator on the action then required. Any proceeds of disposal of such Materials shall be credited to the Operating Account.

ARTICLE 7 – SUMS RECEIVED FROM THIRD PARTIES

All sums received by Contractor from any third party in compensation for the use of facilities utilized by Operator for Petroleum Operations shall be credited to the Operating Account.

ARTICLE 8 – BASIS OF ACCOUNTING

The Operating Account may be maintained on an accrual basis, that is, costs shall be recorded and entered in the Operating Account when the liability thereto first arises, and revenues shall be recorded and entered in the Operating Account when the title thereto is acquired.

However, for the purposes of cost recovery as per Article 19 of this Contract, the relevant calculations shall be made on a cash basis, that is, costs shall be considered only when paid and revenues only when collected.

ARTICLE 9 – PAYMENT OF SERVICE FEES AND SUPPLEMENTARY FEES

Contractor shall, pursuant to Article 19 of this Contract, render to ROC as promptly as practical but not later than forty five (45) days after the end of the last Month of a Quarter, an invoice of due and payable Service Fees and Supplementary Fees for the Quarter based on the Operating Account and showing the following details:

9.1 Due Service Fees and Supplementary Fees brought forward from the previous Quarter, if any;

9.2 Service Fees and Supplementary Fees during Quarter;

9.3 Total Service Fees and Supplementary Fees for the Quarter (9.1+9.2);

9.4 Service Fees and Supplementary Fees received and/or quantity and value of Export Oil lifted by Contractor for the Quarter according to the lifting procedure as referred to in Addendum Four;

9.5 Amount of Service Fees and Supplementary Fees to be carried forward into the succeeding Quarter if any (9.3~9.4), and

9.6 Excess, if any, of the value of Service Fees and Supplementary Fees received and/or Export Oil lifted by Contractor over Service Fees and Supplementary Fees due for the Quarter (9.4~9.3). Such excess shall be set off in the next calculation of Contractor's outstanding Service Fees and Supplementary Fees payable in the immediately succeeding Quarter in accordance with Article 19 of this Contract.

ARTICLE 10 – NON – RECOVERABLE COSTS

The following list of items shall be treated as non-recoverable costs for the purpose of cost recovery:

10.1 Except for the period when ROC is Operator, costs incurred as a result of any proven Gross Negligence or Wilful Misconduct of Contractor/Operator including any amount paid in settlement of any claim alleging Gross Negligence or Wilful Misconduct whether or not Gross Negligence or Wilful Misconduct is admitted or whether such sum is stated to be paid on an ex-gratia or similar basis;

10.2 Any expenditure incurred directly or indirectly in connection with the raising of money to finance Petroleum Operations and other incidental costs and charges related thereto by whatever method raised; such expenditure includes, but is not limited to, interest, commissions, fees and brokerage;

10.3 Any costs, charges or expenses including donations relating to public relations or enhancement of Contractor's corporate image and interests, unless expressly approved by the JMC and endorsed by ROC;

10.4 Any expenditure incurred which is not related to Petroleum Operations or on matters or activities beyond the Delivery Point(s);

10.5 Corporate income tax;

10.6 Training, Technology and Scholarship Fund; and,

10.7 Any other expenditure which is stated elsewhere in this Contract to be non-recoverable expenditure.

ARTICLE 11 – CONTROL STATEMENTS AND MAJOR ACCOUNTS

11.1 Contractor shall annually prepare, from the statements of expenditure prepared pursuant to Article 1.4 of this Annex C a statement showing for the relevant Year the excess or deficit in development expenditure compared to the Minimum Work Obligations. Such statement shall be rendered to ROC not later than ninety (90) days following the end of such Year.

11.2 For the purpose of classifying costs, expenses and expenditures for cost recovery and Minimum Work Obligations, costs, expenses and expenditures shall be recorded in major accounts including Capital Cost and Operating Cost.

ARTICLE 12 – TRANSFER PROCEDURE FOR THE OPERATING ACCOUNT

12.1 In accordance with this Contract, when the FOD becomes the Operator, the ROC shall transfer to the FOD all the accounting records relating to the Operating Account.

12.2 In conducting the transfer of the books of account and inventory and check of all properties in accordance with the provisions of this Accounting Procedure, the implementation procedure for the transfer and verification, the accounting files to be transferred and accounting matters to be settled as well as other details, shall be agreed upon through consultation in advance between the ROC and the FOD. The transfer procedure shall be completed within the period agreed upon by the Parties. Thereafter, owing to the needs of any Party, FOD shall allow such Party's staff access to the books of accounts within the relevant periods and provide them with duplicates of the relevant accounting records, if necessary.

ARTICLE 13 – EXTERNAL AUDITOR'S CERTIFICATE

Contractor shall provide ROC with a certificate from the external auditor of Lead Contractor's head office evidencing that the charges and the rates applied pursuant to to Articles 2.1(a) to 2.5(c) of this Annex C represent actual costs.

ADDENDUM ONE–HEADS OF JOINT OPERATING AGREEMENT

This Addendum One is attached to and made part of the Technical Service Contract for the __________ Field ("Contract"). Terms defined in the Contract shall have the same meanings for the purpose of this Heads of Agreement. The parties to the Joint Operating

Agreement are the Companies and the State Partner.

ARTICLE 1 – SCOPE

This Heads of Agreement is to provide for the basic principles to be included in a Joint Operating Agreement ("JOA") to be executed among the Companies and the State Partner (hereinafter referred to individually as "Participant" or collectively as "Participants").

ARTICLE 2 – PARTICIPATING INTEREST

Each Participant shall have the undivided percentage interest determined under this Contract and/or as agreed by the Participants ("Participating Interest"), provided that each Participant's Participating Interest shall not be less than three point seven five percent (3.75%). The Companies shall participate in proportion to their respective Participating Interest in all costs, expenses and liabilities incurred pursuant to this Contract or JOA and shall own, in the same proportion, the Contractor's rights under this Contract and the Participants' rights under the JOA.

ARTICLE 3 – LEAD CONTRACTOR

3.1 The Lead Contractor appointed in accordance with the Contract shall act for the Participants.

3.2 The Lead Contractor may, at any time resign as such by giving the Participants notice in writing. The Lead Contractor shall cease to be Lead Contractor if: (a) it dissolves, liquidates or terminates its legal existence; (b) it becomes insolvent, bankrupt or is placed in receivership; (c) its Participating Interest is reduced to less than twenty two point five percent (22.5%); or (d) it takes no action within thirty (30) days after notification to it by a Participant to remedy a material breach of the JOA. Pursuant to Article 9.4 of this Contract, replacement of the Lead Contractor shall be subject to the prior approval of the ROC.

ARTICLE 4 – OPERATING COMMITTEE

4.1 An Operating Committee composed of representatives of the Participants shall be established and shall act for the entire duration of JOA to make decisions and establish joint policies and make proposals to be submitted to ROC or the JMC, as well as to make any other decisions necessary or expedient for the orderly supervision and direction of the Petroleum Operations.

4.2 The decisions of the Operating Committee on all matters shall be made by the affirmative vote of the representatives of Participants having a combined voting right of at least seventy percent (70%), each Participant being entitled to have and to exercise through its representatives a voting right equal numerically to its Participating Interest. The Operating Committee shall also decide upon Contractor's representation in the JMC provided that Lead Contractor shall have at least one (1) of the members provided to Contractor and the State Partner shall have one (1) member.

ARTICLE 5 – WORK PROGRAMS AND BUDGETS

For each Calendar Year, the Lead Contractor shall prepare and submit to the Participants Work Programs and Budgets not later than the first day of August of the preceding Year. Each such Work Program and Budget shall set out in a reasonably detailed manner the work to be carried out and shall include an itemized estimate of the corresponding expenditures. The Operating Committee shall review and discuss the Work Program and Budget submitted by Lead Contractor for the following Calendar Year and shall adopt, not later than August 30, a Work Program and Budget to be submitted to the Operator for further study and possible modification before referring to the JMC pursuant to Article 12.2 of the Contract.

ARTICLE 6 – COSTS AND EXPENSES

All costs and expenses of the Contractor for Petroleum Operations shall be borne by the Companies in proportion to their respective Participating Interest. All costs and expenses that are incurred in the conduct of operations under this JOA shall be determined and recorded according to an accounting procedure (without prejudice to Annex C of the Contract), generally accepted accounting practices used in the international petroleum industry and shall be subject to periodic inspection and audit.

ARTICLE 7 – DEFAULTS

7.1 Any Company that fails to pay when due its Participating Interest share of costs and expenses shall be in default (hereinafter referred to as "Defaulting Company"). The Operator shall as soon as practicable notify all Participants of such default and the Operator shall keep the Participants informed thereafter of material events in relation thereto. The amount not paid by the Defaulting Company shall bear interest from the date due until fully paid. After any default has continued for thirty (30) days, the Defaulting Company shall not be entitled to attend Operating Committee meetings or to vote on any matter coming before the Operating Committee during the period such default continues. Non-Defaulting Companies shall pay the defaulted amount on behalf of the Defaulting Company, in proportion to their Participating Interests or in any other proportion they may agree upon.

7.2 The Defaulting Company shall have the right to remedy the default at any time prior to forfeiture, as hereinafter provided, by payment in full to the Operator or, if the Non-Defaulting Companies have paid any amounts under Article 7.1, to the Non-Defaulting Companies, in proportion to the amounts so paid by them, of all amounts which the Defaulting Company has failed to pay together with interest thereon on a day to day basis at the rate of LIBOR plus five percent (5%) per annum.

If a Defaulting Company has not remedied the default by the thirtieth (30th) day, then, during the continuance of such default, the Defaulting Company shall not be entitled to its Participating Interest share of Service Fees and Supplementary Fees, as applicable, which shall vest in and be the property of the Non-Defaulting Companies. The Service Fees due to the Defaulting Company shall proportionately be paid to the Non-Defaulting Companies, which Fees shall be credited against all monies advanced by such Non-Defaulting Companies on behalf of the Defaulting Company. The balance of such fees, if any, shall be paid to the Defaulting Company when such default has been remedied.

7.3 State Partner shall be carried by the Companies for its Participating Interest share of Petroleum Costs and Supplementary Costs. The amount so paid by the Companies on behalf of State Partner shall be fully recovered by the Companies from the Petroleum Costs and Supplementary Costs paid under the Contract.

7.4 In no event shall State Partner be considered in default.

ARTICLE 8 – WITHDRAWAL

After the Minimum Work Obligations have been fulfilled, any Company may elect, and subject to ROC's prior written consent, by giving notice to the other Participants, to withdraw from the Contract and the JOA. Each of the other Participants may also give notice that it desires to withdraw from the Contract and the JOA. Should all Participants give such notice of withdrawal, the Participants shall proceed to abandon the Contract Area and terminate the Contract and JOA. If less than all of the Participants give such notice of withdrawal, then the withdrawing Participants shall execute and deliver all necessary instruments and documents to assign their Participating Interest to the non-withdrawing Companies, without any compensation whatsoever. Such assignment to the non-withdrawing Companies shall be in proportion to their Participating Interests, unless otherwise agreed among them. The non-withdrawing Companies shall take the assignment of all of the withdrawing Participants' Participating Interests; otherwise, all Participants shall be deemed to have decided to withdraw from the Contract and the JOA.

ARTICLE 9 – ASSIGNMENT

Each Participant may assign, subject to any requirement under the Contract, all or part of, its Participating Interest to an Affiliate without the consent of the other Participants; provided that such Participant shall remain responsible for the performance of the financial and other obligations under the Contract and the JOA to the same extent as if the transfer had not occurred and provided further that the assigning Participant shall timely notify the other

Participants of any such assignment.

Without prejudice to the provisions of the Contract, no assignment of any interest under the Contract and the JOA to third parties may be made by any Participant without the written consent of the other Participants which consent shall not be unreasonably withheld. The assignment by a Participant of its interest under the Contract and the JOA to third parties shall be subject to ROC's approval and its pre-emptive right and to the preferential rights of the other Participants. The assignee shall be bound by the Contract and the JOA.

ARTICLE 10 – RELATION OF THE PARTICIPANTS

The rights, duties, obligations and liabilities of the Participants under this Heads of Agreement and the JOA shall be individual, not joint or collective. It is not the intention of the Participants to create, nor shall this Heads of Agreement or the JOA be deemed or construed to create a mining or other partnership, joint venture, association or trust, or as authorizing any Participant to act as an agent, servant or employee for any other Participant for any purpose whatsoever except as explicitly set forth in the JOA.

ARTICLE 11 – GOVERNING LAW AND ARBITRATION

The JOA shall be governed by, construed, interpreted and applied in accordance with the Law. Any dispute, controversy or claim arising out of or in relation to or in connection with the JOA or the operations carried out thereunder, including without limitation any dispute as to the validity, interpretation, enforceability or breach of the JOA, shall be settled by arbitration in Paris, France in accordance with the Rules of Conciliation and Arbitration of the International Chamber of Commerce conducted in the manner contemplated in Article 37 of the Contract.

ARTICLE 12 – EFFECTIVE DATE AND TERM

This Heads of Agreement shall come into force on the Effective Date and shall continue in effect until the Contract terminates, or expires upon the Participants entering into the JOA, whichever is the earlier.

ARTICLE 13 – JOINT OPERATING AGREEMENT (JOA)

Within six (6) Months from the Effective Date, the Participants shall enter into the JOA which shall embody the principles stipulated in this Heads of Agreement and it may include such other provisions as customarily used by international petroleum industry and shall continue in effect as long as the Contract is in effect.

〈표 4-4〉 양허계약, 생산분배계약, 위험용역계약간 비교38)

	Risk assignment	Managerial control	Profit sharing
CC	concessionaire	Concessionaire	royalty and tax
PSC	contractor	Gov't (in theory)	65 : 35-90 : 10 gov't take's favor
RSC	contractor	Gov't (mostly)	100% gov't take

5. 참여계약39)

자원보유국 또는 그 NOC와 IOC간 합작투자사업으로서 석유탐사가 이루어지는 경우 합작투자사업당사자간 권리의무를 정한 계약서를 참여계약이라 부른다. 과거 전통적 양허계약을 산유국이 점진적으로 수정하여 가면서 종국적으로는 NOC가 IOC의 지분을 매입하였고 결과적으로 많은 국가에서 참여계약의 형태로 자원개발이 이루어지고 있다. 최근에는 IOC가 NOC와 특정 유전개발을 위한 JVC를 설립하는 것을 전제로 JVC와 국가 또는 NOC간 계약이 체결되는 경우가 많다. 최근 Venezuela는 기존의 계약에 반하여 탐사개발업자에게 60%지분을 NOC에 이전할 것을 요구하면서 참여계약을 강요하여 국제적 분쟁을 야기하였다.40)

참여계약은 IOC와 NOC가 합작투자법인을 설립하여 이 법인이 석유탐사의 주체가 되는 구조와 독립된 법인을 설립함이 없이 조합이 사업주체가 되는 두 가지 형태가 있을 수 있다.41) 모든 합작투자에서 당사자간 합의되어야 하는 중요한 사항은 합작당사자간 의사결정 권한의 분배이다. 주식회사라면 이사회의 구성과 정족수를 통하여, 조합이라면 업무집행조합원을 통하여 의사를 결정하지만, 문제는 의견이 다른 경우 합작투자 당사자간 어떻게 해결할 것인지, 어느 시점에 제3자의 판단으로 분쟁을 전이할 것인지 등 주요논점은 제5장에서 논의하는 공동개발운영계약상의 법적인 문제와 상당히 유사하다. 특히 석유를 발견하였으나 상업성이 없어서 개발할 필요가 없다는 결정에 대하여 다른 합작투자 상대방이 동의할 수 없다면 독자적 개발추진권을 부여할 것인지가 중요한 협상논점이다. 통상의 합작투자와 다른 점은

38) Gao, 위 주 14 상게서, 205 표 7. 1.

39) 참여계약 대신 미국의 lease계약을 하나의 유형으로 설명하기도 한다. 윤상직, 국제석유개발계약의 이해, 95 (2010).

40) Brandon Marsh, *Preventing the Inevitable: The Benefits of Contractual Risk Engineering in Light of Venezuela's Recent oil Field Nationalization*, 13 STAN. J.L. Bus. & Fin. 453 (2007-08).

41) 이는 모든 합작투자에 해당되는 고려사항으로 우리나라 외국인투자촉진법은 합작투자법인의 설립을 요구하고 있고 과거 외국환관리법에 따른 조합의 수익송금가능성이 명확하지 않아서 조합형 합작투자의 조세절약가능성에도 불구하고 실제는 거의 사례가 없다.

자원보유국 내지 그 NOC는 자본 내지 조합지분을 출자하지 않고 합작투자사업이 이연비용으로 가지고 가다가 탐사의 결과 분배할 이익이 나는 경우 이와 상계한다는 점이다. 합작투자사업의 탐사결과를 어떻게 나눌지는 원래의 양허계약이나 생산분배계약상의 합의에 따르는 것으로 통상의 양허계약이나 생산분배계약과 다르지 않다.[42] 참여계약의 연혁 때문에 UAE는 통상의 양허계약에 이를 참여계약으로 바꿀 수 있는 선택권을 포함시킨다.

6. 주요공통계약조항[43]

석유탐사·개발·생산을 위한 계약을 위에서 본 몇 가지 유형으로 구분할 수 있지만, 실제는 이들 여러 유형의 복합체인 경우가 많으며 개별국가나 입찰라운드에 따라서 다른 특징을 지니고 있다. 그럼에도 불구하고 통상적으로 들어가는 몇 가지 조항을 아래에서 논한다.[44]

가. 국내자원사용의무조항

자원보유국은 자원개발을 통하여 장단기 국가운영에 필요한 재원을 확보하고 개발과 생산에 따르는 공적 자금의 위험을 최소화하며 국내 자원에 대한 외국기업의 지배를 관리함과 동시에 국민경제발전에 필요한 기술과 인적 자원을 육성하고자 할 것이다. 이는 일반적인 외국인투자유치의 목적이기도 하다. 따라서 자원개발계약의 일부로 일정한 금액의 펀드를 설립하거나 자원보유국의 인적·물적 자원을 우선적으로 사용할 것을 요구하는 조항이 들어가는 경우가 많으며[45] 한걸음 더 나아가서 자원개발권을 입찰에 붙이는 경우 소위 국내자원사용비율이 입찰자들의 제안을 평가하는 요소 중 하나로 고려되기도 한다. 이는 또한 모든 국제조달에 있어서의 일반적인 실무이기도 하다.[46]

---

42) Smith, 위 주 1-4 상게서, 493-501에 의하면 1955년 Italy가 이집트와 이란의 석유탐사에 참여하면서 참여계약을 맺었으며 Columbia도 통상 참여계약을 요구한다고 한다. Barrows Company는 전세계 석유탐사계약의 database를 유지하고 있으므로 이를 통하여 전세계의 E&P계약을 열람할 수 있다.

43) 탐사, 개발, 생산에 관한 조항 이외에 자료의 소유권, 자산의 소유권, 양도, 지배주주변경, 수출입, 판매, 석유의 평가 등에 관하여는 Claude Duval/Honore Le Leuch/Andre Pertuzio/Jacqueline Lang Weaver, INTERNATIONAL PETROLEUM EXPLORATION AND EXPLOITATION AGREEMENTS: LEGAL, ECONOMIC & POLICY ASPECTS, ch. 19, 349-78 (2nd ed. 2009).

44) 최소한의 탐사의무, 탐사지역 반환의무, 환경보존의무, 개발종료시 정리의무(Decommissioning), 부패방지법규 준수의무 등도 공통.

45) Suleiman, 위 주 5 논문, 15.

46) 특히 군수물자의 입찰시 OFFSET PROGRAM이라 하여 기술이전의 정도, 국내부품공급업자의 사용비율이 중요한 평가요소가 된다. 방위사업철 지침 제2012-1호 절충교역지침서 제11조.

나. 탐사정보이전 및 비밀유지조항

일반적으로 비밀유지조항은 영업비밀이 제3자에 의하여 사용되는 경우 영업비밀이 지적재산권으로서 보호, 유지되기 위하여 필요하며 그런 경우 비밀로 유지되는 정보의 범위, 기간, 사용허락의 목적 등을 고려할 때 그 의무의 범위는 경우에 따라 다를 것이다. 기술실시허여계약하에서의 사용권자가 제3의 다른 기업에 흡수합병되거나 영업을 양도하고자 하는 경우 영업비밀을 제공한 자가 이를 저지할 수 있는지 여부는 실제 거래성사 여부를 결정하는 심각한 조건이 될 수도 있다.[47] 또한 IOC가 E&P 계약하의 탐사개발권 일부를 제3자에게 매각하고자 하는 경우 통상적인 M&A거래가 그러하듯이 투자자에게 혼란을 야기하지 않고 거래를 성사시키기 위하여 거래의 협상 사실 자체를 대외비로 유지하는 것이 바람직할 수 있다.[48] 또한 고용자와 근로자의 관계에서 근로자는 고용자인 기업의 이익을 위하여 일하여야 하며 고용계약에 기초하여 얻은 정보를 자신의 이익을 위하여 이용할 수 있는 데에는 한계가 있다. 석유나 천연가스 등 에너지자원의 개발도 지질학자의 탐사결과에 의존하므로 근로자가 기업을 떠나서 독자적인 탐사활동을 하는 경우 고용자인 기업과 대외비밀유지조항의 위반여부가 문제될 수 있다.[49] 그러나, NOC와 IOC 사이에서는 IOC가 NOC에 탐사정보를 이전하며 이를 대외비로 유지할 의무를 규정한다.

인천지법 2004. 11. 19. 선고 2001가합2507 판결

1. 기초사실

가. 원고 회사와 피고 회사의 관계 및 소외 정갑렬이 원고 회사에서 퇴사하여 피고 회사를 설립하기까지의 경위

(1) 원고 회사(보성전자 주식회사에서 상호변경)는 전기전자 부품, 음향기기 부품 등의 제조, 판매업을 목적으로 1987. 8. 5. 설립된 회사이고, 피고 회사는 정갑렬이 원고 회사를 퇴사하여 프로용 피에이 음향시스템 · 정보통신용 음향부품 · 방송장비 및 통신기기 부품 · 방송수

---

47) *M.D.Mark, Inc. v. Nuevo Energy Co.*,988 S.W.2d 463 (Tex. App.-Houston [1st Dist.] 1999)

48) AIPN Model Form Confidentiality Agreement (2007). AIPN은 석유가스산업에 종사하는 자들이 만든 단체로서 그 가장 중요한 사업이 표준계약서 양식을 제공하는 것이다. aipn.org에서 이들 표준계약서 열람가능. AIPN 이외에도 많은 석유가스 사업자단체에서 표준양식을 제공하고 있으며 이들이 협상의 출발점으로서 도움이 될 것이나, 이들이 해결책은 아님을 명심하여야 한다.

49) *Hunter v. Shell Oil Co.*, 198 F.2d 485 (5th Cir. 1952); *Chevron Oil Co. v. Tlapek*, 407 F.2d 1129 (8th Cir. 1969); *Amoco Production Co. v. Laird*, 622 N.E.2d 912 (Ind. 1993).

신기 및 음향기기 제조업 등을 목적으로 2000. 7. 10. 설립한 회사이다.

(2) 정갑렬은 북한에서 일렉트릿 마이크로폰의 연구·개발 등의 업무에 종사하다가 1996. 4.경 귀순한 음향 기술자로서 1996. 12.경부터 전자부품종합기술연구소 선임연구원으로 근무하다가, 1997. 8.경 원고 회사에 영입되어 2000. 6.경까지 원고 회사의 전기음향연구소장으로 재직하면서, 콘덴서 마이크로폰의 제품연구, 제품소재 개발, 생산설비 개발업무, 관리업무 등을 총괄하였다.

(3) 정갑렬은 1998. 12.경부터 원고 회사의 대표이사인 소외 박진수에 대하여 자신에 대한 대우를 조정해 달라고 요구하였고, 이에 따라 원고 회사는 1999. 1. 20. 정갑렬과의 사이에, 원고 회사는 정갑렬에게 특별상여금과 격려금조로 40평 이상 아파트와 현금 10억 원을 지급하고, 프로마이크 전문제조회사를 설립하며, 정갑렬은 위 연구소의 연구개발계획에 따른 연구를 진행하되, 이와 관련된 모든 설비 및 지적소유권은 원고 회사 소유로 하고, 정갑렬이 연구소 재임시 개발한 연구실적은 원고 회사에게 속하며 그와 관련된 업무상 기밀 및 기술사항은 다른 곳에 응용·사용할 수 없으며 또한 보안을 유지하기로 약정{갑 제3호증(갑 제12호증의 17 및 을 제6호증과 같음)}하였는바, 원고 회사는 정갑렬에게 위 약정에 따라 아파트을 제공하고 금 5억 원을 지급하였다.

(4) 2000. 5. 29.경 정갑렬과 박진수는 위 1999. 1. 20.자 약정의 내용을 구체화하고, 정갑렬의 원고 회사에 대한 기여에 대한 보상차원에서 원고 회사의 주식을 정갑렬에게 지급하는 문제 등에 관하여 서로 협상을 하였으나 양측의 의견차이를 좁히지 못하여 결국 실패하였고, 그에 따라 정갑렬은 2000. 6.경 원고 회사를 퇴사하여 2000. 7. 10. 피고 회사를 설립하고 대표이사로 취임하였다.

(5) 한편, 정갑렬은 원고 회사에 근무하던 2000. 4.경 당시 원고 회사가 생산하고 있던 백 일렉트릿 콘덴서 마이크로폰(Back-type Electret Condenser Microphone, 이하 'BECM'이라고 한다)의 제조 공정에 관한 자료를 부하직원들로부터 CD에 담아서 보고할 것을 요구하여 이를 제출받은 후 자신의 집에 보관하고 있다가, 박진수로부터 형사고소를 당하여 수사를 받는 과정에서 그 CD가 발견되어 압수당하였는데, 그 CD에는 별지 제4목록 기재와 같은 내용의 BECM 제조 공정 중 일부에 관한 내용이 담겨 있었다.

(6) 정갑렬은 2000. 7. 10. 피고 회사를 설립한 후 현재까지 원고 회사의 생산품과 동일한 종류의 BECM을 제조하여 판매하고 있다.

2. 원고 회사의 주장

원고 회사는 피고 회사가 원고 회사의 영업비밀을 침해하여 원고 회사의 제조 공정과 유사하거나 동일한 방식으로 원고 회사가 생산하는 제품과 동일한 BECM을 제조하여 판매하고 있어 자신의 영업상의 이익이 침해되고 있으므로 피고 회사를 상대로 영업비밀 침해행위에 대한 금지 등을 구하고 있는바, 그 주장의 요지는 다음과 같다.

가. 별지 제1목록 기재의 각 기술정보는 원고 회사가 BECM의 제조와 관련하여 보유하고 있던 기술정보로서 그 내용은 피고 회사에 의해 침해되기 전까지 비공지성, 경제적 유용성, 비밀관리 노력 등의 요건을 구비하고 있어서 부정경쟁방지및영업비밀보호에관한법률(이하 '영업비밀보호법'이라고 한다)에서 보호되고 있는 영업비밀에 해당한다.

나. 정갑렬은 원고 회사에서 근무하면서 알게 된 위 영업비밀에 대하여 원고 회사와의 관계에 있어서 계약상의 혹은 신의칙상의 비밀유지의무를 부담하고 있음에도 불구하고, 위 영업비밀 중 일부의 내용을 CD에 담아서 절취하여 피고 회사에 공개하고, 위 의무에 반하여 자신이 알고 있던 위 영업비밀을 사용하거나 공개하였고, 피고 회사는 정갑렬의 이러한 영업비밀 침해행위를 알고서도 그 영업비밀을 취득하여 이를 사용하여 BECM을 제조하여 원고 회사의 위 영업비밀을 침해하였다.

3. 피고 회사의 주장

원고 회사의 위 주장에 대한 피고 회사 주장의 요지는 다음과 같다.

가. 원고 회사가 정갑렬의 영업비밀침해행위의 하나로서 주장하고 있는 CD 부분은 정갑렬이 원고 회사에 근무하면서 부하 직원들로부터 보고받는 내용들이 서면으로 보고하기에는 너무 많고, 또 보고받은 내용을 퇴근하여 집에서도 검토할 필요가 있어서 CD로 보고받았던 것으로서 이를 집에 보관하고 있던 상태에서 박진수와의 사이가 나빠지고 원고 회사를 퇴사하는 과정에서 반환할 기회가 없어 보관하고 있었을 뿐이며 이를 절취한 것은 아니다.

나. 원고 회사가 자신의 영업비밀로서 주장하는 내용들의 대부분은 정갑렬이 원고 회사에 입사하기 전부터 이미 지득하고 있는 내용이거나, 원고 회사에 근무하면서 스스로 개발한 것으로서 그것이 영업비밀로서의 가치를 갖는다고 하더라도 이는 정갑렬에게 귀속되는 것이다.

다. 가사 그렇지 않다고 하더라도, 원고 회사와 정갑렬 사이에서의 비밀유지약정이 포함된 1999. 1. 20.자 계약은 원고 회사 및 피고가 모두 해제를 주장하고 있으므로 당사자간의 의사합치에 의해 해제되었다고 할 것이어서 위 계약 및 그 내용의 일부인 정갑렬의 비밀유지약정은 더 이상 효력을 가지지 않는다고 할 것이다.

라. 또한, 원고 회사가 영업비밀이라고 주장하는 내용의 대부분은 이 사건 BECM과 같은 제품을 자동화 공정을 통해 생산함에 있어 누구나 쉽게 설계하여 사용할 수 있는 기술로서

이미 업계에 공지된 것이어서 특별한 영업비밀로서의 가치를 가지지 않는 내용들이거나, 역설계를 통해 쉽게 생각해낼 수 있는 것들이므로 이를 두고 영업비밀보호법에서 보호하고 있는 영업비밀이라고 볼 수 없다.

4. 판　　단

가. 정갑렬이 원고 주장의 영업비밀에 대한 비밀유지의무를 부담하는지 여부에 대한 판단

살피건대, 영업비밀보호법 제2조 제3호 (라)목 및 (마)목에서는 계약관계 등에 의하여 영업비밀을 비밀로서 유지하여야 할 의무가 있는 자가 부정한 이익을 얻거나 그 영업비밀의 보유자에게 손해를 가할 목적으로 그 영업비밀을 사용하거나 공개하는 행위와 영업비밀이 위 규정에 의하여 공개된 사실 또는 그러한 공개행위가 개입된 사실을 알거나 중대한 과실로 알지 못하고 그 영업비밀을 취득하는 행위 또는 그 취득한 영업비밀을 사용하거나 공개하는 행위를 영업비밀침해행위의 하나로서 규정하고 있는바, 위 '계약관계 등에 의하여 영업비밀을 비밀로서 유지하여야 할 의무가 있는 자'에는 명시적인 문언에 의한 비밀유지약정을 체결한 경우뿐만 아니라, 인적신뢰관계의 특성 등에 비추어 신의칙상 또는 묵시적으로 그러한 의무를 부담하기로 약정하였다고 보아야 할 경우도 포함된다고 할 것이다. 따라서 계약의 문언에 의해서 혹은 신의칙에 비추어 비밀유지의무를 부담하고 있는 자가 그에 반하여 비밀을 사용하거나 공개하는 행위 및 이를 알거나 혹은 중대한 과실로 알지 못하고 그 영업비밀을 취득, 사용, 공개하는 행위 등은 영업비밀침해행위에 해당한다고 할 것이다.

이 사건에 관하여 보건대, 원고 회사가 정갑렬과 사이에 1999. 1. 20.자 약정을 체결한 사실 및 그 약정에 따른 의무로서 정갑렬이 원고 회사에 재직중 취득한 영업비밀을 유지하기로 약정한 사실과 정갑렬이 원고 회사에 재직하면서 개발한 기술 등에 관한 권리를 원고 회사에 귀속시키기로 약정한 사실은 앞에서 본 바와 같다.

그러나 을 제154호증의 1, 2, 제155호증의 1, 3의 각 기재 및 변론의 전취지에 의하면, 원고 회사와 정갑렬은 공히 1999. 1. 20.자 계약의 해제를 주장하다가, 원고 회사가 정갑렬 등을 상대로 인천지방법원 2001가합5506호로 제기한 손해배상청구소송에서 원고는 위 약정의 해제를 주장하는 서면에 의한 의사표시를 하였고, 그 의사표시가 2001. 5. 21. 정갑렬에게 도달하였으며, 정갑렬도 원고 회사에 대하여 인천지방법원 2001가합1399호로 제기한 부당이득반환청구소송에서 위 약정의 해제를 인정하는 의사표시를 하고 그 의사표시가 2001. 2. 7. 원고 회사에게 도달한 사실은 인정할 수 있으므로 원고 회사와 정갑렬 사이의 1999. 1. 20.자 계약은 당사자 사이의 의사합치에 의해 해제되었다고 할 것이므로, 정갑렬은 더 이상 1999. 1. 20.자 약정에 기한 비밀유지의무는 부담하지 않는다고 할 것이다.

그러나 위와 같이 고용주와 근로자 사이에서 약정에 따른 비밀유지의무가 인정되지 않는다고 하더라도 앞에서 본 바와 같이 영업비밀보호법의 입법 취지와 근로계약 및 비밀유지의무의 성질 등을 고려하면 근로자는 퇴직 후에도 그 고용주 또는 영업비밀의 보유자를 해하지 아니할 신의칙상의 의무를 가진다고 할 것이므로, 정갑렬은 원고 회사에 근무하는 도중에 지득한 영업비밀에 대해서는 원고 회사로부터 퇴직한 이후에도 신의칙상 상당한 기간 동안은 영업비밀유지의무를 부담한다고 할 것이다(정갑렬이 원고 회사에 대하여 신의칙상의 영업비밀 유지의무를 부담하는 이상, 그가 CD 속의 원고 회사 영업비밀을 사용하거나 공개하였다면, 그가 그 CD를 절취한 것인지 여부는 그의 영업비밀유지의무의 존부 및 영업비밀침해행위에의 해당 여부에 영향을 미치지 않는다고 할 것이다).

피고는 나아가 원고 주장의 이 사건 영업비밀은 정갑렬이 원고 회사에 입사하기 이전부터 보유하고 있던 기술이거나 원고 회사에 입사한 이후에도 정갑렬 자신에 의해서 창출된 것이므로 이는 정갑렬에게 귀속된다고 할 것이어서 정갑렬에게는 그에 대한 비밀유지의무가 존재하지 않는다거나, 원고 회사와 정갑렬 사이의 계약은 동업계약관계이므로 종업원과 고용주 사이의 관계에 따른 신의칙상의 영업비밀 유지의무가 발생하지 않는다고 주장하므로 살피건대, 피고 제출의 각 증거들만으로는 위 각 주장사실을 인정하기에 부족하고 달리 이를 인정할 증거가 없으므로 피고의 이 부분 주장은 받아들이지 아니한다.

나. 별지 제1목록 기재 기술정보의 영업비밀 해당 여부에 대한 판단

(1) 별지 제1목록 기재 기술정보의 내용은 원고 회사가 BECM을 제조하는 공정 중에서 스퍼터링 공정, 스트레칭 공정, UV본딩 공정, 진동막 푸쉬백 쉬트 제작공정, 라미네이팅 공정, 전하주입 공정, 조립 공정, 계측 및 분류 공정, 무향실 측정 공정, PDE 조립공정에 관한 기술정보들이다.

(2) 한편, 갑 제4, 5, 13, 18, 34, 35, 36, 45, 46, 51, 52, 53, 63, 64, 65, 66, 70, 71, 80호증, 을 제7, 8, 9호증(각 가지번호 포함)의 각 기재와 감정인 이전국, 문성욱, 프로그램심의조정위원회 작성의 각 감정 결과 및 이 법원의 프로그램심의조정위원회에 대한 사실조회 결과에 변론의 전취지를 종합하면 다음과 같은 사실을 인정할 수 있다.

(가) 원고 회사는 현재 국내 콘덴서 마이크로폰 시장 점유율 1위를 차지하고 있는 회사로서 1997년에 정갑렬을 영입하여 박형 BECM 제조 기술을 새롭게 개발하고 제조 공정을 자동화하는 부문에 많은 투자를 한 끝에 BECM 제조에 관한 현재의 기술을 갖추게 되었는바, 1997년 당시 구형 ECM의 생산·판매를 통해 총 70억 원 정도의 매출을 올렸으나, 정갑렬 영입 이후 박형 BECM제품을 세계 최초로 개발하여 생산함으로써, 1999년에는 연매출 350억 원, 2000년에는 연매출 1,000억 원에 달할 정도로 비약적인 성장을 하여 결국 앞에서 본 바

와 같이 국내 콘덴서 마이크로폰 시장에서 1위를 차지하게 되었고, 세계 시장에서도 30%의 점유율을 가지게 되었다.

(나) 원고 회사가 위와 같이 비약적인 성장을 하게 된 것은, 당시까지 일본 기업들이 독점적으로 사용하고 있었던 백타입 일렉트릿(Back Electret)용 각종 Laminate 소재들을 국산화하는 데 성공하였고, 자동전하주입 공정에 있어서 Aperture Control Charge Injection 방식을 발전적으로 도입하였으며, 양산 체제를 위한 초정밀 자동 조립기(Batch Auto Machine)를 개발하였고, 일본으로부터의 수입에 의존하던 진동판용 필름을 한국의 협력 회사와 진공스퍼터링 방식으로 공동개발하고 양산시스템을 구축하여 국산화에 성공하였으며, 또한 진동판의 장력을 임의로 조절·통제하고 균일성을 부여하는 정밀 스트레칭 머신을 고안함으로써 ECM의 품질을 개선함은 물론, 품종분류의 중요인자인 지향특성을 정밀하게 임의로 조절하여 품종확대에 기여하게 하는 등의 기술개발에 성공하였기 때문이다.

(다) 별지 제1목록 기재 각 기술정보들은 원고 회사가 위와 같은 기술개발의 노력 끝에 2000. 6. 정갑렬이 원고 회사에 퇴직할 당시 보유하게 된 각 기술정보들인데, 원고 회사는 위 각 기술정보를 사용하여 BECM을 제조함으로써 생산성 향상, 불량률 감소, 인력 절감 효과, 손실방지 효과, 공정안정화 및 감도 개선 효과 등의 성과를 거둘 수 있게 되었다.

(라) 원고 회사는 위 기술정보 개발 및 이를 이용한 제품 생산과정에서의 영업비밀의 누설을 막기 위하여 외부 업체와 협력하여 생산설비 및 프로그램 등을 제작하거나 개선할 때에는 해당 업체들로부터 비밀유지서약서를 수령하여 공증을 하였고, 하청업체에 제공된 원고 회사의 설계도면은 모두 회수할 수 있도록 노력하였으며, 회사 내부적으로도 직원들에게 보안계약서, 서약서 등을 작성하여 제출하도록 하였고, 카드키를 사용하도록 하여 각 생산설비별로 해당 부서의 직원만이 당해 설비가 설치되어 있는 작업실에 출입할 수 있도록 하는 등 영업비밀에 대한 보안을 유지하려는 노력을 하였다.

(마) 한편, 피고 회사는 별지 제1목록 기재 각 기술정보(정갑렬이 원고 회사로부터 퇴직하면서 반환하지 않고 보유하고 있던 CD에 저장되어 있던 기술정보 및 정갑렬이 원고 회사에 근무하면서 지득하게 된 기술정보)를 사용함으로써 회사 설립 후 불과 3-4개월의 짧은 기간 안에 원고 회사가 생산하고 있던 것과 동일한 종류의 BECM을 양산할 수 있을 정도의 생산설비 및 기술정보를 갖추게 되었고, 현재까지 위 각 기술정보들을 사용하여 BECM을 생산하고 있다.

(3) 살피건대, 영업비밀보호법 제2조 제2호의 '영업비밀'이라 함은, 공연히 알려져 있지 아니하고 독립된 경제적 가치를 가지는 것으로서, 상당한 노력에 의하여 비밀로 유지된 생산방법·판매방법 기타 영업활동에 유용한 기술상 또는 경영상의 정보를 말하며, 영업비밀을 보호하는 목적은 그 영업비밀 자체의 보호에 있는 것이 아니고, 비밀로 관리되고 있는 타인의 정보를 부정한 수단으로 취득하여 경쟁상 유리한 지위를 차지하려는 행위를 막아 건전한

경쟁질서를 유지하고자 함에 있으므로, 비록 기계 및 생산설비의 전체적인 작동원리나 구성이 이미 공연히 알려져 있어서 그 자체는 영업비밀에 해당한다고 할 수는 없다고 하더라도, 기계 및 생산설비를 구성하는 개개 부품의 규격이나 재질, 가공방법, 그와 관련된 설계도면 등이 공연히 알려져 있지 아니하고 독립된 경제적 가치를 가지는 것으로서, 상당한 노력에 의하여 비밀로 유지된 생산방법이나 그에 관한 정보라면 영업비밀에 해당한다고 할 것(대법원 1998. 11. 10. 선고 98다45751 판결 등 참조)인바, 앞에서 본 사실관계에 의하면, 원고 회사의 BECM 제조 공정에 관한 별지 제1목록 기재 각 기술정보들은 비공지성, 경제성, 비밀유지노력 등 영업비밀로서의 요건을 모두 갖추었다고 봄이 상당하므로, 위 영업비밀은 영업비밀보호법 소정의 보호의 대상이 되는 영업비밀에 해당된다고 할 것이고, 피고 회사가 위 영업비밀을 사용하여 기계설비를 제작하고 원고 회사와 동일한 종류의 BECM을 제조하여 판매하고 있는 이상, 이로 인해 원고의 이 사건 영업비밀이 침해되고 있다고 할 것이므로 특별한 사정이 없는 한, 이 사건 영업비밀의 보유자인 원고는 위 영업비밀의 침해를 중단시키기 위하여 피고에 대하여 위 영업비밀침해행위의 금지와 침해행위를 조성한 물건의 폐기, 침해행위에 제공된 설비의 제거 기타 침해행위의 금지 또는 예방을 위하여 필요한 조치를 청구할 수 있다고 할 것이다.

피고는 이에 대하여 피고 회사의 생산설비 및 그 운용을 위한 프로그램 등은 그 구조 및 작동방식에 있어서 원고 회사의 것과는 상이하며, 피고 회사가 채택하고 있는 기술정보 중에서 원고 회사의 것과 동일 또는 유사한 부분이 있다고 하더라도 이는 이미 특허공보 등을 통해서 공개된 공지의 내용이라거나, 해당 업계에서 필수적으로 채택하고 있는 자동화요소의 단순한 조합이라거나, 원고 회사의 도면 또는 프로그램을 참조함이 없이 피고 회사가 자체적으로 역설계를 통하여 제조한 것이라는 등의 주장을 하고 있으나, 갑 제66, 81호증, 을 제14호증, 제17호증의 5, 6, 제23, 25, 27, 36, 57, 65, 71, 77, 97, 105, 107, 116, 118, 123, 135, 139, 140, 142호증(각 가지번호 포함)의 각 기재, 감정인 이전국, 문성욱의 각 일부 감정 결과 및 이 법원의 프로그램심의조정위원회에 대한 일부 사실조회 결과만으로는 위 각 주장사실을 인정하기에 부족하고 달리 이를 인정할 증거가 없을 뿐만 아니라, 앞서 본 각 증거들에 의하면, 원고 회사는 별지 제1목록 기재 각 기술정보를 엄격한 비밀로 유지하면서 회사 내부에서 사용하고 있었고, 피고 회사는 해당 업계에서 사용하고 있는 위 기계와 유사한 기계를 분석, 평가하여 제작도면, 생산방법 등을 취득한 것이 아니라, 원고 회사에 대하여 비밀유지의무를 부담하고 있는 정갑렬을 통하여 원고 회사에서 사용하고 있는 위 기술정보를 용이하게 취득한 것으로 보이는바, 그렇다면 피고 회사가 원고 회사에 근무하던 정갑렬이 가지고 있던 정보를 바탕으로 역설계를 통해 자신의 기계 설비를 설계하였다고 하더라도, 피고 회사는 위 기계 설비에 대한 비밀유지의무가 있는 자로부터 영업비밀을 취득한 경우에 해당하여 그 부당성이 역설계에도 남는 것이고, 또한 가사 원고 회사의 기술정보가 없는 상태에서도 이 사건 BECM 제조를 위한 기계 설비의 역설계가 가능하고 그에 의하여 원고 주장의 영업비밀과 동일한 내용의 기술정보의 획득이 가능하더라도 그러한 사정만으로 별지 제1목록 기재 각 기술정보를 영업비밀로 보는 데는 지장이 없다고 할 것이므로 피고 회사의 이 부분 주장은 이유 없다.

다. 영업비밀의 보호기간에 대한 판단

(1) 한편, 앞에서 영업비밀로서 인정된 별지 제1목록 기재 각 기술정보에 대한 침해금지기간에 관하여 보건대, 영업비밀이 영업비밀보호법에 의하여 보호되는 시간적 범위는 침해행위자가 침해행위에 의하여 공정한 경쟁자보다 유리한 출발, 시간절약이라는 부당한 이익을 취하지 못하게 함으로써 공정하고 자유로운 경쟁을 보장하기 위해 필요한 시간적 범위 내로 제한되어야 하고, 그 범위를 정함에 있어서는 영업비밀인 정보의 내용, 영업비밀 보유자의 그 정보취득에 소요된 기간과 비용, 영업비밀의 유지에 기울인 노력과 방법, 침해자들이나 다른 공정한 경쟁자가 독자적인 개발이나 역설계와 같은 합법적인 방법에 의하여 그 기술정보를 취득하는 데 필요한 시간, 침해자가 종업원인 경우에는 사용자와의 관계에서 근무기간, 담당업무나 직책, 영업비밀에의 접근 정도, 영업비밀보호에 관한 내규나 약정, 종업원이었던 자의 생계 활동 및 직업선택의 자유와 영업활동의 자유, 지적재산권의 일종으로서 존속기간이 정해져 있는 특허권 등의 보호기간과의 비교, 기타 변론에 나타난 당사자의 인적·물적 시설 등을 고려하여 합리적으로 결정하여야 할 것이다(대법원 1998. 2. 13. 선고 97다24528 판결 등 참조).

(2) 그런데 앞에서 본 사실관계 및 변론의 전취지에 의하면, 원고는 1987. 8. 5.에 설립되었으나 1997. 8. 20. 정갑렬을 영입하기 전까지는 BECM에 비해 현저히 떨어지는 수준의 마이크로폰을 생산하는 단계에 불과하였으나, 정갑렬 영입한 후 그의 도움을 받아서 현재의 BECM 제조기술을 보유하게 된 사실, 그럼에도 불구하고, 원고 회사가 정갑렬에게 그의 기여도에 상응하는 보상을 하지 않는 것에 불만을 품고 정갑렬이 원고 회사를 퇴사하여 피고 회사를 설립하게 된 사실 등을 인정할 수 있는바, 그 사실관계에다가 BECM을 포함한 휴대폰 부품 제조기술은 아주 급속도로 발전하는 과정에 있는 점, 근로자의 퇴직 후의 영업비밀유지기간을 지나치게 장기간으로 정할 경우 경제적 약자인 근로자의 직업선택의 자유 및 영업의 자유를 제한하고 경쟁의 제한에 의한 부당한 독점상태를 초래할 가능성도 있는 점 등 이 사건 변론에 나타난 제반 사정을 종합하여 보면, 정갑렬 등이 원고 회사를 퇴직한 2000. 6.경을 기준으로 하여 앞에서 인정된 원고 회사의 영업비밀이 보호될 수 있는 기간은 길어야 1년 정도로 봄이 상당하다.

(3) 한편, 이 사건에서 위와 같은 영업비밀침해 금지기간의 기산점은 정갑렬이 그 영업비밀 취급업무에서 이탈한 때인 퇴직시점을 기준으로 산정하는 것이 합리적이라고 할 것인 바(대법원 1998. 2. 13. 선고 97다24528 판결, 2003. 7. 16.자 2002마4380 결정 등 참조, 퇴직 시점을 기산점으로 삼는 경우에는 이 사건과 같이 소송 진행 과정에서 영업비밀침해금지기간이 경과하여 영업비밀침해사실이 인정되더라도 그 금지를 구할 수 없게 되는 결과가 발생하기도 하지만, 그렇다고 해서 기산점을 판결 확정일로 하는 경우에는 당해 영업비밀 자체의 성질, 거래사정 등과 무관한 판결 확정이라는 우연적이고 외부적인 요소에 의하여 영업비밀 보호기간이 달라지게 되고, 사실심법원으로서는 향후 판결 확정시점을 추정하여 금지기간을 설정하여야 하여, 경우에 따라서는 판결 확정이 지체되는 경우에는 판결 확정시에 이미 영업비밀성을 상실하여 보호되지 말아야 할 정보에 대해서도 금지를 하게 되는 불합리가 발생할 여지가 있는 점, 영업비밀 보호의 취지에 비추어 볼 때 그 침해금지기간은 공정하고 자유로운 경쟁을 보장하기 위해 필요한 시간적 범위 내로 제한할 필요가 있는 점 등을 고려하면 판결 확정일을 기산점으로 삼는 것은 부당하다고 할 것이고, 퇴직시점을 기산점으로 삼는 것이 상당하다고 할 것이다), 그 퇴직시점인 2000. 6.경으로부터 기산하여 이미 4년 이상의 기간이 경과한 현 단계에서 정갑렬 및 피고 회사에 대한 영업비밀침해금지의무가 더 이상 유지된다고 볼 수 없기 때문에, 원고 회사가 정갑렬 및 피고 회사에 대하여 그 영업비밀침해로 인한 손해의 배상을 구하는 것은 별론으로 하고, 피고 회사에 대하여 영업비밀침해금지의무가 부과되고 있음을 전제로 하는 원고의 이 사건 청구는 더 나아가 살펴볼 것 없이 이유 없다.

다. 안정화조항

IOC는 경제, 정치적 상황에 관하여 일정한 가정을 하고 이를 전제로 투자의 경제성을 판단하여 결정한 것이므로 이러한 판단의 가정이 바뀔 경우 보호받기를 원한다. 자원보유국의 정부가 갑자기 석유사업에만 적용되는 특별세금을 부과한다거나 석유사업에만 적용되는 환경규율이 강화되는 것이 그 예이다. 이는 석유사업이 자원보유국의 귀중한 천연자원추출에 관계되는 것이고 환경에 민감한 것이기 때문이기도 하지만, 석유개발계약이 상당히 장기간에 걸치기 때문이기도 하다.[50]

크게 두 가지 유형이 있다. 하나는 정부의 행동에 제약을 가하여 이러한 행동이 계약상 권리의무에 아무런 영향을 미치지 않는다고 합의하는 것이다. 상황을 동결시킨다는 의미에서 동결조항(freeze-out clause)이라고도 한다. 그러나, 이러한 조항이 과연 집행가능한 것인지 의문이며 국제법상으로도 국유화조치와 관련하여 그 효력이 인정되지 않고 있다.[51] 집행가능

50) 장기계약을 협상하다 보면 온갖 상황이 법률가와 사업가의 상상력을 자극한다. 따라서, 단순히 상대방이 계약상 의무를 이행하지 않는 경우라는 전형적 경우뿐만 아니라 계약당사자가 통제할 수 없는 제3자의 행동이 걱정되기 시작한다.

51) 뒤 9장에서의 논의 참조.

성에 대한 의문을 해소하기 위하여 정부의 행동이 제약되는 범위를 최소화하여 합의하는 예도 있다.[52)]

또 다른 유형은 입법권을 포함한 국가주권이나 법의 적용에 제한을 가하는 표현을 하기보다는 계약의 기초를 이루는 경제적 사정에 중대한 변화를 가져오는 국가권력의 행사가 있는 경우 새로운 경제적 균형을 반영하는 새로운 계약조건을 재협상할 의무를 규정하는 경제적 균형조항(economic equilibrium clause)이다. 경제적 균형이 깨진 상황이 무엇인지와[53)] 그런 상황이 발생한 경우 계약당사자의 의무는 무엇인지에 관한 합의는 물론 새로운 경제적 균형점을 찾아가는 절차 등에 관한 합의가 필요하다는 점에서 문제를 해결하려다가 문제를 더 복잡하게 만들 가능성도 있다. 실제 자원보유국이 정치적으로 안정되어 있거나 협상력이 월등한 경우에는 IOC가 안정화조항을 제기한다는 것 자체가 협상상대방에 대한 불신의 표시로 보아질 수도 있기 때문인지 거의 사용되지 않고 거꾸로 자원보유국이 자신의 협상력을 강화하기 위하여 또는 법규가 IOC에 유리하게 변경된 경우 재협상의 필요성 때문에 제기할 수도 있을 것이다.

안정화조항의 예[54)]

Offshore Oil License Agreement dated 10 January 1978 between Government of Ghana & Offshore Hydrocarbons Corporation (Later Transferred to Agri-Petco)[55)]

(1) The Licensees shall be liable to pay to the Government an income tax computed in accordance with clause 64 of this Agreement in respect of its income arising from its operations under this Agreement and no tax shall be imposed under any other Act or law on such income or dividends or remittances paid out of such income or upon the export of petroleum produced by and belonging to the Licensees.

(2) The Licensees shall be free from all other taxation, charges, duties and fees payable to the Government or to any governmental authority in Ghana in relation to

52) Peter D. Cameron, INTERNATIONAL ENERGY INVESTMENT LAW, 68-74 (2010).

53) 기업인수계약에서 중대한 악영향과 유사한 개념이다. 실제 Angola의 석유개발계약은 유사한 표현을 사용하고 있다. 중대한 악영향은 통상 산업전체에 영향을 주는 경제사정의 변경 등은 포함되지 않는 반면 경제적 균형의 파괴는 세법의 개정이나 국유화 등 석유산업 전반에 영향을 주는 것도 포함되는 점에서 차이가 있다. Smith, 주 1-4 상게서, 510.

54) Barrows Company의 동의를 받아서 전재. R. Doak Bishop/James Crawford/W.Michael Reisman, FOREIGN INVESTMENT DISPUTES 290-92 (2005). 상황변화에 따른 재협상의무에 관한 조항은 같은 책 303-304쪽에 나와 있는 계약서 조항 참조.

55) 58 Basic Oil Laws & Concession Contracts: South & Central Africa 22 (1980). Barrows Company의 동의를 받아서 게재하였으며 Bishop, 주 4-54 상게서 290-92에서 전재. 이하 동일하게 적용.

such petroleum operations except payments which would be made in accordance with this Agreement and the application of the Mineral Oil Taxation Ordinance as amended, as provided for in clause 64 of this Agreement, and charges and fees for services rendered by governmental authorities on request or to the public generally provided that such charges and fees are reasonable and non-discriminating.

Amoco Group Agreement dated 14 December 1996 on the Exploration, Development & Production Sharing for Prospective Structures for Ashrafi Dan Ulduzu & Area Adjacent in the Azerbaijan Sector of the Caspian Sea.[56)]

Art. 22.1

Upon approval by the Parliament of the Azerbaijan Republic of this Agreement, this Agreement shall constitute a law of the Azerbaijan Republic and shall take precedence over any other current or future law, decree or administrative order (or part thereof) of the Azerbaijan Republic which is inconsistent with or conflicts with this Agreement except as specifically otherwise provided in this Agreement.

Oman Model Exploration & Production Sharing Agreement of 2002[57)]

26.2 In the event that any provisions contained in the laws, rules or regulations of the Government are inconsistent with the terms and conditions of this Agreement, the Government shall take such action as is necessary to relieve the Company from any loss, liability or jeopardy as a result of such inconsistency and shall also take such action as may be necessary to maintain the economic equilibrium existing between the Parlies on the Effective Date of this Agreement.

Restated LNG Development & Production Sharing Agreement for the North Field Gas dated 31 January 1993 between the Government of the State of Qatar and (as Contractor) Qatar General Petroleum Corporation, et al.[58)]

Article XXIV — Flag and Applicable Laws

B. The laws and regulations of the State of Qatar shall apply to the exercise by the Government and the Contractor of their rights under this Agreement.

C. Without prejudice to the foregoing, if any restrictions are imposed by a law. regulation or administrative order countervailing the provisions hereof so as to prejudice the Contractor's rights and interest hereunder, the Parties shall enter into negotiations in good faith to define an equitable remedy thereto, including amending the terms hereof.

---

56) 52 Basic Oil Laws & Concession Contracts: Russia & NIS 1 (Supplement 24) (2003).

57) www.barrowscompany.com, Basic Oil Laws & Concession Contracts: Middle East (2003)에 게재되어 있다고 함.

58) 58 World LNG Contracts: Qatar 1 (2003).

Agip/BP/Etal Production Sharing Agreement dated 18 November 1997 in respect of the North Caspian Sea (Kashagan) among Agip Caspian Sea B.V., et al.[59)]

Section 40.2 — Change of Law

Without prejudice to rights of Contractor under Article 9 of the Investment Law of the Republic and Article 57 of the Petroleum Law of the Republic, if at any time after the signing of this Agreement there is (a) a change in the Laws of the Republic (or of any subdivision or governmental instrumentality thereof), whether through amendment of existing Laws or enactment of new Laws, or a change having the force of law in the interpretation or application thereof by any judicial, arbitral or administrative body or (b) any binding adjudication by any judicial, arbitral or administrative body that any provision of this Agreement is rendered invalid by reason of the Petroleum Law, the Customs Code or the Tax Code, and such change or adjudication has a materially adverse effect on the economic benefits (including those resulting from the fiscal regime provided by this Agreement) accruing to Contractor hereunder or provided hereunder to accrue to Contractor during the term of this Agreement, the Parties shall amend this Agreement or take such other action as is appropriate or necessary so as to restore the overall economic benefit (including the economic effect resulting from the fiscal regime provided by this Agreement) to Contractor; provided, however, that no amendment to this Agreement shall be required hereunder as the result of (i) changes to Laws concerning health, safety or environmental protection that cause such Laws to be consistent with international standards for insurance and are applied on a non-discriminary basis.

라. 불가항력 조항

안정화조항 없이 보다 간단하게 불가항력조항을 통하여 상황을 해결할 수도 있을 것이나 자연적 재해가 아닌 법률의 변경이 언제나 불가항력으로 포함되지 않는다는 것이 문제이다. 반대로 계약을 하나의 법안으로 만들어서 국회에서 승인할 수도 있으나 그러한 절차가 안정화조항의 집행력을 얼마나 강화할 수 있는지에 관하여도 의문이 있다. 단순한 계약조항에 더하여 정부간 투자협정이나 다자협정을 체결하면 계약의 집행력이 보다 강화될 것이다. 실제 Baku-Tbilisi-Ceyhan을 연결하는 원유파이프라인건설프로젝트에서 Georgia, Azerbaijan, Turkey 3국의 정부가 다자간 협정으로 법과 제도의 안정성을 보장하고 이러한 보장에 위반하였을 경우 건설컨소시엄에 피해를 보상할 것을 약정한 예도 있다.[60)]

59) 52 Basic Oil Laws & Concession Contracts: Russia & NIS 1 (Supplement 39) (2003).

60) Abigail S. Reyers, *Protecting the 'Freedom of Transit of Petroleum: Transnational Lawyers Making (Up) International Law in the Caspian,* 24 BERKELEY J. INT'L L. 842, 858 (2006).

노트와 질문

물건을 제조하는 데 필요한 기술과 지질조사의 결과가 달리 취급되어야 한다면 그 이유는 무엇일까? 신의칙상 상당한 기간을 산정하기 위한 요소로서 열거된 것 중 어떤 것이 지질학정 정보와 관련이 있을까? 구제책은 어떤 것들이 있을까?

7. 투자결정

가. 재무구조

자원보유국의 입장에서는 어떤 재무구조를 제시하여 가장 효과적으로 자원탐사·개발을 할 것인가가 중요한 정책적 과제라고 할 수 있다. 위에서 설명한 계약형태에 따라 누가 어떤 결정권한을 가지며 어떤 위험을 부담하는지가 결정되지만 실제 운용에 있어서 IOC와 NOC가 상호 협조하는 한 커다란 차이가 나지 않을 수도 있으며 결국은 자원보유국과 IOC간 투자의 성과를 어떻게 나눌 것인가라는 재무구조가 가장 중요할 것이다.[61] 물론 재무구조가 전부는 아니다. 모든 투자유치가 그러하듯이 투자에 대한 경제적인 보상을 크게 하여야 할 뿐 아니라 이러한 보상의 가능성을 결정하는 자원보유국의 법과 정책를 정비하여 투자회수의 확실성을 보장하여야 할 것이다. IOC의 입장에서는 투자의 기회를 투자의 비용과 비교하여 예상수익률이 자본조달비용보다 높을 경우 투자결정을 할 것이며 예상수익률을 결정하는 것은 탐사계약상 재무구조와 지질학적 위험일 것이기 때문에 이의 분석이 필요할 것이다. 또한 자원보유국의 과거의 외국인투자에 대한 정책과 현재 및 미래의 정치상황이 투자에 대한 위험을 초래할 것이기에 이들도 고려되어야 함은 물론이다.

C.R.K. Moore, Perspectives on the Valuation of Upstream Oil and Gas Interests: An Overview, 2 J. WORLD ENER. L & BUS. 24 (2009)

1. Introduction

In any business endeavour, quantifying value is important. Investment decisions are

61) Silvana Tordo, FISCAL SYSTEMS FOR HYDROCARGONS: DESIGN ISSUES (World Bank No. 123, 2007).

made on the basis of the perceived value to be generated. Assets, indeed entire businesses, are bought and sold regularly. Legal and commercial disputes arise for which the appropriate remedy is either compensation or damages, which must be quantified. All these situations require a consistent rational approach in determining value. Valuing upstream oil and gas interests faces particular challenges because of the high probability of failure (in the exploration phase), the extreme ranges of uncertainty in technical performance and the significant differences in other, non-technical risks. Appropriate valuation techniques should be theoretically sound and must also take into account the practice in the market and explain observed behaviour. Because of the nature of the assets, historical and current performance is useful only to the extent it allows extrapolation to future performance. The value should be based on the future performance, which is why discounted cash flow (DCF) analysis is not only the most appropriate, but also the most widely used starting point.

This paper provides some perspectives on issues surrounding industry approaches to DCF analysis and argues for particular approaches for adjusting the initial results to account for risk.

2. Empirical determination of fair market value

The rights to explore for and produce oil and gas from the subsurface are obtained in the first instance from the host government, with the notable exception of private lands in the US where ownership was vested in the landowner. Such rights are generally not in perpetuity, but terminate after a fixed period of time. Subject to applicable laws, regulations and contractual arrangements between right-holders, these rights may be assigned to third parties. The consideration for the purchase of a participating interest may be cash, an undertaking to pay future costs (either a specified amount or an unlimited amount to cover a specific operation, drilling a well, for example), or rights over a different area. A participating or working interest (WI) is an interest which bears a share of costs and receives a share of revenues, subject to applicable laws and contracts. Other types of interests exist, such as overriding royalties, net profit interests and carried WIs, where the owner does not contribute directly to the costs. All of these interests are traded in a worldwide marketplace.

The details of such transactions are frequently made public. This is especially true of relatively small public companies whose stock exchanges require them to disclose the details of material transactions. With these details, it is generally possible to calculate the cash equivalent of even the most complex farm-in. It should be noted that a promise, for example, to fund 100 percent of a $120 million exploration programme to earn a 75 percent WI does not mean that the interest is valued at $120 million. In this case, $90 million of the programme is for the account of the company farming in. The result would be identical if the company farming in pays $30 million in cash to the company farming out. Both companies then pay their own WI shares of the future programme. The cash transaction is thus $30 million to purchase a 75 percent interest, valuing 100 percent WI at $40 million.

Where transactions include reserves, companies are often required to file third-party reserves' reports compiled under either standardised or explicit and transparent assumptions. Actual purchase prices may be compared to such evaluations. Analysis of thousands of such transactions provides actual fair market value (FMV) data for particular interests. It is tempting to use these as comparable sales in valuing other interests. However, extreme caution is required in defining a 'comparable' interest. A checklist for determining what is comparable is daunting (date, location, contractual terms, life cycle stage, geologic risk, reserves and contingent or prospective resources, etc). Indeed it may be argued that the only truly comparable interest is another WI in the same petroleum right, provided that there have been no material economic or technical changes since the prior transaction (and there are no differences in the WIs' rights. both are non-operators). One only has to look at the difference in bids for adjacent tracts in US Gulf of Mexico lease sales to see that values vary significantly over

Fig.1 profiles of different measures of value through the life cycle of an oil and gas asset

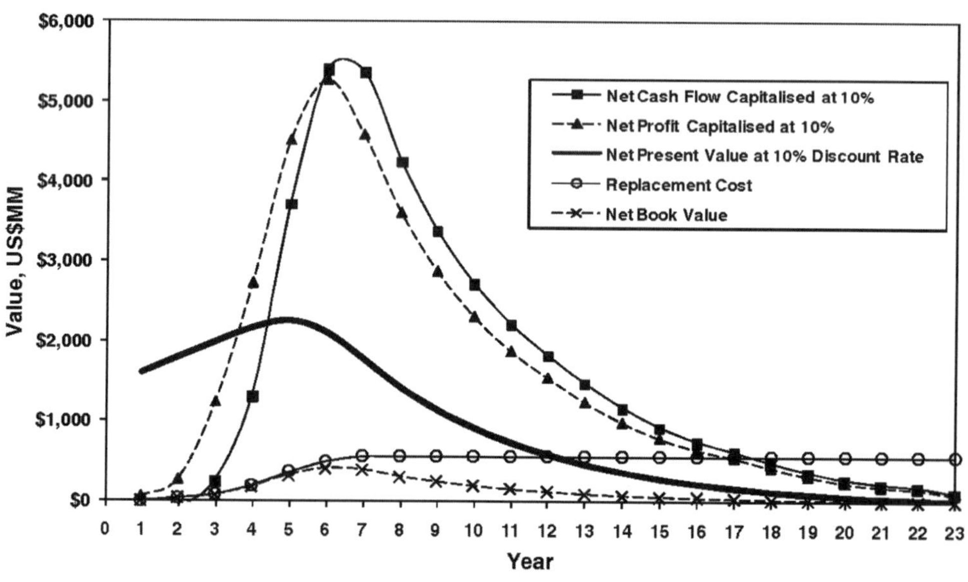

short distances.

Despite this limited applicability in determining absolute value, analysis of comparable transactions provides market information to assist in determining FMV. Normalised metrics (value per acre or value per unit reserves or unit production) are frequently quoted and are useful, both as a reality check on values determined analytically and in determining the relation between FMV and expected present value (EPV). Comparables can also provide other useful informations. They can provide evidence for the premium, if any, being offered for interests with control or a veto (operatorship or a large WI). They can provide evidence of either a premium or a discount for a small WI (both have been observed). Finally, the general terms being offered for comparable farm-ins (such as two-for-one or a third for a quarter) can provide a useful starting point for valuing other exploration opportunities.

3. Characteristics of oil and gas interests and their impact on valuation methods

The character of an oil and gas asset changes over its life cycle. Before drilling takes place, its value depends on estimates of its potential to contain commercially viable hydrocarbon accumulations. After a discovery, its value is based upon estimates of its economic performance if the accumulation is developed. After development, its value is based on estimates of how the accumulation will continue to perform. The risk (here, chance of failure) and uncertainty (here, range of quantitative outcomes) are reduced significantly through the life cycle. Nevertheless, an accurate account of its economic performance is not available until it is abandoned.

An important characteristic of oil and many gas fields is that the production naturally declines from some peak value usually reached early in the life of the field. There may be opportunities to accelerate production with additional investment, or to invest in secondary or tertiary recovery. Nevertheless, production will still decline naturally after project implementation. Eventually, it will terminate either because the deposit no longer generates positive cash flow, or the period of the right to produce (the lease, concession, contract, etc) terminates. This has important consequences for the valuation method. Of course, an individual interest may include numerous individual assets, and may simultaneously include declining mature fields and opportunities for growth (exploration opportunities). Ultimately, however, decline is inevitable.

Valuation techniques based on either replacement cost or net book values are wholly unsuited to the valuation of oil and gas interests as can be seen from Fig.1. While the amount of sunk costs may affect future revenue streams, sunk costs alone are poor predictors of total future revenues. Similarly, capitalising current year profit or free cash flow should not be used to value oil and gas interests. Their unsuitability should be obvious from the shape of the cash flow profile because of the inevitable post-peak decline in future performance compared to current measures.

4. DCF analysis and EPV

The most widely used and preferred method for valuing oil and gas interests is DCF analysis. This form of analysis was the method preferred by 88 percent of respondents to the most recent Society of Petroleum Evaluation Engineers' survey. DCF analysis involves forecasting the future costs and revenues to which the interest holder is entitled. Each future year's cash flow is reduced by a discount factor to account for the time-value of money. The sum of these discounted annual cash flows over the life of the project is here called the net present value (NPV). The forecast cash flows are typically obtained from a spreadsheet model or a software package with a model built-in. Input to this model comprises a discount rate, forecasts of oil and gas production schedules, product prices, inflation, exploration and development costs and schedules, operating costs and other costs. All of these forecasts are uncertain, even for producing fields with a long history.

Similar techniques are used for both producing properties and exploratory rights. The approach used to value exploration properties is to carry out DCF analysis of one or more defined prospects. Representative but hypothetical outcomes are modelled, based on the technical assessment of the probable size of the accumulations. The results of these analyses are combined to give the value of the success 'leg'. The discounted cost of an unsuccessful programme, the 'failure leg', is also estimated. The EPV for an exploration prospect is calculated by multiplying the success leg NPV by the probability that a commercial field will be discovered, and subtracting the discounted cost of failure multiplied by the probability of failure.

5. Issues in DCF analysis: Subsurface evaluation

The evaluation of geologic risk (chance of success) remains a largely subjective exercise dependent only on the experience of the expert. Success rates may be used to validate subjective assessments. However, this comparison is much like using comparable sales to determine FMV—truly comparable analogue data sets are rarely available.

Estimation of reserves, well and field production performance is subject to significant uncertainty, although the range of uncertainty diminishes substantially through the life cycle of the asset. Techniques of varying sophistication are used to account for this uncertainty, including statistical and analytical techniques, which combine alternative outcomes or cases (from as few as two or more usually three, to as many as several thousands in a computer simulation). Where large numbers of cases are analysed, it is customary (and statistically correct) to quote and use the average or mean value (where a single point of reference is required). Where a single case is used, it is customary to use a case representative of the central tendency. Use of probabilistic approaches is increasing, according to the SPEE survey, up from 46 percent in 2007 to 54 percent in 2008.

There continues to be some confusion, perhaps even controversy, over the choice of mean or median case in representing the central tendency. This is important because, with a wide range of uncertainty and the skewed nature of the probability distribution, the median may be significantly lower than the mean. The more useful and appropriate measure is the mean, and this is more properly the 'best estimate'. However, the industry standard now equates the best estimate of reserves to Proved plus Probable ('2P') Reserves but defines this as the median value when probabilistic approaches are used. The mean value should be used in valuations, despite this being different from (greater than) the more widely reported and accepted 2P value.

This assertion is consistent with the widely reported phenomenon of reserves' growth. If the mean estimate were correct, and remained constant throughout the life cycle of the asset, both the Proved (90th percentile) and 2P (median) reserves must increase as the variance of the distribution is reduced through time. Both converge to the mean at abandonment.

In cases where probabilistic approaches are not employed, particularly in producing fields, three deterministic reserve cases are generally used: Proved, Proved plus Probable (2P) and Proved plus Probable plus Possible (3P). The problem then remains of how to combine these. The most common approach, according to the SPEE survey, is to use reserve adjustment factors. These are fractional multipliers applied to each separate category of reserves. The survey results are reported specifically for those used in acquisition valuations. The fractions may be thought of in two ways. Firstly, they may incorporate the chance that the reserves do not exist or will not be developed. An alternative view is that the fractions are weights to be used in calculating the mean value, in the same way that Swanson's rule is used as a method of deriving the mean of a lognormal distribution. It is instructive to look at the result if the reserves follow a lognormal distribution and the deterministic reserve cases are similar to their probabilistic equivalents (noting that this is not a requirement of the current guidelines). The survey results may be slightly misleading as they are presented as if each factor is independent.

Fig.2 Weighted averages using common industry reserve adjustment factors for a range of reserves' uncertaninty, shown as a proportion of the true mean value for lognormally distributed reserves

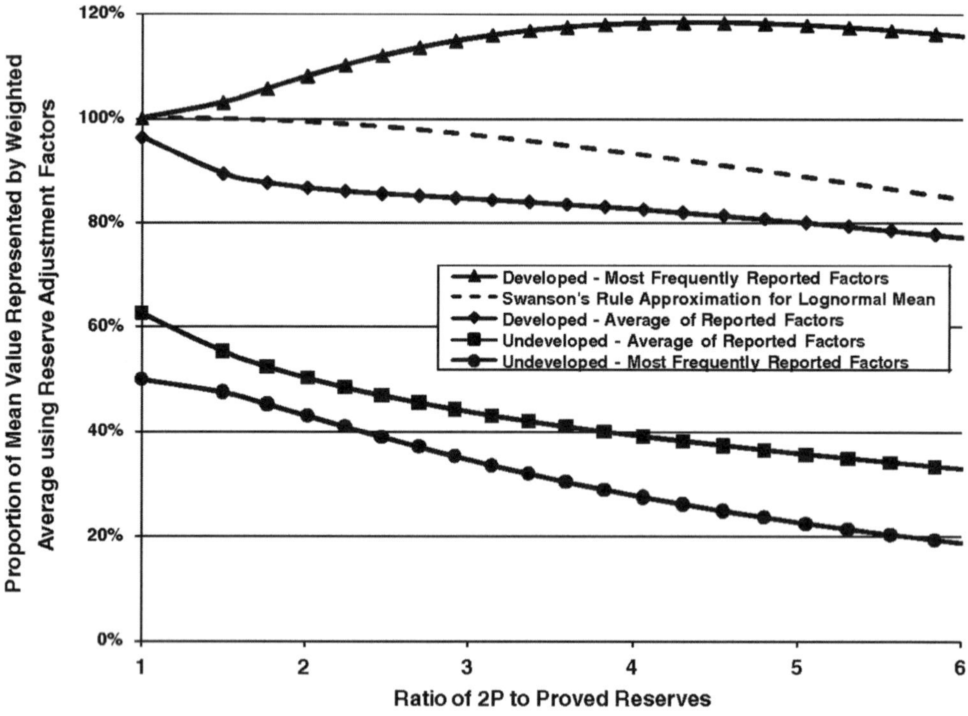

Four cases are shown in Fig.2. The proportion of the true mean value obtained by using the factors to obtain a weighted average is plotted against the ratio of 2P to Proved reserves. This ratio is a function of the variance of the distribution, but is probably easier to relate to than the variance itself. Note that a ratio of unity is where there is no uncertainty and all the reserves are Proved. The results using the Swanson's rule approximation are also shown. Although most fields contain a mix of producing, shut-in, behind pipe and undeveloped reserves, two simple end members are shown. One has only developed producing reserves and the other has only undeveloped reserves. For each case, two sets of Reserve Adjustment Factors have been taken from the survey results-the mean factor for each category, and the most frequently used factor. For developed reserves, the mean factors are 96.4 percent for Proved, 42.9 percent for Probable and 30.8 percent for Possible; the most frequently used factors are, respectively, 100 percent, 50 percent and 50 percent. For undeveloped reserves, the mean factors are, respectively, 62.7 percent, 34.7 percent and 30.8 percent, while the most frequently used factors are 50 percent, 50 percent and 0 percent respectively. Note that the uncertainty of the reserves is likely to be greater before development than after development, and the developed fields are more likely to plot towards the left of the diagram.

It is not clear what to conclude from this data. It is tempting to suggest that the results for developed reserves are attempts to find the mean. The reduction in calculated value at high variance is because the approximation of the mean is deteriorating (as it does with Swanson's rule). If so, the results for undeveloped reserves can be explained to be similar to (parallel to) the results for developed reserves, but undeveloped reserves are reduced by the chance that the development will occur.

An alternative view is that the discounts to the mean are real and intentional, and they represent an increasing aversion to paying full value for an asset as both its risk (here, chance of not occurring) and uncertainty increases. If so, some evaluators may be surprised to learn that the most frequently used Reserve Adjustment Factors for producing reserves yield a value that represents a substantial premium to the implied mean value. Moreover, the premium increases with increasing uncertainty across the range of variance associated with producing fields.

The use of statistical and analytical techniques where a mean value is calculated is preferred. However, FMV is, at least in part, determined according to what is done by those supplying the buyers with evaluations. Practice among those evaluators cannot be ignored.

6. Issues in DCF analysis: Operational and development plans, costs and schedules

As a general rule, operational and development plans, costs and schedules in such analyses represent best-in-class scenarios, executed flawlessly and trouble-free. This is not necessarily an inappropriate initial analysis, but it is misleading to regard this as the expected case. Delays and cost overruns are far more likely than project acceleration or cost savings if the base case is best-in-class performance. The probability distribution about the plan is therefore severely skewed towards value reduction, but this is rarely incorporated into the analysis. It is believed that this systematic bias is an agency effect, due to experts' experience providing scenarios in internal capital allocation competitions in earlier corporate careers. A better approach is to include allowances for expected delays and cost increases (other than inflation, treated separately).

A second issue is whether the plan is consistent with a business plan, either that of the right-holder or that of a hypothetical 'prudent operator'. The most flagrant abuse of this requirement is valuing exploration portfolios as if all wells will be drilled, immediately and simultaneously. In practice, a prudent business plan would recognise operating and budgetary constraints, rig availability and other practical limits, and incorporate some limit on the number of wells to be drilled based on an appropriate dry hole tolerance.

7. Issues in DCF analysis: Fiscal terms

It is assumed that the DCF model accurately takes into account even the most complex fiscal terms. Where the particular interest is not 'ring-fenced', its value to the owner may be affected by fiscal positions generated by its other interests. This is usually an issue with tax/royalty regimes, but may also apply for cost recovery under production sharing arrangements. However, the value in the marketplace will be determined by the potential buyer's position. Indeed it may be argued that FMV will be determined by buyers able to take advantage of tax efficiencies, since they will offer the most, other things being equal.

A well-known example is used to illustrate this. The 1983 UK budget removed the ring fence for the deduction of exploration for Petroleum Revenue Tax (PRT), then at a 5 percent rate. This dramatic reduction in failure leg exploration costs for those paying PRT gave those firms a significant competitive advantage. This resulted in the marketing by British Petroleum (BP) of PRT-paying Forties Field units, which enabled even the smaller explorers to acquire tax efficiency. From then on, it was unrealistic to determine the FMV of exploration opportunities in the UK North Sea without recognising the PRT benefit, even if it was not available to the owner of a particular interest. This is also an interesting example of a situation where a very small WI was valued at a premium to the entire interest. Without that premium, there would have been no incentive for BP to sell.

8. Issues in DCF analysis: Leverage

It is assumed that there is agreement that the DCF value should be based on free cash flows after tax excluding the effect of debt financing. This ignores the capital structure of the company, which is taken care of in the discount rate. However, there are some situations where it may be appropriate to include benefits from debt financing. Interest expense is cost recoverable under some production sharing contracts. Moreover, this may extend to parent company loans to subsidiaries at arm's length rates, even if the parent company does not incur actual interest costs on any external debt. In this and similar cases, the interest cost benefit should be included (but not the drawdown or repayment of principal).

9. Issues in DCF analysis: Surface risk

'Surface risk' is used here to describe the variety of political, environmental, logistical, commercial or bureaucratic issues that may impact project performance, particularly by causing delays. It includes low probability but catastrophic events such as expropriation or natural disaster. It is synonymous with 'country risk', which covers the same issues but implies, incorrectly, a uniform application throughout a particular country. It can be argued that the US Gulf of Mexico shelf is relatively free of surface risk, due to the extensive infrastructure, efficient spot markets for oil and natural gas, widespread availability of services and people, and a transparent and well-established business framework. Nevertheless, it is not risk-free, as demonstrated by the ravages of recent hurricane seasons and threats of a windfall profit tax. Similarly, the UK North Sea shares many of the positive characteristics of the Gulf of Mexico, and is less prone to catastrophic natural disasters, but has historically had an extremely unstable fiscal regime for oil and gas companies. Surface risk differences within countries may be illustrated in Nigeria, where deep water offshore developments do not share the operating difficulties onshore in parts of the Niger Delta. It would be preferable to incorporate these risks into the DCF analysis by adjusting the cash flows. Some elements may be incorporated into the development plans where there is historical data to support project performance forecasts, such as elapsed time for development projects. However, most surface risk remains unpredictable, with respect to both timing and scope. In these circumstances, an alternative approach is required. There have been a number of attempts to use an adjustment to the discount rate to account for surface risk. Objections to using increased discount rates to account for any type of risk are discussed below. The empirical observation that the FMV in a 'risky' place is less than the FMV of a similar project in a less risky place does not by itself imply the use of a higher discount rate. The same is true while considering the use of different discount rates for different reserve categories.

10. Issues in DCF analysis: Price forecasts

There does not appear to be a consensus on incorporating price uncertainty into valuations. In contrast to the statistical techniques used to manage subsurface uncertainty, price uncertainty is frequently treated by preparing arbitrary 'upside' and 'downside' sensitivities. While apparently useful to those making investment decisions, these sensitivities cannot be incorporated into the valuation unless they are associated with some probability. If the expected price case is used, the result will be the required mean NPV. However, the variance of the result will be understated if price uncertainty is not quantified.

Much has been written about the poor track record of price forecasts, from the 'hockey sticks' of the early 1980s to sub-$20 flat-real-for-ever in the early 2000s. It is important to note that for market value purposes, it does not matter whether these predictions are ultimately correct or woefully short-sighted. What matters is the consensus in the market as this determines market values.

About five years ago, there was a trend of companies moving from arbitrary corporate planning forecasts to the use of forward price strips such as New York Mercantile Exchange (NYMEX) Sweet Light Crude forward contracts based on West Texas Intermediate (WTI) crude oil. Hedging had become more common such that companies were often realizing strip prices. There appeared to be consensus about long term prices, as the end of the forward strip tended to regress towards a mean.

In Fig.3, the thicker spiky line shows the WTI spot price. Thin lines show the NYMEX forward strip for the first day of each quarter. Note the tendency of the NYMEX futures curves to be rising when the spot price is low, and falling when the spot price is high. Longest dated NYMEX prices were confined to a relatively narrow band. The

Fig.3 Daily spot WTI with NYMEX Sweet Light Crude forward contract strips at the start of each quarter, January 1996 to December 2002

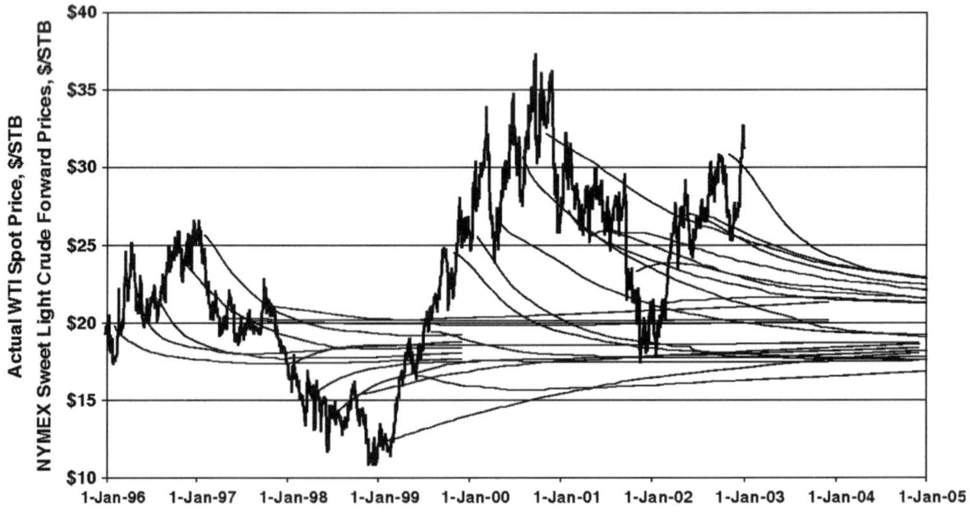

Fig.4 Spot WTI and that day's longest dated NYMEX Future Prices, for the first business day of each month. Nominal $ is quoted price, 'Real' $ are deflated using 2 per cent annual inflation for the period to the longest date

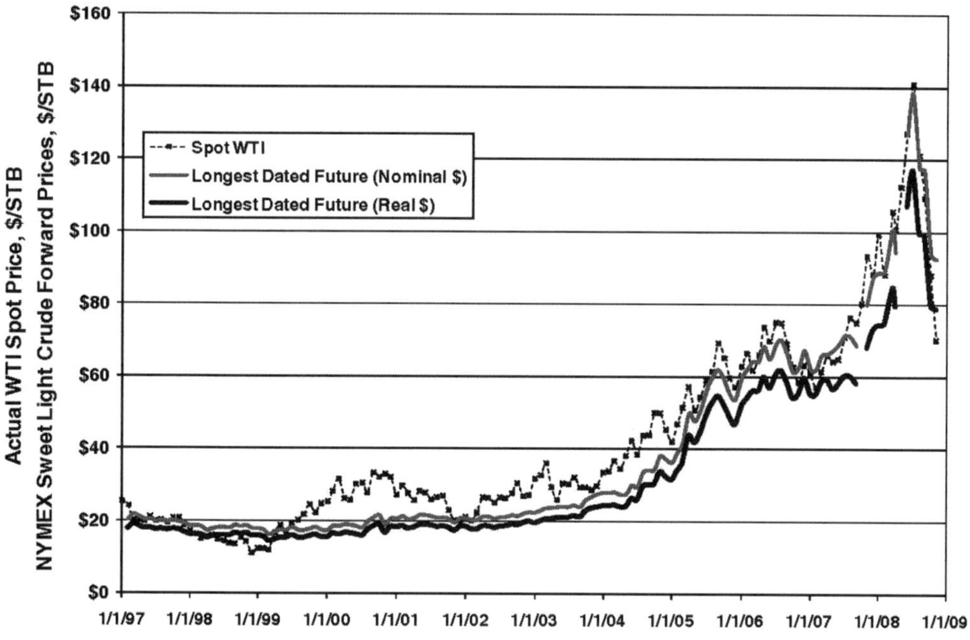

consistency of the longest dated futures prices until 2003 is shown in Fig.4.

More recent history has demonstrated that there is no longer the same stability in the futures strip (Fig.4). A gradual rise in the long-term price started in 2003, and accelerated in 2005. The longest dated futures have more recently mirrored the volatility in spot prices. It is argued that the volatility in long-term price outlook is real and is accompanied therefore by real volatility in asset values. If true, the effective date of a valuation becomes very important. The forecast (future strip) from that date should be used even if current forecasts are substantially different.

Beyond the strip, it is argued that a neutral and justifiable approach is to maintain prices flat in real terms. Thus, prices beyond the strip are escalated at the assumed US$ inflation rate. As an aside, it is interesting to note that despite record oil prices in 2008, for the most part the NYMEX strip continued to show declining nominal oil prices for the duration of the strip. This backwardation is counter-intuitive if the cause of the record prices was fear of future demand significantly outstripping supply. Indeed since mid-1999, the longest dated future contract has consistently implied falling real prices.

11. Issues in DCF analysis: Inflation and foreign exchange rates

The effect of inflation on product prices is assumed to be incorporated into the price forecast expressed in money of the day. Estimates of future costs are assumed to be provided in current money, and so an inflation adjustment is required. The alternative (deflating revenues and discounting at a real rather than a nominal discount rate) still requires an explicit inflation forecast. Explicit inflation forecasts may (with appropriate justification) vary through time, in which case a single real discount rate cannot be employed. One area where this may be important enough to incorporate is the observation that significant real increases in oil and gas prices may be accompanied by significant real increases in the cost of oil field services and equipment. The converse may be true for real price decreases. This dampens the impact of price swings in both upside and downside cases.

Foreign exchange and local inflation rates are required if there are significant elements of the cash flow denominated in a local currency. Two approaches are possible. With no change in purchasing power, future exchange rates are determined by differential inflation. There will be no difference between the results of carrying out the analysis in local currency with local inflation and, say, US$ and US$ inflation. No local exchange rate/inflation forecast is required. The second approach (recognising future changes in purchasing power) requires a forecast.

12. Issues in DCF analysis: Discount rates

It is assumed that any project adds value to a firm if the internal rate of return (IRR) exceeds the firm's weighted average cost of capital (WACC). In these circumstances, the NPV calculated from DCF analysis using the WACC as the discount rate will be positive. This sum equals the surplus cash generated over and above the return on capital required, adjusted for its time value. A firm is supposed to be indifferent in carrying out the project or having the NPV in the bank today and investing in different projects. Note that the cash flows are not assumed to be risk-free in this approach. The perceived risk is priced into the cost of equity component of the WACC. The return on equity required by investors in a firm with one single risky asset should completely account for all risks associated with the cash flows. The value obtained by discounting at the WACC that includes that return on equity should require no further adjustment for risk.

Although theoretically sound, there are practical difficulties in determining WACC, particularly for private companies. A more intractable problem is that the capital structure of a company may reasonably be expected to vary through the asset life cycle.

It is unlikely that a pure exploration company will have access to corporate debt. If successful, however, it will undoubtedly attempt to finance a development with as much debt as the quality of the asset allows. However, it is argued that the WACC of the owner is not relevant in the determination of FMV. What matters is the discount rate used by the market. This will be either the discount rate used by the highest bidder (the lowest discount rate in the market, other things being equal) or some generally accepted discount rate used throughout the industry.

A consensus industry standard is appropriate. The recent SPEE survey results showed that 71 percent of respondents used a cost-of-capital discount rate in the range 9 percent to 11 percent, with an average of 10.4 percent. It appears that 10 percent is the rate most frequently quoted since (a) US companies are required to report Standardized Measures of Oil and Gas (SMOG) values to the Securities Exchange Commission (SEC) using a discount rate of 10 percent and (b) it approximates to US companies' after federal income tax WACC.

The practice of using a higher discount rate to account for risk is widespread but not pervasive; 48 percent of SPEE respondents used a higher Risk Adjusted Discount Rate (RADR) to account for a profit or expected rate of return for the buyer, and any risk/uncertainty that the evaluator may choose to impute to the asset. There are two variations to this approach, used about equally. One group used the RADR to account for all risks, including reserves' uncertainty. The second group used the RADR for all risks excluding reserves' uncertainty, for which they used reserve adjustment factors. These are fractional multipliers used to reduce the reserves or value for different categories of reserves. Their use was explored in the earlier section on subsurface evaluation. The mean RADR for the first group was 12.9 percent. The mean RADR for the second group was higher, 15.3 percent, despite the fact that this group had already applied a fractional multiplier to reduce the values. This illogical result is attributed to the arbitrary nature of this approach.

There are several problems with increasing the discount rate to account for risk. Firstly, the relation between discount rate and present value is nonlinear and the method has some intuitively inappropriate effects. Secondly, attempts to quantify the higher rate are entirely arbitrary. This is apparent not only from the RADR survey data, but also from attempts to justify the rates in the literature. Thirdly, it does not provide a value system consistent with behaviour.

Fig.5 is a plot of NPV v discount rate for success cases for three large gas projects. Measured by the NPV at a 10 percent discount rate (NPV10), Project A has the highest NPV10 but the lowest IRR (the discount rate at which NPV equals zero). The development is to supply an LNG facility and is characterised by a long delay to

Fig.5 NPV v Discount Rate for three success case gas field developments

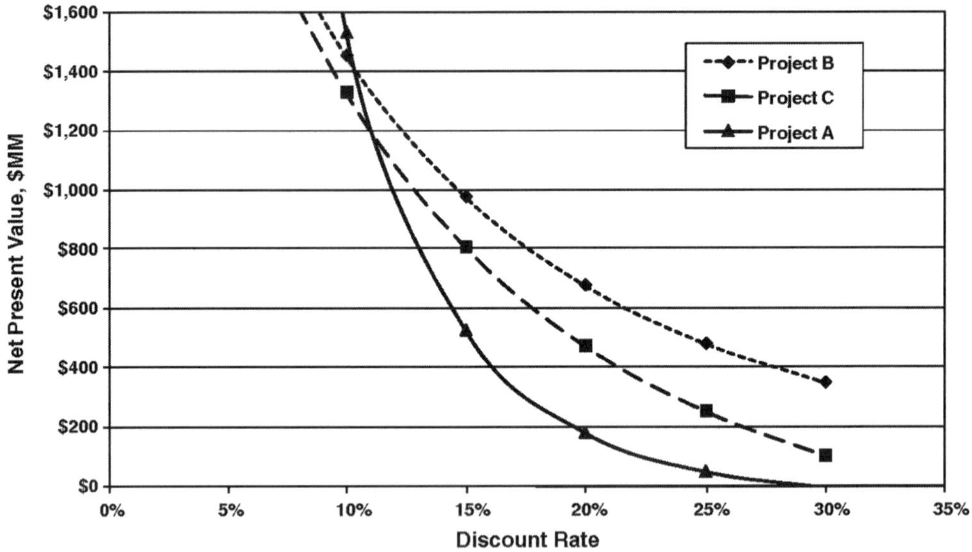

development sanction and a long, flat production profile. Project B is an onshore development in a spot market. The production profile has a rapid rise to a much higher plateau rate (as a proportion of reserves) and then a very rapid decline. Moreover, early cash flow covers much of the incremental development costs. The NPV10 of Project B is 5 percent lower than that of Project A, but the IRR is dramatically higher (off-scale on the plot at 130 percent). This very large value is a reminder of a more general problem with IRR as a measure. The return on investment of a project only equals the IRR if all the proceeds are re-invested at that rate. If, for example, the excess cash flow is re-invested at the marginal rate for other projects (the WACC), the resulting growth rate of return is 31 percent. Project C is a hypothetical offshore project, identical to Project B except that the development drilling and most of the spending on facilities are accelerated to occur prior to production startup. The resulting NPV10 is lowered, but only by 9 percent, but the IRR drops dramatically to 35 percent, and the growth rate of return drops, although less dramatically, to 17 percent.

At a 15 percent dscount rate, Project A's NPV has dropped by two-thirds, but those of Projects B and C have dropped by much less, 33 percent for Project A and 39 percent for Project C. If the 15 percent discount rate is being used to account for comparable levels of, for example, surface risk, the impact should affect each comparably. Here, it affects A much more than B or C. This is because the impact is a function of the particular shape of the cash flow profile, a characteristic that has little to do with surface risk or subsurface risk. Indeed it may be argued that the subsurface risk in Project A is likely to be less than that in Project B because of unusually high level of reserves' certainty required to support or finance an LNG project. The use of a higher discount rate simply introduces a bias against long-lived projects, which is not only unwarranted, but also counter-productive. The disparity increases with discount rate — note that at a 30 percent discount rate, Project A has a negative value (its IRR is 27 percent), Project B's NPV30 is 24 percent of its NPV10 and Project C's NPV30 is 8 percent of its NPV10.

The proponents of the use of higher discount rates argue that some decision-makers make decisions based on higher discount rates and this logically dictates valuing them at the higher discount rate. This is misleading. In the author's experience, decision-makers expect, based on history, projects to underperform against evaluation scenarios. They attempt to compensate by setting higher hurdle rates. A much better approach is to demand more realistic projections for project timing, costs and technical performance. Note that there is no evidence that the same decision-makers are attempting to incorporate surface risk by using higher hurdle rates.

13. The Disparity between EPV and FMV

Despite the issues discussed above, present values derived from DCF analysis are widely accepted evaluation yardsticks. Experts' detailed reports containing these analyses, usually with precision that cannot be justified by the underlying uncertainties, are required and accepted by stock exchanges and tax authorities as well as arbitration panels and courts. However, these reports, at least for stock exchanges, generally feature a prominent disclaimer that the results do not represent an opinion as to the market value of the property.

Analysis of transactions involving exploration and production assets shows a substantial difference between FMV and EPV, usually a discount and frequently a large discount. This may be explained as the application of a fractional multiplier, either to the underlying cash flows or the EPV itself or the use of a higher discount rate. An early quantitative approach to valuing interests at substantially less than EPV came from competitive bidding analysis. Because of the significant uncertainties in exploration risk and resource estimation, different evaluators will often generate substantially different results. It may be assumed that the true value is best estimated by the average of a set of independent unbiased estimates. In any competitive bid situation, therefore, the highest bid will be an overestimate compared to the true value. Competitive bidding models were developed to determine an appropriate fraction of the EPV to bid to avoid 'winner's curse'. The limitation of this approach is that it presumes that the true EPV is the true value to the owner. Any valuation system must be able to account for observed behaviour. A particular characteristic of oil and gas company behaviour is the frequency with which companies deliberately limit their WI of less than 100 percent. The reduced risk of total failure from participating in five identical but independent prospects with a 20 percent WI compared to the one with 100 percent WI is quantifiable (17 percent v. 70 percent for a 30 percent chance of success). However, the EPV of both holdings are identical. For any given single asset, maximum value occurs at 100 percent WI. Moreover, the same is true if the EPV is reduced by an arbitrary fractional multiplier or a higher discount rate.

The behaviour is due to risk aversion. An intuitively acceptable technique that explains these behaviours is available from preference theory. Risk adjusted values (RAVs), derived from present value calculations using an exponential utility function, provide a value system that incorporates risk aversion. The method also predicts a WI that maximises value. This is frequently, but not always, less than 100 percent.

A feature of early work on applying RAV to oil and gas interests focused on defining the firm's RT(Risk Tolerance), which proved to be difficult or at least

Fig.6 RAV v WI for a variety of RTs

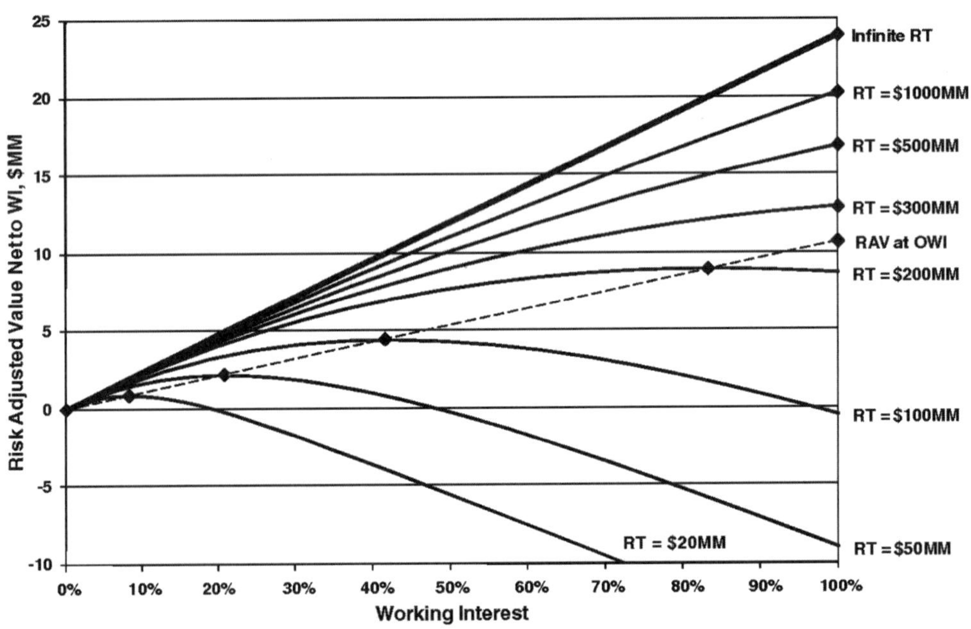

inconsistent. This is, with hindsight, intuitive. Firms have different levels of enthusiasm for different types of projects independent of any particular project EPV. This is reflected in substantial variation in RT depending on the nature of the project and its location. This is partly to compensate for surface risk, and partly to reflect the firm's strategic focus (preferred types and locations of projects). It explains why large firms will totally ignore small opportunities that would clearly be attractive if the only consideration was the firm's financial RT. By setting rigorous strategic requirements to concentrate on specific core areas or core activities, the firm is setting a much higher RT for those activities. Conversely, the behaviour of some large firms in some theatres is consistent with an extremely low RT.

A powerful feature of the method is that if it is assumed that the firm's WI is at OWI, both RT and RAV may be determined. It may be argued that firms do not fine-tune their WIs, and factors beyond their control contribute to the initial WI level. This is true, but the error in the assumption is believed to be within the accuracy of value determinations generally. When WIs become significantly different from OWI, firms acquire or divest interests. Indeed the corollary is that acquisitions and divestments of interests are driven entirely by changes in OWI (as EPV evolves or following a change in strategic direction and thus RT).

A valid criticism of using RAV as a proxy for FMV is that the method is not in widespread use. Instead firms rely on the experience of the decision-makers to

Fig.7 Cumulative RAV of a portfolio of prospects. Gray area indicates additional value above the sum of the individual prospects

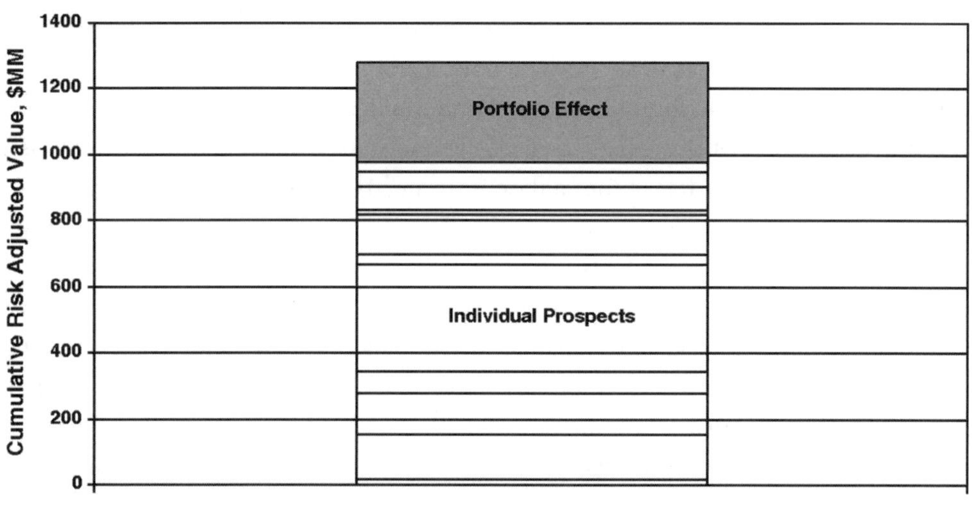

determine the preferred WI and the appropriate discount to EPV. This author's limited experience has been that these decisions and valuations are nevertheless consistent with calculated RAV, in line with other research in this area.

15. Portfolio effect

A further benefit of the RAV approach is that it can be used to explain the value of a portfolio. The EPV of a portfolio is the sum of the EPV of its constituent projects. However, the RAV of a portfolio is greater than the RAV of the constituents. This is because the value is dominated by the product of the chance of failure and the cost of failure. The overall chance of total failure of the portfolio is much less than the chance of failure of each component, while the overall cost of failure remains constant.

The method is approximate because it requires a single overall RT. The example shown in Fig.7 uses the average RT for all portfolio members. It can be argued that the value of an individual project should be calculated as the difference between the portfolio with the project and the portfolio without the project, rather than the stand-alone project RAV. However, the difference may not be significant when compared with the uncertainty in the underlying analysis.

16. Problems with an RAV approach

The traditional application of RAV, assumed above, is based on a simple lottery with all successful outcomes represented by the mean success case. This is a simplification but is appropriate where risk averse behaviour is dominated by the desire to avoid total loss, as in a dry hole in exploration. Setting the chance of failure to zero in this formulation yields an RAV equal to the EPV.

The failure of this measure to account for the underlying uncertainty (the underlying probability distribution of the value of successful outcomes) has been raised but has not attracted any attention, as far as the author is aware. However, it becomes crucial if the concept of RAV is to be extended to projects where there is considerable uncertainty but no significant likelihood of total loss.

A very simple approach is to assume a normal distribution of value. The RAV is then the EPV minus a discount equal to the variance of the underlying distribution divided by twice the RT. The formula is simple yet accurate, but its use is limited to situations where a normal distribution is realistic, possibly approached only by very mature fields. Development projects are usually characterised by lognormal distributions. Work continues on the search for a simple yet robust approach for these more complex distributions.

A further difficulty with this expanded approach is that the risk discount is independent of WI, and so RT cannot be determined from the data. Guidelines for RT have been suggested for exploration projects. At present the author is unaware of any systematic studies relating the ratio of FMV to NPV to the underlying variance for development and production assets. This would provide the basis for guidelines. Since RT varies between groups of exploration projects within a firm, it may be expected to vary between groups of assets in later life cycle stages. There may also be differences between classes of projects based on their position in the life cycle.

17. Application of EPV, RAV and FMV in expert determinations

If EPV and RAV can be determined, it raises some interesting questions about their application, particularly in expert determinations. The author is not a legal expert and this is not intended to be a legal opinion.

For a fair trade to occur, the Buyer's RAV must be greater than or equal to the Seller's RAV. Since an actual transaction takes place, the FMV is the Buyer's RAV and the Buyer's RT may be determined. The Seller's RAV and RT remain undetermined but are largely of academic interest. For identical EPV, the Seller's RT must be less than the Buyer's.

One may be required to determine FMV where there is no actual fair trade. This might be for valuation purposes for an intra-company transfer or as part of dispute resolution. The expert determines the 'Seller's' RAV and the Seller's RT is also determined. However, the hypothetical Buyer's RAV is likely to differ from the Seller's RAV. From here, there are perhaps two valid approaches.

The first argument is that the FMV is the Seller's RAV (since the latter is the minimum Buyer's RAV). Any incremental value is speculative because there is no direct evidence that a Buyer with a higher RT exists in the market. It is noted that there is no 'winner's curse' overbid possibility because the existence of a Buyer with an EPV exceeding that of the expert is also speculative. This argument offers the advantage that the FMV is not subjective because the RAV is determined explicitly. However, it fails to take into account the market information.

The second argument is that the FMV is different from the Seller's RAV and the issue to be determined is the Buyer's RT (since the expert's EPV applies equally to both). Although this appears speculative, it mimics the determination of FMV using comparable transactions. Comparable transactions will have been priced according to the RT of active buyers in the market, and may provide cmpelling evidence of Buyers' RT.

A weaker argument in the absence of comparable transaction data is to estimate RT based on the nature of the project and the likely range of Buyers' RT using guidelines. In either case, it should be noted that the FMV could be less than the Seller's RAV if the Seller's RT is the highest in the market. Thus, the likelihood is that the FMV so determined exceeds the Seller's RAV, but this is not necessarily so. This is an improvement on the previous approach which ignored the market, but becomes more subjective as the availability of good market data diminishes.

Finally, it should be noted that the EPV is the best estimate of future economic performance taking into account the time value of money. FMV (whether or not it is determined using the RAV approach) represents the exchange of a risky future cash flow for certain cash today. To the extent that firms are risk averse, FMV will therefore be at a discount, and perhaps a substantial discount, to EPV. It is not necessarily appropriate to equate lost or damaged economic performance with FMV. If an EPV is required, several of the FMV assumptions may require revision (WACC, business plan considerations). In the determination of FMV, these were taken to be those of the market, not the owner. Experts require careful instruction on the proper analysis to undertake, based on a legal opinion of what is appropriate.

나. 정치적 위험

Christopher M. Blanchard, *Iraq: Oil and Gas Legislation, Revenue Sharing, and U.S. Policy* (Congressional Research Service,[62] Nov. 3, 2009)

Summary

Development in Iraq's oil and natural gas sector is proceeding, in spite of continuing delays in agreeing to hydrocarbon sector and revenue sharing legislation to define new terms for the management of the country's significant oil and natural gas resources. Both the Bush Administration and the 110th Congress considered the passage of oil and gas sector framework and revenue sharing legislation as important benchmarks that would indicate the Iraqi government's commitment to promoting political reconciliation and providing a solid foundation for long-term economic development in Iraq. Obama Administration officials and some Members of the 111th Congress have expressed similar views. In the absence of new Iraqi legislation, interim revenue sharing mechanisms have been implemented, while both the national

62) CRS는 우리나라 국회 입법조사처에 해당.

government and the Kurdistan Regional overnment have signed oil and natural gas contracts with foreign firms.

The central importance of oil and gas revenue for the Iraqi economy is widely recognized by Iraqis, and most groups accept the need to create new legal and policy guidelines for the development of the country's oil and natural gas resources. However, Iraq's Council of Representatives (parliament) has not taken action to consider proposed legislation to date because of ongoing political disputes. In September 2009, U.S. Ambassador to Iraq Christopher Hill predicted that proposed legislation would not be considered prior to national elections planned for early 2010. The chairman of the Iraqi parliament's oil and gas committee also recently expressed doubt that the legislation will be considered by the current parliament.

Iraqi critics and supporters of various proposed solutions differ strongly on a number of key issues, including the proper role and powers of federal and regional authorities in regulating oil and gas development; the terms and extent of potential foreign participation in the oil and gas sectors; and proposed formulas and mechanisms for equitably sharing oil and gas revenue. Concurrent, related discussions about the administrative status of the city of Kirkuk and proposed amendments to articles of Iraq's constitution that outline federal and regional oil and gas rights also are highly contentious. In October 2009, the Council of Ministers prepared its proposed 2010 budget, which includes a deficit of more than $15 billion for the second straight year because of lower global oil prices and stagnant production and export levels in Iraq. Iraq is seeking a loan from the IMF to cover a portion of the expected 2010 deficit, as U.S. officials continue to warn that reduced Iraqi revenues and spending jeopardize investments needed to stabilize the country.

The military strategy employed by U.S. forces in Iraq has sought to create a secure environment in which Iraqis can resolve core political differences as a means of ensuring national stability and security. However, it remains to be seen whether proposed oil and gas legislation and ongoing interim efforts to development Iraq's energy resources will promote reconciliation or contribute to deeper political tension. U.S. policymakers and Members of Congress thus face difficult choices with regard to engaging Iraqis on various policy proposals, related constitutional reforms, and oil and natural gas development contracts, while encouraging Iraqi counterparts to ensure that the content of proposed laws, amendments, and contracts reflects acceptable political compromises. This report reviews policy proposals and interim contracts, analyzes the positions of various Iraqi political actors, and discusses potential implications for U.S. foreign policy goals in Iraq. See also CRS Report RL31339, Iraq: Post-Saddam Governance and Security, by Kenneth Katzman.

Contents

Background

Oil exploration and production in Iraq began in the 1920s under the terms of a wide-ranging concession granted to a consortium of international oil companies known as the Turkish Petroleum Company and later as the Iraq Petroleum Company. The nationalization of Iraq's oil resources and production was complete by 1975. From 1975 to 2003, Iraq's oil production and export operations were entirely state operated. However, from the early 1980s until the toppling of Saddam Hussein's government in 2003, the country's hydrocarbon infrastructure suffered from the negative effects of war, international sanctions, a lack of investment and technology, and, in some cases, mismanagement.

According to the Oil and Gas Journal, Iraq has 115 billion barrels of proven oil reserves, the world's third-largest. Other estimates of Iraq's potential oil reserves vary, and the U.S. Department of Energy's Energy Information Administration notes that current estimates "have not been revised since 2001 and are largely based on 2-D seismic data from nearly three decades ago." In April 2007, oil industry consultants IHS estimated that Iraq's proven and probable reserves equal 116 billion barrels, with a potential additional 100 billion barrels in largely unexplored western areas. The U.S. Geological Survey's median estimate for additional oil reserves in Iraq is approximately 45 billion barrels. In August 2004, Iraq's then-Oil Minister Thamer al Ghadban stated that Iraq had "unconfirmed or potential reserves" of 214 billion barrels. Iraq's current proven reserves are concentrated largely (65% or more) in southern Iraq, particularly in the southernmost governorate of Al Basrah. Large proven oil resources also are located in the northern governorate of Al Tamim near the disputed city of Kirkuk. (For a map of Iraq's oil resources, see Figure 1, below.)

At present, crude oil is the source of over 90% of Iraq's domestic energy consumption and oil exports generate over 90% of Iraq's government revenue. Declines in global oil prices from their 2008 high and reduced oil production led Iraqi leaders to amend their 2009 and 2010 revenue and budget assumptions from projected surpluses to projected consecutive $15 billion deficits. Official U.S. assessments stress that continued fluctuations in oil prices and production could jeopardize Iraq's fiscal stability and the sustainability of its reconstruction and development plans, with uncertain follow-on effects on stability. Current Iraqi plans call for the expansion of oil production to the level of 4 million barrels per day (mbd) by 2013 and then upward to six mbd by 2017. In support of those goals, Iraqi officials have opened an international bidding process for service contracts and renegotiated a series of Saddam-era oil production agreements, including the transformation of a production sharing agreement into a service contract for Ahdab oil field with China National Petroleum Corporation (CNPC).

Table 1. Key Oil Indicators

Oil Production (current weekly avg.)	Oil Production (pre-2003)	Oil Exports (current)	Oil Exports (pre-2003)	Oil Revenue (2007)	Oil Revenue (2008)	Oil Revenue (2009, to date)
2.50 million barrels per day (mbd)	2.50 mbd	1.96 mbd	2.20 mbd	$41 billion	$61.9 billion	$28.5 billion

Source: U.S. Department of State "Iraq Weekly Status Report," October 28, 2009.

Note: Oil export revenue is net of a 5% deduction for reparations to the victims of the 1990 Iraqi invasion and occupation of Kuwait, as provided for in U.N. Security Council Resolution 1483.

Recent Developments

On June 30, 2009, Iraq opened a long-awaited first bidding round for 20-year service contracts on six of its largest oil fields and two large, undeveloped natural gas fields. Iraq pre-qualified 41 international companies to participate in the bidding process. In the run-up to the bidding round, political scrutiny of Iraqi Oil Minister Hussein Al Shahristani intensified as members of Iraq's Council of Representatives (Parliament) voiced strong concerns about the terms of the contracts on offer and about Shahristani's management of the oil sector to date. Calls for a vote of no confidence in Shahristani were rebuffed, although the Oil and Gas Committee in parliament has moved forward with plans to question the minister, with a session scheduled for mid-November.

The first bidding round reflected international interest in and apprehension about the terms of potential investment in Iraq and prevailing political and security conditions. At the close of the bidding round on June 30, only one field bid had been accepted by Iraq's Oil Ministry. The joint bid by U.K. oil giant BP plc and China National Petroleum Corporation (CNPC) was chosen for the service contract for Rumaila, Iraq's largest oil field. Iraq's cabinet subsequently approved the proposed terms of the Rumaila bid and parliamentary leaders stated their desire to review any related contract before its signature. Bids for the other five oil fields on offer in the first round demonstrated wide differences in negotiating positions between international oil companies and Iraqi officials. Iraq sought per barrel service payments at far lower dollar-per-barrel levels than nearly all bidders were prepared to accept, in some cases bids exceeded Iraq's offered terms by ratios of up to ten to one. Subsequent negotiations between Iraqis and international oil companies reportedly have demonstrated some flexibility on both sides, as Iraqis relaxed some production expectations and companies agreed to lower per barrel terms. A consortium bid led by Italy's ENI reportedly was initialed on November 2, 2009, and will now be sent for review by the Iraqi cabinet. The bid, which includes U.S. oil company Occidental Petroleum, was amended to accept Iraq's original offer of a $2 per barrel remuneration fee, subject to taxation.

Iraqi officials, for both political and economic reasons, are seeking to maximize both the overall amount of production in order to meet planned expansion targets and increase the revenue that will accrue to the federal government to meet the country's considerable investment needs. Iraq's Federation of Oil Unions and its Southern Oil Company have publicly opposed the bidding process, and government officials appear to be seeking to address popular nationalist concerns about the participation of foreign firms in Iraq's energy sector. International investors are seeking contract terms that will balance the attractiveness of Iraq's relatively easy-to-produce, plentiful oil with persistent uncertainties surrounding the country's legal and tax regime and security conditions. These differences were also apparent during previous service contract negotiations over potential contract terms during 2008 and early 2009. The date for a planned second round of bidding is tentatively set for mid-December 2009, but may be delayed until early 2010.

The first bidding round took place in an atmosphere marked by several unresolved policy questions. Draft hydrocarbon legislation remains stalled in Iraq's Council of Representatives, without a pending resolution in sight. In September 2009, U.S. Ambassador to Iraq Christopher Hill predicted in testimony before the House Foreign Affairs Committee that proposed energy sector legislation would not be considered prior to national elections planned for early 2010.1) The chairman of the Iraqi parliament's oil and gas committee also has recently expressed doubt that the legislation will be considered by the current parliament.2) Iraqi critics and supporters of legislation proposed to date have differed strongly on a number of key issues, including the proper role and powers of federal and regional authorities in regulating oil and gas development; the terms and extent of potential foreign participation in the oil and gas sectors; and proposed formulas and mechanisms for equitably sharing oil and gas revenue. Concurrent, related disputes about the administrative status of the city of Kirkuk and proposed amendments to articles of Iraq's constitution that outline federal and regional oil and gas rights also remain highly contentious.

Disagreements between officials in the national government and the Kurdistan Regional Government (KRG) continue to flare concerning the legality and terms of each government's oil contracts with international investors (see "Interim Arrangements and Contracts" below). Although the national government has agreed to the export of some oil produced under KRG contracts with foreign firms, Baghdad maintains that the KRG is responsible for paying its foreign partners and that KRG contracts signed after February 2007 are considered "illegal" until reviewed and approved by the national Oil Ministry. KRG officials in turn argue that the Baghdad government is responsible for paying the foreign partners because the exports utilize national pipeline infrastructure and the oil ultimately belongs to the Iraqi people. In October 2009, KRG officials indicated that oil production for export in KRG territory would be halted until a resolution of the payment dispute is reached. KRG officials have criticized the national government's service contract bidding process as suboptimal from an economic point of view and have opened controversial negotiations for the potential future export of natural gas via the Nabucco pipeline.

Small-scale U.S. government efforts continue to encourage development of legal and regulatory frameworks for the oil sector and to offer assistance to improve Iraqi budget execution. However, major U.S. programs to assist in the rehabilitation and security of Iraqi oil infrastructure are reaching completion. According to the most recent report of the Special Inspector General for Iraq Reconstruction (SIGIR, issued October 30, 2009), "as of September 30, 2009, the United States had allocated $2.06 billion, obligated $1.92 billion, and expended $1.91 billion to rehabilitate the oil and gas sector in Iraq."3) The SIGIR has reported that Iraq's operational funds for its Oil Ministry have increased over 800% in 2009 to $950 million, while investment funds have remained roughly static at $2.2 billion. Both the SIGIR and the U.S. Department of Defense report that the security of Iraq's oil infrastructure has improved markedly since 2007 because of the introduction of an infrastructure protection system that includes several Pipeline Exclusion Zones (PEZs), many of which are in their final stages of construction.

Key Issues

Draft Hydrocarbon Legislation

A package of proposed hydrocarbon sector and revenue sharing legislation proposed in 2007 remains stalled amid ongoing disputes among Iraqis about broader political questions. The legislation would define the terms for the management and development of the country's significant oil and natural gas resources and was viewed by the Bush Administration and the 110th Congress as an important benchmark that would indicate the current Iraqi government's commitment to promoting political reconciliation and providing a sound basis for economic development in Iraq. Obama Administration officials and some Members of the 111th Congress have expressed similar views.

Compromises reached in early 2007 allowed the legislative package to move forward toward formal consideration by Iraq's parliament, but continuing disagreements about the relative powers of regional and national government authorities have precluded further progress in adopting the new laws. The legislative package preliminarily agreed to in 2007 included a draft hydrocarbon framework law that outlined a regulatory and policy development framework for future oil and gas exploration and production in Iraq. Three companion laws completed the package by establishing terms and mechanisms for revenue sharing, creating the Iraq National Oil Company, and reorganizing Iraq's Ministry of Oil. At present, it remains unclear whether Iraqi officials intend to consider the proposed legislation in its current form or whether they will renegotiate key elements of their original compromise. As noted above, some U.S. officials and Iraqi politicians have expressed doubt that the Council of Representatives will consider the legislation prior to planned national elections in early 2010. For more detailed analysis of the legislation proposed in 2007, see the Appendix.

The main points of contention among Iraqi politicians and citizen groups with regard to energy policy include the proper roles and authorities of federal and regional bodies, the terms and extent of potential foreign participation in oil and gas production and development, and potential formulas and mechanisms for equitably sharing oil and gas revenue. In addition, some Iraqi labor groups and elected officials have challenged the transparency and inclusiveness of legislative drafting and contract negotiation processes thus far. Some blocs within Iraq's Council of Representatives have opposed and/or attempted to significantly amend elements of proposed legislation and contracts to reflect their priorities (see "Players and Positions" below). Concurrent negotiations regarding constitutional amendments have had direct implications for the hydrocarbon legislation debate, particularly efforts to clarify the specific authorities granted to federal and regional governments to regulate oil and gas development and export activities under Articles 111 and 112 of the Iraqi constitution.

Overall, Iraqi, U.S., and other international observers have expressed concern that the violence and political tension that have prevailed in Iraq in recent years have not been conducive to careful consideration of detailed hydrocarbon sector legislation or new national oil and natural gas contracts. In 2008, the Chairman of the Council of Representative's Oil and Gas Committee reportedly decided that the committee will not proceed with a first reading of draft hydrocarbon legislation until the federal government and the KRG reach a political agreement on the management of the sector.4) The June 2009 U.S. Defense Department report on security and stability in Iraq states that "fundamental differences remain over federal and regional authorities in contracting and management of the oil and gas sector."5) As the campaign season for Iraq's 2010 national elections unfolds, candidates' positions on oil and natural gas related policy questions are likely to receive considerable scrutiny from voters, and candidates may be inclined to defend uncompromising positions to garner popular support.

Interim Arrangements and Contracts

In the absence of new oil legislation and regulation, both the Ministry of Oil and the KRG have moved forward with hydrocarbon sector investment and development processes. In turn, new national government and KRG contracts have contributed to the persistence of an atmosphere of political controversy surrounding the hydrocarbon sector, as each side has questioned the validity and wisdom of the other's agreements with investors. In spite of these conditions, several international companies have chosen to pursue investment opportunities in Iraq in an uncertain legal and political environment.

Kurdistan Regional Government (KRG) Contracts

In late 2007, the KRG finalized its own regional oil and gas investment law and signed new production sharing agreements with several international companies, including U.S.-based Hunt Oil.6) The KRG opposes proposals to require federal approval of its existing or future contracts, but notes that it is committed to revenue sharing as defined in the constitution and draft revenue sharing law. In September 2007, a State Department spokesman stated the Bush Administration's view that the KRG deals "elevate tensions between the Kurdish regional government and the Government of Iraq," and were not "particularly helpful" to the extent that they were hindering consideration of a national oil law.7)

Many Iraqi government officials have reacted negatively to the impasse between the national government and the KRG and have condemned the KRG's contracting activities. In November 2007, Oil Minister Al Shahristani warned international oil companies that the national government would not allow the export of oil produced under KRG contracts, and the export ban persisted until June 2009. 8) The Ministry of Oil has since refined its position slightly to emphasize its firm opposition to contracts signed by the KRG after February 2007, when the initial compromise on hydrocarbon legislation was reached between the KRG and Baghdad. According to Shahristani, contracts signed before February 2007 with firms currently producing oil for domestic consumption would be considered valid after review and potential amendments. In May 2009, the Oil Ministry agreed to allow the KRG to export a limited quantity of oil using the national oil pipeline infrastructure from two fields, Tawke and Taq-Taq, for which KRG contracts were signed prior to February 2007. Under the terms of the recent agreement, the revenue from the sales accrues to the national government, but a dispute has emerged over the compensation of the foreign partners in the production operations: Baghdad is insisting that compensation is the KRG's responsibility. The KRG announced in October 2009 that it intends to block further production from the fields for export purposes until the compensation dispute is resolved.9)

KRG officials have long accused Minister Shahristani of mismanaging the Oil Ministry and have consistently stated their opinion that the KRG contracts are constitutional, legal, and "in the best interests of Iraq."10) In January 2008, at least 120 members of the Council of Representatives from a wide range of political parties endorsed a joint statement underscoring their opposition to the KRG contracts.11) The cross-sectarian and cross-party opposition appears to be motivated by concerns about the production sharing model used in the KRG contracts and the precedent set by KRG demands for regional autonomy in oil and revenue decision-making.

Ministry of Oil Contracts

In an effort to improve the output of Iraq's currently producing oil fields, the Ministry of Oil opened negotiations with major international oil companies on two-year technical service contracts (TSCs), but decided in September 2008 to drop further negotiations. Potential partners reportedly included Royal Dutch Shell, Chevron, BHP Billiton, Anadarko, ExxonMobil, BP and Total SA. Under the terms of the TSCs, international firms would have provided technology, equipment and services to increase the total output of currently producing Iraqi oil fields by 500,000 barrels per day.12) The technical contracts reportedly were to be based on studies that international oil companies completed for the Iraqi government under the terms of existing memoranda of understanding.13)

Instead, Minister Al Shahristani has proceeded with licensing rounds for long-term service contracts in a number of oil fields. In January 2008, the Ministry launched a pre-qualification review process for potential international investors. Oil companies interested in bidding on oil extraction and service licenses issued by Iraq's national government were required to submit a pre-qualification form to the ministry's Directorate of Petroleum Contracts and Licensing by February 18, 2008.14) In March 2008, Minister Al Shahristani reported that approximately 150 companies had made submissions, and, by June 2008, 35 companies had been pre-qualified to bid for long-term service contracts.

The first bid round opened on June 30, 2009, and covered Iraq's main oil fields at Rumaila, Kirkuk, Zubair, West Qurna (Stage I), Bai Hassan, and Maysan, along with natural gas fields at Akkaz and Mansouriyah. According to Middle East Economic Digest, "although there was strong competition for phase one of the West Qurna field and the southern Zubair oil field, there was just one bid each for the Bai Hassan, Missan, Kirkuk and Akkas fields."15)

As noted above (see "Recent Developments"), only one bid originally was accepted by Iraqi authorities.a joint bid by BP plc and China National Petroleum Corporation (CNPC) for the Rumaila service contract. Cabinet approval is being sought for long-term contracts in the absence of a hydrocarbon framework law, and the cabinet reportedly approved the Rumaila bid in July 2009, paving the way for contract negotiations. The Federation of Oil Unions of Iraq and the Federation of Workers Councils and Unions in Iraq are protesting the bidding process in general and the Rumaila proposal in particular.

A second bidding round is scheduled for mid-December 2009 or early 2010 to include eleven discovered but currently non-producing fields, including the major fields at Halfaya, Majnoon, East Baghdad, and West Qurna (Stage II). Interest reportedly remains high in the proposed bidding round, although industry executives are watching intently for signals from Baghdad about its plans to negotiate service contracts for the remaining fields from the first round, perhaps by including them in a rescheduled second round for an earlier date. The misalignment of Iraq's proposed compensation fees and the bids offered by international oil companies in the first round suggested a need for serious consultation among Iraqi officials and between them and their prospective partners. Subsequent reported agreements with consortia for the Rumaila and Zubair fields indicated that some parties on both sides are willing to be flexible in the interest of reaching agreements.

Prospects for Revenue Sharing and Current Arrangements

Outside observers and Iraqi experts have emphasized the importance of proper oil revenue management and equitable oil revenue sharing as requirements for economic development and political reconciliation in Iraq. The Iraq Study Group recommended that oil revenue accrue to the central government and not to regions (Recommendation 28). This principle appears to have been included in the draft hydrocarbon framework and draft revenue sharing legislation, which would create central accounts for oil and gas revenues. Under the drafts, revenue sharing would reflect a population-based system for revenue allocation, with automatic monthly distributions to regional and governorate authorities. Potential obstacles to revenue sharing on those terms include the lack of recent, reliable national census data and uncertainty over the terms of communal representation on hydrocarbon policy decision making and implementation bodies.

Current revenue sharing arrangements are outlined in Articles 17 through 20 of Iraq's 2009 Budget Law. The budget prioritizes so-called "sovereign expenditures" for the Council of Representatives, the administration of the national Cabinet, the Ministry of Foreign Affairs, the Ministry of Defense, oil export production, and other national government functions. After these expenditures are provided for, 17% of the remaining budget is allocated to the Kurdistan Regional Government, and the rest is allocated for use by national ministries in other governorates on the basis of population percentages and specific needs. The law calls for the auditing of KRG government revenue to determine any funds that should be transferred to the national treasury and provides for the potential withholding of proportionate amounts of national budgetary funds from transfer to the KRG in the event of non-payment by the KRG of revenues due to the national government. Article 20 of the law states that the percentages of the budget allocated to the KRG and the governorates were to be "reconsidered" based on the results of a nationwide census to be held no later than December 31, 2009. As of November 2, 2009, no schedule for a nationwide census had been announced. ...

Oil Revenue and Security Concerns

Revenues from the sale of oil resources are the engine of Iraq's national economy and the lifeblood of its national budget. Iraq's state-owned oil production and marketing system ensures that revenue from the export and sale of Iraqi oil accrues to the Iraqi government, and the Iraqi people's elected representatives are now responsible for administering that revenue to meet the country's considerable development needs. The U.S. Department of the Treasury and the International Monetary Fund have expressed confidence that, over time, Iraq's oil revenues are likely to be sufficient to meet the country's development needs, if underlying conditions remain favorable for the expansion of oil production and if revenues are managed effectively. However, according to U.S., Iraqi, and international observers, shortcomings in Iraqi financial management capacity have prevented capital investment budgets from being spent effectively thus far and may continue to hinder reconstruction progress if left unaddressed. Changes in security conditions, Iraqi political reconciliation, and international supply and demand may affect the Iraqi oil sector's ability to fund Iraq's reconstruction over the medium to long term.

Revenues and Arrangements

Current Arrangements

Iraq's State Oil Marketing Organization (SOMO) remains responsible for the sale and export of Iraqi crude oil. Under the terms of United Nations Security Council resolution (UNSCR) 1483 (and renewed through subsequent Security Council resolutions), revenue from Iraq's oil exports is deposited into an Iraq-controlled account held at the Federal Reserve Bank of New York (FRBNY). Five percent of the funds are reserved for a United Nations Compensation Fund for reparations to the victims of the 1990 Iraqi invasion and occupation of Kuwait. The remaining 95% is deposited into a Development Fund for Iraq (DFI) account at the FRBNY and is then transferred to an Iraqi Ministry of Finance account at the Central Bank of Iraq for further distribution to Iraqi government ministries. Iraq has sought to reduce the percentage paid to Kuwait to 1%. However, as of October 2009, a proposal to channel paid reparation funds into joint investment projects has been rejected by Kuwaiti parliamentarians.

Under the terms of UNSCR1546 (and renewed by subsequent resolutions), the DFI is monitored by an International Advisory and Monitoring Board (IAMB), which provides periodic reports on Iraq's oil export revenue, Iraq's use of its oil revenues, and its oil production practices. According to the IAMB, as of December 31, 2007, $23.43 billion had been disbursed from the United Nations Compensation Fund; Iraq owed $28.95 billion to the Fund. In 2008, Iraq contributed an additional $3 billion. As of mid-2008, the IAMB estimated that "at the present rate of Iraqi oil sales, it would take approximately 17 years for the compensation award to be fully paid." Significant declines in the price of oil since that time have likely altered that estimate, although the IAMB has not issued a revised date.

U.N. Security Council Resolution 1859 (December 22, 2008) extends the IAMB authority only until December 31, 2009, making reference to a 2009 "transition to successor arrangements" for the DFI and the IAMB, to Iraqi-led auditing processes. In October 2006, the Iraqi cabinet approved the creation of an oversight body known as the Committee of Financial Experts (COFE) to monitor oil revenue collection and administration. The president of the COFE inaugurated its activities in April 2007, and it currently is working alongside the IAMB on audit procedures. The establishment of an audit oversight committee for the DFI and oil export revenues is a structural benchmark under Iraq's Stand-by Arrangement (SBA) with the International Monetary Fund currently satisfied by the extension of the IAMB arrangement and the creation of the COFE. The signing of the SBA was a requirement for Iraq's debt reduction agreements with the members of the Paris Club. In April 2009 the IAMB stated that Iraq's Committee of Financial Experts "is ready and capable to succeed the IAMB and conduct competent and independent oversight of the DFI." A similar finding was reported to the UN Security Council in August 2009.

Immunity provisions contained in standing UN Security Council resolutions prevent Iraqi funds deposited in the DFI from being subject to property attachment motions in lieu of legal judgments rendered against the former Iraqi regime. President Bush issued a continuation of the U.S. legal protections for the DFI and other Iraqi assets under Executive Order 13303 through May 20, 2009, and President Obama extended the protections through May 2010. Article 26 of the U.S.-Iraq security agreement commits the United States to continue to assist Iraq with its request to the UN to extend related protections for energy proceeds and the DFI.

Oversight of Oil Production and Revenue Management

From its creation in May 2003 through December 31, 2007, the DFI had received over $121.7 billion in oil proceeds and other deposits. Audit results found that an additional $58.8 billion in net export proceeds were received in 2008. Periodic audits conducted under the auspices of the IAMB have routinely found irreconcilable discrepancies in oil production and export figures and DFI account receipt and distribution amounts. A lack of reliable oil output measurement has proven to be a fundamental and persistent problem. Oil production and exports were conducted without metering equipment throughout the Coalition Provisional Authority (CPA) period. A May 2007 GAO report confirmed that reliable metering in Iraq's oil fields remained lacking and contributed to the lack of reliable data on Iraq's oil production and related revenue. A January 2008 IAMB report stated that Iraq's Ministry of Oil "does not have in place a full operational loading and metering system at production and loading points in order to determine produced and loaded quantities [of oil] accurately." A June 2008 IAMB report confirmed that "some metering has been installed at oil terminals, but there continues to be no metering in the oil fields." In August 2009, the UN Secretary General reported to the Security Council that "much remains to be done before a fully operational control and measurement system over oil production, distribution and export sales can be comprehensively implemented," and added that, "Indications from the Ministry of Oil point to implementation by 2011 at the earliest."

Completed financial audits through December 2005 found that "no comprehensive financial and internal controls policies and procedures manuals" were present in Iraqi ministries that were spending oil export proceeds delivered through the DFI system. On June 12, 2007, the IAMB released a statement on its 2006 findings, noting that the audits demonstrated that "the overall financial system of controls is deficient." The audits found that there was "no overall comprehensive system of controls over oil revenues," and that "basic administrative procedures" were "outdated and ineffective." These conditions may have facilitated the type of widespread corruption that has been alleged against a number of Iraqi ministries spending distributed oil export revenue, often associated with weak contracting and cash management policies. The IAMB's preliminary findings for 2007 recognized Iraqi government's efforts to respond to IAMB recommendations, but found that "the overall financial system of controls in place in the spending ministries, the U.S. agencies in respect of outstanding commitments using DFI resources, and the Iraqi administration of DFI resources remain deficient." The 2008 preliminary assessment, released in April 2009, concluded that "much remains to be done before a sound financial management system is operating effectively in Iraq." In July 2009, the IAMB stated that the completed 2008 audit, "continues to highlight key issues of concern regarding weaknesses in controls over oil extraction and use of the resources."

1) Testimony of U.S. Ambassador to Iraq Christopher Hill before the House Foreign Affairs Committee, September 10, 2009.

2) Ben Lando, "Oil laws not likely before January election" Iraq Oil Report, September 15, 2009.

3) Special Inspector General for Iraq Reconstruction (SIGIR), Quarterly Report to the United States Congress, October 2009.
4) U.S. Department of Defense, Measuring Stability and Security in Iraq -June 2008, Report to Congress in accordancewith the Department of Defense Appropriations Act 2007 (Section 9010, P.L. 109-289), p. 3.
5) U.S. Department of Defense, Measuring Stability and Security in Iraq . June 2009, p. 4.
6) Bloomberg News, "Dallas Oil Company Approved to Drill in Kurdistan," September 10, 2007. The KRG law isavailable at http://www.krg.org/uploads/documents/Kurdistan%20Oil%20and%20Gas%20Law%20English_2007_09_06_h14m0s42.pdf.
7) U.S. Department of State Daily Press Briefing, Tom Casey, Deputy Spokesman, Washington, DC, September 28, 2007.
8) Platts Commodity News, "Iraq's Shahristani Says Hydrocarbon Law not Expected Soon," November 15, 2007.
9) KRG Oil Minister Ashti Hamrawi reportedly stated that the KRG and the companies operating the fields, "have jointly agreed that no free oil will be pumped for export, and payments have to be made. We will only resume exports with guaranteed payments." Nassir Shirkhani, "KRG stops oil exports," Upstream, October 16, 2009.
10) Ben Lando and Alaa Majeed, "Load 'em up: fields in Iraqi Kurdistan begin," Iraq Oil Report, June 1, 2009.
11) Ned Parker, "Iraqi Political Factions Jointly Pressure Kurds," Los Angeles Times, January 14, 2008; and, UPI, "IraqFactions Join Against Kurd Oil Deals," January 15, 2008.
12) Mariam Karouny, "Oil firms line up for contracts in Iraq," Reuters, March 1, 2008.
13) Vahe Petrossian, "Iraq Opens Door to Foreign Input," Upstream, March 28, 2008.
14) Faleh al Khayat, "Iraq Prepares Oil Licensing Round Without Federal Oil Law," Platts Commodity News, January 9,2008. An Arabic and English version of the form is available at http://www.oil.gov.iq/pcld.pdf.
15) Perry Williams, "A crushing blow to Baghdad's plans," Middle East Economic Digest, July 10, 2009.

노트와 질문

KNOC은 Kurdistan 주정부와 PSC를 체결하였다가 Iraq 정부로부터 blacklist에 올랐고 따라서 앞으로 Iraq 석유개발계약을 체결할 자격을 상실하였다. 사전에 이러한 위험을 최소화할 방안이 있었을까?

제 5 장

공동입찰 · 운영계약

1. 투자의 분산과 표준계약서의 개발

국제적인 석유 · 가스탐사프로젝트는 투자금액의 크기로 보나, 투자의 성격으로 보나, 이해관계당사자의 복잡성으로 보나 상당한 위험이 따른다. 이를 줄이는 방법 중 하나는 투자금액을 줄이고 투자조건을 명확히 하는 것이다.[1] 따라서, NOC와 특정 block의 탐사개발을 위한 계약을 체결한 IOC는 계약체결 직후부터 또 다른 투자자들을 구하며 이는 또한 NOC가 원하는 바이기도 하다. 그리하여 실제 탐사가 시작하는 단계에 들어가면 거의 예외없이 탐사를 위한 투자자 컨소시엄이 구성되며 이들간의 관계를 규정한 공동운영계약이 체결된다. 물론 NOC에의 입찰단계에서부터 여러 IOC가 하나의 컨소시엄을 구성, 입찰을 준비하는 경우도 많다. 본 장에서는 IOC가 공동으로 입찰하거나 운영을 하는 경우 당사자간 법률관계를 살핀다. 공동입찰을 위하여는 컨소시엄계약을, 공동운영을 위하여는 공동운영계약("JOA")을 체결하므로 결국 이들 계약의 작성과 해석에 관한 논의이다.

한 가지 흥미로운 것은 많은 사업자단체에서 표준계약서를 개발하여 거래비용을 줄이고 계약서의 해석을 둘러싼 다툼의 여지를 줄이고 있다는 것이다. AIPN,[2] RMMLF,[3] AAPL,[4] CAPL[5] 등이 그 예로서 이들은 JOA를 비롯하여 여러가지 다양한 표준계약서를 제시하고 있

1) Stephen V. Arbogast, *Project Financing & Political Risk Mitigation: The Singular Case of the Chad-Cameroon Pipeline,* 4 TEX. J OIL & GAS ENER. L. 269, 273 (stake reduction과 terms clarification을 위험분산의 기술로 열거) (2008-09).

2) AIPN는 JOA, Accounting Procedure, Confidentiality Agreement, Lifting Agreement, Farmout Agreement, Service Contracts, Study and Bid Group Agreement, Unitization and Unit Operating Agreement 등 거의 모든 종류의 표준계약서를 가지고 있고 계속 수정하여 나가고 있다. http://aipn.org/ 회원에게 제공.

3) RMLLF 역시 계속적인 세미나와 표준계약서 개정작업을 하고 있다. https://www.rmmlf.org에서 회원에게 제공.

4) www.landman.org에서 JOA나 Master Land Services Contract 등을 제공.

5) www.landman.ca에서 Operating Procedure, Natural Gas Lease, Farmout and Royalty Procedure 등 출판물 목록정보 열람가능.

다. 물론 표준계약서는 하나의 샘플에 불과하므로 개개의 거래실정에 맞추어 수정되어야 하는 것이기는 하지만, 계약서 작성과 협상시 구체적인 논점과 대안을 제시하고 있으므로 이를 준비하고 마무리짓는 데 필요한 노력과 시간을 줄이는 데 커다란 도움이 된다. 표준계약서를 제시하려면 이달 단체내부의 합의가 필요한바, 합의가 쉽게 이루어지는 이유 중 하나는 몇 개의 사업자단체는 그 구성원이 공통된 이해관계를 가지고 있다는 것이며 학술단체의 경우에는 이들이 비교적 중립적인 입장에서 표준계약서에 이해관계의 균형을 유지하려고 노력하였기 때문으로 짐작된다.

처음부터 컨소시엄을 구성, 공동입찰을 통하여 탐사·개발권을 취득한 경우 물론 JOA가 필요하지만, 단독으로 탐사계약을 체결한 IOC가 제3의 IOC에게 자신의 지분을 매각한 경우에도 JOA가 필요하다. 따라서, 이 장에서 JOA 전단계로서 IOC간 지분의 양수도, 즉 IOC의 M&A도 논의하기로 한다.

이들 계약관계는 국제적인 거래당사자간 합의에 따라 형성되는 것이지만, 우리나라에서 동업관계에 관한 일반법이라고 할 수 있는 조합에 관한 법리와 비교하여 봄으로써 보다 그 실체에 대한 이해를 높일 수 있을 것이다. 그러나 일반적으로 조합은 보다 지속적이고 광범위한 사업을 위하여, 계약형 합작투자는 단기간 제한된 목적의 사업을 위하여 체결된다는 점에서 양자는 구별된다. 그런 이유에서 조합원간 권리의무는 공동사업자 상호간의 권리의무와도 구별될 것이다.[6] 광구공동운영(unitization)시에도 JOA와 유사한 관계가 형성된다. 어쨌든 우리는 JOA에 관한 판례가 없는 까닭에 동업관계나 다른 유사관계에 관한 판례를 살펴보는 것이 도움이 될 것이다.

2. 탐사이전단계: 공동입찰계약

여러 회사가 하나의 팀을 구성, 입찰에 응하고자 할 때 통상 컨소시엄계약이 체결된다. 우리나라에서도 특정산업에서 새로운 면허가 주어지는 경우 이를 대비하여 국내외 기업간 컨소시엄이 구성된 사례가 적지 않다.[7] 마찬가지로 국제적인 석유탐사개발권 입찰이 있는 경우 공동연구 및 입찰계약을 체결한다.

컨소시엄 구성단계에서 구성원 모두의 참여비율이 확정되어 있지는 않더라도 주된 구성

---

6) Robert Prichard, *The Use of Joint Ventures in FDI*, in ECONOMIC DEVELOPMENT, FOREIGN INVESTMENT, AND THE LAW 175, 180-81 (Robert Prichard ed. 1996)는 joint bidding agreement, production sharing agreement, joint operation agreement 등을 대표적인 계약형 합작투자의 예로 들고 있다.

7) 과거 제2이동통신이나 보다 최근 종편 및 보도전문채널면허가 그 예이다. 정부의 면허가 아니더라고 기업의 매각과 관련하여 하나의 기업이 매수대금 전부를 조달할 수 없는 경우 또는 여러 기업이 공동인수하면 시너지가 예상되는 경우 컨소시엄을 구성하여 입찰에 참여하기도 한다.

원과 그들의 참여비율은 정하여져 있어야 할 것이고 이 비율은 컨소시엄이 입찰을 준비하기 위하여 발생한 비용의 분담비율이기도 할 것이다. 입찰규정에 따라서 다르겠지만, 통상 입찰규정은 언제나 바뀔 수가 있는 것이기에 컨소시엄이 원하는 출자비율과 다르게 면허가 주어졌다고 하여도 컨소시엄은 이를 충족시켜야 할 것이다.

대법 2008. 2. 14. 선고 2006다18969 판결

2. 원심은, 그 채용 증거들을 종합하여 판시와 같은 사실을 인정한 다음, 건영의 회사정리절차를 관할하는 서울중앙지방법원은 정리회사의 재무구조를 개선하고 정리채무를 조기에 변제함과 아울러 새로운 지배주주를 확보함으로써 정리절차를 조기에 종결하기 위하여 정리회사의 관리인으로 하여금 M&A를 적극적으로 추진하도록 하여 왔고, 건영의 관리인도 정리법원의 방침에 따라 M&A를 추진하여 2002. 9. 5. 원고를 포함한 시데코-레마코 컨소시엄과 구속력 있는 이 사건 양해각서를 체결한 점, 이후 자산부채실사를 거쳐 최종 인수대금이 1,940억 원으로 합의되었으나 위 컨소시엄은 일부 구성원들의 탈퇴와 인수자금 조달의 어려움으로 투자계약을 체결하지 못하였고 이에 건영의 관리인은 그 체결기한을 당초의 '2002. 9. 30.까지'에서 '2002. 11. 5.까지'로 연장하였다가, 다시 '2002. 11. 12.까지'로 거듭 연장해 주었음에도, 위 컨소시엄 또는 이를 승계한 오현-레마코 컨소시엄은 계약금을 완납하지 못한 사실, 이후 건영의 관리인은 2002. 11. 18. 마지막으로 투자계약 체결기한을 2002. 11. 25.까지로 연장해 주면서 원고 등과 이 사건 부제소특약을 하였던 점, 이 사건에서 몰취된 이행보증금은 합의된 인수대금 1,940억 원의 5% 남짓에 불과하고, 이 사건 양해각서상으로도 '인수인의 귀책사유에 의하여 양해각서가 해제되는 경우 이행보증금은 발생이자와 함께 위약벌로서 정리회사에 귀속되는 것으로 한다'는 취지가 이미 명시되어 있었던 점, 원고의 주장과 같이 컨소시엄 구성원들이 분담하여야 할 이행보증금을 원고 혼자서 부담하였고, 컨소시엄 다른 구성원들의 탈퇴가 계약금을 마련하지 못한 원인이 되었다는 것은 컨소시엄의 내부적인 사정에 불과할 뿐이라는 점 등을 감안하면, 위 부제소특약이 선량한 풍속 기타 사회질서에 위반되는 법률행위라거나 원고의 궁박한 사정을 이용한 현저하게 공정을 잃은 법률행위라고 볼 수 없고, 달리 이를 인정할 증거가 없다고 판단하였는바, 관련 법리와 기록에 의하여 살펴보면, 원심의 위와 같은 사실인정과 판단은 정당하고, 거기에 상고이유로 주장하는 바와 같은 심리미진, 법리오해 등의 위법이 있다고 할 수 없다.

3. 탐사개발권 M&A 거래

탐사개발권 또는 이를 가진 기업을 M&A하려는 경우도 통상의 M&A와 크게 다르지 않다. 자산거래와 주식거래 각각의 장단점이 있다. 자산거래는 매수할 자산을 선별할 수 있고 따라서 인수후 잠재적 위험요소를 통제할 수 있는 반면 거래구조가 보다 복잡할 것이다. 계약문서의 복잡함이나 매도인의 이월결손금이 매수인에게 이용가능하지 않은 것도 자산거래의 단점이다. 특정 광구에 대한 탐사개발권을 인수하려는 경우 다른 공동운영자의 우선매수권이나 산유국 정부의 승인을 전제로만 가능한 경우가 대부분일 것이다. 주식거래는 거래구조는 비교적 간단한 반면 대상 기업이 보유하는 모든 자산을 인수하여야 함에 따르는 위험이 있다.[8] 또한 지배주주의 변경에 따른 다른 계약들의 갱개 내지 양도에 필요한 동의가 있을 수 있다.[9] 자산거래이건 주식거래이건 상대방 계약당사자 이외에도 정부의 인가나 제3자의 동의가 필요한지, 필요하다면 동의를 얻는 데 장애사유는 없는지를 점검하여야 할 것이다.[10]

오정환, 원유가스탐사개발권의 취득에 관한 법적 연구 40-48, 50-55 (2010 한양대학교 박사학위논문)

第 3 節 探査開發權의 M&A

Ⅰ. 序 言

2008년 세계경제가 派生金融商品의 危險으로 인해 크게 위축돼 原油가스探査開發權에 대한 去來가 많이 감소되었던 것이 사실이다. 세계경제의 침체로 多國籍石油會社들은 유동성확보에 많은 어려움을 겪을 수밖에 없었고, 이로 인해 探査開發事業이 다소 주춤할 수밖에 없었다. 信用度가 낮고 負債比率이 높아 외부자금조달이 어려운 中小石油會社들의 경우

8) Anthony Jennings, 주 4-12 상게서, 252-71 Sale and Purchase와 Farm-in 두 가지를 설명.

9) Geoffrey Picton-Turberville, *Oil and Gas Acquisition Agreements* in UPSTREAM OIL AND GAS AGREEMENT (Martyn R. David ed. 1996) 187, 190-94. 자산거래의 경우 탐사자료의 이전문제를 지적. 졸저, 기업인수 4G (2010)도 참조.

10) 에너지기업 내지 탐사권의 매수라고 M&A 실사사항이 다르지는 않겠지만 아무래도 해당 산업에 특수성에 대한 고려가 필요할 것이다. 실사에 관하여 Alex Ritchie/John Davis, *The Due Diligence Process and Its Impact on the Deal: A Primer on Bayoneting the Wounded* (Due Diligence in Oil and Gas Transactions) (RMMLF May 2011); W. Paul Loyd/Jane Fleck Romanov, *Business Overview of a Sale Transaction* (Oil and Gas Agreements: Sales and Financings) (RMMLI May 2006).

특히 資源開發事業의 어려움이 컸다고 볼 수 있다. 이에 따라 石油會社들, 그 중 中小石油會社들을 중심으로 그들이 보유하고 있는 비핵심의 探査開發權을 市場에 賣物로 내놓게 되었다. 이에 따라 探査開發權의 去來가 낮은 가격으로 이루어지게 되었고 中國 등의 일부國家에서는 賣物로 나온 探査開發權을 집중적으로 引受하는 노력을 기울였다. 이렇듯 일부국가에 편중되었던 探査開發權移轉에 대한 관심은 2009년 아시아開發途上國들을 중심으로 세계경제가 다시 살아나면서 보다 많은 國家와 國營會社들로 확산되었고, 에너지안보에 대한 경각심이 새롭게 조명되고 探査開發權의 重要性이 더욱 부각됨에 따라 대부분의 國家들과 대다수의 石油會社들은 探査開發權을 취득하기 위하여 다시 힘을 경주하고 있는 실정이다.

探査開發權은 앞서 살핀 바와 같이 資源保有國으로부터 原始的으로 취득할 수 있다. 그러나 原油가스에 대한 探査開發權이 100여 년 동안 여러 契約형태로 多國籍石油會社나 國營會社에게 부여되다 보니 원시적 취득의 기회가 점차 사라지고 있다. 이제는 探査開發이 비교적 손쉬운 육상이나 대륙붕 등의 많은 지역에서는 새로운 探査開發權을 취득할 만한 곳을 찾기 너무 어려워졌다. 그러다 보니 기왕에 발생한 探査開發權에 대한 去來, 즉 探査開發權의 M&A에 대해 관심이 모아질 수밖에 없게 되었고, 그에 대한 去來가 늘어나게 되었던 것이다. 최근 들어 이러한 探査開發權의 M&A 去來가 대폭 증가하고 있는 이유 중 하나를 원시적 探査開發權의 부족에서 찾을 수 있다. 中國의 CNPC, CNOOC, PetroChina, Sinopec 등과 같은 國營石油會社들은 政府의 적극적 지원에 힘입어 세계금융위기로 인해 資産價値가 폭락한 探査開發權이나 이를 보유하고 있는 石油會社의 持分을 적극적으로 引受하고 있다. 한국석유공사가 2009년 2월경 페루의 Petro-Tech의 50% 지분을 引受하고, 같은 해 말경 캐나다 Harvest Energy와 카자흐스탄의 Sumbo를 引受한 것과 2010년 11월 현재진행중인 英國石油會社 DanaPetroleum에 대한 敵對的 M&A도 같은 맥락에서 이해할 수 있다.

探査開發權을 賣渡하는 이유는 여러 가지 있을 수 있으나, 아무래도 探査開發에 많은 資金이 소요되고 그 危險이 적지 않기 때문에 자금부담과 투자위험을 줄일 목적으로 대부분 이루어진다. 반대로 探査開發權을 引受하는 이유는 資源保有國으로부터 직접 취득할 수 있는 探査開發權이 제한적이고 그런 상황에서 原油가스의 資源을 사전에 확보할 수 있는 유일한 방안이기 때문일 것이다. 일반적인 M&A의 動機처럼 引受의 時間節約, 危險分散, 租稅節減 등의 이유도 있을 것이다. 지금은 資源保有國들이 대부분 國營石油會社들을 보유하고 있고 자국의 原油가스田의 開發生産을 國營石油會社 중심으로 수행하는 것이 많다 보니 新規의 探査開發權을 취득하는 것이 극히 제한적일 수밖에 없다. 그러다 보니 資源이 부족한 國家들은 자국의 國營石油會社 또는 民間大型石油會社들을 통하여 자국에 필요한 原油가스를 사전에 확보하기 위해 探査開發權의 移轉取得을 도모할 수밖에 없게 되었다. 그리고 探査開發權의 移轉取得이 자국의 에너지安保에 매우 중요하기 때문에 대부분 特別法 등을 통해 이를 적극 지원하고 있다. 資源의 民族主義현상이 근래 더욱 뚜렷해짐에 따라 각국은 探査開發權획득을 통해 原油가스의 安保를 지키고자 하는 것이다.

探査開發權의 取得은 앞서 살핀 바와 같이 資源保有國 등으로부터 리스 또는 라이센스의 讓許, 政府參與의 合作投資, 生産物分配契約, 서비스契約 등을 통해 원시적으로 취득하는 방법이 있고, 다음으로 위와 같은 절차를 통해 探査開發權을 취득한 자로부터 그 전부 또는 일부를 事後에 移轉取得하는 방법이 있다. 전자의 방법은 앞서 살핀 바와 같이 資源保有國이 직접 또는 國營石油會社들을 통해 探査開發事業에 참여함으로써 상당히 제한적으로만 가능한 실정이고, 후자의 방법은 현재 세계경제침체로 인한 資産價値의 하락에 따라 비교적 활발하게 去來되고 있는 실정이다.

原油가스의 探査開發權을 M&A를 통해 移轉取得하는 방법으로는 크게 探査開發權의 전부 또는 일부를 직접 引受하는 資産引受의 방법이 있고, 探査開發權을 보유한 石油會社의 株式을 讓受하여 探査開發權을 간접적으로 취득하는 방법이 있으며, 探査開發權을 相互交換하는 방법이있다. 또한 國內에 비교적 알려지지 않고 제대로 활용되지 않고 있는 방안으로서, 探査開發權者가 farmor가 돼 farmee의 일정한 給付 또는 資金供與의 義務履行을 條件으로 探査開發權의 일부를 farmee에게 양도하는 farmout 또는 farmin의 방법이 있다.

한편 farmout에 의한 探査開發權取得이 M&A의 한 類型으로 분류할 수 있는지 여부에 대해 논의가 있을 수 있는데, farmout 給付履行후 探査開發權取得을 목적으로 하는 去來, 즉 資産의 讓受를 위한 去來라는 점에서 넓은 槪念의 M&A에 포함시켜 이해할 수 있을 것이다. 더욱이 給付履行후 farmee가 100%의 探査開發權을 취득하고 費用回收기간이 지난 뒤에도 farmor가 最優先로열티권을 포기하지 않는한 100%의 資産取得에 변화가 발생하지 않으므로 일반적인 M&A 類型인 資産讓渡와 다르지 않다고 본다. 또한 探査開發權 중심으로 特殊目的會社(special purpose company, SPC)가 설립되므로 探査開發權의 全部讓受는 會社의 讓受에 해당할 수도 있으므로 farmout去來를 M&A의 한 방식으로 보는 데 무리가 없다고 본다.

아래에서는 각각의 探査開發權移轉取得의 方法에 대해 장단점을 중심으로 그 特徵들을 살펴보고자 한다.

II. 探査開發權 M&A의 主要類型

1. 資産讓渡

探査開發權者의 探査開發權에 대한 資産配分의 構造는 일반의 投資資産에 대한 配分

構造와 크게 다르지 않다. 그러므로 探査開發權의 資産配分의 적정성은 주기적으로 평가하고 검토돼야 하고, 다른 投資資産과 마찬가지로 探査開發權의 일부 또는 전부를 매각 또는 매수하여 적정한 포트폴리오를 유지해야 한다. 이러한 去來의 必要性은 探査開發의 段階가 성숙하면 할수록 더욱 늘어나게 된다. 探査開發權 포트폴리오의 일환으로 資産讓渡가 이용될 수 있음은 물론이다. 앞서 논의한 바와 같이 探査段階의 資産讓渡거래는 開發生産段階보다 덜 빈번한 것이 사실이다. 그러나 探査段階의 資産引受가 여전히 그 필요성이 적지 않은 이유는 探査資産의 危險을 관리하는 한 방법이 될 수 있기 때문이다. 石油會社의 개별입장에 따라 달라질 수 있지만, 探査開發權의 50%를 양도하여 探査에 필요한 자금을 지출할 義務를 輕減하고자 할 수 있다. 논리적으로 보면, 探査鑛口의 일부가 生産鑛口의 처분에 도움이 되기 때문에 함께 처분되는 경우가있고, 반대로 도움이 되지 않아 生産鑛口 처분이전에 처분대상에서 배제하기 위해 探査鑛口의 일부를 처분하는 예도 있을 수 있다.

探査段階의 資産讓渡에 관한 契約은 生産段階의 資産讓渡에 관한 契約보다 단순하다. 관련資産의 價値가 크지 않을 뿐만 아니라 探査와 관련된 許可權의 수도 적고, 관련契約들의 條件과 內容도 많을 필요가 없기 때문이다. 그러므로 偶發的 責任의 문제도 적고 擔保나 免責관련구조도 상대적으로 단순하다. 그러나 단순한 구조에도 불구하고 때론 복잡한 문제를 야기할 수 있는데 多數의 資産을 동시에 讓渡하는 경우에 더욱 그러하다.

한편 生産物分配契約上의 探査開發權은 契約上의 地位로서 다른 資産의 성격과 다르기 때문에 契約上의 地位를 양도하는 방법으로 資産讓渡를 할 수밖에 없다. 政府와의 合作投資나 서비스契約上의 資産讓渡도 역시 契約上 地位를 양도하는 방식으로 이루어져야 할 것이다. 그러한 차이로 인하여 去來構造 또한 그 特性들을 반영하여 만들어져야 할 것이다.

2. 探査開發權의 交換

資産의 取得이나 處分시 賣買의 방법을 이용하여 대상鑛口에 대한 探査開發權을 讓受渡하는 것이 일반적이지만, 당사자의 의사에 따라 交換의 방법이 활용되기도 한다. 資産의 交換은 대체로 資産引受와 같은 契約內容으로 이루어지고 있지만, 통상 현금의 대가가 수수되지 않기 때문에, 당사자들의 權利나 義務, 擔保나 責任에 대한 規定들이 상호 동일하게 交換的으로 적용되도록 하는 특징을 갖고 있다. 양 당사자는 매도자인 동시에 매수인의 지위를 갖고 있고, 同一한 內容의 權利를 갖는 동시에 동일한 내용의 義務를 부담한다. 일방당사자가 부담하는 免責의 範圍나 擔保의 內容도 타방당사자에게도 동일한 내용으로 효력이 미쳐야 한다. 그러므로 양 당사자의 모든 契約上의 權利나 義務는 相互的이고 交換的일 수밖에 없다. 交換은 앞서의 상호교환적 특성 때문에 資産讓渡나 株式讓渡와 달리 협상이 용이하다. 資産讓渡나 株式讓渡의 경우에는 우월적 지위에 있는 어느 일방이 타방에게 무리한 내용의 權利나 義務를 강제할 여지가 있지만, 交換의 경우에는 상호교환적이기 때문에 그럴 가능성이 크지 않으므로 협상이 용이할 수밖에 없다. 그러나 交換의 경우에도 探查開發權 내지 관련鑛口의 권리하자정도, 우발채무의 발생가능성의 크기, 경제적 가치의 차이 등에 따라 어느 일방당사자가 보다 우월한 지위에서 협상을 진행할 수 있음은 물론이다. 交換對象의 探查開發權 및 관련鑛口의 경제적 가치에 차이가 있을 때에는 交換對象의 探查開發權에 대한 정당한 가치를 산정할 필요가 있고, 그 차액을 현금 등으로 정산토록 해야 할 것이다. 交換되는 資産들의 경우 그 본질적 성격이 探查開發權의 內容에 따라 상호간 상이할 수 있다. 예를 들어 라이센스를 내용으로 하는 探查開發權鑛口와 리스契約상의 探查開發權鑛口를 교환하는 경우 相互交換되는 資産의 性格이 판이할 수밖에 없다. 재산적 가치가 있는 權利라고 하여 모두 交換의 對象이 될 수 없는데, 生産物分配契約上 權利나 서비스契約上 일정生産物에 대한 특정權利는 교환대상으로 적합하지 않을수 있다. 交換은 두 개의 資産讓渡가 동시에 이루어지는 경우와 같다. 그러므로 實査에 들이는 努力이나 費用이 두 배가 됨은 물론 去來의 問題 또한 두 배가 되는 경우가 많다. 探查開發權의 制限이나 擔保(encumbrances) 등의 문제나 訴訟이나 偶發債務 발생가능성 또한 일반의 거래보다 두 배나 많을 수 있다. 앞서 살핀 바와 같이 交換對象의 探查開發權의 條件이나 內容에 차이가 많다면 그 조정의 문제로 인해 時間과 費用이 單純去來보다 두 배 이상 소요될 수 있다. 그런 측면에서 交換에 의한 探查開發權의 讓渡는 일반적으로 활용할 수 있는 去來構造로는 미흡한 점이 없지 않다.

3. 株式讓渡

石油會社가 探查開發權資産을 소유하는 경우 資産자체의 양도가 아닌 그 會社의 株式을 양도함으로써 探查開發權의 去來가 간접적으로 이루어질 수 있다. 株式讓渡방식에 의한 探查開發權去來는 주로 어느 한 會社가 여러 探查開發權을 보유하고 있을 때 그 會社를 處分함으로써 이루어진다. 물론 會社處分은 그 會社의 자산의 양도가 아닌 株式을 讓渡함으로써 이루어지게 된다. 어떤 會社의 株式讓渡가 이루어진다는 것은 그 會社가 讓受會社의 子會社가 된다는 의미를 갖는다. 그러므로 株式讓渡로 인해 讓渡會社의 資産이 간접적으로 讓受會社의 資産이 되는 것이다. 探查開發權 내지 관련鑛口 등 讓渡會社의 資産에 대한 處分은 讓受會社가 株式을 引受함으로써 실질적으로 이루어지게 된다. 株式讓渡가 資産讓渡의 대체거래방법이 되기 위해 극복해야 할 문제가 여러 가지 있다. 우선 會社가 讓渡對象의 資産 이외의 資産들을 보유하고 있는 경우이다. 이때 株式讓渡가 이루어지기 전에 관련없는 資産들을 모두 처분해야 한다. 이러한 去來방식은 복잡할 뿐만 아니라 과세문제도 뒤따를 수 있으므로 유의해야 한다. 그 외에도 株式讓渡로 會社에 대한 處分이 이루어질 때

讓渡會社의 資産뿐만 아니라 會社債務와 責任도 함께 移轉한다는 것을 기억해야 한다. 讓受會社의 입장에서는 債務와 責任까지 引受하는 것을 원치 않을 것이다. 그런 경우 별도의 會社를 세워 원치 않는 資産과 債務, 責任 등을 모두 引受하게 하고, 讓受會社가 원하는 資産만을 보유한 讓渡會社의 株式을 讓受함으로써 去來의 목적을 달성해야 할 것이다. 그러나 이와 같은 去來構造를 구성하여 이행하는 데에는 많은 복잡한 문제들이 뒤따를 수 있다. 우선 讓渡會社의 資産을 子會社에게 양도하고 그 子會社의 株式을 讓受會社에게 讓渡하는 방식으로 이루어지는 去來는 讓渡會社의 資産讓渡에 제한을 가하는 共同事業者의 優先買受權(preemptive right)을 회피하기 위한 방안으로 종종 활용된다. 대부분의 共同運營契約(joint operating agreement, JOA)에서는 子會社 등 關係會社에 대한 資産處分을 제한하지 않고 오직 제3자에 대한 資産處分만을 제한하고 있으며, 株式去來를 制限去來의 對象에서 排除하고 있다는 점을 참작하여 이루어지는 去來構造이다. 그러나 시간상 여유가 없다고 한다면 많은 시간이 소요되는 이러한 去來構造도 활용하기 어려울 수 있을 것이다. 株式讓渡는 探査開發權의 처분방식으로 매력이 크지 않은데, 특히 探査段階에 있을 때는 더욱 그러하다. 株式讓渡는 앞에서 살핀 바와 같이 偶發債務와 責任도 떠안을 수 있는 構造이기 때문에 資産讓渡때보다 더 주의를 기울여야 한다. 이런 이유로 去來節次가 보다 복잡하고 상세한 實査(due diligence)의 필요성이 크다. 그만큼 時間과 費用이 많이 소요되는 去來構造이고 이슈에 대한 체계적 분석이 요구된다. 그러므로 優先買受權의 회피수단으로 유용하다고 하여도 探査開發權 내지 관련鑛口의 처분방식으로 활용도가 높지 않다. 앞서의 사례에서 보았듯이 優先買受權을 회피하기 위해 부득이 이용할 수밖에 없는 경우에 한해 유용한 探査開發權의 처분방식이라고 할 수있다.

4. Farmout에 의한 讓渡

原油가스의 探査開發權을 讓渡하는 방법으로 farmout 契約構造가 있다. 나중에 자세히 살피겠지만, farmout은 探査開發權의 讓渡가 讓受人인 farmee가 일정한 義務를 이행하는 것을 先行條件으로 하여 이루어지는 특성을 갖고 있다. 거래대가로 現金이나 資産을 讓渡人인 famror에게 지급하지 않고, 오직 farmee가 farmout 契約에서 정하고 있는 探査 등의 給付를 이행함으로써 探査開發權을 취득하게 된다. 향후 farmee의 일정給付履行을 조건으로 探査開發權이 이전하지만, farmout 契約체결시점에 farmee가 대상광구의 점유를 이전받고 이에 대한 探査開發을 직접 수행한다는 점이 특이하다고 볼 수 있다. Farmout 去來는 앞서의 절차에 따라 探査開發權이란 資産을 취득하므로 일응 資産讓渡의 일종으로 볼 수도 있으나 去來節次나 方法이 일반의 資産讓渡와 다르므로 구별되는 去來構造이다.

이러한 構造적 특성으로 인해 farmout 去來가 다른 일반의 株式讓渡와 資産讓渡와 같이 賣買(sale and purchase)의 性格을 갖는지 아니면 매매와 전혀 다른 合作投資에 불과한 것인지에 대해 논의가 있다. 만약 資産讓渡와 같이 매매의 성격을 갖는다고 본다면 양도에 따른 세무적 효과가 따르고, 合作投資로서 지분의 투자방식으로 farmout 構造가 단순히 활용된다고 본다면 讓渡所得稅 등의 세무적 문제가 전혀 발생하지 않기 때문이다. 개별國家마다 차이가 있는데, 美國이나 캐나다는 farmout을 일반의 資産讓渡와 전혀 다르게 인식하여 讓渡所得稅 등의 세무문제가 야기되지 않고 있고, 반면 英國은 일종의 매매로 보기 때문에 讓渡所得稅 등 관련稅金이 발생한다.

Farmout 去來에서는 farmee의 探査井의 試錐가 farmee의 義務인지 아니면 探査開發權取得을 위한 단순한 條件인지 여부를 신중하게 판단해야 하고, farmee의 給付의 內容에는 구체적으로 무엇을 포함시킬 것인지 분명히 정해야 하며, 최종적으로 farmor가 讓渡하는 探査開發權의 구체적 범위 및 그 내용에 대해서도 면밀한 검토가 이루어져야 한다. 이러한 차원에서 farmout은 다른 去來類型과 구별되는 固有한 去來構造를 띠고 있다고 볼 수 있다.

5. 優先買受權

探査開發權의 移轉에 있어 가장 큰 危險 중 하나는 優先買受權의 존재이다. 優先買受權은 探査開發權의 일부를 보유한 共同事業者의 1인이 그 지분을 제3자에게 매도하고자 할 때 다른 共同事業者가 동일한 매도조건으로 우선 매수할 수 있는 權利를 의미한다. 優先買受權規定이 있는 경우 제3자에 대한 자유로운 지분매각이 어려워지므로 共同事業者의 持分讓渡의 自由를 제한하는 기능을 한다. 이러한 優先買受權은 통상 共同運營契約이나 共同入札契約의 양도규정에서 발견되므로, 探査開發權 去來 이전에 그 존재여부를 먼저 살펴야 한다. 일반적으로 共同入札契約은 향후 체결될 共同運營契約의 내용들을 요약하여 규정하고 있기 때문에, 優先買受權에 대한 요건들을 두기도 한다. 그러나 共同入札契約의 優先買受權은 共同運營契約이 효력을 발생해야 비로소 행사할 수 있는 것이 원칙이므로, 入札에 성공하여 探査開發權을 획득하였지만 아직 共同運營契約이 성립하기 이전이라고 한다면, 優先買受權의 제한없이 探査開發權의 讓受渡가 가능할 수 있다. 共同運營契約상의 優先買受權規定에 의하면 일반적으로 讓渡會社의 子會社 등 關係會社에 대한 讓渡를 허용한다. 그러나 제3자에 대한 양도는 共同探査開發權者들에게 양도조건과 더불어 양도승낙요청서를 보내야 한다. 그리고 共同探査開發權者들로 하여금 통상 30일 내지 60일의 기간 내에 동일조건에 따라 探査開發權 내지 관련資産을 讓受할 수 있는 기회를 부여해야 한다.

優先買受權이 존재하는 경우 그 적용범위를 확정하거나 특정去來에 대한 적용여부를 결정하는 데 많은 어려움이 있을 수 있다. 優先買受權의 대상이 되는 去來의 條件이 너무도 다양하기 때문에 이를 모두 포섭하여 優先買受權규정을 정할 수 없기 때문이다. 물론 문언의 의미가 너무 포괄적이기 때문에 본래 의도가 반영되기 어려운 경우도 있다. 예를 들어 探査開發權을 매도할 의사가 있는 때에는 共同探査開發權者들에게 通知를 한다는 규정이 있다고 할 경우 '賣渡할 意思'자체가 너무 抽象的이고 不確定한 概念이므로 통지의 기준시점으로 하는 데 많은 어려움이 있다. 引受會社와 협상도 제대로 되지 않고 去來條件도 합의된 바 없지만, 讓渡會社가 探査開發權을 양도할 의사가 있으면 그때 통지해야 한다는 견해가 있을 수 있고, 적어도 去來條件을 모두 合意한 때 매도의 의사가 확정될 수 있으므로 그때 통지해도 된다는 견해가 있을 수 있기 때문이다.

통상 優先買受權을 행사할 수 있는 共同探査開發權者에게는 修正提案을 할 權利가 없다. 引受會社와 讓渡會社 사이에 합의된 내용과 동일한 또는 상당정도로 동일한 去來條件대로 우선매수를 할 것인지 여부의 선택문제만 남는 것이다. 그런데 farmout처럼 현금去來가 아닌 試錐 등의 給付를 대가로 探査開發權이 去來된다거나, 交換처럼 자산이 대가로 지급되는 경우에는 優先買受權者에게 동일한 去來條件으로 優先買受할 것을 강제하기 어렵다. 그러므로 이 경우에는 試錐 등의 給付와 交換對象의 資産을 現金價値로 환산하여 優先買受權者가 이를 지급함으로써 優先買受權을 行使할 수 있도록 하여야 할 것인데, 당사자 사이에 그 價額에 대한 합의가 용이치 않을 것이고, 專門家判斷(expert decision) 등과 같은 제3자에 의한 해결방안을 둔다고 하여도 원만한 優先買受權行使로 이어지기 어려울 것이다.

探査開發權 移轉取得의 契約類型의 측면에서 優先買受權의 제한정도를 살펴보면, 株式讓渡나 資産讓渡는 단순히 現金을 대가로 이루어지는 去來이므로 優先買受權者가 용이하게 去來에 개입하여 契約關係에서 引受候補會社를 배제시킬 수 있다. 그러나 앞서 살펴본 바와 같이 farmout과 交換의 契約類型에서는 優先買受權을 행사하는 데 많은 제약이 있다. 특히 farmout의 경우에는 farmee가 부담하는 試錐 등의 給付를 優先買受權者가 그대로 떠안거나 그 給付를 현금가치로 환산하여 讓渡會社에 지급해야 할 것인데, 양자 모두 매우 복잡하고 합의가 쉽지 않으므로 優先買受權의 현실적 행사가 더욱 용이치 않을 것이다. 그러므로 探査開發權者가 優先買受權의 제한을 회피하기 위하여 farmout에 의한 양도를 선택하는 것도 고려해 볼 만하다. 한편 farmee로부터 權利를 讓受한 제3자(third party purchaser)가 다시 再讓渡하는 경우에도 優先買受權이 인정될 수 있는지가 문제되는데, 法院에서는 직접적인 契約關係(privity of contract) 존부와 관계없이 이를 인정한 바 있다.

6. 共同探査開發權者의 同意

共同探査開發權者들 사이에는 통상 共同運營契約이 체결되는데, 그 契約條項 중 하나가 探査開發權의 전부 또는 일부 양도시 共同探査開發權者의 事前同意를 얻어야 한다는 것이다. 共同事業者사이에 사전동의를 필요로 하는 취지는 探査開發의 共同事業을 처음 시작할때 探査開發을 위한 충분한 기술력과 재정능력이 있는지 여부를 따져 보았으므로, 探査開發權의 移轉取得을 통해 共同事業에 참여하고자 하는 자도 동일 또는 유사한 기술력과 재정능력이 있는지 여부를 동의절차를 통해 판단받아야 한다는 것이다.

讓渡會社가 지배 내지 통제하는 子會社 등의 關係會社(affiliate)에 대한 讓渡는 원칙적으로 共同事業者의 同意를 요구하지 않는다. 왜냐하면 探査開發에 필요한 기술력이나 재정능력에 있어 讓渡會社와 關係會社를 일괄하여 판단하기 때문이다. 비록 讓受會社가 별개의 法人格을 갖추고 있으나 그 지배 및 운영이 母會社에 의해 이루어지므로 讓受會社의 義務와 責任의 履行能力을 염려할 필요가 없다. 그리고 현실去來에 있어서는 引受를 받는 關係會社가 探査開發을 위해 특별히 설립한 特殊目的法人으로 資産이 충분치 않은 경우에는 讓渡會社가 그 기술력과 재정능력을 보증하는 것이 일반적이다.

探査開發權을 引受하고자 하는 會社가 讓渡會社의 기술력 내지 재정능력과 무관한 제3의 會社인 경우에는 共同運營契約상의 동의절차를 거쳐야 함은 앞서 살핀 바와 같다. 그러므로 探査開發權 및 관련鑛口의 일부資産을 引受하여 共同事業에 참여하고자 하는 會社의 경우 다른 共同事業者들의 동의를 얻어야 할 것이다. 그러나 株式讓渡의 경우에는 支配權의 變動(change of control)이 발생하지 않는 한 동의를 필요로 하지 않는 것이 일반적이므로, 資産讓渡나 交換에 비해 共同探査開發權者들의 동의권행사로 인한 제한으로부터 상대적으로 자유롭다. 한편 farmout의 경우에도 共同探査開發權者들의 同意를 요구하지만, 豫備讓受者인 farmee가 그의 기술력과 재정능력을 통해 探査試錐 등의 給付를 이행한 다음 探査開發權을 引受하는 것이므로, 共同探査開發權者들의 同意를 얻는 데 좀더 용이하다고 볼 수 있다. …

Farmout의 選擇[11)]

앞서 살핀 바와 같이 秘密遵守, 優先買受權의 制限, 共同事業者의 同意, 稅制 등 에 있어 farmout은 다른 契約類型에 비교하여 많은 장점이 있다. 그러한 이유로 美國과 캐나다를 중심으로 1960년대 이후 많은 探査開發權移轉取得의 類型으로 애용되고 있다. 探査開發權 移轉取得의 類型으로서 farmout은 다른 契約類型처럼 探査開發權者가 보유하고 있는 探査開發權 및 관련鑛口를 처분하여 자신의 資産목록에서 除去한다는 의미가 없다. 오히려 보유하고 있는 資産을 引受會社인 farmee의 기술과 자금력을 이용하여 그 가치를 증대시키고 探査開發의 危險을 分散시킨다는 측면이 강하다. 만약 引受會社가 探査試錐 등을 하여 경제성없는 鑛口로 판단된다고 하여도 讓渡會社에게는 전혀 損害될 것이 없다. 探査試錐에

11) farmout은 미국세법의 고려상 발달된 탐사권거래라고 한다. John S. Lowe, *Analyzing Oil and Gas Farmout Agreements,* 41 SW. L. J, 759, 765-78.

讓渡會社의 努力과 費用을 전혀 들이지 않았기 때문이다. 그러므로 farmout은 讓渡會社의 探査開發에 따른 附加價値를 확대시키는 기능을 한다고 볼 수있다.

引受會社의 입장에서도 株式이나 資産을 직접 引受하는 경우에는 대규모의 資金이 필요한데, farmout은 1년 내지 3년에 걸쳐 探査試錐 등에 필요한 자금을 작업일정에 따라 조달하면 되므로 경제적으로 부담이 적을 뿐만 아니라, 探査開發權의 原始的 取得 없이도 引受會社가 보유하고 있는 人的·物的資源을 활용하여 探査開發事業에 참여할 수 있기 때문에 人的·物的資源의 효율적 운영 등에도 유리하게 작용할 수 있다. 또한 farmout의 기간 동안 脫退權(right of withdrawal)을 확보하여, 주기적으로 原油가스의 상업적 발견가능성을 판단하여, 그 가능성이 없다고 판단하는 경우 farmout으로부터 탈퇴하여 자금의 추가투입을 줄일 수 있는 효과를 거둘 수 있다. 만약 株式이나 資産引受를 통해 探査開發事業에 참여하였다면 일시에 자금을 모두 引受代價로 지급해야하기 때문에 farmout과 같은 자금절약의 기회를 갖는 것이 불가능하다.

探査開發權의 移轉取得의 목적과 조건에 따라 여러 類型의 移轉契約 중 하나를 선택할 수 있을 것이다. 그러나 앞서 살핀 여러 가지의 주요문제들에 직면한 계약유형별 長短點을 고려하건대, farmout의 選擇은 그 의미가 있다 할 것이고, 이러한 이유로 앞으로 farmout 去來構造를 통한 探査開發權의 移轉取得이 더욱 활성화될 것을 기대해 본다.

노트와 질문

1. 우리의 사업구조는 KNOC이 해외탐사개발권을 취득하여 국내 자원개발업체에 일부를 양도하는 경우도 많은데, 이러한 경우 KNOC과 국내자원개발업체, 그리고 국내자원개발업체와 외국의 NOC간 법률관계는 어떻게 처리될까?
2. 입찰단계에서 탐사개발권의 취득가격이 정하여졌으니 탐사개발권의 일부를 양도하는 경우에는 그 가격 산정에 커다란 어려움이 없을까? 탐사개발권의 가격에는 탐사가 성공적이어서 생산하게 될 자원의 현재가격도 포함하여야 할까?
3. 우리 민법상 조합의 업무집행자 선임과 조합의 업무집행방법결정에 관한 규정을 이유로 조합계약상 지분의 양도를 허용하고 있다고 하더라도 일부의 양도까지 허용하고 있다는 취지로 해석할 것은 아니라는 판례로 비추어 조합지분의 일부양도는 언제나 조합원 전원의 동의를 요하는 것으로 보아야 할까?[12]
4. 에너지개발업체의 주식이나 개발탐사권의 일부 지분을 취득하는 경우 사전에 실사절차를 통하여 확인하여야 할 사항은 어떤 것들이 있을까? NOC나 운영자의 동의를 필요로 하는 경우 동의를 얻을지 여부가 불확실한 상황에서 어떻게 계약협상을 진행하여야 할까?

12) 대법 2009. 4. 23. 선고 2008다4247 판결.

4. 공동운영계약(Joint Operation Agreement, JOA)

공동운영계약은 참여계약이나 farmout계약, 탐사광업권의 매매 등으로 하나의 광구를 여러 사업자가 운영할 경우 이들간의 관계를 정하는 계약이다.[13] 조합계약에 견주어 생각하면 운영자는 업무집행조합원으로 비운영자는 비업무집행조합원으로 비유될 수 있고 주식회사에서는 이사와 주주간 관계에 견줄 수 있을 것이다. 업무집행조합원은 조합원 전체의 이익을 위하여 업무를 집행하며 모든 조합원은 조합 전체의 비용을 분담하여야 할 것이다. 운영자와 비운영자간 이견시 운영자의 권한을 박탈하거나 독자적으로 위험을 부담하면서 사업을 진행할 권리는 통상의 합작투자에서는 발견하기 어려운 특이한 조항이다. 해외에서 엄청난 자금이 필요하고 결과가 불확실하며 정치적으로도 위험한 합작투자사업을 같이 하려면 온갖 상황을 다 감안하여 동업자간 자세한 합의가 필요한 것은 어찌 보면 당연하다. 이하 주로 AIPL 표준계약서상의 문언을 중심으로 설명한다.

가. 운영자의 권리의무

1) 면 책

운영자는 합리적이고 신중하게 산업관행에 따라서 개발권을 근면하고 안전하며 효율적으로 운영하여야 하지만, 비운영자에게 고의나 중과실 여부를 불문하고 책임을 지지 않는 것이 실무례이다.[14] 우리법의 경우 자신의 고의나 중과실로 인한 손해에 대하여까지 면책을 합의할 수 있는지 의문이 있다. 실제 복잡한 공장시설의 운영과 관련하여 개인의 아닌 법인의 과실과 중과실간 구분이 명확하지 않을 수 있다는 이유로, 또는 각자 자신의 근로자와 재산에 대하여 책임을 지는 것을 전제로, 계약상대방의 과실 전반에 관하여 상호면책을 합의하는 예는 있을 수 있다.[15]

2) 충실의무

운영자에게 자신의 이익보다 비운영자의 이익을 우선하여 업무집행을 할 의무가 있는지 여부에 관하여 운영자는 비운영자로부터 업무를 수탁받아 처리하는 지위에 있다는 이유로, 또는 합작투자의 구성원이라는 이유로 이를 인정하는 견해가 다수인 것으로 보인다.[16] 그러

---

13) 국제적인 운용은 계약적인 측면이 전부이겠지만 원래 공동소유자간 관계라는 물권적 연원에 관하여는 David Pierce, *Transnational Evolution of Operating Agreements in the Oil and Gas Industry, in* OIL AND GAS AGREEMENTS: JOINT OPERATIONS (Mar. 2008, RMMLI).

14) 그러나, AIPN Model Form JOA Art. 4.6 (C) 참조.

15) 약관법 제7조 제1호.

16) 예를 들면 *Leck v. Continental Oil Co.*, 1989 OK 173, 800 P.2d 224; *Johnston v. America Cometra,*

나, 우리 상법은 조합의 업무집행조합원은 선량한 관리자로서의 주의의무를 지고 있으며[17] 다만, 회사의 이사나[18] 금융투자업상 집합투자업자,[19] 수탁자에게만[20] 충실의무를 부과하고 있는 것을 감안하면 일반적으로 운영자에게 충실의무를 인정할 수 있을지는 의문이다.

대법 2008. 12. 23. 선고 2007도6463 판결

횡령죄는 타인의 재물을 보관하는 자가 그 재물을 횡령하거나 반환을 거부하는 것을 내용으로 하는 범죄로서, 횡령죄의 주체는 타인의 재물을 보관하는 자이어야 하고, 여기서 보관이라 함은 위탁관계에 의하여 재물을 점유하는 것을 의미하므로, 결국 횡령죄가 성립하기 위하여는 그 재물의 보관자가 재물의 소유자(또는 기타의 본권자)와 사이에 법률상 또는 사실상의 위탁신임관계가 존재하여야 하며(대법원 2005. 6. 24. 선고 2005도2413 판결, 대법원 2007. 5. 31. 선고 2007도1082 판결 등 참조), 이러한 위탁신임관계를 발생시키는 명의신탁관계는 반드시 신탁자와 수탁자 사이의 명시적 계약에 의하여서만 성립되는 것이 아니라 묵시적 합의에 의하여서도 성립될 수 있다(대법원 2001. 1. 5. 선고 2000다49091 판결 참조). 그리고 명의신탁에 대한 묵시적 합의가 있었는지 여부는 위탁자와 수탁자 사이의 관계, 수탁자가 그 재물을 보관하게 된 동기와 경위, 위탁자와 수탁자 사이의 거래 내용과 태양 등 모든 사정을 종합하여 사회통념에 비추어 합리적으로 판단하여야 한다.

원심판결 이유에 의하면, 원심은 피고인이 피해자 공소외 1로부터 받은 아람파이낸셜서비스주식회사(이하 '아람파이낸셜'이라고 한다) 증자대금 39억 3,000만 원으로 증자를 하면서 위 피해자를 위하여 피고인 명의로 신탁받아 보관하던 아람파이낸셜 주식 786,000주의 반환요구를 거부하여 이를 횡령하고, 또한 피해자 공소외 1로부터 79억 5,000만 원 및 피해자 안신물류로부터 40억 원을 받아 신호제지 주식회사(이하 '신호제지'라고 한다)의 주식 1,877,358주를 매입하여 피고인이 대표이사인 아람파이낸셜 명의로 신탁받아 보관하던 중 위 피해자들의 반환요구를 거부하여 이를 횡령하였다는 공소사실에 대하여, 판시 사정만으로는 피고인과 공소외 1, 안신물류 사이에 각기 위와 같은 명시적 또는 묵시적 명의신탁 약정이 이루어졌다고 단정할 수 없다고 하여 위 각 공소사실에 대하여 유죄를 인정한 제1심판결을 파기하여 무죄를 선고하였다.

Inc., 837 S.W.2d 711 (Tex. App. Austin 1992, writ denied).

17) 대법 2008. 10. 23. 선고 2007도6463 판결.

18) 상법 제382조의3.

19) 자본시장과 금융투자업에 관한 법률 제79조.

20) 신탁법 제33조.

그러나 이러한 원심의 판단은 이를 그대로 수긍할 수 없다.

기록에 의하면, 공소외 1은 공소외 2와 함께 피고인의 도움을 받아 피고인이 대표이사로 있는 기업구조조정전문회사인 아람파이낸셜을 통하여 기업개선작업이 종료될 예정인 신호제지를 인수하여 경영할 목적으로 피고인에게 아람파이낸셜의 증자대금으로 39억 3,000만 원을, 신호제지 주식의 매입대금으로 안신물류와 함께 99억 5,000만 원을 각 지급하였을 뿐만 아니라 주도적으로 아람제1호구조조정조합(이하 '아람조합'이라 한다) 및 아람컨소시엄을 구성한 반면, 피고인은 위 자금으로 아람파이낸셜을 증자하고 아람파이낸셜 명의로 신호제지 주식을 인수한 것 외에는 별다른 기여를 한 것으로 보이지 아니한 점, 아람파이낸셜은 이 사건 당시 자본금의 부족으로 기업구조조정전문회사의 등록을 반납한 상태이어서 신호제지를 인수하기 위한 기업구조조정전문회사로 등록하기 위해서는 50억 원의 증자대금이 필요하였고 공소외 1은 이 중 39억 3,000만 원을 조달한 점, 신호제지의 신채권단은 2004. 11. 23. 신호제지와 사이에 1,450억 원 및 미화 1억 달러를 대출하는 약정을 체결하면서 아람파이낸셜과 아람조합의 신호제지에 대한 지분비율을 33% 이상으로 유지할 것을 조건으로 하였고, 또한 아람컨소시엄에 150억 원을 투자하여 신호제지 주식 2,830,188주를 매수한 한국캐피탈주식회사 및 70억 원을 투자하여 1,320,754주를 매수한 신한캐피탈 주식회사(신한조합 명의 포함)가 아람컨소시엄에 참여하는 조건으로 아람파이낸셜에게 담보제공을 요청하였기 때문에 아람파이낸셜은 이러한 요구를 충족하기 위하여 그 명의로 신호제지 주식을 취득하여야 할 사정이 있었던 점, 구 채권단은 아람컨소시엄에게 신호제지의 구 사주인 공소외 2 및 그의 특수관계인과 관련된 자금을 주식인수대금에 투입하지 않을 것을 요청한 까닭에 공소외 2의 지인인 공소외 1 명의로는 아람파이낸셜 또는 신호제지 주식을 취득하기 어려운 사정이 있었던 점, 공소외 1이나 안신물류, 공소외 3 등은 모두 피고인에게 금원을 보내기 전에 피고인과 사이에 금원에 대한 이자나 변제기한 등을 정하거나 피고인으로부터 차용증 등 서류나 담보를 제공받은 사실이 없고 사후에 자금관계 출처에 관한 증빙 등으로 사용하기 위하여 피고인과 사이에 무보증 사모사채인수계약서나 금전소비대차계약서를 작성한 점, 피고인은 공소외 1과 안신물류가 조성하여 지급한 자금으로 신호제지 주식을 인수하면서 공소외 2에게 그 자금에 해당하는 주식 수를 기재한 신호제지 투자자명단을 작성하여 교부한 점, 공소외 1과 안신물류 및 아람조합에 참여한 신호제지 협력업체 등이 자금을 투입한 것은 신호제지의 인수와 경영권 유지를 위한 것이지 피고인에게 대여하여 이자 등 금전적인 이익을 수취하기 위한 것이었다고는 보기 어려운 점, 공소외 1이 공소외 3 및 동문건설, 동양고속건설로부터 높은 이율로 차용한 자금을 피고인의 주장과 같이 그보다 나쁜 조건으로 다시 아람파이낸셜에게 대여한다는 것은 경험칙상 인정하기 어렵고 공소외 1이 그렇게 하여야 할 만한 특별한 이유도 없었던 점, 아람컨소시엄이 신호제지를 인수한 후 공소외 2는 회장으로, 공소외 1은 부회장으로 취임하면서 공소외 1이 공소외 4를 대표이사로 추천하여 선임되게 하는 등 신호제지에 대한 실질적인 경영권을 행사하였던 점 등을 알 수 있다.

위 법리와 이러한 사정에 비추어 보면, 공소외 1과 공소외 2는 신호제지 주식을 취득하는 방식으로 신호제지를 인수하여 운영하기 위하여 피고인에게 인수를 대행하게 하였고, 이에 따라 공소외 1과 안신물류가 피고인에게 인수자금을 지급하고, 피고인이 위 자금을 이용하여 아람파이낸셜을 증자하고 신호제지의 주식을 취득한 것이라고 할 것이므로, 피고인과 공소외 1, 안신물류 사이에는 위 아람파이낸셜의 증자주식을 피고인 명의로, 신호제지의 주식을 아람파이낸셜 명의로 각 신탁하기로 하는 묵시적인 합의가 있었음을 충분히 인정할 수 있고, 따라서 피고인이 직접 명의수탁자로서 또는 명의수탁자인 아람파이낸셜의 대표이사로서 보관 중이던 위 주식에 대한 반환요구를 거부한 행위는 횡령에 해당한다고 할 것이다.

그럼에도 불구하고, 이와 달리 판단한 원심의 조치에는 묵시적 명의신탁관계에 대한 법리오해 및 채증법칙 위배 등의 위법이 있고 이러한 위법은 판결 결과에 영향을 미쳤다고 하지 않을 수 없다. 이 점을 지적하는 상고이유의 주장은 이유 있다.

2. 상고이유 제2점에 대하여

산업발전법상 기업구조조정조합은 구조조정대상기업에 대한 투자, 인수 등을 목적으로 하여 결성되고(산업발전법 제15조 제1항), 기업구조조정조합은 업무집행조합원과 업무감독조합원을 두되 기업구조조정전문회사가 업무집행조합원이 되는 것으로 하고 있으며(같은 법 제15조 제4항), 업무집행조합원은 기업구조조정조합에 출자되는 자금을 선량한 관리자의 주의로써 출자자의 이익을 위하여 관리하도록 규정하고 있으므로(같은 법 제15조의3 제1항), 기업구조조정조합은 기업구조조정업무에 전문성을 갖춘 기업구조조정전문회사의 권한과 책임하에 운영된다고 할 것이나, 기업구조조정조합의 조직과 운영에 관하여 필요한 사항은 대통령령으로 정하도록 하고 있고(같은 법 제15조 제7항), 기업구조조정조합도 그 법률적 성질은 민법상 조합으로서 산업발전법 및 그 시행령에 위배되지 아니하는 범위에서는 민법상 조합에 관한 규정이 적용된다고 할 것이므로, 산업발전법의 규정 취지상 업무집행조합원인 기업구조조정전문회사의 조합재산에 대한 관리·운용권 자체를 박탈할 수는 없다고 하더라도, 조합규약이나 조합원총회의 결의에 의하여 업무집행조합원이 조합재산을 처분함에 있어 조합원총회의 결의를 거치게 하는 등의 제한은 할 수 있다고 보아야 한다.

원심판결 이유에 의하면, 원심은 피고인이 아람조합의 업무집행조합원인 아람파이낸셜의 대표이사로서 아람조합 명의로 신호제지 주식 3,262,055주를 업무상 보관하던 중, 피해자 안신물류 등 아람조합원들이 2005. 10. 7. 조합원총회의 결의로 업무집행조합원의 대리권을 제한할 수 있도록 조합규약을 변경하여 피고인의 신호제지 주식의 매각에 대한 반대의사를 명백히 하였음에도 불구하고, 그 업무상의 임무에 위배하여 신호제지 주식 중 2,739,010주를 매각하여 횡령하였다는 공소사실에 대하여, 업무집행조합원의 조합재산 관리 · 운용권에 대한 산업발전법령의 규정은 강행규정으로서 조합규약이나 조합원총회의 결의에 의하여 일체 변경할 수 없으므로, 피고인이 신호제지 주식을 매각한 것은 아람조합 업무집행조합원의 업무상의 임무에 위배한 것이라는 전제에 선 위 공소사실은 범죄의 증명이 없다는 이유로 제1심의 유죄판결을 파기하여 무죄를 선고하였다.

그러나 기록에 의하면, 아람조합의 조합원들이 2005. 10. 7. 임시 조합원총회에서 총 조합원 35명 중 출석한 32명(의결권의 기준이 되는 총출자좌수의 약 85%) 전원의 찬성으로, 아람조합의 투자업체의 임원변경, 정관변경, 영업양수도, 경영위탁 등 주주총회 결의사항에 대한 조합의 주주권(의결권 포함) 행사 및 투자자산의 처분을 새로운 조합원총회의 결의사항으로 신설하고(신설된 조합규약 제20조 제1항 제9호), 업무집행조합원의 업무집행권한 및 대리권을 일부 제한하여 조합원총회가 조합규약에서 총회의 권한으로 정한 사항의 집행을 위하여 필요한 경우 업무감독조합원 중에서 그 총회 결의를 집행할 자를 지정할 수 있으며, 이 경우 업무집행조합원의 대리권은 소멸되고 총회가 지정한 업무감독조합원이 조합 명의로 조합원들을 대리하여 이를 집행할 수 있도록 규정(신설된 조합규약 제25조 제1항 단서)한 사실을 알 수 있다.

앞서 본 법리를 이러한 사실에 비추어 보면, 조합원총회의 권한으로 정한 사항의 집행을 위하여 필요한 경우 업무감독조합원 중에서 그 총회 결의를 집행할 자를 지정하도록 하면서, 이 경우 업무집행조합원의 대리권 자체를 배제할 수 있도록 한 규정은 산업발전법 제15조 제4항의 규정 취지에 비추어 무효라고 할 것이지만, 투자자산의 처분 등을 조합원총회의 결의사항으로 한 것은 업무집행조합원의 대리권 행사 방법을 제한한 것에 불과하여 무효라고 할 수는 없으므로, 피고인이 위와 같은 아람조합의 조합규약 및 조합원들의 의사에 반함을 알면서도 업무집행조합원인 아람파이낸셜의 대표이사로서 보관 중이던 위 신호제지의 주식을 처분하였다면, 이러한 피고인의 행위는 횡령에 해당한다고 할 수 있고, 위와 같은 사정에 비추어 횡령의 범의 역시 충분히 인정된다고 보아야 할 것이다.

그럼에도 불구하고, 이와 달리 본 원심의 판단에는 산업발전법상 기업구조조정조합에 대한 법리오해 및 횡령죄의 성립과 그 범의 등에 대한 법리오해의 위법이 있고, 이는 판결 결과에 영향을 미쳤다고 하지 않을 수 없다. 이 점을 지적하는 상고이유의 주장도 이유 있다.

대법 2000. 10. 10. 선고 2000다28506, 28513 판결

원심은, 한국토지개발공사(뒤에 한국토지공사로 이름이 바뀌었다)로부터 고양시 덕양구 화정동 소재 화정택지개발지구 내의 토지를 분양받아 그 지상에 지하 2층, 지상 7층 규모의 상가건물(아래에서는 "이 사건 상가건물"이라 한다)을 신축하여 분양·임대할 목적으로 1994. 3. 26. 창립총회를 열어 결성된 삼원상가조합(아래에서는 "이 사건 조합"이라 한다)이 이 사건 소송 계속중인 1999. 11. 12. 임원회를 개최하여 그 조합원으로서 이 사건 상가건물 중 106호와 107호 점포를 분양받은 피고 이병의에 대하여 갖고있는 그 분양잔대금채권 85,900,441원(아래에서는 "이 사건 채권"이라 한다)을 원고에게 양도하는 결의를 하였고, 2000. 3. 20. 위 피고에게 위 채권양도사실을 통지한 사실을 인정하면서도, 이 사건 조합은 위와 같은 동업사업을 위하여 조합원 각자의 지분에 따라 사업자금을 출자하고 손익분배를 하기로 하는 내용의 동업계약을 체결한 조합원들로 구성된 동업체로서, 이 사건 조합이 이 사건 상가건물의 신축공사에 관한 도급계약이나 조합원 개개인과의 분양계약 내지 원고와 사이에 업무대행계약을 체결할 때 전 조합원들이 그 당사자로 되었던 점, 이 사건 조합의 정관 제14조에 의하면 조합원의 비용부담과 징수방법, 상가건축 및 분배처분 계획과 방법 등은 반드시 조합원총회의 결의를 거치도록 규정되어 있는 점 등에 비추어 보면, 이 사건 조합이 그 조합재산인 이 사건 채권을 원고에게 양도함에 있어서는 조합원 전원의 동의가 필요하거나 적어도 조합원총회의 결의가 있어야 하는데, 이 사건 채권의 양도에 있어서는 그와 같은 조합원 전원의 동의나 조합원총회의 결의가 없었으므로 이 사건 조합 임원회의 결의에 의한 이 사건 채권양도는 무효라고 판단하고, 나아가 "사업의 주관과 모든 의사결정권은 임원회에서 하기로 한다."라고 규정하여 마치 이 사건 조합의 임원회에 위와 같은 조합채권의 양도결의를 할 수 있는 것처럼 보이는 이 사건 조합의 동업계약서 제6조의 취지는 이 사건 상가건물의 신축공사와 관련된 사업과 그에 따른 1차적인 의사결정권을 임원회에 위임하는 내용에 불과하고, 이에 더하여 실제적으로 이 사건 조합의 사업과 관련된 사업부지의 결정, 토지대금의 납부, 조합원의 변경, 도급계약, 분양계약, 업무대행계약, 건축공사비의 정산 등 주된 사항들은 모두 조합원총회의 결의를 거치고 있는 점에서 보더라도 이 사건 조합의 임원들을 업무집행조합원으로 선임하는 내용이거나 조합재산의 처분 또는 변경을 임원회의 결의에 따라 할 수 있도록 하는 내용이라고 보기 어려우며, 만약 위 동업계약서의 내용을 위와 같이 해석하지 않는다면 위 동업계약서는 이 사건 조합의 대내적 및 대외적인 권리의무관계를 근본적으로 변경하는 내용을 갖고 있어 실질적으로 정관의 내용 자체를 변경하는 것이라 할 것인데 위 동업계약서는 조합원총회의 결의 없이 제정된 것이어서 정관의 변경은 반드시 조합원총회의 결의를 거치도록 한 이 사건 조합 정관에 위반되므로 이 또한 무효라고 판단하였다.

그러나 이 사건에서 보면 이 사건 조합의 정관에서도 임원의 종류, 인원, 선임절차 및 직무권한 등에 대하여 규정하고 있는데, 조합장은 조합을 대표하여 회무를 통리하고 총회의 의장이 되며, 매입대상 토지선택 및 신청권, 계약체결권, 토지대금납부, 토지사용승낙 등 토지계약 체결에 따른 모든 권리의무행사 이행권, 건축허가신청권, 조합원변경신청권 및 기타 정관시행약관에서 정하는 사항의 업무를 행하고(정관 제10조 제1항), 이사 및 총무도 정관시행약관이 정하는 바에 따라 조합의 업무를 분장하며(정관 제10조 제3항), 총회에서 선임한 임원들로 구성된 임원회에서는 임원의 선임 및 변경, 정관의 제정 및 변경, 조합원의 부담비용과 징수방법, 사업시행계획의 변경, 필요한 경우 사업시행 대행업체 또는 건축시공업자에게 건축비용의 일부 또는 전부를 부담하게 하고 건축된 상가의 일부로 동 부담금을 변제할 수 있도록 하는 결정, 상가건축 및 분배·처분계획, 조합원의 제명처분에 대한 결정을 제외하고는 총회의 권한을 대행할 수 있도록 규정하고 있으므로(정관 제16조), 총회에서 선임된 임원들은 위 동업계약서의 유·무효에 상관 없이 위와 같은 정관 규정에 따라 이 사건 조합의 업무집행조합원이라고 보아야 할 것이다. 그리고 조합재산의 처분·변경에 관한 행위는 다른 특별한 사정이 없는 한 조합의 특별사무에 해당하는 업무집행이며, 업무집행조합원이 수인 있는 경우에는 조합의 통상사무의 범위에 속하지 아니하는 특별사무에 관한 업무집행은 민법 제706조 제2항에 따라 원칙적으로 업무집행조합원의 과반수로써 결정하는 것이므로(대법원 1998. 3. 13. 선고 95다30345 판결 참조) 위와 같이 이 사건 조합의 업무집행조합원들의 의사결정기관인 임원회의 과반수 결의로 이루어진 이 사건 채권의 양도는 다른 특별한 사정이 없는 한 유효한 업무집행이라 할 것이다(물론 조합의 업무집행 방법에 관한 위와 같은 민법 규정은 임의규정이므로 당사자 사이의 약정에 의하여 조합의 업무집행에 관하여 조합원 전원의 동의 또는 조합원총회의 결의를 요하도록 하는 등 그 내용을 달리 정할 수는 있으나, 원심에서 들고있는 조합원의 비용부담과 징수방법, 상가건축 및 분배처분 계획과 방법 등은 반드시 조합원총회의 의결을 거쳐야만 한다는 이 사건 조합 정관 제14조 규정을 보더라도 이 사건 채권양도로 인하여 이미 결정된 조합원의 비용부담과 징수방법에 변경을 가져오거나 상가건축 및 분배처분 계획과 방법에 어떠한 영향을 미치는 것도 아니므로 위 규정이 이 사건 채권양도와 관련한 조합의 업무집행방법에 관하여 그 일반원칙과 달리 조합원총회의 결의를 요하도록 규정한 것은 아니라 할 것이고, 이 사건 조합이 이 사건 상가건물의 신축공사에 관한 도급계약이나 조합원 개개인과의 분양계약 또는 원고와 사이에 업무대행계약을 체결할 때 전 조합원들이 그 당사자로 되었던 것은 조합에 법인격이 인정되지 않기 때문에 그러한 방식을 취한 것이다).

그럼에도 원심은 이와는 다르게 이 사건 조합이 그 조합재산인 이 사건 채권을 원고에게 양도함에 있어서는 조합원 전원의 동의가 필요하거나 적어도 조합원총회의 결의가 있어야 하며 이와 같은 요건을 결한 채 이 사건 조합 임원회의 결의만에 의한 이 사건 채권양도는 무효라고 판단하였으니, 결국 원심판결에는 채증법칙을 위반하거나 조합의 업무집행에 관한 법리를 오해하여 판결에 영향을 미친 위법이 있다고 인정된다. 따라서 이 점을 다투는 상고이유는 이유가 있다.

나. 비운영자의 권리의무

1) 비용분담의무

탐사개발계약은 대부분 작업계획과 최소한의 과제를 정하고 있으며 이에 따라서 공동운영계약도 예산작성과 비용할당에 관한 규정을 두고 있다. 또한, 운영자는 일정한 규모 이상의 지출시 사전에 비용승인신청을 통하여 비운영자의 동의를 받는다. 그러나, 비용승인신청은 하나의 추정치에 불과하며 이를 초과하는 지출이라는 이유로 비운영자가 이의 갹출을 거절할 수는 없다. 실제 비용갹출의 비율은 지분에 비례하지 않는데, 그 이유는 NOC의 비용은 이연되기 때문이다. 만약 비용을 제때에 갹출하지 않는 경우에는 프로젝트의 진행에 중대한 지장을 초래하기 때문에 비용을 갹출하지 아니한 비운영자는 그 지분을 상실하거나 다른 공동운영계약의 당사자들에게 매각할 의무를 부과하기도 한다.

대법 1992. 7. 3 . 자 92마244 결정

재항고이유를 본다.

원심결정 이유에 의하면 원심은, 서울지방법원 서부지원 91가합933 임료청구사건의 피고 유한회사 렌사(이하 피고 회사라고 한다)는 한국에서의 고급호텔의 건설 및 관광숙박업 등을 목적으로 하여 설립되어 그 회사의 대표이사인 원고 소유의 토지위에 호텔을 건립하던 중 1986. 5. 8. 그 사건의 원고인 재항고인(이하 원고라고 한다) 소외 이우진, 피고보조참가신청인인 스위스에어어소시에이티드컴퍼니리미티드(이하 보조참가인이라고 한다), 및 소외 네슬레리미티드와 사이에 외자도입법에 따라 보조참가인과 위 네슬레리미티드를 사원으로 받아들여 공동으로 위 토지 위에 스위스호텔을 포함한 호텔단지를 건설, 운영하기 위한 합작투자계약을 체결함에 있어 (1) 보조참가인과 위 네슬레리미티드는 그 계약에서 정한 조건들이 충족될 것을 조건으로 하여 위 피고 회사의 사원이 되기로 합의하고 (2) 원고는 금 4,050,000,000원으로 평가된 부지를 회사에 출자하기로 하여 위 호텔부지의 일부토지에 대하여는 감정회사의 감정 후 그 소유권을 위 피고 회사에 이전하고 나머지 부지에 대하여는 위 피고 회사와의 사이에 경영계약에 규정된 임대차계약을 체결하기로 하되 그 임대차계약서에서 기간은 개업일로부터 시작하여 위 경영계약에 규정되어 있는 경영계약 기간까지로 하고 연간임대료는 금 3억원을 초과하지 아니하고 개업일 이후 매년 금 180,000,000원(18,000,000원의 오기로 보인다)을 초과하지 아니하는 금액만큼 인상하고 위 임대료 중 1/3은 발생 즉시 지급하되 나머지 임대료는 발생 후 위 피고 회사가 매회계연도에 보조참가인과 위 네슬레리미티드에게 기발생 1순위 누적적 우선배당금으로 각 금 2,212,500,000원의 10퍼센트에 해당하는 금원을 지급한 후 이용가능한 현금 중에서 지급한다는 점 등을 규정하기로 하고 (3) 보조참가인과 위 네슬레미티드는 앞서 본 바와 같은 상대방의 현물출자 및 임대차계약체결 등의 약정사항이 충족되는 것을 조건으로 하여 피고 회사에 금 3,500,000,000원 상당의 미화를 현금출자하기로 약정한 사실, 그 후 1986. 9. 29. 위 합작투자계약의 당사자들 사이에 원고 및 보조참가인 등의 위 출자금액에 관한 사항 등 위 합작투자계약의 내용을 일부 수정하는 계약을 체결하고 같은 달 원고는 위 합작투자계약상의 약정이행으로서 위 피고 회사와의 사이에 원고 소유의 서울 서대문구 홍은동 201의 1 토지 외 11필지에 관한 임대차계약을 체결함에 있어서 그 연간임료액 및 임료상한액, 임료의 지급방법 등을 위 합작투자계약상의 약정내용과 동일하게 약정한 사실, 위 합작투자계약에 따라 위 피고 회사의 총자본금은 금 23,895,000,000원으로 되었고 현재 그 사원들의 지분비율은 원고가 50퍼센트, 위 이우진이 10퍼센트, 보조참가인과 위 네슬레리미티드가 각 20퍼센트로 된 사실 및 위 서부지원 91가합933 사건은 원·피고간에 1986. 9. 26. 체결한 위 임대차계약상의 임료액이 그간의 경제사정변경 등으로 인하여 상당하지 아니하게 되었음을 이유로 1990. 12. 6 .부터 같은 달 31.까지의 기간에 대한 임료증액분 중 금 21,369,863원의 지급을 구하는 것인 사실을 각 확정하였다.

원심이 확정한 사실에 의하면 이 사건 소송은 원고와 피고 회사 사이에 1986. 9. 29. 체결한 위 임대차계약상의 임료액이 그간의 경제사정변경 등으로 인하여 상당하지 아니하게 되었음을 이유로 1990. 12. 6 .부터 같은 달 31.까지의 기간에 대한 임료증액분의 지급을 구하는 것이며 원고와 피고 회사 사이에 체결된 위 임대차계약은 원고와 피고 회사 및 보조참가인등 사이에 1986. 5. 8. 체결된 합작투자계약에서 보조참가인 등이 투자를 하는 전제조건으로 약정된 사항들을 기초로 한 것이므로 보조참가인으로서는 당초의 합작투자계약의 한쪽 당사자로서 그 다른 당사자인 원고가 제기한 위 소송의 결과에 대하여 피고 회사와 이해관계를 같이 하는 법률적인 이해관계에 있어 위 소송에 피고 회사를 위하여 보조참가를 할 수 있다고 할 것이다.

원심의 이유설시는 다소 미흡한 점이 있으나 보조참가인에게 법률상 이해관계가 있다고 본 원심의 판단은 그 결론이 정당하고 거기에 소론이 주장하는 바와 같은 심리미진이나 보조참가요건에 있어서의 법률상 이해관계에 관한 법리를 오해한 위법이 없으므로 논지는 이유 없다.

그러므로 재항고를 기각하기로 하여 관여 법관의 일치된 의견으로 주문과 같이 결정한다.

2) 단독위험운영권리

탐사개발권자가 작업계획을 사전에 정치하게 작성한다고 하여도 실제 탐사작업의 진행 속도나 범위는 상당한 판단이 필요한 것으로 탐사작업을 진행하면서 공동운영계약의 당사자들에게 참여여부를 결정할 기회를 주기도 한다. 소극적으로 다수에 의하여 채택된 탐사작업에의 참여거부권을 줄 수도 있고, 반대로 적극적으로 다수에 의하여 거부된 탐사작업의 독자적 추진권을 줄 수도 있다. 전자의 경우 참여거부에 대한 벌로서 당초 갹출금액의 수배를 지급하여야 하며 후자의 경우 독자적 추진에 반대한 나머지 공동운영계약 당사자들에게 일체의 면책을 약속하여야 한다.[21)]

3) 운영자자격박탈권리

운영자의 중대한 채무불이행의 경우 비운영자나 운영위원회의 결정으로 이를 치유할 일정한 기간을 통지하고 그 기간내에 치유가 되지 않는 경우 운영자의 자격을 박탈할 수 있다. 운영자의 자격을 박탈하는 것과 새로운 운영자를 선임하는 것은 다른 결정이므로 운영자의 자격박탈을 정하였다면 이어서 새로운 운영자선임절차에 관한 규정을 추가로 두어야 한다.[22)] 운영자의 파산시 자동자격상실조항을 두기도 하지만 이러한 조항의 유효성은 각국의 파산법에 따라서 다를 것이다. 우리는 합작투자계약의 약정해지와 관련하여 판결이 나온 바 있다.[23)]

Clifford D. Johnson, *Non-Operator's Rights Under the CAPL Operating Procedure,* 28 ALTA. L. REV. 1 (1989-90)

A. OPERATORSHIP

1. Removal or Replacement of Operator

One of the most basic and fundamental principles set forth in the 1981 CAPL ("Procedure"), as with its predecessors, pertains to operatorship and the selection of one

21) 발전소 시설의 일부 주식매매를 협의하면서 추가수요시 새로운 발전소건설에 대한 합의가 불가능한 경우 합작투자회사의 일방 당사자의 독자적 진행에 협조할 의무를 계약서에 추가한 적이 있으나, 공동운영계약처럼 일반적인 단독위험운영권한을 규정한 합작투자계약서는 보기 어렵다.

22) AIPN Arts. 4. 9와 4. 11.

23) 김성용, 도산조항의 효력, 4 사법 215(2008); 임채웅, 도산격리의 연구 12 한국민사소송법학회지 422(2008). 운영자자격박탈은 단순한 OJA해석의 문제로 삼아도 무방할 듯하다.

joint-operator to perform that role on behalf of all joint-operators. Conduct of operations in such a manner is obviously felt to be the most expedient for all concerned. It may be noted that this is not the usual approach for the operation of units or major facilities such as gas plants, where the operator conducts operations directly under the supervision of an operating committee comprised of representatives of the owners. This latter approach has the potential to give non-operators a more effective say in operations than that available to them under the operating procedure. However, the establishment of an operating committee for operations carried out under the operating procedure would be impractical in most circumstances, particularly where minimal lands are involved.

In the 1981 Procedure, the basic functions and duties of the operator are described in Article III, with the limitations on liability and the right of indemnification of the operator described in Article IV. Assuming the operator complies with its basic obligations, as set out in Clause 301 in particular, its ability to maintain its position as operator is virtually assured.

Substantial concerns for non-operators arise in circumstances where it is believed that the operator is not adequately performing its obligations, or where the operator is in financial difficulty (with the attendant requirement of non-operators to nonetheless advance money to the operator to fund operations) or where the operator is receiving funds from third parties to which the non-operators are entitled. Moreover, the priorities for exploration and development of the joint lands may be different for the individual joint-operators at various times. When the attention of the operator is focused on other lands, or is otherwise disinterested or distracted from such matters, whether because of budgetary constraints, bankruptcy or insolvency or otherwise, the non-operators may feel a change of operators is appropriate. The non-operators face difficulties in effecting the removal of the operator if it chooses to resist such removal.

Under the 1981 Procedure there is a limited range of options available to the non-operators in this regard. The applicable provisions are set forth in Article II, entitled "Appointment and Replacement of Operator". Clause 202 is of potential application in the aforementioned situations. However, as straightforward as its provisions appear, their application is not without difficulty. Under Paragraph 202(a), the operator is to be replaced immediately in any one of the following circumstances:

(i) if the operator becomes bankrupt or insolvent or commits or suffers any act of bankruptcy or insolvency, or makes any assignment for the benefit of its creditors, or causes any judgment to be registered against its participating interest;

(ii) if the operator assigns or purports or attempts to assign its general powers and responsibilities of supervision and management as operator hereunder.

The first situation appears to be relatively straightforward, but this has not proven to be the case in practice. The terms "bankruptcy" and "insolvency" are undefined in the 1981 Procedure. They are often used synonymously, although perhaps incorrectly, as the "inability to pay one's debts." Nonetheless, the legal status of a person in each case is quite different. Since the *Bankruptcy Act* is a codification of the common law of bankruptcy and insolvency, its provisions would seem to be appropriate for the interpretation that the provisions of an agreement that reflect an intention that they apply. It is submitted that the framers of the 1981 Procedure and its predecessors evidenced such an intention through utilizing the appropriate terminology.

A "bankrupt" is defined in section 2 of the *Bankruptcy Act* as "a person who has made an assignment or against whom a receiving order has been made". An "assignment" is effected by the voluntary application of an "insolvent person" to the provisions of the *Bankruptcy Act* by making an assignment for the benefit of his creditors. If all the formalities are met and the assignment is filed with the official receiver, it becomes an official record of the court. A "receiving order" is an order made in respect of a person who is involuntarily petitioned into bankruptcy by one or more creditors. Under subsection 71(1) of the *Bankruptcy Act,* the "bankruptcy" is deemed to have commenced upon a receiving order being made or an assignment being filed with the official receiver. Whether or not an assignment or receiving order has been made by or in respect of an operator is a question of fact. If it has occurred in respect of an operator, such operator is subject to "immediate replacement".

An "insolvent person" is defined in the *Bankruptcy Act* to mean "a person who is not bankrupt and who resides or carries on business in Canada, whose liabilities to creditors provable as claims under this Act amount to one thousand dollars," and:

"(a) who is for any reason unable to meet his obligations as they generally become due;

(b) who has ceased paying his current obligations in the ordinary course of business as they generally become due; or

(c) the aggregate of whose property is not, at a fair valuation, sufficient, or, if disposed of at a fairly conducted sale under legal process, would not be sufficient to enable payment of all his obligations, due and accruing due."

This definition is consistent with the import of the common law definition noted above, namely that such a person is unable to pay its debts. However, there is an added prospective element described in subsection (c) above which may not have been caught by the common law definition. It is a "liquidation value" test which would be difficult to assess in any given circumstances with any degree of certainty.

If an actual bankruptcy has not yet occurred, and it is unclear whether or not an insolvency exists, the next determination to be made in respect of the potential application of Paragraph 202(a) is whether or not the operator has committed or suffered any "act of bankruptcy or insolvency". The references to acts of bankruptcy or insolvency appear to refer to the situation where a person has committed an act of bankruptcy, but has not yet been rendered (either voluntarily or involuntarily) subject to the *Bankruptcy Act* with the resultant status of a bankrupt or insolvent person. Subsection 42(1) of the *Bankruptcy Act* lists ten situations in which a debtor is deemed to have committed an act of bankruptcy. The most notable for present purposes is as set forth in Paragraph 42(1)(j), which applies to a person "if he ceases to meet his liabilities generally as they become due". The supplementary words "or makes any assignment for the benefit of itscreditors" in Paragraph 202(a) of the 1981 Procedure are somewhat superfluous in that such an event would in and of itself constitute an act of bankruptcy under the *Bankruptcy Act*.

The last element of Sub-paragraph 202(a)(i) of the 1981 Procedure of potential application is where the operator causes any judgment to be registered against its participating interest." It is questionable whether the filing of a judgment is an appropriate event to trigger a change in operatorship, since the judgment could affect or relate to only a portion of the lands and a minor share of the relevant participating interests. Further, it could apply only to a "carved out" interest, rather than to the entire or even a portion of the relevant working interest. However, a non-operator having found a writ of execution filed against the title to the lands as a result of a judgment against the operator would appear to have found the grounds to have the operator removed, although it is highly unlikely that such an operator would voluntarily resign.

Even if, in the particular circumstances, one could conclude that the operator is either bankrupt or insolvent, this conclusion will not necessarily determine the issue. A non-operator approaching the operator with the news that the operator is going to be replaced will often be invited to prove the bankruptcy or insolvency. In the case of a bankruptcy this may not be all that difficult as the appropriate searches would confirm that fact. However, in the case of insolvency, a great deal of information may be required to prove that the operator is in fact insolvent. In this latter circumstance, the non-operator may have no choice but to proceed with court action to effect removal of the operator if its cooperation in that regard is not forthcoming.

Assuming that the facts in support of a bankruptcy or insolvency are established, one could infer from the positive language of Clause 202 that the change of operator is to happen immediately upon such occurrence. There are three cases that have dealt with the issue of removal of the operator pursuant to the provisions of Article II of the 1981

Procedure, the *Tri-Star* case,[1] the *Oakwood* case,[2] and the *Rimoil* case.[3]

In the *Tri-Star* case, the court was considering the rights of the parties under an operating agreement entered into among a number of companies in 1984 governing certain lands, to which the 1981 Procedure was appended. A proposal was made by J.C. International in July of 1986 under the *Bankruptcy Act* and Mr. Justice Dixon granted an order on July 24th, 1986 appointing Clarkson Gordon Inc. as interim receiver. The plaintiffs Tri-Star and Copetrex each argued that, pursuant to the terms and conditions of their respective operating agreements, it was now the operator *pro tem* and sought a declaration naming it as operator. Mr. Chief Justice Moore noted that the Royal Bank of Canada had security on virtually all of the assets of J. C. International for a debt which far exceeded the value of those assets. Mr. L.C. Cole, President of J.C. International had also stated in an affidavit sworn on July 22nd, 1986, that the company owed the sum of $24 million, more or less, to the Royal Bank and that this debt was secured by both debenture and *Bank Act* security covering substantially all the assets of the company. In addition, he stated that the company owed approximately $2.5 million to its preferred and ordinary creditors, was insolvent and possessed assets of a value less than its debts.

The respondent Clarkson Gordon submitted that the relief sought should be denied since there were triable issues to be determined, in particular, the question of insolvency. It argued that the company may not have been insolvent since:

(i) some of its debts had been paid with additional funds advanced by the Royal Bank,

(ii) the plaintiffs were estopped in their cause by virtue of representations made by officers of Tri-Star to the effect that no steps would be taken to remove J.C. International as operator,

(iii) in a separate joint application of Tri-Star and Copetrex there were seven parties with working interests, with no guarantee that Copetrex or Tri-Star would be named to represent such working interests as operator, and

(iv) the bank, who had appointed Clarkson Gordon as its agent to take custody of the assets of J.C. International pursuant to its security, would refuse to continue to fund the proposal and bankruptcy would follow.

Through various transactions, J.C. International had obtained a 55% working interest in the relevant lands prior to the proposal being filed. Copetrex and Tri-Star had both

---

1. *Tri-Star Resources Ltd. v. J.C. Int. Petroleum Ltd.* (1986), 48 Alta. L.R. (2d) 355 (Q.B.) [hereinafter *Tri-Star]*.
2. *Norcen Energy Resources Limited v. Oakwood PetroleumsLtd.* (1988), 63 Alta. L.R. (2d) 361 (Q.B.) [hereinafter *Oakwood]*.
3. ***he Rimoil*** *Corporationv. HexagonGas Ltd., DynamarEnergy Limited andBranniganResources CanadaLtd.,* May 5, 1989 (unreported) [hereinafter *Rimoil]*.

notified J. C. International in accordance with their separate respective operating agreements, each incorporating the 1981 Procedure, that pursuant to Paragraph 206(b) thereof, each was the new operator thereunder and that pursuant to Clause 207 thereof, all well data and other facilities, equipment and documents were to be delivered to them.

On the first argument, Mr. Chief Justice Moore held that:

> ... there is no issue to be tried on the question of "insolvency". The company, by Mr. Cole's own admission as stated in his Affidavit of 22nd July, was unable to meet its obligations and was insolvent. Black's Law Dictionary defines "insolvency" as an "inability to pay one's debts". Surely when the President of the company under oath states that the company is unable to pay its debts, there can be no further argument on the question.

On the question of estoppel, he further concluded that the equitable remedy of estoppel could not be relied upon in view of the specific wording of Clause 202 which was for the protection of the non-operators having regard to the fact that the company was already in a state of insolvency. Moreover, he stated that the mandatory nature of the words "shall be replaced immediately" dictated that J.C. International should be replaced by the party having the next greatest interest in accordance with the provisions of Paragraphs 206(b) and (d) of the 1981 Procedure. The court then granted the separate applications, declaring Tri-Star and Copetrex as the new operators under the two operating agreements, and further directed that the respondents comply with the provisions of Clause 207 of the 1981 Procedure which governs the transfer of property on a change of operator.

In the *Oakwood* case the first question requiring resolution was whether or not Oakwood was insolvent within the meaning of the 1981 Procedure. Mr. Justice Forsyth applied the test set forth in the *Tri-Star* case and concluded that the affidavit of an executive vice-president of Oakwood, which contained numerous admissions that Oakwood was unable to pay its debts, was sufficient to establish the fact of insolvency.

The basic issue under consideration in the *Oakwood* case was whether or not Oakwood should be afforded the protection of the *Companies' Creditors Arrangement Act* as being a debtor company within the meaning of the CCAA. Mr. Justice Forsyth expressed the view that it would be difficult to argue on one day that you are insolvent and that you deserve the protection of the CCAA for one purpose and then argue on another day, for another purpose, that you are not insolvent within the meaning of the relevant operating procedure. The Royal Bank had argued that Oakwood was "commercially solvent" even though it may have been "legally insolvent", apparently on the basis that it was meeting day to day obligations though not long-term obligations.

The Court rejected this argument and concluded that insolvency was to be given its normal meaning under the agreement and could not be interpreted as being restricted only to the meeting of day to day expenses and making payments to the other joint-operators. The court also noted that under Clause 306 of the 1981 Procedure one of the duties of the operator is to pay all trade debts, and that under Clause 605 there is an obligation upon the operator to distribute income to those entitled to it. Finally, he concluded that "by the bringing of its CCAA application, Oakwood has declared itself insolvent and thus Clause 202 of its operating agreement came into play".

The second issue, which may be of more concern for non-operators, was whether or not the fact of insolvency created an automatic ejection of Oakwood from its operatorship or whether some further action in that regard was required by Norcen. Notwithstanding the provisions of Paragraph 206(d) which called for immediate replacement of the operator, the court concluded that its effect was simply that no waiting or notice period was required. This was also considered in the context of Paragraph 206(a), which provides that if there are only two joint-operators, the other joint-operator would have the right to become the operator, a consideration found to be most important in these circumstances. In his reasons for judgement, Mr. Justice Forsyth stated:

> It appears to be worded in the future tense suggesting that at some point following insolvency another party may become the operator if appropriate measures are taken. There is some positive election required on Norcen's part indicating that it wants to exercise its right to become the operator.

If faced with a situation where the facts would appear to support the non-operators' position that they have the right to remove an operator, the operator could choose to seek the protection of the CCAA. This could be a risky step for an operator to take since in order to do so, insolvency is necessarily admitted and, upon termination of any stay of proceedings which is granted (as in respect of a bankruptcy), the non-operators would appear to win the day. Norcen raised this issue in its arguments before the court and suggested that if the stay were allowed, its right to become operator could be adversely affected, since during that period of time Oakwood might cure its insolvency. The Court did not decide whether the ability of Oakwood to cure its insolvency did adversely affect Norcen, although Mr. Justice Forsyth noted that he was mindful of this concern and its implications for Norcen.

It seems arguable on one hand that any curing of the insolvency during a stay imposed pursuant to CCAA should not adversely affect the ability of the non-operators to have the operator removed, since it is the fact of insolvency or an act of bankruptcy or insolvency at the time that it occurs which is important and relevant for purposes of the 1981 Procedure. If the non-operators have, acted expeditiously in initiating proceedings to exercise their rights and have the insolvent operator removed, and such proceedings are affected by a stay, the non-operators should not have their rights prejudiced on a permanent basis. To allow the insolvency to be cured, thereby defeating the rights of the non-operators to have the operator replaced, would suggest a form of relief against forfeiture of a right which may be inappropriate in such circumstances.

From the point of view of the insolvent operator and its creditors, it may be argued that the precise intention of the CCAA is to allow the insolvent party interim relief to permit it to put its affairs in order. It may also be argued that there is a greater intrinsic value if a sale or other disposition could be made of the insolvent operator as a going concern, which would have greater benefits for all concemed, including non-operators which may be adversely affected by a bankruptcy. If the insolvent operator cures its insolvency, it could be argued that it should be able to defeat any challenge to its operatorship that might be made on that basis. However, it may be suggested that this argument does not address a fundamental issue for non-operators, namely that operatorship is at least not intended to be financially based, since it is not intended that operatorship serve as a centre of profit. However, it is also clear that an operator does receive a benefit through the use of the non-operator's funds while in its possession, and may well benefit financially by serving as operator.

The appropriate balancing of interests in the type of situations that may arise would depend on a number of factors, such as the presence of any specific and unique knowledge that the operator's employees might have with respect to operation of the relevant lands which could be lost if they were terminated, the current status of the lands as an exploration, development or mature operation, the general capabilities of the operator as an operator, the abilities of one or more of the non-operators to assume operatorship should they wish to do so and the potential financial recovery for all concerned if some form of reorganization of the operator is achieved. It would seem that each situation must be examined on the basis of its own special merits, and generalizations may be inappropriate.

Mr. Justice Forsyth did grant the stay in the *Oakwood* case, presumably accepting Oakwood's evidence that if Oakwood were removed as operator this would be fatal to attempts to restructure the company. Since the Court found that Section 11 of the CCAA was to be given a wide interpretation, it was concluded that the stay could extend to and interfere with contractual obligations, whether or not the parties being interfered with creditors in fact or in effect. It is perhaps unfortunate that this case was not appealed to confirm whether or not this interpretation settles the issue. Whether or not the non-operators could successfully continue with proceedings for removal of an operator which has, in one form or another, cured its insolvency during a stay that was granted, is an open question, since it is understood Norcen did not pursue this matter after the stay was lifted and apparently accepted the successor to Oakwood as operator. This decision would appear now to be the law applicable in Alberta, although it may be subject to further refinement by the courts, since this case could be found to be confined in application to its own particular facts.

One issue that is not specifically dealt with in Clause 202 of the 1981 Procedure are the implications attendant on a "receivership" of the operator. As a receivership order is a natural consequence of a successful petition for bankruptcy, there should be no issue as to whether or not such a party is bankrupt or insolvent since the order issued is predicated on a determination of that very issue. However, it is possible for a private receivership to take place pursuant to a debt instrument such as a debenture, which does not necessarily include a court order to this effect, although it is understood that the usual practice is to obtain a confirming court order. The standard debenture, whether or not in the nature of a demand, will provide that the security evidenced by the instrument shall become enforceable upon the event of a default, such as the failure to make payments to the secured party when due. It should be noted that such an event may not, in and of itself, be sufficient to prove that the operator is insolvent, or that it has committed an act of bankruptcy or insolvency. Failing to make payments when due under a debt obligation secured by a debenture would arguably constitute an act of bankruptcy or insolvency. However, a non-operator advancing such a claim will very likely be invited to prove this to be the case. Short of court action, it is highly unlikely that the non-operator will have sufficient information available to it to prove its case and effect a change of operator. Further, it is possible, although unlikely, that the operator will survive the receivership and regain control of its own destiny. For the 1988 Procedure a proposed amendment to Paragraph 202(a) provides for immediate replacement of the operator if it is either placed in receivership or makes a proposal to creditors pursuant to section 33 of the *Bankruptcy Act*. However, this amendment may not adequately address all potential problems. It may be appropriate for the 1988 Procedure to consider the implications of an operator making an application under the CCAA and whether this should entitle the non-operators to effect a removal of the operator, although the courts may not enforce such a provision, given the broad interpretation afforded to section 11 of the CCAA. If the Procedure is to address such matters, it may be appropriate to provide for elections by the non-operators, rather than to provide for automatic ejectment of the operator, to permit the affected parties to review the matter and the implications of their actions.

It is sometimes difficult to understand the preoccupation with keeping the operator in that position in the circumstances outlined above. One could suggest that it is usually easier to sell properties of the bankrupt if operatorship is maintained and can be transferred to the purchaser. However, it may be noted that under the 1981 Procedure, operatorship does not automatically follow in a disposition of an interest subject to an operating agreement, although that usually will be the case if the largest participating interest is involved in such a disposition. On the negative side, a receiver may only be concerned with the short term goal rather than any long term strategy or investment potential and thus development may come to a standstill in a receivership situation. From the point of view of costs, an operator faced with bankruptcy or receivership may also be able to reduce its overhead costs significantly if it did give up operatorship, through reduction in operating staff and the like. A lean organization may be more attractive to some buyers who do not want the added burden of staff who may well turn out to be redundant.

In Sub-paragraph 202(a)(ii) of the 1981 Procedure, it is stated that an act by the operator of assigning or purporting or attempting to assign its general powers and responsibility of supervision and management constitutes grounds for removal. It appears that this provision is intended to preclude the operator from entering into agreements for contract operation of the joint lands which would effectively remove the operator for all intents and purposes from the management of such joint lands. It may also address a cost concern, since the operator may attempt to charge the third party costs incurred to the joint account, and such costs would likely be greater than the operator would otherwise be entitled to charge under the accounting procedure.

It is common practice for operators to enter into well operating contracts and similar agreements with other operators for convenience or other reasons in areas where such other operators have significant operations. If there are no imminent plans for development of the joint lands, day to day supervision and management may well be appropriately undertaken by a contract operator rather than by the operator itself. Entitlement to replace the operator in such circumstances may not have been the intended result of entering into such an arrangement. If the relevant operating procedure is applied to one section of land upon which a sole gas well was located, the entering into of a contract well operating agreement presumably could be sufficient to place the operator in violation of this provision and entitle the non-operators to take the position that the operator is to be replaced. However, it may be noted that such contract well operating agreements usually have termination clauses of short duration so the situation could be easily resolved by the operator. Further, the operator could argue that the ultimate responsibility has not been surrendered, which would likely be the case.

In the *Rimoil* case, the plaintiff Rimoil claimed a right to be appointed operator in the place and stead of the existing operator on the basis that it had breached the provisions of Paragraph 202(b) of the 1974 Procedure by assigning its general powers of supervision and management as operator. Although it is difficult to ascertain the precise (and all relevant) facts from the reasons for judgment, it appears that Hexagon, a subsidiary of Dynamar, was the named operator under a number of operating agreements. In May of 1985 it purported to assign operatorship to Dynamar. By May of 1988 Dynamar was insolvent. The Royal Bank had debenture security against the assets of Dynamar and a receiver-manager was appointed. After the receiver-manager of Dynamar was unable after several attempts to sell its assets for what was considered by the Royal Bank to be an adequate price, such assets were, with the approval of the Court, conveyed by the receiver to Brannigan, a wholly-owned subsidiary of the Royal Bank. On January 18, 1989 Hexagon purported to assign its operatorship to Brannigan. On February 14, 1989 Brannigan, Hexagon and the receiver-manager for Dynamar gave written notice to the working interest owners under the various operating agreements of a meeting intended for proper novation of all appropriate working interest owners into their operating agreements, and to appoint or confirm appointment of operator. At the meeting held on March 2, 1989, the requisite majority vote was only obtained in respect of one operating agreement. Nonetheless, it is apparent that Brannigan continued in the role of operator for all of the operating agreements in question.

The Court accepted the fact that breaches of Paragraph 202(b) had occurred, but did not accept that Rimoil had the right to become operator without a vote, particularly in view of the interim vote taken at the March 2 meeting, at which Rimoil had voted. The Court concluded that a meeting must be called to effect a change of operator pursuant to Paragraph 206(a). If the requisite majority cannot be obtained, then pursuant to Paragraph 206(b), the joint-operator with the greatest participating interest will act as operator *pro tem*. In this situation the Court found that Rimoil would have to prove its entitlement under Paragraph 206(b) in respect of those operating agreements where the requisite majority had not been obtained, but that in any event Brannigan had been validly appointed under the one operating agreement.

Paragraph 202(b) of the 1981 Procedure provides two additional situations in which the operator can be removed, although it is not a requirement that this removal occur immediately. The first is where the operator ceases to hold or represent at least 10% of the participating interests. This provision would seem to be the automatic result of a disposition by the operator of all of its interest in and to the joint lands. However, the operator and the purchasing party may provide in their purchase and sale agreement that the operator will continue to represent the interest pending the execution and delivery by all parties of an assignment and novation agreement, in which the transfer to the purchaser of the interest in the lands and the relevant operating agreement is recognized by all affected parties. It is doubtful if the 10% rule would become operative in such circumstances. This is obviously an undesirable situation from the point of view of the non-operator, since an operator ceasing to have a beneficial interest in the joint lands will clearly not have the interests of the non-operators at heart. The most desirable result in the circumstances of a disposition by an operator of its interests will, of course, depend on the particular situation, making it difficult to draft appropriate provisions of general application.

If there is an existing non-operator having a substantial interest in the relevant lands, it may well be desirable for that party to assume operatorship. For avariety of reasons the other non-operators may not want the purchasing party to assume conduct of operations and may refuse to execute an assignment and novation agreement that attempts to have this effect or otherwise confirm the purchaser as the new operator. In such circumstances the non-operators would be well within their rights since operatorship does not automatically transfer to the purchaser on an operator's disposition of its interest in the relevant lands and operating agreement. However, if the purchaser will be assuming a significant participating interest which exceeds that of the other non-operators and is an experienced and reliable operator with a good track record, it may be desirable for such a party to assume operations immediately for the benefit of all of the joint-operators.

Perhaps appropriately, the 1981 Procedure does not address all the various situations that can develop in a disposition, and it is often possible for stalemates to occur. In the event of a permitted disposition, it is in the interests of all concerned that a suitable assignment and novation agreement be entered into. Such an agreement does not and perhaps should not release the operator from obligations it may have assumed while it was the operator. However, it would be useful to provide that a vote be held for the appointment of a new operator or confirmation of the purchaser as operator within a reasonable period of time after closing of the disposition, whether or not the operator is said to continue to represent the interest being disposed of. It is reasonable for the non-operators to have the opportunity to address the question of operatorship upon a disposition, or perhaps even on a periodic basis, such as every few years, particularly when it is so difficult to remove an operator once appointed.

The proposed changes for the 1988 Procedure reflect a direct approach and simply state that the operator may be replaced by the affirmative vote of two or more joint-operators representing a majority of the participating interest. This suggested change will resolve many multiple ownership situations, but not the situation where the existing operator holds 50% or more of the relevant participating interest. There are also situations where there are only two joint-operators, each holding an undivided 50% participating interest, with the non-operator potentially being more qualified than the operator at the relevant time to conduct operations for the joint account, but without apparent ability to effect a change other than pursuant to a challenge of operator.

The second additional provision which may result in the removal of the operator is described in Sub-paragraph 202(b)(ii) of the 1981 Procedure. This is where the operator defaults in its duties or obligations and does not commence to rectify the default within 30 days after written notice from a majority in interest of the joint-operators (excluding the operator) specifying the default and requiring the operator to remedy it. The primary duties and obligations of the operator are as set forth in Article III, which appears to set the reference point for any challenge that might be made on this basis. If a non-operator can find a described obligation that is not being satisfied by the operator, it could utilize such a provision to attempt to effect a change in operator. However, it is clear that the operator could also commence to remedy the default within the specified time and thus defeat the challenge. It may also be noted that the provision does not require the operator, after commencing to remedy the default, to act diligently or even continue with such remedy until completed. Although this could be considered an implied term, it would appear to be a defect requiring appropriate rectification.

2. Challenge of Operator

Clause 203, entitled "Challenge of Operator", is one of the more controversial and for the most part ineffective provisions through which a non-operator might gain control of operations. A non-operator may issue a "challenge notice" to all joint-operators to the effect "that it is ready, able and willing to conduct operations for the joint account on more favorable terms and conditions". It is a condition precedent to the right to issue a challenge notice that the existing operator has been in place for at least two years. If that requirement is satisfied, the challenge notice may then be issued. The issue that arises in this context is what constitutes "more favorable terms and conditions", since no reference point is provided. To the writer's knowledge this provision has not been specifically tested in the courts.

However, the Appellate Division of the Supreme Court of Alberta in the *Permo Gas* case considered the meaning of the words "upon terms more favorable" in the context of a favoured nations clause in a gas purchase contract. The Court focused on the word "terms" as requiring interpretation in the context of this case, and stated:

> ... if it means a difference in one item of several making up the computation of the sale price, the appellant is entitled to succeed. If, however, "terms" has a broader meaning, requiring that the contract as a whole, or at least several

> clauses of it, must be looked at to determine if its terms are more favourable, then the interpretation which the appellant asks to put upon these words must be rejected. "Terms" is expressed in the plural. It does not follow that a single term may not be sufficient to bring favoured condtions clause into operation. For instance, if all terms of two agreements except one are the same, one more favourable term would make the "terms" of that agreement "more favourable".

It may be argued this is precisely the question that arises in reference to Clause 203 of the 1981 Procedure. All terms of the agreement under which the challenging non-operator would function will be similar, except for those it asserts performed on a more favorable basis. There are no express restrictions on the terms founding a non-operator's challenge. Although the normal challenge would be financially based, a challenge may be predicated on operational viability, such that the requirements of all of the parties are satisfied.

There is no specific guidance as to what magnitude of change will be sufficient to satisfy the "more favorable" requirement, but it is submitted that a court would likely apply a reasonable test requiring the effect to be more than nominal, and if financially based, to at least represent a material economic benefit for the other joint-operators. A challenge based on improved operations may be more difficult to establish, but is no less important from a non-operator's perspective. If a non-operator does decide that it wishes to challenge the operator, it should first carefully weigh the potentially adverse consequences of doing so, since whatever the result, it may be difficult for the parties to continue to carry on joint operations. The negative feelings generated by such actions may also carry over into other operations in which the operator and non-operator are jointly involved.

Thus, if a non-operator elects to issue a challenge notice, it should at least be reasonably certain that it has a good chance of success on the merits and be prepared to accept the possible negative consequences. If a challenge notice is issued, the operator has a positive obligation to respond within 60 days and to advise the non-operator either that it is prepared to operate on the terms and conditions set out in the notice and, if so, must forthwith proceed to do so, or that it is unable or unwilling to operate on such terms and that it will resign as operator effective not later than 90 days following the aforementioned 60-day notice period. If the operator fails to respond to the notice within the 60 day notice period, he shall be deemed to have elected to resign.

Two observations can be made about the potential implications of the operatorship challenge. First, the operator may accept the terms and conditions, and if he does he is entitled to continue as operator. Secondly, if he elects not to do so, and the challenge notice has been given near the beginning of a month, a period of time close to 180 days may pass before the change of operatorship will be effected, and potentially longer if there is resistance by the operator. In neither circumstance will the non-operator likely have met its immediate objective assuming conduct of operations in a timely manner. It may also be noted that it is very likely that the charges to which the operator is entitled under the accounting procedure may be of far less benefit than the utilization of cash it holds from time to time that properly belongs to the non-operators, such that it may well elect to operate on the proposed terms to retain any advantage it may have been enjoying in this latter regard. Therefore, if after an assessment of the situation, it may reasonably be expected that an operatorship challenge notice will not be successful, the non-operator may be better served by looking to the independent operations provisions of the 1981 Procedure as a means of effecting an increased level of activity in respect of the joint lands.

서울중앙지법 2004. 10. 22. 선고 2003가합78569 판결

1. 기초사실

다음의 각 사실은 당사자 사이에 다툼이 없거나, 갑 제1 내지 13호증, 을 제1 내지 4호증(각 가지번호 포함), 을 제6호증의 각 기재에 변론 전체의 취지를 종합하여 이를 인정할 수 있다.

가. 당사자의 지위

원고는 영국 법률에 의하여 설립된 법인으로 주류관련 제품을 제조·판매하는 회사이고, 회사정리절차 개시전의 주식회사 진로(이하 '진로'라 한다)는 주류 및 발효제품의 생산 매매업 등을 목적으로 설립된 회사이다.

나. J. Lyons, Inc.와 진로의 합작투자계약 및 원고의 계약 인수

(1) 원고가 지분 전부를 소유하고 있는 J. Lyons, Inc.와 진로는 1999. 9. 17. 주류의 제조·유통 및 판매 등을 목적으로 하는 합작회사를 설립하기로 하면서 다음과 같은 계약을 체결하였다(이하 '이 사건 합작투자계약'이라 한다).

제4조 제1항 합작투자회사의 설립시 회사의 총자본, 즉 각 당사자가 보유할 주식의 총수 및 각 당사자의 주식보유비율은 아래와 같다.

J. Lyons, Inc.: 보통주 1,340,500주 및 우선주 12,064,500주(각 주당 액면가 10,000원)로서 134,050,000,000원, 총발행주식의 70%

진로: 보통주 574,500주 및 우선주 5,170,500주(각 주당 액면가 10,000원)로서 57,450,000,000원, 총발행주식의 30%

제4조 제2항 J. Lyons, Inc.와 진로는 1차 종결일에 J. Lyons, Inc.가 합작투자회사에 134,050,000,000원을 인수대금으로 현금지급하고 진로가 현물출자를 완료함으로써 제4조 제1항의 규정에 따라 합작투자회사의 주식을 인수한다.

제10조 제12항 진로가 합작투자회사의 주식에 질권 또는 기타 담보를 설정하고자 하는 경우(이하 '담보주식'이라 한다), 진로는 다음을 이행하여야 한다

제1호 질권설정과 관련된 차입거래에 대한 상세한 내용 및 질권자로 예정된 자의 신원을 J. Lyons, Inc.에게 통보하여야 한다

제2호 질권자가 담보주식에 대하여 합작투자계약 제10, 12, 13 및 24조에 기속된다는 약정을 J. Lyons, Inc.와 체결할 수 있도록 합리적인 노력을 다하며, 만약 질권자가 위 계약을 거부하는 경우에는 질권자의 질권행사시 J. Lyons, Inc.에게 담보주식에 대한 우선매수권을 부여한다.

제3호 위 제2호의 노력이 실패할 경우, J. Lyons, Inc.에게 J. Lyons, Inc.나 J. Lyons, Inc.가 허용하는 질권자가 상기 1항에 기재된 조건과 같은 조건으로 진로에게 자금대여가 이루어지도록 주선할 것을 요청한다.

제4호 위 제3호의 제안이 실패할 경우, 진로는 제1호에서 언급한 거래의 목적을 위하여 질권자에 대하여 담보주식에 질권을 설정하고, 그에 관련된 권리와 의무에 관한 자세한 내용을 J. Lyons, Inc.에게 통보한다. 다만, 질권계약서에 규정된 바를 제외하고는, 진로는 최종종결일전에 합작투자회사 주식에 질권 또는 기타 담보를 설정할 수 없다.

제12조 제1항 진로는 원고의 매수권 행사요건을 인지하자마자 그 원고의 매수권 행사 요건을 J. Lyons, Inc.에게 통지하여야 한다. 진로의 그러한 통지를 받은 날로부터 30일 이내에 또는 J. Lyons, Inc.가 진로의 통지없이 그러한 매수권 행사요건을 알게 된 후 J. Lyons, Inc.는 다음과 같은 권리를 가진다.

제1호 제12조 제2항 제1호에 있어서 새로운 지배주주가 J. Lyons, Inc.의 경쟁회사인 경우나 제12조 제2항 제2호의 경우, 진로의 주식 전부를 매수할 수 있는 권리(이하 '매수권'이라 한다)를, J. Lyons, Inc.는 매수권 행사의사를 서면으로 진로에게 통지함으로써 행사한다. 매수권은 공정한 시장가격에 행사된다. 제10조 제12항에 규정된 질권 또는 기타 담보로 인하여 매수권 행사시 그리고 매수권 이행완료시 진로가 주식을 인도할 수 없는 경우 J. Lyons, Inc.는 일방적으로 본 정관을 수정할 수 있으며, 나아가 J. Lyons, Inc.는 합작투자계약을 해지할 수 있다. 단 J. Lyons, Inc.는 진로가 주식을 인도할 수 있

게 되자마자 매수권을 행사한 당시의 위에 언급된 공정한 시장가격으로 매수권 행사를 완료하여야 한다.

제2항 "원고의 매수권 행사요건"이란 다음 각 호의 사건이 발생한 경우를 의미한다.

제2호 (a) 합작투자계약일 현재 존재하는 화의상태를 제외하고, 진로 또는 진로의 채권자들이 진로의 해산, 청산, 회사정리, 파산 또는 화의를 신청하는 경우

(b) 진로의 재정상태가(1999. 9. 17.과 비교하여) 더 악화된 후에 기업구조조정촉진을 위한 금융기관 협약에 따라 진로의 채권자들과 부채 재조정 계획이 개시되는 경우

제23조 제2항 다음의 각 호의 경우에는, 일방 당사자가 상대 당사자에게 서면통지를 함으로써 본 계약을 해지할 수 있다.

제1호 제22조에 의한 경우를 제외하고, 일방 당사자의 본 계약서상 중대한 의무위반에 대해서 타방 당사자가 그 위반행위의 치유를 요구하는 통지서를 발송한 날로부터 30일 이내에 그 위반행위가 치유되지 아니한 경우

제3호 J. Lyons, Inc.만이 해지할 수 있는 경우로서, 제12조 제2항 제2호의 사유가 발생하고, 180일 이내에 그 사유가 소멸되지 않은 경우

제24조 제3항 본 계약이 제23조 제2항 제1호, 제3 내지 5호에 의하여, J. Lyons, Inc.에 의해 해지된 경우에는

제2호 J. Lyons, Inc.는 진로의 비용으로 제22조 제4항에 따른 합작투자회사 주식에 대한 공정시장가격의 감정을 요구할 권리가 있다. 감정이 종료된 직후, J. Lyons, Inc.는 진로에 대하여 진로 소유의 합작투자회사 주식 전부를 J. Lyons, Inc. 또는 J. Lyons, Inc.가 지명하는 자에게 공정시장가격으로 매각할 것을 요구할 권리가 있다. 다만 진로 소유 주식의 공정시장가격이 6억 스털링 상당의 한국 원화 가액을 초과하는 경우, J. Lyons, Inc.는 진로의 주식 중 이를 초과하는 부분에 대한 매수의무를 부담하지 아니한다.

(2) 진로와 J. Lyons, Inc.는 1999. 12. 14. 이 사건 합작투자계약에 따라 진로발렌타인스 주식회사(이하 '진로발렌타인스'라 한다)를 설립하였고, 진로는 별지 목록 기재 주식(이하 '이 사건 주식'이라 한다)을 소유하게 되었다.

(3) 원고는 2002. 12. 23. J. Lyons, Inc.와 사이에 J. Lyons, Inc.로부터 J. Lyons, Inc.가 소유한 진로발렌타인스의 주식 전부를 양수받고, 이 사건 합작투자계약에 따른 당사자의 지위를 인수하기로 하는 계약을 체결하였으며, 진로는 같은 날 위 계약 체결에 동의하였다.

다. 진로의 이 사건 주식에 대한 질권 설정 경위

진로는 1999. 12.경 진로발렌타인스와의 사이에 진로가 토지, 건물, 구축물, 기계장치 및 공기구 비품 등을 현물출자하기로 하는 현물출자계약을 체결하였으나, 위 계약에 따른 현물출자 대상인 이천공장에는 주식회사 한빛은행 명의의 근저당권이 설정되어 있었으므로 위 근저당권을 해지하기 위하여 주식회사 한빛은행에게 100억 원을 지급하였고 이 사건 주식 중 250만 주에 대하여 질권을 설정하여 주었으나, 이 사건 합작투자계약 제10조 제12항에서 정한 절차를 이행하지 않았다.

라. 진로에 대한 회사정리절차개시 및 원고의 정리채권 신고

(1) 한편, 1997년 초경부터 자금사정이 악화되어 온 진로는 1997. 9. 9. 부도로 인하여 은행으로부터 거래정지 처분을 받았고, 1997. 9. 8. 서울지방법원에 화의개시신청을 하여 1998. 2. 3. 위 법원으로부터 화의개시결정을 받았으며, 1998. 3. 19. 화의인가 결정을 받았다.

(2) 그런데, 진로는 위 화의인가결정 이후로도 자산이 계속적으로 감소하고 부채는 계속적으로 증가하여 결국 진로의 채권자인 세나 인베스트먼트 (아일랜드) 리미티드가 2003. 4. 3. 진로에 대하여 회사정리절차개시신청을 하였고, 2003. 5. 14. 서울지방법원 2003회9호로 진로에 대한 회사정리절차개시결정이 내려지게 되었으며, 위 법원은 진로에 대한 회사정리절차 개시결정 당시에 이원을 진로의 관리인으로 선임하였는데, 2004. 4. 30. 그의 임기가 만료되자 피고를 진로의 관리인으로 새로이 선임하였다.

(3) 원고는 정리채권 신고기한 내인 2003. 6. 28. 27,450,000,000원(=액면가 10,000원×이 사건 주식 2,745,000주)을 정리채권으로 신고하였으나, 정리회사 주식회사 진로(이하 '정리회사'라 한다)의 관리인은 2003. 9. 24. 개최된 정리담보권과 정리채권의 일반조사기일에서 위 채권 전부에 대하여 '주식인도청구사유 미발생'을 이유로 이의를 제기하였다.

2. 주장 및 판단

가. 원고 주장의 요지

(1) 진로는 이 사건 주식에 대하여 질권을 설정하거나 그 외의 방법으로 담보를 제공할 경우에는 이 사건 합작투자계약 제10조 제12항에서 정한 절차를 이행하여야 함에도 불구하고 위 절차를 이행하지 아니한 채 이 사건 주식에 대하여 주식회사 한빛은행에게 질권을 설정하여 주었는바, 이는 이 사건 합작투자계약 제23조 제2항 제1호 소정의 '중대한 의무위반'에 해당하므로 원고는 정리회사에 대하여 위 약정 조항에 의하여 이 사건 합작투자계약을 해

지할 수 있다.

(2) 또한, 진로의 채권자가 2003. 4. 3. 진로에 대한 회사정리절차개시신청을 하였고, 그로부터 180일이 경과한 2003. 9. 29.까지도 진로의 회사정리사유가 치유되지 않았으므로, 원고는 정리회사에 대하여 이 사건 합작투자계약 제23조 제3호에 의하여 이 사건 합작투자계약을 해지할 수 있다.

(3) 그리고, 위 (1), (2)항의 사유로 이 사건 합작계약이 해지된 경우에는 위 합작투자계약 제24조 제3항 제2호에 의하여 원고 또는 원고가 지명하는 자에게 정리회사 소유의 이 사건 주식의 매도를 청구할 수 있는 권리가 있다.

(4) 따라서, 원고는 정리회사에 대하여 위 해지권 및 주식매도청구권의 행사를 조건으로 이 사건 주식의 인도를 청구할 정지조건부 정리채권을 가진다.

나. 판 단

(1) 이 사건 합작투자계약 제23조 제2항 제1호 소정의 해지권 발생 여부

살피건대, 진로가 1999. 12.경 진로발렌타인스와 사이에 진로가 토지, 건물, 구축물, 기계장치 및 공기구 비품 등을 현물출자하기로 하는 현물출자계약을 체결하였으나, 위 계약에 따른 현물출자 대상인 이천공장에는 주식회사 한빛은행 명의의 근저당권이 설정되어 있었으므로 위 근저당권을 해지하기 위하여 주식회사 한빛은행에게 100억 원을 지급하였고 이 사건 주식 중 250만 주에 대하여 질권을 설정하여 주고도 이 사건 합작투자계약 제10조 제12항에서 정한 절차를 이행하지 않은 사실은 앞서 본 바와 같으나, 한편 을 제6호증의 기재에 변론 전체의 취지를 종합하면 원고와 J. Lyons, Inc.가 진로와 이 사건 합작투자계약을 체결할 당시 진로에 대한 장기간의 실사로 이천공장에 설정된 근저당권 해지의 필요성에 대한 충분한 이해가 있었고, 또한 진로가 주식회사 한빛은행에게 이 사건 주식에 대한 질권을 설정하여 줄 무렵 진로의 대리인이던 변호사 김양훈이 원고와 J. Lyons, Inc.의 대리인 데이빗 루카스에게 질권 설정에 관한 설명을 한 사실을 인정할 수 있는바, 위 인정사실과 같이 진로가 이 사건 합작투자계약에 따라 이천공장을 현물출자하기 위하여 이 사건 주식에 질권을 설정한 점, 진로가 원고 및 J. Lyons, Inc.에게 위 질권설정에 관한 설명을 하여 원고 및 J. Lyons, Inc.가 그러한 사정을 알고 있었던 점에 비추어 보면 진로가 이 사건 주식에 질권을 설정하고도 이 사건 합작투자계약 제10조 제12항에서 정한 절차를 이행하지 않았다고 하여 그러한 사유만으로 위 합작투자계약 제23조 제2항 제1호 소정의 "중대한 의무위반"에 해당한다고 볼 수 없고, 달리 이를 인정할 만한 증거가 없으므로, 위 약정 조항에 해당함을 전제로 한 원고의 위 주장은 더 나아가 살펴 볼 필요 없이 이유 없다.

(2) 이 사건 합작투자계약 제23조 제2항 제3호 소정의 해지권 발생 여부

(가) 원고의 주장에 관한 판단

앞서 인정한 사실에 의하면 진로의 채권자인 세나 인베스트먼트 (아일랜드) 리미티드가 2003. 4. 3. 진로에 대한 회사정리절차개시신청을 하여 2003. 5. 14. 진로에 대한 회사정리절차개시결정이 내려졌고, 위 신청일인 2003. 4. 3.부터 180일이 경과한 2003. 9. 29.까지도 진로의 회사정리사유가 치유되지 아니하였으므로, 특별한 사정이 없는 한, 이 사건 합작투자계약의 계약인수인인 원고는 위 합작투자계약에 따라 정리회사에 대하여 위 합작투자계약을 해지하고, 위 합작투자계약 제24조 제3항 제2호에 의하여 원고 또는 원고가 지명하는 자에게 정리회사 소유의 이 사건 주식의 매도를 청구할 수 있는 권리가 있다 할 것이어서, 원고는 정리회사에 대하여 위 해지권 및 주식매도청구권 행사를 조건으로 이 사건 주식의 인도를 청구할 정지조건부 정리채권을 가진다고 할 것이며, 이에 대하여 피고가 이의를 제기한 이상 원고는 소로써 위 정리채권이 있음의 확정을 구할 수 있다고 할 것이다.

(나) 피고의 주장에 관한 판단

이에 대하여 피고는, 회사정리절차개시신청이 있을 것을 대비하여 약정해지권을 유보한 이 사건 합작투자계약 제23조 제2항 제3호는 쌍무계약에 관하여 정리회사의 관리인에게 계약의 이행 또는 해제의 선택권을 부여한 회사정리법 제103조 제1항의 취지를 몰각시키는 규정이므로 무효인 조항이라고 주장한다.

먼저 이 사건 합작투자계약이 회사정리법 제103조 제1항에서 규정하고 있는 '쌍무계약'에 해당하는지에 관하여 살피건대, 회사정리법 제103조 제1항 소정의 쌍무계약이라 함은 쌍방 당사자가 상호 대등한 대가관계에 있는 채무를 부담하는 계약으로서, 쌍방의 채무 사이에는 성립 · 이행 · 존속상 법률적 · 경제적으로 견련성을 갖고 있어서 서로 담보로서 기능하는 것을 가리키는 것인데(대법원 2000. 4. 11. 선고 99다60559 판결 참조), J. Lyons, Inc.와 진로가 1999. 9. 17. 주류의 제조 · 유통 및 판매 등을 목적으로 하는 합작투자회사를 설립하기로 하면서 J. Lyons, Inc.와 진로는 1차 종결일에 J. Lyons, Inc.가 합작투자회사에 134,050,000,000원을 인수대금으로 현금지급하고 진로가 현물출자를 완료함으로써 이 사건 합작투자계약 제4조 제1항에 따라 합작투자회사의 주식을 인수하기로 약정한 사실은 앞서 본 것과 같은바, 위 인정사실에 의하면 이 사건 합작투자계약은 J. Lyons, Inc.와 진로가 합작투자회사 설립이라는 공동의 목적을 달성하기 위하여 J. Lyons, Inc.가 134,050,000,000원을 현금지급하고, 진로가 현물출자를 하기로 약정한 일종의 발기인 조합계약이어서 J. Lyons, Inc.와 진로 쌍방이 상호 대등한 대가관계에 있는 채무를 부담한다고 볼 수 없고, 따라서 이 사건 합작투자계약은 회사정리법 제103조 제1항 소정의 '쌍무계약'에 해당하지 않는다 할 것이므로, 이와 다른 견해를 전제로 하는 피고의 위 주장은 이유 없다.

가사, 이 사건 합작투자계약이 위 '쌍무계약'에 해당한다고 하더라도, 갑 제10호증, 을 제1호증, 을 제2호증의 1, 2의 각 기재에 변론 전체의 취지를 종합하면, 이 사건 합작투자계약에 따라 진로발렌타인스가 1999. 12. 14. 설립되어 현재까지 운영되고 있고, 또 진로는 1999. 12. 27.경 진로발렌타인스에게 이천공장을 현물출자하였으며, J. Lyons, Inc.도 그 무렵 진로발렌타인스에게 합작투자회사의 주식 인수대금 134,050,000,000원을 현금 지급한 사실을 인정할 수 있는바, 위 인정사실에 의하면 진로 및 J. Lyons, Inc.는 이 사건 합작투자계약에 따라 진로발렌타인스에 대한 현물출자 및 현금지급의무를 모두 이행한 것이어서 위 합작투자계약 제23조 제2항 제3호에 대하여는 "회사와 그 상대방이 모두 회사정리절차개시당시에 아직 그 이행을 완료하지 않았음"을 전제로 한 회사정리법 제103조 제1항이 적용될 수 없다 할 것이므로, 결국 피고의 위 주장은 어느 모로 보나 이유 없다.

4. 결 론

그렇다면, 원고의 청구는 이유 있어 이를 인용한다.

서울고법 2005. 6. 10. 선고 2004나87017 판결

1. 기초사실

이 법원이 이 부분에 관하여 설시할 이유는 제1심 판결문 이유 중 해당 부분 기재와 같으므로 민사소송법 제420조에 의하여 이를 그대로 인용한다.

2. 주장 및 판단

나. 회사정리절차신청부 해지특약에 관하여

(1) 당사자 주장의 요지

원고는, 진로의 채권자가 2003. 4. 3. 진로에 대한 회사정리절차개시신청을 한 이래 그로부터 180일이 경과한 2003. 9. 29.까지도 진로의 회사정리사유가 치유되지 않았고, 따라서 원고는 정리회사에 대하여 이 사건 합작투자계약 제23조 제3호에 의하여 이 사건 합작투자계약을 해지할 수 있으며, 또한 위 합작투자계약 제24조 제3항 제2호에 의하여 원고 또는 원고가 지명하는 자에게 정리회사 소유의 이 사건 주식의 매도를 청구할 수 있는 권리가 있으므로, 정리회사에 대하여 위 해지권 및 주식매도청구권의 행사를 조건으로 이 사건 주식의 인도를 청구할 정지조건부 정리채권을 가진다고 주장한다.

이에 대하여 피고는, 회사정리절차개시신청이 있을 것을 대비하여 약정해지권을 유보한 이 사건 합작투자계약 제23조 제2항 제3호는 회사정리절차의 취지에 반하여 무효이고, 이를 전제로 한 주식매도청구권은 발생될 수 없다 할 것이므로 위 정지조건은 성취될 수 없고, 따라서 위와 같은 해지권 및 주식매도청구권의 발생을 정지조건으로 하는 정리채권은 존재하지 않는다고 주장한다.

(2) 판 단

회사정리제도는 재정적 궁핍으로 파탄에 직면하였으나 경제적으로 갱생의 가치가 있는 주식회사에 관하여 채권자, 주주 기타 이해관계인의 이해를 조정하며 그 사업의 정리재건을 도모함을 목적으로 하는바(회사정리법 제1조 참조), 회사정리법은 특정 이해관계인의 일방적 권리행사를 원칙적으로 금지시키고 정리회사와 그 채권자 및 주주로 구성되는 이해관계인 전체의 관리자로서 일종의 공적수탁자인 관리인으로 하여금 회사정리법에 따라 주식회사를 재건시키기 위하여 작성된 계획 즉 정리계획의 수행에 의하여 정리절차가 진행되도록 하고 있고, 회사정리절차가 개시된 경우 회사재산에 대한 관리처분권은 관리인에게 전속하게 되므로(회사정리법 제53조), 채권자들을 포함한 이해관계인들의 권리는 정리계획에 정한 바에 의하여 관리인이 정리회사의 사업을 경영하고 그 재산을 전속적으로 관리, 처분한 결과에 따라 실현되어질 수밖에 없고, 이와 같은 권리의 제한이 정당화될 수 있는 것은 비록 현재 재정적인 파탄에 직면하고 있을지라도 향후의 계속기업가치를 따져 경제적으로 갱생의 가치가 있다고 인정되는 때에는 법원의 감독 아래 채권자 등 이해관계인의 이해관계를 조정해 가면서 사업을 계속하게 하여 종국적으로 기업을 재건하고자 하는 것이 사회경제적으로 이익이 되고 나아가 채권자 기타의 이해관계인들에게도 이익이 되기 때문이다.

따라서 계약의 일방 당사자인 주식회사에 대하여 회사정리절차개시신청이 있음을 원인으로 하여 이 사건 합작투자계약을 해지할 수 있다는 약정은 위와 같은 회사정리절차의 취지에 반하고 또한 회사정리법상 관리인의 회사재산에 대한 관리처분권을 침해하는 것으로서 무효라고 할 것이며, 비록 이 사건과 같이 해지권이 발생하기 위하여, 회사정리절차개시신청의 사유가 발생한 사실 이외에 180일 이내에 그 사유가 소멸되지 않을 것을 추가요건으로 하고 있다 하더라도 위와 같은 결론에는 아무런 영향이 없다.

더욱이, 이 사건 합작투자계약 해지 후의 주식매도청구권에 관한 약정은 이 사건 합작투자계약관계를 청산하기 위한 별개, 독립의 약정이라고 볼 것이지 이 사건 합작투자계약에 의한 주식회사의 설립 또는 주식인수약정 등과 일체로서 불가분의 관계에 있는 것으로 볼 수는 없고, 한편 원고는 아직 위 계약해지권 및 주식매도청구권을 행사하지 아니한 채, 정리법원에 대하여 위 해지권 및 주식매도청구권의 행사를 조건으로 이 사건 주식의 인도를 청구할 정지조건부 정리채권이 있음을 신고하였고, 피고는 위 채권에 대하여 '주식인도청구사유 미발생'을 이유로 이의를 제기하였음은 앞서 본 바와 같은바, 원고가 위 약정에 기하여 정리절차 개시 후에 관리인에 대하여 주식매도청구권을 행사한 경우일지라도 그와 같은 주식매도청구권의 행사에 의하여 이 사건 주식에 대하여 매매계약이 이루지게 되어 그 매매계약에 따라 매수인인 원고는 매도인인 관리인에 대하여 이 사건 주식매매대금을 지급하여야 하고, 관리인은 위 주식을 인도하여야 할 의무를 부담하게 되므로, 이와 같이 정리절차 개시당시에 주식매매계약을 체결할 권리가 존재하였고 정리절차가 개시된 이후에 비로소 상대방의 권리행사에 의하여 주식매매계약이 체결된 경우에 관하여도 관리인으로서는 회사정리법 제103조의 규정을 유추하여 위 매매계약을 해제하거나 계약이행의 청구를 선택할 수 있다고 보아야 할 것이고, 그 이전에 상대방인 원고가 임의로 관리인에게 위 매매계약의 이행을 청구할 수는 없다고 할 것이다.

따라서, 위 해지약정이 무효인 이상 이에 기한 주식매도청구권 역시 발생될 수 없다 할 것이므로 위와 같은 해지권 및 주식매도청구권의 발생을 정지조건으로 하는 정리채권은 존재하지 않는다고 할 것이다.

대법 2007. 9. 6 . 선고 2005다38263 판결

1. 계약의 당사자들 사이에 채무자인 회사의 재산상태가 장래 악화될 때에 대비하여 지급정지, 회사정리절차의 개시신청, 회사정리절차의 개시와 같이 도산에 이르는 과정상의 일정한 사실이 그 회사에 발생하는 것을 당해 계약의 해지권의 발생원인으로 정하거나 또는 계약의 당연 해지사유로 정하는 특약(이하 '도산해지조항'이라고만 한다)을 두는 경우가 있는데, 민법은 몇 가지 계약 유형에 관하여 일방 당사자에게 선고된 파산이 계약에 미치는 영향에 관한 규정을 두고 있을 뿐(민법 제599조, 제614조, 제637조, 제663조, 제674조, 제690조, 제717조 등 참조) 도산해지조항의 효력과 관련하여서는 별다른 규정을 두고 있지 아니하고, 구 회사정리법(2005. 3. 31. 법률 제7428호로 제정된 채무자 회생 및 파산에 관한 법률 부칙 제2조로 폐지, 이하 '회사정리법'이라고만 한다)이나 그 후속 입법에 해당하는 현행 채무자 회생 및 파산에 관한 법률에서도 도산해지조항을 일반적으로 금지하는 규정은 찾아볼 수 없다. 그리고 도산해지조항의 적용 결과가 정리절차개시 후 정리회사에 미치는 영향이라는 것은 당해 계약의 성질, 그 내용 및 이행 정도, 해지사유로 정한 사건의 내용 등의 여러 사정에 따라 달라질 수밖에 없다. 따라서 도산해지조항을 일반적으로 금지하는 법률이 존재하지 않는 상태에서 그와 같은

구체적인 사정을 도외시한 채 도산해지조항은 어느 경우에나 회사정리절차의 목적과 취지에 반한다고 하여 일률적으로 무효로 보는 것은 계약자유의 원칙을 심각하게 침해하는 결과를 낳을 수 있을 뿐만 아니라 상대방 당사자가 채권자의 입장에서 채무자의 도산으로 초래될 법적 불안정에 대비할 보호가치 있는 정당한 이익을 무시하는 것이 될 수 있다. 이와 같은 사정과 아울러 회사정리법상 관리인은 정리절차개시 당시에 존재하는 회사 재산에 대한 관리처분권을 취득하는 데에 불과하므로 채무자인 회사가 사전에 지급정지 등을 정지조건으로 하여 처분한 재산에 대하여는 처음부터 관리처분권이 미치지 아니한다는 점을 생각해 보면, 도산해지조항이 회사정리법에서 규정한 부인권의 대상이 되거나 공서양속에 위반된다는 등의 이유로 효력이 부정되어야 할 경우를 제외하고, 도산해지조항으로 인하여 정리절차개시 후 정리회사에 영향을 미칠 수 있다는 사정만으로는 그 조항이 무효라고 할 수는 없다.

그리고 쌍방 미이행의 쌍무계약의 경우에는 계약의 이행 또는 해제에 관한 관리인의 선택권을 부여한 회사정리법 제103조의 취지에 비추어 도산해지조항의 효력을 무효로 보아야 한다거나 아니면 적어도 정리절차개시 이후 종료시까지의 기간 동안에는 도산해지조항의 적용 내지는 그에 따른 해지권의 행사가 제한된다는 등으로 해석할 여지가 없지는 않을 것이다. 그러나 회사정리법 제103조에 정한 쌍무계약이라 함은 쌍방 당사자가 상호 대등한 대가관계에 있는 채무를 부담하는 계약으로서, 본래적으로 쌍방의 채무 사이에 성립·이행·존속상 법률적·경제적으로 견련성을 갖고 있어서 서로 담보로서 기능하는 것을 가리키는 것이므로(대법원 2000. 4. 11. 선고 99다60559 판결, 2002. 5. 28. 선고 2001다68068 판결 등 참조), 위 규정이 적용되려면 서로 대등한 대가관계에 있는 계약상 채무의 전부 또는 일부가 이행되지 아니한 것을 의미한다. 그런데 이 사건의 경우에 도산해지조항이 문제된 합작투자계약은 둘 이상의 당사자가 모여 상호출자하여 회사를 설립·운영하는 것을 목적으로 하는 계약으로서 본질적으로 조합계약에 해당하고, 계약당사자들로서는 상호 출자하여 회사를 설립함으로써 조합구성에 관한 채무의 이행을 마쳤으며 그에 따라 계약에서 정한 바에 의하여 설립된 회사에 관한 의결권의 행사 또는 이사회의 구성 등을 위하여 서로 협조하여야 하는 의무 등이 남게 되었는바, 이러한 의무는 성립·이행·존속상 법률적·경제적으로 견련성을 갖고 있어서 서로 담보로서 기능한다고 할 수 없어 서로 대등한 대가관계에 있다고 보기 어려우므로 회사정리법 제103조가 적용된다고 할 수 없고, 또한 일반적인 재산상의 계약과는 달리 서로 간의 고도의 신뢰관계를 전제로 하므로 일방 당사자에게 지급정지 등의 사유가 발생하고 회사정리절차가 개시되어 장차 계약 당사자가 아닌 제3자인 관리인이 상대방으로 될 것으로 예상되는 경우에는 다른 당사자로서는 그로 인하여 초래될 상황에 대비할 정당한 이익을 갖는다고 보아야 할 것이며, 따라서 위와 같은 사유에 의한 도산해지조항을 약정한 경우에는 이를 무효라고 단정하기 어렵다 할 것이다.

그럼에도 불구하고, 이와 달리 이 사건 합작투자계약의 성질, 그 내용 및 이행 정도, 해지사유로 정한 사건의 내용 등 여러 사정에 비추어 도산해지조항의 적용 결과가 정리절차개시 후 정리회사에 실질적으로 어떠한 영향을 미치는지를 세밀히 심리하지 아니한 채 합작투자계약의 일방 당사자인 주식회사 진로에 대한 회사정리절차 개시신청을 약정해지권 발생사유로 정한 이 사건 도산해지조항이 회사정리절차의 목적과 취지에 반하고 또한 회사정리법상 관리인의 회사재산에 대한 관리처분권을 침해하는 것이라는 이유로 무효라고 한 원심의 판단에는, 도산해지조항의 효력에 관한 법리를 오해한 위법이 있다고 할 것이다.

2. 그러나 회사정리법 제102조의 정리채권이라 함은 의사표시 등 채권 발생의 원인이 정리절차개시 전의 원인에 기해 생긴 재산상의 청구권을 말하는 것이므로, 원래 채권 발생의 원인이 정리절차개시 전의 원인에 기한 것인 한 그 내용이 구체적으로 확정되지 아니하였거나 변제기가 정리절차개시 후에 도래하더라도 정리채권으로 될 수 있지만, 채권의 발생원인이 쌍방 미이행의 쌍무계약에 해당하는 경우에는 회사정리법 제103조 및 제104조의 규정이 적용되어 관리인이 이행 또는 해제를 선택하기 전에는 관리인에게 그 이행을 청구할 수 없고 나아가 관리인이 이행을 선택하면 공익채권으로 취급되어 정리채권의 신고 대상이 아니며 반대로 관리인이 해제를 선택하면 채권 자체가 소멸되어 역시 정리채권의 신고 대상이 되지 못하고 단지 그 해제권 행사로 인한 손해배상청구권을 정리채권으로 신고할 수 있을 뿐이므로, 어느 경우에나 위 채권은 정리채권이 될 수 없다. 그리고 이와 같은 법리는 정리절차개시 당시에 매매계약을 체결할 권리가 존재하였고 정리절차가 개시된 이후에 비로소 상대방의 권리행사에 의하여 매매계약이 성립되거나 장차 매매계약이 성립될 수 있어 아직 쌍방의 채무가 이행되지 아니한 경우에도 유추적용된다고 보아야 할 것이다.

이 사건에서 원고는 이 사건 합작투자계약상의 도산해지조항에 따른 계약해지권 및 주식매수청구권을 행사하지 아니한 채 정리법원에게 그 행사를 정지조건으로 이 사건 주식의 인도를 청구할 정리채권이 있음을 신고하였는바, 위 정지조건부 주식인도청구권은 원고가 정리절차개시 이후에 이 사건 도산해지조항에 따른 계약해지권을 행사한 다음 다시 이 사건 합작투자계약에 따라 주식매수청구권을 행사할 경우에 성립하는 장래의 매매계약에 관한 권리이므로, 위에서 본 쌍방 미이행의 쌍무계약에 관한 법리에 따라 관리인이 이행을 선택할 경우나 반대로 관리인이 해제를 선택할 경우에 모두 정리채권으로 될 수 없으므로, 위 정지조건부 주식인도청구권을 정리채권으로 신고하여 확정을 구할 수는 없다.

노트와 질문

현행 채무자회생 및 파산에 관한 법률("도산법")은 채무자 또는 채권자의 회생절차개시의 신청으로 개시되며[24] 법원은 보전처분이나 다른 절차의 중지를 명할 수 있고 개시결정이 있게 되면 다른 절차는 자동적으로 중지되며 관리인에 채무자의 업무수행과 재산관리권이 전속한다. 도산법 및 진로판결을 고려하여 운영자권한박탈조항을 둔다면 어느 시점에 어떤 절차를 통하여 권한이 박탈당하는 것으로 할 것인가?[25]

다. 공동운영계약당사자간 우선매수청구권[26]

공동운영계약의 일방당사자가 자신의 이익을 매각하려는 경우 다른 계약당사자는 이를 우선 매수할 권리가 있는 것으로 합의하는 것이 통상의 관행이다. 공동운영계약의 당사자들은 서로의 기술능력과 자금사정, 경영능력 등을 신뢰하여 공동운영을 하기로 한 이상, 신뢰관계가 없는 제3자나 경쟁자가 계약상의 당사자로서 들어오는 것을 당연히 꺼리기 때문이다. 통상 합작투자계약서에서 합작투자상대방이 자신의 주식을 제3자에게 매각하기에 앞서 합작투자상대방에게 이를 먼저 매수할 기회를 줄 것을 규정하고 있는 것과 유사한 메커니즘이다.

우선매수청구권도 여러가지 변형이 가능하여 우선 협상할 권리와 우선 청약을 할 권리로 나누어 볼 수 있다.[27] 우선 협상할 권리는 공동운영계약의 일방당사자가 자신의 지분을 매각하기를 원하는 경우 우선 이러한 의사를 다른 계약당사자들에게 통지하고 일정한 기간 이내에 선의로 협상할 의무를 부과하는 것이다. 우선 매수할 권리는 공동운영계약의 일방당사자가 자신의 지분 매각에 관하여 제3자와 협상, 합의를 한 후에 이를 다른 계약당사자들에게 알리고 이보다 우월한 조건으로 청약을 할 수 있는 권리를 부여하는 것이다.

매각의 의미에 관하여도 논란의 여지가 있다. 공동운영계약의 당사자가 제3의 회사에 흡수합병되는 경우 지분의 매각이라고 볼 수 있을까?[28] 계약해석의 불명확성을 미연에 방지하기 위하여는 매각의 의미에 관한 자세한 규정을 두어야 한다. 통상 계열사에 대한 매각은

---

24) 채무자회생 및 파산에 관한 법률 제34조 이하.

25) 캐나다에서의 논의에 관하여는 Clifford D. Johnson, *Non-Operators' Rights Under the CAPL Operating Procedure*, 24 ALTA. L. REV. 1, 9 (1989-90)는 CALP Operationg Procedure의 개정은 논하면서 운용자가 채권자와 회생절차개시신청에 관한 협의를 시작하는 시점과 같이 가장 이른 시점에 자동적으로 자격을 상실하는 조항을 제안.

26) 권리의 구체적인 내용에 따라서 right of first refusal과 right of first offer로 나뉘고 통틀어 preferential right to purchase라고도 한다.

27) AIPN Model Form JOA. Art. 12. 2.

28) *Fina Oil & Chemical Corp. v. Amoco Production Co.*, 673 So.2d 668 (La. App. 1996) (Amoco는 자신이 소유하고 있던 탐사개발권 50% 지분을 자회사에 양도한 후 자회사의 주식을 제3자에게 양도하자 나머지 50% 지분 보유자가 우선매수권을 주장).

우선매수권 대상이 되지 않는 것으로 합의하며 또한 너무 작게 나누어 매각하는 것을 막기 위하여 일정한 비율 이상의 매각만 가능하도록 합의하기도 한다. 공동운영계약의 당사자가 다수인 경우 절차적인 메커니즘이 복잡하여질 수 있고 또한 지분소유자가 너무 많아져서 공동운영 자체가 어려워질 수 있기 때문이다.

노트와 질문

운영계약의 당사자간 일방 당사자가 장래 추가적인 탐사권을 얻은 경우 이를 서로 나누기로 합의하는 AMI조항을 넣기도 한다. 이러한 합의는 운영계약의 당사자가 계약상 지위를 제3자에게 양도한 경우 양수인에게도 적용되는가?[29]

29) *CNOOC Southeast Asia Ltd. v. Paladin Resources (Sudan) Limited,* 222 S.W.3d 889 (Tex. App.-Dallas 2007).

제 6 장

운영자와 지질조사, 시추 등 용역계약자

1. 표준계약서의 개발

석유탐사개발업체가 석유탐사권을 취득, 탐사를 시작하면서 실제 많은 하도급업체가 각자의 도구를 가지고 탄성파 자료취득, 전산처리, 해석, 지질조사, 탐사시추조사, 물리검출 등 여러 작업을 진행한다.[1] IADC,[2] IAGC,[3] AIPN, LOGIC[4] 등 사업자단체들이 표준계약서를 제시하고 있고 사업자들도 내부적으로 표준양식을 가지고 있다.[5] 통상의 계약서와 마찬가지로 기술적인 사양을 특정하고 양 당사자의 제한된 진술과 보장, 제공하여야 할 용역의 내용과 이에 대한 용역대가의 지급, 용역의 제공시기, 용역의 적용법규준수, 채무불이행시 구제수단, 위험분담, 준거법과 분쟁해결수단을 포함하고 있다. 작업장에의 적용법규는 경제적 낭비를 막기 위한 과대투자방지, 석유의 낭비를 막기 위한 석유잔존방지와 누수방지, 환경보존을 정책목표로 한다. 이하에서는 대가의 지급과 위험의 배분이라는 두 가지 주제에 맞추어 계약관행과 분쟁사례를 살펴본다.

2. 대가지급유형

용역대가의 지급방식은 크게 두 가지로 나누어 볼 수 있다. 하나는 총액계약으로 일괄수

---

1) 기술적인 측면에 관하여는 AMERICAN PETROLEUM INSTITUTE, INTRODUCTION TO OIL AND GAS PRODUCTION (1983); William C. Lyons et al, STANDARD HANDBOOK OF PETROLEUM & NATURAL GAS ENGINEERING (2005).

2) http://www/iadc/org에서 Footage Drilling Contract, Daywork Drilling Contract(미국, 국제, 해저, 육지별 구분), Turnkey Drilling Contract, Master Service Contract 등 출판물정보열람가능.

3) http://www.iagc.org contract manual, data licensing 등 출판물정보열람가능.

4) http://www.logic-oil.com/standard-contracts/documents에서 표준계약서 열람가능.

5) 모법계약서의 장단점에 관하여는 A.Timothy Martin, *Model Contracts: A Survey of the Global Petroleum Industry,* 22 J. OF ENERG. & NAT'L L. 281, 284 (2004). A. Timothy Martin/J. Jay Park, *Global Petroleum Industry Model Contracts Revisited: Higher, Faster, Stronger,* 3 J. WORLD ENER. L & BUS. 4 (2010).

주(턴키)계약과 같이 일정한 용역을 제공하는 데 대한 대가가 미리 고정되어 있는 것이다. 탐사시추의 예를 들면 용역제공자는 일정한 깊이까지 시추작업을 하면 그만이며 실제 석유나 천연가스를 발견하는 것도, 탐사공을 폐쇄하는 것도 용역제공자의 의무가 아니다.

일당계약은 용역제공자에 보다 유리한 것으로 진행에 관계없이 하루의 용역제공에 대하여 보수를 지급하는 것이다. 북미의 실태를 보면 일당계약이 대부분이며 총액계약이나 시추의 깊이에 따라서 foot당 용역대가를 지급하는 계약은 드물다고 한다. 일종의 인센티브로서 비용에 미리 정한 수익률로 또는 일의 성공여부나 완성에 필요한 시간에 따른 보너스를 지급하는 경우도 있다고 한다.[6]

3. 위험의 배분수단[7]

가. 면책조항

1) 제3자의 손해배상청구

통상적인 작업장의 풍경은 운영자와 함께 여러 하도급업자들이 동시에 작업을 진행하고 있는 것이다. 이들은 자신의 도구로 각자 또는 서로 협업하여 작업을 하면서 도구를 잃어버릴 위험도 있고 사고가 나면 여러 사람이 목숨을 잃을 수도 있다. 이들간 계약은 서로의 위험한계를 정하는 중요한 도구이다. 계약에 더하여 위험을 분산하기 보험사와 보험계약을 체결할 수도 있다.

계약상 서로의 위험을 분할하는 조항이 면책조항이다. 위험은 그 위험을 가장 잘 관리하거나 부보할 수 있는 자가 부담하는 것이 이상적이지만, 실제 계약상 면책조항은 협상에 따라서 결정된다. 위험을 부담할 수 없는 계약당사자가 위험을 부담하게 되면 파산에 이를 수 있고 거꾸로 위험을 부담할 수 있는 계약당사자가 위험을 부담하게 되면 당사자들의 전체 위험수위를 낮추어서 계약체결을 촉진할 것이다.

면책조항은 크게 3가지로 나뉜다. 첫째, 누구에게 귀책사유가 있느냐에 따라서 위험을 분할하는 방식이다. 특별한 계약상 합의가 없더라도 계약법이나 불법행위법의 일반원칙에 따라 귀책사유가 있는 자가 손해를 부담하겠지만 소송비용의 보상이 가능한 점에서 의미가 있다. 둘째, 누구의 행위인가에 따라서 위험을 분할하는 방식이다. 예를 들면 탐사구역 A의 운영권자 AA사가 필요상 탐사구역 B의 운영권자 BB사의 플랫폼을 이용하는 경우 BB사는 AA

6) Smith, 주1-4 상게서, 652-53.

7) 아래의 논의는 Smith, 주1-4 상게서 670-86에 요약되어 있는 Donald P. Butler, The Master Service Agreement 2000이라는 논문을 주로 참고. Donald P. Butler, The Master Service Agreement, *in* ENERGY CONTRACT MANAGEMENT IN OIL AND GAS (Barclay Nicholson ed. 2011).

사에게 플랫폼의 이용에 관한 일체의 면책을 요구할 것이다. 셋째, 누가 관리 내지 지배관계에 있는가에 따른 위험분할방식이다. 손해발생에 과실이 있었는지, 과실에 대한 면책조항이 유효한지에 관계없이 인력 내지 도구를 지배 내지 관리하는 자가 위험을 부담하기로 합의하는 것이다. 이는 과실책임에 따르는 과다한 보험부보의 가능성이나 과실여부의 판단을 위한 쟁송의 필요성이 없으니 효율적이고 또한 도구를 관리하고 근로자와 지배관계에 서 있는 자가 위험을 가장 잘 예측하고 방지조치를 취할 수 있는 위치에 있다는 점에서 합리적이다.

지배관계에 따른 위험분담의 경우 운용자와 하도급업자는 통상 각자의 직원과 도구에 대하여 위험을 분담하는 것으로 합의한다.[8] 보다 어려운 협상은 운용자의 다른 하도급업자나 하도급업자의 하도급업자와 같은 제3의 손해를 누가 부담할 것인가에 관한 것이다. 이들에 대하여 아무런 합의가 없은 경우 제3자에 대한 손해배상책임을 제3자에게 이전시키지 못하고 운용자가 중간에서 책임을 지는 사태가 일어날 수 있다.

[그림 6-1] 운영자와 용업업자간 거래구조도

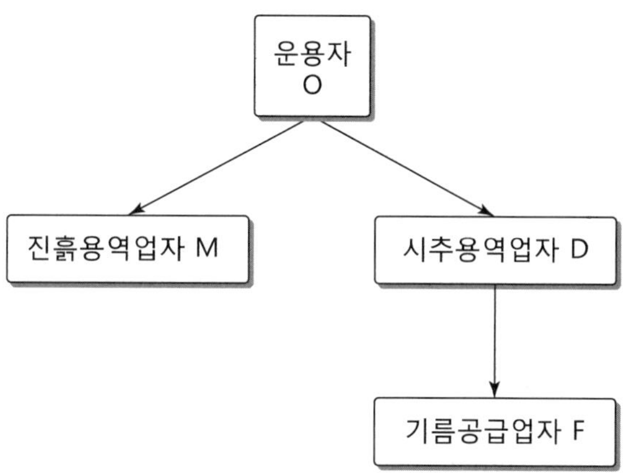

O-M, O-D, D-F 3개의 계약은 제3자의 책임에 대하여 합의한 바 없이 각자 자신의 지배관계에 관하여 책임을 합의하였는데, O의 과실로 M, D, F가 손해를 입은 경우 M과 D는 면책조항에 따라서 O에게 손해배상을 청구하지 못한다. 그러나, F의 근로자가 손해를 입은 경우 또는 F가 재산상 손해를 입은 경우 이들은 O에게 그 배상을 청구할 수 있다. O가 이런 상황을 피하는 방법은 상대방이 면책하여 줄 손해의 범위를 확대하든가, 아니면 용역업체와 하도급업체간 면책조항에 자신이 피면책자의 범위에 포함되는 것이다.

8) 발전시설을 운영하는 자가 수처리장치, 가스공급장치, 전기공급장치를 운영하는 자들과 각자 지배하는 범위내에서 책임을 분담하기로 합의하는 것과 유사하다.

O는 O-D 면책조항에서 O는 D에게 D뿐만 아니라 D의 하도급자인 F의 손해에 대하여도 면책하여 줄 것을 요구할 수 있다. 그런 면책조항하에서 F가 O을 상대로 손해배상청구를 하는 경우 O는 이를 지급하고 D에게 면책을 요구할 수 있고 따라서 결국 D가 F의 손해를 부담하게 된다.

O-D 면책조항에 관계없이 D-F 면책조항에서 D가 F에게 D뿐만 아니라 D의 다른 용역업체, 즉 O나 M에게까지 면책하라고 요구할 수 있다. 이런 면책조항하에서 F가 O에게 손해배상청구를 하는 경우 O은 D-F 면책조항이 제3자를 위한 계약이며 이에 대한 수익의 의사표시를 하고 D-F 면책조항을 직접 원용하여 F의 손해배상 청구를 거절할 수 있다. 결국 M, D, F 모두 각자의 손해를 떠맡는 결과가 된다.

O-M, O-D, D-F 3개의 계약은 제3자의 책임에 대하여 합의한 바 없이 각자 자신의 지배관계에 관하여 책임을 합의하였는데, F의 과실로 D. O, M이 손해를 입은 경우 F는 D의 손해배상청구에 대하여는 면책조항을 근거로 배척할 수 있으나, O, M의 손해배상청구에 대하여는 자신이 떠 맡아야 한다.

그러나, D-F 면책조항에서 D가 F뿐만 아니라 O, M까지의 손해도 책임지기로 한다면, F가 O와 M에게 손해를 배상하여 주고 D에게 면책책임을 추궁할 수 있다. D가 이를 다시 O에게 청구하려면 D-O면책조항에서 O가 D의 손해를 D뿐만 아니라 하도급자인 F의 손해까지 면책하여 주기로 합의하여야 한다. D-O간 면책조항의 내용을 모르는 단계에서 F는 D에게 면책의 손해와 피면책자 모두를 광범위하게 요구하는 것이 가장 바람직할 것이다.

Foreman v. Exxon Corporation, 770 F.2d 490 (5th Cir. 1985)

[Exxon은 운용자로서 Diamond M과는 시추용역계약을, Offshore와는 유정파이프용역계약을 별도로 체결하였다. Offshore의 근로자가 Exxon과 Diamond M을 상대로 손해배상을 청구, 법원은 Exxon : Diamond M : Offshore가 10 : 55 : 35로 과실이 있으니 Exxon은 Diamond M과의 면책계약에 따른 55를, Offshore는 Exxon과의 면책계약에 따른 45를 지급하라고 판단, Exxon은 Offshore을 상대로 Exxon이 Diamond M에게 부담한 면책책임 55에 대하여도 보상하여 달라고 주장했다.]

IV. Offshore's Indemnity Obligation for Exxon's Contractual Liability to Diamond M

The district court determined that Offshore was not required to indemnify Exxon for amounts Exxon owed pursuant to Exxon's contract of indemnity with Diamond M. On cross-appeal, Exxon argues that the first paragraph of the indemnity provision of the contract between Exxon and Offshore unambiguously provides for such indemnity and in the alternative that the parties intended to provide for such indemnity.[1] In doing so, Exxon relies upon *Mills v. Zapata Drilling Co.*, 722 F.2d 1170 (5th Cir.1983), and attempts to distinguish *Corbitt v. Diamond M. Drilling Co.*, 654 F.2d 329 (5th Cir.1981). Because we conclude that *Corbitt* is controlling and *Mills* is distinguishable, we affirm the district court's determination that Exxon is not entitled to indemnity for amounts for which it is liable to Diamond M pursuant to their indemnity agreement.

Our interpretation of the terms of the Exxon-Offshore contract leads us to conclude that, as in Corbitt, the parties did not intend to provide Exxon indemnification for Exxon's contractual liability to Diamond M.

In *Corbitt* the issue before this Court was identical to the issue presented here: whether Shell was entitled to indemnification from its contractor (Sladco) pursuant to a Shell-Sladco indemnity agreement contained in a purchase order for amounts Shell was required to pay Diamond M pursuant to a Shell-Diamond M indemnity agreement. The Shell-Sladco indemnity agreement provided in pertinent part that:

> Contractor [Sladco] shall indemnify and defend Shell Oil Company and its employees and agents against all claims, suits, liabilities and expenses on account of injury or death of persons (including employees of Shell or Contractor, and sub-contractor and their employees) or damage of property arising out of or in connection with performance of this Order, and not caused solely by Shell's negligence without any contributory negligence or fault of Contractor or any sub-contractors. *Corbitt*, 654 F.2d at 351.

Affirming the district court's judgment that Shell was not entitled to such indemnification, this Court stated that "express notice is required where a party seeks to shift his contractual liability to indemnify a third party" and then went on to state that:

> The Purchase Order, however, does not expressly provide that Sladco will indemnify Shell for Shell's contractual liability to third persons. The Sladco-Shell agreement simply provides for indemnity 'against all claims, suits, liabilities and expenses on account of personal injury....'(emphasis in original).

---

1. The first paragraph of the indemnity provision provides that: Contractor further agrees to protect, indemnify, and hold harmless Exxon, its agents, servants and employees, from and against all claims, demands and causes of action of every kind and character arising in favor of Exxon's employees or third parties (third parties being defined for purposes of this provision as any party other than employee of Exxon or an employee of Contractor) for injury to or death or illness of persons or loss of or damage to property in any way resulting from the willful or negligent acts or omissions of Contractor, Contractor's agents, employees, representatives, or subcontractors, whether or not such personal injury, illness, death or loss of or damage to property arose out of the joint and/or concurrent negligence of Exxon, its agents, employees, or representatives and/or the unseaworthiness of any vessel.

But Shell's liability to Diamond M is not on account of personal injury. Rather, it is on account of its agreement to indemnify Diamond M.... Since the Purchase Order does not specifically provide that Sladco assumes claims arising from Shell's own separate contractual obligations, such indemnification is not required. *Corbitt*, 654 F.2d at 333.

Similarly, the agreement between Exxon and Offshore provides for indemnity "against all claims, demands and causes of action ... for injury to or death or illness of persons ... in any way resulting from the willful or negligent acts or omissions of Contractor...." (emphasis added) Exxon's argument that the language of the indemnity provision unambiguously provides that Offshore must reimburse Exxon for Exxon's contractual liability to Diamond M ignores the limiting language "for injury to or death or illness of persons." This language is identical, as a practical matter, to the limiting language in *Corbitt* — "on account of personal injury" — and should be accorded the same meaning and force. Both limit the indemnitees to indemnity for claims based upon tortious, not contractual, injuries.

Further, Exxon argues that Offshore's agreement to indemnify it against "all claims, demands, and causes of action of every kind and character arising in favor of ... third parties" includes Diamond M's "third party" contractual claim against Exxon. (emphasis added) This argument ignores the fact, however, that in *Corbitt* we declined to read the phrase "all claims" to include contractual claims when that phrase was limited by language requiring some claim based "on account of personal injury."[2] In *Corbitt*, we stated that "Shell's liability to Diamond M is not on account of personal injury. Rather, it is on account of its agreement to indemnify Diamond M...." Id. Similarly, Exxon's liability to Diamond M is not "for injury to ... persons;" rather, it is for, or the result of, its agreement to indemnify Diamond M. We find *Corbitt* indistinguishable from this action. *Marathon Pipe Line Co. v. Drilling Rig Rowan/Odessa*, 527 F.Supp. 824, 835-36 (E.D.La.1981), aff'd, 699 F.2d 240 (5th Cir.1983).

In addition, we find the reasoning in *Corbitt* equally applicable to the instant case. There, we stated:

> Nor can it be said that Shell's contractual duty to indemnify Diamond M is the kind of liability which the parties to the Purchase Order intended to include within the scope of Sladco's duty to indemnify Shell. Apart from any contractual undertaking to the contrary, Sladco's exposure to liability for injuries sustained by its own employees would be limited by the relevant workers' compensation scheme. If Shell

---

2. [t]he obligation to indemnify is to be strictly construed, and the status of indemnitee is also interpreted narrowly. *Gulf Oil Corp. v. Mobile Drilling Barge or Vessel Margaret*, 441 F.Supp. 1 (E.D.La.1975), aff'd, 565 F.2d 958 (5th Cir.1978). Additionally, an indemnity agreement will be held to benefit a particular party only when it is express in that effect, and reflects the clear intent of the parties. *Day v. Odeco*, 353 F.Supp. 1350 (E.D.La.1973).

> had intended that Sladco forego its limited liability for such injuries, Shell should have said so in clear, specific terms. In the absence of such explicit language, it is unreasonable to assume that Sladco intended to undertake such an unusual and surprising obligation. *Corbitt*, 654 F.2d at 733.

Similarly, we find no indication in the Exxon-Offshore contract that Offshore has accepted this unusual extension of its normal obligations.

Exxon also contends that our disposition of this appeal is controlled by *Mills*, supra. *Mills*, like this case, involved a contractual indemnity issue relating to an injury that occurred on the outer continental shelf off the Louisiana coast. The plaintiff in *Mills* was employed by Louisiana Casing Crew & Rental Tool Corporation (Louisiana) while working on a Shell rig. CNG was the operator of the rig and the plaintiff was killed by an employee of Zapata, a subcontractor of CNG. At issue in *Mills* was the effect of an indemnification provision in a contract between CNG and Louisiana which provided in pertinent part that:

> Contractor [Louisiana] agrees to indemnify and hold harmless ... any or all co-lessees of CNG [i.e., including Zapata] ... and any or all ... invitees ... of CNG [including Zapata] ... against any and all claims ... in which such co-lessees ... or ... invitees ... of CNG [including Zapata, which was a co-lessee as well as an invitee of CNG] may be named party defendant ... by any employee [Arland Mills] of Contractor [Louisiana], ... or the legal representative [Vicki Mills] ... of any such employee, in anywise arising out of or incident to the work to be performed under this contract....*Mills*, 722 F.2d at 1174.

Exxon argues that just as Zapata is identified as an "invitee" or "co-lessee" in *Mills*, so also is Diamond M identified as a "third party" in the indemnity provision at issue in this case. We decline to accept such an argument.

In *Mills*, unlike the indemnity agreement in this action, Zapata, as an "invitee" of CNG, was specifically named as an indemnitee of Louisiana. As we stated in Mills, "the Louisiana-CNG contract specifically provides ... that 'contractor [Louisiana] shall be responsible and CNG shall never be liable' for damages recoverable by an employee of Louisiana, or his representative, on account of an injury caused by the negligence of an employee of Zapata." *Mills*, 722 F.2d at 1175. Diamond M, even if considered a "third party" as defined in the Exxon-Offshore contract, is not an indemnitee under the terms of the indemnity provisions here. Accordingly, we find *Mills* distinguishable in fact.[3]

---

3. To the extent that the contract in Mills expressly provided that Zapata, as an invitee, was entitled to indemnity, Mills supports this Court's conclusion that the parties must expressly provide for indemnity of another's contractual indemnity exposure. Here, the contract between Exxon and Offshore evidences no such intent.

We conclude that Offshore's obligation to indemnify Exxon for Exxon's contractual liability to Diamond M may arise only from the plainly expressed intention of the parties, spelled out in unambiguous terms. Louisiana law is clear that a contract of indemnity for one's own negligence can not be allowed unless the parties specifically, clearly and expressly agree to such. *Rivers v. Schlumberger Well Surveying Corp.*, 389 So.2d 807 (La.App.3d Cir.1980). In *Corbitt* we addressed this same requirement for indemnity of one's own negligence and we extended it to a case similar to ours. There we stated:

> A contract to indemnify another for his own negligence imposes an extraordinary obligation. Thus an indemnitor is entitled to express notice that under his agreement, and through no fault of his own, he may be called upon to pay damages caused solely by the negligence of his indemnitee. For the same reasons express notice is required where a party seeks to shift his contractual liability to indemnify a third party. 654 F.2d at 333 (emphasis added). See also *Scherff v. Missouri-Kansas-Texas Railroad Co.*, 449 F.2d 23 (5th Cir.1971). This reasoning applies with equal force to the issue before us under Louisiana law.

We believe that the district court properly interpreted the intent of the parties to this contract, and that it properly concluded that the parties failed to clearly and expressly provide that Offshore indemnify Exxon for Exxon's contractual liability to Diamond M.

Generally, Louisiana law requires the Court to give legal effects to agreements, according to the true intent of the parties. The true intent of the parties is to be determined by the clear and explicit terms of the agreements. *Leenerts Farms, Inc. v. Rogers*, 421 So.2d 216, 218 (La.1982); La.Civ.Code Ann. art. 1945 (West 1977). Because we conclude that *Mills* is not dispositive here, and because we agree that the parties to this contract, like the parties to the contract in *Corbitt*, did not intend to shift to Offshore the contractual indemnity exposure of Exxon to Diamond M, we reject Exxon's cross-appeal.

노트와 질문

Exxon이 Offshore와 용역계약을 어떻게 수정하였더라면 본건 Diamond M에 대한 책임에 대하여서도 면책책임을 추궁할 수 있었을까?

2) 피면책자의 과실

면책조항의 또 다른 중요한 논점은 피면책자의 과실이 면책조항의 효력에 어떠한 영향을 주는가의 문제이다. 지배에 기초한 위험범위를 분할하는 조항은 피면책자의 과실의 유무에 관계없이 언제나 유효할까? 우리 법제는 중대한 과실이나 고의의 경우를 제외하고 자기과실에 대한 면책조항은 유효한 것으로 보고 있는 것같다.[9] 미국 몇몇 주에서는 자기과실에 대한 면책조항을 엄격하게 해석하여야 하며 그러한 면책조항는 현저하게 표시되어야 하고[10] 또한 정책적 필요성이 있는 경우 그 효력이 부인된다는 법규[11] 내지 판례가 확립되어 있다.[12]

El Caledonia Ltd. v. Orbit Valve Co., [1994] 2 Lloyd's Rep. 239

[원고 EE Occidental Ltd.는 북해 Aberdeen 북동쪽 110마일 해상의 Piper Alpha구조물을 운영하면서 1988. 6. 7. 피고 Orbia Valve사와 플랫폼상의 밸프제거작업용역계약("본건 계약")을 체결하였다. 1988. 7. 6 . 플랫폼상 화재가 발생, 피고의 근로자 Terrence Quinn이 목숨을 잃었고 Quinn은 원고를 상대로 손해배상의 소를 제기, 승소하였다. 이에 원고는 본건계약 제10조의 면책조항에 근거, 피고에게 면책책임을 추궁하자 피고는 화재의 원인은 원고 근로자의 과실이므로 면책조항이 적용되지 않는다고 항변하였고 하급심을 이를 받아들여서 원고의 면책청구를 기각하였다.]

Art. 10
(a) Non-Compliance with Laws
The Contractor shall comply, and cause its employees to comply with all laws, ordinances, rules, regulations and orders directly or indirectly applicable to the WORK, including but not limited to the labour employed on the WORK, the safety and security of the WORK, and the preservation and public health and safety. The Contractor shall indemnify and hold harmless the Company and its affiliates against all liability arising from non-compliance with any such provisions.
(b) Company's and Contractor's Employees and Property
Each party hereto shall indemnify, defend, and hold harmless the other, provided that the other party has acted in good faith, from and against any claim, demand, cause of action, loss, expense or liability (including the cost of litigation) arising by reason of any injury to or death of an employee, or damage, loss or destruction of any property, of the indeminifying party, resulting from or in any way connected with the performance of this Order.
(c) Third party Employees and Property..

---

9) 약관규제에 관한 법률("약관법") 제7조 제1호.

10) *Ethyl Corp. v. Daniel Construction Co.,* 725 S.W.2d 705 (Tex. 1987). 약관법 제3조 제1항도 "부호, 색채, 굵고 큰 문자 등으로 명확하게 표시하여 알아보기 쉽게" 할 것을 요구.

11) 예를 들면 N.M. Stat. Ann. § 56-7-2; La. Stat. Ann. §9: 2780.

12) *EE Caledonia Ltd. v. Orbit Valve Co.*, 1995 1 All. ER 174, 1994 WLR 1515, 1994 2 Lloyd's Rep. 239, Court of Appeal; *Cazadrilling (California), Inc. v. Teg Oil & Gas U.S.A.,Inc.*, 142 Cal. App. 4th 452, 48 Cal. Rptr. 3d 271 (2006).

It will be useful to consider the scheme of Article 10(a) imposes obligations only on the contractor (the defendants). It provides that the contractor shall comply with all statutory obligations applicable to the work. It creates a contractual right in favour of the company (the plaintiffs) for it to be indemnified against all liability arising from non-compliance by the contractor with statutory duties. Article 10(b) is a bilateral provision: it creates reciprocal rights and duties. The rationale of the clause is that, in each case, the liability shall be borne by the owner of the property or the employer of the perosn killed or injured. While it is helpful to bear in mind this objective, it does not by itself answer the first or second questions. The question still remains: what is the scope of Art. 10(b)? It is further important to observe that Art. 10(b), whatever its scope may be, allocates and distributes risks. It does so in two ways. In relation to property, it operates as an exception clause: it provides a defence to a claim by the other party. In relation to death or personal injury, it gives a cause of action for a contractual indemnity against the other party.

The first question: Does Art. 10(b) cover negligence? The question before us is not to divine what the parties in fact intended. Our task is to determine what the words of Art. 10(b) mean. The plaintiffs argue that the language of Art. 10(b) covers negligence. The Judge accepted the defendants' submission to a contrary effect. Our task is to decide which is the best interpretation.

The starting point must be the language of Art. 10(b). It contains no express reference to negligence. It contains no words synonymous with negligence, or words which in the case law have acquired a status equivalent to a reference to negligence: *Canada Steamship Lines Ltd. v. The King*, [1952] 1 Lloyd's Rep. 1 at p. 8; [1952] A.C. 192 at p. 208.

Mr. Aikens said that the words "including the cost of litigation" in Art. 10(b) by itself indicated that the indemnity covered cases where negligence was alleged but none had occurred. I consider that Mr. Aikens attributes greater force to this subsidiary provision than is justified. Like the Judge I reject this contention. Article 10(b) also does not contain any reference to a breach of statutory duty. The only express qualification of the potentially extravagant scope of Art. 10(b) are those flowing from the words "provided that the other party has acted in good faith" and the words of causation at the end of Art. 10(b) restricting its scope to liability, and so forth, "resulting from or in any way connected with the performance of this Order". The concluding words of Art. 10(b) are an obvious restriction and tell us nothing about the first question. The Judge held that the words "provided that the other party has acted in good faith" refer not to the origin of the liability but to the handling of any claim, the incurring of expense and the acceptance of liability. I agree. But even if that were wrong, this provision falls markedly short of a clear indication that the clause was intended to cover negligence. Since Mr. Aikens, Q.C., who appeared on behalf of the plaintiffs, did not argue that the words in question were apt to indicate that negligence is covered, I need not pursue the point.

Article 10(b) is a truly elliptical provision. Naturally one turns to parts (a) and (c) of the clause to ascertain whether these provisions throw light on the meaning of (b). Mr. Aikens sought comfort in these provisions. He emphasized the wide wording of (a) and (c). That is so. But (a) deals specifically with the contractor's duty to comply with "laws", i.e. statutory duties. That cannot help in construing (b). For my part I cannot see that (c) helps. While (b) is intended to deal with the "Company's and the Contractors Employees and Property", as the heading indicates, (c) is referable to "Third Party Employees and Property", as the heading indicates. Mr. Aikens pointed out that Art. 10(c) contains no reference to third parties in the text of the provision. But the heading of 10(c), as contrasted with the heading and text of 10(b), is relevant. I would hold that the intended operation of Art. 10(c) is as indicated by the heading. The Judge held that the resort to the other two parts of Art. 10 did not ultimately assist on the question whether Art. 10(b) covers negligence. For my part I am also persuaded that there is no meaningful assistance to be gained either way from Art. 10(a) and (c) on the question before us.

That leaves the question whether in construing Art. 10(b) assistance can be gained from other parts of the agreement. In argument two further clauses were explored. Article 11 imposes a contractual obligation to insure on the contractor only. It is sometimes right to take into account an obligation to insure in construing an indemnity or exception clause. That is so because that context may reveal an allocation of risks which are insurable and expected to be insured. On reflection Mr. Aikens conceded that Art. 11 cannot assist his interpretation. I agree. Article 12 is a clause providing that an exclusion of liability for consequential loss in favour of both parties. Even if it is assumed that this provision is apt to cover negligence, it does not assist. It is a limitation of liability provision with its own special wording.

And the law is more indulgent towards such clauses than towards exemption clauses and indemnities: *Ailsa Craig Fishing Co. Ltd. v. Malvern Fishing Co. Ltd.*, [1983] 1 Lloyd's Rep. 183; [1983] 1 W.L.R. 964; *George Mitchell (Chesterall) Ltd. v. Finney Lock Seed Ltd.*, [1983] 2 Lloyd's Rep. 272; [1983] 3 W.L.R. 163. Since Mr. Aikens did not rely on Art. 12 I need not pursue the point.

That brings me to the approach of our law to exemption clauses and indemnities. The classic statement of the duty of a Court is that of Lord Morton of Henryton in *Canada Steamship Lines Ltd. v. R*, [1952] 1 Lloyd's Rep. 1 at p. 8, col. 1; [1952] A.C.

192 at p. 208. Lord Morton said:

> (1) If the clause contains language which expressly exempts the person in whose favour it is made (hereafter called "the proferens") from the consequence of the negligence of his own servants, effect must be given to that provision ...
>
> (2) If there is no express reference to negligence, the court must consider whether the words used are wide enough, in their ordinary meaning, to cover negligence on the part of the servants of the proferens ...
>
> (3) If the words used are wide enough for the above purpose, the court must then consider whether "the head of damage may be based on some ground other than that of negligence," to quote again Lord Greene in the *Alderslade* case. The "other ground" must not be so fanciful or remote that the proferens cannot be supposed to have desired protection against it; but subject to this qualification, which is no doubt to be implied from Lord Greene's words, the existence of a possible head of damage other than that of negligence is fatal to the proferens even if the words used are *prima facie* wide enough to cover negligence on the part of his servants.

These propositions were, of course, formulated in an opinion of the Judicial Committee of the Privy Council in a Canadian appeal. They correctly state the law of England, and were indeed applied by the House of Lords in *Smith v. South Wales Switchgear Co. Ltd.*, [1987] 1 W.L.R. 165. Mr. Aikens does not demur. But he asked us to bear in mind the judgments in the Court of Appeal in *The Raphael*, [1982] 2 Lloyd's Rep. 42 where the Court of Appeal emphasized the need always to have regard to the particular wording of each contract. Mr. Aikens particularly emphasized the following passage in the judgment of Lord Justice May at p. 50):

> With respect to both sides in this appeal, I think that this is an over-legalistic approach to this problem. When two commercial concerns contract with one another, they do not, neither should they be deemed to, concern themselves with the legal subtleties of the law of private nuisance or the like. They in fact approach the problem, and so should the Courts, with a much broader brush. They consider, or must be deemed to have in mind, their respective responsibilities one to another more from a factual standpoint than from a legalistic one. In seeking to apply Lord Morton's third test, we should not ask now whether there is or might be a technical alternative head of legal liability which the relevant exemption clause might cover and, if there is, immediately construe the clause as inapplicable to negligence. We should look at the facts and realities of the situation as they did or must be deemed to have presented

> themselves to the contracting parties at the time the contract was made, and ask what potential liabilities the one to the other did the parties apply their minds, or must they be deemed to have done so.

For my part I am not convinced that these observations add much to what was inherent in what Lord Morton said. But I willingly accept Lord Justice May's gloss on Lord Morton's third test. Ultimately, the third test is not a rigid or mechanical rule. It simply is an aid in the process of construction. And the ordinary meaning of the words in their contractual setting is the dominant factor.

But this citation of *The Raphael* does not assist in the present case. In Art. 10(b) there is no reference to negligence nor words to a like effect. It is plain that neither the other parts of Art. 10 nor the rest of the agreement assist the plaintiffs' interpretation. That brings me back to Art. 10(b). Given that the words of Art. 10(b), although not indicative of an intent to cover negligence, are nevertheless wide enough to cover negligence of the parties, Lord Morton's second proposition is satisfied. Lord Morton's third proposition must therefore be considered. The question is whether liability may be based on some other ground than negligence. The answer is plainly "yes". But that leaves the question whether such other heads of liability were fanciful or remote. The Judge dealt with this matter: *E.E. Caledonia Ltd. (formerly Occidental Petroleum (Caledonia) Limited v. Orbit Valve Co. Europe*, [1993] 2 Lloyd's Rep. 418. The Judge said (at p. 423):

> In Art. 10(b) there is no express reference to negligence; therefore there is no express provision that the right to an indemnity should cover a liability arising out of negligence of the party seeking the indemnity. However the words used are wide enough potentially to cover a liability arising from negligence. The words are "any claim ... or liability". Clearly such liability could, and will often be, a liability which has arisen from the negligence of the party liable or of those for whom he is responsible. But the liability need not arise from such negligence. It could arise as a result of a breach of a statutory duty which has occurred without any negligence of the party liable or his servants. This could be the situation with regard to both the company and the contractor; both are subject to statutory duties which could give rise to civil liabilities for death or personal injury. The examples are not fanciful; in an environment such as an off-shore platform in an oil field where a strict statutory regime operates, the possibility of a strict liability arising is a real one and is directly within the contemplation of this contract.

Accordingly it is clear that Art. 10(b), like (a) and (c), is capable of applying to situations where there has been no actual negligence of the relevant party or his own servants. This could have been the situation in the present case. The breaches of the regulations could in fact have been solely those of the employees of independent contractors working on the platform. In fact the disaster was also a result of the actual negligence of one of the plaintiff's own servants.

Mr. Aikens has unambiguously conceded that the other heads of strict liability to which the Judge referred are not in any way fanciful or remote. It follows that the Lord Morton's third proposition is applicable. Reading Art. 10(b) against this well established aid to construction, it seems to me that Art. 10(b) should be construed as not covering the consequences of the negligence of the parties and their servants.

Mr. Aikens argued that the fact that Art. 10(b) contains reciprocal indemnities and exceptions takes it outside the scope of Lord Morton's third proposition. Rightly Mr. Aikens said that the rationale of this aid to construction, which is equally applicable to indemnities and exceptions, is the *prima facie* implausibility of a party agreeing to release the other from liability for negligence or assuming liability for the consequences of the other's negligence. The argument is that, if the reason for the aid to interpretation ceases, the "rule" ceases. If the premise of the argument was right, I would accept Mr. Aiken's argument. But in my judgment even in the case of a bilateral clause, such as the one before us, it is *prima facie* implausible that the parties would wish to release one another from the consequences of the other's negligence and agree to indemnify the other in respect of such consequences. The point is a matter of first impression and not capable of elaboration. But I would hold that Lord Morton's third proposition equally applies to a bilateral clause such as Art. 10(b).

If one assents to Mr. Aiken's invitation, relying on Lord Justice May's dictum in *The Raphael*, to have regard to the realities of the situation as they must have been in the minds of the parties at the time of contracting, the position becomes even clearer. While it is true that reciprocity is inherent in Art. 10(b) it does not follow that, if Art. 10(b) is interpreted to cover negligence, there is equal treatment of the parties. Leaving aside other contractors' employees, we know that the defendants had one engineer on board while the plaintiffs had 38 employees on board. The task of the defendants' one employee was limited to overhauling some 13 valves. By contrast the functions of the plaintiffs employees were multifarious. As a matter of common sense the anticipated risk of death or injury through the negligence of the defendants' employee must have been of a lesser order than the risk of death or injury through the negligence of the plaintiffs' employees. There is either an inequality or imbalance inherent in the plaintiffs' interpretation, which is therefore *prima facie* implausible, or at the very least it has not been demonstrated that there is not such an implausibility.

There is one further matter to be considered. The third "rule" of Lord Morton is horn-book construction law. The printed conditions in the agreement in this case were plainly drafted by a lawyer. Why was an express reference to negligence not inserted? Similar questions have been posed on a number of occasions. Why do draftsmen not take note of the impact of a clear and consistent line of judicial decisions? For my part I have no doubt that the draftsman to whom such a question was addressed would say "one does not want to frighten off one or other of the parties". Omissions of express reference to negligence in contracts drafted by lawyers tend to be deliberate.

Ultimately, the only material question is the meaning of the words in Art. 10(b) read in the context of well established construction law. Taking into account the very general words of Art. 10(b), I am satisfied that the Judge came to the right conclusion on the first question.

But I would add that this interpretation also better matches the reasonable expectations of the parties than the somewhat technical approach of the plaintiffs. Given that Art. 10(b) must be construed as not covering negligence, the Judge's interpretation is in my view the more reasonable interpretation. After all, it is inherently improbable even in a bilateral clause such as Art. 10(b) that a party would be willing to assume a risk of loss caused by the negligence of the other, notably when there is probably an imbalance and inequality in the risks of negligence by the one employee of the defendants and the many employees of the plaintiffs.

Cazadrilling (California), Inc. v. Teg Oil & Gas U.S.A., Inc., 142 Cal. App. 4th 452, 48 Cal. Rptr.3d 271 (2006)

[Teg은 유정 Yule 6의 운영자로서 시추용역업체인 Caza에게 시추작업을 시키던 중 시추공이 폭발, Caza의 근로자가 사망하고 수명이 부상당하였으며 유정이 완전히 파괴되었다. Teg은 Caza에게 blowout은 Caza의 과실과 법규상 안전의무위반으로 인한 것이니 유정의 파괴로 인한 손해, 청소 및 현장보구비용과 사업상손해 등을 배상하여 줄 것을 청구하였다.]

[계약서조항내용]

Daywork Drilling Contract

The 2002 Daywork Drilling Contract consists of a standardized form agreement with a number of blanks for the name of the operator, the contractor, the location of the well, the commencement date of drilling operations, the rates to be charged for various tasks, and other items. TEG was designated the "Operator" and CAZA was described as the "Contractor." The contract begins with a statement that "Operator [TEG] engages

Contractor [CAZA] as an Independent Contractor to drill the hereinafter designated well or wells in search of oil or gas on a daywork basis" and that "Contractor shall furnish equipment, labor, and perform services as herein provided, for a specified sum per day under the direction, supervision and control of Operator." "Daywork basis" is defined to mean that "Contractor shall furnish equipment, labor, and perform services as herein provided, for a specified sum per day under the direction, supervision and control of Operator (inclusive of any employee, agent, consultant or subcontractor engaged by Operator to direct drilling operations)." The contract also provides that: "When operating on a daywork basis, Contractor shall be fully paid at the applicable rates of payment and assumes only the obligations and liabilities stated herein. Except for such obligations and liabilities specifically assumed by Contractor, Operator shall be solely responsible and assumes liability for all consequences of operations by both parties while on a daywork basis, including results and all other risks or liabilities incurred in or incident to such operations."

Paragraph 8, entitled "DRILLING METHODS AND PRACTICES" includes the following pertinent subparagraphs: "8.1 Contractor [CAZA] shall maintain well control equipment in good condition at all times and shall use all reasonable means to prevent and control fires and blowouts and to protect the hole. [¶] ... [¶] 8.3 Each party hereto agrees to comply with all laws, rules, and regulations of any federal, state or local governmental authority which are now or may become applicable to that party's operations covered by or arising out of the performance of this Contract."

Paragraph 14 governs "RESPONSIBILITY FOR LOSS OR DAMAGE, INDEMNITY, RELEASE OF LIABILITY AND ALLOCATION OF RISK." Under subparagraph 14.1, the contractor (CAZA) "assume[s] liability" for "damage to or destruction of Contractor's surface equipment," unless the damage fell under paragraph 10, which requires the operator (TEG) to prepare a "sound location" to support the drilling rig, or subparagraph 14.3, which requires the operator to assume liability for damage to or destruction of the contractor's equipment "caused by exposure to highly corrosive or otherwise destructive elements, including those introduced into the drilling fluid." Subparagraph 14.2 requires the operator to assume liability for "damage to or destruction of Contractor's in-hole equipment."

Subparagraph 14.4 requires the operator (TEG) to assume liability "for damage to or destruction of Operator's equipment ... regardless of when or how such damage or destruction occurs," and to "release Contractor of any liability for any such loss or damage." Similarly, under subparagraph 14.5, the operator is to "be solely responsible for ... damage to or loss of the hole, including the casing therein" and the operator is to "release Contractor [CAZA] of any liability for damage to or loss of the hole" and in addition "protect, defend and indemnify Contractor from and against any and all claims, liability, and expense relating to such damage to or loss of the hole."

In subparagraph 14.6, the operator releases the contractor from liability for, and agrees to indemnify the contractor from and against claims "on account of injury to, destruction of, or loss or impairment of any property right in or to oil, gas, or other mineral substance or water" unless "reduced to physical possession above the surface of the earth," and for "any loss or damage to any formation, strata, or reservoir beneath the surface of the earth."

Subparagraphs 14.8 and 14.9 require the parties to indemnify each other for claims based on injuries to their own employees "without regard to the cause or causes thereof or the negligence of any party or parties."

Subparagraph 14.10 states that the operator is liable "for the cost of regaining control of any wild well, as well as for cost of removal of any debris."

The parties focus particular attention on subparagraph 14.11. Entitled "Pollution and Contamination," it provides:

"Notwithstanding anything to the contrary contained herein, except the provisions of Paragraphs 10 and 12, it is understood and agreed by and between Contractor and Operator that the responsibility for pollution and contamination shall be as follows: [¶] (a) Unless otherwise provided herein, Contractor [CAZA] shall assume all responsibility for, including control and removal of, and shall protect, defend and indemnity Operator from and against all claims, demands and causes of action of every kind and character arising from pollution or contamination, which originates above the surface of the land or water from spills of fuels, lubricants, motor oils, pipe dope, paints, solvents, ballast, bilge and garbage, except unavoidable pollution from reserve pits, wholly in Contractor's possession and control and directly associated with Contractor's equipment and facilities.

"(b) Operator [TEG] shall assume all responsibility for, including control and removal of, and shall protect, defend and indemnify Contractor from and against all claims, demands, and causes of action of every kind and character arising directly or indirectly from all other pollution or contamination which may occur during the conduct of operations hereunder, including, but not limited to, that which may result from fire, blowout, cratering, seepage of any other uncontrolled flow of oil, gas, water or other substance, as well as the use or disposition of all drilling fluids, including, but not limited to, oil emulsion, oil base or chemically treated drilling fluids, contaminated cuttings or cavings, lost circulation and fish recovery materials and fluids. Operator shall release Contractor of any liability for the foregoing."

Subparagraph 14.12 provides that neither party is liable to the other for "special, indirect or consequential damages resulting from or arising out of this Contract, including, without limitation, loss of profit or business interruptions including loss or delay of production, however same may be caused."

Finally, subparagraph 14.13 entitled "Indemnity Obligation" provides: "Except as otherwise expressly limited herein, it is the intent of parties hereto that all releases, indemnity obligations and/or liabilities assumed by such parties under terms of this Contract, including, without limitation, Subparagraphs 14.1 through 14.12 hereof, be without limit and without regard to the cause or causes thereof (including preexisting conditions), strict liability, regulatory or statutory liability, breach of warranty (express or implied), any theory of tort, breach of contract or the negligence of any party or parties, whether such negligence be sole, joint or concurrent, active or passive."

[본안에 대한 판단: 14조의 의미]

We now turn to the merits. According to the 2002 Daywork Drilling Contract, "[e]xcept for such obligations and liabilities specifically assumed by [CAZA], [TEG] shall be solely responsible and assume liability for all consequences of operations by both parties." This was the provision chiefly relied upon by CAZA in seeking summary judgment. Preliminarily, appellants contend this general language cannot control over more specific provisions of subparagraphs 8.1, requiring CAZA to use "all reasonable means" to prevent fires and blowouts, and 8.3, requiring that both parties comply with all federal, state, and local laws, rules, and regulations.

Appellants are correct that when general and specific provisions are inconsistent, the latter control. (Code Civ. Proc., § 1859; 1 Witkin, Summary of Cal. Law (10th ed. 2005) Contracts, § 754, p. 845.) However, as we have seen, the general provision just quoted is not the only provision in the agreement relating to allocation and limitation of liability. Paragraph 14 describes in detail the parties' respective "RESPONSIBILITY FOR LOSS OR DAMAGE, INDEMNITY, RELEASE OF LIABILITY AND ALLOCATION OF RISK." Under its terms, each party was to be liable for damage to its own equipment, with certain limited exceptions, and for injury to its own employees. Responsibility for damage to the hole and the underground minerals and for regaining control of a "wild well" was fixed on the operator. Liability for "Pollution and Contamination" was allocated between the parties depending on the cause. Neither party was to be liable for the other's consequential damages. These provisions are more specific with respect to allocation and limitation of liability than the language cited by appellants.

Beyond that, we do not believe that the allocation and limitation of liability provisions are contradicted by subparagraphs 8.1 and 8.3. The latter describes CAZA's duties under the contract. To the extent TEG can establish that CAZA failed to perform these duties, it is entitled to raise that breach as a defense to CAZA's claim for payment under the 2002 Daywork Drilling Contract. The provisions of paragraph 14 are intended to limit contract damages by excluding consequential damages and allocating liability for tort damages for injuries to persons or property in the case of negligence. There is nothing inherently inconsistent in a party to a contract agreeing to do "X," but stating that if it does not, the other party may not recover consequential damages or stating that if negligence occurs during the performance of "X," liability will be limited.

The authorities upon which appellants rely — *Woodall v. Wayne Steffner Productions* (1962) 201 Cal.App.2d 800, 20 Cal.Rptr. 572 and *Continental Mfg. Corp. v. Underwriters at Lloyds London* (1960) 185 Cal.App.2d 545, 8 Cal.Rptr. 276 — were decided before the Supreme Court's seminal decision in *Tunkl v. Regents of University of California* (1963) 60 Cal.2d 92, 32 Cal.Rptr. 33, 383 P.2d 441 (*Tunkl*), which we discuss more fully below. Their conclusion that a party cannot limit its liability for a duty it has undertaken to perform by contract when that duty is negligently performed does not represent the current state of the law in this area.

Appellants also contend that the provisions of the various subparagraphs of paragraph 14 cannot be read as excluding liability for negligence because negligence was not specifically mentioned in every subparagraph. It is true that '[f]or an agreement to be construed as precluding liability for "active" or "affirmative" negligence, there must be express and unequivocal language in the agreement which precludes such liability' and that "[a]n agreement which seeks to limit liability generally without specifically mentioning negligence is construed to shield a party only for passive negligence, not for active negligence." (*Burnett v. Chimney Sweep* (2004) 123 Cal.App.4th 1057, 1066, 20 Cal.Rptr.3d 562, quoting *Salton Bay Marina, Inc. v. Imperial Irrigation Dist.* (1985) 172 Cal.App.3d 914, 932-933, 218 Cal.Rptr. 839.) But it is equally true that "[w]hether an exculpatory clause 'covers a given case turns primarily on contractual interpretation, and it is the intent of the parties as expressed in the agreement that should control. When the parties knowingly bargain for the protection at issue, the protection should be afforded. This requires an inquiry into the circumstances of the damage or injury and the language of the contract; of necessity, each case will turn on its own facts.' " (Id. at p. 1066, 20 Cal.Rptr.3d 562, quoting *Rossmoor Sanitation, Inc. v. Pylon, Inc.* (1975) 13 Cal.3d 622, 632, 119 Cal.Rptr. 449, 532 P.2d 97.)

Subparagraph 14.13 specifically states that the allocations of liability set forth in subparagraphs 14.1 through 14.12 are "without limit" and "without regard to the cause or causes thereof," including "regulatory or statutory liability," "breach of contract or the negligence of any party or parties, whether such negligence be sole, joint or concurrent, active or passive." Read as a whole, the provisions of paragraph 14 make clear the parties' intent — to limit "the Operator's" ability to recover for injury resulting from accidents, even those caused by the negligence of "the Contractor." As a matter of contractual interpretation, there is nothing to hinder a "voluntary transactions in which one party, for a consideration, agrees to shoulder a risk which the law would otherwise have placed upon the other party." (*Tunkl*, supra, 60 Cal.2d at p. 101, 32 Cal.Rptr. 33, 383 P.2d 441.) Such an agreement may, however, run afoul of section 1668, to which we now turn.

[14조의 효력여부]

Section 1668 provides that "[a]ll contracts which have for their object, directly or indirectly, to exempt any one from responsibility for his own fraud, or willful injury to the person or property of another, or violation of law, whether willful or negligent, are against the policy of the law." As explained in *Tunkl*, early interpretations of this provision expressed the view that section 1668 absolutely prohibited a party from limiting its liability for its own negligence. (*Tunkl*, supra, 60 Cal.2d at p. 95, 32 Cal.Rptr. 33, 383 P.2d 441, citing *England v. Lyon Fireproof Storage Co.* (1928) 94 Cal.App. 562, 271 P. 532.) In *Mills v. Ruppert* (1959) 167 Cal.App.2d 58, 333 P.2d 818, however, the court pointed out that "the only use of the word negligent in said section is in a restrictive sense and only in connection with violations of law." (Id. at p. 62, 333 P.2d 818.) It necessarily followed that " 'contracts seeking to relieve individuals from the results of their own negligence are not invalid as against the policy of the law as therein provided, and hence are neither contrary to public policy nor expressed provision of the law....' " (Id. at p. 63, 333 P.2d 818; accord, *Werner v. Knoll* (1948) 89 Cal.App.2d 474, 475-476, 201 P.2d 45.)

In *Tunkl*, the Supreme Court limited the holding in *Mills v. Ruppert*. The court concluded that exculpatory clauses relieving a party from the consequences of its own negligence cannot be enforced where the public interest was involved, even if the conduct did not involve a violation of law. The court described factors or characteristics which identify a transaction implicating the public interest: (1) the transaction "concerns a business of a type generally thought suitable for public regulation"; (2) "[t]he party seeking exculpation is engaged in performing a service of great importance to the public, which is often a matter of practical necessity for some members of the public"; (3) "[t]he party holds himself out as willing to perform this service for any member of the public who seeks it, or at least for any member coming within certain established standards"; (4) "[a]s a result of the essential nature of the service, in the economic setting of the transaction, the party invoking exculpation possesses a decisive advantage of bargaining strength against any member of the public who seeks his services"; (5) "[i]n exercising a superior bargaining power the party confronts the public with a standardized adhesion contract of exculpation, and makes no provision whereby a purchaser may pay additional reasonable fees and obtain protection against negligence"; and (6) "[a]s a result of the transaction, the person or property of the purchaser is placed under the control of the seller, subject to the risk of carelessness by the seller or his agents." (*Tunkl*, supra, 60 Cal.2d at pp. 98-101, 32 Cal.Rptr. 33, 383 P.2d 441, fns. omitted.)

Appellants contend these factors are present here. We disagree. Although the Supreme Court did not specifically exclude contracts between relatively equal business entities from its definition of contracts in the public interest, it is difficult to imagine a situation where a contract of that type would meet more than one or two of the requirements discussed in *Tunkl*. With respect to the second and third factors, for example, CAZA did not hold itself out as performing services for the public, but only for the small number of entities that happened to be oil field operators. While the production of oil is of great importance to the public, the drilling of a particular oil well is generally only important to the party who will profit from it. With respect to the fourth and fifth factors, appellants' argument that it was forced into an adhesion contract boils down to this: "Although two provisions in the agreement were altered during negotiations, we did not know we could alter any provisions during negotiations." The fact that TEG found itself backed into a corner in late 2002 as a result of failure to plan ahead and had no choice but to deal with the only company that had a suitable drill rig available at that specific point in time, is not the sort of unequal bargaining power to which the court in *Tunkl* referred.

Appalachian Ins. Co. v. McDonnell Douglas Corp. (1989) 214 Cal.App.3d 1, 262 Cal.Rptr. 716, where commercial entities similarly tried to undercut contractual limitations on liability by reliance on *Tunkl*, is instructive. In that case, a rocket manufactured by defendant McDonnell Douglas Corp. failed to boost a communications satellite to the required orbit. As a result, the satellite had to be written off as a total loss. The insurers of the satellite owner sought to recoup their loss from McDonnell Douglas, contending that limitation of liability provisions in the parties' agreement were contrary to public policy. With regard to plaintiffs' argument that McDonnell Douglas's services were open to any member of the public and provided a service of great importance to some members of the public, the court stated: "[T]he provision of space hardware and launch services is of practical necessity to no individual member of the public; it is of 'practical necessity' only to a few, very large commercial and governmental entities dealing in highly specialized fields such as telecommunications." (*Appalachian Ins. Co. v. McDonnell Douglas Corp.*, supra, at p. 29, 262 Cal.Rptr. 716.) Further, "all [sales] were to large, sophisticated commercial and governmental entities." (Id. at p. 30, 262 Cal.Rptr.

716.) With regard to the supposedly 'essential nature' of the services, the court stated: "*Tunkl*'s focus was on whether the service was 'essential' to individual members of the public. Here, the service is 'essential' only to a small number of large corporations and governmental entities; it 'is not a compelled, essential service' but 'a voluntary relationship between the parties.' (*Okura v. United States Cycling Federation* [(1986)] 186 Cal.App.3d 1462, 1468 [231 Cal.Rptr. 429].) Finally, this case does not involve a 'decisive advantage of bargaining strength [used] against any member of the public who seeks [the] services.' ([*Tunkl*], supra, 60 Cal.2d [at p.] 100 [32 Cal.Rptr. 33, 383 P.2d 441].) This case does not involve a large entity using its bargaining strength against an individual member of the public. This case involves two large, sophisticated corporations with relatively equal bargaining power who negotiated the terms of a voluntary agreement." (Ibid., fn. omitted.)

The same is true here. CAZA's services may have been essential to TEG, but the agreement between the parties did not implicate the public interest in the way required to abrogate exculpatory provisions limiting liability for negligence under *Tunkl*.

[하도급업자의 실정법 위반]

If *Tunkl were* the only basis raised by appellants for the applicability of section 1668, we could end our analysis. However, in their cross-complaint and their opposition to the motion for summary judgment, appellants contend that CAZA violated various statutes and regulations in performing drilling activities. They argue that section 1668 invalidates any exculpatory language that would relieve CAZA of liability for performing drilling operations in violation of law "without regard to whether any public interest [was] involved." They cite for support this court's recent decision in *Capri v. L.A. Fitness International, LLC* (2006) 136 Cal.App.4th 1078, 39 Cal.Rptr.3d 425 (*Capri*).

The plaintiff in *Capri* had joined a health club, signing a membership agreement which contained a release and waiver of liability for injuries caused by the club's negligence. Plaintiff was using the club's outdoor swimming pool when he slipped and fell on the pool deck. After the accident, he noticed an accumulation of algae around the drain in the area where the accident occurred. In defense to plaintiff's personal injury suit, the club raised the release. However, in his complaint, plaintiff had alleged that the club violated Health and Safety Code sections 116040 and 116043, which require operators of public swimming pools to maintain them in a sanitary, healthful, and safe manner. Section 116065 of that code made violation of these provisions a crime. In reversing summary judgment in favor of the club, we held that because plaintiff had alleged that the club violated Health and Safety Code sections 116040 and 116043, and that the violation of these laws was the cause of his slip and fall, the limitation on liability "falls squarely within the explicit prohibition in section 1668 against contractual exculpation for a 'violation of law' and is invalid." (*Capri v. L.A. Fitness International, LLC*, supra, 136 Cal.App.4th at p. 1085, 39 Cal.Rptr.3d 425.)

We found support for our conclusion in *Hanna v. Lederman* (1963) 223 Cal.App.2d 786, 36 Cal.Rptr. 150, where tenants suffered property damage after fire system sprinklers flooded their leased premises. The landlord allegedly had failed to install the kind of sprinklers require by the municipal code. The appellate court held that "[s]ince the claim for damages because of negligence embodied in the first cause of action of each tenant was predicated upon the alleged violation of section 94.30312 of the Municipal Code, the exculpatory provision could not be a defense to that cause of action if the evidence showed such violation to be a proximate cause of the tenant's loss." (Id. at p. 792, 36 Cal.Rptr. 150.) Similarly, in *Halliday v. Greene* (1966) 244 Cal.App.2d 482, 53 Cal.Rptr. 267, plaintiffs were injured in a fire to their apartment building while exiting down the only available staircase. Plaintiffs provided evidence of a general industry safety order requiring two escape exits from a work area. The Court of Appeal reversed a nonsuit in favor of defendant, holding that plaintiffs were entitled to the benefit of the safety order, and hence that the exculpatory clause in the lease agreement was ineffective under section 1668. (*Halliday*, at pp. 487-490, 53 Cal.Rptr. 267.)

Capri is significantly different from the present case because it involved personal injury to a consumer. Here, the contract was between two business entities and the damages claimed are entirely economic. In only one recent case has a court applied section 1668 to invalidate provisions in a contract between business entities: *Health Net of California, Inc. v. Department of Health Services* (2003) 113 Cal.App.4th 224, 6 Cal.Rptr.3d 235 (Health Net). The agreement at issue there was between Health Net and the Department of Health Services (DHS), and stated that remedies for noncompliance with laws not expressly incorporated into the contract "shall not include money damages." (Id. at p. 229, 6 Cal.Rptr.3d 235, italics omitted.) In an action against DHS under the agreement, Health Net claimed that DHS had violated a provision of the Welfare and Institutions Code. The trial court agreed and issued an injunction, but refused to award monetary damages because of the limitation of liability provision in the contract. The trial court thought that section 1668 did not apply since the transaction did not affect the public interest within the meaning of *Tunkl*. On review, that decision was reversed because "section 1668 prohibits the enforcement of any contractual clause that seeks to exempt a party from liability for violations of statutory and regulatory law, regardless of whether the public interest is affected." (*Health Net*, supra, at p. 235, 6 Cal.Rptr.3d 235.)

The holding in *Health Net* does not apply to this case because, as the court explained, the exculpatory clause at issue in that case "prohibit [ed] ... the recovery of any damages at all for DHS's statutory for regulatory violations" and "exempt[ed] DHS completely from responsibility for completed wrongs." (113 Cal.App.4th at pp. 240-241, 6 Cal.Rptr.3d 235, italics added.) The court believed that even in a commercial case, "an exculpation of any liability for any damages for any statutory violation surely rises to the level of an 'exempt[ion] from responsibility' within the meaning of the plain language of section 1668." (Id. at p. 239, 6 Cal.Rptr.3d 235.) The provisions at issue here do not exempt CAZA from all liability, but merely limit its responsibility with respect to economic damages. The court in *Health Net* expressly declined to decide whether "some contractual limitations over the scope of available remedies" would "necessarily run afoul of section 1668." (see *Farnham v. Superior Court* (1997) 60 Cal.App.4th 69, 74, 70 Cal.Rptr.2d 85 ["Although exemptions from all liability for intentional wrongs, gross negligence and violations of the law have been consistently invalidated [citations], we have not found any case addressing a limitation on liability for intentional wrongs, gross negligence or violations of the law"].)

Although it did not reach the issue, the court in *Health Net* cited *Klein v. Asgrow Seed Co.* (1966) 246 Cal.App.2d 87, 54 Cal.Rptr. 609 as an example of a case where the court invalidated a provision in a commercial contract that merely limited liability. Plaintiff in Klein was a farmer who had purchased mislabeled seed that came with a disclaimer of liability limiting the buyer's damages to the price of the seed. The Court of Appeal upheld a different measure of damages: the difference between the reasonable market value of the crop as actually produced and the value of the theoretical crop that would have been produced had the seed been as labeled. The court concluded that the limitation on liability ran afoul of section 1668 because a provision of the Agricultural Code made the sale of mislabeled seed an unlawful act. (*Klein*, supra, at p. 100, 54 Cal.Rptr. 609.)

The court in *Health Net* did not point out that the decision in *Klein* represented something of an anomaly. In the majority of commercial situations, courts have upheld contractual limitations on liability, even against claims that the breaching party violated a law or regulation. (See, e.g., *Nunes Turfgrass, Inc. v. Vaughan-Jacklin Seed Co.* (1988) 200 Cal.App.3d 1518, 1534-1539, 246 Cal.Rptr. 823 [court upheld a contractual provision precluding consequential damages although a violation of law occurred when a seed seller mislabeled packages of grass seed misrepresenting the percentage of annual rye grass because "[t]he California Uniform Commercial Code expressly allows the limitation or exclusion of consequential damages for commercial loss unless the limitation or exclusion is unconscionable"].) A relatively early case, *Delta Air Lines, Inc. v. McDonnell*

Douglas Corporation (5th Cir.1974) 503 F.2d 239, involved the purchase of an aircraft from the manufacturer by a major airline. The purchase agreement contained an exculpatory clause limiting damages in the case of the manufacturer's negligence. The airline suffered economic damage when the nose gear of the aircraft collapsed during a landing because a part had allegedly been incorrectly installed. On appeal, the airline contended that the limitation of liability clause was "in clear violation of the public policy of California," pointing to section 21.165 of the Federal Aviation Administration (FAA) regulations "which provides in effect that an airplane manufacturer must determine that any airplane proposed for certification is in a condition for safe operation." (*Delta*, at pp. 243-244.) Applying California law, the Fifth Circuit disagreed that the alleged violation of the regulation rendered the limitation of liability clause invalid under section 1668: "[The airline] ... confuses a negligence theory of action, under which violation of a law or a regulation may be evidence of negligence, [citation], with the liability that may be imposed by law. [The manufacturer] is still answerable to the FAA and third parties for any responsibility established by the regulation, and any statutory right of action that might be given to [the airline] by FAA regulations has not been abrogated. But none of these causes of action are involved in an action based on common law negligence. We are unable to agree that the contract between two industrial giants fixing the dollar responsibility for [the manufacturer's] alleged negligence would be void under California law, any more than would be an insurance contract which might be written for the same purpose." (Id. at p. 244.)

Nearly a decade after the Fifth Circuit decision in *Delta Air Lines, Inc. v. McDonnell Douglas Corporation*, the Ninth Circuit addressed the identical issue and reached the same result. (*Airlift Intern., Inc. v. McDonnell Douglas Corp.* (9th Cir.1982) 685 F.2d 267.) Again seeking to invalidate a contractual limitation on liability, the airline specifically argued that "the exculpation clause was vitiated under state law by [the manufacturer's] violation of federal air regulations." (Id. at p. 269.) The court rejected that argument based on the authorities enforcing such clauses in similar situations. (Ibid.)

Continental Airlines v. Goodyear Tire & Rubber Co. (9th Cir.1987) 819 F.2d 1519 is to the same effect. That case also involved a limitation of liability provision in a contract for the sale of an aircraft. The airline argued that the exculpatory clause was "unenforce-able to the extent that it bars [the airline] from showing that [the manufacturer] violated federal aviation regulations, which violations allegedly caused the accident." (Id. at p. 1527.) The Ninth Circuit disagreed: "The exculpatory clause does not permit [the manufacturer] to violate the federal regulations with impunity; it merely bars suit by [the airline] on this ground. Other sanctions remain in place. As we have said in a similar case, 'nothing inhibits the operation of the regulation[s] in question through [passengers'] suits ... or sanction imposed by the [FAA].' " (Ibid., *quoting S.A. Empresa de Viacao Aerea Rio Grandense v. Boeing Co.* (9th Cir.1981) 641 F.2d 746, 753.)

This line of authority was followed in *In re Air Crash Disaster, Detroit Metro. Airport* (E.D.Mich.1989) 757 F.Supp. 804, where the court, applying California law, upheld an exculpatory clause in a contract between an airline and an aircraft manufacturer even though some of the airline's claims were based on violation of FAA regulations because "[t]he preclusion of [the airline's] claim would not fully vindicate [the manufacturer] from the adverse repercussions that could result from a violation of federal aviation regulations." (Id. at p. 811.) "To the extent that [the manufacturer] violated any federal aviation regulations, it may be held accountable in the form of civil judgments and/or FAA sanctions. The mere fact that [the airline] is contractually precluded from similarly pursuing [the manufacturer] does not violate the spirit of section 1668." (Id. at p. 812.)

While no reported California case has expressly relied on this federal precedent, a similar issue was addressed in *Delta Air Lines, Inc. v. Douglas Aircraft Co.* (1965) 238 Cal.App.2d 95, 47 Cal.Rptr. 518. There, the court upheld a limitation of liability provision in a contract for the sale of an aircraft against a claim that it involved the public interest as defined by *Tunkl*. The court did not resolve whether a violation of law on the part of the manufacturer would have rendered the provision invalid under section 1668 because it concluded that no such violation had been established. (*Delta*, supra, at pp. 105-106, 47 Cal.Rptr. 518.) Although the lack of a proven violation of law precluded the court from reaching section 1668, in its discussion of the *Tunkl* public interest issue, it indicated that the outcome of the appeal would not have been substantially different had such a violation occurred: "The fact that [the airline] is a regulated enterprise and carries passengers has no relevance to the present decision. The upholding of the exculpatory clause will not adversely affect rights of future passengers. They are not parties to the contract and their rights would not be compromised. They retain their right to bring a direct action against [the manufacturer] for negligence. [Citation.] Also, their right to bring an action against [the manufacturer] for breach of implied warranty would not be interfered with because the passengers were not a party to the contract containing the exculpatory clause. [¶] In short, all that is herein involved is the question of which of two equal bargainers should bear the risk of economic loss if the product sold proved to be defective. Under the contract before us, [the airline] (or its insurance carrier if any) bears that risk in return for a purchase price acceptable to it; had the clause been removed, the risk would have fallen on [the manufacturer] (or its insurance carrier if any), but in return for an increased price deemed adequate by it to compensate for the risk assumed. We can see no reason why [the airline], having determined, as a matter of business judgment, that the price fixed justified assuming the risk of loss, should now be allowed to shift the risk so assumed to [the manufacturer], which had neither agreed to assume it nor been compensated for such assumption." (*Delta*, supra, at pp. 104-105, 47 Cal.Rptr. 518 fns. omitted.)

The same public policy issue was addressed more recently in *Philippine Airlines, Inc. v. McDonnell Douglas Corp.* (1987) 189 Cal.App.3d 234, 234 Cal.Rptr. 423, and, once again, the same result obtained. There, alleged negligence in the manufacture of an airplane led to a crash during takeoff and personal injury to a number of the airline's passengers. The passengers filed a lawsuit against the airline, and the trial court ruled that the limitation of liability clause in the airline's contract with the manufacturer barred the airline's cross-complaint for indemnity. Although it did not point to any specific law or regulation, the airline argued on appeal that the provision created a disincentive for manufacturers to produce safe aircraft and was thus directly contrary to California public policy. The appellate court disagreed: "[C]ontractual allocations of risk in nonconsumer commercial settings are routinely upheld. The reason, we think, lies with our laws of negligence and products liability, and with the economic realities of the marketplace. It may be true, as [the airline] argues, that the ultimate consumer — here the passenger — is provided with a streamlined remedy against the [airline] carrier [and therefore may never have incentive to sue the manufacturer directly]. Given, however, the realities of litigation, and the possibility that [an airline] carrier might have insufficient resources to cover what might be extensive liability should an aircraft malfunction, it would make little economic sense for a manufacturer to place on the market a defective product on the belief that it somehow would be insulated from the personal injury claims of passengers. Moreover, and aside from its potential liability to passengers, a manufacturer whose defective products caused its customers to be sued would not long remain in business. And a manufacturer ... is still answerable to the Federal Aviation Commission. We are thus of the opinion that the argued 'disincentive' to produce safe aircraft resulting from a finding that the disclaimer of liability at issue is valid, is largely illusory." (Id. at p. 242, 234 Cal.Rptr. 423, fn. omitted.)

Based on these authorities, we conclude that the challenged provisions in the 2002 Daywork Drilling Contract represent a valid limitation on liability rather than an improper attempt to exempt a contracting party from responsibility for violation of law within the meaning of section 1668. CAZA did not seek or obtain complete exemption from culpability on account of its potential negligence or violation of any applicable regulations. It merely sought to limit its liability for economic harm suffered by TEG. The parties foresaw the possibility that a blowout could occur and agreed between themselves concerning where the losses would fall. Significantly, the agreement required CAZA to accept responsibility for damage to its equipment, injury to its employees, and certain pollution and contamination removal and control activities. Thus, the limitation of liability provisions did not adversely affect the public or the workers employed by CAZA. As appellants concede, CAZA accepted liability for the bodily injury that occurred as the result of the blowout, and has defended and indemnified appellants, through its carrier, in the Currington litigation. Under these facts, we agree with the federal courts and the court in *Delta Air Lines, Inc. v. Douglas Aircraft Co.*, supra, 238 Cal.App.2d 95, 47 Cal.Rptr. 518: where the only question is which of two equal bargainers should bear the risk of economic loss in the event of a particular mishap, there is no reason for the courts to intervene and remake the parties' agreement.

나. 보 험

다수당사자간 면책조항은 면책대상인 손해나 피면책자에 있어서 계약당사자의 손해를 넘어서는 그룹개념이 도입되어야 함은 물론 손해의 범위에 관하여 최대한이 정하여져 있거나 징벌적 손해배상에 대한 면책책임의 배제 등 면책의 범위가 상이하여서는 아니 되며 무엇보다도 당사자들이 실제 면책채무를 이행할 재정적 능력이 있어야만 각자의 지배범위내 손해에 대한 위험분담이 완벽할 것이다. 이런 이유에서 보험은 면책조항을 보완하는 측면이 있으며 거꾸로 보험상품이 불가능하거나 이용가능하지 않은 손해에 대하여 면책조항이 필요하다는 점에서는 거꾸로 면책조항이 보험을 보완하는 측면이 있다. 보험과 면책조항이 중첩적으로 적용될 경우 누가 우선적 책임을 질 것이지, 보험자가 대위권을 행사할 수 있도록 할 것이지 등 추가적인 고려사항이 필요함은 물론이다. 통상 용역공급자가 체결하여야 할 보험을 계약에서 지정하고 운영자가 추가적인 피보험자로 지정되며 보험사업자는 변제자대위권을 포기할 것을 요구하고 있다.

서울고법 2003. 10. 22. 선고 2003나36722 판결[13)]

1. 기초사실

아래와 같은 사실은 당사자 사이에 다툼이 없거나 갑 제1호증의 1, 2, 갑 제2 내지 5호증, 갑 제6호증의 3(을 제6호증의 1과 같다), 6, 갑 제7호증의 6(을 제6호증의 2와 같다), 9(을 제6

13) 대법 2005. 3. 10. 선고 2003다61580 판결로 확정.

호증의 3과 같다) 내지 16, 갑 제8호증, 을 제5호증의 1, 2, 을 제6호증의 4의 각 기재에 변론의 전취지를 종합하면 이를 인정할 수 있다.

가. 서규석은 '일신양행'이라는 상호로 부천시 원미구 심곡2동 188-3 지상 건물(이하 '심곡동 건물'이라고 한다)을 사업장으로 사용하면서 자동차용 락카 등을 판매하던 중, 1998. 6.경 사업장을 시흥시 미산동 237-5 지상 철근벽돌에이치(H)빔조 스레트즙 평가건 1동 200평(이하 '이 사건 건물'이라고 한다)으로 이전하여 계속하여 자동차용 락카 등을 판매하다가 1999. 6. 15. 같은 곳에서 위와 같은 영업을 목적으로 하여 주식회사인 피고 회사를 설립하여 운영하여 왔다.

나. (1) 서규석은 1998. 3. 4. 원고 보험회사와 사이에 보험계약자 및 피보험자를 서규석으로 하여 아래와 같은 내용의 화재보험계약을 체결하였다.

① 보험기간: 1998. 3. 4.~2003. 3. 4.

② 보험목적물의 소재지: 부천시 원미구 심곡2동 188-3

③ 보험목적물: 심곡동 건물내의 사무실 비품 및 진열대 일체, 상품 일체

④ 보험가입금액: 300,000,000원(사무실 비품 및 진열대 일체 10,000,000원, 상품 일체 290,000,000원)

(2) 또한 서규석은 1998. 5. 28. 원고 보험회사와 사이에 보험기간을 1998. 5. 28. ~ 2003. 5. 28., 보험가입금액을 210,000,000원(사무실 비품 및 진열대 일체 10,000,000원, 상품 일체 200,000,000원)으로 하는 외에는 위와 같은 내용의 화재보험계약을 체결하였다.

다. 그 후 서규석이 위와 같이 사업장을 이전하고 사업체를 법인으로 조직을 변경함에 따라, 1998. 7. 6. 이 사건 보험계약 중 ① 보험목적물의 소재지가 '시흥시 미산동 237-5'로, ③ 보험목적물이 '이 사건 건물 내의 사무실 비품 및 진열대 일체, 상품 일체'로 변경되었고, 1999. 7. 19. 보험계약자 및 피보험자가 '피고 회사'로 변경되었다.

라. 피고 회사의 이사로 등기되어 있는 권오광은 2002. 7. 18. 17 : 00경 이 사건 건물 부근에서 담배를 피우기 위해 라이터를 켜다가 마침 자신의 휴대폰에 묻은 페인트를 닦으려고 가지고 있던 인화성 물질인 솔벤트를 적신 헝겊에 불이 붙자 이를 솔벤트가 담겨 있는 비이커 속에 떨어뜨리게 되어 비이커에서 불이 솟아오르자 당황한 나머지 비이커를 발로 차 약 50㎝ 떨려져 있는 비닐하우스에 불이 붙게 하였고 이어서 그 불이 이 사건 건물로 옮겨 붙게 됨으로써 이 사건 건물(건물 내의 사무실 비품 및 진열대 일체, 상품 일체 포함)이 전소되었다.

마. 이 사건 보험계약에 적용되는 보통약관에 의하면, ① 보험계약자, 피보험자(법인인 경우에는 그 이사 또는 법인의 업무를 집행하는 그 밖의 기관) 또는 이들의 법정대리인의 중대한

과실(제6조 제1호), ② 피보험자에게 보험금을 받도록 하기 위하여 고용인 또는 피보험자와 생계를 같이 하는 친족의 고의(제6조 제2호)로 인해 화재가 발생한 때에는 그로 인한 손해는 보상하지 아니한다고 규정되어 있다.

2. 판 단

가. 원, 피고의 주장

원고는, 위 화재는 권오광의 중대한 과실로 인하여 발생하였는데 권오광은 이 사건 보험계약의 피보험자인 피고 회사의 이사이므로 원고의 피고 회사에 대한 이 사건 보험금지급채무는 위 보험약관 제6조 제1호에 따라 면책된다고 주장함에 대하여, 피고는 권오광이 피고 회사의 실질적의 이사가 아니라 피용자에 불과하므로 원고의 위 면책 주장은 이유 없다고 다툰다.

나. 판 단

우선 위 보험약관의 면책조항에서 정하는 법인의 이사 또는 법인의 업무를 집행하는 그 밖의 기관이 실질적인 이사 또는 업무집행기관에 한하는 것인지에 관하여 살피건대, 보험계약자 등이 보험에 가입하였다는 이유만으로 고의로 보험사고를 일으키거나 중대한 과실로 보험사고가 발생하도록 방치하는 것은 보험사고의 우연성에 어긋날 뿐만 아니라 보험계약자 등을 일종의 도덕적 위험에 빠뜨리게 하므로 이를 방지하기 위하여 보험약관에 위와 같은 면책조항을 둔 것이므로, 위 면책조항에서 피보험자의 범위에 포함된다고 정하고 있는 법인의 이사 또는 업무집행기관은 피보험자와 동시할 수 있을 정도의 권한과 책임을 가지는 실질적인 이사에 한한다고 보아야 할 것이다.

그러므로 나아가 권오광이 피고 회사의 실질적인 이사인지에 관하여 살피건대, 갑 제6호증의 3(을 제6호증의 1과 같다), 갑 제7호증의 6(을 제6호증의 2와 같다), 9(을 제6호증의 3과 같다) 내지 11, 을 제1호증의 1, 2, 을 제2호증, 을 제3호증의 1 내지 11, 을 제4호증, 을 제6호증의 4의 각 기재에 변론의 전취지를 종합하면, 이 사건 화재 당시 피고 회사는 대표이사인 서규석을 포함하여 6명이 근무하였는데 그 중 권오광은 영업부장이라는 직책으로 서규석의 지휘 감독 하에 제품보관창고를 관리하는 업무를 담당하여 왔고 매월 서규석으로부터 일정한 급여를 받으면서 갑종근로소득세를 납부하여 왔으며 다른 종업원 4명과 함께 고용보험에 가입되어 매월 고용보험료를 납부하여 온 사실을 인정할 수 있는바, 위 인정사실에다가 위에서 인정한 바와 같은 피고 회사의 설립경위, 운영형태 및 그 규모 등에 비추어 보면, 권오광은 실질에 있어서는 임금을 목적으로 종속적인 관계에서 근로를 제공하는 고용자일 뿐이지 피고 회사로부터 위임받은 사무를 처리하는 실질적인 이사라고 볼 수 없다.

그렇다면, 권오광이 위 면책조항에서 정하는 법인의 이사에 해당됨을 전제로 한 원고의 위 주장은 나아가 살필 필요 없이 이유 없다.

노트와 질문

IADC의 국제해저시추서비스표준계약 일부는 아래와 같다. 이를 AIPN 표준시추용역계약서와 비교하여 보면 어떤 점이 다른가? 제3자의 손해배상청구 중 손해는 징벌적 손해나 특별손해를 포함하는가? 제3자의 손해배상청구가 불법행위나 특별법상의 제조물책임에 기초한 경우도 포함하는가? 면책범위를 계약서하의 용역대가나 보험료지급금으로 정할 수는 없을까?

IADC, Model Drilling Contract Indemnity Clause

605. Drilling Site and Access

Operator will be responsible for providing all necesuary rights of ingress and egress to drilling locations, as well as selecting, marking, and clearing access routes and drilling locations, for providing proper and sufficient certificates, including, without limitation, all consents, licences, approvals, permits or permission necessary pursuant to applicable laws, rules and regulations to enter upon and operate on the drilling locations, and for notifying Contractor of any obstructions, impediments, faulty bottom conditions or hazards to operations in the area of each drilling location or within the anchor pattern, including but not limited to wellheads, platforms, pipelines, cables, boulders, and mud filled depressions. Should Contractor be denied free access to a location, any time lost by Contractor as a result of such denial shall be paid for at the Standby Rate. ***

Notwithstanding any other provision of this Contract, should there be any obstructions, impediments, faulty bottom conditions or hazards to operations in the access route to a drilling lacation or at or within the area of a drilling location, including the anchor pattern, and these obstructions, impediments, faulty bottom conditions or hazards to operations damage Comtractor's Items, or Contractor's Items damage these obstructions or impediments, or if seabed conditions prove unsatisfiactory to properly support or moor the Drilling Unit during operations hereunder, Operator will be responsible for and hold harmless and indemnify Contractor for all resulting damage, including payment of the Standby Rate during required repairs, but Operator will receive credit for any physical damage insurance proceeds received by Contractor as a result of any damage to the Drilling Unit. All expenses assoeiated with improvements to the seabed and repositioning of the Drlling Unit at the drilling location under this Paragraph 605 shall be for Operator's account.

606. Custom or Excise Duties, Taxes and Fees

Operator shall pay all import and export/charges, customs and excise duties, levies, assessments, taxes and fees including, without limitation, clearing agent's fees, or other similar taxes or fees that are levied on Contractor's and/or Operator's Items(collectively, "Customs Fees"). If Contractor is nessessed and/or pays any such Customs Fees,

Operator agrees to be responsible for and hold harmless and indemnify Contractor from any and all cost, liability, expense, loss or claims with respect to such Customs Fees.

607. Taxes

Except as otherwise provided in Appendix A, Operator shall be responsible for all taxes, levies, and assessments imposed on Contractor, Contractor's Items or expatriate, members of Contractor's Personnel arising out of or in connection with Contractor's performance under this Contract, including, without limitation, corporate and personal income taxes, gross receipts taxes, sales taxes, use or compensating taxes, ad valorem property taxes, value added taxes, stamp duties and any other taxes imposed by the government of the country of operations or any political subdivision thereof, and shall at all times be responsible for and hold harmless and indemnify Contractor from any and all claims and liabilities with resped thereto.

901. Equipment or Property

(a) Except as specifically provided herein to the contrary, Contractor shall at all times be responsible for and hold harmless and indemnify Operator from and against damage to or loss of Contractor's property, Contractor's Items, and the property, equipment, material and services of Contractor's Affiliated Companies, partnerships, and limited liability companies, and its and all of their co-owners, partners, co-venturers, joint owners, and its contractors and subcontractors of any tier and the officers, directors, employees, agents, assigns, representatives, managers, consultants, insurers and subrogees of each of the foregoing. To the extent that the proceeds from Contractor's insurance as made available to Contractor do not compensate Contractor therefor.

(1) Operator shall be responsible for and hold harmless and indemnify Contractor for loss or destruction of or damage to Contractor's drill pipe, drill collars, subs, reamers, bumper subs, stabilizers and other in-hole equipment when such equipment is being used in the hole below the rotary table, normal wear excepted. Abnormal wear and/or damage for which Operator shall be responsible hereunder shall include, but not be limited to, wear and/or damage resulting from the presence of H_2S or other corrosive elements in the hole including those introduced into the drilling fluid, excessive wear caused by sandcutting, damage resulting from excessive or uncontrolled pressures such as those encountered during testing, blowout, or in a well out of control, excessive deviation of the hold from vertical, dog-leg severity, fishing, cementing or testing operations, and from any unusual drilling practices employed at Operator's request. Operator's responsibility for such abnormal wear and/or damage as referred to herein shall include abnormal wear and/or damage to Contractor's choke hoses and manifolds, BOP and other appurtenant equipment, Operator shall pay the cost of repairing damaged equipment if repairable. In the case of equipment lost, destroyed or damaged beyond repair, Operator shall reimburse Contractor an amount equal to the then current replacement cost of such equipment delivered to the Drilling Unit.

(2) Operator shall be responsible for and hold harmless and indemnify Contractor for damage to or loss of Contractor's subsea and mooring equipment, including without limitation, chains, anchors, the riser, slip joint, choke and kill lines, flexible hoses, hydraulic hoses and guidelines, subsea BOP, shackles, pendant lines and buoys, and shall reimburse Contractor an amount equal to the then current replacement cost of such equipment delivered to the Drilling Unit, or the repair cost, whichever is applicable.

(3) Operator shall be responsible for and hold harmless and indemnify Contractor for loss or destruction of or damage, including corrosion and contamination, to Contractor's surface equipment resulting from the presense of H_2S, CO_2 or other corrosive elements introduced into the drilling fluid (including elements introduced from the hole), or the presence of naturally occurring radioactive materials (NORM). Operator shall pay the cost of repairing and/or decontaminating damaged equipment if repairable. In the case of equipment lost, destroyed, damaged or contaminated beyond repair,

Operator shall reimburse Contractor an amount equal to the then current replacement cost of such equipment delivered to the Drilling Unit. In addition, notwithstanding the provisions of Paragraph 706 of this Contract, the Standby Rate shall apply with respect to any downtime that may accur or result from such loss or damage, including decontamination operation.

(4) Operator shall be responsible for and hold harmless and indemnify Contractor for damage to or loss of the Contractor's Items caused by Operator funished helicopters, tugs, supply or service vessels. In addition, notwithstanding the provisions of Paragraph 706 of the Contract, the Standby Rate shall apply with respect to any period of time required to repair Contractor's Items downtime that may occur or result from such loss or damage.

(b) Contractor's operating practices require the BOP stack to be operated at one (1) degree or less from vertical to avoid abnormal wear and damage. In the event the stack angle exceeds one (1) degree from vertical, Operator shall be reponsible for and hold harmless and indemnify Contractor for loss or damage to contractor's subsea and in-hole equipment which may result. Operator shall reimburse Contractor an amount equal to the then current replacement cost of such equipment delivered to the Drilling Unit. In addition, notwithstanding the provisions of Paragraph 706 of this Contract, the Standby Rate shall apply with respect to the period of time required to repair or replace Contractor's subsea and in-hole equipment that may occur or result from such loss or damage.

(c) Operator shall at all times be responsible for and hold harmless and indernnify Contractor from and against damage to or loss of Operator's property, Operator's Items, and the property, equipment, material and services of Operator's Affiliated Companics, partnershipes, and limited liability companies, and its and all of their co-owners, co-lessees, farmors, farmees, partners, co-venturers, joint owners, and its contractors and subcontractors of any tier (with the exception of Contractor and its subcootractors of any tier) and the officers, directors, employees, agents, assigns, representatives, managers, consultants, insurers and subrogees of each of the foregoing.

902. The Hole

In the event the hole should be lost or damaged at anytime, Operator shall be responsible for and hold harmless and indemnify Contractor and its suppliers, contractors and subcontractors of any tier from such damage to or loss of the hole, including all downhole property therein.

903. Contractor's Personnel

Contractor shall at all times be responsible for and hold harmless and indemnify Operator from and against all claims, demands and causes of action of every kind and character on account of bodily injury, illness or death of Contractor's Personnel or Contractor's invitees or damage to their property.

904. Operator's Personnel

Operator shall at all time be responsible for and hold harmless and indemnify Contractor from and against all claims, demands, and causes of action of every kind and character on account of bodily injury, illness or death of Operator's Personnel or Operator's invitees or damage to their property.

905. Pollution and Contamination

Notwithstanding anything to the contrary contained herein, the responsibility for pollution or contamination shall at all times be as follows:

(a) Contractor shall be responsible for and hold harmless and indemnify Operator for control and removal of pollution or contamination which originates above the surface of the water from spills of fuels, lubricants, motor oils, normal water base drilling fluid and attendant cuttings, pipe dope, paints, solvents, ballast, bilge and garbage wholly in

Contractor's possession and control and directly associated with Contractor's equipment and facilities.

(b) Operator shall be responsible for and hold harmless and indemnify Contractor and its suppliers, contractors and subcontractors of any tier against all claims, demands, and causes of action of every kind and character (including control and removal of the pollutant involved) arising directly or indirectly from all pollution or contamination (including radioactive contamination), other than that described in Paragraph 905(a) above, which may occur including, but not limited to, that which may result from fire, blowout, cratering, seepage or any other uncontrolled flow of oil, gas, water or other substance, as well as the use or disposition of lost circulation and fish recovery materials and fluids, oil emulsion, oil base or chemically treated drilling fluids and attendant cuttings, and drilling fluids other than "normal water base drilling fluid.

(c) In the event a third party commits an act or omission which results in pollution or contamination for which either the Contractor or Operator for whom such party is performing work is held to be legally liable, the responsibility therefore shall be considered, as between the Contractor and Operator, to be the same as if the party for whom the work was performed had performed the same.

906. Debris Removal and Cost of Control

Operator shall be responsible for and hold harmless and indemnify Contractor for the cost of removal of debris (including Contractors's Items) to the extent that proceeds from Contractor's insurance as made available to Contractor do not compensate Contractor therefore. Operator shall at all time be responsible for and hold harmless and indemnify Contractor for the cost of regaining control of any wild well.

907. Underground Damage

Operator shall at all times be responsible for and hold harmless and indemnify Contractor and its suppliers, contractors and subcontractors of any tier from and against any and all elaims on account of injury to, destruction of, or loss or impairment of any property right in or to oil, gas or other mineral substance or water, if at the time of the act or omission causing such injury, destruction, loss, or impairment, said substance had not been reduced to physical possession above the seabed, and for any loss or damage to any formation, strata, or reservoir beneath the seabed.

908. Patent Liability

Contractor shall at all time be responsible for and hold harmless and indemnify Operator from and against any and all loss or liability arising from infringement of patents of the United States covering equipment furnished by Contractor. Operator shall at all time be responsible for and hold harmless and indemnify Contractor from and against any and all loss or liability arising from infringement or alleged infringements of patents covering the property, equipment, methods or processes furnished or directed by Operator.

909. Consequential Damages

Subject to and without affecting the provisions of this Contract regarding the payment rights and obligations of the parties or the risk of loss, relesse and indemnity rights and obligations of the parties, each party shall at all times be responsible for and hold harmless and indemnify the other party from and against its own special, indirect or consequcntial damages and the parties agree that special, indirect or consequential damages shall, notwithstanding any interpretation under applicable law to the contrary, be deemed to include, whether direct or indirect, without limitation, the following: loss of profit or revenue; costs and expenses resulting from business interruptions; loss of or delay in production; loss of or damage to the leasehold, concession, production sharing contract or other similar rights; loss of or delay in drilling or operation rights; cost of or loss of use of property, equipment, materials and services, including, without limitation those provided by contractors or subcontractors of every tier or by third parties.

Operator shall at all times be responsible for and hold harmless and indemnify Contractor from and against all claims, demands and causes of action of every kind and character in connection with such special, indirect or consequential danages suffiered by Operator's co-owners, co-venturers, co-lessees, farmors, farmees, partners and joint owners.

910. Termination of Location Liability

Notwithstanding any other provisions of this Contract, once the Driling Unit is under way from the drilling location, Operator shall be responsible for and hold harmless and indemnify Contractor for loss or damage to property, personal injury or death of any person which occurs thereafler as a result of the condition of the well or the location and Contracot shall be relieved of such liability.

911. Indemnity Obligation

(a) The parties intend and agree that the phrase "be responsible for and hold harmless and indemnify" in Paragraphs 605, 606, 805 and 901 through 910 hereof means that the indemnifying party shall release, indemnify, hold harmless and defend (including payment of reasonable attorney's fees and costs of litigation) the indemnified party from and against any and all claims, demands, causes of action, damages, judgments and awards of any kind or character, without limit and without regard to the cause or causes thereof, including, claims, liabilities, demands, and cause of action arising out of operation of, or in connection with, any vessel or vessels (including the Drilling Unit), including ingress and egress to the drilling location, and loading and unloading of personnel and cargo, and also including preexisting conditions, defect or ruin of premises or equipment (whether such coaditions, defect or ruin be patent or latent), the unseaworthiness of any vessel or vessels (including the drilling unit), breach of representation or warranty (express or implied), breach of duty (whether statutory, contractual or otherwise), strict liability, any theory of tort, breach of contract, fault, regulatory or statutory liability, products liability, the negligense of any degree or character (including without limitation sole, joint or concurrent, active, passive or gross negligence) of any person or persons, including such negligence of the party seeking the benefit of a release, indemnity or assumption of liability, or any other theory of legal liability.

(b) An indemnifying party's obligations contained in this Contract shall extend to the indemnified party and shall inure to the benefit of such party, its Affiliated Companics, and their co-owners, co-venturers, co-lessees, farmors, farmees, and joint owners, and the officers, directors, stockholders, partners, managers, representatives, employees, consultants, agents, servants and insurers of each, and to actions against the Drilling Unit, its legal and beneficial owners, whether in rem or in personam.

(c) Except as otherwise provided herein, the terms and provisions of Paragraphs 605, 606, 805 and 901 through 910 shall have no application to claims or causes of action asserted against Operator or Contractor which arise solely by reason of any agreement of indemnity with a person or entity not a party hereto. Except as otherwise provided herein, nothing contained herein shall confer any rights upon any third party beneficiary.

제03편

국제에너지자원—시장

제3편은 제2편에서 논의된 여러 가지 유형의 탐사개발계약조건에 따라서 산유국에서 IOC가 탐사, 개발하여 생산한 원유와 천연가스는 시장에서 실제 어떻게 거래되는가에 관한 것이다.

제7장은 원유시장에 관한 것이다. 원유의 경우 과거 IOC가 양허계약하에서 탐사, 생산해낸 원유는 IOC의 또 다른 계열사인 정유사에 장기공급계약하에서 매각되었다. IOC가 점차 과점적 생산자로서의 지위를 상실하고 산유국의 NOC가 다운스트림화하여 석유소비국의 정유시설에도 투자하면서 선물시장이 출현하게 되었고 나아가 이러한 상품들은 표준화되어 거래소에서 거래되는 금융상품이 되었다. 제7장은 이러한 변화과정과 국제적인 매매계약에서의 일반조항에 관하여 살펴본다.

제8장은 천연가스시장에 관한 것이다. 천연가스는 특별한 운송수단을 필요로 하므로 그러한 저장, 운송시설이 없는 경우 과거 대부분 산유지에서 공중소각되었다. 요즈음은 국제적인 파이프라인 건설이 추진되면서 PNC로, 액화·운송·저장시설의 건설이 추진되면서 LNC로, 천연가스시장이 활성화되었다. 제8장은 이러한 천연가스시장의 변화과정과 천연가스 장기공급계약의 일반조항에 관하여 살펴본다.

제 7 장

원유거래시장

1. 연혁 및 구조

석유메이저들이 세계의 석유시장에서 석유의 생산과 정유, 유통을 주름잡던 시대는 석유메이저들이 정유사나 유통사를 계열사로 세우고 이들간 장기공급계약의 형태로 원유가 공급되었다. 따라서, 원유 또는 정유시장이라는 것이 별로 필요가 없었다. 공급자 독점상황이었기 때문에 불가능하기도 하였다.

그러나, 1940년대 이후 중동의 산유국이 독립, 자원민족주의가 고조되고 또한 구 소련연방지역의 국가들도 산유국으로 나타나면서 1960년대부터 시장상황이 바뀌기 시작하였다. 1960년 석유메이저들이 중동의 산유국에 지급하던 로열티를 줄이기 위하여 공시가를 일방적으로 낮추자 산유국은 바로 OPEC을 구성하여 가격통제기구를 구성하기에 이르렀다.[1)]

1960년대와 70년대 많은 산유국들이 점진적인 협상을 통하여 양허계약을 참여계약으로 바꾸어 나갔고[2)] 일부 국가들은 국유화조치를 단행하기도 하였다.[3)] 또한 일부 NOC들은 단순한 로열티수입의 증가뿐만 아니라 다운스트림 사업을 확대하기도 하였다. 또한 고유가는 많은 새로운 진입자를 만들었고 이들은 현물시장(spot market)에서 오일탱커카고를 현금지불, 즉시인도하는 거래에 뛰어들기 시작하였다. 이와 같이 NOC와 독립생산자가 현물시장을 만들어 나가면서 현물시장가격이 장기공급가격보다 높게 형성되었고 따라서 석유메이저들도 장기공급계약부분을 줄여나가기 시작했다. 또한 70년대 고유가는 구 소련연방과 그 위성국가간 구상무역으로서의 석유거래를 출현하게 하였다.

1980년대부터는 현물거래가 장기공급계약을 대신하여 국제적 원유거래의 주된 방법이 되었으며 NYMEX가 WTI 선물을 제공하기 시작하면서 선물거래, 옵션거래 등 원유에 기초한

1) Luis E. Cuervo, *OPEC from Myth to Realty,* 30 HOUST. J. INT'L L. 433, 64 (2007-08). Yergin, 위 주 4-1 상게서 514-23 (1991)도 참조.

2) 위 주 4-10 상기 논문 참조.

3) 국유화조치로 인한 대표적 국제중재판정에 관하여는 제9장 참조.

파생상품의 거래 또한 활발하게 되었다.[4] 따라서 1980년말대 이후 원유가는 원유의 생산자와 원유의 수요자가 아니라 원유가격의 움직임에 경제적 운명을 거는 많은 중간거래자들에 의하여 결정되었고 가격의 변동폭은 점차 확대되어 갔으며 그 변동원인 역시 수요와 공급이 아닌 중동의 불확실한 정치적 상황 등 경제외적 요소로 옮겨 갔다.[5]

2. 원유판매권계약의 일반적 조항

탐사개발권을 부여하는 계약은 자원보유국이 생산된 원유의 일부를 IOC로부터 로열티로 또는 정부보유분(government take)이라는 이름으로 가져가는 부분을 언제 어떻게 산정할지에 관하여 여러 가지 다른 방식을 정하고 있지만,[6] 이들 계약은 IOC에게 생산된 원유를 판매할 권리를 부여하며 그 대가를 산정할 기준을 정하고 있다는 면에서는 공통된다. 이들 공통된 조항을 열거하여 보면, 우선 탐사개발권은 생산된 원유를 판매촉진하며 수출할 권리를 포함한다. 계약에 따라서는 IOC가 일정 부분의 원유를 산유국 내에서 판매할 의무나 또는 산유국에게 우선 매도할 의무를 정하기도 한다. 이들 계약에는 지하의 원유를 지표로 표출시키는 절차 및 이들 원유에 대한 권리를 확정하는 절차에 관한 규정이 있고 원유도 여러가지 다른 품질의 것이 있으니 이들의 정의와 품질에 따른 가치를 정하는 방법을 정한 규정이 있다.[7]

3. 장기공급계약

IOC는 탐사개발계약하의 독점적 판매권을 행사하여 대개의 경우 실제 구매자와 장기공급계약을 체결한다. 장기공급계약은 일정한 기간 동안 일정한 수량의 원유를 구매자에 공급하기 위한 계약이다. 가격은 대개 일정한 지표에 연결되어 선적때마다 결정되며 WTI나 Brent와 같은 특정품질 석유의 현물시장가나 이들의 집합가와 연결되기도 한다. 매수인이 가격결정방식을 적용할 시기를 정할 수 있는 방식도 있을 수 있다.[8]

---

4) 거래조건에 관하여는 http://www.cmegroup.com/trading/energy/crude-oil 참조. NYMEX 이외에도 Dubai Mercantile Exchange가 Oman 원유를 거래하고 있다. http://www.dubaimerc.com/참조.

5) OPEC의 생산량할당과 구성원의 속임수에 대한 유혹에 관하여는 James M. Griffin/Weiwen Xiong, *The Incentive to Cheat: An Empirical Analysis of OPEC,* 40 J.L.& ECON. 289 (1997). OPEC 이외의 산유국 비중이 증가하고 카르텔을 유지할 수 있는 제재력의 한계로 OPEC의 가격결정에 대한 영향력은 감소하였다. OPEC을 미국 독점금지법위반으로 소송을 제기할 가능성에 대하여는 Spencer Weber Waller, *Suing OPEC,* 64 U. PITT. L. REV. 105 (2002-03).

6) 제4장 참조.

7) Smith, 주 1-4 상게서 895-97 Granting Instrument에 대한 설명 참조.

8) 실제 많은 분쟁은 운송계약을 둘러싸고 일어나는바 본서에서 이 부분에 대한 논의는 생략한다. Smith,

CHARTER CRUDE OIL COMPANY v. PETROLEOS MEXICANOS (U.S. Bankruptcy Court, M.D. Florida) 93 B.R. 286 (1988)

1. On January 1, 1980, Pemex and Charter International Oil Company ("CIOC") entered into an Agreement for the Sale of Crude Oil. CIOC assigned its rights under the Pemex contract to CCOC (the "Pemex/CCOC Contract") in January of 1981.

2. The Pemex/CCOC Contract contains the following provisions material to this adversary proceeding:

ARTICLE 3: Quality/Quantity of Crude Oil
i) The quantity of crude oil delivered hereunder shall average 13,000 barrels per day, plus/minus five percent at BUYER's/SELLER's option by mutual agreement to be lifted relatively evenly in full cargoes in accordance with the provisions of Article 7, hereof....
ARTICLE 4: Price
i) BUYER shall pay PEMEX for each quantity of crude oil which has been certified as loaded FOB tank vessel after deduction of all BS & W as shown in the certificate of quality on actual base selling price(s) established in accordance with the procedures set out in paragraph v) of this Article.
v) The price for the crude oil(s) in the Agreement may be adjusted for each calendar quarter subject to mutual agreement and renegotiation.
If the agreement is suspended for two consecutive quarters, and no price agreement is reached for the third quarter, this agreement shall be automatically terminated on the last day of the second suspended quarter.
vi) In regard to price application, if loading commence last day of any specific quarter prior to a price variation, the price to be applied for that specific cargo is the price in force when cargo has been commenced and such price will be applied for the full cargo in spite of that finishing of loading falls in the next price period.

In addition, Article 8 of that agreement provides that a laytime of 36 hours would be allowed before demurrage liability would begin to accrue.

3. The Pemex/CCOC Contract was similar to crude oil sales contracts which Pemex had in 1981 with approximately 20 other United States oil companies. Pursuant to these contracts, Pemex adjusted its posted prices on a quarterly basis depending upon world oil market conditions.

4. Through a series of telex exchanges beginning April 6, 1981, Pemex and CCOC agreed that the price of crude oil for the second quarter of 1981 would be $38.50 per barrel for Isthmus crude oil and $32.00 per barrel for the Maya crude oil. The telex from Pemex read as follows:

Re crude oil export prices for second quarter 1981 following our conversations concerning crude oil prices for second quarter 1981, with this telex Pemex gives notice that:

Id., Ch. 12. International Crude Oil Sales, 939-1021의 판례와 설명 참조.

1-For Istmo 34 G. API, price will be 38.50 dollars per barrel.
2-For Maya 23 G. API, price will be 32.00 dollars per barrel.
3-Both prices will be FOB loading point with payment terms 30 days after bill of lading date.
4-These prices are to be effective as of April 1, 1981.
5-If market conditions change, these prices could be revised within the quarter.

The CCOC telex in response read as follows:

Ref: Prices for Maya and Isthmus crude oil for second quarter 1981.
We accept the pricing format as set out in your telex dated April 4, 1981.

The prices established by Pemex pursuant to this April 6, 1981 agreement were paid by CCOC with respect to two liftings of crude oil commenced April 1, 1981, and April 29, 1981.

On May 12, 1981, CCOC notified Pemex by telex that CCOC intended to lift a third order of crude oil from Pemex during this quarter. On May 13, 1981 Pemex notified CCOC by return telex that its proposed nomination was accepted and on May 22, 1981, Pemex informed CCOC that the loading could commence on or after May 28, 1981.

On May 29, 1981, the vessel chartered by CCOC, the Amoco Savannah, arrived outside the docking facilities of Pemex at Coatzacoalcos, Mexico. The Amoco Savannah tendered its "Notice of Readiness" upon Pemex at 8:22 a.m. that same day.

At 9:00 p.m. on the evening of May 31, 1981, the loading of Maya crude oil commenced. At 10:10 p.m. that same evening the loading stopped "due [to a] shore request" and did not resume until after midnight June 1, 1981. The loading was finally completed June 2, 1981.

On June 2, 1981, the loading of Isthmus crude oil commenced at 10:15 a.m. By 2:00 a.m. the next day, the loading was completed.

The total volume of crude oil delivered between May 29, 1981, and June 3, 1981 was 34,018 metric tons of Maya crude oil and 22,423 metric tons of Isthmus crude oil. Using the prices in effect for the second quarter of 1981, Pemex calculated the amount due under the contract to be $13,780,237.00 and thereafter billed CCOC for this amount. Payment was due July 3, 1981, thirty (30) days from loading.

On June 3, 1981, Pemex issued a telex to CCOC stating that Pemex "has decided to adjust" its crude oil prices for the third quarter of 1981 "effective June 1, 1981" to reflect a price reduction in the amount of $4.00 per barrel for both Maya crude oil and Isthmus crude oil. The telex also requested confirmation of acceptance from CCOC. The decision by Pemex to reduce its crude oil prices was described by Pemex as "a major decision" which "reflected the oversupply situation and the [high prices] which purchasers of Mexican crude had been complaining [of]."

CCOC considered the new prices to be unacceptable and by telexes dated June 12 and June 24, 1981, it informed Pemex that it was suspending its liftings under the Pemex/CCOC Contract for the third quarter of 1981. CCOC then requested that the prices for the liftings in the fourth quarter of 1981 be renegotiated in accordance with Article 4(v) of the Pemex/CCOC Contract. The telex dated June 12, 1981, read as follows:

> Appreciate greatly your U.S. dollars 4.00 reduction in crude posting and do understand your new pricing concept. Unfortunately, this price still does not enable Charter to run profitably at either Freeport or Houston refineries. Your new program of immediate price changes may work to our betterment or detriment and is unknown at this time. Therefore, we must reluctantly inform you that your new prices are unacceptable. However, we would welcome and may consider favorably a further reduction of prices on third quarter allocations. We appreciate your understanding of our position.

> CCOC's telex of June 24, 1981 stated:

> Regarding your recent telex requesting that Charter International Oil Company (+CIOC+) submit nominations for July, 1981 purchases, please be advised that pursuant to Article 4, Paragraph (v) of the referenced Agreement, by telex dated May 29, 1981, CIOC requested a renegotiation of prices for the calendar quarter beginning July 1, 1981, and offers to meet with your representatives to begin these negotiations during the week of June 1-5, 1981. No agreement was reached by June 16, 1981, as required by Article 4, Paragraph (v) of the Agreement, with respect to prices for the quarter beginning July 1, 1981. Accordingly, pursuant to Article 4, Paragraph (v) of the Agreement, liftings are suspended for such quarter and, therefore, nominations are unnecessary.
> We would like to meet with you at your convenience to discuss the resumption of liftings at a mutually acceptable price for the quarter beginning October 1, 1981, or at the earliest mutually agreeable date prior to October 1, 1981.

13. On June 23, 1981, CCOC responded to the invoice sent by Pemex and suggested that the proper amount of the Pemex invoice for the May 29, 1981, through June 3, 1981, lifting should have been $12,190,933.00 to reflect the prices which went into effect June 1, 1981. On July 3, 1981, CCOC tendered $12,190,933.00 to Pemex.

On November 13, 1981, Pemex sent a telex to CCOC demanding payment of the $1,589,304 balance still due under the invoice.

On December 2, 1981, CCOC again notified Pemex by telex that the Pemex invoice was overstated by $1,589,304 and requested a credit memo in that amount from Pemex. Pemex responded to that telex and again demanded payment of $1,589,304.

In a separate dispute, CCOC issued an invoice dated January 6, 1981 to Pemex in the amount of $34,352.96 for the 294,078 days of demurrage incurred by CCOC in connection with the loading of the Amoco Savannah. Soon afterwards, Pemex and CCOC began negotiating the settlement of all demurrage claims between the parties. In January,

1982, an agreement was reached and all disputed accounts were settled.

On April 18, 1986, CCOC filed a complaint with this Court seeking the turnover of the demurrage debt from Pemex. Pemex contends that the January, 1982 settlement encompassed this debt.

On June 30, 1986, Pemex rediscovered its $1,589,304 claim against CCOC and filed a motion with this Court for authorization to file an untimely proof of claim. On December 29, 1986, the Court entered an order granting Pemex's motion for enlargement of time to file a proof of claim and on January 28, 1987, Pemex filed its claim in the amount of $1,639,432.96. The $1,639,432.96 includes the $1,589,304 debt owing under the Pemex/CCOC Contract as well as a $50,120.96 claim against Charter International Sales Corporation.

19. By order of this Court entered October 16, 1987, this adversary proceeding was consolidated for trial with the Debtors' objections to the Pemex proof of claim. At trial, Pemex withdrew its $50,128.96 claim against Charter International Sales Corporation.

CONCLUSIONS OF LAW

[1] The Pemex/CCOC Contract states that "[t]his Agreement shall be governed by and interpreted in accordance with the laws of Mexico." Hence, the parties were required to present sufficient proof to establish the principles of foreign law which they contend are applicable. Otherwise, it is to be presumed that the law of the foreign state is the same as that of the present forum. *Symonette Shipyards, Ltd. v. Clark*, 365 F.2d 464 (5th Cir.1966); *Seguros Tepeyac, S.A., Com pania Mexicana v. Bostrom*, 347 F.2d 168 (5th Cir.1965).

[2] In this case, the defendant offered the expert testimony of Mr. Adolfo Grana, a professor of Mexican law and an attorney licensed to practice law in that country. His testimony reveals the following principles of Mexican law:

(i) a written contract cannot be modified by a course of conduct between the parties;

(ii) a contract can only be modified by following exactly the same formalities by which the original contract was created (for example, if the original contract was in writing and executed by the parties, it cannot be amended unless such an amendment is also made in writing with the requisite "formalities"); and

(iii) an agreement or course of conduct between the two parties which, due to the absence of the same formalities, does not qualify as an amendment to the original contract, is a new and separate contract.

The Court is satisfied that Mr. Grana has given an accurate statement of Mexican law and, without testimony to the contrary, it will analyze this proceeding in accordance with that testimony.

The primary issue in this proceeding is whether there was a mid-quarter change in prices which would have effected the amount due and owing for the May 29, 1981 through June 3, 1981 lifting. CCOC contends that there was and that such change became effective upon simple notice. To support this contention, CCOC points to prior conduct and the Pemex telex dated April 6, 1981, which states: "If market conditions change, these prices could be revised within the quarter."

CCOC suggests that by accepting Pemex's pricing format by return telex dated April 6, 1981, an agreement to make mid-quarter changes in price was made. CCOC then argues that such a change occurred automatically when Pemex announced a change in prices effective June 1, 1981.

CCOC has also pointed out an incident which occurred on or about June 25, 1980 to support its position. There, Pemex gave notice of a mid-quarter change in prices and, without waiting for a response, required CCOC to pay the increased fee even though a CCOC chartered vessel had commenced loading prior to the change.

Although that situation is fairly similar to the one presented here, the Court finds such evidence immaterial to the decision at hand, for under Mexican law, a contract cannot be modified by a course of conduct between the parties. Thus, the parties are bound by the terms of the original contract even though they may have chosen to informally modify the contract on other occasions. Because the original contract indicates that prices could only be adjusted on a quarterly basis, the parties are so bound.

Secondly, even if a mid-quarter change in prices could be made, the evidence indicates that no such agreement was reached in this case. More specifically, by telex dated June 12, 1981, CCOC unequivocally rejected Pemex's June 6, 1981 offer and suspended liftings for the remainder of the quarter. Therefore, the terms of this transaction are left to be governed by the agreement reached April 6, 1981 which set prices at $38.50 per barrel for Isthmus crude oil and $32.00 per barrel for Maya crude oil. Using these figures, the amount owing from CCOC to Pemex for crude oil delivered between May 29, 1981, and June 3, 1981, is $13,780,237.00.

Finally, and again assuming that mid-quarter changes in price were permitted under the contract, such changes could only be effectuated upon compliance with the same formalities by which the original contract was made. Such formalities included joint signatures, initials on each page, etc. In the instant proceeding, the only evidence offered by CCOC that a change in prices had been made is the exchange in telexes between the parties. This hardly equates to the formalities under which the original contract was created and is ineffective to modify the contract.

Having found that there was no change in prices for the second quarter of 1981, the Court need not address the issue of whether the price in force when loading commenced is to be applied for the full cargo when loading falls within the next quarter.

[3] As for the $34,362.96 demurrage claim asserted by CCOC against Pemex, the Court finds that the January, 1982 settlement between the parties was intended to encompass this transaction. CCOC's claim is barred by the doctrine of accord and satisfaction and CCOC is not entitled to any recovery on its demurrage claim.

CONCLUSION

The Court finds that Mexican law and the terms of the Pemex/CCOC Contract govern the instant transaction, that the Pemex/CCOC Contract cannot be modified by course of conduct, and that CCOC unequivocally rejected Pemex's mid-quarter change in prices. Accordingly, CCOC is liable to Pemex in the amount of $1,589,304. CCOC's claim for demurrage relating to the Amoco Savannah is barred by the doctrine of accord and satisfaction and CCOC is not entitled to any recovery on this claim.

The Court will enter separate orders overruling CCOC's objection to Pemex's proof of claim and awarding final judgment in favor of Pemex in accordance with these findings.

FINAL JUDGMENT Upon Findings of Fact and Conclusions of Law separately entered, it is

ORDERED as follows:

Judgment is entered in favor of the defendant, Petroleos Mexicanos, and against the plaintiff, Charter Crude Oil Company.

The Complaint Seeking Turnover of a $34,362.96 demurrage claim is DISMISSED.

노트와 질문

1. 계약 당사자 일방의 법이 적용된다고 합의할 수도 있지만 국제물품매매에 관하여는 국제적 협약으로서 Convention on International Sale of Goods가 있다. 동 협약에 따르면 위의 결론은 달라지는가?
2. CISG는 계약당사자간 합의에 의하여 그 적용을 배제할 수 있으며 그럴 경우 어느 나라의 법에 따라서 계약문구를 해석하여야 하는가?

4. 현물시장에서의 카고화물계약

현물시장에서는 하나의 카고선에 선적되어 있는 또는 선적될 원유 또는 그 일부를 현물로서 사고 판다. 가격은 고정되어 있으며 이를 할인하여 또는 프리미엄을 붙여서 하나의 화물을 둘러싸고 많은 계약들이 순차적으로 체결된다. 계약은 하나의 카고를 다른 카고와 교환하는 계약일 수도 있고 장래의 일정시점에 카고의 인도를 약속하는 선도계약일 수도 있다. 예를 들어 A사는 즉시 인도가능한 파이프라인상 원유가 있고 B사는 북해에서 휴스톤으로 수송중인 원유가 있으며 B사는 즉시 원유를 필요로 하는 경우 대가를 지불하고 A사와 계약을 교환할 수 있다. 구상무역에서는 A사가 B사에게 설탕을 인도하고 B사로부터 원유를 인도받기를 원할 수도 있다. 선도계약은 계약체결시점으로부터 일정기간이 경과한 후에 정하여진 가격으로 원유를 인도할 것을 약속하는 것으로 원유공급자는 앞으로의 원유가격변동에 관계없이 일정한 가격을 받을 수 있고 원유를 필요로 하는 사업체도 원유의 공급을 미리 확보할 수 있다. 통상 일정한 항구에서 일정한 기간에 선적되는 일정한 품질의 원유를 대상으로 선물계약이 체결되며 실제 선적기간은 추후에 특정된다.

서울행법 2006. 6. 16. 선고 2005구합16611 판결[9)]

1. 처분의 경위

가. 원고는 2000. 7. 12.부터 2002. 5. 3.까지 원유를 수입하면서 피고에게 별지 표 수입신고번호 난 기재와 같이 80건의 수입신고(이하 이 사건 수입이라 한다)를 하였다.

나. 원고는 이 사건 수입을 하면서 원고의 싱가폴 현지법인 Hyundai Oil Refinery (Singapore) Pte., Ltd.(이하, 싱가폴 현대정유라고 한다)에게 수입품인 원유가격을 지급하면서 싱가폴 현대정유가 포페이터(forfeiter)에게 지급한 포페이팅 이자를 지급하였음에도 포페이팅 이자 상당액(이하 이 사건 쟁점금액이라 한다)이 관세법 및 관세법시행령에 정한 연불이자에 해당한다는 사유로 관세 과세가격에서 이를 공제하여 신고하였다.

다. 피고는 원고에 대한 관세사후심사를 한 뒤, 원고가 지급한 이 사건 쟁점금액이 연불이자에 해당하지 아니하여 이를 과세가격에서 공제할 수 없다는 이유로 2002. 7. 12.부터 2002. 11. 25.까지 7회에 걸쳐 이 사건 수입에 관하여 별지 표 기재 관세, 부가가치세 및 가산세 란 기개 각 해당금액을 부과하는 이 사건 처분을 하였다.

9) 서울고법 2007. 2. 16. 선고 2006누16009 판결을 거쳐 대법 2007. 6. 14. 선고 2007두6267 판결로 확정. 할당관세율 적용에 관하여는 chosun.com 2008. 2. 24.자 울산지법 판결에 관한 보도 참조.

2. 처분의 적법 여부

가. 원고의 주장

이 사건 수입에서 싱가폴 현대정유가 형식상 판매자로 되어 있으나 실질적으로는 원유 공급계약이 원유의 원공급자와 원고 사이에 체결되었고 싱가폴 현대정유는 단지 자금융통을 위하여 거래의 중개자 역할을 한 것에 불과하여 실질과세원칙상 원공급자와 원고와의 거래라 할 것인데, 이 사건 포페이팅 이자는 원고가 수입한 유류의 대가와는 상관없이 단지 대금지급을 연지급한 것이어서 유류의 구매와 관련하여 발생한 금융비용에 해당할 뿐, 이를 '실제 지급하였거나 지급하여야 할 가격'으로서 과세가격에 포함시킬 수 없고, 이 사건 쟁점금액은 관세법 및 WTO 평가협약상 과세대상에서 공제되는 연불이자로서의 요건을 충족하고 있으므로 관세법 제30조 제2항 제4호에 정한 연불이자로 과세대상가액에서 공제되어야 한다.

따라서 이와 반대로 이 사건 쟁점금액을 과세가격에 포함하여 과세한 이 사건 처분은 위법하다.

나. 관계법령

별지 관계 법령 기재와 같다.

다. 인정사실

(1) 원고는 2000. 1. 20. Petrolian Nasional Berhad(이하, 'PETRONAS'라 한다)와의 사이에 계약기간은 2000. 1. 1.부터 2000. 12. 31.까지로 하여 말레이시아 산 원유 8,052,000배럴 ±10%(판매자 옵션)을 공급받되, 대금은 원칙적으로 각 선하증권 발행 후 30일 이내에 지급한다는 내용으로 FOB 방식의 장기구매계약을 체결하였고, 2001. 2. 14.에도 PETRONAS와의 사이에 위와 유사한 내용으로 그로부터 말레이시아산 원유 8,037,300배럴 ±10%(판매자 옵션)을 공급받기로 하는 내용의 장기구매계약을 체결한 것을 비롯하여 사우디아라비아 국영석유회사인 ARAMCO, 이란의 국영석유회사인 NIOC, 아랍에미리트연합 아부다비의 국영석유회사인 ADNOC, 쿠웨이트의 국영석유회사인 KPC 원유공급자와의 사이에 같은 방식으로 원유의 장기구매계약을 체결하였다.

(2) 싱가폴 현대정유는 원고가 100% 출자한 회사로 싱가폴에 사업장을 두고 1990. 4. 20. 설립되어 사업자등록을 한 회사로서, 당기순이익이 2000. 3. 기준으로 543,625미국달러, 2001. 3. 기준으로 888,152미국달러, 2002. 3. 기준으로 274,671미국달러 상당이 발생하였고, 현재까지 현대정유의 안정적인 원유공급 등의 목적을 위하여 실질적인 영업활동을 수행하면

서 존속하는 회사이다.

(3) 원고가 위와 같은 원유 공급자들 사이에 원유의 장기구매계약을 체결하면서 원유 공급자에 대하여 싱가폴 현대정유를 구매자인 원고의 지불대리인으로 명시적으로 규정하였거나 원고의 대금지급 목적만을 위하여 구매계약자의 지위를 싱가폴 현대정유로 양도하기도 하였으며, 공급자들은 명시적으로 약정하지 아니한 채 원고의 지불대리인으로서 싱가폴 현대정유에게 원유공급대금의 지급청구서를 발송하기도 하였다.

(4) 원고는 이 사건 수입을 하면서 다음과 같은 절차로 수입대금을 결제하고 수입신고를 이행하였다.

(가) 원고는 국내에 소재하는 특정은행에 의뢰하여 싱가폴 현대정유를 수익자로 하는 취소불능신용장을 개설하면서 싱가폴 현대정유에 대하여 이 사건 수입과 관련한 대금지급기일의 연장을 요청하였고, 싱가폴 현대정유는 위 신용장 개설은행을 인수은행으로 하면서 수입하는 원유의 가액에 포페이팅 비용 등을 포함하여 결정한 액면가액으로 수출환어음을 발행한 후 정리회사에 대하여 그 액면가액을 총 금액으로 하여 '선적자'를 싱가폴 현대정유로 기재한 잠정적인 상업송품장을 발행하였으며, 위 수출환어음을 싱가폴 소재 은행인 The Toronto-Dominion Bank 등 포페이터로부터 무소구 조건으로 할인하는 포페이팅 거래를 하여 지급받은 대금으로 원공급자와의 사이에 체결한 위 원유공급계약상 대금지급기일인 선적 후 30일 내에 원공급자에게 원유대금을 지급하여 왔다.

(나) 그 후 싱가폴 현대정유는 포페이터로부터 위 수출환어음 등이 매입되었다는 통지와 함께 고정이자율로 할인·지급시 제공하는 신용공여액에 대한 이익인 포페이팅 이자 등 포페이팅 거래의 대가인 포페이팅 비용 및 이에 기한 어음할인액을 기재한 청구서를 받아, 이를 기초로 원고에게 포페이팅 이자 등을 명시하여 실제 구매자인 원고로부터 지급받을 금액을 총 금액으로 하여 확정적으로 최종적인 상업송품장을 발행하였다.

(다) 원고는 수입신고를 하면서 공급자를 싱가폴 현대정유로 하고 수입자를 원고로 하여 발행된 상업송품장에 기재된 잠정적인 가격으로 과세가격을 신고한 후, 싱가폴 현대정유로부터 추후 최종적으로 작성된 상업송품장을 재차 교부받아 확정통관사유서를 첨부하여 위 최종적인 상업송품장에 기재된 금원 중 포페이팅 비용인 포페이팅 이자를 수입물품의 과세가액에서 차감하고, 가산요소인 운임과 보험료를 가산한 금액을 총 과세가액으로 하여 확정적으로 수입신고를 하였다.

(라) 확정통관 사유서(갑 제9호증)에는 이 사건 수입의 원유의 공급가격에 포페이팅 이자 등 금융비용 및 이자비용을 더해서 결정된다고 되어 있다.

라. 판 단

(1) 이 사건 수입에서 '판매자'를 누구로 볼 것인지에 관하여

이 사건 수입에서 원유의 판매자(수출자)가 싱가폴 현대정유인지, 아니면 원고의 주장대로 원공급자인지에 관하여 보건대, 위 인정사실에 나타난 제 사정, 즉 ① 원고는 이 사건 수입을 위하여 싱가폴 현대정유를 수익자로 한 신용장을 발행하였고, 수입신고서상에도 공급자는 싱가폴 현대정유로 기재되어 있는 등 관련서류에 싱가폴 현대정유가 수출자로 기재되어 있는 점, ② 싱가폴 현대정유는 이 사건 수입을 위한 매 거래시마다 원고에 대하여 구매자를 원고로, 판매자를 싱가폴 현대정유로 기재하였고 그 대금의 지급에 있어서도 원고에 대하여 이 사건 수입이 이루어진 원유의 단가로 원유대금과 포페이터 비용 이외에 신용장 개설비용 등 여타 부대비용으로 수출 항차별로 2000. 8. 이전은 500미국달러, 2000. 9. 이후는 700미국달러를 신용장에 포함시켰던 점, ③ 싱가폴 현대정유는 현재까지 모회사인 원고와는 별개로 독자적인 수익을 내면서 존속하고 있는 회사인 점을 종합하면, 이 사건 수입에 있어 수출자는 신용장이나 수입신고서에 기재된 바대로 싱가폴 현대정유라 할 것이다.

따라서 이에 반하는 원고의 주장은 이유 없다.

(2) 포페이팅 비용이 과세가격에 포함되는지 여부에 관하여

(가) 일반적으로 수입물품에 대한 관세의 과세가격은 우리나라에 수출하기 위하여 판매되는 물품에 대하여 당해 수입물품의 대가로서 구매자가 실제로 지급하였거나 지급하여야 할 가격으로서, 간접적인 지급액을 포함한 총 금액이고, 명백히 구분할 수 있는 공제금액을 빼고 가산요소를 가산하여 조정한 거래가격이다{관세법 제30조 제1항, 제2항 및 구 관세법(2000. 12. 29. 법률 제6305호로 개정되기 전의 것, 이하 '구 관세법'이라 한다) 제9조의 3 제1항, 제2항 참조}. 여기서, 관세의 과세가격인 '실제로 지급하였거나 지급하여야 할 가격'이라 함은 무역거래 당사자가 무역계약을 체결할 때에 합의한 가격으로 구매자에 의하여 수입물품에 대한 대가로서 지급되기로 합의가 이루어진 후 계약내용대로 이행되어 지급한 가격 또는 계약내용대로 이행하기 이전에 지급의무를 부담하는 가격을 말한다. 또한, 과세가격에 포함되는 '간접적인 지급'이라 함은 구매자가 판매자에게 구매대금을 직접 지급한 것은 아니지만 판매자의 이익을 위하여 판매자와 구매자간에 채권자 채무를 상계하는 것 또는 판매자 아닌 제3자에게 지급하는 것 등을 의미하는데, 관세법시행령 제20조 제6항 제4호는 기타의 간접적인 지급액으로서 '기타 일반적으로 판매자가 부담하는 금융비용 등을 구매자가 지급하는 경우 그 지급급액'이라고 규정하고 있고, 여기서 '일반적으로 판매자가 부담하는'의 의미는 판매자의 이익을 위하여 금융서비스의 이용이 이루어지고 이에 따라 금융비용의 부담자는 판매자인데 판매자와 구매자간의 합의에 의하여 이를 구매자가 부담하기로 특약한 후 특약에 따라 금융

비용을 지급하는 것을 의미한다고 보아야 할 것이다.

(나) 관세가격과 관련하여 금융비용이 문제되는 것은 물품의 수입대금의 결제와 관련하여 자금의 융통이 일어나는 경우로서, 수출자(판매자)가 포페이팅 방식에 의하여 수출채권을 현금회수하는 경우와 거래당사자가 팩토링 방식에 의하여 매매대금을 후지급하기로 하는 경우 등에 발생하고, 그 중 포페이팅(forfeiting)이라 함은 수출거래에 따른 환어음이나 약속어음을 소구권 없이 고정이자율로 할인하여 신용판매를 현금판매로 전환시키는 금융기법의 일종으로, 포페이팅 비용은 포페이터가 수출자에게 환어음이나 약속어음을 소구권 없이 고정이자율로 할인·지급할 때 제공하는 신용공여액에 대한 이익인 '포페이팅 이자'와 포페이터가 수출자를 위하여 서비스를 제공하는 데 따른 대가로서 약정수수료와 옵션수수료 등으로 구성되는 '포페이팅 수수료'로 나눌 수 있다. 이와 같은 포페이팅은 판매자가 수출채권의 만기 도래시 대금회수불능의 위험을 회피하기 위하여 불소구조건부의 어음할인금융인 포페이팅 서비스를 이용하는 경우와 구매자의 자금융통의 편의를 제공하기 위하여 이루어지는 경우로 나뉘며, 판매자의 이익을 위한 전자의 경우 그 비용부담자는 포페이팅 서비스를 통하여 위험을 회피하게 되는 판매자여서 그 비용이 매매대금에 포함되면 그 전액이 과세가격이 된다 할 것이나, 수입자인 구매자의 이익을 위한 후자의 경우 원래 그 비용부담자는 수입자라 할 것이어서 이러한 경우에는 앞서 본 간접적인 비용에 관한 법리상 포페이팅 비용을 과세가격에 포함시킬 수는 없다 할 것이다.

(다) 이와 같이 관세법시행령 제20조 제6항 제4호의 규정에 의하여 '기타의 간접적인 지급액'으로서 과세가격의 포함 여부가 문제되는 '금융비용'과는 별도로, 관세법 제30조 제2항 제4호(구 관세법 제9조의 3 제2항 제4호)에는 과세가격인 실제로 지급하였거나 지급할 가격에서 공제되는 요소로서 '연불이자'에 관하여 규정하고 있고, 여기서 '연불이자'라 함은 연불조건의 수입 또는 후지급조건의 수입에서 구매자가 대금지급을 늦추는 대신 동 대금을 이용한 대가로서 구매자에 의하여 지불되는 이자를 말한다. 위에서 살펴본 바와 같이 포페이팅 비용은 포페이팅 거래가 구매자의 이익을 위하여 행하여지는 경우 연불이자와 마찬가지로 구매자의 대금지급을 늦추기 위한 목적에서 이루어지는 것이기는 하나, 구매자의 자금융통을 위하여 판매자가 포페이터로부터 수출환어음 등을 소구권 없이 할인받는 금융기법의 일종인 포페이팅 거래를 하면서 포페이터에게 결국 그 대가로서 포페이팅 이자 및 수수료 등 포페이팅 비용을 지급하는 형태를 가진다는 점(포페이팅 이자도 대금에 대한 이자가 아니라 대금 및 포페이팅 비용 등을 포함하는 환어음 등의 액면가액에 대한 이자로서, 판매자가 어음할인시 액면가액에서 이를 공제한 나머지 금액만을 지급받게 된다)에서 연불이자와는 구별되는 금융비용으로 관세법 제30조 제2항 본문(구 관세법 제9조의 3 제2항), 관세법시행령 제20조 제6항 제4호에 의하여 과세대상 여부를 결정하여야 할 것이다.

(라) 위와 같은 전제에서 위 인정사실을 살펴보면, ① 이 사건 쟁점금액은 이 사건 수입과 관련하여 포페이터가 싱가폴 현대정유로부터 포페이팅 거래의 대가로서 지급받은 포페이팅 비용으로서 금융비용인 점, ② 싱가폴 현대정유가 이 사건 수입과 관련하여 포페이터와의 사이에 포페이팅 거래를 하게 된 것은 판매자인 싱가폴 현대정유가 회수불능의 위험을 회피하기 위한 것이 아니라, 구매자인 원고의 요청에 의하여 원고의 자금융통의 편의를 제공하기 위한 목적에서 포페이팅 비용 일체를 원고가 부담하기로 한 약정에 기하여 이루어진 점, ③ 비록 최종적인 상업송품장에는 포페이팅 비용을 포함한 거래가격이 기재되어 있기는 하나, 그 기재상으로도 포페이팅 이자를 구별하여 기재하고 있는 점을 종합하여 보면, 이 사건 쟁점금액은 당해 수입물품인 원유에 대한 대가로서 약정이 이루어져 지급된 금원과는 구별되어, 구매자인 원고의 자금융통을 위한 포페이팅 거래에서 발생한 금융비용으로 원고가 당연히 부담하여야 하는 비용에 불과하여, 이 사건 쟁점금액을 관세법 제30조 제2항 본문(구 관세법 제9조의 3 제2항 본문) 소정의 '구매자가 실제로 지급하였거나 지급하여야 할 가격'에 해당한다거나, 이에 포함되는 가액으로서 관세법시행령 제20조 제6항 제4호의 '기타 일반적으로 판매자가 부담하는 금융비용 등을 구매자가 지급하는 경우 그 지급금액'에 해당한다고 볼 수 없다.

따라서 이 사건 쟁점금액을 수입물품의 과세가격에 포함시킬 수 없음에도 불구하고, 이와 반대의 전제에서 한 피고의 이 사건 처분은 위법하다.

3. 결　　론

그렇다면 원고의 청구는 이유 있으므로 이를 인용하기로 한다.

Voest Alpine Intertrading G.m.b.H. v. Chevron International Oil Co., Ltd., [1987] 2 Lloyd's Rep. 547 (Queen's Bench, 1987)

Brent forward market.

The nature and characteristics of this market are very important matters in the case, and are described with single clarity by Meg Annesley, a consultant of acknowledged authority in this field, in a report which is accepted as accurate by both parties. I cannot do better than quote it in full:

THE BRENT MARKET

SUMMARY

The Brent Forward Market is a paper market in which rights to receive or deliver cargoes of Brent crude oil arise in a future month. The rights for purchase and sale are for physical delivery of cargoes of 600,000 barrels of crude oil, under reasonably standard terms, and for delivery in a specified calendar month.

The exact delivery timetable is determined within the standard contracts and specifies particularly that the seller has the obligation to advise the buyer of a 3 day lifting range during the month of the contract, fifteen days prior to the first date of the lifting range. It is at this point that the contracts have physical oil assigned to them. Since many forward deals are concluded for each delivery month, at the point of oil being assigned to the contracts chains of sellers and buyers form, known as "daisy-chains".

HISTORICAL EVOLUTION

STANDARDISED CONTRACT

The Brent Market evolved from what we could call a "normal" market, in which individual cargoes of oil are bought and sold on non-standard terms, either for one cargo at a time, called spot sales, or for a series of sales described as a term contract. Such normal markets exist for all the grades of crude oil in international trade, and are more or less active depending on the exact commercial circumstances surrounding the grade of crude oil in question.

The "normal" spot markets have a disadvantage in that they are inflexible to producers, refiners and traders. This derives from a lack of uniformity in their contracts, this in turn inhibits companies selling the grades short, because of the difficulty of ensuring matching contract terms when and if a seller wishes to buy in a cargo to cover. The low level of activity in normal spot markets results also in a short seller taking time to cover a cargo, this delay increases the seller's risk and reduces the attraction of the short sale. Short sales are inhibited and market flexibility suffers. This problem is only important when market prices are weak, or volatile.

From about 1981 crude oil prices were tending to weakness rather than strength, and the Government selling prices of the producers which were fixed and inflexible became increasingly risky for oil companies and traders to sustain. Although the futures markets were being developed, they lagged behind a need by oil companies and traders to sell short, hedge price risks and otherwise improve their performance, during a time of uncertain prices. From about 1982/3, the concept of standardising the contracts in the "normal" spot market around a set of principles that would meet both buyers and sellers requirements began to find interest and favour.

The benefit afforded by a standardised and gradually active market was principally in aiding price management by having the short sale ability as well as that of being long. The need for a high volume of deals to activate decisions on price hedging also favoured one type of crude oil being used to concentrate the market activity rather than dilute it over several grades.

THE BRENT MARKET

Short Seller Choice.

The Brent market was the obvious choice for standardisation as it offered the least risk for short sellers:

a) Brent crude oil, like all North Sea production, was owned by oil companies, who in practice always maximised production. By contrast OPEC production was subject to wildly fluctuating production, depending on whether their prices were competitive in the market or not.
b) The production derived from several fields, co-mingled into a common stream and delivery point, at Sullom Voe Terminal in the Shetland Islands, and the production was the highest of the North Sea grades. The differing ownerships of the several fields meant that in practice there were always several potential suppliers to the market, thereby reducing the likelihood of a shortage of supplies.
c) Further flexibility of supply was guaranteed because, at this time, the British National Oil Corporation (BNOC) had entitlement to dispose of 51% of the total production of all North Sea grades, under Government statute. Since they had no refineries the oil had to be supplied to the market. Brent was the highest volume of production therefore the BNOC availability was similarly high.
d) The U.K. tax regime benefited arms-length sales by integrated oil companies, particularly when prices were weak, thus ensuring a reasonably steady supply commitment by the producers.

Long Buyers Choice.

For companies who bought cargoes, ease of disposal was desirable. The quality of Brent was well regarded and acceptable to a wide range of refiners, both in Europe and the USA. This latter factor gradually increased the participation in the market adding to its liquidity and attraction.

THE STANDARD CONTRACT
GRADE: Brent Blend Crude Oil
QUANTITY: 600,000 barrels, plus or minus 5% operational tolerance
DELIVERY: A Calendar Month. Seller to advise buyer of a three day loading range by 5.00 p.m. London time 15 days prior to the first day of the loading range.
LOCATION: FOB Sullom Voe Oil Terminal, Shetland Island, UK.
PAYMENT: 30 DAYS from bill of lading date (against letter of credit)
etc., etc.

THE FORWARD MARKET

Around 1983 with the standardised contract reasonably established and short selling a frequent activity together with growing trader participation the concept of selling forward gradually found favour.

This activity appealed to refiners who could hedge their future feedstock requirements when prices were low; but particularly, to the oil producers who were able to hedge their forward production; but most importantly, gained greater flexibility on limiting high tax payments on their production. It was this latter benefit that eventually gave the market its great volume and prominence.

The Brent Forward Market is an informal market in which the buyers and sellers act as principals to the oil contracts. There is no Exchange or other body to provide contract supervision, rules, margins to market price or other security. The market is therefore a collection of buying and selling commitments, all very similar, and in effect interchangeable, for delivery at some stage in the future. Importantly the delivery was always defined by a calendar month, and prices for different calendar months of delivery were invariably different, as is usual in a formal Exchange futures market, to which the Brent Forward Market is often likened.

By 1985 the forward market had attracted such a level of participation that activity had reached some 400 deals per month on average. Trading was heavy for 3 months forward, and forward trading up to 4/5 months ahead was common. Although some months would be more favoured for forward dealing than others, an average 400 deals being contracted meant 400 deals for delivery in each month. Bearing in mind that there were only about 45 cargoes available for the physical delivery of these cargoes, the delivery process inevitably resulted in a series of buyers and sellers being involved in the same cargo delivery.

DELIVERY/DAISY CHAINS

The procedure adopted to specify the delivery date of the cargo within the predefined delivery Month was that the seller must give 15 days notice of a three day date range in which the vessel has to present for loading at Sullom Voe. In effect as the producers advised their buyers of these 3 day ranges, they were passed on to that buyer's own customer, and so on, until a company decided to elect to take the cargo and deliver it to his own refining system. By that time many companies could be involved as buyers and sellers in the same cargo, and what became known as a "daisy chain" had formed. Daisy chains were the series of buyers and sellers of matched contracts for delivery cargo.

An important feature of the market was that prices for the cargoes bought and sold would vary in line with the evolution of market prices. Each company that was active in the market would have a portfolio of interchangeable contracts struck at differing times which were therefore at varying prices. Because all the contracts for any delivery month were interchangeable, companies had alternatives as to which company to pass a date to when they received it. Certain strategies evolved in deciding which cargo to pass to whom. For instance if a trader had a high profit level by matching a certain seller and a buyer, and the buyer and seller were good performers, he had an incentive to go that route. Alternatively a poor performer could be matched in a loss making way so that if delivery was frustrated by the poor performer, then the trader would actually benefit in the short term, although litigation could result.

BOOKOUTS, PAPER CONTRACTS

The manipulation of the daisy chains led to poor performance and difficult operational problems for market practitioners. This factor greatly encouraged the development of a bookout procedure in an effort to reduce the numbers in the daisy chains, improve performance and facilitate the delivery process generally. The practice of bookouts was clearly inspired by the other commodity markets such as the grain market, and was used in oil in the Russian gasoil forward market, prior to its use for Brent. By 1985 the practice was widespread but not formalised into the contracts for sale.

To effect a bookout, the first requirement was to have a company twice in the same delivery daisy chain, this formed a "loop" or "circle". Once the delivery chain was identified, which was usually only when the 3 day date range was passed from seller to buyer and so on, the delivery could bypass the loop. Oil was not necessary to the performance of the deal to the companies in the loop as the oil flow could bypass the loop.

FOR EXAMPLE:

ESSO-SHELL-BP-TRADAX-SUN-CONOCO-BP-PHIBRO-ELF

In the above delivery chain a "loop" exists between BP's two appearances. The "loop" could be booked out leaving the delivery and the flow of oil as:

ESSO-SHELL-BP-PHIBRO-ELF

It was also possible for chains to exist, which were entirely dry, and had no oil associated with them, because the grouping of buyers and sellers were complete.

FOR EXAMPLE:

MARC RICH-SHELL-BP-NESTE-TWO-MARC RICH

In circumstances of a loop being identified bookouts were often attempted. Both the brokers to the deals and the dealers themselves attempted the process which was hindered often by the desire to frustrate performance in the hope of avoiding a loss, and by the lack of uniformity in each company's preferred practice and legal requirements for bookouts.

As the money involved in each deal was around $15-18 million (in 1985) in practice bookouts also attempted to minimise costs, particularly banking costs of letters of credit, often used within contracts to ensure the buyer's financial performance. Thus the practice of trying to determine a commonly acceptable reference price evolved as a means of reducing the cash flow, the banking costs of letters of credit, and the risk of default in the flow of funds. If a base price could be mutually agreed, then each of the differing contract prices, of each and of the members of the loop, would be referenced to this base price which then determined the cash flow between the parties to achieve the same result as if the full contract value was passed round the loop. The delivery of the oil was not necessary, the contracts were fulfilled by the cash transactions. Each bookout was individually negotiated as there were no standard contracts, the agreement to the base price was also negotiable, as was the financial requirements, such as letters of credit to ensure the cash flow round the loop.

PARTICIPANTS IN THE MARKET

The participants in the forward market can be categorised, some companies having a dual or multiplicity of roles.

a) Producers who wish from time to time to hedge their future production. Producers who hedge need not be Brent producers, but could be producers of any grade. Their interest would not be for delivery during the delivery month, but in a financial hedge through use of a paper sale matched later with a paper purchase. Producers of Brent could either hedge or deliver, as commercial circumstances dictated.
b) Refiners wishing to hedge their future feedstock requirements. Like producers they would have flexibility either to hedge through matched paper contracts, or by taking delivery of the physical oil to their refinery as a direct refinery supply.
c) Traders who speculate on price movements, who hedge their other activities in the oil market, and who arbitrate forward Brent with other oil markets particularly the Exchange futures markets.

However the distinction of the trader has become blurred, particularly during the last 4/5 years. After the oil price began falling in 1981, the oil companies sought to improve their profitability, and many set up trading activities. Some of these were independently operated from their production and refining interests and were motivated only by profit. Others combined the functions of their organisations, their traders hedging production on one deal while speculating on the next. As a consequence the oil companies have become as active as the independent traders in the Brent forward market. Obviously the active participation of the oil companies has helped to maintain the Brent Forward Market's credibility during the various performance problems that these informal markets encounter from time to time, and have contributed to its durability.

In expansion of this report in her evidence, Meg Annesley stated that the futures dealings dominate the Brent market so that, in effect, the tail now wags the dog: that these forward deals start some six months ahead, with the main activity taking place one-two months ahead; and that it is essentially a month by month market.

Main narrative.

The daisy-chain.

The relevant contracts, whose chronological order is completely immaterial for present purposes, and each of which was an April contract on terms according with the standard contract as described by Meg Annesley, were as follows:

(i) Delta sold to Rheinoel on Feb. 27 at U.S.$26.50 per barrel.
(ii) Rheinoel sold to Shell on Mar. 13 at U.S.$27.00 per barrel.
(iii) Shell sold to Voest as one of two cargoes on Mar. 20 at U.S.$27.88 per barrel.
(iv) As already noted, Voest sold to Chevron on Apr. 11 at U.S.$28.75 per barrel.
(v) On the same day Chevron sold to Delta at U.S.$28.80 per barrel.

It will be noted that by and large throughout the period February to April there was a rising market, and that Delta's sale to Rheinoel was at some $2 below the mid-April market price at which they bought from Chevron. In other words, in order to close their open position for April, Delta had to buy at a very disadvantageous price.

Phibro Energy A.G. v. Nissho Iwai Corporation and Bowar Oil, Inc., [1990] 1 Lloyd's Rep. 38 (C.A. 1990)

Before I set out the relevant terms of the contracts between the parties, it will be convenient to say something about the market in Dubai crude oil and about the marine terminal at Fateh from which Dubai crude is shipped.

[Dubai 원유시장]

Oil was first discovered in Dubai in 1966. By 1985 production came from three fields. The mix of crude oil from these fields was exported from the Fateh marine terminal which consisted of two offshore loading buoys. The terminal was under the operational control of Conoco. Production was in the hands of six equity participants who in addition to the Ruler consisted of several oil companies, including Texaco and Hispanoil.

The fact that the loading facilities available at Fateh were very limited made it necessary to have a system whereby the dates for the lifting of parcels of oil sold by the individual participants were allocated in such a way as to achieve fairness between the participants and a constant and orderly progress of tankers through the terminal. The allocation of dates was therefore put in the hands of a co-ordinator for tanker scheduling, known as the Dubai co-ordinator.

Since 1973 the Dubai co-ordinator had been Mr. Robbie Robinson. He was an employee of Conoco but he had sole control of the allocation of dates. He was stationed at Houston in Texas. In his CEA statement he stated that the scope and nature of his duties and responsibilities were to consult with the equity participants and the representative of the ruler of Dubai to establish a monthly programme for the lifting of Dubai crude oil from the terminal. He further stated that the programme for each month was limited to the volumes of Dubai crude oil allocated for delivery during that month.

The practice as explained by Mr. Robinson in his statement was for the participants and the representatives of the Ruler to submit nominations by the 5th of the month preceding the month of delivery.

Nominations in respect of crude oil sold by the representative of the Ruler of Dubai could be received direct from the representatives of the Ruler or from the buyer of that oil. All other nominations would be received from an equity participant. By the 15th of the month preceding the month of delivery the loading programme for the terminal for the month of shipment would be issued. Sometimes the programme would be slightly delayed if the 15th occurred on a weekend and no doubt there were sometimes other reasons for delay. It now seems clear that the programme for January, 1986 was not issued until Dec. 18, 1985.

The nominations received by the co-ordinator could be for a five-day range during the month of shipment and the vessel could be described as TBN (to be nominated). The loading programme issued by the co-ordinator, however, limited the layday range to a three-day period except for the last cargo of the month for which a two-day loading range was given. The nomination of a five-day range was treated as an indication that any three-day period within the five days would be acceptable.

It will be obvious that not all the nominations received by the co-ordinator could be accepted by him. There were bound to be overlaps. It was his duty to make allocations of dates which would be fair. Though we were not given any details on this matter, it seems clear that the number of nominations in a particular month that could be made by each participant was a matter which was agreed beforehand between them and the Ruler.

If the Ruler's representative or customer or the equity participant were not satisfied with the layday range allotted to him in the programme, he could make a further nomination. The co-ordinator could then look at the matter again and might be able to make some rearrangement. If no rearrangement were possible, the final decision rested with the co-ordinator and the date which he gave had to be treated as a fixed slot.

The general conditions which apply to the sale of Dubai crude are the Conoco terms which are set out in a document called "General Terms and Conditions for FOB oil sales" (June 1984 edition). Clause 4 of the General Terms and Conditions deals with the nomination of vessels. So far as is material, this clause provides as follows:

4.01 Prior to any delivery the Vessel(s) which are to load oil hereunder shall be nominated by Buyer to Seller by written notice. Such notice shall specify: (a) The name, size, draft and dimensions of the Vessel(s) nominated by Buyer, the designation TBN may be substituted herein but the information required must be provided to Seller at least 5 days prior to the expected date of arrival first given to Seller hereunder in sub-paragraph (c); (b) the approximate quantity to be loaded on each Vessel; (c) the expected date of arrival (within a three-day range) of each vessel at the load port; and (d) full instructions regarding Vessel, the make-up and disposition of bills of lading and other documents and order for port(s) of discharge. Unless otherwise agreed, such notice shall be given by Buyer on or before the first day of the month preceding the month in which delivery is scheduled.

4.02 By the fifteenth day of the month preceding the month in which delivery is to be made, or within five days of receipt of Buyer's nomination made after the tenth day of that month, Seller shall, by written notice to Buyer, accept or reject each such nomination but may not unreasonably reject any nomination. If Seller rejects a Vessel nomination, Buyer shall as soon as possible nominate an alternate Vessel, giving the information required in sub-paragraphs 4.01(a) through (d) herein.

4.03 Buyer may substitute for any previous nomination a Vessel of similar size and draft, provided Buyer gives written notice to Seller at least five days before the scheduled date of arrival at Load Port of the Vessel originally nominated, specifying the information required in sub-paragraph 4.01(a) through (d) herein; provided, however, that the scheduled date of arrival of the substituted Vessel and quantity to be lifted shall not, without prior written consent of Seller, differ from the firm scheduled date and quantity accepted by seller.

15.01 All notices or communications to buyer or seller shall be directed in writing and sent by mail, telegraph, telex or cable to the address indicated in the Special Terms.

[본 사안에서 문제가 된 계약]

I can come now to the relevant contract between Phibro and Nissho.

The contract between Phibro and Nissho was one of a chain of contracts between a number of oil companies and traders for the sale of a parcel of 500,000 barrels of Dubai crude f.o.b. Fateh for delivery in January, 1986. It seems probable that at the bottom of the chain was a company called Lucky Goldstar which required the oil for its refinery at Honam in Korea. The chain extended upwards through C. Itoh in Japan to Tradax/Cargill and then through the U.S. office of the Japanese group Marubeni to Bomar, Nissho and Phibro. For the purposes of the present appeal, however, it is not necessary to make many detailed references to the other companies in the chain.

The contract between Phibro and Nissho was on the terms set out in the telex dated Dec. 18, 1985 from Phibro in Zug in Switzerland to the Singapore branch of Nissho (CB 70), as amended by the telex from Nissho to Phibro dated Dec. 26 (CB 143) and as finally accepted by Phibro on Jan. 17, 1986 (CB 290). The relevant terms were as follows:

4 QUANTITY: 500,000 net US bbls plus/minus 5 pct operational tolerance.
5 DELIVERY: FOB Fateh terminal, Dubai one or two cargo lots during January 1986. Buyer's nomination shall be subject to acceptance by loadport terminal operator and shall conform to all rules and regulations for shipments therefrom. Layday range will be narrowed to date or date range in accordance with usual practice of the loadport.
11 LAYTIME: 36 hours plus 6 hours from NOR or when vessel is all fast at berth, whichever first occurs, pro rata for part cargoes.
12 DEMURRAGE: In accordance with charterparty terms and conditions — pro rata for part cargoes ... demurrage is payable only to the extent that it is recoverable from Seller's supplier. If demurrage is caused through the fault/negligence of Seller, then Seller to remain fully liable for said demurrage even if same not recoverable from prime supplier ...

In addition it was provided that the contract should be governed and constructed in accordance with the laws of England and that the High Court in London should have non-exclusive jurisdiction. The contract further provided:

Where they are not in conflict with the foregoing then Conoco general terms and conditions of FOB Sales of crude oil will apply (latest edition).
This last provision was in conformity with cl. 14.03 of Conoco's general terms and conditions which provided:
To the extent any conflict exists between the terms and conditions of these General Terms and the Special Terms the terms and conditions of the Special Terms shall control.

The terms in the telex of Dec. 18, were plainly special terms within sub-par. 1.18 of the definition section of the general terms.

The contract between Nissho and Bomar was also made on Dec. 18, 1985. So far as is material it contained the following provisions:

QUANTITY: 500,000 net US barrels plus or minus an operational tolerance of 5 percent at Buyer's option.
DELIVERY: Loading in one or two cargo lots FOB Fateh terminal subject to terminal acceptance during the period 1-31 January 1986 subject to terminal acceptance. Normal nomination procedure to apply.
Buyer's nomination shall be subject to acceptance by the loadport terminal operator and shall conform to all rules and regulations for shipments therefrom ...

On the following day, Dec. 19, Nissho made their nomination by a telex in the following terms (CB 96):

We submit our vessel nomination for the above transaction as follows:
Vessel: TBN
ETA: January 15-20 1986
Quantity: 500 MB plus/minus at vessel's option
Quality: Dubai crude oil
Destination: To be advised later
Please confirm acceptance at your earliest convenience.

This telex was from Mr. Mitsuhashi of Nissho in Tokyo on behalf of Nissho in Singapore and was addressed to Mr. Tashiro of Phibro in Tokyo.

It will be remembered that under cl. 4.02 of the general terms it was the obligation of the seller to accept or reject that nomination by written notice to reach the buyer within five days of its receipt by the seller. By Dec. 24, however, Nissho had not had any notice from Phibro, and they were being pressed for a response by Bomar (CB 130), who were themselves under pressure from Marubeni (CB 128). It will be appreciated that lower down the chain the equivalent periods of five days had or might have expired before Dec. 24, because of earlier nominations. In the absence of any response from Phibro Mr. Mitsuhashi spoke on the telephone to Mr. Tashiro. At the trial there was a conflict of evidence as to what was said in the course of this conversation. The Judge preferred the evidence of Mr. Mitsuhashi and stated his conclusion as follows (15C):

I find that Mr Tashiro told Mr Mitsuhashi that the terminal would be accepting 20th-25th and that there was a possibility that the terminal would be prepared to advance this parcel to 15th-20th January.
It also appears that on the same day (Dec. 24) Mr. Tashiro gave a similar oral assurance to Mr. Matsuzawa of C. Itoh (see J.8D), though it is to be observed that in his CEA statement Mr. Matsuzawa said that on Dec. 24, Mr. Tashiro - ... confirmed that the terminal had indeed just advised to him a loading range of 20th-25th January. (G.250, par. 8).

These assurances were non-contractual as they were not in writing and they have no direct relevance to the issues between Phibro and Nissho. But they proved later to be a source of confusion and dismay lower down the chain.

On Dec. 27, Nissho sent a further telex to Phibro in which they passed on the complaint which they had had from Bomar. The quotation from the telex from Bomar concluded as follows (CB 149):

You are obligated to confirm to us your acceptance of alternate date range of our nomination within five days allowance. We, therefore, strongly request you to provide us with your acceptance of alternate date range most urgently. Otherwise we hold you responsible for any damage and costs as a consequence of not responding to our nomination and also hold a right to cancel our contract between you and us. We have been informed from end buyer that not only are they facing potential shortage of crude oil for their refinery, but they are also facing substantial potential dead freight on the vessel if they allow this situation to continue. We are awaiting your reply for this matter.

Later that day Phibro replied (CB 155):

Further to your telex number 193 of today we are pleased to advise acceptance of your TBS for loading about 500,000 bbls Dubai crude oil for destination Japan during December 27-31.
Please urgently let us have your firm vessel nomination and documentary instructions.

The reference to December was corrected on Jan. 3, (CB 175).

It may be convenient to take stock at this stage. The position on Dec. 27, can be summarized as follows. (a) Nissho had nominated for Jan. 15-20, (CB 86). (b) Phibro had given an assurance that the terminal would be accepting Jan. 20-25, and that it was possible this might be advanced to Jan. 15-20, (J 15D). (c) As a result of a telephone call on Dec. 24, Bomar were under the mistaken impression that the terminal had confirmed Jan. 20-25. It seems from the judgment that the mistake was that of Mr. Dilkes of Bomar (J 16A.). Mr. Dilkes set out what he understood to be the position in a telex to Nissho in Tokyo (CB 145). (d) In their telex of Dec. 27, (CB 155 as corrected) Phibro were putting forward dates which had not been mentioned previously-Jan. 27-31. (e) In fact Phibro had neither an available parcel of oil, nor an available slot accepted by the terminal, for any of the dates that had been mentioned. Earlier in December Phibro had bought 500 mbs from Petronor, but it seems that on Dec. 20, this parcel was sold to Mobil. However that may be, it is quite clear that on Dec. 27, Phibro were short of one parcel of 500 mbs for January delivery.

For the next 10 days very little happened. This may have been due to the Japanese New Year. It was not until Monday, Jan. 6, that Nissho passed on to Bomar the acceptance contained in the telex from Phibro of Dec. 27. On that date Mr. Mitsuhashi sent the following telex to Bomar (CB 182):

We are pleased to advise acceptance of your TBN for loading about 500,000 bbls Dubai crude oil for destination Japan during January 27-31.
Please urgently let us have your firm vessel nomination and documentary instructions.

On the same day Bomar sent a telex in similar terms to Marubeni (CB 185).

The new dates, Jan. 27-31, caused concern lower down the chain. It had been thought that the range Jan. 20-25 was either acceptable to the terminal or had in fact been accepted by the terminal. It is sufficient to refer briefly to the telex from Marubeni to Bomar dated Jan. 8, which concluded (CB 192):

We therefore regret to advise you that we are unable to accept your revised acceptance of Jan 27-31 86 and strongly request you to maintain your previous acceptance of Jan 20-25 86.

This telex also contained a vessel nomination of Honam Jade and an e.t.a. Jan. 23-25 1986. It resulted in a revised nomination from Bomar to Nissho (CB 195) and the important telex from Nissho to Phibro dated Jan. 9 (CB 198):

We nominate following against above-mentioned lifting:
Vessel: Honam Jade/sub.
Quantity: Approximately 500,000 bbls
ETA: January 23-25, 1986
Destination: Korea
Please advise terminal acceptance of this nomination.

It is to be noted that in this telex Nissho asked specifically to be advised of terminal acceptance.

On Monday Jan. 13, 1986 Mr. Tashiro replied (CB 220):

We are pleased to confirm VSL "Honam Jade" has been accepted to load ABT 500 MB Dubai during Jan 29th-31st.

It will be noted that these dates were a three-day range within the range given in the telex of Dec. 27, (CB 155, as corrected by CB 175).

The information contained in this telex was passed on to Bomar on the same day (CB 222).

In the course of the argument our attention was drawn to internal telexes which were passing between various branches of Phibro during the period between Jan. 9, and 13. On Jan. 10, the Singapore branch sent a telex stating that they had checked around the market and found that the only possible parcel of oil still available in January was about 300 mb ex Conoco. The telex (CB 209) concluded:

This means we have no possibility to cover our short position in Jan, which means we must keep Turavent's nomination to Feb 1-3 and confirm Nissho's nomination for end Jan.

In addition our attention was drawn to a series of telexes passing between Turavent (an associated company of Phibro), the ruler's representative and the Dubai co-ordinator in Houston relating to a parcel of oil bought from the ruler with laydays Feb. 1-3. This series concluded with a telex from the Dubai co-ordinator to Turavent dated Jan. 15, 1986 in these terms:

Confirm vessel "Honam Jade", 500 MB crude oil laydays Feb 1-3.

It is to be observed (as the Judge noted in his judgment (17D)) that in the nomination from Turavent dated Jan. 13, (CB 231) the vessel's present e.t.a Fateh was said to be "January 30/31".

It is clear that by the middle of January at the latest the companies lower down the chain had become concerned that what they considered to be the contractual range of Jan. 23-25, might be in doubt. As Mr. Matsuzawa of C. Itoh in Tokyo explained in his CEA statement, as far as he was concerned — ... at close of business on 6th January [Itoh] had a contract with Tradax for shipment on 23-25 January.

It is convenient to refer therefore to the following paragraphs in his statement (G251):

15. On 16th January in the evening we received a telex from Lucky Goldstar via Singapore threatening to cancel the contract unless confirmation was received by 1700 hours on 17th that the shipment would take place within the contractual period. I passed this telex on to Tradax and when Mr. Saito, the Section's senior trader, returned to the office that afternoon passed the file to him for assistance ...

17. At about midnight Tokyo time I telephoned Mr. Yamada of our New York office and requested him to make inquiries of Conoco in New York as to the position. He reverted to the effect that Conoco stated that they had received no nomination for the "Honam Jade" and that all cargoes scheduled from the terminal for the rest of the month of January were already committed. I advised Mr. Saito accordingly.

The news of Mr. Matsuzawa's discovery reached Phibro within a few hours. At 08 51 G.M.T. on Jan. 17, Phibro in Tokyo sent a telex to Phibro in Zug which concluded as follows (CB 256):

We have been informed by Nissho Iwai today that "Honam Jade" is not in the programme for Jan. It will only be a matter of time before everyone finds out that the "Honam Jade" has been nominated for Feb 1-3 stem. The final receiver is threatening to cancel this contract which is probably a good possibility if they feel they have a breach of contract.

We see two possible solutions for this potential problem. The Ruler nominates end Jan as contracted (we understand from the Co-ordinator that there is no ship loading Jan 29-31) or we do an exchange with TWO who we believe have 800,000 MB (sic) loading Jan 22-24 and still have not nominated a VSL.

We believe this is a very urgent matter and we should react quickly.

Meanwhile telexes continued to pass between Phibro and Nissho. On Jan. 17, Nissho in Tokyo sent a telex to Phibro in Zug to advise them that Nissho could not accept the load range Jan. 29-31, and to request urgently Phibro's confirmation and acceptance of Jan 23-25. The telex concluded (CB 267):

We have been informed by end buyer that not only they are facing potential shortage of crude oil for their (Honam) refinery, but they are also facing substantial potential loss on other CRU cargo at next port if she cannot load in date range of Jan 23-25, and also informed they are ready to cancel this loading (ie to cancel contract). Awaiting your reply for the above.

Phibro replied at once (CB 273):

We are afraid that you misunderstand the contract and in particular the Conoco terms and conditions when you refer to a loading range of 23-25 January. We are however prepared to accept your nomination of Honam Jade with ETA between 23-25 January 1986.

On the same day, however, Turavent had been told by the Dubai co-ordinator (CB 277) that "based on current production/lifting schedules" the terminal should be able to berth the Honam Jade sometime on Jan. 31, with completion of loading on Feb. 1, if the vessel arrived at Fateh on Jan. 31.

It would appear that by Monday Jan. 20, if not before, other companies in the chain in addition to C. Itoh had made inquiries as to what the true position was as to the terminal acceptance. On Jan. 20, Marubeni sent a telex to Bomar in New York quoting a telex which they had received from Tradax as follows (CB 327):

We have investigated the fact with regard to our nomination of Honam Jade. We found that our nomination had not reached the terminal as of today and all the cargoes scheduled to be lifted in 1986 have been committed to other users. We hereby protest to the fact as stated above.

On Jan. 21, Mr. Mitsuhashi sent a telex to Zug asking Phibro to furnish Nissho most urgently with their official acceptance telex of the nomination Honam Jade with e.t.a. between Jan. 23-25, 1986 (CB 333).

Later that day Phibro replied (CB 333):

We confirm that the vessel Honam Jade is acceptable by the port authorities. With regard to ETA we do not have a problem with your nominated range of January 23-25 1986. Port authorities will permit vessel to stay at anchor awaiting berthing turn.

With regard to loading range we repeat what we have said in our earlier telex messages, namely that loading is confirmed with the range of January 29-31 1986. In view of your early arrival we would obviously make best efforts to arrange for earlier loading.

By now, however, Nissho had been notified by Bomar (CB 317) of the contents of the telex they had received from Marubeni (CB 317). On Jan. 22, Nissho in London communicated the contents of these telexes to Phibro (CB 385).

On Jan. 23 Phibro sent an urgent telex to Mr. Mitsuhashi in Tokyo (CB 401):

In order to try and solve your operational problem we have reshuffled our Dubai programme and have nominated the Honam Jade to load in the time frame for Jan 26-28. This re-allocation will make the oil available a few days earlier than we have already confirmed. Futhermore, in case some other vessels may slip, we will push the terminal to try and load the Honam Jade upon its arrival.

We are pleased that we have been able to help you in this operational problem and we look forward to continual cooperation between our two companies.

But the telex was too late. On the same day Mr. Mitsuhashi sent a telex to Phibro in Zug again quoting the telex which had been received from Bomar (CB 375). The telex from Mr. Mitsuhashi began (CB 402):

We are forced to declare the cancellation of this contract.

Phibro replied at once. Their telex also was dated Jan. 23, 1986 (CB 441). In this telex Phibro asserted that the telex from Nissho (CB 402) represented an unjustified repudiation of Nissho's contractual obligation and stated:

We are holding written confirmation from our supplier that the Honam Jade is in the Dubai programme and that the oil in question is available for lifting 28/30 Jan with best efforts to provide earlier loading when the Honam Jade gives notice of readiness.

Later in this telex Phibro threatened legal action if Nissho did not confirm immediately that they would load the oil.

Nissho, however, continued to treat the contract as cancelled. On Jan. 27, Phibro sent a message to Nissho to say that the oil had been re-sold.

[소송 개시]

On the following day, Jan. 28, 1986, Phibro issued a writ claiming damages for repudiation.

In April, 1986 Nissho served a defence and counterclaim claiming that it was Phibro who had repudiated the contract. It is to be noted that the defence and counterclaim in its original form contained no plea that the acceptance required by the contract was an acceptance by the terminal. This plea was added by par. 9A of an amended pleading served in draft on Nov. 18, 1988 and formally re-served on Dec. 2, 1988, just before the trial began.

With this introduction of the facts I can now turn to the issues with which the Court is presently concerned.

[쟁점]

The issues

The issues which were raised in the notice of appeal fall under three main headings: (A) The correct construction and effect of the contract between Phibro and Nissho; (B) Which party was in breach; and (C) Damages.

5. 선물계약과 옵션, 스왑 등의 에너지관련 파생상품 출현

에너지관련 선물계약의 거래소에서의 등장은 1970년대 후반 난방유로부터 시작, 1980년대이후 NYMEX,[10] CBT, LIPE[11] 등 주요상품거래소에서 원유선물이 거래되고 있다. 선물거

10) 미국에서의 에너지파생상품 종류와 규율에 대하여는 Alexia Brunet/Meredith Shafe, *Beyond Enron: Regulation in Trading,* 27 NW. J. INT'L L & BUS 665, 669-76 (2007).

래는 가격등락의 위험을 헤지하려는 목적도 있지만 가격등락에 따른 수익실현을 기대하는 투기의 목적도 있다. 실수요자인 항공사가 항공유를 필요로 하여 20,000배럴을 배럴당 100불에 6월에 인도받는 계약을 체결하면서 가격이 100불 이상 오를 경우를 대비하여 매도선물계약으로 long hedge하는 것이 전자의 예이다. 후자의 예는 A가 배럴당 $99.50에 9월 인도할 원유 10단위를 매도함과 동시에 9월에 인도받을 원유 10단위를 배럴당 $90불에 매수하였다면, A는 거래소로부터 두 계약의 차액만큼만 정산하면 되며 실제 원유의 인도는 없다는 점에서 투기이다. 거래소에는 선물계약뿐만 아니라 옵션도 거래되고 있다. 옵션은 원유를 배럴당 정하여진 가격에 사거나 팔 수 있는 권리로서 선물과 마찬가지로 헷지 내지 투기목적으로 거래된다. 따라서, 선물·옵션 등 파생상품은 각국이 법으로 규율하고 있으며 정부기관이 이를 집행하고 있다. 미국의 상품거래소법과[12] CFTC가, 영국의 1986년 금융서비스법과 LIPE가 그것이다.

거래소에서 거래되는 파생상품의 경우 표준화, 거래플랫폼, 청산제도를 제공하는 반면, 거래당사자의 개별적 수요를 충족하지 못하는 문제점이 있기 때문에 실제 거래소외에서 당사자간 개별적으로 거래되는 OTC 에너지파생상품이 거래소 파생상품보다 그 거래량에서 더 크다. 원칙적으로 OTC 에너지파생상품은 상품거래소법의 규율을 받지 않지만 사기방지와 시세조정방지를 위하여 제한적인 규율권한을 가진다.[13] 그러나, 무엇이 상품에 기초한 파생상품인지에 대하여는 정확한 정의가 없다.

미국에서는 1990년 Burmuda의 석유회사가 미국의 메이저석유회사를 상대로 이들의 Brent 원유선물거래가 상품거래소법 위반과 독점금지법 위반한다는 이유로 손해배상의 소를 제기한 사례가 있다.[14] 미국법원은 Brent 원유선물거래가 상품거래소법에 따라 면제되는 현금선도계약라는 주장을 배척하였고 CFTC는 행정해석으로 Brent 원유의 거래가 상품거래소법 위반이 아니라고 판단하였으며[15] 곧 이어서 상품거래소법을 개정, 순자산이 5백만불 이상인 회사간 거래는 상품거래소법의 적용대상에서 제외하였다.[16] 한편 FERC가 미국 천연가스와 전기시장에서의 시세조정행위를 조사, 처벌할 권한을 가지고 있으며 2000년 California 사태의 원인을 분석함에 있어서 에너지거래의 현황과 문제점을 조사한 바 있다.[17]

에너지시장의 규제는 전통적으로 시장지배력의 통제를 목적으로 하는 경쟁법과 공공재 공급계약조건의 규율이라는 공공재 규율법에 기초하였으나, 상품거래소나 OTC에서 거래되

11) Peter Ottino, *Crude Oil Futures and Options in London,* 7 OGLTR 179 (1988/89).
12) Commodity Exchange Act ("CEA"), 7 U.S.C. §§ 1-25.
13) Alexia Brunet et al, 각주 8 게재논문, 673-76.
14) 738 F. Supp. 1472 (S.D.N.Y. 1990).
15) 55 Fed. Reg. 39188 (Sept. 25, 1990).
16) Futures Trading Practices Act of 1992, Pub. L. 102-546, 106 Stat. 3590.
17) FERC, Final Report on Price Manipulation in Western Market (Docket No. 9402-2-000)(Mar. 2003).

는 에너지파생상품의 중요성이 점차 커져가면서 사기방지와 가격조작방지라는 유가증권규율의 철학이 필요하게 되었고 앞으로도 이런 추세는 계속될 것이다.[18] 그렇다고 정유사들의 시장지배력에 기초한 경쟁제한적 행태에 대하여 규율을 게을리하여서는 아니 되며 보다 경쟁적 산업구조를 만들어나가기 위한 정책이 필요하여 보인다.[19]

우리나라 정유사 중 GS칼텍스, S-Oil는 해외투자자와 장기공급계약이 있을 것이고 SK에너지의 경우도 수입물량의 상당부분을 장기공급계약에 의존하고 있는 것으로 짐작된다. 일찍부터 해외석유선물시장을 활용하여 원유도입원가를 줄이자는 주장이 제안된 바 있으며 현재 적극적으로 활용되는 것으로 짐작된다.[20] 최근 한국거래소는 정유사들과 수출입업자, 대리점 등이 휘발유와 경우를 2만리터 단위로 매매하는 시장을 개설한 바 있으나 아직 걸음마단계로 보인다.[21]

서울중앙지법 2008. 8. 29. 선고 2008가합2338 판결

가. 원고는 피고의 의정부 중앙지점과 거래하여 오던 중, 2007. 5. 7. 위 지점의 부지점장인 C로부터, 피고가 판매하고 B자산운용 주식회사가 운용하는 수익증권인 “B오일 파생상품투자신탁 제5호”(이하 ‘이 사건 펀드’라 한다)에 가입할 것을 권유받고, 같은 날 이 사건 펀드에 가입하여 300,000,000원을 투자하였다.

나. 이 사건 펀드는 투자기간이 6개월(2007. 5. 9.부터 2007. 11. 5까지)이고, 기초자산을 WTI(West Texas Intermediate, 서부텍사스 중질유) 원유 선물로 하여, 6개월 동안 기초자산 가격이 최초 기준 가격(2007. 5. 9.)에 대비하여 40% 초과 상승하지 않으면 연 9.3%의 수익을 지급하나, 40% 초과 상승한 적이 한번이라도 있는 경우 중 만기시가격(2007. 11. 5.)이 최초 기준가격에 대비하여 상승한 때에는 ‘원금×(100%－WTI 원유 선물 가격 상승률＋4.65%)’로 계산한 금원을 지급하게 되어 원금 손실이 발생하게 된다. 그리고 환매방법은 17시 이전에 환매를 청구하는 경우에는 그날로부터 제4영업일의 기준가격을 적용하여 제6영업일에 환매대금을 지급하고, 17시 이후에 환매를 청구하는 경우에는 그날로부터 제5영업일의 기준가격을

18) David B. Spence/Robert Prentice, *The Transformation of American Energy Markets and the Problem of Market Power,* 53 B.C.L.Rev. 131 (2012).

19) 정유사의 군납유가격담합 관련 판결은 서울중앙지법 2007. 1. 23. 선고 2001가합10682; 서울고법 2009. 12. 30. 선고 2007나25157 판결; 대법 2011. 7. 28. 선고 2010다18850 판결.

20) 변윤성, 해외석유선물시장의 효율적 활용방안에 관한 연구, 1 선물연구 99 (1993); 윤원철, 해외선물을 활용한 국내수입원유의 조달헤징, 8 선물연구 57 (2000).

21) 이데일리 2012. 3. 30. 석유현물전자상거래, 단 1건 거래..‘첫술에 배 부르랴’. www.edaily.co.kr에서 열람가능.

적용하여 제7영업일에 환매대금을 지급하게 되어 있다.

다. 원고는 이 사건 펀드 가입 당시 C로부터 위와 같은 설명이 요약되어 있는 상품설명서와 수익증권거래통장을 교부받았는바, 수익증권거래통장 앞면에는 C가 '연 9.3%, 중도해지 불가, 미국 유가 40% 이상 상승 않으면 세후 11,800,000원'이라고 기재하였다.

라. 원고가 이 사건 펀드에 가입할 당시의 WTI 원유 선물 가격은 배럴당 미화 64달러 정도였는데, 그 후 유가가 계속 상승하여 2007. 10. 16.경에는 배럴당 미화 89달러에 이르러 그 상승률이 최초 기준 가격 대비 40%를 초과함으로써 이 사건 펀드는 원금 손실이 발생하였고, 결국 원고는 만기상환금 지급일인 2007. 11. 9. 피고로부터 160,636,667원만을 상환받아 139,363,333원의 원금 손실을 입게 되었다.

2. 원고 주장의 청구원인사실에 대한 판단

가. 당사자의 주장

원고는, 이 사건 청구원인사실로서, 이 사건 펀드는 투자기간 만료 전의 환매가 가능함에도 불구하고, C가 원고에게 이 사건 펀드 가입을 권유하면서 중도 환매가 불가능한 것처럼 설명하는 등 고객보호의무 및 설명의무 등을 위반하여 원고로 하여금 환매할 시기를 놓치게 하여 위와 같은 원금 손실을 입게 하였으므로, 피고는 C의 사용자로서 C가 그 사무집행에 관하여 원고에게 가한 위 원금 손실 상당액 및 그 지연손해금을 배상할 책임이 있다고 주장함에 대하여, 피고는 C가 이 사건 펀드 가입 당시 원고에게 중도 환매가 가능하다고 설명하였을 뿐만 아니라 원고에게 교부한 상품설명서에도 중도 환매가 가능함을 명시하고 있으며, 수익증권거래통장에 기재한 '중도해지 불가'의 문구는 이 사건 펀드를 중도 환매하는 경우 다른 펀드들에 비해 원금 손실이 크게 발생한다는 것을 상기시키는 차원에서 기재한 것이므로 고객보호의무 및 설명의무를 위반한 바 없다고 주장한다.

나. 판 단

가) 손해배상책임의 발생

살피건대, 증권회사 임직원이 고객에게 적극적으로 투자를 권유하였으나 투자 결과 손실을 본 경우에 투자자에 대한 불법행위책임이 성립되기 위하여는 이익보장 여부에 대한 적극적 기망행위의 존재까지 요구하는 것은 아니라 하더라도 적어도 거래경위와 거래방법, 고객의 투자상황(재산상태, 연령, 사회적 경험 정도 등), 거래의 위험성 및 이에 대한 설명의 정도 등을 종합적으로 고려한 후, 당해 권유행위가 경험이 부족한 일반 투자자에게 거래행위에 필연적으로 수반되는 위험성에 관한 올바른 인식형성을 방해하거나 또는 고객의 투자상황에 비추어 과대한 위험성을 수반하는 거래를 적극적으로 권유한 경우에 해당하여, 결국 고객에 대한 보호의무를 저버려 위법성을 띤 행위인 것으로 평가될 수 있는 경우라야 할 것인바(대법원 2003. 1. 10. 선고 2000다50312 판결 등 참조), 이는 피고와 같이 은행이 간접투자자산 운용업법에 기하여 투자자에게 투자상품인 수익증권 등의 매입을 권유하는 경우에도 마찬가지로 적용된다고 할 것이다.

이 사건으로 돌아와 살피건대, 앞서 인정한 바와 같이 원고가 이 사건 펀드에 가입할 당시 C는 원고에게 '중도해지 불가'라고 기재한 수익증권거래통장을 교부하였는바, 간접투자자산 운영업법 제57조 제1항 제4호는 '판매회사 및 판매회사에서 판매업무를 담당하는 임·직원은 허위표시 또는 중요한 사항에 대하여 오해를 유발할 수 있는 표시행위를 하여서는 아니 된다'라고 규정하고 있고, 이와 같은 펀드상품의 경우 환매 시기를 결정하는 것은 투자자의 입장에서 매우 중요한 사항이라고 할 수 있다. 그런데 C가 통장에 '중도해지 불가'라고 기재함으로써 원고에게 이 사건 펀드의 경우 중도 환매가 불가능한 것으로 오해할 여지를 제공하였고, 비록 원고가 교부받은 상품설명서에 중도 환매가 가능함을 적시하고 있다고 하더라도 원고와 같은 투자자의 입장에서는 판매업무를 담당하는 자가 명시적으로 기재한 내용에 더 의존하게 되는 것이 보통이므로, 이러한 행위는 투자행위의 중요한 사항에 대하여 올바른 인식형성을 방해한 행위로서 원고에 대한 보호의무를 위반한 것이라 할 것이다. 따라서 피고는 C의 사용자로서 C의 위와 같은 불법행위로 인해 원고가 입은 손해를 배상할 책임이 있다.

나) 손해배상의 범위

나아가 그 손해배상의 범위에 관하여 살피건대, 원고가 위 불법행위로 입은 손해는 이 사건 펀드가입시의 원금 300,000,000원에서 피고로부터 상환받은 160,636,667원을 공제한 139,363,333원이라고 할 것이다.

다만, 위 인정사실 및 증인 C의 일부 증언에 의하여 인정되는 다음과 같은 제반사정들, 즉 원고가 이 사건 펀드의 상품설명서를 세밀히 검토하였더라면 중도 환매가 가능하다는 것을 충분히 알 수 있었음에도 C가 적은 '중도해지 불가' 문구만을 믿고 중도 환매가 불가능하다고 생각한 점, 원고는 2007. 6.경 C에게 이 사건 펀드의 해지가 가능한지 문의하였고, 이에 대해 C는 원고에게 중도 환매가 가능하지만 환매할 경우 원금 손실이 크다고 하면서 다른 펀드를 환매하도록 권유하였는바, 이와 같이 원고는 이 사건 펀드에 가입한 지 1달 후에 중도 환매가 가능함을 알았음에도 만기시까지 환매요청을 하지 않아 원고의 손해가 더 증가한 점(2007. 6.경 WTI 원유 선물 가격은 미화 70달러 정도였음) 등 원고에게도 이 사건 펀드의 중도 환매가 가능함을 알 수 있었음에도 이를 확인하지 아니한 과실 및 그로 인한 손해의 확대를 방지할 수 있었음에도 적절한 조치를 취하지 않은 과실이 인정되는바, 원고의 이러한 과실은 이 사건 펀드로 인한 손해의 발생 및 그 확대의 한 원인이 되었다 할 것이므로, 피고가 원고에게 배상할 손해액을 정함에 있어 위와 같은 원고의 과실을 참작하기로 하되, 그 비율은 위에서 본 사실관계에 비추어 60% 정도로 봄이 상당하다 할 것이므로, 결국 피고가 배상할 원고의 손해액은 55,745,333원(=139,363,333원×40%, 원 미만 버림)이 된다.

3. 결 론

따라서, 피고는 원고에게 사용자 손해배상책임의 이행으로 55,745,333원 및 이에 대하여 이 사건 펀드가입일 이후로서 원고가 구하는 바에 따라 2007. 11. 9.부터 피고가 그 이행의무의 존부와 범위에 관하여 항쟁함이 상당한 이 판결 선고일인 2008. 8. 29.까지는 민법이 정한 연 5%의, 그 다음날부터 다 갚는 날까지는 소송촉진 등에 관한 특례법이 정한 연 20%의 각 비율에 의한 지연손해금을 지급할 의무가 있다 할 것이므로, 원고의 이 사건 청구는 위 인정 범위 내에서 이유 있어 이를 인용하고 나머지 청구는 이유 없어 이를 기각하기로 하여 주문과 같이 판결한다

6. 구상무역

1985년 Interbras와 MITCO간 계약이나 1992년 러시아와 쿠바간 계약처럼 원유를 물품과 교환하는 바터로서의 구상무역은 극히 예외적이고 대부분의 구상무역은 매매대금이 현금으로 지급되는 2개의 매매계약간 이루어진다. 이는 평가는 물론이고 별개의 자금조달이나 보증, 대금지급의 편의때문이다. 다만, 수입대금이 구상무역계약에 따라서 상계되는 비율은 미리 정하는 것이 보통이다.

구상무역은 대개 국제결제통화에의 접근이 제한된 국가가 많이 사용한다. 대가를 지급하는 방법은 직접보상과 같이 선진국이 기술을 수출하고 이에 대한 대가로서 완제품을 구입하는 경우와 같이 원래의 인도제품과 구상무역에 따라서 반대로 인도하는 제품이 직접 관련되어 있는 경우, 간접보상과 같이 원래의 인도제품과 구상무역이 관련성이 없는 경우, 역구상무역과 같이 원래의 계약에 따라서 수출자가 구입하는 제품의 대금이 상계처리되는 경우로 나누어 볼 수 있다. 광물의 경우 일본이 페루에 기술을 제공하고 구리의 일부를 받아가는 계약이나 독일이 필리핀에 기술과 인력을 제공하고 철광석의 일부를 받아가는 계약이 직접보상형식의 구상무역이다. 일본이 이라크와 카타르에서 건설공사를 수행하고 원유를 받거나 한국이 리비아에서 건설공사를 수행하고 원유를 받아가는 것이 간접보상형식의 구상무역이다.

노트와 질문

우리나라는 중동지역으로부터 우리가 필요로 하는 원유의 대부분을 수입하는 반면 이들 국가에 대한 수출은 제한적인바, 이러한 무역적자를 해소할 방안으로서의 구상무역 형태를 통한 수출은 가능할까?

제 8 장

천연가스거래시장

1. 천연가스의 수요와 공급[1]

천연가스는 통상 원유와 함께 발견되지만 독자적으로 존재하는 경우도 있다.[2] 천연가스도 원유와 같이 그 품질이 다양하여 rich, sour, sweet 등으로 구분된다.[3] 전통적으로 천연가스는 원유보다 수송하는 비용이나 기술적 어려움 때문에 산유국에서 소각되는 경우가 대부분이었다. 그러나 가스를 이용한 발전수요와 환경오염에 대한 우려, 그리고 신흥국들의 에너지수요 때문에 천연가스가 세계에너지공급원에서 차지하는 비중은 급격히 증가, 2025년에는 25% 이상이 될 것으로 예측한다. 수요의 증가에 따른 공급의 증가는 파이프라인 또는 액화천연가스의 국제거래를 증가시켜서 2002년 전세계 천연가스 생산량의 23%가 국제적으로 거래되었으며 1995년부터 2002년사이 파이프라인을 통한 거래는 46%, 액화천연가스거래는 62% 증가하였다. 천연가스운송의 기술적 어려움, 운송을 위하여 필요한 막대한 인프라건설 비용때문에 천연가스의 거래는 과거 생산국 인근 지역에 국한되었으나 이제는 점차 국제적인 거래영역을 확장하고 있다.

2. 천연가스의 생산과 이동

가. 탐사생산계약상 가스

전통적으로 천연가스는 원유에 비하여 서자취급을 받았기 때문에 탐사계약에서도 지극

1) Smith, 주1-4 상게서, 1022 이하 참조.

2) 셰일가스와 fracturing을 둘러싼 최근의 논의에 관하여는 민관합동 셰일가스대응책 마련 나섰다. 2012. 7. 11. 머니투데이.

3) 천연가스를 측정하는 방법도 열량을 기준으로 joules, BTU, Cal를 사용할 수 있는가 하면 부피나 무게를 사용할 수 있다. KOGAS는 2012. 7.부터 부피가 아닌 열량을 기준으로 요금부과하기로 변경. 유재준, 7월 천연가스 열량제도 시작, 2012. 7. 2. 한국가스신문. KOGAS는 천연가스공급규정을 변경하여 이를 시행중이다.

히 간단하게 처리되었다. 예를 들어 1935년 카타르와 Anglo-Persian Oil Co.간 체결된 양허계약에는 천연가스에 관한 아무런 조항도 없고 단지 동 계약이 원유와 천연가스를 대상으로 한다는 언급이 전부였다. 이러한 추세는 최근까지 계속되었으나 2000년대에 들어와서 계약의 양상이 바뀌기 시작, 2007년 카메룬이 체결한 PSC는 천연가스에 대한 6페이지에 걸친 독자적 계약조항을 가지고 있다. 그리하여 과거 확실한 수요에 기초한 파이프라인건설이나 액화시설 건설비용의 조달이 가능하지 않은 이상에는 천연가스의 탐사나 개발을 중시하지 않던 것과는 달리 몇몇 나라는 천연가스에만 초점을 둔 탐사개발계약을 체결하기 시작하고 있다.[4)]

나. 파이프라인

1) 건설프로젝트

여러 국가를 통과하는 파이프라인 건설은 여러 가지 장애를 극복하여야 한다. 우선 국가간 정치적인 이견은 파이프라인 건설을 무산시키거나 지연시킬 수 있다. 예를 들면 이란이 시리아를 통과하여 건설하려던 파이프라인은 아랍 바트당 내 정치적인 이견으로 지연되었다. 이란-인도 파이프라인은 인도와 파키스탄간 분쟁으로 시작도 못하고 있다. 볼리비아가 칠레쪽으로 건설하려던 파이프라인은 19세기 국경분쟁때문에 무산, 페루쪽으로 건설계획중이다.[5)] 이와 같이 파이프라인이 통과하여야 하는 국가간 합의는 애당초 이루기도 어렵지만 그 이후 이를 지속적 효력을 가지게 하는 것도 만만치 않다. 우리나라가 러시아와 러시아로부터 직접 또는 중국이나 북한을 통한 파이프라인을 통한 천연가스공급가능성을 상당히 오랜 동안 논의하고 있음에도 불구하고 별로 보이는 진전이 없는 이유도 이러한 정치적 불안정이 그 주요한 원인으로 보인다.

정치적인 이견은 파이프라인건설을 원하는 IOC와 가스생산국간 발생할 수도 있다. 가스생산국은 정치적인 이유에서 생산된 가스를 우선 국내 수요자에게 공급하고 잔여분만을 파이프라인을 통한 수출할 것을 바랄 수 있는 반면 IOC는 생산, 운송, 판매 모든 측면에서 독자적인 결정을 하기를 바랄 수 있다. 페루 카미시아지역개발을 둘러싼 Shell Mobil과 페루정부간 다툼이 그 예이다.

국가간 이견은 경제적인 이유에서도 발생할 수 있다. 통과의 조건이나 수익과 렌트간의

4) 천연가스 E&P계약의 회계적 분석에 관하여는 허은녕, *Natural Gas Exploration and Production Contracts: Past, Present and Future* in 2011 자원·에너지법제연구회 311 이하 참조.

5) 파이프라인통과국간 다자조약의 성공적 사례로는 카스피해파이프라인에 관한 Abigail S. Reyes, 위 주 5-49 상기논문, 참조. 통과국의 개별적 파이프라인 소유와 문제점은 Blanche Sas, *Legal and Contractual Issues Relating to Interstate Gas Pipelines in Emerging Nations,* 2002 INT'L ENER. L. & TAX. REV. 70, 73 (2002)(그 예로 Transmediterranean 파이프라인이 튀니지, 알제리, 이태리 회사가 각자 소유하고 있는 형태이고 Maghreb-Europe 파이프라인도 유사한 소유구조라고 한다).

이익분배조건에 관하여 합의에 이르기 어려울 수도 있고 파이프라인 프로젝트 당사자간, 예를 들면 사기업과 국영기업간, 수직적으로 계열화된 기업집단과 개별기업간에도 경제적인 측면에서 이견이 발생할 수 있다. 파이프라인관리기업을 IOC로부터 분리하여 다국적기업이나 국제기구화함으로써 경제적인 이해상충을 다소 완화할 수는 있을 것이다.

파이프라인건설은 엄청난 비용이 들기 때문에 이들 자금을 적기에 조달할 수 있는지 여부에 대한 불확실성 역시 천연가스개발의 커다란 장애이다. 프로젝트자금조달이 가능하려면 새로운 수송로의 건설에 따른 수익의 창출이 건설비용을 조달하기에 충분하여야 하는데, 이는 언제나 가능한 것은 아니다. 더구나 수익이 현지통화에 기초하는 경우 환율변동에 대한 불안과 태환가능성에 대한 의문까지 겹치면 자금조달의 어려움은 더할 것이다. 자금조달가능성은 경제적인 수익률뿐만 아니라 위험의 예측과도 연결되는 것으로서 국가 내지 국가의 정책금융기관의 지지가 필수적일 것이다.

설사 파이프라인이 건설된다고 하여도 그 사용은 통과국내 정치적 소요사태나 자연적 재해시 즉시 중단될 위험이 있다. 설사 그런 사태까지 이르지 않은 상황에서도 렌트를 올리기 위하여 중간의 통과국이 사용중단을 선언할 수도 있다. 실제 러시아와 우크라이나간, 러시아와 조지아간 파이프라인이 중단된 예가 있다. 따라서, 여러 국가를 통과하는 파이프라인은 공급의 안정성 면에서 우려할 만한 상황이 언제나 발생할 수 있다.

파이프라인 통과국간 법과 정책이 상이함으로 인한 중단가능성 역시 무시할 수 없다. 파이프라인은 일종의 자연적 독점이고 이를 공공재로서 규율할 필요성이 없지 않지만, 이를 공공재로서 규정하여 각국이 규율하는 경우 이는 천연가스의 수입규제와 맞물려서 파이프라인이 애당초 계획과는 달리 원할하게 사용되지 못할 가능성을 증가시킨다. 알래스카 파이프라인을 둘러싼 캐나다와 미국 역시 환경정책면에서의 이견이 프로젝트 추진에 커다란 장애로 작용하고 있다.

2) 장기가스판매계약

천연가스의 운송을 위한 대규모투자는 생산자와 수요자간 장기공급계약이 없이는 불가능하다. 따라서 천연가스개발프로젝트는 가스공급계약(Gas Sales Contract)으로부터 출발한다.[6] 마치 민자발전사업자가 전기공급계약으로부터 출발하는 것과 유사하다. 수요자의 자금능력에 의문이 있는 경우 선급금, 구상무역, 신용장이나 은행/모회사보증, 정부보증이 요구된다. 산업관행에 따라서 전형적인 조항이 들어가고 2006년 AIPN이 모델계약서를 만들었다.

6) 자원보유국의 내국법규나 시장상황에 따라서 생산자와 수요자의 직거래계약거래구조가 아닐 수도 있다. 예를 들면 인도네시아는 생산자가 Pertamina와, Pertamina가 수요자와 back-to-back으로 계약을 맺는다. Smith, 각주 1-4 상게서, 1049.

이하 AIPN model을 살핀다.

기간과 관련하여 가스공급계약은 특정가스전의 수명이 다할 때까지 체결하는 소진계약(depletion contract; life-of-the-field contract)과 수요량계약의 두 가지 유형으로 나누어볼 수 있다. 두 계약유형간 차이는 가스전의 생산량이 예상보다 적을 위험을 누가 부담할 것이가에 있다. 전자의 경우 그 위험을 수요자가 부담하며 후자의 경우는 생산자가 부담한다. 전자의 경우 생산자가 합리적이고 신중한 운영자로서 가스전의 수명이 다하였다고 판단, 이를 수요자에게 통지함으로써 계약이 해지되는 반면, 후자의 경우 수요자가 총수요량을 구입함으로써 계약이 해지된다.

계약기간은 통상 20년에서 30년으로 장기이며 기간은 몇 개의 단계로 나누인다. 체결이후 일정한 조건이 충족되면 효과를 발생하나 효력발생일 이후 운송에 필요한 제반 공사를 완공하여 최초로 가스가 배달된 후에도 시설의 시운전을 위한 기간이 필요하다. 본격적인 공급기간도 초기의 축적기, 평탄기, 감축기로 나누어질 수 있다.

[그림 8-1] 천연가스 Delivery Diagram

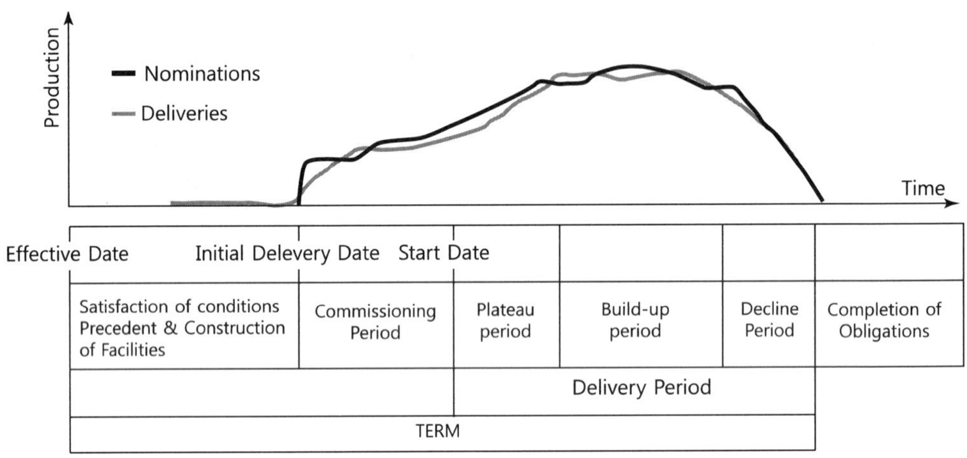

* Commissioning Period can extend beyond "Start Date", but ideally the Start Date is the day following the end of the Commissioning Period

공급기간이 장기이므로 가격의 조정방법이 간단하지 않다. 공급자는 장기간의 안정적 투자회수를 기대하고 투자한 만큼 시장에서의 가격이 적시에 반영되기를 원하고 수요자는 가스와 다른 에너지원의 비교가치가 수시로 반영되기를 원한다. 통상 기준치(base price)를 정하고 몇가지 지표, 예를 들면 다른 연료나 운영비, 운송비 등과[7] 이들 지표의 각 가중치를

7) Niall Trimble, *Gas Sales Agreement,* 주 4-8 상게서, 165, 173-75는 원유생산지가격(북해가스의 경우

정하여 일정한 기간 동안의 변화를 반영, 조정한다.

가장 분쟁이 발생하기 쉽고 또한 어려운 문제가 구매수량이다. 통상 생산자가 수요자에게 공급량에 대한 약속을 하면 원칙적으로 생산자는 제3자에게 천연가스를 판매하지 못하며 수요자 역시 생산자 이외의 제3자로부터 구입하지 못한다. 그 대신 수요자는 주기적으로 구매량을 공급자에 통지하고 공급자는 일정한 오차 범위 내에서 이를 공급하며 초과공급이나 미달공급에 대하여 수요자의 손해를 배상한다. 이를 delivery-or-pay라 한다. 반대로 수요자는 계약에서 합의한 범위 내의 가스공급은 무조건 구매하여야 하며 실제 구매량이 최소구매량을 밑돌 때에는 공급자의 손해를 배상한다. 이를 take-or-pay라 한다. 수요자가 이를 이행하지 않은 경우 공급자에게 보상하거나 수요자가 다음해로 이월할 수 있는 것이 통상의 계약 예이다. 공급자의 손해는 최소구매량과 실제구매량의 차액으로 수요자는 구매하든지 아니면 손해를 배상하여야 한다는 면에서 take-or-pay조항에 따른 수요자의 공급자에 대한 지급액의 법적 성격을 손해배상액의 예정으로 보고 있지는 않다.8)

미국에서는 1970년대 파이프라인 사업자들이 생산자들로부터 가스를 공급받기 위하여 의무구매량의 비율을 높였으나 1980년대에 들어와서 가스산업에 대한 규율이 완화되고 현물시장이 생겨나면서 가스의 수요가 급감하자 파이프라인 사업자들은 의무구매량조항에 따른 엄청난 책임을 지게 되었다. 이를 피하기 위하여 구매자가 불가항력이나 이행불능을 주장하였지만 법원이 받아들인 예는 거의 없다.9)

이러한 사태를 방지하기 위한 계약상 장치는 Price Break Clause 또는 Price Review Mechanism을 두는 것이다. 즉 2-3년에 한 번씩 계약서에서 정한 합의한 상황변화가 발생한 경우 가격을 재검토하기로 합의하는 것이다. 다른 대안은 경제적 곤경(economic hardship)을 선언하면 가격을 재협상하는 의무를 부과하는 것이다. 실제 계약조항자체의 협상이 어렵고 또한 실제 이러한 규정에 따라서 재협상절차가 시작되는 경우 합의나 이견조정이 상당한 시간이 걸린다는 것이 단점이다.10)

광주고법 1987. 11. 27. 선고 87나118(본소) 87나119(반소) 판결

원고와 피고는 1982. 12.경 원고가 각 낙농업자들로부터 수집한 원유(우유)를 매일 일정

Rotterdam price), 원유소비지가격, 전기료, 석탄가, 가스소비자가격, 가스생산지가격, 물가상승률 등을 들고 있다. 2004. 6, POSCO가 Tangguh와 체결한 LNGSPA는 일본의 수입가격에 연동된다.

8) *Prenalta Corp. v. Colorado Interstate Gas Co.,* 944 F.2d 677 (10th Cir. 1991).

9) *Lenape Resources Corporation v. Tennessee Gas Pipeline Company,* 925 S.W.2d 565 (1996).

10) 주 4 상게서, 176-78.

량씩 피고에게 공급하면 피고는 이를 수매하기로 하여 같은 해 12. 8.에 맺은 최초의 계약에서는 원고가 공급하는 원유량을 1일 5톤 내지 6톤으로 약정하였다가 1983. 1.의 계약에서는 1일 3톤 이상으로, 같은 해 4.의 계약에서는 1일 5톤 이상으로 각 원유공급량을 수정하면서 공급계약을 유지하여 온 사실, 그런데 원고와 피고는 모두 우유가공·판매업자들로서 우유제품의 성수기인 매년 4월부터 11월까지는 양자가 모두 많은 양의 원유를 필요로 하는 반면, 비수기인 매년 12월부터 3월까지는 모두 원유의 필요량이 줄어드는 관계로, 성수기에는 원고가 약속한 물량을 제대로 공급하지 못하게 되고 비수기에는 피고가 원고의 공급물량을 제대로 수매하지 못하는 사례가 빈번하여 서로 많은 불편과 손해가 있어 온 사실, 따라서 원고와 피고는 상호 위와 같은 의무불이행을 없도록 하기 위하여 위 1983. 1.의 공급계약에서부터 "원고는 약정물량을 성수기·비수기를 막론하고 피고에게 공급하어야 하고 피고는 이를 수매해야 한다"는 의무조항을 신설하고 상호간 이를 이행하지 아니하였을 경우 이로 인한 손해배상을 예정하였으며, 위와 같은 의무조항과 손해배상의 예정은 위 1983. 4.의 공급계약에서도 그대로 유지되었는데, 그 후 원고가 전국적인 원유부족현상으로 인하여 피고에게 위 공급계약상의 물량을 제대로 공급하지 못하게 되자 피고는 같은 해 6. 8. 원고에게 약정물량의 공급을 촉구하는 내용증명을 보내고 원고는 이에 대하여 같은 해 8. 10.과 9. 30. 2회 결쳐 "원유의 집유량이 자연 감소되어 약속된 공급물량을 제대로 이행할 수 없다"는 취지의 답변을 하는 등 상호 시비가 일어나고 이로 인한 손해배상문제까지 거론되었던 사실, 그리하여 원고와 피고는 1984. 4. 30.에 다시 원유공급계약을 체결하면서 그 내용을 "계약기간은 1984. 5. 1.부터 1985. 4. 30.까지로, 가격은 지방률이 3.4퍼센트의 경우는 1킬로그램당 금 313원으로 하되 지방률 0.1퍼센트 증감에 따라 1킬로그램당 금 7원80전씩 증감하기로 하며 다만 정부고시가격이 변동되면 그에 따르고, 원유의 집유, 냉각, 검사 등의 수수료로 피고가 1킬로그램당 금 30원씩을 부가하여 지급하기로 한다. 원고가 피고에게 공급할 원유량은 매일 최소 4톤 이상으로 하며 원고는 위 약정량을 성수기나 비수기를 막론하고 피고에게 공급하고 피고는 이를 수매하여야 한다. 원유는 원고의 집유장에서 피고가 직접 인수하되 피고의 차량으로 수송한다. 벌칙으로 쌍방이 위 계약을 이행하지 아니할 때에는 그로 인하여 상대방이 입은 손해액의 배액을 배상한다"로 정한 사실, 원고는 별지1 기재와 같이 1984. 5.부터 각 낙농업자들로부터 매입한 원유를 위 약정대로 매일 4톤 이상씩을 피고에게 공급하고 피고는 같은 해 12. 21.까지는 원고가 공급하는 원유 전량을 수매하였으나 같은 해 8.부터 시작된 전국적인 원유공급과잉으로 인하어 같은 해 12. 22.부터 1985. 3. 17.까지는 위 약정을 어기고 1일 약 4톤씩만을 수매하고 그 나머지 공급량에 대하여는 수매를 거절하였던 사실, 이에 앞서 원고는 1984. 12. 12.과 1985. 1. 7.에 피고에게 원고의 공급물량을 계약만료일인 1985. 4. 30.까지만이라도 전량 수매하여 줄 것을 촉구하면서 그렇지 않으면 손해배상을 청구하겠다는 취지의 내용증명을 발송하였고, 이에 대하여 피고는 1985. 1. 11.과 같은 해 1. 16.에 원고의 위 주장을 일축하면서 전국적인 원유공급과잉으로 인하여 1일 4톤 이상은 수매할 수 없다고 맞서 온 사실, 한편 위 1984. 12. 22.부터 1985. 3. 17.까지의 기간 동안 원고가 공급한 원유를 피고가 수매하지 아니한 총 잉여원유량은 별지2 기재와 같이 합계 770,070킬로그램이고 이의 가격은 위 약정한 내용에 따라 계산하여 합계 금 277,421,451원인 사실, 원고는 위 잉여분에 관하여 달리 처리할 방법이 없어 하는 수 없이 분유로 가공판매하기로 결정하고, 원고회사에는 분유제조시설이 없기 때문에 분유제조가 가능한 유업회사에 임가공을 의뢰하여 위 잉여원유 전량으로, 소외 롯데유업에서 9,520킬로그램, 남양유업에서 2,463킬로그램, 해태유업에서 77,402킬로그램 분유를 각 생산하였고, 원고가 그들에게 지급한 ...

(2) 원고는, 피고가 원고공급의 1일 4톤 이상의 원유를 전량수매하지 아니함으로써 위 1984. 4. 30.자 원유공급계약을 위반하였고, 따라서 피고가 수매하지 아니하여 발생하게 된 위 잉여원유 770,070킬로그램으로 인하여 발생한 원고의 손해를 배상할 책임이 있다고 주장함에 대하여, 피고는 원고와의 위 원유공급계약에서 그가 수매하기로 한 '원유량 4톤 이상'의 의미는 상호간 최소한의 공급·수매량을 뜻하는 것으로서, 피고에게는 1일 4톤 정도의 원유만 수매할 의무가 있고 따라서 원고가 매일 4톤 이상의 원유를 무제한 공급하더라도 피고가 반드시 이를 전량 수매하여야 할 의무는 없으므로 원고주장의 위 잉여량 770,070킬로그램에 대하여 아무런 책임이 없다고 다투므로 살피건대, 위에 든 각 증거에 의하면, 원고와 피고간의 1984. 4. 30.자 위 원유공급계약에서 원고의 원유공급량과 피고의 수매량을 1일 4톤 이상으로 정한 의미는 앞에서 설사한 바와 같이 성수기 비수기를 막론하고 상호간에 일정량의 원유를 확보하여 거래하고자 하는 데에 있었던 점, 또한 별지1 기재와 같이 1984. 5. 1.부터 같은 해 12. 21.까지는 원고로부터 피고에게 1일 4톤을 훨씬 상회하는 양의 원유가 공급되었으나 피고로부터 아무런 이의가 없었던 점, 원고의 피고에 대한 원유공급량은 1984. 12.에 280,930킬로그램(피고수매량 216,770킬로그램+잉여량 64,160킬로그램), 1985. 1.에 402,090킬로그램(피고수매량 139,800킬로그램+잉여량 262,290킬로그램), 같은 해 2.에 397,740킬로그램(피고수매량 109,210킬로그램+잉여량 288,530킬로그램), 같은 해 3.에 296,990킬로그램(피고수매량 141,900킬로그램+잉여량 155,090킬로그램)으로서, 1985. 1.과 같은 해 2.에는 평소보다 다소 많은 양의 원유가 공급되었으나 그 양이 지나치게 과다하다고는 볼 수 없으며 1984. 12.와 1985. 3.은 평소와 비슷한 정도의 원유가 공급된 점 및 원고와 피고간의 위 공급계약기간이 비교적 단기간인 1년인 점을 알 수 있으므로 이러한 점 등과 위 계약조항에 비추어보면, 위 계약상의 4톤 이상의 의미는 그 공급량의 최소한을 규정한 것이고 원고가 피고에게 공급하는 원유는 그 양이 지나치게 과다한 것이 아닌 한 피고로서는 위 계약기간 내에는 적어도 이를 전량수매하여야 할 의무가 있다고 해석함이 상당하다고 인정되고, 이에 어긋나는 제1심증인

×××, 당심증인 ×××의 각일부증언은 믿지 아니하는바, 그렇다면 위 잉여원유량 770,070 킬로그램으로 인하여 발생한 원고의 손해에 대하여는 피고에게 그 책임이 있다 할 것이다.

대법 1989. 2. 14. 선고 88다카60, 88다카61 판결

1. 피고 소송대리인의 상고이유 제1점을 본다.

(1) 원고와 피고 사이에 1984. 4. 30.자로 체결된 원유공급(수매)계약서(갑제1호증) 제2조 제3항 및 제3조는 원고는 피고에게 매일 최소 4톤 이상의 원유량을 공급하되 위 원유량을 성수기, 비수기를 막론하고 피고에게 공급하여야 하고 피고는 이를 수매하여야 하도록 규정하고 있는바, 위 각 조항의 규정에 의하면, 피고는 원고가 공급하는 매일 최소 4톤 이상의 원유량을 모두 수매할 의무가 있다고 해석되므로 같은 취지로 판단한 원심판결은 정당하다.

논지는 위 계약조항에서 규정한 매일 최소 4톤은 원고가 성수기에 공급할 의무량의 한계를 규정함과 동시에 비수기에 피고가 수매하여야 할 한계량을 정한 것이며 또 이와 같이 해석하는 것이 형평과 정의에 합치되므로, 피고는 매일 4톤을 수매할 의무는 있을지언정 그 이상을 수매할 의무는 없다고 주장한다.

그러나 원심이 적법하게 배척한 증거 외에 위와 같이 해석할 근거가 없을 뿐 아니라, 성립에 다툼이 없는 을 제2호증, 같은 3호증의 1의 각 기재에 의하면 이 사건 원유공급(수매)계약보다 앞서 원고와 피고 사이에 1983. 1. 및 1983. 4.에 체결된 바 있는 각 원유공급(수매)계약에서도 원고는 1일 최소 3톤 또는 5톤 이상을 성수기, 비수기를 막론하고 공급하며 피고는 이를 수매하여야 한다고 규정하면서 연중수급계획량을 정하고 있는데, 그 수급계획량을 보면 비수기인 12월부터 3월까지의 수급량은 성수기에 비하여 훨씬 많은 양을 예정하고 있는 사실이 인정되므로 이에 의하면 위에서 규정한 1일 최소 3톤 또는 5톤이란 피고가 수매할 의무가 있는 한계량을 정한 것이라고 해석할 여지가 없는바, 이러한 종전의 거래내용에 비추어 보면 이 사건 원유공급(수매)계약에 있어서도 원고가 공급해야 할 1일 최소 4톤은 원고가 공급해야 할 최소 한계량을 정한 것일 뿐 피고가 수매할 의무가 있는 한계량을 정한 것이라고는 볼 수 없으니 위 논지는 이유없다.

(2) 다만 이 사건 원유공급(수매)계약에 의하여 피고는 원고가 공급하는 1일 4톤 이상의 원유를 수매할 의무를 진다고 하더라도 원고가 공급하는 4톤 이상의 원유량이 얼마가 되든 피고는 무제한으로 이를 모두 수매할 의무가 있다고 볼 수는 없고, 종전의 거래실적과 수매능력 등에 비추어 당사자 사이에 수매를 예정한 것으로 볼 수 있는 한도 내의 원유량에 한하여 수매할 의무가 있다고 보아야 할 것이다.

그런데 원심이 채용한 갑제2호증의 기재에 의하면, 원고 스스로 피고에게 1984. 12. 12.자로 비수기에는 원유의 공급수매량을 1일 12,900킬로그램으로 예정한 바 있음을 이유로 이 원유량의 수매를 최고한 사실이 인정되므로, 이에 의하면 원고로서도 1일 12,900킬로그램 이상의 공급을 예정하고 있지 않았음이 명백한바, 원심이 확정한 사실에 의하면 1985. 1.분의 원유잉여량은 262,290킬로그램으로서 그 달의 피고수매량 139,800킬로그램과 합치면 원유총량은 402,090킬로그램이 되어 1일 평균량은 12,970킬로그램이 되고, 또 1985. 2.분의 원유잉여량은 288,530킬로그램으로서 그 달의 피고수매량 109,210킬로그램과 합치면 397,740킬로그램이 되고 1일 평균량은 14,205킬로그램이 됨이 명백하므로, 위 1985. 1.분 및 2.분의 각 원유총량은 당초에 예정한 1일 평균공급수매량 12,900킬로그램을 초과하고 있어 특단의 사정이 없는 한 이 초과부분에 대하여는 피고의 수매의무를 인정할 수 없다고 볼 여지가 있다.

이 점에서 원심판결은 증거판단의 소홀과 심리미진으로 판결에 영향을 미친 위법이 있고 이 범위 내에서 논지는 이유있다.

2. 같은 상고이유 제2점을 본다.

원심판결 이유에 의하면, 원심은 피고가 이 사건 원유공급(수매)계약을 위반하여 원고의 공급원유를 수매하지 않음으로써 발생한 총잉여원유량 770,070킬로그램을 원고가 이를 분유로 가공판매하는 외에 달리 처리할 방도가 없었으므로, 원고가 분유로 임가공하는 데에 소요한 생산원가 합계 338,601,442원과 이 분유를 1킬로그램당 2,500원 및 2,700원에 소외 주식회사 유일양행에게 판매한 대금 합계 233,689,900원과의 차액인 104,911,542원이 피고의 수매의무불이행으로 원고가 입은 손해액이라고 판단하고, 위 판매가격이 부당하게 저렴하다는 피고의 주장에 대하여 분유는 그 품질, 거래시기, 거래당사자의 사정 등에 따라 그 판매가격이 반드시 일정한 것이 아님은 경험칙상 명백하므로 위 판매가격을 부당하게 저렴하다고 볼 수 없다하여 위 피고주장을 배척하였다.

그러나 성립에 다툼이 없는 을제6호증의2 및 1심증인 최백진의 증언에 의하여 진정성립이 인정되는 을제7호증의 1 내지 5 기재에 의하면 1981. 6.경의 전지분유의 공장도가격은 1킬로그램당 3,875원이었던 사실과 피고는 실제로 1984. 12. 및 1985. 1.경 소외 주식회사 삼립유지 등에게 전지분유를 1킬로그램당 3,875원의 가격으로 판매한 실적이 있은 사실이 인정되므로, 특단의 사정이 없는 한 1984. 12. 및 1985. 1.경의 전지분유의 공장도시가는 1킬로그램당 3,875원으로 추정되고, 따라서 원고가 소외 주식회사 유일양행에게 판매한 1킬로그램당 2,500원 및 2,700원의 가격은 시가보다 현저하게 저렴한 가격이라고 하지 않을 수 없다.

그렇다면 원고가 위와 같이 시가보다 현저하게 저렴한 가격으로 판매하지 않을 수 없었던 부득이한 사정이 있었음을 주장 입증하지 않는 한 위 판매가격은 정당한 판매가격이라고 볼 수 없으므로 이를 기초로 손해액을 산정할 수는 없다고 할 것인바, 위와 같은 부득이한 사정이 있었음을 인정할 만한 아무런 자료가 없음에도 불구하고 원심이 분유는 그 품질, 거래시기, 거래당사자의 사정 등에 따라 그 판매가격이 반드시 일정한 것이 아님은 경험칙상 명백하다는 이유만으로 위 판매가격이 부당하게 저렴하다고 볼 수 없다고 판단하였음은 채증법칙을 위반하여 증거판단을 그르친 위법을 저지른 것이라고 하지 않을 수 없고, 이는 소송촉진등에 관한 특례법 제12조 제2항 소정의 파기사유에 해당하므로 이 점 논지는 이유있다.

S. Scott Gaille, *The Use of Quantity Terms to Improve Efficiency and Stability in International Gas Sales & Purchase Agreements,* 29 ENER. L.J. 645 (2008)

Ⅲ. THE PROBLEM OF SEASONAL DEMAND AND ITS USUAL EXTERNAL SOLUTIONS

When the Seller is responsible for managing the Buyer's seasonal capacity needs, it can be forced to reserve sufficient production, processing, and pipeline capacity for the Buyer's peak demand, even if these facilities are only utilized on one day. This type of inefficiency is illustrated in Figure 1 below, which shows a hypothetical gas project with a peak demand of 300 mmscf/day (million standard cubic feet). The "Stranded Capacity" represents quantities that could have been produced and/or transported using the same facilities, thereby spreading the cost of the facilities across more gas molecules (and lowering the gas price).

This is the dilemma that nations in the Middle East face. For example, in Dubai, United Arab Emirates, the average high temperature ranges from seventy-three degrees in January to 103 degrees in August. Between these months, electricity demand more than doubles from the winter low of approximately 2300 MW and the summer peak of 4736 MW. Such dramatic demand differences pose considerable challenges for the region's governments and its gas suppliers.

One of those gas suppliers is Dolphin Energy, which produces approximately two billion cubic feet of natural gas per day in Qatar and transports the gas across the Persian Gulf through a subsea pipeline to the United Arab Emirates, where the gas is sold to three government-owned customers: (1) Abu Dhabi Water & Electricity Company, an Abu Dhabi government entity that purchases an average volume of 929 mmscf/day; (2) Dubai Supply Authority, a Dubai government entity that purchases an average of 730 mmscf/day; and (3) Oman Oil Company, an Omani government entity

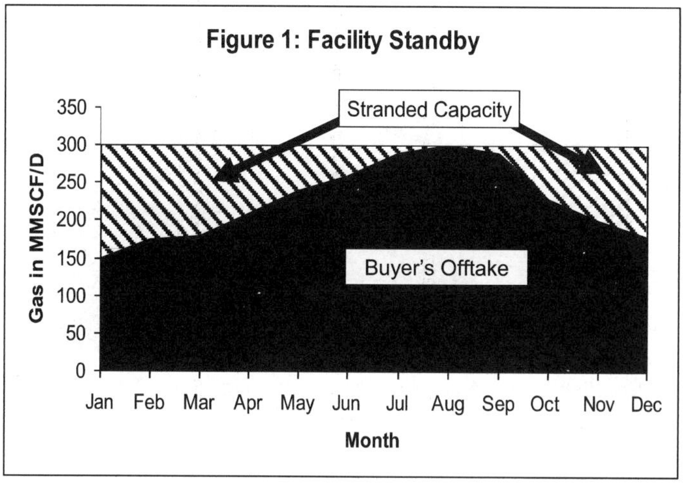

that purchases an average of 200 mmscf/day. Most of this purchased gas is used by the respective governments for electricity production, which is subject to the large variances mentioned above.

Notwithstanding being faced with a seasonal demand variation similar to that in Figure 1, Dolphin Energy only reserves about seven percent of its capacity to meet its customers' "peak requirements." Companies with such a challenge usually rely upon external solutions, such as counter-swing customers, peaking gas, and storage, which often require the cooperation of third parties.

A. Counter-Swing Customers

The ideal scenario for managing the Buyer's seasonal swing is to identify a second customer that can utilize the capacity when the first Buyer does not ("Counter-Swing Customer"). The Counter-Swing Customer may have gas needs that are inverse to the first Buyer's needs (e.g., under-utilized Middle East winter production might be sold as liquefied natural gas (LNG) to Asia during its cold winter). Other times, a customer may be able to take gas whenever it is available (e.g., oil fields that are in need of injection gas and industrial facilities with the capability to switch fuels and that usually burn more expensive liquid fuels).

Figure 2 illustrates how Counter-Swing Customers can manage seasonal swing. The Seller's facilities are optimized when gas is sold on a flat basis of 300 mmscf/d. The Seller's principal customer ("Customer #1") has a demand that ranges from 150 mmscf/d in January to 300 mmscf/d in August. The Counter Swing Customers purchase the difference between the 300 mmscf/d and Customer #1's actual gas consumption.

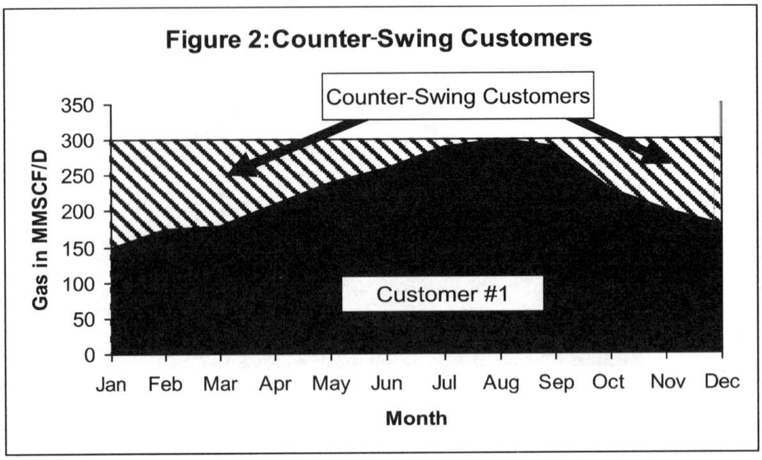

B. Peaking Gas from a Second Gas Source

The Seller may also consider using peaking gas to manage the Buyer's seasonal swing. A peaking gas arrangement usually involves two GSPAs from two production sources, one with a flat, predictable offtake, and a second that manages the swing, the "Peaking GSPA". Figure 3 illustrates how peaking gas can be used to manage a Buyer's seasonal swing. The Seller produces 150 mmscf/d every day of the year, which represents the Buyer's minimum natural gas consumption in January ("Baseload Gas"). As the Buyer's gas consumption increases over the course of the year, the 150 mmscf/d of Baseload Gas is supplemented with gas purchased from a second source until the Buyer's gas consumption needs are met ("Peaking Gas").

Peaking gas sources include associated gas from crude oil fields and condensate stripping operations, which may have the ability to reinject gas that is not sold. In the United Arab Emirates, oil production has been negatively impacted by the practice of diverting gas from crude oil fields (gas is injected in oil fields "to boost reservoir pressure and increase crude recovery rates") to electricity customers as peaking gas "during the summer, when governments scramble to keep the lights on and air conditioners cranking." Peaking gas also might be available from smaller, economically marginal gas fields that lack the capability to sustain customers on a long-term basis. If the Peaking GSPA is an obligation of the Seller, the additional costs of the Peaking GSPA are usually passed on to the Buyer. Alternatively, the Buyer may contract directly with the producer supplying the Peaking Gas.

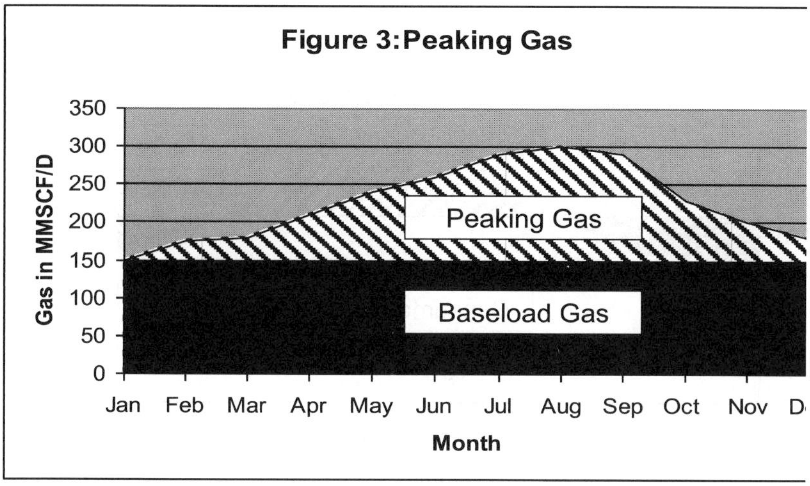

C. Storage

Swing can also be efficiently managed with storage. For example, the Seller might transport the same quantity of gas to the Buyer's geographic region each day. The Buyer consumes as much as it can, and the unconsumed quantities are injected into a depleted gas reservoir. These stored quantities are later withdrawn and consumed during the Buyer's peak period. In the United States, this use of storage capacity is common:

> [S]torage can substitute for expanded delivery capacity upstream of the storage facility, effectively becoming part of the distribution system's peak-day delivery capacity. For instance, a distributor serving a market area with highly seasonal demand might receive a steady flow of gas year round, putting much of that flow during low-demand months into storage and then using storage withdrawals in combination with upstream supply to meet demand in peak months. By using storage this way, the distributor can purchase less peak-day pipeline delivery capacity to bring gas to the distribution system. In this case, storage serves as part of the distribution system's peak-day delivery capacity.

Figure 4 illustrates the use of storage to manage seasonal swing. The Seller produces a flat quantity of 225 mmscf/d every day of the year. During the winter period, the Buyer's needs are less than 225 mmscf/d. The difference between the Buyer's actual daily gas consumption and the 225 mmscf/d of production is delivered into storage ("Stored Gas"). When the Buyer's demand exceeds the Seller's production of 225 mmscf/d, the Seller withdraws stored quantities to meet the Buyer's needs ("Withdrawn Gas"), which is also consumed.

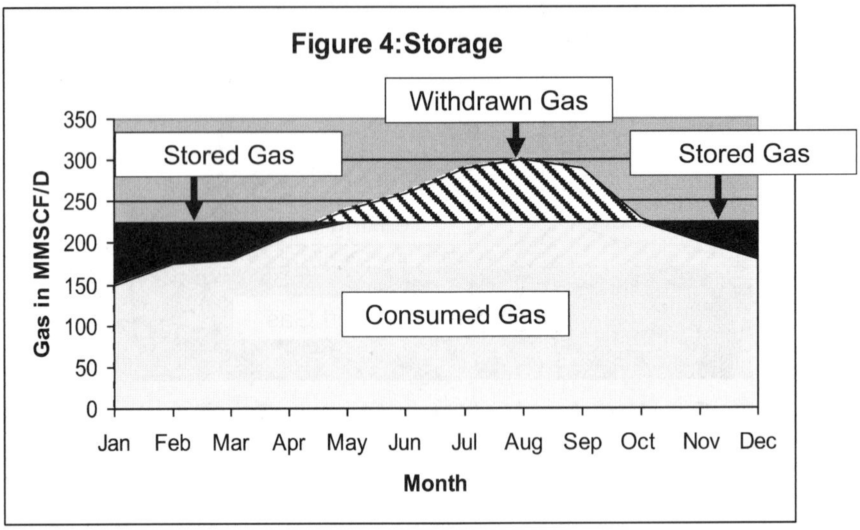

Ⅳ. USING QUANTITY TERMS TO MANAGE SEASONAL SWING INTERNALLY

In addition to the external solutions described above, it also is possible to design the contractual terms of the principal GSPA in a manner that mitigates the counter-swing, peaking or storage quantities required, or that reduces the amount of capacity that needs to be reserved. While the overriding goal for the selection of quantity provisions in a GSPA should be to meet the Buyer's demand needs as narrowly as possible, this can be difficult to achieve in a country with a developing gas market. There may be only one gas producer, and/or only one gas buyer. Even if there is more than one producer, the other producers' gas supplies may be committed to other customers, and therefore not realistically available. In a developing gas market, the limited availability of counter-swing customers, peaking gas suppliers, or gas storage facilities increases the likelihood of construction of excess project capacity and higher gas prices.

As previously discussed, just because the Buyer is willing to pay a higher gas price does not mean this is in the long-term best interest of the Seller. The Seller's ability to recover its costs and rate of return over twenty to thirty years requires contractual stability. The difference between a narrowly tailored gas price and one inflated with excess capacity could affect the country's growth rate or its ability to compete with its neighbors, or simply make the contract's terms more vulnerable to normal economic cycles. This section provides an overview of the quantity terms associated with the Seller's delivery obligation and the Buyer's purchase obligation and then explains how these terms can be adjusted in ways to minimize excess capacity, thereby improving the efficiency and stability of GSPAs.

A. Quantity Terms Associated with the Seller's Obligation to Deliver Gas

1. Annual Contract Quantity

GSPA quantity negotiations typically commence with an analysis of how much gas the Buyer will need on an annual basis. The Annual Contract Quantity (ACQ) is the Buyer's annual entitlement to gas, or to put it another way, the maximum quantity of gas that the Buyer has a right to take during a year. The ACQ is usually expressed as a firm annual number in standard cubic feet ("mmscf") or British Thermal Units (BTUs). Over the course of the GSPA, the Seller may agree to deliver quantities in excess of the ACQ, but it has no contractual obligation to do so. As such, the Buyer will want to ensure that the ACQ is sufficient to meet its realistic demand expectations over the course of the GSPA.

A GSPA may have one ACQ that applies to every year of the contract, or it may provide for different ACQs in different years. For example, if a Buyer's electricity market is growing, it might seek to escalate the ACQ over time, reflecting expectations of increasing gas consumption by its power plants. Such a phased approach could call for facility additions over time, which costs would only be factored into the gas price in the later years. Since these capital expenditures are delayed, the increase in the ACQ, and the construction of the additional facilities can be an option for the Buyer.

2. Daily Contract Quantity

Once the parties are comfortable with how much gas the Buyer needs on an annual basis, the next question is usually how much it needs on a daily basis. The Daily Contract Quantity (DCQ) represents the typical, or average, amount of gas that the Buyer expects to purchase on a given day under the GSPA. If the Buyer expects to purchase the same quantity every day of the year, the DCQ is usually expressed as the ACQ divided by 365. In a situation of seasonally changing demand it is possible for the Buyer's DCQ to vary over the course of a year. The GSPA typically addresses this problem by forecasting the Buyer's average gas consumption for each month and then specifying these figures as monthly DCQs in an appendix.

3. Maximum Daily Quantity

The Maximum Daily Quantity (MDQ) is the daily equivalent of the ACQ. It represents the maximum quantity that the Buyer has a right to take, or have delivered, during a given day. While the Seller may agree, at its discretion, to deliver quantities in excess of the MDQ, the Seller usually has no obligation to do so. The MDQ is expressed as a percentage (typically 105 percent to 120 percent) of the DCQ. If the

DCQ is the same throughout the year, the MDQ usually will be the same every day; if the DCQ varies, the MDQ percentage is likely to vary, as well.

4. Additional Gas

One risk that the Buyer may wish to address in the GSPA is the possibility of exhausting the ACQ before the end of the year. The GSPA may provide for the Buyer's right to request quantities above the ACQ ("Additional Gas" or "Excess Gas") and specify the price that the Buyer will need to pay if the Seller agrees to provide the Additional Gas (typically 105 percent to 130 percent of the ACQ gas price). While the Seller is under no obligation to provide Additional Gas, the negotiated price premium provides the Buyer with an incentive to do so. Including such a term in a GSPA may provide the Buyer with some comfort that the Seller will at least use its reasonable commercial efforts to supply additional volumes in the event that demand forecasts used to establish the ACQ fall short in a future year.

5. Bank Gas

An alternative to Additional Gas (which is only sold to the Buyer at the Seller's discretion) is a firm commitment from the Seller to provide certain quantities of gas above the ACQ ("Bank Gas"). Under such an arrangement, should the Buyer exceed the ACQ, it would be entitled to call on, and the Seller would be obligated to deliver, specific quantities of up to x mmscf per year. The GSPA can also provide for a right to Bank Gas on a specific day should the MDQ be exceeded. For example, the Buyer could be entitled to receive up to an additional ten mmscf per day in addition to the MDQ. In either case, there may be a price premium attached to Bank Gas. As described further below, the use of Bank Gas terms in GSPAs can often help the parties to tailor other quantity terms more narrowly, such as the MDQ, in situations of seasonally changing demand.

6. Total Contract Quantity

Total Contract Quantity is the Buyer's entitlement to gas over the entire life of the GSPA, that is, the maximum quantity that the Buyer has a right to take during the term of the GSPA. The Total Contract Quantity usually represents the amount of gas that can be withdrawn from the reservoir before the Seller is uncertain of its capability to meet the ACQ and MDQ thresholds in the GSPA. Thus, although a Seller may be able to deliver Additional Gas, or Bank Gas, over the course of a GSPA, such deliveries may count against the Total Contract Quantity and shorten the term of the GSPA.

7. Liquidated Damages and Guaranteed Delivery Quantities

The consequences for the Seller's failure to deliver a quantity that a Buyer is entitled to receive vary greatly. The severity of the penalty for delivery failure also may dictate what flexibility a Seller is willing to agree upon with respect to such terms as the MDQ and Bank Gas. The greater the penalty for delivery failure, the more conservative the Seller is going to be with respect to its commitments.

Some GSPAs provide that the Seller's only penalty for a delivery failure is a reduction in the Buyer's obligation to purchase gas (the take or pay). More typically, a GSPA dictates a liquidated damages credit or payment, which is usually expressed as a percentage of the gas price (e.g., thirty percent). For example, if the Seller failed to deliver 100 mmscf, the next 100 mmscf delivered to the Buyer would be subject to a thirty percent discount.

The Seller also will usually seek to negotiate limits on the amount of liquidated damages. One common term is a maximum liability cap, which limits the Seller's liquidated damages at a sum certain during any single year and over the entire term of the GSPA. Liquidated damages provisions also may be limited to the positive difference, if any, between the Buyer's cost of replacement fuel and the gas price. This protects the Seller from the situation where the Buyer incurs little, or no, actual damages.

The quantity of the delivery failure can be factored into the liquidated damages calculation as well. For example, liquidated damages can be set at five percent of the gas price for any portion of a delivery failure of up to ten percent of the DCQ but then rise to thity percent of the gas price for delivery failures of greater than ten percent of the DCQ. A variation of this approach is the exemption of minor shortfalls from liquidated damages altogether. This is usually accomplished by creating daily and annual "Guaranteed Delivery Quantities," which are less than the DCQ and ACQ, respectively. If the Guaranteed Delivery Quantities were ninety percent of the DCQ and ninety percent of the ACQ, the Seller would only incur liquidated damages if the quantities it made available for delivery failed to meet those somewhat lower thresholds. The controlling principle in the negotiation of any delivery failure provision is not making the Buyer whole but preventing the Seller from engaging in opportunism. The Buyer should consider whether the delivery failure mechanism is strong enough to discourage the Seller from selling the gas to another customer. Depending on the maturity of the gas market, this risk may be precluded altogether by geography or law (perhaps, for instance, there is no other entity to which the gas can be sold). It also may be useful for the GSPA to distinguish delivery failures that are intentional in nature, such as the Seller's decision to sell the gas to a different customer at a higher price.

Occasionally, the Buyer will seek "make whole" damages in the form of the cost differential for replacement fuel, or, if no replacement fuel is available, all damages it may suffer. As a general rule, the economics of a gas project cannot sustain the burden of insuring a Buyer's electricity or industrial businesses. If the gas processing plant is damaged, it may be months before gas deliveries can be resumed. To mitigate such risks, it is important for the Seller to place a quantitative limit (in the form of liquidated damages) on its worst case exposure under a GSPA.

Gas Sales Agreement between JV Seller and Buyer[11)]

Table of Contents

11) KOGAS의 동의를 받아서 전재. 거래구조전반에 관하여는 위 제3장 제4절 [그림 3-1] 수르길거래구조도 참조.

14. INDEMNIFICATION

14.1. Injury to Persons and Damage to Property

1) If there shall occur any death or injury to any Person (other than employees of Buyer or Seller) or loss of or damage to any property in relation to the performance by Buyer of its obligations under this Agreement, Buyer shall be liable for and shall indemnify Seller Indemnitees against all such claims arising in connection therewith to the extent that such death or personal injury or loss or damage to property was caused by the act or omission, the negligence or breach of duty of Buyer, its servants or agents.

2) If there shall occur any death or injury to any Person (other than employees of Buyer or Seller) or loss of or damage to any property (excluding Buyer's property) in relation to the performance by Seller of its obligations under this Agreement, Seller shall be liable for and shall indemnify Buyer Indemnitees against all such claims arising in connection therewith to the extent that such death or personal injury or loss or damage to property was caused by the act or omission, the negligence or breach of statutory duty of Seller, its servants or agents.

14.2. Accidents or Injury to Employees

1) Buyer shall indemnify Seller Indemnitees against all claims arising in connection with the death of or injury to any Person employed by Buyer for the purposes performing its obligations under this Agreement. This indemnity shall not apply to the extent that any death or injury results from any wilful act or default of Seller, its servants, agents or employees.

2) Seller shall indemnify Buyer Indemnitees against all claims arising in connection with the death of or injury to any Person employed by Seller for the purposes performing its obligations under this Agreement. This indemnity shall not apply to the extent that any death or injury results from any act or default of Buyer, its servants, agents or employees.

14.3. Loss or Damage to Property of a Party

1) If there shall occur any loss or damage to any property owned by Seller, Buyer shall be liable for the costs of rectification or replacement of such property to the extent that such loss or damage to Seller's property was caused by the act or omission, the negligence or breach of statutory duty of Buyer, its servants or agents.

2) If there shall occur any loss or damage to any property owned by Buyer, Seller shall be liable for the costs of rectification or replacement of such property to the extent that such loss or damage to Buyer's property was caused by the act or omission, the negligence or breach of statutory duty of Seller, its servants or agents.

14.4. Indemnification for Breach of Laws Buyer shall indemnify Seller Indemnitees against all claims with respect to failure of Buyer or any of its servants, agents or employees to comply with Applicable Laws in the performance of its obligations under this Agreement.

14.5. Conduct of Proceedings

1) In the event of any claim being made or brought against Buyer Indemnitees and/or Seller Indemnitees arising out of the matters referred to in this Clause 14, the

indemnifying Party shall be promptly notified thereof and may at its own expense conduct all negotiations for the settlement of the same, and any litigation that may arise therefrom. The Parties shall not, unless and until the indemnifying Party has failed to take over the conduct of the negotiations or litigation within 14 Days of notification thereof, and otherwise complied with its obligations hereunder, make any admission which might be prejudicial thereto.

2) The conduct by the indemnifying Party of such negotiations or litigation shall be conditional upon the indemnifying Party having first given Buyer Indemnitees and/or Seller Indemnitees, as applicable, such security as shall from time to time be required by such Buyer Indemnitees and/or Seller Indemnitees to cover the amount ascertained, agreed or estimated, as the case may be, of any compensation, damages, expenses and costs for which such Buyer Indemnitees and/or Seller Indemnitees may become liable.

3) The Parties shall, at the request of the other Party, afford all reasonably available assistance for the purpose of contesting any such claim, and shall be repaid all expenses and costs (including overheads and financing costs) reasonably incurred in so doing. The Parties shall at the request of the other Party, keep it reasonably informed of the progress of negotiations and litigation referred to in this Clause 14.5.

3) 가스수송계약

가스공급계약과는 별도로 파이프라인사업자가 생산자 또는 수요자와 가스수송계약을 체결할 수도 있다. 가스거래가 발달된 미국이나 북유럽, 영국에서는 에너지당국이 경쟁을 위하여 가스수송을 엄격하게 규율하며 따라서 많은 법규가 있지만 기본적인 계약구조는 가스공급계약과 유사하다. 선적자가 파이프라인사업자에게 수송량을 통지하며 최소수송량을 맞추지 못한 경우 파이프라인사업자에 ship-or-payment를 지급하여야 한다. 공급계약과 마찬가지로 선적자는 이를 보완하거나 다음기간으로 넘길 수 있다. 2009년 AIPN는 파이프라인 건설을 예정하는 단계와 이미 파이프라인이 건설되어 있는 단계에서의 표준 가스수송계약을 제시하였다.

4) 현물시장

파이프라인망이 잘 발달된 미국의 경우 단기공급계약 내지 현물시장이 가능하다. 1980년대 가스수요가 급감하자 미국에너지위원회(FERC)는 파이프라인사업자는 단순한 가스수송수단을 제공하는 역할만을 허용하고 가스거래자로서의 역할을 금지시켰다.[12] 따라서, 파이프라인사업자는 생산자와 수요자에게 가스의 수송수단만을 제공하는 공공사업자가 되었다. 또한 파이프라인사업자는 생산자와 수요자가 상호 의사소통을 할 수 있는 전자게시판을 게재하여야만 하며 파이프라인사업자는 수송서비스의 가격을 투명하게 제시하여야만 한다. 이러한 법적 규율의 변화로 미국 내 약 50여 곳의 허브가 조성되어 단기공급 내지 현물거래가 이

12) 한전으로부터 GRID를 별도의 회사 LGU+로 분리, 매각한 것과 유사한 개념이다. 대한국유관공사와 정유사, 철도시설관리공단과 철도사업자간 관계와 유사.

루어지게 되었다. 그리하여 1980년대 말에는 현물거래가 미국 전체가스소비의 반 이상을 차지하게 되었다.

현물거래 초기에는 사업자들이 각자의 계약서를 사용하다가 1996년 North American Energy Standards Board(NAESB)가 현물거래를 위한 선도계약서 양식을 만들면서 산업표준이 되었다. 이는 3부분으로 구성되어 있는데, 첫번째 부분은 2페이지로 가격, 인도조건 등 주요 거래조건이, 두번째 부분은 10페이지로 일반계약조건이, 그리고 마지막 부분은 거래조건 확인이다.[13)]

현물시장은 바로 거래소에서의 가스선물거래로 이어졌으며 그 중 NYMEX의 Louisiana, Henry Hub에서 인도되는 10,000MMBtus단위 가스선물이 가장 널리 거래되고 있다. 이 외에도 옵션이나 스왑 등 천연가스나 그 가격, 지수등을 기초로 한 다양한 파생상품이 거래소에서 거래되고 있다.[14)]

3. 액화천연가스 (LNG)

가. 액화천연가스의 수요와 공급

LNG의 국제거래는 1990년대 폭발적으로 증가하여 2006년 7.5TCf가 수출되었으며 이 중 일본과 한국이 전세계 LNG수요의 55%를 점하고 있다. 그리고 이러한 LNG의 국제거래는 탱커, 액화시설, 기화시설, 그리고 저장탱크 등 거대한 인프라에 의하여 뒷받침되고 있다.

나. 프로젝트구조[15)]

프로젝트의 크기, 각 과정의 상호의존성, 관계당사자의 다양성 때문에 LNG프로젝트는 가장 복잡한 에너지벤처이다. 거래구조의 출발점은 프로젝트회사를 설립하는 것이고 회사 이외에 비법인합작투자형과 문지기회사형이 있다.

프로젝트회사구조는 이해관계당사자가 가스생산국에 프로젝트회사에 출자하여 이를 설립하여 이 회사를 통하여 자금을 조달하고 플랜트를 소유하게 하는 것이다. 프로젝트회사는 업스트림의 가스생산자로부터 이를 구매하여 액화하여 수요자에게 공급한다. 이 구조는 트리니다드 토바코, 나이지리아 등에서 사용되었으며 KOGAS의 우즈베키스탄 수르길 프로젝트

13) 이는 통상 장외에서 선물을 거래할때의 양식이기도 하다. KIKO거래서류 참조.

14) 우리나라는 해외에서의 장기공급계약에 따른 수입에 전량의존하고 있고 있는데, 하계절과 동계절사이의 수요의 차를 국제천연가스선물 및 옵션시장에서의 거래로서 가격안정을 이룰 수 있을 것이라는 견해는 곽상장/곽수종, 천연가스 선물 및 옵션거래를 이용한 최적 헤징전략, 10 선물연구 29(2002).

15) 이하 Philips R. Weems, *Overview of Issues Common to Structuring, Negotiating and Documenting LNG Projects,* 8 INT'L ENERG. L & TAX. REV. 189 (2000) 주로 참조.

[그림 8-2] LNG 거래 흐름

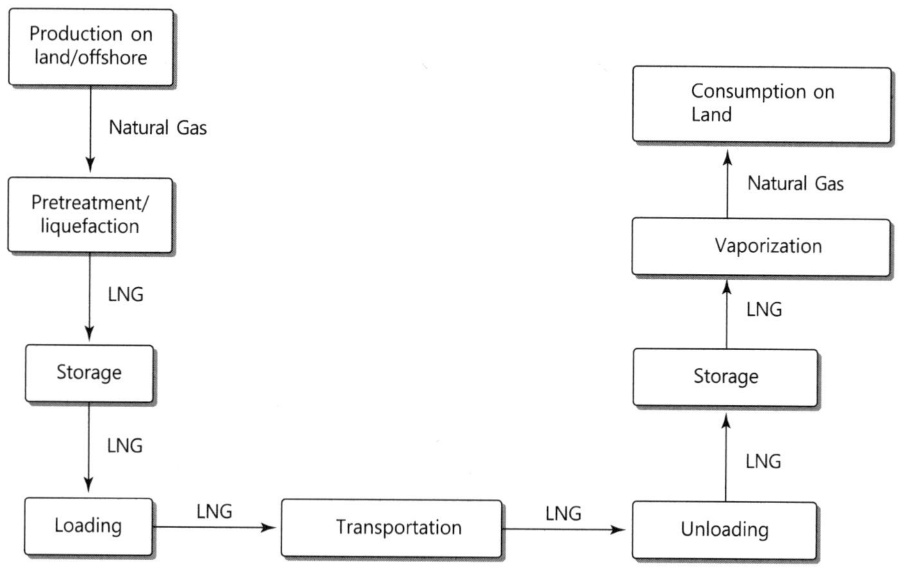

도 이와 유사한 것으로 보인다. LNG시설이 별도의 회사에 의하여 소유, 운용되고 있으므로 자금조달에 편리한 점이 있는 반면 최초 일정한 규모의 시설을 상정하여 프로젝트를 시작하였으나 이를 확장하려면 다양한 주주들이 합의에 이르러야 한다는 점에서 어려움이 있을 수 있다.

비법인합작투자형은 호주와 알래스카에서 시행된 것으로 통상 비법인합작투자형은 업스트림이 아닌 다운스트림에서는 희귀한 것이지만 국가가 소극적인 역할을 하고 있고 비법인합작투자에 대한 법제도가 확립되었다면 제3자로부터의 자금조달 없이 사업자들끼리 합작투자계약을 체결, 출자하고, 운용자를 정하고, 이익을 분배하기로 합의할 수 있다. 호주 Northwest Shelf Project는 6개의 회사가 각 6분의 1씩 출자하고 Woodside Petroleum이 운용하며 수익은 6분의 1씩 분배받는 구조이다.

문지기회사형은 1973년 인도네시아에서 LNG프로젝트가 시작될 때 당시의 특수한 국내사정때문에 구상된 것으로 LNG의 소유와 운용마케팅은 업스트리임의 Pertamina와 PSC를 체결한 IOC가 수행, 이들에게 이익이 귀속되는 형식이다.

[그림 8-3] Trinidad and Tobago 회사조직도

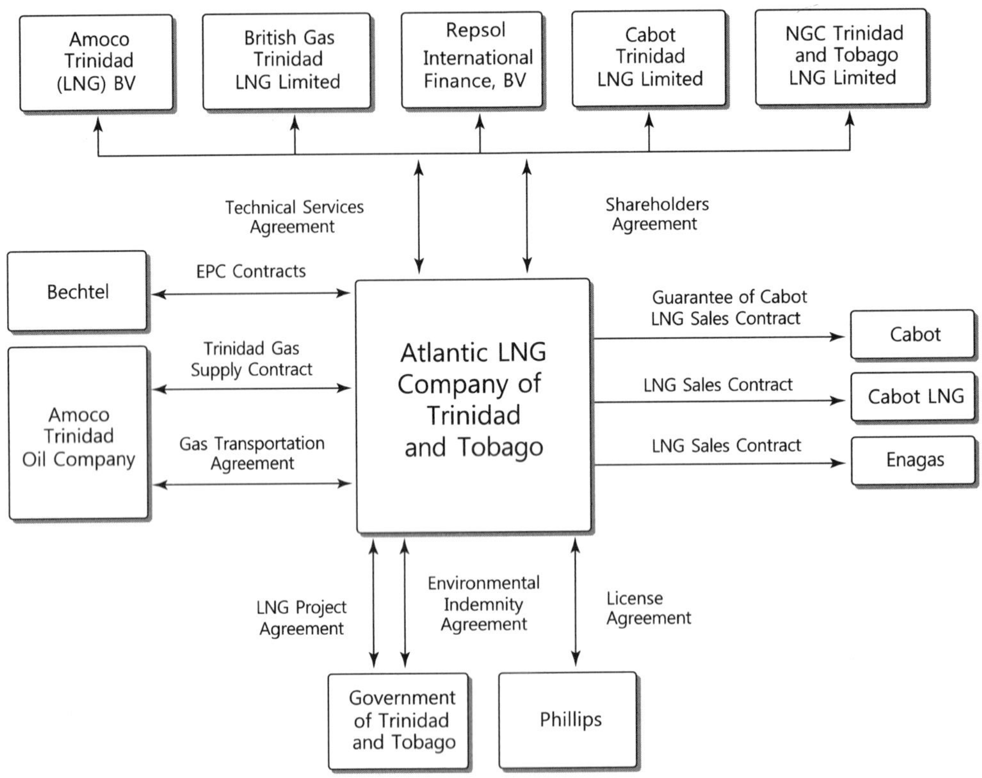

다. LNG 판매계약

Package V Supply Agreement (1995 – 1999): LNG Sales between PERTAMINA et al. and KOGAS[16)]

ARTICLE 1 EFFECTIVE DATE AND DURATION

This Supply Agreement shall be effective as of September 30, 1994, and shall terminate on the date when all rights and obligations of Contractors hereunder have been satisfied.

ARTICLE 2 SUPPLY COMMITMENT AND QUANTITY

2.1 Net Gas Requirement. The total quantity of net Natural Gas required to be supplied and delivered out of proved recoverable reserves of Natural Gas in East

16) Barrows Company의 동의를 받아서 전재.

Kalimantan for liquefaction and sale as LNG under the MOA is estimated to be .3243 trillion standard cubic feet ("t.s.c.f."). Such quantity is herein referred to as the "MOA Net Gas Requirement". The MOA Net Gas Requirement is based on the Fixed Quantities which Buyer has committed to purchase pursuant to the terms of the MOA.

2.2 VICO Contract Gas. PERTAMINA and Contractors hereby commit and agree to supply and deliver from proved economically recoverable reserves of Natural Gas in specific fields within the VICO Contract Area sufficient Natural Gas (and LNG resulting from the liquefaction thereof) to meet a portion of the MOA Net Gas Requirement over the term of this Supply Agreement consisting of 0.0700 ts.c.f., or 21.5956% thereof. Such quantities of net Natural Gas committed to be supplied pursuant to this Supply Agreement are herein referred to as the "VICO Contract Gas", and the above-stated percentage is herein referred to as the "Producers' Percentage". The specific fields from which the VICO Contract Gas will be committed are identified in the supplemental memorandum entered into among PERTAMINA, Contractors and the production sharing contractors in the Other Contract Areas pursuant to the Memorandum of Understanding Re: Supply Agreements and Package V Sales dated October 5, 1994 (the "Package V Supplemental Memorandum"). The VICO participating fields and the quantities in each field comprising the VICO Contract Gas are as follows:

<TABLE>
Participating Fields Quantity of Gas (t.s.c.f.)

The quantities committed from each field are subject to revision from time to time, as the reserves from the fields may be updated, and as additional data from deliverability studies and otherwise become available.

2.3 Other Contract Gas. To meet the balance of the MOA Net Gas Requirement, constituting 0.2543 t.s.c.f., or 78.4044% thereof, sufficient Natural Gas (and LNG resulting from the liquefaction thereof) will be committed for supply and delivery by PERTAMINA and its production sharing contractors from proved economically recoverable reserves of Natural Gas in the Other Contract Areas by separate supply agreements, similar hereto and compatible herewith, executed and delivered concurrently herewith (such amounts are herein collectively referred to as the "Other Contract Gas"). The specific fields from which the Other Contract Gas will be committed are also identified in the Package V Supplemental Memorandum.

2.4 DeGolyer and MacNaughton Certification. The amounts of net Natural Gas constituting the VICO Contract Gas and the Other Contract Gas are part of the estimates of proved recoverable reserves of Natural Gas as certified by the independent consultant firm of DeGolyer and MacNaughton in written statements based on data available on May 31, 1994. The quantities for the VICO Contract Gas and the Other Contract Gas set forth in Sections 2,2 and 2.3 hereof and the Producers' Percentage were established by PERTAMINA at a meeting on May 29, 1995 of the East Kalimantan Gas Reserves Management Committee.

ARTICLE 3 COORDINATION OF GAS SUPPLY

The VICO Contract Gas and the Other Contract Gas may be produced from participating fields at times and production rates which may change from time to time during the term hereof so as to secure the optimal ultimate recovery of Natural Gas. The supply of Natural Gas from the VICO Contract Area and the Other Contract Areas will be coordinated by PERTAMINA so as to conserve and permit full utilization of such Natural Gas. The sources of supply, producing rates, quality of gas, metering and related matters shall be matters for study by the East Kalimantan Gas Reserves Management Committee, consisting of representatives from PERTAMINA, VICO, TOTAL Indonesie and Unocal

Indonesia Company.

ARTICLE 4 ADMINISTRATION, INSURANCE AND CONSULTATION

4.1 MOA. PERTAMINA shall be responsible for the due and prompt administration of the MOA for the benefit of PERTAMINA and Contractors. All matters which affect the MOA or the sale, transportation and delivery of LNG thereunder will be administered by a representative to be appointed by PERTAMINA and the representative appointed by Contractors under Article 9 hereof. It is understood, however, that it will be necessary from time to time for PERTAMINA, as seller under the MOA, to take certain administrative and operational actions without prior consultation where immediate action is required. Contractors will be promptly advised of any such action.

4.2 Insurance. PERTAMINA shall ensure that the interests of it and each Contractor in respect of each ex-ship cargo of LNG transported by PERTAMINA from the Bontang Plant to Buyer shall be adequately insured pursuant to arrangements mutually agreed to by PERTAMINA and each Contractor. PERTAMINA and each Contractor shall be entitled to receive its Production Sharing Percentage of the Producers' Percentage of any proceeds paid under a marine insurance policy covering an ex-ship cargo of LNG being transported from the Bontang Plant. Such proceeds shall be remitted by the insurer directly to the bank designated as Trustee pursuant to Article 6 hereof.

4.3 Consultation. PERTAMINA and Contractors agree to consult with each other freely on all matters relating to the MOA. PERTAMINA and Contractors shall confer and agree as to any amendment to the MOA or to any permitted action or election thereunder which constitutes a material adjustment in the quantities of LNG to be sold and delivered thereunder or a change in the terms thereof. At the request of any party hereto, a memorandum evidencing any such agreement shall be prepared as soon as feasible and signed by each party hereto.

ARTICLE 5 TITLE, DELIVERY AND INVOICING

5.1 Title. PERTAMINA will cause the LNG resulting from the liquefaction of the VICO Contract Gas and the Other Contract Gas to be delivered to Buyer at the "Delivery Point" as that term is defined in the MOA. Title to each Contractor's share of the LNG resulting from the liquefaction of the VICO Contract Gas shall pass to PERTAMINA at the same time as the passage of title from PERTAMINA to Buyer pursuant to the MOA.

5.2 Delivery and Invoicing. At the time of delivery of each cargo of LNG to Buyer at the relevant "Delivery Point", PERTAMINA will furnish Contractors with appropriate documentation to evidence the quantity and quality of LNG delivered, together with copies of the invoices to Buyer in respect of the sale of LNG in question. PERTAMINA will also furnish Contractors with a copy of each invoice or billing delivered to Buyer on account of interest or other payment obligation of Buyer pursuant to the MOA concurrently with its being furnished to Buyer. Calculation of the Contract Sales Price as provided for in the MOA, the amount of sales invoices and other billings to Buyer, and any adjustments, shall be reviewed and approved by PERTAMINA and Contractors prior to presentation to Buyer.

ARTICLE 6 ENTITLEMENT AND PAYMENT

6.1 Contractor Entitlement. The amounts to be paid to each Contractor for its share of the LNG resulting from the liquefaction of Natural Gas to be supplied under this Supply Agreement shall be its Production Sharing Percentage of the Producers' Percentage of the sum of:

(a) all amounts to be paid by Buyer to PERTAMINA for LNG sold and delivered

under the MOA;
(b) all other amounts which Buyer shall become obligated to pay pursuant to the MOA with regard to deliveries of LNG thereunder including, but not limited to, any interest accruing on overdue invoice payments;
(c) amounts payable by insurers in respect of LNG resulting from the liquefaction of the VICO Contract Gas and the Other Contract Gas; and
(d) interest earned on any of the amounts referred to in this Section

6.2 PERTAMINA Assignment of Contractor Percentage Share. In order to arrange for the receipt by each Contractor of the payments to which such Contractor is entitled under Section 6.1 hereof, PERTAMINA hereby assigns to each Contractor that Contractor's Production Sharing Percentage of the Producers' Percentage of all amounts referred to in Section 6.1 hereof.

6.3 Method of Payment. Throughout the term of this Supply Agreement, all those payments referred to in Section 6.1 hereof shall be paid in U.S. Dollars, directly to BankAmerica International in New York City (or such other leading bank in the United States as shall be selected by PERTAMINA and approved by Contractor) pursuant to a Trustee and Paying Agent Agreement the parties to which shall be PERTAMINA, Contractors, the production sharing contractors in the Other Contract Areas and the Trustee thereunder. Amounts so received by the Trustee shall be used for payment of: (i) Financing Costs; (ii) an agreed portion of Plant Operating Costs; (iii) Transportation Costs in respect of the ex-ship cargos; and (iv) other costs approved by PERTAMINA and Contractors. Amounts received by the Trustee, to the extent that they are not used for payment of the costs referred to in the preceding sentence, shall, insofar as they are applicable to the VICO Contract Gas, be disbursed to PERTAMINA and each Contractor in accordance with its Production Sharing Percentage at a bank or banks of its choice.

6.4 Contractors' Right to Payment. The right of Contractors to the payments provided for in this Article 6 shall extend throughout the term of this Supply Agreement and shall not be affected by the production rates or sources of Natural Gas supplied from the VICO Contract Gas or the Other Contract Gas from time to time during the term hereof.

ARTICLE 7 DELIVERABILITY

7.1 Oversupply of VICO Contract Gas. If the quantities of net Natural Gas produced from the participating fields within the VICO Contract Area and delivered pursuant to this Supply Agreement exceed in the aggregate the quantity of the VfCO Contract Gas, the Producers' Percentage (and the percentage of the revenues to be paid to PERTAMINA and Contractors hereunder) will not be increased, and Contractors, together with PERTAMINA, will be credited with and have the right to receive revenue from future marketing opportunities in respect of a quantity of net Natural Gas from reserves in the Other Contract Areas equal to such excess quantities.

7.2 Shortfall of VICO Contract Gas. If the quantities of net Natural Gas produced from the participating fields within the VICO Contract Area and delivered pursuant to this Supply Agreement are in the aggregate less than the quantity of the VICO Contract Gas, the Producers' Percentage (and the percentage of the revenues to be paid to PERTAMINA and Contractors hereunder) will not be reduced, and the production sharing contractors in the Other Contract Areas have the right to receive revenue from future marketing opportunities in respect of a quantity of net Natural Gas from reserves in the VICO Contract Area equal to excess quantities delivered from sources within the Gas Supply Area.

ARTICLE 8 ARBITRATION AND GOVERNING LAW

8.1 Arbitration. All disputes arising in connection with this Supply Agreement shall be finally settled by arbitration conducted in the English language in Paris, France, by three arbitrators under the Rules of Arbitration of the International Chamber of Commerce. Judgment upon the award rendered may be entered in any court having jurisdiction, or application may be made to such court for a juridical acceptance of the award and an order of enforcement, as the case may be.

8.2 Governing Law. This Supply Agreement shall be governed by and interpreted in accordance with the laws of the State of New York, United States of America,

ARTICLE 9 CONTRACTORS'REPRESENTATIVE

VICO is designated representative by Contractors for performance on behalf of Contractors of their obligation under Section 4.1 hereof and for the giving of notices, responses or other communications to and from Contractors under this Supply Agreement. Such representative may be changed by written notice to such effect from Contractors to PERTAMINA.

ARTICLE 10 NOTICES

ARTICLE 11 MISCELLANEOUS

11.1 Amendment. This Supply Agreement shall not be amended or modified except by written agreement signed by the parties hereto.

11.2 Successors and Assigns. This Supply Agreement shall inure to the benefit of, and be binding upon PERTAMINA and each Contractor, their respective successors and assigns, provided that this Supply Agreement shall be assignable by a Contractor only if such Contractor concurrently assigns to the same assignee an equal interest in the Production Sharing Contracts.

11.3 Exclusivity. The parties to this Supply Agreement shall be the only persons or entities entitled to enforce the obligations hereunder of the other parties hereto, and no persons or entities not parties to this Supply Agreement shall have the right to enforce any of the obligations hereunder of any of the partieshereto.

11.4 Headings and Subheadings. The Article headings and subheadings used herein are for convenience of reference only.

IN WITNESS WHEREOF, PERTAMINA and Contractors have caused their duly authorized representatives to execute this Supply Agreement as of the day and year first written above.

* * * * *

LNG 판매계약(LNG Sale and Purchase Agreement)은 개개의 경우에 따라서 다른 내용을 가지지만, 공통으로 발견되는 규정은 파이프라인 가스장기공급계약과 유사하다.

기간은 20-25년으로서 장기공급계약은 LNG시설(train)을 건설하는 데 필요한 막대한 자금조달에 필수적이다. 공급개시일은 통상 LNG프로젝트가 green field프로젝트이기 때문에[17)]

17) 이에 대비되는 용어는 brownfield로서 기존의 시설을 개비하거나 업그레이드하는 프로젝트이다. 기존시

최초 LNG가 공급되는 시점을 의미한다. 수송과 관련된 비용 및 화물의 위험 이전시점은 INCOTERMS상의 FOB, DES, CIF 등이 주로 사용된다.

구입수량은 연단위로 특정되지만(ADQ) 시운전기와 구축기에 특별한 합의가 있을 수 있고 upward flexibility, downward tolerance, make-up 양도 정한다. 또한 ADQ를 정하기 위한 절차와 시기 등에 관한 일정규정을 둔다. 파이프라인 가스장기공급계약과 마찬가지로 의무구매량(Take-or-pay)는 LNG가스공급계약에서도 반드시 들어가는 바, ADQ의 몇 퍼센트가 될지는 당사자간 협상에 달려 있고 TOP를 지불하면 미구입수량은 미래시점으로 이전, 구매할 수 있는 make-up은 통상 허용된다. 1980년대 미국에서의 가스수요감소 때문에 파이프라인업자가 TOP를 거절하였듯이 LNG공급자도 유사한 상황에 처한 경험이 있는 만큼[18] 시장상황에 대비한 계약규정이 필요하다.

가격이 제일 어려운 문제로 다른 경쟁적 연료가격을 지수화하여 이들의 변동에 따른 가격조정을 예정하고 있지만 언제나 만족스러운 것도 아니고 분쟁을 예방할 수 있는 것도 아니어서 가격재협상규정(price reopener)이나 시장상황을 이유로 한 해지규정(market-out)을 두기도 한다.

모든 장기계약과 마찬가지로 불가항력규정은 지극히 예민한 부분이다. 불가항력이 발생한 경우의 계약당사자의 의무나 절차도 중요하지만 요는 특정상황 내지 사건이 불가항력을 구성하는 것인지 여부가 언제나 다툼의 여지가 있는 만큼 조심스럽게 접근하여야 할 것이다.

계약상 채무불이행의 경우 장기공급계약에서는 여러 가지 상황을 고려하여야 하기 때문에 그 구제책 역시 다양하여야 할 것이다. TOP는 일정한 금액의 지급을 보상하면 되지만 그 이외의 경우 단순히 채무불이행의 통지와 해지만으로는 불충분한 경우가 많을 것이다.

계약상 공급자와 구매자간 권리의무의 균형점은 결국 시장에서의 LNG의 경쟁력에 따라서 결정될 것이다. 2009년 AIPN은 LNG공급계약 모델을 제시하였으며 Master Agreement와 확인메모로 구성되어 있다. 다른 AIPN모델계약과 마찬가지로 표준적인 규정과 함께 여러가지 optional provisions, alternatives를 제시하고 있다. 예를 들면 불가항력의 정의는 아래와 같다.

AIPN Model GPA Force Majeure Clause[19]

14.1.2 Force Majeure means for a Party that has acted as a Reasonable and

설에 의하여 이미 오염되었다는 의미에서 brown이라는 단어를 사용한다.

18) *Societe Nationale Algerienne v. Distrigas Corp.*, 80 B.R. 606 (D.C. Mass. 1987).

19) AIPN의 동의를 받아 전재.

Prudent Operator, any act, event, or circumstance, whether of the kind described herein or otherwise, that is not reasonably within the control of the Party and that prevents or delays the Party's performance of any obligations affecting (1) Seller's Facilities; (2) LNG Tankers; and (3) Buyer's Facilities, or otherwise.

14.1.2.1 By way of illustration and subject to satisfaction of the conditions specified in the foregoing paragraph of this Article 14.1.2, Force Majeure may include circumstances of the following kind:

(a) fire, flood, atmospheric disturbance, lightning, storm, hurricane. cyclone, typhoon, tidal wave, tornado, earthquake, volcanic eruption, landslide, soil erosion, subsidence, washout, epidemic, or other natural disaster or act of God;
(b) acts of war (whether declared or undeclared), invasion, armed conflict, embargo, revolution, rebellion, sabotage, acts or threats of terrorism, riot, civil war, blockade, insurrection, acts of public enemies, civil disturbances, or sanctions on the import or export of goods, services or technology;
(c) chemical contamination, ionizing radiation or contamination, or radioactivity from any nuclear fuel or from nuclear waste or from the combustion of nuclear waste, or the combustion of nuclear, radioactive, toxic, explosive, or other hazardous properties of any explosive assembly or nuclcar component;
(d) strike, lockout, or other industrial disturbances;
(e) any change in Law after the Confirm Date, or a change in the interpretation or application of existing Law after the Confirm Date, subject to Article 14.1.2.2(d); and
(f) acts or omissions of a Governmental Authority, subject to Articles 14.1.2.2(e) and 14.1.2.2(0)

14.1.2.2 Notwithstanding the foregoing, Force Majeure does not include:

(a) the ability of Buyer or Seller to obtain better economic terms for LNG from an alternative supplier or buyer, as applicable;
(b) any change in the market or demand for LNG or Natural Gas or events primarily affecting individual downstream customer facilities;
(c) events effecting any individual pipeline or ancillary facility that is not part of a Connecting Pipeline;
(d) any change in Law after the Confirm Date or a change in the interpretation or application of existing Law after the Confirm Date that does not prevent performance, but merely renders such performance more costly;
(e) the following acts or omissions of a Governmental Authority related to a Governmental Approval: (1) the original or any amended terms of any Governmental Approval; (2) any action or inaction by a Governmental Authority pursuant to any Governmental Approval; or (3) the failure to obtain or the withdrawal of any Governmental Approval, in each case of which the Person claiming Force Majeure was aware (or should have been aware acting as a Reasonable and Prudent Operator) as of the Confirm Date of the relevant Confirmation Memorandum, to the extent such Person could have applied for, obtained, maintained, or extended any such Governmental Approval;

OPTIONAL PROVISION

(f) acts of a Governmental Authority that affect solely or primarily the affected Party and are not generally applicable to public and private entities doing business in the same country;

OPTIONAL PROVISION

(g) natural depletion or the absence of economically recoverable Natural Gas from, the Gas Supply Area; and

OPTIONAL PROVISION

(h) loss of, damage to. failure of, or unavailability of the Upstream Facilities.

14.1.3 SELECT ONE ALTERNATIVE

ALTERNATIVE 1

Notwithstanding Article 14.1.2.1, any act, event, or circumstance causing nonperformance by a Third Party of obligations owed to a Party that causes such Party to be unable to perform pursuant to this Agreement shall be a Force Majeure event hereunder for such Party, if and to the extent that it is of a kind or character that, if it had happened to that Party, would have been Force Majeure hereunder.

ALTERNATIVE 2

For the purposes of this Article 14.1.2, an event will not be considered to be beyond the reasonable control of Seller or Buyer unless

14.1.3.1 in the case of Seller, it is beyond the reasonable control of Seller and the Seller Control Entities; or

14.1.3.2 in the case of Buyer, it is beyond the reasonable control of Buyer and the Buyer Control Entities.

14.1.4 A force Majeure shall not relieve a Party of its obligation to pay sums of money due or that might become due pursuant to an Agreement except to the event expressly provided in this Agreement.

제04편

국제에너지자원 분쟁

제4편은 국제에너지자원의 개발을 위한 탐사, 운영, 판매거래와 관련하여 발생한 분쟁에 대한 개관이다. 국제에너지개발의 주체는 국가 또는 국가가 설립한 특수법인이기 때문에, 에너지개발이란 행위의 성격은 국가공권력 행사로 볼 수도 있는 까닭에, 그리고 자원보유국의 특수한 법전통 때문에 에너지개발계약의 해석을 둘러싼 많은 분쟁이 있었다.

제9장은 과거 양허계약을 체결하였던 자원보유국이 이들 자원을 국유화 내지 잠행성 국유화를 단행하면서 기존의 양허계약하에서 투자한 외국인을 어떻게 보상할 것인지에 대한 논의가 주된 내용이다. 또한, 자원보유국에서의 정치적 변화로부터 에너지개발계약을 보호하기 위하여 어떤 조치가 가능한 것인지에 대하여도 논의한다.

제10장은 자원탐사나 개발을 위한 계약의 당사자는 자원보유국 내지 자원보유국내 국영기업이라는 점에서 이들과 국제적 에너지개발프로젝트에 투자한 IOC간 계약의 해석 내지 이행여부와 관련하여 다툼이 발생한 경우 어떤 특수한 법적 문제가 발생할지와 구체적으로 이러한 분쟁을 해결할지에 대한 구체적 계약조항을 어떻게 합의할 것인지에 대한 논의이다. 분쟁해결방법은 크게 중재와 소송이 있을 것인데, 각각의 장단점도 살펴본다.

제11장은 자원보유국 내지 자원보유국내 국영기업이 계약당사자라는 점은 이들 국가가 자원개발 내지 계약해석에 관한 자세한 법제도를 가지지 못한 경우도 많다는 점과 더불어 준거법의 선택을 계약협상의 예민한 문제점으로 떠오르게 만든다. 과거 준거법선택조항은 어떠한 예들이 있고 분쟁시 어떻게 해결되었는지 구체적인 사례를 중심으로 살펴보고 협상시 어떠한 합의가 가능한지, 어떻게 예측가능성을 높일 수 있을지도 살펴본다.

제 9 장

외국인투자와 정치경제적 위험

1. 국유화의 법적 근거

모든 국제거래에는 계약상대방이 계약상 의무를 이행하지 않을 위험뿐만 아니라 정부당국의 일방적 조치로 인하여 투자의 전제가 흔들릴 위험도 있다. 자원개발을 위한 국제거래는 계약의 상대방이 바로 정부라는 점과 석유자원이라는 개발대상의 특성상 자원 내지 탐사권 자체의 국유화나 이에 가까운 법적 조치의 위험을 내포하고 있으며 실제 이들 위험이 현실화된 많은 사례가 있다. Mexico가 1938년 헌법개정과 함께 국유화조치를 취한 이래 1951년 이란이 Anglo-Iranian Oil Company를 국유화하였고 1970년대에는 Lybia와 Kuwait가, 가장 최근에는 Venezuela가 국유화조치를 취한 바 있다. 국유화에 대비되는 접근방법은 Saudi Arabia와 UAE의 협상을 통한 지분확대이었다.

국가주권의 행사로서의 자원국유화는 주권의 정당한 행사로서 그 적법성이 국제사회에서 누차 확인되었다. 1962년 UN총회 결의 1803은 석유자원은 공공재로서, 안보상 또는 국가의 이익을 위하여 국유화가 가능하다고 선언하고 있으며 이는 1974년 결의 3201(NIEO)과 결의 3281(Charter)로서 재차 확인되었다. 그러나, 국유화가 적법하기 위하여는 그 목적에 있어서 공공의 이익을 위하여[1] 행하여진 것으로서 그 방법이 비차별적 · 비자의적이어야[2] 한다.

1) Martin Domke, *Foreign Nationalzations: Some Aspects of Contemporary International Law*, 55 AM. J. INT'L L. 585 (1961).

2) A.F.M. Maniruzzaman, *Expropriation of Alien Property and the Principle of Non-Discrimination in International Law of Foreign Investment: An Overview*, 8 J. TRANSNAT'L L & POL'Y 57 (1998).

United Nations General Assembly Resolution 1803 (XVII) of 14 December 1962, Permanent Sovereignty over Natural Resources

The General Assembly, ...

Bearing in mind its resolution 1314 (XIII) of 12 December 1958, by which it established the Commission on Permanent Sovereignty over Natural Resources and instructed it to conduct a full survey of the status of permanent sovereignty over natural wealth and resources as a basic constituent of the right to self-determination, with recommendations, where necessary, for its strengthening, and decided further that, in the conduct of the full survey of the status of the permanent sovereignty of peoples and nations over their natural wealth and resources, due regard should be paid to the rights and duties of States under international law and to the importance of encouraging international co-operation in the economic development of developing countries,

Bearing in mind its resolution 1515 (XV) of 15 December 1960, in which it recommended that the sovereign right of every State to dispose of its wealth and its natural resources should be respected,

Considering that any measure in this respect must be based on the recognition of the inalienable right of all States freely to dispose of their natural wealth and resources in accordance with their national interests, and on respect for the economic independence of States, ...

Declares that:

4. Nationalization, expropriation or requisitioning shall be based on grounds or reasons of public utility, security or the national interest which are recognized as overriding purely individual or private interests, both domestic and foreign. In such cases the owner shall be paid appropriate compensation, in accordance with the rules in force in the State taking such measures in the exercise of its sovereignty and in accordance with international law. In any case where the question of compensation gives rise to a controversy, the national jurisdiction of the State taking such measures shall be exhausted. However, upon agreement by sovereign States and other parties concerned, settlement of the dispute should be made through arbitration or international adjudication.

United Nations Declaration on the Establishment of a New International Economic Order (U.N.G.A. Res. 3201 (1974))

Solemnly proclaim our united determination to work urgently for the Establishment of a New International Economic Order based on equity, sovereign equality, interdependence, common interest and cooperation among all States, irrespective of their economic and social systems which shall correct inequalities and redress existing injustices, make it possible to eliminate the widening gap between the developed and the developing countries and ensure steadily accelerating economic and social development and peace and justice for present and future generations, and, to that end, declare:

4. The new international economic order should be founded on full respect for the following principles:

a. Sovereign equality of States, self-determination of all peoples, inadmissibility of the acquisition of territories by force, territorial integrity and non-interference in the internal affairs of other States; ...

d. The right of every country to adopt the economic and social system that it deems the most appropriate for its own development and not to be subjected to discrimination of any kind as a result;

e. Full permanent sovereignty of every State over its natural resources and all economic activities. In order to safeguard these resources, each State is entitled to exercise effective control over them and their exploitation with means suitable to its own situation, including the right to nationalization or transfer of ownership to its nationals, this right being an expression of the full permanent sovereignty of the State. No State may be subjected to economic, political or any other type of coercion to prevent the free and full exercise of this inalienable right;

f. The right of all States, territories and peoples under foreign occupation, alien and colonial domination or apartheid to restitution and full compensation for the exploitation arid depletion of, and damages to, the natural resources and all other resources of those States, territories and peoples; ...

h. The right of the developing countries and the peoples of territories under colonial and racial domination and foreign occupation to achieve their liberation and to regain effective control over their natural resources and economic activities;

i. The extending of assistance to developing countries, peoples and territories which are under colonial and alien domination, foreign occupation, racial discrimination or apartheid or are subjected to economic, political or any other type of coercive measures to obtain from them the subordination of the exercise of their sovereign rights and to secure from them advantages of any kind, and to neo colonialism in all its forms, and which have established or are endeavouring to establish effective control over their natural resources and economic activities that have been or are still under foreign control;

United Nations Charter of Economic Rights and Duties of States (U.N.G.A. Res. 3281 (1975))

Chapter II. Economic Rights and Duties of States

Article 1. Every State has the sovereign and inalienable right to choose its economic system as well as its political, social and cultural systems in accordance with the will of its people, without outside interference, coercion or threat in any form whatsoever.

Article 2.

(1) Every State has and shall freely exercise full permanent sovereignty, including possession, use and disposal, over all its wealth, natural resources and economic activities.

(2) Each State has the right:

(a) To regulate and exercise authority over foreign investment within its national jurisdiction in accordance with its laws and regulations and in conformity with its national objectives and priorities. No State shall be compelled to grant preferential treatment to foreign investment;

(b) To regulate and supervise the activities of transnational corporations within its national jurisdiction and take measures to ensure that such activities comply with its laws, rules and regulations and conform with its economic and social policies. Transnational corporations shall not intervene in the internal affairs of a host State. Every State should, with full regard for its sovereign rights, cooperate with other States in the exercise of the right set forth in this subparagraph;

(c) To nationalize, expropriate or transfer ownership of foreign property, in which case appropriate compensation should be paid by the State adopting such measures, taking into account its relevant laws and regulations and all circumstances that the State considers pertinent. In any case where the question of compensation gives rise to a controversy, it shall be settled under the domestic law of the nationalizing State and by its tribunals, unless it is freely and mutually agreed by all States concerned that other peaceful means be sought on the basis of the sovereign equality of States and in accordance with the principle of free choice of means.

2. 국유화에 대한 보상

천연자원의 국유화가 주권의 일부라는 것에 대하여는 국제사회가 공통된 의견을 나누고 있으나 그러한 조치의 결과로서 투자자산을 상실한 투자자를 어떻게 보상하여야 하는지에 관하여 국가간 이견이 지속되고 있다. Charter가 적정 보상(appropriate compensation)을 언급하고 있지만 Charter의 채택에 찬성하지 않은 많은 투자국이 있고 또한 이들이 국제규범으로서의 적정보상을 인정한다고 하더라도 적정보상이 과거 PCIJ나[3] 투자국의 입장인[4] 공정보상과 동일한 것인지, 아니면 새로운 기준으로서의 적정보상이 무엇을 의미하는 것인지에 대하여 이견이 있을 수 있다. 따라서, 보상의 기준에 관하여는 많은 다툼이 있다.[5] 물론 보상의 기준 이전에 보상의 방법으로서 계약상대방인 국가에게 원래 계약하의 채무이행을 구하거나 원래 상태로의 복귀를 명할 수 있는지 여부가 이론상 문제가 될 수 있으나 실제 이를 명한 사례는 극히 드물다.[6] 아래 리바아와 쿠웨이트 관련 중재판정에 나타난 보상의 기준에 관한 의견부분을 살핀다.[7]

BP Exploration Co. (Lybia) Ltd. v. The Government of the Libyan Arab Republic (1973)[8]

[리비아는 1955년 Concession 65로 미국인 헌트에게 50년 독점탐사개발권을 부여하였

3) Factory of Chorzow (Ger. v. Pol) ¶ 124 "just price of what was expropriated," 1928 PCIJ No. 17 (Judgment of Sept. 13, 1928).

4) ALI, RESTATEMENT (THIRD) OF THE FOREIGN RELATIONS LAW OF THE UNITED STATES. § 712 (1) "just compensation."

5) 2차대전후 자본수출국과 과거 식민지지배를 받았던 자원보유국간 대이념논쟁(Great Ideological Debate)에 관하여는 Patrick M. Norton, *A Law of the Future or a Law of the Past? Modern Tribunals and the International Law of Expropriation,* 85 AM. J. INT'L L. 474 (1991).

6) reparation의 일반적 한계에 관하여는 R. Doak Bishop, 위 주 4-54 전게서, 1246-52.

7) Res. 1803 이전 "*Premodern*"사건에 관하여는 Patrick M. Norton, *A Law of the Future or a Law of the Past? Modern Tribunals and the International Law of Expropriation,* 85 AM. J. INT'L L. 474-476 (1991).

8) 53 I.L.R. 297.

고 1960년 BP Lybia는 헌트로부터 50% 지분을 매수하였다. 리비아는 1971. 12. 7. BP Lybia의 모든 자산을 국유화하고 이어 1973. 9. 1. 9개 다른 IOC의 51% 지분을 국유화하였으며 1974. 2. 11. 9개사 중 3개사의 나머지 49% 지분마저 완전히 국유화하였다. 이들 세 번에 걸친 국유화조치와 관련하여 3개의 중재판정이 내려진 바 있다.[9)]]

Clause 28 of the Concession provided for the settlement of disputes by arbitration and stated that the Concession shall be governed by and interpreted in accordance with the principles of law of Libya common to the principles of international law and in the absence of such common principles then by and in accordance with the general principles of law, including such of those principles as may have been applied by international tribunals.

3. Applicable Law

Paragraph 7 of Clause 28 of the BP Concession, quoted in Part I above, stipulates which law is to govern the agreement. While the provision generates practical difficulties in its implementation, it offers guidance in a negative sense by excluding the relevance of any single municipal legal system as such. To the extent possible, the Tribunal will apply the clause according to its clear and apparent meaning. Natural as this would be in any event, such an interpretation is the more compelling as the contractual document is of a standardised type prescribed by the Respondent. The governing law clause moreover was the final product of successive changes made in the Libyan petroleum legislation in the decade between 1955 and 1965 by which the relevance of Libyan law was progressively reduced.

[49] In paragraph 7 of Clause 28, reference is made to the principles of law of Libya common to the principles of international law, and only if such common principles do not exist with respect to a particular matter, to the general principles of law. The Claimant argues, in the first of three alternative submissions, that international law alone is applicable.

This argument has two aspects.

(a) After indicating that a relevant distinction exists between "principles" and "rules"

9) Libya관련 중재판정 3개의 비교분석은 Robert B. von Mehren/P. Nicholas Kourides, *International Arbitrations Between States and Foreign Private Parties: The Libyan Nationalization Cases,* 75 AM. J. INT'L L. 476 (1981).

— a line of reasoning which is not further pursued in this connection — the Claimant states:

... the acceptance of a principle must he supported by both Libyan and international law if it is to govern the Concession. Therefore if the conduct of a parry to the Concession cannot be justified by the principles of both Libyan law and international law, it is not justifiable under the Concession. It is justifiable only if the principles of both systems of law — Libyan and international — support it. Thus conduct which is a breach of the principles of international law must necessarily be a breach of the Concession, even if not in breach of the principles of Libyan law.

This reasoning is dearly incomplete since it entirely leaves out of the picture the direction which follows from paragraph 7 of Clause 28 that conduct etc. in the last analysis should be tested by reference to the general principles of law. It is not correct to say that "a principle must be supported by both Libyan law and international law [in order to be] justifiable under the Concession" and that conduct "is justifiable only if principles of both systems of law — Libyan and international — support it". The principle may still be acceptable, and the conduct justifiable, if supported by the general principles of law. To take a few examples, one system may prescribe that payments shall be made in one currency and the other system that payment shall be made in a different currency. Clearly, in such a case, under paragraph 7 of Clause 28 the general principles of law must provide the answer to the question what currency is to be used. If one system imposes automatic, obligatory limitation after the lapse of a given period, but the other does not, again the general principles of law will be resorted to for the purpose of determining whether a claim is barred by the lapse of time. Similarly, if one system contains the principle that any default by a debtor entitles a creditor to accelerate payment of principal and interest with immediate effect, but the other system does not offer the creditor such a remedy, the general principles of law will govern the issue respecting the availability of that remedy. And so the situation must be also in regard to breach of contract. If a particular action by a party amounts to breach of contract under one system but not under the other, the issue is one which can only be decided by reference to the general principles of law. Thus, die first part of the Claimant's argument must be rejected. It is not sufficient for the Claimant to show that the conduct of the Respondent is a breach of international law as a basis for maintaining a claim based on breach of contract. In the event that international law and Libyan law conflict on that issue, the question is to be resolved by the application of the general principles of law.

(b) Secondly, The Claimant argues that since the Parties have expressly excluded the direct and sole application of Libyan law, but have made reference to the general principles of law, and since "a" system must govern, "the only system that is left is public international law".

The Tribunal cannot accept the submission that public international law applies, for paragraph 7 of Clause 28 does not so stipulate. Nor does the BP Concession itself constitute the sole source of law controlling the relationship between the Parties. The governing system of law is what that clause expressly provides, viz. in the absence of principles common to the law of Libya and international law, the general principles of law, including such of those principles as may have been applied by international tribunals.

4. Breach of Contract

No elaborate reasons are required to resolve the third issue in this case. The BP Nationalisation Law, and the actions taken thereunder by the Respondent do constitute a fundamental breach of the BP Concession as they amount to a total repudiation of the agreement and the obligations of the Respondent thereunder, and, on the basis of rules of applicable systems of law too elementary and voluminous to require or permit citation, the Tribunal so holds. Further, the taking by the Respondent of the property, rights and interests of the Claimant clearly violates public international law as it was made for purely extraneous political reasons and was arbitrary and discriminatory in character. Nearly two years have now passed since the nationalisation, and the fact that no offer of compensation has been made indicates that the taking was also confiscatory.

The real issues of substance which require a resolution by the Tribunal are novel in character and scope in that they have not previously been scrutinised judicially. While certain trends in the law are discernible, there are no precise and clear rules that provide an obvious answer to any of the issues. The facts must be appraised and the law interpreted and applied in a balanced consideration of the intrinsic merits of the case and the de facto position of the Parties.

An expropriation, nationalisation or talcing, if and when implemented in full, is an act of finality where a State has exercised its sovereign territorial power to expel a foreign enterprise and appropriate its property and other rights. No State has ever reversed such an action by granting *restitutio in integrum*, and it is unlikely that any State exercising diplomatic protection of its nationals will demand such a reversal without offering or eventually accepting the alternative remedy, exercisable at the option of the defaulting State, of reparation in the form of monetary compensation. It has rarely been suggested that the subject-matter in dispute is not property rights and interests of a purely economic nature on which, thus, a financial value can be put. It has only been argued doctrinally that, where damages are not an adequate remedy (meaning where the State demonstrably is insolvent or incapable of discharging its proper obligations), *restitutio in integrum* should be considered. The Claimant has made no submission to such effect. At times it has been indicated, also, that damages may be difficult to calculate in respect of the value of an abrogated long term contract. However, such difficulties arc not insurmountable.

The consequences of holding that a concession agreement continues in effect indefinitely despite a nationalisation which amounts to a total repudiation of the agreement by the grantor State and which partakes of the aforesaid character of finality, are complicated and perplexing in a long term perspective. Theoretically, the alleged rights of the concessionaire are not subject to limitation (the imposition by an arbitral tribunal of a rule of extinctive prescription would be purely discretionary and without an established legal basis), and hence the submissions of the Claimant in this arbitration could be made for the first time in 10, 20 or 30 years from now. Assuming that the enterprise has been carried on actively during all that time, the claim of the concessionaire eventually would not appear realistic. Even in a purely municipal law context, such an action would not be admissible since an order for turning the clock back would upset the current position too profoundly and would have unforeseeable practical consequences. The situation is the same if an award were given now to the effect that the BP Concession continues in full force and effect until terminated by the Claimant. So long as the present position in fact continues to exist, such a declaratory award would remain valid and outstanding but with the passage of time necessarily would acquire a quality of increasing absurdity. This is simply the result of what Georg Jellinek so aptly termed "die normative Kraft des Faktischen"; an acceptance of the realities of the contemporary international community.

A rule of reason therefore dictates a result which conforms both to international law, as evidenced by State practice and the law of treaties, and to the governing principle of English and American contract law. This is that, when by the exercise of sovereign power a State has committed a fundamental breach of a concession agreement by repudiating it through a nationalisation of the enterprise and its assets in a manner which implies finality, the concessionaire is not entitled to call for specific performance by the Government of the agreement and reinstatement of his contractual rights, but his sole remedy is an action for damages.

For these reasons, the Tribunal cannot accept the Claimant's principal proposition with respect to the issue now under consideration, and the Claimant cannot be granted the relief asked for in the requested Declarations Nos. 2, 3 and 4 (see Part V above); the requested Declaration No. 6, being predicated on Nos. 2 and 3, also cannot be made. The BP Concession can be said to remain in force and effect as a contractual instrument only in the sense that it forms the basis of the jurisdiction of the Tribunal and of the right 1981 of the Claimant to claim damages from the Respondent before the Tribunal.

Texaco Overseas Petroleum Co./California Asiatic Oil Co. v. The Government of the Libyan Arab Republic (1977)[10)]

86. ... As this Tribunal has already indicated, the legal value of the resolutions which are relevant to the present case can be determined on the basis of circumstances under which they were adopted and by analysis of the principles which they state:

— With respect to the first point, the absence of any binding force of the resolutions of the General Assembly of the United Nations implies that such resolutions must be accepted by the members of the United Nations in order to be legally binding. In this respect, the Tribunal notes that only Resolution 1803 (XVII) of 14 December 1962 was supported by a majority of Member States representing all of the various groups. By contrast, the other Resolutions mentioned above, and in particular those referred to in the Libyan Memorandum, were supported by a majority of States but not by any of the developed countries with market economics which carry on the largest part of international trade.

87. (2) With respect to the second point, to wit the appraisal of the legal value on the basis of the principles stated, it appears essential to this Tribunal to distinguish between those provisions stating the existence of a right on which the generality of the States has expressed agreement, and those provisions introducing new principles which were rejected by certain representative groups of States and having nothing more than a *de lege ferenda* value only in the eyes of the States which have adopted them; as far as the others are concerned, the rejection of those same principles implies that they

10) 17 I.L.M. 3 (1978).

consider them as being *contra legem*. With respect to the former, which proclaim rules recognized by the community of nations, they do not create a custom but confirm one by formulating it and specifying its scope, thereby making it possible to determine whether or not one is confronted with a legal rule. As has been noted by Ambassador Castaneda, "[such resolutions] do not create the law; they have a declaratory nature of noting what does exist" (129 R.C.A.D.L 204 (1970), at 315).

On the basis of the circumstances of adoption mentioned above and by expressing an *opinio juris communis*, Resolution 1803 (XVII) seems to this Tribunal to reflect the state of customary law existing in this field. Indeed, on the occasion of the vote on a resolution finding the existence of a customary rule, the States concerned clearly express their views. The consensus by a majority of States belonging to the various representative groups indicates without the slightest doubt universal recognition of the rules therein incorporated, i.e., with respect to nationalization and compensation the use of the rules in force in the nationalizing State, but all this in conformity with international law.

90. ...From this point of view, even though Article 2 of the Charter does not explicitly refer to international law, this Tribunal concludes that the provisions referred to in this Article do not escape all norms of international law. Article 33, paragraph 2, of this Resolution states as follows: "2. In their interpretation and application, the provisions of the present Charter are interrelated and each provision should be construed in the context of the other provisions". Now, among the fundamental elements of international economic relations quoted in the Charter, principle (j) is headed as follows: "Fulfillment in good faith of international obligations".

Analyzing the scope of these various provisions, Ambassador Castaneda, who chaired the Working Group charged with drawing up the Charter of Economic Rights and Duties of States, formally stated that the principle of performance in good faith of international obligations laid down in Chapter I(j) of the Charter applies to all matters governed by it, including, in particular, matters referred to in Article 2. Following his analysis, this particularly competent and eminent scholar concluded as follows:

> "The Charter accepts that international law may operate as a factor limiting the freedom of the State should foreign interests be affected, even though Article 2 does not state this explicitly. This stems legally from the provisions, included in other Articles of the Charter which should be interpreted and applied jointly with those of Article 2." ("La Charte des Droits et Devoirs Economiques des Etats. Note sur son Processus d'Elaboration", 20 A.F.D.I. 31 (1974), at 54.)

From this point of view, even though Article 2 of the Charter does not explicitly refer to international law, this Tribunal concludes that the provisions referred to in this Article do not escape all norms of international law. Article 33, paragraph 2, of this Resolution states as follows: "2. In their interpretation and application, the provisions of the present Charter are interrelated and each provision should be construed in the context of the other provisions". Now, among the fundamental elements of international economic relations quoted in the Charter, principle (j) is headed as follows: "Fulfillment in good faith of international obligations".

Analyzing the scope of these various provisions, Ambassador Castaneda, who chaired the Working Group charged with drawing up the Charter of Economic Rights and Duties of States, formally stated that the principle of performance in good faith of international obligations laid down in Chapter I(j) of the Charter applies to all matters governed by it, including, in particular, matters referred to in Article 2. Following his analysis, this particularly competent and eminent scholar concluded as follows:

> "The Charter accepts that international law may operate as a factor limiting the freedom of the State should foreign interests be affected, even though Article 2 does not state this explicitly. This stems legally from the provisions, included in other Articles of the Charter which should be interpreted and applied jointly with those of Article ("La Charte des Droits et Devoirs Economiques des Etats. Note sur son Processus d'Elaboration", 20 A.F.D.I. 31 (1974), at 54.)

91. Therefore, one should note that the principle of good faith, which had already been mentioned in Resolution 1803 (XVII), has an important place even in Resolution 3281 (XXIX) called "The Charter of Economic Rights and Duties of States". One should conclude that a sovereign State which nationalizes cannot disregard the commitments undertaken by the contracting State: to decide otherwise would in fact recognize that all contractual commitments undertaken by a State have been undertaken under a purely permissive condition on its part and are therefore lacking of any legal force and any binding effect.

97. (a) International case law and practice

This Tribunal should, first and foremost, recall the often cited principle laid down by the Permanent Court of International Justice in one of its judgments delivered in the *Chorzow Factory* case ([1928] P.C.I.J., Ser. A, No. 17, p. 47):

> "The essential principle contained in the actual notion of an illegal act — a principle which seems to be established by international practice and in particular by the decisions of arbitral tribunals — is that reparation must, as far

as possible, wipe out all the consequences of the illegal act and reestablish the situation which would, in all probability, have existed if that act had not been committed. Restitution in kind, or, if this is not possible, payment of a sum corresponding to the value which a restitution in kind would bear____

98. It could be claimed that, in the case where the above-mentioned principle was laid down, the principle had only the value of an *obiter dictum* and not of a true *ratio decidendi* since restitution in kind was not formally requested and the impossibility of restitution in kind had been established by agreement between the parties. But the fact remains that the principle was expressed in such general terms that it is difficult not to view it as a principle of reasoning having the value of a precedent: the very numerous quotations of this part of the opinion in doctrinal writings confirm, if this were necessary, that all authors see in it a declaration of principle. Moreover, one could mention here the explanation given by Sir Gerald Fitzmaurice as a preliminary to his individual opinion given in relation to the judgment delivered by the International Court of Justice in the *Barcelona Traction* case ([1970] ICJ. 3, at 05):

> "Although these comments can only be in the nature of '*obiter dicta*', and cannot have the authority of a judgement, yet since specific legislative action with direct binding effect is not at present possible in the international legal field, judicial pronouncements of one kind or another constitute the principal method by which the law can find some concrete measure of clarification and development...."

Libyan American Oil Company (LIAMCO) v. The Government of the Libyan Arab Republic (1977)[11]

In response to the invitation proferred by the Arbitral Tribunal, the Claimant consented on the resolutions of the U.N. General Assembly bearing on the subject matter in a Memorial which it submitted to the Tribunal at its meeting of 11 January 1977. Referring to Resolution No. 1803 of 1962, the Memorial concluded that it specifically provided for the respect of foreign investment agreements, and was in contemplation of the Parties when they entered into their Agreements of 1965. As to the Economic Charter contained in Resolution No. 3281 of 1974, it does not represent a consensus of nations and cannot be Invoked as a source of international law.

In this connection, the Arbitral Tribunal has reached the conclusion that the said

11) 20 I.L.M. 1 (1981).

Resolutions, if not a unanimous source of law, are evidence of the recent dominant trend of international opinion concerning the sovereign right of States over their natural resources, and that the said right is always subject to the respect for contractual agreements and to the obligation of coopensation, as will be explained in a later section.

This general principle is also common to international law, in which *restitutic in integrum* is conditioned by the possibility of performance, and consequently hindered by its impossibility. Such impossibility is in fact most usual in the international field. For this reason, it has been asserted that "it is impossible to compel a State to make restitution, this would constitute in fact an intolerable interference in the internal sovereignty of States" (V/ Friedman, op. cit., p. 214).

However, the controversial question in this connection is the scope of compensation and the manner of its determination as regards the incorporeal property of the concession rights *per se*, and whether or not that determination should include the loss of profits (*lucrum cessans*). On this important question there were substantial divergences of view between municipal law and some international assertions in theory and rulings in practice.

"prompt, adequate and effective" compensation for the nationalised property of an alien. This is the formula adopted by the U.S. State Department in its various statements to which it was alluded in a previous section. "Adequate" compensation, in particular, had to include "*lucrum cessans*, namely the loss of future profits from property such as invested capital or a concessionary right granted for a specific number of years" (V. White, op. cit., p. 15).

This classical doctrine was not always accepted neither in the inter-war period nor after World War II. Adequate compensation as including loss of profits, such as was awarded in the old above mentioned arbitral decisions (e.g. *in Delogoa* and *Shufeldt* cases), was no more acceptable as an imperative general rule. It retains only the value of a technical rule for the assessment of compensation, and a useful guide in reaching settlement agreement, as was well and justly asserted (V. White, op. cit., p.l8). It stands only as a maximum rarely attained in practice (V. Katzarov, op. cit., p.447).

In conclusion, it may be safely laid down that it is lawful to nationalize concession rights before the expiry of the concession term, provided that the measure be not discriminatory nor in breach of treaty, and provided that compensation be duly paid.

American Independent Oil Company (AMINOIL) v. Government of the State of Kuwait (1982)[12)]

[쿠웨이트정부는 1948년 AMINOIL과 양허계약을 체결하였다. 1961년 독립한 쿠웨이트는 1974년 쿠웨이트 내 다른 석유사 KOC와 AOC의 60% 주식과 양허계약상 60% 지분을 취득하였고, 1975년 KOC의 나머지 40% 주식과 지분도 국유화하였다. 따라서 AMINOIL이 쿠웨이트 내 유일한 민간석유사업자가 되었다. 쿠웨이트정부과 AMINOIL은 수년에 걸친 양허계약의 재협상에 실패, 쿠웨이트 정부는 1977년 명령으로 양허계약을 해지하였다.]

144. The Tribunal considers that the determination of the amount of an award of "appropriate" compensation is better carried out by means of an enquiry into all the circumstances relevant to the particular concrete case, than through abstract theoretical discussion. Moreover the Charter of the Economic Rights and Duties of States, even in its most disputed clause (Article 2, paragraph 2c) — and the one that occasioned reservations on the part of the industrialized States-recommended taking account of "all circumstances" in order to determine the amount of compensation — which does not in any way exclude a substantial indemnity.

152. On behalf of Aminoil, it has been shown that there was a choice between two methods:

(i) a method based on the sum total of the anticipated profits, reckoned to the natural termination of the Concession, but discounted at an annual rate of interest in order to express that total in terms of its "present value" on the day when the indemnification is due; and without taking account of the value of the assets that would have been transferred to the concessionary Authority, "free of cost", upon that termination;

(ii) a method whereby total anticipated profits are counted and discounted in the same way over a limited period of years only, but taking countervailing account of the value of the assets (for this, Aminoil furnished examples of results calculated over ten year periods).

153. Subject to what is stated later as to the system for determining the annual profits involved, the Tribunal agrees in principle that both of the methods suggested by Aminoil are acceptable, and can be checked against each other. But, while aware that the first method may have been adopted in certain arbitrations, the Tribunal considers

12) 21 I.L.M. 976 (1982).

that in effecting a general evalutation, it is preferable to employ a combination of methods, according to the different factors that have to be taken into account. Moreover, the Tribunal disagrees with Aminoil's assumptions and calculations on two basic points. In this connection the Company has furnished an estimate on the lines of the principle of a *restitutio in integrum* founded on the assumption that the Concession should have continued for its full term under the contractual conditions fixed in 1961, without modification. This calculation is based on a projection of the quantities of oil recovered, the prices, the costs of production, and the operations to be undertaken until the end of concession. The Company has also produced its estimate of the value of the assets, in case the Tribunal should choose the second method.

154. The two basic points on which the Tribunal differs from Aminoil's position are as follows:

(a)-First, in respect of the foundation for the calculation of anticipated profits, which Aminoil takes as being exclusively the financial arrangements of 1961, the Tribunal has already found in Section IV above, both that the 1973 Agreements were valid, and that something is owing to the Government on Abu Dhabi account. Not only is no refund due of moneys paid to the Government under the 1973 arrangements, but the latter are also a component of the present "legitimate expectations" of the Company. Even more pertinent, the negotiations between the Parties about the application of the Abu Dhabi Formula involved a recognition of the principle of a monetary obligation to the Government, and of a modification for the future of the financial relations of the Parties. It is therefore on a combination of these data, not on those of 1961, that the indemnification of the Company must be proceeded to.

(b)-Next-and this constitutes the second aspect of the difference between the Tribunal's and Aminoil's positions — the Tribunal cannot accept the projections as to the future of the petroleum industry based on the consultations of experts that the Company has relied upon. These have been criticized by the Government. If, however, the Tribunal does not accept them, this is not because they include speculative elements, since all methods of assessment, whatever they may be, will do that. It is because the Tribunal thinks that in the present case, as will be shown later, the Parties adopted a different conception in the course of their relations and negotiations, — namely that of the reasonable rate of return. This it is, therefore, that must guide the Tribunal. —

노트와 질문

1. Res. 1803과 NIEO/Charter가 다른 법적 성격을 가지는 이유는 무엇인가? 법적인 성격이 다르기 때문에 보상금액을 결정함에 있어서 실제 차이를 가져오는가?
2. 가장 최근 국유화조치를 취한 국가는 Venezuela로 1990년대 외국인투자에 호의적이던 정책이 2001년 새로운 지도자가 나오면서 점차 로열티율과 법인세율을 높이고 PDVSA의 51% 최소지분율을 요구하는 입법이 시행되었다. 대부분의 IOC는 이에 순응하여 양허계약서를 변경하고 일부 지분을 PDVSA에 매각하였으나, ConocoPhilips와 ExxonMobile은 모든 지분을 포기하면서 그 보상을 PDVSA에게 요구하였다. PDVSA는 장부가를, ExxonMobile은 시장가를 협상카드로 제시, 2007년 ICSIC 중재에 들어갔으며 일부 ICC중재사건도 걸려 있다. 장부가와 현금흐름의 현재가 중 어느 것이 보다 적정한 보상에 가까울까?[13]

3. 다툼을 대비한 조치[14]

가. 국가간 조약

1) BIT(투자보장협정)

국가간 양자조약인 투자보장협정으로 투자보호의 또 다른 측면인 국유화의 요건이나 효과에 관하여 별도의 합의를 할 수 있을 것이다. 예를 들면 미국 국무성은 모델 투자보장협장 제6조에서 아래 보는 바와 같이 국유화의 효과에 관하여 자세하게 정하고 있다. 우리나라가 체결한 2011. 12. 당시 92개국과 체결한 투자보장협정도 대부분 국유화에 관한 규정을 두고 있다.[15] 과거 FCN조약(우호통상항해조약)이 그 대상이 광범위하여 합의하기가 어렵고[16] 또한 전반적 내국민대우가 신흥국이 쉽게 수용할 수 없다는 사정하에서[17] 1950년대 말부터 협상의 대상을 투자에 국한하여 특수한 분쟁해결방법을 규정한 투자보장협정이 나타나기 시작하였다. 1970년대 UN에서의 결의로 자원민족주의가 강화된 것도 투자보장협정이 활성화된 원인이다.[18] 투자보장협정은 FCN과 마찬가지로 내국민대우와 최혜국대우를 요구하지만, 나아

13) Thomas R. Stauffer, *Valuation of Assets in International Takings,* 17 ENER.L.J. 459 (1996).
14) 졸고, 우리 기업의 중동 이슬람지역 진출에 따른 법적 위험 관리방안, 32 한국중동학회논총 73 (2012).
15) http://www.mofat.go.kr/webmodule/htsboard/template/read/korboardread.jsp?typeID=6&boardid=13422&seqno=340548의 첨부파일 참조.
16) Herman Walker, Jr., *Modern Treaties of Friendship, Commerce and Navigation,* 42 MINN. L. REV. 805, 808 (BIT의 OUTLINE)(1957-58).
17) Kenneth J. Vandevelde, *The Bilateral Investment Treaty Program of the United States,* 21 CORN. INT'L L. J. 201, 208 (1988).
18) Jeswald W. Salacuse, *The Emerging Global Regime for Investment,* 51 HARV. INT'L L J. 427, 432 (주도권을 행사하기 위한 것이라는 설명과 협조가 피차에게 도움이 된다는 판단에 따른 것이라는 두 가

가서 국유화, 송금규제와 함께 투자자가 상대방 정부를 상대로 직접 손해배상을 구하기 위한 중재절차를 규정하기 시작한 것이 커다란 특징이다.[19)]

2004 US State Department Model Treaty Concerning the Reciprocal Encouragement and Protection of Investment

Article 6: Expropriation and Compensation

1. Neither Party may expropriate or nationalize a covered investment either directly or indirectly through measures equivalent to expropriation or nationalization ("expropriation"), except:

(a) for a public purpose;
(b) in a non-discriminatory manner;
(c) on payment of prompt, adequate, and effective compensation; and
(d) in accordance with due process of law and Article 5 [Minimum Standard of Treatment] (l) through (3).

2. The compensation referred to paragraph 1(c) shall:

(a) be paid without delay:
(b) be equivalent to the fair market value of the expropriated investment immediately before the expropriation took place ("the date of expropriation");
(c) not reflect any change in value occurring because the intended expropriation had become known to her: and
(d) be fully realizable and freely transferable.

3. If the fair market value is denominated in a freely usable currency, the compensation referred to in paragraph 1(c) shall be no less than the fair market value

지 설명)(2010). BIT가 안정화에 도움이 되지만 국가정책의 건전성에 따라서 생산성향상에 언제나 도움이 되지 않을 수도 있다는 경고는 Kenneth J. Vandevelde, *Investment Liberalization and Economic Development: The Role of Bilateral Investment Treaties,* 36 COLUM. J. TRANSNAT'L L. 501 (1998). BIT를 개발도상국의 입장에서 분석한 것으로 Andrew T. Guzman, *Why LDCs Sign Treaties That Hurt Them: Explaining the Popularity of Bilateral Investment Treaties,* 38 VA. J. INT'L L. 639 (1998).

19) 구체적인 BIC하에서의 ICSID 투자중재절차 및 구체적 사례에 관하여는 Bishop, 주 4-54 상게서, 318-92.

on the date of expropriation, plus interest at a commercially reasonable rate for that currency, accrued from the date of expropriation until the date of payment.

4. If the fair market value is denominated in a currency that is not freely usable, the compensation referred to in paragraph 1(c) — converted into the currency of payment at the market rate of exchange prevailing on the date of payment - shall be no less than:

(a) the fair market value on the date of expropriation, converted into a freely usable currency at the market rate of exchange prevailing on that date, plus
(b) interest, at a commercially reasonable rate for that freely usable currency, accrued from the date of expropriation until the date of payment.

5. This Article does not apply to the issuance of compulsory licenses granted in relation to intellectual property rights in accordance with the TRIPS Agreement, or to the revocation, limitation, or creation of intellectual property rights, to the extent that such issuance, revocation, limitation, or creation is consistent with the TRIPS Agreement.

6. Article 6 [Expropriation] shall be interpreted in accordance with Annexes A and B.

2) 자유무역협정(FTA)

투자보장협정에서 한 걸음 더 나아가 보다 광범위한 경제협력단계로 진입하기 위하여는 통상 FTA를 체결하는바, FTA 역시 국유화와 분쟁해결에 관하여 유사한 규정을 두고 있다. 예를 들어 NAFTA는 Ch. 11(investment), 1110조는 공공의 목적, 비차별적 취급, 적법 절차, 그리고 공정시장가격의 지급을 조건으로 국유화를 허용하고 있다.

3) 에너지헌장조약(Energy Charter Treaty)[20]

1990년 동유럽 붕괴이후 유럽에서는 에너지자원에 대한 공동의 해결을 모색하기 위하여 1991. 12. 유럽에너지헌장를 체결하여 에너지공동체를 설립하고 분쟁해결절차를 규정하였으며, 이러한 헌장은 전 CIS 국가에도 확대되어 1994. 12. 에너지헌장조약으로 확대, 발전되었다.[21]

20) BIT/FTA하의 투자분쟁해결절차에 관하여는 뒤 10장 1절 참조.
21) 김성수, 국제에너지 · 자원법 175(2002).

나. 당사자간 계약조항

국유화를 포함한 보다 광범위한 제한을 양허계약의 일부로서 산유국과 IOC간 합의할 수 있으며 이를 안정화조항이라 부름은 전에서 보았다.[22] 이러한 조항의 효력 내지 의미에 관하여는 *Aminoil* 중재판정에서 의견이 개진되고 있다.[23]

American Independent Oil Company (AMINOIL) v. Government of the State of Kuwait (1982)[24]

88. ...Article 17 of 1948 provided as follows:

> "The Shaikh shall not by general or special legislation or administrative measures or by any other act whatever annul this Agreement except as provided in Article 11. No alteration shall be made in the terms of this Agreement by either the Shaikh or the Company except in the event of the Shaikh and the Company jointly agreeing that it is desirable in the interest of both parties to make certain alterations, deletions or additions to this Agreement."

Finally, Article 7(g) of the Supplemental Agreement of 1961 provided for the deletion of Article 11 of 1948 and the substitution for it of a new Article 11. This new version, after indicating in a first paragraph (A) certain events (not here relevant) in which the Ruler of Kuwait would be entitled to terminate the Concession, went on in a second paragraph (B) to state

> "(B) Save as aforesaid this Agreement shall not be terminated before the expiration of the period specified in Article 1 thereof except by surrender as provided in Article 12 or if the Company shall be in default under the arbitration provisions of Article 18."

---

22) 제4장 제6절 다. 참조.

23) 본 판정을 이 조항에 대한 균형잡힌 해석으로 보는 견해는 Fernando R. Teson, *State Contracts and Oil Expropriations: The Aminoil-Kuwait Arbitration,* 24 VA. J. INT'L L. 323, 344 (1984).

24) 중재합의 및 준거법에 관하여는 Martin Hunter/Anthony C. Sinclair, *Aminoil Revisited Reflections on a Story of Changing Circumstances, in* INTERNATIONAL INVESTMENT LAW AND ARBITRATION 347, 355-357 (Todd Weiler ed. 2005).

These clauses combined, but especially Article 17, constituted what are sometimes called the "stabilisation" clauses of the contract. A straightforward and direct reading of them can lead to the conclusion that they prohibit any nationalisation. Such is the view maintained by the Company. The Government of Kuwait on the other hand, in a series of arguments the merits of which the Tribunal must now consider, maintained that, on the contrary, these clauses did not prevent a nationalisation.

89. The Tribunal will begin by discarding two arguments which it does not consider reliable.

Firstly, the more radical one consists in affirming that these clauses do no more than embody general principles of contract law, and that in consequence the legal regime of the Concession is the same as that of any contract, and that these clauses add nothing to what would in any event be the legal position. This argument cannot be accepted, for it is a well-known principle of the interpretation of contractual undertakings (and indeed of all juridical instruments) that the interpretation to be adopted must be such as will give each clause a worth-while meaning or object. In the present case, as Aminoil has pointed out, that object resides precisely in the fact that one of the Parties, being a State, had available to it all the powers of a public Authority and, by using them, could take those steps against which it was the very object of these clauses to protect the concessionaire.

Secondly, according to an initial Government contention, these provisions had a "colonial" character and were imposed upon Kuwait at a time when that State was still under British protectorate, and not in possession of its full sovereign powers. On this basis tbe stabilisation clauses were devoid of value. However, quite apart from any attempt to enquire into the factual circumstances in which these clauses were adopted, this contention cannot be upheld, for they were expressly confirmed on the occasion of the 1961 revision of the Concession after the attainment of complete independence by Kuwait, and again in 1973 when the text of the "1973 Agreement" was put into operation.

90. Other Government arguments were as follows:

(1) It was contended that the stabilisation clauses — initially valid and effective — were annulled by the emergence of a subsequent factor in the shape either of the Kuwait Constitution of 1962, or of a public international law rule of *jus cogens* forming part of the law of Kuwait. The relevant provisions of the Kuwait Constitution were those registering the permanent sovereignty of the State over its natural resources, and in

particular Articles 21 and 152 which provided as follows (translation from the Arabic taken from AM Vol. VII, Exh. 13)

> Article 21: "All of the natural wealth and resources are the property of the State. The State shall preserve and properly exploit those resources heedful of its own security and national economy requisites."
> Article 152: "Any concession for the exploitation of a natural resource or of a public utility shall be granted only by Law and for a determinate period. Preliminary measures shall guarantee the facilitation of exploration and discovery and shall ensure publicity and competition."

However, it does not appear from these provisions that they in any way prevented the State from granting stabilisation guarantees by contract. Even if they should be interpreted as doing so, it was the State's duty towards its co-contractant to notify the latter of the putting into force of the resulting constitutional modifications to current contracts. This was not done; nor was it done either at the time of the revision of 1961, or of that of 1973.

(2) Equally on the public international law plane it has been claimed that permanent sovereignty over natural resources has become on imperative rule of *jus cogens* prohibiting States from affording, by contract or by treaty, guarantees of any kind against the exercise of the public authority in regard to all matters relating to natural riches. This contention lacks all foundation. Even if Assembly Resolution 1803 (XVII) adopted in 1962, is to be regarded, by reason of the circumstance of its adoption, as reflecting the then state of international law, such is not the case with subsequent resolutions which have not had the same degree of authority. Even if some of their provisions can be regarded as codifying rules that reflect international practice, it would not be possible from this to deduce the existence of a rule of international law prohibiting a State from undertaking not to proceed to a nationalisation during a limited period of time. It may indeed well be eminently useful that "host" States should, if they so desire, be able to pledge themselves not to nationalise given foreign undertakings within a limited period; and no rule of public international law prevents them from doing so.

(3) Another argument advanced by the Government of Kuwait requires consideration. According to this, Aminoil's Concession belonged to the general category of "administrative contracts" in respect of which — as much by Kuwait law as on the

basis of general legal principles — special faculties were reserved to the State, of which account must be taken in the interpretation of the stabilisation clauses.

91. The "administrative contract", as it was originally developed in French law, and subsequently in other legal systems such as those of Egypt and Kuwait, is based on the idea that certain contracts concluded by the State, or by public entities, are governed by special rules, the two principal ones being as follows:

(i)- The public Authority can require a variation in the extent of the other party's liabilities (services, payments) under the contract. This must not however go so far as to distort (unbalance) the contract; and the State can never modify the financial clauses of the contract, — nor, in particular, disturb the general equilibrium of the rights and obligations of the parties that constitute what is sometimes known as the contract's "financial equation". This characteristic is also to be found in certain ordinary private law contracts, and respect for the equilibrium of reciprocal undertakings is a fundamental principle of the law of contracts. But in the present case it has to be realized that the main difficulties that arise are not about respect for the financial equation that reflects the contractual equilibrium, but about the method of applying Article 9, — that is to say not over respect for the original equilibrium, but over the search for a new, equitable, equilibrium.

(ii)-The public authority may proceed to a more radical step in regard to the contract, namely to put an end to it when essential necessities concerning the functioning of the State ("operation of public services") are involved. It is with this second aspect of the notion of an administrative contract that the present case could in theory be concerned. Yet even if Aminoil's Concession belonged to this category of contract, it would still be necessary that exigencies connected with essential State functioning should be such as to justify Decree Law n° 124.

92. In order to find an answer to this question, in connection with that of the effect of the stabilisation clauses of the Concession, the matter has to be seen in its historical perspective.

93. It seems fair to say that what the Parties had in mind in drafting the stabilisation clauses in 1948 and 1961, was anything which, by reason of its confiscatory character, might cause serious financial prejudice to the interests of the Company. Thus, as mentioned earlier, Article 7(g) of 1961, instituting a new revised Article 11 of 1948, enumerated and strictly limited all the instances in which the Concession can terminate through a forfeiture of the concessionair's rights (for failure in its obligations), but is silent as to all acts that would lead to the ending of the Concession without having a confiscatory character. It can be held that the case of nationalisation is precisely one of those acts, since as a matter of international law it is subject, *inter alia,* to the payment of appropriate compensation.

94. The case of nationalisation is certainly not expressly provided against by the stabilisation clauses of the Concession. But it is contended by Aminoil that notwithstanding this lacuna, the stabilisation clauses of the Concession (Articles 17 and revised 11) are cast in such absolute and all-embracing terms as to suffice in themselves — unconditionally and in all circumstances — for prohibiting nationalisation. That is a possible interpretation on the purely formal plane; but, for the following reasons, it is not the one adopted by the Tribunal.

95. No doubt contractual limitations on the State's right to nationalise are juridically possible, but what that would involve would be a particularly serious undertaking which would have to be expressly stipulated for, and be within the regulations governing the conclusion of State contracts; and it is to be expected that it should cover only a relatively limited period. In the present case however, the existence of such a stipulation would have to be presumed as being covered by the general language of the stabilisation clauses, and over the whole period of an especially long concession since it extended to 60 years. A limitation on the sovereign rights of the State is all the less to be presumed where the concessionaire is in any event in possession of important guarantees regarding its essential interests in the shape of a legal right to eventual compensation.

96. Such is the case here, — for if the Tribunal thus holds that it cannot interpret Articles 17 and 7(g)-revised 11—as absolutely forbidding nationalisation, it is nevertheless the fact that these provisions are far from having lost all their value and efficacity on that account since, by impliedly requiring that nationalisation shall not have any confiscatory character, they re-inforce the necessity for a proper indemnification as a condition of it.

97. There is another aspect of the matter which has weighed with the Tribunal. While attributing its full value to the fundamental principle of *pacta sunt servanda*, the

Tribunal has felt obliged to recognize that the contract of Concession has undergone great changes since 1948: changes conceded — often unwillingly, but conceded nevertheless — by the Company. These changes have not been the consequence of accidental or special factors, but rather of a profound and general transformation in the terms of oil concessions that occurred in the Middle-East, and later throughout the world. These changes took place progressively, with an increasing acceleration, as from 1973. They were introduced into the contractual relations between the Government and Aminoil through the play of Article 9, or else as the result of at least tacit acceptances by the Company, which entered neither objections nor reservations in respect of them. These changes must not simply be viewed piece — meal, but on the basis of their total effect, — and they brought about a metamorphosis in the whole character of the Concession.

98. This Concession — in its origin a mining concession granted by a State whose institutions were still incomplete and directed to narrow patrimonial ends — became one of the essential instruments in the economic and social progress of a national community in full process of development. This transformation, progressively achieved, took place at first by means of successive increases in the financial levies going to the State, and then through the growing influence of the State in the economic and technical management of the undertaking, particularly as to the control of pricing policy, taken over in 1973, and the regulation of works and investment programmes. The contract of Concession thus changed its character and became one of those contracts in regard to which, in most legal systems, the State, while remaining bound to respect the contractual equilibrium, enjoys special advantages.

99. In relation to Aminoil's undertaking therefore, the State thus became, in fact if not in law, an associate whose interests had become predominant. Moreover, in spite of its unfinished, and in certain ways improvised character, the text of the projected Agreement of July 1973, made applicable by the 22 December, 1973 Letter, bears witness to this evolution.

100. The faculty of nationalising the Concession could not thenceforward be excluded in relation to the regime of the undertaking as it resulted from the sum total of the considerations relevant to its functioning. This conclusion concerning the interpretation of the stabilisation clauses, as being no longer possessed of their former absolute character, which the Tribunal has thus reached, is in harmony with that regime as it stood in 1977, — and a contrary interpretation would, in addition, disregard its other contractual components.

101. The Tribunal wishes however to stress here that the case is not one of a fundamental change of circumstances (*rebus sic stantibus*) within the meaning of Article 62 of the Vienna Convention on the Law of Treaties. It is not a case of a change involving a departure from a contract, but of a change in the nature of the contract itself, brought about by time, and the acquiescence or conduct of the Parties.

102. The Tribunal thus arrives at the conclusion that the "take-over" of Aminoil's enterprise was not, in 1977, inconsistent with the contract of concession, provided always that the nationalisation did not possess any confiscatory character

다. 보 험

1) OPIC

미국은 1971년 이래 OPIC을 통하여 미국의 해외투자자가 정치적 소유사태, 국유화, 통화의 불태환성, 특수위험의 4개 측면에서 손해를 입을 경우 이를 $250M까지 보상하는 제도를 시행하고 있다. 다만, 보험금의 지급은 미국의 투자자가 합리적인 범위 내에서 가능한 모든 구제수단을 취한 후에만 가능하다.[25] 구체적인 국유화관련 보험금지급청구와 관련하여서도 정부의 행위와의 관련성, 정부의 행위와 투자자 손해와의 인과관계를 입증하여야 하며, 이에 대하여 OPIC은 부패를 포함하여 투자자의 행위에 기인한 것 또는 투자기업에 대한 채권자, 주주 등의 자격으로서 권리를 행사한 것이라는 항변을 제기할 수 있다. 잠행성 국유화와 같이 양허계약을 취소하거나 주주의 본질적 권리침해, 건설대금지급거절, 투자수익송금부인도 역시 국유화로 보아서 보험금을 지급한다.[26]

2) MIGA

국제적인 투자위험의 보험을 위하여는 1985년 세계은행이 MIGA를 설립, 국제적 투자 중 금융분야, 추출산업, 인프라산업, 농상공서비스 4개의 분야에 따르는 비상업적 위험 중 불태환성이나 송금제한, 국유화, 전쟁, 계약위반, 국가채무불이행으로 인한 손해에 대한 보증을

---

25) http://www.opic.gov/insurance 참조.

26) Pablo M. Zylberglait, *OPIC's Investment Insurance: The Platypus of Governmental Programs and Its Jurisprudence,* 25 L. & POL'Y INT'L BUS. 359, 379-386 (1993-94). 초기 OPIC의 국유화를 이유로 한 보험금청구결정의 분석은 Vance R. Koven, *Expropriation and the "Jurisprudence" of OPIC,* 22 HARV. INT'L L. J. 269 (1981).

제공하고 있다.[27] MIGA가 투자자에게 손해를 지급한 후에는 투자자의 host country에 대한 손해배상청구권을 대위할 수 있다. 그러나, 언제나 구상권을 행사하는 것은 아니고 MIGA의 정책적 판단에 따른다. 지급여부에 대한 다툼은 ICSID 중재절차에 따라서 해결된다. 구상권 행사시의 다툼 역시 협상을 거쳐서 ICSID 중재절차에 따라서 해결된다.[28]

3) 한국무역보험공사

우리나라도 한국무역보험공사에서 다양한 수출보험을 제공하고 있으며 이와 별도로 해외자원개발투자전문회사가 해외자원개발사업에 투자하여 비상위험 내지 신용위험으로 인하여 입는 손실의 일부를 보상하는 정책적 보험을 제공하고 있다.[29]

대법 2009. 7. 23. 선고 2008다88030 판결

원심은 그 채택 증거에 의하여, 2002. 6. 24. 원고와 피고는 단기수출보험 포괄보험특약(이하 '이 사건 특약'이라고 한다)을 체결하고 이 사건 특약 및 단기수출보험약관(이하 '이 사건 약관'이라고 한다)에 따라 보험계약이 체결된 수출거래에서 원고가 입게 되는 손실에 대해 피고가 보상하기로 하였는데, 이 사건 특약 제2조 제4항은 적용대상거래를 "일반수출거래, 가공무역거래, 중계무역거래(L/C At Sight 거래 포함, 본지사거래 제외)"라고, 제8조 제1항은 "원고는 제2조에 규정된 적용대상거래로서 다음 각 호의 1에 해당되는 경우를 제외하고는 제17조에 규정된 특약의 유효기간 중에 이루어지는 모든 수출거래에 대해서 빠짐없이 수출한 날의 다음달 20일까지 원·피고가 정하는 절차에 따라 수출사실을 통지해야 합니다. 다만, 피고가 상당한 이유가 있다고 인정하는 경우에는 수출한 날의 다음달 20일을 경과하여 통지할 수 있습니다."라고, 제9조 제1항은 "원고가 제2조에 규정된 적용대상거래에 해당되는 물품을 수출하고, 제8조에 따라 수출통지한 경우에는 수출한 날부터 보험관계가 '성립'되는 것으로 합니다."라고 각 규정하고 있으며, 이 사건 약관 제2조 제2항 제1호는 이 사건 특약의 적용이 제외되는 거래로서 "신용장방식 수출거래에서 신용장조건으로 명시된 서류가 당해 신용장조건

27) http://www.miga.org/ 참조. Christopher K. Dalrymple, *Politics and Foreign Direct Investment: The Multilateral Investment Guarantee Agency and the Calvo Clause,* 29 CORN. INT'L L. J. 161, 172-77 (1996).

28) Ibrahim F.I. Shihata, *The Multilateral Investment Guaranty Agency (MIGA) and the Settlement of Disputes,* 477 PLI/Comm. 345 (Oct. 1988). 김대순, 국제법론 757-761(15th ed. 2010) 참조.

29) www.ksure.or.kr 참조. 경영공시에 따르면 2011년 182조원을 인수, 8175억원의 보험금을 지급하였으며 수출보험활용률은 무려 23%에 이른다. 현재 무역보험법은 과거 강제가입주의에 관한 규정은 없으나 제7조의2에서 포괄보험의 실시가능성을 규정하고 있다.

에 일치하더라도 그와 별도로 신용장 개설은행의 대금지급책임이 면제 또는 경감될 수 있는 내용을 포함하고 있는 경우"를 규정하고 있는 사실, 몽골 포스트 뱅크(Mongol Post Bank, 이하 '몽골은행'이라고 한다)는 2003. 6. 30.경부터 2003. 10. 31.경까지 몽골 소재 회사인 한브로이(Khan Brau Co.,Ltd) 또는 모바일(Mobil Co.,Ltd)의 요청에 의해 3회에 걸쳐 주식회사 ○○(이하 '○○'이라고 한다)을 수익자로 한 신용장을 개설하였으며, 그 무렵 ○○은 몽골은행과 "신용장 수익자(○○)가 신용장의 상환과 관련된 모든 위험을 부담하고, 수입자가 의무를 이행하지 않을 경우 은행에 갚아야 할 일체의 지불금액을 신용장 수익자가 책임지며, 은행은 신용장 수익자에게 아무런 책임을 부담하지 않는다."는 취지의 이면계약을 체결한 사실, 이 사건 제1신용장이 개설된 후인 2003. 7. 16.경 ○○은 원고와 "수출대행의뢰자(○○)가 자신의 명의로 신용장을 수취한 후 수출대행자(원고)에게 그 신용장을 양도하되 수출물품의 생산 또는 조달에 대한 일체의 책임은 수출대행의뢰자(○○)가 부담하고, 원고는 ○○ 또는 제3자가 공급하는 제품에 대해, 원고 또는 원고가 지정하는 검사기관을 통하여 선적 전 검사를 실시할 수 있다."는 내용의 신용장양도방식에 의한 단순수출대행계약을 체결하였으며, 이 사건 제2, 3신용장이 개설된 이후인 2003. 8. 27.과 2003. 12. 22.에도 ○○과 원고 사이에 위와 같은 취지의 단순수출대행계약이 체결되었고, 위 각 수출대행계약 체결 후 원고는 각 수출대행계약에 따라 ○○으로부터 이 사건 각 신용장을 양수한 사실, ○○은 이 사건 각 신용장이 개설되자 위 각 수출대행계약에 따라 원고를 수출자로 하여 신용장 조건에 부합하게 선적서류 등을 위조하거나, 허위로 작성한 후 이를 원고에게 교부하였고, 원고는 수출물품의 검사 등을 실시하지 않은 채 보험종목을 '단기수출보험-일반수출'로, 대행구분을 '직접수출'로 하여 ○○으로부터 받은 선적서류 등을 토대로 한 내용으로 5회에 걸쳐 피고에게 수출통지를 한 사실, 그러나 일부 수출에 있어서는 실제 거래금액이 원고가 피고에게 통지한 수출금액의 1.9%, 4.2%, 1.2%에 불과하였고, 일부 수출의 경우 수출물품이나 거래당사자마저 달랐던 사실, 원고는 수출대행계약에 기하여 ○○으로부터 이 사건 각 신용장을 양수한 후, 위 각 신용장을 제일은행 또는 중국은행(Bank of China)에게 매도하였고, 제일은행과 중국은행은 각 신용장을 매수한 후 신용장 관련 수출서류를 신용장 개설은행인 몽골은행에 송부하였는데, 몽골은행은 위 수출서류를 이의 없이 수령한 후 만기에 지급할 것을 확인한 사실, 그런데 이 사건 각 신용장의 만기가 도래하여 매입은행인 제일은행과 중국은행은 몽골은행에 신용장대금 지급청구를 하였으나, 몽골은행은 '○○과 사이의 이면계약 존재, 신용장 조건의 불충족, 선적서류의 위조 등'을 이유로 신용장대금 지급을 거절하였으며, 이에 위 매입은행들은 원고에게 수출환어음 환매청구를 하여 원고는 매입은행들에게 수출환어음 환매대금을 지급한 사실 등을 인정하였다.

나아가 원심은 위 인정사실에 기초하여, 보험자인 피고와 사이에서는 원고가 보험계약자의 지위에 있고, 이 사건 각 신용장에 따른 수출을 사실상 진행한 ○○은 원고의 수출대리인 또는 이행보조자의 지위에 있다고 볼 것인데, 실제 수출 품목, 금액, 수출자 및 수입자 등에 비추어 볼 때 원고가 수출통지한 내용이 실제 수출거래와 달라, 원고의 수출통지 내용에 의해 이 사건 특약에 따른 수출보험이 적용되는 수출보험계약이 성립되었다고 볼 수 없다고 판단하였다.

원심이 인정한 사실관계를 관련 법리에 비추어 보면, 이 사건 특약은 보험계약자가 일정기간 사이에 성립된 수출계약 전부를 보험계약에 부보하겠다는 예약의 성질을 가지고 있어 보험계약자가 개별적 수출계약마다 수출통지라는 예약완결권을 행사함으로써 한국수출보험공사와의 보험계약이 체결되는 것이라고 할 것이므로, 그 조건에 합치하는 모든 수출계약에 대하여 보험자인 한국수출보험공사의 책임이 자동적으로 발생하는 것은 아니라 보험계약자가 한국수출보험공사에게 수출통지를 함으로써 비로소 이에 대한 보험관계가 성립되는 것으로 해석하여야 할 것이고(대법원 2000. 11. 14. 선고 99다52336 판결 참조), 한편 수출대행업자인 원고가 직접 피고와 이 사건 특약을 체결하였다면 위탁자인 ○○과의 내부관계는 별론으로 하고 원고가 보험계약자로서 이 사건 특약 및 약관에 의한 개별적인 보험계약의 성립요건을 충족시켜야 할 지위에 있다고 할 것인데, ○○에 의해 실제 실행된 각 수출에서의 수출 품목, 금액, 수출자 및 수입자 등에 비추어 볼 때 원고가 피고에게 수출통지한 바와 같은 내용의 '직접수출' 거래가 있었다고 볼 수는 없다.

원심이 같은 취지에서 원고의 수출통지 내용에 의해 이 사건 특약에 따른 수출보험이 적용되는 수출보험계약이 성립된 것으로 볼 수 없다고 판단한 것은 정당하고, 거기에 수출보험계약의 성립 등에 관한 법리오해 등의 위법이 없다. 이 점에 관한 상고이유의 주장은 받아들일 수 없고, 나머지 상고이유의 주장은 수출보험계약이 적법하게 성립되었음을 전제로 하는 것이어서 나아가 살펴 볼 것 없이 모두 이유 없다.

4) 사 보 험

우리나라에서 정치적 위험을 위한 사보험은 제공되지 않은 듯하고 외국에서도 그 시장의 규모나 시장의 구조, 정보의 제한, 외국환 시장에서의 제한, 재보험시장의 부재, 수익성의 한계 등 사유로 지극히 제한적이라고 한다.[30)]

---

30) Elizabeth A. Kessler, *Political Risk Insurance and the Overseas Private Investment Corporation: What Happened to the Private Sector?* 13 N.Y.L. SCH. J. INT'L & COMP. L. 203 (1992); Paul E. Comeaux & N. Stephen Kinsella, *Reducing Political Risk in Developing Countries: Bilateral Investment Treaties, Stabilization Clauses, and MIGA & OPIC Investment Insurance,* 15 N.Y.L. SCH. J. INT'L & COMP. L. 1, 47 (보험료가 비싸지만 고객의 수요에 따라 개별화된 보험이 가능함을 지적). 우리나라의 무역보험은 수출보험법에 따라서 국가가 제공하지만, 대외거래에 따른 보험은 반드시 무역

4. 민영화조치

국유화조치때문에 NOC의 지분이 IOC에 비하여 올라가는 반면, 민영화조치는 이와 반대로 NOC의 지분을 떨어뜨리기 위한 것이다. 기존의 NOC 지분을 매각할 수도 있지만, 새로운 석유사업자의 진입을 허용함으로써 민영화가 가능할 수도 있다. 동기는 다양하겠지만 NOC는 공기업으로서의 운영효율상 한계가 있으니 민간기업의 자금을 유입, 효율성을 높이기 위한 것일 수도 있고 국가가 국가재정운영을 위한 재원을 필요로 한 경우일 수도 있다. 어쨌든 1990년대부터는 전세계의 많은 NOC가 민영화의 길을 걸었으나 2000년대로 돌아서서는 남미의 예에서 보듯이 시장경제의 능률에 대한 신뢰가 떨어지면서 민영화의 열기가 많이 식었다.[31]

천연자원개발사업은 경제전반의 방향을 이끌고 초기투자의 위험을 부담하기 위하여 국영기업(state-owned enterprise)이 영위하는 것이 적정하지만, 한편으로 공기업을 사회안전망으로 활용하면 국가재무건정성과 자본배분의 효율성을 해할 가능성이 다분히 존재한다. 따라서, 국가채무가 심각하여 공기업의 지분을 할 수 없이 매각하는 상황에 이르기 전에 국가채무의 수준과 자원배분의 비효율성이 초기투자의 위험부담 필요성을 초과하는 시점부터 민영화는 하나의 대안으로 고려되어야 할 것이다. 민영화방안은 통상의 기업구조재조정과 마찬가지로 주식매각, 자산매각, 구조개편, 합작투자, 경영위탁 등 다양한 방안이 가능할 것이다. 또한 주식매각의 경우에도 기업공개를 할지, 해외에 예탁증서를 매각할지, 아니면 지배주식을 매도할지 여러 가지 대안이 고려되어야 한다.

우리는 KNOC가 에특자금으로 투자를 선도하고 국내의 민간 에너지업체들이 그 투자기회나 투자이익을 나누어 가지는 형태로 되어 있다. 해외에너지탐사사업에 대한 충분한 인력과 기술이 축적된 시점이라고 판단되면 KNOC의 선도자적 역할은 시장에 넘기고 보다 제한되고 특화된 사업분야로 그 활동범위를 좁히는 것이 바람직할 수도 있다. 이런 점에서 과거 BNOC가 에너지거래와 탐사를 두개의 별도 회사조직으로 나눈 것이 참고가 될 것이다.

보험법에 따라 설립된 한국무역보험공사만 제공할 수 있는 것으로 보이지는 않는다. 동법 제2조의 정의 규정 참조.

31) 우리나라의 공기업 지배구조와 예산에 관하여는 졸고, 공기업의 지배구조와 기업금융, 32 강원법학, 469 (2011).

노트와 질문

1. 현재 KOGAS는 정부가 다수의 지분을 소유하고 있고 거래소에 그 주식이 상장되어 있다는 의미에서 민영화되어 있다. 다음 단계의 민영화를 위하여는 어떤 준비가 필요한가? 에너지기업으로서의 다른 공공기관들 현재의 상황과 민영화의 필요성은 어떠한가?
2. 현재 KNOC은 100% 정부출자기관으로 해외자원개발에 필요한 자금을 국민의 세금으로 지원받고 있는바, IOC를 출자자로 끌어 들여서 해외자원개발에 필요한 자금부담의 일부를 떠맡길 뿐만 아니라, 기술과 경영 노하우를 얻을 수 있는 기회로 활용할 수는 없을까? 적어도 현재의 지배구조에서 좀더 투명한 의사결정절차와 공시기준을 도입할 가능성은 없을까?

제10장

분쟁해결의 방법

1. 원고 적격

일반적으로 국가가 아닌 개인이 타국과 맺은 계약의 해석이나 이행과 관련하여 분쟁이 발생한 경우 국내법에 따른 구제절차를 이행한 후에만 자신의 국가를 통하여 상대방 국가를 상대로 국제법상 구제절차를 취할 수 있었다.[1] 그러나, 개인이 타국과 분쟁이 발생한 경우 자신의 정부를 통하여 상대방 국가에게 압력을 행사, 이를 해결하려는 상황에서 강대국이 약소국을 상대로 일방적인 분쟁의 해결을 요구하기도 하였기 때문에 1868년 아르헨티나 법학자 Calvo는 Calvo clause를 양허계약에 포함할 것을 주장한다. 따라서, Calvo clause는 개인의 분쟁에 국가를 개입시키지 않으며 외국인은 내국인과 동일한 권리를 보유함을 명시한다. 이러한 주장의 근거는 모든 주권은 평등하다는 것이다.

그러나, Calvo clause는 20세기에 들어와서 점차 그 설득력을 잃었고[2] 도리어 투자국들은 개별국가와의 BIT를 통하여 투자자 개인이 직접 외국 정부를 상대로 분쟁의 해결을 위한 ICSIC에서의 중재절차의 개시가 가능함을 요구하였고 실제 많은 BIT가 이러한 규정을 두게 되었다. 또한 NAFTA를 비롯하여 많은 FTA 역시 동일한 중재절차를 통하여 투자자의 분쟁해결이 가능하도록 규정하고 있다. 그러나, 이러한 특별한 합의가 없는 이상, 국제법의 일반원칙은 개인이 국내법적 구제절차를 모두 밟아야 할 의무가 있고 그럼에도 불구하고 구제가 주어지지 않는 경우 개인은 국가에 자신의 권리보호를 요구할 수 있고 그런 경우 비로소 국가는 자국민의 권리보호를 위하여 나설 수 있다.

국제에너지관련투자와 관련하여 분쟁해결방법을 정리하면 에너지탐사개발계약은 국가 또는 국가의 대리인이 직접 계약당사자가 되는 특징상 계약상 분쟁도 계약이 정한 바에 따라

1) 김대순, 위 주 9-28 상게서, 668-77.

2) Wenhua Shan, *From "North-South Divide" to "Private-Public Debate": Revival of the Calvo Doctrine and the Changing Landscape in International Investment Law,* 27 NW. J. INT'L L. & BUS. 631, 633 (2007).

서 이들을 상대로 소송 내지 중재로 해결하여야 할 것이다. 그러나, 자원보유국과 BIT나 FTA가 체결되다면 이들 조약이 정하고 있는 특정한 투자분쟁의 경우 예를 들어 자의적 차별적 국유화나 송금의 제한 등의 경우에 이들 조약에 따라서 계약당사자가 직접 국가를 상대로 ICSID에서의 중재나[3] 기타 여타의 중재절차를 통한 특수한 분쟁해결방법의 동원이 추가적으로 또는 대안적으로 가능할 것이다.

최원목, 해외자원개발에 따른 투자분쟁방지 및 해결을 위한 지침, 2010 자원·에너지법제연구회 연구논문집 11

4-1. 양자 투자보장협정상의 절차

양자 투자보장협정에서는 대부분 국가간 중재재판 절차를 마련하고 있다. 즉 분쟁이 일정기간 해결되지 아니하면 일방당사국의 요청에 의하여 중재재판에 회부된다. 중재판정부는 각 당사국 1인의 재판관을 임명하고, 양국의 합의로 3번째 재판관을 임명하게 된다. 이러한 임명이 일정한 기간 내에 이루어지지 못하는 경우, 당사국의 요청에 의해 국제사법재판소장이 임명할 수 있다. 중재판정부는 다수결에 의해 결정을 내리며, 이러한 결정은 최종적이고 양당사국에 대해 구속력을 지니게 된다. 각 당사국은 각자의 중재인 비용을 부담하며, 재판장의 비용은 균등하게 분담한다.[1]

이와는 별도로 일방 당사국과 타방 당사국의 투자자간 분쟁해결 절차(즉, 투자자-정부 분쟁해결)를 마련하고 있는 경우도 있다. 한-카자흐스탄, 한-인도, 한-우크라이나 투자보장협정에 따르면, 먼저 분쟁당사자간의 교섭과 국내구제조치를 진행해야 한다. 분쟁이 서면 통보를 제기한 때로부터 6개월 이내에 해결되지 않으면, 양 당사자의 합의에 의해, 투자를 허가한 당사국의 법률에 따라 그 사법당국에 회부될 수 있다. 이러한 합의가 성립되지 않으면, 일방당사자의 요청에 따라, 국제 중재재판에 회부할 수 있는데, 중재재판 절차는 (i) 양 당사국 모두 국가와 타방국가의 국민간의 투자분쟁해결에 관한 협약(ICSID협약)의 당사자인 경우에는 국제 투자 분쟁해결 본부(ICSID), 그렇지 않은 경우에는 (ii) 국제 투자 분쟁해결본부의 조정, 중재 및 사실 판정 절차에 대한 추가의정서, 또는 (iii) 1976년 국제연합 국제상거래위원회의 중재규칙에 따른 임시 중재재판소에 회부하여 해결된다.

---

3) 김대순, 위 주 9-28 상게서, 751-57. BIT나 FTA에서의 ICSID 중재절차의 문제점에 관하여는 서철원, 역사적 관점에서 본 국제투자법, 20 법학논총 133, 147-48(2008).

1. 한-쿠웨이트 투자보장협정 제9조 한 모로코 투자보장협정 제9조, 한-카자흐스탄 투자보장 협정 제19조, 한-이란 투자보장협정 제13조, 한-말레이시아 투자보장협정 제10조 한-우즈베키스탄 투자보장협정 제10조, 한-인도네시아 투자보장협정 제10조, 한-우크라이나 투자보장협정 제10조.

한-이란 투자보장협정도 위와 유사한 투자자-정부 분쟁해결 절차를 규정하고 있으나, 차이점은 서면 통보후 6개월 이내에 분쟁이 해결되지 않으면 중재재판 절차로 이행할 수 있다고만 규정되어 있어, 당사자의 합의에 의한 투자유치국의 사법당국 회부 절차를 명시하지 않고 있다. 다만 "투자유치국의 법원에 회부된 분쟁이 계류중인 한, 당사자간 합의에 의하지 아니하고는 중재재판에 회부될 수 없으며, 최종판결이 내려진 경우에는 중재재판에 회부될 수 없다"는 규정을 두어, 투자자가 국내법원을 선택했다가 자의적으로 중재재판으로 이행하는 형태(forum shopping)를 제한하고 있다.

한-말레이시아 투자보장협정은 "3개월간" 분쟁이 해결되지 않으면, 중재재판으로 이행할 수 있다고 규정하여 기한을 단축하고 있으며, ICSID절차로 이행하기 위해서는 당해 투자자가 이를 서면으로 동의해야 하며, 국내재판절차에 제소하지 않을 것을 조건으로 이행할 수 있다. 반면 한-인도네시아 협정은 "12개월"을 우호적 분쟁해결 기간으로 설정하고, 그 후 ICSID절차로 이행할 수 있음을 규정하고 있다.

한-우즈베키스탄 협정은 6개월간 분쟁이 해결되지 않는 경우, 분쟁당사자가 달리 합의하지 않는 한, 중재재판은 "1976년 유엔상거래위원회 중재규칙에 따라 행해진다"고 규정하여, 단일 중재재판 절차만을 상정하고 있다. 한-리비아 협정도 6개월 협상기간 이후 임시중재재판 절차만을 상정하고 있다.

4-2. FTA에서의 분쟁해결 절차

우리가 맺은 FTA는 대부분 정부간 분쟁해결 절차를 마련하고 있다. 즉 한-아세안 FTA를 예로 들면, "이 협정에 달리 규정되지 아니하는 한, 이 협정의 해석, 이행 또는 적용에 관한 분쟁이 발생할 경우 기본협정 하의 분쟁해결제도에 관한 협정에 기재된 절차 및 제도를 통해 해결된다."고 규정하여 국가간 분쟁해결 절차를 마련하고 있다. 한-아세안 FTA 분쟁해결제도에 관한 협정에 따르면, 일반적으로 FTA 분쟁해결절차에서 볼 수 있는 바와 같은 사전 협의(consultations), 중재패널(arbitral panels)구성, 패널판정 및 이행에 관한 절차를 상세하게 규정하고 있다.

그러므로, 한-아세안 FTA 투자협정상의 각종 의무의 해석, 이행 및 적용에 관한 분쟁은 국가 대 국가의 FTA분쟁해결 절차에 해당 당사국이 제기할 수 있는 것이다. 다만, 투자협정 자체가 주국 투자자가 투자자-국가 중재에 문제를 회부한 분쟁에 관하여 외교적 보호를 부여할 것을 금지하고 있으므로, 투자자-국가 중재에 회부된 사안에 대해서는 국가 대 국가 분쟁해결절차가 진행되지 못한다고 해석된다.

한-미 FTA의 경우는 이 점을 명확히 하기 위해, 투자자-국가 중재를 제기하기 위해서는 청구인이 피청구국의 사법 또는 행정재판소는 물론 "그 밖의 분쟁해결절차(other dispute settlement procedures)”를 개시하거나 계속할 권리를 사전에 서면으로 포기할 것을 요구하고 있다. 다만, 먼저 국가 대 국가 분쟁해결절차가 진행되었더라도, 투자자가 투자자-국가 중재를 진행시키는 것은 특별히 이것을 금지하는 조항이 존재하지 않고, 택일방식(fork-in-the-road approach)을 포함한 전제조건에도 반하지 않으므로, 가능하다고 판단된다.

한편, FTA에서는 이러한 국가대 국가 분쟁해결절차와는 별도로 투자자-국가 분쟁해결절차를 마련하고 있다. 아래에서는 한-아세안 FTA 투자협정을 예로 들어 이를 설명하기로 한다.

4-2-1. 의　　의

적용대상 투자의 경영, 영업, 매각, 처분과 관련하여, 한-아세안 FTA 투자협정상의 일정한 의무(내국민대우, 최혜국대우, 투자에 대한 일반적 대우, 고위경영진 및 이사회 구성 제한 금지, 송금, 수용 및 보상, 손실보상) 위반으로 인해, 적용대상 투자나 그 투자자에 손실(loss) 또는 손해(damage)가 야기된 때, 당해 투자자와 당사국간에 일정한 중재절차를 통해 분쟁을 해결할 수 있도록 한 것이다.

전통 국제법의 원칙에 따르면, 국가간에 체결되는 조약이나 협정의 위반은 당사자인 국가가 상대방 국가를 상대로 하는 국가간 분쟁해결제도를 통해서만 해결하도록 되어 있고, 체결국에 속한 개인은 상대방 국가를 상대로 직접 청구를 하지 못하는 것이 원칙이다. 또한, 국제 상사분쟁에 있어서도 개인이 외국을 상대로 당해 외국 이외의 국가 법원에 소송을 제기할 경우 그 국가는 주권면제특권을 누리는 경우가 많아 개인이 국가를 외국법원에서 직접 상대로 소송을 제기하는 데에는 한계가 있다. 투자자와 국가간 분쟁해결제도는 이러한 일반적인 원칙과는 달리 투자자에 관한 한 투자자가 직접 국가를 상대로 분쟁을 제기할 수 있도록 허용하여 분쟁을 신속하게 해결하는 데 중요한 의미가 있다.

투자자가 투자유치국을 상대로 그 유치국의 법원에서 소송을 하자면 투자자 입장에서 공정한 재판을 기대하기 어렵다고 생각할 것이고, 투자자의 국적국의 법원에 제소하게 되면 이번에는 투자유치국 입장에서 공정성에 대한 의문을 제기할 수 있다. 더구나, 국가의 입장에서는 투자협약과 관련한 국제법적 이슈에 대하여 국내 법원의 재판을 받는다는 것이 적절하지 않다는 인식도 가질 수 있다. 이러한 점들을 고려하여 투자자와 국가간의 분쟁해결은 통상 국제중재의 방식을 채택하고 있는 것이다. 국제중재는 서로 다른 국가에 속한 당사자 간의 국제거래에서 발생하는 분쟁의 해결수단으로서 점차 이용도가 높아지고 있다. 그 주된 이유로는 중재기관, 중재규칙 및 중재인을 당사자가 선택할 수 있으며, 판정주체의 전문성을 보장받을 수 있으며, 기밀성을 보장받을 수 있다는 점을 들 수 있다. 또한 당사자들이 서로 다른 국가의 법원에서 재판을 받기를 상호 꺼려하는 경향이 있고, 국제중재의 경우에는 국제적으로 통용되는 일반적인 절차를 기대할 수 있으며, 송달에 있어서 중재가 소송보다 편리하며, 판정의 집행측면에서도 중재의 경우 뉴욕협약이 있어 협약에 따라 집행이 보장된다는 점 등이 중재의 커다란 장점이다.

4-2-2. 청구 주체 및 요건

투자자-국가 분쟁해결을 청구할 수 있는 주체는 "분쟁투자자(disputing investor)"라 불리며, 적용대상 투자의 투자자를 말한다. 단, 당사국의 국적 또는 시민권을 소유한 자연인은 그 당사국에 대하여 청구를 제기할 수 없으며, 투자(investment)는 그 자체로 청구를 제기할 수 없다.

투자자의 국적을 기준으로 청구 주체의 자격이 인정되는바, 실질적인 투자자는 제3국인임에도 불구하고 특정 투자협정의 보호를 받기 위해 형식적인 회사를 설립하여 투자자 요건을 갖추는 경우 이를 투자자로 인정해서 보호할 것인가가 문제된다. 이러한 "조약 쇼핑(treaty shopping)"의 문제는 "혜택의 부인(denial of benefits)" 조항에 의해 해결될 수 있다. 즉, 해당 투자법인이 구성되거나 조직된 당사국의 법에 따라 그 당사국의 영역 내에서 실질적인 영업활동(substantial business activities)이 없고, 비당사국 또는 혜택을 부인하는 당사국의 투자자가 그 법인을 소유하거나 통제(own or control)하는 경우, 해당 법인 투자자와 그 투자자의 투자에 대하여 FTA상의 혜택을 부인할 수 있으므로, 이에 따라 투자자-국가 중재절차의 청구 자격도 부인할 수 있다.

청구의 대상요건과 관련하여, 한-아세안 FTA 투자협정은 "적용대상 투자의 경영, 영업, 매각, 처분과 관련하여, 협정상의 내국민대우, 최혜국대우, 투자에 대한 일반적 대우, 고위경영진 및 이사회 구성 제한 금지, 송금, 수용 및 보상, 그리고 손실보상 의무의 위반으로 인해, 적용대상 투자나 그 투자자에 손실(loss) 또는 손해(damage)가 야기된 때"라 규정하고 있다. 투자협정상의 일정한 의무 위반에 한해 중재절차에 제소할 수 있도록 한 점에서, 협정상의 의무 위반에 더해 투자인가(investment authorization)나 투자계약(investment agreement)상의 의무 위반의 경우까지 청구의 대상요건으로 포함시키고 있는 한-미FTA 보다는 제한적이라 볼 수 있다. 한-싱가포르 FTA나 한-칠레 FTA의 경우에도 이러한 제한적인 방식을 채택하고 있다.

4-2-3. 협의 절차

우선 투자자와 정부는 우호적인 해결에 도달하기 위하여, 협의(consultation) 및 협상(negotiation)을 통해 가능한 한 분쟁을 해결해야 한다. 이러한 협의 및 협상의 요청은 서면으로 이루어져야 한다.

협의 요청일로부터 6개월의 기간 내에 해결되지 아니한 분쟁은 분쟁당사국의 법원이나 행정법원이 동 청구에 대해 관할권을 갖고 있다면 동 법원이나 행정법원에, 또는 중재에 회부될 수 있다. 이때, 투자자가 분쟁 당사국의 법원이나 행정법원 또는 중재제도에 해당 분쟁을 회부하면, 그 법정에 대한 선택은 "최종적(final)"이다.

국내 법원절차와 중재절차가 동시에 진행되거나 중복되어 사용되는 경우, 서로 상충되는 결정이 내려질 가능성이 있다. 또한, 분쟁 당사자가 "포럼쇼핑(forum shopping)"을 남용하는 문제점도 발생할 수 있다. 이러한 문제점을 방지하기 위한 방법으로는 소위 "택일방식(fork-in-the-road approach)"과 "포기방식(waiver approach)"이 그동안 투자협정에 채택되어 왔다. 전자는 투자자가 어느 한 가지 분쟁해결 절차를 선택하도록 하고 일단 절차가 시작되었으면 다른 절차를 선택하지 못하도록 한 것이다. 한편, ICSID협약이나 한-미FTA 등의 경우에는 후자의 방식이 채택되어 투자자가 일단 국내법원에 제소한 경우에도 이를 취소하고 국제중재절차로 이행할 수 있는 길을 열어두고 있다. 물론 국제중재로 이행하는 경우 국내절차는 포기(waiver)한다는 서면포기서를 제출해야 한다.

이러한 두 가지 방식 중에서 한-아세안 FTA는 택일방식을 채택하고 있는 것으로 해석된다. 국내법원과 중재제도 중 하나를 선택하면 그것이 "최종적"이라는 것은 어느 하나만 선택할 수 있고, 일단 국내법원을 선택했다가 다시 중재로 이행할 수는 없다는 의미이기 때문이다.

한편, 한-아세안 FTA 투자협정은 "세금의 부과(taxation)"와 관련된 투자분쟁이 발생한 경우에 대한 사전협의 의무의 특칙을 규정하고 있다. 투자분쟁이 과세조치일 수 있는 조치에 관련된 경우, 분쟁당사국 및 투자자의 국적국은 그들의 조세당국의 대표를 포함하여, 문제의 조치가 과세조치인지 여부를 결정하기 위한 협의를 개최해야 한다. 분쟁투자자가 분쟁당사국이 과세조치를 채택 또는 집행함으로써 수용 및 보상의무를 위반하였다고 주장하는 경우, 양국 정부는 분쟁당사국이 요청 시 문제의 과세조치가 수용 또는 국유화의 동등한 효과를 가지는지 여부에 대한 결정을 하기 위하여 협의를 개최한다. 이러한 협의를 통해 양 당사국간 결정이 내려진 경우, 이러한 결정은 모든 법원이나 중재 재판소에 의해 "심각한 고려(serious consideration)"가 부여되어야 한다. 양국이 이러한 협의를 개시하는 데 실패하거나, 또는 협의 요청 후 180일의 기간 내에 그러한 공동 결정을 내리는 데 실패한 경우, 분쟁투자자는 그의 청구를 중재에 회부하는 것이 금지되지 아니한다.

4-2-4. 중재절차와 효력

중재에 회부될 경우, 투자자는 다음 중에서 선택권을 가진다.

(i) 분쟁 당사국과 비분쟁당사국이 모두 국제투자분쟁해결센터(ICSID) 협약의 당사자인 경우, 국제투자분쟁해결센터 협약과 국제투자분쟁해결센터 중재절차의 절차규칙

(ICSID Rules of Procedure for Arbitration Proceedings)

(ii) 분쟁당사국 및 비분쟁당사국 중 하나만이 국제투자분쟁해결센터 협약의 당사국인 경우, 국제투자분쟁해결센터의 추가절차규칙(ICSID Additional Facility Rules)

(iii) 유엔국제무역법위원회 중재규칙(UNCITRAL Arbitration Rules) 또는

(iv) 분쟁당사자들이 그렇게 동의할 경우, 그 밖의 중재규칙에 따른 그 밖의 중재기관

ICSID는 1966년 10월에 발효되고 우리나라가 1967년 3월 23일 조약 234호로 가입한 "국가와타방국가국민간의투자분쟁의해결에관한협약(Convention on the Settlement of Investment Disputes between States and Nationals of Other States: ICSID협약)"에 의하여 세계은행에 의해 설립된 중재기관이다. 국가간의 국제법 분쟁을 처리하는 국제사법재판소(ICJ)와는 달리 개인투자자와 국가간의 분쟁을 처리하는 중재기관이 탄생한 것이다. ICSID협약에 가입했다고 하더라도 모든 체약국에 대하여 ICSID의 관할권에 복종하기로 합의한 것은 아니다. 협약국에 대하여 ICSID의 관할권이 인정되기 위해서는 양 당사국이 서면으로 동의를 하여야 한다. 또한 동의를 하면서 조건을 부가하거나 제한을 가할 수도 있다. 한-아세안 FTA 투자협정은 분쟁투자자의 일방적 선택에 의해 ICSID가 중재관할권을 가진다는 점을 한국과 아세안국가들간에 서면으로 사전에 합의한 의미가 있는 것이다.

UNCITRAL은 유엔에서 각국의 서로 다른 법률로 인한 무역의 장애를 줄이기 위한 목적으로 1966년 설립한 산하기구로 UNCITRAL에서는 별도의 중재기관은 설립하지 않고 국제중제규칙만을 만들어 누구든지 이용할 수 있도록 한 대표적인 임의중재라고 할 수 있다. 임의중재의 경우에는 중재기관의 개입으로 인한 행정비용이나 절차의 지연 등을 피할 수 있는 이점이 있을 수 있으나 중재절차는 물론 중재비용의 예납, 중재인보수의 지급에 이르기까지의 모든 행정업무를 당사자 합의하에 중재판정부가 수행해야 한다는 점에서 불편한 점이 있고, 한 쪽 당사자가 비협조적일 경우 절차가 매우 지연될 수 있다는 문제점이 있다.

이러한 ICSID나 UNCITRAL 중재규칙 이외에 당사국이 합의하에 선택할 수 있는 대표적 중재절차, 기관으로는 ICC(International Chamber of Commerce)의 ICA(International Court of Arbitration), LCIA(London Court of International Arbitration), ICDR(International Center for Dispute Resolution; AAA) 등이 있다. 우리나라의 대한상사중재원이나 그 국제중재규칙도 당사자들이 선택할 수 있음은 물론이다.

이러한 분쟁의 중재 회부를 위한 전제조건으로는 해당 의무 위반 및 손실 또는 손해를 분쟁투자자나 알았거나, 합리적으로 알 수 있었던 날로부터 3년이 경과하지 않아야 한다. 이것은 중재회부에 있어서의 일종의 제소기한을 설정한 것이라 이해할 수 있다. 이상의 장기간이 경과하였는데도 과거의 일로 인해 투자유치국 정부를 언제라도 제소할 수 있다면, 투자자가 해당 정부를 끊임없이 괴롭히는 수단으로 남용될 여지가 있기에 이를 방지하기 위한 의미

도 있다.

또 하나의 전제조건으로, 분쟁투자자는 중재에 대한 청구를 제기하기 최소 90일 전에 분쟁을 그러한 중재에 회부한다는 의사, 중재판정부 선택, 분쟁 당사국의 의무 위반 주장 및 적용대상투자와 관련한 투자자 또는 적용대상투자에 초래되었다고 주장하는 손실 또는 손해의 간단한 요약을 분쟁 당사국에서 서면으로 통보해야 한다. 투자자가 중재회부 시기를 일방적으로 선택할 수 있는 상황에서, 투자유치국 정부에게 최소한의 준비기간을 부여해야 공정한 법정 논쟁이 가능하기 때문이다.

당사국은 분쟁투자자가 그의 권리 및 이익의 보전을 위하여, 중재판정부에서 절차를 개시하기 전에 분쟁당사국의 법원 또는 행정 재판소에서 손해배상의 지급 또는 분쟁사안의 실체적인 해결을 수반하지 아니하는 "잠정 보호조치(interim measures of protection)"를 구하는 것을 금지하지 아니한다.

당사국은 자국 투자자 및 그 밖의 당사국 중 하나가 이 조항에 따라 중재에 회부하기로 동의하였거나 또는 회부한 분쟁에 관하여 외교적 보호(diplomatic protection)를 부여하거나 국제소송을 제기하여서는 안 된다. 중재절차와 외교적 보호 절차가 중복되어 진행되는 것을 막기 위한 것이다. 다만, 중재절차가 완료되어 판정이 내려졌으나, 패소국 판정을 준수하지 않는 경우에는 승소한 투자자의 청구권을 보호하기 위해 투자자의 국적국이 외교적 보호권을 행사할 필요가 있으므로, 이러한 경우에는 외교적 보호권 행사가 가능함은 물론이다. 다만 오직 분쟁해결 촉진만을 목적으로 하는 비공식적인 외교적 의견교환은 언제나 가능하다.

재판소에 의해 내려진 중재판정은 최종적이며 분쟁당사자를 구속한다. 중재판정은 분쟁당사자간 그리고 그 특정 사건에 관한 것을 제외하고는 구속력을 가지지 아니한다.

이러한 양자투자협정 및 FTA상의 투자분쟁 해결 방식은 우리의 해외자원 개발투자에 대한 분쟁이 발생한 경우 유용하게 활용할 수 있는 법적 해결절차이므로 충분히 그 내용과 의의를 숙지해 두어야 한다. 분쟁이 발생하면, 각 협정상의 제소요건 및 조건 그리고 절차에 따라 적극적이고 유효한 공격과 방어가 이루어질 수 있도록 해야 할 것이다.

한-미 FTA Ch. 11, Sec. B: Investor-State Dispute Settlement

Article 11.15: Consultation and Negotiation

In the event of an investment dispute, the claimant and the respondent should initially seek to resolve the dispute through consultation and negotiation, which may include the use of non-binding, third-party procedures.

Article 11.16: Submission of a Claim to Arbitration

1. In the event that a disputing party considers that an investment dispute cannot be settled by consultation and negotiation:

(a) the claimant, on its own behalf, may submit to arbitration under this Section a claim
  (i) that the respondent has breached
    (A) an obligation under Section A,
    (B) an investment authorization, or
    (C) an investment agreement; and
  (ii) that the claimant has incurred loss or damage by reason of, or arising out of, that breach; and
(b) the claimant, on behalf of an enterprise of the respondent that is a juridical person that the claimant owns or controls directly or indirectly, may submit to arbitration under this Section a claim
  (i) that the respondent has breached
    (A) an obligation under Section A,
    (B) an investment authorization, or
    (C) an investment agreement; and
  (ii) that the enterprise has incurred loss or damage by reason of, or arising out of, that breach,

provided that a claimant may submit pursuant to subparagraph (a)(i)(C) or (b)(i)(C) a claim for breach of an investment agreement only if the subject matter of the claim and the claimed damages directly relate to the covered investment that was established or acquired or sought to be established or acquired, in reliance on the relevant investment agreement

2. At least 90 days before submitting any claim to arbitration under this Section, a claimant shall deliver to the respondent a written notice of its intention to submit the claim to arbitration (notice of intent). The notice shall specify:

(a) the name and address of the claimant and, where a claim is submitted on behalf of an enterprise, the name, address, and place of incorporation of the enterprise;
(b) for each claim, the provision of this Agreement, investment authorization, or investment agreement alleged to have been breached and any other relevant

provisions;

(c) the legal and factual basis for each claim; and

(d) the relief sought and the approximate amount of damages claimed.

3. Provided that six months have elapsed since the events giving rise to the claim, a claimant may submit a claim referred to in paragraph 1:

(a) under the ICSID Convention and the ICSID Rules of Procedure for Arbitration Proceedings, provided that both the respondent and the non-disputing Party are parties to the ICSID Convention;

(b) under the ICSID Additional Facility Rules, provided that either the respondent or the non-disputing Party is a party to the ICSID Convention;

(c) under the UNCITRAL Arbitration Rules; or

(d) if the claimant and respondent agree, to any other arbitration institution or under any other arbitration rules.

4. A claim shall be deemed submitted to arbitration under this Section when the claimant's notice of, or request for, arbitration (notice of arbitration):

(a) referred to in paragraph 1 of Article 36 of the ICSID Convention is received by the Secretary-General;

(b) referred to in Article 2 of Schedule C of the ICSID Additional Facility Rules is received by the Secretary-General;

(c) referred to in Article 3 of the UNCITRAL Arbitration Rules, together with the statement of claim referred to in Article 18 of the UNCITRAL Arbitration Rules, are received by the respondent; or

(d) referred to under any arbitral institution or arbitral rules selected under paragraph 3(d) is received by the respondent.

A claim asserted by the claimant for the first time after such notice of arbitration is submitted shall be deemed submitted to arbitration under this Section on the date of its receipt under the applicable arbitral rules.

5. The arbitration rules applicable under paragraph 3, and in effect on the date the claim or claims were submitted to arbitration under this Section, shall govern the arbitration except to the extent modified by this Agreement.

6. The claimant shall provide with the notice of arbitration:

(a) the name of the arbitrator that the claimant appoints; or
(b) the claimant's written consent for the Secretary-General to appoint that arbitrator.

Article 11.17: Consent of Each Party to Arbitration

1. Each Party consents to the submission of a claim to arbitration under this Section in accordance with this Agreement.

2. The consent under paragraph 1 and the submission of a claim to arbitration under this Section shall satisfy the requirements of:

(a) Chapter II (Jurisdiction of the Centre) of the ICSID Convention and the ICSID Additional Facility Rules for written consent of the parties to the dispute, and
(b) Article II of the New York Convention for an "agreement in writing."

2. 외국정부를 피고로 하는 소송의 특수성

가. 주권면책이론

어느 국가의 사법부이건 외국정부를 상대로 재판을 할 수 없다는 것은 주권면책이론에 기초한 확립된 국제법이다.[4] 국가의 공권력의 행사가 아닌 상업적 활동에는 주권면책이론이 적용되지 아니한다.[5] 그 구체적인 적용범위는 사법부의 누적된 판례에 의존할 수도 있고 미국처럼 실정법에서 정할 수도 있다.[6] 법규로 정한 경우에도 이의 해석과 관련하여 많은 의문이 제기되고 있다. 예를 들어 국가기관은 국제기구를 포함하는가? 묵시적 주권면책포기는 어떤 경우에 인정되는가? 상업적 행위인지 여부는 어떻게 판단하는가? 외국정부의 외국에서의 행위가 자국에 직접적 효과를 가진다는 의미는 무엇인가? 통상의 인적, 물적 관할권 존재여부에 관한 판단은 필요없는가?

---

4) United Nations Convention on Jurisdictional Immunities of States and Their Property, U.N. G.A. Res. 59/38 on Dec. 2, 2004. 자세한 것은 김대순, 주 9-28 상게서 436-86 참조.

5) *S.T.Tringali Co. v. The Tug Pemex XV,* 274 F. Supp. 227 (S.D.Tex. 1967) (PEMEX의 선박에 대하여 압류가능). 산유국정부가 양허계약하에서 미국의 석유회사에 대하여 가지는 로열티와 채권의 법적 성질에 관하여는 논란의 여지가 있다.

6) Foreign Sovereign Immunity Act 28 U.S.C. §§ 1330 et seq. (1976).

Carey v. National Oil Corporation, 592 F.2d 673 (2d Cir. 1979)[7)]

Appellant New England Petroleum Corporation ("NEPCO") is a New York company which sells residual fuel oil in the eastern United States. One of the sources for this residual oil is a refinery company located in the Bahamas, the Grand Bahama Petroleum Company, Ltd. ("PETCO"). PETCO is a wholly-owned subsidiary of NEPCO. Appellant Carey is an assignee of PETCO.

In 1968, PETCO entered into a long-term contract to purchase crude oil from Chevron Oil Trading ("COT"), a branch of a petroleum company which held 50 per cent of an oil concession in Libya. The oil obtained under this contract was to be refined and sold to NEPCO. Libyan crude oil was particularly attractive to NEPCO because its low sulphur content aided compliance with United States air pollution standards.

In September, 1973 the Socialist People's Libyan Arab Jamahirya ("Libya") nationalized several foreign-owned oil concessions in that country, including that of the company of which COT was a part. This caused COT to suspend all crude oil deliveries to PETCO and to terminate its contract with PETCO.

In order to obtain the oil supplies it needed, PETCO entered into new contracts in September, 1973 with the National Oil Corporation ("NOC"), a company wholly owned by the Libyan government. These new contracts were at a substantially higher price than the canceled one with COT.

The following month, Libya imposed an embargo on oil exports to the United States, the Netherlands, and the Bahamas. Accordingly, NOC canceled its contracts with PETCO. World oil prices rose and available supplies declined. NOC then accepted bids on new contracts to supersede the ones effective until that time. In order to fulfill its contracts for the sale of refined oil in the United States, PETCO entered into a new contract with NOC for crude oil to be refined in Italy (during the embargo) and the Bahamas. In January, 1974 the contract was executed, calling for a price per barrel of oil more than three times the previous price.

In December, 1973 another subsidiary of NEPCO, Antco Shipping Company, agreed to charter two tankers owned by a Libyan government-owned entity. NEPCO claims that these were chartered at excessive rates as a condition of delivering oil to PETCO.

This suit attempts to recover damages for NOC's failure to deliver oil under the September, 1973 contract, for breaches of the 1974 contract, and for overcharges on the charter parties. The damages sought total approximately. $1.6 billion. Because we find

---

7) 프랑스판례 *Societe Iranienne du Gaz v. Societe Pipeline Service,* 80 Rev. Critique de Droit International Prive 140에 관하여는 Georges R. Delaume, *Sovereign Immunity — Nature of the Act Teest for Commercial Activity,* 85 AM. J. INT'L L. 696 (1991)에서 정리.

that this court has no jurisdiction in this case, we do not reach the merits of these claims.

Foreign states are immune from suit in the courts of the United States for many of their acts, and thus federal courts have no jurisdiction in disputes involving such public acts. Specific exceptions to this general grant of immunity were carefully mapped out by Congress in the Foreign Sovereign Immunities Act of 1976, 28 U.S.C. s 1330 and ss 1602-11.

Appellants claim, most relevantly, that the events involved in this case come within the exception to immunity which allows U.S. jurisdiction where a claim is based on "an act outside the territory of the United States in connection with a commercial activity of the foreign state elsewhere and that act causes a direct effect in the United States." 28 U.S.C. s 1605(a)(2). [FN3] We find no direct effect in the United States here.

We assume that Congress chose the language in the act purposefully. Section 1605(a)(2) speaks of acts which have a "direct" effect in the United States. The legislative history of this section makes clear that it embodies the standard set out in International Shoe Co. v. Washington, 326 U.S. 310, 316, 66 S.Ct. 154, 158, 90 L.Ed. 95 (1945), that in order to satisfy due process requirements, a defendant over whom jurisdiction is to be exercised must have "certain minimum contacts with (the forum state) such that the maintenance of the suit does not offend 'traditional notions of fair play and substantive justice.' " That standard has not been met here.

PETCO is a Bahamian corporation. Though a subsidiary of NEPCO, it was a separate corporate entity, and we will not here "pierce the corporate veil" in favor of those who created that veil. The cancellation of the contracts between NOC and PETCO, and the overcharge on the charters, had a direct effect on PETCO as a party to those contracts, but not in the United States. Similarly, while there was an admitted effect on NEPCO, an American company, that effect can only be deemed indirect, through NEPCO's relations with PETCO and Antco, whose dealings with NOC were entirely outside the United States.

At no time did NOC or Libya "purposely avail itself of the privilege" of conducting business in the United States. The product which was destined for the United States, the refined oil, was a different substance than the crude oil sold by NOC to PETCO, so there was no real entering of the marketplace in the United States.

The appellants claim that the Libyan government and NOC were aware that the refineries in the Bahamas were being used primarily to channel oil into the United States. Appellants also contend that the Libyan oil embargo was expressly aimed at affecting the United States. Even if these allegations are true, they do not fulfill the "minimum contacts" requirement of International Shoe, and thus cannot reach the level of "direct" effects described in the statute. The claims concerning the charter parties fail for the same reason.

The judgment of the district court dismissing for lack of jurisdiction is affirmed.

Interpetrol Bermuda v. Trinidad & Tobago Oil Co., 135 Misc.2d 160, 513 N.Y.S.2d 598 (N.Y.Sup. 1987)

This case presents an issue of first impression whose resolution requires consideration of both the Foreign Sovereign Immunities Act, 28 U.S.C. § 1602 et seq. (1976) (the "FSIA") and New York statutory scheme concerning prejudgment attachments, N.Y.C.P.L.R. 6201 et seq. The question, put most simply, is whether the postattachment nationalization of a defendant and its property requires, as a matter of statutorily created sovereign immunity, the denial of the plaintiff's motion for an increased attachment and/or the vacating of the prior attachment. For the reasons discussed below the motion is denied and the prior attachment vacated.

FACTS

The underlying action involves a contract for the sale of various petroleum products by defendant Trinidad & Tobago Oil Co., Ltd. (Trintoc) to plaintiff Interpetrol Bermuda Ltd. (Interpetrol). An action was commenced on December 1, 1977 by order to show cause with a TRO against the transfer of assets by plaintiff and two garnishees.[1] A subsequent order to show cause brought on an attachment proceeding, and on May 19, 1978 an order confirming the attachment was entered.[2] At that time, it was conceded that defendant, incorporated under the laws of the United Kingdom, was "a foreign corporation not qualified to do business in the state", one of the four grounds for attachment set forth in CPLR 6201.

Subsequent to the order, the parties entered into various negotiations concerning alternatives to the attachment, not relevant here, but including an offer by defendant to establish a letter of credit to be drawn on by plaintiff in the event it ultimately prevailed in the lawsuit.[3] The offer was rejected, and the attachment, in the amount of

---

1. As a result of the TRO, Tesoro Petroleum Corp. withheld more than $300,000 in accounts receivable, and Citibank withheld some $300,000 in defendant's checking account.
2. The order included the requirement that a $50,000 bond be posted by plaintiff and provided that in the event that it was determined that Interpetrol was ultimately not entitled to the attachment, Interpetrol "shall pay to [Trintoc-U.K.] all costs and damages, including reasonable attorney's fees, which may be sustained by reason of the restraint".
3. Defendant argued that this would be less costly to it, allowing the use of the frozen funds, inter

$471,640.18, continued.

After some activity, in around 1981, plaintiff ceased to prosecute the action. No discovery was conducted, no depositions taken and no communications were had with defendant for a period of five years. On January 10, 1986 defendant filed a demand, pursuant to CPLR 3216, for Interpetrol to resume prosecution or have its case dismissed. Plaintiff, with new counsel, filed a note of issue and on September 23, 1986 moved for an order of additional attachment in the amount of $357,849.92, representing interest on the judgment sought. Defendant opposed and cross-moved to vacate the 1978 order of attachment on the grounds, inter alia, that in December 1980, the government of Trinidad and Tobago had, by legislative act[4] (Vesting Act), transferred the assets of defendant Trintoc-U.K. to a new corporation Trinidad and Tobago Oil Co. Ltd., Trinidad and Tobago (Trintoc-Trinidad) organized under its domestic laws. The new corporation, like the old, was wholly owned by the Republic of Trinidad and Tobago. As such, defendant argued its property was immune from prejudgment attachment under the FSIA, most particularly section 1609. Additionally, defendant argued that under New York law, the attachment must be vacated since Interpetrol has failed to show need for its continuation and because it is unduly burdensome. These grounds will be considered seriatim.

IMMUNITY UNDER THE FSIA

The FSIA, passed by Congress in 1976, provides a comprehensive and uniform statutory scheme defining and preserving sovereign immunity in the courts — State and Federal — of the United States. In addition to its jurisdictional provisions, the act provides as follows: "Subject to existing international agreements to which the United States is a party at the time of enactment of this Act the property in the United States of a foreign state shall be immune from attachment arrest and execution except as provided in sections 1610 and 1611[5] of this chapter." (28 USC s 1609.)

Under section 1603 of the act, a "foreign state" includes an organ of a foreign sovereign which is wholly owned by the foreign sovereign (e.g., *S&S Mach. Co. v*

---

alia, to earn interest, and to the plaintiff who would be spared the expense of a bond. It is not clear why this offer was rejected.

4. This was the Trinidad and Tobago Oil Company Limited Vesting Act (the Vesting Act) enacted by the Fifth Session, First Parliament of the Republic of Trinidad and Tobago, passed by both houses and asserted to in December 1980. Following the acquisition of Trintoc-U.K.'s assets by Trintoc-Trinidad, the original U.K. Corp. was voluntarily wound up.

5. Section 1611 involves special immunities accorded central bank and military property and is inapplicable to this case.

Masinexportimport, 706 F2d 411 [2d Cir], cert denied 464 U.S. 850 [1983] [trading company wholly owned by government of Romania]; *Carey v National Oil Corp.*, 592 F2d 673 [2d Cir 1979] [State-owned oil company]). Since the Vesting Act, it cannot be denied and is not disputed that Trintoc-Trinidad is a foreign State within the meaning of the FSIA. As such, its property is absolutely immune from prejudgment attachment except where there has been an explicit waiver of immunity by the foreign sovereign,[6] as provided in section 1610 (d) (e.g., *Schwartz v Merchants Bank,* 109 AD2d 108 [1st Dept 1985]; see also, *O'Connell Mach. Co. v M.V. "Americana",* 734 F2d 115, 117 [2d Cir 1984]; *S&S Mach. Co. v Masinexportimport*, supra, at 416).

WAIVER

A. JUDICIAL INTERPRETATION

The requirement of explicit waiver under the Immunities Act was designed by Congress to avoid inadvertent or implied waivers. (*Schwartz v Merchants Bank*, 109 AD2d, at 111,supra; *Libra Bank v Banco Nacional de Costa Rica*, 676 F2d 47, 49 [2d Cir 1982].) Congress recognized that prejudgment attachment is "an extraordinary and harsh remedy not to be lightly waived." (*New England Merchants Natl. Bank v Iran Power Generation & Transmission Co.*, 502 F Supp 120, 126 [US Dist Ct, SD NY 1980].) As the Second Circuit has explained: "the asserted waiver must demonstrate unambiguously the foreign state's intention to waive its immunity from prejudgment attachment in this country. We do not take lightly the congressional demand for explicitness. It would be improper for a court to subvert this directive by substituting a judicially reconstituted gloss or a facially unclear document for an unequivocal waiver by the foreign state." (*S&S Mach. Co. v Masinexportimport*, 706 F2d, at 416,supra).

The question thus becomes whether under this rigorous standard the government of Trinidad-Tobago has "explicitly" waived its immunity from prejudgment attachment by the language of the Vesting Act.

That act has two relevant provisions. Section 4 (1) (h) provides: "(h) any security provided by or for the Company that immediately before the appointed day was held as security for the payment or discharge by the Company of a debt or liability or obligation (whether present or future, actual or contingent) shall be held by and be available to a

6. Another section, 28 USC s 1610 (a)-(c), permits both explicit and implicit waivers in the case of postjudgment attachments. The distinction and higher burden of waiver for prejudgment attachment reflects the "inherently burdensome" nature of those attachments since they "encumber property before a final adjudication of the action on the merits" (Raji v Bank Sepha-Iran, 131 Misc 2d 158, 162 [Sup Ct,NY County 1985].) It is, of course, the "explicit waiver" standard of section 1610 (d) which governs here.

holder as security for the payment or discharge by Trintoc of that debt or liability or obligation; and any such security which extends to future advances or liabilities shall on and from the appointed day, be held by and be available to the holder as security for future advances to, and future liabilities of, Trintoc in the same manner in all respects as future advances to or liabilities of the company were secured thereby immediately before the appointed day".

Under the Vesting Act, provision was also made that judgments or awards against Trintoc-U.K. would be enforceable against Trintoc-Trinidad. Section 4 (1) (i) of the Vesting Act provides: "(i) any judgment or award obtained by or against the company and not fully satisfied shall be enforceable by or against Trintoc".

By these provisions plaintiff argues that the Republic of Trinidad and Tobago has "explicitly waived" its immunity with regard to prejudgment attachment in this litigation. Since the enactment of the FSIA, a number of cases have considered whether language in varying documents and in treaties reaches the high, congressionally mandated standard of "explicit" waiver. The leading group involved interpretation of the U.S.-Iran Treaty of Amity, which contained the following language: "No enterprise of either High Contracting Party, including corporations, associations, and government agencies and instrumentalities, which is publicly owned or controlled shall, if it engages in commercial, industrial, shipping or other business activities within the territories of the other High Contracting Party, claim or enjoy, either for itself or for its property, immunity therein from taxation, suit, execution of judgment or other liability to which privately owned and controlled enterprises are subject therein." (Treaty of Amity, art XI, para 4, 8 UST 899, 909 [1957]; emphasis added.)

Almost uniformly the Federal and State courts confronted with this language held it was not an explicit waiver of prejudgment immunity as required by section 1610 (d)(e.g., *New England Merchants Natl. Bank v Iran Power Generation & Transmission Co.*, 502 F Supp 120, 125-126 [U.S. Dist Ct, SD NY 1980], supra; *American Intl. Group v Islamic Republic of Iran*, 493 F Supp 522 [U.S. Dist Ct, DC 1980]; *E-Systems, Inc. v Islamic Republic of Iran,* 491 F Supp 1294 [U.S. Dist Ct, ND Tex 1980]; *Behring Intl. v Imperial Iranian Air Force,* 475 F Supp 383 [U.S. Dist Ct, D NJ 1979]; *Raji v Bank Sepha-Iran*, 131 Misc 2d 158, 164;see also, Pre-Judgment Attachments of Iranian Assets in the United States: Waiving Sovereign Immunity, 13 NY U J of Intl L & Politics 675, 684, 701; Prejudgment Attachment of Frozen Iranian Attachments, 69 Calif L Rev 837, 841, n 28, 846).

In considering similar language in a U.S.-Romanian trade agreement waiving immunity "from suit an execution of judgment or other liability" (Agreement on Trade Relations Between United States and Romanian Government, Apr. 2, 1975, art IV, para 2,

26 UST 2305, 2308-2309, TIAS No. 8159), the Second Circuit has held that "the 'other liability' language does not unequivocally express the will of the parties to waive immunity from prejudgment attachment" (*S&S Mach. Co. v Masinexportimport*, supra, at 417).

In the only case where explicit waiver was found, a borrower and lender expressly agreed in writing that the borrower was subject to suit and "[did] not have any right of immunity" (supra, 676 F. 2d, at 49; emphasis added). In addition, the borrower executed four promissory notes stating that he "irrevocably and unconditionally waives any right or immunity from legal proceedings" (supra, at 49). Based on this unconditional language, speaking directly to the question of immunity, the Second Circuit found an explicit waiver. (*Libra Bank v Banco Nacional de Costa Rica,* supra, 676 F2d, at 49-50.)

On their face, the provisions of the Vesting Act relied upon by plaintiff do not rise to the stringent standard of explicitness required by the FSIA. Section 4 (1) (h) and (i) does not clearly and unambiguously evince an intent on the part of Trintoc-Trinidad or the Republic of Trinidad and Tobago to waive any right of immunity from prejudgment attachment. Indeed, unlike the language in *Libra Bank* (supra), and even unlike that in *S&S Mach.* (supra), the Vesting Act contains no reference to immunity at all.

B. THE VESTING ACT AND TRINIDADIAN LAW

Consideration of the context of the Vesting Act and of Trinidadian law compels the same conclusion. In an unrebutted affidavit by a member of the Trinidad Bar, defendant explains that the purpose of the Vesting Act was to enable Trintoc-Trinidad to acquire certain assets, liabilities and obligations of Trintoc-U.K. Significantly, at the time of the adoption of the Vesting Act, there was no procedure under the laws of Trinidad and Tobago for prejudgment attachment.

Thus, it is clear that the legislature of Trinidad and Tobago did not intend to waive — and could not have waived — its immunity from prejudgment attachment. (See, *Reading & Bates Corp. v National Iranian Oil Corp.,* 478 F Supp 724, 729 [U.S. Dist Ct, SD NY 1979] [rules of construction dictate that in interpreting an alleged waiver of immunity from prejudgment attachment the "paramount consideration for a Court ... is to give effect to the intent of the parties"].)

If the Trinidad and Tobago legislature intended to explicitly waive Trintoc-Trinidad's immunity from prejudgment attachment, it would have done so in section 4 (1)(i) of the Vesting Act, the only provision which directly refers to litigation. Under section 4 (1)(i), "any judgment or award obtained by or against the company and not fully satisfied shall be enforceable by or against Trintoc." The omission in this paragraph of any mention of waiver of immunity clearly demonstrates that no waiver of immunity was intended.

Finally, defendant has submitted the affidavit of Seunarine Jokhoo, Acting Permanent Secretary in the Ministry of State Enterprises of the Republic of Trinidad-Tobago,7 who states that: "attachment of the assets of Trintoc-Trinidad is inconsistent with principles of international comity ...

and is against the interest of the Republic of Trinidad and Tobago." While this affidavit, originally submitted as proof of Trintoc-Trinidad's status as a "foreign state" does not speak directly to the issue of immunity, it is additional evidence that no waiver was ever intended by enactment of the Vesting Act.

대법 1998. 12. 17. 선고 97다39216 전원합의체 판결[8)]

1. 원심판결 이유에 의하면, 원심은 원고가 미합중국 산하의 비세출자금기관인 '육군 및 공군 교역처'(The United States Army and Air Force Exchange Service)에 고용되어 미군 2사단 소재 캠프 케이시(Camp Cacey)에서 근무하다가 1992. 11. 8. 정당한 이유 없이 해고되었다고 주장하면서 미합중국을 피고로 하여 위 해고의 무효확인과 위 해고된 날로부터 원고를 복직시킬 때까지의 임금의 지급을 구함에 대하여, 원래 국가는 국제법과 국제관례상 다른 국가의 재판권에 복종하지 않게 되어 있으므로 특히 조약에 의하여 예외로 된 경우나 스스로 외교상 특권을 포기하는 경우를 제외하고는 외국을 피고로 하여 우리나라의 법원이 재판권을 행사할 수는 없다고 할 것인데, 미합중국이 우리나라 법원의 재판권에 복종하기로 하는 내용의 조약이 있다거나 미합중국이 위와 같은 외교상의 특권을 포기하였다고 인정할 만한 아무런 증거가 없으므로, 이 사건 소는 우리나라의 법원에 재판권이 없어 부적법하다고 판단하였다.

2. 국제관습법에 의하면 국가의 주권적 행위는 다른 국가의 재판권으로부터 면제되는 것이 원칙이라 할 것이나, 국가의 사법적 행위까지 다른 국가의 재판권으로부터 면제된다는 것이 오늘날의 국제법이나 국제관례라고 할 수 없다. 따라서 우리나라의 영토 내에서 행하여진 외국의 사법적 행위가 주권적 활동에 속하는 것이거나 이와 밀접한 관련이 있어서 이에 대한 재판권의 행사가 외국의 주권적 활동에 대한 부당한 간섭이 될 우려가 있다는 등의 특별한 사정이 없는 한, 외국의 사법적 행위에 대하여는 당해 국가를 피고로 하여 우리나라의

---

7. This is the ministry responsible for the functioning of all State enterprises including Trintoc-Trinidad.

8) 김태천, 외국국가의 재판권면제 — 그 법적근거와 범위에 관하여 —, 34 저스티스 276, 290(고용계약은 목적과 성질 중 어느 기준으로 보더라도 주권적 행위로 보기 어려우며 청구원인에 따라서 판단할 문제는 아니라고 본다). 고용계약의 특수성을 인정하는 견해는 석광현, 2000 법조 290, 307.

법원이 재판권을 행사할 수 있다고 할 것이다. 이와 견해를 달리한 대법원 1975. 5. 23.자 74마281 결정은 이를 변경하기로 한다.

따라서 원심으로서는 원고가 근무한 미합중국 산하 기관인 '육군 및 공군 교역처'의 임무 및 활동 내용, 원고의 지위 및 담당업무의 내용, 미합중국의 주권적 활동과 원고의 업무의 관련성 정도 등 제반 사정을 종합적으로 고려하여 이 사건 고용계약 및 해고행위의 법적 성질 및 주권적 활동과의 관련성 등을 살펴본 다음에 이를 바탕으로 이 사건 고용계약 및 해고행위에 대하여 우리나라의 법원이 재판권을 행사할 수 있는지 여부를 판단하였어야 할 것이다. 그럼에도 불구하고 이 사건 고용계약 및 해고행위의 법적 성질 등을 제대로 살펴보지 아니한 채 그 판시와 같은 이유만으로 재판권이 없다고 단정하여 이 사건 소가 부적법하다고 판단한 원심판결에는 외국에 대한 재판권의 행사에 관한 법리를 오해하고 심리를 다하지 아니한 위법이 있다고 할 것이다. 상고이유 중 이 점을 지적하는 부분은 이유 있다.

대법 2011. 12. 13. 선고 2009다16766 판결

1. 우리나라의 영토 내에서 행하여진 외국의 사법적 행위가 주권적 활동에 속하는 것이거나 이와 밀접한 관련이 있어서 이에 대한 재판권의 행사가 외국의 주권적 활동에 대한 부당한 간섭이 될 우려가 있다는 등의 특별한 사정이 없는 한, 외국의 사법적 행위에 대하여는 해당 국가를 피고로 하여 우리나라의 법원이 재판권을 행사할 수 있다(대법원 1998. 12. 17. 선고 97다39216 전원합의체 판결 등 참조).

그런데 채권압류 및 추심명령은 집행법원이 일방적으로 제3채무자에게 채무자에 대한 채무의 지급금지를 명령하고 피압류채권의 추심권능을 집행채권자에게 부여하는 것으로서 이에 따라 제3채무자는 집행채무자에게 채무를 지급하더라도 집행채권자에게 대항할 수 없어 여전히 추심명령을 받은 집행채권자에게 채무를 지급하여야 할 의무를 부담하게 된다. 이와 같이 채권압류 및 추심명령은 제3채무자 소유의 재산에 대한 집행이 아니고 또한 제3채무자는 집행당사자가 아님에도, 채권압류 및 추심명령이 있으면 제3채무자는 지급금지명령, 추심명령 등 집행법원의 강제력 행사의 직접적인 상대방이 되어 이에 복종하게 된다. 이와 같은 점을 고려하면 제3채무자를 외국으로 하는 채권압류 및 추심명령에 대한 재판권 행사는 외국을 피고로 하는 판결절차에서의 재판권 행사보다 더욱 신중히 행사될 것이 요구된다. 더구나 채권압류 및 추심명령이 제3채무자에 대한 집행권원이 아니라 집행채권자의 채무자에 대한 집행권원만으로 일방적으로 발령되는 것인 점을 고려하면 더욱 그러하다. 따라서 피압류채권이 외국의 사법적 행위를 원인으로 하여 발생한 것이고 그 사법적 행위에 대하여 해당

국가를 피고로 하여 우리나라의 법원이 재판권을 행사할 수 있다고 하더라도, 피압류채권의 당사자가 아닌 집행채권자가 해당 국가를 제3채무자로 한 압류 및 추심명령을 신청하는 경우, 우리나라 법원은, 해당 국가가 국제협약, 중재합의, 서면계약, 법정에서 진술 등의 방법으로 그 사법적 행위로 부담하는 국가의 채무에 대하여 압류 기타 우리나라 법원에 의하여 명하여지는 강제집행의 대상이 될 수 있다는 점에 대하여 명시적으로 동의하였거나 또는 우리나라 내에 그 채무의 지급을 위한 재산을 따로 할당해 두는 등 우리나라 법원의 압류 등 강제조치에 대하여 재판권 면제 주장을 포기한 것으로 볼 수 있는 경우 등에 한하여 그 해당 국가를 제3채무자로 하는 채권압류 및 추심명령을 발령할 재판권을 가진다고 볼 것이다. 그리고 이와 같이 우리나라 법원이 외국을 제3채무자로 하는 추심명령에 대하여 재판권을 행사할 수 있는 경우에는 그 추심명령에 기하여 외국을 피고로 하는 추심금 소송에 대하여도 역시 재판권을 행사할 수 있다고 할 것이고, 반면 추심명령에 대한 재판권이 인정되지 않는 경우에는 추심금 소송에 대한 재판권 역시 인정되지 않는다고 봄이 상당하다.

한편 대한민국과 아메리카합중국 간의 상호방위조약 제4조에 의한 시설과 구역 및 대한민국에서의 합중국군대의 지위에 관한 협정(이하 '한미행정협정'이라 한다) 제23조 제5항은 공무집행 중인 합중국 군대의 구성원이나 고용원의 작위나 부작위 또는 합중국 군대가 법률상 책임을 지는 기타의 작위나 부작위 또는 사고로서 대한민국 안에서 대한민국 정부 이외의 제3자에게 손해를 가한 것으로부터 발생하는 청구권의 처리절차에 대하여 규정하고 있는데 위와 같은 청구권이라고 하더라도 그것이 계약에 의한 청구권(contractual claim)인 경우에는 제23조 제5항의 적용 대상에서 제외한다고 규정하고 있고, 한미행정협정 제23조 제6항은 대한민국 안에서 불법한 작위 또는 부작위로서 공무집행 중에 행하여진 것이 아닌 것으로부터 발생한 합중국 군대의 구성원 또는 고용원에 대한 청구권의 처리절차에 대하여 규정하면서 합중국 군대의 고용원이더라도 대한민국 국민이거나 대한민국에 통상적으로 거주하는 고용원인 경우에는 제23조 제6항의 적용대상에서 제외한다고 규정하고 있다. 그리고 2001. 1. 18. 체결된 대한민국과 아메리카합중국 간의 상호방위조약 제4조에 의한 시설과 구역 및 대한민국에서의 합중국군대의 지위에 관한 협정과 관련 합의의사록에 관한 양해사항(이하 '양해사항'이라 한다)은 한미행정협정 제23조 제5항 및 제6항과 관련하여 '합동위원회는 대한민국 법원에 의한 민사재판권의 행사를 위한 절차를 제정하여야 한다.'고 규정하고 이에 따라 제정된 협정 제23조 비형사재판절차에 관한 합동위원회 합의사항 제1호(이하 '합의사항'이라 한다) 제4조의 ㈑에서는 '합중국 정부가 합중국 군대의 구성원, 군속 또는 고용인에게 지급할 금원은 합중국 법률이 허용하는 범위 내에서 압류 기타 대한민국 관할법원에 의하여 명하여진 강제집행의 대상이 될 수 있다'고 규정하고 있다. 이와 같은 규정의 체계 및 그 문언에 의하면 위 합의사항은 한미행정협정 제23조 제5항 또는 제6항에 따른 청구권의 실행 절차 등에 관한 규정이라고 할 것이다.

2. 원심판결 이유 및 기록에 의하면, 소외인은 대한민국에 거주하는 자로서 주한미군사령부에서 고압전기기사로 근무하는 자인 사실, 원고와 소외인 사이에 서울지방법원 99나85700호 손해배상(자) 사건의 판결에 따라 원고가 소외인에게 가지급물반환채권을 가지는 사실, 원고는 서울지방법원 동부지원에 채무자를 소외인, 제3채무자를 피고로 하여 소외인이 피고에 대하여 가지는 퇴직금 및 임금 등에 대하여 채권압류 및 추심명령을 신청하고, 위 법원은 이를 받아들여 서울지방법원 동부지원 2001타기3495호로 채권압류 및 추심명령(이하 '이 사건 채권압류 및 추심명령'이라 한다)을 발령한 사실을 알 수 있다.

위 사실관계를 앞서 본 법리에 비추어 보면, 먼저 원고와 피고 사이에는 아무런 사법적 계약관계가 없어 원고가 피고를 상대로 제기한 이 사건 소에 대하여 우리나라 법원이 당연히 재판권을 행사할 수 있는 것은 아니다.

나아가 우리나라 법원이 원고가 소외인에 대하여 가지는 가지급물반환채권의 만족을 위하여 소외인이 피고에 대하여 가지는 임금 등 채권에 대하여 피고를 제3채무자로 한 채권압류 및 추심명령을 발령할 재판권을 가지는가에 관하여 본다. 원고가 소외인에 대하여 가지는 가지급물반환채권은 한미행정협정 제23조 제5항 및 제6항에서 규정하는 고용인의 불법한 작위 또는 부작위로 인하여 발생한 청구권이 아닐 뿐만 아니라 소외인은 한미행정협정 제23조 제6항에서 그 적용 배제사유로 규정하고 있는 대한민국에 거주하는 자이어서 원고가 소외인에 대하여 가지는 가지급물반환채권은 한미행정협정 제23조 제5항 또는 제6항에서 규정하는 청구권에 해당하지 않는다. 따라서 한미행정협정 제23조 제5항 또는 제6항에 따른 청구권의 실행 절차에 관한 규정인 위 합의사항은 원고가 소외인에 대하여 가지는 가지급물반환채권의 만족을 위한 강제집행에는 적용되지 않는다고 할 것이다. 그 외 피고가 고용원인 소외인에게 부담하는 임금 등 채무에 대하여 압류 기타 우리나라 법원에 의하여 명하여지는 강제집행의 대상이 될 수 있다는 점에 대하여 명시적으로 동의하였다거나 또는 우리나라 내에 그 채무의 지급을 위하여 재산을 따로 할당해 두는 등 우리나라 법원의 압류 등 강제조치에 대하여 재판권 면제 주장을 포기하였다고 볼 아무런 자료가 없으므로 결국 우리나라 법원은 피고를 제3채무자로 한 이 사건 채권압류 및 추심명령을 발령할 재판권을 가지지 못한다고 할 것이다. 따라서 이 사건 채권압류 및 추심명령은 재판권이 없는 법원이 발령한 것으로 무효라고 할 것이고, 우리나라 법원은 이 사건 추심금 소송에 대하여도 재판권이 인정되지 않는다고 할 것이다.

그렇다면 이 사건 소는 우리나라 법원에 재판권이 없어 부적법하다고 본 원심판결은 결론에 있어서 정당하고 거기에 상고이유에서 주장하는 바와 같은 법리오해 등의 위법이 없다.

노트와 질문

외국정부가 추심명령의 제3채무자인가, 원고의 직접적 계약상대방인가, 또는 원고에게 불법행위를 행한 손해배상채무자인가에 따라서 사법부의 재판권 존부가 달라져야 하는가?

대법 1962. 3. 15. 선고 4294민상1083 판결

원고 소송 대리인의 상고 이유는 이 판결서 끝에 매어진 상고 이유서에 쓰여져 있는 것과 같다.

생각하건대 국가 배상법에 규정한 국가 또는 공공 단체의 손해배상 책임은 공권력의 행사에 있어서 공무원이 그 직무 수행에 당하여 고의 또는 과실로 법령을 위반하여 타인에게 손해를 보게 하였을 때에 한하여 있는 것이고 같은 법 제2조의 적용이 있는 경우에 있어서는 민법상 사용자의 배상 책임에 관한 규정(민법 제756조)은 적용이 배제된다 할 것이다. 이 사건에 있어서 기록에 의하면 이 청구의 원인 되는 계약은 원고와 휼병감 김근배 간의 사병 플라스틱 명찰에 관한 매매 계약으로서 이는 휼병감으로서 공권력의 행사에 속하는 직무 수행이 아니고 순전이 대등한 지위에 있어서의 사 경제관계로 인한 계약임이 분명하므로 원고로서는 피고에 대하여 국가배상법의 규정에 의한 배상책임을 물을 수 없다 할 것이다. 그리고 국가 또는 공공 단체는 국가배상법상의 배상책임이 없는 경우에 있어서 민법 제756조 사용인의 배상책임에 관한 규정에 의한 배상책임은 있다고 할 것이나 원판결의 이유에 의하면 휼병감 김근배가 이 사건에서 문제가 되는 계약을 맺음에 있어서 그 계약체결이 폐지된 재정법에 정한 절차에 의한 것이 아니므로 그 매매에 대하여 피고가 그 매매로 인한 채무를 부담하지 않는다는 것을 원고 자신이 충분히 알고 있었다고 인정되며 따라서 휼병감 김근배와의 매매 행위로 인하여 원고는 피고에 대하여 권리를 취득할 수 없다는 것을 알고 있는 이상 원고의 권리가 위법하게 침해되었다고 인정할 아무런 사유를 발견할 수 없는 바이니 피고로서는 민법상 사용주의 배상책임에 관한 규정에 의한 책임도 없음이 스스로 명백하다 할 것이다. 끝으로 이 사건 기록에 의하여 원고의 청구 원인을 살펴보면 휼병감 김근배의 채무 불이행에 의한 손해배상을 청구한 뜻으로도 해석할 수 있는바 기록에 의하면 원고는 이 계약이 예산집행 행위가 아니라는 사실을 스스로 인정하고 있는 터이므로 원고 자신이 휼병감과 사병 푸라스틱 명찰매매계약에 있어서 피고가 매수인으로서의 책임을 지지 않는다는 정을 알았다고 할 것이므로 휼병감의 채무 불이행으로 인한 손해배상을 피고에게 청구할 수 없다 할 것이다.

대법 2009. 12. 24. 선고 2009다51288 판결

1. 원심은 그 채택 증거에 의하여, 원고가 2001. 10. 23. 독일 ○○사(이하 '소외 회사'라고 한다)와 사이에 분뇨 및 축산폐수처리시설과 관련한 비알디(BRD)공법에 관한 기술협약을 맺고 위 공법의 국내에서의 독점사용권을 취득한 사실, 피고는 2002. 4. 3. 원고와 사이에 피고가 분뇨처리시설보강 및 축산폐수공공처리시설공사사업(이하 '이 사건 사업'이라고 한다)을 함에 있어 소외 회사의 위 공법을 채택하기로 하고, 관계 법령에 의거한 설계작업이 완료된 후 원고와 위 공법을 이용한 시설공사(이하 '이 사건 공사'라고 한다)계약을 체결하기로 하되, 원고는 공사기간 단축을 위하여 기계장비(이하 '이 사건 기계장비'라고 한다)를 미리 주문·제작하며 피고측의 사정으로 시설공사계약이 체결되지 아니하는 경우에는 피고는 선발주 기계설비 대금 등 원고의 손해를 배상하기로 하는 내용의 기술공동개발협약(이하 '이 사건 협약'이라고 한다)을 체결한 사실, 피고는 2002. 5. 28. 금호엔지니어링 주식회사에게 이 사건 사업의 타당성 조사, 기본 및 실시설계 용역을 발주하여, 2003. 12. 12. 설계도서를 최종 보고받은 후 2004. 7. 6.부터 2005. 1. 7.까지 사이에 충청남도에 3차례에 걸쳐 분뇨처리시설 보강사업 변경 및 축산폐수공공처리시설 설치승인을 신청하였으나, 모두 반려되거나 보완요구를 지시받은 사실, 한편 원고는 2002. 5. 2. 신용장을 개설하는 등 이 사건 기계장비의 주문·제작을 위한 절차를 진행하여 이 사건 기계장비가 2002. 11. 11. 부산항을 통하여 수입된 사실, 이후 피고는 원고로부터 시설공사계약의 체결을 독촉받자 피고측의 사정으로 사업이 지연되고 있으나 조속한 시일 내에 절차를 추진할 것이라고 통보하여 오다가, 2005. 1.경 이 사건 사업과 관련하여 특혜의혹이 있다는 언론보도가 나오고 관련 공무원들에 대한 경찰수사가 개시되자, 이후 이 사건 사업을 더 이상 추진하지 못한 채 원고와의 계약체결을 거부한 사실 등을 인정한 다음, 피고의 귀책사유로 이 사건 시설공사계약이 체결되지 못하였으므로 피고는 이 사건 협약에 따라 원고가 이 사건 기계장비를 수입하여 보관하는 데에 지출한 비용 상당의 손해를 배상할 책임이 있다고 판단하였다.

2. 그러나 원심의 판단은 다음과 같은 이유에서 그대로 수긍할 수 없다.

구 지방재정법(2005. 8. 4. 법률 제7663호로 개정되기 전의 것, 이하 같다) 제63조는 지방자치단체를 당사자로 하는 계약에 관하여 이 법 및 다른 법령에서 정한 것을 제외하고는 '국가를 당사자로 하는 계약에 관한 법률'의 규정을 준용한다고 규정하고 있고, 이에 따른 준용조문인 '국가를 당사자로 하는 계약에 관한 법률' 제11조 제1항, 제2항에 의하면 지방자치단체가 계약을 체결하고자 할 때에는 계약의 목적, 계약금액, 이행기간, 계약보증금, 위험부담, 지체상금 기타 필요한 사항을 명백히 기재한 계약서를 작성하여야 하고, 그 담당공무원과 계약상

대자가 계약서에 기명·날인 또는 서명함으로써 계약이 확정된다고 규정하고 있는바, 위 각 규정의 취지에 의하면 지방자치단체가 사경제의 주체로서 사인과 사법상의 계약을 체결함에 있어서는 위 법령에 따른 계약서를 따로 작성하는 등 그 요건과 절차를 이행하여야 할 것이고, 설사 지방자치단체와 사인 사이에 사법상의 계약 또는 예약이 체결되었다 하더라도 위 법령상의 요건과 절차를 거치지 아니한 계약 또는 예약은 그 효력이 없다고 할 것이다(대법원 2004. 1. 27. 선고 2003다14812 판결, 대법원 2005. 5. 27. 선고 2004다30811, 30828 판결 등 참조).

그런데 이 사건 협약서(갑 제1호증) 제1항 1.은 '피고는 이 사건 공사에 독일 ○○사의 비알디(B.R.D) 공법을 채택하기로 하고, 관계 법령에 의거 설계작업이 완료된 후 원고측의 공법시행 협약이 포함된 공동시설 공사계약을 체결하기로 협약한다', 제1항 2.는 "피고는 원고측의 기술개발에 필요한 부지와 기존 건물을 제공하며 비알디(B.R.D) 시스템 기계설비에 관한 비용은 성공급으로 지급한다. 단 계약은 '국가를 당사자로 하는 계약에 관한 법률'에 의거 시행하고 원고측은 공사기간 단축을 위하여 기계장비를 미리 주문 제작하며 피고측 사정으로 시설공사계약이 체결되지 아니하는 경우 선발주 기계설비 대금 등 원고측의 손해를 배상한다"고 규정하고 있을 뿐, 이 사건 공사의 대금이나 이를 확정할 방법과 기준 등에 관한 아무런 규정이 없고, 피고측의 사정으로 시설공사계약이 체결되지 아니하는 경우에 피고가 배상하기로 한 기계설비 대금 등 원고측의 손해액이 얼마인지 정해져 있지 않을 뿐 아니라 이를 특정할 기준이나 방법도 정해져 있지 않다. 그렇다면 이 사건 협약서는 구 지방재정법이 준용하는 '국가를 당사자로 하는 계약에 관한 법률'에서 정한 요건과 절차를 거치지 아니한 계약 또는 예약으로서 앞서 본 법리에 따라 그 효력이 없다고 봄이 상당하다.

그럼에도 불구하고 원심은 이 사건 협약서가 유효함을 전제로 하여 피고의 손해배상책임을 인정하고 말았으니, 원심판결에는 구 지방재정법 제63조 및 국가를 당사자로 하는 계약에 관한 법률 제11조에 관한 법리를 오해하여 판결에 영향을 미친 위법이 있다고 할 것이다. 이 점에 관한 상고이유의 주장은 이유 있다.

나. 정치문제이론

Occidental of Umm Al Qaywayn, Inc. v. A Certain Cargo of Petroleum, 577 F.2d 1196 (5th Cir. 1978)

A. Geography.

The scene for this political drama is the exotic Persian Gulf, once noted for the

Arabian nights, now famous and important as a source of oil to light those nights. On the southern "lip" of the mouth of the Gulf lie the Trucial Sheikhdoms of Umm al Qaywayn (hereafter Umm), Sharjah, and Al Ajiman. Situated near the mouth of the Gulf, about 40 miles northwest of Umm, is the tiny island of Abu Musa. The island is also approximately 50 miles due south from Iran, the country with the largest contiguous border on the Gulf.

B. History, relatively ancient.

For almost a century, Great Britain had been the "protectorate" of the Trucial Sheikhdoms, including Umm and Sharjah. Pursuant to the treaty establishing this relationship, the United Kingdom was responsible for the Sheikhdoms' international relations, defense, and internal relations among the individual states. This protectorate jurisdiction included all the territories and territorial waters of the Sheikhdoms and territorial waters. As provided by the treaty, the protectorate ended in November 30, 1971.

During the course of this protectorate, a dispute over the sovereignty of Abu Musa had existed between Great Britain as agent of Sharjah, and Iran. For example, the India Survey Map of 1897 represented the island in the colors of Persia (now Iran), as did the Viceroy's unofficial map of 1892. Later, in April of 1904, the dispute flared as the Persian government placed custom officials on the island and flew the Persian flag. This establishment of sovereignty was short-lived, however, and the evidence was quickly removed at the demand of the British government. Persia did not abandon its claim with this setback, however. In 1923, Persia reasserted its claim to Abu Musa by protesting the leasing, by Great Britain, of mineral rights to the island. In 1930, Great Britain and Persia discussed settlement of the dispute, but no accord was reached.

C. Modern History.

In the early 1960's, because of rising worldwide energy demands and the growth of offshore drilling technology, the Persian Gulf was becoming hot property. In 1964, perhaps as a response to this increased demand, Umm and Sharjah entered into an agreement, under the auspices of the British, establishing their territorial waters and continental shelf borders. This treaty not only established the territorial waters of the parties, but also established their respective continental shelf. The agreement was embodied in an admiralty map establishing the continental shelf of Umm as extending to the three-mile territorial waters of Abu Musa, recognized by the British as Sharjah's possession, giving Umm 37 miles of the intervening continental shelf.

On November 18, 1969, appellant and the Ruler of Umm contracted that appellant would have the exclusive right to explore for and extract oil within Umm, its continental shelf, and its territorial waters for forty years. The boundaries to this concession conformed to those established for Umm by the treaty with Sharjah of 1964. The British Foreign Office ratified the concession agreement, as a condition precedent required under the protectorate. A month later, Sharjah granted Buttes Oil Company, appellees' predecessor, a similar concession to extract oil from its territories. The boundaries of the Buttes concession also conformed to the 1964 treaty and the agreement was subsequently ratified by the British Foreign Office.

No conflict existed between the parties until March 25, 1970, when Buttes Oil and Gas Company notified the British representative to the Sheikhdoms that Buttes intended to drill for oil within the Occidental concession area, approximately 31 miles from Umm, 9 miles east of Abu Musa. Indeed, the drilling location coincided with that suggested by Occidental's exploratory testing. Also at that time, the British agent was made aware of a Sharjah decree purporting to extend its territorial waters from three to twelve miles, including those of Abu Musa. Of course, this unilateral decree did substantial violence to the 1964 treaty, and the British Foreign Office rejected the subsequent amendment of Buttes' concession agreement with Sharjah to reflect the extension. Additionally, the Buttes' request to drill was also denied by the British Government. Although the Foreign Office considered the unilateral action in violation of international law, it strove to bring about an amicable solution. Although Umm and Sharjah were persuaded by the United Kingdom to mediate their claims, mediation failed when Umm refused to abide by the mediator's decision.

Meanwhile, to further muddy the political waters, in a letter dated May 28, 1970, appellant was informed by the National Iranian Oil Company that it should desist all drilling operations in its concession area. The stated basis for this demand was that because Abu Musa was an Iranian possession, and because Iran recognizes twelve mile territorial limits, Occidental concession was within Iran's territories. Faced with the probability of intervention by Iran, the British Government maintained the suspension of all drilling in the disputed area.

On November 26, 1971, the dispute between Iran and Sharjah over Abu Musa was settled, at least practically and prospectively. This agreement between Iran and Sharjah occurred only four days prior to the expiration of the British protectorate over the Trucial Sheikhdoms. Pursuant to this agreement, the island was essentially divided, and Sharjah's concession with Buttes was ratified and the future royalties were split between the sovereigns. On November 30, 1971, Iranian troops landed on Abu Musa, and the Iranian navy began patrolling the waters of the island. Shorn of the protection of the

British Government, Umm had no means to protect its territories as defined under the 1964 agreement, and Occidental was without protection as well. Buttes began drilling immediately with salutory results. Buttes later sold interests in the oil to appellees, Ashland Oil Inc., Kerr McGee Corp., Skelly Oil Company, and Cities Service Company. Each was put on notice of Occidental's claim. In 1974, appellants began extracting oil from the disputed concession area, and among the shipments of this oil to the United States were those aboard the "Dauntless Colocotronis," "Lykavitos," and the "Anglo-Maersk," which were seized in proceedings.

At least among the sovereigns, the rights to the royalties from the area were definitely settled. Some time after the Iranian occupation of Abu Musa, the Rulers of Umm and Sharjah agreed to divide royalties payable to Sharjah with Umm receiving thirty percent. Appellant suffered its final political reverse when in June of 1973, the Ruler of Umm terminated Occidental's concession for failure to pay rentals due under the contract.

D. History of the Case.

Prior to analysis of the case, a brief legal history of the dispute is helpful. The appellants and appellees' predecessors have once before litigated the underlying basis of their dispute. In *Occidental Petroleum Corporation v. Buttes Gas and Oil Co., 331 F.Supp. 92 (C.D.Cal. 1971)*, aff'd, 461 F.2d 1261 (9th Cir. 1972), cert. denied, 409 U.S. 950, 93 S.Ct. 272, 34 L.Ed.2d 221, appellants brought an antitrust action against Buttes, and Clayco Petroleum Company and certain officers of the corporations alleging a conspiracy among the defendants to oust appellant from its concession. This action was filed more than eight months prior to the Iranian occupation of Abu Musa, and years prior to the exportation of oil. The district court held, and the court of appeals affirmed, that the court was precluded from piercing the veil of sovereign action by the "act of state" doctrine and granted summary judgment. Although appellee contends that the Ninth Circuit case is res judicata for the case sub judice, we need not decide the question because we hold that we lack jurisdiction.

Actions No. 74-1192 and No. 75-0033 were brought as diversity actions. Action No. 74-868 was brought as an in rem action in admiralty. The district court granted appellee's motion for summary judgment in the diversity actions holding that because the actions of foreign sovereigns were called into dispute, the "act of state doctrine" required the court to refrain from deciding on the merits. See *Banco Nacional de Cuba v. Sabbatino*, 376 U.S. 398, 84 S.Ct. 923, 11 L.Ed.2d 804 (1964). Moreover, the district court concluded that, under the circumstances, the Hickenlooper Amendment, 22 U.S.C.A. 2370(e) (2) (Cum.1977), did not prevent such abstention. The district court dismissed the admiralty action holding that admiralty jurisdiction was absent because if any conversion occurred, it occurred at the well-head not on the seas. Because we hold that no case or controversy exists, we dismiss all three claims for want of jurisdiction, but on the common ground that a resolution would involve a political question.

A political question clearly emerges under the proper analysis. Although, whether a political question is present and the court lacks jurisdiction are issues committed to federal law, we need to address such questions only if they would arise in the diversity action framework. See *Baker v. Carr*, 369 U.S. 186, 82 S.Ct. 691, 7 L.Ed.2d 663 (1962). Therefore, we must analyze appellant's claim as it would be tried, to determine whether a political question will emerge. Shorn of its factual complexity, appellants claim a tortious conversion of oil. Because this is a diversity case, we apply the law of the forum, Louisiana, to the claim. *Erie R. Co. v. Tompkins*, 304 U.S. 64, 58 S.Ct. 817, 82 L.Ed. 1188 (1938). Additionally, because the operative facts occurred outside of Louisiana, we must also apply Louisiana's conflicts principles to determine which forum's law to apply. *Klaxon v. Stentor Mfg. Co.*, 313 U.S. 487, 61 S.Ct. 1020, 85 L.Ed. 1477 (1941). Applying these principles, we find that to successfully maintain its tortious conversion action, appellant would have to establish its right to possess the oil at the time of conversion. Appellant apparently contends that the conversion occurred when appellant was supplanted by Buttes through the intervention of Iran, sometime after November 30, 1971. Because, as a matter of international law, one who receives an interest in land which is in dispute between sovereigns takes subject to the dispute, *Coffee v. Groover*, 123 U.S. 1, 29-30, 8 S.Ct. 1, 31 L.Ed. 51 (1887); *Poole v. Fleeger*, 36 U.S. 185, 9 L.Ed. 680 (1837), appellant must necessarily develop Umm's right to undisputed possession of the portion of the continental shelf where the oil was extracted at the time the interest was passed, 1969. It is evident from the record, however, that the sovereignty, Abu Musa, and, derivatively, its continental shelf was in dispute between Iran and Sharjah (through Great Britain). Therefore, in order to resolve appellant's right to possess the oil, we would have to resolve the dispute over Abu Musa. The resolution of a territorial dispute between sovereigns, however, is a political question which we are powerless to decide.

Throughout the history of the federal judiciary, political questions have been held to be nonjusticiable and therefore not a "case or controversy" as defined by Article III. In *Ware v. Hylton*, 3 Dall. 199, 300, 1 L.Ed. 568 (1796), the Supreme Court recognized that in the realm of foreign relations policy considerations render issues incompetent for a decision by the court. In *Marbury v. Madison*, 1 Cranch 137, 164-166, 2 L.Ed. 60 (1803), Chief Justice Marshall acknowledged the existence of a class of cases which involve a "mere political act of the executive" and which were placed by the

Constitution in the hands of the executive. The Supreme Court therefore appreciated that the genesis of the political question is the constitutional separation and dispersement of powers among the branches of government. In *Coleman v. Miller,* 307 U.S. 433, 59 S.Ct. 972, 83 L.Ed. 1385 (1939), the Supreme Court clearly recognized that the political question doctrine partakes not only of the existence of separation of powers, but also of the limitation of the judiciary as a decisional body. The Court stated: "In determining whether a question falls within (the political question category), the appropriateness under our system of government of attributing finality to the action of the political departments and also the lack of satisfactory criteria for a judicial determination are dominant considerations." The Court was merely admitting that they were not tribal wisemen dispensing divinely or theoretically inspired judgments, but were a court limited to the application of predetermined law.

In *Baker v. Carr*, 369 U.S. 186, 82 S.Ct. 691, 7 L.Ed.2d 663 (1962), the Supreme Court extensively reviewed the history and evolution of the political question. As a result of this survey, the Court identified a number of basic characteristics or considerations relevant to the existence of a political question. The Court held that the inextricable presence of one or more of these factors will render the case nonjusticiable under the Article III "case or controversy" requirement, and therefore, the Court would be without jurisdiction. In this most definitive pronouncement, the Court identified the following factors as relevant to the affirmative determination of the existence of a political question:

(1) "a textually demonstrable commitment of the issue to a coordinate political department"
(2) "a lack of judicially discoverable and manageable standards"
(3) "the impossibility of deciding without an initial policy determination of a kind clearly for nonjudicial discretion"
(4) "the impossibility of a court's undertaking independent resolution without expressing lack of the respect due coordinate branches of government"
(5) "an unusual need for unquestioning adherence to a political decision already made"
(6) "the potentiality of embarrassment from multifarious pronouncements by various departments on one question"

369 U.S. at 217, 82 S.Ct. at 710. In the instant case, nearly every one of the factors is present and the vitality of the political question in the arena of foreign relations is abundantly demonstrated.

The ownership of lands disputed by foreign sovereigns is a political question of foreign relations, the resolution or neutrality of which is committed to the executive branch by the Constitution. As has been demonstrated, to determine whether a tortious conversion has occurred, it is necessary to determine the sovereign ownership of the portion of the continental shelf from which the oil was extracted. Although sovereigns are not directly involved, a judicial pronouncement on the sovereignty of Iran or Sharjah would be unavoidable. Such a determination is constitutionally reserved to the executive branch, however. Just as the judiciary will follow an executive determination as to which nation has sovereignty over a disputed area, *United States v. Klintock*, 5 Wheat. 144, 149, 5 L.Ed. 55 (1820), so must the judiciary refuse to decide the dispute in the absence of executive action because of that absence of direction. That is, in the language of Baker v. Carr, supra, the question of sovereignty is committed to the executive branch by the Constitution, and decision of the issue is impossible in the absence of the executive policy decision. Additionally, we are persuaded that a judicial determination would reflect a lack of respect for the executive branch, particularly the State Department. Contained in the Government's amicus brief is a letter from the State Department indicating the importance of neutrality in the politically and economically sensitive Middle East. A decision in this case, the State Department warns, would seriously impinge on executive neutrality. Therefore, we are convinced that the issue of sovereignty over disputed territory is a political question reserved to the executive branch.

On cross-appeal, we are asked to review the decision of the district court refusing to grant cross-appellant's motion for an injunction against all pending and further litigation, both in state and federal courts. The result of the immediate imposition of this injunction would serve to deprive the appellant of its statutory remedy of seizing further shipments of oil. On the other hand, appellees have a right to a speedy determination of this issue to avoid endless seizures that may amount to a major nuisance if this action is not finally determined on appeal. We therefore grant the injunction in order to protect the appellee, and stay the injunction pending disposition by the Supreme Court, in order to protect the appellant and promote a speedy resolution of this problem. Should the appellant fail to appeal this judgment, the stay shall expire with the time limit for filing the appeal.

대법 2004. 3. 26. 선고 2003도7878 판결

가. 입헌적 법치주의국가의 기본원칙은 어떠한 국가행위나 국가작용도 헌법과 법률에 근거하여 그 테두리 안에서 합헌적·합법적으로 행하여질 것을 요구하며, 이러한 합헌성과

합법성의 판단은 본질적으로 사법의 권능에 속하는 것이다.

다만, 국가행위 중에는 고도의 정치성을 띤 것이 있고, 그러한 고도의 정치행위에 대하여 정치적 책임을 지지 않는 법원이 정치의 합목적성이나 정당성을 도외시한 채 합법성의 심사를 감행함으로써 정책결정이 좌우되는 일은 결코 바람직한 일이 아니며, 법원이 정치문제에 개입되어 그 중립성과 독립성을 침해당할 위험성도 부인할 수 없으므로, 고도의 정치성을 띤 국가행위에 대하여는 이른바 통치행위라 하여 법원 스스로 사법심사권의 행사를 억제하여 그 심사대상에서 제외하는 영역이 있다.

그러나 이와 같이 통치행위의 개념을 인정한다고 하더라도 과도한 사법심사의 자제가 기본권을 보장하고 법치주의 이념을 구현하여야 할 법원의 책무를 태만히 하거나 포기하는 것이 되지 않도록 그 인정을 지극히 신중하게 하여야 하며, 그 판단은 오로지 사법부만에 의하여 이루어져야 하는 것이다.

나. 원심판결 이유에 의하면, 원심은 그 채택 증거를 종합하여, 피고인 김윤규, 임동원은 1심 공동피고인 최규백, 정몽헌, 박지원 등과 공모하여, 재정경제부장관에게 신고하지 아니하고(권한 위탁에 따라 '지정거래외국환은행장'에게 신고하지 아니하고), 2000. 6. 9. 국가정보원 기획조정실 지출관 공소외 1 등의 도움을 받아 현대상선 주식회사(이하 '현대상선'이라 한다)가 박지원, 이기호의 도움으로 한국산업은행으로부터 대출받은 2,240억 원을 미화 2억 달러로 환전하여 현대아산 주식회사(이하 '현대아산'이라 한다)의 북한 통천지역 경공업지구 조성부지 사용권 등 7대 경제협력사업의 대가 명목으로 북한 조선아시아태평양위원회(이하 '아태위원회'라 한다)가 지정하는 계좌로 송금하여 이를 지급하고, 피고인 김윤규는 정몽헌, 이익치, 김재수(현대건설 관리본부장) 등과 공모하여, 재정경제부장관에게 신고하지 아니하고(권한 위탁에 따라 '지정거래외국환은행장'에게 신고하지 아니하고), 2000. 6. 9.경 위 협력사업의 대가 명목으로 1억 5,000만 달러를 현대건설 런던지사와 싱가포르 지점을 통하여 아태위원회가 지정한 계좌들로 송금하는 방법으로 지급하고, 피고인 김윤규, 임동원은 정몽헌, 박지원, 이익치 등과 공모하여, 남북한의 법인·단체가 공동으로 협력사업을 시행하고자 할 때에는 매 사업마다 통일부장관의 승인을 얻어야 함에도 불구하고, 통일부장관의 협력사업 승인을 얻지 아니하고, 2000. 5. 3. 09 : 00경 중국 베이징에서 현대아산이 북한의 아태위원회와 잠정합의안을 체결하고, 그 대가 명목으로 2000. 6. 9.경부터 2000. 6. 12.경까지 사이에 아태위원회가 지정하는 계좌로 합계 4억 5,000만 달러를 송금하여 협력사업을 시행하였다는 공소사실을 모두 유죄로 인정하였다.

다. 그리고 원심은, 위 공소사실을 유죄로 인정하면서, 위 피고인들의 대북송금행위 및 이에 수반된 각 행위들은 남북정상회담에 도움을 주기 위한 시급한 필요에서 비롯된 이른바 통치행위로서 사법부에 의한 사법심사의 대상이 되지 않는다는 피고인들의 주장에 대하여,

남북정상회담의 개최는 고도의 정치적 성격을 지니고 있는 행위라 할 것이므로 특별한 사정이 없는 한 그 당부를 심판하는 것은 사법권의 내재적·본질적 한계를 넘어서는 것이 되어 적절하지 못하지만, 남북정상회담의 개최과정에서 위 피고인들이 공모하여 재정경제부장관에게 신고하지 아니하거나 통일부장관의 협력사업 승인을 얻지 아니한 채 위와 같이 북한측에 사업권의 대가 명목으로 4억 5,000만 달러를 송금한 행위 자체는 헌법상 법치국가의 원리와 법 앞에 평등원칙 등에 비추어 볼 때 사법심사의 대상이 된다고 판단하였는바, 원심의 위와 같은 판단은 앞서 본 법리에 비추어 정당한 것으로 수긍되고, 거기에 주장과 같은 이른바 헌법상 통치행위에 대한 법리오해의 위법이 있다고 할 수 없으므로, 피고인 김윤규, 임동원의 이 부분 상고는 이유 없다.

대법 1997. 4. 17. 선고 96도3376 전원합의체 판결

위 피고인들의 변호인들은 이 사건 피고인 전두환 등에 대한 공소사실이 반란과 내란에 해당한다고 하더라도, 피고인들이 그러한 반란과 내란의 과정을 거쳐 확고히 정권을 장악하고 헌법개정절차 등을 통하여 구법질서를 무너뜨리고 새로운 법질서를 수립하는 데에 성공하였으니 피고인들의 행위를 새로운 법질서 아래에서는 처벌할 수 없는 것이라고 주장한다.

생각건대, 우리나라는 제헌헌법의 제정을 통하여 국민주권주의, 자유민주주의, 국민의 기본권보장, 법치주의 등을 국가의 근본이념 및 기본원리로 하는 헌법질서를 수립한 이래 여러 차례에 걸친 헌법개정이 있었으나, 지금까지 한결같이 위 헌법질서를 그대로 유지하여 오고 있는 터이므로, 피고인들이 공소사실과 같이 이 사건 군사반란과 내란을 통하여 폭력으로 헌법에 의하여 설치된 국가기관의 권능행사를 사실상 불가능하게 하고 정권을 장악한 후 국민투표를 거쳐 헌법을 개정하고 개정된 헌법에 따라 국가를 통치하여 왔다고 하더라도 피고인들이 이 사건 군사반란과 내란을 통하여 새로운 법질서를 수립한 것이라고 할 수는 없다. 우리나라의 헌법질서 아래에서는 헌법에 정한 민주적 절차에 의하지 아니하고 폭력에 의하여 헌법기관의 권능행사를 불가능하게 하거나 정권을 장악하는 행위는 어떠한 경우에도 용인될 수 없는 것이다.

그러므로 피고인들이 그 내세우는 바와 같이 새로운 법질서를 수립하였음을 전제로 한 주장은 받아들일 수 없다.

다만 피고인 전두환 등이 이 사건 내란을 통하여 정권을 장악한 다음 헌법을 개정하고 그 헌법에 따라 피고인 전두환이 대통령에 선출되어 대통령으로서의 직무를 행하였고, 다시 그 헌법에 정한 절차에 따라 헌법을 개정하고 그 개정된 헌법(현행 헌법)에 따라 피고인 노태우가 대통령에 선출되어 그 임기를 마치는 등 그 동안에 있었던 일련의 사실에 비추어 마치 피고인들이 새로운 법질서를 형성하였고 나아가 피고인들의 기왕의 행위에 대하여 이를 처벌하지 아니하기로 하는 국민의 합의가 이루어졌던 것처럼 보일 여지가 없지 아니하나, 국회는 헌정질서파괴범죄에 대하여 형사소송법상의 공소시효의 적용을 전면적으로 배제하는 헌정질서파괴범죄의공소시효등에관한특례법(이하 '헌정질서파괴범죄특례법'이라 한다)과 바로 그 헌정질서파괴범죄에 해당하는 이 사건 군사반란과 내란행위를 단죄하기 위한 5 · 18민주화운동등에관한특별법(이하 '5 · 18특별법'이라고 한다)을 제정하였으며, 헌법재판소는 5 · 18특별법이 합헌이라는 결정을 함으로써, 피고인들이 이 사건 군사반란과 내란을 통하여 새로운 법질서를 수립한 것이 아님을 분명히 하였을 뿐만 아니라, 헌법개정 과정에서 피고인들의 행위를 불문에 붙이기로 하는 어떠한 명시적인 합의도 이루어진 바가 없었으므로, 특별법이 제정되고 그에 대한 헌법재판소의 합헌결정이 내려진 이상, 피고인들은 그들의 정권장악에도 불구하고, 결코 새로운 법질서의 수립이라는 이유나 국민의 합의를 내세워 그 형사책임을 면할 수는 없는 것이라고 할 것이다.

이 사건 군사반란 및 내란이 사법심사의 대상이 되지 아니한다는 대법관 ×××의 반대의견

이 사건에서 군형법 및 형법 위반의 죄로 각 공소가 제기된 군사반란 및 내란행위에 관련된 피고인들에 대하여는 법원이 그 가벌성 여부에 관하여 재판할 수 없다고 생각되므로, 이와 반대의 견해를 전제로 한 다수의견에 대하여는 찬동할 수 없다. 그 이유는 다음과 같다.

기록에 의하면, 피고인들이 이 사건 군사반란 및 내란행위에 의하여 군권 및 정권을 사실상 장악하고 이를 토대로 하여, 피고인 전두환이 1980. 9. 1. 대통령에 취임한 다음, 1980. 9. 29. 구 정치질서로부터 결별하고 새로운 정치질서를 형성하기 위하여 정당을 해산하고 국회를 새로 구성하며 대통령도 새로 선출할 것 등을 내용으로 하는 헌법의 전문 개정안을 제안하여, 그 개정안이 국민투표를 거쳐 제5공화국의 헌법으로 확정되고 1980. 10. 27. 대통령이 이를 공포함으로써 그 날부터 발효하게 된 사실, 제5공화국 헌법에 따른 절차에 의하여 피고인 전두환이 대통령으로 당선되어 1981. 3. 3. 그 직에 취임하고, 그 직후 실시된 국회의원선거에서 피고인 등이 주도하여 창당한 정당이 국회의 다수의석을 차지한 이래, 그들을 중심으로 한 정치세력이 통치권의 중추를 담당하여 국정을 운영하여 왔고, 피고인 전두환은 대통령으로서의 임기를 마치고 퇴임하였으며, 다시 국회의 의결과 국민투표를 거쳐 1987. 10. 29. 전문 개정된 현행 헌법에 따른 대통령 직접선거에서 피고인 노태우가 대통령에 당선되어 5년의 임기를 마치고 퇴임하였고, 다른 피고인들도 그 동안 대부분 정부의 각료나 국회의원으로 종사한 사실 등을 인정할 수 있다.

위와 같이 헌법상 통치체제의 권력구조를 변혁하고 대통령, 국회 등 통치권의 중추인 국가기관을 새로 구성하거나 선출하는 내용의 헌법개정이 국민투표를 거쳐 이루어지고 그 개정 헌법에 의하여 대통령이 새로 선출되고 국회가 새로 구성되는 등 통치권의 담당자가 교체되었다면, 이는 과거의 헌정질서와는 단절된 제5공화국의 새로운 헌정질서가 출발하였고 국민이 이를 수용하였음을 의미한다고 할 것인바, 피고인들의 이 사건 군사반란 및 내란행위는 국가의 정치적 변혁과정에서 국민이 수용한 새로운 헌정질서를 형성하는 데에 기초가 되었다고 보지 않을 수 없다.

그렇다면 피고인들의 이 사건 군사반란 및 내란행위는 국가의 헌정질서의 변혁을 가져온 고도의 정치적 행위라고 할 것인바, 위와 같이 헌정질서 변혁의 기초가 된 고도의 정치적 행위에 대하여 법적 책임을 물을 수 있는지 또는 그 정치적 행위가 사후에 정당화되었는지 여부의 문제는 국가사회 내에서 정치적 과정을 거쳐 해결되어야 할 정치적·도덕적 문제를 불러일으키는 것으로서 그 본래의 성격상 정치적 책임을 지지 않는 법원이 사법적으로 심사하기에는 부적합한 것이고, 주권자인 국민의 정치적 의사형성과정을 통하여 해결하는 것이 가장 바람직하다 할 것이다.

현대 법치주의의 원리는 원칙적으로 국가사회 구성원의 모든 행위에 대하여 법원이 그 합법성 여부를 심사할 것을 요청받고 있기는 하나, 그렇다고 해서 반드시 모든 행위가 사법적 심사의 대상이 되어야만 하는 것을 의미하지는 않는다. 법원은 구체적인 사안에 따라서는 당해 행위가 가지는 정치적 측면과 법적 측면을 비교하고 그 행위에 대한 규범적 통제의 정도 및 사법제도의 본질적 특성을 감안하여 무엇보다도 그 행위에 대한 사법심사가 국가사회에 미치는 영향을 고려하여 사법심사를 자제하여야 하는 경우가 있는 것이다. 이 사건의 경우가 그러한 경우에 해당한다고 할 것이다.

그러므로 이 사건 군사반란 및 내란행위가 비록 형식적으로는 범죄를 구성한다고 할지라도 그 책임 문제는 국가사회의 평화와 정의의 실현을 위하여 움직이는 국민의 정치적 통합과정을 통하여 해결되어야 하는 고도의 정치문제로서, 이에 대하여는 이미 이를 수용하는 방향으로 여러 번에 걸친 국민의 정치적 판단과 결정이 형성되어 온 마당에 이제 와서 법원이 새삼 사법심사의 일환으로 그 죄책 여부를 가리기에는 적합하지 아니한 문제라 할 것이므로, 법원으로서는 이에 대한 재판권을 행사할 수 없다고 보아야 할 것이다.

그럼에도 불구하고 이 사건 군사반란 및 내란행위에 관련된 피고인들에 대한 각 해당 공소사실에 대하여 실체관계에 나아가 유죄 또는 무죄의 판단을 한 원심판결은 잘못이라고 할 것이므로, 원심판결 중 이 부분을 파기하고, 이에 대하여는 재판권이 없음을 이유로 공소기각의 판결을 선고하여야 할 것이다.

서울지법 남부지원 1999. 2. 25. 선고 98가합15904 판결

대의제 민주주의 헌법질서하에서 국회는 그 소속 의원들을 통하여 국민들 사이에 존재하는 다원적 의견과 제반 이익을 입법과정에 공정하게 반영하고 의원들 간의 자유스러운 토론을 통하여 그것을 조정하며 궁극적으로는 다수결의 원리에 의한 통일적인 국가의사를 형성하는 역할을 부담하는 것이므로 국회의원들에게는 다양한 국민의 의사를 수렴·반영하고 국민 전체의 복지실현을 목표로 하여 행동하는 것이 요청되는데, 대의제 민주주의가 적정하고 효율적으로 기능하기 위하여는 국회의 개회 여부(개회된 국회 의사일정의 진행도 포함한다) 등의 입법과정을 국회의원 각자의 정치적 판단에 일임하고, 그 당부는 종국적으로 자유언론과 선거과정에 의한 정치적 평가에 맡기고 있는 것이므로, 결국 우리 헌법질서 내에서 국회의 입법행위는 본질적으로 정치적인 것이고 그 성격상 실정법적 규제로부터 자유로운 것이며 그러기에 소속 국회의원들 개개인에게 선거 등에 의하여 정치적 책임을 추궁하는 것을 넘어서서 실정법질서의 관점에서 입법행위 또는 그 부작위에 대하여 법적 책임을 귀속시키는 것은 원칙적으로 가능하지 않다고 볼 것이다.

다만 국회의원이 이념적 통일체로서의 전체 국민을 대표하고 전체 국민에 대하여 법적인 의무를 부담하여 개별 국민에 대하여는 어떠한 구체적인 법적 책임을 부담하지 않는 것이 원칙이라고 할지라도 국회의 입법형성권도 헌법에 의하여 부여된 것이기 때문에 헌법질서 내에서만 그 정당성이 인정되는 것이므로 헌법에서 기본권 보장을 위하여 법령에 명시적인 입법위임을 하였을 때, 헌법해석상 특정인에게 구체적인 기본권이 생겨 이를 보장하기 위한 국가의 행위의무 내지 보호의무가 발생하였을 때에는 입법권자인 국회에게 헌법상의 입법의무가 부여되었다고 할 수 있는 예외적인 경우에는 헌법에 의하여 부여된 입법의무를 행하지 않는 입법부작위가 위헌 내지 위법한 것으로 평가될 수 있다 할 것이다.

다. 국가행위이론(act of state doctrine)[9]

외국정부의 국유화조치는 국가행위이론에 근거하여 법원에서의 적법성 판단대상에서 벗어 나는 경우가 많다. *Banco Nacional de Cuba v. Sabbatino,* 376 U.S. 398 (1964)에서 원고는 쿠바정부에 의하여 압수당한 자산의 회수를 구하였으나 미국대법원은 삼권분립을 이유로 외국의 통치행위에 대한 사법부의 판단을 거절하였다. 이는 1964년 Hickenlooper수정안을[10] 초래하였고 또한 국가행위이론은 상사채무의 이행거절과 같은 공법적 행위가 아닌 사

9) 김대순, 주 9-28 상게서, 494-513 참조. 헌법학자들은 통치행위라는 단어를 사용한다.
10) 22 U.S.C. § 2370(e)(2).

법적 행위에는 적용되지 아니된다는 것이 강조되었다.[11]

Hunt v. Coastal States Gas Producing Co., 583 S.W.2d 322 (Tex. 1979)

[Hunt는 리비아정부와 양허계약을 체결하였던바, 리비아정부가 국유화 이후 제3자에게 석유를 매각하자 동 행위가 제3자의 채권침해로서 불법행위이므로 이를 원인으로 한 손해배상청구의 소를 제기하였다.]

In 1957 the Government of Libya granted Hunt a concession which gave him the right, for fifty years, to explore, drill and extract oil in an area now identified as the Sarir field. Hunt assigned a one-half undivided interest in this concession to British Petroleum Exploration Company, Ltd. (British Petroleum) in 1960. Oil was discovered in the concession area in 1961 and, by 1967, it was produced in marketable quantities. In September 1969, Colonel Mu'ammar al-Qadhafi assumed power in Libya under a new government, the Revolutionary Command Council, and commenced making changes in the existing contractual relations with the various oil producers holding concession agreements with Libya. In 1971, the Libyan Government nationalized the operations and interest of British Petroleum in the Sarir field and transferred its rights to the Arabian Gulf Exploration Company (AGECO). AGECO is a corporation whose entire capital stock is owned by the Libyan Government.

On June 20, 1973, by Libyan Law No. 42 of 1973, the Libyan Government nationalized all the rights and assets of Hunt in the concession agreement and assigned these rights to AGECO. Although Libya agreed to pay compensation, the amount was to be determined by a committee designated by the State. In response to this action, Hunt published notices in newspapers throughout the world claiming that the Libyan nationalization violated international law and threatened suit against anyone who came into possession of Sarir oil. In May 1973, Coastal States entered into a contract with AGECO to purchase oil from the Sarir field and it continued to purchase oil under this contract despite Hunt's claims against Libya and threatened suits. This oil was transported by Coastal States to a refinery in Italy where it was processed and sold to third parties. It was stipulated that a portion of the products derived from this oil was subsequently taken to the United States, although it was not stipulated that Coastal States transported or caused any of such products to be brought here. Nevertheless, Coastal

11) 외국중재판정의 승인과 집행 역시 국가행위이론을 이유로 거절되어서는 아니 된다. 9 U.S.C. § 15. *W.S. Kirkpatrick & Co., v. Environmental Tectonics Corp.*, 493 U.S. 400 (1990) 참조.

States is domiciled in the United States and, at least, the net proceeds derived from the Sarir oil were brought here and are the basis of Hunt's suit for conversion.

British Petroleum was a party to the controversy with Coastal States at one time, but it subsequently entered into a full settlement with the Libyan Government after arbitration of its claim and it does not now assert any claim against Coastal States. In May 1975 Hunt entered into a settlement agreement with the Libyan Government whereby, for the sum of approximately $19,000,000, it released any and all claims against the Libyan Government arising out of the nationalization of the Sarir field. Coastal States was not a party to this agreement and Hunt now seeks to recover the proceeds realized by Coastal States from oil allegedly purchased from AGECO prior to the May 1975 settlement.

Both the trial court and the court of civil appeals concluded that the trial court was foreclosed from inquiring into the validity of the Libyan nationalization of Hunt's interest in the Sarir field by the Act of State Doctrine. These courts further concluded that as a matter of law, Hunt's actions in giving notice of his claim to oil from the Sarir field did not violate either state or federal law and would not support Coastal States' claim for damages for tortious interference. Hunt and Coastal States both filed applications for writ of error and complain of the take-nothing judgment entered on the claim of each.

APPEAL BY HUNT

Hunt's claim against Coastal States is necessarily based upon the assertion that Libya's expropriation was invalid so that Coastal States acquired no title from AGECO. The critical question involved in Hunt's appeal is the applicability of the Act of State Doctrine and more precisely, whether Hunt's suit comes within the exception to the doctrine created by the Hickenlooper Amendment, 22 U.S.C. s 2370(e)(2). The lower courts have held that the doctrine bars inquiry by a Texas court into the validity of acts done by a foreign sovereign.

The Act of State Doctrine is a judicially created doctrine of restraint. The landmark case of Banco Nacional de Cuba v. Sabbatino, 376 U.S. 398, 84 S.Ct. 923, 11 L.Ed.2d 804 (1964) reaffirmed the doctrine as originally articulated in Underhill v. Hernandez, 168 U.S. 250, 18 S.Ct. 83, 42 L.Ed. 456 (1897) in the following language:

"Every sovereign State is bound to respect the independence of every other sovereign State, and the courts of one country will not sit in judgment on the acts of the government of another, done within its own territory. Redress of grievances by reason of such acts must be obtained through the means open to be availed of by sovereign powers as between themselves."

In Sabbatino it was stated that the doctrine "arises out of the basic relationships between branches of government in a system of separation" and the courts prior recognition of the doctrine "expresses the strong sense of the Judicial Branch that its engagement in the task of passing on the validity of foreign acts of state may hinder rather than further this country's pursuit of goals both for itself and for the community of nations as a whole in the international sphere."

In Hunt v. Mobil Oil Corp., 550 F.2d 68 (2d Cir. 1977), Cert. denied, 434 U.S. 984, 98 S.Ct. 608, 54 L.Ed.2d 477, the Act of State Doctrine was held to bar Hunt's inquiry into the validity of Libya's nationalization of Hunt's concession. In holding that the trial court properly dismissed Hunt's claim against seven major oil producers in the Persian Gulf area for damages under the anti-trust statute, the circuit court said:

"We conclude that the political act complained of here was clearly within the act of state doctrine and that since the disputed pleadings inevitably call for a judgment on the sovereign acts of Libya the claim is non-justiciable."

This final judgment against Hunt in that case controls his present suit for conversion unless it comes within the exception to the Act of State Doctrine created by the Hickenlooper Amendment. Benson v. Wanda Petroleum Company, 468 S.W.2d 361 (Tex.1971).

The Hickenlooper Amendment was enacted by Congress in 1964 shortly after the Sabbatino holding and in obvious reaction to it. It provides in part:

"(N)o court in the United States shall decline on the ground of the federal act of state doctrine to make a determination on the merits giving effect to the principles of international law in a case in which a CLAIM OF TITLE OR OTHER RIGHT TO PROPERTY is asserted by any party including a foreign state ... based upon (or traced through) a confiscation or other taking ... by an act of that state in violation of the principles of international law ...." (Emphasis Added) 22 U.S.C. s 2370(e)(2). It must be recognized at the outset that this exception which was adopted over the objections of the Executive Department of the United States has been narrowly construed by our courts. Occidental of Umm Al Qay., Inc. v. Cities Serv. Oil Co., 396 F.Supp. 461 (D.C.La.), Aff'd in part, 577 F.2d 1196 (5th Cir. 1978), Petition for cert. filed, — U.S. —, 99 S.Ct. 1276, 59 L.Ed.2d 491 (1978); Occidental Petroleum Corp. v. Buttes Gas & Oil Co., 331 F.Supp. 92 (D.C.Cal.) Aff'd, 461 F.2d 1261 (9th Cir. 1972), Cert. denied, 409 U.S. 950, 93 S.Ct. 272, 34 L.Ed.2d 221; United Mexican States v. Ashley, 556 S.W.2d 784 (Tex.1977).

The statute enumerates three requirements which must exist in order to avoid the Act of State Doctrine under the Hickenlooper Amendment: 1.Expropriated property must come within the territorial jurisdiction of the United States; 2.The act of the expropriating nation must be in violation of international law; and 3.The asserted claim must be a claim of title or other right to property. 22 U.S.C. s 2370(e)(2). The court of civil appeals concluded, without consideration of the first two requirements, that the Hickenlooper Amendment is not applicable to this case because Hunt acquired only a contract right by the agreement with Libya. We agree with this conclusion and therefore limit our consideration to the third requirement stated above.

Since Libya is both the place of the contract's execution and performance as well as the location of the subject matter, Libyan substantive law governs the interpretation and construction of the rights conferred to Hunt by the Concession Agreement. Cantu v. Bennett, 39 Tex. 304 (1873).

The Concession Agreement expressly provides that the applicable law is the Libyan Petroleum Law No. 25 of 1955 and this law provides in part:

"(1) All petroleum in Libya in its natural state in strata is the property of the Libyan State.

"(2) No person shall explore or prospect for, mine or produce petroleum in any part of Libya, unless authorized by a permit or concession issued under this Law."

The expressed intent of the Concession Agreement was to grant Hunt the Right to search for and to extract oil within the defined area for the stated term. It did not grant Hunt title to the oil in the strata. Under Libyan law, title to the oil passed at the wellhead. In 1966 Hunt and Libya voluntarily amended the 1957 Concession Agreement. Clause 16 of the amended agreement states:

"(1) The Government of Libya will take all the steps necessary to ensure that the Company enjoys all the rights conferred by the Concession. The CONTRACTUAL RIGHTS expressly created by this concession shall not be altered except by mutual consent of the parties.

"(2) This Concession shall throughout the period of its validity be construed in accordance with the Petroleum Law and the Regulations in force on the date of the execution of the agreement of amendment by which this paragraph (2) was incorporated into this concession agreement. Any amendment to or repeal of such Regulations shall not affect the CONTRACTUAL RIGHTS of the Company without its consent." (Emphasis added)

This language is significant in that it not only refers to Hunt's rights as "contractual," but it also recognizes Libya's ownership of the oil. We conclude that Hunt obtained only a contractual right under the Concession Agreement.

The Hickenlooper Amendment by its express terms applies only to a claim of title or other right to property. This construction was made abundantly clear in 1965 when Congress added the words "to property" following the phrase "claim of title or other right." Thus this exception to the Act of State Doctrine has no application here where only a contractual right was expropriated from Hunt. See Occidental of Umm Al Qay.,

Inc. v. Cities Serv. Oil Co., supra; French v. Banco Nacional de Cuba, 23 N.Y.2d 46, 295 N.Y.S.2d 433, 242 N.E.2d 704 (1968); Menendez v. Saks and Company, 485 F.2d 1355 (2nd Cir. 1973), Cert. denied, 425 U.S. 991, 96 S.Ct. 2201, 48 L.Ed.2d 815 (1976); Present v. U. S. Life Ins. Co., 96 N.J.Super. 285, 232 A.2d 863, Aff'd, 51 N.J. 407, 241 A.2d 237 (1968). We have been cited to no case, and have discovered no case, holding to the contrary.

The trial court and the court of civil appeals did not err in concluding that the Act of State Doctrine bars judicial inquiry into the validity of Libya's actions.

대법 1985. 1. 29. 선고 74도3501 전원합의체 판결

×××의 의견

법원은 이 사건 긴급조치의 실효를 판단할 권한이 있는가 하는 점을 살펴보기로 한다.

가. 다수의견은 이 사건 긴급조치의 근거규정인 구 헌법 제53조의 긴급조치권은 현행 헌법 제51조의 비상조치권과 현저한 차이가 있어 제5공화국의 국가이념이나 그 헌법정신에 위배되는 것이므로 이 사건 긴급조치는 현행 헌법하에서 그 계속효를 부인할 수밖에 없어 결국 현행 제정시행과 더불어 실효되었다고 판단하고 있다.

그러나 이러한 입론은 구 헌법상의 긴급조치권과 현행 헌법상의 비상조치권과의 동일성 분석을 통하여 이 사건 긴급조치가 현행 헌법에 위배된다는 결론에 이른 것으로서 결국 이 사건 긴급조치의 실효근거를 현행 헌법에 위배된다는 점에 둔 것이라고 볼 수밖에 없는바, 현행 위헌법률심사제도하에서 과연 법원이 위와 같은 위헌판단을 할 수 있는가 하는 문제에 부딪치게 될 것이다.

나. 나는 이 사건 긴급조치는 구 헌법의 폐지에 따라 당연히 실효된 것으로서 그 효력의 종료사유는 구 헌법이 폐지된 데에 있고 현행 헌법에 위배된 데에 있는 것이 아니라고 보므로, 위와 같이 헌법의 폐지에 따른 효력의 종료여부를 심사판단하는 일은 현행 헌법을 기준으로 위헌여부를 심사하여 그 효력의 존부를 판단하는 위헌판단과 다른 것으로서 법원은 위와 같은 효력의 종료를 판단할 권한이 있다고 본다.

앞에서 언급한 바와 같이 이 사건 긴급조치가 헌법적 효력을 가진 것이라고 하여도 구 헌법의 폐지에 따라 그 효력이 종료된 여부를 판단하는 일이 법원의 권한에 속하는 것에는 차이가 없다.

다. 다음에 이 사건 긴급조치를 대통령의 통치행위라고 볼 때 이러한 통치행위의 실효여부를 법원이 심사판단할 수 있는가 하는 점이 문제될 수 있다.

일반적으로 통치행위는 고도의 정치성을 띤 국가행위로서 법원은 그 합법성을 심사할 수 없다는 것이 지배적인 견해이긴 하나, 통치행위라고 할지라도 헌법의 폐지에 따른 그 효력의 상실여부와 같은 사항은 법원의 심사대상이 된다고 보아야 할 것이다.

특히 통치행위 중에서도 이 사건 긴급조치와 같이 국민의 기본권 제한과 관련된 조치인 경우에는 기본권보장과 헌법보장의 책무를 진 법원으로서는 당연히 그 효력의 존속여부를 심사판단할 권한이 있다고 보아야 한다.

종래에 통치행위를 사법심사에서 제외하는 이론적 근거로 권력분립에서 오는 내재적 한계를 들어 법원은 오로지 사법문제만을 심사할 수 있고 정치문제는 입법부나 행정부에 맡겨진 것으로서 사법권의 한계 밖에 있다는 견해가 주장되어 왔으며, 이러한 견해에 따르면 위에서 본 바와 같은 통치행위의 실효여부도 사법부의 심사권한 밖에 있는 것이라는 반론이 나올 수 있을 것이다.

그러나 입헌적 법치주의국가의 기본원칙은 모든 국가행위나 국가작용이 헌법과 법률에 합치할 것을 요구하며 이러한 합법성의 판단은 본질적으로 사법부의 권능에 속하는 것이다. 다만 통치행위와 같은 고도의 정치행위에 대하여 정치적 책임을 지지 않는 법원이 정치의 합목적성이나 정당성을 도외시한 합법성의 심사를 감행함으로써 정책결정이 좌우되는 일은 결코 바람직한 일이 아니며 법원이 정치문제에 개입되어 그 중립성과 독립성을 침해당할 위험성도 부인할 수 없으므로, 고도의 정치성을 띤 통치행위에 대하여 법원은 스스로 사법심사권의 행사를 억제함으로써 그 심사대상에서 제외하고 있을 따름인 것이다.

그러므로 통치행위라고 할지라도 이 사건 긴급조치와 같이 국민의 기본권과 관련된 조치에 대하여 그 실효여부를 심사판단하는 일은 법원이 가지고 있는 본래의 사법심사권을 행사하는 데에 지나지 않으며, 결코 사법권의 한계 밖에 있는 일을 하는 것이라고는 볼 수 없다.

노트와 질문

우리 대법원은 국내정치상황에 관련된 것이기는 하지만 정치문제이론이나 통치행위이론을 받아들이지 않고 있는 듯하다. 외국정부의 공권력 행사로서의 국유화나 점진적 국유화조치로서의 특별세금의 부과, 외국인의 지분제한 등에 대하여는 어떤 태도를 취할까?

3. 소송 대 중재

가. 장 단 점

국제거래에 따르는 분쟁을 중재에 관한 합의가 없는 경우 통상의 소송에 의하여 해결하여야 한다. 자원개발계약의 경우 상대방이 국가 또는 그 기관이므로 위에서 언급한 사법권의 행사에 대한 제한이 있을 수 있다. 국가 또는 그 기관이 중재에 합의한 경우에는 이러한 제한을 주장한 권리를 포기한 것인지, 중재판정이 언제나 집행가능한 것인지에 대하여 약간의 의문이 있을 수 있으나 다수의 견해는 긍정적으로 답한다.

전속적 합의관할에 관한 합의가 없는 경우 다수당사자가 관여된 국제계약에서 분쟁이 발생하는 경우 각 당사자가 각자에게 가장 편하고 유리할 것같은 법원에 다른 당사자보다 먼저 소송을 제기하거나 동시에 소송이 중복 계속될 가능성이 많다. 물론 각국의 법원은 각각의 소송법에 따라서 물적 · 인적 관할권의 행사를 위한 요건구비여부에 관하여 판단하겠지만, 여러 법원이 서로 상반된 판결을 내리면 분쟁은 더욱 해결되기 어려워질 것이다.

전속적 관할법원을 합의할 수도 있으나 관할법원은 대개 국제계약 당사자 일방의 법원이지, 제3국의 법원이 아니라는 점에서 합의의 가능성이 크지 않을 수도 있다. 또한 이러한 합의에 대하여는 각국의 사법부가 다른 태도를 가지며 따라서 언제나 집행가능한 것인지 불확실하다. 이러한 문제는 제3국에서의 중재제도에 합의함으로써 해결될 수 있다.

국제거래에 관련된 다수당사자간 분쟁을 법원이 신속하게 그리고 경제적으로 전문성을 가지고 해결할 수 있는지 여부에 대하여도 의문이 제기된다. 특히 미국에서의 소송시 전제가 되는 discovery제도는 그 시간과 비용면에서 개선할 점이 많다. 물론 중재라고 하여 과연 언제나 신속하고 비용이 저렴한지에 대하여는 반론도 만만치는 않다. 그러나, 적어도 당사자나 중재기관에서 전문성을 가진 중재인을 선정할 수 있다는 점에서 법원보다는 우월한 측면이 있다.

증거조사나 절차의 진행에 있어서 소송은 공개적으로 엄격한 형식적 규정에 따라야 하는 반면, 중재는 비공개이며 비형식적이므로 이 또한 중재가 선호될 수 있는 또 하나의 이유이다. 국제거래시 분쟁 발생의 사실 자체부터 그 해결에 이르기까지 국가나 그 상대방은 조용히 그리고 우호적으로 해결하고자 할 것이며 따라서 소송에 따르는 공개법정에서의 변론과 상대방 당사자와의 대치적 상황은 국제계약 당사자들이 소송을 분쟁해결의 방법으로 선택하는 것을 주저하게 만든다.

마지막으로 집행상의 편의를 들 수 있다. 소송의 종국적 결과물은 판결의 경우 외국판결의 집행에 관한 일반적 조약은 없고 따라서 집행의 필요성이 있는 국가의 외국판결의 효력과 집행에 관한 규정에 따라서 그 효과가 다르다. 중재의 경우에는 세계의 대다수 국가가 가입한 중재판정의 승인 및 집행에 관한 뉴욕협약(1958 UN Convention on the Recognition and Enforcement of Foreign Arbitral Awards)에 따라서 집행국의 법원에서 중재상대방이 제기할 수 있는 항변이 제한되어 있으며 따라서 보다 효과적인 집행이 가능하다.

협상의 실질을 보면 소송의 경우 당사자국의 법원이 아닌 제3국의 법원을 관할법원으로 합의하기는 피차 불편하며 따라서 상대방당사자국의 법원이 아니면 자신의 국가법원을 관할법원으로 합의하여야 하는데, 법원의 중립성에 대한 우려나 법제도에 대한 비친근성, 자신의 제도에 대한 자신감 등때문에 합의에 이르기 쉽지 않다. 한편, 중재는 제3국에서 중립적 절차에 따라 진행할 수 있으므로 당사자가 보다 쉽게 합의할 수 있다.

그러나, 중재 역시 여러가지 문제점이 있다. 비용이나 시간에 대한 논란을 제외하고도 우선 단심이며 그 결과를 예측하기 어렵다는 것은 가장 심각한 문제이다. 법과 형평에 따라서 해결책을 제시한다는 중재제도의 핵심은 엄격한 법원칙에 따른 분석의 어려움을 피할 수 있는 반면, 형평이라는 이름으로 양 당사자의 입장을 적당히 절충하는 해결책에 그칠 가능성이 있다.

또한, 중재는 강행법규가 적용되는 분야에서의 해결책이 될 수 없다는 것이 통설이다. 독점금지법이나 증권거래법 위반에 기초한 손해배상청구가 문제가 되는 경우 중재절차가 이러한 문제까지 다룰 수 있는 것인지에 관하여 논란이 많았다. 이들 강행법 제정의 취지를 살리려면 이러한 논점은 중재대상에서 제외되어야 한다는 주장이 한때 강하였으나, 이제는 모두 중재절차를 통하여 해결할 수 있다는 데 대하여 별로 이견이 없다.

제3국에서의 중재는 거래의 실질보다 합의의 편의에 기초한 측면이 있고 따라서 사실확정에 필요한 증거나 증인 등이 당사자 국가에 소재하는 경우 증거조사에 어려움이 있고 또한 제3국에서의 중재가 적용법규에 얼마나 정통한지에 대한 우려도 있을 수 있다. 그러나, 전술한 바와 같이 계약의 일방당사자가 상대방 당사자에게 굴복하는 모양새를 피할 수 있으며 또한 중재판정의 독립성과 중립성의 확보라는 측면에서도 도움이 될 수도 있기 때문에 실제 많이 이루어진다.

국제에너지탐사계약의 경우에는 계약당사자의 특성상 소송시 예상되는 어려움이 많으며 — 물론 당사자가 주권면책의 특권을 포기할 수 있다고 하지만 그 범위나 방법에 관하여 추후 분쟁이 발생할 수도 있기 때문에 — 따라서 제3국에서의 중재가 하나의 표준적 분쟁해결 방법으로 자리잡았다.

나. 중재의 합의

중재는 중재에 관한 합의가 있는 경우에만 가능한 분쟁해결절차이다. 중재에 관한 합의가 유효하기 위한 요건은 중재판정부가 중재절차가 진행되는 국가의 법규에 따라 결정한다. 우리나라는 1999. 12. 31. UNCITRAL 모델중재법을 참고하여 새로운 중재법을 제정하였다. 동법은 총칙에서 적용범위와 법원의 권한, 기존조약과의 관계를 규정하고 제2절에서 중재합의 요건에 관하여 규정하고 있다. 통상 중재의 대상, 중재 장소, 중재절차, 중재인의 수, 중재인 선정방법, 중재시 언어 등에 관한 합의가 필요하다. 이들에 관한 자세한 합의가 없이도 중재기관을 특정하면 이들 중재기관의 중재규칙이 이러한 합의의 부재를 보완할 수 있다. UNCITRAL이나 ICC, ICSID가 대표적인 중재기관이며 우리나라에는 대한상사중재원이 있다. 이들 중재기관은 각자의 모델중재조항과 중재절차, 중재비용 등을 제시하고 있으므로 이러한 모델조항을 활용하여 볼 수도 있다.

중재조항의 예[12)]

Angola Model Production Sharing Agreement for Deep Water Blocks (February 1992)[13)]

Article 42-Arbitration

1. Any disputes, differences, or claims arising out of this Agreement or relating thereto, or relating to the breach, termination, or invalidation of the same, which it has not been possible to resolve amicably shall be finally and exclusively settled by arbitration, in accordance with the UNCITRAL Rules of Arbitration of 1976 as existing on the Effective Date.
2. The number of arbitrator shall be three (3). They shall be appointed in accordance with the above-mentioned UNCITRAL rules of arbitration. The appointing authority shall be the International Chamber of Commerce, acting in accordance with its relevant rules.
3. The arbitration tribunal shall decide according to Angolan substantive Law.
4. As prescribed in the law in force, the arbitration tribunal shall be set up in Luanda and the language of arbitration shall be Portuguese.
5. The Parties agree that this arbitration clause is an explicit waiver of immunity against validity and enforcement of the award or any judgment thereon and that the award or judgment thereon, if unsatisfied, shall be enforceable against any Litigant in any court having jurisdiction in accordance with its laws.

Trinidadian & Tobagon Model Production Sharing Contract for Deep Water Areas[14)]

Article 33-Consultation, Expert Determination and Arbitration

33.1 The Parties shall make their best effort to settle amicably through consultation any dispute arising in connection with the performance or interpretation of any provision hereof.

12) Barrows Company의 승인을 얻었음.

13) 156 Basic Oil Laws & Concession Contracts: South & Central Africa I (Supplement 141) (2004).

14) Bishop, 주 4-54 상게서, 230-39. T&T계약은 IHS Energy, Petroleum Economics and Policy Solutions (PEPS) Database at http://www.ihsenergy.com에 있다고 하나 아마도 유료서비스인듯.

33.2 If any dispute referred to under this Article has not been settled through such consultation within ninety (90) days after the dispute arises, either Party may by notice to the other Party propose that the dispute be referred either for determination by a sole expert or to arbitration in accordance with the provisions of Article 33.

33.3 Following the giving of notice under Article 33.2, the Parties may, by mutual agreement, refer the dispute for determination by a sole expert to be appointed by agreement between the Parties. Such sole expert shall be an internationally recognised specialist in the interpretation of the subject under dispute. If the Parties are unable to agree on designation of the expert within thirty (30) days following the giving of notice under Article 33.2, the expert shall be named by an internationally recognised organisation to be agreed by the Parties.

33.4 As an alternative to the procedure described in Article 33.3 and if agreed upon by the Parties, such dispute shall be referred to arbitration by an agreed sole arbitrator.

33.5 (a) If the Parties fail to refer such dispute to a sole expert under Article 33.3 or to a sole arbitrator under Article 33.4. within sixty (60) days of the giving of notice under Article 33.2, the dispute shall be referred to arbitration. The arbitration shall be conducted by three (3) arbitrators in accordance with the UNCITRAL Rules in effect on the Effective Date of the Contract.

(b) Where arbitration is resorted to either by the sole arbitrator under Article 33.4 or arbitral tribunal, the Arbitration Rules of the United Nations Commission on International Trade Law (UNCITRAL Rules) in effect on the Effective Date of the Contract shall be used.

33.6 The English language shall be the language used in the expert or arbitral proceedings. All hearing materials, statements of claim or defence, award and the reasons supporting them shall be in English.

33.7 The place of the expert determination or arbitration shall be in Trinidad and Tobago.

33.8 In the ease of a request by Contractor pursuant to Article 17.6(e) for final determination by an expert of whether a disputed charge is subject to cost recovery such expert shall be an internationally recognised specialist in interpretation of Petroleum Operations. If the Parties are unable to agree on designation of the expert within thirty (30) days after Contractor's request under Article 17.6(e) for the expert determination, the expert shall be named by the International Chamber of Commerce. The waiting period required by Article 33.2 shall not apply to this type of expert determination.

33.9 (a) Any decision by the expert determination, sole arbitrator or arbirtal tribunal shall be final and binding upon the Parties. Such decision shall be rendered within sixty (60) days after the completion of the expert determination or arbitration proceedings.

(b) Judgement for execution of any award rendered by the expert determination, sole arbitrator or arbitral tribunal may be entered by any court of competent jurisdiction without review of the merits of such award.

Production Sharing Contract dated 29 June 1992 between the Republic of Equatorial Guinea & United Meridian International Corp.[15]

Section 13-Arbitration

13.1 The Parties agree to submit any dispute, controversy, claim or difference arising out of or in connection with this Contract to arbitration under and in accordance with the Arbitration (Additional Facility) Rules in force on the Effective Date ("Facility Rules") of the International Center for Settlement of Investment Disputes ("Center"). As of the Effective Date, the State is not a Contracting State as that term is defined in the Convention on the Settlement of Investment Disputes between States and Nationals of Other States which entered into force on October 14, 1966 ("Convention"). Under this Contract, the Parties waive all exemptions with respect to arbitration and to all proceedings and actions that enforce the arbitral award, and the State hereby waives any right of sovereign immunity as to it and its property in respect of the enforcement and execution of any award rendered by an arbitral tribunal constituted pursuant to this Contract.

13.2 Each of the Parties agrees to and hereby gives its consent to the jurisdiction of the Center under Article 25 of the Convention in the event that the jurisdictional requirements "ratione personae" of this Article shall have been met at the time when arbitration proceedings are instituted under this Contract. In such event, the Parties agree to submit any dispute, controversy, claim or difference arising out of or in connection with this Contract to the Center in accordance with the Arbitration Rules in force on the Effective Date set forth by the Convention.

13.3 In the event of any dispute, controversy, claim or difference arising out of or in connection with this Contract, the Parties shall endeavor to settle such dispute amicably. If within thirty (30) days after a notice of such a dispute the Parties have not reached a settlement, the dispute shall at the request of either Party be referred to arbitration in accordance with this Section 13.

13.4 It is hereby agreed that the consent to the jurisdiction of the Center expressed above shall equally bind any successor in interest to the present Government of the Republic of Equatorial Guinea and to the Contractor to the extent that the Center can assume jurisdiction over a dispute between such successor and the other Party.

13.5 It is hereby agreed that the right of the Contractor to request the settlement of a dispute by the Center or to take any step as a party to a proceeding pursuant to this Agreement shall not be affected by the fact that the Contractor has received partial compensation on the conditional or an absolute basis, from any third party (whether a private person, a state, a government agency or an international organization), with respect to any loss or injury that is the subject of the dispute; Provided, that the Republic of Equatorial Guinea may require evidence that such third party agrees to the exercise of those rights by the Contractor.

13.6 Any arbitral tribunal constituted pursuant to this Contract shall apply the law of the Republic of Equatorial Guinea and generally accepted principles of international law. Such arbitral tribunal constituted pursuant to this Contract shall have the power to decide a dispute ex aequo et bono.

15) 135 Basic Oil Laws & Concession Contracts: South & Central Africa 1 (1998).

13.7 Any arbitration under this Section 13 shall be conducted by a tribunal constituted by three (3) arbitrators who shall not have the same nationality as the Parties. The arbitration shall be held in Geneva, Switzerland using the Spanish and English languages.

AGIP/BP/ETAL Production Sharing Agreement Dated 18 November 1997 in respect of the North Caspian Sea (Kashagan) among Agip Caspian Sea B.V., et al.[16)]

Section 38.4-Expert Determination

(a) Where, pursuant to an express provision of this Agreement, a dispute between any of the Parties or any of the Parties and any other person is to be referred for expert determination in accordance with this Section 38.4, such dispute shall not be subject to the provisions of Sections 38.1 and 38.2 but upon written demand of any such Party or Person shall be referred to a Person of international repute having extensive experience of international oil and gas operations, and with acknowledged expertise in the matters in dispute, to be appointed by agreement between the Parties concerned and, failing such agreement within thirty (30) calendar days of such written demand, to be appointed by the President of the International Court of Justice at The Hague.

(b) The person appointed pursuant to the foregoing (the "Expert") shall act as an expert and not as an arbitrator, shall determine its own procedure and shall, with due care and expedition, after making such investigation as it may consider proper, either (i) settle such dispute and issue a written certificate containing its determination and the reason therefore (sic), such determination being conclusive and binding upon the Parties concerned or (ii) make its recommendations in written form, as the case may be, as contemplated in the relevant provisions of the Agreement pursuant to which this section is invoked. The Parties shall cooperate with the Expert in obtaining any and all information required by the Expert with respect to any such certification or recommendation. Each of Contractor and Authority shall have the right to make a submission on its own behalf for consideration by the Expert.

(c) Notwithstanding subsection (b) above, the Expert shall be instructed to observe all instructions, considerations or guidelines set forth in the relevant provisions of the Agreement pursuant to which this Section is invoked and to reach a determination consistent with any criteria set out in such relevant provisions and, in the absence of such criteria, consistent with International Good Oil Field Practice.

(d) The Expert shall be instructed to settle or make recommendations, as the case may be, in respect of any dispute among the Parties or among any Party or any other Person that is referred to it hereunder by certification within sixty (60) calendar days of such referral.

(e) Any fees charged or expenses incurred by an Expert appointed pursuant to this section shall be borne equally by the Parties concerned and shall not be eligible for cost recovery pursuant to Article XIV.

16) 52 Basic Oil Laws & Concession Contracts: NIS 2 (Supplement 39) (2003).

다. 외국판결과 중재판정의 승인과 집행

1) 외국판결

전술한 바와 같이 외국판결의 승인과 집행에 관하여는 국제조약이 없이 각국의 소송법에 기초하여 집행되고 있다. 다만 유럽의 경우 Brussels Convention of 27 Sept. 1968 on jurisdiction and the enforcement of judgments in civil and commercial matters와[17] Lugano Convention on 16 Sept. 1988이[18] 체결되어 있고 Hague Conference on Private International Law에서 Convention of 1 Feb. 1971 on the Recognition and Enforcement of Foreign Judgments in Civil and Commercial Matters를 제안하고 있을 뿐이다.[19]

우리나라는 루가노협약에의 가입을 진지하게 검토하고는 있지만[20] 아직은 가입하지 않았고 따라서 외국의 판결은 민사소송법 제217조에 정한 요건이 충족되는 경우 민사집행법 제27조에 의한 집행판결을 통하여 집행된다.[21] 집행판결을 위한 요건 중 하나는 외국법원의 국제재판관할권이 인정되어야 하는바, 외국법원에의 전속적 합의관할에 관한 합의의 효력에 관하여는 민사소송법 제29조가 적용된다.[22] 이하 외국법원에의 전속적 합의관할의 효력과 외국판결의 집행에 관한 판결을 소개한다.

대법 2010. 8. 26. 선고 2010다28185 판결[23]

대한민국 법원의 관할을 배제하고 외국의 법원을 관할법원으로 하는 전속적인 국제관할

17) 유럽의회의 website curia.europa.eu에서 열람가능.
18) Id.에서 열람가능.
19) www.hcch.net에서 열람가능. 2005. 6. Convention on Choice of Court Agreement도 동일 취지.
20) 법원행정처, 외국판결의 승인·집행에 관한 국제규범과 우리의 대응방안, 309-10(2010).
21) 외국에서의 송달 및 증거조사에 관하여는 졸저, 기업+(준)법, 제15장 참조.
22) 우리 법원의 국제적 재판관할에 대하여는 국제사법 제2조가 적용되는바, 실질적 관련성에 관하여는 대법 2008. 5. 29. 선고 2006다71908,71915 판결(원고가 매도인인 한국기업이고 매수인이 일본기업이 중국에 제기한 소는 각하된 상황); 대법 2005. 1. 27. 선고 2002다59788 판결(한국기업인 원고가 미국기업이 제기하여 미국내 도메인이름 분쟁해결기관의 결정에 대하여 불복하는 상황). 국제사법 시행전 판결로 대법 1995. 11. 21. 선고 93다39607 판결과 대법 2012. 5. 24. 선고 2009다22549 판결 참조.
23) 대법 2004. 3. 25. 선고 2001다53349 판결, 대법 2011. 4. 28. 선고 2009다19093 판결도 마찬가지로 합리적인 관련성을 요구. 특허권의 성립에 관한 것이거나 특허권의 유무효 또는 취소는 등록국 법원의 전속관할. 합리적 관련성을 이유로 외국법원의 전속적 관할합의조항이 무효로 판단된 경우는 대법 1997. 9. 9. 선고 96다20093, 서울지법 2002. 12. 24. 선고 2002가합32672 판결, 대법 2004. 3. 25. 선고 2001다53349 판결이 있으나 두 개의 대법판결은 내국법인들끼리 운송계약관련 외국의 전속적 관할조항에 합의한 것으로 본 경우로 특히 그러한 합의에 특히 엄격한 요건을 요구한 것은 아니고 2002가합32672 판결은 본문 대법 2010. 8. 26. 선고 2010다28185 판결의 1심판결로 파기된 것임. 서울지법 2003. 12. 5. 선

의 합의가 유효하기 위해서는, 당해 사건이 대한민국 법원의 전속관할에 속하지 아니하고 지정된 외국법원이 그 외국법상 당해 사건에 대하여 관할권을 가져야 하는 외에, 당해 사건이 그 외국법원에 대하여 합리적인 관련성을 가질 것이 요구된다고 할 것이고, 그와 같은 전속적인 관할 합의가 현저하게 불합리하고 불공정하여 공서양속에 반하는 법률행위에 해당하지 않는 한 그 관할 합의는 유효하다 할 것이다(대법원 1997. 9. 9. 선고 96다20093 판결 참조). 한편 국제사법 제27조에서 소비자 보호를 위하여 준거법 지정과 관련하여 소비자계약에 관한 강행규정을 별도로 마련해 두고 있는 점이나 약관의 규제에 관한 법률(이하 '약관규제법'이라 한다)의 입법목적을 고려하면, 외국법을 준거법으로 하여 체결된 모든 계약에 관하여 당연히 약관규제법을 적용할 수 있는 것은 아니다.

원심판결 이유에 의하면, 원심은 원고와 피고들이 2003. 8. 1. 원고가 캐나다 법에 의하여 설립된 회사인 피고들의 제품을 국내에서 배급·판매대리 하는 내용의 이 사건 계약을 체결하면서 그 준거법을 캐나다 온타리오 주의 법률에 의하도록 약정한 사실, 이 사건 계약 당시 계약해지사유 중의 하나로서 특별한 사유가 없더라도 전적으로 계약을 해지하려는 당사자의 편의에 따라 60일 전에 사전 통보를 함으로써 계약을 해지할 수 있도록 약정한 사실(이하 '이 사건 해지조항'이라 한다), 그 후 원고가 이 사건 계약에 기하여 피고들의 제품을 국내에서 배급·판매대리하는 영업을 하여 오다가 피고들이 2007. 3. 20.경 원고에게 이 사건 해지조항에 기하여 이 사건 계약을 해지한다고 통보한 사실을 기초 사실로 인정한 다음, 이 사건 계약이 캐나다 온타리오 주법을 준거법으로 정함으로써 현저하게 불합리하거나 불공정한 결과가 초래된다고 볼 근거가 없어 그 준거법 약정은 유효하다는 전제하에 피고들의 위와 같은 해지통보에 따라 위 통보일로부터 60일이 경과한 날에 이 사건 계약이 해지되었다고 판단한 후, 이 사건 해지조항은 약관규제법에 따라 무효로 보아야 한다는 원고의 주장에 대하여는, 외국의 법률이 준거법으로 지정되어 있는 이 사건 계약의 경우에는 우리나라의 약관규제법이 적용될 여지가 없다는 이유로 이를 배척하였다.

앞서 본 법리에 비추어 기록을 살펴보면, 원심의 위와 같은 판단은 정당한 것으로 수긍이 가고, 거기에 상고이유로 주장하는 바와 같은 준거법 및 약관규제법의 적용에 관한 법리오해의 위법이 없다.

2. 상고이유 제2점에 대하여

외국적 요소가 있는 법률관계에 관하여 적용될 외국법규의 내용을 확정하고 그 의미를

고 2003가합43945 판결은 가맹사업거래의 공정화에 관한 법률위반을 원인으로 구하는 손해배상에 관한 한 합의관할의 효력을 부인. 본문 대법 2010. 8. 26. 선고 2010다28185 판결이 준거법이 외국법임을 이유로 약관규제법에 관하여 그 적용을 부인할 수 있다고 하고 있으니 가맹사업거래의 공정화에 관한 법률의 적용도 거부할 있다고 볼 가능성도 있다.

해석함에 있어서는 그 외국법이 그 본국에서 실제로 해석·적용되고 있는 의미와 내용에 따라 해석·적용되어야 하고, 그 본국 최고법원의 법해석에 관한 판단은 특별한 사정이 없는 한 존중되어야 하지만, 소송과정에서 그에 관한 판례나 해석 기준에 관한 자료가 충분히 제출되지 아니하여 그 내용의 확인이 불가능한 경우 법원으로서는 일반적인 법해석 기준에 따라 법의 의미와 내용을 확정할 수밖에 없다(대법원 2007. 6. 29. 선고 2006다5130 판결 등 참조).

캐나다 온타리오 주에서는 Tilden Rent A Car Co. v. Clendenning 사례 이래로 계약을 체결함에 있어 계약자에게 계약 내용을 충분히 심사숙고할 수 있는 시간이 부여되지 않았다는 점과 그 계약 내용이 부당하거나 형평을 잃었다는 점이 인정될 경우에는 약관조항의 효력을 부인할 수 있다는 원칙이 수립되어 있는바, 위와 같은 법리에 비추어 원심이 인정한 사실을 살펴보면, 원고의 대표이사가 피고들과의 계약 체결에 앞서 1년 4개월 동안의 트레이닝 기간을 거친 후에 이 사건 계약을 체결하였고, 이 사건 계약이 이 사건 해지조항을 비롯하여 해지사유를 구체적으로 열거하면서 해지사유별로 재고반품 등 배급·판매대리점인 원고의 보호규정을 별도로 마련하여 놓고 있는 점에 비추어 볼 때, 원고가 이 사건 해지조항의 내용을 제대로 읽어보지 않거나 이해하지 못한 상태에서 이 사건 계약을 체결하였다거나 이 사건 해지조항이 원고에게만 불리하여 그 계약 내용이 부당하다고 보기 어렵다.

원심의 판시는 그 설시가 부적절하기는 하나 이 사건 해지조항의 효력을 부인할 수 없다고 판단한 결론은 정당하므로, 거기에 상고이유의 주장과 같은 외국법의 해석 적용 등에 관하여 법리를 오해하여 판결 결과에 영향을 미친 위법이 있다고 할 수 없다.

부산지법 2009. 1. 22. 선고 2008가합309 판결[24)]

가. 망 소외인(이하 '망인'이라 한다)은 1998. 1. 8. 미합중국 캘리포니아주 비스타 소재 이코노 플라스틱사의 공장에서 피고 회사가 제작한 프로맥스 호라이즌탈 인젝션 몰딩 머신 4000씨 시리즈(Promax Horizontal Injection Molding Machine, 4000C Series, 이하 '이 사건 사출성형기'라 한다)에 몰드를 설치하는 작업을 하다가 실린더와 벽 사이에 머리가 끼이는 사고(이하 '이 사건 사고'라 한다)를 당하여 사망하였고, 원고들은 그 처와 자녀들이다.

나. 피고 회사는 사출 성형기 등 기계류를 제조·판매하는 대한민국 회사로서 미합중국 법인인 프로맥스 플라스틱 머쉬너리 잉크(Promax Plastic Machinery Inc., 이하 '프로맥스사'라 한

24) 징벌적 손해와 외국판결의 집행에 관하여는 서울지법 동부지원 1995. 2. 10. 선고 93가합19069 판결(징벌적 손해배상이 포함되어 있다고 볼 수는 없지만 우리나라에서 인정될 만한 상당한 금액을 현저히 초과하는 손해배상분에 한하여는 공서양속에 반한다고 보아 승인거절). 이 외에도 대법 1997. 9. 9. 선고 96다47517 판결, 대법 1992. 7. 14. 선고 92다2585 판결 참조.

다)에 이 사건 사출성형기를 수출하였고, 프로맥스사는 위 사출성형기를 이코노 플라스틱사에 판매하였으나, 피고 회사가 이 사건 사고 당시 미국 현지에 지사나 영업소를 두고 있지는 아니하였다.

다. 원고들은 1998. 7. 22. 이 사건 사출성형기를 판매한 프로맥스사는 물론 위 사출성형기를 제조한 피고 회사 등을 상대로 미합중국 캘리포니아주 샌디애고 카운티 슈피어리어 법원 북부지원(이하 '이 사건 미국법원'이라 한다)에 손해배상청구소송(이하 '이 사건 손해배상청구소송'이라 한다)을 제기하였고, 피고 회사는 1999. 6. 3. 위 소송에 관한 소장, 변경된 소장, 소환장 등을 송달받은 다음 캘리포니아주 샌디에고시 소재 로펌인 Seltzer Caplan Wilkins & McMahon을 선임하여 위 소송에 응소하였다(그 후 위 로펌이 2000. 8. 31. 피고 회사의 수임료 미지급 등의 사유로 변호인 사임계를 제출하자, 피고 회사는 다시 Nam & Cha 로펌을 선임하여 위 소송에 응소하였다).

라. 이 사건 손해배상청구소송은 2001. 11. 30. 이 사건 미국법원의 사브로(Dana M. Sabraw) 판사가 담당하게 되었고(사건번호 N78688), 사브로 판사는 12명의 배심원을 선임하여 이 사건 사고에 대해 엄격제조책임(strict product liability)을 인정할 수 있는지 여부에 대하여 심리를 하게 하였는데, 배심원단은 이 사건 사고가 이 사건 사출성형기의 설계상 하자 및 그 하자에 대한 미경고로 인하여 발생하였고 망인의 사망으로 인한 총 손해액을 미화 5,058,294달러(경제적 손해: 미화 808,294달러, 비경제적 손해: 미화 4,250,000달러)라고 평결(verdict)하였다.

마. 그 후 사브로 판사는 2002. 1. 23. 위와 같은 배심원단의 평결을 승인하면서 프로맥스와 피고 회사가 연대하여(jointly and severally) 원고들에게 위 총 손해액 미화 5,058,294달러와 소송비용 상환액 미화 19,085.18달러를 합하여 미화 5,077,379.18달러와 이에 대하여 2002. 1. 23.부터 다 갚는 날까지 연 10%의 이자를 지급을 명하는 배심재판 후 판결(judgement after jury trial, 이하 '이 사건 미국 판결'이라 한다)을 선고하였고, 그 무렵 이 사건 미국 판결은 법원 서기에 의해 판결책(judgement book)에 등록(entered)되었다.

바. 이 사건 미국 판결이 위와 같이 등록된 이후 프로맥스사는 위 배심원의 평결에 관하여 평결파기신청(motion for Judgement Notwithstanding Verdict)을 하였으나 위 신청이 받아들여지지 않았고, 피고 회사는 이 사건 미국 판결에 대하여 상소를 제기하지 않았다.

2. 집행판결의 요건에 대한 판단

외국 법원에 의하여 선고된 판결이 우리나라에서 승인되기 위하여는 먼저 위 판결이 확정되어 있어야 하는 이외에 민사소송법 제217조 각 호의 요건을 구비하고 있어야 하는바, 이하에서는 이 사건 미국 판결이 위와 같은 요건을 구비하였는지 여부에 관하여 보기로 한다.

가. 이 사건 미국 판결의 확정 여부 (민사집행법 제27조 제2항 제1호)

판결의 확정이라 함은 그 판결을 한 외국의 절차에 있어 통상의 불복방법으로는 더 이상 불복할 수 없는 상태를 의미하고, 무엇이 통상의 불복방법에 해당하는가는 당해 판결국법에 의하여 결정할 문제라고 할 것인바, 갑 제20호증의 각 기재에 변론 전체의 취지를 종합하면, 미국 캘리포니아 주법(Code of Civil Procedure, 이하 '이 사건 미국법'이라 한다)과 같은 주의 법원 규칙(California Rules of Court, 이하 '이 사건 미국 법원규칙'이라 한다)에 의하면 특별한 사정이 없는 한 판결은 선고 즉시 법원서기에 의하여 판결문서철(judgement book)에 등록(entered)되어야 하고, 그 판결에 대한 항소기간(time to appeal)은 판결 등록 후 180일 또는 법원서기가 판결이 등록되었음을 당사자에게 고지하는 서면을 우편으로 발송한 후 60일로 정하여진 사실(이 사건 미국법 제668조, 제668.5조, 이 사건 미국 법원규칙 제2조)을 인정할 수 있고, 이 사건 미국 판결이 그 선고일인 2002. 1. 23. 무렵 등록되었는데 피고 회사가 이에 대하여 위 항소기간 내에 항소를 제기하지 않은 사실은 앞서 본 바와 같으므로 이 사건 미국 판결은 이 사건 미국법 및 법원규칙이 규정하는 상소기간이 경과함으로써 더 이상 통상의 불복방법으로써는 다툴 수 없게 되어 확정되었다고 할 것이다.

나. 상호보증 여부 (민사집행법 제27조 제2항 제2호, 민사소송법 제217조 제4호)

민사소송법 제217조 제4호는 우리나라만이 입을 수 있는 불이익을 방지하고 국제관계에서 형평을 도모하기 위하여 외국 판결의 승인요건으로서 상호보증이 있을 것을 요구하고 있지만, 판결국에 있어서 외국 판결의 승인요건이 우리나라의 그것과 모든 항목에 걸쳐 완전히 동일하거나 오히려 관대할 것을 요구하는 것은 지나치게 외국 판결의 승인 범위를 협소하게 하는 결과가 되어 국제적인 교류가 빈번한 오늘날의 현실에 맞지 아니하고 오히려 외국에서 우리나라의 판결에 대한 승인을 거부하게 만드는 불합리한 결과를 초래한다는 점을 고려할 때, 우리나라와 외국 사이에 동종 판결의 승인요건이 현저히 균형을 상실하지 아니하고 외국에서 정한 요건이 우리나라에서 정한 그것보다 전체로서 과중하지 아니하며 중요한 점에서 실질적으로 거의 차이가 없는 정도라면 민사소송법 제217조 제4호에서 정하는 상호보증의 요건을 구비하였다고 봄이 상당하고, 또한 이와 같은 상호의 보증은 외국의 법령, 판례 및 관례 등에 의하여 승인요건을 비교하여 인정되면 충분하고 반드시 당사국과의 조약이 체결되어 있을 필요는 없으며, 당해 외국에서 구체적으로 우리나라의 동종 판결을 승인한 사례가 없더라도 실제로 승인할 것이라고 기대할 수 있는 상태이면 충분하다 할 것이다(대법원 2004. 10. 28. 선고 2002다74213 판결 등 참조).

갑23, 24호증의 각 기재에 변론 전체의 취지를 더하면, 미국 캘리포니아주에서 채택하고 있는 통일외국금전판결승인법(Uniform Foreign Country Money-Judgements Recognition Act, 이하 '승인법'이라 한다)은 외국 판결의 승인 및 집행에 관한 요건으로 적법절차 조항에 어긋나지 않는 공평한 재판을 거칠 것, 재판관할권의 존재, 적법한 송달, 사위의 방법에 의하여 취득한 판결이 아닐 것, 공서에 반하지 않을 것 등을 요건으로 하고 있는 사실을 인정할 수 있는바, 위 승인법이 정한 동종 판결의 승인요건은 현저히 균형을 상실하지 아니하고 우리나라 민사소송법이 정한 그것보다 전체로서 과중하지 아니하며 중요한 점에서 실질적으로 거의 차이가 없는 정도라고 할 것이므로 이 사건 미국 판결은 민사소송법 제217조 제4호에서 정하는 상호보증의 요건을 구비하였다고 봄이 상당하다.

다. 재판관할권의 구비 여부 (민사집행법 제27조 제2항 제2호, 민사소송법 제217조 제1호)

섭외사건의 국제재판관할에 관하여 일반적으로 승인된 국제법상의 원칙이 아직 확립되어 있지 아니하고, 이에 관한 우리나라의 성문법규도 없는 이상 섭외사건에 관한 외국 법원의 재판관할권 유무는 당사자 간의 공평, 재판의 적정, 신속을 기한다는 기본이념에 따라 조리에 의하여 이를 결정함이 상당하다 할 것이고, 이 경우 우리나라의 민사소송법의 변론관할에 관한 규정 또한 위 기본이념에 따라 제정된 것이므로 피고가 외국 법원에서 해당 재판이 관할 위반이라고 항변하지 아니하고 본안에 대하여 변론을 하였다면 특별한 사정이 없는 한 그 외국 법원에 재판관할권이 있다고 봄이 상당하다고 할 것이다.

이 사건에 관하여 보건대, 위 인정 사실에 의하면, 피고 회사는 1999. 6. 3. 이 사건 미국 법원에 제기된 피고 회사에 대한 손해배상소송에 관한 소장 등의 서류를 송달받고 그 무렵 미국 로펌을 선임하여 위 소송에 응소하였고, 위 로펌이 위 손해배상소송 진행 과정에서 피고 회사를 위해 다수의 답변서, 준비서면 등을 제출한 점을 알 수 있으므로 피고 회사는 이 사건 미국 법원에 계속중이던 위 손해배상소송에서 본안에 관한 변론을 하였다고 봄이 상당하고, 달리 위 소송과정에서 관할 위반의 항변이 있었음을 인정할 자료도 발견되지 아니하므로 이 사건 미국 법원은 위 손해배상소송에 관하여 재판관할권이 있다고 할 것이다.

라. 적법한 송달 등 구비 여부 (민사집행법 제27조 제2항 제2호, 민사소송법 제217조 제2호)

민사소송법 제217조 제2호는 외국 판결 승인요건의 하나로서 패소한 피고가 대한민국 국민인 경우에 공시송달에 의하지 아니하고 소송의 개시에 필요한 소환 또는 명령의 송달을 받거나 또는 받지 아니하고 응소했을 것을 요구하고 있는데, 피고 회사가 1999. 6. 3. 위 소송에 관한 소장, 변경된 소장, 소환장 등을 송달받은 사실은 위에서 인정한 바와 같으므로, 이 사건 미국 판결은 위 요건을 구비하고 있다.

마. 공서양속 위반 여부 (민사집행법 제27조 제2항 제2호, 민사소송법 제217조 제3호)

(1) 피고 회사의 주장

① 이 사건 미국 판결에서 원고들의 비경제적 손해액으로 미화 425만 달러를 인정한 것은 사실상 영미법에서 인정되는 징벌적 손해배상에 해당하고 그와 같이 징벌적 손해배상을 명한 외국 판결을 승인하는 것은 대한민국 손해배상제도의 기본이념에 부합하지 아니하므로 대한민국의 공서양속에 반하는 것이고, 설령 위와 같은 비경제적 손해액이 징벌적 손해배상에 해당하지 않는다고 하더라도 대한민국 손해배상제도의 법리에 비추어 그 손해액이 지나치게 많고 그 근거도 박약하므로 위와 같은 비경제적 손해 부분을 승인하여서는 안 되며, ② 이 사건 미국 판결에서 인정한 경제적 손해액 역시 그 금액이 지나치게 많을 뿐만 아니라 이 사건 사고는 망인 또는 제3자의 부주의한 기기 조작으로 인하여 발생한 것이므로 위 경제적 손해액 중 대한민국 공서양속에 반하는 부분은 승인될 수 없다.

(2) 판 단

(가) 민사집행법 제27조 제1항은 '집행판결은 재판의 옳고 그름을 조사하지 아니하고 하여야 한다'고 규정하여 외국 판결에 대한 실질적 재심사를 금지하고 있기는 하지만, 외국 판결에 대하여 실질적 심사를 하지 않는다는 것은 당해 판결의 법적 당부를 심사하지 않는다는 것을 의미하는 것일 뿐 우리나라의 공서에 반하는지를 조사하는 것까지 금지하는 것은 아니라고 할 것이고, 대한민국 국제사법 제32조 제4항은 "제1항 내지 제3항의 규정에 의하여 외국법이 적용되는 경우에 불법행위로 인한 손해배상청구권은 그 성질이 명백히 피해자의 적절한 배상을 위한 것이 아니거나 또는 그 범위가 본질적으로 피해자의 적절한 배상을 위하여 필요한 정도를 넘는 때에는 이를 인정하지 아니한다"는 저촉규정을 둠으로써 우리나라에서 재판이 이루어지는 섭외적 법률관계에 있어 외국법의 적용을 일정한 한도로 제한하는 등 우리나라 손해배상법의 지침적 기능을 인정하고 있으므로 위와 같은 저촉규정의 적용 여부를 판단함에 있어서는 외국 판결의 기초가 된 사실관계와 우리나라와의 연결, 즉 사건의 내국관련성의 정도가 그 중요한 고려요소가 된다고 할 것인데, 이 사건에 있어 피고 회사는 사출성형기를 대한민국에서 생산하여 미국에 수출하는 대한민국 법인이므로 이 사건 손해배상소송에 관하여 대한민국에도 재판관할권이 있는 점, 이 사건 사출성형기를 수입한 미국의 프로맥스사는 미국 법인으로서 피고 회사의 지사나 영업소 혹은 판매 대리점이라고 볼 수 없고, 독자적인 계산과 책임 아래 피고 회사로부터 수입한 사출성형기를 미국 내에서 판매하여 온 점, 이 사건 손해배상소송이 제기될 당시 피고 회사는 미국 내에 별도로 현지 법인 등을 두고 있지 않아[디마 잉크(DIMA INC.)사는 이 사건 미국 판결이 선고된 이후에 설립되었다] 피고 회사가 위 소송에 응소하기는 하였으나, 그 변론 및 입증에 상당한 어려움을 겪었을 것으로 보

이는 점, 이 사건 미국 판결에서 인정된 손해배상액이 현저히 고액임에도 불구하고 다른 공동피고들이 위 판결에 따른 손해배상액을 전혀 지급하지 않고 있어(이 사건 손해배상소송의 대표 피고였던 프로맥스사는 이 사건 미국 판결 직후 파산하였다) 위 손해배상액 전부에 대한 집행을 승인할 경우 피고 회사의 한국에서의 사업기반이 파탄에 이를 우려가 있는 점 등에 비추어 볼 때, 사건의 내국관련성의 정도가 상대적으로 강하다고 봄이 상당하다고 할 것이어서 위 규정의 지침적 기능을 참작할 수 있다고 할 것이고, 이러한 경우에는 헌법상의 법치국가원리로부터 파생되는 원칙으로서 민사법질서에 있어서도 그대로 타당하다고 할 수 있는 이른바 비례의 원칙을 적용하여 우리나라 손해배상법에서의 기준에 비추어 볼 때 비정상적으로 고액이라고 보이는 부분 전부를 승인하지 아니하고, 우리나라에서 인정될 만한 상당한 금액을 현저히 초과하는 부분에 한하여 우리나라의 선량한 풍속 기타 사회질서에 반한다고 보아 승인을 제한할 수 있다고 봄이 상당하다.

위와 같은 관점에서 출발하여 결론적으로 외국 판결의 승인 여부를 판단함에 있어서는, 우리나라 실질 사법적 정의의 보호측면에서, 집행될 내용 및 당해 사안과 우리나라와의 관련성 등에 비추어 보아 당해 외국 판결의 집행을 용인하는 것이 손해의 전보, 손해의 공평·타당한 분담이라고 하는 대한민국 손해배상법의 기본원칙 내지 사회 일반의 법 감정상 도저히 참을 수 없는 가혹한 결과를 가져오지는 않는지 여부 등 제반 요소를 참작하고 이와 아울러 민사집행법 제27조 제1항이 규정하는 실질재심사 금지의 원칙을 관철하여 국가간 파행적 법률관계의 발생을 억제하고 법적 안정성을 기함으로써 외국 판결의 존중이라는 승인제도의 본래의 취지를 살린다는 측면을 상호 비교·형량하여 구체적, 개별적으로 타당한 결론을 도출함이 상당하다.

(나) 갑1, 3, 20, 21호증의 각 기재 및 변론 전체의 취지를 종합하면, 원고들은 이 사건 손해배상소송의 제2차 청구원인 변경서(second amended complaint)에서 손해배상책임의 근거로 부주의로 인한 과실(negligence) 및 과실추정칙(res ipsa loquitur) 책임을 포함하여 여러 가지 청구원인을 적시하였는데, 그 중 5번째 청구원인으로 피고 회사를 포함한 모든 피고들에 대해 엄격 책임(strict liability)에 따른 징계적 또는 징벌적 손해배상(exemplary or punitive damages)을 구하였던 사실, 이 사건 미국 판결에는 과실 및 과실추정칙에 근거한 청구가 기각되었음을 밝히면서 배심원들이 남은 단 하나의 청구원인(the single remaining cause)인 엄격제조책임(strict product liability)에 대한 것만 청취하고 평결을 하기로 선서한 것으로 기재되어 있는 사실, 원고들의 대리인이었던 허드슨(Richard B. Hudson) 변호사의 진술서에서도 엄격책임에 근거한 청구는 피고들에 대한 잠재적인 징벌적 손해배상청구를 수반한다고 진술하고 있는 사실, 이 사건 미국법원의 승인된 배심안내책자(BAJI, Book of Approved Jury Instruction)에 의하면 경제적 손해(economic damages)란 치료비나 수입의 상실 등과 같이 객관적으로 측

정할 수 있는 금전적 손실을 의미하고, 비경제적 손해(non-economic damages)란 정신적 고통, 모욕감과 같은 주관적인 비금전적 손실을 의미한다고 기술되어 있는 사실, 이 사건 소송에 소환된 전문가 증인인 베르그마크(Bergmark)는 망인과 그 아내인 원고 1의 연간 수입과 가동연한(worklife expectancy), 생계비(personal consumption) 등을 토대로 원고들의 전체 경제적 손해액을 미화 740,958달러(=Total Past 미화 150,305달러+Total Future 미화 590,653달러)로 초안(Draft)하였다가 그 후 미화 67,336달러가 증액된 미화 808,294달러를 경제적 손해액이라고 증언한 사실 등을 인정할 수 있다.

위 인정 사실에서 알 수 있는 바와 같이, 이 사건 미국 판결에서 명시적으로 징벌적 손해배상을 언급하고 있지는 않지만, 원고들은 당초 엄격제조책임을 근거로 하여 그에 대한 징벌적 손해배상청구를 하였고(그 후 위와 같은 징벌적 손해배상청구가 철회되었는지 여부는 기록상 불분명하다), 이 사건 미국 판결에서는 그와 같은 엄격제조책임에 관한 변론만을 청취한 배심원들이 손해배상액을 결정하였으므로 손해액 결정과정에서 징벌적 손해에 대한 고려를 포함시켰을 여지가 많은 점, 이 사건 미국 판결이 원고들의 손해액을 경제적 손해와 비경제적 손해로 나누어 그 손해액을 산정하면서 원고들에게 비경제적 손해액으로 미화 425만 달러라는 엄청난 금액의 손해배상을 인정하는 것이 합리적이라고 판단될 만한 아무런 이유도 제시하고 있지 아니하고 원고들이 제출한 자료에서도 이를 확인할 수 없는 점, 이 사건 미국 판결에서 원고들의 경제적 손해액을 산출해내는 방식은 일응 합리적인 기준과 방법에 의한 것으로 보이지만, 원고들의 비경제적 손해액을 그와 같이 거액의 금액으로 인정한 것은 단지 판결의 편의나 피해자의 이익만을 지나치게 고려한 데 따른 것으로 보이고, 그 중 어느 정도의 금액을 정신적 고통에 대한 보상으로 볼 것인지 특정할 수도 없는 점 등을 종합하여 보면, 이 사건 미국 판결에서 인정된 경제적 및 비경제적 손해액을 전부 승인하는 것은 손해의 공평·타당한 분담이라고 하는 대한민국 손해배상법의 기본원칙 내지 사회 일반의 법 감정상 도저히 참을 수 없는 가혹한 결과를 가져올 수 있다고 할 것이고, 대한민국에서 인정될 만한 상당한 금액을 현저히 초과하는 부분에 한하여는 우리나라의 선량한 풍속 기타 사회질서에 반한다고 보아 승인을 제한해야 할 것이다.

따라서 이 사건 미국 판결에서 인정한 손해액 중 합리적 근거 없이 과도하게 산정된 비경제적 손해액을 제외하고 경제적 손해액 부분만을 승인함이 타당하므로 결국, 이 사건 미국 판결은 경제적 손해배상액 미화 808,294달러에 이 사건 손해배상소송의 소송비용 미화 19,085.18달러를 합한 미화 827,379.18달러(=미화 808,294달러+미화 19,085.18달러)와 이에 대한 이 사건 미국 판결의 선고일인 2002. 1. 23.부터 다 갚는 날까지 연 10%의 비율로 계산한 지연손해금의 범위 내에서만 원고들의 피고 회사에 대한 우리나라에서의 집행을 허가해야 할 것이다.

노트와 질문

1. 대법 2004. 10. 28. 선고 2002다74213 판결은 우리나라와 미합중국자치령 북마리아나제도사이에 상호보증이 존재하는지 여부에 대한 심리미진을 이유로 파기하는 한편, 대법 2009. 6. 25. 선고 2009다22952 판결은 우리나라와 캐나다 온타리오주 사이에 상호보증이 있다고 보았다. 무엇이 서로 다른 결론에 이르게 만들었을까?[25)]
2. 위조·변조 내지는 폐기된 서류를 사용하였다거나 위증을 이용하는 것과 같은 사기적인 방법으로 외국판결을 얻었다는 것이 집행판결을 거부할 사유가 되는가? 처벌받을 사기적인 행위에 대하여 유죄의 판결이 있다면 어떠한가?[26)] 일제강점기에 일본정부에 의하여 강제징용되어 일본국 기업에서 강제노동에 종사한 자의 일본 기업을 상대로 불법행위로 인한 손해배상청구에서의 패소확정판결을 승인하는 것은 공서양속에 반하는가?[27)]

2) 외국의 중재판정

외국에서의 중재는 New York Convention에 가입한 국가의 경우[28)] 당사자가 동 조약 제5조 제1항의 사유를 주장·입증하는 경우와 제5조 제2항의 사유가 있는 경우 법원이 직권으로 그 승인 및 집행을 거절할 수 있으나 그 이외의 어떠한 사유도 외국중재판정의 승인 또는 집행의 거절사유가 될 수 없다. 집행거절의 사유가 있다고 하더라도 승인 내지 집행판결이 있어야만 중재판정이 효력을 발생하는 것은 아니며 설사 중재판정취소의 소송이 제기되었다고 하더라도 효력이 정지되는 것은 아니다.[29)] 실제 공공질서위반이 가장 많이 다투어지는 집행거절의 사유이다.[30)]

---

25) 중국에 관하여는 석광현, 한국법원에서 제기된 중국법의 쟁점, 51 법학 181, 221에서 인용된 서울지법 1999. 11. 5 . 선고 99가합26523 판결 참조.

26) 대법 2004. 10. 28. 선고 2002다74213 판결 참조.

27) 부산고법 2009. 2. 3. 선고 2007나4288 판결과 대법 2012. 5. 24. 선고 2009다22549 판결 비교.

28) 가입한 국가의 명단, 가입일자, 가입시 유보사항 등에 관하여는 http://www.uncitral.org/uncitral/en/uncitral_texts/arbitration/NYConvention_status.html 참조. 우리나라는 외국에서 한국법상 상사적 법률관계에 관하여 내려진 중재판정에만 적용됨을 유보하였고 1973. 8. 2 . 가입, 동년 9. 5.부터 효력을 발생하였다. 뉴욕협약 이외에도 지역적으로 유효한 조약으로 Inter-American Convention on International Commercial Arbitration (Panama Convention) Done at Panama City, 30 Jan. 1975; Entered into Force, 16 Jun. 1976와 European Convention on International Commercial Arbitration Done at Geneva, 21 Apr. 1961; Entered into force, 7 Jan. 1964.

29) *Southern Pacific Properties (Middle East) Limited v. Arab Republic of Egypt,* 86 I.L.R. 494 (1984) 참조.

30) 이호원, *Recognition and Enforcement of Foreign Arbitral Award,*27 RITSUMAIKAN. L. REV. 101 (2010); 최성수, 우리나라 판례에 나타난 외국중재판정집행거부사유, 22 법학논총 197(2010). OECD뇌물방지협약과 국제중재판정에 관하여는 William Fox, *Adjudicating Bribery and Corruption Issues in Internatoinal Commercial Arbitration,* 27 J. ENER. & NAT. RES. L. 487(2009).

대법 2003. 4. 11. 선고 2001다20134 판결[31)]

1. 원심판결의 요지

원심은 내세운 증거들을 종합하여, 피고가 제작하여 공급한 자수기에 하자가 있음을 원인으로 원고가 피고를 상대로 베트남 상사중재원에 제소한 이 사건 중재사건에서 1999. 2. 6., 피고는 원고에게 그 판정일로부터 30일 이내에 동일한 성능의 새로운 자수기를 교체·설치하고(주문 제1.1항), 손해배상으로 미화 17,010.88$를 지급하며, 기계교체의무와 배상금지급의무를 연체하는 경우 베트남 은행의 대출이율에 의한 지연손해금을 지급하고(주문 제1.2항), 아울러 중재판정비용 미화 5,336$를 지급하라(주문 제2항)는 내용의 중재판정이 내려진 사실, 이에 따라 피고는 같은 해 3. 13. 원고에게 손해배상금 미화 17,010.88$ 및 중재판정비용 미화 5,336$ 합계 미화 22,346.88$를 송금하였고, 이어 교체용 자수기를 생산하여 같은 달 26. 베트남으로 수송한 다음 수입통관 절차를 밟고 나서 같은 해 5. 17. 자수기를 교체·설치하고자 교체용 자수기 및 소유권이전에 필요한 수입서류 등을 가지고 원고의 공장으로 찾아갔으나, 원고가 수입절차상의 하자 등을 문제삼아 기계의 교체·설치를 거절한 사실, 그 후로부터 현재까지 교체용 자수기는 소유권이전용 서류와 함께 피고가 지정한 베트남의 수입대행사가 보관중인 사실을 인정한 다음, 피고가 같은 해 5. 17. 이 사건 중재판정에 따라 적법하게 이행제공을 하였고 그 이후에도 수입대행사를 통하여 교체용 자수기 및 소유권이전용 서류를 계속 보관하고 있는 이상 피고는 이 사건 중재판정에 따른 기계교체의무를 이행하였다고 봄이 상당하다는 이유로, 중재판정 중 이행되지 아니한 부분, 즉 같은 해 3. 9. 이후 기계교체의무 및 손해배상금지급의무가 각 이행된 날까지의 지연손해금 부분이 포함된 중재판정문 제1.2항의 집행만을 허용하고, 이미 모두 이행된 제1.1항의 기계교체 부분 및 제2항의 중재판정비용 지급 부분에 대하여는, 중재판정 이후 청구이의의 사유가 발생하였고 중재판정의 성립 이후 집행에 이르기까지의 제반 사정에 비추어 그 집행이 권리의 남용으로서 뉴욕협약 제5조 제2항 (나)호의 공공질서 위반에 해당한다는 이유로 허용하지 아니하였다.

2. 상고이유에 대한 판단

가. 이 사건 중재판정의 주문 제1.1항에 대하여

(1) 이 사건 중재판정은 외국중재판정의승인및집행에관한협약(이하 '뉴욕협약'이라 한다)의 적용을 받은 외국중재판정이므로, 중재법 제37조 제1항, 제39조 제1항에 따라 그 집행은

31) 이 판결에 대한 평석은 장상균, 외국중재판정에 대한 집행재판과정에서의 청구이의사유의 주장, VI 상사판례연구 620(2006).

뉴욕협약을 적용하여 집행판결에 의하여야 한다. 뉴욕협약 제5조에서는 집행의 거부사유를 제한적으로 열거하고 있는데, 그 중 제2항 (나)호에 의하면 중재판정의 승인이나 집행이 그 국가의 공공의 질서에 반하는 경우에는 집행국 법원은 중재판정의 승인이나 집행을 거부할 수 있는바, 이는 중재판정의 승인이나 집행이 집행국의 기본적인 도덕적 신념과 사회질서를 해하는 것을 방지하여 이를 보호하려는 데 그 취지가 있다 할 것이므로, 그 판단에 있어서는 국내적인 사정뿐만 아니라 국제적 거래질서의 안정이라는 측면도 함께 고려하여 제한적으로 해석하여야 할 것이고, 해당 중재판정을 인정할 경우 그 구체적 결과가 집행국의 선량한 풍속 기타 사회질서에 반할 때에 승인이나 집행을 거부할 수 있다고 할 것이다(대법원 1990. 4. 10. 선고 89다카20252 판결, 1995. 2. 14. 선고 93다53054 판결 참조).

그리고 집행판결은 외국중재판정에 대하여 집행력을 부여하여 우리나라 법률상의 강제집행절차로 나아갈 수 있도록 허용하는 것으로서 그 변론종결시를 기준으로 하여 집행력의 유무를 판단하는 재판이므로, 중재판정의 성립 이후 채무의 소멸과 같은 집행법상 청구이의의 사유가 발생하여 중재판정문에 터잡아 강제집행절차를 밟아 나가도록 허용하는 것이 우리 법의 기본적 원리에 반한다는 사정이 집행재판의 변론과정에서 드러난 경우에는, 법원은 뉴욕협약 제5조 제2항 (나)호의 공공질서 위반에 해당하는 것으로 보아 그 중재판정의 집행을 거부할 수 있다 할 것이다. 이와 같이 해석하는 것이 집행판결의 확정 이후에 별도의 청구이의 소송을 통하여 다투도록 하는 것보다 소송경제에 부합할 뿐만 아니라, 변론을 거친 판결의 형식에 의하여 집행판결을 하도록 정한 우리 법제에 비추어 타당하기 때문이다.

(2) 그런데 이 사건 중재판정 주문 제1.1항의 기계교체의무와 관련하여 살펴보면, 원심이 인정한 사실은 피고가 기계교체의무이행의 제공을 하였으나 원고의 수령거절로 이 사건 자수기가 교체·설치되지 못하였고 현재 수입대행사에 의해 보관되고 있다는 것인바, 이와 같은 사실만으로는 피고가 적법한 이행제공을 함으로써 원고를 수령지체에 빠뜨렸다고 볼 수 있을지는 별론으로 하고 이로써 기계교체의무의 이행이 완료되어 기계교체의무가 소멸하였다고 볼 수 없으니 청구이의 사유가 될 수 없고, 기록을 살펴보아도 달리 청구이의 사유가 발생하였다는 사실이 인정되지도 아니한다.

그럼에도 불구하고, 원심은 이 사건 중재판정 주문 제1.1항의 기계교체의무와 관련하여 청구이의의 사유가 발생하였음을 전제로 하여 뉴욕협약 제5조 제2항 (나)호의 공공질서위반 조항을 적용하였는바, 거기에는 채증법칙을 위반하여 사실을 오인하고 뉴욕협약 제5조 제2항 (나)호의 '공공질서위반'에 관한 법리를 오해하여 판결에 영향을 미친 잘못이 있다. 이 점을 지적하는 상고이유 주장은 이유 있다.

서울고법 2001. 2. 27. 선고 2000나23725 판결

1. 기초 사실

가. 당사자 간의 관계

(1) 소외 켁심 베트남 리싱 씨오 엘티디{Kexim Vietnam Leasing Co., Ltd., 이하 '켁심(Kexim)'이라 한다}는 1997. 5. 3. 피고가 생산하는 자수기 SWF/A-WD920(550×300) 2대(이하 '이 사건 자수기'들이라 한다)를 원고에 리스하기 위한 목적의 수입임을 분명히 하고 수입대행업자인 소외 제네랄 임-엑스포트 앤드 서비스 씨오알피{GENERAL IM-EXPORT AND SERVICE CORP., 이하 '제트라니멕스(GETRANIMEX)'라 한다}와 이 사건 자수기들에 관한 수입위탁계약을 체결하였다.

(2) 소외 제트라니멕스(GETRANIMEX)는 1997. 5. 3. 피고와 이 사건 자수기들을 대당 단가 미화 68,000달러($) 합계 미화 136,000달러($)에 매수하면서 위 매매계약에 관련하여 발생하는 모든 분쟁은 양자가 우호적으로 해결하되, 우호적 해결이 어려울 경우에는 베트남 상공회의소 내의 베트남 국제중재원(이하 '베트남 상사중재원'이라 한다)의 중재판정에 의하며, 이 중재판정은 최종적이며 당사자에게 구속력을 갖는다고 약정하였다.

(3) 소외 켁심(Kexim)은 1997. 5. 30. 원고에게 이 사건 자수기들에 관하여 기간은 1997. 5. 30.부터 2002. 5. 30.까지, 리스사용료는 미화 3,227.14달러($)로 정하여 리스하는 내용의 리스계약을 체결하였다.

나. 이 사건 자수기들에 대한 분쟁발생과 베트남 상사중재원의 중재판정

(1) 피고가 1997. 5. 16. 위 매매계약, 수입위탁계약 및 리스계약에 따라 원고에게 이 사건 자수기들을 인도하였으나 원고가 이 사건 자수기를 사용하는 동안 이 사건 자수기들이 작동하지 않는 문제가 발생하였고, 피고는 그 수리를 위한 전문가를 보냈으나 위 자수기들은 여전히 작동하지 않았으며, 그 후 피고는 원고에게 1998. 1. 4.까지 수리를 완료하여 줄 것과 40일간의 기계 미작동에 대한 보상으로 미화 29,202.14달러($)를 배상하기로 약속하였으나 미화 4,302.85달러($)만을 배상하고 기계수리를 중지하였다.

(2) 그 후 위 제트라니멕스(GETRANIMEX)는 트라니멕스코(TRANIMEXCO)로 상호를 바꾸었고, 위 소외 회사가 피고에 대하여 갖는 이 사건 자수기들에 관한 손해배상 등 분쟁해결의 모든 권리를 켁심(Kexim)에게 위임하고 베트남 상사중재원의 중재판정은 피고와 켁심(Kexim) 사이에 효력이 있다는 위임장을 작성하여 베트남 상사중재원에 제출하였고, 위 켁심(Kexim)

은 원고에게 위 권리를 재위임한다는 위임장을 작성하여 베트남 상사중재원에 제출하였다.

(3) 원고는 1998. 8. 4. 베트남 상사중재원에 중재판정을 신청하였고, 원고측에서는 원고의 사장 박종학이, 피고측에서는 피고의 베트남 주재 한국 지사장인 천해우가 각 참석하여, 원고측에서는 베트남 변호사 보 낫 탕(Vo Nhat Thang)을, 피고측에서는 베트남 변호사 누옌 충(Nguyen Chung)을 각 중재인으로 지명하였고, 이들에 의해 베트남 상사중재원 중재인인 베트남 변호사 부 후 투(Vu Huu Tuu)가 중재위원장이 되어 중재판정부를 구성하였다.

(4) 위 중재판정부는 1998. 11. 7. 중재판정부의 설립을 당사자에게 통지하였고 원고와 피고는 이에 대하여 어떠한 이의도 제기하지 아니하였으며, 중재판정부는 1999. 2. 6. 원고가 신청한 중재사건에 관하여 별지목록 기재와 같은 중재판정(이하 '이 사건 중재판정'이라 한다)을 하였다.

2. 피고의 본안전 항변에 관한 판단

가. 베트남 상사중재원의 중재판정에 관하여 국내에서의 집행판결을 구하는 원고의 이 사건 소에 대하여, 피고는 이 사건 중재판정의 당사자로 되는 중재판정 신청인은 소외 제트라니멕스(GETRANIMEX)이므로 원고는 이 사건 집행판결을 신청할 당사자적격이 없어 이 사건 소는 부적법하다고 항변한다.

그러나 위에서 인정한 바와 같이 원고는 이 사건 자수기들의 실수요자로서 위 자수기들의 매매계약에 있어 실질적인 매수인인 위 제트라니멕스(GETRANIMEX)로부터 이 사건 손해배상 및 분쟁해결의 모든 권한을 위임받은 켁심(Kexim)으로부터 재위임을 받아 위 중재에 참석하였고, 피고는 원고와의 중재시 원고의 자격에 관하여 아무런 이의를 제기하지 아니하였을 뿐만 아니라, 갑 제1호증, 갑 제15호증의 1 내지 4, 갑 제16호증의 1, 2의 각 기재에 의하면 이 사건 중재판정의 결정문에도 원고가 신청인으로 기재되어 있음을 인정할 수 있다.

그렇다면 원고는 위 제트라니멕스(GETRANIMEX)와 켁심(Kexim)으로부터 이 사건 자수기와 관련한 분쟁해결에 관한 권한을 위임받아 이 사건 중재판정의 당사자가 되었다고 볼 수 있을 뿐만 아니라, 위 베트남 상사중재원의 중재시 피고가 원고의 자격에 관한 어떠한 이의도 하지 아니함으로써 적어도 위 중재판정시에는 원고와 피고 간에 원고와 피고 간의 분쟁을 위 중재판정부의 중재에 따라 해결하기로 하는 의사가 있었다고 할 것이므로, 피고의 위 항변은 이유 없다.

나. 피고는 다시 위 제트라니멕스(GETRANIMEX)와 켁심(KEXIM)이 원고에게 위임한 권한은 베트남 상사중재원의 판정이 있을 때까지만 유효하다고 하였으므로 원고에게는 이 사건 집행판결을 신청할 당사자적격이 없다고 항변한다.

그러나 외국 중재판정에 있어서의 당사자는 당연히 국내에서 이를 집행하기 위하여 그 집행판결을 신청할 당사자적격을 갖는다 할 것이고, 이는 비록 소외 제트라니멕스(GETRANIMEX)와 켁심(KEXIM)이 원고에게 위임한 권한이 중재판정이 있을 때까지 유효하다는 위 제트라니멕스(GETRANIMEX) 및 켁심(KEXIM)과 원고 사이의 약정(이러한 약정의 취지는 이 사건 자수기들에 관한 분쟁해결의 권한만을 위임한 것으로 보아야 할 것이지 원고가 이 사건 중재판정 이후 그 집행판결을 청구하는 것을 금지하는 취지는 아니라고 할 것이다)이 있었다고 하여도 달리 보아야 할 것은 아니라 할 것이므로 피고의 위 항변도 이유 없다.

3. 원고의 집행판결 청구에 관한 판단

베트남은 외국중재판정의승인및집행에관한UN협약{뉴욕협약: 1958. 6. 10. 뉴욕에서 채택, United Nations Convention on the Recognition and Enforcement of Foreign Arbitral Awards (New York, 10 June 1958), 이하 '뉴욕협약'이라 한다}에 당사국으로 가입하였고 우리나라는 대한민국 법상 상사관계의 분쟁에 한해서 위 협약을 적용할 것으로 유보하고 위 협약에 가입(1973. 2. 17. 조약 제471호)하였으며, 베트남에서 우리나라 중재판정이 집행되기 위한 조건은 우리나라와 같으므로 위 협약에 의하여 이 사건 중재판정은 우리나라에서도 그 효력이 인정되어 그 집행이 허용된다 할 것이다.

4. 피고의 주장에 관한 판단

가. 피고의 주장

피고는 이 사건 중재판정 이후 그 결정내용에 따라 성실하게 이행 내지 이행의 제공을 하였음에도 불구하고 원고가 이를 거절하였으므로 원고가 구하는 이 사건 중재판정의 집행판결은 거부되어야 한다고 주장하고, 이에 대하여 원고는 피고가 주장하는 사유는 뉴욕협약에서 정한 외국중재판정의 승인이나 집행을 거부할 수 있는 경우에 해당하는 것이 아니므로 중재판정에서 확정된 권리관계는 집행판결 절차에서는 다툴 수 없고, 이에 관한 항변도 제출할 수 없으며, 중재판정에 취소사유가 있는 경우 중재법에 따라 그 취소소송을 제기할 수 있을 뿐이고, 가사 위 피고 주장의 사유가 외국중재판정의 집행을 거부할 수 있는 사유에 해당한다고 하더라도 피고는 그 주장과 같은 이 사건 중재판정에 따른 적법한 이행을 한 사실이 없으므로 위 피고의 주장은 어느 모로 보나 이유가 없다는 취지로 다툰다.

나. 청구이의의 사유가 뉴욕협약의 규정에 의하여 집행거부의 사유가 되는지 여부

뉴욕협약 제1조 제1호에서는 이 협약은 그 승인 및 집행의 요구를 받은 국가(이하 '집행국'이라 한다) 이외의 국가의 영토에서 내려진 중재판정 및 집행국에서 내국판정이라고 인정되지 아니하는 중재판정의 승인 및 집행에 적용한다고 규정하고 있고, 제5조에서는 중재합의의 당사자가 무능력자이었거나 합의가 무효인 경우, 당사자에게 중재절차에 관하여 적절하게 통지하지 아니한 경우, 중재판정이 중재합의의 범위를 벗어난 사항에 관한 것인 경우, 중재판정부의 구성이나 중재절차가 당사자 간의 합의와 합치하지 아니하는 경우, 중재판정이 내려진 국가의 권한 있는 기관이나 법령에 의거하여 중재판정이 취소 또는 정지된 경우에 해당한다는 증거를 당사자가 제출하면 중재판정의 승인 및 집행을 거부할 수 있으며(제1항), 집행국의 권한 있는 기관이 스스로 중재판정의 대상이 된 분쟁이 그 국가의 법에 따라 중재로 해결될 수 없는 사항이거나 중재판정의 승인이나 집행이 그 국가의 공공의 질서에 반한다는 것을 인정하는 경우에도 중재판정의 승인과 집행을 거부할 수 있도록(제2항) 규정하고 있다.

피고는 중재판정 이후에 자신이 중재판정에 따라 이행의 제공을 하였으므로 이는 위 뉴욕협약 제5조 제2항 (나)목 소정의 국가의 공공질서에 반하는 경우{2. Recognition and enforcement of an arbitral award may also be refused if the competent authority in the country where recognition and enforcement is sought finds that: (a) 생략 (b) The recognition or enforcement of the award would be contrary to the public policy of that country}에 해당하고, 따라서 원고의 이 사건 집행판결 청구는 기각되어야 한다고 주장하므로 위 피고가 주장하는 사유가 위 뉴욕협약 소정의 국가의 공공질서에 반하는 경우에 해당하는지에 관하여 본다.

위 뉴욕협약 제5조에서 열거하고 있는 외국중재판정의 승인 및 집행의 거부사유는 예시적인 것이 아니라 한정적인 것으로서 같은 조 제2항 (나)호에 규정된 재판정의 승인이나 집행이 그 국가의 공공의 질서에 반하는 경우에 집행국 법원이 중재판정의 승인이나 집행을 거부할 수 있도록 규정하고 있는 것은 중재판정의 승인이나 집행이 집행국의 기본적인 도덕적 신념과 사회질서를 해하는 것을 방지하여 이를 보호하려는 데 그 취지가 있다 할 것이므로, 그 판단에 있어서는 국내적인 사정뿐만 아니라 국제적 거래질서의 안정이라는 측면도 함께 고려하여 제한적으로 해석하여야 하며, 외국중재판정에 적용된 외국법이 우리나라의 실정법상 강행법규에 위반된다고 하여 바로 승인거부의 사유가 되는 것은 아니고, 해당 중재판정을 인정할 경우 그 구체적 결과가 우리나라의 선량한 풍속 기타 사회질서에 반할 때에 한하여 승인 및 집행을 거부할 수 있다고 할 것으로서(대법원 1995. 2. 14. 선고 93다53054 판결, 대법원 1990. 4. 10. 선고 89다카20252 판결 참조) 결국, 외국판결의 집행청구에 관한 민사소송법 제203조 소정 공공질서의 개념보다는 좁게 해석되어야 할 것이다.

위와 같은 기준에 비추어 청구이의의 사유가 위 뉴욕협약상 국가의 공공질서에 반하는 경우에 해당하는지에 관하여 살펴보면, 비록 확정된 외국에서의 중재판정이라고 하더라도 그 권리의 행사는 신의에 좇아 성실히 행사되어야 하고 그 판정에 기한 집행이 권리남용이 되는 경우에는 허용되지 않는다고 할 것인데, 중재판정 이후 그 판정에 따라 판정의 상대방이 성실하게 그 내용을 이행하여 결과적으로 그 집행을 구하고자 하는 내용이 실체적 권리관계에 배치되는 경우 그 중재판정에 의하여 집행할 수 있는 것으로 확정된 권리의 성질과 그 내용, 판정의 성립 경위 및 판정 성립 후 집행에 이르기까지의 사정, 그 집행이 당사자에게 미치는 영향 등 제반 사정을 종합하여 볼 때, 그 확정된 중재판정에 기한 집행이 현저히 부당하고 상대방으로 하여금 그 집행을 수인하도록 하는 것이 정의에 반함이 명백하여 사회생활상 용인할 수 없다고 인정되는 경우에는 그 집행은 권리남용으로서 허용되지 않는다고 할 것이고 (확정판결에 기한 권리행사의 경우에 대한 대법원 1997. 9. 12. 선고 96다4862 판결, 대법원 1984. 7. 24. 선고 84다카572 판결 각 참조), 따라서 위와 같은 제한적인 경우에 한하여 청구이의의 사유는 위 뉴욕협약에서 정한 외국중재판정의 집행거부사유에 해당한다고 봄이 상당하다(이와 같은 청구이의사유를 집행판결을 구하는 소송과정에서 상대방 당사자가 제한적으로나마 항변으로 주장할 수 있도록 하는 것이 이미 구속력 있는 판결·중재판정의 강제집행절차의 한 과정인 집행판결절차에서 집행판결 후 청구이의의 소 등으로서만 다투게 하는 것보다는 당사자에게 편리하고 경제적인 측면도 있다).

다. 뉴욕협약상 중재판정의 일부에 대한 집행판결이 가능한지 여부

피고가 이 사건 중재판정에 따라 원고에게 이행을 한 것이 중재판정의 각 조항에 따른 완전한 이행이 되지 아니하고, 일부 이행이 된 부분과 이행이 되지 아니한 부분으로 나누어지고, 그 일부 이행이 된 부분에 대한 집행이 위와 같은 사유로 뉴욕협약에서 정한 집행거부사유인 국가의 공공질서에 반하는 경우 그 부분에 한하여서만 중재판정에 따른 집행판결을 거부하고, 나머지 이행이 되지 아니한 부분에 한하여 집행판결을 할 수 있는지의 문제에 관하여 살펴본다.

살피건대, 원칙적으로 집행판결의 경우 집행법원은 중재판정의 형식적 요건만을 심사하여야 하고, 집행판결은 외국중재판정의 전부에 대하여 집행력을 부여하는 형성판결이므로 그 판정 주문 중 일부분에 대해서만 집행판결을 할 수는 없다고 보아야 할 것이지만, 뉴욕협약 제5조 제1항 (c) 단서는 중재인이 권한을 벗어나 내린 판정도 그 권한 내에 속하는 부분만을 승인하여 주거나 집행을 해 줄 수 있음을 규정하고 있고(Article V 1. Recognition and enforcement of the award may be refused, at the request of the party against whom it is invoked, only if that party furnishes to the competent authority where the recognition and enforcement is sought, proof that: (a), (b) 생략, (c) The award deals with a difference not contemplated by or not falling within the terms of the submission to arbitration, or it contains decisions on matters beyond the scope of the submission to arbitration, provided that, if the decisions on matters submitted to arbitration can be separated from those not so submitted, that part of the award which contains decisions on matters submitted to arbitration may be recognized and enforced;), 이는 집행판결을 하는 법원의 재량에 맡겨진 것이라 할 것인데, 위와 같은 뉴욕협약의 규정은 단지 그 제5조 제1항 (c)항의 경우에 한하여 부분 집행의 가능성을 열어둔 것으로 해석할 것이 아니라 위 제5조 제1, 2항 모두에 대하여 부분 집행의 가능성을 열어둔 것이라고 해석하는 것이 상당하고, 다만 위 (c)항의 경우에는 더 제한적으로 해석하여 한 개의 집행주문 중에서도 나누어 집행을 허가할 수 있도록 하였다고 보는 것이 상당하다.

따라서 위와 같은 뉴욕협약 규정의 취지에 비추어 보건대, 판정 주문이 여러 개의 항으로 나누어져 있고, 그 중 판정 주문에 따른 이행이 완료된 부분에 관한 주문의 항과 이행이 되지 아니한 주문의 항이 명백하게 나누어져 있는 경우에 그 중재판정 중 위 이행이 완료된 주문의 항에 한하여 집행을 거부할 사유가 있는 경우에는 그 부분에 한하여 집행판결을 하지 않을 수 있고, 나머지 이행이 되지 아니한 부분의 주문 항에 한하여 집행을 허가할 수도 있다고 봄이 상당하고, 다만 한 개의 주문 항에 이행이 된 부분과 이행이 되지 아니한 부분이 함께 기재되어 있는 경우(예를 들면, 원금과 지연손해금의 지급을 함께 명하는 주문의 1개 항 중 원금의 지급만이 이행이 된 경우)중에는 집행의 명료성을 위하여 그 부분 항 전체에 대하여 집행판결을 하는 것이 타당하다고 할 것이다.

라. 피고가 이 사건 중재판정에서 정한 의무를 이행하였는지 여부

(1) 다음의 각 사실은 갑 제17, 18호증, 을 제6호증의 1 내지 3, 을 제10호증의 1 내지 17, 을 제11호증의 6, 을 제13, 14호증의 각 1 내지 4, 을 제15호증, 을 제19 내지 21호증의 각 기재와 원심증인 박정주의 증언(단, 뒤에서 일부 믿지 않는 부분 제외), 당심증인 김장택, 이규훈(단, 뒤에서 일부 믿지 않는 부분 제외), 천해우의 증언에 변론의 전취지를 종합하면 이를 각 인정할 수 있고, 위 인정에 일부 반하는 듯한 원심증인 박정주, 당심증인 이규훈의 일부 증언은 믿지 아니하며 달리 반증이 없다.

(가) 피고는 이 사건 중재판정 이후 1999. 2. 13.자로 작성된 중재판정문을 1999. 2. 19. 수령한 뒤, ① 1999. 3. 13. 원고에게 중재판정문 제1.2항에 기재된 배상금 미화 17,010.88$ 및 제2항 기재 중재판정비 미화 5,336$ 합계 금 미화 22,346.88$를 원고 대표이사 구좌로 송금하고, ② 중재판정문 제1.1항에 기재된 내용대로 즉시 이 사건 자수기들을 신제품으로 교체하기 위한 생산에 들어가 1999. 3.경 그 생산을 완료하였으며 그 시경 현대상선을 통하여 베트남으로 이 사건 자수기들의 최초 수입대행사인 제트라니멕스(GETRANIMEX)를 수하인으로 하여 교체용 자수기들을 운송하였다.

(나) 교체용 자수기들은 1999. 3. 26. 베트남에 도착되어 피고측 현지 지사장 천해우는

켁심 사무실에 교체용 자수기가 도착한 사실을 통보하였으나, 선하증권상 수하인인 제트라니멕스(GETRANIMEX)가 이미 상호를 트라니멕스코로 변경하여 통관이 되지 않았고, 트라니멕스코는 위 교체용 자수기들을 통관하는 것에 대한 협조를 거부하자 피고는 다시 베트남 정부가 운영하는 봉타우사(VUNG TAU SERVICES & SHIPPING COMPANY, 이하 '봉타우'라 한다)를 수입대행사로 하여 수입대행계약을 체결한 후 봉타우를 수하인으로 한 선하증권을 현대상선으로부터 교체, 발부받았다.

(다) 위 천해우는 1999. 4. 9. 켁심측에게 켁심이 붕타우에 수입을 위임한다는 위임계약서, 제트라니멕스(GETRANIMEX)가 봉타우에 계약을 위임한다는 위임계약서, 붕타우와 피고 사이의 구입계약서, 제트라니멕스(GETRANIMEX)가 피고와 봉타우 사이의 계약을 동의한다는 계약서를 1999. 3. 5.로 날짜를 소급해서 작성한 다음 이에 서명해 줄 것을 요구하였으나, 켁심측은 이를 거절하였다(위 천해우의 요구는 중재판정문상의 기계교체 지연으로 인한 지연손해금의 지급을 면하고, 통관을 용이하게 하기 위하였던 것으로 보인다).

(라) 피고측은 봉타우를 통하여 이 사건 교체용 자수기 2대에 관하여 세금을 모두 부담하는 일반통관절차를 밟았고, 그 과정에서 관세로 미화 13,000$를 부담하고, 1999. 4. 26. 통관을 완료하였다.

(마) 피고측 천해우는 1999. 5. 17. 직접 원고측에게 이 사건 교체용 자수기를 전달하기 위하여 운송업체에 의뢰하여 교체용 자수기를 싣고 이에 대한 선적서류 및 소유권을 봉타우로부터 넘겨받기 위하여 필요한 빨간색 영수증을 지참하여 피고측 변호사 및 중재위원과 함께 원고 회사의 신규공장으로 갔으나, 원고측은 기계인수에 대한 켁심측의 동의를 요구하면서 기계인수를 거절하였고, 켁심측에서도 원고의 이의를 문제삼아 협조를 거부하여 결국 현재 이 사건 교체용 자수기는 그 관련 선적서류와 빨간색 영수증과 함께 봉타우가 보관중이다.

(2) 피고는 위 인정 사실에서 본 바와 같이 중재판정에 따른 금전의 지급 및 새로운 기계의 인도 등 모든 의무를 이행하였으나, 원고측의 비협조로 새로운 자수기가 인도되지 아니하였을 뿐이므로 이 사건 원고의 집행판결 청구는 이유가 없다고 주장하고, 원고는 이 사건 중재판정에서 명한 교체용 자수기의 인도는 그 수입과정을 이전의 자수기를 수입한 대행사인 트라니멕스코(구상호 제트라니멕스)에 의하여 대행되어야 함에도 불구하고, 피고측이 임의로 수입절차를 진행하여 통관이 지연되었을 뿐 아니라 베트남에서는 중재판정에 따라서 새로운 기계를 반입하고, 구기계를 반출할 경우에는 상무성의 반입반출 허가를 받도록 되어 있는데, 피고측은 이러한 절차를 거치지 않아 구기계를 적법하게 반출하는 것이 불가능하게 되었으므로 피고가 위와 같이 교체용 자수기를 원고측에 인도하려 한 것은 중재판정에 따른 적법한 이행이 아니므로 위 피고의 주장은 이유 없다고 주장한다.

(3) 피고가 주장하는 바와 같은 이행 및 이행의 제공이 중재판정에 따라 적법하게 이루

어진 것인지에 관하여 살펴본다.

(가) 우선 이 사건 중재판정문의 적법한 번역문인 갑 제15호증의 3의 기재에 의하면, 이 사건 중재판정은 중재의 양 당사자가 출석한 가운데 1999. 2. 6. 결정되었고, 중재위원회는 그 결정 내용을 피고가 위 결정일로부터 30일 내인 1999. 3. 8.까지 이행하도록 명한 사실을 인정할 수 있고, 피고는 1999. 3. 13. 중재판정문 제1.2항 및 제2항에서 정한 배상금 원금 및 중재판정비를 원고에게 송금한 사실은 위에서 본 바와 같으므로 피고는 위 배상금 원금에 대한 1999. 3. 9.부터 1999. 3. 13.까지의 지연손해금을 제외하고, 금전 배상 부분은 모두 이행하였다고 할 것이다.

(나) 다음으로 중재판정문 제1.1항에 기재된 기계인도부분에 관하여 살피건대, 동산의 인도에 관하여 이 사건 중재판정의 준거법인 베트남법에 의하면 적법한 동산인도채무의 이행제공이 어느 정도인지는 분명하지 않고, 이러한 경우와 같이 섭외적 사건에 관하여 적용될 외국법규의 내용을 확정하고 그 의미를 해석함에 있어서는 그 외국법이 그 본국에서 현실로 해석·적용되고 있는 의미·내용대로 해석·적용되어야 하는 것인데, 소송과정에서 적용될 외국법규에 흠결이 있거나 그 존재에 관한 자료가 제출되지 아니하여 그 내용의 확인이 불가능한 경우 법원으로서는 법원에 관한 민사상의 대원칙에 따라 외국 관습법에 의할 것이고, 외국 관습법도 그 내용의 확인이 불가능하면 조리에 의하여 재판할 수밖에 없는바, 그러한 조리의 내용은 가능하면 원래 적용되어야 할 외국법에 의한 해결과 가장 가까운 해결 방법을 취하기 위해서 그 외국법의 전체계적인 질서에 의해 보충 유추되어야 할 것인데{대법원 2000. 6. 9. 선고 98다35037 판결 참조}, 갑 제12호증의 1 내지 3의 각 기재에 의하면, 베트남국 민법은 동산의 소유권이전시기에 관하여 동산이 실질적으로 인도된 때로 규정하고 있는 것으로 보이고, 이러한 소유권이전을 위한 모든 절차가 마쳐진 경우에는 동산인도의 이행제공이 있었다고 보는 것이 조리상 상당하다고 보여진다.

따라서 위 인정 사실에서 본 바와 같이 피고가 1999. 5. 17. 이 사건 교체용 자수기들에 대한 통관절차를 모두 마친 후 원고 공장에 소유권을 양도받을 수 있는 관련 서류와 함께 인도하려 하였고, 원고측이 이를 거부하여 해당 기계를 원고의 공장에 설치하지 못하였고, 수입대행사가 그 자수기 및 소유권 관련 서류를 보관하고 있는 이상 피고는 위 중재판정과 베트남법에 따른 기계인도 및 설치의무를 이행하였다고 봄이 상당하다.

원고가 주장하는 바와 같은 사유, 즉 교체용 자수기의 수입을 이전의 자수기를 수입한 대행사를 통하지 아니하였고, 구기계의 반출을 위한 상무성의 허가가 없다는 사유는 위 중재판정문의 주문에서 인도의 조건으로 제시하고 있지 않을 뿐 아니라 원고측이 이 사건 교체용 자수기의 소유권을 취득할 수 있는 여건이 모두 갖추어진 이상 피고의 위 중재판정에 따른 의무를 모두 이행하였다고 할 것이고, 나아가 위 원고가 주장하는 바와 같은 사유로 구기계의 반출 등 그 처리와 관련하여 원고에게 추가적인 비용이 발생할 경우 이는 위 중재판정과는 별도로 피고에게 그 배상을 구할 수도 있음은 별론으로 하고 이를 이유로 위 피고의 이행제공이 중재판정에 따라 이루어지지 않았다고 주장하면서 위 자수기들의 인수를 거부한 것은 부당하다고 보여지므로 위 원고의 주장은 이유 없다.

따라서 기계의 인도와 관련하여 피고는 원고에게 1999. 5. 17. 이 사건 중재판정에 따른 의무의 이행제공을 하였고, 그 이후 이행의 제공이 계속되고 있다고 보여지는 이상 중재판정문 제1.1항은 피고에 의하여 모두 이행이 되었고 다만, 위 중재판정문 제1.2항에서 명한 기계의 지연인도시 지연손해금(1999. 3. 9.부터 1999. 5. 17.까지) 부분은 이행되지 않았다고 할 것이다.

마. 소 결 론

따라서 위에서 지적한 바와 같이 외국중재판정의 국내집행에 있어 주문이 명백하게 분리되어 그 일부 집행이 가능한 한도 내에서 원고와 피고 간의 이 사건 중재판정 중 제1.2항(금원지급 및 지연배상을 명한 부분)에 대하여 집행을 구하는 원고 청구 부분만 이유 있고, 그 나머지 청구는 이유 없다고 할 것이다.

대법원 1990. 4. 10. 선고 89다카20252 판결[32)]

가. 중재조항에 관한 논지

기록에 의하면, 우리나라가 1973. 5. 9. 가입하여 그때부터 조약 제471호로서 국내법과 같은 효력을 가지는 "외국중재판정의승인및집행에관한협약"(Convention on the Recognition and Enforcement of Arbitral Awards, 이하 뉴욕협약이라 한다) 제1조 제1항에 의하면, 이 협약은 그 승인 및 집행의 요구를 받은 국가(이하 집행국이라 한다) 이외의 국가의 영토에서 내려진 중재판정 및 집행국에서 내국판정이라고 인정되지 아니하는 중재판정의 승인 및 집행에 적용한다고 규정하고 있고, 우리나라는 위 협약가입시 같은 협약 제1조 제3항의 유보 조항에 따라 타체약국의 영토내에서 내려진 중재판정의 승인과 집행에 한하여, 또 계약적 성질의 것이거나 아니거나 불문하고 국내법상 상사상의 것이라고 인정되는 법률관계로부터 발생하는 분쟁에 한하여(즉 상사중재판정에 한하여) 위 협약을 적용한다고 선언하였음을 알 수 있다.

따라서 뉴욕협약의 체약국인 영국의 영토내에서 내려지고, 그 성질상 상사분쟁임이 분명한 이 사건 분쟁에 관하여 내려진 이 사건 외국중재판정의 대한민국에 의한 승인 및 집행

32) 이 판례에 관한 평석은 목영준, 외국중재판정의 집행거부사유인 공공질서, V 상사판례연구 413(2005).

에 관하여는 뉴욕협약이 우선적으로 적용되어야 하는 것이다.

그런데 뉴욕협약 제2조에는 각 체약국은 중재에 의하여 해결이 가능한 사항에 관한 일정한 법률관계에 대한 분쟁을 중재에 부탁하기로 하는 취지의 당사자간의 서면에 의한 합의(계약문 중의 중재조항 또는 당사자간에 서명되었거나 교환된 서신이나 전보에 포함되어 있는 중재의 합의를 포함한다)를 승인하여야 한다고 규정하고 있으며 그 제3조에서는 각 체약국은 위의 중재판정을 다음 조항에 규정한 조건하에서 구속력있는 것으로 승인하고 그 판정이 원용될 영토의 절차규칙에 따라서 그것을 집행하여야 한다고 규정하고 제4조에서는 전조에서 언급된 승인과 집행을 얻기 위하여 승인과 집행을 신청하는 당사자는 신청서에 ㉮ 정당하게 인증된 중재판정원본 또는 정당하게 증명된 그 등본, ㉯ 제2조에 규정된 합의의 원본 또는 정당하게 증명된 그 등본 및 공증된 이들의 번역문을 제출하여야 한다고 규정하고 있는데 이는 뉴욕협약에 따른 외국중재판정의 집행을 위한 적극적 요건으로서 위 중재판정의 승인 및 집행을 신청하는 당사자가 그 입증책임을 부담한다고 할 것이다.

기록에 의하면, 원고는 영국 런던중재법원의 1981. 5. 1.자 중재판정서의 정당하게 증명된 등본 및 그 인증된 번역문(갑제4호증의 1)과 서면에 의한 중재합의서의 증명된 등본 및 그 인증된 번역문이라면서 원고와 피고 회사를 대리한 소외 이상준 사이에 작성된 것으로 되어 있고 중재조항이 포함되어 있는 각 매매계약서의 등본과 그 번역문(갑제4호증의 2 내지 4)을 제출하였으므로 집행국법원으로서는 위 각 매매계약서 중 중재조항이 뉴욕협약 제2조 소정의 서면에 의한 중재합의에 해당하는지 아니면 논지의 지적과 같이 단순히 부동문자로 인쇄된 이른바 예문에 불과한지의 여부를 판단하여야 할 것이다.

이에 관하여 원심이 채용한 위 갑제4호증의 2 내지 4의 각 기재에 의하면, 원고와 피고 회사의 대리인이라 칭하는 소외 이상준 사이에(그 대리행위의 효력유무는 뒤에서 본다) 작성된 이 사건 강철봉 매매계약서 앞면 좌측상단에는 “뒷면의 조건에 따라 공급하여 주십시오(Please supply, subject to conditions overleaf)”라고 부동문자로 인쇄되어 있고, 뒷면의 조건 중 제13조에는 “본 계약의 효력, 해석 및 이행은 영국법에 따라 규율되며, 그 효력, 해석 및 이행을 포함하여 본 계약하에서 또는 그와 관련하여 발생하는 모든 분쟁은 본 계약일의 런던중재법원규칙에 따라 중재에 의하여 결정된다.......”라고 기재되어 있으며, 원심이 적법하게 인정한 바와 같이 위 이상준은 그 조항의 내용을 충분히 이해하고서 위 매매계약서에 서명한 사실을 알 수 있다. 그렇다면 이 사건 매매계약서 뒷면에 기재된 중재조항은 위 뉴욕협약 제2조 제2항 소정의 “계약문 중의 중재조항”으로서 같은 조 제1항 “분쟁을 중재에 부탁하기로 하는 취지”의 서면에 의한 중재합의에 해당한다고 할 것이다.

따라서 위 중재조항을 뉴욕협약상의 서면에 의한 중재합의로 본 원심의 판단은 그 판단의 순서 및 이유설시에는 다소 미흡한 점이 있으나 결론에 있어서는 정당하고, 위 중재조항이 이른바 예문에 불과하다는 논지는 이유없다.

논지는 나아가, 이 사건 매매계약서 뒷면에 기재된 중재조항에는 중재장소, 중재기관 및 준거법 등이 명시되어 있지 아니하여 당사자 사이에 유효한 중재합의가 있는 것으로 볼 수 없다고 하나 뉴욕협약 제2조에 의하면 같은 협약이 적용되는 중재합의는 "분쟁을 중재에 부탁하기로 하는 서면에 의한 합의"로서 족하고 중재장소나 중재기관 및 준거법까지 명시할 것을 요건으로 하고 있지는 아니할 뿐 아니라 위 중재조항에 의하더라도"......본 계약하에서 또는 그와 관련하여 발생하는 모든 분쟁은 본 계약일의 런던중재법원규칙에 따라 중재에 의하여 결정된다......."라고 되어 있어, 중재장소와 중재기관 및 중재절차의 준거법이 한꺼번에 모두 명시되었다고 볼 것이므로 이점에 관한 논지도 이유없다. ...

가. 뉴욕협약 제5조 제1항 나호에 관한 논지

뉴욕협약 제5조 제1항 나호에 의하면, 중재판정이 불리하게 원용되는 당사자가 중재인의 선정이나 중재절차에 관하여 적절한 통고를 받지 아니하였거나 또는 기타 이유에 의하여 방어할 수 없었던 경우에는 집행국 법원이 중재판정의 승인 및 집행을 거부할 수 있게 되어 있는바, 이 규정의 취지는 위와 같은 사유로 당사자의 방어권이 침해된 모든 경우를 말하는 것이 아니라 그 방어권 침해의 정도가 현저하여 용인할 수 없는 경우만으로 한정되는 것이라고 해석되고, 또 중재당사자의 방어권 보장은 절차적 정의실현과 직결되어 공공의 질서의 일부를 이루는 것이므로 이는 집행국 법령의 기준에 의하여 판단하여야 할 것이니 우리나라의 법령을 기준삼아 피고에 대한 중재절차 통고의 흠결로 인한 방어권침해여부에 관하여 본다.

원·피고 사이의 중재조항인 이 사건 매매계약서(갑제4호증의 2 내지 4)의 뒷면에 기재된 조건 제13조에 의하면, 이 사건 중재절차에 있어서의 통지는 계약서에 표시된 당사자의 주소에서 행한 송달로써 충분하다고 되어 있는바, 갑제39호증(영국내 외국회사등기부 등본)의 기재에 의하면 피고 회사 런던사무소의 주소가 위 계약서상의 주소와 동일하게 기재되어 있고 그 송달영수인은 위 런던사무소의 책임자인 소외 이상준으로 신고되어 있음을 알 수 있다.

한편 원심이 확정한 사실에 의하면, 피고 회사는 1979. 1. 5. 위 이상준을 대한민국 본사에서 근무하도록 발령하고 그 후임자를 파견하지 아니하여 직접 위 중재법원이 위 런던사무소로 보낸 중재절차상의 통지를 받지 못하였고 중재절차에도 참석하지 아니한 것은 사실이나, 원심이 채용한 갑제2호증의 3 내지 5(등기편지), 갑제35 내지 37호증(등기우편으로 보낸 통지서), 각 기재와 원심증인 정 윤석의 증언을 종합하여 보면, 런던 중재법원이 1980. 9. 23. 임명한 중재인 폴 시그하트 당사자들 사이의 위 중재합의에 따라 피고 회사 런던사무소에 중재절차에 관한 통지를 수차 등기우편으로 보내었으나 피고가 출석하지 아니하고 서면도 제출하지 아니하므로 1981. 4. 15. 심리를 종결하고 같은 해 5. 1. 이 사건 중재판정을 내린 사실,

피고 회사 런던사무소는 위 이상준이 1979. 1. 5. 대한민국 본사로 발령난 후 같은 해 9.21. 사실상 폐쇄되고, 그날 같은 장소에 피고 회사가 100퍼센트 주식을 소유하는 자회사인 코벤(Koben)이 현지법인으로 설립되어 외국회사 등기소에 등기를 마쳤으며 피고 회사의 직원인 소외 장영재, 이철재 등 2명이 파견나와 근무하고 있었고 위 피고 회사 런던사무소는 외국회사등기소에 1981. 8. 26.자로 말소등기가 된 사실을 알 수 있고, 기록상 위 발송우편물이 반송된 점은 엿보이지 아니하므로 위 중재절차에 관한 통지는 피고 회사 런던사무소에 송달되었다고 추정되고, 더욱이 위 갑제7호증의 16, 17, 갑제9호증의 2, 4, 갑제8호증의 1(합의각서), 갑제9호증의 3의 각 기재에 의하면 원고는 피고 회사 본사와 사이에 이 사건 매매계약에 따른 분쟁으로 인하여 여러 차례 텔렉스로 교신하고, 1979. 10. 9.에는 원고 회사를 대리한 드러리 및 커닝햄이 직접 서울에 와서 피고 회사의 한 병일 이사 및 이훈 지배인과 절충끝에 합의각서를 작성하는 등 원만한 타협을 모색하였으나 피고 회사 이사회의 승인을 얻지 못하여 결국 결렬되자 1980. 5. 19.에는 수주일 이내에 피고 회사에게 런던 중재법원의 절차개시통고가 될 것이라고 통지까지 하여 주었음을 엿볼 수 있으니 피고 회사로서는 이 사건 중재절차에 관하여 원고로부터 본사에서 직접 사전통고를 받았고, 런던사무소 및 그 후신격인 코벤회사에 근무중이던 자기회사 직원들로부터 중재절차 진행중에 중재법원으로부터의 각종 통지들을 충분히 전달받았으리라고 추정됨에도 불구하고 스스로 위 절차진행중 필요한 서면을 제출하거나 심리기일에 출석하여 의견으로 진술하는 등 방어권을 행사하지 아니하였고, 또 원심이 적법하게 채용한 갑제3호증의 기재에 의하면 피고 회사 본사가 중재판정서 사본을 원고 회사로부터 송달받고도 영국법에 따른 불복절차를 전혀 취하지 아니하였음을 알 수 있으니 이러한 사정을 종합하여 보면 이 사건 중재절차에 있어서 그것이 적절히 통고되지 아니하여 피고의 방어권이 부당하게 박탈되었다고 볼 수는 없다 할 것이다.

따라서 이와 같은 취지의 원심판단은 옳고 이 점에 관한 논지는 이유없다.

나. 뉴욕협약 제5조 제1항 라호에 관한 논지

뉴욕협약 제5조 제1항 라호에 의하면, 중재기관의 구성이나 중재절차가 당사자간의 합의와 합치하지 아니하는 경우 또는 이러한 합의가 없는 경우에는 중재를 행하는 국가의 법령에 합치하지 아니하면 중재판정의 승인과 집행을 거부할 수 있게 되어 있다.

논지는 이 사건 매매계약서에 기재된 중재조항에는 그 중재기관의 구성이나 중재절차에 관하여 당사자 사이에 유효한 합의가 없으므로 결국 이 사건 중재기관의 구성이나 중재절차는 중재지법인 영국법에 따라야 할 것인데 원심이 이 점에 관한 영국법의 조사를 거치지 아니한 채 원고 제출의 일부 서증에 의하여 이 사건 중재기관의 구성 및 중재절차가 영국의 법령에 합치한다고 판시한 것은 위 제5조 제1항 라호에 위반된 것이라고 함에 있으나 이 사건 매매계약서(갑제4호증의 2 내지 4) 뒷면 조건 제13조에 "......이 계약하에서 또는 그와 관련하여 발생하는 모든 분쟁은 이 계약일 당시의 런던중재법원의 규칙에 따라 중재에 의하여 결정된다"고 기재되어 있는 것은 전형적인 중재조항으로서 중재장소는 영국 런던, 중재기관은 런던중재법원, 준거절차법은 런던중재법원의 규칙(즉 영국법)으로 정한 당사자 사이의 합의라고 해석되고 이 사건 중재판정은 위 중재기관 및 중재절차에 관한 원·피고 사이의 합의에 따라서 내려진 것임이 갑제4호증의 1(중재판정)의 기재에 의하여 명백하므로 같은 취지의 원심판단은 정당하고 위 논지도 이유없다.

다. 뉴욕협약 제5조 제2항 나호에 관한 논지

뉴욕협약 제5조 제2항 나호에 의하면 중재판정의 승인이나 집행이 그 국가의 공공의 질서에 반하는 경우에는 집행국 법원은 중재판정의 승인과 집행을 거부할 수 있게 규정하고 있는바, 이는 중재판정이나 승인이 집행국의 기본적인 도덕적 신념과 사회질서를 보호하려는데 그 취지가 있다 할 것이므로 그 판단에 있어서는 국내적인 사정뿐만 아니라 국제적 거래질서의 안정이라는 측면도 함께 고려하여 제한적으로 해석하여야 할 것이다.

논지는 이 사건 중재판정에 있어서 피고가 불출석한 채 원고의 일방적인 출석으로 심리를 종결하였고, 중재법원은 피고가 원고에게 배상할 금액을 결정함에 있어서 논리와 합리적 고려를 도외시함으로써 당초의 매매대금보다 더 큰 배상금액을 인정하였을 뿐 아니라 그 지연이자 계산에 있어서도 뚜렷한 근거없이 준거법인 영국의 법정이율로 하지 아니하고 고율인 미국의 우대금리를 적용하였으며, 중재판정문에 이유를 붙이지 아니하였으니 위 중재판정의 승인이나 집행은 대한민국의 공공질서(이자에 관한 법질서)에 반하므로 원심으로서는 그 승인을 거부하였어야 할 것임에도 불구하고 이 점에 관한 피고의 주장을 제대로 판단하지 아니한 채 위 중재판정을 승인함으로써 판단을 유탈하여 이유를 갖추지 못하고 뉴욕협약 제5조 제2항 나호의 법리를 오해한 위법을 저질렀다는 것이다.

기록에 의하여 살펴보면, 원심의 판단에는 위와 같은 주장을 배척한 취지가 포함되어 있다고 볼 수 있고, 이 사건 중재절차에 있어서 통지에 관한 특약이 우리나라의 법 원리에 반한다고 볼 수 없는 이상, 앞에서 본 바와 같이, 설시의 사유로 피고가 참석하지 못한 가운데 이 사건 중재판정이 내려졌다 하여 그 집행이 우리나라의 공공질서에 반하는 것은 아니며, 중재법원이 인정한 배상금액에 관한 집행이 우리나라의 공공질서에 반한다고 볼 근거가 없고, 한편 국제 상거래에 있어서 일방당사자의 채무불이행에 관하여는 일반적으로 승인된 적절한 국제금리에 따른 지연손해금의 지급을 명함이 관행이라 할 것인데 영국 런던중재법원이 피고에 대하여 일반적으로 적용되는 국제금리인 미국은행 우대금리(그 최고이율도 연 2할 5리로서 우리나라 이자제한법의 제한범위내이다)에 따른 지연손해금의 지급을 명한 것은 상당하고, 중재판정서에 자세한 이유기재가 없다 하더라도 그것만으로는 우리나라의 공공질서에 반한다고 볼 수 없으니 같은 취지의 원심판단은 정당하고 이 점에 관한 위 논지는 모두 이유 없다.

노트와 질문

1. 금전채무의 지급을 명하는 중재판정의 근거가 기존의 대법원판례와 상반되는 경우는 공공질서위반인가?33) 외국중재판정이 사기적 방법에 의하여 편취되었음을 이유로 외국중재판정의 집행이 공공질서위반이라고 주장할 수 있는가?34) 중재판정이 성립하기 전에 상대방에 대하여 중재합의의 대상이 되는 별개의 채권을 내세워 상계주장을 하였으나 그 상계주장이 받아들여지지 않은 것도 청구이의사유로서 공공질서위반인가?35) 지적재산권 침해여부에 관한 분쟁은?36)
2. 당사자간 서면에 의한 중재의 합의가 없음에도 불구하고 내려진 중재판정이라는 항변에 대하여 집행을 요구받은 법원의 중재의 합의 여부를 어느 나라 준거법에 기초하여 판단하여야 하는가?37)
3. 우리나라가 외국과 체결한 BIT중 ICSID 중재절차에 따른 분쟁해결을 규정하고 있는 것이 있다. 이런 경우 ICSID 중재판정은 우리나라에서 또는 상대방국가에서 어떤 요건하에 어떤 절차에 따라서 집행가능한가?38)

---

33) 대법 2010. 6. 24. 선고 2007다73918 판결 참조.

34) 대법 2009. 5. 28. 선고 2006다20290 판결(동해펄프사건) 참조. 이 판결에 대하여는 석광현, 사기에 의해 획득한 외국중재판정의 승인과 공서양속, 법률신문 2010. 10. 14. 제3880호. 동해펄프에 관하여는 대법 2003. 2. 26. 선고 2001다77840 판결도 참조(동해펄프의 중재판정취소의 소에 대한 소각하판결).

35) 대법 2010. 4. 29. 선고 2010다3148 판결 참조.

36) 대법 1995. 2. 14. 선고 93다53054 판결(DHV사건) 참조. 김갑유, 외국중재판정의 집행과 중재약정의 실효, 2006. 9. 25. 법률신문 제3493호는 집행판결을 구하는 원고가 중재합의를 포함한 노하우실시계약상의 지위를 제3자에게 양도되어 애당초 중재를 신청할 권한이 없었는지 여부는 NY협약 제5조 제1항(a)의 사유로 집행판결의 신청을 받은 법원이 판단하여야 한다고 비판.

37) 대법 1988. 2. 9. 선고 84다카1003 판결, 서울민사지법 1984. 4. 12. 선고 83가합7051 판결 참조. 중재합의의 해석에 관하여는 대법 2003. 8. 22. 선고 2003다318 판결(판결 또는 중재라는 선택적 중재조항은 무효); 대법 2001. 10. 12. 선고 99다45543 판결(축협과 스위스회사간 축협의 입찰과 계약에 관한 일반조항에 따른 중재합의효력인정). 이 판결에 대한 평석은 김갑유, 중재합의 유효성판단과 그 준거법, VI 상사판례연구 603 (2006). 서울지법 2002. 10. 24. 선고 2002가합8808 판결도 참조(중재후 법원최종판단 역시 무효). 한편 대법 2000. 12. 8. 선고 2000다35795 판결은 중재합의에 중재장소나 중재기관에 대하여 합의가 없었지만 매도인이자 원고인 중국기업이 매수인이자 피고인 한국기업을 상대로 중국내 중재위원회에 제기한 중재신청에 대하여 피고가 아무런 이의없이 중재절차를 진행한 경우 중재합의의 부재를 이유로 원고의 집행판결신청에 대한 거부사유를 주장할 수 없다고 판시.

38) Bishop, 주 4-54 상게서, 1542-62.

제11장

분쟁해결의 준거법

1. 국내법 체계

국제거래는 상대방당사자에 대한 최소한의 신뢰와 당사자의 권리의무를 규정한 계약서에 기초한다. 계약서에 장래의 여러 가지 상황을 감안하여 당사자의 권리의무를 정하지만 이들이 의미하는 바에 대하여 다른 의견이 있을 수 있고 또한 계약서에서 미리 예견하지 못한 상황이 발생할 수도 있다. 이런 이유로 계약서는 통상 그 말미에 분쟁해결의 방법과 준거법 조항을 둔다. 계약서의 말미에 있지만 이는 이 조항이 협상에서 중요하지 않기 때문이 아니라 상대방 당사자의 자존심을 건드릴 수 있는 예민한 사항이기 때문에 마지막에 논의하자는 취지일 것이다.

관할법원이나 중재지에 관한 합의는 분쟁발생시 증거조사방법에 관한 절차법이나 중재합의의 존부에 대한 판단의 근거법을 정한다는 면에서 준거법의 선택이라는 측면이 없는 것은 아니다. 하지만 통상 준거법의 선택이라 함은 계약서의 해석을 통한 당사자의 권리의무를 정하는 법의 선택이라는 면에서 관할법원이나 중재지에 관한 합의와는 아무런 관련이 없고 따라서 관할법원이나 중재지의 합의를 근거로 준거법에 관한 묵시적 합의를 추정하거나 가정하는 것은 불합리하다.

국제거래의 특정분야에 적용될 모든 국가에 공통된 법규범이 존재한다면 특정국가의 법체계를 선택할 이유가 없을 것이다. 또한, 모든 국가의 국내법이 동일하다면 역시 특정국가의 법체계를 선책할 이유가 없을 것이다. 따라서, UNCITRAL이나 UNIDROIT 같은 단체에서 계속 국제거래에 적용될 조약초안이나 국내법으로서 모델법을 만들어내고 있다. 예를 들어 UNCITRAL 모델 중재법은 우리나라를 비롯하여 많은 국가에서 중재법을 만들 때 참고하여 성공적인 프로젝트의 하나로 평가받고 있다. 또한, 국제매매협약(Convention on International Sale of Goods)도 국제매매거래에서 실제 많이 활용되고 있는 중요한 국제규범이라고 할 수 있다. 이들 국제기구나 단체들은 그 효력면에서 법규범에 미치지 못하지만 하나의 기준으로서 소위 soft law로서 best practice나 행동강령을 제시하여 국제규범의 통일에 많은 기여를 하고 있다.

그러나, 아직 역사적·문화적인 이유로 몇개의 상이한 법체계가 있으니 이하 이를 간단히 살펴본다. 다만, 아래의 설명은 지역적 구분에 기초한 것으로 지극히 일반적이고 간략하다. 오늘날 국제화의 시대에 모든 국가에 공통된 법규범 내지 soft law가 끊임없이 만들어지면서 상호 영향의 정도는 과거와 비교할 수 없을 만큼 지대하여졌다. 이제는 과거처럼 몇몇 국가가 해외에 식민지를 개척하면서 하나의 법체계가 다른 국가 내지 지역에 이식되는 시대가 아니라 모든 국가가 공통된 법규범을 만들기 위하여 서로 협의하면서 상호 영향을 주고받는 시대라고 할 수 있을 것이다. 그러나, 세계화가 언제나 바람직한 것만은 아닐 것이다.

가. 영미법 체계[1)]

영미법은 영국에서 유래한 법체계로서 법이란 다른 진리와 마찬가지로 개별적인 사안에 타당한 선례의 집적을 통하여 점진적으로 만들어지는 것이라는 지적 전통에 기초한다. 사법부의 적극적인 법발견자로서의 역할을 기대하여 판결은 결론에 대한 자세한 이유를 설명하고 선례와 비교, 분석하며 법원으로서의 가치를 가진다. 물론 분야에 따라서는 국회에서의 제정법이 필요하며 이를 기초로 특정 법체계를 발전시키기도 하지만 원칙적으로 모든 경우에 언제나 타당한 법원칙을 법규로서 성문화하기 위한 노력이 가지는 의미에 대하여 회의적이다.

나. 대륙법체계[2)]

대륙법은 유럽대륙에서 유래한 법체계로서 로마법의 성문화처럼 모든 경우에 언제나 타당한 법규를 선험적으로 만들 수 있다는 지적 전통에 기초한다. 입법부의 역할을 중시하고 사법부에는 단순히 이를 해석하고 적용하는 소극적인 역할을 기대한다. 성문법규는 완벽하기 때문에 이에 대한 해석은 사법부가 아닌 법학자들의 역할이며 구체적인 사안에서의 판단은 아무런 선례적 가치가 없다. 따라서, 판례는 아무런 법적인 구속력이 없고 체계적으로 축적, 논의될 필요도 없다.

다. 이슬람법체계[3)]

이슬람법(sharia)은 이슬람교에 근거한 법체계로서 법적인 규범이 종교적인 믿음에서 유래한다는 면에서 다른 법체계와 구별된다. 대부분의 이슬람국가는 헌법 내지 기본법에서 이

1) JANE. C. GINSBURG, LEGAL METHODS, 65-73 (3rd ed. 2008).
2) VON MEHREN/JAMES GORDLEY, THE CIVIL LAW SYSTEM(1977), part one, Historical and Institutional Background.
3) 이원삼, 이슬람법사상(아카넷 2001); 이원삼 등, 이슬람법이론 및 금융법제(한국법제연구원 2009).

슬람법이 최고의 또는 유일한 법원임을 선언하고 있으며 따라서 이슬람법에 어긋나는 성문 법규나 계약은 그 효력이 없다고 볼 수 있다. 다만, 이슬람교가 법상 또는 사실상 국가의 지배적 종교인 경우에도 언제나 이슬람법이 절대적으로 지배하는 것은 아니고 구 소련연방하의 CIS국가의 경우에는 러시아의 지배를 받으면서 법체계가 세속화되어 이슬람법이 지배한다기보다는 러시아와 유사한 성문법체계라고 할 수 있다.[4]

이슬람법은 신의 말씀인 코란, 신의 전달자인 예언자 마호메트의 언행을 기록한 순나, 법률가들의 학설(usal-al-fiqh), 개별적 사안에서의 판단(fiqh)로 구성되어 있으며 우리가 이해하는 통상의 법규범보다 추상적이고 일반적이다. 더구나, 이슬람법이 지배하던 중동·북아프리카 지역은 유럽제국주의의 확장속에서 근대화를 위한 개혁의 과정으로서 유럽의 성문법체계를 받아들여 민법과 상법 등을 제정하였기 때문에 이들 성문법규와 이슬람법에서 금지하고 있는 특정행위가 상호 충돌되는 것으로 보이기도 한다. 예를 들어 도박이나 사행행위를 금하는 Gharar나 상대방의 경제적 궁핍을 이용한 이자를 금하는 Riba가 현대의 금융기법의 구축이나 석유탐사계약의 해석에 어떠한 영향을 미치는지 명확하지 않다. 그러나, 많은 법률가들은 이슬람법의 적용범위를 가족이나 상속에 국한하며 이슬람법과 현대의 자원개발이나 금융을 위한 계약과의 관련성을 제한적으로 해석한다.

2. 준거법의 합의

국제거래시 준거법 선택에 관한 국제조약은 아직 존재하지 않는다. 유럽의 경우 Convention on the Law Applicable to Contractual Obligations on 19 Jun. 1980 (Rome Convention)이 있으며[5] 미국의 경우 Restatement에서 판례를 정리하였고[6] Hague Convention of Private International Law에서 입양, 신탁, 혼인, 대리 등 몇몇 특수분야에서 준거법에 관한 조약안을 제시하고 있다.[7]

우리나라는 이들 국제적인 움직임을 반영, 과거의 섭외사법을 전면 개정한 국제사법을 2001. 7. 1 .부터 시행하였다. 준거법 선택의 기본원칙은 당사자자치이며[8] 당사자간 합의가 없을 경우 계약과 가장 밀접한 관련이 있는 국가의 법이 적용된다.[9] 실제 국제거래의 협상시

4) 김한칠, 법·제도 요인으로 분석한 투자매력도, 중앙아시아 국가들의 투자매력도 분석과 한국의 진출방안(대외경제정책연구원 2010), 241-72.
5) eur-lex.europe.eu에서 열람가능.
6) RESTATEMENT OF THE LAW (2nd): CHOICE OF LAW, §188 (ALI, 1986).
7) hcch.net.
8) 국제사법 제25조.
9) 동법 제26조. 국가의 관할권을 기초로 한 준거법 선택에 대한 비판은 Paul B. Stephan, *The Politial Economy of Choice of Law,* 90 GEO. L. J. 957 (2002).

준거법과 분쟁해결을 위한 법정지 내지 중재지를 서로 하나씩 선택하는 경우도 많다. 그러나, 관할법원이나 중재인들이 자기들 소재지가 아닌 제3국의 법에 따라서 분쟁을 해결하여야 한다면 가장 이상적인 선택이 아닐 수도 있다. 물론 실제 분쟁을 제기함에 곤란함이 많은 분쟁해결방법과 준거법을 계약에서 규정함으로써 계약 당사자들이 분쟁을 일으키는 것을 꺼려하게 만드는 것이 가장 바람직한 합의라고 판단할 수도 있다.

이러한 준거법 선택의 일반이론이 언제나 국가가 소유하고 있는 석유자원의 탐사, 개발을 위한 계약에는 그대로 적용될 수가 없다. 왜냐하면 계약당사자가 국가 내지 국가의 NOC이기 때문이다. 산유국의 국가주권이 관련된 문제이기도 하고 또한 산유국의 협상력이 월등히 우월하기 때문이다. 따라서 국제탐사계약에서는 통상 IOC 설립의 준거법인 미국이나 유럽법이 준거법으로 선택된 예는 많지 않은 것같다. 기본적으로 자원보유국의 법을 지정하고 이를 국제법이나 법의 일반원칙으로 제한하거나 아니면 자원보유국의 법을 전면적으로 배제하고 국제법이나 법의 일반원칙만을 준거법으로 지정하고 있다.

준거법조항의 예[10)]

UMC Production Sharing Contract dated 29 June 1992 between the Republic of Equatorial (Guinea) & United Meridian International Corp.[11)]

Section 16-Laws and Regulations

16.1 For purposes of this Contract the laws of the Republic of Equatorial Guinea as existing and in force on the Effective Date of this Contract and generally accepted principles of international law shall govern this Contract.

Oil Concession Agreement dated 13 October 1980 between the Government of Abu Dhabi & Amerada Hess Petroleum Abu Dhabi Ltd.[12)]

Art. 35 (G)

This Agreement shall have the force of law. It shall be given effect and shall be interpreted and applied in conformity with the principles of law normally recognized by civilized states in general including those which have been applied by International Tribunals.

10) T&T 조항을 제외하고 모두 Barrows Company로부터 동의를 받아서 전재.

11) 135 Basic Oil Laws & Concession Contracts: South & Central Africa 1 (1998).

12) 75 Basic Oil Laws & Concession Contracts: Middle Fast 2 (1982).

Pennzoil/Lukoil Group Agreement dated 10 November 1995 on Production Sharing for the Karabakh and Area Adjacent in the Azerbaijan Sector of the Caspian Sea between the State Oil Co. of the Azerbaijan Republic (Socar) and Lukoil International, et al.[13]

This Agreement shall be governed and interpreted in accordance with principles of law common to the law of the Azerbaijan Republic and English law, and to the extent that no common principles exist in relation to any matter then in accordance with the principles of the common law of Alberta, Canada (except for laws regarding conflicts of laws). This Agreement shall also be subject to the international legal principle of *pacta sunt servanda* (agreements must be observed).

Texaco Exploration Pakistan Petroleum Concession Agreement dated 6 November 1990 between the Islamic Republic of Pakistan, Oil & Gas Development Corp., & Texaco Exploration Pakistan Inc.[14]

Art. 29.5

This Agreement shall be governed and interpreted in accordance with and shall be given effect under the laws of Pakistan to the extent that such laws and interpretations are consistent with generally accepted standards of International law including principles as may have been applied by international tribunals.

Trinidadian & Tobagon Model Producion Sharing Contract for Deep Water Areas[15]

Article 32-Applicable Law

32.1 The validity, interpretation and implementation of the Contract shall be governed by the laws of the Republic of Trinidad and Tobago.

---

13) 52 Basic Oil Laws & Concession Contracts: Russia & NIS 1 (Supplement 23)(2003).

14) 116 Basic Oil & Concession Contracts: Asia & Australia 1 (1993).

15) Bishop, 주 4-54 상게서, 255-56. T&T계약은 IHS Energy, Petroleum Economics and Policy Solutions (PEPS) Database at http://www.ihsenergy.com에 있다고 하나 아마 유료서비스인 듯하다. Petroconsultants사가 1996년 IHS로 넘어가면서 자료도 이전된 듯하다.

3. 구체적 분쟁사례

Petroleum Development (Trucial Coast) Ltd. v. Sheikh of Abu Dhabi (1951)[16)]

[아부다비왕은 1939. 1. 11. Petroleum Development(Trucial Coast) Limited에게 아부다비 일정지역내 독점적 석유탐사권을 부여하는 권리를 부여하였다. 동 계약은 중재조항을 포함하고 있으며 제17조는 "they base their work in this Agreement on goodwill and sincerity of belief and on the interpretation of this Agreement in a fashion consistent with reason"이라고 규정하고 있다. 1949년 아부다비왕은 영해를 넘어선 대륙붕에 관하여 탐사권이 있음을 선언하였다. 동사는 1939년 양허계약하의 탐사권이 아부다비 본토와 섬뿐 아니라 영해의 해저, 그리고 아부다비왕의 주권 내지 석유탐사권이 미치는 영해 밖의 연장된 해저, 즉 대륙붕에 대하여도 미침을 주장하였다.]

(b) What is the 'Proper Law' applicable in construing this contract. This is a contract made in Abu Dhabi and wholly to be performed in that country. If any municipal system of law were applicable, it would prima facie be that of Abu Dhabi. But no such law can reasonably be said to exist. The Sheikh administers a purely discretionary justice with the assistance of the Koran; and it would be fanciful to suggest that in this very primitive region there is any settled body of legal principles applicable to the construction of modern commercial instruments. Nor can I see any basis on which the municipal Law of England could apply. On the contrary. Clause 17 of the Agreement, cited above, repels the notion that the municipal Law of any country, as such, could be appropriate. The terms of that Clause invite, indeed prescribe, the application of principles rooted in the good sense and common practice of the generality of civilised nations — a sort of 'modern law of nature' I do not think that on this point there is any conflict between the old ties.

---

16) 18 I.L.R. 144 (1951). UAE의 탐사권 역사에 관하여는 Dr. Atef Suleiman, 주 4-4 상게논문, 6 참조. 1973년 25% 지분 양도합의후 1974년 60%로 상향합의하고 또한 85% 소득세 부과. ADNOC가 이들 주식의 소유를 통하여 ADPC를 경영하고 있다. 이 중재판정에 대하여는 Edwi J. Cosford, Jr., *The Continental Shelf and the Abu Dhabi Award,* 1 MCGILL. L. REV. 109 (1953) 참조. Dr. Khaled Mohammed Al-Jumah, *Arab State Contract Disputes: Lessons from the Past,* 17 ARAB LAW QUARTERLY 215, 233-34 (2002)(영국법은 19세기 산업혁명이후 광업법을 발전시켰지만 이슬람법은 그 전부터 훨씬 효과적인 광업법이 있었다고 주장하면서 아래 중재판정을 내린 영국인 Lord Asquith of Bishopstone과 Sir Alfred Buckill의 무지를 지적).

but, albeit English Municipal Law is inapplicable as such, some of its rules are in my view so firmly grounded in reason, as to form part of this broad body of jurisprudence — this 'modern law of nature' instance, while in this case evidence has been admitted as to the nature of the negotiations leading up to, and of the correspondence both preceding and following the conclusion of the Agreement, which evidence as material for construing the contract might, according to domestic English Law, be largely inadmissible, and to this extent the rigid English rules have been disregarded; yet on the other hand the English rule which attributes paramount importance to the actual language of the written instrument in which the negotiations result seems to me no mere idiosyncrasy of our system, but a principle of ecumenical validity. Chaos may obviously result if that rule is widely departed from: and if, instead of asking what the words used-mean, the inquiry extends at large to what each of the parties meant them to mean, and how and why each phrase came to be inserted.

The same considerations seem to me to apply the same principle *expressio unius est exclusio auerius*.[17] I defer entirely to the warnings given by Wills J. and Lopes L.J. in the case of Colquhoun v. Brooks (19 Queen's Bench Division 400 at p. 406: and 21 Q.B.D. 52 at p. 65) as to the possibilities (and indeed the frequency) of its misapplication. But confined within its proper borders it seems to me mere common sense. (If I have a house and a garden and two hundred acres of agricultural land and if I recite this and let to X my house and garden it seems obvious that the two hundred acres are excluded from the lease.)

Much more dubious to my mind is the application to this case of certain other English maxims relied on by one or the other party in this case For instance, verba chartarum fortius accipiuntur contra proferentem: or the rule that grants by a sovereign are to be construed against the grantee. The latter is an English rule which owes its origin to incidents of our own feudal polity and royal prerogative which are now ancient history; and its survival, to considerations which, though quite different, seem to have equally little relevance to conditions in a protected State of a primitive order on the Persian Gulf.

---

17) Mentioning one thing may exclude another thing.

Ruler of Qatar v. International Marine Oil Company, Ltd. (1953)[18)]

[카타르왕은 1949. 8. 5. 앞으로 설립될 International Marine Oil Company, Ltd.("회사")를 대리한 Central Mining and Investment Corporation/Superior Oil Company와 Principal Agree- ment를 체결하였다. 계약서 체결 이후 위 양사의 동 계약상의 권리의무는 회사에 양도되었다. 동 계약서 제4조에 따르면 회사는 계약서 체결시 왕에게 어떤 경우에도 돌려받을 수 없는 50만 루피를 지불하여야 하며 또한 동 계약서 제5조는 회사는 왕에게 계약서 체결후 연간 백만 루피를 지불하여야 하며 최초의 지급은 계약서 서명후 1년이 되는 시점으로 한다고 정하고 있다. 또한, 상업적 생산이 가능한 석유가 발견되면 연간 임차료의 지급은 중단되며 그 이후 회사가 왕에게 지불하여야 할 금액은 어떠한 경우에도 백만 루피보다 적지 않은 금액으로 정하였다. 1949. 6. 25. 25만 루피가 왕에게 지급되었고, 계약서명일인 동년 8. 5. 계약서에 정한 계약체결시 지급하여야 할 50만루피 중 선급금 25만 루피를 공제한 나머지 25만 루피와 왕이 계약서를 서명한 데 대한 대가 20만 루피 총 45만 루피가 지불되었다. 1950. 8. 2. 회사는 왕에게 계약서에 따라서 계약서 체결시점으로부터 일년이 경과한 때에 지불하여야 할 백만 루피를, 그로부터 1년 후인 1951. 8. 5. 역시 백만 루피를 지불하였다. 1952. 5. 3. 회사는 계약의 종료를 왕에게 통지하면서 1952. 8. 5. 왕에게 아무런 채무가 없다고 주장하였다. 왕은 1950. 8. 5. 지급한 백만 루피는 1949. 8. 5.부터 1950. 8. 5.까지의 탐사에 대한 지급이므로 회사는 1951. 8. 5.부터 1952. 8. 5.까지의 기간에 대한 백만 루피를 지급하여야 한다고 주장하였다. 카타르왕과 회사간 계약은 왕이 1935. 5. 17. Anglo-Persian Company에게 75년간 카타르전역에 대한 독점적 탐사권계약과 상치되는 바가 있었고 1946년 Anglo-Persian Company로부터 동 계약상의 권리를 양수한 Petroleum Development Qatar Limited('PDQ')가 1949년 중재절차를 개시하자 1950. 8. 5. 회사는 카타르왕에게 동 중재절차상의 일체의 비용을 보상하여 주는 별도의 계약도 본계약과 동시에 맺은 바 있다. 중재인단은 1950. 3. 27. PDQ사의 1935년 계약서상의 탐사권은 카타르의 영해 연장선상의 페르시아만 대륙붕을 포함하지 않는다고 판정하였다.][19)]

The Referee said: "In the absence of any stipulation to the contrary, it seems to me that 'the principles of justice, equity and good conscience' on which the Respondent Company relies in their pleaded Answer require that the rent should not be payable in advance. It was admitted that, in Islamic Law, which is based on the principles of equity, rent always accrues in theory from second to second. Surely equity does not call

18) 20 I.L.R. 534 (1953).

19) 1951 I.L.R. Case No. 38.

on a tenant to pay a sum in advance for what he has not received, or to pay in advance for a chattel before it is delivered to him. In the absence of any other arrangements, payment and delivery should be concurrent. Some such principle seems to be the motive power which led the British Parliament to pass the Apportionment Acts. A passage from Hill & Redman's Law of Landlord and Tenant, 10th Edition, page 262, was cited to me wherein appear these words: Rent, whether reserved or made payable under an instrument in writing or otherwise, is considered as accruing from day to day and is apportionable in respect of time accordingly. (See the Apportionment Act, 1870, Section 2.) At Common Law there was no apportionment of rent in respect of time, since the rent only became payable on the expiration of the full quarterly or other period in respect of which it was reserved. It is interesting to note that the Preamble to the Apportionment Act of 1870 states that rents and some other periodical payments are not at Common Law apportionable in respect of time, and for the remedy of some of the mischiefs and inconveniences thereby arising, etc., diverse statutes have been passed, and it is expedient to make provision for the remedy of all such mischiefs and inconveniences etc.; and Section 2 of the Act states: From and after the passing of this Act all rents, annuities, dividends and other periodical payments in the nature of income ... shall be considered as accruing from day to day and shall be apportionable in respect of time accordingly.

On this crucial point, therefore, I have come to the conclusion that unless there is anything in the documents which points the other way, I must decide that the annual payments of Rupees 1,000,000 under Article 5 were intended by the parties to be payments for the rights conceded to the Respondent Company in the preceding 12 months. But, on behalf of the Respondent Company, it was argued that the agreement by the Company that these payments should be irrecoverable pointed strongly to the interpretation that they were payments in advance. What would be the point, it was said, in stipulating that they shall be irrecoverable if they were intended to be payments in arrear. They would naturally be irrecoverable. This point impressed me, until the arbitrator for the Claimant pointed out that when the Principal Agreement was signed in August 1949 it was uncertain whether the Ruler had a legal right to make the grant, because of the earlier P.D.Q. Agreement in 1935. In the absence of this agreement about irrecoverability, if the Arbitrators decided against the Ruler in, say, September 1950, the Respondent Company might fairly have demanded repayments of the million rupees paid in August 1950 under Article 5 of the Principal Agreement and that whether the payment was in respect of the preceding or ensuing year. I do not know that this contention would have succeeded, but equity would seem to say so.

Therefore, the Ruler, being acquainted with Islamic law and equitable principles, wished to make certain that the 'rent' should not be recoverable in any event, and insisted upon the supplemental agreement signed on the 5th August, 1949. This supplemental agreement in terms refers to the impending arbitration between the Ruler and P.D.Q., and indicates that the Ruler had in his mind the possibility of a decision against him when he made this stipulation, and intended it to refer to such payments whether by way of rent in advance or in arrear.

Moreover, it is difficult to see why this supplemental agreement was needed, apart from a possible adverse decision in the P.D.Q. Arbitration. Once a million rupees had been paid, whether in advance or in arrear, it would seem to be irrecoverable under normal conditions. It was the fear of what the decision in the P.D.Q. Arbitration might be which, in my opinion, caused the Ruler to insist on these payments being irrecoverable, whether they were paid in advance or in arrear.

The first question was whether the proper law to to be applied in the construction of the Principal Agreement is Islamic law or the principles of natural justice and equity. On this point the remarks of Mr. Justice Hardy, a Member of the Supreme Court of Oklahoma, in the case of *Bearman v. Dux Oil Co.,* decided in 1917, and quoted to me, are apt. The case concerned an oil concession, and Mr. Justice Hardy, in the course of his judgment, said: 'On the construction of contracts, it is the duty of the Court to place itself as far as possible in the situation of the parties at the time their minds met upon the terms of the agreement, and from a consideration of the writing itself ascertain their intention, and if this cannot be done by the instrument itself, the circumstances under which it was made and the subject matter to which it relates may be considered, and with these aids, it is the duty of the Court so to interpret the contract as to give effect to the mental intention of the parties as it existed at the time of contracting, so far as that intention is ascertainable and lawful.'

There is nothing in the Principal or Supplemental Agreements which throws a clear light upon the intention of the parties on this point. If one considers the subject matter of the contract, it is oil to be taken out of ground within the jurisdiction of the Ruler. That fact, together with the fact that the Ruler is a party to the contract and had, in effect, the right to nominate Qatar as the place where any arbitration arising out of the contract should sit, and the fact that the agreement was written in Arabic as well as English, points to Islamic law, that being the law administered at Qatar, as the appropriate law.

On the other hand, there are at least two weighty considerations against that view. One is that in my opinion, after hearing the evidence of the two experts in Islamic law, Mr. Anderson and Professor Milliot, there is no settled body of legal principles in Qatar applicable to the construction of modern commercial instruments to quote and adapt the words of Lord Asquith of Bishopstone in his award as Referee in an Arbitration in 1951 in which the Shaikh of Abu Dhabi, a territory immediately adjacent to Qatar and in fact much larger than Qatar, was a party, and the Arbitration concerned the interpretation of words in an oil concession contract. I need not set out the evidence before me about the origin, history and development of Islamic law as applied in Qatar or as to the legal procedure in that country. I have no reason to suppose that Islamic law is not administered there strictly, but I am satisfied that the law does not contain any principles which would be sufficient to interpret this particular contract.

Arising out of that reason is the second reason, which is that both experts agreed that certain parts of the contract, if Islamic law was applicable, would be open to the grave criticism of being invalid. According to Professor Milliot, the Principal Agreement was full of irregularities from end to end according to Islamic law, as applied in Qatar. This is a cogent reason for saying that such law does not contain a body of legal principles applicable to a modern commercial contract of this kind. I cannot think that the Ruler intended Islamic law to apply to a contract upon which he intended to enter, under which he was to receive considerable sums of money, although Islamic law would declare that the transaction was wholly or partially void. Still less would the Ruler so intend, and at the same time stipulate that these sums when paid were not to be repaid under any circumstances whatever. I am sure that Sir Hugh Weightman and Mr. Allan did not intend Islamic law to apply. In my opinion neither party intended Islamic law to apply, and intended that the agreement was to be governed by 'the principles of justice, equity and good conscience' as indeed each party pleads in Claim and Answer, alternatively to Islamic law, in the case of the Claimant.

It is interesting to note that in the Agreement which the Ruler made on the 17th May, 1935, to which I have referred, there is this express stipulation: "The Shaikh and the Company declare that they base action upon this Agreement on the basis of good faith and pure belief and upon the interpretation of this Agreement in a manner consistent with reason.

Saudi Arabia v. Arabian American Oil Company (Aramco) (Aug. 23, 1958)[20)]

[1923년 사우디왕은 British Eastern and General Syndicate에 탐사권을 주었으나 기간 경과로 종료되었다. 1933. 5. 29. Standard Oil Company of California(Socal)에 사우디 동부 지역에 대한 독점적 탐사권을 60년간 부여하였고 이는 1933. 7. 7. Royal Decree No. 1135로 승인되었으며 Socal 이사회 역시 1933. 7. 5. 동 계약을 승인하였다. 1933. 11. 8. Socal은 California-Arabian Standard Oil Company(Casoc)를 설립하였으며 1944. 1. 31. Casoc는 회사명을 Arabian American Oil Company (Aramco)로 바꾸었다. Aramco는 그 후 몇 차례 수정계약을 체결하였고 1938년 석유탐사에 성공하여 원유를 생산, 판매하고 있었는데, 사우디정부가 1954. 1. 20. 오나시스에게 30년 동안 석유수송권을 부여하는 계약을 체결하자, 사우디정부의 계약위반을 이유로 중재절차를 시작하였다.]

a. The law to be applied.

The dispute being of a purely legal character, the first question to be decided by the Arbitration Tribunal is what law is to be applied to the relationship existing between the Parties.

[중재합의상 준거법에 관한 조항]

The decision on this point is made somewhat easier by the Arbitration Agreement, whose Article IV contains the following solution, accepted by both Parties:

> The Arbitration Tribunal shall decide this dispute
> (a) in accordance with the Saudi Arabian law as hereinafter defined in so far as matters within the jurisdiction of Saudi Arabia are concerned; Saudi Arabian law, as used herein, is the Muslem Law (1) as taught by the school of Imam Ahmed ibn Hanbal: and (2) as applied in Saudi Arabia.
> (b) in accordance with the law deemed by the Arbitration Tribunal to be applicable, in so far as matters beyond the jurisdiction of Saudi Arabia are concerned:

This agreement regarding the law to be applied is in conformity with the rules of private international law adopted in most civilized States and it must be observed by the

20) Stephen M. Schwebel, *The Kingdom of Saudi Arabia and Aramco Arbitrate the Onassis Agreement,* 3 J. WORLD ENEG. L. & BUS. 245, 256 (양허계약에 관한 한 주권의 한계를 지적한 중요한 판정으로 평가. 사우디는 판정에 따라 오나시스계약을 취소하고 1973년부터 10년에 걸쳐 Aramco의 지분을 취득)(2010).

Arbitration Tribunal. However, the Parties did not stipulate the application of a single law to their dispute but also envisaged the application of a law to be determined by the Arbitration Tribunal in so far as matters beyond the jurisdiction of Saudi Arabia were concerned.

The method of drawing a distinction between matters within the jurisdiction, and matters beyond the jurisdiction of Saudi Arabia may well be, and has actually been, the subject of controversies.

The Tribunal cannot accept the suggestion that Clause (b) of Article IV (which empowers it to decide what law is applicable) has a subordinate character in relation to Clause (a) (which provides for the application of Saudi Arabian law, i.e., Muslem law as taught by the Hanbali school and as applied in Saudi Arabia). Both Clauses are legally on the same level and both Parties, when introducing this distinction into Article IV of the Arbitration Agreement, were fully aware of the fact that various systems of law must be applied to the different matters connected with the operation of an oil concession.

[중재합의의 해석]

In the Tribunal's opinion, the delimitation between the domains of those legal systems must be made according to two criteria: the legal nature of the matters under consideration, combined with the principles of private international law.

The Tribunal considers that this delimitation cannot be made on the basis of the jurisdiction of Saudi Arabia's Courts, since the arbitration Clause of the Concession Agreement (Article 31) provides that, in default of agreement between the Parties, the arbitrators shall meet in another country, namely, at The Hague, Holland. Article V of the Arbitration Agreement, however, which constitutes a special agreement about the seat of the Tribunal, reads as follows: 'The Arbitration Tribunal shall meet in Lucerne, Switzerland by an Amendment dated 13 September 1955, corresponding to 26 Moharram 1375, the Parties agreed to establish the seat at Geneva. The arbitration is to take place, in all cases, outside Saudi Arabia. It is obvious, therefore, that the law to be applied to this institution is not the law of Saudi Arabia, since the Parties have intended from the very beginning to withdraw their disputes from the jurisdiction of local tribunals. This is an essential provision of their agreements, as the concessionaire wished to secure the guarantee of a neutral judge.

Although the present arbitration was instituted, not between States, but between a State and a private American corporation, the Arbitration Tribunal is not of the opinion that the law of the country of its seat should be applied to the arbitration.

The jurisdictional immunity of States (the principle *par in parem non habet jurisdictionem*) excludes the possibility, for the judicial authorities of the country of the seat, of exercising their right of supervision and interference in the arbitral proceedings which they have in certain cases. In all civilized States, ordinary Courts possess by law such powers of supervision and interference. The Courts can sometimes appoint the arbitrators or the umpire directly by virtue of the law, particularly when one Party violates the arbitration agreement or fails to designate its arbitrator. They can also require that the award, in order to be valid, should be filed with the registry of the court. They can declare the nullity of the award in various circumstances: sometimes the law of the State lays down special grounds for annulment of arbitral awards; sometimes, 'cassation' proceedings are open on the same grounds as in the case of judicial decisions of the Courts; sometimes an appeal can be lodged against arbitral awards, either *ipso jure* or by virtue of a special reservation in the compromis or in the arbitral Clause; sometimes a 'revision' of arbitral awards is permitted and the matter is referred back for determination to the arbitral tribunal itself or to the Courts of the State; sometimes a special organ is given the power to declare the nullity of the award. In certain cases, this acknowledged power of the judicial authorities of the State to interfere may go as far as the substitution of the arbitrators chosen by the Parties by such authorities.

The Courts of Geneva have applied the law of Geneva to arbitrations between foreign corporations which, in the 'compromis' had established the seat of their arbitration tribunal in Geneva (in the case *Telefunken v. Philips*, the Tribunal of Geneva appointed an umpire, pursuant to Article 374 of the Genevese Code of Procedure, following the failure of one of the Parties to co-operate in doing so, and notwithstanding a contrary clause of the Arbitration Agreement which provided for the appointment of the umpire, should the Parties fail to agree, by the President of the Federal Tribunal, who had declined this mission; cf. *Semaine Judiciaire* 1953, p. 417). The question of the applicability of Swiss law to an arbitration in Switzerland to which a foreign State is a Party does not appear to have ever been decided by the Courts of Geneva or by Swiss Courts.

Considering the jurisdictional immunity of foreign States, recognized by international law in a spirit of respect for the essential dignity of sovereign power, the Tribunal is unable to hold that arbitral proceedings to which a sovereign State is a Party could be subject to the law of another State. Any interference by the latter State would constitute an infringement of the prerogatives of the State which is a Party to the arbitration. This would render illusory the award given in such circumstances. For these reasons, the Tribunal finds that the law of Geneva cannot be applied to the present arbitration.

It follows that the arbitration, as such, can only be governed by international law, since the Parties have clearly expressed their 'common intention that it should not be governed by the law of Saudi Arabia, and since there is no ground for the application of the American law of the other Party. This is not only because the seat of the Tribunal is not in the United States, but also because of the principle of complete equality of the Parties in the proceedings before the arbitrators. It is true that the practice of the Swiss Courts has limited the jurisdictional immunity of States and does not protect that immunity, in disputes of a private nature, when the legal relations between the Parties have been created, or when their obligations have to be performed, in Switzerland. The Arbitration Tribunal must, however, take that immunity into account when determining the law to be applied to an arbitration which will lead to a purely declaratory award. By agreeing to fix the seat of the Tribunal in Switzerland, the foreign State which is a Party to the arbitration is not presumed to have surrendered its jurisdictional immunity in case of disputes relating to the implementation of the 'compromis' itself. In such a case, the rules set forth in the Draft Convention on Arbitral Procedure, adopted by the International Law Commission of the United Nations at its fifth session (New York 1955), should be applied by analogy.

In considering that the arbitration, as such, is governed by the Law of Nations, the Arbitration Tribunal does not intend to apply this Law to the merits of the dispute, since the law governing the merits is independent of the law governing the arbitration itself.

[국제사법상 합의존중: 준거법에 관한 합의가 있는지?]

It is a principle universally admitted in private international law that the law governing relations which were not established between States, is to be determined by resorting to the conflict rules of the *lex fori*. But, for an arbitration tribunal which is directly subject to public international law as a result of the jurisdictional immunity of States, there is no *lex fori* to indicate what conflict rules should be used, since general public international law does not contain any such rules.

The Arbitration Tribunal holds, therefore, that it has to ascertain the law to be applied to the merits according to the indications given by the Parties and, failing adequate indications of the Parties, to determine this law by taking all the circumstances of the case into consideration.

In the present instance, the agreement of the Parties does not relate to one single system of law. In so far as the Tribunal is empowered to determine the law to be applied, it will do so by resorting to the general doctrine of private international law. To perform this task, the Tribunal must first ascertain what is, in municipal law, the legal nature of a concession, as the Law of Nations does not contain any principle regarding the characterization of this legal institution.

As was pointed out in the Memorial of the Reparations Commission in the arbitral proceedings which took place between that Commission and Germany, with regard to the interpretation of Article 260 of the Treaty of Versailles, and which ended in the award of 3 September 1924, 'the concept of the concession is very wide and varied; it may extend, according to the legislation and the doctrines concerned, from the grant of titles of nobility or of a burial ground to that of certain public functions involving, for instance, the right to expropriate or the right to regulate (*Annual Digest of International Law Cases*, 1923-1924, pp. 341 ff.; translation).

Even the legal nature of economic concessions is not the same in the case of public service concessions, or of pure public works concessions, or of concessions for the occupation of the public domain or the exploitation of State resources, or of port concessions, or of concessions of water works or of land, for instance in the colonies, or, lastly, of mining concessions. It does not seem possible to subsume all these various concessions under a common concept; this was recognized by the French Conseil d'État in its Opinion of 19 and 26 December 1907 about various questions relating to mining concessions (*Dalloz périodique,* 1908, 3rd part, p. 46). Finally, the legal nature of the concession is not the same in the different systems of law.

An oil concession is a mining concession. It possesses the characteristic feature of the latter concession, i.e., its operation destroys the very substance of the concession. The products of the enterprise are not, therefore, fruits or income, but a part of the capital. This is aptly expressed by Planiol:

> What is extracted from a mine or from a quarry is not a product of the soil; it is the soil itself which is being extracted; the "exploitation" inevitably results in the exhaustion of the mine.' (*Traité élémentaire de droit civil*, vol. I, 3rd ed.. No. 3590, p. 173; translation.)

The same is true of petroleum, by the nature of things. The distinctive feature of any oil concession is thus to be an 'exploitation which attacks the very substance of its object. Such is the first factor of all legal relations resulting from an oil concession, the 'initial fact to use the words of Roguin, i.e., the fact governed by a rule of law (*La Science juridique pure*, 1923, vol. I, p. 82. and vol. II, pp. 200 ff.). This fact is to be found in all legislation relating to mining concessions, whatever the system of law to be applied or the legal theories put forward to explain them.

[합의가 없다면 세계각국에서의 양허계약의 법적 성격을 규정하여 준거법 결정]

It is thus necessary to determine the legal nature of the oil concession, starting from this 'initial fact' and resorting not only to comparative law and to the general principles of law, but also to pure jurisprudence, which purports to ascertain by analysis the permanent elements of a legal institution, whatever the particularities of the systems of law and of the legal doctrines prevailing in the various States of the world.

In a concession regime, any mining 'exploitation' implies an authorization by the State; as the resources of the subsoil affect the public interest, the State is anxious to prevent them from being misused or wasted. According to the general principles of law recognized by civilized States, even the owner of the soil — and consequently also of the subsoil — cannot grant to a third party the right to exploit the resources found in his land and cannot exploit them himself, without an authorization of the State.

This State intervention is justified in two ways: either by instituting in its favour public rights of a proprietary nature to all useful minerals, including oil; or by subjecting mines to the administrative intervention of the State, acting by virtue of its sovereignty.

A mining concession necessarily operates a transfer of title, because it is only the right of ownership which gives a person the faculty to dispose of the thing by consuming it or by transforming its substance. This is clear, for instance, in Article 7 of the French Statute of 1810 on Mine Concessions, which provided: 'the concession confers the perpetual ownership of the mine Since the French Act of 1919 on mines, replaced by the Mining Code of 16 August 1956, mining concessions are no longer perpetual in France, but they create, even in favour of the owner of the surface of the soil, a 'real' right which is distinct from the ownership of the surface and which may be mortgaged independently of any mortgages existing on the land. It follows that the rights granted to the concessionaire are analogous to a temporary ownership. Even assuming that the concessionaire no longer possesses property rights in the mine, it must nevertheless be recognized that he has a proprietary right in an immovable, a right capable of being mortgaged (Planiol, op. ext., No. 3805, p. 1235). The concessionaire has always the right, therefore, to deal with the substance of the mine which is to revert to the State at the end of the period fixed by the concession. He becomes the owner of what is extracted from the mine, by himself and even by unauthorized third parties. The Swiss Civil Code adopts a similar conception in its Article 655, which refers to property in immovables and defines them as follows: 'Immovables within the meaning of the present Code are: ... 3° Mines'.

Such is the double character of the concession; it involves, first, a State act, and, second, rights of ownership vested in the concessionaire. This State intervention does not assume the same legal nature in all States; it may be noted that the various distinctions to be made according to the nature of the concession are frequently unknown.

In the laws of Switzerland and of Germany, the concession is viewed as a unilateral act of the conceding State. The term 'concession agreement' is, nevertheless, usual in these States, but is considered as inexact and misleading; it refers only to the procedure of granting the concession (Ruck, Schweizerisches Verwaltungsrecht, 1934, p. 74; Fleiner, *Les Principes généraux du droit administratif allemand*, trad. Eisenmann, 1933. pp. 213 and 233; *Institutionen des deutschen Verwaltungsrechtes,* 1939, 9th ed., pp. 346 to 350, 380 note 54, and 381). The concession remains a unilateral act of the State even when it results from an exchange of wills between the State and the individual. It produces between them rights and obligations of public law, whose content is determined by the concession. This instrument has the character of a kind of constitution and must be strictly observed by the parties. In this way the concessionaire becomes the holder of subjective rights of a public law character, which cannot be taken away from him as long as he fulfils his obligations, unless the State is specifically authorized to do so by the concession Agreement under conditions set forth in the instrument, for instance when a right of repurchase has been reserved to it. In those systems of law, the concession is not of a contractual character, because it is effective against third parties. The concessionaire is elevated, so to speak, into the realm of public law and public power, and the private rights of third parties must yield to the rights granted to him. Sometimes he has the right of expropriation. He is bound to create and operate the enterprise. The State keeps a special right of supervision — which is juxtaposed to police supervision — as regards the organization and operation of the conceded enterprise, in order to watch over the execution of the concessionaire's obligations. In the exercise of this right of supervision, the State may impose upon the concessionaire new duties, but only in order to maintain or improve the enterprise. It cannot infringe the concessionaire's subjective rights of public law, which are irrevocable so long as the conditions of the concession are observed and within the limits defined therein.

In France, the concession is also considered as a unilateral administrative act by Professor Jeze, who thinks that the fact of its having been solicited by the grantee does not suffice to turn it into a contract. He holds the view that the concession is an 'act-condition' which subjects the concessionaire to an objective and impersonal legal regime, a fact which implies the existence of laws and regulations pursuant to which the concession was granted. The majority of judicial decisions and doctrinal writings in France consider that any concession is contractual in character. However, certain distinctions must be drawn between various categories of concessions. This point needs to be stressed owing to the lengthy developments concerning French law in the Government's argument during the present proceedings. The following types of concession are usually distinguished:

(a) The public service concession, by virtue of which the concessionaire undertakes to manage a public service and receives his reward in the form of the charges paid by the users of the services.

Concessions in this category can be purely contractual. They are, first, looked upon as contracts between the State and the concessionaire, and then as stipulations in favour of third parties, in so far as a right to benefit by the concession is recognized to future users. The conceding State is assumed to have stipulated in favour of the users, and the concessionaire has the same legal position as a promisor.

The public service concession is sometimes considered as having a dual legal nature: it is viewed as a contract between the grantor and the concessionary; as against users, it is looked upon as a public law regulation which is the law of the service. This conception has the disadvantage of attributing to the same juridical act a different character depending on what persons it is applied to.

The public service concession is also considered as a mixed act, partly contractual and partly regulatory. The distinction between these two elements is drawn here according to the category of clauses included in the concession and the cahier des charges, and no longer according to the category of persons subjected to these clauses. Purely contractual clauses must be distinguished in each particular case, in concreto. They do not interest users, but are related to the financial or other advantages granted by the State to the concessionaire. The regulatory clauses are generally included in the cahier des charges. They concern the organization and the functioning of the service and interest the users as well as the concessionaire.

(b) The pure public works concession, by virtue of which the concessionaire undertakes to build, maintain and manage public works, while deriving his remuneration from the results of this exploitation.

The French Conseil d'Etat has recognized that hydroelectric concessions are not public service concessions (22 June 1928, in the case *De Sigalas v. Société hydro-electrique et métallurgique du Palais*: *Sirey*, 1928, 3.113); this is the case, for instance, when the concessionaire uses in its own factories the electric current produced as a result of the hydro-electric concession. It may be mentioned that the public works concession is frequently linked with a public service concession and may present the various features of this latter concession.

(c) Mining concessions, including oil concessions.

Speaking of this type of concessions in its opinion previously quoted (see above)

157 ot 19 and 2b December 1907 on several questions relating to mining concessions, the French Conseil d'etat said: 'There is no analogy between the public service concession, by which an administrative authority grants to a private corporation the management of a public service under definite conditions and for a limited period, and the mining concession, by which the public authority creates a perpetual ownership governed by the regime of the Statutes of 21 April 1880 and 27 July 1880 This statement remains true for mineral products under the regime of the new French legislation, which abolished this perpetual character. Only temporary concessions are recognized under the new law, since the complete ownership of the mine reverts to the State at the end of the concession.

Mining and oil concessions are not public service concessions because they do not include any provision in favour of users. To use the words of Planiol: 'The mine is not destined to public use and is exploited by the concessionaire in his own private interest' (op. ext., vol. I, No. 3803, p. 1234). The concessionaire enjoys a nearly total freedom, and is neither bound by clauses concerning maximum tariffs for sales nor by prohibitions of preferential tariffs, which are the usual features of the cahiers des charges in public service concessions. Mining concessions are not public works concessions either, because the mineral deposits become the property of the concessionaire who, at the end of his concession, will have to return them to the State with their exploitable substance diminished and sometimes even exhausted.

In conclusion, it may be said that a mining concession in French law is an act *sui generis*, which cannot be completely assigned to any other category. It is an act which partakes of the nature of a unilateral act in that it depends on the authorization of the State and of that of a contract in that it requires an agreement of the respective wills of the State and of the concessionaire.

In English law, a mining concession can be viewed as a lease or as the creation of a *profit á prendre*. This question was discussed by Whyatt, C.J., of the Supreme Court of Singapore, in the case *N.V. Bataafsche Petroleum Maatschappij and Others v. War Damage Commission* (Case No. 29/X955), relating to oil concessions in Indonesia.

According to the most generally accepted doctrine in private international law. since the time of the works of Kahn (Latente Gesetzes Kollisioncn, *Iherings Jahrbücher* 1891, XXX, pp. 107 ff.) and Bartin ('De 1'impossibilité d'arriver á la solution définitive des conflits de lois', *Journal Clunet*, 1897, pp. 225-255, 466-495 and 720-728, *Etudes de droit international privé*, 1899, pp. 1-82), the characterization or classification, *i.e.*, the determination of the legal nature of a juridical relationship, is given by the *lex fori*. As the Arbitration Tribunal does not have a *lex fori*, it considers as decisive — according to an exception to the *lex fori* principle which is universally admitted in classical private international law — the legal notions of the *lex situs*. This is because the Tribunal is concerned here with legal relations involving immovable property situated in Saudi Arabia. The Tribunal is thus led to examine the law of Saudi Arabia in order to ascertain whether an oil concession, granted by the Government with respect to the subsoil of its territory, should be characterized as a unilateral act of public law, or as a public or administrative contract, or as a contract of private law, or as a lease, or as a profit a prendre, or as an institution *sui generis,* partly public and partly private. This question must be solved according to the principles of Moslem law, as taught by the Hanbali school.

Aramco contends, however, that Moslem law, as taught by the Hanbali school, is law which is not sufficiently developed to determine the legal nature of the operations involved in the exploitation of petroleum. It maintains that, because of its international connections, the oil concession must be delocalized' and assimilated to an international treaty, governed by the Law of Nations. It maintains, further, that the general principles of law recognized by civilized nations, mentioned in Article 38 of the Statute of the International Court of Justice, should be applied by analogy to its concession.

According to the doctrine and the information submitted by both Parties to the Tribunal, Saudi Arabia belongs to one of the great legal systems of the world, namely Moslem law, in which several rites or schools are distinguished. The principle Sunni schools are the Hanafi, the Maliki, the Shaffei, and the Hanbali school; they do not differ in fundamentals but disagree in several points of detail.

The Hanbali school is followed by the Wahabis of Saudi Arabia. It is the school of Imam Ahmed ibn Hanbal (164-211 a.h., corresponding to 745-792 of the Christian era). Its fundamental principles were developed mainly by the jurist Ibn Taimiya (Arminjon, Nolde and Wolff, *Traité de droit comparé*, vol. II, 1952, p. 402 ff.; Laoust, *Essai sur doctrines sociales el politujues de Taki-D-Din Ahmad B. Taimiya*, Cairo, 1939).

Saudi Arabia is a kingdom of a theocratic character, in which the King is Imam of the Moslem community (Laoust, op. cit.; Book III, chap. II, pp. 606 ff. of his work, on Ibn Taimiya and the Wahabi theocracy; Nallino, *Raccolta di Scritti editi e inediti*, vol. I, *l'Arabia Sa'udiana,* Pubblicazioni dell'Istituto per 1'Oriente, Roma, 1939, p. 9). Hanbali law, like the other schools in Moslem law, is dominated by the principles of the Koran and of the 'Sunna' (*i.e.*, the tradition of the Prophet Mohamed), which are of Divine Revelation and which constitute the Shari'ah; purely legal principles in these sources have been developed by the science of Fikh (jurisprudence), which might be called a kind of Moslem common law. The interpretation of the jurisprudence ('Fikh') is given by the Ulemas or doctors in theological and legal matters. The legislative power left to the Monarch is therefore limited to those matters which are not included in the 'Fikh' because they are not clearly connected with Divine Revelation or with the practice of the first two or three generations of Moslems. The Ruler enjoys an exclusive jurisdiction over a considerable part of the administration of the State in so far as the decrees issued by him are in conformity with the Shari'ah (Nallino, op. cit., p. 10).

There has been no 'reception complete or partial, of French public or administrative law in Saudi Arabia. The only Code ever put into effect in Saudi Arabia is the Code of Commerce of 15 Muhar-ram 1350, corresponding to 1 June 1931. After 1933, the year of the Aramco Concession, the law of the State continued to be based on the traditional principles of the Shari'ah.

The regime of mining concessions, and, consequently, also of oil concessions, has remained embryonic in Moslem law and is not the same in the different schools. Principles of one school cannot be introduced into another, unless this is done by an act of authority. Hanbali law contains no precise rule about mining concessions and a fortiori about oil concessions.

Owing to this lacuna in Moslem law, as taught by the Hanbali school, the Imam, i.e., H.M. the King, in his capacity of theocratic Ruler, has the power to adopt such solutions as he deems most appropriate to the general interest. To this end, he can resort to a regime of mining concessions, in specie of oil concessions, based on a contract, provided that this solution is not contrary to the rules of the Shari'ah. The concession contract does not conflict with these rules, since it is in conformity with two fundamental principles of the whole Moslem system of law, i.e., the principle of liberty to contract within the limits of Divine Law, and the principle of respect for contracts. The first principle is stated by Ibn Taimiya as follows: 'The following rule shall be obeyed: men shall be permitted to make all the transactions they need, unless these transactions are forbidden by the Book or by the Sunna' (Laoust, *Le Traité de droit public d'Ibn Taimiya,* traduction annotée de la Siyasa Sar'iya, Beyrouth, 1948. p. 167; Milliot, op. cit., p. 205, who stresses the principle of freedom to contract, as one of the basic rules of the Law of Obligations in Islam). The second basic rule, in Ibn Tiamiya's opinion, results from the fact that Moslem law does not distinguish between a treaty, a contract of public or administrative law and a contract of civil or commercial law. All these types are viewed by Moslem jurists as agreements or pacts which must be observed, since God is a witness to any contract entered into by individuals or by collectivities; under Moslem law, any valid contract is obligatory, in accordance with the principles of Islam and the Law of God, as expressed in the Koran: 'Be faithful to your pledge to God. when you enter into a pact' (Laoust, Essai sur les doctrines sociales et politiques de Taki-D-Din Ahmad B. Taimiya, Cairo, 1939, p. 445). These rules clearly demonstrate that the oil Concession of Aramco has a contractual character.

According to the Government's Memorials and to the oral hearings, Aramco's Concession must be considered as an 'unnominated' contract *sui generis*. This conception of Saudi Arabian law is related to that which is accepted in many other civilized States, but with one distinctive feature: the contractual character of the concession in Saudi Arabian law is unquestionable.

Particularly strong reasons support the idea of the contractual nature of the Concession granted by the Government of Saudi Arabia to Aramco. This is apparent in the very name of the instrument granting the Concession, the constant use in the text of the word 'Agreement' and especially the provision requiring the contract not only to be approved by H.M. the King, but also to be ratified, within fifteen days after receipt of the document, by the competent organs of the Company at its seat in the United States of America, before the Agreement signed by the Minister of Finance of Saudi Arabia and the representative of the Concessionary Company becomes effective. Such a requirement, rather unusual in the case of concessions, emphasizes the contractual character of the concession in Saudi Arabia. This feature prevails over its unilateral character, which would presuppose laws and regulations not to be found in Saudi Arabia.

The contractual nature of the Concession does not conflict in the least with the present state of comparative law, of the general principles of law and of pure legal science. It is normal to consider that the Concession is based upon an agreement between the grantor and the grantee, even in those legal systems which do not characterize the Concession as a contract, since it is never imposed upon a concessionaire. The latter, by the mere fact of his having applied for the Concession, has expressed his intent to accept it. Numerous are the legal systems where this exchange of declarations of will, made with a view to creating a legal relationship between grantor and grantee, is considered as basically contractual.

Even if the Concession were characterized, *arguendo*, as a unilateral act of the State, because of the ratification of the 1933 Concession Agreement by Royal Decree No. 1135, it would not follow that the Concession could be considered as what is known in French law as a public service Concession, for there are no users of a service. Aramco has undertaken no obligation whatsoever to allow the public to use and benefit by its petroleum and petroleum products. Its reward does not consist in charges or dues paid by the users to the Company. It has no other duty in this connection than to sell its products, while making certain deliveries to the Government. No cahier des charges is annexed to the Concession. It follows that Saudi Arabia cannot subject the Company to any of the regulations established by French law and which are unknown in Moslem law.

The Government maintains that the sovereignty of the State which is a Party to the

Concession is a decisive factor in the determination of the legal nature of the Concession. This contention finds no support in Moslem law. On the contrary, no distinction is drawn by Ibn Taimiya between State treaties, contracts of public or administrative law, and contracts of civil or commercial law. All have the same validity. The rule pacta sunt servanda is fully recognized by Moslem law.

[계약해석의 준거법?]

Now that the legal nature of the Concession has been ascertained, in accordance with the Hanbali school of Moslem law, the law to be applied to this contract remains to be determined.

It is obvious that no contract can exist in *vacuo*, i.e. with out being based on a legal system. The conclusion of a contract is not left to the unfettered discretion of the Parties. It is necessarily related to some positive law which gives legal effects to the reciprocal and concordant manifestations of intent made by the parties. The contract cannot even be conceived without a system of law under which it is created. Human will can only create a contractual relationship if the applicable system of law has first recognized its power to do so.

As the Agreement of 1933 has not been concluded between two States, but between a State and a private American corporation, it is not governed by public international law. As was said by the Permanent Court of International Justice in the Serbian Loans Case:

> Any contract which is not a contract between States in their capacity as subjects of international law, is based on the municipal law of some country.' (Judgment of July 12, 1929. case regarding the *Payment of Certain Serbian Loans Issued in France, P.C.I.J., Series* A, No. 20, p. 41.fa In the same sense Jessup, *Transnational Law*, p. 83.)

In order to determine what law is to be applied, resort must be had to the principles of private international law known as that of the autonomy of the will. According to this principle, in any contract presenting an international character, the law expressly chosen by the parties should first be applied. Second, failing any choice of law. the law presumably intended by the parties is applicable. But this choice of a subsidiary law is not interpreted in the same way by the legal writings and the practice of the various States. Sometimes reference is made to the common lex patriae of the parties, or to the lex loci contractus, or to the lex domicilii debitoris, or to the lex loci executionis, or to the law of the country with which the contract has the closest connection, or to the law of the contract as determined objectively without resorting to the presumed intention of the parties, or to the law indicated by presumptions more or less absolute in character, or to the lex fori. Sometimes the contract is split into different parts by legal practice and doctrines: capacity is governed by the lex patriae or the lex domicilii of the parties, the form of the contract by the law of the place where it is made, its essential validity by the lex loci contractus and its effects by the lex loci solutionis. Elsewhere this division of the contract is rejected and the whole contract is governed by a single law. Some authors and some case laws require that the matter should have a reasonable connection with the law chosen by the parties, while others consider the choice of law by the parties to be free from any restrictions.

As the Parties to the Arbitration Agreement left to the Arbitrators a broad discretion in this respect, the Tribunal is free to choose one or the other of these multiple theories, provided its choice is objective and is justified by the circumstances of the dispute submitted to it.

Since the Parties themselves declared that the Concession was not to be governed by a single law, the Tribunal can justifiably split the contract into parts, to be governed by several laws.

The Tribunal wishes to point out that the Parties, inasmuch as they left to it the duty to determine what law should be applied to matters beyond the jurisdiction of Saudi Arabia, have undoubtedly examined the question of the applicable law and have failed to find a solution. For this reason the Tribunal is unable to determine what law was tacitly chosen by the Parties. The Arbitration Tribunal is thus called upon to reconstruct, not the choice of law which the Parties might have had in mind or intended, but, in an abstract manner, the choice of law which reasonable persons would have made and intended. In other words, the Tribunal must resort to objective criteria in order to connect certain matters regulated by the contract with a specified place and a specified legal system.

[사우디법]

The Aramco Concession Agreement signed by the Government of Saudi Arabia and an American corporation has, because of its Parties and of its ramifications, an international character. The law expressly chosen by the Parties must be taken into consideration, therefore, provided this choice is reasonable, that is to say, provided the Parties have selected a legal system connected with their transaction. This is undoubtedly so here, for many reasons. The contract was signed at Jeddah, Saudi Arabia; the *lex loci contractus*, then, is the law of that State. Further, the effective date of the contract was fixed by Article 54 of the Concession as the date of its publication in Saudi Arabia, following its ratification by the Company. Lastly, the contract is, for the most part, to be performed in this State. Its performance entails the exploitation, in a direct manner, of the hidden wealth of the subsoil of Saudi Arabia and the creation of proprietary rights in immovables situated in the territory of that State.

The law in force in Saudi Arabia should also be applied to the content of the Concession because this State is a Party to the Agreement. as grantor, and because it is generally admitted, in private international law, that a sovereign State is presumed, unless the contrary is proved, to have subjected its undertakings to its own legal system. This principle was mentioned by the Permanent Court of International Justice in its Judgments of July 12th, 1929 concerning *the Serbian* and *Brazilian Loans* (Judgment No. 14, P.C.I.)., Series A. No. 20. p. 42, and Judgment No. 15. P.C.I.J., Series A, No. 21, p. I2i).

As for the law to be applied to matters which are not governed by the law expressly chosen by the Parties, according to Article IV of the Arbitration Agreement, the Tribunal adopts the following solution. Influenced by the most progressive teachings in that part of private international law which deals with the autonomy of the will, the Tribunal decides to follow the solutions prevailing in British and Swiss practice and to apply the law which corresponds best to the nature of the legal relationship between the Parties, without looking for the tacit or presumed intention of the contracting parties. This is the law of the country with which the contract has the closest natural and effective connection, unless another law is designated by the conclusive conduct of the parties. Relying on objective considerations, the Tribunal believes that the governing law should coincide with the economic milieu where the operation is to be carried out.

Guided by this criterion, the Arbitration Tribunal comes to the conclusion that some of the effects of the Concession Agreement cannot be governed By the law of Saudi Arabia, both because of objective considerations and because of the subsequent conduct of the Parties.

The Concession Agreement of 4 Safar 1352, corresponding to 29 May 1933, derives therefore its judicial force from the legal system of Saudi Arabia, the Shari'ah, the Divine Law of Islam, supplemented by Royal Decree No. 1135. of 14 Rabie al Awal 1352, corresponding to 17 July 1933. It came into force on the date of its publication, pursuant to Article 2 of the said Royal Decree, and it forms the basis of all subsequent Agreements, as well as of the letters exchanged by the Parties, in which their respective rights and obligations were more precisely defined, modified or supplemented. This is the standpoint which the late King, H.M. Ibn Saud, adopted when he declared to a representative of Aramco: 'You advise your people to abide by your Concession contract and they will abide by the law of Saudi Arabia' (text cited during the Jeddah negotiations, Verbatim Rec ord of meeting held on 27 January i955. P. 65).

[양허계약상 내용]

Inasmuch as the law in force in Saudi Arabia did not contain any definite rule relating to the exploitation of oil deposits, because no such exploitation existed in that State before 1933, this lacuna was filled by the 1933 Concession Agreement, whose validity and legality under Saudi Arabian law are not disputed by either side. The present dispute only concerns the effects of the provisions contained in the Agreement.

The Concession Agreement is thus the fundamental law of the Parties, and the Arbitration Tribunal is bound to recognize its particular importance owing to the fact that it fills a gap in the legal system of Saudi Arabia with regard to the oil industry. The Tribunal holds that the Concession has the nature of a constitution which has the effect of conferring acquired rights on the contracting Parties. By reason of its very sovereignty within its territorial domain, the State possesses the legal power to grant rights which it forbids itself to withdraw before the end of the Concession, with the reservation of the Clauses of the Concession Agreement relating to its revocation. Nothing can prevent a State, in the exercise of its sovereignty, from binding itself irrevocably by the provisions of a concession and from granting to the concessionaire irretractable rights. Such rights have the character of acquired rights. Should a new concession contract incompatible with the first, or a subsequent statute, abolish totally or partially that which has been granted by a previous law or concession, this could constitute a clear infringement, by the second contract, of acquired rights or a violation, by the subsequent statute, of the principle of non-retroactivity of laws, with the only exception of rules of public policy. This is because a legal situation acquired by virtue of a previous special statute cannot be abrogated by a subsequent statute — *generalia specialibus non derogant* — unless the legislator has expressly given retroactive effect to such statute, which the State cannot do in respect of concessions, without engaging its responsibility.

[법의 일반원칙]

In so far as doubts may remain on the content or on the meaning of the agreements of the Parties, it is necessary to resort to the general principles of law and to apply them in order to interpret, and even to supplement, the respective rights and obligations of the Parties.

The Arbitration Tribunal relies, by analogy, on the precedent of the *Lena Goldfields Arbitration* between the U.S.S.R. and a British corporation, with respect to mining concessions, and on the award given in that case on 3 September 1930. According to Article 75 of the concession contract, the concessionary company was subject to the whole present and future legislation of the U.S.S.R., but with the following important reservation: 'in so far as special provisions are not contained in the present agreement Further, under Article 76, the Government had undertaken not to modify the contract in any way, by order, by decree or by any other unilateral act, without the approval of the Lena Goldfields Ltd. The arbitrators (in the absence of the Government's arbitrator who refused to take part in the proceedings) adopted the following standpoint, in conformity with the submissions of the plaintiff:

> "... On all domestic matters in the U.S.S.R., the laws of Soviet Russia applied except in so far as they were excluded by the contract, and accordingly that in regard to performance of the contract by both parties inside the U.S.S.R. Russian law was the 'proper law of the contract' "
>
> But ... for other purposes the general principles of law such as those recognised by Article 38 of the Statute of the Permanent Court of International Justice at The Hague should be regarded as the 'proper law of the contract'

The latter solution seemed justified to the arbitrators because several provisions in the Concession called for the application of international law rather than that of municipal law (Cornell Law Quarterly, vol. 36, 1930, p. 50).

A similar decision is found in the Arbitral Award given by Lord Asquith of Bishopstone, in August 1951, in the case of *Abu Dhabi*. Looking for the law to be applied, the Arbitrator noted that the law of Abu Dhabi was applicable *prima facie*, as an oil concession was involved, but that this law did not contain any rules on the subject. Having, on the other hand, excluded the application of English law, as unwarranted, the Arbitrator held, therefore, that he had to resort to the general principles of law, as a kind of 'modern law of nature' (*Petroleum Development [Trucial Coast] Ltd. v. The Shaikh of Abu Dhabi: International and Comparative Law Quarterly*, vol. I [4th series] 1952, p. 247lIJ).

This award has been relied upon by both Parties in the present arbitration (Government's Memorial, No. 36-37, pp. 26-27 Aramco's Second Memorial, No. 238, p. 125).

This same character of public rights inevitably mixed with the grant of private rights to the concessionaire is to be found in the Aramco Concession Agreement.

Matters pertaining to private law are, in principle, governed by the law of Saudi Arabia but with one important reservation. That law must, in case of need, be interpreted or supplemented by the general principles of law, by the custom and practice in the oil business and by notions of pure jurisprudence, in particular whenever certain private rights — which must inevitably be recognized to the concessionaire if the Concession is not to be deprived of its substance — would not be secured in an unquestionable manner by the law in force in Saudi Arabia.

This solution results directly from the interpretation of Article 35 of the Concession Agreement; although this Article only provides that the English text shall prevail in all cases relating to the obligations of the Company, it supports this solution as follows:

> "Inasmuch as most of the obligations hereunder are imposed upon the Company and inasmuch as the interpretation of the English text, especially as regards technical obligations and requirements relating to the oil industry, has been fairly well established through long practice and experience in contracts such as the present one, it is agreed that while both texts shall have equal validity, nevertheless in case of any divergence of interpretation as to the Company's obligations hereunder, the English text shall prevail.'

In the Tribunal's opinion, this provision is an unequivocal recognition by the Parties of the established custom and practice of the oil industry; such custom and practice can therefore supplement an incomplete legal system.

[수출할 권리]

Aramco's right of ownership in the oil it extracts and the oil derivatives it produces is not expressly mentioned in the 1933 Concession Agreement and it has been questioned by the Government, although the latter admits that the Company does possess private rights of a sacred character. (Answering Memorial No. 46, p. 56.)

In the course of the oral hearings, the Government claimed that this omission was intentional and that neither one nor the other Party had any absolute right of ownership in the oil. Aramco has no such right, it was argued, because it is not entitled to enjoy and dispose freely of the object of the Concession. Under Moslem law, it cannot base its alleged right of ownership on the fact of prior discovery and extraction of the oil because the right of the first discoverer in Hanbali law is not an exclusive right and is only attributed to Moslems and to non-Moslems who are among the residents of the Moslem State (Ahl al Dar); Aramco, it was further argued, cannot claim to be the first discoverer of the oil by virtue of its exclusive right to explore the vast area reserved to it in the Concession for the following reason: as no one else had the right to explore and prospect, Aramco's privilege would destroy the rules of Hanbali law according to which the first discoverer cannot prevent others from taking their needs of the mineral resources he has discovered.

But these rules, evolved some centuries ago in respect of mineral deposits other than oil, have precisely been supplemented by the 1933 Concession Agreement, ratified by Royal Decree No. 1135 in the proper exercise of the powers vested, under Hanbali law, in the Ruler of the State. The right to sell the products of the conceded oil deposits is not disputed by the Government, for it is explicitly mentioned in Article I of the 1933

Concession, as follows: 'It is understood, however that such right does not include the exclusive right to sell crude or refined products within the area described below or within Saudi Arabia.'

It follows, by an inescapable argument *a contrario*, that the concessionaire has the exclusive right to sell outside Saudi Arabia. This right of sale, which entails a transfer of title, implies a recognition of Aramco's right of ownership in the oil and oil products.

The arguments proffered in order to dispute the concessionaire's ownership are all the more devoid of foundation since this very right of ownership has been recognized several times in the Government's correspondence and, during the proceedings, in the Government's Memorials (Answering Memorial of the Government, No. 53-54, pp. 63-65). The proof of this statement can be found in the letter, dated 10 July 1954, corresponding to 9 Zul Quada 1373, from the Minister of Finance to Mr. Davies, Chairman of Aramco's Board of Directors, where Aramco's property right is recognized in the following words:

If it is admissible that the oil produced within the area which the second article of the Agreement delimits is by principle the property of Aramco, and that to the Government (there belong only) the royalty and taxes, nevertheless this statement requires clarification ... The idea is then expressed that this property right is subject to the laws and decisions of the Government and is inferior in rank to the supreme right of the State in respect of properties and persons within its territorial borders. The same view is expressed in the Government's Answering Memorial (No. 53-57, pp. 63 to 67). The reservations accompanying this recognition in principle of Aramco's property right are not such as to weaken its force. The Company claims nothing more than the respect of its acquired rights, which cannot be unilaterally altered by the State, both Parties being on an equal footing from a contractual standpoint.

In conclusion, this analysis shows that, in Saudi Arabian law as in the laws of Western Countries, the oil concession is an institution which implies an authorization by the State, on the basis of a statute or of a contract, and necessarily entails the grant to the concessionaire of property rights in the oil. As a result of this, the Concession, even in the absence of an express clause to that effect, confers upon Aramco the right to dispose of the oil. Because of this fundamental similarity, the Tribunal will be led, in the case of gaps in the law of Saudi Arabia, of which the Concession Agreement is a part, to ascertain the applicable principles by resorting to the world-wide custom and practice in the oil business and industry; failing such custom and practice, the Tribunal will be influenced by the solutions recognized by world case-law and doctrine and by pure jurisprudence.

As regards the international effects of the Concession, such as the effects of the sale and transport of the oil and oil products to foreign countries, and in particular the f.o.b. sales, the Tribunal holds that these effects are governed by the custom and practice prevailing in maritime law and in the international oil business.

Because of the American nationality of the concessionaire, a particular importance must be ascribed, in this connection, to the custom and practice followed by producers in the United States and their buyers all over the world. This does not mean that American law, as the law of the nationality and of the domicile of one of the Parties, should be given any priority in relation to the law of Saudi Arabia, as the national law of the grantor and the law of the place of exploration. What the Tribunal intends to take into account is only the world-wide practice adopted in the oil industry and business.

Lastly, the Tribunal holds that public international law should be applied to the effects of the Concession, when objective reasons lead it to conclude that certain matters cannot be governed by any rule of the municipal law of any State, as is the case in all matters relating to transport by sea, to the sovereignty of the State on its territorial waters and to the responsibility of States for the violation of its international obligations.

Texaco Overseas Petroleum Co./California Asiatic Oil Co. v. The Government of the Libyan Arab Republic (1977)

C. Meaning and scope of the internationalization of the contracts in dispute

46. The Tribunal must specify the meaning and the exact scope of internationalization of a contractual relationship so as to avoid any misunderstanding: indeed to say that international law governs contractual relations between a State and a foreign private party neither means that the latter is assimilated to a State nor that the contract entered into with it is assimilated to a treaty.

This distinction is worth making, because the situation of individuals, and more generally private persons, in respect of international law, has recently been the subject matter of important doctrinal debates on the occasion of which excessive positions sometimes may have been stated. Thus, for some:

> "The rules of economic international law concern not only States but directly the individuals; because economic and social progress has as its objective to assure its direct application to those concerned. The result is that individuals

are directly the subjects of economic or social international law." (P. Vollas, 1 *Droit International Économique et Social* (1965), at 30.)

47. This Tribunal will abstain from going that far: it shall only consider as established today the concept that legal international capacity is not solely attributable to a State and that international law encompasses subjects of a diversified nature. If States, the original subjects of the international legal order, enjoy all the capacities offered by the latter, other subjects enjoy only limited capacities which are assigned to specific purposes. The proposition which has just been stated is in conformity with the statement by the International Court of Justice in its *Advisory Opinion on Reparations of 11 April 1949* under which "the subjects of law, in any legal system, are not necessarily identical in their nature or in the extent of their rights and their nature depends on the needs of the community" ([19-19] I.C.J. 174, at 178). In other words, stating that a contract between a State and a private person falls within the international legal order means that for the purposes of interpretation and performance of the contract, it should be recognized that a private contracting party has specific international capacities. But, unlike a State, the private person has only a limited capacity and his quality as a subject of international law does enable him only to invoice, in the field of international law, the rights which he derives from the contract.

48. This is what is noted by Professor I. Seidl-Hohen-veldern who, when referring to tho work of Professor Bock-stiegel, writes ("Contrats entre Etats et Personnes Privées Etrangères: The Theory of Quasi-International and Partly International Agreements", Rev. Beige D.L 5C7 (1975), at 570):

> "If it is possible to recognize international organisations, insurgents, etc. as subjects of international law and if some authors at least consider that even individual human beings under certain circumstances may be subjects of international law, why should a State be prevented from recognizing its partner to such a contract as a subject of international law? Of course such recognition does not mean that the State recognizes its partner to such a contract as a subject enjoying all rights and duties due to a State. The private partner is recognized as a subject of only those rights and duties, as are embodied in the contracts concerned."

Or, as stated by Professor Garcia Amador ("International Responsibility", 2 Y.B. Int'l. Comm'n 1, U.N. Doc. A/CN.4/119 (1959), at 32):

"... In the matter of contracts, the international personality and capacity of the individual [that is to say the private person, natural or fictitious] depend on the recognition granted to them by the State in its legal relations with him. Agreements which provide in one form or another for the application of a legal system or of principles alien to municipal law, or for the settlement of disputes by international means and procedures, differ from those governed exclusively by municipal law in that the contractual relation between a State and a private person is raised to an international plane, thus necessarily conferring upon that person the necessary degree of international personality and capacity."

Thus, the internationalization of certain contracts entered into between a State and a private person does not tend to confer upon a private person competences comparable to those of a State but only contain capacities which enable him to act internationally in order to invoke the rights which result to him from an internationalized contract.

49. The above quotation from Mr. Garcia Amador is all the more appropriate as it refers to the conclusion of agreements which are "governed exclusively by municipal law", implying thereby that some agreements may be governed both by municipal law and by international law. It is precisely this latter kind of hypothesis which is to be found in the case under consideration since the clause of the contracts under dispute relating to the applicable law refers to the "principles of Libyan law which are common to the principles of international law". It is significant in this respect that, in a formula in which it must be assumed that each term has been weighed, the parties concerned referred not to Libyan law itself, but to "the principles of Libyan law". Indeed, the parties thereby wanted to demonstrate that they intended the Arbitral Tribunal to base itself on the spirit of the Libyan law as expressed in the fundamental principles of that law, rather than by its roles which may be contingent and variable since these rules depended, in the last instance, on the unilateral will — even arbitrariness — of one of the contracting parties: hence, the reference which is also made to the principles of international law.

It follows that the reference made by the contracts under dispute to the principles of Libyan law does not nullify the effect of internationalization of the contracts which has already resulted from their nature as economic development agreements and recourse to international arbitration for the settlement of disputes. The application of the principles of Libyan law does not have the effect of ruling out the application of the principles of international law, but quite the contrary: it simply requires us to combine the two in verifying the conformity of the first with the second.

50. The Tribunal must in this respect make two observations in order to clarify the scope of the internationalization of the contracts in dispute:

– in the first place, the national law (that is: the principles of Libyan law) can be raised to the level of the international legal order: in other words, the national law is incorporated into the international legal order as a body of substantive law (*"règles les matérielles"*), by reason of its normative content which becomes a set of rules to be applied by the International Tribunal. The grounds of its applicability does not result from the automatic operation of the sovereignty of the contracting State, but from the common will of the parties: the national law of the contracting State is therefore regarded as *lex contractus* by incorporation. This is what Professor Weil expressed in the following terms ("Les Clauses de Stabilisation ou d'Intangibilité Insérées dans les Accords de Développoment Économique," in Mélanges Offerts à Charles Rousseau 301 (1975), at 319-320):

  "... Municipal law does not therefore apply in itself but as a law of renvoi. The presence in the contract of a provision referring to the municipal law of the host State does not therefore necessarily mean that internationalization "must be ruled out: if such internationalization results from the other characteristics of the contract — and this is the case with most economic development agreements — the contract will nonetheless be internationalized, and national law will therefore be applicable as a law of renvoi on the basis of the choice of the parties as authorized by the international law applicable in the field of contracts...."

– in the second place, the municipal law of the contracting State itself includes principles of international law: every municipal law is a vehicle for the general principles of law as provided for under Article 38 of the Statute of the International Court of Justice. Under this generic name of general principles of law, reference is made in fact to contain principles common to the legal systems of the various States of the world. They constitute a source of international law which originates in the various municipal laws: therefore, the application of municipal law does not exclude the application of the general principles of law which themselves are part and parcel of the principles of international law.

51. Applying the principles stated above, the Arbitral Tribunal will refer:

(1) On the one hand, as regards the principles of Libyan law: regardless of the source of Libyan law taken into consideration, whether we refer to the Sharia, the Sacred Law of Islam (a special reference should be made to Surah 5 of the Koran which begins with the verse: "0 ye believers, perform your contracts!") or to the Libyan Civil Code which includes on this point two basic articles illustrating the value which Libyan law attaches to the principle of the respect of the word given:

- Article 147, under which "The contract makes the law of the parties. It can be revoked or altered only by mutual consent of the parties or for reasons provided by the law";

- Article 148, under which "A contract must bo performed in accordance with its contents and in compliance with the requirements of good faith", one is led to the same conclusion, that is: that Libyan law recognizes and sanctions the principle of the binding force of contracts.

(2) On the other hand, as regards the principles of international law: from this second point of view, it is unquestionable, as written by Professor Jessup in concluding his opinion (p. 71) that the maxim " 'pacta sunt servanda' is a general principle of law; it is an essential foundation of international law".

No international jurisdiction whatsoever has ever had the least doubt as to the existence, in international law, of the rule *pacta sunt servanda*: — it has been affirmed vigorously both in the *Aramco* award in 1958 and in tho *Sapphire* award in 1963. One can read, indeed, in the *Sapphire* award, that "it is a fundamental principle of law, which is constantly being proclaimed by international Courts, that contractual undertakings must be respected. The rule 'pacta sunt servanda' is the basis of every contractual relationship" (35 Int'l L.R. 136 (1963), at 181). This Tribunal cannot but reaffirm this in its turn by stating that the maxim *pacta sunt servanda* should be viewed as a fundamental principle of international law.

52. The conformity, on this essential point, of the principles of Libyan law with the principles of international law relieves the Tribunal from discussing the matter further — in particular from going to the second part provided for subsidiarily in Clause 28 of the Deeds of Concession — and enables it to conclude that the Deeds of Concession in dispute have a binding force.

대법 2010. 3. 25. 선고 2008다88375 판결

(1) 원고는 2005. 1. 27. 중국의 위너 글로벌 지앙수 컴퍼니 리미티드(Winner Global Jiangsu Co., Ltd. 이하 '위너 글로벌 지앙수'라고 한다)에게 오토크실렌(Ortho-Xylene) 3천 메트릭 톤(이하 '이 사건 화물'이라고 한다)을 매도하였다. 위너 글로벌 지앙수는 이 사건 화물의 대금을 지급하기 위하여 2005년 2월 중순경 홍콩 스탠다드 차타드 은행 등으로부터 각 취소불능 신용장을 개설받았다.

(2) 원고는 이 사건 화물의 운송을 위한 선박을 구하다가 사정이 여의하지 아니하자 매수인인 위너 글로벌 지앙수에게 선박의 용선을 부탁하였고, 위너 글로벌 지앙수는 다시 운송주선업 등을 영위하는 위너 글로벌 베이징 컴퍼니 리미티드(Winner Global Beijing Co., Ltd. 이하 '위너 글로벌 베이징'이라고 한다)의 업무담당자인 소외인에게 선박의 용선을 의뢰하여 여러 운송중개인의 중개 등을 거쳐 피고 소유의 선박인 닝화406호(Ninghua 406. 이하 '이 사건 선박'이라고 한다)를 용선하였다.

(3) 원고는 2005. 2. 26. 이 사건 화물을 네 그룹으로 분류하여 이 사건 선박에 선적하고 그 각각에 대하여 피고로부터 선하증권 4통(이하 모두 합하여 '이 사건 각 선하증권'이라고 한다)을 발행·교부받았다. 이 사건 선박은 선적항인 울산항을 출항하여 2005. 3. 1. 목적지인 중국 난징항에 도착하였다.

(4) 소외인은 발행일이 2005. 2. 28.로 기재된 위너 글로벌 베이징 명의의 '보상장(Letter of Indemnity)' 4장(이 사건 각 선하증권에 대응하는 것이다)을 발행한 다음, 팩시밀리 전송의 방법으로 이를 이 사건 선박의 용선에 관여하였던 아시아벌크차터링 컴퍼니 리미티드, 흥아해운 주식회사, 켄오스를 각 순차로 통하여 피고에게 2005. 3. 2. 12 : 55경 전달하였다.

한편 소외인은 원고에게 원고 명의의 보상장을 발행해 줄 것을 요청하면서 팩시밀리로 위너 글로벌 베이징 명의의 위 각 보상장과 동일한 내용의 보상장 서식 4장을 전송하였고, 이에 응하여 원고는 2005. 3. 2. 13 : 43경 위 각 서식에 서명·날인하여 이를 소외인에게 팩시밀리로 전송하였다(이하 이들 보상장을 '이 사건 보상장'이라고 한다. 이들 보상장의 발행일은 2005. 2. 28. 또는 2. 29.이다). 이들 보상장의 주된 내용은 다음과 같다. 즉 ① 원고는 피고가 이 사건 각 선하증권 원본을 제출받음이 없이 이 사건 화물을 위너 글로벌 지앙수에게 인도하여 줄 것을 요청한다. ② 피고가 위 요청에 따를 경우, 원고는 피고 및 그 고용인과 대리인 등에게 이 사건 화물의 인도로 인하여 발생하는 모든 손해(소송비용, 선박가압류 등의 해제를 위한 보상금 등 포함)를 보상하여 준다. ③ 이 보상장에 관한 준거법은 영국법이다.

(5) 피고는 2005. 3. 3. 15 : 30부터 3. 5. 16 : 00까지 사이에 이 사건 화물을 양하하여 이 사건 각 선하증권상의 통지처인 위너 글로벌 지앙수에게 이를 인도하였다.

2. 원고는 자신이 이 사건 보상장에 기하여 피고에 대하여 손해배상책임 기타 일체의 채무를 부담하지 아니한다고 주장한다. 이에 대하여 원심은 이 사건 보상장에 기한 원·피고 사이의 계약의 성립 및 유효성도 이 사건 보상장에 관한 준거법인 영국법에 의하여 정하여진다고(국제사법 제29조 제1항 참조) 전제한 후, 그 계약이 유효하게 성립하였는지에 관하여 다음과 같이 판단하였다.

이 사건 보상장상의 의사표시가 원고를 구속하기 위하여는 그 청약의 의사표시가 피고에게 도달하고 피고가 이를 승낙하여 상호간에 '의사의 합치(agreement)'가 있을 것이 필요하다. 보상장에 관한 당사자의 합의 역시 일종의 계약이라고 할 것이므로, 그것이 성립하기 위하여는 영국법에 의하더라도 우리나라 법과 마찬가지로 청약(offer)과 승낙(acceptance)이라는 두 가지 요소가 갖추어져야 할 것이다. 그런데 이 사건 보상장에 나타난 원고의 의사표시는 반드시 이 사건 보상장 원본 또는 사본이 피고에게 도달하여야 청약으로서의 효력을 가지는 것이 아니라 어떠한 방법으로든 그와 같은 의사표시가 피고에게 도달하면 청약으로서 효력을 가진다고 할 것이고, 또 피고의 승낙의 의사표시 역시 반드시 명시적으로 원고에게 표시되어야 할 필요 없이 원고의 청약에 따른 행위를 피고가 실행하는 방법으로 묵시적으로 표시하여도 무방하다는 것이다.

이러한 법리를 적용하여 원심은 피고가 소외인으로부터 이 사건 보상장이 발행되었다는 통지를 받고 이 사건 화물을 인도한 이상 이 사건 보상장에 기한 계약이 유효하게 성립하였다고 인정하고, 결국 원고의 이 사건 채무부존재확인청구를 기각하였다.

3. 그러나 원심의 위와 같은 판단은 수긍할 수 없다.

가. 섭외적 사건에 관하여 적용될 준거법으로서의 외국법은 여전히 사실이 아니라 법으로서 법원은 직권으로 그 내용을 조사하여야 하고, 그러한 직권조사에도 불구하고 그 외국법의 내용을 확인할 수 없는 경우에 한하여 조리 등을 적용할 것이다(대법원 1990. 4. 10. 선고 89다카20252 판결, 대법원 2000. 6. 9. 판결 98다35037 판결 참조). 한편 섭외적 사건에 관하여 적용될 준거법인 외국법의 내용을 확정하고 그 의미를 해석함에 있어서는 그 외국법이 본국에서 현실로 해석·적용되고 있는 의미 또는 내용에 좇아야 하고, 소송과정에서 그 외국의 판례 등 해석기준에 관한 자료가 제출되지 아니하여 그 내용이 확인이 불가능한 경우에만 일반적인 법해석기준에 따라 법의 의미·내용을 확정할 수 있는 것이다(대법원 1991. 2. 22. 선고 90다

카19470 판결, 대법원 2010. 1. 28. 선고 2008다54587 판결 참조).

나. 그런데 원심은 위와 같이 이 사건 보상장에 기한 계약의 성립 및 유효성에 관한 준거법이 영국법임을 인정하면서도, 영국법이 이 사건 보상장과 같은 '보상장'에 기한 계약이 유효하게 성립하기 위한 요건에 관하여 어떻게 정하고 있는지, 또는 그에 관한 영국법이 그 본국에서 현실적으로 어떠한 의미 또는 내용으로 해석·적용되고 있는지에 관하여 심리하거나 직권으로 조사하였다고 볼 만한 자료를 기록상 찾을 수 없다. 그리하여 원심이 위와 같이 이 사건 보상장에 기한 계약의 유효한 성립요건에 관하여 판시한 바가 영국법에서의 어떠한 법적 근거에 의한 것인지가 파악되지 아니한다.

따라서 원심에는 이 사건 보상장의 유효한 성립에 관하여 그 준거법인 영국법의 내용에 대하여 심리를 다하지 아니하고 또 그 판단의 이유를 제대로 갖추지 못하여 판결 결과에 영향을 미친 위법이 있다고 할 것이다. 이 점을 지적하는 상고이유 제2점의 주장은 이유 있다.

대법 2010. 1. 28. 선고 2008다54587 판결[21)]

가. 외국적 요소가 있는 법률관계에 관하여 적용될 외국법규의 내용을 확정하고 그 의미를 해석함에 있어서는 그 외국법이 그 본국에서 현실로 해석·적용되고 있는 의미·내용대로 해석·적용하는 것이 원칙이며, 소송 과정에서 그 외국의 판례나 해석기준에 관한 자료가 제출되지 아니하여 그 내용의 확인이 불가능한 경우에만 일반적인 법해석 기준에 따라 법의 의미·내용을 확정할 수 있는 것이다(대법원 1991. 2. 22. 선고 90다카19470 판결, 대법원 2007. 7. 12. 선고 2005다39617 판결 등 참조).

나. 원심판결 이유와 기록에 의하면, 주식회사 대우(이하 '대우'라고 한다)는 1997. 3. 26. 총 발행금액 미화 5,500만 달러, 만기 2007. 12. 31.인 제F-9회 기명식 해외전환사채(이하 '이 사건 사채'라고 한다)를 영국법을 준거법으로 하여 발행하면서, 체이스 맨해튼 트러스티즈 리미티드(Chase Manhattan Trustees Limited, 이하 '체이스 맨해튼'이라고 한다)를 장래 이 사건 사채를 취득할 사채권자를 위한 수탁자로 선임하고, 체이스 맨해튼과 이 사건 사채권자 및 이 사건 사채에 관한 이해관계인들의 권리의무관계에 관하여 규정하는 신탁계약(Trust Deed)을 체결한 사실, 이 사건 사채에 관한 신탁계약서와 사업설명서에는 「(1) 유럽포괄사채권(유럽포괄사채권. European Global Certificate)이 발행되는 이 사건 사채는 기명사채이다. 사채권자(사채권자, Bondholder)는 사채권자 명부에 사채의 소지자로 등록된 자를 의미한다. (2) 이 사건 사

21) 허항진, 외국법을 준거법으로 발행한 포괄사채권(Global Certificate)의 사채권자와 사채권의 행사주체, 23 상사판례연구 171(2010) 참조.

채를 표창하는 유럽포괄사채권은 청산기관(clearing system)인 유로클리어(Euroclear)와 세델 은행(Cedel Bank, societe anonyme)의 공동예탁기관(common depositary) 또는 그를 위한 피지명인(nominee)의 이름으로 발행되고, 그의 명의로 사채권자 명부에 등록된다. (3) 유럽포괄사채권은 유로클리어와 세델 은행의 공동예탁기관인 체이스 맨해튼 은행(The Chase Manhattan Bank)에 예탁된다. (4) 사채권(사채권, Title to Bond)은 사채권자 명부에 사채소지자로 등록하여야만 이전되고, 적정하게 등록된 사채권자만이 유럽포괄사채권에 의하여 표창되는 사채에 관하여 지급받을 권리를 갖는다. (5) 사채권을 청산기관이 지명한 자가 아닌 다른 이름으로 등록하는 것은 소정의 예외적인 경우를 제외하고는 허용되지 아니한다. (6) 청산기관의 계좌에 기입된 형태로 존재하는 이 사건 사채에 관한 권리(Title to book-entry interest in the Bonds)는 청산기관이 정한 절차에 따라 그 계좌상 기입된 명의를 변경하는 방법으로 양도한다」는 취지의 규정이 있는 사실, 위 각 규정에 따라 대우는 18개 국내외 금융기관으로 구성된 인수단으로부터 주간사 회사(Lead Manager)를 통하여 사채대금을 납입받음과 동시에 이 사건 사채 전액에 관하여 유럽포괄사채권을 발행하였고, 발행된 유럽포괄사채권은 체이스 노미니즈(Chase Nominees Limited) 명의로 이 사건 사채권자 명부에 사채권자 등록이 이루어졌으며, 그 실물은 등록대리인(Registrar)이자 공동예탁기관인 체이스 맨해튼 은행에 보관된 사실, 이 사건 사채의 인수단을 구성하는 금융기관들이 유로클리어와 세델 은행에 개설한 각 해당 계좌들에는 이 사건 사채 중 해당 액면금이 표시된 금액이 각 기입되었고, 그 계좌이체로 유럽포괄사채권에 관한 권리에 대한 유통이 시작되었는데, 유로클리어와 세델 은행에 계좌를 보유하는 자는 통상적으로는 기관투자자들이며, 그 기관투자자로부터 사채에 관한 권리를 매입하는 개인들은 기관투자자에게 다시 자신의 계좌를 개설하게 되는 사실, 원고들은 1998. 12. 14. 미국 베어스턴스 증권회사(Bear, Sterns Securities Corporation, 이하 '베어스턴스 증권'이라고 한다)로부터 베어스턴스 증권이 이 사건 사채와 관련하여 유로클리어의 계좌(계좌번호 생략)를 통하여 보유하고 있던 미합중국통화(이하 '미화'라고 한다) 96만 달러 상당의 이 사건 사채에 관한 권리 중 미화 30만 달러 상당 부분을 매입하고, 베어스턴스 증권에 원고들 명의의 계좌를 개설하여 그 내용을 기입한 사실 등을 알 수 있다.

다. 앞에서 본 법리와 위 사실관계에 비추어 보면, 이 사건 신탁계약과 이 사건 사채는 준거법인 영국법, 특히 영국의 신탁법리에 기초하여 그에 따라 이 사건 사채의 발행회사인 대우와 이 사건 사채권자 및 이 사건 사채에 관한 이해관계인들의 권리의무관계를 규율하는 구조로서, ① 청산기관인 유로클리어와 세델 은행의 공동예탁기관 또는 그를 위한 피지명인 명의로 이 사건 사채를 표창하는 유럽포괄사채권이 발행되고 그 명의인이 사채권자 명부에 사채소지자로 등록되어 있는 동안에는, 그 명의인만이 이 사건 사채의 유일한 사채권자가 되고 그 사채권은 원칙적으로 수탁자에 의하여만 행사되도록 되어 있는 한편, ② 청산기관에 계좌를 개설한 기관투자자 등과 같은 계좌보유자들은 곧바로 이 사건 사채를 취득하거나 사채권자로서의 지위를 취득하는 것이 아니라 이 사건 사채에 관한 수익적 권리를 취득하며, ③ 나아가 이러한 계좌보유자들과 다시 계좌를 개설한 개인 투자자 등은 그 계좌보유자들이 취득한 이 사건 사채에 관한 권리에서 파생하는 수익적 권리를 계좌보유자와의 계약을 통하여 취득하게 된다.

따라서, 이 사건 사채의 유일한 사채권자는 사채권자 명부에 사채소지자로 등록된 체이스 노미니즈로서, 원칙적으로 체이스 노미니즈 혹은 그 수탁자인 체이스 맨해튼만이 사채 발행회사인 대우에 대한 관계에서 권리의무관계를 맺고, 이 사건 사채의 청산기관인 유로클리어나 세델 은행에 계좌를 개설하여 미화 96만 달러 상당의 이 사건 사채에 관한 권리를 취득한 베어스턴스 증권에 다시 계좌를 개설함으로써 그 중 미화 30만 달러 상당의 이 사건 사채에 관한 권리에서 파생하는 수익적 권리를 취득한 원고들은 발행회사인 대우에 대하여 사채권자의 지위에 있다거나 직접 미화 30만 달러 상당의 금전지급청구권이 있음을 주장할 수 없다.

그렇다면, 구 증권거래법(2007. 8. 3. 법률 제8635호로 공포되어 2009. 2. 4. 시행된 자본시장과 금융투자업에 관한 법률 부칙 제2조로 폐지되기 전의 것) 제174조의3, 제174조의4의 규정과 같이 증권예탁결제원의 예탁자계좌부와 예탁자의 고객계좌부에 기재된 자를 각각 예탁된 유가증권의 점유자로 보고 그 예탁유가증권에 대한 공유지분을 갖는 것으로 추정하는 법리나 해석론은 이 사건 신탁계약 및 이 사건 사채에 관한 권리의무관계를 해석하는 데 적용될 여지가 없는 것이다.

대법 2008. 1. 31. 선고 2004다26454 판결

가. 국제사법 제1조가 '이 법은 외국적 요소가 있는 법률관계에 관하여 국제재판관할에 관한 원칙과 준거법을 정함을 목적으로 한다'고 규정하고 있으므로, 거래 당사자의 국적·주소, 물건 소재지, 행위지, 사실발생지 등이 외국과 밀접하게 관련되어 있어 곧바로 내국법을 적용하기보다는 국제사법을 적용하여 그 준거법을 정하는 것이 더 합리적이라고 인정되는 법률관계에 대하여는 국제사법의 규정을 적용하여 준거법을 정하여야 한다.

원심이 인정한 사실을 종합하여 보면, 이 사건은 필리핀국 국립노동위원회(National Labor Relations Commission)가 시행한 경매절차에서 필리핀국 법인인 필립스 엑스포트 인더스트리즈 아이엔씨(Philips Export Industries. Inc., 다음부터 '필립스사'라고만 한다)에 대한 채권자로서 필리핀국 국민인 해고근로자들이 필리핀국 내에 있던 이 사건 기계를 낙찰받은 것이 유효한지, 그 뒤 필리핀국 내에서 이 사건 기계에 대하여 순차로 체결된 위 해고근로자들과 내국인인 신청외인 사이의 매매계약, 신청외인과 채무자 사이의 매매계약의 효력은 어떤지가 문제되는 사건으로서, 위와 같은 각 매매계약이 체결된 후 우연한 사정에 의하여 이 사건 기계가 국내로 반입되었고, 이 사건 채권자와 채무자가 모두 내국인이라고 하더라도 그 전에 이루어진 모든 외국적 요소를 무시한 채 국제사법의 규정에 따르지 않고 곧바로 내국법을 적용하는 것은 합리적이라고 할 수 없다.

한편, 국제사법 제19조는 "동산 및 부동산에 관한 물권 또는 등기하여야 하는 권리는 그 목적물의 소재지법에 의한다(제1항). 제1항에 규정된 권리의 득실변경은 그 원인된 행위 또는 사실의 완성 당시 그 목적물의 소재지법에 의한다(제2항)"고 규정하고 있는바, 위 각 매매계약이 체결된 당시 목적물인 이 사건 기계가 필리핀국 내에 있었으므로 위 각 매매계약에 관하여는 필리핀국법을 적용하여 그 법률효과를 판단하여야 한다.

그런데도 원심은, 이 사건 당사자인 채권자와 채무자가 모두 국내 법인이거나 자연인이고 소유권 유무가 다투어지는 이 사건 기계가 이미 필리핀국에서 반출되어 국내로 반입된 만큼 이를 섭외사건으로 규율하기보다는 국내법에 따라 해결함이 상당하다는 이유로, 채무자가 이 사건 기계의 소유권을 취득하였는지에 관하여 국내법을 적용하여 판단하였는바, 원심판결에는 외국적 요소가 있는 법률관계에 관한 준거법 결정에 대한 법리를 오해한 잘못이 있고, 이에 관한 상고인의 지적은 타당하다.[22]

노트와 질문

최근의 대법원 판례는 준거법이 외국법인 경우 외국법의 확인은 법원의 직권조사사항이라고 하면서 준거법인 외국법에 대한 보다 자세한 확인을 요구하여 너무나 쉽게 국내법이나 조리에 따른 판단으로 넘어가는 것을 경고하고 있다.[23]

서울고법 2001. 2. 27. 선고 2000나18863 판결

다. 채무불이행 사실을 적시한 서류의 제시가 이 사건 보증금 지급청구의 요건인지 여부

(1) 준 거 법

위 인정 사실에서 본 바와 같이, 이 사건 제1차 보증서의 준거법은 사우디아라비아왕국

22) 매매계약을 언급한 것은 잘못이라는 지적은 석광현, 외국소재동산소유권이전준거법과 대법원판결들의 오류, 2011. 8. 17. 법률신문.

23) 선박사건에서는 보다 자유롭게 일반적인 법해석기준에 따른 외국법 내용확정을 허용. 대법 2007. 6. 29. 선고 2006다5130 판결 참조.

의 법령이고, 특히 위 왕국 재정경제부 1408. 2. 4.(해지라력) 공고 규정번호 16/67의 보증서 규정에 의하게 되어 있는데, 위 사우디아라비아의 보증서규정에 의하면, 이 사건과 같은 독립적 은행보증(first demand bank guarantee)의 경우에 과연 원칙적으로 채무자의 채무불이행 사실의 통지가 필요한지 여부와 그것이 지급청구의 요건인지 여부는 분명하지 않다(기타 다른 사우디아라비아의 관련 법령에 관하여는 기록상 자료가 없다).

나아가, 위 보증서규정은 이 사건의 경우 보증서의 문언에 나타난 바와 같이 "절대적인 판단에 따른 최초의 서면통지(your first written notice … according to your absolute judgment of a failure…)"가 채무자의 채무불이행 사실을 담고 있어야만 채권자의 보증서에 기한 청구가 적법하게 되는 은행보증의 유형에 해당하는지에 관하여도 규정하고 있지 않으며, 이 점에 관한 다른 사우디아라비아의 관련 자료도 보이지 않는다.

이러한 경우와 같이 섭외적 사건에 관하여 적용될 외국법규의 내용을 확정하고 그 의미를 해석함에 있어서는 그 외국법이 그 본국에서 현실로 해석·적용되고 있는 의미·내용대로 해석·적용되어야 하는 것인데, 소송과정에서 적용될 외국법규에 흠결이 있거나 그 존재에 관한 자료가 제출되지 아니하여 그 내용의 확인이 불가능한 경우 법원으로서는 법원(법원)에 관한 민사상의 대원칙에 따라 외국 관습법에 의할 것이고, 외국 관습법도 그 내용의 확인이 불가능하면 조리에 의하여 재판할 수밖에 없는바, 그러한 조리의 내용은 가능하면 원래 적용되어야 할 외국법에 의한 해결과 가장 가까운 해결 방법을 취하기 위해서 그 외국법의 전체계적인 질서에 의해 보충 유추되어야 할 것이고{대법원 2000. 6. 9. 선고 98다35037 판결[공2000하, 1593] 참조}, 그러한 의미에서 사우디아라비아의 전체적인 법체계에 비추어 조리에 기한 판단이 필요하다고 할 것이다(다만, 피고의 주장과 같이, 국제적인 은행거래관습에 비추어 위와 같은 표현을 쓰는 경우, 은행보증의 유형 중 채무자의 채무불이행 사실의 통지를 요하는 유형에 해당하는 것으로 보는 것이 상당하다고 보여진다).

(2) 사우디아라비아 금융분쟁조정위원회의 결정내용

(가) 채무불이행 사실을 적시한 서류의 제시가 이 사건 제1차 보증금 지급청구의 요건인지 여부에 관하여, 아랍파이프와 원고 사이의 보증금 청구사건에 대한 사우디아라비아 금융분쟁조정위원회의 결정(을나의 제7호증 영문번역본을 기준)은 다음과 같다.

"…이 사건 보증서가 절대적이고 무조건적이며, 수익자의 절대적인 재량에 따라 첫 번째 서면통지가 지급을 요청하는 서류로서 제시되었기 때문에, 피고 회사가 이 사건 지급청구가 보증서의 요건에 따라 이루어지지 않았다고 주장하는 것은 보증서의 양식을 불합리하게 강조하는 것이다. 이 사건 은행보증서에 있어 위와 같은 의무의 표현은 단지 이행을 보다 용이하게 하기 위한 보증서의 유형에 대한 설명에 불과하고, 그것이 지급 요청을 위한 조건이나 혹은 지급 요청시 반드시 제시되어져야 하는 서류로 간주되어서는 아니 된다."(을나 제7호증 영문번역본에 대한 피고 제출의 국문번역본은 오역으로 보인다).

(나) 즉, 사우디아라비아 금융분쟁조정위원회는 이 사건 제1차 보증서에 기한 지급청구시 채무자의 채무불이행 사실을 명시한 서류의 제시가 지급청구의 요건사실인지 여부에 관하여 부정적으로 해석하고, 아랍파이프에 대하여 원고 은행의 무조건적인 지급을 명하였다.

(다) 갑 제5 내지 7, 9호증의 각 기재에 변론의 전취지를 종합하면, 위 사우디아라비아 금융분쟁조정위원회는 사우디아라비아 금융청 산하에 동 왕국 내에서 금융기관과 고객과의 분쟁을 조정하기 위하여 1407(H) 7월 10일자 칙령 제729/8호에 의하여 설립되어 위 왕국 내에서 금융기관 간, 또는 금융기관과 그 고객 사이의 금융관련 분쟁에 관하여 전속적인 관할권을 가지고, 그 결정은 법원의 판결과 마찬가지의 사법적 효력과 집행력을 가지며, 당사자들에 대하여 최종적이고 기속적인 사실을 인정할 수 있고, 이에 반하는 듯한 을가 제4호증의 3, 을가 제6호증의 각 기재는 믿지 아니하며, 을가 제3호증의 기재는 위 인정에 방해가 되지 아니한다.

(라) 그런데 위에서 본 바와 같이 사우디아라비아의 관련 법령에 의하여 이 사건 보증서와 같은 경우 채무자의 채무불이행 사실을 명시한 서류의 제시가 지급청구의 요건사실인지 여부에 관하여 자료가 없는 이상, 위와 같은 금융분쟁에 관하여 최종적인 판단 권한을 가진 사우디아라비아 금융분쟁조정위원회는 자국의 관련 법령에 따라 적법하게 위 보증서의 문언을 해석한 것으로 추정할 수 있다고 봄이 상당하다.

(3) 따라서 이 사건 제1차 보증서에 기한 아랍파이프의 청구에는 그 준거법인 사우디아라비아의 법령에 의하면, 피고가 지적하는 바와 같은 채무자의 채무불이행 사실을 적시한 서류의 제시가 보증금 지급 청구의 요건이라고 볼 수 없다고 할 것이고, 나아가 가사 사우디아라비아의 법령과 국제적인 표준은행관습에 비추어 아랍파이프의 제1차 보증서에 기한 청구가 그 요건을 갖추지 못하였다고 하더라도 원고가 소외 아랍파이프에게 이 사건 보증서에 대하여 독립적 은행보증거래에 있어 국제적인 표준은행관행(international banking standard)에 따라 엄격하게 심사한 후 위와 같은 금융분쟁조정위원회의 결정에 따라 그 보증금을 지급한 것을 두고 수익자의 보증서에 기한 지급 청구가 그 요건을 갖추지 못하였음을 명백히 알았거나 알 수 있었던 경우에 해당한다고 볼 수 없으므로 결국, 피고의 위 아랍파이프의 청구가 지급의 요건을 갖추지 못하였고, 이를 원고도 알고서 지급에 응하였다는 피고의 주장은 받아들이지 아니한다.

(4) 나아가 국제적인 표준은행관행에 비추어 이 사건과 같은 독립적 은행보증을 둘러싼 거래의 경우 보증신용장(Standby Letter of Credit)과 유사한 기준과 법리가 적용되어야 함이 상당하고, 위와 같은 은행보증의 유형 중 간접보증의 경우 제1차 보증서의 보증인(이 사건 원고)

이 제2차 보증서의 보증인(이 사건 피고)에게 제1차 보증서상 수익자의 청구에 기하여 제2차 보증서의 보증금 지급청구를 한 경우 제2차 보증서의 보증인으로서는 제1차 보증서의 보증인(이 사건 원고)이 정하여 통보한 기간 또는 그 기간이 상당하지 아니하다면 국제적 은행관행에 비추어 상당한 기간 내에 그 청구가 요건을 갖추었는지 여부를 심사하여 만약 하자가 있으면 그 하자가 치유될 수 있는 성질의 것이면 그 하자를 보완하도록 요구하고, 보완이 불가능한 것이면 하자의 내용을 적시한 후 즉시 지급을 거절하는 통지를 하여야 할 것이고, 만약 그와 같은 통지를 하지 아니하고 하자도 주장하지 아니한 경우에는 차후에 그와 같은 하자를 이유로 제1차 보증서의 보증인인 원고의 청구를 거절할 수는 없다고 봄이 상당하다{은행보증에 관한 통일규칙(Uniform Rules for Demand Guarantees, 줄여서 URDG라 한다, ICC Pub. No. 458, 1992. 4.)은 이에 관하여 규정하고 있지 않으나, 제5차 신용장통일규칙(UCP 500: The Uniform Customs and Practice for Documentary Credits, 1993 Revision, ICC Pub. No. 500, Effective January 1, 1994) 제14조는 "신용장 개설은행이 제시된 서류의 불일치를 이유로 서류의 수리를 거절하고자 하는 경우에 지체 없이 제시인에게 그 불일치 사항을 통지하고 서류를 반송하는 등의 조치를 취하지 아니하면 개설은행은 그 서류가 신용장의 조건과 일치하지 않는다는 주장을 할 수 있는 권리를 상실한다."는 취지의 규정을 담고 있고, 국제적인 은행거래에서 이와 같은 표준관행이 자리잡고 있는 것으로 보아 이러한 논리를 독립적 은행보증의 경우에도 원용할 수 있다고 봄이 상당하다}.

돌아와 이 사건의 경우 위 인정 사실에서 본 바와 같이 피고는 1996. 12. 26. 원고로부터 pay or extend의 요청을 받고, 원고가 정한 시한인 1996. 12. 28.까지 아무런 응답을 하지 않다가 1997. 1. 3.과 같은 달 15. 원고에게 아랍파이프가 무슨 이유로 연장을 원하는지 알고 싶으며, 보조참가인은 이 사건 계약에 따른 의무를 모두 이행하였고, 불이행 부분은 보조참가인의 책임이 아니라는 취지의 답신을 보냈을 뿐 지금 이 사건 소송에서 주장하는 바와 같이 채무자의 채무불이행 사실을 적시한 문서가 은행보증서의 지급청구 요건으로서 제시되지 아니하였다는 주장을 하지 아니한 사실이 인정되고, 따라서 위와 같이 지급청구 과정에서 피고가 원고에게 통지하지 아니한 하자는 차후에 따로 주장하지 못한다고 봄이 상당하다고 할 것이어서 이 점에 관하여 보아도 위 피고의 주장은 이유 없다고 할 것이다.

노트와 질문

위 판결은 다행히도 동일한 논점에 관하여 다른 당사자간 분쟁이 사우디 당국에 의하여 해결된 경우로서 사우디법 입증이 비교적 용이하였다고 할 수 있을 것이나 그 이외 사우디법에 관한 입증이 필요한 경우 어디서부터 출발하여야 할까? 어느 정도 입증을 다한 후에 국내법이나 법의 일반원칙으로 이동하여야 할까?

제05편

국제에너지자원—미래

국제에너지개발이 과거 현지 주민들의 이해관계에 대한 진지한 고려 없이 개발이라는 이름으로 일방적으로 추진된 측면이 있었다. 이제 개발은 지금 당장 개발자와 현지의 일부 권력자에게 경제적인 풍요를 가져올지 모르지만 후일 엄청난 대가를 치를 수도 있다는 것이 인식되면서 현지 주민들의 참여와 이들의 인권, 경제적 개발에 따를 수 있는 사회적 환경적 폐해에 대한 고려가 요구되고 있다. 이러한 사회적 요구는 현재의 법규범을 바꾸어야만 수용가능한 것이라는 점에서 제5편에서 논의되는 주제가 언제나 현재의 법규범은 아니지만, 앞으로 자원개발 프로젝트의 중요한 일부가 될 것이다. 제5편에서는 원주민의 경제적 참여 내지 보상권, 자원보유국 주민의 보편적 인권, 부패방지와 기후변화를 논한다.

제12장

새로운 법의 형성

1. 원주민과 개발

가. 원주민의 권리

Aboriginal은 통상 호주 원주민을 말하지만, 캐나다, 미국, 남미, 남아프리카, 파푸아 뉴기니 등 여러 나라의 인디언도 원주민의 개념에 속한다. 이들이 지금 또는 앞으로 어떤 요건이 충족되면 자원개발에 관한 어떤 권리를 주장할 수 있는지, 이러한 권리가 석유나 가스의 탐사개발권까지 포함하는지 여부는 불분명하지만 1992년 호주의 High Court가 MABOII사건에서 획기적인 판결을 내렸고 그 이후 Native Title Act가 만들어지게 되었다. UN도 2007. 9. 총회에서 원주민의 권리에 관한 선언을 채택한 바 있다.[1)]

Mabo v. State of Queensland, [1992] HCA 23, (1992) CLR 1 (3 Jun. 1992)

[호주 Queensland주 소유 Murray섬 지역에 거주하는 원주민들이 Mer섬 토지 일부에 대한 소유권을 주장하였다. Murray섬이 영연방의 일부로 편입되기 전의 상태에 기초한 주장이다. Queensland주 의회는 1985년 Queenslands Coast Islands 소유권확립법을 통과, 소송을 저지하였고 이에 대하여 호주법원은 이 법이 민족차별적 입법이므로 무효라고 선언했다. 이에 따라 Meriam 원주민들은 문제의 토지에 대한 소유권자, 점유권자, 또는 사용할 권리가 있는 자로 선언하여 달라는 소송과 함께 Murray Islands는 영연방에 토지소유권을 귀속시키는 입법의 대상이 아니었고 Queensland주 정부는 Meriam 원주민의 권리를 박탈할 권리가 없다는 확인을 구하였다.]

---

1) http://www.un.org/apps/news/story.asp?NewsID=23794 참조.

RECEPTION OF THE COMMON LAW

The means by which the municipal laws of England, including the common law, became the law of a country that had been outside the King's dominions were stated by Blackstone as follows:

> "Plantations or colonies, in distant countries, are either such where the lands are claimed by right of occupancy only, by finding them desert and uncultivated, and peopling them from the mother-country; or where, when already cultivated, they have been either gained by conquest, or ceded to us by treaties. And both these rights are founded upon the law of nature, or at least upon that of nations. But there is a difference between these two species of colonies, with respect to the laws by which they are bound. For it hath been held, that if an uninhabited country be discovered and planted by English subjects, all the English laws then in being, which are the birthright of every subject, are immediately there in force. But this must be understood with very many and very great restrictions. Such colonists carry with them only so much of the English law, as is applicable to their own situation and the condition of an infant colony; ... What shall be admitted and what rejected, at what times, and under what restrictions, must, in case of dispute, be decided in the first instance by their own provincial judicature, subject to the revision and control of the king in council: the whole of their constitution being also liable to be new-modelled and reformed by the general superintending power of the legislature in the mother-country. But in conquered or ceded countries, that have already laws of their own, the king may indeed alter and change those laws; but, till he does actually change them, the ancient laws of the country remain, unless such as are against the law of God, as in the case of an infidel country. Our American plantations are principally of this latter sort, being obtained in the last century either by right of conquest and driving out the natives (with what natural justice I shall not at present inquire) or by treaties. And therefore the common law of England, as such, has no allowance or authority there; they being no part of the mother-country, but distinct (though dependent) dominions. They are subject, however, to the control of the parliament."

According to Blackstone, English law would become the law of a country outside England either upon first settlement by English colonists of a "desert uninhabited" country or by the exercise of the Sovereign's legislative power over a conquered or ceded country. Blackstone did not contemplate other ways by which sovereignty might be acquired. In the case of a conquered country, the general rule was that the laws of the country continued after the conquest until those laws were altered by the conqueror. The Crown had a prerogative power to make new laws for a conquered country although that power was subject to laws enacted by the Imperial Parliament. The same rule applied to ceded colonies, though the prerogative may have been limited by the treaty of cession. When "desert uninhabited countries" were colonized by English settlers, however, they brought with them "so much of the English law as [was] applicable to their own situation and the condition of an infant colony". English colonists were, in the eye of the common law, entitled to live under the common law of England which Blackstone described as their "birthright". That law was not amenable to alteration by exercise of the prerogative. The tender concern of the common law of England for British settlers in foreign parts led to the recognition that such settlers should be regarded as living under the law of England if the local law was unsuitable for Christian Europeans. This rule was applied even to English residents in Eastern countries which were not under British sovereignty.

When British colonists went out to other inhabited parts of the world, including New South Wales, and settled there under the protection of the forces of the Crown, so that the Crown acquired sovereignty recognized by the European family of nations under the enlarged notion of *terra nullius*, it was necessary for the common law to prescribe a doctrine relating to the law to be applied in such colonies, for sovereignty imports supreme internal legal authority. The view was taken that, when sovereignty of a territory could be acquired under the enlarged notion of *terra nullius*, for the purposes of the municipal law that territory (though inhabited) could be treated as a "desert uninhabited" country. The hypothesis being that there was no local law already in existence in the territory, the law of England became the law of the territory (and not merely the personal law of the colonists). Colonies of this kind were called "settled colonies". Ex hypothesi, the indigenous inhabitants of a settled colony had no recognized sovereign, else the territory could have been acquired only by conquest or cession. The indigenous people of a settled colony were thus taken to be without laws, without a sovereign and primitive in their social organization. In *Advocate-General (Bengal) v Ranee Surnomoye Dossee* Lord Kingsdown used the term "barbarous" to describe the native state of a settled colony:

> "Where Englishmen establish themselves in an uninhabited or barbarous country, they carry with them not only the laws, but the sovereignty of their own State; and those who live amongst them and become members of their

community become also partakers of, and subject to the same laws."

In *Campbell v Hall* Lord Mansfield suggested that Jamaica should be regarded as a settled colony because the English colonists arrived after the Spaniards had left, the negro inhabitants presumably being of no significance. In *Cooper v Stuart* Lord Watson proffered the absence of "settled inhabitants" and "settled law" as a criterion for determining whether inhabited territory had been acquired by "settlement" under English law:

> "The extent to which English law is introduced into a British Colony, and the manner of its introduction, must necessarily vary according to circumstances. There is a great difference between the case of a Colony acquired by conquest or cession, in which there is an established system of law, and that of a Colony which consisted of a tract of territory practically unoccupied, without settled inhabitants or settled law, at the time when it was peacefully annexed to the British dominions. The Colony of New South Wales belongs to the latter class. In the case of such a Colony the Crown may by ordinance, and the Imperial Parliament, or its own legislature when it comes to possess one, may by statute declare what parts of the common and statute law of England shall have effect within its limits. But, when that is not done, the law of England must (subject to well-established exceptions) become from the outset the law of the Colony, and be administered by its tribunals. In so far as it is reasonably applicable to the circumstances of the Colony, the law of England must prevail, until it is abrogated or modified, either by ordinance or statute."

As the settlement of an inhabited territory is equated with settlement of an uninhabited territory in ascertaining the law of the territory on colonization, the common law which the English settlers brought with them to New South Wales could not have been altered or amended by the prerogative-only by the Imperial Parliament or by the local legislature. (This principle raises some doubts about the validity of the exercise of legislative power by the Governor of New South Wales before a Legislative Council was established in 1823, but we need not pause to consider that question.) In a settled colony in inhabited territory, the law of England was not merely the personal law of the English colonists; it became the law of the land, protecting and binding colonists and indigenous inhabitants alike and equally. Thus the theory which underpins the application of English law to the Colony of New South Wales is that English settlers brought with them the law of England and that, as the indigenous inhabitants were regarded as barbarous or unsettled and without a settled law, the law of England including the common law became the law of the Colony (so far as it was locally applicable) as though New South Wales were "an uninhabited country ... discovered and planted by English subjects". The common law thus became the common law of all subjects within the Colony who were equally entitled to the law's protection as subjects of the Crown. Its introduction to New South Wales was confirmed by s. 24 of the Australian Courts Act 1828 (Imp)(94). As the laws of New South Wales became the laws of Queensland on separation of the two Colonies in 1859(95) and, by the terms of the Queensland Coast Islands Act 1879 and the Governor's Proclamation, the Murray Islands on annexation became subject to the laws in force in Queensland, the common law became the basic law of the Murray Islands. Thus the Meriam people in 1879, like Australian Aborigines in earlier times, became British subjects owing allegiance to the Imperial Sovereign entitled to such rights and privileges and subject to such liabilities as the common law and applicable statutes provided. And this is so irrespective of the fact that, in 1879, the Meriam people were settled on their land, the gardens were being tilled, the Mamoose and the London Missionary Society were keeping the peace and a form of justice was being administered.

THE BASIS OF THE THEORY OF UNIVERSAL AND ABSOLUTE CROWN OWNERSHIP

It is one thing for our contemporary law to accept that the laws of England, so far as applicable, became the laws of New South Wales and of the other Australian colonies. It is another thing for our contemporary law to accept that, when the common law of England became the common law of the several colonies, the theory which was advanced to support the introduction of the common law of England accords with our present knowledge and appreciation of the facts. When it was sought to apply Lord Watson's assumption in *Cooper v Stuart* that the colony of New South Wales was "without settled inhabitants or settled law" to Aboriginal society in the Northern Territory, the assumption proved false. In *Milirrpum v Nabalco Pty. Ltd.* Blackburn J. said:

> "The evidence shows a subtle and elaborate system highly adapted to the country in which the people led their lives, which provided a stable order of society and was remarkably free from the vagaries of personal whim or influence. If ever a system could be called "a government of laws, and not of men', it is that shown in the evidence before me."

Faced with a contradiction between the authority of the Privy Council and the evidence, his Honour held that the class to which a colony belonged was a question of law, not of fact:

> "Whether or not the Australian aboriginals living in any part of New South Wales had in 1788 a system of law which was beyond the powers of the

settlers at that time to perceive or comprehend, it is beyond the power of this Court to decide otherwise than that New South Wales came into the category of a settled or occupied colony."

The facts as we know them today do not fit the "absence of law" or "barbarian" theory underpinning the colonial reception of the common law of England. That being so, there is no warrant for applying in these times rules of the English common law which were the product of that theory. It would be a curious doctrine to propound today that, when the benefit of the common law was first extended to Her Majesty's indigenous subjects in the Antipodes, its first fruits were to strip them of their right to occupy their ancestral lands. Yet the supposedly barbarian nature of indigenous people provided the common law of England with the justification for denying them their traditional rights and interests in land, as Lord Sumner speaking for the Privy Council said in In re Southern Rhodesia:

> "The estimation of the rights of aboriginal tribes is always inherently difficult. Some tribes are so low in the scale of social organization that their usages and conceptions of rights and duties are not to be reconciled with the institutions or the legal ideas of civilized society. Such a gulf cannot be bridged. It would be idle to impute to such people some shadow of the rights known to our law and then to transmute it into the substance of transferable rights of property as we know them."

As the indigenous inhabitants of a settled colony were regarded as "low in the scale of social organization", they and their occupancy of colonial land were ignored in considering the title to land in a settled colony. Ignoring those rights and interests, the Crown's sovereignty over a territory which had been acquired under the enlarged notion of terra nullius was equated with Crown ownership of the lands therein, because, as Stephen C.J. said, there was "no other proprietor of such lands". Thus, a Select Committee on Aborigines reported in 1837 to the House of Commons that the state of Australian Aborigines was "barbarous" and "so entirely destitute ... of the rudest forms of civil polity, that their claims, whether as sovereigns or proprietors of the soil, have been utterly disregarded". The theory that the indigenous inhabitants of a "settled" colony had no proprietary interest in the land thus depended on a discriminatory denigration of indigenous inhabitants, their social organization and customs. As the basis of the theory is false in fact and unacceptable in our society, there is a choice of legal principle to be made in the present case. This Court can either apply the existing authorities and proceed to inquire whether the Meriam people are higher "in the scale of social organization" than the Australian Aborigines whose claims were "utterly disregarded" by the existing authorities or the Court can overrule the existing authorities, discarding the distinction between inhabited colonies that were terra nullius and those which were not.

The theory of *terra nullius* has been critically examined in recent times by the International Court of Justice in its Advisory Opinion on Western Sahara. There the majority judgment read:

> "'Occupation' being legally an original means of peaceably acquiring sovereignty over territory otherwise than by cession or succession, it was a cardinal condition of a valid "occupation' that the territory should be *terra nullius* — a territory belonging to no one — at the time of the act alleged to constitute the 'occupation' (cf. Legal Status of Eastern Greenland, P.C.I.J., Series A/B, No. 53, pp. 44 f. and 63 f.). In the view of the Court, therefore, a determination that Western Sahara was a "terra nullius' at the time of colonization by Spain would be possible only if it were established that at that time the territory belonged to no-one in the sense that it was then open to acquisition through the legal process of 'occupation'." 80.

Whatever differences of opinion there may have been among jurists, the State practice of the relevant period indicates that territories inhabited by tribes or peoples having a social and political organization were not regarded as terrae nullius. It shows that in the case of such territories the acquisition of sovereignty was not generally considered as effected unilaterally through "occupation' of terra nullius by original title but through agreements concluded with local rulers. On occasion, it is true, the word "occupation' was used in a non-technical sense denoting simply acquisition of sovereignty; but that did not signify that the acquisition of sovereignty through such agreements with authorities of the country was regarded as an "occupation' of a "*terra nullius'* in the proper sense of these terms. On the contrary, such agreements with local rulers, whether or not considered as an actual "cession' of the territory, were regarded as derivative roots of title, and not original titles obtained by occupation of terrae nullius."

Judge Ammoun, Vice-President of the Court, delivered a separate opinion in which he commended as penetrating the views expressed on behalf of the Republic of Zaire which he restated as follows:

> "Mr. Bayona-Ba-Meya goes on to dismiss the materialistic concept of *terra nullius*, which led to this dismemberment of Africa following the Berlin Conference of 1885. Mr. Bayona-Ba-Meya substitutes for this a spiritual notion: the ancestral tie between the land, or "mother nature', and the man who was born therefrom, remains attached thereto, and must one day return thither to be united with his ancestors. This link is the basis of the ownership of the soil, or

> better, of sovereignty. This amounts to a denial of the very concept of terra nullius in the sense of a land which is capable of being appropriated by someone who is not born therefrom. It is a condemnation of the modern concept, as defined by Pasquale Fiore, which regards as terrae nullius territories inhabited by populations whose civilization, in the sense of the public law of Europe, is backward, and whose political organization is not conceived according to Western norms. One might go still further in analyzing the statement of the representative of Zaire so as to say that he would exclude from the concept of terra nullius any inhabited territory. His view thus agrees with that of Vattel, who defined terra nullius as a land empty of inhabitants."

He concluded that "the concept of *terra nullius*, employed at all periods, to the brink of the twentieth century, to justify conquest and colonization, stands condemned." The court was unanimously of the opinion that Western Sahara at the time of colonization by Spain in 1884 was not a territory belonging to no-one *(terra nullius)*.

If the international law notion that inhabited land may be classified as *terra nullius* no longer commands general support, the doctrines of the common law which depend on the notion that native peoples may be "so low in the scale of social organization" that it is "idle to impute to such people some shadow of the rights known to our law" can hardly be retained. If it were permissible in past centuries to keep the common law in step with international law, it is imperative in today's world that the common law should neither be nor be seen to be frozen in an age of racial discrimination.

The fiction by which the rights and interests of indigenous inhabitants in land were treated as non-existent was justified by a policy which has no place in the contemporary law of this country. The policy appears explicitly in the judgment of the Privy Council in In re Southern Rhodesia in rejecting an argument(5) that the native people "were the owners of the unalienated lands long before either the Company or the Crown became concerned with them and from time immemorial ... and that the unalienated lands belonged to them still". Their Lordships replied(6):

> "the maintenance of their rights was fatally inconsistent with white settlement of the country, and yet white settlement was the object of the whole forward movement, pioneered by the Company and controlled by the Crown, and that object was successfully accomplished, with the result that the aboriginal system gave place to another prescribed by the Order in Council."

Whatever the justification advanced in earlier days for refusing to recognize the rights and interests in land of the indigenous inhabitants of settled colonies, an unjust and discriminatory doctrine of that kind can no longer be accepted. The expectations of the international community accord in this respect with the contemporary values of the

Australian people. The opening up of international remedies to individuals pursuant to Australia's accession to the Optional Protocol to the International Covenant on Civil and Political Rights brings to bear on the common law the powerful influence of the Covenant and the international standards it imports. The common law does not necessarily conform with international law, but international law is a legitimate and important influence on the development of the common law, especially when international law declares the existence of universal human rights. A common law doctrine founded on unjust discrimination in the enjoyment of civil and political rights demands reconsideration. It is contrary both to international standards and to the fundamental values of our common law to entrench a discriminatory rule which, because of the supposed position on the scale of social organization of the indigenous inhabitants of a settled colony, denies them a right to occupy their traditional lands. It was such a rule which evoked from Deane J.(8) the criticism that:

> "the common law of this land has still not reached the stage of retreat from injustice which the law of Illinois and Virginia had reached in 1823 when Marshall C.J., in *Johnson v McIntosh*, accepted that, subject to the assertion of ultimate dominion (including the power to convey title by grant) by the State, the "original inhabitants' should be recognized as having "a legal as well as just claim' to retain the occupancy of their traditional lands."

However, recognition by our common law of the rights and interests in land of the indigenous inhabitants of a settled colony would be precluded if the recognition were to fracture a skeletal principle of our legal system. The proposition that the Crown became the beneficial owner of all colonial land on first settlement has been supported by more than a disregard of indigenous rights and interests. It is necessary to consider these other reasons for past disregard of indigenous rights and interests and then to return to a consideration of the question whether and in what way our contemporary common law recognizes such rights and interests in land.

나. 사회영향평가 — World Bank OD 4.2와 계약서 조항

우리의 환경영향평가법이 일정한 사업의 경우 지역주민과의 공청회 등을 통하여 의견수렴을 하여야 하며 환경영향평가서를 사업승인 신청시 제출하게 하고 있는 것처럼[2] World Bank는 1991년 이래 개발프로젝트가 현지주민에 미치는 사회적 영향평가의 일환으로 현지발전계획을 제시하게 하고 있으며[3] 이러한 평가가 자원탐사·개발계약상 Contractor의 의무

2) 환경영향평가법 제14조(의견수렴 및 평가서 초안의 작성).

3) http://www.bicusa.org/en/Issue.Resources.24.aspx에서 제반 자료 열람가능.

의 하나로 포함시킬 것도 제안되고 있다.[4)]

2. 인권법과 에너지개발

가. Alien Tort Claims Act

IOC가 산유국의 억압적 정치체제에 영합하면서 현지의 권력자와 자원개발사업을 벌이는 경우 자원보유국 내 다수국민의 인권은 개발이라는 이유로 짓밟힐 수도 있다. 물론 중동의 산유국 중 다수가 아직도 절대왕정 내지 독재체제를 유지하고 있는 마당에 억압적 정치체제가 무엇을 의미하는지 근본적인 의문은 남아 있다. 어쨌든 미국은 1789년 연방법원의 관할과 관련하여 외국인이 미국 밖에서 국제법 또는 미국이 체결한 조약에 위반되는 불법행위를 당한 경우 미국 연방법원에 손해배상청구를 할 수 있다는 법을 만든 바 있는데,[5)] 이 조문에 근거하여 1980년대부터 외국인들이 미국법원에 해외자원개발사업을 벌이는 IOC를 상대로 손해배상청구소송을 제기하기 시작하였다. 많은 소송이 각하되거나 소송상 화해로 기각되었지만 일부 최종판결까지 가서 승소한 경우도 있고 금전적 보상은 받지 못하더라도 IOC의 해외자원개발실상을 널리 알리는 효과는 있었다.

Doe I v. Unocal Corp., 395 F.3d 932 (9th Cir. 2002)

[미얀마인이 미얀마정부, Total, Unocal 등을 상대로 ATCA위반을 이유로 손해배상을 구한 사안에서 1심은 이들 모두를 약식판결로 기각하자 항소한 사안]

FACTUAL AND PROCEDURAL BACKGROUND

A. Unocal's Investment in a Natural Gas Project in Myanmar.

Burma has been ruled by a military government since 1958. In 1988, a new military government, Defendant-Appellee State Law and Order Restoration Council ("the Myanmar Military"), took control and renamed the country Myanmar. The Myanmar Military established a state owned company, Defendant-Appellee Myanmar Oil and Gas Enterprise ("Myanmar Oil"), to produce and sell the nation's oil and gas resources.

In 1992, Myanmar Oil licensed the French oil company Total S.A. ("Total") to produce, transport, and sell natural gas from deposits in the Yadana Field off the coast

4) Smith, 주 1-4 상게서, 804-06.

5) 28 U.S.C. § 1350.

of Myanmar ("the Project"). Total set up a subsidiary, Total Myanmar Exploration and Production ("Total Myanmar"), for this purpose. The Project consisted of a Gas Production Joint Venture, which would extract the natural gas out of the Yadana Field, and a Gas Transportation Company, which would construct and operate a pipeline to transport the natural gas from the coast of Myanmar through the interior of the country to Thailand.

Also in 1992, Defendant-Appellant Unocal Corporation and its wholly owned subsidiary Defendant-Appellant Union Oil Company of California, collectively referred to below as "Unocal," acquired a 28% interest in the Project from Total. Unocal set up a wholly owned subsidiary, the Unocal Myanmar Offshore Company ("the Unocal Offshore Co."), to hold Unocal's 28% interest in the Gas Production Joint Venture half of the Project. Similarly, Unocal set up another wholly owned subsidiary, the Unocal International Pipeline Corporation ("the Unocal Pipeline Corp."), to hold Unocal's 28% interest in the Gas Transportation Company half of the Project. Myanmar Oil and a Thai government entity, the Petroleum Authority of Thailand Exploration and Production, also acquired interests in the Project. Total Myanmar was appointed Operator of the Gas Production Joint Venture and the Gas Transportation Company. As the Operator, Total Myanmar was responsible, *inter alia,* for "determin[ing] ... the selection of ... employees [and] the hours of work and the compensation to be paid to all ... employees" in connection with the Project.

B. Unocal's Knowledge that the Myanmar Military Was Providing Security and Other Services for the Project.

It is undisputed that the Myanmar Military provided security and other services for the Project, and that Unocal knew about this. The pipeline was to run through Myanmar's rural Tenasserim region. The Myanmar Military increased its presence in the pipeline region to provide security and other services for the Project. A Unocal memorandum documenting Unocal's meetings with Total on March 1 and 2, 1995 reflects Unocal's understanding that "[f]our battalions of 600 men each will protect the [pipeline] corridor" and "[f]ifty soldiers will be assigned to guard each survey team." A former soldier in one of these battalions testified at his deposition that his battalion had been formed in 1996 specifically for this purpose. In addition, the Military built helipads and cleared roads along the proposed pipeline route for the benefit of the Project.

There is also evidence sufficient to raise a genuine issue of material fact whether the Project *hired* the Myanmar Military, through Myanmar Oil, to provide these services, and whether Unocal knew about this. A Production Sharing Contract, entered into by Total Myanmar and Myanmar Oil before Unocal acquired an interest in the Project, provided that "[Myanmar Oil] shall ... supply[ ] or mak[e] available ... security protection ... as may be requested by [Total Myanmar and its assigns]," such as Unocal. Unocal was aware of this agreement. Thus, a May 10, 1995 Unocal "briefing document" states that "[a]ccording to *our contract,* the government of Myanmar is responsible for protecting the pipeline." (Emphasis added.) Similarly, in May 1995, a cable from the U.S. Embassy in Rangoon, Myanmar, reported that Unocal On-Site Representative Joel Robinson ("Unocal Representative Robinson" or "Robinson") "stated forthrightly that *the companies have hired* the Burmese military to provide security for the project." (Emphasis added.)

Unocal disputes that the Project hired the Myanmar Military or, at the least, that Unocal knew about this. For example, Unocal points out that the Production Sharing Contract quoted in the previous paragraph covered only the off-shore Gas Production Joint Venture but not the Gas Transportation Company and the construction of the pipeline which gave rise to the alleged human rights violations. Moreover, Unocal President John Imle ("Unocal President Imle" or "Imle") stated at his deposition that he knew of "no ... contractual obligation" requiring the Myanmar Military to provide security for the pipeline construction. Likewise, Unocal CEO Roger Beach ("Unocal CEO Beach" or "Beach") stated at his deposition that he also did not know "whether or not Myanmar had a contractual obligation to provide ... security." Beach further stated that he was not aware of "any support whatsoever of the military[,] ... either physical or monetary." These assertions by Unocal President Imle and Unocal CEO Beach are called into question by a briefing book which Total prepared for them on the occasion of their April 1996 visit to the Project. The briefing book lists the "numbers of villagers" working as "local helpers hired by battalions," the monthly "amount paid in Kyats" (the currency of Myanmar) to "Project Helpers," and the "amount in Kyats" expended by the Project on "food rations (Army+Villages)."

Furthermore, there is evidence sufficient to raise a genuine issue of material fact whether the Project directed the Myanmar Military in these activities, at least to a degree, and whether Unocal was involved in this. In May 1995, a cable from the U.S. Embassy in Rangoon reported:

> [Unocal Representative] Robinson indicated ... Total/Unocal uses [aerial photos, precision surveys, and topography maps] to show the [Myanmar] military where they need helipads built and facilities secured .... Total's security officials meet with military counterparts to inform them of the next day's activities so that soldiers can ensure the area is secure and guard the work perimeter while the survey team goes about its business.

A November 8, 1995 document apparently authored by Total Myanmar stated that "[e]ach working group has a security officer ... to control the army positions." A January 1996 meeting document lists "daily security coordination with the army" as a "working procedure." Similarly, the briefing book that Total prepared for Unocal President Imle and Unocal CEO Beach on the occasion of their April 1996 visit to the Project mentions that "daily meeting[s]" were "held with the tactical commander" of the army. Moreover, on or about August 29, 1996, Unocal (Singapore) Director of Information Carol Scott ("Unocal Director of Information Scott" or "Scott") discussed with Unocal Media Contact and Spokesperson David Garcia ("Unocal Spokesperson Garcia" or "Garcia") via e-mail how Unocal should publicly address the issue of the alleged movement of villages by the Myanmar Military in connection with the pipeline. Scott cautioned Garcia that "[b]y saying *we* influenced the army not to move a village, you introduce the concept that they would do such a thing; whereas, by saying that no villages have been moved, you skirt the issue of whether it could happen or not." (Emphasis added.) This e-mail is some evidence that Unocal could influence the army not to commit human rights violations, that the army might otherwise commit such violations, and that Unocal knew this.

C. Unocal's Knowledge that the Myanmar Military Was Allegedly Committing Human Rights Violations in Connection with the Project.

Plaintiffs are villagers from Myanmar's Tenasserim region, the rural area through which the Project built the pipeline. Plaintiffs allege that the Myanmar Military forced them, under threat of violence, to work on and serve as porters for the Project. For instance, John Doe IX testified that he was forced to build a helipad near the pipeline site in 1994 that was then used by Unocal and Total officials who visited the pipeline during its planning stages. John Doe VII and John Roe X, described the construction of helipads at Eindayaza and Po Pah Pta, both of which were near the pipeline site, were used to ferry Total/Unocal executives and materials to the construction site, and were constructed using the forced labor of local villagers, including Plaintiffs. John Roes VIII and IX, as well as John Does I, VIII and IX testified that they were forced to work on building roads leading to the pipeline construction area. Finally, John Does V and IX, testified that they were required to serve as "pipeline porters"-workers who performed menial tasks such as such as hauling materials and cleaning the army camps for the soldiers guarding the pipeline construction.

Plaintiffs also allege in furtherance of the forced labor program just described, the Myanmar Military subjected them to acts of murder, rape, and torture. For instance, Jane Doe I testified that after her husband, John Doe I, attempted to escape the forced labor program, he was shot at by soldiers, and in retaliation for his attempted escape, that she and her baby were thrown into a fire, resulting in injuries to her and the death of the child. Other witnesses described the summary execution of villagers who refused to participate in the forced labor program, or who grew too weak to work effectively. Several Plaintiffs testified that rapes occurred as part of the forced labor program. For instance, both Jane Does II and III testified that while conscripted to work on pipeline-related construction projects, they were raped at knife-point by Myanmar soldiers who were members of a battalion that was supervising the work. Plaintiffs finally allege that Unocal's conduct gives rise to liability for these abuses.

The successive military governments of first Burma and now Myanmar have a long and well-known history of imposing forced labor on their citizens. *See, e.g., Forced labour in Myanmar (Burma): Report of the Commission of Inquiry appointed under article 26 of the Constitution of the International Labour Organization to examine the observance by Myanmar of the Forced Labour Convention, 1930 (No. 29)* Parts III.8, V.14(3) (1998) (describing several inquiries into forced labor in Myanmar conducted between 1960 and 1992 by the International Labor Organization, and finding "abundant evidence ... showing the pervasive use of forced labour imposed on the civilian population throughout Myanmar by the authorities and the military"), http://www.ilo.org/public/english/standards/relm/gb/docs/gb273/myanmar.htm. As detailed below, even before Unocal invested in the Project, Unocal was made aware-by its own consultants and by its partners in the Project-of this record and that the Myanmar Military might also employ forced labor and commit other human rights violations in connection with the Project. And after Unocal invested in the Project, Unocal was made aware-by its own consultants and employees, its partners in the Project, and human rights organizations-of allegations that the Myanmar Military was actually committing such violations in connection with the Project.

Before Unocal acquired an interest in the Project, it hired a consulting company, Control Risk Group, to assess the risks involved in the investment. In May 1992, Control Risk Group informed Unocal that "[t]hroughout Burma the government habitually makes use of forced labour to construct roads." Control Risk Group concluded that "[i]n such circumstances UNOCAL and its partners will have little freedom of manoeuvre." Unocal's awareness of the risk at that time is also reflected in the deposition testimony of Unocal Vice President of International Affairs Stephen Lipman ("Unocal Vice President Lipman"):

[I]n our discussions between Unocal and Total[preceding Unocal's acquisition of an interest in the Project], we said that the option of having the [Myanmar] [M]ilitary provide protection for the pipeline construction and operation of it would be that they might proceed in the manner that would be out of our control and not be in a manner that we would like to see them proceed, I mean, going to excess.

On January 4, 1995, approximately three years after Unocal acquired an interest in the Project, Unocal President Imle met with human rights organizations at Unocal's headquarters in Los Angeles and acknowledged to them that the Myanmar Military might be using forced labor in connection with the Project. At that meeting, Imle said that "[p]eople are threatening physical damage to the pipeline," that "if you threaten the pipeline there's gonna be more military," and that *"[i]f forced labor goes hand and glove with the military yes there will be more forced labor."* (Emphasis added.)

Two months later, on March 16, 1995, Unocal Representative Robinson confirmed to Unocal President Imle that the Myanmar Military might be committing human rights violations in connection with the Project. Thus, Robinson wrote to Imle that he had received publications from human rights organizations "which depicted in more detail than I have seen before the increased encroachment of [the Myanmar Military's] activities into the villages of the pipeline area." Robinson concluded on the basis of these publications that "[o]ur assertion that [the Myanmar Military] has not expanded and amplified its usual methods around the pipeline on our behalf may not withstand much scrutiny."

Shortly thereafter, on May 10, 1995, Unocal Representative Robinson wrote to Total's Herve Madeo:

From Unocal's standpoint, probably the most sensitive issue is "what is forced labor" and "how can you identify it." I am sure that you will be thinking about the demarcation between work done by the project and work done "on behalf of" the project. Where the responsibility of the project ends is *very important.*

This statement is some evidence that Unocal knew that the Myanmar Military might use forced labor in connection with the Project. In June 1995, Amnesty International also alerted Unocal to the possibility that the Myanmar Military might use forced labor in connection with the Project. Amnesty International informed Unocal that comments from a Myanmar Department of Industry official "could mean that the government plans to use 'voluntary' labor in conjunction with the pipeline." Amnesty International went on to explain that "what they call 'voluntary' labor is called forced labor in other parts of the world."

II.
ANALYSIS

A. Liability Under the Alien Tort Claims Act.

1. Introduction

The Alien Tort Claims Act confers upon the federal district courts "original jurisdiction of any civil action by an alien for a tort only, committed in violation of the law of nations." 28 U.S.C. § 1350. We have held that the ATCA also provides a cause of action, as long as "plaintiffs ... allege a violation of 'specific, universal, and obligatory' international norms as part of [their] ATCA claim." *Papa v. United States,* 281 F.3d 1004, 1013 (9th Cir.2002) (quoting *In re Estate of Ferdinand E. Marcos, Human Rights Litig.,* 25 F.3d 1467, 1475 (9th Cir.1994) ("*Marcos II*")). *See also Marcos II,* 25 F.3d at 1474-75. Plaintiffs allege that Unocal's conduct gave rise to ATCA liability for the forced labor, murder, rape, and torture inflicted on them by the Myanmar Military.

[1] The District Court granted Unocal's motion for summary judgment on Plaintiffs' ATCA claims. We review a grant of summary judgment *de novo. See Lopez v. Smith,* 203 F.3d 1122, 1131 (9th Cir.2000) (en banc). We must determine whether, viewing the evidence in the light most favorable to the nonmoving party, there are any genuine issues of material fact and whether the district court correctly applied the relevant substantive law. *See id.*

[2][3][4] One threshold question in *any* ATCA case is whether the alleged tort is a violation of the law of nations. We have recognized that torture, murder, and slavery are *jus cogens* violations and, thus, violations of the law of nations. *See United States v. Matta-Ballesteros,* 71 F.3d 754, 764 n. 5 (9th Cir.1995). Rape can be a form of torture. See *Farmer v. Brennan,* 511 U.S. 825, 852, 854, 114 S.Ct. 1970, 128 L.Ed.2d 811 (1994) (Blackmun, J., concurring) (describing brutal prison rape as "the equivalent of" and "nothing less than torture"); *Kadic v. Karadzic,* 70 F.3d 232, 242 (2d Cir.1995) (describing allegations of "murder, rape, forced impregnation, and *other forms of torture*" (emphasis added)); *In re Extradition of Suarez-Mason,* 694 F.Supp. 676, 682 (N.D.Cal.1988) (stating that "shock sessions were interspersed with rapes and *other forms of torture*" (emphasis added)); *see also generally* Evelyn Mary Aswad, *Torture by Means of Rape,* 84 Geo. L.J. 1913 (1996). Moreover, forced labor is so widely condemned that it has achieved the status of a *jus cogens* violation. *See, e.g.,* Universal Declaration of Human Rights, G.A. Res. 217(A)III (1948) (banning forced labor); Agreement for the Prosecution and Punishment of the Major War Criminals of the European Axis, and Charter of the International Military Tribunal, Aug. 8, 1945, art. 6, 82 U.N.T.S. 280 (making forced labor a war crime). Accordingly, all torts alleged in the present case are *jus cogens* violations and, thereby, violations of the law of nations.

[5] Another threshold question in any ATCA case *against a private party,* such as Unocal, is whether the alleged tort requires the private party to engage in state action for ATCA liability to attach, and if so, whether the private party in fact engaged in state action. In his concurrence in *Tel-Oren v. Libyan Arab Republic,* 726 F.2d 774 (D.C.Cir.1984), Judge Edwards observed that while most crimes require state action for

ATCA liability to attach, there are a "handful of crimes," including slave trading, "to which the law of nations attributes *individual liability,*" such that state action is not required. *Id.* at 794-95 (Edwards, J., concurring) (emphasis added). More recently, the Second Circuit adopted and extended this approach in *Kadic*. The Second Circuit first noted that genocide and war crimes-like slave trading-do not require state action for ATCA liability to attach. *See* 70 F.3d at 242-43. The Second Circuit went on to state that although "acts of rape, torture, and summary execution," like most crimes, "are proscribed by international law only when committed by state officials or under color of law" to the extent that they were committed *in isolation,* these crimes "are actionable under the Alien Tort [Claims] Act, without regard to state action, to the extent that they were committed *in pursuit of genocide or war crimes.*" *Id.* at 243-44 (emphasis added). Thus, under *Kadic,* even crimes like rape, torture, and summary execution, which by themselves require state action for ATCA liability to attach, do *not* require state action when committed in furtherance of other crimes like slave trading, genocide or war crimes, which by themselves do not require state action for ATCA liability to attach. We agree with this view and apply it below to Plaintiffs' various ATCA claims.

2. Forced Labor

a. Forced labor is a modern variant of slavery to which the law of nations attributes individual liability such that state action is not required.

[6] Our case law strongly supports the conclusion that forced labor is a modern variant of slavery. Accordingly, forced labor, like traditional variants of slave trading, is among the "handful of crimes ... to which the law of nations attributes *individual liability,*" such that state action is not required. *Id.* at 794-95 (Edwards, J., concurring). *See supra* section II.A.1.

b. Unocal may be liable under the ATCA for aiding and abetting the Myanmar Military in subjecting Plaintiffs to forced labor.

Plaintiffs argue that Unocal aided and abetted the Myanmar Military in subjecting them to forced labor. We hold that the standard for aiding and abetting under the ATCA is, as discussed below, knowing practical assistance or encouragement that has a substantial effect on the perpetration of the crime. We further hold that a reasonable factfinder could find that Unocal's conduct met this standard. *Unocal may be liable under the ATCA for aiding and abetting the Myanmar Military in subjecting Plaintiffs to murder and rape, but Unocal is not similarly liable for torture.*

노트와 질문

1. 국제법 위반 중 어떤 행위가 연방법상 불법행위를 구성하는지에 대하여는 *Sosa* 판결 이전에 ATCA jurisprudence를 연 1980년 *Filartiga* 판결부터[6] 문제가 되었다. 해적행위, 노예무역, 고문, 환경훼손, 질병야기?
2. 기업이 국제법을 위반한 국가의 공동불법행위자로서 ATCA상 책임을 지려면 어떠한 정도로 자원보유국의 행위에 참여하여야만 하는가?
3. 자원보유국 주민의 인권문제는 우리 기업과도 관련이 있다. EarthRight는 2008. 10. 미얀마에서 가스전 개발에 참여하고 있는 대우인터내셔날과 KOGAS가 OECD의 다국적기업행동규범에 어긋하는 행동을 하고 있다는 고발장을 OECD 한국사무소에 제출한 바 있다.[7]

나. 미국무성의 행동강령, World Bank EIR과 UN 보고서

ATCA 소송은 실정법에 근거하여 법원에서의 다툼으로 문제를 해결하려는 노력이라면, 미국무성과[8] World Bank,[9] UN은[10] 기업의 자발적 참여로서 산유국에서의 자원개발필요와 현지에서의 안전상황, 그리고 현지인의 인권을 조화시키려 하고 있다. 미국무성은 2000. 12. 20. 미국과 영국의 대표적 IOC들과 현지에서의 위험을 평가하고 국가의 안전요원이나 사설 안전요권과의 안전을 위한 연락업무원칙을 자발적 참여형식으로 합의하였다. World Bank는 2000. 6. 회의에서 IFC가 개발도상국의 석유와 가스, 광업프로젝트에 자금을 지원하면서 이들 추출산업이 개발도상국의 환경과 인권에 미치는 영향에 대한 충분한 고려가 없다는 지적에 따라서 보고서를 제출하고 향후 현지주민과의 사전협의, 효과의 공개, 지역사회 경제발전에의 기여 등을 감안하여 자금을 지원하기로 하였다. UN 특별대표 Ruggie는 2005년부터 국가와 사업체가 지켜야 할 인권에 관한 조사를 시작, 2011. 3. 최종보고서와 guiding principles를 제시하였고 2011년부터 UN은 Working Group과 Forum을 통하여 이 원칙의 집행을 추진하고 있다.

---

6) 630 F.2d 881 (1980).
7) http://www.earthrights.org/campaigns/burma-project/korean-government-rejects-oecd-complaint-against-daewoo-international-and-ko에서 고발장 열람가능.
8) http://www.state.gov/www/global/human_rights/001220_fsdrl_principles.html.
9) http://web.worldbank.org/WBSITE/EXTERNAL/TOPICS/EXTOGMC/0,,contentMDK: 20306686~menuPK: 592071~pagePK: 148956~piPK: 216618~theSitePK: 336930~isCURL: Y,00.html에서 EIR보고서와 경과, work shop자료를 열람가능.
10) http://www.business-humanrights.org/media/documents/ruggie/ruggie-guiding-principles-21-mar-2011.pdf 보고서 열람가능.

3. 부패방지와 에너지개발

Lucinda A. Low/Thomas K. Sprange/Milos Barutciski, *Global Anti-corruption Standard and Enforcement: Implications for Energy Companies,* 3 J. WORLD ENER. L & BUS. 166 (2010)

1. Introduction

While every country has laws, usually of a criminal nature, prohibiting bribery-particularly in the public sector-until recently, laws prohibiting foreign bribery were relatively rare. The US Foreign Corrupt Practices Act (FCPA) stood for almost 20 years as the only transnational bribery statute in the world, focusing only on the 'supply side' of the bribery equation, and leaving the 'demand side' and lower-level corruption, to domestic enforcement. The last 10 years have, however, seen dramatic changes in this landscape. With the adoption of a series of international treaties, some highly targeted and others far-reach-ing, today dozens of countries have laws criminalizing the bribery of foreign public officials in international business. Some of these countries have extended their laws to purely commercial conduct as well. Moreover, these treaties create a legal infrastructure to facilitate cross-border investigations and enforcement. International financial institutions such as the World Bank, which previously turned a blind eye to corruption in projects they financed, are now investigating and sanctioning firms and their personnel found to have engaged in improper practices. As exemplified by the Siemens case, multijurisdictional investigations are on the rise, as are the penalties for violations, particularly where so-called 'grand' corruption is concerned.

Although enforcement is still quite uneven across countries, where there is the political will and capacity to enforce, the level of enforcement activity is rising rapidly. In the United States, enforcement of the FCPA is at an all-time high, with cases focusing not only on grand corruption in the procurement or business development context, but in many cases on lower-level operational corruption, in dealings with customs, tax, immigration and other regulatory authorities. In the last year, the United Kingdom went from being an enforcement laggard to apparent aggressive regulator and enforcer engaged in close cooperation with the United States.

And even on the 'demand' side in countries that are recipients of investment activity there are signs of a new era, whether from Lesotho's prosecution of multinational engineering companies involved in the Lesotho Highlands Water Project, to the Nigerian

Economic and Financial Crimes Commission's activities, to Indonesia's Corruption Eradication Commission.

Fig.1 Extractive industry FCPA prosecutions

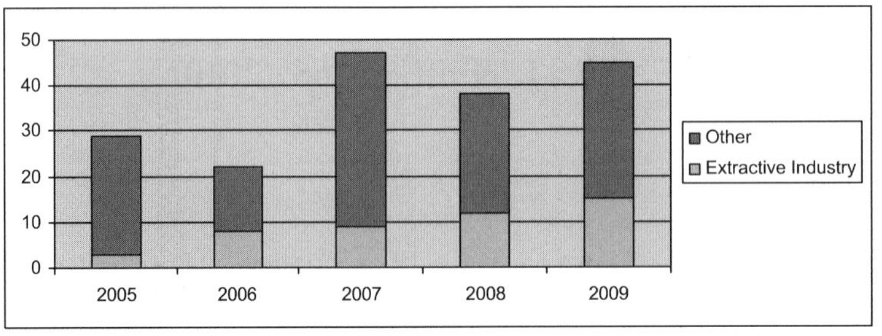

These efforts are spotty. For each example of enforcement, other countries that have failed to act can be identified. And yet despite the uneven picture, movement in the direction of greater harmonization and increased enforcement is unlikely to abate.

These developments affect extractive industries and their contractors and suppliers to perhaps a greater extent than any other group of industries. The natural resource industry cannot choose where to locate its core operations, but mast go where the resources are. And in many cases those resources are in places that are among the most challenging -with weak and frequently changing governments, underdeveloped and often opaque laws and institutions, and inadequate government resources. Extractive companies, while not traditionally thought of as regulated industries, must deal with 'government' (as defined in transnational bribery laws) at every turn-in the process of securing the basic rights to a resource, and in developing and operating the business as well as in exiting it. They tend to intersect with all branches of government-the executive, the legislative, the courts and the security forces-and at all levels, as well as with state-owned enterprises such as national oil and mining companies.

The last few years in the United States have seen a high number of enforcement actions against energy-related companies and their personnel, from the record penalties against a US company ($579 million US) in the Halliburton/KBR case in 2009, to the multijuris-dictional cases such as Statoil, to the Oil-for-Food cases that have snared energy and non-energy companies alike, to the cases (with more to come) involving service companies and suppliers.

Table 1. Number of extractive industry FCPA prosecutions

	2005	2006	2007	2008	2009
Extractive industry	3	8	9	12	15
Other	26	14	38	26	30

International financial institutions

Also significant in the expanded enforcement picture is the adoption by the World Bank and other international financial institutions (IFIs) and other public bodies engaged in procurement of new anti-corruption rules applicable both to Bank personnel and to outside contractors and consultants in connection with Bank-financed projects. These rules are being applied and enforced, resulting in sanctions, including debarment leading to losses of business opportunities and criminal referrals to national authorities.

Within the World Bank Group, the International Development Association (IDA) and the International Bank for Reconstruction and Development (IBRD) have issued revised guidelines for procurement under IBRD loans and IDA credits and for the use of consultants by borrowers that included anti-corruption provisions.147 The procurement guidelines delineate immediate and specific consequences for violations. Upon discover)' of fraudulent or corrupt conduct by a bidder or, once financing has been granted, by a borrower the guidelines state that the Bank will reject the bidder's proposals for awards, cancel the remaining portions of loans already granted to the borrower, and debar the borrower from future World Bank financing, either for a specified time period or indefinitely. To help Bank officials in policing possible corrupt activities, the guidelines give the Bank the right to inspect the books and records of any suppliers and contractors involved in the performance of a bank-financed contract, and to submit the records to outside auditors appointed by the Bank. Similar requirements are created by the consultant guidelines, which include provisions for canceling financing to borrowers if it is determined that their consultants engaged in corrupt or fraudulent behavior.

The International Finance Corporation and other IFIs involved in project lending also have adopted, or are adopting in this area, new rules and contractual standards to enforce these rules. For example, during its first year of operation, the Office of Institutional Integrity of the Inter-American Development Bank (IDB) handled more than 200 active cases. Most of the allegations received by that office in 2004 related to fraud or corruption. The IDB also has established a sanctions committee to impose penalties on those persons found to have violated the IDB standards.

Siemens, as noted above, entered into a comprehensive settlement with the Bank in July 2009 that was designed to prevent it from being informally sanctioned. As part of that settlement, it voluntarily agreed to a 2-year stand-down. Other cases have resulted in sanctions proceedings, following on the heels of investigations and referrals to the sanctioning body of the Bank. Some of the highest-profile sanctions cases have involved the Lesotho Highlands Water Project in Southern Africa. In that case, civil proceedings in Lesotho against an official who had headed the project for a number of years led to Swiss bank accounts and the discovery of evidence of payments to that official by agents of project contractors, and sometimes by the contractors directly. This led in turn to criminal prosecutions in Lesotho and to investigations by the World Bank of those project contractors who had received Bank-financed contracts. Although initial proceedings before the Bank against several contractors resulted in a finding of insufficient evidence of corrupt practices to justify the imposition of a sanction, two of the contractors, Acres International Ltd and Lahmeyer International GmbH, subsequently were convicted of bribery in Lesotho. The Bank reopened its proceedings, and both companies have been debarred for periods of time. Other major companies have been sanctioned by the World Bank as well.

5. Compliance

The increased enforcement of anti-corruption laws in the last decade has prompted a greater focus on programs to prevent violations of law. In the U.S., listed companies have focused on ethics and comliance programs and internal controls with new urgency since the enactment of the Sarbanes-Oxley legislation in2002 and amendments to the Federal Sentencing Guidelines for Corporations (which took effect in November 2004) that provide substantial new detail regarding the US Government's view of an 'effective compliance program'. At the same time, foreign companies, especially those with publicly traded stock in the United States, have devoted increased attention to FCPA compliance in the wake of the first enforcement actions against them and the beginnings of the FCPA's counterpart laws in foreign countries.

Standards for compliance programs have been developed by a number of different institutions, including Transparency International, the International Chamber of Commerce and Industry-specific bodies. A significant number of major multinational companies have subscribed to the Business Principles for Countering Bribery, among others, which provide a framework for compliance program development.

With laws imposing liability based on willful ignorance for the acts of another, companies increasingly are adopting measures to prevent violations and mitigate the risk of violations. Third-party relationship-whether partners, agents, consultants, lobbyists, brokers, finders or contractors-remain a significant source of potential liability. Risk-mitigation strategies for third parties may include limiting their use or limiting their activities, or, where they are used, conducting pre-engagement due diligence, ensuring that the relationship is governed by a contract containing significant anti-corruption safeguards, and monitoring and overseeing performance, including responding to any red flags that may be presented.

For a company's own employees, risk-mitigation strategies typically include the establishment of policies and procedures (tailored to the particular risks and structure of the company), controls, training, monitoring and oversight. For multinational companies operating in multiple foreign jurisdictions through subsidiaries, affiliates and branches, this is not a small undertaking. For extractive industry companies, the challenges of the operating environments they confront make the undertaking even more substantial.

With the costs of violations growing-Siemens is reported to have spent in excess of US$1 billion on investigations and remediation, in addition to the fines and penalties reported above-many companies arc concluding that prevention, although not inexpensive, is the most cost-effective approach.

4. 기후변화와 에너지개발

James A. Holtkamp/Richard M. Saines, *North American Approaches to Climate Change: Greenhouse Gas Emission Control Strategies,* 51 ROCKY MT. MIN. L. INST. 2005

§ 2.01 Introduction

Climate change is emerging as the most significant environmental issue of the 21st century, and some would suggest it is one of the most pressing issues of any kind, ranking with global poverty and war as threats to the well-being of the global community. Although vigorous debate over the causes, intensity, and impacts of climate change continues, there is no question that it is a political and legal reality. Today's climate change policy can rapidly become passi, however, with a change in government administration, a judicial decision, or a climate catastrophe.

This article addresses the varied climate change requirements in place and under development in the United States and Canada. The national governments in each country have adopted radically different approaches to climate change. The states and provinces have also rolled out climate change programs ranging from energy efficiency programs for government buildings to strict requirements on emissions of greenhouse gases (GHGs) and GHG trading systems.

This article also examines corporate responses to the climate change issue, particularly by energy companies and companies that require significant amounts of energy for their goods and services. The various government GHG programs on a national and state/provincial level present increasingly bewildering requirements for companies that operate in more than one jurisdiction. In addition, major shareholder blocs, including large pension funds, are demanding more disclosure of projected liabilities from corporate GHG-producing activities and more proactive steps to mitigate GHG emissions. On top of all of that, the potential is looming for liability for damages from events related to climate change under common-law theories. The political and legal reality is that GHG-producing enterprises will have to address GHG mitigation and liability sooner rather than later.

§ 2.02 Climate Change

[1] Causes of Climate Change

While debate over climate change policy continues, the questions of whether climate change is real and whether humans are contributing to it are fairly settled. The Intergovernmental Panel on Climate Change (IPCC), a scientific body created by the World Meteorological Organization and the United Nations Environment Programme, issued its first assessment report in 1990. The 1990 IPCC report warned that global warming is real and contributed to by human activity. The 1990s and early 2000s have seen growing acceptance within the scientific community that global warming is a real and serious threat. In 2001, the Bush Administration commissioned the National Academy of Science (NAS) to prepare its own assessment of the state of climate change science. The NAS confirmed the prior IPCC findings that the concentration of GHGs in the atmosphere is increasing due to human activities. The Bush Administration has now formally acknowledged links between human activity and climate change. As recently as July 8, 2005, President George W. Bush signed the G8 Gleneagles Communiqué, which commits the G8 countries to put themselves "on a path to slow and, as science justifies, stop and reverse the growth of greenhouse gases."

GHGs are defined by the United Nations Framework Convention on Climate Change (UNFCCC) as "those gaseous constituents of the atmosphere, both natural and anthropogenic, that absorb and re-emit infrared radiation." In other words, these gases are referred to as "greenhouse" gases because, like the glass roof of a greenhouse, they trap heat. Although many gases would fit this definition, including water vapor, the most commonly characterized suite of GHGs for purposes of climate change is that identified in the Kyoto Protocol: carbon dioxide (CO2), methane (CH4), nitrous oxide (N2O), perfluorocarbons (PFCs), hydrofluorocarbons (HFCs), and sulfur hexafluoride (SF6).

The IPCC reports that the amount of CO2 has increased by 31% since 1750, a rate that has not been exceeded during the last 420,000 years. There has been nearly a 20% increase since 1959 alone. About three-fourths of the man-made contribution of increased CO2 in the last part of the 20th century was due to fossil fuel burning, with the rest due primarily to land use changes, mostly consisting of deforestation. There is little question that the natural levels of GHGs are being rapidly supplemented by the combustion of fossil fuels, by agricultural activities and other changes in land use, and by certain industries generating industrial gases that do not occur naturally. As a result of human activities, computer climate models estimate that the average global temperature will rise by 1.4° to 5.8° C by the year 2100. The average temperature of the earth's surface has risen by 0.6° C since the late 1800s. Even if the minimum predicted increase takes place, it will be larger than any century-long trend in the last 10,000 years.

The scientific debate has shifted largely away from the question of whether anthropogenic activities have increased GHGs or whether there are climatic changes under way. The question of the day is now whether the climate change models are accurate and whether the predictions of dire consequences from climate change are reliable. Climatology is a particularly complex discipline, and the interrelationships between atmospheric, oceanic, solar, terrestrial, and other conditions are less than perfectly understood. Some suggest that the stakes are so high and the risks so great that GHG mitigation and reduction measures need to be implemented now. Others argue that the economic costs of significant GHG controls are not justified based on the uncertainties inherent in trying to predict the consequences of continued increases in human-caused GHG emissions.

[2] Kyoto Protocol

Although considered imperfect (indeed, ineffective) by some, the Kyoto Protocol is now international law. The Kyoto Protocol directly influences Canadian climate change policy by virtue of the fact that Canada ratified the Protocol and is now subject to its requirements. The Protocol also indirectly influences U.S. climate change policy notwithstanding the official repudiation of the Protocol by the Bush Administration.

The Kyoto Protocol was established under the authority of the 1992 UNFCCC. The UNFCCC, ratified by both the United States and Canada, established a goal for all signatory countries to stabilize their GHGs at 1990 levels by 2000:

The ultimate objective of this Convention and any related legal instruments that the Conference of the Parties may adopt is to achieve, in accordance with the relevant provisions of the Convention, stabilization of greenhouse gas concentrations in the atmosphere at a level that would prevent dangerous anthropogenic interference with the climate system. Such a level should be achieved within a time-frame sufficient to allow ecosystems to adapt naturally to climate change, to ensure that food production is not threatened and to enable economic development to proceed in a sustainable manner.

The UNFCCC Conference of the Parties, including the United States, negotiated and signed the Kyoto Protocol in 1997. However, in March 2001, President Bush formally made clear that the United States would not support the Protocol. Nonetheless, the Protocol entered into force in February of 2005 after ratification by Russia. Canada ratified the Protocol in late 2002 after much debate, with the energy-rich western Canadian provinces opposed to ratification on the grounds that it would put them at a disadvantage relative to their U.S. competitors.

The Kyoto Protocol establishes legally binding GHG emission reduction commitments for industrialized state Parties (known as "Annex I" countries because they are listed in Annex I to the UNFCCC). The overall commitment is a reduction in GHG emissions of 5% below 1990 levels during 2008-2012 (the Compliance Period). Each Annex I country is assigned a reduction percentage based on its 1990 levels of GHG emissions. Developing countries, including notably China and India, are exempt from GHG reduction requirements under the Protocol.

In subsequent Conferences of the Parties, rules and procedures for meeting the reduction commitments under the Protocol have been established. Pursuant to these procedures, an Annex I country may meet its reduction obligations under the Protocol through a combination of:

(1) direct reductions of its own domestic GHG emissions; each industrialized state will be assigned a limited number of Assigned Amount Units for its GHG emissions which reflect its allowable GHG emissions during the 2008-2012 commitment period;
(2) limited offsets against emissions through Sequestration, which will be initially limited to projects beginning on or after 1990 to increase carbon uptake and storage through agriculture and forestry;
(3) credits generated through Joint Implementation projects, which are projects occurring after 2000 undertaken between two industrialized states that generate emission reductions occurring after 2008 to be shared by both states;
(4) credits generated through Clean Development Mechanism projects, which are projects undertaken in a non-industrialized state, either unilaterally by such state or by an entity from an industrialized state; and
(5) Emissions Trading (in part), in which credits may be transferred from a country that has more reductions than is required to achieve its commitment to a country that has fallen short.

Because the United States is not a Party to the Protocol, it cannot be a participant in these various mechanisms.

The Parties to the UNFCCC are now engaged in preliminary discussions on requirements for future commitment periods beyond 2012, which will include discussion of whether and to what extent developing countries, most notably China and India, should take on reduction commitments of their own.

[3] Response to Climate Change

Although the UNFCCC and the Kyoto Protocol are both ostensibly global approaches to climate change, and although the Kyoto Protocol has entered into force, there is not yet a unified or consistent multinational response to climate change. This is attributable in part to the design of the international regime, which places the ultimate burden of developing the response to climate change at the national level. Under Kyoto, individual state Parties have the responsibility to implement policies and laws to achieve their reduction commitments. The difficulties experienced by the members of the European Union in developing their National Allocation Plans for reductions in industrial emissions and actually achieving those reductions is emblematic of the gap between the international support for addressing climate change and the realities of industrial economies.

There are many other climate change regimes in place throughout the world, some of which operate across national boundaries. Others are domestic national programs or private mechanisms. As described in more detail below, there are also an increasing number and variety of climate change programs at the state and local level in the United States.

The United States' repudiation of Kyoto, while enabling short-term deferral of response measures for U.S. companies, has complicated global response strategies for companies with operations in multiple jurisdictions. It has become increasingly apparent to energy companies that successfully navigating the complex and sometimes contradictory welter of climate change policies and requirements is not only necessary from an operating perspective, but may ultimately be a matter of long-term survival.

국내판례목록

외국판례/중재판정 목록

저자소개

서울대학교 법과대학, 대학원 졸업
행정고시 제24회 합격, 사법시험 제23회 합격, 사법연수원 제13기 수료
미국 컬럼비아 법과대학원 LL.M./J.D.(Parker School Recognition with Honor)
Baker & McKenzie, Chicago 변호사, 법무법인 우방·율촌 변호사
Columbia Law School Board of Visitors Member
GW's Center for Law, Economics & Finance Fellow
한국형사정책연구원 감사
국회 입법지원위원 / 국회사무처 행정심판위원회 위원
청와대 방송정보통신정책 자문위원
총리실 금융기관감독제도 혁신T/F 위원
기획재정부 법률고문
기획재정부 IFRS 도입자문단 위원
금융위원회 금융발전심의위원회 자본시장분과 / 정책분과 위원
금융위원회 공공금융기관 경영예산심의위원회 위원
조달청 행정발전위원회 위원
연세대학교 법학전문대학원 교수
현 법무법인 에어펙스 대표변호사

주요저서 및 논문

기업+(준)법 (박영사 2012. 1)
기업인수 4G (박영사 2010. 8)
대법 2012. 3. 15. 선고 2008두4619 판결에 대한 평석: 금융위 적기시정조치에 대한 사법적 통제의 한계, 금융법연구 제 9 권 1호(2012. 8)
우리 기업의 중동이슬람지역 진출에 따른 법적 위험관리방안, 한국중동학회 제32권 3호(2012. 2)
Finance and Corporate Governance for New Decade in Korea Considering 2000/2003 World Bank/IMF Reports, Jindal Global Law Review (Apr. 2011)
Legal Compliance and Korea Financial Services Market, Pacific Rim Law & Policy Journal (Apr. 2011)
Hostile Takeovers in Korea: Turning Point or Sticking Point for Policy Directions? Asia Pacific Law Review (June 2010)
Korean Legal Education for the Age of Professionalism: Suggestions for More Concerted Curricula, East Asia Law Review (June 2010)
Impending Amendments to Korean Corporate Laws in 2009: A Mystic Mix, Asian Journal of Comparative Law (May 2009)

국제거래법

2012년 9월 15일 초판 인쇄
2012년 9월 25일 초판 발행

저 자 정 영 철
발행인 안 종 만
발행처 (주) 박영사
서울특별시 종로구 평동 13-31번지
전화 (733) 6771 FAX (736) 4818
등록 1959. 3. 11. 제300-1959-1호(倫)

저자와 협의하여 인지첩부를 생략함

www.pybook.co.kr e-mail: pys@pybook.co.kr

정 가 49,000원 ISBN 978-89-6454-858-5